P9-AFT-858

Contemporary Literary Criticism

Guide to Gale Literary Criticism Series

When you need to review criticism of literary works, these are the Gale series to use:

If the author's death date is:	You should turn to:
After Dec. 31, 1959 (or author is still living)	*CONTEMPORARY LITERARY CRITICISM* for example: Jorge Luis Borges, Anthony Burgess, William Faulkner, Mary Gordon, Ernest Hemingway, Iris Murdoch
1900 through 1959	*TWENTIETH-CENTURY LITERARY CRITICISM* for example: Willa Cather, F. Scott Fitzgerald, Henry James, Mark Twain, Virginia Woolf
1800 through 1899	*NINETEENTH-CENTURY LITERATURE CRITICISM* for example: Fedor Dostoevski, George Sand, Gerard Manley Hopkins, Emily Dickinson
1400 through 1799	***LITERATURE CRITICISM FROM 1400 TO 1800 (excluding Shakespeare)*** for example: Anne Bradstreet, Pierre Corneille, Daniel Defoe, Alexander Pope, Jonathan Swift, Phillis Wheatley
	SHAKESPEAREAN CRITICISM Shakespeare's plays and poetry
Antiquity through 1399	*CLASSICAL AND MEDIEVAL LITERATURE CRITICISM* for example: Dante, Plato, Homer, Sophocles, Vergil, the Beowulf poet *(Volume 1 forthcoming)*

Gale also publishes related criticism series:

CHILDREN'S LITERATURE REVIEW

This ongoing series covers authors of all eras. Presents criticism on authors and author/illustrators who write for the preschool to junior-high audience.

CONTEMPORARY ISSUES CRITICISM

This two-volume set presents criticism on contemporary authors writing on current issues. Topics covered include the social sciences, philosophy, economics, natural science, law, and related areas.

ISSN 0091-3421

Volume 35

Contemporary Literary Criticism

Excerpts from Criticism of the Works of Today's Novelists, Poets, Playwrights, Short Story Writers, Scriptwriters, and Other Creative Writers

Daniel G. Marowski
EDITOR

Roger Matuz
Jane E. Neidhardt
ASSOCIATE EDITORS

Gale Research Company
Book Tower
Detroit, Michigan 48226

STAFF

Library of Congress Catalog Card Number 76-38938
ISBN 0-8103-4409-2
ISSN 0091-3421

Computerized photocomposition by
Typographics, Incorporated
Kansas City, Missouri

Printed in the United States

Contents

Preface

The last thirty years have brought about a type of literature which is directed specifically to a young adult audience. These works recognize the uniqueness of young adult readers while preparing them for the subjects, styles, and emotional levels of adult literature. Much of this writing has also had a definite appeal for adult readers and a discernible influence on their literature. Because of the importance of this subject matter and its audience, *Contemporary Literary Criticism (CLC)* devotes periodic volumes to writers whose work is directed to or appreciated by young adults. Until now, a collection of opinion has not existed which has centered on writers for the junior high to junior college age group. These special volumes of *CLC*, therefore, are meant to acknowledge this genre and its criticism as an important and serious part of recent literature.

In these special volumes we have broadened the definition of young adult literature to include not only such writers as John Donovan and M.E. Kerr, who fit the classic young adult mode, but also such authors as Langston Hughes and Carl Sandburg, whose works are received enthusiastically by the young even though they were not originally the intended audience. In the latter category are writers whose works have such relevance for the young adult sensibility that they have achieved mass appeal. A distinctive feature of these special volumes is the inclusion of criticism on writers whose work is not restricted to book form. The works of many lyricists, for instance those of John Lennon and Paul McCartney, have been critically analyzed and accepted as serious literary creations. Since young people look to television and the theater to expand their knowledge and reflect their world view, the young adult volumes also feature criticism on television producers, scriptwriters, and dramatists who appeal to the young, including Steven Bochco, Michael Kozoll, and Thornton Wilder in the present volume. Such authors of science fiction as Arthur C. Clarke and Frank Herbert, whose works are read by young adults for both entertainment and social comment, are also included.

Each periodic special volume on young adult literature is designed to complement other volumes of *CLC* and follows the same format with some slight variations. The list of authors treated is international in scope and, as in the other *CLC* volumes, includes creative writers who are now living or who died after December 31, 1959. Since this volume of *CLC* is intended to provide a definitive overview of the careers of the authors covered, the editors have included approximately forty-five writers (compared to fifty-five authors in the standard *CLC*) in order to devote more attention to each writer.

Criticism has been selected with the reading level and interests of the young adult in mind. Many young adult authors have also written for younger children. Criticism on these works has been included when it is felt the works may be of interest to the young adult.

Format of the Book

Altogether there are about 900 individual excerpts in each volume—with an average of about 20 excerpts per author—taken from hundreds of literary reviews, general magazines, scholarly journals, and monographs. Contemporary criticism is loosely defined as that which is relevant to the evaluation of the author under discussion; this includes criticism written at the beginning of an author's career as well as current commentary. Emphasis has been placed on expanding the sources for criticism by including an increasing number of scholarly and specialized periodicals. Students, teachers, librarians, and researchers frequently find that the generous excerpts and supplementary material provided by the editors supply them with all the information needed to write a term paper, analyze a poem, or lead a book discussion group. However, complete bibliographical citations facilitate the location of the original source as well as provide all of the information necessary for a term paper footnote or bibliography.

A *CLC* author entry consists of the following elements:

- The **author heading** cites the author's full name, followed by birth date, and death date when applicable. The portion of the name outside the parentheses denotes the form under which the author has most commonly published. If an author has written consistently under a pseudonym, the pseudonym will be listed in the author heading and the real name given on the first line of the biographical and critical introduction. Also located at the beginning of the introduction to the author entry are any important name variations under which an author has written. Uncertainty as to a birth or death date is indicated by a question mark.

• A **portrait** of the author is included when available.

• A brief **biographical and critical introduction** to the author and his or her work precedes the excerpted criticism. However, *CLC* is not intended to be a definitive biographical source. Therefore, *cross-references* have been included to direct the reader to other useful sources published by the Gale Research Company: *Contemporary Authors* now includes detailed biographical and bibliographical sketches on more than 82,000 authors; *Children's Literature Review* presents excerpted criticism on the works of authors of children's books; *Something about the Author* contains heavily illustrated biographical sketches on writers and illustrators who create books for children and young adults; *Contemporary Issues Criticism* presents excerpted commentary on the nonfiction works of authors who influence contemporary thought; *Dictionary of Literary Biography* provides original evaluations of authors important to literary history; and the new *Contemporary Authors Autobiography Series* offers autobiographical essays by prominent writers. Previous volumes of *CLC* in which the author has been featured are also listed in the biocritical introduction.

• The **excerpted criticism** represents various kinds of critical writing—a particular essay may be normative, descriptive, interpretive, textual, appreciative, comparative, or generic. It may range in form from the brief review to the scholarly monograph. Essays are selected by the editors to reflect the spectrum of opinion about a specific work or about an author's literary career in general. The excerpts are presented chronologically, adding a useful perspective to the entry. All titles by the author featured in the entry are printed in boldface type, which enables the reader to easily identify the works being discussed.

• A complete **bibliographical citation** designed to help the user find the original essay or book follows each excerpt. An asterisk (*) at the end of a citation indicates the essay is on more than one author.

Other Features

• A list of **Authors Forthcoming in *CLC*** previews the authors to be researched for future volumes.

• An **Appendix** lists the sources from which material in the volume has been reprinted. Many other sources have also been consulted during the preparation of the volume.

• A **Cumulative Index to Authors** lists all the authors who have appeared in *Contemporary Literary Criticism, Twentieth-Century Literary Criticism, Nineteenth-Century Literature Criticism,* and *Literature Criticism from 1400 to 1800,* along with cross-references to other Gale series: *Children's Literature Review, Authors in the News, Contemporary Authors, Contemporary Authors Autobiography Series, Dictionary of Literary Biography, Something about the Author,* and *Yesterday's Authors of Books for Children.* Users will welcome this cumulated author index as a useful tool for locating an author within the various series. The index, which lists birth and death dates when available, will be particularly valuable for those authors who are identified with a certain period but whose death date causes them to be placed in another, or for those authors whose careers span two periods. For example, F. Scott Fitzgerald is found in *Twentieth-Century Literary Criticism,* yet a writer often associated with him, Ernest Hemingway, is found in *Contemporary Literary Criticism.*

• A **Cumulative Index to Critics** lists the critics and the author entries in which their essays appear.

Acknowledgments

The editors wish to thank the copyright holders of the excerpted articles included in this volume for permission to use the material and the photographers and other individuals who provided photographs for us. We are grateful to the staffs of the following libraries for making their resources available to us: Detroit Public Library and the libraries of Wayne State University, the University of Michigan, and the University of Detroit. We also wish to thank Anthony Bogucki for his assistance with copyright research.

Suggestions Are Welcome

The editors welcome the comments and suggestions of readers to expand the coverage and enhance the usefulness of the series.

Authors Forthcoming in *CLC*

To Be Included in Volume 36

Vicente Aleixandre (Spanish poet and essayist)—The recent publication of *A Longing for Light: Selected Poems by Vicente Aleixandre* has increased appreciation of this Nobel laureate's work.

J. G. Ballard (English novelist and short story writer)—A distinguished science fiction writer, Ballard often explores the implications of new developments in science and technology for contemporary society. His recent novel, *Empire of the Sun,* evidences Ballard's concern with humanity's struggle for survival and its potential for self-destruction.

Norman Dubie (American poet)—Dubie's poetry, which is distinguished by its imaginative and intellectual complexity, is collected in five volumes, including his recent *New and Selected Poems.*

Marian Engel (Canadian novelist, short story writer, essayist, and nonfiction writer)—One of Canada's most respected contemporary writers, Engel won the Governor General's award for her novel *Bear*. Her recent novel, *Lunatic Villas,* offers a satiric view of life in Toronto.

Nicolas Freeling (English novelist, short story writer, and nonfiction writer)—A prolific author of suspense and crime novels, Freeling created Inspector Peter Van der Valk, a sensitive and logical detective who appears in several works, including the award-winning *King of a Rainy Country.*

Allen Ginsberg (American poet and editor)—The publication of *Collected Poems: 1947-1980* has prompted reevaluation of the entire career of this controversial literary figure.

Joseph Heller (American novelist, dramatist, and scriptwriter)—*God Knows,* an irreverent account of the life of King David of Israel, displays the wit, inventiveness, and insight that distinguished earlier Heller novels, including *Catch-22* and *Something Happened.*

Andrea Lee (American novelist, short story writer, and nonfiction writer)—Lee is best known as the author of the novel *Sarah Phillips,* a sensitive depiction of an intelligent and independent young black woman, and the nonfiction work *Russian Journal,* a highly praised view of life in the Soviet Union.

Edna O'Brien (Irish novelist, short story writer, dramatist, and scriptwriter)—Among the works that will be covered in this prolific author's entry are *Virginia,* a play about the life of Virginia Woolf, and *The Fanatic Heart: Selected Stories.*

George Plimpton (American nonfiction writer, journalist, and editor)—Often described as a "professional amateur," Plimpton is well regarded for his humorous accounts of his adventures in various sporting activities.

Michel Tournier (French novelist, short story writer, and essayist)—Considered one of France's most important contemporary writers, Tournier is widely praised for his philosophically speculative fiction. His entry will cover several works, including his recently translated short story collection, *The Fetishist.*

Lanford Wilson (American dramatist)—Wilson is best known for *The Hot l Baltimore* and for his series of plays about the Talley family, including *Talley's Folly,* for which he won the Pulitzer Prize.

To Be Included in Volume 37

Breyten Breytenbach (South African poet, novelist, and nonfiction writer)—Breytenbach is an important Afrikaans writer whose two recent works, *Mouroir: Mirrornotes of a Novel* and *The True Confessions of an Albino Terrorist,* were inspired by his seven-year imprisonment under South Africa's Terrorist Act.

William F. Buckley, Jr. (American novelist, essayist, nonfiction writer, and editor)—Editor of the *National Review* and author of books on conservative political thought, Buckley has also gained attention as a writer of spy fiction, including the recent *See You Later, Alligator.*

Donald Hall (American poet, essayist, dramatist, critic, and editor)—A prolific writer, Hall is best known for his poems, many of which are narrative reminiscences of his childhood and family. His latest works include *To Keep Moving* and *Fathers Playing Catch with Sons.*

Nella Larsen (American novelist)—The author of the novels *Quicksand* and *Passing,* Larsen was an important figure of the Harlem Renaissance whose work has undergone substantial critical reevaluation in recent years.

Primo Levi (Italian novelist, short story writer, and poet)—Many of Levi's books are based on his experiences as an inmate and survivor of Auschwitz. Recent translations of his work include *The Periodic Table* and *If Not Now, When?*

John Metcalf (Canadian short story writer, novelist, essayist, and editor)—An established author of short fiction, Metcalf recently published a collection of essays, *Kicking Against the Pricks,* which attacks the Canadian literary community.

V. S. Naipaul (Trinidadian-born English novelist, short story writer, essayist, and travel writer)—Naipaul's works are noted for their skillful, compelling depiction of the changing cultures of the Third World. His latest works, *Among the Believers: An Islamic Journey* and *Finding the Center: Two Narratives,* recount his travels through Iran, Pakistan, Malaysia, and Indonesia.

Robert Pinget (Swiss-born French novelist, dramatist, short story writer, and journalist)—Often compared to Samuel Beckett and Alain Robbe-Grillet, Pinget writes novels and plays bearing the influence of both the New Novel movement and concepts of the Theater of the Absurd.

Barbara Pym (English novelist and autobiographer)—Pym's witty and perceptive novels of British manners are enjoying renewed interest with the posthumous publication of her autobiography, *A Very Private Eye.*

Gay Talese (American nonfiction writer, journalist, and essayist)—Among the most highly regarded practitioners of New Journalism, Talese is best known for *Honor Thy Father,* a portrait of the private life of a Mafia member, and *Thy Neighbor's Wife,* a history of sexuality in the United States.

Hugh Whitemore (English dramatist and scriptwriter)—Whitemore's first work to be performed on Broadway, *Pack of Lies,* recently introduced to American theater the author of the acclaimed play *Stevie.*

Elie Wiesel (Rumanian-born American novelist, short story writer, essayist, and journalist)—Wiesel is considered among the most powerful writers of Holocaust literature and an eloquent spokesperson for contemporary Judaism. His recent works include *The Golem* and *The Fifth Son.*

C(arole) S(chwerdtfeger) Adler

1932-

American novelist and author of books for children.

Adler's novels for young adults focus on adolescent characters who overcome stressful situations through communication with and understanding of others. Most of Adler's works touch on problematic family relationships; these may be at the center of a novel, or they may be one element in a mystery or romance story. Adler spent ten years as a schoolteacher in New York State. From this, she says, "I learned what complex emotional creatures children are and was touched by their frequently helpless situations in life and their difficulty in communicating with the adults who wield power over them."

***Down by the River* (1981), *Some Other Summer* (1982), and *Roadside Valentine* (1983) are romances which explore adolescent love. In *Down by the River,* a girl who has been involved with a boy since childhood finds that his interest in her is superficial. Realizing the difference between infatuation and love, she finds her ideal family-oriented man living across the street. Adler's mystery novels dwell less upon interpersonal problems but still center on family conflict. *Footsteps on the Stairs* (1982), *The Evidence That Wasn't There* (1982), and *Shadows on Little Reef Bay* (1984) are among Adler's mystery titles. In *Footsteps on the Stairs,* two stepsisters gain insight into their own conflicts when confronted by the ghosts of two sisters who had failed to resolve their rivalry forty years earlier.**

Serious family problems are the subject of Adler's recent young adult fiction. In *The Shell Lady's Daughter* (1983), Kelly feels guilty and abandoned when her mother is institutionalized after a mental breakdown, but she is able to offer love and support when she understands that her mother has been living with feelings of inadequacy and depression for most of her life. Shari, the misfit protagonist of *Fly Free* (1984), is the victim of an abusive mother. With the help of her stepfather and a neighbor, she gains confidence in herself and some understanding of her mother's problems.

(See also *Contemporary Authors,* Vols. 89-92 and *Something about the Author,* Vol. 26.)

Photograph by Arnold Adler. Courtesy of C. S. Adler

ZENA SUTHERLAND

Since [***Down By the River***] opens with an italicized passage in which it is clear that Marybeth is married, this isn't about whether or not girl gets boy, although it is equally clear that Marybeth, whatever else happens in the course of the book, wants only the stability and security of love and marriage. It's just her choice of a husband that is out of the usual love-story pattern, for after a long and painful period in which she realizes that the boy she's always loved . . . cares for her only superficially, Marybeth adjusts; she even learns to care for the rock-steady older man who is a young [single] father . . . and she marries him. There are other relationships to balance the love interest: a growing understanding of her sometimes cranky mother, a deep and proud affection for a younger sister with cerebral palsy. . . . The writing style gets a bit florid occasionally, but not often enough to be obtrusive and mar the flow of the story.

Zena Sutherland, in a review of "Down by the River," in Bulletin of the Center for Children's Books, *Vol. 35, No. 1, September, 1981, p. 1.*

SYMME J. BENOFF

[In ***Down by the River*** Marybeth] is in love with childhood sweetheart Peter, who wants her love and his freedom. The plot moves along as lazily as the river near Marybeth's house. At least the river is going somewhere. The only character development is Marybeth's painfully slow realization that Peter doesn't want commitment and that she can get what she wants—a house, a man and babies by the river—with someone else. Moments of sexual tension between Marybeth and Peter are realistic and titillating; readers empathize with her difficult decisions about lovemaking, but may lose patience with her obsequiousness. There is no sense of emotional depth in supporting characters. While Adler does present different viewpoints about marriage and family life, she doesn't show the ambivalent feelings *within* characters. Instead, they are almost caricatures. . . . (pp. 69-70)

Symme J. Benoff, in a review of "Down by the River," in School Library Journal, *Vol. 28, No. 4, December, 1981, pp. 69-70.*

HILDAGARDE GRAY

It has arrived! A love story in which the man and woman learn to need and like each other and have concern for each other long, long before the meeting of bodies in delicate heart-felt, better than heat-felt, physical love.

Marybeth, sixteen at the . . . beginning [of ***Down By the River***], dreams of a future as wife and mother in a home by her beloved river. . . . Peter, her boy friend since sixth grade, pushes for sexual intimacy with subtle hints of "other girls" as a ploy to pressure her. Urged on by her very natural inclination, she feels the tug of innate common sense pulling her back. The story's resolution is an unusual one, emphasizing maturity as a question of emotional, not physiological, growth.

Normal adolescent feelings are explored in a manner close to earning the description "classy." Peter's weakness (he is a user of people for sympathy, support, admiration and sex) reveals itself gradually. The real hero moves even more imperceptibly to the foreground.

The nest-building urge *is* more common among women than feminists may acknowledge. Here it is given a dignity and status of a career choice acted upon by a heroine neither simple nor saccharine, but rather ordinary and appealing. ***Down By the River*** is contemporary enough to attract young-adult readers and they may not even spot the impressive philosophy hidden in the story. (pp. 400-01)

Hildagarde Gray, in a review of "Down by the River," in Best Sellers, *Vol. 41, No. 10, January, 1982, pp. 400-01.*

M. KAY HELLER

[In ***Down by the River***] Marybeth begins the story as a young married woman but we do not know the name of her husband. The author takes us back into Marybeth's life using flashback scenes where the present-day is indicated by the use of italics. . . .

Marybeth is a character who seems very mature in her thinking about many things and aspects of life. She has a basic loving, giving nature as she shows in dealing with her sister, Lily, who has cerebral palsy, and in her concern for the family next door. . . .

Teens will find this interesting despite the tendency to pat answers and stock characters. It does give an accurate picture of the difference between infatuation and love.

M. Kay Heller, in a review of "Down by the River," in Voice of Youth Advocates, *Vol. 4, No. 6, February, 1982, p. 28.*

ILENE COOPER

Dodie and Anne join forces in pursuit of two ghosts that haunt their summer home [in ***Footsteps on the Stairs***]. The supernatural elements work just fine, and the mystery of why two teenage girls haunt the house promotes lots of page turning. Less successful are the psychological snippets that give only superficial insights into the family dynamics. A quick, enjoyable read, this is like the ghosts themselves, short on substance but still a little scary.

Ilene Cooper, in a review of "Footsteps on the Stairs," in Booklist, *Vol. 78, No. 16, April 15, 1982, p. 1091.*

DREW STEVENSON

[Two] sisters investigate ghostly ***Footsteps on the Stairs*** . . . in the middle of the night, phenomena they believe to be connected to the history of the house itself. What emerges is the tale of two sisters of another era who are also at odds with one another, odds that ultimately led to their drowning deaths in the marsh. The present-day sisters are able to put the ghosts to rest while learning about themselves and their relationships to their parents. There's little mystery here, but the strong characterizations are at the heart of the plot, particularly that of humorously self-critical Dodie.

Drew Stevenson, in a review of "Footsteps on the Stairs," in School Library Journal, *Vol. 28, No. 9, May, 1982, p. 83.*

ELIZABETH PORGES WATSON

Footsteps on the Stairs by C. S. Adler is . . . ominously disastrous. The tiresome Dodie, who is distressed, and with reason, by her own general unattractiveness and by the fact that her new step-father seems fond also of his own daughter, tells what there is of a story. There are a couple of teenage ghost-sisters, *c*1944 vintage, being equally self-centred over a GI who . . . was stringing them both along. This is no doubt intended as a significant parallel to Dodie's own situation, but, as handled here, it merely doubles its fatuity. (p. 34)

Elizabeth Porges Watson, "Fantasy and Reality," in Books and Bookmen, *No. 322, July, 1982, pp. 33-4.**

DOROTHY NIMMO

[In ***Footsteps on the Stairs***] Dodie is one of those refreshingly energetic, quirky American heroines, a compulsive eater, an eccentric dresser, and a great disappointment to her widowed mother. . . . Dodie overcomes her step-sister Ann's initial coldness in the search for an explanation [of the ghostly footsteps they hear], but the ghost story is immaterial. It is the relationships between the characters which are the heart of the book. Dodie's resentment of her mother's expectations, her jealousy of Ann's relationship with her father and his obligations towards his divorced wife, Ann's resentment of her father's new wife—these are problems into which one is given a lot of insight and which must face a great many children in the aftermath of divorce. Here they are presented with sensitive lightheartedness through Dodie's defensive ebullient narrative.

Dorothy Nimmo, in a review of "Footsteps on the Stairs," in The School Librarian, *Vol. 30, No. 3, September, 1982, p. 249.*

DREW STEVENSON

The villain in . . . ***The Evidence That Wasn't There,*** is Malcolm Davis Orlop, who runs a genealogy scam conning people into the belief that they are heirs to a vast fortune. Kim and her friend Morey realize from the beginning that Orlop is a crook, however, their friends the Davises have been taken in . . . and ignore all warnings. When Orlop discovers that Kim may have a piece of evidence that could convict him, he begins a campaign of terror . . . that doesn't let up until the final pages. Deirdre Davis' reluctance to take a firm hand to stop her mother's disastrous folly and Kim's reluctance to confide in her own mother when she is scared to death seem unbelievable.

Despite these weaknesses, this is a good suspense novel with interesting characters and plenty of page turning chills.

Drew Stevenson, in a review of "The Evidence That Wasn't There," in School Library Journal, *Vol. 29, No. 4, December, 1982, p. 80.*

ILENE COOPER

In ***The Magic of the Glits*** . . . , 12-year-old Jeremy helped young Lynette overcome the death of her mother. Now, five years later [in ***Some Other Summer***], Jeremy is spending the summer at the ranch where Lynette lives with relatives. Lynette, who has romanticized Jeremy, expects the same devotion he once showed her, and she is disappointed when he exhibits more interest in her attractive teenage cousin. . . . The unhappiness this engenders in the "ever-good" Lynette causes her bad side to show, but the fact that her adoptive family can accept her imperfections gives her a serenity that puts Jeremy's indifference into a new perspective for her. Readers will be pulled into the situation, and their frustration at Jeremy's behavior will rival Lynette's own. Adler manages a real resolution that satisfies without being fairy-tale-like and, as usual, presents a polished story worth telling.

Ilene Cooper, in a review of "Some Other Summer," in Booklist, *Vol. 79, No. 7, December 1, 1982, p. 495.*

ZENA SUTHERLAND

In [***Some Other Summer***], a sequel to ***The Magic of the Glits*** . . . Lynette is now twelve, living on her uncle's ranch but always fearful that she isn't loved and may be sent away. . . . Not a great deal happens here, but what happens is important; the perceptive development of Lynette's maturation is part of the broader insight with which Adler handles her characters and their relationships. Characterization and dialogue are strong, the writing style competent.

Zena Sutherland, in a review of "Some Other Summer," in Bulletin of the Center for Children's Books, *Vol. 36, No. 81, January, 1983, p. 81.*

ILENE COOPER

[***The Evidence That Wasn't There*** is a] chilling yet totally plausible thriller. . . . When Malcolm Davis Orlop enters the Davises' lives, Kim knows he's trouble right from the beginning. . . . And when Orlop turns nasty because he thinks Kim has a letter of his, Kim has reason to be frightened. Unlike many mysteries, Adler's does not rely on coincidences to move the story along. Her characters are efficiently drawn and the plotting cagily planned. It will be hard for readers to put this down.

Ilene Cooper, in a review of "The Evidence That Wasn't There," in Booklist, *Vol. 79, No. 10, January 15, 1983, p. 672.*

FRANK PERRY

In writing [***Some Other Summer,*** a] sequel to ***The Magic of The Glits,*** C. S. Adler adroitly avoids producing a mirror image of her award-winning novel. Instead she switches the scenery from New Mexico to New York state, advances Lynette to a young teen and Jeremy to an old one. The result is a solid story which sings when 13-year-old Lynette rides her horse, Penny, or when she recalls that other summer when Jeremy, now 18, helped her overcome the trauma of her mother's death. Yet it spears holes into the myth that Prince Charmings always ride white horses and are eternally faithful. . . .

As with the Glits, Adler provides an amicable and unpretentious solution. When Lynette learned, with Jeremy's help, to trust in the future without her mother, now she learns to trust her own judgments and to accept the present. This is one story which readers will not just accept; they will embrace it.

Frank Perry, in a review of "Some Other Summer," in Voice of Youth Advocates, *Vol. 6, No. 1, April, 1983, p. 35.*

KIRKUS REVIEWS

[In ***The Shell Lady's Daughter,*** when] Kelly Allgood's sunny, enthusiastic mother has a mental breakdown, 14-year-old Kelly is peremptorily deposited by her business-pilot father with his rich, aloof parents in Palm Beach: in current juvenile fiction, practically a cliché. The protagonists are not usually so strong-spoken, however, nor so well matched. Kelly had been a little worried by her mother's vacant, recessive moods—but she didn't want the burden of being her mother's "best friend" any longer. . . . [It's] Kelly's share of Allgood iron will that brings the book to a four-square windup. Kelly learns that her mother tried suicide, and discovers (by making a forbidden call) that she's seriously depressed. She hears (from "dynamic," crippled lawyer Evan) that "love and support" are what her mother needs most—and fears she let her mother down. But she also learns about the feelings of unworthiness her mother had to overcome from childhood, relieving her (and her father) of guilt. And she sees in her grandmother's stubborn refusal to leave her senile husband an instance of "love and support" that she emulates, when her mother is released, by refusing to go away to boarding school. . . . There's wisdom in the handling of Kelly's mother's condition, and plenty of backbone in the story.

A review of "The Shell Lady's Daughter," in Kirkus Reviews, *Vol. LI, No. 7, April 1, 1983, p. 379.*

ZENA SUTHERLAND

[In ***The Shell Lady's Daughter***] Kelly's father is a pilot, away more than he's home; she calls him in a panic when her mother begins to act peculiar, but she's totally unprepared for the fact that that behavior was only a signal for a deep, suicidal depression. Packed off to stay with her ramrod grandmother in Florida, Kelly is worried, lonely, and resentful because she is told that she cannot even telephone her mother. Periodically, she remembers one of the "shell lady" stories Mother had told her, and wonders why they were always sad. Gradually, talking to her grandmother and father, and to a sympathetic neighbor, Kelly begins to understand her mother's problem, to feel convinced that love and support are needed; she announces she . . . will go home to be with her mother, who needs her. She has come to understand herself better: she is the king of the sea, the rescuer in all her mother's shell lady stories. Trenchant and touching, this is a book written with insight and compassion; the story has a natural flow and tight structure, and the few characters are sharply-etched and psychologically intricate and believable.

Zena Sutherland, in a review of "The Shell Lady's Daughter," in Bulletin of the Center for Children's Books, *Vol. 36, No. 10, June, 1983, p. 181.*

RUTH CLINE

[In ***The Shell Lady's Daughter***] Kelly feels guilty when her mother suffers a nervous breakdown, overdoses on sleeping pills, and is taken to the psychiatric unit of the hospital. . . . The title comes from the sad little stories the mother tells Kelly about the spirits who live in sea shells, revealing to Kelly, in retrospect, the truth about the mother's unhappy childhood. Well-written, good characterization of Kelly and the Grandmother, and a believable plot will make this book a favorite of young girls who are coping with unexpected events in their own lives. Values of family over material wealth are part of the theme.

Ruth Cline, in a review of "The Shell Lady's Daughter," in Voice of Youth Advocates, *Vol. 6, No. 3, August, 1983, p. 144.*

MARGARET C. HOWELL

[In ***The Shell Lady's Daughter,*** when] Kelly's mother is hospitalized for severe depression, [Kelly] is sent to live with her grandparents in Florida. . . . She remembers her mother's sad shell lady stories, in which the woman in the story always dies and is kept in a sea shell. These tales, scattered throughout the book, shed light on her mother's problems and help Kelly (and readers) understand that the seeds of depression were always there. The relationship between Kelly and her grandmother grows stronger as Kelly appreciates her grandmother's sacrifice to care for her senile husband, and the crippled man next door helps Kelly realize that love and support for her mother are important. When her mother returns home, Kelly decides to care for her. . . . One wonders why this decision was agreed upon when originally no one would tell Kelly, a mature 14-year-old, what was wrong with her mother. Too many themes and relationships detract from the story line and hinder the character development. (pp. 129-30)

Margaret C. Howell, in a review of "The Shell Lady's Daughter," in School Library Journal, *Vol. 30, No. 1, September, 1983, pp. 129-30.*

NANCY C. HAMMOND

Underneath a layer of contemporary problems—fortunately not belabored—lies a buoyant story of friendship and love between two vulnerable, appealing teenagers [***Roadside Valentine***]. Seventeen-year-old Jamie, a lonely boy living in a sleek condominium with his work-addicted father, renews a friendship with Louisa, his confidante in the fourth grade, who now struggles to be less bossy and more feminine than she used to be. Wary of alienating her boyfriend, she welcomes Jamie into her life on a strictly platonic basis. While he enjoys her large, animated family, . . . he begins . . . a playful but serious campaign for Louisa's affection. Nevertheless, . . . Louisa resolutely rebuffs Jamie's overtures. To break away from his father, Jamie acquires a job and an apartment; his increased self-respect and independence foster a new, awkward, but promising, relationship with his father. And Jamie's admiration and example help Louisa gain self-confidence and end her restraining romance. In Jamie, Louisa, and [Louisa's younger sister] May the author proves her ability to create well-drawn characters; yet, as if distrusting the reader's insight, she overemphasizes her points and almost caricatures Jamie's father and Louisa's boyfriend.

Nancy C. Hammond, in a review of "Roadside Valentine," in The Horn Book Magazine, *Vol. LIX, No. 6, December, 1983, p. 714.*

ZENA SUTHERLAND

[In ***Roadside Valentine***] Jamie has two big problems. One is that his father, a busy and taciturn doctor, doesn't communicate with him, . . . and can't ever forget that after Jamie's mother had walked out the boy had turned first to drugs and then to alcohol. . . . The other problem is Louisa, the girl Jamie loves; she's in love with someone else, and when Jamie carves a roadside valentine of snow, it precipitates a quarrel between Louisa and her swain. . . . Louisa, desperate because Jamie has ignored the signals she's given, rivals his valentine; she takes out a newspaper ad, "Louisa loves Jamie." It is the smooth style, strong characterization, and perceptive depiction of relationships that enlist the reader's sympathy to such an extent that the sweet ending doesn't seem sugary.

Zena Sutherland, in a review of "Roadside Valentine," in Bulletin of the Center for Children's Books, *Vol. 37, No. 5, January, 1984, p. 81.*

DREW STEVENSON

[In ***Shadows on Little Reef Bay***] 14-year-old Stacy loves living in a hotel on a beautiful Caribbean island with her mother, who is on sabbatical. Then she learns that Gladston, one of her native friends, has been arrested for drug smuggling. Convinced that the old man is innocent, Stacy sets out to help him. The number of suspects mounts as Stacy slowly begins to unravel the illegal operations. . . . Although she faces several brushes with death, Stacy's determination to get to the bottom of things and help her friend remains strong until the culprits are captured. Savvy mystery fans aren't going to believe much of these island shenanigans. The strength of Adler's novel is the tropical locale, which is ripe for adventure. ***Shadows on Little Reef Bay*** is breezy escapist entertainment to be enjoyed strictly for the fun of it all.

Drew Stevenson, in a review of "Shadows on Little Reef Bay," in School Library Journal, *Vol. 30, No. 9, May, 1984, p. 103.*

ZENA SUTHERLAND

[In ***Fly Free***] sensitive thirteen-year-old Shari, "Ape Face" to her abusive mother, Charlotte, feels loved only by her father, Zeke (who is away trucking much of the time) and by her younger brother, Peter. . . . When Peter is injured in a fall, Charlotte blames Shari, beats her in a rage, and reveals that Zeke is not Shari's father. Shari is helped through the crisis by Zeke and by Mrs. Wallace, an older woman who appreciates Shari and involves her in a bird-banding project. The family scenes are well-drawn, especially the tension of the abused child who suffers a parent's frustration and resentment. But the narrative is slow and sometimes simplistic: Shari's purity and Mrs. Wallace's home-baked bread and refinement opposed to common Charlotte "with a cigarette dangling from her sulky mouth" as she opens cans of spaghetti for dinner.

Zena Sutherland, in a review of "Fly Free," in Bulletin of the Center for Children's Books, *Vol. 37, No. 10, June, 1984, p. 179.*

BILL ERBES

Though Jamie's past involves problems with drinking and drugs, [***Roadside Valentine***] deals with his unrequited love for Louisa, and his deteriorating relationship with his father. Jamie and Louisa have been school chums for years, but now Jamie has become more interested in romance. . . . Jamie tries everything he can think of to win her over, and eventually, of course, he does. Along the way, though, he has a serious falling-out with his father and he moves into his own apartment.

I found Jamie and Louisa likeable. There is warmth and humor here, and, though a bit predictable, the story held my interest. Jamie's relationship with his father is not examined deeply enough, nor are Jamie's drug and alcohol problems. Still, this is a pleasant book. . . .

Bill Erbes, in a review of "Roadside Valentine," in Voice of Youth Advocates, *Vol. 7, No. 2, June, 1984, p. 94.*

KAREN STANG HANLEY

[In ***Shadows on Little Reef Bay,*** one] month into her art teacher mother's sabbatical on a small Caribbean island, Stacy's enthusiasm for the venture has waned considerably. . . . Stacy has made few friends, none of her own age, so she takes a personal interest when one of her acquaintances, Gladston, is jailed under suspicion of drug smuggling. Gladston, an elderly islander, is opinionated and ill educated, but Stacy instinctively feels that he is innocent. Determined to help her friend, she does some casual sleuthing around Little Reef Bay. . . . Proficient plotting and a convincing, fast-paced narrative distinguish this down-to-the-wire thriller. Adler's sensitive portrayal of Stacy's relationship with her innocently childlike mother lends depth and substance, while the well-realized Caribbean island setting . . . will capture readers who like their mysteries leavened with local color.

Karen Stang Hanley, in a review of "Shadows on Little Reef Bay," in Booklist, *Vol. 80, No. 19, June 1, 1984, p. 1395.*

GRETCHEN S. BALDAUF

[In ***Shadows on Little Reef Bay***] Stacy is convinced that her friend, Gladston, is innocent of smuggling drugs on a Caribbean resort island and vows to find the evidence necessary to clear him. . . . The Caribbean setting captured here is as common as a yellowbird sipping sugar; the island cadences in speech seem genuine. Clues to the real culprits are offered along the way for the astute reader. The characterization is generally good and the conclusion is plausible and satisfying.

Gretchen S. Baldauf, in a review of "Shadows on Little Reef Bay," in Children's Book Review Service, *Vol. 12, No. 13, July, 1984, p. 139.*

ILENE COOPER

[In ***Fly Free,*** Shari is] a misfit who is happier in the company of birds than she is being with people, and only her youngest brother and her father, Zeke, serve as buffers against her mother's biting words and cruel actions. . . . When the girl is befriended by Mrs. Wallace, a sympathetic neighbor who also loves birds and the wilderness, Shari finds the courage to deal with her feelings—and her mother—head on. Smoothly written, the story nimbly handles the complex dynamics of this family's relationships, though Charlotte, Shari's mother, is such a harridan that she borders on caricature. The metaphor of flight that links Shari's real father (a pilot), the girl's love of birds, and her own yearning to fly free is well woven into the story—clear yet not intrusive. An affecting, vivid novel.

Ilene Cooper, in a review of "Fly Free," in Booklist, *Vol. 80, No. 22, August, 1984, p. 1622.*

ETHEL R. TWICHELL

[In ***Fly Free,*** all but one of Shari's] brothers virtually ignore her; Charlotte, her emotionally unstable mother, occasionally abuses her; and her adored father Zeke is too often away on his trucking jobs. . . . If the portrait of Charlotte is sometimes overdrawn, her behavior and its effect on the family are dramatically pictured. In an otherwise appealing and sensitive story conversations occasionally become stilted lectures on birding or on the virtues of family love. But Shari's growth from timid isolation toward confidence and greater expectations is both believable and absorbing.

Ethel R. Twichell, in a review of "Fly Free," in The Horn Book Magazine, *Vol. LX, No. 4, August, 1984, p. 471.*

KAREN K. RADTKE

[In ***Fly Free,*** an] emotionally draining story, 13-year-old Shari keeps her hurt and resentment locked inside, her only way of defending herself from her unhappy, abusive mother. When she learns that her real father ran away before she was born, she is shattered, and the emotional strength she has built up begins to crumble. . . . [Her] love for her step-father and younger brother and her hope for a better future with her mother convince her to remain at home. Solid, realistic incidents remove the topic of physical and emotional abuse from the realm of the sensational and into the sadly commonplace. The characters' actions and feelings further this believability. . . . Her mother is given another chance, but she is neither forgiven nor excused by Shari or the author.

Karen K. Radtke, in a review of "Fly Free," in School Library Journal, *Vol. 31, No. 2, October, 1984, p. 153.*

Joan (Delano) Aiken

1924-

English novelist, short story writer, author of books for children, dramatist, and poet.

Aiken creates suspenseful, fast-moving, entertaining works for readers of all ages. Her stories are characterized by imaginative settings, intricate plots, rich detail, and bizarre incidents. Horror plays a significant role in her stories, with monsters, witches, and demons often contributing to a sinister tone. Aiken typically combines elements from such diverse genres as fairy tales, historical fiction, and gothic romance, resulting in an innovative approach. As Mary Cadogen and Patricia Craig declare: "There is nothing original about her plots, but she has brought to bear upon them a sensibility which *is* original, if only because of its ability to assimilate, re-channel, enliven, send up, make good use of elements and conventions already traditional." Aiken's infusion of humor into desperate situations also distinguishes her originality. Her characters battle such evils as the poverty of London's slums, kidnappings, and murderous villains, yet these terrors are presented on such an extreme level that they become less real, and therefore less threatening and more comic. Some critics contend that Aiken's skill lies in her ability to make absurd plots both believable and affecting, while others argue that exaggeration keeps readers from taking her plots seriously.

Some of Aiken's novels have been termed "unhistorical" because of their mixture of historical events with fantastic situations. Patricia Craig notes that "with her unhistorical romances, [Aiken] has created a new genre which far outdoes its conventional counterpart in inventiveness and wit." The settings of many of Aiken's "unhistorical" works is early nineteenth-century England. In some of these novels, a fictitious Stuart king reigns over a country beset by constant threats, including wild wolves and a violent group of Hanoverian rebels determined to assassinate him. This setting recurs throughout a series of novels: *The Wolves of Willoughby Chase* (1963), *Blackhearts in Battersea* (1964), *Nightbirds on Nantucket* (1966), *The Cuckoo Tree* (1971), and *The Stolen Lake* (1981). These books resemble nineteenth-century melodrama in their clear definition of good and evil. The fiesty heroine, Dido Twite, is featured in the majority of these works, and like many of Aiken's characters she is capable of fighting and overcoming enormous odds. Aiken received an Edgar Allan Poe Award for her mystery novel *Night Fall* (1969).

(See also *Children's Literature Review*, Vol. 1; *Contemporary Authors*, Vols. 9-12, rev. ed.; *Contemporary Authors New Revision Series*, Vol. 4; and *Something about the Author*, Vols. 2, 30.)

Photograph by Rod Delroy. Courtesy of Joan Aiken

SCHOOL LIBRARY JOURNAL

[***Died on a Rainy Sunday***] is advertised as a juvenile but could equally well be considered an adult gothic romance reminiscent of the book-length novels of suspense and terror included in women's magazines. Jane Drummond's architect husband, Graham, insists that she take back her old job temporarily to help meet spiraling expenses on the beautiful country home which he has just built. Jane hates to leave her two young children, but Graham hires Mr. and Mrs. McGregor as gardener and housekeeper and Jane dutifully begins commuting to London every day. She soon discovers that little Caroline is terrified of sadistic Mrs. McGregor, but spinelessly puts up with the situation because Graham refuses to fire her. . . . Readers will undoubtedly enjoy this romance-mystery, but a few may want to shake some sense into Jane.

A review of "Died on a Rainy Sunday," in School Library Journal, *an appendix to* Library Journal, *Vol. 18, No. 9, May, 1972, p. 92.*

ZENA SUTHERLAND

Joan Aiken, with her usual skill, builds an atmosphere of mounting terror [in ***Died on a Rainy Sunday***]. The McGregors are as convincingly nasty a pair as ever appeared in print, and the plot moves steadily toward its denouement, to disclosure and death.

Zena Sutherland, in a review of "Died on a Rainy Sunday," in Saturday Review, *Vol. LV, No. 21, May 20, 1972, p. 83.*

GEORGESS McHARGUE

A thriller by Joan Aiken is like an ice cream cone. Both must be consumed at a single sitting and both leave a cold but pleasurable feeling in the pit of the stomach.

Consider the situation [in **"Died on a Rainy Sunday"**] of Jane Drummond, wife of a successful architect, mother of two, former film writer, just moved into a beautiful modern house in rural Kent. All serene and typical. If Jane's husband Graham is worried about paying for their new abode, unable to make financial plans, a bit of a social climber, growing more and more remote from his wife and children, well, that's hardly unusual either. *Just half a turn of the screw, please.*

Now, if Jane accepts a temporary job with her old firm because of the unpaid bills and has to face all the oft-rehearsed conflicts of the working mother; and if Mrs. McGregor, the "local" who comes in to see to the children, is not only sly, cold and repressively neat but also (Jane suspects) malicious, cruel, and a poison-pen artist, what have we after all but another Mad Housewife? *Tighten a little more now . . . .*

Far be it from us to tell more. Or to reveal what goes on in the finale of **"Died on a Rainy Sunday."** Joan Aiken's triumph with this genre is simply that she does it so much better than most other practitioners. In this case, there is the added attraction of an intelligent, self-questioning heroine, rather than the ninny so often encountered in Modern Gothic.

Don't get the impression that the book is more than it claims to be: it lacks the scope and intricacy of the author's historical fantasies, such as **"The Cuckoo Tree."** This time round, Miss Aiken has given us a simon-pure chiller, delicious to the end. But then, so is a double-dip fudge mocha cone with nuts and jimmies.

Georgess McHargue, in a review of "Died on a Rainy Sunday," in The New York Times Book Review, *July 23, 1972, p. 8.*

THE JUNIOR BOOKSHELF

Librarians who know Joan Aiken's books written for children will be interested in this collection of short stories [***A Bundle of Nerves***] written for adults in magazines and offered to a younger readership. Most teenagers have a taste for the macabre, the horrific and the downright nasty. They are well catered for, with a little cannibalism, a teacher who murders one of his pupils and a mild case of lycanthropy. . . . The shock often comes in the last sentence and might even be missed by a careless reader. (pp. 169-70)

A review of "A Bundle of Nerves," in The Junior Bookshelf, *Vol. 40, No. 3, June, 1976, pp. 169-70.*

MARY CADOGAN AND PATRICIA CRAIG

[Joan Aiken's "unhistorical" adventure stories] have an exuberance, a pantomimic largeness which is . . . effective. There is nothing original about her plots, but she has brought to bear on them a sensibility which *is* original, if only because of its ability to assimilate, re-channel, enliven, send up, make good use of elements and conventions already traditional. She has effected a fusion of Gothic with Baroque, set off by a manneristic flair for detail, both idiomatic and ornamental. Her books have reputable antecedents in *Uncle Silas,* the novels of Thomas Love Peacock, Dickens, the Brothers Grimm, *Treasure Island* and John Masefield's "Kay Harker" stories. But Joan Aiken's Nightmare Abbeys are all her own, her "Midnight Folk" are given an unexpected location—they are ***Night Birds on Nantucket,*** "Hanoverian" plotters, whose drastic design is to fire a gun across the Atlantic which will slaughter the English king Jamie III at St James's Palace.

Joan Aiken has created, for her own purposes, a period in English history which never existed: the time is around 1832, but she has placed a Stuart king on the throne, infested the countryside with wolves and disgruntled Hanoverians, and erected a castle, a folly along the lines of the Brighton Pavilion, in Battersea Park. This device has a great economy: events which take place in an imaginary era obviously are not governed by restrictions of plausibility, either social or temperamental. The period's non-existence serves mainly to emphasize that the stories are not meant to be pegged to the ground, their purpose is to take off as stylishly as possible. In a time that never happened anything *can* happen: wild dashes by air balloon; encounters with flirtatious pink whales; rides to London on an elephant named Rachel.

In the first book, ***The Wolves of Willoughby Chase*** (1962), the Gothic mood predominates. . . . The principal girls in this story, Bonnie and Sylvia, are spirited but uninspired. Things happen to them, they have to deal with wolves and wicked governesses and suffer awful privations in an orphanage, but their characters are not developed, they lack the sheer perverse charm of the back-chatting urchin Dido Twite, whose appearance (in ***Black Hearts in Battersea***) is unheralded by the conventional build-up for a heroine. Dido "was a shrewish-looking little creature of perhaps eight or nine, with sharp eyes of a pale washed-out blue and no eyebrows or eyelashes to speak of. Her straw-coloured hair was stringy and sticky with jam and she wore a dirty satin dress two sizes too small for her." She is, however, an archetypal scene-stealer, but the author *has* built up qualities in her which make for an expansion of this rôle. She is emphatically not a cute or beaming child in the Shirley Temple tradition. She is forthright, scornful, tough; knowing in the usual way of a London street-child; completely "modern" in her lack of emotional encumbrances. She has no use for her relatives, just as they have none for her. She is resourceful, intolerant of any kind of dithering, and prone to encounter and get the better of a whole cast of villains, including a spidery West Indies witch and a sinister "Mr Mystery". Miss Slighcarp, the awful governess of ***The Wolves of Willoughby Chase,*** turns up again in ***Night Birds on Nantucket;*** she is passing herself off as the timid Pen's Aunt Tribulation, and sits up in bed exactly in the manner of Red Riding Hood's wolf. Pen (short for Dutiful Penitence), befriended by Dido on board a whaling ship, is a slender-reed type of person who needs the irrepressible, sensible Dido to prop her up.

Joan Aiken's one failure is with Simon, the central figure of ***Black Hearts in Battersea.*** Simon has a whole pastoral tradition behind him, which to some extent has had a flattening effect. He is a type of rustic, noble-natured boy who has made a success of bringing himself up in a wood, living on chestnuts, who turns out to be a prince—or at least the Duke of Battersea. With Simon there is a slackening of the author's controlling amusement; she almost presents him seriously. She has given him no quirks of temperament, no interesting rough edges. He is an amalgam of Dick Whittington, a babe in the wood who survived (his sister survived too, as it turns out) and Oliver Twist. He sets out for London with a donkey and a kitten, to study art at Dr Furneaux's Academy in Chelsea, and is embroiled at once in a situation of Hanoverian intrigue. He is, however, played off the stage by Dido Twite, whose heart he has won, incidentally, by providing her with a new dress, a replacement for the dirty satin one, "two sizes too small". The new dress serves its purpose, is ruined in a shipwreck, and Dido takes to dressing like a sailor boy. By now her character has evolved sufficiently to fit this costume. She and Simon lose sight of one another for a couple of years, but are reunited up a Cuckoo tree—a scene, however, which is left to the reader's imagination.

The richness of the books is underlined by their dramatic contrasts. There is opulence on the one hand and squalor on the other, and the characters are subjected to the most extreme experience of each. ***Midnight is a Place*** (1974) has its Midnight Court, a vast, stately, gentleman's residence set in a park, from which its hero, the boy Lucas Bell, goes out to work in the sewers of Blastburn. There is of course a comic sense, an unseriousness, which informs even the most horrific of Joan Aiken's events: horror is all on an extravagant level, which makes it less threatening, though it continues to stimulate. The books have a fairground kind of grotesqueness which is forceful and decorative. The fantasy which these stories contain is in no sense personal or nostalgically retrogressive; they are fanciful in a way that is formal, lucid and objective. (pp. 357-60)

Mary Cadogan and Patricia Craig, " 'Time Present and Time Past . . .'," in their You're a Brick, Angela! A New Look at Girls' Fiction from 1839 to 1975, *Victor Gollancz Ltd., 1976, pp. 355-72.**

BRIGITTE WEEKS

[***Go Saddle the Sea*** is a] formidable action suspense novel with carefully constructed historical background, set in early 19th-century Spain and England. Felix Brooke, born under mysterious circumstances into an aristocratic Spanish family, runs away and sets off to England to look for his dead father's family. His progress is picaresque indeed, perhaps too many dramas not to strain the practical sense of young readers, but it's all very exciting and fast moving if rather loosely strung together.

Brigitte Weeks, "Pharaohs, Horses, and Owls," in Book World—The Washington Post, *January 8, 1978, p. E6.**

SHIRLEY WILTON

[In ***Go Saddle the Sea***] Felix Brooke, orphaned and mistreated in the gloomy house of his Spanish grandfather, sets off to find the origins and family of his English father. Whether falsely accused of murder and imprisoned or kidnapped on the high seas by desperadoes who plan to transform him into a carnival freak and sell him, Felix remains the young Candide, an innocent journeying in a wild world and managing to survive a lifetime's share of trials and terrors. Aiken may not add anything new to the form of the 18th-Century English novel that she adopts here, but its style and conventions are faithfully reproduced with a full measure of suspense and humor.

Shirley Wilton, in a review of "Go Saddle the Sea," in School Library Journal, *Vol. 24, No. 6, February, 1978, p. 62.*

NAOMI LEWIS

Though the picaresque takes the place of magic in this rich and elegant yarn [**'Go Saddle the Sea'**], where is the line between? Orphaned Felix (father an English captain in the Peninsular Wars, mother a highborn Spaniard) is brought up by bitter Spanish relatives. But *is* he illegitimate, as they aver? No, says Bob the groom before he dies handing over the indecipherable letter. Move on and find your people, advises old Bernadine. So to the journey—precipice, duellists, convent, echoes of 'The Bible in Spain' and of Hugo's frightful 'L'Homme qui rit,' if I don't mistake. But the whole thing has a verve and tension that place it high among [Aiken's] full-length works.

Naomi Lewis, in a review of "Go Saddle the Sea," in The Observer, *March 26, 1978, p. 25.*

MARGERY FISHER

The details of Stuart Hughes's jacket (aggressive swan, snake-entwined clock, background patterned with skulls) announce powerfully the mood of these elegantly artful and brilliantly crafted tales [collected in ***A Touch of Chill***]. . . . [The] occasions for the tales are as ingenious as their atmosphere. Joan Aiken's prose has the relaxed air of reminiscence but it is in fact very concentrated and the necessary effects of suspense and strangeness are all the more telling for being unexpected. There are handsome rewards here for the alert and attentive reader.

Margery Fisher, in a review of "A Touch of Chill," in her Growing Point, *Vol. 18, No. 3, September, 1979, p. 3577.*

IRMA PASCAL HELDMAN

These 15 finely-honed, horrific tales [collected in **"A Touch of Chill"**] come from the pen of a sorcerer who spins her stories as easily as a spider spins webs. The ingredients are innocuous (cats who need tender loving care, an electrical storm, a birthday present, apple pie, a dentist's chair, a schoolroom before recess), and the situations both perennial and ordinary (extra guests for lunch, growing old in the century of the young and the bullying, a little girl's fantasy world). What Joan Aiken has done is to render them extraordinary, by adding just enough supernatural to an otherwise tranquil landscape to entice, then fascinate, and ultimately scare us.

I say "us," because it has long been known that Aiken country is not for young adults only. The atmosphere she creates is at first blush unbelievable but, on second thought, all too possible. The young tend to swallow her whole and clamor for more. They know, and she knows they know, that there is more to the outermost corners of all our lives than meets the eye. Adult readers, on the other hand, become disoriented. She creates a need in "grown-ups" to ground themselves in "reality" after reading her. . . .

It's been said that Joan Aiken writes rather like "Iris Murdoch gone into partnership with Agatha Christie." In the case of a macabre tale called **"Elephant's Ear"** and of another goody, **"It's a Long Way to Swim,"** both of which defy description, my own sense is that she writes more like Roald Dahl conspiring with Alfred Hitchcock or Daphne du Maurier. It's a good game; she's not easy to pigeonhole. . . .

Joan Aiken is witty, classy and original. She's worth losing sleep over.

Irma Pascal Heldman, in a review of "A Touch of Chill," in The New York Times Book Review, *April 27, 1980, p. 52.*

NATALIE BABBITT

Joan Aiken is so competent and experienced a writer, so sure of her language, her characters, her situations, that often it seems this should be enough, that the reader should and could ask for nothing more. These 15 stories [in ***A Touch of Chill***] . . . are as competent as should be expected; smooth, strong, sure writing, and a varied meal of moods. None of them particularly lingers in the imagination after the book is closed, none reflects the dismal brilliance of a genuinely macabre imagination, and yet they are very good.

They do not, any of them, go in much for the blood and gore that passes for horror in the movies these days, nor do any of them deal flat-out with the supernatural, also a common movie gimmick. Rather they run on the gray edge between order and chaos called so aptly the "twilight zone" by the old television series. . . .

What Aiken may lack of the aforementioned macabre imagination she makes up for to some degree by her mastery of scene setting and characterization. Throughout these stories, whatever their degree of success as suspenseful tales, the people seem real and move through beautifully detailed, evocative worlds both commonplace and bizarre. Aiken describes with equal skill the feel of a ship crowded to the gunnels with immigrants, and a dark house on a lonely moor. The reader feels she must have seen and known them all, that nothing is invented.

Yet, in spite of the author's skill, one comes away finally untouched, and it is extremely difficult to say why. There are ghost stories, read recently or long ago, that live on and on in the memory, never losing their power to raise gooseflesh. I wonder if these stories must not spring from minds that are bruised somewhere, that come to the edge of madness insofar as they seem thoroughly to believe, themselves, in the stories they tell—that they are haunted, themselves, and write for their own relief rather than to entertain a prospective reader. Perhaps an author must be himself struck with horror, to transmit that horror effectively to the reader. Poe's "The Tell-Tale Heart" is unforgettable. Even his poor old "Raven" still has the power to chill. There is a northwoods tale called "The Wendigo" (author unknown to me) that I would dearly love to forget. Coleridge's "caverns measureless to man" and even the lonely sea of his "Ancient Mariner" are permanent parts of the gloomy landscape of nightmares. And our own nightmares, swimming up from Heaven knows where, can leave us terrified.

Joan Aiken is perhaps too literate, and too sane, to bring this kind of story off supremely well. True horror has no sense of humor, that crowning attribute of sanity. Though Poe and his fellows were certainly gifted writers, their work seems to have rushed full-blown and shuddering from its dark inspirations; one would never think first of competence with them as one does with Aiken in this collection. For though the reader feels she must have known her settings, that nothing in that area was invented, still there is a definite sense of invention in her gooseflesh, a sense of conscious craftsmanship, a sense of manipulation rather than participation. In short, Joan Aiken seems not to be on the edge of madness. And perhaps that is the final sieve separating the sweat of hard work from the sweat of horror, making the final all-important difference.

These are finely crafted stories, but they won't keep anyone awake. Maybe that is all to the good. We have more than enough already to keep us awake these nights.

Natalie Babbitt, "Stories That Go Bump in the Night," in Book World—The Washington Post, *July 13, 1980, p. 8.*

JOHN ROWE TOWNSEND

A manual for beginning children's writers might well include the advice "Don't fool around with major legend", to which could be added, "especially Arthurian". The pitfalls are huge, and have been fallen into again and again. You can hardly hope to avoid anticlimax, trivialization of the material, and lack of credibility; and your efforts are likely to seem weak and ephemeral in contrast with the power and durability of the original.

Joan Aiken is no beginner, and there would be no point in warning her not to fool around with anything. She is a consummate fooler-around and getter-away-with-it. But does even Miss Aiken get away with reviving King Arthur in her new novel ***The Stolen Lake***? I'm not sure that she does. If you bring King Arthur to life, you not only have to make him sufficiently kingly; you have to provide him with a task and triumph of sufficient magnitude. Miss Aiken's Arthur is (understandably) depressed to find a fat, sinister, 1,300-year-old Guinevere waiting for him; he manages to reject her as a "selfish, wicked woman", to capture the city of Bath Regis without a battle and to organize its defences against a volcanic eruption; but even so, he doesn't really match up to the splendour of his reputation.

It would be unfair however to concentrate solely on the Arthurian element of ***The Stolen Lake.*** This is a novel with a vast amount of assorted content. It's an addition to the shamelessly unhistorical sequence which began with ***The Wolves of Willoughby Chase,*** set at a time when King James III is on the throne of England and Hanoverians are plotting on behalf of Bonnie Prince Georgie. Its heroine is the resourceful Cockney waif Dido Twite, and the action takes place mainly in New Cumbria.

New Cumbria is high in the Andes. It was founded in 577 A.D., when Romans and Britons fleeing from the invading Saxons set sail across the Atlantic and arrived in what is now Roman America. Peasants there speak Latin. New Cumbria is Britain's oldest ally, and when its Queen seeks help in recovering Lake Arianrod, stolen from her by King Mabon of neighbouring Lyonesse, the mission is entrusted to Captain Hughes of H.M.S. Thrush, who wisely takes Dido with him. . . .

Audacity and invention are Joan Aiken's stocks-in-trade, and she has unlimited supplies of both. ***The Stolen Lake*** is as wild and whirling a story as its predecessors, and if one feels a little less of the former breathless delight it may be merely because one is no longer astonished by anything Miss Aiken thinks up. Or perhaps, for me, it's the *lèse-majesté* involved in projecting poor King Arthur into all this schemozzle.

Some readers may wonder how you steal a lake. No problem. You wait until it's frozen and carry it away in blocks.

John Rowe Townsend, "Lèse-Majesté?" in The Times Educational Supplement, *No. 3389, June 5, 1981, p. 37.*

PATRICIA CRAIG

Joan Aiken, who remains unequalled as a purveyor of the preposterous, cheerfully rearranges history and geography to fit the requirements of her splendidly elaborate intrigues. In a time that never happened (the reign of King James III), of course, anything can happen: plots to fire a gun across the Atlantic; reunions up cuckoo trees. Like the other books in this exuberant series (after the first one) ***The Stolen Lake*** . . . has Dido Twite, 11 years old, to put paid to various kinds of conspiracy and nastiness; few readers, I think, will fail to relish the Cockney agility of Joan Aiken's engaging heroine. With her unhistorical romances, this author has created a new genre which far outdoes its conventional counterpart in inventiveness and wit.

Patricia Craig, "Blyton Punk," in New Statesman, *Vol. 102, No. 2646, December 4, 1981, p. 20.**

BRYNA J. FIRESIDE

Dido Twite, that feisty lass from the slums of London, first appeared in Joan Aiken's **"Black Hearts in Battersea"** and then reappeared as the heroine of **"Nightbirds on Nantucket."** Dido has surfaced once again. The adventure Miss Aiken has dished up for the intrepid 12-year-old in **"The Stolen Lake"** is zanier and more devilishly fiendish than ever.

A genius at mixing history and mythologies from diverse cultures, the author can make her readers believe anything is possible. This time her cast of characters includes a ship's steward who turns out to be King Arthur, reborn, and Queen Guinevere, who fled England after the Battle of Dyrham in 577 to "Roman America" and set up the kingdom of New Cumbria in exile. Now, nearly 1,300 years later, she still awaits the return of her husband. How has the Queen managed to defy death all these years? Why, by dining on the ground-up bones of young maidens. One young maiden's bones, we are told, is good for six months of life. . . .

Even though Miss Aiken has a penchant for trussing her heroine in gunnysacks and occasionally lapses into repetitiveness, **"The Stolen Lake"** is a novel that will keep good readers turning pages and less able ones scurrying to the dictionary. And the rare kid who knows Celtic myth, the Bible and Arthurian legend will chuckle even through the most gruesome episodes.

Bryna J. Fireside, in a review of "The Stolen Lake," in The New York Times Book Review, *February 14, 1982, p. 28.*

ANTHONY THWAITE

What Joan Aiken seems to have been after in **'The Young Lady From Paris'** is an attempt to blend elements of 'Villette' (Madame Beck is alluded to in a prefatory note) with George Eliot and Thomas Hardy, and to harness them to a strong redemptive plot.

The time is the late 1850s. Ellen is separated from her family, first in a pensionnat in Brussels, then in a 'situation' in Paris. At home, her widowed father retreats deeper into his gloomy recognition of his own lost promise and present failure. A shepherd wrongly imprisoned at his initiative has just been released after a long sentence. Turns and counterturns at last bring Ellen home, in the end to fulfilment.

The slow, dignified manner of much of the book is too overfurnished, especially in the Paris episodes, with tiny vignettes of Flaubert, Gautier and the like; and there is far too much play of the 'Oh, là là' and 'Eh bien' sort to show that though we are reading English the people are really speaking French.

Anthony Thwaite, "A Course in Creativity," in The Observer, *April 18, 1982, p. 31.**

BRYN CALESS

If a prodigious output is any indication of a successful writing formula then surely Joan Aiken has found it, for [***The Young Lady from Paris***] is her forty-fifth book, her eighteenth for adults. It also means that she will have established a devoted audience, whom criticism will not sway. It is therefore to the 'floating' reader that I address myself. Ellen (alias Hélène, alias Ellie) is the subject of the limerick-like title and heroine of this latest novel, and you would not believe the things that happen to her! I didn't. She is a teacher in Paris in the early 1860s, having previously been in Brussels and before that in Petworth. Her star is in the ascendent, as is her travelling. Beloved by, in order, Professor Bosschére, Raoul Ferté, Lawyer Wheelbird and Handsome Benedict, Ellen remains the serene heroine of magazine fiction. Not a hair out of place, always poised and virtuous, she persists through a series of escapades (which would have sent most real people to a nursing home), surviving the attentions of the least convincing of lesbians and a propensity on the part of characters to die in her vicinity. . . .

Ms Aiken writes the kind of prose to make you wince: French speakers (speaking in English) just have to throw in a *bon mot* or two in French to remind you who they are; coincidence abounds . . . ; and there's even a Great-Aunt Fanny to make all complete. 'My romances are quite intellectual' remarks one Parisian loftily—if only Joan Aiken's were, we'd all sleep sounder in our beds o' nights.

Bryn Caless, in a review of "The Young Lady from Paris," in British Book News, *August, 1982, p. 510.*

THE JUNIOR BOOKSHELF

Much as I admire Joan Aiken's towering baroque romances, the short-story form seems to suit the classical side of her genius. Here is the power which comes from economy of materials and firm, disciplined control of them.

The thirteen tales in this present collection [***A Whisper in the Night***] are all about the border country between common reality and the supernatural. They may be funny, pathetic, macabre, but always intriguing, always concealing a sting in the tail. One or two have been met before—notably ***She was afraid of upstairs*** which is a masterly and unsentimental story of child-death—but all call for several re-readings. . . . Nothing here calls for nightmares but plenty for thought and for the exercise of such emotions as pity and sympathy.

A review of "A Whisper in the Night," in The Junior Bookshelf, *Vol. 46, No. 5, October, 1982, p. 1921.*

DOROTHY NIMMO

[***A Whisper in the Night: Stories of Horror, Suspense and Fantasy***] is Joan Aiken's third collection of stories; one suspects they may be the ones she thought went a bit far. More stomach-turners than spine-chillers, they move from the titillating whisk-round-the-corner, dark-below-the-stairs into something altogether more cruel. The bear eats the baby and then its mother; the man buries it under the inscription 'Sultan, a Friend', and it isn't the bear's ghost that kills Mrs Cadell, who rents the old house, it is her husband. A hiker, working for his supper in the remote Highlands, uncovers a hidden door in the turret room and an old corpse falls on him. . . . These stories are too cruel for children and too cruel for adults, but I suspect fifteen-year-old monsters may enjoy them very much.

Dorothy Nimmo, in a review of "A Whisper in the Night: Stories of Horror, Suspense and Fantasy," in The School Librarian, *Vol. 30, No. 4, December, 1982, p. 355.*

MARJORIE KAISER

Bridle the Wind thrusts the reader immediately both into the mind of courageous thirteen-year-old Felix and into an amazing and complex adventure tale set in the 1820's in France and Spain. . . .

As in her other works, Ms. Aiken skillfully creates a masterful and rich plot while highlighting the unique characters that come alive on every page through realistic dialogue and sharp nature imagery. Good and evil are clearly delineated here, and readers will thrill at the bizarre and frightening events that ultimately lead to the destruction of evil. The novel in its archetypal and simple beauty will attract readers from age twelve on up. And every reader, male or female, will be in for a lovely surprise at the conclusion of the tale.

Marjorie Kaiser, in a review of "Bridle the Wind," in The ALAN Review, *Vol. 11, No. 2, Winter, 1984, p. 25.*

MARGERY FISHER

The heady atmosphere of ***Bridle the Wind . . .*** over-rides the necessity for more than a minimal knowledge of the facts of the Peninsular War. It is more of a help, in fact, to have read the earlier ***Go Saddle the Sea*** so as to be acquainted with the young hero, Felix Brooke, who, after ending a desperate journey in search of his English parentage, is now on his way back to a more secure home with his aristocratic Spanish grandfather. The second book can of course stand on its own. Felix's character is fully established during his second gruelling journey across Spain, this time in company with a skinny but determined youth, dramatically cut down from a gibbet, whose true identity is guessed more quickly by the reader than by perplexed Felix. Not only must the two lads guard against bandits, hunger and severe weather, but their path is dogged by the evil, tormented Father Vespasian, whose monastery, a haven for shipwrecked Felix, turned out to be a prison. The evil spirit which prolongs the monk's cruelty matches the sense of wild superstition and the atmosphere of the uncivilised corners of France and Spain through which the companions make their perilous way. Joan Aiken's pictorial, energetic prose, her unique mixture of bizarre humour and suspense, are at their best in this entertaining yarn of boyish loyalty and endeavour. (pp. 4180-81)

Margery Fisher, in a review of "Bridle the Wind," in her Growing Point, *Vol. 22, No. 5, January, 1984, pp. 4180-81.*

JENNY WOOLF

Surely aspiring writers must look upon Aiken's work and despair. And ***Bridle The Wind*** (a sequel to ***Saddle The Sea,*** only better) is up to her top standard. It tells of young Felix's terrifying flight across the nineteenth-century Pyrenees, with shadows of horror, evil and black magic in pursuit; and of how Felix's baffling companion Juan—first seen as a ghost—becomes only too four-dimensionally alive by the end of the book. Written with the wit, verve and conviction that characterises Aiken's work, ***Bridle The Wind*** is an imaginative tour-de-force.

Jenny Woolf, in a review of "Bridle the Wind," in Punch, *August 15, 1984, p. 45.*

Lloyd (Chudley) Alexander

1924-

American novelist, nonfiction writer, and translator.

A prominent author of fantasy fiction, Alexander is best known for his series of young adult novels collectively titled *The Prydain Chronicles*. Although these works contain classic fantasy themes, including the conflict between good and evil, they also address such concerns as the search for identity and the problems young people face growing up in a world with uncertain values.

Five books comprise *The Prydain Chronicles: The Book of Three* (1964), *The Black Cauldron* (1965), *The Castle of Llyr* (1966), *Taran Wanderer* (1967), and *The High King* (1968). These works, which are often compared to J.R.R. Tolkien's novels, are loosely based on the *Mabinogion*, a collection of ancient Welsh fables and myths. The central protagonist, Taran, is an impressionable young boy who becomes involved with an assortment of characters endowed with magical powers. Throughout the series, Taran and his friends embark on many dangerous adventures and battle evil forces that threaten their kingdom. Critics especially praise Alexander's realistic portrayal of Taran as a fallible individual who, in the course of the novels, matures from a naive assistant pig-keeper to the powerful and wise King of Prydain. Alexander has also written several novels for children that revolve around some of the minor characters first introduced in *The Prydain Chronicles*. His first fantasy for children, *Time Cat* (1963), relates the adventures of a cat with the power to travel through time.

With his recent trilogy, *Westmark* (1981), *The Kestrel* (1982), and *The Beggar Queen* (1984), Alexander began incorporating political and philosophical themes into his fantastic settings. He centers on the importance of human rights and explores consequences that arise from the misuse of political power for personal gain. These novels are set in the kingdom of Westmark and concern a group of freedom fighters who attempt to overthrow Westmark's oppressive government. Some critics fault Alexander for excessive didacticism, but others find convincing his insight into human character, and several note the parallels of Westmark and certain eighteenth-century European monarchies. Alexander's numerous literary awards include the 1969 Newbery Medal for *The High King*, a 1971 National Book Award for *The Marvelous Misadventures of Sebastian*, and a 1982 American Book Award for *Westmark*.

(See also *Children's Literature Review*, Vols. 1, 5; *Contemporary Authors*, Vols. 1-4, rev. ed.; *Contemporary Authors New Revision Series*, Vol. 1; and *Something about the Author*, Vol. 3.)

Photograph by Alexander Limont. Courtesy of Lloyd Alexander

HAROLD U. RIBALOW

Much has been written about John Brown, the famous Abolitionist, but little is known about the men who rode with him. One of them was a Jewish pioneer from Kansas, named August Bondi. How Bondi met John Brown and was fascinated by his personality; how Bondi risked his life for freedom and eventually settled down to become a distinguished citizen make up the material of Lloyd Alexander's [**"Border Hawk"**]. There is a great deal of warfare and bloodshed in **"Border Hawk."** Nevertheless, the author manages to inject—painlessly and usefully—thoughts about liberty, Americanism and the values of Judaism.

Harold U. Ribalow, "Fighters for Freedom," in The New York Times Book Review, *March 23, 1958, p. 36.**

ELLEN LEWIS BUELL

[**"Time Cat"**] is a provocative fantasy about Jason and his cat Gareth. Gareth takes Jason back into nine periods of time, with stops in ancient Egypt, medieval Japan, seventeenth-century Germany in the days of witch-hunters and New England in April, 1775. Filled with excitement and humor the book also leaves the receptive reader with some interesting reflections on human conduct.

Ellen Lewis Buell, in a review of "Time Cat," in The New York Times Book Review, *April 14, 1963, p. 56.*

MIRIAM S. MATHES

The Time Cat takes his young master on a journey into nine lives: Egypt: 2700 B.C., Rome and Britain: 55 B.C., Ireland:

411 A.D., Japan: 998 A.D., Italy: 1468, Peru: 1555, The Isle of Man: 1588, Germany: 1600, America: 1775. Each story is suspenseful and accurate in information, e.g., the British did wear bearskin helmets at the Battle of Lexington and Concord. The strong point of [**"Time Cat"**] is its good delineation of the character of the peoples living in the various historical periods. However, the episodic treatment fails to sustain excitement throughout, but this will appeal to good readers who enjoy an occasional fresh, humorous insight into history.

Miriam S. Mathes, in a review of "Time Cat: The Remarkable Journeys of Jason and Gareth," in Library Journal, *Vol. 88, No. 12, June 15, 1963, p. 2548.*

RUTH HILL VIGUERS

Welsh legends and mythology are the inspiration for [***The Book of Three***], a fast-paced chronicle of the imaginary land of Prydain. Some of the characters stem from legendary figures, but they have undergone metamorphoses to make them more integrated components of a completely new story. . . . Following the tradition of the great writers of fantasy, Mr. Alexander introduces his readers to a new and complete world. Time will tell how satisfying boys and girls will find the chance to live for a while in Prydain. I believe that the book will wear well, and that the children will be eager for other stories in which Taran may yet learn the meaning of heroism.

Ruth Hill Viguers, in a review of "The Book of Three," in The Horn Book Magazine, *Vol. XL, No. 5, October, 1964, p. 496.*

JANET ADAM SMITH

Though Lloyd Alexander's ***The Book of Three*** is fantasy rather than history, it too is firmly based on knowledge—this time, of the Welsh legends of the Mabinogion. In the splendidly realized country of Prydain, the boy Taran of Caer Dallben searches for a magic pig with his allies Gwydion, Elionwy, Fflewddur the Bard and Gurgi the creature of alliterative talk. Spied on by the dread bird gwythaints, captured by the Cauldron-Born, who are warriors of the evil Arawn, beset by wolves, confronted by the terrible Horned King whose head is a stag's, Taran comes at last to safety, and home, and the end of his youth. Here too the tone of the narrative is brisk and down-to-earth; as in T. H. White, voices of today echo in a fabulous world of dwarfs and warriors and talking creatures. It is a book to suit all who delight in *The Sword in the Stone*. (p. 16)

Janet Adam Smith, "Engines of Mischief: "The Best Children's Books of 1964," in The New York Review of Books, *Vol. III, No. 8, December 3, 1964, pp. 13-14, 16.**

BOOK WEEK—THE SUNDAY HERALD TRIBUNE

In writing of a land of Faerie called Prydain which he half-invented and half-borrowed from Welsh folklore, Lloyd Alexander has attempted in both [***The Black Cauldron***] and his previous one, ***The Book of Three,*** to be as "subcreative" as Tolkien in his *Lord of the Rings* trilogy. There is a sense of genuine enthusiasm for old Welsh Faerie in his books, an ability to fashion an interesting plot with magical elements and a fine style but so far he seems to us to have not quite brought it off. The characters and adventures are real enough but they are fitted into a legendary world that only half-exists for the reader, a world invoked more by the magic of the Welsh names than by any picture created by the author.

This story, however, seems more closely-knit and effective than the earlier one. Taran, the young assistant pig-keeper, sallies forth on a quest announced by Prince Gwdion, to snatch the black cauldron from the hellish kingdom of Arawn, lord of the Land of Death, in order to prevent the creation of more cauldron-born, immortal and evil fighters. Taran and his friends endure great hardships, learn the meaning of sacrifice and that a vainglorious braggart can become a hero, and a mighty king can turn traitor before the quest ends. (pp. 12, 14)

"A Touch of Faerie," in Book Week—The Sunday Herald Tribune, *May 9, 1965, pp. 12, 14.**

RUTH HILL VIGUERS

The chronicles of Prydain, begun in ***The Book of Three,*** are continued [in ***The Black Cauldron***] but each book is complete in itself. . . . At the beginning of the new book, a council of warriors meets and determines to find and destroy the great cauldron in which are created from the stolen bodies of the slain the dread Cauldron-Born, "the mute and deathless warriors" who serve the evil Lord of Annuvin. . . . The same kind of engagingly fantastic nonsense lightens this story as it did the first one; but the overtones here are more truly heroic. The reader's involvement is intense as the excitement leads up to the climactic meeting of tragedy and triumph. An exalting experience for the fortunate children whose imaginations are ready for great fantasy.

Ruth Hill Viguers, in a review of "The Black Cauldron," in The Horn Book Magazine, *Vol. XLI, No. 3, June, 1965, p. 274.*

RUTH HILL VIGUERS

[In ***The Castle of Llyr***] the Princess Eilonwy is captured and bewitched by the wicked enchantress Achren. Joining Taran, Fllewddur, Gurgi, and Kaw on the hazardous journey to rescue Eilonwy is Prince Rhun of the Isle of Mona, who expects eventually to marry Eilonwy. Rhun is well-meaning but quite lacking in judgment, and his bungling complicates and endangers the mission, plunging the loyal group into underground caverns where they must outwit the giant Glew and the tremendous cat Llyan. The story reaches dramatic heights with the struggle against the magical powers of Achren to restore Eilonwy to reality. Although this third book showing the growth of Taran, the young Assistant Pig-Keeper, toward noble manhood may not reach the powerful heights of ***The Black Cauldron,*** it has its own strong identity. . . . [Readers] will look forward to further adventures, for Taran and Eilonwy still have room to grow. (pp. 304-05)

Ruth Hill Viguers, in a review of "The Castle of Llyr," in The Horn Book Magazine, *Vol. XLII, No. 3, June, 1966, pp. 304-05.*

JEAN FRITZ

[Lloyd Alexander's Prydain series] is fantasy in the great tradition. Created by the tension between the good and evil forces in the world, it is wonderfully impossible on the one hand and utterly true on the other. The cast of characters is large: giants, princes, dwarves, sorceresses, kings good and bad. Each one, no matter what shape he assumes or what role he plays, is real and in very human ways.

Most important are the Companions. They are the ones who carry the burden of the story, and on three different quests save Prydain from disaster. Leader of the group is Taran, Assistant Pig Keeper, who is impatient to test his manhood. With him are Princess Eilonwy, who refuses to be left out of an adventure; Fflewddur Fflam, an unofficial bard with a flair for exaggeration; Gurgi, a perpetually hungry creature with hair like an owl's nest; and, finally, Doli of the Fair Folk, whose ears ring uncomfortably every time he becomes invisible. It is a brave company. They give Mr. Alexander an opportunity to mix humor with heroism, to explore what heroism is and to conclude that "For each of us comes a time when we must be more than what we are."...

While each of the books is a complete chronicle in its own right—exciting, highly imaginative and sometimes profound—the trilogy is a unit with a cumulative effect. The reader should, like this reviewer, plunge from one to another and pause only to praise.

Jean Fritz, in a review of "The Book of Three," "The Black Cauldron" and "The Castle of Llyr," in The New York Times Book Review, *June 19, 1966, p. 36.*

MARGARET SHERWOOD LIBBY

[Evil is personified] fairytale fashion, in ***The Castle of Llyr*** in which Lloyd Alexander continues his series about the fabulous kingdom of Prydain. . . . Although in imaginative depth and inventiveness they are a far cry from Tolkien's stories, they do combine in a lively manner elements from Welsh folklore with elaborately mythical adventures of odd and comical, if somewhat stilted, characters, quite to the taste of those just beyond the earliest fairy-tale age who enjoy complicated magical mixtures.

Margaret Sherwood Libby, "Types of Fantasy," in Book Week—The Washington Post, *August 21, 1966, p. 11.*

JEAN FRITZ

A former traveler returning to Lloyd Alexander's land of Prydain will welcome another quest with his hero, Taran, and will wonder if these new adventures [in **"Taran Wanderer"**] can possibly match those in the three earlier books. They do. This time Taran hopes to find out who he is by discovering the secret of his parentage. As usual, he meets danger on a grand and epic scale. . . .

In the end, through his own experience of failure and with the help of four master craftsmen, Taran learns that the secret lies not in his parentage but within himself. Like all men, he is both strong and weak, courageous and fearful; but at the same time he is an individual, different from everyone else.

Lloyd Alexander's triumph is that while his plots follow a slashing heroic pattern, his quest is into the subtleties of manhood itself. It is rare that high excitement yields such quiet wisdom.

Jean Fritz, in a review of "Taran Wanderer," in The New York Times Book Review, *April 9, 1967, p. 26.*

RUTH HILL VIGUERS

[Of the four books about Prydain, ***Taran Wanderer***], it seems to me, can most quickly capture the younger reader's interest, so soon is he plunged into excitement, as Taran and Gurgi start off for the Marshes of Morva to face the enchantresses of Orddu, Orgoch, and Orwen, from whom nothing is hidden, hoping to learn from them the truth about his lineage. . . . When a lie destroys Taran's dream of noble birth, he discovers how false, after all, were his hopes. Knowledge of his parentage could not reveal to him the secret of his own worth or his true place in life. As Taran begins seriously to examine his dreams and hopes, the story becomes more philosophical, but so deeply is the reader involved that there is no lessening of interest. Taran, who in the other books is the usual two-dimensional fairy-tale hero, in this story is more completely realized, so that the rather mature, thoughtful ending is very satisfying.

Ruth Hill Viguers, in a review of "Taran Wanderer," in The Horn Book Magazine, *Vol. XLIII, No. 3, June, 1967, p. 341.*

LILLIAN N. GERHARDT

[***The High King***] is a tremendously satisfying finish to what was so well begun in ***The Book of Three*** four years ago. . . . Here, Taran, the ambitious assistant pigkeeper who has grown from childhood throughout the series, becomes High King of Prydain, Princess Eilonwy becomes his queen, the predictions of Taran's wizard guardian Dallben are fulfilled, and the forces of black magic led by Arawn, Lord of Annuvin, Land of the Dead, are vanquished forever. These final battles are the fiercest and fastest in Prydain's history, and they cost Taran the death of companions like Coll, the warrior-farmer, and Rhun, the clumsy, well-intentioned young king. Victory also means the end of all the powers of white magic and the predestined departure from Prydain of all the men of Don, who exile themselves to eternal life in the Summer Country, which Taran and Eilonwy reject to assume responsibilities and mortality. The longstanding questions of orphaned Taran's heritage and the difference between royalty and nobility are adroitly handled. The author dedicates this book to ". . . the boys who might have been Taran and the girls who will always be Eilonwy" and that takes in just about all the confirmed romantic readers today . . . and all the readers to come for the strongest high fantasy written for children in our times.

Lillian N. Gerhardt, in a review of "The High King," in School Library Journal, *an appendix to* Library Journal, *Vol. 14, No. 6, February, 1968, p. 86.*

JEAN FRITZ

Reading the five books of the Prydain cycle is like listening to the movements in a symphony separately over an interval of time. Now with **"The High King,"** the concluding book to the cycle, one wants to stand up and shout, Bravo!

This time an enchanted sword stolen by Arawn, the Death-Lord, upsets the balance of power between the good and evil forces in Prydain. . . . Not until every magic resource on both sides has been exhausted and evil has been unmasked as good and good as evil does Taran, the recaptured sword in hand, slay Arawn and becomes victor over death itself.

Then comes Mr. Alexander's master stroke: the revelation of Taran's true destiny, a secret so well kept . . . , yet a secret so inevitable that the whole epic becomes a spiritual adventure with a new dimension. Bravo, indeed.

Jean Fritz, in a review of "The High King," in The New York Times Book Review, *March 24, 1968, p. 38.*

ELEANOR CAMERON

Lloyd Alexander is a perfect example of one who, before he could come into his own as a writer, had to discover that place which was, for him, the spiritual symbol or expression of something hidden. Geographical place most certainly exerted a power over it, and the experience of childhood was related. In an article, "The Flat-heeled Muse," an exploration of the necessity for logic and consistency in fantasy, he writes:

> Surely everyone cherishes a secret, private world from the days of childhood. Mine was Camelot, and Arthur's Round Table, Malory, and the *Mabinogion*. The Welsh research brought it all back to me. Feeling like a man who has by accident stumbled into an enchanted cavern lost since boyhood, both terrified and awestruck I realized I would have to explore further. Perhaps I had been waiting to do so all these years, and some kind of moment had come.

If one is to judge by public reaction to ***The Book of Three, The Black Cauldron, The Castle of Llyr*** and ***Taran Wanderer***, possibly it had. . . . Here at last he entered the enchanted cavern and thus could be wholly happy and released because he was writing about what was intimately related to childhood, to what he had loved as a child. The cavern returned him to a private country of the mind which was, in a way, a geographical place but, even more potently, the habitation of Arthur, the landscape and atmosphere of Arthur, which so possessed him that out of it he could write four books in five years, the Prydain cycle, which children, apparently, have taken to with delight despite the strangeness and difficulty of the y-fraught names. (pp. 185-86)

Eleanor Cameron, "A Country of the Mind," in her The Green and Burning Tree: On the Writing and Enjoyment of Children's Books, *Atlantic-Little, Brown, 1969, pp. 163-202.**

MARGARET A. DORSEY

[***The Marvelous Misadventures of Sebastian*** is a] solid adventure story with likeable protagonists, set in the imaginary kingdom of Hamelin-Loring. Sebastian is a young fiddler, not overly dedicated but enjoying his relatively easy life in a country baron's household. But the kingdom is growing uneasy under politically and financially repressive rule of the Regent Grinssorg, as Sebastian discovers when he loses his place with the baron and must seek his future elsewhere. When he meets the runaway Princess Isabel, his wanderings take on a new purpose: to help the orphaned girl escape forced marriage to the Regent. Sebastian and Isabel are befriended by mild-mannered Nicholas, who turns out to be the chief organizer of popular resistance to the Regent; they join a circus, and Sebastian acquires a strange fiddle which produces music of unearthly beauty and power and which eventually helps him to decide on his future course. The action—both physical (a multitude of narrow escapes) and psychological (the gradual humanization of haughty Isabel)—will hold young readers' attention; and the characters, whether sympathetic, like Nicholas, or villainous, like the bloodthirsty barber who dogs Sebastian's steps, are similarly involving. When he's not trying to be profound and epic, as in the Prydain books, Mr. Alexander writes a jolly good story and still manages to provide his readers with plenty of food for thought.

Margaret A. Dorsey, in a review of "The Marvelous Misadventures of Sebastian," in School Library Journal, *an appendix to* Library Journal, *Vol. 17, No. 3, November, 1970, p. 104.*

PAUL HEINS

In form, [***The Marvelous Misadventures of Sebastian***] suggests an eighteenth-century roadside novel, the chapters being typically headed by such titles as How Sebastian Had a Bucket on His Head, or How Sebastian Reached for the Moon. The characters are puppetlike but full of animation—in the manner of Dickensian or Hogarthian caricatures: the murderous barber in the pay of the tyrannical Regent of Hamelin-Loring; Isabel, the princess who can rarely forget the formality of her court speech and her upbringing; Sebastian himself, a Chaplinesque character, forever picking himself up after each disaster and forging on to what life has next to offer.

But up and above the lively episodes and the lively characters, soar the melodies of Lelio's violin, which comes into Sebastian's possession when he and Isabel join the Gallimaufry-Theatricus, a group of strolling entertainers. The strangely enchanted and enchanting instrument is more player than played upon and catches up both listener and performer alike in the magic of its music. More than once the "unbearable beauty" of the "song of the violin" threatens death to Sebastian and more than once is he called back to himself by Presto, his faithful cat. For the beauty of the violin's voice is as fatally enticing as the Sirens' song or as the voice of the Lorelei.

The story is a comic fantasy, successfully combining eighteenth-century briskness with romantic "moonshine." It can be read as an exciting series of adventures, of which many of the chapters end with a suspense line. Or it can be read as an allegory on the ambivalent power of beauty. Or—best of all—it can be read as the story of Sebastian's apprenticeship to life.

Paul Heins, in a review of "The Marvelous Misadventures of Sebastian," in The Horn Book Magazine, *Vol. XLVI, No. 6, December, 1970, p. 628.*

SIDNEY LONG

[**"The Cat Who Wished to Be a Man"**] is a mock medieval adventure complete with a crotchety wizard, a naive and good-hearted hero, a spirited heroine, a trusty, phrase-making friend, and a pair of unscrupulous villains. They are variations of characters the author has dealt with so often that he probably could have written the book in his sleep. Even in spite of all the last-minute, last-sentence-in-the-chapter surprises, it is filled with the kind of predictability that can result when a writer is too much in control of the developing action. . . .

Instead of a fantasy about a cat in a man's form, the story is really just another version of a country boy up against some city slickers. As such, it is beautifully written and eminently readable, but it is a concoction rather than a creation. It doesn't end so much as disappear, leaving the reader to wonder if it isn't Lloyd Alexander rather than the wizard Stephanus who has mastered sleight-of-hand.

Sidney Long, in a review of "The Cat Who Wished to Be a Man," in The New York Times Book Review, *September 30, 1973, p. 10.*

ETHEL L. HEINS

Transforming animals into men offers all sorts of challenging opportunities to a born storyteller. George Selden's dog-turned-man in *The Genie of Sutton Place* . . . combined many winning characteristics of both creatures. An equally amusing metamorphosis occurs in [***The Cat Who Wished to Be a Man***], when a high wizard's cat is granted human shape. It was Lionel, himself, who, given the power of speech by his master, begged for a brief fling in the world of men. . . . [Alexander] blends some of his favorite ingredients to produce a savory mixture. In the style of classical comedy he makes full use of broadly exaggerated stock characters: Pursewig, the greedy Mayor; Swaggart, the villainous Captain of the Watch; Dr. Tudbelly, the bombastic, Latin-quoting *"Medicus illustrius"*; and the comely Mistress Gillian, the innkeeper, for whom Lionel joyfully renounces his feline nature and becomes a total human being. A comic and ebullient fantasy; just right for reading aloud. (pp. 463-64)

Ethel L. Heins, in a review of "The Cat Who Wished to Be a Man," in The Horn Book Magazine, *Vol. XLIX, No. 5, October, 1973, pp. 463-64.*

JEAN FRITZ

Bard, wizard, founder of the kingdom of Prydain, Lloyd Alexander displays all his skills as he returns to the scene of his famous chronicles [in **"The Foundling and Other Tales of Prydain"**]. He comes now primarily, it seems, as a master weaver to pick up threads in his tapestry, to fill in scattered bits of background. The characters are familiar to those of us who have adventured before in Prydain, but in this book we journey further back both in time and mystery.

Who, for instance, really was Dallben? [A] three-hundred-and seventy-nine-year-old enchanter when we first met him, he must, of course, have an extraordinary history. And so in the first of these six tales Mr. Alexander explains that Dallben was a foundling, abandoned in a basket at the edges of the evil Marshes of Morva, home of the three hags who guard so much of the country's magic. And Doli of the Fair Folk? No mystery here, but it is a pleasure to have him back, short-tempered, in trouble as usual, soured on humankind and small wonder. Even in this early encounter, Doli found man to be a bumbling creature, sighing for the gift of eternal youth instead of settling on something useful like a cook pot. In other stories we learn the history of Drynwyn, the magic sword—all powerful if used in a good cause; we meet Princess Eilonwy's mother, who had the good sense to recognize a true magician when she saw one; we see the Lord of Death, disguised as usual, tempting man, succeeding often but not always.

Although the time frame of these stories is not far removed from the chronicles themselves, it is as if Lloyd Alexander were reaching deep into the cauldron where first stories simmer to find a mythic underpinning for his mythic world. . . . Yet in their final form the tales are pure Alexander and true to Prydain. And the winners in this world? They are the poets, of course, and the lovers. Those who know the magic words. Those who, like Lloyd Alexander himself, are able "to see around the edges of things."

Read these tales before or after the chronicles, or independently—no matter. The important thing is to go to Prydain. (pp. 48, 50)

Jean Fritz, in a review of "The Foundling and Other Tales of Prydain," in The New York Times Book Review, *November 4, 1973, pp. 48, 50.*

KIRKUS REVIEWS

[***The Foundling and Other Tales of Prydain***] demonstrates both the author's special talent for spinning this kind of story and the extent of his need to borrow plots and motifs on which to build. The foundling of the title story is the enchanter Dalben as a child, adopted by three hags who send him off with his chosen gift of wisdom after he (recalling Taliesin) acquires knowledge by licking the fingers he has burned while stirring their magic potion. The other five stories are more generally familiar and their connection with Prydain more gratuitous. . . . [They are all] worth another hearing as Alexander tells them, but hardly an important contribution to a mythological landscape. (pp. 1308-09).

A review of "The Foundling and Other Tales of Prydain," in Kirkus Reviews, *Vol. XVI, No. 23, December 1, 1973, pp. 1308-09*

BRIAN ATTEBERY

Despite my love of fantasy and of all the shining figures of myth and romance, I tire of meeting Arthur and Merlin and their Celtic forerunners in story after story. I would not grow weary, however, if these stories breathed new life into their heroes and wizards: if, like T. H. White in *The Once and Future King*, they boldly reinvented the whole Arthurian sequence. A step below White, certainly, but genuinely interesting are the children's fantasies by Lloyd Alexander known as the ***Chronicles of Prydain.***

The Chronicles take place, not in an Arthurian setting, but in the mythological Wales that preceded Arthur, altered a bit to make it conform to the Tolkienian pattern. It has an Aragorn figure called Gwydion, a Gandalfish wizard called Dallben, a dwarf named Doli, a softened Gollum called Gurgi, and a boy hero, Taran, who is hobbitlike because of his comic innocence and small size. The first story, ***The Book of Three,*** is no more than a clever imitation of Tolkien, lighter in tone than its model and based primarily on Welsh myth, rather than a combination of Northern motifs. By the last two books, however, Taran has grown up, the land of Prydain has taken on a degree of solidity, and the author has found in his story an outlet for some real philosophical exploration.

Interestingly enough, the ***Chronicles of Prydain*** become most engaging when Taran reveals himself to be a hero in the American grain. In the fourth book, ***Taran Wanderer,*** he becomes, as the title indicates, a wanderer, an experimenter, a seeker after an identity that always seems to lie over the next hill. In his metamorphoses and in his restlessness he resembles Hawthorne's Holgrave, Cooper's Leatherstocking, and that other orphan, Twain's Huckleberry Finn. And in the final volume, ***The High King*** . . . , Taran finds his identity, as Americans have throughout our literary tradition, in the future rather than the past. Without ties or ancestry, and with a wife who renounces her own heritage, he becomes King of Prydain and leads it into a new, unmagical age. Like the nameless couple in Hawthorne's short story, "The Maypole of Merrymount," Taran and Eilonwy stand together at the end of the story, shorn of the trappings and enchantments of a lost age, ready to move together into a soberer world. It is a moving ending and an appropriate one, an ending which is the natural flowering of the cross between alien motifs and the author's own culture. (pp. 156-57)

Brian Attebery, "After Tolkien," in his The Fantasy Tradition in American Literature: From Irving to LeGuin, *Indiana University Press, 1980, pp. 154-86.**

JEAN FRITZ

Lloyd Alexander is obviously a bard who has traveled the roads of many kingdoms, perfecting the art of storytelling and becoming ever more wise in the ways of humankind. Like a juggler, he keeps four stories going at once in [**"Westmark"**]: tossing them lightly apart, calling them together, crisscrossing their paths until at last he has described a complete circle. Of course there is always the danger that power-hungry Cabbarus, chief minister to a grieving, ineffective king, will bring the other stories crashing down to an evil end. He comes close to it many times. . . .

The wisdom of the book lies in its difficult solution: good does not triumph over evil simply because it *is* good. Theo, the printer's apprentice, may think so at first when he wants to face his accusers and confront injustice head-on. Yet is he himself completely innocent? He had always believed in his own good nature, but he finds himself lying, swindling, even trying to kill. He may be acting in the cause of justice, but still—"What kind of person does that make me?" he asks.

"No different from anyone else," he is told.

Lloyd Alexander does not answer questions; he raises them. Who can be certain what he'll do in any given situation? Can right even exist in a pure form? As grave as these considerations are, Mr. Alexander keeps his adventures spinning and in the end we are happy at how it all turns out.

Jean Fritz, in a review of "Westmark," in The New York Times Book Review, *May 10, 1981, p. 38.*

ETHEL L. HEINS

[***Westmark,*** the] author's most inventive book in many years is both a picaresque novel and an energetic cloak-and-dagger tale with a climax as breathtaking as that of a Douglas Fairbanks film. . . . [The] author maneuvers the crisscrossing threads of his complex, but brilliantly controlled, plot, which is filled with bloodshed, intrigue, ghostly apparitions, disguises, and trickery. Lacing the storytelling with incisive epigrammatic wit, he presents the reader with the age-old perplexities of right and wrong, human weakness and decency, the temptation of power, and the often unclear call of conscience. (pp. 428-29)

Ethel L. Heins, in a review of "Westmark," in The Horn Book Magazine, *Vol. LVII, No. 4, August, 1981, pp. 428-29.*

DENISE M. WILMS

[Readers of ***Westmark*** will welcome ***The Kestrel,*** a] brimming continuation of the story of Theo, Mickle, and their colorful comrades. Here Westmark finds itself at war when King Augustine dies and the neighboring kingdom of Regia invades. At issue is the direction Westmark will take with Mickle, now Queen Augusta, on the throne. Her democratic sympathies and social conscience threaten the aristocracy, who are in collusion with their Regian counterparts to dethrone their "Beggar Queen." What happens to Theo and Mickle is too complicated to detail; suffice it to say that the moral dilemmas Theo faced in ***Westmark*** are compounded here, and that the cruelties of war transform him into an uncharacteristically aggressive fighter whose soul is in profound despair at the conflict's end. The story's pace flags a bit as war logistics unfold, but not for long; there's always a quick turn in store, and some hard questions to ponder between the lines. The tale is an ambitious one, more complex and slightly less nimble than its predecessor, but ultimately no less satisfying.

Denise M. Wilms, in a review of "The Kestrel," in Booklist, *Vol. 78, No. 16, April 15, 1982, p. 1091.*

HAZEL ROCHMAN

The high adventure and picaresque comedy of ***Westmark*** [moves in its sequel, ***The Kestrel,***] into a more realistic and complex narrative form as the struggle for power in the kingdom erupts into betrayal, war and foreign invasion. The fast-paced plot, subtleties of character, ironic wit, quiet understatement and pervasive animal imagery—all work with superb concentration to undercut the heroics of war, its slogans, uniforms and myths of comradeship and glory. . . . Alexander's range is wide, and he moves easily from the brutality to the absurdity of war. Peace is brought about, not by any battle, but by a combination of accident and the Queen's clear-eyed acceptance that there has to be a compromise, since neither side can win. (p. 64)

Hazel Rochman, in a review of "The Kestrel," in School Library Journal, *Vol. 28, No. 8, April 15, 1982, pp. 64-5.*

GEORGESS McHARGUE

There are not many political novels for young people, so we should probably be glad when a new one comes along. . . .

[**"The Kestrel"**] brings its characters face to face with a number of ethical and political dilemmas. Is unenlightened monarchy any better than enlightened despotism? Should the press be free to criticize the good as well as the bad? How can there be peace unless one is ready to kill for it?

There is a lot going on in **"The Kestrel,"** some of it quite exciting as adventure literature, but the story loses vitality because Lloyd Alexander seems determined to make issues come before character, language, atmosphere or even emotion. Poor Theo, in his journey from printer's devil to bloodthirsty tyrant, is a tool for instruction rather than a character we can care about. Even his constant self-questioning seems less a trait of character than a means of discussing issues. The big scene in which he shoots at and wounds Mickle seems patently contrived.

No one can fault Mr. Alexander for his commitment to ideas, but the hand of the puppeteer is a little too much in evidence here.

Georgess McHargue, "A Political Education," in The New York Times Book Review, *April 25, 1982, p. 47.*

SPENCER G. SHAW

[Lloyd Alexander] has given invaluable gifts to the world of literature for children in his treasure trove of creative works of fantasy. Recognizing a need for an active process of "hopeful dreaming" rather than a passive, isolated dependence upon "wishful thinking," this skilled author offers opportunities to his youthful followers to engage in never-ending quests. They adventure through the ***Prydain Chronicles*** with Taran, the Assistant Pig-Keeper, perceive the subtle humor in ***The Town Cats and Other Tales,*** delight in the antics of ***The Cat Who Wished to Be a Man.*** They wander wonderingly through the interconnecting twists and turns of good and evil in ***Westmark*** and ***The Kestrel.*** . . . In his multiple works with an infusion of myth, fantasy, and reality, Lloyd Alexander shares with eager readers a needed catalyst "to explore the infinities of the inner spirit, to seek to transplant understanding, compassion, and love from one person to another." Lloyd Alexander, we thank you for your priceless literary gifts. (pp. 471-72)

Spencer G. Shaw, "Laura Ingalls Wilder Award Presentation," in The Horn Book Magazine, *Vol. LIX, No. 4, August, 1983, pp. 471-73.**

KAREN STANG HANLEY

[The chronicle begun in ***Westmark*** and carried through in ***The Kestrel***] is brought to a brilliant climax in [***The Beggar Queen,***] a novel that skillfully completes this landmark, award-winning trilogy. The consular government established by Florian at the end of the war with Regia is already threatened from within when it is violently overthrown by the officer corps, who recognize onetime prime minister Cabbarus as director of a new "egalitarian" regime. . . . Justin, the embittered revolutionary, angrily retires to the countryside with his band of partisans; and Mickle, Westmark's much-loved "beggar queen," with her fighter/fiancé, Theo, engineer a bloody resistance movement from the district of Marianstat known as The Shambles. The fast-paced, intricately plotted, and often surprising narrative deftly balances violence and death with love, loyalty, and deep friendship; ironies are gently tempered with drollery and wit. Some old friends from previous books meet their ends, while others move closer to center stage. . . . Considered as a unit, the trilogy has a remarkable depth and symmetry, and while the political and philosophical overtones are pronounced, they never dominate the story.

Karen Stang Hanley, in a review of "The Beggar Queen," in Booklist, *Vol. 80, No. 16, April 15, 1984, p. 1186.*

MARY M. BURNS

The concluding volume of the ***Westmark Trilogy*** [***The Beggar Queen***] resolves the fates of the characters through a surprising, carefully wrought climax. Although references to earlier events are smoothly integrated into the text, they cannot fully convey the skill of the author's complicated, fully realized characterizations. Emphasis on action and dialogue rather than explanation heightens tension and intensifies the final drama of Westmark's political evolution but would perhaps confuse those unacquainted with its earlier history. . . . Despite the conflicting theories of the leaders, the fate of Westmark is ultimately determined by its citizens—not by ideologues. Justin dies in battle; Florian survives to become part of the new country; but, ironically, Mickle and Theo, for the common good, must choose exile. Yet, as Mickle sagaciously observes, they have each other and "all the rest of the world"—a reassuring conclusion to a panoramic, romantic adventure story of epic proportions. In creating a country of the mind the author offers a commentary on the dynamics of revolution and insight into the tragic flaws of leaders like Justin whose concentration on the attainment of an ideal overrides a concern for humanity—represented in all its facets by a varied and memorable cast of heroes, rogues, charlatans, and scholars. Some are larger than life; others quite ordinary; but each character is unique and important.

Mary M. Burns, in a review of "The Beggar Queen," in The Horn Book Magazine, *Vol. LX, No. 4, August, 1984, p. 472.*

DIANE C. DONOVAN

War and revolution in a compact, small society often bring a lasting sense of social unrest not easily quelled by dictator, monarch or democracy: this fact is revealed [in ***The Beggar Queen***] when the scheming Cabbarus seizes control of Queen Mickle's kingdom, forcing her and her colleagues into exile. . . .

The reader follows the exploits of several of the Queen's colleagues of the lower class gutter snipes Weasel and Sparrow, whose street knowledge allows them intimate insights into the underlying feelings of the people; Justin, Florian and Theo, political opposites who both intentionally and unintentionally use the public for political gain; and other, lesser characters whose goals and sacrifices are made for the good of social causes. . . .

The Beggar Queen concludes Alexander's ***Westmark Trilogy,*** following the political changes and choices of a kingdom and the exploits of Mickle and her friends. Readers already familiar with ***Westmark*** and ***The Kestrel*** will find this concluding title more satisfying than would a newcomer to the series; and while casual young adult readers might tire of the political struggles of the protagonists, those interested in issues of political control, social unrest, and the politics and morals of war will find this a thought-provoking story.

Diane C. Donovan, in a review of "The Beggar Queen," in Best Sellers, *Vol. 44, No. 6, September, 1984, p. 228.*

Maya Angelou

1928-

(Born Marguerite Johnson) American autobiographer, poet, short story writer, scriptwriter, dramatist, nonfiction writer, composer, and editor.

Best known for *I Know Why the Caged Bird Sings* (1970), the first of her series of autobiographies, Angelou has led a highly diverse career. In addition to writing poetry and prose, Angelou has performed as a singer and dancer, she has written, directed, and acted in plays and films, and she has composed musical scores. She has also been active in the fight for black civil rights. With the film *Georgia, Georgia* (1972) she became the first black woman to have an original script produced. Largely due to the success of the first volume of her autobiography, both Angelou's life and her writings have elicited great interest. She is widely respected as a dynamic individual who has overcome many of the obstacles faced by black American women. Her life is a testimony to her stated belief: "You may encounter many defeats, but you must not be defeated."

I Know Why the Caged Bird Sings chronicles the early childhood of Angelou and her brother Bailey, spent mainly with their grandmother in Stamps, Arkansas, a rural southern town "no bigger than its own squint-eyed view of the world," as Lynn Darling describes it. In the process of depicting a child's perspective of the bewildering world of adults, Angelou creates a poignant account of a black girl's coming-of-age. The book also provides insights into the social and political tension which characterized the 1930s. Critical reception to this work has been almost unanimously positive. Annie Gottlieb asserts that "Angelou accomplishes the rare feat of laying her own life open to a reader's scrutiny without the reflex-covering gesture of melodrama or shame. And as she reveals herself so does she reveal the black community, with a quiet pride, a painful candor and a clean anger." Reviewing the recently released British publication of *I Know Why the Caged Bird Sings,* Paul Bailey declares, "If you want to know what it was like to live at the bottom of the heap before, during and after the American Depression, this exceptional book will tell you."

The next three volumes of Angelou's autobiography—*Gather Together in My Name* (1974), *Singin' and Swingin' and Gettin' Merry Like Christmas* (1976), and *The Heart of a Woman* (1981)—follow her as she emerges out of a painful and oppressive childhood to become a leading figure in the political and literary movements of contemporary American society. Her personal and political involvement with civil rights, her evolving relationship with her illegitimate son, and her probing insights into herself and her life are recurrent themes throughout the series. Although these subsequent volumes have not received the acclaim awarded *I Know Why the Caged Bird Sings,* critics continue to praise Angelou's narrative skills and her impassioned response to challenges in her life.

Angelou's poetry, like her prose, is highly rhythmic, reflecting the dialects of her heritage. Her collections consist of *Just Give Me a Cool Drink of Water 'Fore I Diiie* (1971), *Oh Pray My Wings Are Gonna Fit Me Well* (1975), *And Still I Rise* (1978), and *Shaker, Why Don't You Sing?* (1983). Although her poetry has contributed to her reputation, most critics reserve their

Gamma-Liaison

highest praise for her prose. The short lines, easy diction, and heavy dependence on rhythm and rhyme in her poetry has led several critics to cite it as overly simplistic or slight. Nevertheless, as R. B. Stepto notes, "a good Angelou poem has what we call 'possibilities.' One soon discovers that she is on her surest ground when she 'borrows' various folk idioms and forms and thereby buttresses her poems by evoking aspects of a culture's written and unwritten heritage." Her poems convey those struggles, triumphs, and self-affirmations that are revealed in her autobiographical works and are likewise praised for their honesty and moving sense of dignity.

(See also *CLC*, Vol. 12 and *Contemporary Authors,* Vols. 65-68.)

PUBLISHERS WEEKLY

Her many talents aside, the secret of Maya Angelou's rise to celebrity may lie in her strong note of self-affirmation. "I'm a woman / Phenomenally. / Phenomenal woman, / That's me," she writes in one of the most enjoyable poems in [***And Still I Rise***]. . . . Hers is not a major poetical voice; she seldom dazzles—or tries to—and at times her addiction to rhyme betrays her to banality. But her human warmth, honesty, strength and deep-rooted sense of personal pride—call it defiance—come through in almost every word she sets down. There are certain love poems here that are, in a true sense, as intimate as any by her sister poets of any race; yet they are uniquely Angelou, totally innocent of any exploitation or shock value.

A review of "And Still I Rise," in Publishers Weekly, *Vol. 214, No. 5, July 31, 1978, p. 87.*

CAROL GARGAN

We all have to convince ourselves of our own self-worth. The majority of poems, even the title of this volume of poetry [***And I Still Rise***], centers on that theme. There is a consistent problem with the conviction pursued. . . . Nothing has happened in [**"Phenomenal Woman,"** for example,] . . . to make me believe in some phenomenal being. It's clear the poem wants me to believe it, but everything has been generalized—the situation, the men, even "Phenomenal woman." Personal experience has not been examined, it has been turned into a sort of propaganda. The metaphors are trite—"swarm around a hive of honey bees," "It's the fire in my eyes," and "the joy in my feet."

Unfortunately these characteristics predominate in all of the poetry in this volume. Easy reading—not so easily believed.

Carol Gargan, in a review of "And Still I Rise," in Best Sellers, *Vol. 38, No. 12, March, 1979, p. 404.*

R. B. STEPTO

And Still I Rise is Angelou's third volume of verse, and most of its thirty-two poems are as slight as those which dominated the pages of the first two books. Stanzas such as this one,

In every town and village,
In every city square,
In crowded places
I search the faces
Hoping to find
Someone to care. . . .

cannot but make lesser-known talents grieve all the more about how this thin stuff finds its way to the rosters of a major New York house while their stronger, more inventive lines seem to be relegated to low-budget (or no-budget) journals and presses. On the other hand, a good Angelou poem has what we call "possibilities." One soon discovers that she is on her surest ground when she "borrows" various folk idioms and forms and thereby buttresses her poems by evoking aspects of a culture's written and unwritten heritage. **"One More Round,"** for example, gains most of its energy from "work songs" and "protest songs" that have come before. In this eight-stanza poem, the even-number stanzas constitute a refrain—obviously, a "work song" refrain. . . . At the heart of the odd-number stanzas are variations upon the familiar "protest" couplet "But before I'll be a slave / I'll be buried in my grave," such as the following: "I was born to work up to my grave / But I was not born / To be a slave." The idea of somehow binding "work" and "protest" forms to create new art is absolutely first rate, but the mere alternation of "work" and "protest" stanzas does not, in this instance, carry the idea very far.

Other poems, such as **"Willie,"** cover familiar ground previously charted by Sterling Brown, Langston Hughes, and Gwendolyn Brooks. Indeed, Angelou's Willie, despite his rare powers and essences ("When the sun rises / I am the time. / when the children sing / I am the Rhyme"), approaches becoming memorable only when he is placed in that pantheon where Brooks's Satin-Legs Smith and Brown's Sportin' Beasly are already seated. Similarly, **"Through the Inner City to the Suburbs," "Lady Luncheon Club,"** and **"Momma Welfare Roll"** bear strong resemblances to several poems of Brooks's pre-Black Aesthetic period in *Annie Allen* and *The Bean-Eaters*.

Up to a point, **"Still I Rise,"** Angelou's title poem, reminds us of Brown's famous "Strong Men," and it is the discovery of that point which helps us define Angelou's particular presence and success in contemporary letters and, if we may say so, in publishing. The poetic and visual rhythms created by the repetition of "Still I rise" and its variants clearly revoice that of Brown's "strong men . . . strong men gittin' stronger." But the "I" of Angelou's refrain is obviously female and, in this instance, a woman forthright about the sexual nuances of personal and social struggle:

Does my sexiness upset you?
Does is come as a surprise
That I dance like I've got diamonds
At the meeting of my thighs?

Needless to say, the woman "rising" from these lines is largely unaccounted for in the earlier verse of men and women poets alike. Most certainly, this "phenomenal woman," as she terms herself in another poem, is not likely to appear, except perhaps in a negative way, in the feminist verse of our time. Where she *does* appear is in Angelou's own marvelous autobiographies, ***I Know Why the Caged Bird Sings*** and ***Gather Together in My Name.*** In short, Angelou's poems are often woefully thin as poems but they nevertheless work their way into contemporary literary history. In their celebration of a particularly defined "phenomenal woman," they serve as ancillary, supporting texts for Angelou's more adeptly rendered self-portraits, and even guide the reader to (or back to) the autobiographies. With this achieved, Angelou's "phenomenal woman," as persona *and* self-portrait, assumes a posture in our literature that would not be available if she were the product of Angelou's prose or verse alone. (pp. 313-15)

R. B. Stepto, "The Phenomenal Woman and the Severed Daughter," in Parnassus: Poetry in Review, *Vol. 8, No. 1, Fall-Winter, 1979, pp. 312-20.**

BILL OTT

Previous volumes of Angelou's remarkable autobiography have dealt with her childhood, her experiences as a teenage mother, and her struggle to break into show business. This fourth installment [***The Heart of a Woman***] carries the story into the early 1960s—a period that saw Angelou heavily involved in civil rights. . . . Her recollections of encounters with Martin Luther King, Malcolm X, James Baldwin, and other black activists capture all the fire and idealism of the era. On a more personal level, she recounts the details of her romance with Vusumzi Make, a South African freedom fighter. If the story of Angelou's adult life lacks some of the inherent drama or terrible poignancy of her childhood in the South (chronicled in the perennially popular ***I Know Why the Caged Bird Sings***), it is nonetheless a stirring record of the complex fabric of a black woman's life.

Bill Ott, in a review of "The Heart of a Woman," in Booklist, *Vol. 78, No. 1, September 1, 1981, p. 1.*

JANET BOYARIN BLUNDELL

[In ***The Heart of a Woman***] Angelou writes of her life in the late 1950s and 1960s. Angelou has seen much and done much—she's been in important places at important times. . . . Her reminiscences of a visit from the failing Billie Holiday and meetings with Martin Luther King, Jr. and Malcolm X are well told and insightful; but it is Angelou's turbulent marriage to an African freedom fighter and her evolving relationship with her son that serve as the emotional center of the book. Although at times too chatty and anecdotal, ***The Heart of a Woman*** is lively, revealing, and well worth the reading.

Janet Boyarin Blundell, in a review of "The Heart of a Woman," in Library Journal, *Vol. 106, No. 17, October 1, 1981, p. 1919.*

DAVID LEVERING LEWIS

Eleven years ago, James Baldwin heralded the autobiographical event, Maya Angelou's ***I Know Why the Caged Bird Sings,*** as marking the "beginning of a new era in the minds and hearts of all black men and women." From a source less canonical, such extraordinary praise might have been adjusted downward for inflation. Since *The Life and Times of Frederick Douglass,* after all, autobiography has been the Afro-American strong suit, a literary form generating maximum compassion and indignation for victims of injustice. By the '60s and early '70s, that outpouring of first-person straight talk (viz., Claude Brown, Eldridge Cleaver, Angela Davis, George Jackson, Malcolm X and Baldwin himself) brought in a high tide of compelling testimony that swept over the public in wave upon candid, coruscating wave, seemingly telling everything like it was in black and white America. To move well beyond this shoreline to new ground, to beat out the first contours of a new era of mind and spirit seems, at first thought, more than the life story of one gifted, determined woman could reasonably be supposed to achieve.

That, nevertheless, is precisely what Maya Angelou has done. She has achieved a kind of literary breakthrough which few writers of any time, place, or race achieve. Moreover, since writing ***The Caged Bird Sings,*** she has done so with stunning regularity, in ***Gather Together in My Name,*** in ***Singin' and Swingin' and Gettin' Merry Like Christmas.*** Now comes her uproarious, passionate, and beautifully written ***The Heart of a Woman,*** equal in every respect to ***Gather Together in My Name*** and only a shade off the perfection of her luminous first volume. As with any corpus of high creativity, exactly what makes Angelou's writing unique is more readily appreciated than analyzed and stated. It is, I think, a melding of unconcerned honesty, consummate craft, and perfect descriptive pitch, yielding a rare compound of great emotional force and authenticity, undiluted by polemic. . . .

From materials as uncaptivating as a series of dumb personal misfortunes and sordid California business deals, and displays of barely possible talent as actress, dancer, singer, or mother, Angelou has rearranged, edited, and pointed up her coming of age and going abroad in the world with such just-rightness of timing and inner truthfulness that each of her books is a continuing autobiography of much of Afro-America. Her ability to shatter the opaque prisms of race and class between reader and subject is her special gift. "Bailey and I," she writes in ***The Caged Bird Sings*** of a childhood dilemma she and her brother confronted in Stamps, "Bailey and I decided to memorize a scene from *The Merchant of Venice,* but we realized that [grand] Momma would question us about the author and that we'd have to tell her that Shakespeare was white, and it wouldn't matter to her whether he was dead or not. So we chose 'The Creation' by James Weldon Johnson instead." In this poignant vignette, the tragedy that was once this nation's two-track culture is illumined with the intensity of lightning. (p. 1)

David Levering Lewis, "Maya Angelou: From Harlem to the Heart of Africa," in Book World—The Washington Post *October 4, 1981, pp. 1-2.*

ELLEN MILLER CASEY

In ***I Know Why the Caged Bird Sings*** (1969), the first volume of Maya Angelou's autobiography, she tells of her early years as a black in Arkansas and of the birth of her illegitimate son when she was seventeen. In ***The Heart of a Woman,*** the fourth volume of that autobiography, Angelou's son Guy grows from an adolescent of twelve to a young man of eighteen while Angelou moves from California to New York to Egypt to Ghana, involved all the time with the fight for black civil rights.

The strength of this book lies in its effective juxtaposition of the public and the personal aspects of Angelou's life. (p. 376)

Angelou stresses that her story is that of a black woman, and, in faithfully recreating her own experience, she provides a vivid picture of a turbulent time. One does wish, however, that she were more self-reflective. It is impossible to know what the Angelou of now thinks of the Angelou of then. In ***The Heart of a Woman*** Angelou is wise about her son but stupid about men in general. . . . As a woman she responds to the sexuality of men while disregarding their other traits; as a black she cannot believe that *any* white could possibly accept a strong black as an equal. One understands why Angelou judges and acts as she does, and one suspects that she recognizes her limitations of twenty years ago. However, because she presents her perceptions and actions without judgment, her book, valuable and interesting though it is, raises more questions than it answers. (pp. 376-77)

Ellen Miller Casey, in a review of "The Heart of a Woman," in Best Sellers, *Vol. 41, No. 10, January, 1982, pp. 376-77.*

ADAM DAVID MILLER

[***The Heart of a Woman***] covers one of the most exciting periods in recent African and Afro-American history. The beginning of a new awareness of Africa on the part of Negroes. It is the period of the early civil rights marches, of Malcolm X and Dr. Martin Luther King, Jr., of the Egypt of Nasser and the Ghana of Nkrumah, and the murder of the Congo's Patrice Lumumba. It is also the period when Maya tries her wings and learns that she can fly, of her brief but important marriage to a South African freedom fighter, and the period when her *wunderkind* son, Guy Johnson, grows into manhood.

As with all her books ***The Heart of a Woman*** can be mined for its riches: instruction, insight, humor, wry wit, lore, and fine writing. From this casebook on successful single parenting, we can see the perils a single mother, in this case a black one, faces in bringing up a black male child in our society, where so many things seem bent on preventing him from reaching adulthood. . . . Maya Angelou shows how one woman succeeds in skirting these dangers and comes out safely on the other side. (pp. 48-9)

As befits a master story teller, Maya Angelou's book is rich with the tight sketch, the apt portrait, the pithy line. Like Thoreau, she builds from the sentence. Throughout her account of her many experiences, I am constantly arrested when she uses just the right sentence to share some insight or fix some conclusion.

While Maya Angelou does many things in ***The Heart of a Woman,*** what she keeps constant throughout the book is that it is the account of a black W-O-M-A-N's life. Her experiences with women, her love and respect for them and theirs for her, her niceness and delicacy in dealing with them, from her mother to her friends, even to mere acquaintances, these could provide a model of conduct for any woman to follow.

Few will come away from this book into Maya Angelou's heart without being moved. (p. 49)

Adam David Miller, in a review of "The Heart of a Woman," in The Black Scholar, *Vol. 13, Nos. 4 & 5, Summer, 1982, pp. 48-9.*

DAISY ALDAN

From a shy child in Stamps, Arkansas, who through emotional shock had lost the power of speech, Maya Angelou had the will and courage to become a uniquely dynamic, internationally known figure. . . .

Outstanding [in the fourth volume of her autobiography, ***The Heart of a Woman,***] are several of her characterizations: of her mother, Vivian Baxter Jackson, depicted in a gem of a scene in Fresno's Desert Hotel; of [her husband] Make, with his strengths as a revolutionary and his idiosyncrasies—custom-tailored clothes, luxurious tastes, deceptions, feelings of male superiority and rigidities of conventional African behavior. Picasso never distorted portraits of his son, and in the same way Guy, Angelou's son, is treated with the utmost finesse and tenderness.

These portraits, however, are in flagrant contrast to the fanatic hostility the author expresses toward all white people. Certainly there is cause for bitterness, but its extremity is sad and unfortunate. In spite of national recognition and success, Angelou cannot seem to learn (at least by the time of the writing of this book) the wisdom in Martin Luther King's counsel when he tells her, "Remember we are not alone. There are a lot of good people in this nation. White people who love right and are willing to stand up and be counted." Instead she seems to agree with Malcolm X, who tells her, "All whites are blue-eyed devils trained to do one thing—take the black man's life." . . .

Her venomous hostility to one and all of the white race . . . is the epitome of stereotype and cliché. She would have compassion and gives none. She would have a world free of prejudice and is herself guilty of a reverse prejudice as violent as that of the psychopathic Southerner of the pre-civil rights days. When she appears in the Jean Genet play *The Blacks,* she wonders why the largely white audience "sits gaping as black actors fling filthy words and even filthier meanings into their faces," only to respond to this ridicule by applauding and shouting "Bravo!" I must admit that as a member of that audience, I recall wondering the same thing, and I assure Angelou that one person there did not join in the applause. Genet proposes that if blacks seize power, they will become as tyrannical and hate-ridden as the whites. Does Angelou not realize that her own attitude substantiates this? Only at the very close of the book does she state, "Sooner or later I am going to have to admit that I didn't understand black men or black boys and certainly not all white men." Let us hope it will be sooner rather than later that she learns that a prayer for mercy itself "doth teach us all to render the deeds of mercy."

Although the book on the whole cannot be called a great artistic or literary achievement, it nevertheless is absorbing, with several scenes narrated skillfully: the demonstration at the United Nations, the performance at the Apollo Theatre, life in Cairo's diplomatic circles, her son's accident—all these are molded by a talented writer who does attempt to be honest. Thereby some insight into the heart of one lusty, creative, bitter yet courageous black woman is gained.

Daisy Aldan, in a review of "The Heart of a Woman," in World Literature Today, *Vol. 56, No. 4, Autumn, 1982, p. 697.*

JANET BOYARIN BLUNDELL

Angelou is best known for her penetrating autobiographies. . . . Unfortunately, this fourth volume of her poetry [***Shaker, Why Don't You Sing?***] is no match for her prose writings. The reader is jarred by stilted, "poetic" language and sing-song, schoolgirlish rhyme. The best poems are those that swing with a touch of the blues, as in **"Weekend Glory."** . . . (p. 746)

Janet Boyarin Blundell, in a review of "Shaker, Why Don't You Sing?" in Library Journal, *Vol. 108, No. 7, April 1, 1983, pp. 746, 748.*

MARY SILVA COSGRAVE

[***Shaker, Why Don't You Sing?***] is a lyrical outpouring of seasoned feelings from the heart and mind. Her **"Family Affairs"** shrewdly encloses centuries of black history in a verse-play on the Rapunzel story; **"Caged Bird"** is a lament for a freedom never known; **"Prescience"** brings to mind Robert Burns's eighteenth-century love song of parting. . . . Writing of the blues, of recovering from passion, of the smells and sounds of Southern cities, of living life right on Saturday night, Angelou is musical, rhythmical, and enchanting.

Mary Silva Cosgrave, in a review of "Shaker, Why Don't You Sing?" in The Horn Book Magazine, *Vol. LIX, No. 3, June, 1983, p. 336.*

CANDELARIA SILVA

Maya Angelou's poetry is easily accessible, relying often on rhythm for its success. The poems are pared down with a sculptor's precision to simple yet elegant lines. She writes about love, beauty, the South, the human struggle for freedom and the incredible dignity black people have maintained against all odds. Her perceptive vision is emphatic and clear. Angelou is best in her poems which rhyme, like **"Weekend Glory"** and **"Impeccable Conception."** Her rhymes never seem awkwardly constructed or contrived. . . . Her sense of music in language, a heritage from her Southern black roots, is not utilized as much [in ***Shaker, Why Don't You Sing?***] as in other volumes, notably ***And Still I Rise.*** . . .

Candelaria Silva, in a review of "Shaker, Why Don't You Sing?" in School Library Journal, *Vol. 30, No. 1, September, 1983, p. 143.*

FIONA MADDOCKS

At the age of eight she was raped by her mother's boyfriend. At 16, she gave birth to a son whose father she scarcely knew. Even without these two shocks, Maya Angelou's autobiography would be remarkable: devoid of bitterness; pungent; funny; with that rare gift for hope in adversity hinted at by the title [of the first volume, ***I Know Why the Caged Bird Sings***].

A singer, dancer and black activist—a household name in the United States—Maya Angelou grew up in the Arkansas and California of the '30s. It is these years that are covered by this first volume of her autobiography. Three subsequent volumes tell of working with Martin Luther King, editing *African Review* and acting in *Roots,* but here Maya is a reasonably well-off black girl, discovering, with slow pain, that the white people's world is not open to her. . . .

Maya brings irresistibly alive the *dramatis personae* of her early years in Stamps, Arkansas—her adored brother; lame Uncle Willie; Mrs Flowers, the town's black aristocrat, with her voile dresses and skin like a black peeled plum. It was she who inspired Maya's love of literature: of Shakespeare (even though he was white) and of women in English novels who drink tea and walk across the moors ('whatever they were'). Indeed, Maya shares with Jane Austen a sharp eye for the world she knows. . . .

With the support of her fierce, Gospel-singing grandmother and, later, her own mother, Maya not only recovers her sense of sexual self respect, but, by the end of this volume, is fighting the white authorities to become the first black ever to work on the San Francisco streetcars. It is astonishing that this country [England] has had to wait so long to read her.

Fiona Maddocks, in a review of "I Know Why the Caged Bird Sings," in New Statesman, *Vol. 107, No. 2758, January 27, 1984, p. 26.*

HILARY BAILEY

Over the past year heart and conscience have sometimes failed to do their stuff in the business of the book about the Strong, Black American woman. There have been a good many of these books celebrating the virtues of women so terribly exploited in the white man's field, on the white woman's floor and over the tub containing the white family's laundry.

In the end you begin to wonder whether it wouldn't be fairer to let their aching bones rest in peace, instead of grinding them up into a powder of pathos and respect for the benefit, now, of the white man's publishing office in New York. . . .

[But] here is the real thing by Maya Angelou. Not an act of filial respect written by a daughter in a quiet room on campus or heavily funded by a honky in New York but the autobiography of a woman who did grow up in a town in the rural South where they'd lynch you soon as look at you.

She was raped in childhood in St. Louis, where her mother worked in gambling parlours, and got to college in San Francisco, where she also, by sheer persistence became the first black streetcar attendant. She also became pregnant at the age of sixteen, solving the problem three weeks before the birth of the baby by leaving a note on the bed saying, "Dear Parents, I am sorry to bring this disgrace on the family, but I am pregnant. Marguerite."

None of this conveys the true strength of the book, where the author manages the feat of describing herself growing up from the outside. She sees everything with an eye full of relish—the life of the rural South. New Orleans during prohibition, wartime San Francisco. There is pain, fear and suffering and there is enjoyment, too, for the life that, described secondhand, can be a grim documentary is, to the individuals involved, just their life, their experience, what made them.

Hilary Bailey, "Growing Up Black," in The Guardian Weekly, *Vol. 130, No. 6, February 5, 1984, p. 21.*

PAUL BAILEY

If you want to know what it was like to live at the bottom of the heap before, during and after the American Depression, this exceptional book [***I Know Why the Caged Bird Sings***] will tell you.

Maya Angelou was born Marguerite Johnson in 1928. When she was three, her parents separated. Marguerite and her brother, Bailey, were put on a train at Long Beach, California, with name-tags on their wrists which said that they were en route to Stamps, Arkansas, where they would be collected by Mrs Annie Henderson. The porter who was entrusted to look after them got off in Arizona, after pinning the children's tickets to Bailey's inside coat pocket.

Marguerite and Bailey—who gave his sister the nickname Maya ('mine')—spent their formative years in Stamps, a small town regularly visited by the Ku Klux Klan. Their paternal grandmother, Annie, ran the local store, and as a consequence was shown a mite more respect by the white community than were her fellow blacks.

And hardly more than a mite it was, as Sister Henderson discovered when she took her suffering granddaughter to the town's sole dentist, to whom she had loaned money. Mr Lincoln refused to extract Maya's two aching teeth. 'Annie,' he told her, 'my policy is I'd rather stick my hand in a dog's mouth than in a nigger's.' . . .

Maya Angelou's portrait of her grandmother is the finest thing in this fine memoir. Annie Henderson is an archetype of those noble, barely educated black women who inspired their children with a faith in themselves against the severest odds. . . .

This first part of a four-volume autobiography ends with Maya giving birth to her son, Guy, in San Francisco at the age of 16. She has to her considerable credit the fact that she has been the only black girl to date—the year is 1944—to find employment as a conductorette for the Market Street Railway Company. ***I Know Why The Caged Bird Sings*** was originally published in America in 1970. It should have appeared here long ago.

Paul Bailey, "Black Ordeal," in The Observer, *April 1, 1984, p. 22.*

Piers Anthony (Jacob)

1934-

English-born American novelist and short story writer.

Anthony writes science fiction and fantasy novels for young adults and is the creator of the best-selling *Xanth* fantasy series. Using puns and wordplay, literary allusions, mythical characters, and whimsical satire, he creates works of light entertainment which include a madcap sense of wondrous discovery. Anthony is praised for his imagination and his inventive brand of philosophical logic that tends toward the humorous.

Anthony's fiction often features people who solve problems that develop in their relationship with the natural universe. *Sos the Rope* (1967), *Var the Stick* (1972), and *Neq the Sword* (1975) comprise *The Battle Circle* trilogy. Set in America in the wake of a nuclear holocaust, the novels contrast a tribe of nomadic barbarians named for the weapons they use with a group of technologically-oriented humans. To avoid another holocaust, the "techies" maintain the warlike nomads as an outlet for human aggression. Anthony thus illustrates the need to acknowledge aggression as a part of human nature. Another series concerning humanity's interaction with nature consists of the novels *Omnivore* (1968), *Orn* (1970), and *Ox* (1976). In *Orn,* a trio of explorers is transported to a prehistoric world threatened by earthquakes and erupting volcanoes. In this world, a great bird is doomed to extinction at the hands of government agents who follow the explorers. Although the wanton destruction of nature is viewed as inevitable in this novel, the heroes nevertheless attempt to protect the planet.

Richard Mathews contends that the *Xanth* series "ranks with the best of American and classic fantasy literature." The series takes place in the distant future in Florida and reveals the fantastic aspects of the natural world. Among the most popular novels in the series are *The Source of Magic* (1979), *Centaur Aisle* (1982), and *Dragon on a Pedestal* (1983). Writing in a fairy-tale tone, Anthony portrays a world populated by such creatures as ogres, magicians, and zombies. Anthony's environmental concern is again evident, though a sense of pure adventure dominates the series.

Two recent series inaugurate what Roland Green calls "Anthony's new 'serious' phase." The first two books of the *Bio of a Space Tyrant* series, *Refugee* (1983) and *Mercenary* (1984), cover the traumatic childhood and the naval career of Hope Hubris, who grows up to become the Tyrant of Jupiter. In the *Incarnations of Immortality* series, characters personifying Death, Time, Nature, Fate, and War do battle with Satan. The novels in both of these series contain touches of Anthony's characteristic humor but are distinguished by the sophistication of the ideas they discuss. Anthony has also written the *Tarot* and *Cluster* series, among others.

(See also *Contemporary Authors,* Vols. 21-24, rev. ed. and *Dictionary of Literary Biography,* Vol. 8.)

Photograph by Cam. Courtesy of Piers Anthony

PUBLISHERS WEEKLY

[The setting of ***Chthon***] is a small hell planet orbiting in the outer edges of the galaxy. The caverns of its steamy interior are used as a prison for incorrigibles, who are forced to mine garnets. Among the prisoners, and the only one who does not accept his fate, is Anton Five. . . . Desperation finally starts Anton on a long trek through the caverns to escape to the surface. . . . Flashbacks fill in the background of Anton's life, his entrapment . . . and his struggles to escape. . . . The background material is as fascinating as the struggle to the surface is full of suspense. A busy and ingenious combination of the elements of myth, poetry, folk song, symbolism, suspense story—a bursting package, almost too much for one book, but literate, original and entertaining.

A review of "Chthon," in Publishers Weekly, *Vol. 191, No. 23, June 5, 1967, p. 180.*

BENEDICT NIGHTINGALE

SF writers often rationalise their desire to handle quasi-mythological themes, or to exploit primitive settings, by postulating a world reduced to near-ashes by the Bomb. So it is [in ***Sos the Rope***]: unnecessarily, in my view. Anthony's story of men fighting for mastery of wandering tribes . . . has its own internal conviction—its own grandeur, even. No subtlety, little finesse, perhaps; but a rigorous, masculine power, rare in any kind of novel nowadays.

Benedict Nightingale, in a review of "Sos the Rope," in The Observer, *January 10, 1971, p. 28.*

PUBLISHERS WEEKLY

[In **"Orn,"** three] reluctant space explorers from Earth are sent to the planet of Paleo, and they find it bears a close resemblance to what Earth was 65 million years ago. . . . [They] struggle to survive, and strangely come to prefer this wild place to "civilized" Earth. Orn, meanwhile, a gigantic flightless bird . . . endowed with racial memory, barely manages to keep alive in his constantly changing world. His path finally crosses that of the Earth men, but too late to save him from an incendiary attack from the civilized planet. The narrative is sometimes slow, but readers who like a lot of science with their fiction—geology, zoology, biology, paleontology—won't mind the frequent breaks for professional shop talk.

A review of "Orn," in Publishers Weekly, *Vol. 199, No. 18, May 3, 1971, p. 58.*

PUBLISHERS WEEKLY

[**"Var the Stick"** is a] followup to Anthony's **"Sos the Rope,"** with that character in a supporting role; it is the same post-holocaust setting, with an America reduced to wandering nomad barbarians (whose men are known by their weapons) and a small underground of technologically knowledgeable types. The techies maintain the nomads as a safety valve for the belligerent strain of humanity, to prevent another blowup. . . . Anthony's invention ranges from trite to intriguing; characterization is above average for SF. (pp. 63-4)

A review of "Var the Stick," in Publishers Weekly, *Vol. 204, No. 16, October 15, 1973, pp. 63-4.*

PUBLISHERS WEEKLY

[In **"Ox"**] Veg, a hot-tempered vegetarian, Cal, a mild-mannered man obliged to subsist . . . on human blood, and Aquilon, a woman painter, explore alternate probability worlds under the direction of the super-efficient android Agents. A dense texture of cross-purposes, ambiguities of time and space, and the gradually manifest presence of a sentient super-computer make this a book for readers willing to put a lot of concentration into reading it. [**"Ox"** is a] sequel to **"Orn."** . . .

A review of "Ox," in Publishers Weekly, *Vol. 210, No. 4, July 26, 1976, p. 78.*

PUBLISHERS WEEKLY

[***The Source of Magic***] is a readable, occasionally gripping fantasy about Bink, a hero too noble and pure to be likable, who is sent by the king of Xanth on a quest for the source of the kingdom's magic. . . . The characters and the prose have a penchant for cuteness; this is the central problem of the book. Nevertheless, the novel is redeemed by its inventiveness and charm. The opening scene, the queen's ball, is especially enchanting. Good fare for teens.

A review of "The Source of Magic," in Publishers Weekly, *Vol. 214, No. 24, December 11, 1978, p. 68.*

PUBLISHERS WEEKLY

Piers Anthony has taken the tarot and dealt a bizarre, uneven novel of a man's journey through the playing cards [with **"The God of Tarot"**]. Brother Paul, of the Holy Order of Vision, is called upon to travel to the planet Tarot to investigate the mystery of the animated cards. . . . Brother Paul's search for the truth leads him into these animations and down a path of wrenching self-discovery. . . . Although it has a rather ponderous midsection, for the most part this is a lively SF-fantasy novel with an audacious and original concept that is well worked out.

A review of "The God of Tarot," in Publishers Weekly, *Vol. 215, No. 6, February 5, 1979, p. 94.*

ROSEMARY HERBERT

[***The Source of Magic***] is Piers Anthony's delightful sequel to ***A Spell for Chameleon.*** This volume takes Bink, a magician whose power lies in the fact that magic cannot harm him, through the magic land of Xanth in quest of the source of all magic. Bink's passive magic is challenged by all manner of inventive ill-intentioned instruments of magic. . . . Although female characterization is almost offensively stereotyped (Bink's wife has two distinct personalities: one "beautiful-stupid" and one "smart-ugly"!), nimble action makes this book a charmer.

Rosemary Herbert, in a review of "The Source of Magic," in Library Journal, *Vol. 104, No. 4, February 15, 1979, p. 515.*

JANET JULIAN

The plot of . . . [***The Source of Magic***] is straightforward enough. Bink (a mortal) and Chester (a centaur) and Crombie (a soldier changed for the occasion into a griffin) and the Good Magician Humfrey all go off to discover the source of magic in Xanth, a country reeking with enchantment. . . . The book suffers from too much cutesie fantasy and becomes an encyclopedia rather than a novel. The pages are littered with Alice-in-Wonderland creatures like . . . a chocolate-chip cookie bush, a water-chestnut tree that gives beverages, bedbugs that snore, etc. The book is worth reading for its curious creatures but don't expect to fall in love with the characters or find a theme.

Janet Julian, in a review of "The Source of Magic," in Kliatt Young Adult Paperback Book Guide, *Vol. XIII, No. 3, April, 1979, p. 15.*

ALGIS BUDRYS

Anthony's loyal following will enjoy this tale of a future Earth [***The God of Tarot***]. Troubled by the depletion of technology and resources in his world, Brother Paul . . . seeks a rational solution. . . . His adventures lead him through a variety of trials and perils, culminating in a climax that is revelation to him and diverting to those readers who appreciate the author's unique brand of logic. (pp. 1481-82)

Algis Budrys, in a review of "The God of Tarot," in Booklist, *Vol. 75, No. 19, June 1, 1979, pp. 1481-82.*

PUBLISHERS WEEKLY

[In ***Split Infinity***] Stile, a top jockey, is a pampered serf on Proton, a super-rich mining planet where life depends on technology. He wants to stay past his tenure there. To do that, he must continue to satisfy his "Citizen" employer and win the athletic / intellectual / artistic contest called "the Game." His chances look good until he is injured by an unknown enemy during a race and loses his job. He avoids exile only by his opportune discovery of Proton's parallel world, Phaze, a natural paradise where magic works. . . . Stile is an interesting hero and there's pleasant diversion in his adventures. This is the first book of what promises to be an entertaining trilogy.

A review of "Split Infinity," in Publishers Weekly, *Vol. 217, No. 7, February 22, 1980, p. 94.*

PUBLISHERS WEEKLY

[In **"Thousandstar"**] Jessica, clone-sister of Jesse, must take her brother's place in a galactic race when he is injured. . . . In this race specie is paired in mind-contact with alien specie, to compete with other odd couples to reach the planet Ggoff, undeveloped prize of the Thousandstar system. Jessica's partner is Heem of Highfalls, a water creature. . . . To lose would mean death for these two, and desperation brings out the extraordinary in them. Before very long the aliens have fallen in love, an almost literally star-crossed situation, but the author makes it work (and work out). Anthony has done a solid job of creating an alien physiology and psychology in this unusual and highly entertaining novel.

A review of "Thousandstar," in Publishers Weekly, *Vol. 217, No. 14, April 11, 1980, p. 76.*

K. SUE HURWITZ

Anthony is at his best in [***Thousandstar,*** a] rollicking examination of the age-old question: Is there anything more alien than the difference between male and female? Jessica of Cappela (humanoid) and Heem of Highfalls (giant alien jellyfish) discover that interspecies misunderstandings are inconsequential when compared with the cosmic differences between the sexes when, in order to be partners on a secret mission, Jessica's mind must share Heem's body. It is unthinkable, impossible, and accidental—an intersex alien mind transfer has never been accomplished before. . . . Once accomplished, it's too late to abort the mission . . . and they soon discover that their collective life hinges on the successful completion of an almost impossible task.

Anthony handles his subject with characteristic wit and aplomb, sending his hero/ines off on a series of misadventures which strip away their pretensions, expose their weaknesses, and make them more aware of and responsive to their innate cultural and sex role conflicts.

K. Sue Hurwitz, in a review of "Thousandstar," in Kliatt Young Adult Paperback Book Guide, *Vol. XIV, No. 6, September, 1980, p. 12.*

PUBLISHERS WEEKLY

[In **"Mute,"** the] slightly lopsided mutant Knot is pressed into service as an agent for the Coordination Computer, the brain of galactic civilization, by the lovely Finesse, with whom Knot finds himself falling unwillingly in love. . . . [Complications] are created by Knot's mutant talent of being literally out-of-mind when out of sight, which makes him very valuable as an agent. Aided by the telepathic weasel Hermine and the telepathic and prescient hermit crab Mit, the two track down the Computer's enemies, led by the malignant Piebald. . . . This intricate, original adventure is perhaps overlong. Its subplot (concerning a couple working out a complex, star-crossed relationship) is more compelling than the main story line.

A review of "Mute," in Publishers Weekly, *Vol. 219, No. 7, February 13, 1981, p. 92.*

TOM EASTON

Piers Anthony gave us a very nice belt in the funnybone early in his career, with ***Prostho Plus.*** Since then, he has moved into fairly mystical territory, telling us that intelligence, identity, and personality reside in Kirlian auras, which can be transmitted from one person to another across interstellar distances. It's a clap-trap premise, but it does allow some interesting situations—what is it like for a human to share an alien body? It also allows wide-ranging stories that duck the Einstein barrier, for . . . aural transmission is (of course) instantaneous.

And that is what we find in ***Thousandstar,*** a tale set in the Thousand-Star Cluster, where an artifact left behind by the mysterious Ancients has been found. Protocol demands that all interested species take part in a race to the artifact, winner to gain custody. The limits of Anthony's technology dictate that each species' specially trained representative must occupy the body of a local sapient, so that the human rep becomes a tenant of an amoeboid energy-eater. However, the human, Jessica, is untrained. . . . Her host, Heem, is both a criminal and male, and the male-female pairing is supposed to be impossible. . . . Yet it happens, and Heem and Jessica find a unique *modus vivendi,* one that hinges on certain peculiarities of Jessica's aristocratic home culture, where she lacks a suitable marriage.

I've read several of Anthony's latest books, and I'm still not sure I like them. They don't grip, but they don't repel, either. What do they do? I confess perplexity. His plots are easy to summarize. . . . The complications are not, for he is given to baroquely ornamented personal histories and interactions that make his SF read more like fantasy. His creatures . . . and his science prove him fey. Perhaps I should simply say that, when I read him, I feel estranged. I witness the man's admittedly marvelous imagination as through a glass, darkly, with all participation in the story barred. Yet I wish for more, and I pick up each of his books in turn, hoping each time that now, finally, the glass will break. It hasn't so far, and I'm about ready to give up. (pp. 167-68)

Tom Easton, in a review of "Thousandstar," in Analog Science Fiction/Science Fact, *Vol. CI, No. 4, March 30, 1981, pp. 167-68.*

PUBLISHERS WEEKLY

In **"Split Infinity"** we were introduced to the twin worlds of Proton and Phaze, the former dependent on technology, the latter on magic. In [**"Blue Adept"**], our hero, Stile, is living in both worlds, striving to rise from serf to citizen in one by winning the all-encompassing Game, while he struggles to become a master of magic in the other—through the new Blue Adept. There's an arbitrary feel to the setup here, the relationship between the parallel worlds is too pat, but those who can suspend their disbelief will be nicely diverted. . . . The original Blue Adept's assassin is discovered, but a greater mystery remains to be resolved in what should be an exciting third book.

A review of "Blue Adept," in Publishers Weekly, *Vol. 219, No. 16, April 17, 1981, p. 52.*

SUSAN L. NICKERSON

[***Blue Adept***] continues the adventures of Stile, who is still seeking the unknown enemy menacing him in both the magic world of Phaze and the adjoining "real" world of Proton. In Proton, aided by the android Sheen, Stile advances in the all-important Game. . . . In Phaze, aided by the unicorn Neysa, he kills a dragon . . . and wins the love of the Lady Blue. Although the alternation of fantasy and sf chapters is rather gimmicky, the story maintains its exciting pace with many unexpected twists, and Anthony's humorous touches continue to delight the reader. Stile's love of horses, women, music, and sports is obviously shared by the author. (pp. 1325-26)

Susan L. Nickerson, in a review of "Blue Adept," in Library Journal, *Vol. 106, No. 12, June 15, 1981, pp. 1325-26.*

PATRICIA HERNLUND

[***Centaur Aisle,*** the] fourth book of [the ***Xanth***] series . . . can be read as a fairly good separate novel. It suffers as a continuation because the hero is inconsistent, but the supporting characters and some of the adventures are good. . . .

Dor is sixteen but often acts too young: in the first third of the book he can't cope with spelling or with the advances of 15-year-old Irene. Then he becomes temporary King while King Trent and Queen Iris go to Mundania. In the second third Dor journeys south to forestall the danger of a new magician, taking with him Chet the Centaur, Grundy the Golem and Smash the Ogre. Irene also goes, seemingly because the author needs to have Dor fall in love with her at the end, by proximity rather than believably. They find the magician is Arnolde, a Centaur whose talent is to have an "aisle" or aura of magic around him. In the last third, this group, with Arnolde replacing a wounded Chet, journey to Mundania to rescue the King, the Queen, and good King Omen.

The book has two other flaws: first, the extensive spelling joke doesn't work because it involves misspelling *spoken* as well as written words. Second, the map at the front, identifying Xanth as Florida (where Anthony lives), isn't needed or used, and it undercuts the creation of a fantasy world.

Patricia Hernlund, in a review of "Centaur Aisle," in Science Fiction & Fantasy Book Review, *No. 2, March, 1982, p. 11.*

JANET JULIAN

The protagonist [of ***Centaur Aisle***] is Dor, hero of the previous novel ***Castle Roogna.*** This time, instead of being a 12-year-old inside the body of a lusty 25-year-old human, Dor is himself, a lusty teenager enamored of the Princess Irene. His troubles begin when Irene's parents, King Trent and Queen Iris, travel back to Mundania (our "real" world). . . . Because their magic does not work in Mundania, they are promptly captured and imprisoned. Dor and Irene go to the rescue with Grundy the Golem, Chet the Centaur, and Smash the Ogre. The rescue entails a good deal of swordplay and adolescent horseplay. . . . There are the usual egregious puns and bizarre creatures. High school students will identify with Dor's sexual yearnings and his inability to spell. The book will delight fans of Piers Anthony. . . . (pp. 18-19)

Janet Julian, in a review of "Centaur Aisle," in Kliatt Young Adult Paperback Book Guide, *Vol. XVI, No. 3, April, 1982, pp. 18-19.*

PAUL GRANAHAN

Juxtaposition, a work which combines both science fiction and fantasy, provides ample opportunity for [Anthony] to demonstrate his skill in each field. . . .

This is the story of Stile, a rather diminutive but eminently resourceful individual, who as a serf on the planet Proton competes in the all-demanding Game, the ultimate prize being Citizenship with its considerable wealth. An unprovoked, mysterious attack transforms Stile's existence into a roller coaster ride of both highs and lows at breakneck speed. He then discovers a way to enter another frame of reality called Phaze, where magic is operative and the laws of physics are not. In Phaze his alternate self, a powerful image known as the Blue Adept, was murdered and Stile, though inheriting his double's mystic abilities, finds himself in mortal danger from his "own" slayers. . . .

As if he weren't busy enough, it is also swiftly approaching the time of Juxtaposition, an apocalyptic event for both worlds in which Stile is prophesied to play an essential role. At that point, the two frames are temporarily to fuse, only forever to separate—but Stile must first accomplish certain tasks to avert total disaster. Romance further complicates matters, for Stile is the beloved of a beautiful female robot, a shape-shifting unicorn/woman, and of the magnificent Lady Blue, his own true love and the widow of his other self.

Although this all sounds too confusing, it somehow fits together and it's a lot of fun. While I sometimes wish Anthony, with his obvious talent, would attempt deeper endeavors, I highly recommend this imaginative series.

Paul Granahan, in a review of "Juxtaposition," in Best Sellers, *Vol. 42, No. 4, July, 1982, p. 135.*

MICHAEL R. COLLINGS

Anthony undertakes several difficult tasks [in ***Viscous Circle***]. First, he sets this novel against the complexity, energy and wit of the earlier Cluster novels. . . . ***Cluster*** (1978), ***Chaining the Lady*** (1978), ***Kirlian Quest*** (1978) and ***Thousandstar*** (1980). Second, the primary conflicts in the novel are emotional and spiritual rather than physical, resulting in extended static passages, such as an episode in which Ronald talks to himself for nearly 12 pages before dispatching a three-headed monster in three short, anti-climactic paragraphs. Third, Anthony creates an alien species, the Banda, who are almost quintessentially good—explicitly "angelic"—and have no conception of war, government or selfishness. . . . And finally, Anthony concentrates on an essentially anti-human bias. It is one thing to show humans/Solarians from alien perspectives, as he did in other Cluster novels; it is another, more dangerous, thing for the human to assume entirely the aliens' attitudes and commit conscious treason against his own species. . . . Utter misanthropy threatens to alienate reader from hero no matter how ideal the alternate society might be.

In addition, ***Viscous Circle*** seems tired. Anthony writes in an author's note that the book was "difficult when it should have been easy, and may lack that spark of wonder that is the essence of this type of writing." He is correct. The lushness of physical, verbal, and contextual invention that characterizes the first Cluster novels is here radically trimmed, chastened, muted. . . . Plot resolution is explained rather than presented. Compared with the climactic permutations in the final chapters of ***Cluster*** or ***Chaining the Lady, Viscous Circle*** seems . . . well, viscous.

Still, in spite of these barriers, the novel is a creditable job. It becomes engaging: and although Rondl/Ronald is far less interesting than Melody of Mintaka or Herald the Healer, he invites empathy. Anthony also continues the pattern of suggesting serious themes in his novels—in this case, he indicts human/Solarian greed and insensitivity. The novel opens slowly, with an amnesiac hero, but the second half is stronger and approaches more closely the intensity one associates with Anthony.

As an isolated novel ***Viscous Circle*** is interesting; as the latest in a long series of impressive novels . . . it seems tired. It lacks the sense of a richly embroidered tapestry, meticulously detailed and re-created, that lies at the heart of Anthony's appeal. The writing is smoother than is usual, with fewer verbal pyrotechnics, fewer ringings of variations on puns—but I think I prefer the old fire to fluidity. (pp. 17-18)

Michael R. Collings, in a review of "Viscous Circle," in Science Fiction & Fantasy Book Review, *No. 6, July-August, 1982, pp. 17-18.*

SISTER AVILA LAMB

[***Blue Adept***] can be read alone; but, it really would be better to read ***Split Infinity*** first as the author frequently refers to incidents and characters of the previous volume without enough explanation. Blue Adept in the frame of Phaze, a magical world, is Stile, a serf in the parallel frame of Proton, a world based on science. He shifts from one world to the other. As the Blue Adept he is the leading magician of Phaze suffering from unrequited love for the widow of the first Blue Adept who was the alternate self of Stile. (Clear?) There he seeks his enemy who has determined to kill him. . . . The author is a neat manipulator of words, as is evident in his choice of names and his skill in shifting from antiquated English to modern. Throughout the story he reveals his wide range of interests and expertise. Well worth reading for pleasure or rumination.

Sister Avila Lamb, in a review of "Blue Adept," in Kliatt Young Adult Paperback Book Guide, *Vol. XVI, No. 6, September, 1982, p. 17.*

GEORGE M. A. CUMMING, JR.

The danger in writing speculative science fiction is that all too easily an author can sail off into a private universe and leave readers behind and bewildered. ***Viscous Circle*** nearly falls into that trap. A human agent's personality is projected into the body of a band, an alien sort of intelligent donut. . . . Rondl, the agent, turns sides in sympathy with the bands, whose society is an anarchist's utopia. The plot is rescued by a vision in which life after death is an imminent fact of existence. . . . Strangely, it is not the novel itself that makes ***Viscous Circle*** well worth reading, but the author's note at the end. Piers Anthony takes you on a guided tour of his life. . . . In 9 pages he has done what most novels don't in 300. That is to poke deep into the heart of one human being and find something to say. It's the kind of reading experience that will rescue you from the clutches of an overrated best seller and leave you wishing for a full-length autobiography. (pp. 146-47)

George M. A. Cumming, Jr., in a review of "Viscous Circle," in School Library Journal, *Vol. 29, No. 1, September, 1982, pp. 146-47.*

LOIS A. STRELL

[***Night Mare***] is the sixth book in a series which centers around the magic world of Xanth and the non-magic world of Mundania. Imbri, a mare of the night who delivers bad dreams, is sent on a mission to the day world to help Xanth ward off an invasion from Mundania. First King Trent, then each succeeding King, loses his soul to the mysterious and evil Horseman. . . . Without a doubt, the book will be grabbed up by science fiction fans. Anthony continues to deliver lighthearted adventure in a tongue-in-cheek satirical manner. Unfortunately, he also laces his book with overt sexism. In [***Night Mare***], beauty in a woman is equated with stupidity, and ugliness with intelligence. . . . Perhaps Anthony is being satirical, but if I found it difficult to determine, a student might miss it completely. The stories are fun, but Anthony ought to clean up his act. (pp. 128-29)

Lois A. Strell, in a review of "Night Mare," in School Library Journal, *Vol. 29, No. 8, April, 1983, pp. 128-29.*

CLAUDIA MORNER

The ogre of this delightful fantasy tale [***Ogre, Ogre***], Smash, is only half ogre as his mother was human. But until he encounters Tandy and the six other females who need his protection, he does not realize his human potential. At the beginning of the story he is tough-guying his way through Xanth. . . . Enroute, Smash has plenty of opportunities to live up to his name as he conquers dragons, night mares, goblins, sea creatures, fire and even the Void. In the process he learns about compassion, loyalty, love and intelligence. Later he realizes that he has become more like a man and less like an evil monster. With lots of puns and jokes and ample doses of fighting, bashing and excitement, this story will delight young adults who enjoy fantasy.

Claudia Morner, in a review of "Ogre, Ogre," in School Library Journal, *Vol. 29, No. 8, April, 1983, p. 129.*

PEGGY MURRAY

[In ***Ogre, Ogre***] Tandy, half-nymph and half-human, runs away from home to escape the amorous attentions of a demon. Assigned to protect her is the ogre Smash, who is quite stupid and ugly and can speak only in rhymes like "Well spoke; no joke" until he tangles with an Eye Queue vine. They have various pulp adventures on their journey, while Smash . . . acquires more and more human sensitivity. In the end, they realize that they love each other. . . .

Those looking for the beauty and subtlety of high fantasy will not find it here, but Piers Anthony's stories, full of sophomoric humor and bad puns, have tremendous appeal with YA fantasy readers.

Peggy Murray, in a review of "Ogre, Ogre," in Voice of Youth Advocates, *Vol. 6, No. 1, April, 1983, p. 44.*

CHRISTY TYSON

[In ***Night Mare,*** the] King of Xanth has been enchanted; his body is there but his mind is gone. Each of his successors must try to avoid a similar entrapment while keeping Xanth free from invasion by barbarians. Each one fails until only Imbri, the night mare (an equine deliverer of bad dreams), stands between Xanth and total defeat. . . . [Newcomers] to Xanth may get lost in the large cast of characters and fail to understand some of the references to past adventures. More discerning readers may find that the humor is becoming just a bit strained and the action just a bit contrived. However, this is fast-paced, funny adventure that will be much appreciated by fans of the series.

Christy Tyson, in a review of "Night Mare," in Voice of Youth Advocates, *Vol. 6, No. 2, June, 1983, p. 99.*

PUBLISHERS WEEKLY

[The world depicted in ***On a Pale Horse*** is] a world very much like ours, except that magic has been systematized and is as influential as science. Satan's war against God is out in the open . . . and abstractions like Time, War, Nature and Fate are real people. No less a real person is Death, as Zane discovers when he kills him while attempting to commit suicide, thereby succeeding to the job himself. . . . Zane slowly comes to understand the importance of his role, the mercy in ending hopeless pain. But he goes on strike when the woman he loves is threatened with an untimely death by Satan's plan for dominion over the Earth. Death, no longer a reluctant draftee, comes into his full powers as he confronts and defies the Devil. Anthony's prose is pedestrian, but his ideas are anything but. The author of the bestselling Xanth series has found a fascinating new direction for his fantasy. . . .

A review of "On a Pale Horse," in Publishers Weekly, *Vol. 224, No. 10, September 2, 1983, p. 72.*

SUSAN L. NICKERSON

[With ***Refugee***, the first volume in the series **"Bio of a Space Tyrant,"**] Anthony tackles a new project: the creation of the ultimate space opera. In five volumes, he will present the biography of Hope Hubris, Tyrant of Jupiter, accused of every crime from mass murder to incest. . . . ***Refugee,*** the story of his horrific and traumatic childhood, explains much of this in gruesome and sickening detail, yet Anthony never loses control and manages to inject telling social comment along the way.

Susan L. Nickerson, in a review of "Refugee," in Library Journal, *Vol. 108, No. 16, September 15, 1983, p. 1811.*

MARY S. WEINKAUF

[***Bio of a Space Tyrant***] is a five-volume, plodding white-wash biography edited by the tyrant's daughter. [***Refugee,*** the] first volume, could be retitled "Wetbacks in Space." The story is of the poor but proud Hispanics' illegal flight from Callisto only to endure raid and rape on a regular basis from pirates. . . . Hope Hubris manages to be responsible [for] murder, cannibalism, transvestism, theft, hijack, incest, prostitution of mother and sisters, and a host of stupid errors which he considers sacrificial deeds. If he were a better person, he concludes, he never would have survived. Who cares?

Mary S. Weinkauf, in a review of "Bio of a Space Tyrant, Volume 1: Refugee," in Science Fiction & Fantasy Book Review, *No. 18, October, 1983, p. 16.*

SUSAN L. NICKERSON

[In ***Dragon on a Pedestal***] Anthony stops straining for every pun and pratfall he can invent, and the result is the best Xanth novel in some time. Three-year-old Princess Ivy, lost in the forest, meets and makes friends with Hugo, son of Good Magician Humfrey. . . . Meanwhile, her distraught mother Queen Irene leads a motley (and familiar) crew of rescuers. Of course, the story still has its madcap moments, but Anthony's restraint allows more depth to both characters and plot. Xanth fans will love it. (pp. 1975-76)

Susan L. Nickerson, in a review of "Dragon on a Pedestal," in Library Journal, *Vol. 108, No. 18, October 15, 1983, pp. 1975-76.*

EUGENE E. LAFAILLE

[In ***Dragon on a Pedestal***] Princess Ivy . . . is lost in the forest. Ivy meets and befriends Hugo (Magician Humphrey and Zora, the Zombie's son) and the youthful and friendly Gap Dragon. Together, they wander throughout Xanth. . . .

Your appreciation or dislike of puns will basically determine your reaction to this work of fantasy. There are many interesting characters, numerous literary allusions, lots of good fun and humor, fine plot pacing, and excellent integration of social commentary into the text. Also, the characters are fully developed and exhibit a wide range of positive and negative human traits.

Eugene E. LaFaille, in a review of "Dragon on a Pedestal," in Kliatt Young Adult Paperback Book Guide, *Vol. XVIII, No. 1, January, 1984, p. 21.*

RICHARD MATHEWS

[***Dragon on a Pedestal***] exudes energy, humor and delightful invention. Anthony seems to have set himself an impossible task in selecting a three-year-old heroine, and he compounds his trials with a zombie as the principle romantic interest, but the book is a success on many levels. (p. 24)

One of the first things to applaud is Anthony's sense of audience. He is aware of writing for a young reader, but he includes enough levels of action and meaning for open-minded adults as well. . . . This, like all the Xanth tales, is episodic in structure, and rich in classic mythic reference. Anthony is assembling, bit by bit, his own *Arabian Nights*.

The novel is entertaining, and it is literate. The puns which invade the book, as in others in the Xanth series, do fall flat upon occasion, but they succeed in communicating the vitality of language, the power of words. Language itself is one of the underlying values affirmed. This affirmation is particularly important for young readers who are being wooed away from books and the literary imagination into a non-verbal world of electronic color and sound.

In one sense, Xanth is a direct descendant of James Branch Cabell's Poictesme. Anthony shares Cabell's ironic humor without his intellectual arrogance. There is something Cabellian in Anthony's use of Florida as the locus for Xanth, and in the ironic play of such chapters as "Ivy League" (Ivy is the 3-year-old heroine, daughter of King Dor and Queen Irene) or "Hugo Award" (Hugo is the somewhat retarded son of the Good Magician Humphrey). Some reviewers previously expressed disappointment that the Florida connection established by Chem Centaur's map of Xanth did not seem integral to the book, but this novel should dispel that criticism. The point for Anthony (as for Cabell) is that the fantastic begins in his own back yard. In ***Dragon on a Pedestal*** Florida figures centrally in the story, from its tropical climate which provides an ideal setting for Irene's plant-magic, to key plot elements like the Fountain of Youth. . . . (pp. 24-5)

Three-year old Ivy turns out to be a charming heroine, and Zora the Zombie is remarkably transformed into a suitable object for romance as bits of her flesh cease falling away and she begins to look almost lovely. Along the way Anthony includes parables of humane idealism which treat such themes as ecology, prejudice, healthy sexuality, and the power of positive thinking. The values, the invention, and the language of this book deserve applause. I have compared it to the *Arabian Nights* and works of Cabell because I think it, and the entire Xanth series, ranks with the best of American and classic fantasy literature. (p. 25)

Richard Mathews, "Xanth Series Extolled," in Fantasy Review, *Vol. 7, No. 2, March, 1984, pp. 24-5.*

WAYNE HOOKS

Anthony is a delightful author whose earlier books such as ***Omnivore*** and ***Orn*** did not have the success they deserve. . . . Anthony's style is typified by its lightheartedness, characterization, and satire. His latest book . . . ***On a Pale Horse*** is hampered by the style which has become an Anthony trademark.

Zane, the main character, does not understand the nature of magic and so is cheated out of love and fortune. . . . The novel begins interestingly enough but bogs down in philosophy and other ponderous subjects halfway through. The Afterword explains Anthony's hospital visit midway through the novel and he mentions a heightened awareness of death after it. This awareness mars the novel, making it change course in midstream. An interesting novel, but it could have been so much more.

Wayne Hooks, in a review of "On a Pale Horse," in Voice of Youth Advocates, *Vol. 7, No. 1, April, 1984, p. 37.*

DAVID SNIDER

Hope Hubris (our 15-year-old hero) must flee his home on Callisto due to an incident involving his 18-year-old sister, Faith, her honor, and an overly lusty aristocrat. . . . [***Refugee***] tells of the long flight which results in Hope's parents being killed by pirates, Faith being raped by pirates, . . . etc. The end of [***Refugee***] finds Hope alone on Jupiter. Obviously, the author has big plans for Hope Hubris because he's billed at length as the Tyrant of Space: unfortunately the reader may not be interested in waiting to see how that happens. Anthony has become interested in death but [***Refugee***] is pretty grim, even worse, it gets boring in all too many places.

David Snider, in a review of "Bio of a Space Tyrant: Refugee," in Voice of Youth Advocates, *Vol. 7, No. 1, April, 1984, p. 37.*

PUBLISHERS WEEKLY

[Anthony's early] books suffered . . . from their brevity and lightness. His current multivolume biography (***Bio of a Space Tyrant***) allows for greater scope and detail. This second entry [***Mercenary***] takes future tyrant Hope Hubris from his teens to 30, describing a meteoric career in the Jupiter Navy. While his archenemy QYV plots against him, Hope rises quickly through the ranks, thanks to his uncanny ability to read and manipulate men. . . . Anthony slows the pace as Hope lectures on hand-to-hand combat and the outrageous sexual practices of the Navy and pirates. But the boldly outlined characters with their jigsaw relationships and violent conflicts keep the reader engrossed.

A review of "Mercenary," in Publishers Weekly, *Vol. 225, No. 19, May 11, 1984, p. 270.*

JACKIE CASSADA

[***Mercenary***] follows Hope's career from a brief stint as a migrant worker to his rise and fall in Jupiter's navy. Hope's daring rescue of Spirit, his sister, and his subsequent success in wiping out the asteroid-based pirate trade offer some excitement for fans of battles in space, but Hope himself remains a thoroughly uninteresting hero. The humor and spontaneity Anthony so capably demonstrates elsewhere is sadly missing in [the ***Bio of a Space Tyrant***] series.

Jackie Cassada, in a review of "Mercenary," in Library Journal, *Vol. 109, No. 11, June 15, 1984, p. 1253.*

PUBLISHERS WEEKLY

[In ***Bearing an Hourglass,*** the second volume in the ***Incarnations of Immortality*** series] a wanderer named Norton, grief-stricken over the suicide of his lover, allows himself to be talked into becoming the Incarnation of Time, Chronos. Now a demigod, Norton engages in cosmic, mind-bending adventuring, witnesses the death and birth of the universe and obstructs the evil workings of Satan. The story, however, never seems to find its proper voice; it begins humorously, a mood that soon becomes inappropriate, switches to space opera parody, then straight adventure, and so on—and it is not a smooth mesh. It is further burdened by *deus ex machina,* an omniscient ring and an hourglass that allows Norton to travel freely through space and time. . . . The reader may also be amused by the concluding Note, in which Anthony opines that writers suffering from writer's block are "pseudo-professionals" and that he, Anthony, is, in fact, a "world-class writer."

A review of "Bearing an Hourglass: Book Two of Incarnations of Immortality," in Publishers Weekly, *Vol. 225, No. 25, June 22, 1984, p. 90.*

ROLAND GREEN

[In ***Bearing an Hourglass***] a grief-stricken Norton assumes the position of the Incarnation of Time but discovers that such a role involves an increasingly deadly duel with Satan. On the basis of this novel and the previous ***On a Pale Horse*** . . . Anthony's new "serious" phase promises well. The author's characters come admirably to life, he does well with the tone of individual scenes, and there is a considerable amount of religious and ethical speculation that even people who may disagree with his ideas will recognize as intelligently rendered.

Roland Green, in a review of "Bearing an Hourglass," in Booklist, *Vol. 80, No. 21, July, 1984, p. 1497.*

MARY S. WEINKAUF

Less repetitive, less full of piratic violence, and more subtle in its allegory than ***Refugee, Mercenary*** makes better reading. Anthony combines political/social allegory with the kind of blood and sex adventure that lures readers to buy the next volume. Living in Florida has obviously sensitized Anthony to the values and problems of Hispanics.

Mary S. Weinkauf, "Space Foreign Legion," in Fantasy Review, *Vol. 7, No. 7, August, 1984, p. 7.*

JACKIE CASSADA

[In ***Bearing an Hourglass***] Norton reluctantly accepts a new mode of existence . . . and locks forces with wily Satan himself in a complex, harrowing struggle to preserve the balance of harmony in the world. Amid weighty and often convoluted speculations about the nature of good and evil, time and space, and magic and science, Anthony's irrepressible humor asserts itself in unexpected ways. Far from being grim—or even allegorical—this sequel to ***On a Pale Horse*** will appeal to Anthony's large readership.

Jackie Cassada, in a review of "Bearing an Hourglass," in Library Journal, *Vol. 109, No. 13, August, 1984, p. 1470.*

NEAL WILGUS

[In ***Bearing an Hourglass***] Chronos, the Incarnation of Time, has or will or might defeat Satan, the Incarnation of Evil. The bad news is that it will or has or could take him so long to do it. Maybe.

The uncertainty here involves the nature of Time and the office of Chronos, according to Norton, the man who recently took over that position. Norton who was formerly an unemployed wilderness-seeker, reports that Time is one of the most powerful of the Incarnations of Immortality, but that the limitations and complications to which it is subject make things very difficult for the office holder.

Norton reports that he has met with the other Incarnations (Death, Fate, War and Nature) and with Satan and that he has already learned a great deal in his short time in office. He has learned to use the hourglass that is the symbol of his position to travel in time / space and perform his duties, but he's also learned that he is doomed to live backward in time, as each of his predecessors will. (pp. 45-6)

There are some critics who complain that the account of Norton's adventures told in Piers Anthony's ***Bearing an Hourglass*** is unnecessarily burdened by the scenes in which Norton battles the Bems and the Eviler Sorceress and that the reversal-of-time scenario was too drawn out. Nevertheless, the Anthony book is a fine piece of writing. . . . (p. 46)

Neal Wilgus, in a review of "Bearing an Hourglass," in Science Fiction Review, *Vol. 14, No. 1, February, 1985, pp. 45-6.*

Jay Bennett

1912-

American novelist, dramatist, and scriptwriter.

Bennett is acknowledged as a leader in the field of young adult mysteries. The protagonists of his novels are usually male high school or college students who unwittingly become entangled in a crime, often murder or theft. In *The Dangling Witness* (1974), a young man who is the sole witness to a murder must decide whether to report what he has seen, thereby endangering his own life. Bennett's novels often have surprising endings which are nevertheless logically contrived. In addition to his mystery novels, Bennett has written two love stories for young adults: *Masks: A Love Story* (1972) and *I Never Said I Loved You* (1984).

Although Bennett's works have occasionally been faulted for underdeveloped characterizations, critics generally commend his ability to sustain a suspenseful mood throughout the story. Bennett has written mysteries for adults, yet says he prefers writing for young adults because they are "alive, questioning, and . . . more decent human beings than their elders." Bennett has won the Mystery Writers of America Edgar Allan Poe Award for best juvenile mystery for both *The Long Black Coat* (1973) and *The Dangling Witness*.

(See also *Contemporary Authors,* Vols. 69-72; *Contemporary Authors New Revision Series,* Vol. 11; and *Something about the Author,* Vol. 27.)

Photograph by Francesca; reproduced by permission of Jay Bennett

GEORGE A. WOODS

[**"Deathman, Do Not Follow Me"** is] a taut suspense novel with the maturity befitting a book for teen-agers. Danny Morgan, the boy in danger because of the switch of a Van Gogh in the Brooklyn Museum, is real life. Loner and high-school junior, he day-dreams, has resentments, reads Playboy (and National Geographic), plays his record player too loudly, likes Bob Dylan and is capable of seeing some of the phoniness of our age. His edges sometimes grate against mother, girl friend and teacher and there's no one in whom he can confide, especially about the "Deathman." The speech is real, too. . . . Victims have real blood, not catchup, and the screams aren't caused by the rocking chair coming down on the cat's tail.

George A. Woods, in a review of "Deathman, Do Not Follow Me," in The New York Times Book Review, *July 7, 1968, p. 16.*

GERALDINE E. LaROCQUE

Deathman, Do Not Follow Me is a gripping story of Danny Morgan, a high school football hero in Brooklyn, whose life is in danger. . . . The author portrays unbearable suspense with a sinister quality, while at the same time he demonstrates a warm recognition of what constitutes the long, long thoughts of a loner like Danny and what characterizes his conversations and personal encounters. A short novel, ***Deathman, Do Not Follow Me*** could be enjoyed by both junior or senior high school boys and girls because of its combination of easy readability and adult content. (pp. 295-96)

Geraldine E. LaRocque, in a review of "Deathman, Do Not Follow Me," in English Journal, *Vol. 58, No. 2, February, 1969, pp. 295-96.*

JOHN W. CONNER

[***The Deadly Gift***] is an exciting memorable reading experience. It contains short, pithy chapters charged with emotion resulting from carefully developed situations. John-Tom Dawes picks up a box containing ten thousand dollars left by a distraught man he encounters on a rainy night as they both wait for a bus. The money is a deadly gift John-Tom is afraid to reveal. . . .

The social issues involved are real as John-Tom wrestles with the problems possession of the money creates. He knows the money is not his, but he is not convinced that the money belongs to the underworld boss who threatens to kill him if he does not return it. The underworld characters are stereotypes, but in the best sense of the word. That is, the characters represent qualities of evil inherent in mankind which John-Tom feels must be defeated or these qualities will defeat him.

Life is very much like the game of chess John-Tom is constantly beginning with his friend, Dave Peng. Because John-Tom is afraid to tell Dave the truth about possessing the money, each time they engage in a game the match is dismissed before either player wins because the players do not have an honest confrontation.

John-Tom's parents and his friend Ruth Elder also exert an influence over his actions. These relationships are briefly stated but help him arrive at a final resolution of the crisis created by the money. ***The Deadly Gift*** will involve an adolescent reader and provide a brief, pleasurable reading experience for him.

John W. Conner, in a review of "The Deadly Gift," in English Journal, *Vol. 59, No. 4, April, 1970, p. 591.*

SARAH LAW KENNERLY

[***The Deadly Gift***] is a brief mystery-melodrama so full of literary gimmicks—stream of consciousness narration, outbursts of formless poetry, fragmentary thoughts, sections written in italics, sections without capitalization, chapters a dozen lines long—that the style almost succeeds in obscuring the sense. It is the tension-filled story of John-Tom Dawes, a Mohawk Indian living in Brooklyn, whose ambition is to win a college scholarship. Football would do it, but Tom won't play a game of such senseless violence. For his refusal, the coach curses him, and Indians, even modern educated ones, take a curse seriously. But Tom's real curse is the deadly gift left him one night by a terrified man at a bus stop—a black brief case containing ten thousand dollars. . . . The money is his, insists Tom, but at what price? There is something almost epic about John-Tom's struggle with himself, and the story is decidedly worth reading in spite of its overly pretentious style. It should have much to say to contemporary teen-agers.

Sarah Law Kennerly, in a review of "The Deadly Gift," in School Library Journal, *an appendix to* Library Journal, *Vol. 16, No. 9, May, 1970, p. 92.*

THE BOOKLIST

[***Masks: A Love Story*** is a] contemporary interracial love story about a white teen-age girl and the son of a dedicated Chinese doctor. . . . Jennifer's parents are deeply disturbed by their daughter's love for Peter Yeng and step in to separate the pair. Family relationships as well as Jennifer's and Peter's romance are sketchily but convincingly drawn. Despite the over-spare, somewhat choppy prose style and well-worn plot the book is easy reading. . . .

A review of "Masks: A Love Story," in The Booklist, *Vol. 67, No. 19, June 1, 1971, p. 829.*

PUBLISHERS WEEKLY

[In **"The Killing Tree,"** Fred Wilk] accepts a carving brought from Sierra Leone to New York by Walter Carlton. . . . Immediately, Fred finds himself in danger of his life as several toughs—for strange reasons—try to make him give up the keepsake. The story is well written—the author knows how to sustain mood, especially in dialogue—but the plot is rather pedestrian and too readily resolved.

A review of "The Killing Tree," in Publishers Weekly, *Vol. 202, No. 7, August 14, 1972, p. 46.*

THE BOOKLIST

Soon after his anthropologist father's death in Africa seventeen-year-old Fred Wilk receives from his father an ancient African wooden statue. . . . Fred's refusal to part with the statue leads him into danger and eventually to the realization that not only is Carlton the master criminal but his father was not the honorable man of his image. Although characterizations are flat and the plot fairly predictable [***The Killing Tree***] is a generally satisfying suspenseful adventure. . . .

A review of "The Killing Tree: A Novel," in The Booklist, *Vol. 69, No. 5, November 1, 1972, p. 242.*

KIRKUS REVIEWS

[***The Long Black Coat*** is a] taut, uncluttered thriller about Brooklynite Phil Brant, first seen at the funeral of older brother Vinnie who—unknown to Phil but revealed to readers in a one-page preface—pulled a bank vault job on the Coast with two accomplices just before the three of them were shipped out to Vietnam. Phil's grief is soon mixed with uneasiness and then displaced by terror as Vinnie's army buddies appear on the scene and begin to close in on Phil, the kid brother to whom they believe Vinnie had confided the whereabouts of the stolen package. . . . [The] tired trick ending . . . [is] preceded by a whole hatful of stock devices, but Bennett makes the efficient most of Phil's feelings for his brother and his growing sense of menace.

A review of "The Long Black Coat," in Kirkus Reviews, *Vol. XLI, No. 7, April 1, 1973, p. 395.*

PUBLISHERS WEEKLY

[In **"The Long Black Coat"**, too] many improbabilites and unanswered questions mar what could be a real thriller. Vinnie Brant and two other thieves had robbed a bank before leaving to serve in Vietnam. When Vinnie is killed, the survivors—Dawson and Madigan—move in on his young brother, Phil. . . . The key to the mystery is hidden in a costly cashmere coat which Vinnie had planned to sport in civilian life. Phil discovers the secret at the same time Vinnie turns up, not dead after all. . . . We wish the author had taken the time and trouble to build a convincing story on these promising elements.

A review of "The Long Black Coat," in Publishers Weekly, *Vol. 203, No. 19, May 7, 1973, p. 65.*

SARAH LAW KENNERLY

Trite, cliché-ridden, and lacking in tension and suspense, ***Shadows Offstage*** . . . does not measure up to Jay Bennett's previous mysteries. At 16, Anna Kowalski left the West Virginia mining country to make her fortune in New York. At twenty-five, having been transformed into the beautiful, talented Cinderella Wharton, she is about to star in a Broadway play. She sends for her 18-year-old brother Peter to share her triumph, but he arrives instead to witness her "suicide." Cindy's friends urge Peter to go back to West Virginia, but he is determined to find out why his sister killed herself. . . . Finally, in what fails to be a shocking climax, Peter discovers that Cindy was murdered.

Sarah Law Kennerly, in a review of "Shadows Offstage," in School Library Journal, *an appendix to* Library Journal, *Vol. 20, No. 9, May, 1974, p. 69.*

PUBLISHERS WEEKLY

[**"Shadows Offstage"** is a] taut, engrossing mystery.... It's soundly structured and baffling, although all the clues are duly offered. Young Pete Kowlaski comes to New York from his home town in the mining country of West Virginia to visit his sister, "Cindy Wharton," née Anna Kowalski.... [One] evening she kills herself, leaving a cryptic note for Pete. The boy believes she was murdered and sets out to find her killer. Among the suspects are a cruel jockey, Cindy's dance instructor, her director, with whom she had quarreled violently, and others. The unmasking is a real surprise and a real shocker.

A review of "Shadows Offstage," in Publishers Weekly, *Vol. 205, No. 22, June 3, 1974, p. 157.*

PUBLISHERS WEEKLY

Mr. Bennett's new novel [**"The Dangling Witness"**] is superior in many ways to **"The Long Black Coat."** ... Featured here is Matthew who's working as an usher in a movie theatre to help pay his college expenses. He witnesses a murder and knows who the criminal is but does nothing about it. Matt is terrified of violence, having inadvertently caused the death of a fellow player in a football game. It takes the friendship of the murdered man's sister, Julie, and the intelligent understanding of a detective, Anderson ... to resolve the crisis of his conscience and the case. The characters are all believable and so is the plot in this solid story. It offers not only entertainment but subtle moral guide lines.

A review of "The Dangling Witness," in Publishers Weekly, *Vol. 206, No. 7, August 12, 1974, p. 58.*

GLORIA LEVITAS

Matthew Garth, the college-aged hero of **"Dangling Witness,"** approaches the threat to his life with a veneer of cold-blooded rationality. An accidental witness to murder, Matthew refuses either to identify the killer or to cooperate with the police in apprehending him. Although his life has been threatened, Matthew's paralysis does not derive from physical cowardice but from emotional turmoil over his relationship with a bitter, disillusioned father and with the powerful, and not unattractive, man behind the killings. Bennett's book promises more than it ultimately delivers, principally because it fails to develop Matthew's relationship with both men into a psychological imperative, but uses it instead as a *deus ex machina*. (p. 10)

Gloria Levitas, "Haunts and Hunts," in The New York Times Book Review, November 10, 1974, pp. 8, 10.*

SARAH LAW KENNERLY

Jay Bennett is back with another of his hard-hitting crime stories. After Fred Corell discovers that his father is head of an underworld syndicate, he disowns him, changes his own name to Morgan, and tries to make a new life for himself. Now a college student, Fred is jolted to receive a mysterious phone call telling him to ***Say Hello to the Hit Man***.... Filled with bitterness and fear, he finally goes to his father who insists on giving him around-the-clock bodyguards. Fred's only escape from constant surveillance is when he is with Callie Ross, the only person he feels he can trust, who saves him from being killed when he inadvertently steps in front of a car. The climax is a shocker, and this murder mystery, brutal as it is, deserves not to be missed.

Sarah Law Kennerly, in a review of "Say Hello to the Hit Man," in School Library Journal, *Vol. 22, No. 9, May, 1976, p. 77.*

GLORIA LEVITAS

[**"Say Hello to the Hit Man"** is not very] successful in its attempt to explore a set of twisted family relationships.... Bennett has used his terse, staccato style to better effect in previous novels. Here his use of allusion rather than statement struck me as coy; and his attempt to make the mundane appear mysterious seemed more crafty than artful. The ingredients of this novel will be familiar to Bennett's readers: a young college student whose only crime is that he is the son of an organized-crime figure, is suddenly threatened with death.... Unfortunately, Bennett clumsily telegraphs the solution to his mystery early in the book. More damaging is that Bennett's allusive cinematic style proves too fragile to support the psychological mysteries he has imposed upon but failed to integrate with character and plot.

Gloria Levitas, in a review of "Say Hello to the Hit Man," in The New York Times Book Review, *May 2, 1976, p. 38.*

PUBLISHERS WEEKLY

[**"The Birthday Murderer"**] earns high grades for its atmosphere of suspense and menace. Shan Rourke's 17th birthday party is shattered by a letter accusing him of murdering another young man at the latter's 17th birthday party 12 years before.... Shan's feeling of inexplicable terror is compounded by what he fears are hallucinations of a figure stalking him. When his potential murderer reveals himself the boy is isolated and terrified. Shan is a deftly drawn, credible character, but his mother is not.... The novel ends on a sad and bitter note. Shan is vindicated, but still feels abandoned by his mother.

A review of "The Birthday Murderer," in Publishers Weekly, *Vol. 212, No. 8, August 22, 1977, p. 66.*

ZENA SUTHERLAND

[In ***The Birthday Murderer***] Shan gets a card that says, "Happy Birthday, Murderer," and the handwriting is his own. He pries out of his mother the fact that he had accidentally caused the death of adolescent George Lambert when he (Shan) was five. His widowed mother is now in love with George's father, and both of them assure him that they feel he is innocent. Shan is convinced that someone is trying to kill him ... that it has to be Lambert.... The ending is sharply dramatic, following a careful building of suspense; although there are some parts of the story that seem over-extended, it is constructed deftly enough to compensate for the uneven pace.

Zena Sutherland, in a review of "The Birthday Murderer," in Bulletin of the Center for Children's Books, *Vol. 31, No. 6, February, 1978, p. 90.*

BOOK WORLD—THE WASHINGTON POST

[***The Birthday Murderer*** is strong] psychological suspense involving a young man whose life is being threatened—it begins with teasing menace and quickly escalates into violence—by a family friend determined to avenge the death of his son years before. Bennett is adroit at establishing mood; here, the reader is forced to participate in the hero's questioning of his own sanity as he faces the seeming unlikelihood of an otherwise respectable adult's madness.

A review of "The Birthday Murderer," in Book World—The Washington Post, *October 7, 1979, p. 15.*

DREW STEVENSON

Jay Bennett deftly draws readers into a web of terror. ***The Pigeon*** . . . is high school senior Brian Cawley, lured to his girlfriend's Greenwich Village apartment only to find her murdered. . . . Suffering from loneliness, loss, and isolation, he turns to his old teacher, Mrs. Fisher, who lives in Soho. Mrs. Fisher helps him disguise himself so that he can go undercover to look for Donna's killers. What he finds is a young band of international terrorists who have set bombs on the Staten Island ferry, and only Brian can avert a massacre. Bennett's dialogue is terse, biting, and effective, while Brian's eventual triumph is realistically bitter-sweet.

Drew Stevenson, in a review of "The Pigeon," in School Library Journal, *Vol. 26, No. 9, May, 1980, p. 86.*

ANN A. FLOWERS

The characterizations [in ***The Pigeon***], especially of the ruthless members of the terrorist gang and of the strong, kindly teacher, lack depth; and it is hard to believe that a seventeen-year-old could show such self-control and resourcefulness in an emergency as Brian does. But the dialogue is taut and spare, the story fast-paced and exciting.

Ann A. Flowers, in a review of "The Pigeon," in The Horn Book Magazine, *Vol. LVI, No. 5, October, 1980, p. 523.*

KENNETH L. DONELSON and ALLEEN PACE NILSEN

Deathman Do Not Follow Me, [Jay Bennett's] first book, begins as a fine study of alienated Danny Morgan. Unhappily, once the reader cares about Danny, a silly mystery intrudes and the book falls apart. But two of his later books [***The Long Black Coat*** and ***The Dangling Witness***] are more successful. . . .

His most hard-boiled work is ***Say Hello to the Hit Man.*** Fred Morgan, an apparently typical college student with a girl friend, a job, and a future, is the son of a crime syndicate leader. Fred dislikes his father and will not acknowledge him. By the second page, we know something is terribly wrong when [Fred gets a telephone call from a stranger telling him he is going to die]. . . . Out of desperation, Fred seeks his father's help, several people become suspects, and, though the ending is vaguely reminiscent of Hammett's *The Maltese Falcon,* it has a character of its own.

Bennett's mysteries more commonly hinge on implied violence and real threats than on actual murders. Active violence, Bennett seems to say, is less threatening than the possibility of imminent violence, and he's right because threats from unknown or shadowy sources are insidious and may go on forever whereas the event, the actual violence, is real and can be handled, assuming, of course, that you are not dead. (p. 239)

Kenneth L. Donelson and Alleen Pace Nilsen, "Excitement and Suspense: Of Sudden Shadows," in their Literature for Today's Young Adults, *Scott, Foresman and Company, 1980, pp. 228-57.**

HILDAGARDE GRAY

[In ***The Pigeon,*** Jay Bennett] uses as leading characters neo-Nazis, terrorists, (yesterday's leather-jacketed rebels under current pseudonyms) and has them decide to eliminate Donna, whose political loyalties have begun to reflect a law-and-order attitude.

To provide the action line, Donna's paramour of another day is fingered as the pigeon, framed by a simple call for help from unwitting Donna. Brian arrives only to find her already dead and the phone ringing, almost demanding to be answered.

The raspy voice tells Brian that he's been deliberately placed at the murder scene with police already on the way.

Suspense and denouncement of violence proceed hand in hand to a timely. . . . climax. The author's claim is to write about violent times while simultaneously entering a plea for non-violence. Doubts must plague the reader, though, who will surely pick up an "end justifies the means" philosophy for the good guys with condemnation of the exact same idea as a tenet of terrorist faith!

Hildagarde Gray, in a review of "The Pigeon," in Best Sellers, *Vol. 40, No. 10, January, 1981, p. 349.*

STEPHANIE ZVIRIN

[In ***The Executioner***] Bennett offers a melodramatic, at times forced, genre piece in which characters and plot take a backseat to mystery and suspense; but he manipulates his elements with unconcerned ease and assembles enough suspected killers to keep armchair detectives enthusiastically guessing to the end.

Stephanie Zvirin, in a review of "The Executioner," in Booklist, *Vol. 78, No. 15, April 1, 1982, p. 1014.*

DREW STEVENSON

[***The Executioner***] is a typical Jay Bennett mystery—plenty of chills with no frills. It begins with an auto accident in which driver Raymond Warner is killed. Of the three surviving teenagers in the car . . . only Bruce knows that it was he who unintentionally caused the car to swerve out of control. Bruce feels intensely guilty and, what's more, suspects that someone holds him, along with Ed and Elaine, personally responsible for Raymond's death. . . . The suspense is heart-stopping before he learns his stalker's identity. Tight, tense and terrifying, as always.

Drew Stevenson, in a review of "The Executioner," in School Library Journal, *Vol. 28, No. 9, May, 1982, p. 84.*

JOHN RUTH

The writing [in ***The Executioner***] is hackneyed, the plot laborious, but teens will more than likely enjoy this book in spite of its flaws because of the very fact that they are unsophisticated readers and have not yet learned to expect, in literature, more than they are given. I was not impressed—especially after reading the author's "professed aim" of using every word he writes to cry out against violence. Bennett, if he's crying out in this book, not only has a weak voice but masks whatever point he tries to make with a less than original, lower than mediocre, simple minded mystery. This is especially distressing when one considers the need for a tell-it-like-it-is, gut level YA novel about young people and alcohol. A supreme disappointment.

John Ruth, in a review of "The Executioner," in Voice of Youth Advocates, *Vol. 5, No. 3, August, 1982, p. 28.*

PUBLISHERS WEEKLY

[In ***Slowly, Slowly I Raise the Gun***] Bennett is back with a tale of intrigue that's anything but melodramatic, as the title suggests. The characters and fraught events compel close attention to the dilemma facing 18-year-old Chris Gordon and those he's involved with. Years after the death of his mother Marian, Chris receives anonymous notes accusing his father Jamie of murdering the woman. . . . Trying to find out if his father is guilty as charged, Chris is influenced by his kind, caring stepmother Ellen, by Marian's sister Rhoda who hates and fears Jamie and by Lisa, the girl Chris loves. When he's sure that he must kill his father, or be killed, the confrontation creates hair-trigger suspense.

A review of "Slowly, Slowly I Raise the Gun," in Publishers Weekly, *Vol. 223, No. 26, July 1, 1983, p. 103.*

SCHOOL LIBRARY JOURNAL

The agony for Chris Gordon [in ***Slowly, Slowly I Raise the Gun***] begins when he receives an anonymous note saying that his deceased mother was murdered and that he too is in danger. It just so happens that Chris is playing *Hamlet* in a local production and throughout the story associates his current predicament with that of Hamlet. Chris suspects that his father Jamie, a former professional football player, killed his mother, who supposedly died of cancer. . . . After a number of tense confrontations with Jamie, Chris discovers the truth about him, about his mother's death and about the source of the anonymous warnings. Bennett is known for his short sharp dialogue but here the conversations are so terse that one is reminded of *Dragnet*. The atmosphere of fear and tension is, as always, sustained from beginning to end, but the plot is far-fetched and disappointing, especially the climax. This latest effort sags under the weight of its own melodrama.

A review of "Slowly, Slowly I Raise the Gun," in School Library Journal, *Vol. 30, No. 4, December, 1983, p. 84.*

DOLORES MAMINSKI

It is unfortunate that Jay Bennett is so popular a YA author, because his name alone will cause teens to pick up this disappointing mystery [***Slowly, Slowly I Raise the Gun***]. A potentially interesting (though not unique) plot is thin and transparent, even to the most inexperienced reader. . . .

The dialogue is so abrupt and choppy that it is irritating to read. One thus tends to skim over entire pages, making the book a very quick read indeed. Characters are developed minimally and excite no interest or concern. Unlike many other Bennett titles, this one is a bore.

Dolores Maminski, in a review of "Slowly, Slowly I Raise the Gun," in Voice of Youth Advocates, *Vol. 6, No. 6, February, 1984, p. 337.*

DENISE L. MOLL

Peter, the narrator [of ***I Never Said I Loved You***] is a Princeton freshman, destined to join his father's law firm. In flashback, readers learn of his relationship with Alice, an intellectual idealist who is something of a romantic. Alice has some very definite plans for Peter, but his plans for himself are not so clear cut. Readers never really know if he chooses law because it appeals to him or because he's following the path of least resistence, a trait that he has acquired from his mother. During their time together, Alice calls the shots, yet it is Peter who makes the final decision to sever the relationship. Characterizations are good, and there are a few genuinely funny moments, but the writing is often heavy-handed.

Denise L. Moll, in a review of "I Never Said I Loved You," in School Library Journal, *Vol. 30, No. 10, August, 1984, p. 80.*

MARY K. CHELTON

Conservative Peter, third generation in line for Princeton and the law, falls in love with classmate free spirit Alice who makes it clear that she has no intentions of staying with somebody who does what is conventional and expected. Peter wavers because he really loves her, but finally decides to follow the traditional family role, and the love story founders. [***I Never Said I Loved You***] begins with Alice's detour en route back to college to see Peter, and ends with his painfully deliberate avoidance of seeing her again. The entire story, told in the first person from Peter's point of view, almost completely in dialogue, without any explicit sex, is utterly heartrending. All the talent previously used by Bennett to evoke mood and plot with an absolute minimum of description in his excellent mysteries is evident here, making this a satisfying read on a complicated topic for a broad range of reading levels. . . . Anyone who lumps this with the series romances is a fool. It is so much better.

Mary K. Chelton, in a review of "I Never Said I Loved You," in Voice of Youth Advocates, *Vol. 7, No. 3, August, 1984, p. 143.*

Steven Bochco

1944?-

Michael Kozoll

1940?-

Photograph furnished by NBC. Courtesy of Steven Bochco

Photograph furnished by NBC. Courtesy of Michael Kozoll

American scriptwriters and television producers.

Bochco and Kozoll are best known as the creators of "Hill Street Blues," a critically acclaimed television series about a group of police officers working in an inner-city precinct. The series realistically depicts the dangers and frustrations of police work, including the tragedy of youths who commit serious crimes and the sometimes indifferent and ineffectual judicial system. While portraying these conditions, many of the episodes also contain comic situations that border on slapstick and the absurd. "Hill Street Blues" premiered in January 1981 and received poor viewer ratings, ranking eighty-seventh out of the ninety-six prime-time television programs aired that season. However, it was nominated for a record twenty-one Emmy Awards and won eight Emmys in both performance and production categories, including the "Outstanding Drama Series" award. Bochco and Kozoll also received Emmys for the teleplay "Hill Street Station" and the Edgar Allan Poe Award and the George Foster Peabody Award for Broadcasting in 1981. Since then, "Hill Street Blues" has attracted a large and faithful audience and is generally considered one of television's more sophisticated and provocative dramas.

The concept of "Hill Street Blues" was originated by Fred Silverman, formerly the president of the National Broadcasting Corporation. He wanted to create a police drama that combined elements of Daniel Petrie's violent film about New York City police officers, *Fort Apache: The Bronx*, with the humor of the police-comedy television series "Barney Miller." Silverman persuaded Bochco and Kozoll, who had been story editors for such popular detective series as "Columbo" and "Quincy," to develop a police drama that focused on the personal lives of its characters. The essence of "Hill Street Blues," according to Bochco, is to dramatize the lives of people "who happen to be cops, as opposed to cops who, in some small corner of their lives, happen to be people." Although several NBC censors thought the pilot episode was "too grim, violent, and sexy," Bochco and Kozoll insisted that these elements were essential to a realistic portrait of urban life and crime.

The popularity and critical reputation of "Hill Street Blues" rests primarily on its unique insight into human character and motivation. Unlike most detective series, which depend on a single superficial hero or heroine, the show features an ensemble of thirteen well-developed individuals of various ethnic backgrounds and idiosyncrasies. "Hill Street Blues" is also recognized for representing the diverse ways in which women function in a predominantly male environment. Fay Furillo depends on the men in her life to make decisions concerning her welfare; Officer Lucy Bates adopts a tough, masculine image while on duty to suppress her sensitivity and vulnerability; and Joyce Davenport typifies the secure white-collar professional whose credibility is sometimes challenged by males. The balance of criminals, police officers, and law-abiding citizens from different upbringings and lifestyles has also been commended.

Another distinguishing feature of "Hill Street Blues" is its format. The scripts contain multiple storylines, some of which are resolved during a single episode, while others extend into several. As in real life, various crises are never resolved. Some critics fault this structure, contending that it makes the show choppy and difficult to follow, but others claim it adds depth to the stories. The technical production of "Hill Street Blues" is considered innovative for television. The combination of handheld cameras and dull lighting, an abundance of minor characters crowding the sets, and the use of overlapping dialogue and background soundtracks adds an authentic sense of confusion to the show. John O'Connor suggests that "the very insistence of 'Hill Street Blues' in being seemingly messy is what gives the show its distinctive personality."

Kozoll left the show after its second season to pursue a career in film. Bochco stayed with "Hill Street Blues" as executive producer until the conclusion of the 1984-85 season. While Bochco and Kozoll are credited with writing scripts that are intelligent and challenging as well as entertaining, some critics contend that the stories are contrived and pretentious. A few reviewers have expressed concern that the clever situations and unusual texture of "Hill Street Blues" may lose its originality and raw energy. Still, the dramatic force and humane quality of "Hill Street Blues" has helped promote similar standards in contemporary television. "Hill Street Blues" won the "Outstanding Drama Series" Emmy award in 1981, 1982, 1983, and 1984.

HARRY F. WATERS

Set in an inner-city police station, [**"Hill Street Blues"**] deftly blends the lunacy of "Barney Miller" with the gritty authenticity of "The Police Tapes," public TV's classic *cinéma vérité* documentary. Headquarters captain Frank Furillo . . . has long ago learned that criminals are the least of his aggravations. He must cope with drop-in sociologists determined to "interface with the police experience"; a Serpico-style detective with a penchant for biting the noses off perpetrators, and the commander of the resident S.W.A.T. team, who thinks he's George Patton. Pleading to blow away some hoods holding hostages, he explains: "My guys need the validation."

Yet the series is anything but a laughing matter. The precinct house is a true war zone, its inhabitants an occupation force treated with equal contempt by those they are serving and those they are fighting. Black hats and blue hats seem almost interchangeable; the only immutable law is the insane randomness of tragedy. This is rough, unconventional video terrain, peopled by all those station-house habitués we welcome into our homes and then lock out as soon as their pain ceases to be sitcom funny. It commands at least a visit.

Harry F. Waters, "The Peacock Lays an Egg," in Newsweek, *Vol. XCVII, No. 2, January 12, 1981, p. 58.**

TOM BUCKLEY

"Ten-thirteen" is the police-radio code for "assist patrolman." Too bad there isn't a signal for "assist writers," because **"Hill Street Blues"** needs help badly. . . .

The writer-producer team of Steve Bochco and Michael Kozoll has tried to present the men of the Hill Street station house in an unidentified metropolis as the kind of oddballs who would be members of the bow-and-arrow squad of any big-city force. That is, not permitted to carry weapons because of emotional instability.

One plainclothes man bites suspects on the ankle or the nose and turns out to have a mother complex. Another is an inept Don Juan. A good ol' boy patrolman wears cowboy boots and a string tie with his uniform. His radio-car partner, inevitably, is a young, well-educated black. The precinct sergeant behaves like a house mother, the captain's alimony checks bounce and the leader of the city's Swat team thinks he's George C. Scott playing Patton.

But **"Hill Street Blues"** veers back and forth between comic situations that aren't funny—serious matters such as the taking of hostages during a robbery and the shooting of two patrolmen—and a romance that is merely silly.

An effort has been made to achieve a sense of gritty reality with tight hand-held camera shots, garish lighting and the technique used by Robert Altman of having the characters frequently step on one another's dialogue, further confusing an already choppy script.

Tom Buckley, "'Hill Street Blues': New NBC Police Series," in The New York Times, *January 17, 1981, p. 48.*

VARIETY

With **"Hill Street Blues,"** NBC-TV has obviously come up with the best-crafted series of the 1980-81 season to date. The question is "do they know what to do with it?"

A series concept that resembles "Lou Grant" in form and style and conjures up memories of the "Marcus-Nelson Murders" pilot for "Kojak" and Joel Oliansky's "The Law," . . . **"Hill St."** nevertheless has an originality of its own. Its style seems to be the slice-of-life kind of approach used on "Grant," adapted to fit the activities of a police precinct in a ghetto area of an unnamed eastern city. . . .

The viewer interest is generated by the conflicting styles and attitudes of the cops involved, ranging from [Captain Frank Furillo's] composed top cop through seasoned sergeant [Phil Esterhaus], gung-ho sergeant [Howard Hunter] and varied other fuzz types. . . .

The pervading flavor of the series' opener was reality (and thus believability), which was laced with a lot more natural humor than one might expect—and it all looked as commercial as all get out. The writing, by exec producers Steven Bochco and

Michael Kozoll, was tight, terse and insightful and Robert Butler's direction permitted an awful lot of activity to go on without the viewer losing track of the story-line continuity. . . . If there was an apparent weak spot in the concept, it would be the secret romance between [Furillo] and attorney [Joyce Davenport]—but that aspect of the premise might work out. . . .

At the moment, **"Hill Street Blues"** looks like a sure winner. . . .

Bok., in a review of "Hill Street Blues," in Variety, *January 21, 1981, p. 80.*

RICHARD CORLISS

[***Hill Street Blues***] is the best new series since *Taxi*.

In the '70s, TV opened its cyclops eye wide enough to recognize that Americans don't spend all of their time on the Ponderosa spread or in suburban kitchens. Some people actually work for a living, and those people became the focus for some of TV's finest series: *Mary Tyler Moore, Taxi, Lou Grant, WKRP in Cincinnati*. . . . In ***Hill Street Blues*** . . . all is motion and commotion; for Hill Street is part of a nameless inner city, and the Blues are the men and women of the local police precinct. Each episode traces a day in the life of the precinct, as the Blues try to defuse street crime, play social worker at knife point, slip out of an octopus stranglehold of red tape, keep their private lives from ending in a singles bar or the divorce court. Sometimes their allies are teenage gang lords who come on like Geronimo crossed with the Blues Brothers; sometimes their toughest adversaries are officers whose tensions threaten to explode in a one-man apocalypse. The show treats those on both sides of the law with respect for their crotchets and obsessions. . . .

In charge of the carnage and chaos is Captain Francis Furillo . . . , a good, strong man breeding an ulcer while trying to do a tough job. At the end of every crisis-strewn day, each superb show, Furillo struggles home in an uneasy truce with his job, his willful woman . . . and himself. . . . Viewers will do . . . themselves a favor by visiting ***Hill Street*** as often as possible.

Richard Corliss, "Midwinter Night's Dreams: 'Hill Street Blues'," in Time, *Vol. 117, No. 4, January 26, 1981, p. 72.*

RICHARD T. JAMESON

Hill Street Blues: Cop show. Thirteen series regulars identified up front, most of them unfamiliar and most of them frozen in slantwise TV grin. Handheld camera, Action News editing, and overlapping mutters on the soundtrack during the morning briefing that opens the show—mannneristic bad signs for the jaundiced viewer, though they did seem to make for an appropriate grab-shot naturalism here. What the hell, give it a chance. . . .

[The characters] have to get identified; even Lou Grant needed half an hour of his first show to get settled in at the *Trib*. And by the time that much of ***Hill Street Blues'*** first episode has gone by, all suspicion of ethnic and cuteness quotas have dissolved, a community has been defined, and these people are simply who they are, neither more nor less "on" than they need to be to lead their professional and personal lives. That's something many TV series—indeed, many feature films—never manage to do. Hand in hand with this achievement goes the series' amazing success at finding a narrative rhythm to accommodate its need to develop shaped dramatic events and at the same time honor the institutional imperative that the precinct's story, and the stories of the individuals in occupational orbit there, must be ongoing, beyond resolution. Over the five episodes televised as of this writing, interest has never flagged; yet I have never encountered another TV program that betrayed less sign of anticipating commercial breaks or straining to tie off tonight's episode. . . .

[The series' creators] generate a density that not only puts standard over-lighted, emptied-out, programmatically-written television drama to shame, but can hold its own against most recent movies.

As the denizens of Hill Street might put it in their verbally unfettered fashion, ***Hill Street Blues*** has texture up the wazoo. Any given space in the precinct house contains more bodies than should humanely be expected to occupy the same vicinity, and the flow of action and movement refuses to respect the conventional television inviolability of the fourth wall. (p. 78)

[The] camera covers this and the endlessly various urban-ghetto milieux with an intricacy and agility that never tips over into visual complication for its own self-displaying sake. We see clearly what we need to see, and at the same time see it in the context of the living flux—social, political, professional, interpersonal—which surrounds and defines it. The backs of shots are often as intriguing as the foregrounds, and there's no predicting when a background element is going to insinuate itself into the foreground. Likewise, the principals in one episode may serve as little more than occupational color, glorified extras, in the next, while an apparent walk-on may unexpectedly become a major focus of dramatic intensification.

There's no telling, either, where the action may lead, or when the comic and the dramatic are going to bleed into each other. In the premiere episode, . . . [officers Hill and Renko] answer a call to settle a violent family squabble. . . . The viewer is still marveling over the matter-of-factness with which incest has wafted into range and out again, when Hill and Renko arrive back at curbside to find their brand new squad car missing. It isn't the first time the cops have been in this absurd position and, the nearby call box having been ripped off as well, they mosey toward a semi-derelict building across the street in search of a public phone. They step through the door, the angle shifts to a dope pusher in the act of making a sale at the rear of the lobby, and before we or the cops can adjust to the surprise, the dealer has pulled a gun and shot both men down.

As it happens, the gunning-down of Hill and Renko (who survive to become the emotional center of a drama of readjustment, mutual estrangement, and rapprochement in subsequent episodes) and the Emergency Action Team shootup of a street-gang siege elsewhere in the same program account for the only shots fired thus far in the series. Neither, mercifully, has there been a single car chase. Instead, ***Hill Street Blues*** has mostly concerned itself with the continuing, volatile complexities of urban peace-keeping, the bureaucratic infighting of various law-enforcement and other governmental agencies, and, above all, the lives and evolving characterizations of the regulars. (pp. 78-9)

Richard T. Jameson, "Quality Up the Wazoo," in Film Comment, *Vol. 17, No. 2, March-April, 1981, pp. 78-9.*

JEAN BERGANTINI GRILLO

Ever since *The Untouchables* appeared in 1959, Italian-Americans have been sensitive about their portrayal on TV. While I would have preferred a profile of William Paca (who signed the Declaration of Independence), the first so-called Itlo I met on the tube was Al Capone, star of the show my nonethnic friends jeeringly called "Cops and Wops." Recent series characters such as Angie, Laverne, *Taxi*'s Tony and all those soap-opera heavies invariably named Vito or Sal aren't exactly inspiring, either. (p. 35)

[***Hill Street Blues,*** on the other hand,] is a thoughtful melting-pot drama. . . . [The] program portrays an inner-city police station with the required ethnic mix: an Italian, a Jew, a Slav, a black, a Hispanic, some Irish. . . . [The significance of ***Hill Street***] is that all of these characters have several different dimensions. Sometimes they're good; other times they blow it. Sometimes they act with feeling; other times they're mean-spirited and unlovable. In short, they're a gathering of *human beings* who just happen to have widely different last names. (You know, like real life.) ***Hill Street Blues*** is the all-too-rare example demonstrating that you *can* have an ethnic drama without the characters being one-dimensional.

Precinct captain, Frank Furillo, the group's leader, is one of the few Italian-American TV creations who could actually be somebody's relative. He is warm but not ridiculously emotional; he's handsome but not flashy; he has humanistic values without being simplistic. Most important, he is a thinker—one of the few media Itlos who doesn't require "street-smart" written before his name. (pp. 36-38)

All of ***Hill Street***'s main characters are so genuine and worthy, it's impossible not to like them. . . .

Does this mean all TV ethnics must be Furillos? Of course not. My belief in the First Amendment prevents me from supporting any pressure group that would censor even lousy shows such as *The Gangster Chronicles*. What is needed is balance. Ethnic pride wouldn't bruise so easily if many other dramas existed highlighting all that is fine in America's immigrant history. The saga of all those who rose out of the ghetto without resorting to crime remains largely untold. (p. 38)

Jean Bergantini Grillo, "Ethnic Slurs Are Back," in TV Guide® *Magazine, Vol. 29, No. 24, June 13, 1981, pp. 35-6, 38.**

RICHARD MEYERS

People don't like things being shoved down their throats. Telling someone that something is good for him will usually have him running for cover. NBC is in danger of doing that with [***Hill Street Blues***]. . . . The publicity campaign aside, the series itself is impressive. Every episode seems an exercise in monumental logistics. Boasting thirteen regular cast members, every scene seems to be awash with movement. In fact, the show can occasionally be tiring to watch, there's so much going on. Otherwise, a strange feeling of *déjà vu* seemed to grip me as I stared at the set. Where had I seen this show before?

I'll tell you where. On *Lou Grant, M*A*S*H, Barney Miller, The Muppet Show,* and *Second City TV*. . . . [The character] Belker borrowed the look of the "Animal" character on *Grant* while borrowing the manner of the "Animal" character of the Muppets (Belker is known for occasionally biting suspects). . . . [Howard Hunter] is merely *M*A*S*H*'s Frank Burns character grown up and trying to be G. Gordon Liddy. He's about as unrealistic as the Frank Burns character was too. And that no-good, no-account cop Johnny LaRue . . . got his name and his evil ways from the Johnny LaRue played by John Candy on the comedy-satire *Second City* program. (pp. 255-56)

[Everybody backstage] has got his heart in the right place . . . , but I don't know what it is. Maybe it's NBC's pushing, but I get the feeling everybody is trying too hard. They're trying too hard for the pathos, they're trying too hard for the drama, and they're especially trying too hard for the comedy. It's disconcerting when a person leaps out of character simply for the sake of humor.

The most glaring example of this I can remember came when intrepid Capt. Furillo . . . was in the middle of delicate negotiations with some hoods holding hostages in a meat locker when beefy Sgt. Esterhaus . . . interrupted with a call trying to save the station-house decorator he had fallen in like with from being fired. Now, the series plays up Esterhaus's unusual sexual tastes, but it was very unlikely the desk sergeant would blow a situation he knew was dangerous for that lame reason.

But perhaps all this is Hill Street hair splitting. I will agree with the majority of the critical establishment: [***Hill Street Blues***] is a worthy, worthwhile series. But these are just a few of the reasons I don't go racing to my set every time the program is on. After all, the name of the media game is to stay on, not to send critics into fits of rapture. (p. 256)

Richard Meyers, in a review of "Hill Street Blues," in The Armchair Detective, *Vol. 14, No. 3, Summer, 1981, pp. 255-56.*

MARK CRISPIN MILLER

America's television critics . . . have cheered [**"Hill Street Blues"**] with an outcry of defensive praise unprecedented in the history of television.

By and large, they like it for two reasons. First of all, it strikes them as very realistic, and so they tend, in their plaudits, to use certain adjectives that suggest the cast of characters in a porno remake of *Snow White:* "gutsy," "gritty," "racy," "raunchy," "punchy," "tough," and "steamy." And yet they also applaud the show's correctness as a liberal statement: the show is good because it contains little violence and no offensive ethnic stereotypes. While its characters are ethnically diverse, enthused one columnist in a recent issue of *TV Guide* [see Grillo excerpt above], they are simply "a gathering of *human beings* who just happen to have widely different last names. (You know, like real life.). . . . All (these) characters are so genuine and worthy, it's impossible not to like them."

Now that's heart-warming, if not very steamy. In "real life," it seems, there are no ethnic traits, nor any such things as national character, regional identity, or class consciousness. And everyone is equally "genuine and worthy." This is gritty realism? In fact, **"Hill Street Blues"** is not both true to life and idealized, because such a combination is impossible. A work might either reflect "real life" or transcend it. As it happens, ***"Hill Street Blues"*** does neither. Although promising at first, the show soon settled down to do little more than promulgate a tired ideology.

Its "realism" is largely the quick result of a few well-worn cinematic devices. A hand-held camera, for example, lends many scenes the jerky immediacy of a documentary. There is also plenty of inner-city texture. The precinct-house is credibly seedy, the producers having worked hard to see that things break down: the furnishings are dim and battered, the heat goes out, the vending machines (a running gag) have to be beaten regularly. The streets are a mess, like many of the characters, who overrun this perfect squalor in endless sleazy multitudes. Actors jam the foreground, background, middle distance, and stream across the frame from points unknown. Surely no cop show has ever seemed this crowded; this is *French Connection III*, directed by Thomas Malthus. Even the soundtrack is cluttered. The background hubbub nearly drowns out the dialogue, which is no mean feat, since the characters generally bellow as if going deaf. (You know, like real life.) Their dialogue also overlaps, charging the action with the sort of rich confusion that we notice every day, in films by Robert Altman.

Although this kind of naturalistic din has suffused many American films since the 1960s, on television it seems like a novelty. The show is also structurally unlike the usual prime-time item. Each episode is more fluid and various than the typical plot-and-subplot arrangement, sustaining at least three unrelated stories at a time. Moreover, things don't wind to a tidy close just before the final credits, but stray into subsequent episodes, as in a soap opera. Such openendedness, and the anarchic milieu, create an impression of hectic vitality. The impression is not lasting. Once we spot the gimmicks, that air of "realism" disappears, leaving a tissue of clichés, artfully modernized.

The old-fashioned cop show, best represented by Jack Webb's early productions ("Dragnet," "Adam-12"), usually would go like this: two stern half-wits drive around Los Angeles, looking for "suspicious behavior." Although technically policemen, these dank prigs seemed more like social workers from beyond the grave, always butting in and moralizing with dead faces. No one could be whiter than these guardians of the norm, who protected their necropolis from the threat of a faint diversity (creeps, crooks, punks).

Such were the TV lawmen of another day, when boys liked girls, skies were blue, and blacks were Negroes. Now, of course, most (some?) of us laugh at those grim squares, preferring a groovier sort of policeman, hip, streetwise, and yet "caring," likably rebellious without losing his authoritative air, 100 percent American and still engagingly ethnic—Kojak, Baretta, Toma, Columbo. Collectively, these cops are not a force of clones, but as diverse an army as any band of bad guys, even as diverse as the very USA.

The Hill Street cops reflect this myth from the top down. The leadership is nicely varied. We have a Spanish-American lieutenant [Ray Calletano] . . . who runs the plainclothes division; the Polish-American sergeant Phil Esterhaus . . . ; and an Italian-American in Captain Frank Furillo . . . , the man in charge. Because this trio is acceptably motley, like the crowd in a United Way commercial, we are supposed to applaud it automatically. And just in case we miss the point, the show includes a built-in satire of the thick-witted WASP in the character of Howard Hunter . . . , commander of a SWAT-type outfit. A large, eager buffoon with an angular jaw and blinding teeth, Hunter is accoutered like Douglas MacArthur and sounds like one of Nixon's henchmen (E. Howard Hunter?), always singing the praises of excessive force in bizarre bureaucratese.

This devaluation of the straight white Hunter would seem to place **"Hill Street Blues"** opposite the likes of "Dragnet," but the shows have much in common. Under the surface of his slight ethnicity, for instance, Captain Furillo is as much a pill as Jack Webb's Sergeant Joe Friday. His heritage is a great device, allowing him the authenticity of being Italian, while letting him overcome the stereotype of being Italian. At first, his looks suggest a perfect synthesis of various street-wise types. (He looks like James Caan wearing Roy Scheider's nose.) But Furillo is no warm and explosive Mediterranean, like Travolta, De Niro, et al. On the contrary, he plays so intently against that type that he seems to be turning to cement right on camera. He never moves his neck, and rarely speaks above a soft, slurred monotone, as if afraid that, if he ever lets go, he might break out into an oily tan and start touching everybody.

Furillo's stiff joints are a sign of integrity. He is, of course, much purer than everyone above him. His superiors are always inviting him out to lunch or breakfast so they can harass him with corrupt advice: he should "play ball," etc. He'll never capitulate, or have a bite, but sits and eyes their loaded plates with monkish disapproval. On the other hand, he unbends slightly among his underlings, sometimes even permitting himself a tight little smirk over their wacky ways.

Furillo's function is to seem superior to everyone around him, so that we can feel superior by identifying with him. This strategy is obvious when it refers to those in power: Frank's various bosses and counterparts in the police establishment are all smooth toadies and pompous fools, easy targets like the overdrawn Hunter. We are meant to look down on them because they are unenlightened. When it comes to the common man, however, the strategy becomes more insidious: through Furillo, we find all the little people—civilians as well as policemen—terribly colorful and cute. Each cop is just an amalgam of certain social and psychological tics, all of them stereotypic. We can look down on these characters because their "foibles" are at once laughable and easy to define.

Belker . . . is a funky maniac who likes to bite off parts of suspects, yet always phones his mother (hostile/Jewish). There is patrolman Andy Renko . . . , a loud-mouthed northerner who puts on a Texas accent and always feels slighted (inferiority complex/"good ole boy"). Through this device, the show can include the obligatory cowboy without having to import a real one. J. D. LaRue has a drinking problem and is always scheming (alcoholic/white trash). They are lovably flawed, unglamorous, and weak, presented with the same affectionate contempt that imbues those TV commercials showing "real people" in all their droll impotence.

Not all the show's characters are so condescendingly drawn. The derision, in fact, is highly selective, expressing the liberal bias that has made the show a critical success. For instance, there is nothing funny about those cops who represent, however obliquely, the third world. There are two black officers, [Hill and Washington]. . . . One is handsome, diligent, brave, and upright, and so is the other one. (Washington is more flamboyant than Hill, and that's the only difference.) Ray, the Hispanic lieutenant, is another paragon, soft-spoken and attractive in a fatherly way.

The women are also the figments of some earnest liberal (male) imagination. Lucy . . . is a policewoman, not good-looking, but with a great personality: able and dedicated, yet vulnerable. On the other hand, high ratings demand a measure of tease, and so we have the well-groomed . . . Joyce Davenport, who spends her days in the Office of the Public Defender and her nights in the sack with the divorced Furillo. We are supposed to see Davenport as a liberated woman because she acts like an unfriendly man. . . . She is supposed to be much preferable to Furillo's ex-wife Fay, a shrill flake whose main function is to assault her ex-husband with labored quips: "Harvey is boiled beef, Frank," she complains of an erstwhile boyfriend. "I want escargot."

All the dialogue is painfully arch and overwritten, no matter who's speaking. Esterhaus's lines are all tortured circumlocution, a bad parody of Damon Runyon. . . . [His] verbal mannerisms, like Fay's or Hunter's, get lost in the general flood of inept repartee. Aside from rank clichés ("I need you!" "I'd hate to see you get hurt." "It's OK to cry," etc.), there are stunningly clumsy attempts at clever banter: "Lots of workaholics, of which I consider you one, break out in hives at the mere thought of a vacation." "If you want to see battle scars, I've got a whole closet-full." A promotion, says Davenport, will give Frank "more time for the better things in life, namely *moi*." It's all meant to sound snappy and intriguing, like *interesting* people saying *interesting* things, but it only sounds like what you'd overhear in a singles bar for retarded television writers.

The show tries to cover its shallowness with these inanities, and with the various naturalistic techniques. So far, the viewers haven't bought it. . . . [The] critics have blamed the bad timeslot . . . , assuming that a better one will make a big difference. It may not. And why? Because American viewers have such high standards, and consider **"Hill Street Blues"** overwritten and badly acted? That may seem unlikely. The millions who watch "Real People" or "The John Davidson Show" are probably not too finicky about dramaturgy. On the other hand, they might reject the show's unmistakable smugness, its air of liberal righteousness, its propagandistic pitch disguised as something "gutsy." That is, they may disagree with all those critics who have been campaigning to save **"Hill Street Blues"** from cancellation. . . . It could indicate a new awareness, because there are still too many shows like this, piously telling us how to think and "feel" while suggesting a subtle elitism. Such a rejection of **"Hill Street Blues"** would not be further evidence of any so-called "turn to the right," but simply the repudiation of something dated and offensive. As network television continues its slow decline, the failure of this show would be one more healthy sign of approaching death. (pp. 27-9)

Mark Crispin Miller, "Off the Prigs," in The New Republic, *Vol. 185, No 3, July 18, 1981, pp. 27-9.*

JOHN J. O'CONNOR

The most frequent criticism of **"Hill Street Blues"** is directed at its juggling of several stories in a single hour. Some are neatly brought to a conclusion; others are left open to be finished in another episode; still others are dropped and then picked up again almost at random. Those programming experts committed to tidy beginning-middle-end television formats are irritated. But the very insistence of **"Hill Street Blues"** in being seemingly messy is what gives the show its distinctive personality. It takes chances. Sometimes, getting overly cute, it falls on its face, but its attempts to break the shackles of standard formats are rarely uninteresting. A representative case in point was the recent episode that garnered the series its highest-to-date ratings.

Written by Jeffrey Lewis and directed by Rod Holcomb, the episode began with Sergeant Esterhaus reminding his morning shift to "be cognizant of" the fact that this was the day for Monday-night football on television, which meant that 15 percent of the night force would not show up for work, thereby requiring double shifts for some of the day people. The football motif was to run throughout the hour, especially with Officer Renko . . . determined to avoid any arrest that might require his appearance in court that evening while the game was on. Captain Furillo was learning from the wife he left that his young son had been arrested for shoplifting. She announced that a psychologist said the boy wanted to be caught by his father the cop. Sergeant Esterhaus, having been informed by his widow friend that she might be pregnant, became excited at the prospect of having a "progeny of our own."

Meanwhile, out on the streets, Detectives Johnny LaRue . . . and Neal Washington . . . were arresting a man suspected of viciously mugging a number of elderly people. Officers Lucille Bates . . . and Joe Coffey . . . rushed to the scene of a gang war where an innocent 10-year-old Hispanic girl had been killed. And Detective Mick Belker . . . was forced to resort to his notorious biting techniques in an effort to subdue a giant shakedown thug. Needless to say, most of the officers, including the heatedly reluctant Renko, wound up in night court with their assorted cases.

Then the football routine became silly as, at one point, the judge and attorneys retired hurriedly to his chambers to watch the cliff-hanging conclusion of the game. That much was overdone, evidently in an effort to counterbalance some of the more serious business at hand with some diversions. It seems Joyce Davenport, the public defender, was upset with the entrapment techniques used to arrest the mugger. . . . [The] judge tossed out the case, sympathetically noting to the detectives that "you bring me something I can live with and I'll throw away the key." This resolution could hardly be popular with the vast viewing audience increasingly upset with crime in the streets, an audience that probably would be more comfortable with the vigilantism being marketed on several other police shows.

The episode could have ended there, but the scene switched to Officer Bates pursuing a suspect in the gang-war killing. Ordered to halt, the suspect turned on her and began firing. She responded, killing him instantly and then discovering that he was nothing but "a kid." Although Captain Furillo, upon arriving at the scene, assured her that it was good work, a stunned Lucy moved to the shadows with tears streaming down her face. "What was it?," asked Joyce, sitting in Furillo's car. "A 14-year-old kid who shot a 10-year-old girl," he answered grimly. **"Hill Street Blues"** regained its special composure. If it can maintain a balance between solid substance and the kind of cute gimmicks that supposedly lure bigger audiences, the show should have a long and prestigious run.

John J. O'Connor, "The 'Hill Street Blues' Lesson," in The New York Times, *December 13, 1981, p. 33.*

JAMES WOLCOTT

The backgrounds in NBC's Emmy-laureled police drama ***Hill Street Blues*** . . . are like the backgrounds in Mort Drucker's movie parodies for *Mad:* crowded and comical, crammed with awkward, quirky details. As two cops sass each other over coffee, behind them, his legs thrashing between their heads, a frothing psycho is subdued by a pack of grunting detectives. The cops don't shift their attention or comment on the flailing turmoil around them; a psycho's outburst is simply another rumble of bad weather, as indigenous to the climate of chaos they wade through as wailing sirens and the pumping music spilled out on the streets by cranked-up ghetto-blasters. In a medium which emphasizes foregrounds, the bustling backgrounds of ***Hill Street Blues*** seem raw and daring, as does the bobbing camera work, patchy lighting, and grit-seamed surfaces—all those lurches and scrapes which give the show its semblance of documentary realism. But for all its battle-worn funkiness, ***Hill Street Blues*** has an air of unreality; it seems to be taking place in a rundown urban amusement park: Fort Apache, U.S.A. Instead of ferris wheels and roller coasters, Fort Apache, U.S.A. offers junkies bouncing off the curb, transvestite hookers twirling their pocketbooks and snapping insolent wads of gum. The cops are our wisecracking tour guides, wheeling us from one bombed-out landmark to another as winos wave their bottles of cheap ripple in mock-salute.

Now that ***Hill Street Blues*** has been around a spell and become a secure hit, its clutter no longer seems richly exotic and its idiosyncrasies are beginning to turn into clever schtick. After missing the show for several weeks, I . . . was stunned at how *cute* the show had become. The joshing rowdiness of the early-morning briefing . . . , the morbid rattlings of Mrs. Furillo on cancer and death, the comicbook heroics of . . . Captain Freedom, the embarrassment of a cop sporting a black eye after being pasted one by a jealous hubbie, the slapstick automobile collisions caused by Renko's reckless behavior—all this was as darling as the down on a duck's behind. Some of the cutenesses even seem borrowed. A drawn-out joke about a pair of baseball fans was one Johnny Carson had used in a monologue several months earlier . . . , and much of the buddy-buddy banter reminded one all too painfully of Starsky razzing Hutch. As for [the exploits of] Captain Freedom: this sort of cavorting foolishness has been done so many times before that squadrons of moths seemed to be fluttering overhead, pursuing Freedom in the hope of a large-scale snack.

Of course, it's difficult for any show to keep its edge week after week, particularly a show which pitches itself in the squalor and strife of an urban hellhole. A bit of humor needs to breathe now and then so that the series won't buckle up with a case of hypertension. But the humor in ***Hill Street Blues*** has become so ponderously fey that it threatens to bury the series under the weight of its whimsy. The only moments I truly enjoy in the show are those in which there isn't teeming looniness in the background or frolicsome twitting in the foreground: the stroking bedroom scenes with Furillo . . . and his haughty lawyer lady-love, Joyce. . . . Stretched out on the sheets, Furillo and Joyce have a pettish, murmurous rapport more maturely erotic than almost anything else on television. (It's the sort of sleepy ease Paul Newman had with Melinda Dillon in *Slap Shot*.) In one cuddle session, [Joyce] . . . lowered her head and showered her co-star with her impressive fall of raven-black hair, a gesture almost Egyptian in its voluptuousness. In its rare moments of tender quiet, ***Hill Street Blues*** lives up to its formidable rep, but once the noise washes in, it loses its charm in a babble of wiseguying chatter. Has success spoiled ***Hill Street Blues***? Not yet, but the first mouse-peeps of deterioration are beginning to be heard.

James Wolcott, "Hill Street Cutes," in The Village Voice, *Vol. XXVII, No. 5, January 27-February 2, 1982, p. 61.*

BRIAN CASE

Everyone sleeps safer in their beds for knowing there's another new cop series on the box; it's the documentaries that keep you awake, worrying. By now, television cops bear . . . little resemblance to the real thing. . . .

Most crimes are solved by dead-ass routine or narks, which would take the carbide out of the inkwell as far as **"Hill Street Blues"** is concerned. It's tempting to take all that overlapping dialogue and in-fighter's camerawork for realism, but it's genre and spin-off genre at that.

"MASH" has been here before—different war, same buddyhood and black humour as the little campfire in the surrounding dark. "How can ya joke at a time like this?" "How can ya NOT joke?" goes the routine, amplified every morning by Sergeant Esterhaus's assembly address: "and let's be damn careful out there."

In fact, it's so bad out there that most of them don't seem to go out much, but hug the nick and talk each other down through emotional problems. "If you have a moment?" is a standing request on The Hill, and precedes closeted cuddles for all ranks. (p. 10)

The embodiment of all this concern is Sergeant Esterhaus, bluff-faced as a doorknob, oozing gentleness from his giant frame with the steadiness of a slow puncture. Big cop heart is contrasted at times with the cynicism of the streets in which junkies overdose and punks remark of fire victims "send that one back to the chef—he ain't done enough."

The saving grace of **"Hill Street Blues"** is the way the comedy comes from character, and undercuts the sentimentality behind this cutesy community. "A precinct house is a tenuously balanced social microcosm," says Esterhaus, laughably addressing this information to the markedly unreflective Renko, who wears his flipper-cap with the peak sideways.

Hand-held camera reeling about between black leather shoulders and stake-out sock hats, long-angle chromium automobile fronts and rain-smeared lights, ***"Hill Street Blues"*** is go-go-go.

Clever lines are almost, but not quite squandered in the adrenalin babble. "Today there is cream of wheat where bone marrow should be," raps the sententious Lieutenant Hunter, patrician leaf-cluster on his peak and Grand Old Party pipe in mouth. (p. 11)

Brian Case, "TV Cops Seen Red," in Melody Maker, *March 6, 1982, pp. 10-11.*

TOM SMUCKER

Hill Street Blues is shot in the other great TV style besides L.A. video bright—New York film dark. Lots of different kinds of shows, from sitcoms to cops have used this style. The "it's a jungle out there" cop shows have used both, sometimes at once. And one of the greatest "New York" shows, *Barney Miller,* was shot in "bright L.A.," combined with an over-crowded, give-me-a-break New York visual clutter. "N.Y. dark" hasn't always signified a certain kind of content.

Hill Street Blues takes that dark New York film style, with *Barney Miller's* clutter (and perhaps cast of characters) and moves it further. To the Midwest and an implied permanent recession. Its visual style becomes a metaphor for realism. *Dallas* is our fantasy about the Sunbelt, and about scarcely controlled ambition. J.R.'s grace is one of greed trying, or forced, to remain functional. ***Hill Street Blues*** is "real," and . . . Captain Furillo is moral grace under a shrinking budget.

Is either show really true to life or accurate? I have my own ideas, but what I'm trying to get at here is that both are successful as acts of imagination. Both have hit on formulas and visual styles that have opened up creative possibilities for the people who have to churn the shows out, and have kept them attention-holding for the audience. Both are fertile metaphors. . . .

J.R. is a trickle-down conservative who's forgotten about, or doesn't want to think about, sin. Lapsed Catholic liberal Furillo is obsessed with sin and he's the one who's realistic, who understands limits, and who has a program and a sense of values. Jack Kemp can get elected in Buffalo, but such an optimistic conservative has not been able to be imagined in the Buffalo of TV, ***Hill Street Blues.***

Tom Smucker, "Deep in the Heart of 'Dallas'," in The Village Voice, *Vol. XXVII, No. 47, November 23, 1982, p. 67.**

TODD GITLIN

[The essay from which this excerpt is taken originally appeared in a different version in American Film, *September, 1981.]*

[***Hill Street Blues,*** an] intelligent, literate ensemble police series with its rough texture and intertangled plots, its complex mix of crime melodrama and absurdist comedy, was commissioned by the same network executive who brought America *Real People, The Brady Brides,* and *Sheriff Lobo.* As the networks scrambled to cash in on the presumed trend toward national discipline, Fred Silverman at NBC wanted a down-and-dirty cop show. . . . [What] Silverman got was ***Hill Street Blues,*** at its best a mature and even brilliant show that violated many conventions, pleased critics, caught the undertow of cultural change, and ran away with the Emmys. . . . But for all its singularity, ***Hill Street*** in the end was also commercial television banging up against its limitations, revealing at the moment of its triumph just how powerful are the pressures and formulas that keep prime time close to dead center. For when network television aspires to be extraordinary, the industry's everyday mentality doesn't dissolve. Breakthroughs in form soon become fossilized as formula. This season's odd characters become next season's stereotypes. The weekly assembly line is not kind to writing, acting, or risk-taking. Thus, the story of the extraordinary ***Hill Street Blues***—the product of "a long series of flukes," as its cocreator Michael Kozoll puts it—underscores not only the possibilities of popular culture, but the industry's most ordinary boundaries. ***Hill Street***'s achievement was first of all a matter of style. . . . [Most] of the episodes were written in four-show blocks, with at least four major stories running concurrently, each starting at a different moment and often not resolving at all. In ***Hill Street*** shop talk, the stories were "knitted." This intercutting, which is characteristic of soap opera, was joined to a density of look and sound that was decidedly un-soap operatic. Quick cuts, a furious pace, a nervous camera made for complexity and congestion, a sense of entanglement and continuous crisis that matched the actual density and convolution of city life, of life in a ghetto police precinct in particular. In one episode, for example, five major stories were set up in the first three minutes. In the course of that two-hour sequence, three more story lines were introduced and two others continued. By the end, at least eight major stories were still unresolved. No wonder many people who watched an episode or two found the series hard to follow. (pp. 273-74)

The language of ***Hill Street*** was also uncommonly quick, smart, and, at least at first, rarely damaged by episodic television's occupational hazard, the sure-shot, trademark line. In bad television, every point is made twice. In mediocre television, an expository line is certain to come once, framed for effect. On ***Hill Street Blues*** at its best, the obvious line was uttered in passing, or not at all. In one core story line in the pilot, two teenagers were holding hostages during a robbery. No one burst into Hill Street Station to announce sonorously, "There's a holdup in progress; they're holding hostages!" Instead, in a rushed moment, Capt. Frank Furillo said over the phone, "It may or may not be a hostage situation in that liquor store. We haven't made contact yet," while his lines overlapped with Sgt. Phil Esterhaus's comically baroque dialogue over another phone: "We don't know that yet, Commander. We won't know that until we've interfaced with the perpetrators." . . .

Hill Street was also a show that knew race and class tear this society apart, that behaving decently under these conditions is an everyday trial, and that there are no blindingly obvious solutions for the accumulated miseries of the ghetto. The show's racial byplay honored the everday street sense of race without sliding into race baiting. And despite the occasional quick fix to move into or out of a segment, the growing number of action stunts to cover over writing problems in later seasons, the growing reliance on predictable character shtick, the payoff in ***Hill Street*** was usually not really a deed done, a criminal caught. Instead it was a provisional sort of knowledge, what Michael Kozoll called "a very Henry Jamesian finish." (p. 275)

As craft, the first season of ***Hill Street*** was as good as series television has gotten. It goes without saying that American commercial television is hostile to the nuance and resonance of art, but ***Hill Street*** demonstrated that the instinct for craftsmanship does not automatically disqualify a show from noticeable, if not epoch-making, popularity. Intelligent writing, it seemed, had its appeals; so did some unusually good acting, the serial form, ensemble work, an interesting texture. Complexity of plot and atmosphere did not intimidate ten or fifteen million American households. But what then?

For those of us who like to speculate about the larger significance of popular culture, the frustrating thing is that whatever we say about a show's appeal, beneath the surface of ratings numbers, amounts to guesswork. But I proceed from the belief that people came to watch the show not only because of its casting and texture, its undoubted and much commented on "chemistry," but because it spoke to, and for, a particular cultural and political moment. ***Hill Street*** "worked" in part because it immersed itself in major popular cross-currents—far more than the law-and-order shows that hit the airwaves at the same moment. The energy swarming through in ***Hill Street*** was the energy of American liberal-middle-class ideology turned on itself, at a loss for direction. Bochco and Kozoll had floated into a maelstrom point of popular consciousness.

At its strongest, ***Hill Street*** was positively rhapsodic about the contradictions built into the liberal world view in the early eighties. It not only acknowledged uncertainties but embraced them. To put it another way, ***Hill Street Blues*** was the first postliberal cop show. I say postliberal and not conservative, because some of the hopes of the sixties did hang on fitfully, in the incarnation of Henry Goldblume. . . . Goldblume was forever trying to negotiate peace in the community where Howard Hunter wanted to send in the heavy artillery. (pp. 307-08)

The pivotal moment in Goldblume's sentimental reeducation came in the fourth episode, when Furillo dispatched him to do something about a suicide threat. By the time he got to the scene, the twenty-year-old black man had jumped. . . . Goldblume seemed to take this stranger's death personally. Driving back to the precinct, he got a flat tire. A gang of black teenagers appeared, took his jack, menaced him. Goldblume demanded the jack, asked to be left alone, played the nice guy, until finally he could take no more. He pulled his gun to get away. Back at the station, he came uncorked. "In twelve years I never so much as unsnapped the holster," he confided to a black cop. "Until Frank found out, I never used to load it." "What's wrong with those people, Alf?" he asked. "Are we past fixing it up between us? I mean—if that's the way it is, what the hell's the sense?"

Nonetheless, in future episodes Goldblume remained the dogged negotiator, the principled understander of social conditions who was, for example, devoted to getting the goods on slum landlords. Goldblume believed in talking criminals into surrender whenever possible, but he always tested his beliefs in the crucible of the streets, unlike the pompous, puffy-faced liberal Chief Daniels, whose "concern" for the community, one gathered, was less a matter of principle than a response to political pressures. If a conservative was a liberal who'd been mugged, as the saying goes, then Goldblume after the flat-tire sequence was the absurd hero who holds to his values not because he expects them to accomplish anything but purely and simply because they are right and they are his. They are right but insufficient. A liberal cop who pulls his gun in a pinch doesn't give up caring how ghetto conditions grind people down, but neither does he flatter himself that his personal compassion can stop switchblades, let alone move mountains. By the third season, Goldblume was fed up enough to manhandle a prisoner, knowing no one would believe it of him. (pp. 308-09)

Goldblume, disillusioned yet hopeful, expressed the society's more widespread separation between political hopes and practical life. (p. 309)

As a culture hero Furillo was inconceivable before the late seventies. He represents a new image of benign authority cultivated in the middle class, especially those in their thirties and forties, especially in California, but now diffused via management training seminars and therapeutic encounters, *Ms.* and *Kramer vs. Kramer,* to the far corners of American culture. As an image of sensitive male authority in contemporary American life, Furillo stands as an alternative to Al Pacino's predatory, power-hungry, paranoid godfather. As a police captain, of course, he also stands apart from Hawkeye's brash, boyish acerbity in *M*A*S*H*. Furillo stands for commanding patience, wry humor, self-control under fire. He manages his men without judging them. He listens to everyone and understands everyone's frailties: the frantic ex-wife, the dangerous cops, the worn out, the self-destroyers. He plays his emotions with a soft pedal; his voice usually stays in the same muted register. (pp. 310-11)

Furillo is almost too good to believe. True, he did bounce a child-support check once, and he does lose his temper now and again, though always for good reason. He is a reformed alcoholic. . . . By the third season, pressures from Chief Daniels compel him to twist some rules to get a conviction. But Furillo's flaws—or rather, our knowledge of the price he has paid for his stability—make him all the more interesting as a hero. There is even the suggestion that his recovery from alcoholism is precisely what enables him to understand other people and exact the best from them. (p. 311)

Furillo is the updated version of an old American hero, the self-remade man. What makes him right for his moment is that he unites the inner with the outer man. This pragmatist is no hot-tub liberal. He shows no sign of sharing Goldblume's social ideals. His realism even displays a social-Darwinist edge. He says, at one point, echoing Bochco's private credo, "It's a dog-eat-dog world, and no dog's going to eat me." In this dog's world, flawed, tense, willful, brutalized and sometimes brutal men and women at risk have to depend on each other for human connections. Furillo prevents them from flying apart. When his men take up baseball bats to go out to bash the "animals" outside, he stops them by reminding them they represent the law. When gang leaders violate a trust, he puts the lid on them, too. When his men's personal lives fall apart (even the saintly Goldblume has an affair and loses his marriage in the second season), he reminds them he's been there. In a crumbling society, all human bonds are provisional; a pragmatist's work is never done. Mediating between Goldblume's community-relations liberalism and Hunter's toughness, coping with Chief Daniels downtown and the goons and gangs all around, Furillo harnesses a powerful emotional charge that drives the show. Only his soft-pedaled embodiment of old-fashioned professional duty, combining self-discipline, service, and care, can stave off the utter, catastrophic dissolution of the social contract. In a world that has lost its rhyme and reason, Furillo's soft authority presides over his raw, needful, quasi-family of cops.

Furillo is always on call, and his private life suffers. Even so, he is rewarded by the companionship of the regal Joyce Davenport, herself as much the New Woman as Furillo is the New Man. Indeed, like the successful professional of the women's magazines, she dresses with enormous style on her public defender's salary. In proper feminist fashion, Davenport fends off Furillo's desire to get married—or at least go public with their "relationship"—with barbed reminders about the importance of her career. Where Esterhaus's Grace Gardner lives for sex and Fay Furillo for marriage and motherhood, Davenport lives for her work and takes offense when Furillo calls it her "job." Yet she is also a connoisseur of whatever pleasures of bed, table, and beach can be snatched from the rigors of Furillo's and her dutiful lives. . . . (pp. 311-12)

Hill Street is indeed a series of holding actions. It occupies a time when the right actions don't lead to grand results. For whatever reasons—poverty, the rules of evidence, or the dissolution of social norms—the police cannot keep the peace. They are ordinary people asked to accomplish something extraordinary. (p. 312)

Hill Street speaks to a larger cultural sense, stretching across political positions, that the major government institutions—education, welfare, health—and the cities as a whole simply do not work. Like *M*A*S*H* and *Barney Miller,* it shows the state to be inept; the best that can be said for top authority is that, quaintly, it tries to keep order. People suffer, and the institutions authorized to redress that suffering fail in their stated purposes. What is left is a creative coping that honors both the suffering and the failure of a society now seemingly beyond remedy, one in which a change in the social structure seems out of the question. (pp. 312-13)

Race issues perfectly illustrated the show's approach to the real world. ***Hill Street*** conveyed the ambivalence of white middle-class feelings about the black and brown underclass, and if it sounds strange to speak of a show carrying conviction about ambivalence, this is because television is ordinarily designed to strip away such complexity and to leave pure feelings glaring in neon splendor. The show's split image of ethnics matches both a split in the mind of the white middle class and a real divide in the black community between respectable, upwardly mobile ethnics and the underclass. Inside the stationhouse stand the embattled cops who engage our sympathies, poised for trouble in the roiling menace of the ghetto. (In one episode, the blues even barricade themselves against an assault from "out there.") "Out there" are the killers, muggers, rapists, and thieves, the street criminals and gang members who make life miserable for everyone else. And it is these small-potato underclass criminals who fire the show's imagination. (pp. 313-14)

A wonderfully powerful show at the end of the first season centered on a scuzzy white narcotics cop named Weeks, who, during a stakeout one night, was fired upon by black youths who were up to some unholy business. Weeks fired back and killed one of the youths. Internal investigation ensued. It turned out that this was the third time Weeks had shot a person of color under suspicious circumstances. Weeks himself was outspokenly racist, and in the early stages of the investigation he could not convincingly explain what he was doing on that stakeout. Community groups clamored for Weeks's indictment and conviction. Even so, the black officer Neal Washington worked to clear Weeks, although Weeks sneered at him and called him "Sunburn." Why? Washington's record had been suffering from the sloppiness of his deteriorating partner LaRue. Washington, Bochco said, needed to restore his self-image as a professional. The message was that professionalism was more important than race-consciousness. If Washington and Hill were the more reliable members of their respective salt-and-pepper teams, the producers argued, this wasn't liberal guilt but reality: Black cops were always busy proving themselves.

The effect, though, was to deepen the rift in image between good blacks, who are professional, and bad blacks, who are criminal or radical or both. The community groups campaigning for Weeks's hide were comprehensible, if insensitive, but they were off camera. As in the standard cop show, it was the police alone who kept the lawless ghetto from sinking into utter barbarism. The community lacked its own forms of solidarity, however tenuous. And in the second season, the rift between police and community deepened. In the opening shows, the central continuing plot revolved around one Jesse John Hudson, the once and future king of a community group called the Black Arrow. Hudson had served time for murder, and was now returning to the streets with a published book, a political program for community self-help, and a political manner that impressed Henry Goldblume if not the warier Furillo. Actually Hudson was hell-bent on constructing a criminal empire. It took the deaths of two people, one an undercover cop, the other a pure innocent, both black, to expose him. Against criticism that the show thereby discredited ghetto movements in general, the producers insisted that there are indeed black gangsters who prey on the ghetto. Only a fool would deny it. But Jesse John Hudson was not comprehended or given any complexity; he was dropped into the story as an unambiguous given. Bad ghetto blacks were not given the benefit of the complicated motives of corrupt cops. The show was, after all, a cop show, the producers argued, and the neighborhood, funny or poignant or poisonous as it might be, remained a backdrop against which the heroes could strut their stuff.

Especially in the second season, social movements had no place in ***Hill Street***'s conception of heroism. Heroism was a lonely, private struggle to light up the darkness. In another important second-season story line, the Black Officers Coalition prevailed upon Bobby Hill to run for vice-president. Hill got time off from regular duties, leaving Renko abandoned by his buddy. An old-line member of the Black Officers Coalition made strong arguments for their political position, but the more powerful emotional force lay with Renko's hurt feelings. . . . In the end, loyalty to his partner mattered to him more than organizing for affirmative action. The private code prevailed.

Around the same time, Fay Furillo threw in with a feminist sit-in organized by a group saddled with the name Women Against Discrimination, or WAD. Functionally, her arrest amounted to another way of hectoring hapless Frank; it also reaffirmed that movements are frivolous and unnecessary. Officer Lucy Bates fought back when her fellow officers treated her as a sex object, but this was again the private code: Women should deal with sexism through personal acts of courage. Despite ***Hill Street***'s claim to realism, Fay at one point referred to WAD's demand for "quota hiring," a term thrown against advocates of affirmative action and rarely if ever used by them. More profoundly, during the same sequence, Joyce Davenport was badly shaken by the killing of a devoted public defender colleague, a black woman—only to see her killer, a snarling black monster, released because of a technical violation in the way the police gathered evidence. Now, as in other episodes as well, she had to confront the real-life consequences of civil-liberties statutes and the rest of her liberal principles. By the end of the season, against Furillo's counsel, she had bought herself a gun.

Davenport's metamorphosis made good drama (and reflected the entry of a lawyer, Jeffrey Lewis, onto the ***Hill Street*** writing staff). Whatever its dramatic use, however, this sequence ratified the conservative drift of ***Hill Street***'s second year. In a single episode, Davenport considered quitting her job in disgust with the springing of the killer; the Black Officers Coalition pulled Hill away from Renko; and Furillo denounced WAD as "radical activists." Yet amid this neoconservative surge, Henry Goldblume got the goods on a bully slumlord who beat up any tenants who got up the nerve to complain (including a Hispanic law student: a major change from the first season's images of street Hispanics). So ***Hill Street*** remained complex. But by season two the defense of liberal values was being left more and more to the liberal cop. A year later, the show dealt with an armored-car holdup-killing by a hard-bitten remnant of sixties radicals, obviously based on Weather Underground holdovers. The sloganeering terrorists were realistic sketches of a self-caricaturing reality, while Goldblume and Davenport wondered aloud whether their onetime idealism was still tenable. . . . But at the same time, the FBI was held up to scorn for shoddy police work. The local police, including former radicals slogging through the reality of the eighties, remained the best hope for humane values.

Obviously, ***Hill Street*** has hardly been a left-wing, even a politically motivated show. None of the writers carries didactic purposes uppermost in his mind, but they are mindful of criticisms that emerged in conversation and in mail; and it seems to me that they have often tried to accommodate. While the show drifted rightward, the liberal conscience stayed alive. (pp. 315-18)

At its best, and its best is very good, ***Hill Street*** honors something of the enormity of urban misery in the United States. At other times, ***Hill Street*** abjectly fails to measure up to the terrible and wonderful territory it claims. For the most part, though, the show wrestles plausibly with the vast burdens of race and class. It bears witness. . . . And that, in the thick of the Reagan years, is itself no small achievement. (p. 319)

Inevitably ***Hill Street*** lost novelty. The stunning look that had leaped out of the screen in the pilot was no longer surprising. Several of the actors seemed to reach the limits of their competence. But ***Hill Street*** remained the liveliest, most open, richest series on the air. I found myself complaining about it, even missing one or two episodes the second season; then found myself turning back to it. Friends whom I had regaled with praise of the show reported to me that they were now addicted to it, just as I was showing them how it was becoming fossilized. Which truth to conclude with, the truth of ingenuity or the truth of fossilization? Let the last word go to Michael Kozoll, as responsible as anyone for the promise of ***Hill Street Blues.*** Halfway through the second season, Kozoll said he had finally found the metaphor for television he had long been seeking. Doing episodic television, he said, is like raising a retarded child. By which he meant that there are only so many things it will ever learn to do, no matter how much you love the child, no matter how much effort and care and intelligence you lavish upon it. It will never shine. One could add: Its little accomplishments are also miraculous. (p. 324)

Todd Gitlin, " 'Hill Street Blues': 'Make It Look Messy'," in his Inside Prime Time, *Pantheon Books, 1983, pp. 273-324.*

JARICE HANSON

[***Hill Street Blues (HSB)***] has ushered in a new format of television which effectively mixes genres which have existed in both daytime and nighttime television for a number of years and more importantly, it elevates the moral question inherent in police procedural drama to the point where the audience is left to decide the value of what the institution of police work and law enforcement have become. For the first time in fictional television, the viewers are asked to balance "private and public issues" and to ask "at what expense do our social institutions operate?" To do this, the producers of ***HSB*** have mixed not only the genres of television, but the cinematic style of the cinema verite documentary tradition and the innovation provided by the popularizer of the police procedural genre, Arthur Conan Doyle. . . . (p. 59)

[In] presenting this mixture, the producers have paid careful attention to making it look realistic. While much of its form stems from classic police procedural drama, ***HSB*** has proven that not all police procedural dramas must have hackneyed cliches and stereotypes. (p. 60)

The writers of ***HSB*** are also careful not to exploit minorities as the usual lawbreakers, as has been done so often. Part of the solution to the potential ethnic problem, was to mix the ethnic types within the station as well as on the street, but whether the individual is law enforcer or law breaker, Producer Steven Bochco says: "we're equal opportunity offenders."

The concept of morality within the police procedural genre stems from another NBC program called *Police Story* which made its debut in 1973. Producers of that show, Liam O'Brien and Stan Kallis felt that it was time to explore "the immorality of a system that forces everything in that system to contribute to that morality." After *Police Story,* the networks took variations on the police procedural theme with *The Streets of San Francisco, Columbo, Ellery Queen, Baretta, Hawaii Five-O, Mannix* and *Kojack,* just to name a few of the more successful shows. However, real police who were asked what show, in their opinion was the most realistic, often cited the sit-com *Barney Miller* as one of the most realistic cop-shows on television. In fact, as producers Steven Bochco and Michael Kozoll discussed the concept of the new show with the NBC network brass, they were told that what NBC wanted was "a little bit of *M*A*S*H,* a little bit of *Barney Miller.*"

The keen ensemble acting of a *M*A*S*H* or a *Barney Miller* emerged from yet another popular genre, the sit-com, which was given new life in the early seventies by people like Norman Lear and the creative staff behind MTM Productions. . . . Lear and MTM introduced controversy to the sit-com and in doing so, also constructed casts which developed over the years. Relationships and philosophies were given birth, matured and occasionally withered under the watchful eye of the public and the result was a new sense of empathy for television characters. (pp. 60-1)

The format of ***HSB*** also borrows from the success of the nighttime soap operas, such as *Dallas, Knot's Landing, Dynasty, Flamingo Road,* and *Falcon Crest.* In writing of *Dallas* and the "Texas-trend," Horace Newcomb has cited the fortuitous casting of the show as one of the keys to its success, and the way the characters talk to us about ourselves as another: ". . . their words come from some of popular culture's most powerful and appealing language. What we get is a sense of place, of tradition, and of true character. And we like what we hear because such qualities are in very short supply these days."

HSB also gives us a sense of place. . . . However, when it comes to language, ***HSB*** is unique. The station personnel *and* the various gang members in the community usually have vocabularies which tend to be more polysyllabic than the norm. Still, the format of one or two major stories with three or four sub-stories woven into the fabric of the episode is common to the nighttime (and daytime) soap.

Stylistically, ***HSB*** also borrows from the genre introduced by the show *Lou Grant,* which has occasionally been called "comdram." *Lou Grant* effectively took the one-hour drama and introduced bits of humor—subtle though it may be. . . . ***HSB*** has constantly used the same approach, only the comedy and drama often occur when the private troubles and public issues interface. Occasionally they take place within the structure of one of the sets of partners on the Hill; at times they influence decisions which have irreversible consequences—but like *Lou Grant*'s cast of characters, the ***HSB*** cast reacts to the pressure created by the two elements.

While all of the genres mentioned so far are common to television, ***HSB*** uses yet one more device which it has borrowed from documentary film. In each Roll Call segment, and occasionally during moments of action, the subjective camera becomes almost one more police officer, finding his or her way to a seat while Sgt. Esterhaus outlines the day ahead and assigns tasks to all. (pp. 61-3)

Throughout the Roll Call, we learn that the police on the Hill are human too, often nursing hangovers, sporting cuts or bruises (unlike the playboy-cops on *CHIPS*), or responding bawdily to Esterhaus' command of the English language. While the evidence of the family unit is apparent on most television programs, the family of ***HSB*** is an extended one. Characterization in general remains mythical, but not clearly segmented, as it has been on other popular shows, such as *M*A*S*H.*

On ***HSB*** the father-figure alternates, depending upon the circumstance, from Frank Furillo . . . , the man of reason, to Sgt. Phil Esterhaus . . . , the passionate intellectual. While both men are viewed as competent and most often ''by-the-book'' cops, each has a personal flaw—Furillo's stemming from the alcoholism he has beaten . . . , and Esterhaus' from his intellect, flawed by his sexual urges, which he finds difficult to control at times. One wonders if Esterhaus could ever appear to become more dominant if he could learn to control his sexual power as well as he controls his baroque rhetoric. It is unlikely the writers would ever let Esterhaus' character deny his sensuality because it serves to keep him in his place—only men who can transcend personal needs make it to Captain. . . . [The] Esterhaus character has . . . introduced the closest character to the sympathetic intellectual in nighttime drama. Prior to ***HSB*** the television audience would not have trusted anyone who they might not be able to understand—or so we have been led to believe.

The other individual men in the cast contribute to the myth of the individual. . . . Henry Goldblume . . . the psychologist, is the idealist who, with his youthful looks and command of the academic discipline of psychology, often shows us how rationality and a cool head helps us deal with crisis. His nemesis, Howard Hunter . . . , is a man who believes that violence is the only solution when dealing with ''your basic non-white lawless types.'' Like his name, Hunter is the man of action and with his foot in Vietnam history, he reminds us, like the characters on *M*A*S*H,* that there are different ways of thinking in the military world.

The myth of the individual is further supported by Detective Mick Belker . . . , who, with his growling, biting and general appearance, presents a character half-man, half-animal. Through him, we are reminded that no matter how individualistic a person may become, he or she faces real problems which transcend individualism. In Belker's case, he must deal with his aging parents and with his attachment to society's misfits. Belker befriends and is often befriended by the people who society has branded as ''different.'' Ironically, in a sample survey of real police officers, it was determined that Belker is the ***HSB*** character with whom most police officers identify.

Ray Calletano . . . may be one of the strongest Hispanic characters on television. . . . Calletano shows us that Hispanics can be loving husbands and devoted family men. His character is competent, and able to cite procedure verbatim. His only character flaw as has been exploited by an episode of ***HSB,*** is his deference to authority and his own lack of leadership qualities. He remains a strong minority member—but is not threatening to the white audience.

The women of ***HSB*** may be introducing a new archetype—that of the ''three faces of Eve.'' Together, these women make up one real woman. Joyce Davenport . . . is the professional woman who knows that her first allegiance is to her job as Public Defender. However, despite her cold ''manly'' approach to her clients, she retains the look of a glamor girl—her hair and clothing not particularly suited to her role. Lucy Bates . . . is the woman who more effectively operates in a traditionally male role. Her effectiveness on the job is only marred by the potential romantic involvement she may have with her partner, ''ladies man'' Joe Coffey. As the most dimensional woman in the cast, Bates often says things which do not sit well with her contemporaries. Like most of us, she sometimes speaks before thinking.

Finally, Fay Furillo . . . epitomizes the airheaded housewife. True, she's a devoted mother, but she's hopeless at making decisions and finds herself deferring to her ex-husband, Frank. She is the stereotype of the woman who cannot function without her man and like Hunter, comes close to being a caricature. The idea that Frank could have gone from a relationship with Fay to one with Joyce asks the audience to stretch their imaginations, but as is typical, the ***HSB*** writers have not run away from this problem, but have addressed it directly in episodes where Fay and Joyce talk about their relationship with Frank, to one another. Two of Eve's three faces meet in the sisterhood of woman. Altogether, the three women portray every stereotype of women imaginable, but in doing so, the audience sees the depth and breadth of womanhood.

The partners set up another interesting set of dynamics. Lucy and her partner Joe . . . portray the fantasy of what may happen when women are paired with men. The suggested sexuality of both are balanced by the traditional concern for primary group members and because they are professionals, they cope with the situation. But because they are humans, the dynamics of the relationship are interesting to watch.

The archetype of the shadow is yet another common image in the remaining partners. Each dyad suggests one partner maintains reason and intelligence, while the other is prone to emotional, sometimes irrational actions. Contrary to historical portrayals, the partners with reason and intellect are black, however this means that the more interesting situations go to the white characters. (pp. 63-6)

[Bobby Hill's partner Renko] portrays the displaced cowboy who treats the urban environment like the frontier. Because he is an ''earthy'' character, Renko often suggests problems which are real, but which television normally would not address, such as the time his full bladder had to wait until a proper arrest had been made before he could get relief. At times Renko is the macho officer, at times he is, like Shakespeare's fool, the comic who speaks the truth.

Neal Washington . . . effectively uses his street-smart ways to deal with his partner J. D. LaRue . . . who, when he is not on duty, breaks, or at least interprets the law broadly. LaRue can be a good cop, but his flaws are in his character. An alcoholic, there is often tension between himself and Furillo, who has overcome alcohol and his own need to succeed despite his failures. LaRue's rogue optimism is balanced by Washington's common sense.

The partners on ***HSB*** are not always in agreement and sometimes the partnerships change for awhile to add interest to the scripts. The irresolute sanctity of partnerships is never exploited and like married couples, these partners have their differences and their need to separate at times.

The private and public issues brought to the audience's attention takes the traditional concept of the police procedural drama, adds style and structure, suggested by other genres, and confronts the audience with a realistic look at urban police work. The various elements such as structure and characterization enable the audience to participate in and judge the ethical and moral problems. The characters are humans with real flaws, who face moral decisions in their line of work and who do not always make the right decisions.

In an award-winning episode called **''Freedom's Last Stand,''** the audience learns that, as in many jobs, the longer one is around, the harder it becomes to separate right from wrong.

In ***HSB,*** the most corrupt individuals are often not the kids on the streets, but the people who have closed their eyes to the wrongs around them. Often the higher a person may be in the police hierarchy, the more temptation there may be to abuse the system. Even more importantly, the more specialized the system becomes, the more we forget the humanistic qualities which separate us from mechanistic solutions to real problems. Corruption often occurs when individuals have more to gain, or more to lose. (pp. 67-8)

Moral questions which arise throughout the episodes are balanced with the immorality of the system of police work and the law. When public defender Davenport is successful in her job and her client is released to return to the streets, Furillo's life becomes complicated by the system of justice. While Furillo becomes law enforcer, his paramour Davenport handles the rights of the criminal. The two characters complement one another, but the harmony in which they work is questioned by the system which puts one against the other in the proper execution of their duties. The resolution, which inevitably occurs in one of the steamy bedroom or bubble bath scenes for which these two characters are known, is a counterpoint to their professional affiliation. The physical intimacy they share is their reward for dealing with the immorality of society. Finally, morality is viewed within the context, and the various perspectives are tempered with realistic, contemporary values.

HSB comes to the viewing audience at a time in history when many of our established institutions are being questioned. As Alvin Toffler says in his book, *The Third Wave,* we are coming out of an orientation where the bureaucracy dominated every institution. We have now begun to realize that values are changing, but the institutions have not kept pace. Through ***HSB*** we learn how the social system's institution of police work and justice have not kept pace with our changing value system. Morality, as it is defined today, requires an individual's approach to passing judgement on an act. The myth of the individual is returning to our lives and as in the case of ***HSB,*** art imitates life. (pp. 68-9)

HSB brings the world of police work and justice into our homes and asks us to participate in the evaluation of the system as well as the deed. . . . It breaks traditions, but not so drastically that we feel helpless during the change and most importantly, it does not side-step issues (as even the news has been doing of late), but faces them with integrity. The adult approach toward television content has rarely ever treated viewers like thinking individuals, but rather like unthinking children. With ***HSB*** the audience sees what we, as society, have become. (pp. 70-1)

Jarice Hanson, ''The View from the Hill: 'Hill Street Blues','' in Clues: A Journal of Detection, *Vol. 5, No. 1, Spring-Summer, 1984, pp. 58-72.*

DAVID FREEMAN

[Unlike those for most TV shows, the scripts for ***Hill Street Blues***] are sprawling and almost aggressively messy. The stories don't have the usual neat beginnings, middles, and ends. A typical script will have several story lines that might go on for four weeks, while others start and end within one episode. The glue that binds it all together is a combination of character and mise-en-scène. . . .

Time is one of the few constants in every show. Each ***Hill Street*** episode runs for one day, from early-morning roll call (when the day's duties are assigned) to late at night. That doesn't mean every problem gets solved in one day—just that time runs out and the characters finally try for some sleep—the unsolved problems to be dealt with another time. Acting and writing on ***Hill Street*** have merged in an extraordinary way. Other cop shows have naturalistic acting, but it's usually on the order of ''Hey, is that a new shirt?'' ''Yeah, you like it?'' Then somebody robs a bank. We are talking about a higher order of things here. Credible and theatrical.

The show is never over when you think it is. Repeatedly, a story line seems to have run its course, when something else happens that makes what precedes it feel like a prologue. Here's an example: A cop's mother pesters her unmarried son to call the daughter of a friend. Eventually he does. The cop is Belker, everybody's favorite mess, the one who bites suspects and is often brutal. Belker obeys his mom. The date is fine at first and maybe Mom was right. God knows Belker could benefit from a steady woman in his life, and Debbie looks like a likely candidate, except then it develops that she's sexually voracious, with a wide masochistic streak. Belker gets enough of hurting people in the streets, so he moves on. First you think it's through when he calls for the date to pacify his mom. Then you think, ''Oh, that's nice, he's met a girl.'' Then she turns out to be weird. Neatly, ironically, that weirdness relates to the aspect of Belker's work he's most famous for—kicking ass—and it makes him unhappy. (p. 80)

If the show has a main artery, it's Captain Furillo, the ultimate adult. . . . Furillo's a good man in a flawed world and a flawed man in an indifferent world. He does his best in a universe that's filled with venality and love, where people have names that end in vowels or *-witz* or*-stein;* his command is a neighborhood where people have accents and are mostly black or Hispanic. Some are good, but many are not. They're all looking for an edge they'll never find. Furillo remains stoic as all day long people try to get a word with him, each person in crisis, each one desperate for a moment of his time. Furillo stays as calm as he can, given the pressure and the chaos; all day he stifles his humor, or at least tries to. At night, in bed, he looks for a little human relief. His feelings are a pretty good model for the way we all feel about ourselves—torn, tired, keeping the world together with the glue of our own put-upon, overworked personalities. And that's why he's a hero even if he doesn't act like Achilles or John Wayne. We can identify with him even if we're not precinct captains. His humanity is ours, or so we would like to think as we flatter ourselves in our secret hearts that we too are trying to avoid the abyss. (pp. 80, 82)

Most action or cop shows on American televison seem to have some pat formula for minority representation. If a bad guy is black, you can bet the next black guy will be a nuclear physicist. If a blond bimbo wanders through, we'll soon be subjected to several supermoms. ***Hill Street*** is one of the few places where blacks are portrayed with genuine diversity and with no apparent scorecard. In its treatment of women, the show is possibly unique. There are three women who are real people. Joyce Davenport. . . , the public defender and once Furillo's clandestine lover, now his wife, is the paradigmatic Eighties woman: a fine, dedicated lawyer who is tough, smart, sexy, and straight. Fay Furillo. . . , Frank's ex-wife, is usually on the edge of hysteria when she's near her ex-husband. You just know she's a better person when Frank's not around, but she keeps coming back for more. Fay is the definition of a well-written, well-acted character: you're certain you know what she's like when she's not on screen. Lucy Bates. . . , the only woman patrol sergeant, has to get along with a lot of rowdy men. She's smart, but not brilliant and certainly not able to articulate the complex problems she faces. The easy way out for Lucy is to be one of the boys. As a result, she's ready to pull her gun and use it if she has to. She's looking for a private life, but mostly she's fixated on her job.

The underlying assumptions that [the] writers bring to characters like Joyce, Fay, and Lucy are postfeminist. These women have lives outside their romances and marriages, but that doesn't mean they don't want men. Of course they do, the same way men want them. The characters rarely talk about feminism. I don't think the ***Hill Street*** staff thinks about it, it just comes out. (p. 82)

There have been many memorable ***Hill Street*** episodes, but the best one, arguably, is **"Trial by Fury."** . . . The script is packed with incident and character. There's a big melodrama—a nun raped and murdered—that leads to a quieter personal drama: Furillo and Davenport's romance coming apart, because of differing legal principles. It has jokes and it has dreams, and for a while it makes one murder feel less important than another—and then of course you realize that's wrong; all murders are important. There are few flashy passages, only a deep look into the guts of the characters.

The script pits Furillo against Davenport. Furillo has the nun's murderer and enough evidence for an indictment, but not a conviction. Outside there's a mob of concerned citizens ready to lynch. Furillo instructs the assistant D.A. to drop charges, which means the killer can go free—right into the arms of the mob. The gentleman reconsiders and finally confesses. Davenport, as the legal defender, is infuriated. She feels Furillo has manipulated the law, something Furillo points out she does all the time. The coda has Furillo walking in the dark to some unnamed place that looks like a prison. There are bars and a face behind them. And Furillo says, "Forgive me, Father, for I have sinned." We might have thought he was right, but he knew in his heart he was wrong enough to feel guilty. So he goes to his own confession. You realize what a good cop he is. And what a fine script this is.

Some ***Hill Street*** scripts are more self-contained than others. The story line of **"Trial by Fury"** unfolds almost entirely within the hour, cathartic within itself. But even with that structure it embodies the paradox of ***Hill Street's*** overall attitude: terrible things happen, and we spend our days trying to cope. Life can be wonderful or grim, but it's never fair. . . . These scripts don't spin inner-city fairy tales—the characters can't walk away easily, not out of their lives or their work, not into the next episode.

There are seventy-eight hours of ***Hill Street Blues*** now, and it all adds up to some vast nineteenth-century novel, teeming with life, full of characters, cliff-hangers, and themes that resonate, one with another—all creating a picture of urban life in the Eighties. If you bear in mind that it's written in week-to-week installments full of big, juicy, sloppy, emotional scenes, the shadow of Dickens is inescapable. ***Hill Street*** exists in a real city with snow and rain and lunatics in the street. This isn't Hollywood backlot, not *CHiPs* southern California, but a world we can live in, at least vicariously, more readily and with greater clarity than the one we actually inhabit. The precinct house here is as totemic of modern urban life as the cathedral was to another century. And when we watch the Hill from our TV privacy, our imagination is led to see the actual world with a deeper perception than before we tuned in. . . . (pp. 82, 85)

David Freeman, "Television's Real A-Team," in Esquire, *Vol. 103, No. 1, January, 1985, pp. 77-80, 82, 85.*

JOYCE CAROL OATES

Hill Street Blues is the only television program I watch with any degree of regularity now, so perhaps it is presumptuous to call it my "favorite" program. In contrast to the lavishly produced BBC productions widely admired here, ***Hill Street Blues*** is unpretentious and unglamorous; simply a consistently rewarding series, intelligently conceived and executed, and performed with remarkable skill. (p. 5)

[***Hill Street Blues***] is one of the few current television programs that is as intellectually and emotionally provocative as a good book. In fact, from the very first, ***Hill Street Blues*** struck me as Dickensian in its superb character studies, its energy, its variety; above all, its audacity. And if, upon occasion, its humor is rather slap-dash and broad, even outrageous . . . , this, too, is in the solid Dickensian tradition. Melodrama, sentiment, defiantly bad taste, high seriousness—all are mixed together here, and nearly always the mixture is just right. (pp. 5-6)

Hill Street Blues tells a profoundly disturbing story by way of numerous small stories that are braided deftly together. So typically rapid-fire is the dialogue, so cleverly interwoven the various tales, so swiftly does one scene cut to another, it is often remarked that new viewers find it difficult to follow any storyline at all. (It is helpful to give oneself two weeks' viewings before making any judgment.) At times one would like to know more about characters' motives and one would certainly like to know more about characters' fates—but the show has a relentless forward motion that mimics, one assumes, the unforgiving nature of "real life" in a city precinct station. This *is* a fair microcosm of the police world, set in a beleaguered urban environment the more convincing for being mysteriously anonymous. . . .

At its most compelling, ***Hill Street Blues*** has the frantic, controlled air of ingenious improvisation. Except in the most extreme comic episodes, one is never conscious of actors "acting"; the performances are consistent but rarely predictable. (p. 6)

Hill Street Blues is most moving when it deals directly with conflicts rising out of personal rather than social (or even criminal) issues. Recent episodes have dealt graphically with material that is surely controversial—police violence, for instance (perpetrated by a trigger-happy young officer under the authority of Lt. Howard Hunter . . . is one case, and by the otherwise gentlemanly Lt. Goldblume himself in another); the inability of police to protect their own witnesses; an on-camera electrocution of a black murderer-rapist (a powerful argument against capital punishment); the suicide by hanging of a young rookie following a crude hazing session; and the insensitivity of the police chief to that suicide. (If there is a dramatic flaw to Chief Daniels . . . , it is simply that he is too one-note and predictable a character: always shallow, self-promoting, venal.)

One of the prevailing themes of the series is the depiction of the violent masculine world in which most of the policemen participate—"masculine" in the stereotypical sense of the word—and their efforts to transcend it, or to define themselves against it. So Renko and Hill are shown going through the considerable stress of breaking up their partnership of many years; Belker is often portrayed as sentimental, even rather sweet, despite the frequent coarseness of his persona; even the somewhat adolescent J. D. LaRue is capable of falling in love—however unwisely. In a recent episode, Joe Coffey is deeply agitated by being forced to arrest (on charges of solicitation) his former high-school football coach—a story that might have deteriorated into crude situation comedy had it not been so sensitively done.

While most of the interlocking stories are satisfactorily resolved, some are merely—minimally—resolved: the Hill Street police are figures of Sisyphus rolling their rocks up the hill and the next day rolling them up again, and again. Human effort and intelligence, action, risk, sudden eruptions of violence, sudden death—yet very little changes. It is always the next morning, it is always roll call.

In tone, ***Hill Street Blues*** is realistic melodrama, but it charts an unmistakably tragic course. Its message seems to be that the institutions of democracy have largely failed. Civilization depends upon a rigorous hierarchy of command—and upon distinctive personalities: men like Capt. Frank Furillo. (Yet Furillo is so clearly a special case: is there anyone else like him?) The precinct does not appear to be supported by the city, but is responsible for, and superior to, the city; the Hill is a region ruled by police, not governed by its own people—who scarcely exist except as victims and criminals.

It is probable that ***Hill Street Blues*** will continue to develop along its iconoclastic, disturbing lines. Are convicted murderers never convicted mistakenly? What of the volatile issues involving abortion, pro and con, in impoverished communities like the Hill? The questionable morality of undercover police work has been explored with commendable subtlety, but the ethics of entrapment need to be further explored: how do Detective Mayo and Sergeant Bates feel about disguising themselves as prostitutes, for instance? (Both these interesting women characters need to be developed in terms of contemporary feminism.)

Because of the high degree of respect it has earned, and its ongoing popularity, ***Hill Street Blues*** is not merely an hour's time slot in the television week, but a forum for provocative, timely issues. And it never fails to be entertaining—in the best, Dickensian sense of the word. (pp. 6-7)

Joyce Carol Oates, "For Its Audacity, Its Defiantly Bad Taste and Its Superb Character Studies," in TV Guide® *Magazine, Vol. 33, No. 22, June 1, 1985, pp. 4-7.*

Larry Bograd

1953-

Photograph by S. Stephen Hicks; reproduced by permission of Larry Bograd

(Also writes under pseudonym of Grady Barrol) American novelist and author of books for children.

In his novels for young adults, Bograd examines contemporary social issues through the lives of teenage protagonists. He discusses such topics as human rights, child abuse, and the ethics of nuclear war while addressing the traditional adolescent themes of loneliness and the search for self. Although some critics contend that his reliance on "exposé and message" obstructs his narratives, most regard Bograd's work as entertaining and informative.

Bograd's first novel for young adults, *The Kolokol Papers* (1981), depicts the difficulties of growing up under an oppressive government. Lev, a Russian teenager, is shunned by his classmates following the arrest of his father, a political activist and critic of the Soviet Union. Lev is later forced to choose between his conformist views and his father's dissident beliefs. Critics especially praised Bograd for his realistic depiction of contemporary Soviet life. *Bad Apple* (1982) is a grim story of juveniles who commit serious crimes. The novel concerns Nicky, a fifteen-year-old boy who is arrested for attempted murder. Through a sequence of flashbacks, Nicky recounts his unhappy childhood as a victim of parental neglect and emotional abuse. His mental state deteriorates through the course of the novel and culminates in his brutal assault of an elderly couple. Although some critics contend that Bograd's sympathetic treatment of Nicky is overwhelming, most consider *Bad Apple* honest and convincing.

In *Los Alamos Light* (1983), Bograd portrays the development of the first atomic bomb as observed by Maggie, the daughter of a scientist assigned to work on this project during World War II. Uprooted from her Boston home, Maggie attempts to adjust to the desert community of Las Alamos, New Mexico, and to her father's preoccupation with his work. Critics praised this novel for its historical authenticity and for encouraging thought about the effects of technological development.

(See also *Contemporary Authors,* Vols. 93-96 and *Something about the Author,* Vol. 33.)

PUBLISHERS WEEKLY

[In **"The Kolokol Papers"** the] young son of Russian-Jewish dissidents, Lev Kolokol, endures isolation in school, the pitiless limelight of the KGB and the world press. The situation of the Kolokol family worsens when the father loses his job but persists in speaking out against violations of human rights. A telegram from the President of the U.S. offers hope to the activists but a bombing, blamed on the dissidents, leads to the father's arrest. . . . Lev's conscience is on trial as he is presented with the choice of "freedom" or punishment by officials who demand that he turn over papers incriminating his father. Bograd's simple, eloquent prose strengthens the effects of his powerful novel.

A review of "The Kolokol Papers," in Publishers Weekly, *Vol. 220, No. 21, November 20, 1981, p. 55.*

STEPHANIE ZVIRIN

Using a rather stiff form of personal memoir [in ***The Kolokol Papers***], Bograd allows Lev to record the development of his political awareness and the incidents surrounding his father's arrest. Characters are wooden and simply sketched, and Lev's naiveté and his ultimate transformation into political activist (he cruises through most of the novel thinking largely about sex) are hard to accept. Despite that, however, Bograd's images of oppressive Soviet life form a sharp and unusual background, and his stark record of human rights violations should be enough to make up, at least in part, for the novel's lack of force.

Stephanie Zvirin, in a review of "The Kolokol Papers," in Booklist, *Vol. 78, No. 11, February 1, 1982, p. 703.*

ZENA SUTHERLAND

[***The Kolokol Papers***] gives a trenchant picture of the harsh tactics used to persecute and punish Lev's father, and eventually Lev himself, and makes clear the dilemma of the individual caught between the danger of cleaving to his own beliefs in a totalitarian state, and the promised comfort of conformity. As Lev's father goes through the mockery of his trial and conviction, he chooses principle over compromise. So does Lev, when his turn comes. Although the characters are clearly defined, the style capable, and the atmosphere vividly evoked, the story line is almost lost in the book's heavy emphasis on exposé and message.

Zena Sutherland, in a review of "The Kolokol Papers," in Bulletin of the Center for Children's Books, *Vol. 35, No. 9, May, 1982, p. 164.*

ANDREA DAVIDSON

[***The Kolokol Papers***] is a grim picture of Soviet life, well done, seen through the eyes of teen-age Lev. His life in Moscow, with his parents constantly talking with Western reporters "underground", is fraught with uncertainties, and the reader is left at the end not knowing what will happen to him. Anyone interested in the lives of the Russians will find this a fascinating, hard to put down story, with many parts that would be good for book discussions.

Andrea Davidson, in a review of "The Kolokol Papers," in Voice of Youth Advocates, *Vol. 5, No. 2, June, 1982, p. 30.*

ROBERT UNSWORTH

Bograd's fictionalized case study of a boy headed for trouble [***Bad Apple***] has a zinger of an opening. Fifteen-year-old Nicky is holding a gun to the head of his sleeping father. He calmly considers killing both his parents, but doesn't. The only reason we're given for his sparing their lives is that his friend Prune is waiting outside the shabby apartment building to take him to a theft in the suburbs. As they drive north to Westchester County from New York City, Nicky has detailed flashbacks of the tormented path that will lead him from neglected child to arrested felon. An unwanted boy, his parents wrongfully blamed him for the tragic death of a favored sister. . . . Nicky is not a good student and to him school is senseless (although, for a change, school is not the "heavy" in the plot). . . . We know from the beginning what to expect. While robbing an elderly couple in their home, Nicky strikes out at them for no apparent reason, almost killing both. He is arrested the next day. The story is convincing, compelling and frightening. It is also, we hope, overstated. The boy is depicted as sensitive and perceptive but without character or soul. He is defenseless as a vegetable and, as depicted, seemingly blameless of any wrongdoing. A thoughtful, provocative novel of social realism with enough quite explicit sex to restrict recommendation for purchase to upper secondary school libraries only.

Robert Unsworth, in a review of "Bad Apple," in School Library Journal, *Vol. 29, No. 4, December, 1982, p. 70.*

STEPHANIE ZVIRIN

[A series of vivid flashbacks used throughout ***Bad Apple*** depicts] the psychological unraveling of a high school sophomore—a boy pushed to the breaking point, unable to withstand continued emotional abuse from his parents, to shoulder unfairly placed blame for his sister's death, deal with increasingly disturbing nightmares, or cope with what he perceives as betrayals by those he trusts. Nicky is portrayed as a seriously troubled teenager, but one whose emotional trauma and innate compassion for others will make him seem peculiarly sympathetic, vulnerable, and disturbing to readers—especially since help does not come to him in time. The author has taken great pains to fit intricate pieces of Nicky's life together to provide the boy with an excuse, so to speak, for his final breakdown. He thoroughly saturates Nicky's environment with ugliness, permeating it with rough language and explicit sex that fit the circumstances. Perhaps it is the feeling that the sordidness of the boy's life simply can't last (or that Nicky's desire to hang on to his sanity will save him in the end) that keeps the basic narrative from being overwhelmed by its own episodic structure or Bograd's pessimism and lack of subtlety. What teenagers will actually come away with after reading the novel is hard to guess. What Bograd seems to convey most emphatically, however, is the frightening, unnecessary waste of human life. And he does so in a powerful, realistic manner that cannot fail to disturb and/or provoke thought among those mature, perceptive teenagers for whom the novel is best suited. (pp. 559-60)

Stephanie Zvirin, in a review of "Bad Apple," in Booklist, *Vol. 79, No. 8, December 15, 1982, pp. 559-60.*

GRETCHEN S. BALDAUF

From its ominously chilling beginning the reader [of ***Bad Apple***] descends into the desperate gray world that Nicky inhabits, complete with switchblades, drugs, prostitutes, porn shops and teenage mothers who abuse their infants in darkened movie theaters. . . . The action shifts back and forth between flashbacks and dreams as Nicky and an accomplice travel to the suburbs to commit a robbery. For those readers strong enough to take it, this is provocative, disturbing reading; there are no happy endings.

Gretchen S. Baldauf, in a review of "Bad Apple," in Children's Book Review Service, *Vol. 11, No. 7, February, 1983, p. 68.*

ZENA SUTHERLAND

[***Bad Apple*** is] almost a case history, but it's less successful as a novel, made choppy by flashbacks to past incidents (not in chronological order) in Nick's life, and written in an uneven style, at times with staccato dialogue or monologue. Nick's is a sordid life, and this has some impact in expressing his situation, but the book is more a collage than a picture that tells a story.

Zena Sutherland, in a review of "Bad Apple," in Bulletin of the Center for Children's Books, *Vol. 36, No. 8, April, 1983, p. 143.*

PRISCILLA LIGGETT

Author Larry Bograd brings out important questions for young readers to explore in [**"Los Alamos Light"**]. . . . He presents such issues as man's relationship with nature and the implications of technological advancement for society. But Bograd doesn't moralize, and the reader is left to reach his or her own conclusions.

Los Alamos is the isolated town where top scientists came together to develop the first atomic bomb. Sixteen-year-old Maggie, the daughter of one of these scientists, tells her own story. It begins when she is wrenched from Boston, with its urban advantages, to live in the sparsely populated Southwest.

Tension soon develops between Maggie's growing love for the arid land, with its traditional cultures, and the approaching atomic age.... Her Pueblo pottery teacher tells her: "Our duty is to earth and clay. We are here to make pots, not to talk of death. Our hope lies with the earth and clay." To Maggie, this idea seems right.

However, after witnessing a tremendous atomic explosion from a distance, (the Trinity test), she realizes that great techno-military advancement is unavoidable. She also begins to see that a reconciliation between society's relationship to nature and technology must take place, if peace is to endure.

Priscilla Liggett, "Growing Up in Los Alamos During WWII," in The Christian Science Monitor, *October 7, 1983, p. B2.*

STEPHANIE ZVIRIN

A scene of children playing war games is a rather obvious opening device for [***Los Alamos Light***], set amidst the activity at Los Alamos in 1943. Its narrator/protagonist, Maggie Chilton, uprooted from her Boston home, has accompanied her scientist father to the desert community, where she finds his constant preoccupation with the secret project and disregard of her both disconcerting and a challenge. Bograd's use of interconnected episodes to demonstrate Maggie's adjustments to her new environment and her progress toward independent thought and action is not entirely effective. Scenes often lack both the drama and the cumulative effect that Bograd handled so well in his recent ***Bad Apple*** ..., and the book's forties setting is a little forced.... [However], Maggie is a credibly ingenuous heroine, and her passage into adulthood a common and compelling theme that should keep teenage readers involved.

Stephanie Zvirin, in a review of "Los Alamos Light," in Booklist, *Vol. 80, No. 4, October 15, 1983, p. 337.*

MARGUERITE M. LAMBERT

[***Los Alamos Light***] is a unique work of historical fiction. There is no other account of this place and time written especially for adolescent readers. The protagonist, 16-year-old Maggie Chilton, must adapt first to her mother's suicide, then to the sudden move from Boston to New Mexico with her scientist father, a colleague of Robert Oppenheimer. She finds herself isolated in wartime Los Alamos far from friends—a serious student in a disorganized high school—and increasingly alienated from her father.... She comes to terms with the war, her relationship with her father and through her friendship with an Indian girl and a Hispanic boy, learns to appreciate the cultures of New Mexico. Maggie Chilton is a sensitive and intelligent young woman who makes mature decisions in difficult situations. The historical, geographical and cultural details of ***Los Alamos Light*** are authentic and illuminating.

Marguerite M. Lambert, in a review of "Los Alamos Light," in School Library Journal, *Vol. 30, No. 3, November, 1983, p. 87.*

MARCUS CROUCH

[***Bad Apple***] calls for ... serious consideration. What are the preoccupations of today's teenagers? Sex, drugs, crime, violence; at least that is what Nicky seems to be concerned with in this ugly picture of American life. We should, I suppose, be sorry for Nicky, who is the product of a dreary environment and a loveless home, but he is too lacking in any positive quality to become the object of sympathy.... Larry Bograd handles the narrative brilliantly, pursuing his main theme ... and filling it in with many back-flashes. Here is a writer of formidable talent, but one with a subject which I hope most readers in this country would reject as irrelevant to their situation and interests. (p. 376)

Marcus Crouch, in a review of "Bad Apple," in The School Librarian, *Vol. 31, No. 4, December, 1983, pp. 375-76.**

NANCY SMITH

[***Los Alamos Light***] is an honest look at the people and forces active at Los Alamos, New Mexico, during the development of the first atomic bomb.... The book raises many ethical questions operating during WWII, but especially focuses on the pros and cons of the development of the bomb and the pressure of government and the military on the scientists working on the project. This would be excellent background material for a discussion of the role of atomic power today and hopefully would provide insight into varying attitudes stemming from the decision to use the bomb on Japan.

Nancy Smith, in a review of "Los Alamos Light," in Voice of Youth Advocates, *Vol. 7, No. 1, April, 1984, p. 28.*

Robin F(idler) Brancato

1936-

American novelist.

Brancato writes realistically of problems encountered by teenagers. Recalling her youth, she states, "I was always poring through the fiction, between the unicorns and the time machines, for the book that could show me literally what I was and what I might become." Brancato's novels, which reflect her preference for realism in literature, portray experiences and crises that adolescents actually confront. Her characters learn of the essential impermanence of their lives as loved ones die, relationships with friends and parents change, and their bodies mature. Brancato also writes of problems not encountered by the typical adolescent: the protagonist of *Winning* (1977) is a high school student paralyzed in a football accident; *Blinded by the Light* (1978) examines the appeal of religious cults; and in *Sweet Bells Jangled Out of Tune* (1980) the protagonist must cope with the drastic mental deterioration of her grandmother. Brancato's characters ultimately survive their hardships and mature as a result. Louise A. DeSalvo comments: "Instead of protecting kids from adversity, the implicit message in each of Brancato's novels is that we need to help them develop their resources for coping with it."

(See also *Contemporary Authors*, Vols. 69-72; *Contemporary Authors New Revision Series*, Vol. 11; and *Something about the Author*, Vol. 23.)

Photograph by Carol Kitman. Courtesy of Robin F. Brancato

PUBLISHERS WEEKLY

[In **"Don't Sit Under the Apple Tree"**] Robin Brancato has captured the somber moments of self-awareness awakening 12-year-old Ellis Carpenter throughout the turbulent summer of 1945. . . . Ellis experiences the joy of true friendship, the enormity and pain of death and the confusions of physical maturing. The children and adults who play parts in the life of the hero are warm and human. The writing evokes a particularly troubled time in America's history with fine detail and accuracy.

A review of "Don't Sit Under the Apple Tree," in Publishers Weekly, *Vol. 207, No. 11, March 17, 1975, p. 57.*

SUSAN TERRIS

"Don't Sit Under the Apple Tree" is packed with all of the now-familiar 1945 trivia details, slightly glamorized by the rosy haze of memory. In her first book, Robin F. Brancato evokes memories of victory gardens, tin can collections, air raid drills, milkweed pod lifejackets, silver-colored pennies, gold star mothers, Jack Benny's radio program, food shortages and gas rationing. These and other features of that year are given to us through the eyes of the first-person narrator, a spirited girl named Ellis Carpenter.

Ellis tells us how it was in Wissining, Pa., the summer World War II was coming to an end. A few crucial things happen that affect her life. . . . In between these important moments, the novel focuses upon the events of a slower, gentler era where children spent their time marching in Fourth of July parades and giving magic shows to raise money for the war effort.

In 1945 a girl like Ellis would have been called a tomboy, but by our current standards she has all the right feminist vibes. . . . I like Ellis. Citizenship awards notwithstanding, she is no goody-goody. Instead, along with most of us, she is a fairly good citizen wrestling to contain all of her bad citizen impulses. I find myself wishing, however, that Robin Brancato had been able to develop and bring alive some of the other characters in this book. The first-person genre does give immediacy, but it can be limiting—particularly in children's fiction. To most self-absorbed pre-adolescents—including Ellis Carpenter—the rest of the world often appears shadowy and two-dimensional.

Susan Terris, in a review of "Don't Sit Under the Apple Tree," in The New York Times Book Review, *March 30, 1975, p. 8.*

CYRISSE JAFFEE

[***Don't Sit Under the Apple Tree*** is a] modest yet satisfying story of a young girl growing up in a small Pennsylvania town as World War II nears its end. Ellis Carpenter learns to deal with death and impermanence, discerns true friendship and the beginnings of a female identity. The historical setting is superficially developed (the war is remote enough for Ellis to say, "There was something special in the air—maybe it was the excitement of V-E Day, or maybe it was just the perfume of lilac bushes."), and there is one unresolved and disturbing incident: the Fourth of July Dance where Ellis feels, for the first time, like a "tomboy" misfit, seems to mark the end of her active and vigorous life. . . . However, Brancato's treatment of characters is sensitive and humorous (except Ellis' one-dimensional father); and, Ellis' close relationship with her German grandmother is nicely drawn, as is her friendship with her classmate Jules.

Cyrisse Jaffee, in a review of "Don't Sit under the Apple Tree," in School Library Journal, *Vol. 21, No. 9, May, 1975, p. 52.*

PAMELA JAJKO

[In ***Something Left to Lose***] Jane Ann, a ninth grader whose thoughts and actions throughout are more appropriate for a 12 year old, tries to work through the usual conflicting loyalties to her friends, her family, and herself. She is concerned with a part in the school play, her first boyfriend, . . . as well as the personal problems of her best friend, Rebbie. . . . The book is well written and is enjoyable to read, but the characterizations are stereotyped and predictable: Rebbie is from an unstable home, therefore she is the odd one; Jane Ann is from a middle-class home, therefore she is average; a third friend, Lydia, is from a home in which both parents are professionals, therefore she is the mature, poised one of the group.

Pamela Jajko, in a review of "Something Left to Lose," in School Library Journal, *Vol. 22, No. 8, April, 1976, p. 84.*

BARBARA ELLEMAN

[***Something Left to Lose*** is] an engrossing story of three freshman girl friends and their loyalties to each other. Impetuous Rebbie, insecure and troubled by her mother's alcoholism, forces a pact on her friends to "follow the trail of friendship . . . wherever it leads." Calm, self-controlled Lydia takes these intensities in stride, but the more easily influenced Jane Ann is caught up in Rebbie's horoscope predictions, illegal joy rides, cigarette smoking, and beer drinking escapades. . . . Only after she questions Rebbie's demands to prove her friendship and comes to grips with where the "friendship trail" has led her is Jane Ann able to assert herself and begin to gain the self-confidence she longs for. Although the story line suffers somewhat from an overload of problems, Brancato handles the emotions, uncertainties, and dialogue with assurance. (p. 1260)

Barbara Elleman, in a review of "Something Left to Lose," in The Booklist, *Vol. 72, No. 17, May 1, 1976, pp. 1259-60.*

PUBLISHERS WEEKLY

[In **"Something Left to Lose"**] Jane Ann is torn between instilled standards of duty and of loyalty to a self-destructive friend. Fat Rebbie idolizes Janis Joplin, sneaks cigarettes and booze, and affects indifference toward her alcoholic mother. A third friend, Lydia, tries to act as a balance wheel but both Jane Ann and Rebbie resent Lydia's cool and her "hip" parents. . . . The story's dramatic culmination and achingly vague conclusion will leave sensitive readers shaken and moved. Throughout the plot, an astrology theme recurs—a deft touch, denoting the adolescent's desperate search for meaningful guidance.

A review of "Something Left to Lose," in Publishers Weekly, *Vol. 209, No. 19, May 10, 1976, p. 84.*

BOOKLIST

[In ***Winning*** a] football accident near the beginning of his high school senior year leaves Gary Madden paralyzed from damage to his spinal column—prognosis: he will never walk again. . . . Concurrent with Gary's story is that of his young, recently widowed English teacher whose involvement with Gary through tutoring helps her come to terms with the loss of her husband. The main thrust of the narrative concerns Gary's struggle to accept his condition; Brancato is, perhaps, too superficial in dealing with Gary's mental anguish and gradual determination to go on with life, but her portrayal of the effect of Gary's condition on his parents, his friends, and his girl, as well as the mutually beneficial relationship between him and his English teacher, is realistic. A generally moving and involving junior novel that avoids being maudlin.

A review of "Winning," in Booklist, *Vol. 74, No. 1, September 1, 1977, p. 30.*

KAREN HARRIS

[In ***Winning***] Brancato explores the ramifications of severe disablement through high school senior Gary Madden who, as the result of a football injury, is left a quadriplegic. . . . Although the characters are not memorable, the treatment of the problems of reduced functioning, damaged self-concept, dependence, unavoidable fears and humiliations are handled honestly and sensitively.

Karen Harris, in a review of "Winning," in School Library Journal, *Vol. 24, No. 2, October, 1977, p. 120.*

PUBLISHERS WEEKLY

[In **"Winning"**] Gary Madden, high school football hero, lies helpless in a hospital. He is permanently paralyzed. . . . In an impeccably constructed and unsentimentalized story, Brancato reveals the effects of the trauma on Gary and others in his life. Among them are his stunned parents, his confused young sweetheart and friends, some of whom desert him. All these characters are realistically portrayed, thoroughly understandable. A standout is Ann Treer, Gary's English teacher. Coming to terms with her own tragedy, the accidental death of her young husband, she pulls Gary up out of suicidal despair. . . . Like Brancato's other novels, this is a superior work.

A review of "Winning," in Publishers Weekly, *Vol. 213, No. 1, January 2, 1978, p. 65.*

BOOKLIST

Infiltrating the Light of the World Church in the hope of saving her brother Jim, college freshman Gail Brower [in ***Blinded by the Light***] finds herself mesmerized by the constant proselytizing combined with lack of food and rest. She is saved from pledging by her lover. . . . Characterizations are two-dimensional, merely acting out their roles in the story, and Brancato oversimplifies the cult experience; but despite her somewhat didactic approach, she manages to convey the frightening ease with which someone, whether particularly impressionable or not, can be converted. Less impressive than the author's ***Winning*** . . . , but nonetheless a tale with popular appeal.

A review of "Blinded by the Light," in Booklist, *Vol. 75, No. 2, September 15, 1978, p. 175.*

C. NORDHIELM WOOLDRIDGE

With only a few weeks left till graduation, Jim Brower [in ***Blinded by the Light***] hooks up with a religious group called the Light of the World, quits school, and disappears. Convinced that she can talk him into coming home, younger sister Gail . . . embarks on a weekend retreat with the L.O.W. . . . Although the rescue (kidnap?) attempt itself fails, Gail does eventually get to talk with Jim—and the author effectively chooses to end her tale at this point. Brancato tries to present both sides of the issue but too obviously sympathizes with the bereaved family. She is also heavy-handed in her manipulation of the characters' dialogue, actions, and thought processes. Despite these drawbacks however, the plot has the magnetism of suspense and the issue confronted is a refreshing change from beleaguered old stand-bys.

C. Nordhielm Wooldridge, in a review of "Blinded by the Light," in School Library Journal, *Vol. 25, No. 2, October, 1978, p. 152.*

PETER S. PRESCOTT

The trend in fiction for teen-agers these days is to write candid, compassionate novels about what adult authors take to be everyday teen-age concerns—impotence, lesbianism, whatever. In ***Blinded by the Light*** . . . Robin F. Brancato offers a brisk, no-nonsense story about a quack religious cult and its nefarious techniques for brainwashing the unsuspecting young. The menace of these cults, insofar as we understood it before the news from Guyana broke, is unstintingly portrayed. Brancato's story involves a girl, a college sophomore . . . , in a search for her older brother who has disappeared into a group that calls itself Light of the World. To discover his whereabouts, she must pretend interest in the cult. . . . This cautionary tale is dramatic and convincing. It ends with matters still unresolved—and that, too, is a trend in this kind of fiction.

Peter S. Prescott, in a review of "Blinded by the Light," in Newsweek, *Vol. XCII, No. 25, December 18, 1978, p. 102.*

HILDAGARDE GRAY

[In ***Blinded by the Light***] Gail Brower tries in every way to contact her brother who has gone off with a "Moonie"-type organization. With the aid of her boyfriend, her parents, and a de-programmer, she makes one last try by infiltrating the Light Of The World ranks. Tension builds page by page and the author is able to create a sense of pressure as it comes down on Gail, almost sweeping her into the maelstrom of cultism. Realism carries the tale as Gail's one chance to "save" Jim, after the accidental (?) death of a fellow L.O.W., is left undetermined, leaving the reader to wonder if Jim will see the truth or twist it to fit his already warped beliefs. Can Gail resolve her own problem as to how much she has the *right* to interfere with her brother's decisions? No final conclusion is reached but the no-man's land of decision making is painted in somber tones, clearly underlining the fact that few situations are all black or all white. (p. 406)

Hildagarde Gray, in a review of "Blinded by the Light," in Best Sellers, *Vol. 38, No. 12, March, 1979, pp. 406-07.*

LOUISE A. DeSALVO

The novels of Robin Brancato mark signposts in the stages that children must live through in learning about adversity, and the way-stations they must pass through in coping with hardship. Her novels, and others like them . . . teach young people about their own capacities for coping with problems without relinquishing the joys that come with living.

Ellis Carpenter, the heroine and narrator of Brancato's first novel, ***Don't Sit Under the Apple Tree,*** is poised somewhere between childhood and adolescence. As the novel opens, having already lived through the greater part of World War II, she has developed both the scars and the special kind of resilience that come from surviving in difficult times. (p. 16)

Even though she has grown up with war bulletins and air raids, with the keeping of a class scrapbook into which "sickening clippings" are regularly pasted, . . . with her best friend's brother, Les, being reported missing in action, Ellis clings to the belief in the sanctity of life and understands all too well its fragile and fleeting nature. The novel opens on V-E Day with the stunning juxtaposition of the report of Hitler's death with Ellis' voice: "The morning rain had washed earthworms onto the sidewalk and I walked on tiptoe so I wouldn't step on any."

But what Ellis has gone through already is nothing compared to what she must yet endure. She must pass from winning a citizenship award to understanding her ambivalent feelings about her own brother—she loses him almost deliberately when they journey into the woods in which they lose their innocence. . . . She must move from looking at adult love and friendship ideally, to learning that lovers are sometimes unfaithful and cruel to one another. . . . She must proceed from learning about death in the abstract from radio bulletins and newspaper clippings to facing the actual deaths of Les and her Grossie.

Ellis must also confront some primal fears and some deeply seated terrors in addition to those engendered by the outside world. What is so vital about this novel is that Brancato understands the relationship between the two. (pp. 16, 18)

Ellis uses Snow White to make sense of her fears of death and nothingness, feelings that she first believes are idiosyncratic but which she validates and verifies through remembering an analogue to her experiences in the literature with which she is familiar. A fear that would otherwise remain inexplicable to her thus becomes manageable. The reference to Snow White also tells us that another of Ellis' primal fears which she will not face until later in the novel is her fear of sexuality—she must give up the safety of her easy and warm relationship with her best friend, Jules, for the complications of adolescence; she passes from sexual innocence to sexual awareness.

This passage into adolescence has been made possible by Ellis' grandmother. In a powerful and poignant scene, Ellis travels to her grandmother's house (the reference to Little Red Riding Hood is intentional) soon before the old woman's death. Ellis learns that facing the reality of the world and its hardships is as possible for her as it has been for her courageous namesake, Mary Ellis, who lived a good life despite the death of her lover during the First World War; she learns that she must "try harder to accept the good things that come to us without feeling guilty." Her grandmother gives Ellis a volume of poems by Emily Dickinson, once owned by Mary Ellis—a volume that will later help Ellis sort out her feelings when Grossie dies, a volume that stands for the healing potential of literature. . . .

Brancato's second novel, ***Something Left to Lose,*** deals with creating a balance between impetuosity, spontaneity and a healthy hedonism on the one hand, and reason, deliberateness, and necessary self-discipline on the other. As the novel opens, Rebbie Hellerman and Jane Ann Morrow seem to represent these poles—Rebbie skips out on responsibility as often as Jane Ann embraces it. In the novel, both of their capacities for dealing with hardship will be tested: Rebbie must face the fact of her mother's alcoholism and her father's death; Jane Ann must face a move to another part of the state that will deny her everything she has come to value.

Rebbie's defiant death-wish is juxtaposed against Jane Ann's timid and almost reluctant life-hold. But Rebbie's obsession with astrology . . . and with knowing obscure details about presidents . . . indicate that beneath her spontaneous facade is a desperate need both to see herself as part of a larger pattern and to relinquish responsibility for what she does.

Jane Ann's anxiety attacks, where she loses her sense of identity and must repeat to herself ritualistically the facts of her identity ("I am Jane Ann Morrow. I live at 814 Oak Street, Windsor, Pennsylvania. My parents are James and Evelyn Morrow.") suggest that the control *she* exerts over feelings and emotions is life-suffocating. Jane loves the stage because it is a place where she can "look like she was doing the right thing, but how come, in everyday living, she was so often unsure of herself?"

The reasons for Rebbie's problems are obvious: she is saddled with an alcoholic mother whom she loves and an uncaring father who escapes the nightmare of his family by working obsessively at his law practice. (p. 18)

The reasons for Jane Ann's problems are less obvious. She has lived out life in a good, normal home with a nurturing mother and a productive reasonable father, but she cannot escape the growing pains that afflict everyone, no matter how well taken care of they are. Brancato knows that adversity is an ordinary, everyday, and *universal* condition: we are delusional if we think that we can banish it by creating isolated paradises of peace and tranquility for our children to grow in. It simply won't work. Life has a way of messing up paradise, as Jane Ann learns.

Instead of protecting kids from adversity, the implicit message in each of Brancato's novels is that we need to help them develop their resources for coping with it. Brancato reminds us that we have made it far too easy for the weakest and most alienated of our children to choose death, or the death of the soul, over life. . . . It is no wonder, then, that Rebbie has adopted Janis Joplin's litany to the troubled of her generation, that freedom is having nothing left to lose: that Jane Ann fears that Rebbie will commit suicide after her mother is hospitalized once again. Jane Ann knows that there is something paradoxical in using the corpses of literature and history to teach kids about survival and loving life, even though death is something that she must face. (pp. 18, 50)

Rebbie helps. She counters that part of Jane Ann which prefers fantasies of perfection and death to the risk of raw reality. And Jane Ann helps Rebbie: she helps her learn about self-control and about both of their capacities for courage. . . .

Winning and ***Blinded by the Light*** expand and amplify Brancato's earlier themes. In ***Blinded,*** Gail Brower engages in a quest for her brother Jim who has entered the Light of the World, a religious cult which demands obedience to a father figure, sexual abstinence, and self-denial. The L. O. W. is successful because it offers its adherents simplistic solutions to life's real problems: it purports to substitute a loving community for parental betrayal, bliss for hardship, happiness for suffering, certainty for chaos, paradise for the real world. . . .

Like *Antigone* (about which Gail writes a college term paper), ***Blinded*** deals with the conflicting claims of family love and loyalty and adherence to a higher authority; like Antigone, Gail must go underground to be reunited with her brother. She participates in a cult initiation weekend and she sees that they "want things to be perfect—by magic. They love *everybody* but no one special person." . . .

Winning is Brancato's finest novel. It recounts the relationship between Ann Treer, a recently widowed English teacher, and Gary Madden, one of her high school students who has become permanently disabled as a result of a football injury. That Brancato calls the novel ***Winning*** is not only an ironic commentary on our national preoccupation with victory at almost any price, it is also a paean to the victory of the human spirit. The novel alternates between Gary's increasing awareness of the meaning of his injury, his denial, anger, depression, and near suicide, and Ann's responses to the opening up of the old wound of her husband's death, which Gary's disability represents. Although she agrees reluctantly to tutor him, she begins to need Gary to reteach herself how to feel, to care passionately, and to love again. And he needs her to teach him to face the reality of his disability with courage, to take the hard and not the easy way out, to face the fact that although he will never walk again, his life is still just beginning. (p. 50)

The special magic of Brancato is that she erects contemporary novels in the very same set of emotive and intellectual principles as those works to which she alludes in her fiction—the fairy tales, the poetry of Emily Dickinson, the *Antigone, Death of a Salesman,* and *Crime and Punishment*—without compromising her ability to speak in a modern voice. It is a voice that young people will profit from hearing. (p. 51)

Louise A. DeSalvo, "The Uses of Adversity," in Media & Methods, *Vol. 15, No. 8, April, 1979, pp. 16, 18, 50-1.*

PUBLISHERS WEEKLY

Not up to **"Blinded by the Light"** or to her other successes, Brancato's new novel [**"Come Alive at 505"**] is crammed with too many digressive plots for conviction. A senior in high school, Dan Fetzer sniffs at college and relies on the gabby tapes he makes incessantly to win him a contest opening the door to a career as a disc jockey. His other two interests are attracting Mimi—a fat girl, new to the local high school—and plotting with her, his friend Marty and a snide kid, George, to elect a nonexistent senior the class president. When Mimi confides in Dan that George had supplied her with the pep pills that had helped her lose weight and then landed her in a hospital, her remarks are accidentally (hmmm) taped. . . . It's odd to find, incidentally, the presumably admirable young characters resorting to profanity and vulgarity to express all their reactions.

A review of "Come Alive at 505," in Publishers Weekly, *Vol. 217, No. 12, March 28, 1980, p. 49.*

KATHLEEN LEVERICH

Danny Fetzer's obsession is radio. . . . As [**"Come Alive at 505"**] opens on his senior year of high school, he wants to scrap his parents' plans for his college education and find himself a job, any job, at a real radio station. . . . Danny wants listeners, life, his future to "come alive," so he organizes an elaborate hoax to shake up the students at Duncan High. . . .

In maneuvering the hoax, he becomes involved with mysterious Mimi Alman, whose weight problem and frosty manner can't disguise her sexy voice, dry wit and beautiful face. Add a half-dozen of the wimps, nice guys, jokers and villains whom we all recognize from high school. Throw in the terrifying anxieties of coming of age in these days of drift—too many possibilities, early disillusionment, drugs, teen-age suicide—and you have a book which the jacket copy touts as "energetic . . . sure to appeal to today's media-oriented generation."

The book does have energy: from Danny's clever radio patter . . . to the tight, action-filled scenes that follow one another as closely as the segments of a successful radio show. Robin Brancato is a terrific DJ whose dialogue never misses: these *are* today's media-oriented kids talking.

But . . . the book's true genre . . . is neither media-oriented, trendy nor Today. What Mrs. Brancato has written to follow such successes as **"Winning"** and **"Blinded by the Light"** is an old-fashioned, optimistic adventure-romance. Whatever your vintage and orientation, it will leave you smiling and all-in from rooting and caring.

Kathleen Leverich, in a review of "Come Alive at 505," in The New York Times Book Review, *April 27, 1980, p. 65.*

STEVE MATTHEWS

High school senior Dan Fetzer [in ***Come Alive at 505***] wants nothing but a career as a radio personality, a goal his parents find unacceptable. With a range of recording equipment set up in his room, Dan records shows, spots, and a winning entry in a New York metro station's "new talent" contest. With the discovery of Mimi Alman, a pudgy but not undesirable classmate with a tremendously sexy voice, the possibilities are broadened. . . . The drug scene, complete with one-dimensional pusher, is presented rather limply. Otherwise, the characters are strong and the dilemmas believable. Dan Fetzer is likable and, while Mimi's background smacks of early afternoon soap, her personality and relationship with Dan spark our sympathy and interest.

Steve Matthews, in a review of "Come Alive at 505," in School Library Journal, *Vol. 26, No. 10, August, 1980, p. 74.*

PUBLISHERS WEEKLY

Affectionate, naive Ellen Dohrmann [in **"Sweet Bells Jangled Out of Tune"**] is struck by the chance sight of her estranged paternal grandmother Eva and wistfully thinks about her childhood visits with the erratic old woman. Her widowed mother had forbidden contacts with Eva years earlier. The elder Mrs. Dohrmann is the town scandal: a compulsive petty thief and given to generally outré behavior. Now Ellen, aware that her grandmother's housekeeper and sole companion has died, is compelled to rescue Eva. The girl's insistence causes tension between her and her mother, Ellen accusing the woman of hypocrisy and rejecting a person in need of help. . . . Admired for realistic novels on social issues, Brancato has produced a topnotch drama about "different" people, its serious theme leavened by flashes of humor, mostly by Josie, Ellen's good buddy and sympathetic ally.

A review of "Sweet Bells Jangled out of Tune," in Publishers Weekly, *Vol. 221, No. 3, January 15, 1982, p. 99.*

ROGER D. SUTTON

For years 15-year-old Ellen has been forbidden to visit her grandmother Eva, who has gradually disintegrated from mild eccentricity into being a genuine bag lady. . . . After talking with her mother and various social-service professionals, Ellen tricks Eva into signing herself into a hospital. [***Sweet Bells Jangled Out of Tune***], told in the present tense, moves quickly and smoothly, and Brancato demonstrates a fine hand with dialogue. One extended conversation between Ellen and a psychiatrist is awkwardly loaded with virtuous information about mental health care, but for the most part the message—in some cases, the end justifies the means—is exposed through action. This is not a particularly thought-provoking novel, but it will grab readers. . . . (p. 67)

Roger D. Sutton, in a review of "Sweet Bells Jangled out of Tune," in School Library Journal, *Vol. 28, No. 9, May, 1982, pp. 67-8.*

RUSSELL H. GOODYEAR

[**"Sweet Bells Jangled Out of Tune"**] is about two child-women. One, into her seventies, lives a life dominated by the ghost of her father. The other, just turned fifteen, struggles to escape the bonds of childhood.

When Ellen, the fifteen year old, renews the special bond between her and her grandmother Eva, she learns realistically to see the dangers in her grandmother's lifestyle. Ellen refuses to view her grandmother as a romantic loner the way her flighty friend Josie does. Josie thinks Eva's eccentricity is entertaining, and she wants to make a game out of visiting the old woman's house. Ellen, however, realizes that Eva has withdrawn from reality and may soon do serious harm to herself or to someone else.

This is an exciting story with a fast-moving plot. Brancato writes with an ease that is a delight to the reader's ear. I was most pleased with how well it read out loud, a trait that unfortunately is not often characteristic of many contemporary adolescent novels. . . .

Ellen is a dynamic, well-developed character. The reader sees her grow into maturity through her relationships with her mother, her girlfriend Josie, and an intriguing boy, Ben Bernhauser, who wears an earring in one ear. What makes the plot especially compelling is the mystery of Eva's life. How did a woman, once rich and envied, end up as a bag lady? Seldom does a writer of adolescent literature provide as much insight into psychological cause and effect as Robin Brancato has.

This fine novel rates a solid "A" and should not be missed.

Russell H. Goodyear, in a review of "Sweet Bells Jangled out of Tune," in Best Sellers, *Vol. 42, No. 3, June, 1982, p. 118.*

ANN A. FLOWERS

Jepson, Dave Jacoby's best friend [in ***Facing Up***], was a bit zany and always in trouble. Dave was a little in awe of him, loved him, and sometimes envied him his freedom and his girl, the beautiful Susan Scherra. When Susan began hinting that she was tired of Jep . . . and that she was interested in Dave, he was consumed by self-disgust for betraying his friend but fell in love with her, anyway. Finally realizing that she was a sensation seeker, Dave stopped seeing her, but Jep found out about their relationship and caused a drunken scene. Driving the unconscious Jep home, Dave had an accident; Jep was killed, and Dave, though cleared of blame, was filled with unutterable guilt. He sank into lethargy and depression and decided to leave home. . . . Dave's struggle to regain his equilibrium is told in a tight, clean narrative that clearly pictures Jep's magnetic personality, Dave's innate decency, and his loving but overprotective parents. Less observant of the social milieu than *The Outsiders* . . . and furnished with more conventional characters than M. E. Kerr's books about high school life, the story of an adolescent friendship and its tragic outcome is nevertheless filled with vitality and interest. (pp. 199-200)

Ann A. Flowers, in a review of "Facing Up," in The Horn Book Magazine, *Vol. LX, No. 2, April, 1984, pp. 199-200.*

CONSTANCE ALLEN

[In ***Facing Up,*** a] teen novel of American high-school students, the emphasis is on cars, dating and drinking. Dave is a model student from a middle-class family and his best friend, Jep, who comes from a broken home is cool, casual and daring. Dave would like to be more like Jep and that includes having the same girlfriend. . . . The present tense format, cliché-ridden dialogue and stereotyped characters are disappointing. It doesn't help to know that Dave rejects Susan when he finally "faces up" to his own values. Nothing memorable here.

Constance Allen, in a review of "Facing Up," in School Library Journal, *Vol. 30, No. 8, April, 1984, p. 122.*

AARON I. MICHELSON

Facing Up is the latest in a long succession of popular, contemporary novels by the well-known young adult writer, Robin Brancato. Among her accolades are no less than three American Library Association "Best Books for Young Adults" awards. Yet to this reviewer, ***Facing Up*** is a rather pulpish teen-age melodrama that exudes schmaltz. It is also written in a style that certainly would not challenge an intelligent young reader. Perhaps its virtue lies in the message that despite horrible personal tragedies, one has to adjust and life must go on.

Aaron I. Michelson, in a review of "Facing Up," in Best Sellers, *Vol. 44, No. 3, June, 1984, p. 115.*

VICTORIA YABLONSKY

[In ***Facing Up,*** a] love triangle arises when high school junior Dave becomes involved with Susan, the girlfriend of his best friend, Jep. . . .

Dave's efforts to learn to live with the consequences of his actions are the focus of the latter part of the novel. In his fight to cope with the grief facing him each day, Dave's character growth is effectively displayed. But while the elements of friendship and responsibility are handled well, the story is unfortunately somewhat marred by the use of some negative female stereotypes.

Victoria Yablonsky, in a review of "Facing Up," in Voice of Youth Advocates, *Vol. 7, No. 4, October, 1984, p. 195.*

Betsy Byars

1928-

American novelist and author of books for children.

Byars's works are noted for their sensitive portrayals of troubled adolescents who suffer from feelings of isolation and loneliness. Her characters undergo realistic emotional growth, and a subtle humor offsets the gravity of her themes. Critics also praise Byars's lack of sentimentality and her direct, accessible prose. *Summer of the Swans* (1970), for which Byars won a Newbery Medal, established her reputation and anticipated the themes and style of her later work. The plot revolves around Sara, who is experiencing an awkward adolescence, and Charlie, her mentally-impaired younger brother. When Charlie becomes lost one night, Sara is forced to reach out to others for help. Through this experience, Sara gains a greater appreciation of her own worth. Critics particularly admired Byars's compassionate approach to mental retardation.

Byars often examines the difficulties of growing up in a broken home. *The Pinballs* (1977) concerns three foster children with backgrounds of neglect and abuse; *The Animal, the Vegetable and John D. Jones* (1982) explores how three children cope with divorce; and *The 2,000 Pound Goldfish* (1982) delineates a young boy's emotional turmoil caused by his mother's abandonment. In these three novels, as in many of her works, Byars skillfully dramatizes the pain her characters experience. As Marilyn Kaye observes, "Betsy Byars has a gift for exposing the soul of the lost child, the damaged, the unloved."

(See also *Children's Literature Review*, Vol. 1; *Contemporary Authors*, Vols. 33-36, rev. ed.; and *Something about the Author*, Vol. 4.)

Courtesy of Betsy Byars

ETHEL L. HEINS

[Seldom] are the pain of adolescence and the tragedy of mental retardation presented as sensitively and as unpretentiously as in [***The Summer of the Swans***] the story of Sara and Charlie, the brain-damaged younger brother she loved so protectively. Sara, in her fourteenth summer, felt the rhythm of her life break down and anger, confusion, and discontent rush in. She experienced a new self-consciousness, a feeling of being clumsy, too tall, and hopelessly unattractive; unwillingly she envied the serenity of her pretty, older sister; and Charlie, dependent and often importunate, seemed to be a constant concern. . . . Then, one warm night, Charlie, unable to sleep, slipped out into the darkness and disappeared; and at the end of an anguished, unforgettable day of searching, Sara knew that she had found even more than a terrified, lost little boy. A subtly told story, echoing the spoken and unspoken thoughts of young people. (pp. 53-4)

Ethel L. Heins, in a review of "The Summer of the Swans," in The Horn Book Magazine, *Vol. XLVII, No. 1, February, 1971, pp. 53-4.*

DEE DEE SIMMONS

[In **"The Summer of the Swans,"** the] heroine Sara is a "tall skinny girl with big feet and a crooked nose" who in the dalliance of her fourteenth summer feels most fashionably "like nothing." . . . Sara's mother is dead, her father absent and distant, and she lives in the charge of an aunt she loves "without finding her coarse," and in the company of an older sister she loves "without envy," and a younger brother she loves "without pity."

The brother is . . . [a] retardate, named almost traditionally, Charlie. One night after he is treated to a visit to a flock of swans, stopping over on a nearby lake during their migration, he leaves his room, walks out of the house, and proceeds to get lost in quest of them in a nearby forest.

The burden of the book is the flight (from Charlie's point of view) and the search (from Sara's point of view) that culminates in Sara's not only finding him but also discovering true happiness for her 14-year-old gangling self: a teen-age boy's inviting her to a party featuring the local electronically amplified rock group.

So much for the plot. There are, to be sure, some insights offered into the life of a retardate: his unusual frustration over an unsewn button, his utter fascination with the moving hands of a watch whose time he cannot read. And also there is the poignancy of a retardate's sibling reacting to the cruel jeers directed at her brother. And there is the abject pathos implicit in having to report to the police a child "who can be lost and afraid three blocks from home and cannot speak one word to ask for help.''

But retardation . . . is an endless problem. There is enough drama in the daily existence of a retarded child to keep his family and siblings fully occupied without his having to wander off into the woods: the simple logistics of fulfilling his special school needs, of anticipating his special routine requirements, of beginning to make provisions for his ''adult'' years: he will simply not grow up and leave home and take care of himself that matter of factly.

These concerns are for the most part sidestepped or overlooked by Mrs. Byars. It can be argued that in a slender book for tender youth there is scarcely room for much coverage in depth. Yet Mrs. Byars moves her story along so slowly, piling narrative trifles upon conventional details in a pace reminiscent of old ''One Man's Family'' radio scripts that one wonders if there oughtn't to have been room for a little more reality.

So, I cannot cheer as loud as I would like to or in fact, as loud as others already have for this book.

Dee Dee Simmons, in a review of ''The Summer of the Swans,'' in The New York Times Book Review, *February 28, 1971, p. 22.*

TOP OF THE NEWS

[***Summer of the Swans***] is a moving and perceptive family story focusing on the relationship of junior high-aged Sara and her younger brother Charlie. In spite of the predictable frustrations of early adolescence, Sara feels protective and defensive about Charlie who is retarded and full of his own unexpressed dreams and fears. Sara is often ambivalent about herself, her friends, and her family, but the bond of trust and affection with Charlie is the strength which forces self-concerns aside. During the summer, Sara takes Charlie to the lake to see the swans and the child is strangely moved by their beauty. Later, he sets out alone to find them and becomes lost in the wooded ravines near home. The story moves dramatically through the suspense of searching, the despair of Charlie's fear and helplessness, Sara's reluctant trust in a boy from school who helps her look for Charlie—to the ultimate relief and elation at finding him.

Throughout this realistic, tender, and sometimes humorous story there is an authentic emotional tension which characterizes the interactions between family and friends. Both Sara and Charlie are realistically portrayed, and the impact of the ''Summer'' on Sara's view of herself comes through with unforgettable poignancy. Betsy Byars, a sensitive writer with an ear and heart attuned to the subtleties of growing up, has created a story of extraordinary understanding and warmth. (p. 241)

''Betsy Byars: Newbery 1971,'' in Top of the News, *Vol. 27, No. 3, April, 1971, pp. 240-41.*

BRIGITTE WEEKS

[In ***The Pinballs,*** three] foster children have individual problems and their parents have failed them—Harvey's most dramatically by driving into him while drunk and breaking both his legs. Carlie, Thomas J, and Harvey come to the Mason household as successors to 17 previous foster children who have used the calm and friendly household as a haven to patch together their bruised minds and bodies. Mrs. Mason seems almost too good to be true in her endless tolerance and cheerful understanding but one is eager and willing to believe in her. Byars has portrayed children in an unenviable situation with good humor and optimism.

Brigitte Weeks, in a review of ''The Pinballs,'' in Book World—The Washington Post, *April 10, 1977, p. E10.*

ETHEL L. HEINS

When Sid Fleischman observed, ''Comedy is tragedy; but it is tragedy in motley'' and ''Comedy . . . is alchemy; the base metal is always tragedy''—he might well have been talking about Betsy Byars' latest book [***The Pinballs***]. The stark facts about three ill-matched, abused children living in a foster home could have made an almost unbearably bitter novel; but the economically told story, liberally spiced with humor, is something of a tour de force. Ideal but never idealized, the foster parents Mr. and Mrs. Mason are modest, patient, and quietly loving; one summer two boys and a girl come to live with them. Thirteen-year-old Harvey arrives in a wheel chair, his legs having been broken when his father, driving in a drunken rage, accidentally ran over him. . . . As a two-year-old toddler, [Thomas J] had been found abandoned near the home of elderly twin sisters. . . . The girl Carlie, repeatedly beaten up by her stepfather, was a cynical, rude teenager, ''hard . . . as a coconut,'' who concealed beneath her brittle exterior a keen mind and a courageous spirit. . . . Goaded into furious action by Harvey's deteriorating condition and impenetrable depression, Carlie finally took matters into her own hands, injecting life into the listless Thomas J as she swept him along in her grim determination. A deceptively simple, eloquent story, its pain and acrimony constantly mitigated by the author's light, offhand style and by Carlie's wryly comic view of life.

Ethel L. Heins, in a review of ''The Pinballs,'' in The Horn Book Magazine, *Vol. LIII, No. 4, August, 1977, p. 437.*

NAOMI LEWIS

'One summer two boys and a girl went to a foster home to live together.' So begins Betsy Byars's **''The Pinballs,''** . . . and as always with this author a serious content is sped along by sleight of wit and inimitable dialogue. How does she do it? If it misses being the best of the Byars books, this is not because of its characters, but because its story, good as it is . . . is just too persuasive a notion.

Naomi Lewis, ''Solitaries and Others,'' in The Observer, *September 25, 1977, p. 25.**

BARBARA H. BASKIN AND KAREN H. HARRIS

[***Summer of the Swans***] is essentially a beautifully written story about a sibling's love and responsibility and how mental retardation affects those feelings. The descriptions of behavior, such as the drawing of Charlie's self-portrait, are both tender and accurate. It is in just such vignettes that Byars' consummate skill is revealed. She can describe scenes revealing limitations in ways that reflect reality and avoid maudlin pity. At the same time, her descriptions of teasing incidents toward Charlie resonate with a vivid sense of reality. For example, Sara, not unashamedly, reports: ''This nice little Gretchen Wyant didn't see me—all she saw was Charlie at the fence—and she said, 'How's the *retard* today?' only she made it sound even uglier, 'How's the *reeeeetard,*' like that. Nothing ever made me so mad. The best sight of my whole life was nice little Gretchen Wyant standing there in her wet Taiwan silk dress with her mouth hanging open." Much information about retardation can be extrapolated from incidents in Charlie's life, but more important is the feeling tone generated by the text and supported by the warm, touching illustrations. Charlie has his own modest literary identity, but his story function is to act as a catalyst in the clarification of values and establishment of self-identity of the heroine. (p. 138)

Barbara H. Baskin and Karen H. Harris, "An Annotated Guide to Juvenile Fiction Portraying the Handicapped, 1940-1975: 'Summer of the Swans'," in their Notes from a Different Drummer: A Guide to Juvenile Fiction Portraying the Handicapped, *R. R. Bowker Company, 1977, pp. 137-38.*

JODY BERGE

[In ***Goodbye, Chicken Little***] Jimmy Little witnesses his uncle's death as he literally walks on thin ice, and it seems yet another example of the world's unreasonable treachery. Jimmy thinks of himself as "Chicken Little" because of his extreme caution in the face of risks. It takes the wisdom of old Uncle C. C. and the healing warmth of a family party to help Jimmy see that his fear is only a cocoon from which he will one day emerge. I finished the book [feeling] . . . that the problem facing the introspective central character is a trifle hard to comprehend, the secondary characters are one-dimensional (though humorously offbeat), and the resolution of the plot is realistic but not wholly satisfying. Jimmy is a thoughtful, sensitive boy, and it will take that sort of reader to appreciate him.

Jody Berge, in a review of "Good-bye, Chicken Little," in Children's Book Review Service, *Vol. 7, No. 9, April, 1979, p. 86.*

PAUL HEINS

[In ***Good-bye, Chicken Little***] Jimmie Little became filled with anxiety the year his father was killed in the coal mine, and he began to call himself Chicken Little. As time went on, he began "to notice that his . . . family drew attention to themselves in the wrong way. They did silly, senseless things that made them look foolish even when they succeeded." But his mother's brother Pete did not succeed when he tried to walk across a frozen river four days before Christmas. He was drowned. After her initial shock Jimmie's mother, who had a strong sense of family solidarity, decided to hold a Christmas party. . . . Jimmie continued to be morosely unappreciative of his mother's activities until it occurred to him that his family was really remembering and honoring Pete, and the boy learned to see each of his relatives as a "unique, one-of-a-kind individual." As in the author's other works, the extended terse dialogue gives the narrative a characteristic quality of understated, often wry humor; but after the realism and the seriousness of the opening incident, the sudden change of mood seems disconcertingly incongruous. Although the author is obviously attempting to account for the transformation of the boy's emotional attitudes, she fails to make a successful transition between the tragic and the comic portions of the story. (pp. 189-90)

Paul Heins, in a review of "Good-bye, Chicken Little," in The Horn Book Magazine, *Vol. LV, No. 2, April, 1979, pp. 189-90.*

JEAN FRITZ

Betsy Byars has always had the capacity to create unique and believable characters. [In **"Good-bye, Chicken Little"** the protagonist, Jimmie Little, has a friend who] says the Littles are crazy. Certainly when Jimmie's mother decides to give a big family party a few days after the tragedy [in which Jimmie's Uncle Pete is killed], it seems, at the least, unconventional, but it is at this party, with everyone toasting Pete and laughing about his antics, that Jimmie feels restored.

It is a moving story and a marvelous family. I'm not likely to forget Jimmie or his mother, but my favorite character is 92-year-old Uncle C. C., who pretends he's 100 so that the Baptist ladies with haystack hairdos who visit his nursing home will make a fuss over him.

Jean Fritz, in a review of "Good-bye, Chicken Little," in The New York Times Book Review, *October 7, 1979, p. 35.*

ZENA SUTHERLAND, DIANNE L. MONSON, AND MAY HILL ARBUTHNOT

Although few of her books are humorous, there is in most of Betsy Byars' writing a quiet, understated sense of humor that children quickly recognize and enjoy. More evident, and just as much appreciated, are her compassion and her understanding of the deepest emotions of children. And, as in ***The Midnight Fox*** (1968) there is an empathy with children's love of animals. (p. 328)

The compassion depicted in [***The Midnight Fox***] . . . appears again in Byars' Newbery Medal book, ***The Summer of the Swans*** (1970), one of the early books about a retarded child. Charlie's sister Sara is loving and protective, terrified when Charlie is lost, and glad of the help of a friend, Joe, in finding him. Sara, fourteen and shy, accepts a party invitation from Joe, and comes to a turning point. Like the swans she and Charlie have watched, she knows for the first time that she will move from a first, awkward flight to the confidence of being in her own element. The book has a tender quality and has enough action to balance the quiet unfolding of a situation.

In ***The Night Swimmers*** (1980) Byars again explores a situation and a turning point in a child's life with insight, again writes with tenderness and grace, again creates a memorable character. Retta is the oldest of three children; motherless, she is a mother to her younger brothers, since their father, a country-western singer, is away at night and asleep for most of the day. Secretly they swim, at night, in a neighbor's pool; it's one of the many ways that Retta tries to keep her brothers busy and happy. She is bereft when they develop other interests, confused by her own reactions of jealousy and resentment. The situation is resolved when a friend of their father's takes over; she's a tough, cheerful woman who's determined to marry Retta's father. Only when she realizes that she can be a child, that somebody else will assume the role of protector, does Retta accept the change in her role, in a story that is touching but never saccharine.

Byars has written some fantasy and some lightly humorous stories, but her strong forte is in depicting troubled children. . . . In all her books, Byars affirms a respect for children's resiliency and strength. (pp. 328-29)

Zena Sutherland, Dianne L. Monson, and May Hill Arbuthnot, "Modern Fiction: 'The Midnight Fox', 'The Summer of the Swans' and 'The Night Swim-

mers'," *in their* Children and Books, *sixth edition, Scott, Foresman and Company, 1981, pp. 328-29.*

MICHELE SLUNG

Divorced parents are as regular a feature of today's books for young readers as consumptive relatives were in the sentimental family fiction of a century ago. In their latest books, both Betsy Byars and E. L. Konigsburg, each a former Newbery Award winner, have chosen the same seasonal theme: summer vacation, and how resentful children cope with single parent holidays. Their approaches to this familiar situation are different, however; Mrs. Byars opts for a low-key normality (squabbling sisters, Dad's new girlfriend and her bratty son) while Mrs. Konigsburg takes another route (a new friend whose mom is a moocher and con artist, a godmother who's a rock star, not to mention Dad's camel, Ahmed). . . .

Betsy Byars's **"The Animal, the Vegetable & John D. Jones"** refers to three children condemned by their parents to share a beach house for two weeks. Clara and Deanie get along about as well as any two early adolescents who happen to be sisters, except when they're fighting for the attention of their divorced father. He, treacherously, has invited another single-parent family, Delores Jones and her son, John D, to join them for their vacation, giving Clara and Deanie scant warning. John D, for his part, likes the arrangements no better, and, upon first encountering them, mentally dubs Clara "the Animal" and Deanie "the Vegetable." . . . [John D is] a brainy, over-imaginative seventh-grader so convinced of his own superiority that he's busy composing a potential best seller based on his own experience, "Simple Ways to Get What You Want." . . .

Learning tolerance is what both of these books are about. They remind us that it's difficult enough to let down our guards and open ourselves to new ideas, places and people without the added burden of worrying whether our parents want us and love us when we don't live with them. Gaining maturity is always an act of juggling old emotions and new ones; divorce certainly complicates it. Mrs. Byars and Mrs. Konigsburg are wise to the ways of fear of loss, adolescent snobbery and conformism, the way kids' antennae are tuned to every nuance of change and difference, and they want their young readers to gain a bit of this wisdom. The message is less baroquely adorned in **"The Animal, the Vegetable & John D Jones,"** which ends in a near tragedy, than in "Journey to an 800 Number," which concludes with a sobering revelation. I think the Byars is the better book because of its simplicity.

Michele Slung, in a review of "The Animal, the Vegetable, & John D. Jones," in The New York Times Book Review, *May 30, 1982, p. 14.*

ZENA SUTHERLAND

Warren, a lonely child, is given to a particular form of daydreaming, although the older sister and grandmother with whom he lives have told him it's not good for him. The goldfish of the title [***The Two-Thousand-Pound Goldfish***] is only one of the many lurid science fiction films he composes, complete with dialogue, and in which he occasionally uses as characters people he knows. Not his mother, never his mother. A political activist wanted by the police, she hasn't been home in years. . . . Warren discovers that his sister occasionally gets a call at a public telephone booth, and he insists he, too, must talk to his mother—but it's not very satisfying, and he turns to his sister for emotional stability for the first time, knowing that his dreams of Mom's return will not materialize, and for the first time he also knows that he must give up the daydreams that have filled the vacuum in his life. Bits of scenarios appear as interpolations throughout the story, which has Byars' usual smooth writing style, well-drawn characters, and a situation in which a child's deep needs are seen with percipience; this does not, however, have the focus and direction that distinguish most of Byars' work.

Zena Sutherland, in a review of "The Two-Thousand-Pound Goldfish," in Bulletin of the Center for Children's Books, *Vol. 36, No. 1, September, 1982, p. 4.*

NANCY K. JOHANSEN

[***The Animal, the Vegetable, and John D. Jones***] would be light and whimsical if one didn't take seriously the children's dilemma, and that's the problem. To find oneself on the way to a vacation at the beach with your father, and discover it's to be shared with his friend, and her son, who you've never met, raise questions immediately about the adults' credibility. All children view some adult behavior as irrational, but in this case the behavior is blatantly insensitive, and although, as the story develops, the adults begin to display evidence of concern, the original, startling impression is difficult to change. But readers will be able to understand and appreciate the developing relationships between two sisters, Deanie and Clara, and John. The innocent bickering, the suspicions based on insecurity and anger, and even changed feelings about each other, will ring true as will the satisfying conclusion.

Nancy K. Johansen, in a review of "The Animal, the Vegetable, and John D. Jones," in Language Arts, *Vol. 59, No. 7, October, 1982, p. 751.*

LINDA BARRETT OSBORNE

[***The Two-Thousand-Pound Goldfish*** explores] with sensitivity and skill the pain and problems of coming to terms with an absent mother. . . .

[It is] the story of a boy's need for love. . . . [Warren Otis] idealizes his mother, as well as the reunion he envisions between them. She is wanted by the FBI for politically motivated bombings, and he imagines her both as a wonder-woman avenger and as a loving mother who spends all of her time thinking about him and who will erase all his loneliness as soon as she returns. In fact, as his older sister points out, his mother did not spend much time with them when they were together, and the life she chooses to live does not center on them.

Warren denies such painful facts by inventing horror movies so vivid to him he can forget the loneliness of his days. The 2,000-pound goldfish is one such fantasy, once flushed down a toilet, exposed to dangerous waste material, now forced to slurp the human beings who cross his path to live. Yet even though the goldfish devours sewer workers and stray dogs, there is something gentle and appealing about him. He is the perfect counterpart to Warren, whose life is also shaped by things he cannot control, and who is gently heroic as he keeps believing in his mother.

When Warren learns that his mother sometimes calls his sister, and has also been in town without meeting with him, however, he must rethink the picture he has of her. For the first time he admits both anger and disappointment. "Suddenly Warren was overcome with the wish that he had a mother who didn't care so much about the world. . . . He wanted one of those mothers he saw . . . standing in line to have their children's pictures made, the children as clean and combed as if they'd just come out of a box." This poignancy is intensified when Warren finally gets to speak to his mother for a few minutes. Should he tell her about his friend or his grades? "These were things you told your mother every day when you got home from school, things you told at the kitchen table while you were having cookies and milk. Tonight he had to tell his mother something so interesting, so fascinating she would not want to hang up. . . ." This conversation helps Warren to accept his mother's absence, and to understand more realistically her character and her feelings.

Through such sensitive observations about a child's need for ordinary life and love, Byars turns an unlikely and grim situation into a moving and sometimes humorous story.

Linda Barrett Osborne, "Learning to Live without Mother," in Book World—The Washington Post, *October 10, 1982, p. 6.**

MARILYN KAYE

Betsy Byars is at her best taking an uncommon situation and treating it to a simple, forthright exploration. **"The Two-Thousand-Pound Goldfish"** is a provocative and compelling example. . . .

[Warren Otis misses his mother] terribly; or, at least, he thinks he does, since he can barely remember her. What he really misses is the *idea* of a mother; someone to hug him, tuck him into bed, bake cupcakes for him—a juvenile ideal of maternal love.

Warren focuses his emotional energies on cows that squirt radioactive milk, and Bubbles, a giant goldfish who lives in a sewer. Imagined disasters distract Warren from his personal ongoing sense of disaster. There is a remarkably skillful blend of imaginative fantasy and reality here. . . .

Mrs. Byars's straightforward narration lets pure gut feelings come through. The rationale for the mother's behavior and her actual motives are never really explored, but that's not important. The impact of Warren's having to cope with the fact that he's not the No. 1 priority in his mother's life *is* important. It's not an easy concept to grasp, but he will eventually accept it, and survive. In the end, he imagines a movie in which his 2,000-pound goldfish is released from the sewer and sent out to sea. With this, his first nondestructive cinematic finale, he takes the first step toward banishing his own demons.

Marilyn Kaye, in a review of "The Two-Thousand-Pound Goldfish," in The New York Times Book Review, *November 28, 1982, p. 24.*

LINDA KAUFFMANN PETERSON AND MARILYN LEATHERS SOLT

Summer of the Swans sensitively presents the pain of growing up and the tragedy of mental retardation in the story of thirteen-year-old Sara Godfrey and her brain-damaged younger brother, Charlie. (p. 181)

This is essentially Sara's story, but it is Charlie's, too. The reader is with Charlie for a part of the time he is lost. Charlie's limited thoughts and perceptions give a concept of the world in which the mentally retarded child dwells. We learn more of this world from his actions and from the conversations the other characters have about him. Mute Charlie provides a contrast to voluble Sara. There is little narration by the author; most of the story is gained from the natural-sounding dialogue. Sara's conversations with her sister Wanda, Aunt Willie, her friends Mary and Joe, and Charlie help to characterize her as do her thoughts. We see all sides of her personality. Even in her misery and anger with herself she can still manage a little humor as she tells Wanda, "I'd like to know who would call me Little One except the Jolly Green Giant." Sara is a convincing character who speaks and acts as a real girl might in the circumstances in which the author places her.

The title has literal significance and it also reflects the theme, as well as a pattern of imagery that appears throughout the book. The family and neighbors will remember the summer when Charlie became lost for that was the year the swans left their home pond at the university and settled for a little while on the pond close to the Godfreys' home. Sara will remember that, and more, too. At the end of her long day of searching, when she finds Charlie, she knows that she has found more than a frightened, lost boy; in some way she has also found herself. Images of swans and ducks call to mind Hans Christian Andersen's story of the ugly duckling. At the beginning of the story, Sara is an ugly duckling: she feels clumsy, too tall, hopelessly unattractive. Her large feet in their orange sneakers remind her of Donald Duck's. At the close, as she dresses for the party, Sara is beginning to feel a bit swanlike. (pp. 181-82)

Linda Kauffmann Peterson and Marilyn Leathers Solt, "The Newbery Medal and Honor Books, 1922-1981: 'Summer of the Swans'," in their Newbery and Caldecott Medal and Honor Books: An Annotated Bibliography, *G. K. Hall & Co., 1982, pp. 181-82.*

NANCY SHERIDAN

[In ***The Two-Thousand-Pound Goldfish***] Warren Otis creates horror movies in his mind; his latest is about Bubbles, an overgrown goldfish living in the sewer, ingesting unknowing victims. . . . Like Harvey in ***The Pinballs*** . . . , he has built up dreams about his mother that are far from true. With his slow acceptance comes the decision to end the movie about Bubbles. "He had had enough. It was all he could do to handle everyday problems." Warren's growth comes about gradually and believably as the author once again handles a painful experience with compassion and insight. The interweaving of the humorous movie plots with day-to-day reality is skillfully done in a subtle and powerful novel.

Nancy Sheridan, in a review of "The Two-Thousand-Pound Goldfish," in The Horn Book Magazine, *Vol. LIX, No. 1, February, 1983, p. 43.*

ANN A. FLOWERS

[***The Glory Girl***], about the Glorys, a family of not very successful gospel singers, is told from the point of view of one of the daughters, Anna, the only one who cannot sing and who feels like an outcast. . . . Mrs. Glory tries to be the peacemaker, the twins Joshua and Matthew are holy terrors, and their sister Angel is beautiful but withdrawn. Learning that his brother Newt has been paroled from prison and needs to stay with them, Mr. Glory is enraged. Believing her uncle to be a fellow misfit, Anna alone feels sympathy for him and keeps an eye out for his arrival. Angel, constantly pursued by boys, is bothered by a vicious pair who follow the bus and force it off the road into a flooding stream. Only the quick, heroic action of Anna and Uncle Newt, who has been wistfully trailing them, saves the lives of the family. Before Uncle Newt leaves to start life elsewhere, he gives Anna her first feeling of self-esteem by praising her kindness and generosity. The book seems to be more like an episode than like a full-length novel. Anna, the clear-minded heroine, contrasts sharply with her father and the rest of her family in a story that clearly portrays a seldom-explored lifestyle. (pp. 569-70)

Ann A. Flowers, in a review of "The Glory Girl," in The Horn Book Magazine, *Vol. LIX, No. 5, October, 1983, pp. 569-70.*

MARIA SALVADORE

[In ***The Glory Girl,*** the] Glory family is not exactly a group of overachievers nor are they especially likable. They are, however, plausible. . . . [Anna, the protagonist,] feels terribly distant from the family to which she longs to be part. A letter from the family outcast, Uncle Newt, upsets the whole family. Anna learns that Newt is being paroled from prison after serving time for a particularly inept bank robbery. Could she, Anna wonders, have found a kindred spirit? Anna finds Uncle Newt an elusive character until the night he rescues the family after an almost fatal traffic accident caused by vicious pranksters. Only then does Anna realize her own mettle as she glimpses her uncle's. Once again Byars has created a likable protagonist who must overcome a difficult situation. Anna's situation, however, is one with which readers are unlikely to readily identify. Not only does the Glory family have an unusual occupation, the book is filled with emotional tension and seemingly endless conflict among characters. The negativism and tension created is unrelieved by the humor characteristic of so many other of Byars' books. Although 12-year-old Anna ultimately gains a sense of self with the too brief support of Uncle Newt, she remains isolated—isolated from unlikable parents and self-absorbed siblings. The total lack of outside friends or interests even further isolates the girl. One only hopes that Anna can grow up and away from the Glory family.

Maria Salvadore, in a review of "The Glory Girl," in School Library Journal, *Vol. 30, No. 3, November, 1983, p. 88.*

MARILYN KAYE

Betsy Byars has a gift for exposing the soul of the lost child—the damaged, the alienated, the unloved. Her stories may not always live up to expectations, but her characters have credibility. They tend to rise above situations and plots.

[In **"The Glory Girl"**] Anna Glory, 12, is the only person in her family who can't carry a tune, a miserable state of affairs when one's family is a gospel singing group. Onstage, her parents and siblings bask in the glow of spotlights and spiritual fervor. Meanwhile, untalented Anna sits in the back of the auditorium and waits to perform the only function for which she's suited—selling Glory family records and tapes. . . .

The rest of the Glorys are vaguely defined. There's the harsh, quick-tempered father and an insipid mother who plays favorites among her offspring. The beautiful sister spends her time setting her hair, while the frenetic twin brothers count the stitches they accumulate through various scrapes. While Mrs. Byars makes no explicit judgments about the family's piety, they do come off as a pretty sleazy bunch. She avoids the religious angle and concentrates instead on a situation in which a young person is made to feel inadequate.

The story is thin, but the tension builds neatly and the writing is polished. The plot, particularly the climax, may carry a hint of contrivance, but **"The Glory Girl"** is rescued by its striking and appealing protagonist. In the end, it's Anna who becomes its salvation.

Marilyn Kaye, in a review of "The Glory Girl," in The New York Times Book Review, *November 27, 1983, p. 34.*

Jim Carroll

1951-

American poet, autobiographer, and songwriter.

Carroll has gained attention for his commentaries on the sordid side of modern urban life. His reputation is largely based on three works: *The Basketball Diaries* (1978), a journal Carroll wrote between the ages of twelve and fifteen; *Living at the Movies* (1973), a collection of poems; and *Catholic Boy* (1981), an album praised for its powerful lyrics and musical diversity. Central to these works are Carroll's experiences growing up on the streets of New York City.

***The Basketball Diaries,* sections of which originally appeared in small press magazines, chronicles with chilling candor Carroll's early experimentation with drugs and sex and the sometimes fatal despair of contemporary adolescents. Although critical recognition was sparse, this work became an underground classic valued for its poignant humor, vivid imagery, and unpretentious style. After reading an excerpt of *The Basketball Diaries,* Jack Kerouac declared that "at the age of 13, Jim Carroll writes better prose than 89 per cent of the novelists working today." As with *The Basketball Diaries, Living at the Movies* attracted interest in the literary circle which included such experimental writers as William Burroughs, Ted Berrigan, and Allen Ginsberg. The collection inspired Berrigan to term Carroll "the first truly new American poet." Prior to this work, Carroll had published two limited edition volumes of poetry, *Organic Trains* (1967) and *Four Ups and One Down* (1970).**

Since the mid 1970s, Carroll has concentrated on songwriting. His debut album, *Catholic Boy,* combines folk music themes, poetry, and hard rock in the tradition of such artists as Patti Smith, Lou Reed, and Jim Morrison. "People Who Died," an outstanding song on the album, exemplifies much of Carroll's work. Both celebratory and lamenting in tone, this song is a tribute to the people Carroll knew who lived hard and died at an early age. Barbara Graustark notes, "not since Lou Reed wrote 'Walk on the Wild Side' has a rock singer so vividly evoked the casual brutality of New York City as has Jim Carroll." Carroll has also recorded two other albums, *Dry Dreams* (1982) and *I Write Your Name* (1984).

(See also *Contemporary Authors,* Vols. 45-48.)

Courtesy of Jim Carroll

FRED KIRBY

Jim Carroll can handle folk and rock material with equal facility and his appearances at Folk City during his first national tour display both styles. His opening selection, **"Scratch Your Head,"** is in folk style with high voice and acoustic guitar. . . .

"I Don't Know" is a good blues with his backing of [lead guitarist David] Spinoza, bass guitarist Rickie Marada and drummer Stevie Woods very much in evidence. **"Mean Mother Mary"** is a gutsy blues. A contrast is **"Porch Song"** with Carroll supplying sole accompaniment on acoustic guitar.

The rockin' **"I Got Plenty"** is a strong finale. Carroll . . . is a firstrate talent as songwriter and performer.

Fred Kirby, "New Acts," in Variety, *November 24, 1971, p. 55.**

BILLBOARD

Obviously perceptive, Carroll emerges [in performance] as more than just a singer of pretty songs. He is a poet of creative and emotional substance; and possesses the expertise to communicate his thoughts to his audience in a manner to which they could readily relate.

[Carroll's] arrangements are good, and his back-up musicians are enthusiastic. Overall, the package is a good one that portends a future of mutual fulfillment between Carroll and his audiences.

"Jim Carroll," in Billboard, *Vol. 83, No. 48, November 27, 1971, p. 13.*

GERALD MALANGA

The great thing about the work of a genuine poet is the atmosphere which it creates in the mind of the reader. This is as difficult to define as it is impossible to miss. It has a great deal to do with technique and with style, but only in so far as they are an integral part of the feeling and thinking that go to make up a poet's work. But it is as equally difficult to fail to realize it, when a writer turns out to be a genuine poet. Jim Carroll at twenty-five is a genuine poet just as surely as Rod McKuen and Rod Taylor are not. In reading Jim Carroll's first full-length book of poems ***Living at the Movies*** it is quite evident to me that he fully understands the nature of poetry because he perceives and follows the nature of his own life, and with that recognition of his nature, he is able to write about it.

Mr. Carroll's poems are populated with people he has loved and crowded with those who love him. His poems are irrigated by friends, by his own kind and consanguinity. He is original without being unique. His technique, however, is in advance of his maturity. At times he is capable of spoiling a good poem by a precious or very sentimental line or phrase, like "and our life is that rusted bottle . . . pointing north", in ***The Distances,*** but never of trying to make one out of any emotion that is not an integral part of his own deep feeling.

The poems seem roughly to group themselves into "general" poems, usually longer, where a subject is viewed from many different angles and states of consciousness, and the "specific," where something is seen whole in a flash. . . . In them the vision is so strong that there is no craftiness and the medium of poetry gives way to an idea that can't wait for doctoring-up to be born a flawless declarative sentence. That fast kind of poetry is always the best kind of writing. I think it's spiritual without being churchy as some of the longer poems seem.

Literature is not a competition. Yet Jim Carroll will invariably be compared by some critics both with some of his contemporaries and with their predecessor Frank O'Hara. Carroll's poems are not so perfect as O'Hara's nor is his vision so intense. While there's nothing extremely deep in the experimental and phenomenological sense, his range is wider than O'Hara's; his feelings not deeper, but made general. . . . (pp. 164-65)

On the whole Jim Carroll has the sure confidence of a true artist, meaning he is confident about the right things. He is steeped in his craft. He has worked as only a man of inspiration is capable of working, and his presence has added great dignity to the generation of poets of the 'seventies to which he belongs. His beginning is a triumph. (p. 165)

Gerald Malanga, "Traveling & Living," in Poetry, *Vol. CXXV, No. 3, December, 1974, pp. 162-65.**

JAMIE JAMES

The Basketball Diaries by Jim Carroll is a literary miracle; a description of the formation of an artistic sensibility written by the artist, not in retrospect, but in the process. It is a portrait of the artist not just as a young man but as a child, written by the child, and thus free of the mature artist's complicated romantic love of himself in pain. It also works engrossingly well as a narrative, *The Catcher In The Rye* for real, for bigger stakes.

The Basketball Diaries is an anecdotal journal kept by Carroll from the age of twelve to fifteen, more or less from the first time he shot heroin until he showed up at Ted Berrigan's poetry workshop, a basketball in one hand and his poetry in the other, when he became something of an overnight sensation. Entries from the ***Diaries*** have been leaked one and two at a time to various poetry magazines over the years, surrounding the work with the atmosphere of legend. Once every couple of years there would be a new rumor that it was being published *in toto;* now, at least, here it is.

It makes a difference, seeing it all together. Reading it in drips and drabs over the years, a rather precious impression was created by Carroll's sharp ear for hip street lingo and the Mark Twainish droll exaggerations. It seemed to be the charming but trivial work of a precociously gifted young writer. The catch was that anyone who had read Jimmy Carroll's poetry (such as the extraordinary collection ***Living At The Movies***) knew it was charming but trivial like *Moby Dick* is charming but trivial. Seeing it all together bears out one's ongoing suspicion that there's more here than the swaggering bravado of a smart kid grown up all wrong.

The tone of the ***Diaries*** is an uncanny blend of almost unnerving self-possession and a gentle, fully developed sense of irony. . . .

The Basketball Diaries is a blow-by-blow account of a season in Hell. By the age of fifteen, he had experienced more in the way of existential vicissitudes and worldly observation than several ordinary middle class lives combined. Despite the adolescent egoism and occasional tendency towards smart-aleckiness, the theme that reverberates through the whole, like the recurring melody of a jazz improv, is the struggle of a boy to hold on to his sense of himself. ***The Basketball Diaries*** is concerned with the ethics, rather than the politics, of survival. . . .

Rimbaud is the name that pops up when people (Ted Berrigan and Patti Smith, for instance) talk about Jim Carroll, and ***The Basketball Diaries*** in particular. It is a useful invocation, for a change. One especially thinks of Rimbaud's remark that "The soul has to be made monstrous." If one word describes what happens in the ***Diaries,*** it is monstrous. The difference is that Rimbaud is talking about a self-conscious, systematic cultivation of the monstrous with the end of becoming a visionary, "the supreme Savant." There is nothing so calculated about Jim Carroll's excursion into the inferno; if there is an organizing principle here, it is not, refreshingly, the design of an artist preparing himself for writing poetry. He is only obliquely aware that he is a writer, which is exactly the genius of it. ***The Basketball Diaries*** functions with the kind of unimpeded sensitivity of observation that sometimes occurs when the writer is in direct, intimate touch with himself when his writing approaches artlessness.

Make no mistake: ***The Basketball Diaries*** is no great work of literature. It is not literature, in the usual sense, at all. It is a great work of storytelling, in the most elemental sense—storytelling as in Homer, the kind of storytelling that happens when two good friends on a cross-country drive find themselves on the interstate in the middle of the night, two hundred miles from nowhere. It suffers from all the faults of the genre, too: some of the stories sound made up, others are stock footage from anyone's adolescence. . . .

The Basketball Diaries is a harmonious blend of funny passages and depressing passages. When it is funny it is hilarious, reminiscent of Lenny Bruce at his best. When it hits a blue note, it is harrowing. . . .

Jamie James, in a review of "The Basketball Diaries," in The American Book Review, *Vol. 2, No. 3, February, 1980, p. 9.*

JACK McDONOUGH

The most obvious reference point for Carroll would be Lou Reed, a comparison Carroll heightened [at a recent concert] with a gutsy encore rendering of "Sweet Jane." Both are consummate New York street poets and both project a similar rawboned attitude on stage with autobiographical songs of urban tension and psychosexual drama.

Whereas Reed, however, has a highly mannered style that sometimes results in dirge-like readings, Carroll is a much more straightforward rocker.

He keeps the pace clean and steady and makes full use of the power provided by his strong and able band. . . .

The set was well-paced, building to the stunning climax provided by his best and most wildly intense song, **"All My Friends Died."**

Jack McDonough, "Jim Carroll Band," in Billboard, *Vol. 92, No. 24, June 14, 1980, p. 50.*

BARBARA GRAUSTARK

Not since Lou Reed wrote "Walk on the Wild Side" has a rock singer so vividly evoked the casual brutality of New York City as has Jim Carroll [on **"People Who Died"**]. . . . Featured on [the album **"Catholic Boy,"** this song] has propelled him from underground status in a literary circle that included Allen Ginsberg, William Burroughs and various minions of Andy Warhol to national attention as a contender for the title of rock's new poet laureate.

Carroll knows whereof he sings. He spent his boyhood hanging out on many of New York's meaner streets. The son of an Irish-Catholic bartender, he sampled speed, codeine cough syrup, LSD and cocaine while still in grade school. By 15 he was a junkie who supported his habit by snatching purses and hustling homosexuals. But he was terrific at basketball and, when he wasn't shooting up heroin, he was shooting hoops. . . . He was also serious about writing. Between 12 and 15, he chronicled his squalid coming of age for an autobiographical novel called **"The Basketball Diaries."** His terse wit, with its archly contrived naïveté, transformed a tale of teen-age rebellion into a contemporary classic. . . . Carroll [also] became a poet of some renown. . . . (pp. 80-1)

But he grew tired of the poetry scene. . . . [He now] has metamorphosed from poet to rocker, following in the footsteps of a former girlfriend, Patti Smith. Says Carroll: "Poets today are all intellect, ya know? But rock can strike at the intellect and the heart, like a wind in your veins or a fist tightening under your chest. When Henry Miller wrote about Rimbaud, he called this 'the inner register.' Even an illiterate could feel the force behind Rimbaud's work."

Filled with imagery that is spiritual, sexual and violent, Carroll's debut album, **"Catholic Boy,"** is something the debauched poet would understand. Like his best known precursors, Smith and Reed, Carroll isn't much of a singer. But his songs of a city morally gone to seed have a raw power. **"When the City Drops (Into the Night)"** describes a surreal world populated by hookers, pimps, drag queens and thieves, itching with fantasies of Sodom and Gomorrah. Another depicts a young girl with "inscrutable poise and nihilist charm [who] gets her sleep through tubes in her arms." . . .

To some, his songs will sound like glorifications of the decadent, and indeed Carroll is carrying on the beat tradition of celebrating lives lived on the edge. But, he insists, "I don't want to glorify junk. Susan Sontag once told me that a junkie has a unique chance to rise up and start life over. But I want kids to know it's not hip to indulge yourself at the bottom unless you're planning on one helluva resurrection." (p. 81)

Barbara Graustark, "Mean Streets," in Newsweek, *Vol. XCVI, No. 10, September 8, 1980, pp. 80-1.*

RICHARD RIEGEL

Jim Carroll's the latest word pusher (as in prose, poetry, you know, the pen-meets-paper thing) to cross the art-will-be-convulsive-or-not-at-all line, into the authentically electric seizures of rock music. And if you appreciated the many jagged gems of word'n'roll hidden among the furious chaos of Patti Smith's attempts to make that same leap of faith, then get set for major acupuncture on your jugular, as you listen to Carroll's debut recording [***Catholic Boy***]. . . .

[Carroll's ***The Basketball Diaries***] earned praise from beatnik godhead Jack Kerouac himself, who, as you must know, died in 1969. Since Carroll's only 29 or so now, you can see what a prodigy he was when St. Jack smiled down on the earliest ***Basketball Dairies.***

Kerouac was right about Carroll, too; ***The Basketball Diaries*** is nothing less than *the* manifestation of many an aware 60's-kid's dream of converting the consciousness-expanding riches of a full life into the creative expression that would open yet more doors to the rich life. ***The Basketball Diaries*** is a disturbingly seamless mixture of fact and fiction, written by Jim Carroll about a "Jim Carroll" character who reflects / cheats his true autobiography in probably equal measure as the tall-tale writhings of Henry Miller's favorite protagonist, "Henry Miller."

And I'm emerald with literary envy that Jim Carroll not only *really might've been* the simultaneous Manhattan child / jock hero / white spade / stud / prehippie drug-fiend / aware hustler / street aesthete he claims in his book, but also that he had the consummate *imagination* to fuse these elements into a wholly convincing narrative, either way.

So how come Jim Carroll didn't get around to the modality of rock 'n' roll until now, if he already saw and knew it all back in '65? . . .

The punch line is that Carroll didn't miss a thing by absenting himself from the rock of the 70's, even as the rest of us were denying the Eagles and celebrating the Sex Pistols. ***Catholic Boy*** confidently takes up that uniquely Eightyish urbanscape right where ***The Basketball Diaries*** left it off in the summer of 1966. The Jim Carroll Band . . . play dynamic, fluid, straight-ahead rock 'n' roll that owes next to nothing to punk and its discontents. Rock music crafted (hell no, *felt*) as a direct challenge to Bruce Springsteen's night-after-night urbancrest melodramas, yet sharing nothing of Springsteen's flair for the eternal homilies.

The influences on ***Catholic Boy*** (if you insist) are more like Lou Reed (but the campus poet Lou Reed who idolized Delmore Schwartz, Reed before he thought of forming the relatively disingenuous Velvet Underground), or maybe even Iggy when he was still an Iguana, prior to making *The Stooges* because he couldn't do otherwise. Jim Carroll phrases with the prophetic bemusement, with the dry and prurient wonder of a true believer Lou Reed. . . .

One song off ***Catholic Boy***'s plenty for weeks of psychotextual analysis, as I hear it tonight, and I've got to go with **"City Drops Into The Night,"** a stern Gotham moonscape beyond the blare of Bobby Keys' sax, but somewhere this side of those horribly-flaming oil tanks I can make out on the apocalyptic Jersey shore. Jim Carroll sees it all, even as the sproinging guitars . . . and the cocksucking sax keep smashing into his vocals to underline / contradict his lyrics: "Before the darkness / There's one moment of light / When everything seems clear / The other side / It seems so nearrr!" . . .

Pardon my critic's disbelief that rock 'n' roll this intense and true has come from what I've always smugly called "a *real* writer," but Jim Carroll's done it, over and over, for sure. And I haven't half-unravelled the intricacies of ***Catholic Boy***'s intimate Patti Smith tribute, **"Crow,"** or of its title cut, a bittersweet storehouse of emotion that Ti Jean Kerouac would be sure to love, if only he and the 60's had never ended. . . .

Richard Riegel, in a review of "Catholic Boy," in Creem, *Vol. 12, No. 9, February, 1981, p. 44.*

STEVEN SIMELS

Jim Carroll works in a fairly circumscribed and generally unfashionable idiom. The very idea of rock-and-roll as Poetry is pretty much a dead issue, and yet Carroll, like Bob Dylan, Jim Morrison, and Patti Smith before him, attempts to take the diction of serious poetry (by way of the French Symbolists and the Fifties Beats), mate it to the diction of traditional rock-and-roll, and then come up with an appropriately neon-lit musical style to go along with it. It's a Sixties concept, to be sure, and the irony is that Carroll, like Smith in 1975, is going to be taken as modernist (New Wave, if you must) simply because his stuff doesn't sound like what's on the radio these days. Nevertheless, his **"Catholic Boy"** is an extremely impressive debut album, flawed and pretentious at times, but also genuinely ambitious, gripping, and believable.

Lyrically, you've heard a lot of this before. Carroll deals with Catholic guilt, drugs, redemptive sex, life and death on the wild side, Rimbaud—in short, the whole Bohemian shopping list. The reasons he gets away with it are twofold. First, he's lived it. . . . Second, and more important, he's a gifted writer. . . . [His book] ***The Basketball Diaries*** is a scary, mordantly funny odyssey along the dark underbelly of the Sixties, a virtuoso performance that ought to be must reading for those who still tend to romanticize the counterculture. In short, Carroll is an Authentic Voice. . . .

[The] most arresting track [on **"Catholic Boy"**] is ***People Who Died,*** and it neatly sums up the conflicting, contradictory impulses that power Carroll's work. An offhand listing of various friends of his who, for whatever reasons, bought it at an early age, the song is simultaneously poignant (Carroll genuinely misses his departed comrades and is appalled by the waste involved) and oddly celebratory: its gospel-derived choruses in the traditional "rock-anthem" manner are so exhilarating that it soon becomes apparent that he *admires* their "romantic" exits, viewing his own survival as a kind of artistic failure. Nothing I know of in the history of rock-and-roll has quite prepared us for this insider's perspective on the "live fast, die young, make a good-looking corpse" brand of adolescent bravado. It's a brutally honest, rather chilling performance.

The rest of the album has its share of lapses (***Crow,*** for example, is a fairly sophomoric tribute to Ms. Smith, and ***Three Sisters*** gets a bit arch about being sexually knowing), but there's no use pretending that Carroll isn't a genuine talent, or that he and his magnificent band haven't made, in **"Catholic Boy,"** some of the most impressive rock of this young decade.

Steven Simels, "Jim Carroll," in Stereo Review Magazine, *Vol. 46, No. 2, February, 1981, p. 40.*

RICHARD GOLD

"There's no one left that I want to imitate," declaims poet-turned-rocker Jim Carroll in one of his urgently driven rock narratives. And, while Carroll's darkly enigmatic lyricism and idiosyncratic presence recall off-beat artists like Jim Morrison, Lou Reed and Patti Smith, his work is a vital reminder that rock and roll at its best can be a refuge for untrammeled individualism.

On his debut LP, **"Catholic Boy,"** and his more recent release, **"Dry Dreams,"** Carroll deals with themes of sin, redemption, drugs, sex and the concrete jungle with free-associating lyrics that are compelling and captivating, if occasionally obtuse. Having chosen electric rock and roll for its theatrical possibilities and populist appeal, the gangly Carroll delivers his cathartic songs with a refreshingly unpolished stage manner whose very vulnerability suggests courage and commitment. Carroll is not much of a singer, as his abysmal rendering of the ballad "Jody" demonstrated, but his biting, fierce rock-rap style was engrossingly powerful on numbers like **"People Who Died"** and **"Work Not Play."**

Richard Gold, "Jim Carroll," in Variety, *June 9, 1982, p. 56.*

MICHAEL GOLDBERG

On his first album, ***Catholic Boy,*** Jim Carroll came off like Lou Reed fronting the Stones—all raunchy guitars and monotone vocals. With ***Dry Dreams,*** he has moved slightly away from those influences, creating a distinctly urban brand of rock & roll that's equal parts New York intellectual and savvy street hipster. Carroll has developed considerably as a vocalist in the year and a half since ***Catholic Boy***. . . .

Carroll is most successful on slower, brooding pieces like **"Rooms"** and "Jody," but he often has trouble when the band tries to rock out—a problem that is particularly obvious on **"Barricades."** Still, the best song here is **"Lorraine,"** which is about kicking junk to form a rock band. "She got straight / She understands / She wanted to die but now she's got plans," he sings. "She want to live / She want to start her band / She swears the stage is God's left hand." For many of us, rock & roll has that kind of power; Jim Carroll does a good job of articulating it.

Michael Goldberg, in a review of "Dry Dreams," in Rolling Stone, *Issue 373, July 8, 1982, p. 50.*

MICHAEL TEARSON

The first album by The Jim Carroll Band got lots of press and attention mostly due to the throat-grabbing intensity of **"People Who Died."** That album's pure drive is matched on ***Dry Dreams,*** although Carroll's songs are not as strong as the previous crop with the obvious exception of **"Jealous Twin,"** the clear standout.

The band has the snap and crackle Carroll's songs need, but however sturdy a group they are, when the lead voice is as limited as Jim Carroll's, the poetry had better be brilliant. This time around, except for the occasional flash and the aforementioned **"Jealous Twin,"** nothing is that remarkable.

Michael Tearson, in a review of "Dry Dreams," in Audio, *Vol. 66, No. 8, August, 1982, p. 23.*

CHRISTOPHER CONNELLY

"Freddy's Store" is Jim Carroll's best song since his necrorock standard, **"People Who Died."** A sassy conga-colored workout about an arms merchant's voluminous warehouse—"it's not exactly hell / It's more like Bechtel / They got only one item to sell"—the song showcases this street-smart poet-turned-dilettante-rocker's talent as a gritty lyricist with a taste for full-throttle rock & roll. Still, his overall abilities remain a mite too slim to carry an album's worth of material. ***I Write Your Name*** has its moments, but overall it's too much of not enough. (p. 74)

It's been four years since Jim Carroll burst on the scene in a hail of hype . . . , and ***I Write Your Name*** shows that he has yet to fulfill his promise. (p. 76)

Christopher Connelly, in a review of "I Write Your Name," in Rolling Stone, *Issue 418, March 29, 1984, pp. 74, 76.*

BRUCE POLLOCK

Everywhere, including the rock world, literacy is dwindling. And conventional wisdom only hampers matters. Where is it written, for instance, that to be a songwriter you have to be a musician in a band? To me, a pungent lyric carries as much or more impact than the average guitar solo. Why, then, is the American listening public the victim of the weightless musings of so many nimble-fingered but addle-brained musicians who dare to think their musical abilities (such as they are) entitle them to dabble in the foreign land of Words?

Will there someday be a place where the literate among us (the few who still prefer rock to country music or TV) can seek solace in a musical form aided and abetted by words worth savoring? I doubt it, but if so, [The Jim Carroll Band's ***I Write Your Name***] would command [its] share of airtime in a world free, for the moment, from Michael Jackson, Duran Duran, and Boy George. (p. 746)

Like Leonard Cohen, Jim Carroll is a poet and a novelist/rocker whose singing plainly is a last resort. Over the course of his three-album career, Carroll has drifted—or been pushed—toward the traditional singer/song writer middle ground, that of a performer/bandleader. For a poet this thought might be ludicrous, had not Lou Reed, Patti Smith, and probably some others accomplished it with much aplomb, though not without some initial embarrassment, one suspects.

For Carroll, on ***I Write Your Name,*** the results are less embarrassing than frustrating. The musical voice in which his rock-like poemsongs are presented is far less interesting (while still a long way from being commercially viable) than his material demands. Though possibly necessary for the adequate performance of these works in concert, the typical rock scores provided for Carroll's lyrics lack the subtlety and power of his best material. He collaborates with seven musicians on the album, suggesting that Carroll, too, was dissatisfied in his search for a complementary musical voice. Ironically, the one song for which he wrote both words and music is no standout either. . . .

On the other hand, the title song is the strongest thing Carroll has written since **"People Who Died,"** the grizzly epic with which he began his career on a profound and disturbing note. **"I Write Your Name"** deserves to be considered as a kind of rock and roll *Howl* of the eighties. Meanwhile, **"Dance the Night Away"** is one of the most haunting songs I've heard this year. (p. 747)

Bruce Pollock, in a review of "I Write Your Name," in Wilson Library Bulletin, *Vol. 58, No. 10, June, 1984, pp. 746-47.*

(Charles) Bruce Catton

1899-1978

American historian and editor.

Catton's lively accounts of historical events helped popularize American history for the nonhistorian and won the respect of many experts in the field. His substantial canon includes many books on the Civil War, the subject with which he is most closely associated. These works are acclaimed for their combination of historical accuracy and lively narrative style. Catton's philosophy of writing history was that it should come alive for readers, involving them in those past events which contributed to shaping the present. Catton regarded history more as a branch of literature than of the social sciences; he believed that professional historians should not limit themselves to writing for other academics but should offer their insights to readers outside the field as well. In order to expand understanding and appreciation of history for the public, Catton often presented his facts from the perspectives of common people rather than well-known figures.

Catton began his career as a journalist. With the outbreak of World War II, he became information director for the War Production Board. His experiences in this position inspired his first book, *The War Lords of Washington* (1948). Catton's first important work, *Mr. Lincoln's Army* (1951), formed with *Glory Road* (1952) and *A Stillness at Appomattox* (1953) a trilogy about the Army of the Potomac, a unit which Catton felt had been overlooked by historians. *A Stillness at Appomattox* was considered responsible for helping renew popular interest in the Civil War and was also Catton's first work to attract a large readership. It won both the Pulitzer Prize for history and a National Book Award. *The Coming Fury* (1961), *Terrible Swift Sword* (1963), and *Never Call Retreat* (1965) formed a second trilogy, *The Centennial History of the Civil War*. These works take into account not only military encounters but the political, social, and economic impact of the war on the lives of people on both sides, particularly the soldiers. *Grant Moves South* (1960), a book about Ulysses S. Grant's Western campaigns, shows some change in Catton's approach. Although he continues to focus on human drama, he begins to include more discussion on the techniques of war. This book and a subsequent volume on Grant, *Grant Takes Command* (1969), complete a three-volume biography begun by Lloyd Lewis, who died after completing the first book, *Captain Sam Grant*.

Catton's sources and methods were untraditional. He preferred to recreate the times rather than analyze them and to present incidents as part of a comprehensive pattern. Instead of relying on accepted texts and manuscripts, Catton used obscure regimental diaries, personal papers, and memoirs to recount the war in the words of those who fought it. Some critics questioned the objectivity of Catton's presentation of his personal heroes, Abraham Lincoln and Ulysses S. Grant. Catton was also accused of misunderstanding and misinterpreting some events and of making sweeping, unsubstantiated generalizations. Nevertheless, his work is generally well regarded by critics. Catton's writing style is consistently praised as unpretentious, even poetic, and is distinguished by his ability to make history an emotional as well as an intellectual experience.

The Bettmann Archive, Inc.

(See also *Contemporary Authors*, Vols. 5-8, rev. ed., Vols. 81-84 [obituary]; *Contemporary Authors New Revision Series*, Vol. 7; *Something about the Author*, Vols. 2, 24; and *Dictionary of Literary Biography*, Vol. 17.)

THOMAS L. STOKES

Much of the confusion and conflict in our domestic scene today has its genesis, as we now recognize, in decisions made in Washington during [World War II] and shortly thereafter. . . . The story of how all this happened is told brilliantly and with warm human interest and intimate personal detail [in **"The War Lords of Washington"**] by Bruce Catton, who saw it all close up and from the inside as assistant director, then director, of information for the War Production Board. . . .

Gradually there unfolds the internal clash that ultimately overshadowed all else, the battle in our multifold war agencies over civilian or military control of the economy. The verdict was not clear and precise, as the lines of battle were not always definite, but eventually the decision was weighted in favor of the "war lords." . . . (p. 3)

The decisions by Washington war agencies in which Mr. Catton reads the origins are thoroughly and carefully documented by the author, who is a veteran and experienced newspaper man.

His book is full of the controversy with which we were familiar in Washington. It will revive that controversy—which is all to the good.

It is *ex parte* in a sense, though done sympathetically throughout with due consideration for human error, and with no absolute heroes or villains. It tells the story from the side of Donald Nelson and those who stood with him, many of them New Dealers, in the fight for civilian as against military control. The chief sin of those days, as the author views it, was the failure to recognize that we were in the midst of a world revolution, whereas the emphasis was on a purely military victory with too little concern for the bigger issues that such a revolution breeds. (pp. 3, 50)

How the pattern was formed, bit by bit, day after day, makes a story as engrossing as a novel because of the human factors involved. . . . And there is grim humor in some of the strange things that some big business executives did in the crisis, such as the red, white and blue trains that Floyd Odlum sent out over the country to show small business what they might build for war, instead of really organizing small business for the part it never got to play. . . .

Americans, [Mr. Catton says], . . . came out of the war "with an inferiority complex and a deep sense of fear" because of the determination that things should remain the same in a world revolution, when they can't remain the same. (p. 50)

Thomas L. Stokes, "Confusion and Conflict," in The New York Times Book Review, *October 17, 1948, pp. 3, 50.*

WILLIAM HARLAN HALE

As the New Deal brought professors into government, so the war brought newspaper men into it—chiefly with the passion of "selling" to Americans their own nation's effort against the Axis. . . .

Bruce Catton, . . . the information director of the War Production Board, is one of those who reacted violently. He saw a good deal, peering as Donald Nelson's confidant into many crannies of high-level war-time back-biting and intrigue, and he has thrown the sum of his anger into [**"The War Lords of Washington"**], a book that is in part personal reminiscence, in part a general history of the war agencies, in part an ideological tract and in part a sardonic dusting-off of palace gossip after the style of "Washington Merry-Go-Round."

So loose a combination is not likely to make for a good book, and much of Catton's is as garish and unfocused as its title. For, just who are the American "war lords" whom he promises to lay out? A jacket blurb proclaims his book to be "The Inside Story of Big Business Versus the People in World War II." It isn't, though. It is less than that—yet it ends up by being considerably more than that. It sets out to describe the reluctance of many reigning industrialists to awaken to the war emergency and their desire to maintain business as usual; but before long Catton shifts his fire from the N.A.M. front and levels it pointblank at the Administration—even to the extent of straddling the White House itself with pot shots—charging that here, too, there was failure to go all out in furthering a people's war.

In spite of the smoke which obscures its own aim, Catton's blast is designed to set up a strong disturbance in the assessment of our recent past. His theme is broad and not to be easily dismissed. It is that the dominant powers of America, confronted by a challenge to this country's order that was social as well as military, chose to fight the Axis for limited or military objectives only. In short, they mistook a revolution for just another war. . . .

This thesis gives point to Catton's many specific charges, some backed by first-hand evidence and others by little more than generalization. He is on strong ground when he recounts the generally admitted failure of the O.P.M. and its dollar-a-year men to mobilize an all-out defense effort during the first eighteen months of crisis. He appears to have a good case when he argues that aggressive men like Nelson, William Batt, Leon Henderson and Robert Nathan had a far clearer initial vision of our war-time production needs and capabilities than had the somewhat bemused brass of pre-Pentagon days. . . .

Catton's book would have been better had it been soberer. But it makes for provocative reading, nevertheless.

William Harlan Hale, "About Our Recent Past," in New York Herald Tribune Weekly Book Review, *October 24, 1948, p. 12.*

HENRY STEELE COMMAGER

The history of the Union Army is not as studded with controversies as that of the Confederate, but the one major controversy that emerges from it is, of course, the controversy over Gen. McClellan. Was he—as he himself thought—the organizer of victory, the saviour of the Union, the man of destiny? Or was he—as his critics thought—a marplot and almost a traitor, prepared to subvert the American principle of the supremacy of the civil over the military, and—withal—a master of defeat? Or was he something less dramatic—simply a competent organizer who was never a very good fighter?

In a sense it is to this ever-fascinating problem that Mr. Catton addresses himself [in **"Mr. Lincoln's Army"**]. Yet it would be misleading to suggest that this lively and dramatic book is merely a rehash of the hackneyed McClelland controversy. What Mr. Catton thinks of McClellan emerges clearly enough before he is through with him, but it emerges as a by-product of the story of the Army of the Potomac.

Let us make clear at once what this book is—and what it is not. It is not a history of "Mr. Lincoln's Army"—whatever that phrase may mean—for the Army of the Tennessee or the Army of the Cumberland was as much Lincoln's Army as the Army of the Potomac. It is a history of that Army roughly from Ball's Bluff through Antietam, of its organization, its character and its leadership.

Mr. Catton feels, quite rightly, that the Army of the Potomac has not had a fair deal at the hands of historians, novelists and poets. . . . What Mr. Catton here gives us is a wonderfully vivid re-creation of the spirit and character of this much-abused Army—the boys and men who made it up, the officers, the weapons, the food, the way it marched and the way it fought. It is a very personal and intimate study: it gets behind the formalities of battle and campaign to the homely and often tragic realities of fighting.

The scene opens on a note almost sinister: the inability of McClellan to support Pope when that hapless general was reeling under the blows of Longstreet and Jackson at Second Bull Run. Was there mismanagement here, or treason perhaps? Mr. Catton does not analyze the causes of McClellan's failure, but he does evoke the atmosphere of the time—an atmosphere heavy with suspicion, jealousy, frustration, plot and counterplot.

The spotlight shifts quickly to the divisions, regiments and even companies engaged in the battle; the method here is that of the kaleidoscope with the miscellaneous pieces all falling together, at the last, to create a colorful pattern. We are presented, that is, not with a blueprint of the battle but with its endless confusions and blunderings, with bravery and cowardice, with disorder and death, and the whole leads up to that retreat which so nearly became a rout. (pp. 1, 8)

Mr. Catton . . . reviews for us—it is a roundabout way to get his effects—the history of McClellan's rise to fame and of the Peninsular campaign. It is clear that he is both fascinated and repelled by McClellan. He sees McClellan's weaknesses: vanity amounting almost to egomania, procrastination, vacillation, a persecution complex, arrogance, and a mind too complex to be bold. He sees his strength, too—his ability as organizer and administrator, and above all, his devotion to his army and his men. That devotion was reciprocated, for reasons hard now to understand.

Like a skillful dramatist Mr. Catton lets the tragedy develop out of its own situation, foreshadowed by innumerable hints. The army was being trained—but for what? Apparently not for fighting, for McClellan was busier fighting the Administration than he was fighting the enemy. Already he was revealing that procrastination—Lincoln called it the "slows"—that was in the end to prove fatal to himself and almost to the Union. . . .

Mr. Catton turns, then, to the third act of his drama—the restoration of McClellan to command after the debacle of Second Bull Run and the Antietam campaign. While the scenery is being shifted Mr. Catton takes time out for a more circumstantial description of the Army of the Potomac, and it is gratifying that he does so, for these are some of the best pages in the book. We are introduced to one regiment after another. . . . As these regiments swing by us . . . we are told something of the way they lived in camp, what they ate, the songs they sang, the jokes they cracked, what they thought of their officers—and of the war. . . .

Finally we come to the Antietam campaign itself—the campaign of lost opportunities. As every one knows, Lee's famous order 191 fell into McClellan's hands—and with it the opportunity to destroy Lee's army piecemeal and end the war. . . .

The final chapter contains what is probably the best Northern account of Antietam in our historical literature. Not, to be sure, in our literature: the best accounts were penned by participants such as that Col. Strother whom Mr. Catton unaccountably neglects, or Col. Livermore, or Gen. Hyde. But Mr. Catton has done a superb job of weaving all these accounts together; no other narrative of the battle gives us such a feeling of the fury and the horror of this bloodiest day of the war. . . .

Mr. Catton's book is so good it may seem carping to call attention to some minor defects. The organization is confusing, and it is to be hoped that in future volumes Mr. Catton will prefer chronology to drama. Even though Mr. Catton's interests are in narrative rather than analysis, it would be well to exploit, far more than he has done, the immense body of monographic literature—and especially the Official Records, mentioned but not used as far as the evidence goes. The system of annotation—if it can be called that—is faulty; references are casual and arbitrary, and it is exasperating not to be given pages for quotations. Finally it is never quite clear whether Mr. Catton is writing about McClellan or about the Army of the Potomac. That army was never as dependent upon McClellan as Mr. Catton implies; it managed pretty well without him after Antietam. If Mr. Catton is primarily interested in McClellan he should give us perhaps a bit more detail on that talent for organization and administration upon which the man's reputation so largely rests. If he is primarily interested in Mr. Lincoln's Army he might give us more of the description which he does so well—shelter, medical services, religious activities, the Sanitary Commission, the technique of marching, and a score of other aspects of army life.

But these are minor blemishes in a book that is, by any standards, one of the most exciting war narratives in our literature. (p. 8)

Henry Steele Commager, "And Still We Go On Learning about Abraham Lincoln," in New York Herald Tribune Book Review, *February 11, 1951, pp. 1, 8.*

OSCAR HANDLIN

The outbreak of the Civil War found those who were to fight it totally unprepared for the kind of war it would be. It took years and the expenditure of enormous resources in money and men before the government in Washington discovered the means for bringing the conflict to a successful conclusion. . . .

If it was a long task to assemble the proper army, it took longer still to find the appropriate commander. . . . For until Grant appeared on the scene, none really understood that the function of the new fighting was total destruction and that gallantry had no place in it. The result was a long period of bungling that involved the useless waste of lives and resources and that left behind the bitterness that poisoned the peace.

It is the great virtue of Catton's [**"Mr. Lincoln's Army"**] that he understands this essential quality of Civil War history. In form his volume is a history of the Army of the Potomac under General George McClellan. In substance it is an enlightening interpretation of the whole course of the conflict.

The book opens with an account of the Second Battle of Bull Run, in which Pope demonstrated his unfitness for command. The story then moves backward in time for a retrospective survey of the organization of the army and of McClellan's relationship to it. Coming back to the aftermath of Bull Run, Catton then carries his narrative on to the climactic battle of Antietam, a battle that McClellan appeared to have won and yet that finally cost him his command.

At first impression, this organization may seem needlessly intricate. But by abjuring the straight chronological treatment Catton has endowed his work with a sense of great authenticity. Too often the military historian, laboring under the compulsion to clarify the events as they occurred, endows the actors in those events with a false consciousness of purpose and with a delusive prescience. This fault Mr. Catton escapes. In a superbly told story he makes clear what did happen and why but without leaving the erroneous impression that the generals knew what would happen or why. On the contrary he makes dramatically plain . . . that the commanders often had not the vaguest idea of the meaning of the unfolding incidents about them.

While Catton has managed to get in the excitement and the thrill of the actual fighting, he has not neglected to fill in the realistic details of the periods between. Nor is he unaware of the political implications of the military events. A clear account of the effects on the military decisions of the background of suspicion and distrust that poisoned the atmosphere of Washington brings the whole picture into focus. Lucidly written and competently put together, this is a splendid example of popular interpretative history and deserves a wide audience.

Oscar Handlin, "Problems of 1861," in The Nation, *Vol. 172, No. 11, March 17, 1951, p. 255.*

DAVID DONALD

Glory, concluded a Pennsylvania private, "consisted in getting shot and having your name spelled wrong in the newspapers." There was reason for his cynicism in that winter "of unrelieved gloom," 1862-63. . . .

With this bleak picture Bruce Catton begins [**"Glory Road"**], the second volume of his history of the Army of the Potomac. In the previous volume entitled **"Mr. Lincoln's Army,"** Mr. Catton described the unhappy career of the Federal forces "under glamorous McClellan" and "braggart Pope." **"Glory Road"** recounts the short and unhappy commands of Burnside, Hooker, and Meade, highlighting the fierce encounters at Fredericksburg, Chancellorsville, and Gettysburg.

Mr. Catton's project is an ambitious one, and since his subject has attracted some of the most distinguished historians of our times, comparisons are inevitable. Unlike Carl Sandburg or J. G. Randall, Mr. Catton is not primarily interested in biography or wartime politics. Unlike Douglas Southall Freeman, he is not making an analysis of personality or of command. Unlike Kenneth Williams, he does not concentrate on high-level strategy and the relative merits of Union generalship.

Of course Mr. Catton has to discuss such matters in part, and on the whole he handles them admirably. Though his Lincoln remains a rather shadowy figure, Mr. Catton has decided opinions on politics and feels strongly about "the coarse, savagely cruel, everlastingly vital . . . Secretary of War Edwin M. Stanton." Mr. Catton knows the Army's high brass, too, and, like the expert newspaper man he is, describes them in all their rococo magnificence. . . .

But none of these is his major concern. "The great anonymous private soldier" is his hero. . . . **"Glory Road"** is the saga of the ordinary Union soldier, a tale of heroism but without heroics. Drawing from little-used and long-forgotten regimental histories, Mr. Catton reconstructs an admirably realistic picture of life in the Army. . . .

If some of the anecdotes are not without exaggeration, if regimental histories recall events as somewhat larger than life, that is the way they should have occurred. For in that year of defeat and lost victory between Fredericksburg and Gettysburg the common soldier was beginning to realize that . . . "the man who would finally get the army through its trials was a profane, weary man with no stars on his shoulders and scant hope of any in his crown, the everlasting high private. . ." Here, then, is Mr. Catton's theme and here is his achievement, for **"Glory Road"** is the dramatic and absorbing biography of an army.

David Donald, "The Trail of Defeat That Ended at Gettysburg," in The New York Times Book Review, *March 16, 1952, p. 7.*

HENRY STEELE COMMAGER

[Some of the songs that were popular with the Army of the Potomac] express what is, in a sense, the theme of [**"Glory Road"**]: that the Army of the Potomac survived and in the end triumphed not so much over Lee and his lieutenants as over their own generals.

"Glory Road" is the story of how the privates retrieved failure and turned it into success.

This second installment of the saga of the Army of the Potomac is better even than its predecessor, **"Mr. Lincoln's Army,"** and that is high praise. . . . Once again regimental histories furnish the raw material, but they are richly supplemented by the Official Records and other sources; once again there is close attention to the hours, the days, the weeks, not given over to fighting, and the material here is fresh and alive; once again Mr. Catton lays about him unsparingly, but there is more depth, more understanding, less cocksureness and cleverness. What we have here is less than a year in the life of the Army of the Potomac—but what a year. It began with Fredericksburg, then on to Chancellorsville, then came to a climax with Gettysburg. Mr. Catton's book is really the story of these three battles as fought by, and seen by, the common soldier in the Union ranks. In between there are sections on discipline, desertion, punishment, medical care and sanitation, and a dozen other aspects of army life. The whole, for all its unpretentiousness, adds up to a study of the American military character—a subject too little understood. . . .

Mr. Catton's description of Chancellorsville is a wonderful piece of writing. Again it is the tactical history, not the strategical, that concerns him: the private's view, and perhaps the captain's, but not the general's. . . .

A hundred historians have broken their pens on Gettysburg; a half dozen accounts seem worthy of that heroic battle, Catton's among them. With what skill does he reconstruct the picture: the peaceful countryside, the Confederates coming in from the west looking for shoes, Buford holding them off and shouting to Reynolds, "There's the devil to pay." . . . Catton's is no Olympian view, encompassing the whole of the great complex battlefield; he sees the battle rather as the soldiers themselves must have seen it and felt it, a piecemeal affair, an endless series of desperately fought out encounters, everywhere the crash as of Arctic ice on ice. . . .

It is the peculiar quality of this book that it re-creates for us the sights and sounds, the feelings and passions of the battlefield, that it deals with simple things in an unpretentious fashion, that it rejects all mock heroics, but that again and again we hear the trumpets sound through its pages. It is a splendid achievement, historical and literary.

Henry Steele Commager, "The Army of the Potomac Licked Its Wounds and Went on Fighting," in New York Herald Tribune Book Review, *April 13, 1952, p. 3.*

DAVID DONALD

"A Stillness at Appomattox" is the story of the final grim twelve months of the war in the East, "the year of the Wilderness and the Bloody Angle, of Cold Harbor and the Crater; the year that killed John Sedgwick and saw Abraham Lincoln under fire; the terrible year when war became total; the year of U. S. Grant." (p. 450)

Grant is the central figure in Mr. Catton's story, and like many a previous student of the Civil War he finds the General a curiously ambiguous character. Grant's grim determination he admires, and he is convinced that his strategic objective was the only correct one. . . . At the same time, though, **"A Stillness at Appomattox"** offers a damning indictment of Grant's tactics, for at Spotsylvania, Cold Harbor, and the Crater it was all too clear that the commander shared his subordinates' belief that the "way to beat the enemy was to pile into him head on, and if a great many men were killed that way it could not be helped because to get killed was the soldier's hard fate and it would never be any other way."

Neither the politician nor the general is Mr. Catton's hero. Where neither politics nor strategy could bring success, he concludes, "the only value that seemed to amount to anything any more was the simple courage of the enlisted man." **"A Stillness at Appomattox"** is a powerful tribute to the American volunteer soldier. . . . (p. 451)

This same theme has been dominant in Mr. Catton's two previous books, **"Mr. Lincoln's Army"** and **"Glory Road,"** which traced the Army of the Potomac from its 1861 beginnings through the terrible climax of Gettysburg. **"A Stillness at Appomattox"** completes the trilogy and makes it clear that Mr. Catton has produced what is unquestionably the best-written military history of the Civil War. The events here described have of course been related by other historians, but never before with such literary skill and such profound sympathy. Mr. Catton's books are in a class by themselves. He has deliberately avoided writing a history and critique of Union strategy, . . . for he feels that neat battle maps and orderly official reports do not reveal the war which the soldiers were actually fighting. . . . Though Mr. Catton's books abound in skilful word portraits as graphic as the photographs of Matthew B. Brady, he has not attempted to write a study of commanders. . . . [And] he has not made a detailed analysis of the political aspects of the war, and some of his incidental pronouncements on Northern war-time politics will not bear close scrutiny.

What Mr. Catton has done is to write the life history of an army. From bulky regimental histories, from soldier diaries, from war-time letters, from official records, he has reconstructed the conflict as soldiers experienced it. Any serious student of the Civil War must read many books, some for their factual content, some for their character portrayals, a few for their new ideas. Mr. Catton's history of the Army of the Potomac deserves reading on all these counts. But these superb volumes are not merely accurate and provocative history; the combination of literary brilliance and deep human compassion makes them a memorable and moving saga of Americans at war. (pp. 451-52)

David Donald, "Life History of an Army," in The Nation, *Vol. 177, No. 22, November 28, 1953, pp. 450-52.*

HENRY STEELE COMMAGER

[At] last the Army of the Potomac has found a historian worthy of it. With **"A Stillness at Appomattox"** Mr. Bruce Catton brings to conclusion his history of this neglected and maligned army, and now that we have all three volumes we can see that this is one of the great achievements in historical literature of our time.

What an army it was, after all—. . . . Under the blows of war it was being hardened into one of the greatest fighting forces of modern history.

All that it needed was leadership, and this at last it was to get in the indomitable Grant. Mr. Catton's volume is a monument to that leadership, not to Grant alone but to his lieutenants. . . .

This third volume tells the story of the last year of the war in Virginia and mostly—though not altogether—of the men in blue. It is the story, really, of five great battles: the Wilderness, Cold Harbor, Petersburg, The Crater, Five Forks and the end at Appomattox. . . .

It is not all fighting, or heroism, that Mr. Catton describes for us. There are those brilliant little vignettes that he does so well of the interior life of the army. . . . But much of this he has given us before, and mostly what he tells here is the fighting.

This final volume of Mr. Catton's trilogy is in many respects the best of the series. It is broader in scope than its predecessors, more concerned with larger questions of strategy; it is less tied to the regimental histories; it gives more attention to that very important ingredient in the history of the Army of the Potomac—Lee and his veterans. It has all the narrative vigor of its predecessors, and it has, too, a reflective quality, the music of sympathy and of pity. For Mr. Catton has grasped what all of us know instinctively and what so few of us can say, that this war was not only a stupendous military drama but a profound spiritual experience, one which touched with fire not that generation alone but succeeding generations, so that a hundred years later we cannot read the story without tears. It is a tribute to Mr. Catton's skill, to his integrity, that he has been able to tell this story honestly and faithfully, without dramatics and without insincerity, and that it turns into the very stuff of poetry and of legend.

Henry Steele Commager, "The Army of the Potomac Marches to Its Last and Greatest Triumph," in New York Herald Tribune Book Review, *November 29, 1953, p. 3.*

BELL I. WILEY

[**"A Stillness at Appomattox"**] like its predecessors, **"Glory Road"** and **"Mr. Lincoln's Army"** is aimed at the general reader. Except for the fact that the author makes only token use of manuscripts, monographs and historical periodicals, he meets fully the standards recognized by scholars. His approach is judicious, his interpretation unbiased and his coverage comprehensive. He has no axe to grind and he resorts to no trickery or cheap sensationalism—not even in the carefully underplayed finale at Appomattox itself just before the actual surrender. . . .

"A Stillness at Appomattox" is a magnificent piece of writing. Some of its passages have the grandeur and beauty of poetry. Through the magic of the author's pen the reader marches to the very scene of battle, senses the anxiety of responsible commanders, feels the gnawing nervousness of the rank and file, welcomes the relief that comes with actual commitment. He smells the smoke of burning powder, listens to the roar of the guns, shares in the tremendous confusion that follows the assault, experiences the exhaustion that comes with prolonged conflict, and witnesses the unspeakable suffering of the wounded.

The account is outstanding for scope and balance. Noncombatant activities receive full attention. Skillful and rapid shifts of focus produce a panorama that is vivid and absorbing. The story never drags. The author never loses control. The reader never has to fumble for location or direction. The epic account of **"Mr. Lincoln's Army"** which this volume completes is a landmark in Civil War literature and an outstanding contribution to military history.

Bell I. Wiley, "A New Chief, a New Spirit," in The New York Times Book Review, *November 29, 1953, p. 3.*

AVERY CRAVEN

Ulysses S. Grant, according to Bruce Catton [in **"U. S. Grant and the American Military Tradition"**], has gone down "in history as an odd combination of things that he was not." As a soldier his great campaigns were built "on speed and deception and military brilliance," yet he has been written off as "a dull plodder who could win only when he had every advantage and need count no cost." . . .

Mr. Catton does not make clear why his hero has been so badly misrepresented. He does, however, explain with unusual skill his reasons for thinking that Grant was such a superb military success and such an excusable failure as President. . . .

Mr. Catton's efforts to soften Grant's fall from the pinnacle of military success to the depths of political failure are praiseworthy but not successful. He succeeds only in making him into a rather pathetic figure, strikingly like that one which came slumping back to Galena a few years earlier. His thesis is that the very qualities which made Grant a great general caused his ruin as President. Yet it is quite clear that if Grant possessed all the virtues and abilities ascribed to him as a person only a few pages back, some of them should have been apparent in civil life as well as in the army. It is quite clear that the study of this phase of Grant's life has not gone far enough when an era of flagrant corruption, of heartless reconstruction and aimless drift can be spoken of as only "disappointing."

Avery Craven, "What Made the Extraordinary Ups and Downs of Grant's Career," in New York Herald Tribune Book Review, *May 30, 1954, p. 7.*

ANTHONY WEST

Mr. Bruce Catton's **"This Hallowed Ground"** . . . is the latest product of the flourishing industry devoted to turning out books on the Civil War. . . . It is painfully clear that we are in for an avalanche of multi-volumed boxed sets of biographies of generals (photographs by Brady), histories of campaigns, and mystical examinations of the meaning of it all. In view of the literary prospect that so implacably looms up ahead, Mr. Catton's book acquires a melancholy interest as an indicator of the tone that is likely to prevail as the centenary closes in upon us.

An early hint that all is not going to be quite as it should be in the present volume is provided by the manner in which Mr. Catton squares up to the business of discussing the fact that Beauregard's Confederate gunners started the war by firing a mortar shell into Fort Sumter at four-thirty on the morning of Friday, April 12, 1861:

> The substance and the shadow went in opposite directions, and it was hard to say which was real and which was no more than a shred of mist blowing from the land of haunted impossible dreams; and there was, meanwhile, a great pentagon of masonry built on a reef at the entrance to the harbor of Charleston, South Carolina, where the orderly sequence of events was about to be crossruffed by exploding violence.

How the appalling landslide into war so brilliantly described in Allan Nevins' definitive "Ordeal of the Union" can be described as an orderly sequence of events it would be hard to say. It is difficult, too, to understand what Mr. Catton means by suggesting that Beauregard's cannonade introduced a new element of violence into the situation. For Mr. Catton has already all too colorfully dwelt upon the beating of Senator Sumner after a speech against slavery, the murderous attack on Lawrence, Kansas, by pro-slavery guerrillas, and John Brown's retaliatory raid on a neighboring settlement, and he has been moved by those events to thoughts almost too deep for tears. . . .

Mr. Catton's prose arouses the suspicion that he does not care much for precision in thought or language. (p. 84)

[Another] suspicion about Mr. Catton's approach to history suggests itself; it is possible that he likes to fatten the bare record of events with drama and intensity. . . . It is not enough for him to tell the story of Grant's build-up for the campaign and of his able conduct of it, packed with political and military lessons though the story is. More has to be added. The command problems Grant had to solve during the winter were how to retain the confidence of Lincoln and his superiors in Washington, and how to keep his army in hand as a fighting force during the long wait for the rains to end and the Mississippi River bottoms to dry out. His other chief problem concerned the natural impatience of the politicians and political soldiers who wanted rapid action for purely political reasons. He surmounted these difficulties—the means he employed, so ably set forth in Kenneth P. Williams' "Lincoln Finds a General," establish his clearest claim to being a military genius—and it is this fact, almost as much as his final complete success in achieving his strategic aims, that gives the campaign its meaning. Grant was the first American, and one of the first soldiers, to solve the command problems created by the structure of a modern state. If his solutions had gone unnoticed at the time, the campaign would have been merely an incident in the war, but Lincoln understood them, and they can be said to have completed Sherman's military education. The American military tradition was founded, and the war, which up till then had been fought with political objectives in mind, such as the security of Columbus, Ohio, or the capture of Richmond by one side or of Washington by the other, became a professionally conducted modern conflict aimed at the systematic reduction of the strategic assets of the South and the remorseless destruction of one nation by another. Mr. Catton seems to be upset because this element of power politics has been injected into American life by the uncontrollable necessities of war, and he tries, one might say desperately, to find other, more reassuring, meanings in the events. . . . (pp. 85-6)

And there appears to be no virtue, either, in Mr. Catton's thesis that the formation of Negro regiments . . . brought about a profound change for the better in the national attitude toward racial discrimination. Even if one believes that the war did not exacerbate racism in the South, it is certainly a fact that it did nothing to prevent the enactment of the Chinese Exclusion Act of 1882. This racist measure was followed by a number of others directed against what seemed to be considered the lesser breeds without the law. An American racist literature was flourishing in the nineteen-hundreds, and its beliefs about the superiority of the Anglo-Saxons, which were enshrined in the Immigration Act of 1917, still rule the present quota system. . . . One can only conclude that to give the experience of the Civil War mystical value, Mr. Catton is attributing to it a broadening of the basis of democracy that, in fact, dates from Andrew Jackson's election in 1828, and a change in feeling about race that is still incomplete and that had its origin in something as recent as America's confrontation with racism in action during the triumph of Fascism between the two World Wars.

Since he has enriched the prelude to the campaign with so much moral gain, it is natural that Mr. Catton should go on to heighten the significance of the campaign itself. This time the war is the agent of economic instead of social progress. . . .

Between the fog of war and poetic prose one detects some questionable history. (p. 87)

One begins to see at Vicksburg what Mr. Catton is up to in investing each successive chapter in the grim history of the war with drama and significance; he is divesting it of its futility. And one begins to appreciate something that, if it is to his credit as a man, is not to his advantage as a historian. His attitude is humane; he cannot bear waste and loss, and it is his purpose to give meaning and dignity to everything in the war. (p. 90)

What happened when Beauregard fired on Fort Sumter was a breakdown of the democratic process. Blood was substituted for argument in settling the issue of whether the nation should exist half slave and half free, and a minority decided to fight the will of the majority. That those who fought for that minority dragged down their home states to ruin for two generations was one result, and that they wasted the lives of enormous numbers of men was another. Many of the men who died had given clear evidence before they went off to battle that they had great contributions to make to the rapidly growing society to which they belonged. Others, the average members of the numberless flock, died undistinguished, deprived simply of the normal chances for happiness. To pretend that the Union was served or enriched by all the slaughter, the waste of treasure and effort, and the lost laughter seems almost perverse.

It is too much to expect that this will be the last Civil War book to present that horrible and wholly sterile disaster as a creative national experience. Its true essence was engraved on the tragic mask that Lincoln's face became in his last years. One could have hoped that even popular historians would outgrow the sentimentality that caused them to wish to shield their readers from sharing the knowledge that shaped that image of sorrow and to offer in its place a consoling legend. Persistent folly made the war inevitable, and cruelty fought it through to the bitter end. It did nothing but hurt to the Union, and the scars exist to this day. What men learn by making war is how to make war. That is what America learned in the Civil War, and that is all. Sooner or later, an American generation will grow up that will be prepared to live with this historical truth. But that generation will have to be raised on a kind of book about the Civil War quite unlike **"This Hallowed Ground."** (p. 92)

Anthony West, "The Hateful Legacy," in The New Yorker, *Vol. XXXII, No. 47, January 12, 1957, pp. 84-6, 89-90, 92.*

D. W. BROGAN

For the American, the Civil War is still *the* war. It has provided the background for what are the two most famous American films, *The Birth of a Nation* and *Gone with the Wind.* It provoked the best American elegiac poetry, Whitman's, and at least one admirable epigram, Timrod's 'Magnolia Cemetery,' and it was illustrated by the two greatest of American orations, the Gettysburg address and the Second Inaugural. 'Civil War buffs' are numbered by the hundred thousand; as a business, writing about the war rivals religion. . . .

Knowing all this, knowing, too, that Mr. Catton is one of the most indefatigable tellers of the oft-told tale, one is tempted to approach [***This Hallowed Ground: The Story of The Union Side in the Civil War***] with some [boredom or irritation]. . . . If such preconceptions put off readers, they impose a very serious loss, for Mr. Catton seems to me to have done a very remarkable thing. He has produced a moving, living, exciting book that is yet worthy of serious attention. This *is* vulgarisation, but high vulgarisation. The reader who thinks he knows too much about the Civil War to waste time reading this, shows, in my opinion, that he doesn't know enough. Of its kind, this is a masterly job.

It is as well to get out of the way certain biases provoked by Mr. Catton's literary methods, methods that have provoked a very *de haut en bas* review from the *New Yorker*. It is a long time since James Russell Lowell damned Augustin Thierry for introducing the picturesque style into history. Mr. Catton is a faithful disciple of Thierry; he has never heard of or disregards Verlaine's counsel to take eloquence and wring its neck. This book is held up, from time to time, by almost comic outbursts of spread-eagle oratory, what used to be called in Ireland 'sunburstery.' But we should remember that the Attic simplicity of Lincoln was not much to the taste of his times. Mr. Catton writes as the orators of the age wrote and his clotted metaphors and inky-white *chiaroscuro* would have been much to the taste of admirers of Edward Everett, George Bancroft and Henry Ward Beecher. He writes as Charles Sumner spouted.

But Mr. Catton has more than a style, he has a point of view. This is the story from the Union side. . . . The right side won. As Augustine Birrell put it, for once 'the great twin brethren, Right and Might,' were on the same side. . . .

This candid partisanship does not seriously distort Mr. Catton's narrative. . . . Mr. Catton is mainly a military historian, but he is a political historian, too. Or rather he is the historian of the politics of the army. He tells us, again and again, how the mere duration of the war changed its temper and objects, how the Northern soldiers got tired of fighting a war and dodging its basic issue, slavery.

D. W. Brogan, "The Birth of a Nation," in The Spectator, *Vol. 198, No. 6726, May 24, 1957, p. 681.*

DAVID M. POTTER

[In **"Grant Moves South"** Bruce Catton] carries Grant's career from the summer of '61 to the summer of '63—two crowning years during which Grant trained the 21st Illinois Volunteers, served for a brief time in Missouri, captured Fort Henry and Fort Donelson, fought the costly battle of Shiloh, suffered eclipse after Shiloh, and emerged again to plan and execute the bold and difficult operations that ended in the capture of Vicksburg with its entire army of 30,000 defenders.

For Civil War enthusiasts the big news of this volume will not be that Grant moves South, but that Catton moves West. As the foremost living historian of the military aspects of that war,

Catton has already written an epic trilogy on the Army of the Potomac, thus falling in with the tradition which regards the Virginia front as the classic theatre. In **"This Hallowed Ground"** he ranged more widely, and in a shorter study of **"U. S. Grant and the American Military Tradition"** Catton turned to his present theme. But **"Grant Moves South"** is his first major treatment of the Western campaigns. As he enters this new field his style of presentation alters somewhat, and the reader finds, to a degree, a new Catton. Heretofore, his forte has been the evocative re-creation of the human experience of the war—how it seemed and what it meant to the men who fought it. He has concentrated more on making the experience live than on analyzing the decisions of the high command. One measure of Catton's achievement in the present volume is that he still re-creates the human impact of the war most vividly, but he now also puts strategy and tactics into sharper focus than ever before. . . .

This dual awareness, both of war as a crucible of human qualities, and of strategy and tactics as a military art, stands Catton in good stead in dealing with a figure who showed rare attributes both as a man and as a general. Grant possessed a simplicity, a humanity, and a courage astonishingly parallel to the same characteristics in Lincoln. Catton's treatment shows these traits well. . . . (p. 15)

Thus the man and the soldier interact, and the experience of the man becomes the shaping of the strategist. In going with Catton from Fort Henry to Vicksburg, the reader follows a guide who uses less detail than Kenneth Williams employed in covering the same ground. Catton's analysis of strategy is not quite so probing as Williams's nor are his verdicts quite so tart. But the truly crucial developments are made to stand out in bolder relief by Mr. Catton, the vital factors are more clearly emphasized, and it is, therefore, somewhat easier to see the overview. Also, where Williams tended, perhaps, to derive the man from the soldier, Catton derives the soldier from the man. . . .

Catton is superb in recreating Grant at the top of his working and fighting form. The reader who looks ahead may wonder what Mr. Catton will do with 1864, when he has to go again over ground that he has already traversed so brilliantly in **"A Stillness at Appomattox,"** or with 1868, when he will be outside the military orbit altogether. But for 1862 and 1863 he proves himself an ideal interpreter of the period of Grant's rise to greatness. In the realm of Civil War literature, there is, notoriously, always a plethora of new titles, but **"Grant Moves South"** goes at once to the head of the line. (pp. 15-16)

David M. Potter, "The Man a Nation Couldn't Spare," in Saturday Review, *Vol. XLIII, No. 6, February 6, 1960, pp. 15-16.*

T. HARRY WILLIAMS

The most striking quality of [**"Grant Moves South"**] is its completeness. This is no mere battle record but a detailed description of all the factors that went into Grant's generalship. Generals do not spend all their time with purely military problems, Catton points out. . . .

Among Grant's problems that Catton deals with are contraband trade, refugee slaves, mails, passes and supplies, and these sections of the book add much to our understanding of Grant and of the whole war. In his devotion to detail, the author even tells us how many yards behind the battle line Grant's headquarters were at Fort Donelson. But it should not be supposed that Catton subordinates the battles. On the contrary, they are presented with high narrative skill. The account of the tangled Vicksburg campaign is a model piece of battle reporting.

Readers of Mr. Catton's previous books will not be disappointed with this one. (p. 1)

Catton best displays his analytical ability in tracing the evolution of Grant to a great general. Most of the first Northern generals believed in "positional warfare." . . . That is, many thought that places rather than armies were the vital objectives. . . . It had the effect of causing a delay after every victory to consolidate the conquest of land.

The story of Grant's development, Catton writes, "is the story of his attempt to break out of this crippling tradition and apply the country's strength in a remorseless, continuing pressure." From the beginning Grant advocated aggressive action to destroy the enemy. (pp. 1, 29)

Always, Mr. Catton emphasizes, Grant learned and grew. He captured Fort Henry easily and thought he could do the same with Fort Donelson. There he learned that an enemy who has yielded in one place may fight in another. At Shiloh he underestimated the initiative of the enemy and found that devotion to the offense must not cause neglect of the defense.

In 1863, at the height of the Vicksburg campaign, he had reached his full powers. He was at last "the Grant who knows precisely what he is about. . . ."

This book is exactly what a military biography should be, a really distinguished work. It has all the color and drama of Mr. Catton's previous books, and more solidity and depth. Like Grant, Mr. Catton keeps getting better. (p. 29)

T. Harry Williams, "The General Marched to Greatness," in The New York Times Book Review, *February 7, 1960, pp. 1, 29.*

DAVID DONALD

Inevitably, in this Civil War centennial year, most of the events Mr. Catton describes [in **"The Coming Fury"**] are familiar to every literate American, but never before has the blundering road to war been traced so surely and so vividly. Though no book can materially change our factual knowledge of the period, the author's vigorous prose and his colorful details give a new dimension to the troubled story of the nominating conventions of 1860, of the ensuing election in which Lincoln was chosen by a minority of the voters, of the secession of the Lower South, of the futile efforts at compromise, of the inept management of James Buchanan's caretaker regime and of the equally unskilled beginnings of the Lincoln Administration, of the firing on Fort Sumter, of the rally to the rival flags, and of the first disastrous major encounter of arms at Manassas.

All these matters—and many others as well—Mr. Catton handles with the accuracy, the impartiality and the literary distinction that readers of his earlier Civil War writings have come to expect in his books. Believing history to be essentially the portrayal of human beings in action, he presents a fascinating portrait gallery of nineteenth-century American leaders in all their strengths and weaknesses. . . .

Few living historians have Mr. Catton's eye for the telling detail. More effective than pages of editorializing about the confusion at the outset of the war is his anecdote of how a group of Federal marines politely requested their commandant to refrain from burning their barracks when he evacuated the naval base at Norfolk in 1861, because "the sergeant of the guard had a hen setting on twelve eggs in the guardroom and he hoped that the brooding fowl might not be disturbed." . . .

A narrative historian in the tradition of Francis Parkman and William Hickling Prescott, the author is more concerned with recapturing the mood of an era than with dissecting its motives. This is not to say that he avoids interpretations, for scattered through his book are dozens of clear, pointed and challenging judgments. Believing that in the antebellum South "the institution of slavery had become comparatively benign," he holds that by 1860 slavery "was beginning to live on borrowed time" and that "it would inevitably come down to manageable proportions if men would only let it do so." He understands, however, that the real difficulty was not slavery but the fact that "slavery was a race problem." Consequently he argues that, by the outbreak of the war, "the issue of slavery had become, as men's emotions then stood, both intolerable and insoluble." (p. 1)

In this volume the author's admiration for Abraham Lincoln is decidedly tempered. The President-elect's silence during the months before his inauguration reflected "the caution perhaps of a lawyer rather than of a statesman"; moreover, Lincoln "fumbled badly" in his ill-advised, unimpressive speeches on his way East. Tending to agree with Seward that Lincoln during his early months in office had "no system, no relative ideas, no conception of his situation," Mr. Catton is certain that the new President "grossly overestimated the amount of Unionist sentiment" in the South.

Once hostilities began, however, Mr. Catton holds that the future course of the war was almost inevitable. Faced with "fundamentally insoluble" economic problems, the Confederate leaders were "a group which knew a little about the modern world but which did not know nearly enough and could never understand that it did not know enough." On the other hand, Lincoln, after seeming "to sway uncertainly with varying breezes," had come to "one of the fateful decisions of the Civil War. He would fight secession with any weapon he could lay his hands on, no matter what the weapon might be." Henceforth "the Yankees had a government that knew exactly what it wanted and would stop at nothing to get it."

It might be said that there is nothing new in any of these interpretations, for they generally echo the best recent scholarship in the field. . . . Furthermore, it must be noted that Mr. Catton does not really argue for these interpretations, as a professional historian would, carefully marshaling his evidence for and against and arriving at a reasoned conclusion. Instead, he offers his interpretations as insights—or perhaps as obiter dicta. It is not want of research which dictates his attitude on this important matter, for the present volume is based upon substantial and accurate investigation of the sources, both printed and unpublished. Nor is it a limitation of space, for he has ample room to develop rather unimportant episodes . . . when he thinks the topic interesting.

The author's handling of the problem of conflicting evidence and interpretation appears instead to stem from his conception of history as a dramatic and personal chronicle, an evocation rather than an analysis, a branch of literature rather than of social science. With this view of the historian's role there can be sharp disagreement, but there can be no doubt that Mr. Catton is a practitioner of romantic narrative history at its finest. **"The Coming Fury"** is the best book he has ever written.

With all the vigor and sympathy of his three-volume work on the Army of the Potomac, Mr. Catton's new book is far broader in scope and more perceptive in interpretation. It has all the awareness of the mystery of the human dilemma and of the complexity of human motives exhibited in **"This Hallowed Ground,"** without the passages of brooding rhetoric that too often clouded the pages of that work. The same restraint and elegance Mr. Catton demonstrated in his text for the **"American Heritage Picture History of the Civil War"** are here; but the present volume is, of course, far more detailed and colorful. In short, **"The Coming Fury"** is a major work by a major writer, a superb recreation of the twelve crucial months that opened the Civil War. (pp. 1, 54)

David Donald, "Stumbling Along the Road to War," in The New York Times Book Review, *October 22, 1961, pp. 1, 54.*

DAVID M. POTTER

No virtuoso of Civil War history now operating has proved able to evoke the stirring sound of bugles with a more certain and a more compelling touch than that seasoned campaigner Bruce Catton. When Catton launches the first volume of a multivolume "Centennial History of the Civil War," it is what the military historians might call a decisive literary engagement. . . .

The real question about [**"The Coming Fury"**], then, is not whether it can bring our past to life but, rather, how does Catton do it, or, as some critics surfeited with the Civil War might ask, how does he get away with it? Here is a writer who has already traversed the Civil War three times—once in one volume (**"This Hallowed Ground"**), once in three (the trilogy ending with **"A Stillness at Appomattox,"** which dealt, to be sure, only with the Army of the Potomac), and once as expert literary accompanist for a book of pictures (**"The American Heritage Picture History of the Civil War"**). Now he is going into round four with every prospect of scoring his most resounding triumph. Will the law of diminishing returns ever catch up with this man, and what is the key to his success?

Whether the law will ever overtake him, whether the nap will ever get completely worn away from the Civil War carpet by the marching feet of all these authors—it is not for this reviewer to say. All we can be sure of is that the war has already stood up under more reiteration than almost any theme in history. But we can ask just what it is about Catton's history that has given it such immense appeal.

Some critics have felt that it was his choice of theme—that battle scenes are naturally, and obviously, pulse-stirring, vivid, dramatic. But there are only two battle scenes (Sumter and First Manassas), occupying thirty pages out of more than 500 in **"The Coming Fury,"** and Catton has demonstrated that his talent is not limited to military history. At times it has seemed, particularly in **"This Hallowed Ground,"** that his style was impressionistic—calculated to evoke a mood rather than clearly to narrate the steps in a sequence of events. But again, **"The Coming Fury"** is loaded with factual information. . . . Moreover, Catton gives considerable attention to the forces at work as well as to events. Although avoiding the terminology of historical theory and analysis, he handles effectively certain analytical topics such as the role of slavery, the progressive narrowing of the range of possible decision, and the separation of the locus of decision from the locus of responsibility. He is less sure-footed with some of these themes than with straightforward events, but most of the interpretation is first-rate, and his account is by no means all narrative.

If he does not achieve his effects by holding his focus on scenes of combat, nor by moving always at a narrative gallop, how does he make his exposition so compelling? He does it, in large part, of course, by plain literary skill and vigor of imagination. His characterizations, for instance, are curt and pungent. (p. 20)

But the quality that Catton seems to possess to an almost unique degree is his capacity to convey the quality of human experience. It is trite to say that he enables the reader to feel again the emotional impact of occurrences in the past, but it is perhaps worth noting some of the devices by which he achieves this result. For one thing, instead of telling what men did in our terms he often tells what they did in their own terms: instead of saying Beauregard wrote a demand for the surrender of Sumter, he says, "Beauregard set about the composition of the formal demand"; instead of saying McClellan was appointed major-general, he says McClellan "found himself, in the middle of May, major-general of volunteers." For another, he shows events not in isolation, but often with a flash to the future or to the past that illuminates them in perspective. (pp. 20-1)

To convey the meaning of experience, the writer may project it directly at the reader, by vivid description. But this technique involves a use of the imagination that is usually unhistorical, and sometimes the reader cannot feel an experience if he has had no equivalent in his own life history. Very often, therefore, we can apprehend the meaning of an experience best, not by receiving a description of the phenomenon, but by receiving a description of its impact upon the persons involved. Catton has sensed this, and he constantly looks at events, not directly but in terms of what they meant to individuals whose feelings we can share. . . .

Catton's history is not primarily a history of facts, although it is better furnished with facts than many factual histories. If it were first of all a factual record, the repetitive quality would be intolerable, for facts do not bear repeating and we would all complain that Allan Nevins has already written on a grand scale all the facts necessary about the year the war began, and that two full-dress histories are one too many. But Catton has seized upon a basic feature of the Civil War, namely that, for some reason, the human factor in history reveals or seems to reveal itself in this conflict far more readily than in most historical situations. . . .

Somehow, the Civil War has been a kind of showcase where we find human experience in a form that we can grasp. Because this is so, the Civil War can turn a poet toward history, as it did Stephen Benét, or turn a historian toward poetry as it has Bruce Catton in some of his finest passages. So long as this is so, it will be vain to propose a moratorium on histories of the Civil War—as vain as to propose that we stop playing Hamlet because the quotations are already familiar, or that no one should tell again the story of the Odyssey because it has been told often enough before. (p. 21)

David M. Potter, "The Sound of Bugles: Prelude to Fratricide," in Saturday Review, *Vol. XLIV, No. 46, November 18, 1961, pp. 20-1.*

T. HARRY WILLIAMS

It was going to be a war that would get out of control, Bruce Catton tells us over and over in [**"Terrible Swift Sword"**], the second volume of his monumental history of the Civil War, which began with **"The Coming Fury."** . . . That it would be such a war was apparent as early as the summer of 1861, says Mr. Catton, which is where the present volume picks up, right after First Bull Run. . . .

The great force in the situation that was twisting men and the whole country into new shapes was not just the fact of war itself, says Mr. Catton. It was, rather, a vague but terribly compelling urge for fundamental change. . . . Mr. Catton writes about this urge again and again and always in moving if sometimes cloudy prose. What he is saying of course, is that, once the conflict settled into the long haul, it had to become an anti-slavery war, if for no other reason than that the Northern people were not going to fight very long to preserve the property of those they were fighting. Mr. Catton recognizes this last factor clearly enough, but he also would like to pull out of the war and its result something deeper, some impulse to freedom in the round that is inherent in the American ethic or spirit.

Nobody can doubt that the impulse was there. But Mr. Catton is no more successful than others who have tried to pinpoint this facet of the war, and sometimes in his pursuit of the idea he seems to contradict himself. Thus he records on the first page his belief that the war was likely to grow to the point where it involved "at last the dignity, equality, and rights of human beings as well as of states," which at least implies that in the South the state was everything. But later we are told that the Confederacy was based upon a concept "wherein the individual was everything and the government was next to nothing," which implies something entirely different. And still later we learn that all Americans would lose one kind of freedom as a result of the war, the freedom of personal independence, but that this could be compensated for if in the process the notion of the importance of "the unattached individual" could "somehow" be consecrated. These ambiguities are doubtless clear in Mr. Catton's mind, and five minutes conversation with him would probably dissolve all of them. The point is that when the historian attempts to set down these complexities of the war on paper he is likely to run into all sorts of semantic difficulties.

These quandaries disappear when the author swings into his main job of describing what happened in the war and why things happened the way they did. Essentially his story deals with the last half of 1861 and all of 1862 except its last month, that month that would witness the battles of Fredericksburg and Stone's River and the beginning of U. S. Grant's drive at Vicksburg. As in his first volume, the author presents a fairly full picture of events. There are good sections on such subjects as diplomacy, trade between the lines, and Washington and Richmond politics. But as before and as always, Mr. Catton is primarily interested in battles, on land and on sea, and all the familiar engagements are here. . . .

They are good battle pieces, too, comparable to the best in Civil War literature, just long enough to tell the story meaningfully but not loaded down with antiquarian or needless detail. And they are related with the high literary skill we have come to expect from Mr. Catton. (p. 7)

It is a mark of Mr. Catton's art that he can capture the whole spirit of the war or a facet of it in one revealing episode. He demonstrates this quality fully in these pages. Thus he tells us of the Missouri farm woman who found a group of Confederate soldiers eating apples from her trees after Wilson's Creek. She told them to help themselves, and then as an afterthought asked the identity of the plunderers: "Are you Lincoln's folk, or Jeff Davis's folk?" All the tragedy of the tortured border, the saddest victim of this civil clash, was in her question.

Some critics have said that Mr. Catton's forte, which has enabled him to render his greatest contribution to the literature of the war, is his ability to afford insight into the meaning of events, to hand down, as it were, inspired guesses. This is not quite fair, as it implies that he does not conduct his research or handle his evidence as a conventional historian would. In recent years Mr. Catton's work has become increasingly "professional," and this book meets professional standards. The author and his research director, Mr. E. B. Long, have turned up many rich new sources . . . and the result enlarges our knowledge and understanding of several aspects of the war. (pp. 7, 29)

It remains true that Mr. Catton's great strength is in his insights, and this is a good quality. He peers around at everything and comes up with some awfully sharp guesses that the academic historian might hesitate to offer. The examples are all through the book and too numerous to cite. Perhaps the best case is the treatment of McClellan and the Army of the Potomac. The sketch of McClellan is devastating—and to this reviewer accurate and unanswerable. McClellan's talent for unreality is documented in damning detail. . . .

The Army of the Potomac took on a mass character that made it distinctive, Mr. Catton suggests. It was around Washington too much and absorbed too much politics into its organization. Like McClellan, it saw the government as an enemy, and, like him, it wanted to define the purposes of the war, to decide what the victory it was supposed to win would mean.

The author throws out many evaluations, pro and con. Robert E. Lee fans are going to be delighted and possibly surprised at his opinion of the great Confederate. These are the kind of judgments that make for good history, and there can be no doubt that Mr. Catton is writing good and very possibly great history. (p. 29)

T. Harry Williams, "A War Out of Control," in The New York Times Book Review, *May 26, 1963, pp. 7, 29.*

EDWARD WEEKS

It is the gift of Bruce Catton, our foremost living historian of the Civil War, that he can make clear to us today realities which were by no means so clearly comprehended at the time, either by the politicians in Washington or Richmond or by the generals at the front. ***Terrible Swift Sword,*** . . . the second volume of ***The Centennial History of the Civil War,*** begins on the Monday after Bull Run and ends with the Emancipation Proclamation, announced after the victory of Antietam in the early autumn of 1862. Mr. Catton is a fine assimilator and a shrewd scrutinizer, a fair judge of men and motives, and a swift idiomatic narrator. He does not use hindsight to make fools of the dead, but when a general like McClellan alters his testimony later in self-defense, Mr. Catton is swift to note. This book is alive with character and with the shared experience of humble men.

One of the first points Mr. Catton makes is the earnest effort with which Lincoln strove to keep this "a limited war." (p. 116)

Mr. Catton, who gives full credit to the brilliant leadership of Jackson and Lee and to the fighting qualities of their ragged, resourceful armies, is equally telling in his analysis of why the Confederate war effort failed. . . .

Some of the liveliest writing is to be found in the portraiture, especially at those turning points when the hard decisions had to be made. . . .

In the long summer of 1862 as he waited patiently for a Union victory, the President, says Mr. Catton, carried on a brooding soliloquy: the Emancipation had been written but not released, and now with a forethought that was characteristic he kept reviewing this fundamental idea. What practical effect would a proclamation have? What about the slaves themselves? "Suppose they could be induced by a proclamation of freedom from me to throw themselves upon us, *what should we do with them?*" That question we are still trying to answer a century later. (p. 118)

Edward Weeks, in a review of "The Centennial History of the Civil War," in The Atlantic Monthly, *Vol. 212, No. 3, September, 1963, pp. 116, 118.*

T. HARRY WILLIAMS

It could not be done, that march that W. T. Sherman proposed to make across Georgia. It "could not be tried, or even thought of rationally," Bruce Catton writes in [**"Never Call Retreat"**], the third and concluding volume of the **"Centennial History of the Civil War."** . . . It seemed insane but it was not, Catton contends. It would work because the Confederacy in the autumn of 1864 was in a state of collapse and powerless. . . .

The trumpets that would never sound retreat were, presumably—Mr. Catton is not quite explicit as to them—the historical imperatives of the war, the determination of the Northern people to preserve the ideal and the reality of nationalism, the moral fervor of the antislavery impulse and the translation of these concepts into military power by leaders such as Lincoln and Grant. Throughout his pages Mr. Catton has a great deal to say about the importance of the moral in this war, and, by implication, in any war.

He has a good deal to say, too, about the stupidity and pointlessness of some of the fighting, underlining that in some engagements men were becoming the slaves of their weapons or tactics; were, for example, firing big guns, not because they hoped to accomplish anything with them, but just because they had the guns and thought they ought to use them. This is a little surprising, coming from a man who is known as a military historian and who has sometimes been accused of exaggerating the violent in war and of glorifying the martial spirit.

The new emphasis very possibly marks a progression in the author's thinking. After years of describing warlike deeds, he may have concluded that they are after all not the things that determine the significance or decide the outcome of a war, that behind the deeds and the flash of the guns there are qualities of the human spirit that are more important.

Or, it may be that Mr. Catton has become impressed with the knowledge that the Civil War settled one great problem, slavery, but spawned another that still awaits complete solution in our own time: the position of the Negro in American society.

Certainly, although in this volume he puts the spotlight on military events, he devotes more attention to politics and the emerging race question than in his earlier writings. . . .

Sometimes Mr. Catton seems to labor to find evidence that the war was a revolution. He quotes an impromptu address in which Lincoln said the Southern rebellion aimed at overthrowing the principle that all men were created equal. When Lincoln talked about equality, as he did frequently, he was talking about opportunity. But Mr. Catton sees much more in the passage. "The war was growing, with a hard logic of its own," he writes. "First it had been a fight to restore the Union, then it became a fight to destroy slavery, and now apparently it was a fight to establish the equality of all men. This was a definition not of war but of a general overturn; a social reconstruction for the North as well as for the South."

Something of this thread of the social significance of the war appeared in the two earlier volumes of this work, **"The Coming Fury"** (1961) and **"Terrible Swift Sword"** (1963). Those volumes took up the story in 1860, with a backward look at some causal events, and carried it to the last months of 1862, but he takes only one volume for the last half. There is possibly a disproportion here. This is a crowded volume, crammed with episodes great and small. . . .

The descriptions of battles are brief in comparison with the accounts in the earlier volumes, and sometimes an important and complicated incident gets very summary treatment. Thus the mental process by which Grant arrived at his decision to attack Vicksburg as he did is not even hinted at. We are told merely that he decided to move. . . .

Short the battle pieces may be, but they always have clarity and vividness, qualities we have come to associate with Mr. Catton's writing. The Catton style appears in the very first pages, which picture Jefferson Davis on his visit to Tennessee and Mississippi in December, 1862, to assess the state of Confederate arms. Mr. Catton proceeds to make his own assessment, and quickly he creates the mood of doom that was hanging over the Confederacy. The South just did not have the human and material resources to go around. (p. 1)

From his review of the situation of the Confederacy, the author swings into a recital of the battles of Fredericksburg . . . and Stone's River. His accounts of the Western campaigns are nearly always better done than those of the Eastern engagements. Perhaps he has become a bit weary of retelling the battles of the Army of the Potomac. Yet descriptions of two Eastern meetings are among the best things in the book. The record of the Federal attack on Charleston and the Confederate defense is excellent, a model summary. The analysis of the blunders of Ben Butler and his subordinates in their advance on the Richmond line in 1864, is as perceptive, and as pitiless a piece of writing as we have in Civil War literature.

Good too are the flashing insights into the meaning of events and into the nature of men, the brilliant quick looks that we have come to expect from Mr. Catton. . . .

At the end Mr. Catton recurs to the theme that the war had moved the nation into a vast future, toward uncharted shores. . . . It is an eloquent ending to one of the great historical accomplishments of our time. Surely this Centennial History (a project begun in conjunction with The New York Times), which compresses the best finding of other scholars, which reveals some findings of its own . . . , and which is both history and literature will have an enduring place in our national records. (p. 33)

T. Harry Williams, "Battle Cry of Freedom," in The New York Times Book Review, *August 29, 1965, pp. 1, 33.*

DAVID DONALD

Among the hundreds of histories and biographies and diaries and memoirs published during the centennial of the Civil War, the books of Bruce Catton occupy a unique place. During these past five years there have, of course, been other excellent books on the war . . . but most of these were begun years ago and their publication at this particular time was fortuitous. But of the writings undertaken expressly to commemorate the war 100 years ago, Mr. Catton's ***Centennial History of the Civil War*** alone ranks as great history written in the grand style. His series got off to a brilliant start in 1961, with the publication of ***The Coming Fury. Terrible Swift Sword,*** published two years later, was an even better book. Now comes the final volume, ***Never Call Retreat,*** which shows some understandable signs of battle fatigue but is nevertheless a distinguished and moving narrative of the last years of the war.

For literary excellence this third volume, like its predecessors, is outstanding. With each succeeding book Mr. Catton's prose has become a more precise and subtle instrument of expression. He has a remarkable gift for writing perfectly constructed sentences which, without seeming to strain, are almost epigrams. He summarizes volumes when he remarks, concerning Lincoln's habit of giving military directives to his generals: ". . . it would seem odd to find this untaught civilian lecturing professional soldiers on elementary points of tactics except for the fact that many of the professionals obviously needed lecturing by somebody." Commenting on the command given John B. Hood to go out and fight, Mr. Catton sums up a whole campaign in one sentence: "This he did, and presently the South lost 20,000 good soldiers, Atlanta, the presidential election, and most of what remained of the war."

More than any other living historian with the exception of Samuel Eliot Morison, Mr. Catton is master of the art of making a point with the specific detail, the precise illustration. Rather than tell us that General Joseph E. Johnston's Confederates fled in haste from Jackson, Mississippi, as Grant's troops approached, he writes: ". . . that night when Grant checked in at a hotel he was given the room Johnston had just vacated." . . .

Gone now are the swirling clouds of words, conveying a mood rather than any precise information, which sometimes marred Mr. Catton's early books. To be sure, the ***Centennial History*** still contains some set battlepieces, but these have a specific stylistic function. (p. 1)

In tone as in style ***Never Call Retreat*** lives up to the high standards set by the previous volumes of ***The Centennial History.*** One of Mr. Catton's greatest gifts as a historian is his charitableness of spirit, his willingness to recognize that humans are fallible, that the varieties of behavior are infinite, and that in any action rational and irrational motives are inextricably intertangled. Throughout his ***Centennial History*** there are few sharp or hostile judgments. . . . Mostly Mr. Catton is willing to meet his characters on their own terms. He is able at the same time to understand the problems of Jefferson Davis, when "the crisis called on him to take a gambler's chance and he did not feel that he ought to gamble,'' and those of his archrival Alexander H. Stephens, whose ''hard fate'' it was ''to see problems so clearly that he became immobilized.'' An admirer of Grant, he has the proper respect for Lee. The fact that Lincoln is his hero does not cause him to blackguard the Radical Republicans.

Mr. Catton and his ''Director of Research,'' E. B. Long, have searched through libraries of printed materials as well as through hundreds of manuscript collections, some of which have rarely if ever been used before. Wherever possible Mr. Catton has dug to the original sources, and he cites them liberally. Most of his quotations, however, are designed to serve as illustrations rather than to prove any new point, for in basic interpretations he closely follows previous Civil War scholars. Except on purely military points he has not been generous in recognizing this debt. . . .

Doubtless a good many . . . omissions can best be explained as the result of war weariness, for ***Never Call Retreat*** is in a number of other ways not so satisfactory as the two previous volumes in the ***Centennial History.*** In large part the problem is that this final volume is obliged to cover too much ground. While ***The Coming Fury*** brought the story only through the first battle of Bull Run and ***Terrible Swift Sword*** covered only a little more than one year after that, ***Never Call Retreat*** is obliged to sweep through the events of more than two years, from December, 1862 through April, 1865. Merely to list the major campaigns and battles would suggest with what breathless speed Mr. Catton has had to pace his narrative. Moreover, time moves faster toward the end of this volume than at the beginning; not until the next to the last chapter does Mr. Catton even get to 1864. Inevitably much has had to be omitted, and ***Never Call Retreat*** lacks the comprehensiveness of its predecessors. Here there is virtually nothing about economic or technological developments in the North or the South, or about social life, whether in the armies or behind the lines, or about intellectual currents. Attention to wartime politics is perfunctory, and diplomacy is slighted. Not even the problems of military administration receive much attention. Instead, much more than either of its predecessors, this is a history of campaigns and battles.

It is, moreover, a history which lacks a unifying theme. ***Terrible Swift Sword,*** by far the best of Mr. Catton's many books, had an artistic and logical coherence because it developed the thesis that ''the government at Richmond in the first . . . years of war was simply the government at Washington transposed to a different key,'' and Mr. Catton skillfully showed how Jefferson Davis and Abraham Lincoln ''met similar problems with similar expedients, faced the same sort of men in Cabinet, in Congress, and in uniform, and if they had different thoughts they at least thought in the same way and related the items thought about to the same basic values.'' But in this concluding volume, as Mr. Catton remarks, ''the war itself had changed.'' Now ''Mr. Lincoln was compelled to look in one direction and Mr. Davis was compelled to look in another direction entirely.'' Trying to follow both leaders, Mr. Catton's book develops a strabismus rather like that of General Butler, and his stories of rival Union and Confederate war efforts seem interleaved rather than unified.

Despite these weaknesses, ***Never Call Retreat*** is a superbly told story which achieves the literary excellence and the breadth of compassion more often associated with good fiction than with history. As one lays down this last volume of ***The Centennial History,*** one has the feeling not so much of having finished a book as of having re-enacted the past. (p. 10)

David Donald, ''Glory, Glory, Hallelujah,'' in Book Week—The Sunday Herald Tribune, *September 5, 1965, pp. 1, 10.*

MICHAEL SCHAFFER

For all its potential weakness, . . . the [Bicentennial State histories] series can succeed, as Bruce Catton proves admirably in . . . [***Michigan***]. Catton is a master of popular history, and he knows exactly how to handle the medium. He realizes that the best approach to the general reader is through a story rather than a semiencyclopedic collection of facts. Catton does not neglect historical data; he weaves them into the fabric of a skilful narrative. He has chosen a manageable theme—man's developing ability to exhaust the seemingly inexhaustible abundance of nature—and traces it through 350 years of Michigan history. Catton wisely ignores the invitation to indulge his personal feelings about Michigan. He is content to work his affection for the land and the people into his narrative. This modesty, along with the universality of the theme and a readable, exciting style, dissolves the problem of relevance to the reading public outside Michigan. With shrewdness and humor, Catton converts one strand of Michigan history into a paradigm of the American experience and thereby points out the potential value of the series. His conclusion, that we *Americans* must abandon prodigal individualism and learn the fine art of what he calls ''associating together,'' is as relevant an application of Revolutionary principles as one can hope to find.

Michael Schaffer, ''State History Series Bows with One Hit, Two Misses,'' in The National Observer, *July 3, 1976, p. 17.**

STANLEY D. SOLVICK

It would have been a pleasure to report that ***Michigan: A Bicentennial History*** makes a significant contribution to the literature of state history; instead, it is largely a disappointing book. The intent of The States and the Nation series, of which this is a volume, does not call for original scholarship. According to the series' editor, ''Bibliographies and footnotes are minimal. We have asked each author for a summing up . . . of what seems significant about his or her state's history.'' . . . The author, however, could have made a little more use of scholarly apparatus. It would have been most helpful if Catton had more often shared his sources with his reader. Even if one did not expect a comprehensive bibliography, his list is disappointing. Neither the bibliography nor the text suggests that the author has used [certain recent works]. . . . (p. 1005)

Errors range from small mistakes to those of an embarrassingly serious nature. For example, the author ignores . . . the prevailing view that Adrien, not Louis, Jolliet canoed from the Soo to Lake Erie. Contrary to Catton's assertion . . . that Congress decided Michigan would receive the Upper Peninsula in return for relinquishing claim to the Toledo strip, Michigan already included the eastern portion of that peninsula. Catton accepts . . . an account of a particular meeting in 1760 between Major Robert Rogers and Pontiac, although Howard Peckham effectively refuted that tradition in 1947. The author describes . . . Henry Hamilton as continuing as the British commandant at Detroit after the Revolution, even though he never returned to Michigan after his capture in 1779. According to Catton,

Hamilton encouraged in the 1780s the infamous Indian raids, which actually occurred in the 1770s.

Although Catton discusses the origins of the automobile industry, alludes briefly to Hazen Pingree, and has a few comments about the plight of Detroit, modern Michigan is almost ignored. . . .

Bruce Catton has produced a well-written account which will doubtless attract many readers who may be encouraged to delve further into Michigan history. Nevertheless, this volume fails to meet expectations raised when a historian of Catton's abilities agreed to do a study of his native state. (p. 1006)

Stanley D. Solvick, in a review of "Michigan: A Bicentennial History," in The Journal of American History, Vol. LXIII, No. 4, March, 1977, pp. 1005-06.

ROBERT M. SENKEWICZ

An entire generation of Civil War buffs has, with reason, acclaimed Bruce [Catton] as one of our best popular historians, while his son, William, has taught for years at Middlebury College. The result of their collaboration, [***The Bold and Magnificent Dream***], is a joy to encounter. This book combines the great strength of popular history, vivid and gripping narrative, with the conceptual sophistication of scholarly research.

The Cattons' account of American colonial life is filled with paradox and ambiguity. We sense, for instance, the theory and practice of the Mayflower Compact. While it was a real step toward popular sovereignty, it was also a political device by which the minority of religious settlers whom we know as the Pilgrims successfully imposed their own orthodoxy on the majority of their unchurched fellow emigrants. We discover that while social mobility did make America a genuine land of opportunity, most indentured servants never achieved anything like economic security or independence. We see how the people of one generation could be sincere ideologists of self-determination and yet vicious persecutors of those who determined to continue their allegiance to the crown. In the same vein, we realize how the relative abundance of cheap land conditioned the American dream of freedom but also nourished the psychic seed of Anglo-American racism.

The above examples are only the tip of the iceberg. The authors range widely over the entire field of American colonial development, and their narrative and interpretations are unfailingly exciting. The Cattons have introduced that rarest of books: a popular book which scholars can read with profit and a scholarly book which the general public can read with pleasure. (pp. 397-98)

Robert M. Senkewicz, "Recapping the Long Tale of a Winter's Dream," in America, *Vol. 140, No. 18, May 12, 1979, pp. 397-98.*

J. M. BUMSTED

For a historian of the academy to review a work of history obviously written for the popular market is always difficult. The task is made even more onerous when the authors of the book in question disarmingly confess . . . that what they have written is not really history at all. They have set out neither to synthesize the latest scholarly writings nor to produce something original. ***The Bold and Magnificent Dream*** is, we are told, "a combination of narrative and interpretive essay" in which the authors "have sought not to break new ground but to impose our own thoughts and order upon conventional historical method." Despite this disclaimer the publishers appear to have assumed that the work is something more than an extended essay of personal opinion—the title page lists it as part of the Doubleday Basic History of the United States and the dustjacket boasts of the meticulous research of its authors. Whomever one chooses to believe, history obviously comes in somewhere.

In fairness to the authors, the early history of America—as any of its academic practitioners can readily attest—does not lend itself easily to the breezy narrative technique at which they excel. . . . This book gets much better when its authors can write about battles and national politics. But those of us who work on the earlier period before 1775 are strangely fond of it, and can be legitimately distressed by what the Cattons have done to a fascinating era.

For this reviewer, the book is stridently overwritten. Two of its more common techniques are the vaguely patronizing aside and an excessive use of hyperbolic foreshadowing. I found the chummy use of contemporary slang and clichés as disturbing as the frequent passages of purple prose. The authors make no attempt to be consistent in their interpretation, except perhaps in the sense that they are whiggish, chauvinistic, and filiopietistic to an extent one would have thought went out in the nineteenth century. This work revels in the frontier and colonial America's middle-class values, even managing to resurrect social Darwinism. . . . George Bancroft still lives. Do Americans really still prefer their popular history in the Bancroft tradition?

J. M. Bumsted, in a review of "The Bold and Magnificent Dream: America's Founding Years, 1492-1815," in The Journal of American History, *Vol. 66, No. 3, December, 1979, p. 629.*

JAMES NUECHTERLEIN

Before his death in 1978, Bruce Catton had earned a reputation with the general public—though not necessarily among professional historians—as the greatest historian of the American Civil War. . . . [**"Reflections on the Civil War"**], compiled by John Lockley from tapes Catton made for educational distribution, adds little new to the Catton canon, but it does provide, along with a capsule overview of the war, evidence of his characteristic strengths and weaknesses.

Catton's discussion of the causes and conduct of the war is competent . . . , but it says nothing that could not be found in any adequate textbook. Still, he at least understands that the war was about slavery and race, a fundamental point that many academic historians, searching for underlying causes of the conflict, somehow manage to talk themselves out of.

Catton demonstrates his mastery of the military history of the conflict . . . through his analysis of the major campaigns, although this section of the book is too summary to suggest fully the depth of his knowledge.

He is at his best, and the book at its most fresh and useful, in the extended discussion of the everyday experience of life during wartime. We get the sense of what the war meant to civilians and to the ordinary soldier. Above all, we are reminded how miserable life was for those who fought on either side. (pp. 16, 18)

To Catton, the Civil War, for all its tragic elements, was not in itself a tragedy. It was worthwhile, he argued, because it both preserved the Union and extended freedom. . . .

Though this is all quite unexceptionable, one wishes Catton had been content to leave it at that. Instead he pushes on to some hopelessly muddled reflections concerning the war's deeper philosophical meanings and mysteries. And of all events in American history, it is surely the Civil War that least requires a pseudophilosophical gloss to lend it significance. (p. 18)

James Nuechterlein, in a review of "Reflections on the Civil War," in The New York Times Book Review, *October 18, 1981, pp. 16, 18.*

Aidan Chambers

1934-

English novelist, nonfiction writer, editor, critic, and dramatist.

Chambers is respected both as a novelist and as an authority on literature for young people. He believes that an appreciation of literature is essential to a complete life and that children should be introduced to reading at an early age and encouraged to develop their skills and tastes independently. His academic works, which include *The Reluctant Reader* (1968) and *Introducing Books to Children* (1973), express this premise, and the fiction Chambers writes and edits is designed to stimulate and challenge young readers. His insight into adolescent thoughts, interests, and behavior is considered exceptional.

A teacher of English and drama, Chambers began his literary career writing plays for his students before turning to fiction writing. A principal figure in Chambers's fiction is the adolescent on the threshold of maturity. In *Cycle Smash* (1967) a young athlete who has sustained a serious injury must learn to accept his diminished physical capabilities without bitterness. In *Marle* (1968) the simple life is extolled when a young man who has gone to the city to find excitement chooses to return to the peace of his island home.

***Breaktime* (1979) is widely considered Chambers's most successful work. Called an adolescent version of James Joyce's *Ulysses* by some critics, *Breaktime* is the journal kept by seventeen-year-old Ditto while on holiday from school. In this novel Chambers deviates from the straight narrative approach used in most literature for young adults, incorporating wordplay, stream-of-consciousness, visual effects, and other stylistic features in a fragmented format. In addition to reproducing the emotions felt by an adolescent at a critical time of his life, *Breaktime* also concerns the nature of literature, since Ditto begins his journal in response to a friend's challenge about the validity of fiction. *Dance on My Grave* (1982), in which Chambers again uses various stylistic techniques, is a frank exploration of love between two young men. Most of the novel is an account of the relationship told by the protagonist to a social worker in order to explain his unusual behavior after his friend's death. Chambers combines this narrative with reminiscences, flashbacks, and notes taken by the social worker. *The Present Takers* (1983) has a school setting and examines the relationship between a class bully and her victims. This novel evokes the pain and intimidation felt by the victims and also suggests causes of the bully's behavior.**

In addition to his work as a novelist and his book-length studies on children's reading, Chambers contributes criticism to periodicals that focus on children's literature. He has acted on his encouragement of good reading habits by compiling anthologies on such subjects of interest to young people as ghosts, crime, and aviation. Chambers has also edited several paperback book series designed to motivate reluctant readers.

(See also *Contemporary Authors,* Vols. 25-28, rev. ed.; *Contemporary Authors New Revision Series,* Vol. 12; and *Something about the Author,* Vol. 1.)

News Ltd., *Sydney*

ADRIAN RENDLE

[***The Chicken Run***] is in two acts and it is that rare phenomenon in the theatre; a well-written and interesting play for young people. . . . [This] is a 'play' in which real events are given dramatic highlight by an author who really knows what he is doing and why. ***The Chicken Run*** concerns itself with one of the major concerns of all young people—courage. To do this the author has taken the raw spirit of the 'tough' living areas and set it round the children who work a paper-round for a newsagent called Len and another older group called the 'mobs' who ride motorbikes and hold ceremonies of fearlessness as their badge of office.

Naturally enough the boys on the paper-round want to graduate to the older group—a sort of gladiatorial promotion and the efforts by one boy in particular to do this makes the main theme of the play. Interwoven with this is the fact that the newsagent's takings are the object of a robbery by another of the 'mobs' and the crime proves both distasteful and punishable by both groups. If this sounds good *Boys' Own* material I am doing the writer an injustice, for like all good drama the plot is there to be illuminated by the characters and these are brilliantly drawn.

The only deplorable moral feature of the play seems to be the misplaced belief in rough and ready justice taking its course. . . .

The play seems to condone an attitude rather than comment on why it has arisen. . . .

[There is] an exquisite scene concerning a young boy borrowing father's razor to shave off the faint whiskers of adolescence. There is also a fight scene that is powerfully conceived between the two protagonists of the groups that has all the fire of Hector and Achilles on the Trojan plain.

This is the stuff of young people's drama.

Adrian Rendle, in a review of "The Chicken Run," in Drama, *No. 91, Winter, 1968, p. 62.*

B. W. ALDERSON

[Aidan Chambers] has been one of the most consistent advocates of "teenage novels", and it is therefore disappointing that his [**"Cycle Smash"**] . . . should set only a very moderate example of his ideas. There is some strength in its opening sections, some suggestion of contemporary concerns to be developed, but the story gets progressively more unreal and finishes up like a second-rate woman's magazine serial.

B. W. Alderson, in a review of "Cycle Smash," in Children's Book News, *Vol. 3, No. 2, March-April, 1968, p. 83.*

B. W. ALDERSON

[**"Marle"** has] potential. Although Aidan Chambers wrote it before **"Cycle Smash"** . . . it is a more credible creation than that book. It depicts the inward-looking life of a small off-shore island on the Northumberland coast, the departure of Susan to the bright lights of Newcastle, her pursuit by Kevin and his subsequent return to Marle. . . . The best parts of the book are in the characterization and in the portrayal of the island, but there is a terrible wanness in the plot.

B. W. Alderson, in a review of "Marle," in Children's Book News, *Vol. 3, No. 4, July-August, 1968, p. 196.*

THE JUNIOR BOOKSHELF

Superficially, [***Marle***] is a convincing story of first love, and the rebellions, despairs and loneliness of adolescence. Dominating the slight but charming plot, however, is the bleak, beautiful island of the title off the Northumberland coast, whose younger people are moving away to find more life on the mainland. The hero Kevin has the sea, the island and boat-building so deeply in his blood that he voices his reactions and experiences . . . in terms of these things. In his case, [after he tries city life], the country wins, and he returns to try to awaken some of the old industries on Marle. The author's plea for country values is obviously deeply felt. There are vivid word pictures of the natural setting and the inside of homes. . . . The plot is well-handled, the death of the old boat-builder, Kevin's grandfather, is moving, and there is no slick happy ending, only pleasurable anticipation.

A review of "Marle," in The Junior Bookshelf, *Vol. 32, No. 5, October, 1968, p. 317.*

MARGERY FISHER

Breaktime is a significant title in more than one way. It indicates the strictly defined period of time of Ditto's break from normality, an extended half-term holiday when this schoolboy of seventeen leaves his home in County Durham to camp near Richmond. It also stands for the fragmented form of the book, breaking strict chronology, its passages of orthodox cursive narration interrupted by Joycean verbal hieroglyphics, letters, dialogue dramatically arranged, quotation, first-person reporting in the historic present, reminiscence and the like. The method is in fact a kind of authorial double bluff. Ostensibly it is the result of an argument between Ditto and his friend Morgan, who argues that fiction is "a sham, no longer useful, effluent, CRAP" because it misses truth by its conventions, its tidy rendering of the untidy fabric of life. Taking up the challenge, Ditto finds it useful as a way of facing his own problems—his deteriorating relations with his father, sad result of divisive education, and his own unresolved sexuality. He plans to invite his girl-friend Helen to join him in Yorkshire and promises Morgan that he will record the events of the "jaunt" not in "the manner of our logical stories" but using any style that seems suitable, with the object of proving that fiction *can* seriously reflect the truth. Clearly at the same time the controlling author, helped by an invisible, suspended narrator who takes over parts of the narrative, is asserting the validity and flexibility of fiction, claiming by implication that the confusions, the bookish absurdities, the need to love and the need to be separate, the whole kaleidoscope of an adolescent's nature at one particular time, can be gathered up and presented to a reader as truth, as reality. Aidan Chambers is far from dogmatic in his experiment. Morgan's comment after reading Ditto's document, "Are you saying I'm just a character in a story", leaves us in the air. But whether Ditto has described a real event or an imaginary one, whether his sexual adventures, or the whole scatty, disturbing enterprise with Newcastle Jack and his mate, happened or not, a particular moment of truth has been reached by and for the boy. With humour and wit, with ingenuity and candour, the author has offered one piece of one kind of truth in a spirit of technical and emotional investigation. (pp. 3418-19)

Margery Fisher, in a review of "Breaktime," in her Growing Point, *Vol. 17, No. 4, November, 1978, pp. 3418-19.*

RICHARD YATES

A 17-year-old English boy leaves home for a few days during spring vacation, determined to acquire worldly experience and to write it all down in the chronicle that comes to form the bulk of [**"Breaktime"**]. It's a nice idea for a young-adult book, and for the most part Aidan Chambers has brought it off. The trouble is that he doesn't seem to trust his talent.

The adventuring schoolboy hero of **"Breaktime,"** whose name is Ditto, comes through as an appealing young man. If he and his friends often sound as pretentious as Stephen Dedalus, it's all right with me, because some children really do talk that way; besides, the nature of Ditto's quest is something any number of readers can take to their hearts. He wants to gain perspective on his failure to get along with his invalid father, and he wants to lose his virginity with an amiable girl who has shown an interest in him. Both themes are convincingly developed and resolved: The father-son material is unforced and poignant, and the love story is a sweet one. I imagine most readers will be persuaded, as I was, that Ditto on coming home is a stronger and more compassionate boy than when he left.

But there is an awful lot of stylistic fooling around in this book. There are breathless "stream-of-consciousness" passages that turn out to be more trouble than they're worth; there is an obtrusive use of tricks such as irregular spacing, scrambled typography, and visual effects derived from comic strips; and there are failing attempts to render simultaneous events by running two or even three columns of print down the page.

All this is too bad, because it comes close to swamping the novel. And you can tell that the author doesn't need his affectations: Whenever he puts them aside he writes well.

Richard Yates, "You Can and Can't Go Home Again," in The New York Times Book Review, *April 29, 1979, p. 30.*

MARILYN KAYE

[***Breaktime*** is] a complex story, told in a complex, and occasionally confusing manner. Switching back and forth from first to third person narrative, frequently making use of a stream of consciousness style, and combining various literary and graphic modes, Chambers tries to present Ditto's story in a way which will reflect the disorder in his mind. It's an intriguing endeavor, and sometimes it's quite effective. The descriptive passages are fine: carefully chosen words sketch images with clarity and precision. Occasionally, however, the heavy use of irony becomes ponderous, and attempts at literary experimentation begin to appear pretentious, even tedious. This is not to say that the book is a failure—it's clever, intense, and very appealing. (p. 71)

Marilyn Kaye, in a review of "Breaktime," in School Library Journal, *Vol. 25, No. 9, May, 1979, pp. 70-1.*

EUGENE V. SULLIVAN, JR.

Will the real Holden Caulfield please stand up. Forgive the cynicism, but each time a youthful adventurer strides across the fictional plain headed toward his or her rendezvous with maturity, a longing for the depth and awareness of Salinger is evoked in this reviewer. . . .

Breaktime is really a rather trite and shallow novel, stereotyping today's youth and lacking the perception and depth hearkened to above. The use of various and sundry illustrative techniques, cartoons, scrawled letters and divided page narrative in the trysting scene (Chambers on the left, Dr. Spock on the right) make the whole work just that much more contrived.

Eugene V. Sullivan, Jr., in a review of "Breaktime," in Best Sellers, *Vol. 39, No. 6, September, 1979, p. 228.*

GERALDINE DeLUCA

Breaktime is Chambers' *Ulysses*. And Chambers makes it clear that his splendidly baroque work is following in Joyce's footsteps. The novel's humble hero "Ditto" calls it to the reader's attention in a footnote on imitation. . . . And it is "with puzzled pleasure," the same response an adult brings to a first reading of *Ulysses,* that one can hope a sophisticated adolescent, in love with language, will approach this work. For it is not only a linguistic *tour de force,* filled with typographical experiments, a few pop-art illustrations, handwritten letters, and Joycean puns; it is also finally an involving story of a young man's attempts to deal with his sick father; his guilt at placing the burden of caring for the father on his mother; his intellectual growth, particularly focused on his need to prove to a friend that literature is not a game but an image of life; and his desire to lose his virginity with a flamboyantly promiscuous young woman aptly named Helen.

His desire to meet Helen, who is living in the English countryside, provides the impetus for Ditto's small odyssey. He takes his trip during spring recess from school—breaktime—intent, along the way, to prove his claims for literature by recording his experiences. During the first day he meets two young men, Jacky and Robbie, and the three discourse, with extraordinary articulateness, on political activism, all this of course being filtered through Ditto's literary sensibility. . . . Having accomplished his goal, Ditto returns home, finds his father doing well, and presents his friend Morgan with his piece of literature—which is ***Breaktime*** itself. When Morgan charges that this isn't literature because it all really happened, Ditto cleverly answers that he is glad Morgan is convinced but that perhaps it hasn't happened at all.

Initially the book's idiosyncrasies are irritating. The opening dialogue, setting forth the challenge between Morgan and Ditto, is overbearingly self-conscious. . . . And there are passages of prose that are pure verbal indulgence, strongly reminiscent of Stephen Dedalus. . . . The work moves slowly, a composite of mannerisms. . . . And by way of establishing Ditto's emotionally charged situation at home, there is some pseudo-scientific description, reflecting his need for clarity, objectivity, an intellectual life. . . . The conversations between Ditto, Robbie and Morgan are laborious to read, and somewhat unreal, translated as they are into the convoluted voice of Ditto. Chambers uses other techniques as well to undercut our involvement in the story as story, asking us, for example, to supply our own character descriptions. . . . Because Chambers withholds standard fictional information and because so much of the book is talk and reflection, the characters take on the quality of disembodied voices. . . . But once one gets used to the work, there is pleasure to be found in it. The book is not meant to be probable or realistic. In fact what Chambers, or his precocious adolescent narrator, is saying is that one must forget about realism and probability in order to approach it more closely, since experience is not perceived as it is written in books. Which is true and not true, but an interesting point and certainly a fresh one for adolescents. (pp. 144-46)

As the work progresses, its experiments seem less and less intrusive and one becomes increasingly involved in Ditto's experience. The mask of the virtuoso falls away and gradually Ditto becomes more honest about his awarenesses. . . . So ultimately, even though the book has its cold spots, its self-indulgent passages, it amply justifies itself as a work of literature, attempting to capture the simultaneity and improbability of human experience, reflecting the mind acting in or out of harmony with an event, and acknowledging the fragmentary and distorted quality of our perceptions. (pp. 146-47)

Since this book is so doggedly about the attempt to record experience in all its complexity, and about how literature draws on and illuminates our lives, the social issues it includes, and there are many, are presented as naturally, and at times bizarrely, as they occur in life. Ditto's sexual experience with Helen, for example, is as graphic as Judy Blume could do. But it is also much more. Chambers presents the encounter in three columns, reflecting Ditto's simultaneous and conflicting reactions. In one column is pure action flavored with myth: all romance, fluid music, a gauzy movie scene; in the second is Ditto's attempt to quiet himself, not to laugh, to relax and give himself up to it; and the third column that moves in toward the end is a pat description of "healthy sex" quoted from Dr. Spock. This is a recording far more true to an adolescent's experience—albeit harder to read—than any descriptions provided by less talented writers.

The book is a long way from standard young adult fare, but we can see, in Ditto's precocity, the same attempt to reflect the adolescent mind that moves other writers for the age group. He is attempting to write a Joycean novel as an adolescent would, with all the energy and none of the moderation of age. The result is certainly not for every adolescent. But for those, like Ditto, with poetic sensibilities and aspirations, it is a gift, and the genre, if one can claim this work as a contribution, is richer for it. (pp. 147-48)

Geraldine DeLuca, "Taking True Risks: Controversial Issues in New Young Adult Novels," in The Lion and the Unicorn, *Vol. 3, No. 2, Winter, 1979-80, pp. 125-48.**

THE JUNIOR BOOKSHELF

The speed and conviction with which Aidan Chambers establishes the parent/child relationship in the early chapters [of ***Seal Secret***] is an immediate indication of his skill. A potentially boring holiday for William is transformed when he meets Gwyn, who owns a calf and wants to buy another. He reveals his secret to William—a seal pup hidden in a cave—and horrifies him with a proposal to farm seals and sell their meat and skins. William plans to save the pup and embarks on a difficult and dangerous mission, doubly important for him because 'for the first time in his whole life he would be on his own'. . . .

The conflicts between the two boys are traced in controlled, conversational prose. . . . William's venture to save the seal is not only a brave reaction to a formidable challenge; it is also a determined step on the path of self discovery.

A review of "Seal Secret," in The Junior Bookshelf, *Vol. 44, No. 5, October, 1980, p. 245.*

JAN KEY

[***Seal Secret***] is a nondescript tale with several promising strands in the plot which could have been effectively explored further, William's relationship with his parents, for example. The style of writing is staccato and irritatingly studded with sentences beginning 'and', 'but' and 'then'. I could not believe in it, and the atmosphere of Wales did not come across well either. Except for the boy Gwyn calling William 'Boyo' all the time, the setting could have been anywhere. Also, would the family have made such persistent efforts to befriend the locals if they were going to be there for only a week?

Jan Key, in a review of "Seal Secret," in The School Librarian, *Vol. 28, No. 4, December, 1980, p. 377.*

MARGERY FISHER

[In ***Dance on My Grave*** there is first] an ordered untidiness of narrative which ensures that the first-person apologia of a boy of sixteen for an act of seemingly irrational and appalling disrespect is not on one consistent time level, which could have seemed artificial, but gradual, dispersed, moving into different areas of time and experience. Flashback, reverie, jottings are organised into sections which mark stages in Hal's sorting process (and so, stages in the readers' understanding of his actions). Then, there is a personal voice, the voice of the author adapted to the natural idiom of a boy in whom coarseness and sensitive feelings are at war, a voice expressing with special clarity the way adolescent boys can in moments of extreme emotion switch to a disconcertingly matter-of-fact detachment. Anyone who believes unisex is an answer to anything may think again: this is the masculine attitude, one of the subtle underlying incitements to the hostility between the sexes. 'Youth's Pact to Dance on Friend's Grave'—the newspaper headline states the plot. From this develops a candid, searching analysis of a homosexual relationship, uneven in age . . . and in intention. . . . This is a serious book, not just the study of a single experience but an attempt to define personality, to encapsulate a stage in growing up, even in an undictatorial way to make a statement of philosophy. It is a book that makes its point through raucous humour and implied feeling, through the sharp observation of a boy and his blundering apprehensions of the way others observe him. If teenage novels are to justify their existence, it will be by this kind of honest, particularised, personal writing.

Margery Fisher, in a review of "Dance on My Grave," in her Growing Point, *Vol. 21, No. 2, July, 1982, p. 3928.*

THE JUNIOR BOOKSHELF

"'You Bore Me!'" Barry yells at Hal at the climax of [***Dance on My Grave***]. I sympathize. Hal bores me too. Mr Chambers is a most sincere and dedicated writer, and no one could question his integrity, but he has found a most unprepossessing hero on whom to spill out his many talents. . . .

The story-line is thin, and everything depends on (1) skill in narrative, and (2) involvement with the hero. Mr Chambers tells the story through the words of Hal in a report to the social worker appointed to examine his case. This device enables him to explore Hal in depth, but it does not make for swift action. Many of the episodes are described twice, as the young man tries to express himself, fails and tries again. Mr Chambers gets into Hal's muddled head most successfully, and speaks in the authentic tones of youth, but the small story is stretched out to intolerable lengths in the process. The writer's skill has not, it seems to me, helped him on this occasion. . . .

I wish that Mr Chambers had found a theme more worthy of his deep understanding and his literary skills.

A review of "Dance on My Grave," in The Junior Bookshelf, *Vol. 46, No. 6, December, 1982, p. 235.*

ZENA SUTHERLAND

[In ***Dance on My Grave***] Chambers tells the story of a homosexual relationship in which one of the partners is dominant and that ends in tragedy. . . . Chambers' style is often staccato, often introspective; this is not an easy book to read. What should appeal to readers are the effective communication of deep and often anguished feelings, the perceptive depiction of relationships, and the depth and consistency of characterization.

Zena Sutherland, in a review of "Dance on My Grave," in Bulletin for the Center for Children's Books, *Vol. 36, No. 10, June, 1983, p. 185.*

GREGORY MAGUIRE

[Hal Robinson, protagonist of ***Dance on My Grave,***] is intelligent, witty, self-deprecating, and somewhat innocent. During his sixteenth summer, friendship and then romance blossom between him and the self-confident Barry Gorman. When Barry dies in a motorcycle crash, Hal is driven to re-creating the events of the summer in a vivid, colloquial account capturing the breathlessness of adolescent love. Hal's first-person narrative has a quirky style that conveys the emotional upheaval he is enduring after Barry's death. . . . A few scenes verge on the slapstick . . . which serves neither as comic relief nor as social satire. But the author is marvelously gifted at suggesting the ecstasy and insecurity that accompany new love—including its emotional and physical, social and spiritual aspects. A major strength of the book, the central conflict hinges not on the lovers being gay, but on their having two idiosyncratic and contradictory personalities.

Gregory Maguire, in a review of "Dance on My Grave," in The Horn Book Magazine, *Vol. LIX, No. 3, June, 1983, p. 308.*

MARGERY FISHER

[In ***The Present Takers***] Aidan Chambers approaches the relationships and encounters of the middle years in a spirit of realism—that is, in the usually accepted use of the word, he describes scenes and people as they really are. But are they? Certainly the girls who persecute Lucy in the school playground . . . can be found in a good many junior schools at one time or another, and the appalling parents who have shaped Melanie's cruelty with their glossy neglect are only too believable in terms of today's society. Uneasiness creeps in when it comes to the teachers. Could Mrs. Harris . . . really have failed to see the reason for Lucy's vagueness in class? Could Mr. Jenkins . . . really have ignored what was going on in the playground? The plot is bitterly plausible, most of all when Lucy and the shaggy, anarchic Angus find a way to expose Melanie to ridicule and end her domination, and beyond the immediate events at school and at home a picture is assembled of a community where adults and children work out their problems partially—and clumsily, in the manner of what we call 'real life'. If there is one inconsistency in this acidly comic piece of fiction it is compensated for, thoroughly, by the incisive dialogue through which a great deal of the feeling comes through. . . .

Margery Fisher, in a review of "The Present Takers," in her Growing Point, *Vol. 22, No. 4, November, 1983, p. 4164.*

THE JUNIOR BOOKSHELF

Despite vociferous denials, bullying of one sort or another does take place in school at all levels and [in ***The Present Takers***] Aidan Chambers' Lucy suffers a particularly nasty example from a gang organised and orchestrated by an unhappily twisted, brassy specimen of primary schoolgirlhood. . . . Prompted by a friendly, moonstruck boy in her class, Lucy struggles to find a solution to her problem without recourse to authority, but she is constantly outnumbered and outmanoeuvred by a gang with a talent for aggravation. The picture is not a pleasant one and the reader must rejoice wholeheartedly when the tables are eventually turned.

A review of "The Present Takers," in The Junior Bookshelf, *Vol. 47, No. 6, December, 1983, p. 255.*

SANDRA HANN

Aidan Chambers poses many questions [in ***The Present Takers***] but offers no easy answers, an approach which takes his readers as seriously as he creates his characters. The bully, Melanie, is shown at home. She is a child who is emotionally neglected, possibly sexually precocious, possibly physically abused. The reader must decide. Lucy, the victim, lives in a caring and loving family; her parents are damaged by the bullying too. . . . Melanie steals not only their daughter's birthday presents but 'the present moment. All they've got.' Hovering on the sidelines is Lucy's friend Angus, angrily powerless to help at first, but gradually seeing a way to help not only Lucy but himself in his relationship with his deserted father.

The book is, at times, a disturbing experience, for Lucy's plan is vividly portrayed. It is a story which offers the reader a wide range of sympathies and the freedom to respond at his or her own level of emotional maturity. (pp. 73-4)

Sandra Hann, in a review of "The Present Takers," in The School Librarian, *Vol. 32, No. 1, March, 1984, pp. 73-4.*

C. J. Cherryh

1942-

(Pseudonym of Carolyn Janice Cherry) American novelist and short story writer.

A prolific and inventive author of science fiction and fantasy, Cherryh creates startling yet believable alien characters and worlds. She explains that her work is "of an essentially anthropological slant—speculations on the essence of humanity and the possibilities of non-human intelligence and non-human society." Many of Cherryh's novels are tales of interstellar or intercultural conflict. Her central characters are usually strong females; they often rule matriarchal societies in which traditional gender characteristics are reversed. The complexity and ambition of Cherryh's work has been praised by many critics, but the same qualities have also led to charges of obscurity.

Photograph by Jay Kay Klein

Cherryh's first novel, *Gate of Ivrel* (1976), is a fantasy that begins her trilogy centering on the enchantress Morgaine. *Well of Shiuan* (1978) and *Fires of Azeroth* (1979) complete the trilogy, which concerns Morgaine's battles to close the gates built for space and time travel by a supernatural alien race called the Qhal. The existence of these gates is thought to destabilize human-populated planets. Morgaine is depicted as a figure of apocalyptic stature attempting to save the universe but perhaps hastening its destruction, since closing the gates may be as dangerous as leaving them open. *Gate of Ivrel* earned Cherryh the John W. Campbell Award for Best New Science Fiction Writer of the Year.

The *Faded Sun* trilogy also centers on a powerful female, Melein, who is the ruler of a warrior race called the Mri. In *The Faded Sun: Kesrith* (1978), the Mri are attacked by the Regul, an opportunistic race that had previously employed the Mri in their war against humans. In *The Faded Sun: Shon'jir* (1978) and *The Faded Sun: Kutath* (1979), Cherryh continues her theme of intercultural conflict as Melein and her brother, the only Mri to survive the Regul attack, are accompanied on a journey to their home planet by a human, Sten Duncan. As the Mri are pursued by both Regul and Earth forces, Duncan attempts to transform himself into a Mri warrior. Other Cherryh novels in which a female defends her race against enemies are *The Pride of Chanur* (1982) and *Chanur's Venture* (1984).

Hunter of Worlds (1977) is the novel that most clearly demonstrates Cherryh's interest in anthropology and linguistics. Three separate alien cultures, each with its own language, history, and psychology, are fully developed in this book. The plot involves the kidnapping of a member of the Kallia, a highly-evolved race, by the Iduve, a predatory species who live in battleships and enslave others throughout the galaxy. The kidnapping is thwarted through the intervention of a third race called the Amaut. *Hunter of Worlds* includes an extensive glossary to aid the reader in understanding the languages of the various aliens.

Downbelow Station (1981), which won the Hugo Award for best novel, is a complex story of interstellar warfare and political intrigue. The novel presents an account of the conflict between a colonizing company and a group of rebellious troops known as the Union. Its sequel, *Merchanter's Luck* (1982), narrows the focus of *Downbelow Station* by concentrating on the transformation of two merchants forced to overcome their distrust of one another through their mutual need for survival.

Like the *Morgaine* trilogy, some of Cherryh's other works combine science fiction and fantasy. *Port Eternity* (1982) relates the story of an heiress in space whose cloned servants have been conditioned to behave like the characters of Arthurian legend. Examples of pure fantasy novels by Cherryh are *The Dreamstone* (1983) and *The Tree of Swords and Jewels* (1983). Both novels are set in ancient times and involve human intrusion into Ealdwood, the last of the faerie realms.

(See also *Contemporary Authors,* Vols. 65-68; *Contemporary Authors New Revision Series,* Vol. 10; and *Dictionary of Literary Biography Yearbook: 1980.*)

ALGIS BUDRYS

Never mind that you never heard of Ms. C. J. Cherryh before. . . . [Cherryh] is a born story-teller.

While not of the "magnitude of Tolkien and Merritt"—blurb-writing makes strange bedfellows—or as intricate a worker as Le Guin, Cherryh produces a "novel of barbarian worlds" [*Gate of Ivrel*], fully worthy of the company of Leigh Brackett or C. L. Moore, far less slapdash than Merritt, considerably less boring than Tolkien, and, while not impossible to put down, very, very easy to return to.

The world of [this] novel might—might not—be Earth; rather, one would guess that Morgaine has come to this world next after leaving Earth behind in her infinite journey through the gates that span the universe. She is the last of her band of a hundred whose mission can only end in death, and again one hears an echo of Camelot, perhaps only because one would like to.

Her story here is told through Vanye the warrior, native outcast of this world, who follows her at first because he has no choice, and then because he has no heart to leave her. Together and sometimes separately, they pursue the road to the Gate of Ivrel through lands with what to me are vaguely Welsh names, among clans and nations which have rightly feared and cursed Morgaine's memory for a hundred years. . . . (pp. 44-5)

There is of course the question of how long Cherryh worked on this manuscript, and how much labor she might expend on the next. Her sense of pacing is not sure; too much is spent on a minor incident, not enough on another. Her ability to create tension is unpracticed; she has only one means of surprising her protagonists, and that is to always underplay. That is not a trick to rely on throughout. And her supporting characters can be seen to be reacting arbitrarily. In particular Erij, Vanye's unhanded brother, weathervanes frantically in response to Cherryh's attempts to depict duality of character, which emerge instead as a rather forced attempt to give Vanye an uncle, a brother, and an enemy all out of the same limited cast. The exotic language, imposed on a society already complicated by caste and clan, acts to eventually bore a reader who began by attempting to follow them. All of these are apprentice faults, listed here because Cherryh's obvious underlying talents—and the immediate rewards of reading ***Gate of Ivrel***—fully justify taking an interest.

If you respond at all to tales of adventure in faerie lands, I can almost guarantee you that ***Gate of Ivrel*** will come as a happy surprise, and that while it ain't no *Silverlock,* with portions of which it compares either directly or as if in mirror image, we can expect a mature Cherryh to be fully an equal of John Myers Myers, or a Brackett. . . . (pp. 45-6)

Algis Budrys, in a review of "Gate of Ivrel," in The Magazine of Fantasy and Science Fiction, *Vol. 50, No. 6, June, 1976, pp. 44-6.*

PUBLISHERS WEEKLY

[In ***Brothers of Earth***] Kurt Morgan, only survivor of a space battle which has destroyed his home-world and the enemy's, lands on a planet populated by humanlike beings, the nemet, and finds that the ruler of Nephane, the city-state he has been taken to, is Djan, a woman officer of the enemy. . . . Morgan's presence and Djan's manipulation trigger a bloody civil war in the city, from which Kurt and a nemet friend flee, only to find themselves in the hands of another ruler who is planning to destroy Nephane, and demands their aid. A final confrontation leaves Morgan the only human on the planet, with a life to make for himself among the nemet. Colorful and active, but sometimes overtalky. (pp. 65-6)

A review of "Brothers of Earth," in Publishers Weekly, *Vol. 210, No. 10, September 6, 1976, pp. 65-6.*

LESTER DEL REY

[***Hunter of Worlds*** is] not a bad book. There's an uncommonly great amount of skill shown in writing a very difficult story and a lot of ingenuity. Behind it all is also a complex and fascinating plot. But I'm sorry to say I'm somewhat disappointed. I think Cherryh has taken a wrong turn off into roads where her talent gets somewhat lost in the brambles along the way.

It all takes place off in space, around worlds beyond human settlement originally, then back to an outpost world of mankind. It seems that there is a proud and mighty race too powerful for any other race to oppose. This race is the Iduve, who exist only in their great ships, handing down decrees to other races and taking slaves as they will. (Well-treated slaves, however.)

The Iduve have an elaborate set of feral cultural traditions. Now it seems one member of the race has violated one of their most inviolate traditions and has escaped onto an outpost world of humanity. One Iduve ship, the Ashanome, takes on a member of the Kallia race and a captured human as slaves. These are brain-coupled by a mechanical mind linkage with a slave who had been brought up in the service of the Iduve. It is the job of these three to locate the ritual-breaker.

And from there, it gets complicated. The human is sent to lead a band of quisling humans who begin slaughtering their fellows in a complicated plan to flush out the fugitive. (pp. 172, 174)

The trouble is, it's all too damned complicated. In her first two books, Cherryh told her story in pretty straightforward fashion, following a single viewpoint character most of the time. . . .

[In ***Hunter of Worlds***] she jumps around like the mad hatter serving tea at the trial. She really has to, to get all the material in, of course; but that doesn't make it any easier for the reader to follow.

She also has evolved languages—not one, but three—for her aliens, which require glossaries in the back of the book. Now, some of the concepts are fairly hard to get without knowing exactly what the words are, but many aren't necessarily that different; yet for both strange and normal concepts, there are the alien terms striking us on every page. Perhaps a reader can skim through it all and get the general story without looking up words; I found it better to keep turning to the glossary. . . .

Maybe I'll like the book better on second reading—if I bother. Even on first reading, there were good spots in plenty. For one thing, the fugitive is a fascinating character. I liked him and wished I could have seen much more of all this from his view; but he was about the only one I really could care about.

As I said, there's a lot of good story buried in the novel, and to pull something like this off at all speaks well for Cherryh's skill. But I wish she'd go back to doing the type of book she can do exceptionally well—a straightforward but rich novel that can be followed without eight pages of vocabularies in the back. (p. 174)

Lester del Rey, in a review of "Hunter of Worlds," in Analog Science Fiction/Science Fact, *Vol. XCVII, No. 8, August, 1977, pp. 172, 174-75.*

ALGIS BUDRYS

C. J. Cherryh is now reaping the benefit of having been overpraised and overweighted with attention. ***Hunter of Worlds*** has elaborated on all her hitherto minor faults. It's as interesting a story as it is only because of her considerable raw talent, and the resourcefulness of an imagination equal to the young Brackett's. Meanwhile, however, it imposes an enormous burden on the reader, who really ought to take notes on the languages Cherryh invents, and make a genealogical chart on which to follow the elaborate politics played out among non-human beings. . . . (p. 26)

Cherryh's chronic problem has been an inability to close with the crucial scene. In the much-praised ***Brothers of Earth,*** she persistently had the crucial action happen offstage, except in cases where it happened on-stage but she did not say so, leaving it for the reader to deduce why everyone's attitude had suddenly changed. In ***Gate of Ivrel,*** in which she used invented language sparingly to good effect, she had usually avoided describing interaction . . . a curious flaw in a broadsword action story.

In other words, someone who showed great promise with her first novel, but needed a clearer understanding of how story-telling works, has now progressed into incomprehensibility in just three books. I blame the people who devoted so many paragraphs to telling her she was without flaw. . . . [If] Cherryh finds herself one day writing entirely to herself, supported only by a small cult of people who dig that sort of thing, and comforted by notices claiming that if only the readers weren't so stupid, she'd be enjoying the fruits she deserves for her intelligence and creativity, it will be too damned bad. Intelligence and creativity are not what readers want. What readers want is the *result,* and I commend you to Brackett. (p. 27)

Algis Budrys, in a review of "Hunter of Worlds," in The Magazine of Fantasy and Science Fiction, *Vol. 53, No. 6, December, 1977, pp. 26-7.*

ALGIS BUDRYS

Those who have been waiting for C. J. Cherryh's next tale of high adventure and swashed bucklers have a particular treat awaiting them with her ***Well of Shiuan.*** Not only is it the pure science fantasy quill, with its roustings of mailed warriors and its tense deeds among the battlements of fortresses never erected on this Earth, but it is the promised sequel to her 1976 first novel, ***Gate of Ivrel.***

The well, like the gate, is a space-time passageway between worlds. Each world is inhabited by humans, but also by the humanoid ancient *qujal,* who are very cold of heart, and possessed of certain secret ways. Through the gates, world after weary world, comes blonde Morgaine, the enigmatic warrior woman, followed by outlaw princeling Nhi Vanye i Chya. She carries the fantastic sword which can . . . unlock and then shut the gates forever behind her.

Cherryh is the best writer of this sort of adventure tale since the earliest days of C. L. Moore and the prime of Leigh Brackett. Morgaine and Vanye fans will be fascinated by this new skein of development in the relationship between the two, as well as by the setting of her tale, so much like Ivrel and yet so different. Any reader who is willing to become lost in an alternate reality will find much to enjoy. (p. F1)

Algis Budrys, "Tales of Time and Space," in Book World—The Washington Post, *March 5, 1978, p. F1-F2.**

LESTER DEL REY

[The world Cherryh depicts in ***Well of Shiuan,*** the sequel to ***Gate of Ivrel,*** is] a dismal world, one where the seas are rising, flooding out the land and ruining what civilization was attained by those who had originally come through a Gate and occupied it. Adding to the chaos of the constant rains and rising sea is the unstable nature of what land remains, beset by frequent earthquakes. And it's a savage place in many ways, with little time for anything except the struggle to survive. The only hope for humanity would be to escape back through the Gate; but everything about the Gate has become a fearful, superstition-haunted legend. (p. 172)

I don't find the world here nearly as interesting as that of the first book; it does not offer the varied possibilities for cultures and backgrounds that the other world had. The scenes are well depicted, the cultures believable, but the grimness of everything makes it all somewhat of a one-mood performance.

The characters are another matter. Jhirun, the girl who flees her hopeless homeland to accompany them—often against their wishes—is fine, as is the seemingly effete, unreliable Kithan, second son of the ruling lord. Morgaine is fascinating and complex, and Vanye grows in character.

Most interesting, however, is a character who is on-stage only briefly. This is Roh—by body, a cousin of Vanye; now he is the body occupied by one of the race that built the Gates, or at least used them to the ill of the universe. As such, he should be completely evil, a creature that has become nearly immortal by moving his essence from body to body in his never-ending quest for power. And yet, there is much of the honest decency of Roh in his actions, whatever his motives.

The book ends satisfactorily, with the threads neatly tied. But I suspect that there will be another book in the series, and I look forward to further revelations of just what Roh's character really is. (pp. 172, 174)

[***Well of Shiuan*** is a] good adventure novel with a lot of color. I enjoyed it. (p. 174)

Lester del Rey, in a review of "Well of Shiuan," in Analog Science Fiction/Science Fact, *Vol. XCVIII, No. 5, May, 1978, pp. 172, 174.*

ALEXEI PANSHIN AND CORY PANSHIN

Like other young writers who came of age in the Sixties, and like so many of the new female writers in particular, Cherryh's impulse is to combine the virtues of traditional science fiction and heroic fantasy. Her roots can be seen to lie in works like *The Lord of the Rings, Dune,* and the early romantic novels of Ursula Le Guin. But ***Hunter of Worlds*** is cast not as sword-and-sorcery or as after-the-bomb melodrama, but as a new sort of galactic adventure, . . . clearly work of a new order.

What is the difference? Perhaps it lies in the fact that humanity is relatively peripheral in this novel, not the central locus of interest, not the lusty muscular rulers of the universe. There are, in fact, no less than three other races of alien beings, each with its own distinct psychology, that stand closer to the center of this story. A situation of this sort would simply not have existed in that earlier era. That it can exist now is token, perhaps, of the passing of American insularity and parochialism. It is an admission that other modes of thought than our own exist, and that some of them may be older and more central than ours. This is underscored by a device that ***Hunter of Worlds*** shares with Neeper's *A Place Beyond Man*—the frequent use of alien terms. (pp. 75-6)

The result is *real,* but it also makes for slow, hard reading. . . . It is another case, perhaps, of a virtue carrying with it its own defect. The alien vocabularies of ***Hunter of Worlds*** are both an evidence of other states of mind and an impediment to full identification, full rapport, with the ongoing story.

The other chief limitation of ***Hunter of Worlds*** is the smallness of the problem posed and resolved, particularly small when compared with the scope of the setting. . . . [At] the end of the story the focal characters are still slaves and the fundamental imbalance between species still remains. Again, not enough. But again, this insufficiency, this inability to resolve problems on the widest scale . . . may be a factor of the cloudiness and uncertainty of the decade in which they were written.

In any case, stick with Cherryh. She's really going to be good. (p. 76)

Alexei Panshin and Cory Panshin, in a review of "Hunter of Worlds," in The Magazine of Fantasy and Science Fiction, *Vol. 54, No. 6, June, 1978, pp. 74-6.*

DAVID A. TRUESDALE

Well of Shiuan has the ancient and powerful Morgaine of the *Qujal* and her sworn servant Nhi Vanye i Chya attempting to close one of the last of the world and time-spanning Gates on the world of Hiuaj/Shiuan. But a problem arises when the people of Shiuan learn of the Gate and attempt a mass exodus through it in order to escape the flooding and breakup of their entire planet. It is their sole hope of survival, and it is Morgaine who has come to seal it from them forever, for the Gates have long ago been determined a terrible evil, threatening by their very existence to disrupt the fabric of time and space.

The main burden of the story is Vanye's catharsis into something more than a man without honor, an outcast from his own people, and the poor peasant girl Jhirun, whose hide-bound determination to leave her homeland sets a great deal in motion. As is obvious from her previous novels, Ms. Cherryh delights in the creation of alien societies and much intricate background detail, so much so in this story that of the 115,000 plus words comprising this adventure, perhaps in only one half-sentence in the whole book is it made clear just *why* the world of Shiuan is a doomed world at all. . . .

Also perceived is a marked lack of action due to much setting of the stage, much mental and verbal maneuvering by the principal characters, again a propensity for extended mood, character and world description that while beautiful to imagine and interesting to read, slows the pace considerably. . . .

Nevertheless, I give a hearty thumbs up to ***Well of Shiuan*** for despite its flaws it is a rich and entertaining work by a gifted and maturing storyteller. . . .

David A. Truesdale, in a review of "Well of Shiuan," in Science Fiction Review, *Vol. 7, No. 3, July, 1978, p. 39.*

LESTER DEL REY

[***The Faded Sun: Kesrith***] is a novel that deals with three races in the aftermath of an interstellar war which has been won by the terrans. The central race in the story is the mri. . . . As long as the mri can remember, they have lived by sending forth their warrior caste to fight all the battles for the regul, who are a trading race, totally incapable of doing their own fighting. . . . To the mri, honor is everything; to the regul, the word has no meaning.

Now the regul have wasted almost all of the mri in their lost war against the terrans, until only one young kel (or warrior) is left on the barren, harsh world that is their home. The regul are abandoning the planet to the terrans as spoils of war, deserting the mri.

Most of the story is seen from the view of Niun, a young mri kel [warrior]. But to his shame, he has never been blooded, never been permitted to go into combat and gain honor that should be his by right of his skills. His people are ruled by his grandmother, a matriarch and priestess who guards the rites and traditions of the mri. She has kept him near her as if he were still a mere child. Yet now it falls on him to take on the task of trying to save all that is left of his people and his way of life, against restrictions that are still imposed by the matriarch and against both terrans and regul.

To complicate things, he is forced to save and protect a human, Sten Duncan, while considering him still a potential enemy.

There's a great deal more to the story, and much more to the involvement of Duncan and Niun. But above all else is the strong development of the fascinating culture and the history of the mri. Cherryh has a splendid talent for making an alien culture real without holding up the story.

Lester del Rey, in a review of "The Faded Sun: Kesrith," in Analog Science Fiction/Science Fact, *Vol. XCVIII, No. 8, August, 1978, p. 174.*

LESTER DEL REY

[In ***The Faded Sun: Kesrith,*** the] *mri* were strange, proud aliens who served as mercenary warriors against the forces of Earth. They lost. And those who still existed were betrayed. . . . [In ***The Faded Sun: Shon'jir***] only two remain—Niun, trained as a warrior but never in battle, and Melein, the priestess-mother-queen who must be obeyed. They are held captive by Earthmen. But Duncan, who lived with them as their somewhat willing captive, manages to free them and get them on a ship, guided by their ancient records toward what may be their home world, incredibly far away.

But no *tsi'mri* (non-mri) may go with the mri. Duncan must accept the rule of Melein and become effectively mri. And during the long voyage, he is forced into the harsh and unyielding discipline and ethic of a *kel*—a warrior of the mri. Somehow he must achieve what no other tsi'mri has ever accomplished, must learn what has taken Niun all his life to master. (pp. 170-71)

Their only hope is to find other mri on the planet toward which the ship heads. What will they find there? Millennia have passed since they left. . . .

And behind come the forces of Earth and the alien regul, ready to seize or destroy whatever may be found on the home planet of the mri.

[***The Faded Sun: Shon'jir***] is a powerful story, bitter and yet somehow inspiring in its determination and feeling of strange loyalties and stranger courage. It sticks in the mind, long after the last page is finished. And there is a resolution to the shaping of Duncan, though much remains to be told. (p. 171)

Lester del Rey, in a review of "The Faded Sun: Shon'jir," in Analog Science Fiction/Science Fact, *Vol. XCVIX, No. 2, February, 1979, pp. 170-71.*

PUBLISHERS WEEKLY

[**"Fires of Azeroth"**] is the third and final novel about the "White Queen," Morgaine kri Chya. The ghal race, ancient enemies of humans, had created a series of gates that connect the stars. Now the humans must close each gate. Morgaine, accompanied by her *ilin,* Vanye, and armed with a magic sword, has the job of closing the last one. . . . This is a rather ponderous work, carefully wrought in a somewhat archaic style. . . .

A review of "Fires of Azeroth," in Publishers Weekly, *Vol. 215, No. 17, April 23, 1979, p. 78.*

MARTIN MORSE WOOSTER

Cherryh is a classicist by profession, and [***The Faded Sun: Shon'jir***] is part of her attempt to raise science fiction to the form and substance of myth. She has a spare, lean style that is always a pleasure to read. Unfortunately, ***Shon'jir*** is not quite as powerful as ***Kesrith:*** Cherryh has set up a triangle of conflict between three forces where the characters are best explained and explored through battle; removing one or more of the actors lessens the drama. Nonetheless, the plot moves smoothly. . . . C. J. Cherryh is one of the best SF writers to appear within the last three years.

Martin Morse Wooster, in a review of "The Faded Sun: Shon'jir," in Science Fiction & Fantasy Book Review, *Vol. I, No. 5, June, 1979, p. 68.*

PUBLISHERS WEEKLY

[In **"The Faded Sun: Kutath,"** the] mri Melein and Niun with Sten Duncan . . . have returned to Kutath, mri ancestral home and final refuge. The proud race has been decimated by the treacherous and repulsive regul, who had previously employed the mri as mercenaries. Now the regul have followed the trio to the home planet to finish the genocide. In this carefully wrought third and final volume of the Faded Sun series . . . Cherryh demonstrates an almost clinical eye for detail, creating an alien race in depth. Her writing, however, like her characterizations, is overly stylized, without passion and ultimately not involving. (pp. 86-7)

A review of "The Faded Sun: Kutath," in Publishers Weekly, *Vol. 217, No. 1, January 11, 1980, pp. 86-7.*

ROSEMARY HERBERT

[***The Faded Sun: Kutath***] is typically complex and linguistically trying, demanding close attention to several voices, including clipped contemporary lingo and mythical-sounding description. Some readers will find that the plot, relying on swift action and lots of adventure, is not substantial enough to be worth the careful reading.

Rosemary Herbert, in a review of "The Faded Sun: Kutath," in Library Journal, *Vol. 107, No. 6, March 15, 1980, p. 748.*

REBECCA SUE TAYLOR

[In ***Serpent's Reach,*** 15-year-old] Raen a Sul haut Meth-maren is the only survivor of an attack that annihilates the Meth-maren clan. She is sheltered and healed by the Majat, the fearsome insect-like race that co-inhabits the planets of Hydri (Serpent's) Reach. Raen swears to revenge her family's death and spends years waiting for the right time. The concept of an ant colony type civilization is not original but is interestingly and fully developed here. Characters are well developed though, sadly, most humans come off as weak or vicious while the insects come off considerably stronger and definitely more intelligent. . . . Recommended for mature readers interested in traditional science fiction.

Rebecca Sue Taylor, in a review of "Serpent's Reach," in Voice of Youth Advocates, *Vol. 3, No. 6, February, 1981, p. 37.*

TOM EASTON

For interesting aliens, try C. J. Cherryh's ***Serpent's Reach.*** In it, she has created what may be the first sympathetic hive mind in SF. The Reach is populated by humans and the Hives [an insect-like race]. Centuries ago, the first humans got themselves accepted by the Hives by pretending to be a Hive of their own. . . . Given immortality by the real Hives, they became the Kontrin. The lab-born, programmed to a Puritan-Ethic subservience, became the Betas and created the cloned azi. Interestingly, the Betas' programs seem to have bred true, a testament to Cherryh's belief in Lamarckian evolution, or perhaps in the power of environment over heredity. . . .

Cherryh's human culture here is strange enough, but her Hive aliens strike me as a considerable success. The [author] has taken features of ant and bee and combined them—elements of the Hives include Warrior, Worker, Drone, and Mother (*not* Queen); communication is by speech and taste/odor. . . . Individuals have a measure of independence in thought and action, but exist only in the context of the Hive. They are *not* cells in a super-organism's body, nor sharers of a single mind. Cherryh has successfully avoided almost all the mystic pseudoscience claptrap inspired in her predecessors by Earth's social insects. She has achieved a Hive intelligence that makes sense. I congratulate her, and I look forward to her attempt to top it.

Tom Easton, in a review of "Serpent's Reach," in Analog Science Fiction/Science Fact, *Vol. CI, No. 2, February 2, 1981, p. 171.*

REBECCA TAYLOR

[In ***Downbelow Station***], Signy Mallory is a hardened starship captain; Damon Konstantin is a senior administrator of Downbelow Station; Satin is a native of the world that orbits Pell's Star; Josh Talley is a prisoner of war who may be more dangerous than anyone realizes. A galactic war between the Earth's colonizing Company and the rebellious Union colonies is drawing toward a decisive battle and these four people's lives become bound together by their struggle to maintain some sanity and responsibility in the midst of the utter insanity of war.

Explored here are themes not unusual to SF: interstellar warfare, contact with intelligent aliens, and responsibility of one human for his fellow man. Here they are explored with a fresh perspective. The well drawn variety of backgrounds and motivations of the characters is the work's strength. The complexity of plot and confusing number of paralleling stories prove to be the book's weaknesses.

Rebecca Taylor, in a review of "Downbelow Station," in Voice of Youth Advocates, *Vol. 4, No. 3, August, 1981, p. 31.*

DIANE C. DONOVAN

[In ***Sunfall,*** six] short stories use the historical backgrounds of major cities as a basis upon which to present visions of city life in Earth's distant future. **"The Only Death in the City"** takes place in Paris, where centuries of reincarnation have prompted boredom among its inhabitants . . . and **"Nightgame"** dwells upon the past and future warriors of Rome.

Sunfall's reliance upon an awareness of the history of each city gives it a unique perspective, though limiting it to more advanced readers whose historical knowledge will enable them to fully appreciate the book's special slant.

Diane C. Donovan, in a review of "Sunfall," in Kliatt Young Adult Paperback Book Guide, *Vol. XV, No. 6, September, 1981, p. 20.*

TOM EASTON

Downbelow Station is a fat book: a long one, perhaps even an epic. Certainly it feels as if it were intended to be an epic, and some people will say it succeeds. Me, I'm not so sure. The book takes almost its first third to provide the background for the eventual action. And an epic really should move pretty briskly right from the start. Shouldn't it?

Cherryh's world, as usual, is our future. She shows us Earth and its nearer colonies, stations orbiting lifeless worlds and Pell, a second Earth whose settlers live downbelow with the charming natives and supply food to Pell Station and the ships that stop there. She shows us the Beyond, settled by malcontents, ruled by the Union and its vat-bred minions. There is war, and refugees clog Pell Station as Union's forces gather for the final battle with Earth's discredited forces. (p. 168)

There is plenty of personal conflict here, but the story itself is impersonal, a confrontation of empires. Union is the monolithic, impersonal, controlling State, and it seems clearly the villain. But Earth is equally monolithic, cocooned in bureaucracy (though there are signs of emergence), perhaps equally a villain. The merchanters are the last reservoir of individualism, and the future may belong to them. The heroes are of Pell, though. They are neutral, and largely lost in the shadows of the superpowers. Cherryh's problems with this story may be the same ones any writer would encounter trying to discuss Switzerland's position as a neutral zone between East and West here and now: The story is there, the protagonists are there, but the focus of the story is necessarily displaced to the zones of power, and it suffers.

This problem of focus may be endemic to ambitious novels. It is, in fact, the issue that prompts that classic advice to the beginning writer: Control the size of your story; keep it small enough not to lose your grip on it. . . . Perhaps ***Station*** would have been better as a trilogy itself, each book taking a different side in the struggle for its focus, or a different period of the story's history.

For all my carping, though, don't let me put you off. . . . For [Cherryh], ambition is a sign that she is not content to write what she has done before, that she struggles to improve her craft, that she strives to grow; and we should welcome that. It bodes well for the future.

For all its problems, in my eyes or yours, ***Station*** *is* a good read, and it will hold you for a long weekend. (pp. 168-69)

Tom Easton, in a review of "Downbelow Station," in Analog Science Fiction/Science Fact, *Vol. CI, No. 10, September 14, 1981, pp. 168-69.*

DEBBIE NOTKIN

C. J. Cherryh, who seems to have been in a very experimental mood recently, has produced a very odd short novel, ***Wave Without a Shore.*** In fact, it is closer to a discourse on (as The Flying Karamazov Brothers say) "Art and Reality—Who's Right?"

Cherryh's protagonist, Herrin Law, is an egotistical artist in a very limited, protective community. . . . As an artist, Law is striving for a range of both literal and figurative vision, and the effort entailed by not seeing the aliens (nor any humans who have crossed the line into the aliens' metaphorical territory) becomes too much for him.

This could be the basis for a fine science fiction novel, but Cherryh has quite consciously chosen to write in the style and structure of a philosophy text. It is still somewhat thought-provoking, but very slow and certainly not a successful novel. Anyone who reads the Book of Job or the Dialogues of Plato for pleasure (this is not wholly facetious—I know there are some of you out there) will probably enjoy it a great deal.

Debbie Notkin, in a review of "Wave without a Shore," in Rigel Science Fiction, *No. 3, Winter, 1982, p. 44.*

TOM EASTON

[***Wave Without a Shore***] concerns a world on which continents (Sartre and Hesse) and towns (Camus and Kierkegaard) are named for existentialist philosophers. Existence is based starkly on the premise that "Man is the measure of all things," . . . and that a superior person is one who can impose his reality on others. . . . [This] world has aliens too, but they are a part of no one's reality and hence no one sees them—they are effectively invisible. (pp. 162-63)

The tale is one of massive denial, to use a term invented by our patent sanforizers. Into this frame Cherryh sets two students, Herrin Law (significant name), budding artist, and Waden Jenks, heir to the planet. They argue over whose reality is stronger and agree to use each other. Jenks assassinates his father to take over the government. Law undertakes a monumental sculpture of Jenks that has the effect of unifying disparate realities. Jenks's reaction is the Divine Right of kings throughout history—he forbids Law to surpass his masterwork, and he has his hands smashed to enforce his decree. . . .

Solipsism is a common theme in SF. When it is treated as explicitly as it is here, it is usually played at least partly for laughs, as in Heinlein's classic "All You Zombies," or as an odd or horrifying interpretation of true reality. Never, to my knowledge, has it been handled in Cherryh's way. She has tried to show how it might work as a philosophy put into practice and in conflict with an external reality with which it refuses to mesh. She has expressed the philosopher's frustration—"It's a nifty idea, but it can't really be"—far more explicitly than anyone else.

Shore is thus a very intellectual novel in its theme. It is so in other ways as well. Cherryh set herself a very difficult task in the portrayal of a superior intellect. I had my doubts at first that she could pull it off, and now I think she wasn't entirely successful, but she did come close. In particular, she conveys a key frustration of the highly intelligent—the title says it: if no one understands you, if no one can reflect your ideas or follow your mind, you are a wave without a shore, never cresting, inevitably fading. . . .

Cherryh also comments on the reception of the artist. . . . The artist, she says, who is greeted by a rejecting fury is far more likely to be expressing valuable truths than one who is universally approved. Great art, perhaps, can be recognized by the heat it kindles. I am sympathetic to this view, even though it says great artists are rarer than even the lit profs say. (p. 163)

What does all this imply for a recipe for art? Art, to be art, must generate argument, but the arguments fail to count if they involve only a few fans or critics. To qualify as art, a novel (for instance) must therefore be widely read, and the heat it kindles must warm some significant fraction of the culture for which and in which it was written. . . .

Does anything in the SF canon qualify? There was Wells, of course, and Orwell and Huxley, but since them there may be no one but Heinlein, with his *Stranger In A Strange Land.* Nothing else has been both read widely enough and controversial enough. And I am fully aware that many other books may be more "artistic" works in the conventional sense. So is Cherryh, for Herrin Law's sculpture makes trouble only after it evokes intense personal reactions in its viewers. Perhaps she would agree with the more conventional view that the intensity of these personal reactions—the degree to which personal realities are changed—is more the key to a definition of art. I would be happier with such a definition myself. . . . Controversy, I suspect, really must be at least a part of any useful definition of art. (p. 164)

Tom Easton, in a review of "Wave without a Shore," in Analog Science Fiction/Science Fact, *Vol. CII, No. 4, March 29, 1982, pp. 162-64.*

K. SUE HURWITZ

Is the comical bipedal creature lurking around the loading docks at Meetpoint Station [in ***The Pride of Chanur***] a loose exotic pet, or a member of a newly discovered spacefaring species? When the crew of the hani ship *Pride of Chanur* take the strange being aboard, it is more because of their open rivalry and hatred of the sadistic "kif" who claim to own it, than for sympathy. But when the Tully-creature—who calls himself a "human"—throws himself on the mercy of the hani ship, he causes a space war that threatens the survival of the entire hani species and the balance of power among the five disparate species who make up the Compact.

This is a rousing good tale, and Cherryh's feisty hani are the most believable alien characters to come down the SF pike in a long time—a warlike, feline species whose social structure can best be called an Amazonian matriarchy. . . . [Older] teen readers will love them!

K. Sue Hurwitz, in a review of "The Pride of Chanur," in Kliatt Young Adult Paperback Book Guide, *Vol. XVI, No. 3, April, 1982, p. 19.*

ALGIS BUDRYS

Cherryh—Carolyn Cherryh—has become "family" [in the speculative fiction] establishment. Her qualities are presumed known and her loyalty is a matter of course. Newer faces, with fresh idiosyncrasies to be explored, attract attention away from the fact that her performance is not only frequent and consistent but also on a level of quality to which few writers will ever attain. If she published one book every two or three years, she'd be far better off in that respect, which tells you something about the correlation between being idolized and being good.

From the beginning of what is now a very long career, measuring in terms of noteworthy production rather than years, it's been obvious that she is possessed of major talent. An elegant prosaist, she is also an uncommonly deft storyteller with a very broad range of education and insight, a characterizer with no visible defects, and, of utmost importance in SF writing, strikingly capable of imagining and then of depicting what she has imagined. (pp. 33-4)

If, like me, you began to shy away from Cherryh's work a little not because it lacked virtues but because of what you told yourself was an inexplicable and undefined reluctance—meaning there were so many little reasons you couldn't come up with a clear one—let me direct you to ***The Pride of Chanur.*** It is an immensely successful piece of art.

Pyanfar Chanur is a merchant captain, a tough veteran of commerce across the gulfs of interstellar space, trafficking with alien races whose nature is far removed from hers. She, like her crew, is female and tigerish. The males of her race are too unstable to leave their home world, where they are constantly aggravated into near-psychosis by the territorial imperatives that have left her society an agglomeration of family holdings under constant internecine aggression.

Told entirely from Pyanfar's viewpoint, the story begins when, at a trading port far from home, she incurs the chillingly energetic enmity of the kif, a gray, self-righteous race. What has happened is that a hitherto unheard-of organism—a white, clawless, nearly hairless male named Tully—has escaped from the kif ship where it was being held captive and has sought shelter on board Pyanfar's vessel. It is helpless, starving, wounded, and unable to communicate in any civilized tongue. Pyanfar might give it back to the kif. But their reaction is so arrogant and so precipitous that this worthless thing takes on worth as a matter of pride.

And from there the story evolves. . . .

The feline alien is of course an SF staple. Frankly . . . , I am not beguiled by this device. As usually done, these aliens relate to actual felines about as well as Doctor Moreau's creations relate to humans. But I commend Pyanfar, and her crew and . . . family . . . to your attention. She would be an alien, yet a consistent and understandable alien, whether she had fur and claws or not. And an admirable one.

That goes without saying. The protagonist of an SF adventure story is bound to be admirable on some level. But how many do you find in the literature about whom you could then go on to write a complete biography? Cherryh does not tell us all that much about her Pyanfar's past or culture in so many words.

What she does do is create a complete being, in a completely realized and understandable social setting, while actually showing us little more than a few days in her life, and furthermore a few days in which she is almost invariably in a totally artificial environment. What Cherryh has done for us in relation to Pyanfar is essentially the obverse of what Pyanfar tries to do with Tully; understand this individual, and deduce empires from him, while at first knowing nothing about his context. (pp. 34-6)

Now this, I submit, is what we mean when we say *tour de force*. We say it too often. This book serves as a measure of how often we ought to say it. This is quintessential SF. Under the hardware and the galactic intrigue, under the fur and claws, under the glossary—measured out deftly now, and always to best effect—under the hurtling storyline brought to a controlled and satisfactory climax—is the probe into what is essential in self-aware life. This need not have been a major work of SF. Perhaps it had no ambitions to be one. . . . It needed only to be a plain tale plainly told. And that is what [***The Pride of Chanur***] is. (p. 36)

Algis Budrys, in a review of "The Pride of Chanur," in The Magazine of Fantasy and Science Fiction, *Vol. 63, No. 1, July, 1982, pp. 33-6.*

TOM EASTON

I don't think Carolyn Cherryh will want to argue with me when she reads this. I'm leading up, you see, to telling you that she has given us an alien psychology story, and she has done it the hard way, and she has done a grand job. It's ***The Pride of Chanur,*** whose sole human being we never really get to know. He's there, yes, but he doesn't speak the language(s) and he show us little more than a ready intelligence and a very arboreal strength. . . . (pp. 125-26)

The story begins at Meetpoint Station, an interspecies trading post, where Pyanfar Chanur's *Pride of Chanur* is docked. A critter sneaks aboard, hairless and clad only in a ragged loin-wrap. Pyanfar shelters the strange being from the barbarous kif, who claim ownership. . . .

[Pyanfar's species, called the hani,] look rather like lions, with their feline heads and golden manes. The likeness is hard to miss, although Cherryh does not make it too obvious. . . . Cherryh deftly understates as she portrays her aliens with her own inimitable skill. The hani are truly alien, for all their Earthly model, and one can indeed identify with them. It is a mark of Cherryh's success that here it is the human who seems the alien, though one gets the feeling that hani and human should get along very well.

But Cherryh has not only done a swell job of alien invention. Tully is also a center of excellence, for his situation rings very true. He and his shipmates were captured by the kif, who killed all but Tully in their effort to learn of Earth. Tully played dumb for them, escaped, found the more sympathetic hani—the only aliens at Meetpoint who laughed—and turned cooperative. At story's end, a foreshadowed *deus ex machina* returns him to his own and promises an era of mutual benefit for humans and hani. Yet Tully is mainly a stimulus for events, not a hero, and the happy ending is none of his devising. He is powerless and desperate among the aliens, and both he and Cherryh know it. It is very much to Cherryh's credit that she refrained from a story of false superheroism of the sort we see too often from other pens.

Need I add that I greatly enjoyed ***The Pride of Chanur***? . . . I think you will enjoy it too. (p. 126)

Tom Easton, in a review of "The Pride of Chanur," in Analog Science Fiction/Science Fact, *Vol. CII, No. 8, August, 1982, pp. 125-26.*

MICHAEL W. McCLINTOCK

Merchanter's Luck is a good representative of Cherryh's craftsmanship, though it's a smaller novel than its predecessor, ***Downbelow Station,*** the 1982 Hugo winner, and hasn't the absorbing complexities of some of her other work, such as the Faded Sun trilogy or ***Wave Without a Shore.*** Set in the same future history as ***Downbelow Station*** but a few years later, ***Merchanter's Luck*** tells of a poor but not especially honest young business man trying to survive amid the chancy politics of a culture in transition. Sandor Kreja, as a child, saw most of his family murdered by the Earth Company fleet, men and ships abandoned by Earth and turned pirate. Managing to retain his own ship, a small tramp freighter, he ekes out a living in the byways of commerce among the great space stations of Union, the interstellar civilization grown independent of Earth. He survives by skill, subterfuge, luck, and a bitter refusal to trust anyone.

But Sandor, lonely and still young, meets Allison Reilly, a favored daughter of a powerful merchanter family. He follows her to Pell Station, the newly independent buffer between Union and Earth. . . . Inadvertently and unwittingly, they become enmeshed in the maneuverings of Signy Mallory, the warship commander working for Pell and fighting her old comrades, the renegade Company fleet. Action ensues.

Part of the interest of reading Cherryh, besides enjoying her abilities in respect of narrative and characterization, arises from the care and intelligence with which she develops details of her settings. That density of specification is the only noteworthy difficulty with ***Merchanter's Luck:*** it's useful, though not strictly necessary, to be acquainted already with ***Downbelow Station.*** But that's hardly an adverse criticism, because it's a pleasure to become acquainted with any and all of Cherryh's novels. (pp. 16-17)

Michael W. McClintock, "Merchanter's Luck," in Science Fiction & Fantasy Book Review, *No. 8, October, 1982, pp. 16-17.*

MARY T. BRIZZI

In early science fiction, female characters were absent or poorly portrayed. Even women science fiction writers created mostly male protagonists while using females as symbols or archetypes rather than interesting, complex identification-figures. But with the recognition that women read science fiction, and that one appeal of the genre is identification with the main character, writers began to use epic heroines as protagonists.

C. J. Cherryh, however, does something novel. She portrays men who, though they have many virtues of their own, are rather more yielding, who defer to their ladies' judgement, who often must be rescued, who are at times used sexually, and who sometimes even worship the lady. . . . Cherryh is making more than a feminist statement about the potentialities of women raised in the expectation of being strong, courageous leaders. She is also making a statement about the complementary nature of feminine and masculine characteristics, showing that a whole human personality must exhibit both types of qualities. (p. 32)

Hunter of Worlds is a densely written study of cultural values, linguistics, and biology. . . . [Moreover], the novel examines the cultural impact of the ecological role a species may have had before it evolved to sentience. Four sentient species interact in the novel: humanity, amaut, kallia, and iduve. Amaut are a phlegmatic farming race. Kallia are blue, with white hair, possessing a highly evolved social structure where propriety and dignity are paramount. Culturally the most alien group—in spite of their feline beauty with amethyst eyes, indigo skin, and superhuman strength—are the masters of the galaxy, the iduve.

Cherryh, whose field is linguistics, devotes most of her nine-page glossary to the iduve language. . . . While human, amaut, and kalliran languages are based on subject-predicate structure, the iduve language is based on Tangibles and Ethicals: what is and what it should become. This reflects the evolutionary origin of the iduve: predators. A result in linguistic terms (Cherryh gives many) is that there is no iduve word for *love*. . . . The nearest approach to *love* is *m'melakhia,* or desire for acquisition. (pp. 32-3)

The iduve live, not planet-bound, but in huge ships, or *akitomei,* which rove the galaxy bringing civilization and terror to the other three races. Chimele, *orithain* (captain) of the *akites Ashanome,* needs to bring vengeance (rough translation of the iduve *vaikka*) upon her stepbrother Tejef. To help her, she kidnaps a kallia aristocrat, Aiela, to flush Tejef out of his hideout on a human-populated world, Priamos. The relationship between Chimele, an epic heroine, and Aiela, a helpful male, clearly reflects role reversal in this novel.

Chimele, the epic heroine, is placed in a natural leadership role. Aiela, the helpful male, is also a spaceship captain, but early in the novel he is stripped of his kalliran prerogatives and made Chimele's bondsman or *nas-kame*. Even Aiela's name creates the initial expectation of a female character, because it ends in *-a,* which is often a feminine suffix in human languages. Aiela's bondage to Chimele is expressed in terms parallel to a wife's bondage in western civilization. He wears the *idoikkhe,* a jeweled bracelet that communicates commands and punishments. Kings historically bestowed neck, finger, and arm rings upon their thanes to symbolize mutual obligation and privilege. . . . Chimele establishes such a bond with an arm ring, except that the roles are reversed: she commands, while he obeys.

Other characteristics are also reversed with respect to our culture's traditional sex roles. Chimele is physically stronger than Aiela, so much so that the sting of the idoikkhe is a protection of Aiela—she uses a shock to punish him, else her blows might cripple or kill. Chimele, like all iduve, is incapable of weeping; Aiela weeps on many occasions. Chimele is more rational than Aiela. She controls those few emotions she shares with humans—anger, for instance. Softer, more "feminine" emotions she lacks entirely. Her race has no concept of romantic love; Aiela, in contrast, carries pictures of the fiancée he will never see again. Nor do the iduve know the maternal instinct. They do experience a kind of insanity, *dhisais,* during late pregnancy, but only in particular females does this last past childbirth, then manifesting in terrifying ways quite alien to maternal feelings in human mothers. (pp. 33-4)

Yet Chimele retains a feminine aura—her beauty and seeming delicacy are emphasized in every physical description. . . . Her gestures are feminine, almost feline: she dismisses people with a wave of her hand; she touches things "with a violet nail"; she raises her brows ironically; she hisses softly.

Aiela, in contrast, is almost a perfect British gentleman, broad shouldered and slim-hipped, with physical courage surprising even Chimele. . . . These techniques build a picture of these two, who reverse traditional role expectations, as biologically male and female. . . .

[***Hunter of Worlds***] illuminates the relation of sex roles to culture, evolution, and language. In consequence, it has convincing texture; the reader gets lost in the reality of Cherryh's characters and her world. This, to my mind, reflects her ability to portray both male and female characters, masculine and feminine personality traits. Role reversal contributes to these effects rather than diluting them. (p. 35)

Among novels of supreme feminine power, ***Serpent's Reach*** surely tops the list. What more matriarchal life forms are there than ants and bees? The dominant life form of the Hydris planets is the majat, large sentients who live in hives ruled by a Mother, with a social structure similar to ants or bees. When humans come to their home planet, the majat are distressed because the death of a single human is the cessation of an individual consciousness, a situation impossible with their group mind. They finally agree to allow one family, the Kontrins, to live in the system and manage trade relations with the Outside. Horrified by the concept of death to sentient memories, the majat use biochemical expertise to grant immortality to each Kontrin. The protagonist, Raen, is the last scion of the most favored branch of the Kontrins. Raen, an epic heroine, embodies many fantasies of feminine power.

As a Kontrin, Raen is potentially immortal. At the beginning of the novel, her immediate family, the Sul-Meth-maren, is wiped out by dissident Kontrins. Only fifteen years old, she leads a retaliatory raid against her enemies, killing some. This act of derring-do fails, but through the intervention of another powerful and scheming Kontrin female, Moth, Raen inherits the enormous wealth of her family and tours the Hydri system.

Almost a female James Bond, she is an expert at all martial arts; the first time we see her, she is practicing her marksmanship. She is cosmopolitan, sophisticated, even a bit jaded, not just a world traveler, but a planet-hopper. . . . Like Bond, she is the object of many assassination attempts, which she foils with humor and ease. Like Bond, she is susceptible to the charms of the opposite sex, but unwilling to regard her exploits as anything more than recreation. Some of her partners are enemies, some simply innocent bystanders. (pp. 35-6)

But there are no goddesses without mere mortals to lord it over. The Kontrin family have tricked the majat by importing millions of human ova to be raised as servants. These are the beta, mortals living in a capitalistic mercantile society not unlike our own. The betas, in turn, created the azi, sterile slaves who die at age forty. . . . Though they are used for any unpleasant work, including soldiering . . . , they generally perform "feminine" tasks: nurturing children, cooking, cleaning, organizing and maintaining a home.

Jim, Raen's helpful male, is an azi. A well-trained entertainer and servant, he is owned by a shipping company and meets Raen as she voyages to Istra. As a male Cinderella figure, he represents the emotional and physical gratifications women generally give to men, except that Jim's and Raen's roles are reversed. (pp. 36-7)

Jim is a fantasy "wife" to Raen. Upon winning him at the gaming tables, she immediately tries him out in bed. Finding him satisfactory, she then amuses herself by buying him expensive adornments. . . . When Raen acquires her new estate, she puts him in charge of the house computer that maintains it. He is condemned through inbred genetic fault to die at forty—but after all, are there any women over forty in James Bond movies? Until then, he is supposed to provide Raen with bedtime companionship.

What goes on in the mind of this wifely paragon? Like the stereotyped repressed female, Jim is awed by Raen. Sex is not important to him, but he craves physical contact. He is terrified that something will happen to this godlike female protector. When she attempts to entertain him with Deepstudy tapes, he tries to memorize them to please her. When she is gone, he winds down like a clockwork doll, catatonic. His training, like that of the traditional super-feminine women, has been directed at making him the perfect slave. . . . You could be sorry for him if his passivity were not so infuriating.

Cherryh does give him one spark of initiative. When Raen leaves to fight evil Kontrins, he sits around wringing his hands until things get out of control. Then he actually disobeys her. She has left certain forbidden tapes, containing sensitive material on Kontrin history. Though previously it has been a big effort for him to overcome his conditioning enough to call her by her first name, he finally audits the tapes and discovers how to protect himself and her from the murderous Pol Hald. (pp. 37-8)

At the end of the book, Raen and Jim are seen as a nouveau Adam and Eve without the Fall, having survived many human generations as an immortal pair. . . . Jim is Raen's carbon copy, except submissive. (p. 38)

In ***Serpent's Reach,*** all the unpleasant tasks traditionally assigned to females have been transferred to azi, leaving Kontrins and rich betas to playboy freedom. When the hives go through the destructive end of their cycle, however, the rich and powerful are destroyed. Life is restored to those that can both command and serve—run farms, work in fields, bear and raise children. . . . Raen gives the message to beta farmers: the slaves will die, never to be replaced. Be independent, have children, and look to the future. Above all, do not enslave yourself or look to masters for salvation. A stratified society of privilege versus slavery will not endure. Only those who can fulfill a variety of roles, both master and servant, both masculine and feminine, will survive in the long run.

Melein, central figure in the Faded Sun trilogy, is the most exalted epic heroine in Cherryh's work. Young, brilliant, gifted with second sight, she leads an entire race, the mri, to salvation. Niun, her brother, follows her in social rank, lacking her vision and knowledge. Sten Duncan, the human who renounces humanity to follow Melein, is another helpful male. At times Melein assumes a Christlike role in ***The Faded Sun: Kesrith, The Faded Sun: Shon'jir,*** and ***The Faded Sun: Kutath.***

The mri are mercenary soldiers who at the beginning of ***Kesrith*** are about to leave the service of the regul, another alien race who have hired them in unsuccessful wars against humanity. Attractive, golden-complexioned humanoids, mri are fierce, proud, and unyielding in war, and secretive about their language and tribal life. The regul, in contrast, are blubbery beings who establish gender only at puberty, about age thirty. Until then, they may be casually killed by a parent or other adult with no sanction. Ethics and imagination are foreign concepts to the regul, but they do have total recall. The regul, having made peace with humankind, cold-bloodedly slaughter all their remaining mri allies, an act of genocide supposedly showing goodwill toward the human victors. Surviving, however, are Melein and Niun, brother and sister, mri priestess (*she'pan*) and warrior (*kel'en*). Given a ship and a human captive, Sten Duncan, they make a journey (*shon'jir*) of over a hundred dead planets to their world of origin, Kutath, where other mri survive. The regul trail them and try to destroy all remaining mri, but ultimately humans save the mri and establish friendship.

Cherryh frequently uses alien civilizations to explore gender-linked role assignment. So with regul and mri. Regul, because they do not know what sex they will be until they reach adulthood and have completed their education, are free of early gender-bound conditioning. Some top regul officials are female. While humans in the abstract are called *man* and referred to as *he,* youngling regul are called *it,* cancelling the sexual bias of language. (pp. 39-40)

Mri have potential for more sympathetic characters. They have a matriarchal civilization, with a she'pan at the head of each house and of the whole race. Under her are the Sen, scholars who can be either sex; the Kel, warriors also of either sex; and the Kath, children and nurturing women. The whole tribe, therefore, is subordinate to a woman. The she'pan and the Sen, because they are the sole repositories of literacy and learning, make all tribal decisions. Unlike the regul, the matriarchal mri are capable of imagination and vision.

Melein is a superwoman. But Cherryh first allows the reader to absorb the regul prejudice against the mri, considered "bloody-handed savages" incapable of learning, trade, or even subsistence farming. Mri civilization is conservative. . . . Sheltered in this "backward" culture of mud towers and illiteracy is the fragile, protected Melein. She and Niun even refuse medical aid when she breaks a rib during the regul attack. . . . Cannily figuring out that she and Niun have been given a ship so that humans and regul can track them to their planet of origin and destroy them all, she takes her only option, brainwashing Duncan, the human, into becoming her kel'en. Thus he, a human agent, becomes an additional weapon in her hands. (pp. 40-1)

Intelligence, risk-taking, and courage are often qualities ascribed more to males than females. And Melein has another "masculine" quality, her aloofness. The rarity of her moments of honor-giving, touching, or kissing make her more male. All these male qualities are underlined by characteristic technique of never using Melein as point-of-view character. Her thoughts are concealed or inaccurately interpreted through Niun and Duncan.

Niun also reverses traditional sex role assignments. Melein is allowed to read and write, but he is not. Though he is the leader of her Kel, he must ask permission to ask permission to ask a question of her. In ***Kesrith,*** he has no idea of her plan for mri destiny. . . . Coupled with this naïveté is humility. He is forbidden to think of Melein as his sister. She is the she'pan, ultimate authority. . . .

Duncan, the human who turns mri, feels even more humble. When Duncan agrees to turn mri, Niun disposes of all his human property, even medical supplies, and forbids him human language and literacy. (p. 41)

Duncan, too, has Christlike qualities. In ***Kutath,*** we learn his middle initial, X, a cross. . . . In ***Shon'jir,*** he is taken to a high place—human ships—and tested, as Christ was . . . in Matthew.

But Melein's Messianic qualities are more extensive. [Her title, she'pan] implies a female (*she-*) Body of Christ (*pan*). Her surname, *Zain-Abrin,* echoes *Zion* and *Abram.* She wears white robes and often sits with her followers at her feet, as in portraits of Christ. Her ritual scars resemble stigmata. (p. 42)

As she'pan, death is taboo to her, as Christ overcame death. Her weeping when she recovers the Pana, with Duncan and Niun waiting, following Intel's "Last Supper" and before her capture has overtones of Gethsemane. Wounded in the side, as Christ was pierced after crucifixion, she lies in a coma, as if dead. When "resurrected," she puts on white robes and becomes leader of all mri. From Duncan she demands, as Christ demanded of his disciples, that he leave everything to follow her. On Kutath, she is accused of consorting with tsi-mri, aliens, as Christ was accused of consorting with publicans and sinners. But before the instruments of Ah'ehon, she is transfigured in light. (pp. 42-3)

Though the strongest of Cherryh's epic heroines, Melein does not overshadow Niun and Duncan. They, too, have strength and ingenuity, strong Hands, though she is Head. Melein has been a member of all three castes, Kath, Kel, and Sen. She encompasses and contains all. But the structure of mri society emphasizes the need for different qualities—"male" and "female"—for a superior personality like Melein's. Divinity itself is not all male, but partakes of the feminine as well. It takes Head, Hand, and Heart to make a whole being.

The medieval romance background of the Morgaine trilogy, ***Gate of Ivrel, Well of Shiuan,*** and ***Fires of Azeroth,*** is suggested in the earth, air, water, and fire in the titles. Cherryh's epic heroine in the trilogy is Morgaine, and her helpful male is Vanye. (p. 43)

Morgaine's heroism is of character, not supernormal powers. Like Melein, she has superior technical knowledge and carries with her a laser gun, antibiotics, and Changeling, a sword which utilizes Gate power to throw things in its field into a distant space-time. She is also quick of apprehension, brave in battle, dedicated, a good horsewoman, and a canny bargainer. . . . She exhibits feminine charm and humor in her fastidious roasting of game, which contrasts amusingly to the studied masculine poses she assumes before her enemies, and her courteous suggestion that Vanye be not "overnice" in sharing her bed reflects cozy companionability. (pp. 43-4)

Like sword-and-sorcery, the trilogy draws on medieval romance, particularly the Grail legend—but in an inverted way. Morgaine and Vanye are knight and squire . . . , but the twist is that the knight or king figure is Morgaine, female. Like King Arthur, she wields a magic sword. . . . Like Gawain, whose name hers echoes, she is on a quest to save the land. (p. 44)

Vanye has qualities traditionally assigned to women. Illegitimate child of a woman dead in childbirth, he has been raised where he is considered second best. He strives to earn adult privileges, but when, in late adolescence, he slays his brother in self-defense, he is cast out by his father when he refuses to save his honor by killing himself. Branded a coward, he is set out with no means of livelihood and finally taken up by Morgaine. Like an unwanted female child in a male-oriented world, he turns to a protector—not a husband, but a female.

Morgaine claims Vanye as ilin by slashing his hand and tasting his blood—a parody of the blood-show of a virginal wedding night. She smears her hearth-ash into the wound, reminder of household duties. He is then bound to obey her. . . . Their role reversal is symbolized in ***Azeroth*** by her riding a stallion and him riding a mare. (pp. 44-5)

Another inversion involves the attitude toward good and evil. Morgaine is really a public-spirited heroine, devoted to saving a whole universe from the disasters of time paradox from the Gates. But everywhere, legends of Morgaine depict her as an evil witch. . . .

The qhal suffer similar bad press, with more injustice. In Ivrel, they are body snatchers, creators of monsters. In Shiuan, they are effete, decadent lords. In Azeroth, however, we see their potential for good—Merir and his court, like good fairies or the Round Table, protect humankind and tend the forest like a garden. . . . The whole movement of the trilogy is from opposing dualities, good and evil, male and female, mad and sane, qual and human, showing that blending or pairing of opposites will result in the best outcome. (p. 45)

[A reconciliation of opposites] occurs in Vanye. At the beginning, Vanye's father hacks off Vanye's hair to show loss of honor. Further humiliation comes with Vanye's service to Morgaine. But at the end of the trilogy, Morgaine helps him braid up the grown-out hair again, restoring honor, and this intimate service makes them more than kin, resolved polarities, male and female in transcendent partnership. . . . (p. 46)

Vivid characterization, indeed the sheer variety and number of characters in each novel, are a keystone to Cherryh's success. And basic to this success is her unconventional treatment of male and female personality traits. Her epic heroines are unswerving, rational, godly, dominant; her helpful males are confused, faulted, submissive, and emotional, opposite to traditional roles. She challenges male and female stereotypes, drawing compellingly original and convincing portraits. Role-reversed pairs make a statement about the complementary nature of "feminine" and "masculine" traits, suggesting that a whole personality must partake of both qualities. A symbol of this type of personal integration occurs in ***Wave without a Shore,*** with the ahnit statue of two lovers, which seems to lack a third figure—but, as Sbi explains, the third figure, the lovers' child, is the viewer himself or herself, who creates his or her own identity and reality out of the polarities of male and female in his or her culture. What appears, in Cherryh's books with epic heroines, to be superficially a feminist statement about the heroic possibilities of females and the helping possibilities of males is actually a more profound, but still feminist, statement about the creative androgyny of the human spirit. (pp. 46-7)

Mary T. Brizzi, "C. J. Cherryh and Tomorrow's New Sex Roles," in The Feminine Eye: Science Fiction and the Women Who Write It, *edited by Tom Staicar, Frederick Ungar Publishing Co., 1982, pp. 32-47.*

PUBLISHERS WEEKLY

[***The Dreamstone***] is set in an ancient time when humans have almost completed their domination of the Earth and magic has all but left the land. One last magic place remains, the forest Ealdwood, which cannot be entered unless the spirits allow it. Into Ealdwood comes Niall Cearbhallain, fleeing for his life from the traitors who have killed his king. And shortly after follows his comrade Caoimhin, to persuade him to return and defend the land for the infant king who is being raised in secrecy. A harpist also comes to the forest, and becomes the companion of Arafel, the guardian of Ealdwood, who has lost her stone of power. The harpist sacrifices his life to regain it. Niall is moved by this to return to the fight, to defeat the traitors that are even then whittling away at Ealdwood. This is a beautifully told tale, reminiscent of Dunsany, and fully the equal of Cherryh's SF.

A review of "The Dreamstone," in Publishers Weekly, *Vol. 223, No. 4, January 28, 1983, p. 83.*

SUSAN L. NICKERSON

In 1981 Cherryh wrote a short fantasy, ***Ealdwood,*** . . . . Expanded to full length as ***The Dreamstone,*** it is the haunting tale of Arafel, last of the Sidhes, and guardian spirit of Ealdwood. . . . Arafel becomes entangled in several mortal affairs, helping men to escape Lord Death, while defending one of the last enclaves of Faery against modern depradations. Cherryh has done a marvelous job of investing her tale with a chilly glamour unlike the kindly magic of most fairytales, and Arafel is a complex and unforgettable character. (pp. 603-04)

Susan L. Nickerson, in a review of "The Dreamstone," in Library Journal, *Vol. 108, No. 6, March 15, 1983, pp. 603-04.*

PAUL GRANAHAN

[A] pure fantasy, [***The Dreamstone***] is a departure for Cherryh but bears forth her talent no less than her science fiction. It is the tale of the last stronghold of Faery against the cold iron of upstart Man, the forest of Ealdwood, and of its lone remaining guardian, Arafel of the Elder Folk, the Daoine Sidhe. Although the rest of her kindred have faded to some other realm sickened by the encroachments of mortals, Arafel stays, unwilling to relinquish her home. . . . Arafel recaptures both joy and heartbreak long forgotten.

Cherryh's versatility is again manifest in this enthralling saga rooted in Celtic lore. Her elves are not diminutive sprites but unearthly powers capable of haughty cruelty and of a nobility alien to human ken. My only complaint is the unfortunate brevity of the novel—the reader is not allowed nearly enough time with her characters and world. On the other hand, the brevity conveys something of Arafel's perspective regarding the fleeting lives of mayfly humans. Cherryh remains a personal favorite whose future works will surely reflect her growing skill.

Paul Granahan, in a review of "The Dreamstone," in Best Sellers, *Vol. 43, No. 1, April, 1983, p. 48.*

TOM EASTON

C. J. Cherryh has tried something interesting, but only partially successful, in ***Port Eternity***. . . . [Lady Dela Kirn] has a fancily decorated starship, the *Maid of Avalon,* staffed with "made people," clones programmed for their duties. She has given them names from Arthurian legend. . . . Her maid, Elaine, is the narrator. At the start, that is as far as the Arthurian parallel goes. But Elaine has borrowed her mistress's taped dramatization of an Arthurian poem. She knows what her name means and the role she stands for. Her fellows are still ignorant.

And then the ship falls into a strange, inescapable place beyond normal space. It docks with a mysterious object that may be a station, for it is festooned with alien ships. Noises assault the hull. Her fellows experience the tape, and conflicts of role, of dream and reality, emerge. In the end, the tape-defined roles help their adaptation to the future.

Strange setting and event interfere here more than they should with what seems clearly meant as a novel of character. (Or is it an allegory of fandom?) The problem, I think, is that the characters do not live as they do in other Cherryh novels. They lack vitality, urgency, motivation. Their pasts are too skimpy, their programming too dominant, at least at first. They are machines (archetypes) groping for life in a way we lack the experience to understand.

If this view is Cherryh's intent, she succeeded. However, I—and presumably you—am not enchanted by tales that, intentionally or not, leave me dissatisfied, groping in a fog of uncertainty or irresolution. As an allegory—and I hesitate to come right out and call it one—it would please me better. (pp. 109-10)

Tom Easton, in a review of "Port Eternity," in Analog Science Fiction/Science Fact, *Vol. CIII, No. 6, June, 1983, pp. 109-10.*

SUSAN L. NICKERSON

Continuing the austere and chilling story begun in ***The Dreamstone,*** Cherryh presents [in ***The Tree of Swords and Jewels***] the further depletion of Faery in the world. Arafel the Sidhe, poisoned by her evil cousin, cannot save the Man whom she had taken under her protection in the earlier novel. Ciaran Cuilean, now lord of Caer Wiell for years, is afraid for the safety of his two children, who, like him, have Elvish blood. . . . Cherryh masterfully invests the narrative with anguish.

Susan L. Nickerson, in a review of "The Tree of Swords and Jewels," in Library Journal, *Vol. 108, No. 14, August, 1983, p. 1506.*

PUBLISHERS WEEKLY

Set in the same future history as 1981's Hugo-winning ***Downbelow Station*** . . . but fully self-contained, [***Forty Thousand in Gehenna***] is a story on the classic theme of human underestimation of the alien. The 40,000 colonists on Gehenna, most of them heavily conditioned, genetically perfected clones, are abandoned for political reasons. . . . Over a period of 200 years, the descendants of the colonists who couldn't impose Terran conditions on Gehenna become a part of Gehennan ecology themselves, by entering a partnership with the planet's native intelligence—the lizardlike, burrowing calibans. Cherryh tantalizes our minds with these enigmatic aliens, captures our hearts with her characters and involves us completely with her mix of broad and narrow views of a new culture's rise. Once again, Cherryh proves herself a consistently thoughtful and entertaining writer. (pp. 51-2)

A review of "Forty Thousand in Gehenna," in Publishers Weekly, *Vol. 224, No. 11, September 9, 1983, pp. 51-2.*

TOM EASTON

Forty Thousand in Gehenna is set in the universe of ***Downbelow Station*** and other novels. Like them, it stands completely alone; the connection is one of history and context. Unlike them, this one spans centuries, for it is the tale of a colony's development. Gehenna is a world to which 452 standard humans and 41,911 lab-born, tape-programmed *azis* are shipped as colonists. There they meet the calibans, dragon-like mound-builders who prove intelligent in a peculiar way: the calibans think less in words than in patterns, and they "talk" by constructing patterns of mounds across the countryside.

The colony is promptly abandoned. . . . The calibans destroy it. The colonists lose their technology. Some struggle on amid the ruins. Some take to the woods. Some, the Weirds, move into the mounds with the calibans. In time, there develops a sort of social symbiosis between the two species, and a new civilization begins to form, built on a new way of processing information. . . . The end product seems a new element for Cherryh's universe, and one she may be able to use to good effect in future books.

Gehenna is long and slow, and I'm sure it will bore many in its present form. Nevertheless, Cherryh has worked out her vision well, with her usual skill at presenting truly alien aliens. She does not always convince me that the calibans' way of thinking would work as well as she says it does, but the book is still satisfying and rewarding. (pp. 163-64)

Tom Easton, in a review of "Forty Thousand in Gehenna," in Analog Science Fiction/Science Fact, *Vol. CIII, No. 11, October, 1983, pp. 163-64.*

PAULA NESPECCA DEAL

[In ***The Tree of Swords and Jewels*** the] powers of darkness and destruction, long ago chained, are escaping and preparing to destroy the human world and the magical forest of Eald. The last daoine sidhe, or fairy folk, Arafel, who guards the forest joins forces with Lord Ciaran Cuilean who once broke her heart. Ciaran must leave his castle, wife and children to battle his jealous brother who has loosed the evil. As Arafel's powers fade, Ciaran struggles to save himself and the world.

This well-crafted story has a fully developed setting, interesting characters, epic battles and believable magic. . . . Since the story can be confusing when the characters travel between worlds and the pace is slow, reserve this for older, better YA readers that are ready for a complex fantasy.

Paula Nespecca Deal, in a review of "The Tree of Swords and Jewels," in Voice of Youth Advocates, *Vol. 6, No. 6, February, 1984, p. 342.*

PUBLISHERS WEEKLY

[***Voyager in Night*** is] a novel of little distinction that reads like a rejected script from some 1960s television show. Instead of describing the aliens or their interplay with the humans they encounter, Cherryh's E.T.s bottle up their three human captives and create replicas of each in order to test and understand them. This means a long, desultory talkfest among the growing company. . . . The aliens themselves are not given names but typographical symbols, which further confuses the story, as they argue over what to do with the humans. This is all thoroughly familiar. (pp. 111-12)

A review of "Voyager in Night," in Publishers Weekly, *Vol. 225, No. 10, March 9, 1984, pp. 111-12.*

CAROLYN WENDELL

[***Voyager in Night***] deals with an alien encounter: a tiny prospector ship is crashed into by a ship so large and inhuman that it is called a "bogey." The three humans are injured, then painfully examined and used by the resident alien.

Cherryh has tried typographical symbols rather than letters to represent alien characters, but by the time you figure out who's who, you don't much care what's what. If her novels occasionally seem to be unsuccessful experiments, we can assume that she will succeed in doing what she has done before—create worlds and beings so vivid that the page cannot contain them. . . . [The] characters and settings of ***Voyager in Night*** remain imprisoned on the page.

Carolyn Wendell, "Cherryh Seduced by Philosophical Abstractions," in Fantasy Review, *Vol. 7, No. 9, October, 1984, p. 26.*

TOM EASTON

C. J. Cherryh's ***Voyager in Night*** is set in her universe of merchants and stations. It begins as Station Endeavour is being built. To the site swarm thousands of tiny, obsolete ships and their hopeful crews. Among them are Rafe and Jillan Murphy and Jillan's husband Paul. As they seek out the ores the growing station needs, they are kidnapped by an alien ship, an intimidating colossus that has been voyaging for 100 millennia and lacks all fleshly crew.

Paul and Jillan die. Rafe lives, and then he meets his sister and brother-in-law again, as holograms. They have been recorded in the ship's computer as "artificial intelligence" programs. Do they deserve the label "human"? This is Cherryh's question. . . . She also considers the question of identity as she shows us multiple hologram characters, copies of the programs, each with its own consciousness, differing only in when the program was made or how long it has been running.

As usual, Cherryh is highly competent, thoughtful, and absorbing. If ***Voyager*** is not one of her better books, that is only because she does so well so often.

Tom Easton, in a review of "Voyager in Night," in Analog Science Fiction/Science Fact, *Vol. CIV, No. 11, November, 1984, p. 167.*

RAYMOND H. THOMPSON

Cherryh is an award-winning author with a talent for portraying the effects of stress upon personality. She typically takes a small group of characters, disrupts their familiar routine by placing them in a crisis situation, then examines how they react under pressure. This is precisely what she does in ***Port Eternity:*** a private space craft is marooned in another dimension where its occupants find themselves threatened by aliens.

Their anxiety is heightened by the nature of the staff and crew of the vessel. They are "made people," cloned from special genetic combinations, then conditioned with "deepteach" tapes to create a special "psych-set." These "made people" are "sold out" to "born people" when ready at sixteen or eighteen, and "put down" when they pass forty years of age. The sole reason for their existence is to serve their owners, and their programming is so tight that they have very little freedom of choice. Thus when confronted with a crisis that is outside their limited range of experience, they have great difficulty in handling it. However, in this it turns out that they are not so different from the born people, who experience equal difficulty in coping with the unexpected. Cherryh thus reveals the extent to which we are all the product of our innate tendencies, developed in certain directions by our specific experience of life. We have little real freedom of choice, because we react as our personalities dictate. . . . (p. 80)

What serves to throw this scrutiny of human conditioning into focus is the Arthurian element. Influenced by Tennyson's *Idylls of the King,* Dela, the wealthy owner of the craft which she named "Maid of Astolat," has decorated the interior "in a strange mix of old fables and shipboard modern.". . . But her fantasy extends beyond furnishings to the made people who serve her. There are seven of them, and all have been modeled upon characters in Tennyson's poem: the pilots are Gawain and Lynette; the engineers are Percivale and Modred; the accountant is Vivien; the household is run by Lancelot; and Lady Dela's personal servant, and the narrator of the novel, is Elaine (of Astolat). On this journey, as on so many others, they "play out the old game" . . . , the familiar and comfortable Arthurian fantasy created by their owner. But this escapist fantasy entangles her as well. . . . Even her born-men guests are drawn into the fantasy. Thus Dela behaves often like an imperious Queen Guenevere, while Griffin, her lover and prospective husband, fills the role of an aggressive Arthur: even his name recalls Pendragon.

This familiar pattern is irrevocably shattered when they find themselves marooned in another dimension, and the crisis is complicated by the made people's discovery of their Arthurian personae. This exerts conscious pressure upon them to act out their traditional roles. . . . Much of this pressure comes because they begin to react to each other as to their legendary namesakes. Thus when Modred advises that they supply the aliens with complete information about themselves, they suspect that he wishes to betray them. . . . And because we tend to become what other people expect us to be, forced into the role by their attitude toward us, the illusion becomes the reality, the Arthurian persona takes over the original person. To survive, the humans need all their resources, but find instead that they are hindered by mistrust of one another, uncertain what to expect. Starting out as illusion, a game, an escapist fantasy, the Arthurian pattern gradually enmeshes the characters, becoming the reality.

Cherryh borrows not only characters from Tennyson's *Idylls of the King,* however, but the quotations that head each chapter also. These help to reveal that the plot structure is based upon an Arthurian pattern. Like Arthur and his court, the humans have achieved success in their world, and settled into a comfortable way of life; this ends abruptly, and they find themselves threatened by external invasion; but their resistance is weakened by internal dissension; they are overwhelmed in the last battle, which ends when their leader is carried off to the other world; he does not die there, but recovers. In this science-fictional Avalon, . . . the humans live out their Arthurian roles: Modred always devising new ideas; Vivien compiling careful records of what she finds out; Percivale discussing philosophy; Gawain and Lynette traveling widely throughout the land; Griffin and Dela (Arthur and Guenevere) living together in their Camelot; Lancelot, who loves them both, living finally with Elaine in a tower by the lake (del Lac?): "Whether we dream, still falling forever, or whether the dream has shaped itself about us, we love . . . at least we dream we do.". . . (pp. 80-2)

This conclusion underlines the final paradox of loss and gain in the novel. On one hand we witness the descent into complete illusion, into another world from which there is no return. Failure to return from the other world bearing the treasure of knowledge is a traditional signal of defeat in legend and folklore, a symbolic death. Thus despite the contentment of being with those one loves, there is also a lack of intensity about life in this other world. The fierce emotions of the struggle for survival prior to entry are gone, replaced by a dream-like detachment in a world outside time where nobody ages—or develops.

Yet Arthurian legend teaches us that this defeat is also a triumph. The aching loss of Arthur's glorious realm is balanced by the heroic achievement of those who strive against all odds to hold back the dark for a while. Their lives become an inspiration to those who follow, "something brighter and more vivid than ourselves.". . . In ***Port Eternity*** the humans rise above their limitations. Armed with only swords and their courage, they resist valiantly to the end, struggling against overwhelming odds and their own weaknesses. . . . Moreover, by conquering fear and doubt, they triumph. Their enemies become friends. From this point of view they have, in fact, become their heroic predecessors, resting in Avalon, the home of legend. . . . This is a complex novel that can be confusing at times, but its achievements are impressive, particularly the tight interdependence of setting, character, plot and theme, and the skilful use of Arthurian legend. (pp. 82-3)

Raymond H. Thompson, "Science Fiction and Science Fantasy," in his The Return from Avalon: A Study of the Arthurian Legend in Modern Fiction, *Greenwood Press, 1985, pp. 77-86.**

Arthur C(harles) Clarke

1917-

English novelist, short story writer, essayist, nonfiction writer, scriptwriter, and scientist.

Clarke is recognized as a major science fiction writer and as a distinguished author of nonfiction books on space travel and technology. All of Clarke's works reflect his expertise in the physical sciences and project his optimistic view that space exploration will yield great benefits for humankind. Like H. G. Wells and Olaf Stapledon, with whom he is often compared, Clarke displays faith that proper use of technology will effect a more harmonious civilization. Accordingly, Clarke's fictional works often present both proper and improper uses of technology. In much of his fiction, including his best-known novels, *Childhood's End* (1953), *2001: A Space Odyssey* (1968), and *2010: Odyssey Two* (1982), Clarke explores such themes as human contact with extraterrestrial life and mystic transcendence of knowledge.

A number of critics observe that Clarke's early science fiction works can be divided into two groups. In several of those works he concentrates on technology and space adventure, and in others he focuses on metaphysical themes. *Childhood's End,* which exemplifies Clarke's metaphysical interests, is generally considered his most significant early work. In this novel Clarke depicts an alien life force called the "Overlords," who visit Earth and serve to further the evolution of human intelligence. In a poignant climax, Clarke portrays the last generation of human children as they transcend their material existence and become part of a universal intelligence known as the "Overmind." Several critics have noted parallels between Clarke's Overmind and various Eastern and Western concepts of transcendentalism.

Photograph by Jay Kay Klein

Clarke gained wide recognition in 1968 with his novelization of the film *2001: A Space Odyssey.* Both the film and the novel are based on Clarke's short story "The Sentinel" (1951). In "The Sentinel" an astronaut speculates that aliens visited Earth in prehistoric times and left behind signalling devices that would advise them of the progress of human evolution. In *2001: A Space Odyssey,* huge black monoliths appear at various crucial stages of human evolution; the monoliths are generally interpreted as alien aids to human development or signalling devices similar to those depicted in "The Sentinel." The film version, on which Clarke collaborated with filmmaker Stanley Kubrick, is widely regarded as a landmark in science fiction cinema. It is praised for its symbolism, its lush images of space and technological gadgetry, and for the sundry implications that arise from Kubrick's disjointed development and deliberate mystification of themes. Clarke's novel, which appeared shortly after the film, has been praised for offering a clearer and more unified presentation of themes. Most critics agree that *2001: A Space Odyssey* will endure as a classic in both genres.

Clarke's later work includes the novels *Rendezvous with Rama* (1973) and *The Fountains of Paradise* (1979). The former centers on human exploration of an alien spacecraft and offers another of Clarke's speculations on the results of human contact with alien life. In *The Fountains of Paradise,* Clarke depicts a Godlike man who combines his intelligence with technological developments.

After having claimed on several occasions that a sequel to *2001: A Space Odyssey* would be an impossible undertaking, Clarke surprised readers and critics by publishing *2010: Odyssey Two.* Critical reception to this sequel is mixed; several critics conclude that Clarke compromises the symbolism and the mystique of his earlier work, in particular by explaining the meaning of the black monoliths. However, Clarke is praised for his inventive integration of new information on the planet Jupiter that had been compiled by NASA's Voyager Space Probe.

Clarke published several nonfiction works during the 1970s, among them *Report on Planet 3 and Other Speculations* (1973), which contains essays on various subjects related to modern physical science, and *The View from Serendip* (1977), a collection of pieces on a variety of topics. Clarke's nonfiction works as a whole, including *The Promise of Space,* which has been revised several times to include new developments in technology, are highly recommended for their clear and dynamic presentation of astronautics and aeronautics. In his recent nonfiction works *1984: Spring; a Choice of Futures* (1984) and *Profiles of the Future,* a revised version of several earlier editions of the same title, Clarke offers more of his intriguing and informed speculations on the future.

Clarke is also respected for his knowledge of physics and mathematics. During the 1940s he proposed a communications satellite that would orbit in synchronization with the rotation of the earth, thus allowing the satellite to maintain a stationary position above the earth. Such satellites are now widely utilized. Clarke is a former chairman of the British Interplanetary Society, and he worked as a commentator for the CBS television network during the Apollo lunar missions.

(See also *CLC*, Vols. 1, 4, 13, 18; *Contemporary Authors*, Vols. 1-4, rev. ed.; *Contemporary Authors New Revision Series*, Vol. 2; and *Something about the Author*, Vol. 13.)

WILLIAM BARRETT

Arthur C. Clarke in ***Profiles of the Future*** . . . seems to have not the least fear of the future as he paints a gaudy panorama of the dazzling technological world of tomorrow. Indeed, his rule seems to be that we can hardly be too imaginative in forecasting the future; what were once the marvels of Jules Verne are pretty prosaic stuff to us now. . . .

Mr. Clarke proceeds to entertain us with a whole circus of future marvels: cities with moving streets; vehicles and houses that ride on air; and degravitation appliances that overcome the force of gravity itself. . . .

Mr. Clarke is a witty and incisive writer, and he makes all these prospects plausible and exciting, until we begin to wonder what will become of man himself. We are not told that until the next to last chapter, whose ominous title, "The Obsolescence of Man," forebodes a catch to all these marvels. Machines are going to be so good, Mr. Clarke warns us, that in any war between man and machine you know who will get beaten. Maybe so; but this book might be a little less chilly if the author, just for the sake of auld lang syne, had thrown in with the losing side.

William Barrett, in a review of "Profiles of the Future," in The Atlantic Monthly, *Vol. 211, No. 4, April, 1963, p. 152.*

ISAAC ASIMOV

There are those to whom science fiction is nothing but a dreary catalogue of papier-maché monsters crunching down on matchstick reconstructions of the Golden Gate Bridge and the Empire State Building. There are others to whom it is but a slightly gaudier version of a western, with galloping spaceships and evil Martian uranium-rustlers. There are also those to whom science fiction offers a look into the murk of the future. To these last, Arthur C. Clarke belongs.

He has a thorough grounding in science, and, in addition, has a nimble and most receptive mind. Nothing reasonable frightens him simply because it seems fantastic, and—equally important—nothing foolish attracts him simply because it seems fantastic.

As concrete proof of his ability as a seer, it is generally accepted that Clarke, in 1948, was the first to suggest the use of satellites for long-distance communications. He did not build or launch Telstar, but he saw it in the sky years before anyone else did.

Now, in [**"Profiles of the Future"**], Clarke brings his mind to bear on the whole range of technological advance, suggesting directions in which it may move and the limits past which (according to the best of our present understanding) it cannot move. He begins in the necessary defensive (human beings being what they are) and devotes two chapters to the queer blind spots of the past. (p. 22)

Succeeding chapters are devoted to fields of technological advance. Transportation, for instance, is covered thoroughly, with consideration of such things as "ground effect machines" (automobiles riding on jets of compressed air), long-distance conveyor-belt roads, and plastic-sausage tankers being towed under the ocean by atomic subs. He does not stop at what, in the light of present-day knowledge, is sheer fairy-tale and magic, for he considers in detail the possibilities of anti-gravity and direct mass-transference. What makes Clarke's treatment so valuable, however, is that he explains just *why* we consider this sort of thing sheer fairytale and magic.

Clarke accepts the impossible, by our present lights, and admits the velocity of light to be an unbreakable limit to the speeds we may attain, and the laws of thermodynamics to set an unbreakable limit to the amount of energy we may obtain and utilize. He finds ample room for advance, however, within the limits of the possible. . . .

Later chapters are given over to the possible developments of robots and computers, which may yet become the intellectual companions as well as the servants of man. A final chart projects Clarke's estimate of the rate of future technological advance. He places planetary landings in 1980, the development of intelligent machines in 2000, with travel to the stars, the development of robots and the control of weather and of heredity by 2030. Past 2100, however, even Clarke doesn't dare try to guess.

With science and society changing as rapidly and as drastically as they are today, it still remains the almost universal tendency to regard the present as somehow fixed. This book offers all of us a chance to raise our eyes from the ground and to contemplate the scenery ahead. It is marvelous scenery indeed, and there could scarcely be a better guide to its landmarks than Arthur Clarke. (p. 24)

Isaac Asimov, "Miracles to Come," in The New York Times Book Review, *April 14, 1963, pp. 22, 24.*

ROBERT JASTROW

Any writer on scientific subjects for the layman must admire [Clarke] enormously for the clarity of his explanations of the technical mysteries of space flight. ***The Promise of Space*** heightens my own admiration; it is a revision of an earlier book [***The Exploration of Space***], augmented by a great deal of fascinating material on the scientific discoveries, technical developments, history and politics of the American and Russian space programs. The discussion of such matters as rocket propulsion, the reasons for building rockets in stages, and the factors that control escape from the earth are as clear as can be found anywhere; and the exposition is enlivened by many anecdotes from Clarke's full store of memories of these last eventful decades. There are excellent chapters on the planets—"children of the sun," Clarke calls them—and the prospects for life elsewhere. The completely nontechnical reader will want to skip over some portions of the chapters on the physics of the solar system and the detailed workings of rockets and satellites, but these are readily spotted and can be passed by without seriously disturbing the book's continuity. (p. 1)

Robert Jastrow, "Baby Steps from the Earth to the Stars," in Book World—The Washington Post, *June 30, 1968, pp. 1, 3.*

WILLY LEY

There are some people, including professors, publishers, reviewers, and N.A.S.A. officials, who feel that there are too many books on space travel. That may be a correct general observation; but the number of good ones is small, and even the good ones become slowly obsolescent. Therefore, notwithstanding the total number of space books, one that is up-to-date and good deserves a warm welcome.

I hardly need to say that Arthur C. Clarke's **"The Promise of Space"** fits this description; it is to be expected from the past activities of the author. . . .

The first section of the book, entitled simply "Beginnings," deals with the principles of rocket propulsion, rocket construction and the motions in space, with a little history thrown in where it illustrates a point. . . .

The sections following the first bear the titles "Around the Earth," "Around the Moon," "Around the Sun." I do not know whether Clarke, by using the "around" as the first word, tried to echo classical Greek treatises, the titles of which always begin with this word. I hope he did, but to readers without a classical background the titles are still meaningful: satellites go around the earth, lunar orbiters around the moon and planetary probes around the sun. All through the book Clarke not only recounts what has been done during the last two decades, but has his eye on both the immediate results and the future.

Naturally this results in a sprinkling of predictions. . . . Speaking of communication satellites he comes to the hopeful conclusion: "In the long run, the Comsat will be mightier than the ICBM." . . .

Since Clarke's book, of necessity, is wide-ranging, it is impossible to touch on every point worth mentioning. However, it is possible to summarize what it does: for the novice to the field it is a very fine introduction; for the "old hand" it contains bits of information and speculation that come as surprises. At any event it is worth the time spent in reading it, even worth the time for several rereadings.

Willy Ley, "Among the Stars," in The New York Times Book Review, *August 25, 1968, p. 10.*

EUGENE M. EMME

[Arthur Clarke's writings] have deep roots. His seminal paper **"Extraterrestrial relays"** (*Wireless World,* Oct. 1945), which he wrote as a recent radarman of the Royal Air Force and as a member of the British Interplanetary Society, well forecast the technical feasibility and utility of communications satellites. His influential ***Prelude to Space*** (1948), an engaging novel whose hero was a historian, was but one of the first of over a dozen nonfiction space and oceanology volumes. . . .

[***The Promise of Space***] provides a historical launching pad for its author's stimulating and biased projection of what today's space capabilities and potential could mean for the intellectual and practical affairs of mankind in the future. Clarke's history is brief, accurate, and vivid. Like James E. Webb, he delights in quoting Daniel Webster, who refused to vote a single cent for the opening up of the American West because it would always be a howling wilderness and no use to anyone but savages. (pp. 874-75)

Clarke is at his best in digesting the "first harvest" of gains in space science and technology during the past decade. . . . His four sections of four chapters each contain the best available summary of scientific and imaginative theory regarding space potentials: Around the Earth; Around the Moon; Around the Sun; and Around the Universe. Collectively they offer a most persuasive rationale, at least to this reviewer, which may be rebutted only with difficulty by critics of the space venture, who might profit most by its reading.

The Promise of Space, Clarke freely admits, was calculated to help restore the long-term view to space mobility recently diminished by the initial cost of capital investment already made and by the temporary sublimation of the international "space race," which characterized the beginning of the space program and may not be required for the future. Clarke's message is clear enough: the U.S. space program, at least in its earlier days, was certainly prodded by "gusts of emotion." . . .

Clarke suggests that every revolutionary idea—in politics, science, art, or whatever—seems to evoke three stages of reaction: (i) "It's completely impossible"; (ii) "It's possible but not worth doing"; and (iii) "I said it was a good idea all along." Whether this volume will "smooth the transition" of astronautics from the second to the third stage in the United States, as Clarke intends, remains for the future historians to determine. (p. 875)

Eugene M. Emme, "Space, Past and Future," in Science, *Vol. 161, No. 3844, August 30, 1968, pp. 874-75.**

BRENDA MADDOX

Science fact could be the death of science fiction. Now, with men trying on the shoes that they will wear on the moon, lunar fantasies are as interesting as last year's travel brochure. The rest of space is still unreal, but, as calculations begin on what to take to Mars, it may have lost its romance as well. And a good thing too. Arthur Clarke has been writing astronautics for the masses for nearly twenty years, and a comparison of his two latest books shows that the real problems of space are a great deal more tantalising than the reveries of imaginary astronauts.

The novel [***2001: A Space Odyssey***] which has been made out of the screenplay by Mr Clarke and Stanley Kubrick has the faults of the film and none of its virtues. The characters still have the subtlety of comic-strip men and, lacking the film's spectacular visual gimmickry—giant stations wheeling majestically in space—the story must propel itself with little gusts of scientific explanation. . . . (p. 877)

There is a great dependence on images of whirling light, luminous star streaks on milky skies, and faint glows of blue, crimson, pink and gold. The most sympathetic character, Hal the computer, is not half so endearing in cold print, without his red light. The novel does shed some light on the nature of the mysterious black slab that, in the film, turns up in prehistoric Africa, on the moon and on a satellite of Saturn. It turns out to be a literary device to hold together a rickety plot.

Mr Clarke's non-fiction effort, ***The Promise of Space,*** is something quite different. It is as good a history as exists of man's effort to leave his planet, and a good cram course in astronomy as well. While it is unflinchingly technical, it is always readable. For example, Mr Clarke worries about the velocity needed to get into orbit around Mars. He compares the alternatives, makes his choice (26,000 miles an hour) and the readers have the splendid illusion of having understood it all.

Most books on rocketry open with an essay on the cosmology of the ancients that is so long and dreary and full of woodcuts that one falls asleep long before the astronauts come in. What a pleasure it is to travel over the same historical ground—from Lucian of Samosata in the second century A.D. to Wernher von Braun—without being dragged heavily through all the Wells and Verne plots. Mr Clarke's anecdotes from the past tend to be relevant to today's space projects. The first artificial earth satellite appears to have been proposed in a 19th-century American work of science fiction by the Reverend Edward Everett Hale (a man who, Mr Clarke observes, was probably the last chaplain of the United States Senate to write science fiction). (pp. 877-78)

What is the promise of space? Mr Clarke expects ports in orbit before very long, and the moon itself to become a kind of petrol station in the sky that will save space ships the bother of coming near the earth's gravitation. By the year 2000 he foresees settlements on Mars with spacemen camping out under little plastic domes like beach huts. Probably not until 2,300 A.D. does he think it will be practical to start thinking about travelling to the stars, and not until then will the practical problems of metaphysics have to be faced. What breed of human being will want to take a 33-year-trip, circumnavigating the universe, only to find that it is 10 billion years later when he gets home? Incidentally, don't look here for any criticism of the Americans' expensive race to the moon. Mr Clarke is a passionate advocate of man in space (he expects to go to the moon by 1980) and believes that those who grumble about cost are like Galileo's accusers, they simply do not comprehend the new world around them. (p. 878)

Brenda Maddox, "Cosmic Thoughts," in New Statesman, *Vol. 76, No. 1971, December 20, 1968, pp. 877-78.**

DIANE ACKERMAN

Teeing off ***Report on Planet Three and Other Speculations*** . . . with a Martian's observations of Earth (largely uninhabitable, ghoulishly colored, and rife with a poisonous gas called oxygen), Arthur C. Clarke speculates eclectically on invasion via radio waves, the possibility of compact energy sources (a chunk of the radioisotope Californium the size of a fountain pen could effect a daily output of *five thousand horsepower of pure heat*), and traveling faster than the speed of light. He offers evocative essays on time, the disinvention of work's effect on our psychological fabric, the elimination of night, and the star of the Magi (a supernova whose light is wreaking havoc perhaps on the religions of yet another solar system).

Since this collection includes essays spanning roughly fifteen years, it seems to reproduce in its entirety the Clarkean universe. In his zeal to be comprehensive as well as up-to-date, Clarke addresses himself several times over to certain vexed questions and thus involves himself in postscripts (which is a bonus) and self-contradictions (which is a nuisance). Jupiter, for example, proffered as the indisputable biological center of the solar system in chapter 7, has life blithely dismissed from it in chapter 8; while what he says about exceeding the speed of light seems equally paradoxical. Most of his cogitations are well-wrought, but too often they are littered with ambiguities.

Diane Ackerman, "Radioisotopes, Robot Brawls, White Light, and Green Flippers," in Book World—The Washington Post, *December 19, 1971, p. 6.**

PETER HENNIKER-HEATON

In discussing edsats, or education satellites, Arthur Clarke [in **"Report on Planet 3 and Other Speculations"**] remarks that with their aid "the whole world may become one academy of learning." If Mr. Clarke is one of its professors, that academy will be an exceedingly exciting and stimulating one.

In one sense this latest anthology of his own talks and articles . . . is an exercise in time travel. Its various chapters were written at different periods over the last 15 years or so, and, as the preface warns us, "there is no particular order in which they need to be read." As a result, the reader finds himself sometimes behind and sometimes ahead of such historic events as the 1969 moon-landing. To avoid chronological disorientation he will need to keep wide-awake.

It is, therefore, a little strange that time travel, or chrononautics, seems to be the only project in technology that Arthur Clarke dismisses with almost total disbelief. After listing what he regards as the six farthest out speculations in the centuries of human thought, he comments: "There is only one of these that I feel certain (well, practically certain!) to be impossible, and that is time travel."

But read this statement along with a speech given in 1967, wherein the author developed what he calls Clarke's three laws. The first reads: "When a distinguished but elderly scientist states that something is possible, he is almost certainly right. When he states that something is impossible, he is very probably wrong." That seems to put time travel right back on the list of realizable projects—but it will almost certainly be achieved in the light of new discoveries about the nature of time and so will be something quite different from what we conceive it might be now.

I have discussed this question of time travel at some length because it most clearly illustrates one of the special delights of the book: its delicate progress along the highwire of the improbable stretched across the cataracts of the impossible. . . .

This anthology is primarily a report on Earth, on Planet 3 of Sol; but its other speculations range to the farthest marches of the space-time continuum. And on almost all the major questions to which scientific ingenuity has addressed itself it has something original to contribute. Which way is up? Is the speed of light an ultimate? How do we greet extraterrestrials? The Star of the Magi? The worlds we can't see? In a society of increasing leisure how do we disinvent work? Arthur Clarke's prophecies, notably his forecasting of comsats or communications satellites, have so often proved right that we neglect them at our peril. . . .

In Arthur Clarke's company the impossible is apt to become possible and the possible probable.

Peter Henniker-Heaton, "Beyond the Limits of the Possible," in The Christian Science Monitor, *February 10, 1972, p. 10.*

STANLEY B. HALL

[**"Rendezvous with Rama"**] involves the appearance of a mysterious "asteroid" on the fringes of the solar system in the year 2130. With the discovery that Rama is not a natural object, but an immense "cylinder of sculptured, ageless metal," 31 miles long, 12½ miles across and with a mass of 10 trillion tons, mankind braces for its first encounter with visitors from an incredibly old and incredibly advanced civilization.

The cautious approach of the space survey ship Endeavor to the "asteroid" and its momentous landing have all the gripping reality of man's first touchdown on the lunar Sea of Tranquillity. Even more gripping is what the earthlings find as the sun's warmth begins to "hatch" the miniworld inside the huge astral artifact.

This is science fiction at its best—explorers grappling with the unknown but equipped with the knowledge that the universe operates according to fixed, dependable laws.

Author Clarke's fiction is based solidly on scientific fact. Indeed, the book includes a substantial "course" in astral, solar, and planetary physics—woven unobtrusively into a first-rate story.

Stanley B. Hall, in a review of "Rendezvous with Rama," in The Christian Science Monitor, *August 8, 1973, p. 9.*

JOHN LEONARD

In **"Rendezvous With Rama,"** Mr. Clarke has not written anything as ambitious as **"Childhood's End."** But he has taken a formal problem in the best sci-fi tradition—the arrival in our area of an alien space craft, Rama, pregnant with enigmas—and worked it like an accordion. It achieves a nice tune.

Mr. Clarke, according to his custom, is benignly indifferent to the niceties of characterization. His (our) Bill Norton, commander of the Endeavour, is as dauntless and as imprecise as Joe Palooka. He talks like an electric typewriter. The only thing startling about Bill is that he has two sets of families in two different worlds, and Xeroxes his letters home. But when, in the year 2130, a 10-billion-ton, 31-miles-long cylinder putt-putts into the solar system to use our sun as a filling station, Bill investigates—by landing Endeavour on Rama and going inside.

Once out of the comic strips and into the Rama, Mr. Clarke is splendid. Rama is more than a ship, it is almost a planet, with a complex topography and lots of important weather. Or it can be thought of as an enormous chemical tank, with cybernetic furniture—a womb, in which chimeras spontaneously combust. As a superior intelligence spins a strange spider-culture out of its bowels, we experience that chilling touch of the alien, the not-quite-knowable, that distinguishes sci-fi at its most technically imaginative.

John Leonard, "Two Tales for the Future," in The New York Times, *August 22, 1973, p. 35.**

THOMAS D. CLARESON

Although it is everywhere apparent that [Clarke's] main concern involves man's encounter with alien intelligence, at the heart of his vision—most obvious throughout his non-fiction and early novels—remains the certainty that the exploration of space and the colonization of the planets of innumerable suns will bring a new Renaissance freeing mankind from the short-sighted prejudices and limitations of earth-bound, modern civilization. Repeatedly he invokes images fusing his voyagers "Across the Sea of Stars" with those explorers who opened up the Earth, as he does in ***Prelude to Space*** (1951), which celebrates preparations for the voyage of the *Prometheus* to the moon and climaxes with the departure of that first ship. (p. 217)

". . . the childhood of our race was over . . .": there is a delightful irony in that line because of the widespread popularity of ***Childhood's End*** (1953), Clarke's only work—fiction or nonfiction—in which *"The stars are not for Man."* Billed as "a towering novel about the next step in the evolution of man," it belongs, most simply, to that group of stories in which vastly superior aliens intrude into the affairs of men—a plot having perhaps its widest vogue during the decade or so after World War II. In this instance the Overlords, who possess the form of Satan, terminate the Soviet-American race for the moon, end the threat of nuclear holocaust, and in fifty years bring about a seeming utopia. . . . Creating an 'Earthly Paradise,' is not, however, the final purpose of the Overlords; they were sent, their leader explains, to act as midwives while the human race evolved psychically preparatory to uniting itself with the cosmic Overmind. . . . The Overlords are racially incapable of taking this evolutionary step and do not comprehend the forces at work; yet while the Overmind triggers and guides the change, they must act as guardians, protecting man from himself, until the last generation of children is ready for the transformation.

The novel ends as a solitary adult watches the children, now joined into a single intelligence, undergo a metamorphosis which not only releases them from their human form but dissolves the Earth itself into the energy necessary to complete the change. . . . Like other galactic races which have completed their probation, mankind has become a part of the Overmind. Although David Samuelson questions the artistic effectiveness of much of ***Childhood's End*** [see *CLC,* Vol. 18], he notes that "we feel the tug of the irrational, in familiar terms. The Overmind clearly parallels the Oversoul, the Great Spirit, and various formulations of God, while the children's metamorphosis neatly ties in with mystical beliefs in Nirvana, 'cosmic consciousness,' and 'becoming as little children to enter the Kingdom of God.'" One might add that its resolution recalls—but does not duplicate—stories by the followers of Madame Blavatsky and John Fiske in the late nineteenth century which sought reconciliation between traditional beliefs and new scientific data, thereby often insisting that the next step in evolution must involve some higher potential of the human spirit. The essentially traditional mysticism of that resolution, as well as the emphasis upon the children as "successors" to mankind with whom their parents would "never even be able to communicate," may well account for much of the appeal of the novel, particularly in the classroom. (pp. 220-21)

Other than ***Childhood's End,*** the longer narratives among his early works divide themselves into two groups, the first strongly didactic, reflecting Clarke's desire to sell astronautics to the public. ***Prelude to Space*** . . . celebrates preparations for the voyage of the *Prometheus* to the moon in 1978 and, as noted, climaxes with the departure of that ship. In the 'Epilogue' Dirk Alexson, the historian who must produce an enduring record of that flight, reflects upon the successful colonization of the moon and the coming of a new Renaissance. Wisely the shifting narrative focus stays primarily with Alexson, thereby making more acceptable the introduction of an abundance of technical detail as he learns about the project. This includes far more than the mechanics of the technology, however, for he readily understands the importance of the program to the future. . . .

Another character summons up what has become a familiar image in Clarke's rebuttal to those who would spurn the venture into space because, properly run, there is no better world than Earth: "The dream of the Lotus Eaters . . . is a pleasant fantasy for the individual—but it would be death for the race." . . . (p. 224)

Prelude to Space has little plot action because there are too many things to describe and talk about, including over-views imagining the ship's departure from the atmosphere and summarizing the diverse, essentially uninformed public attitudes toward space flight. . . . ***Earthlight*** [1955] introduces a spy from Earth into the moon colony of the twenty-second century on the eve of an interplanetary war between Earth and the Triplanetary Federation. (That name alone underscores [Clarke's] intimacy with the older magazine science fiction.) Earth's ex-colonies on Mars, Venus, Mercury, and the moons of Jupiter and Saturn comprise the Federation; the issue concerns raw materials, for only Earth has access to the heavy elements essential to the technologies of all the worlds. (p. 225)

[The] moon becomes the hub of the solar system, her "inexhaustible wealth" supporting all of the inhabitable planets. Again idea dominates. . . . All of this is played out against the backdrop of *Nova Draconis,* the first supernova in this Galaxy since the Renaissance. Its appearance permits reflections upon the fragility of life, but unfortunately it does not attain a unifying symbolic value. Its presence, however, does emphasize how long the phenomenon has teased Clarke's imagination.

The Sands of Mars (1952) makes use of familiar patterns. Its protagonist, a famous science fiction writer, has been invited to be the sole passenger aboard the new spaceliner *Ares* so that he can write a book about its initial voyage. One journeys with him from a space station to Port Lowell, the principal domed city of the Martian colony. When he decides to throw in with the Martian pioneers rather than to return to Earth, his task becomes that of selling the colony to an Earth already weary of supporting it. The novel gains a unity because the point of view remains almost entirely with the protagonist, but apparently in an attempt to make the characters more complex, Clarke has added to the plot the contrived romance between the protagonist's protégé (actually his son by a young woman he loved at the university) and the daughter of the "Chief Executive" of the colony. (pp. 225-26)

However readable these novels are, beyond the circle of science fiction aficionados they have their chief importance, as Clarke suggested of ***Prelude to Space,*** as a means of spreading the "Zeitgeist of Astronautics." They are as much propaganda pieces as is ***The Exploration of Space*** [(1951), a nonfiction work in which Clarke advocates space travel]. Yet they may also say something of the essential nature of science fiction. Even in ***Prelude to Space,*** the protagonists leave familiar settings to venture into unknown worlds, whether extraterrestrial or not. As in ***Earthlight*** and ***The Sands of Mars*** especially, much attention may be given to their technologies. . . . However, the true sense of wonder . . . lies in the exploration of those exotic, often hostile worlds. The protagonists may return or not—often they have come home; often they have created new homes. In Clarke intellectual curiosity may replace such reliable devices as those devastating catastrophes so popular with a writer like John Wyndham, but the result is the same. The issue is man's ability to survive in and comprehend those far lands, whether they are beyond Eden or beyond Jupiter. This mixture of familiarity and otherness, reality and fantasy, has led David Young to refer to science fiction as "our most viable version of the pastoral."

The degree to which he is correct may be seen even more clearly in a second group of Clarke's early narratives. . . . ***Against the Fall of Night*** (1948) and ***The Lion of Comarre*** (1949) are the earliest of those works in which Clarke responds to Campbell's melancholy vision of the twilight of humanity. . . . (pp. 226-27)

Against the Fall of Night has retained a devoted audience, although flawed by its brevity and a reliance upon unembellished conventions from magazine science fiction. Clarke's feeling for it led him to expand it as ***The City and the Stars*** (1956), the only instance in which he has completely revised a published story. Its point of departure echoes Campbell. The immortal populace of Diaspar, the only city remaining amid the deserts of Earth, lives contentedly amid wondrous machines which fulfill their every need and desire. The people have never viewed the world beyond the walls of the city and know of the desert—the nothingness—only by legend; indeed, they are afraid to venture out of Diaspar. Much of their fear stems from a supposed fact of history: half a billion years ago the Invaders drove man from the stars; since then he has confined himself to his dying planet. (Like Triplanetary Federation, the term Invaders links Clarke to the space opera of the 1930's.)

Only Alvin, the young protagonist, the only child born to the immortals in seven thousand years, possesses curiosity and a desire for knowledge. Refusing to accept the "gracious decadence" of Diaspar, he seeks and finds a way into the outer world, where he finds the "Land of Lys," a vast oasis of forest and grass-covered plains protected by mountains from the desert. . . . His discovery precipitates a crisis, for he wishes Lys and Diaspar to cooperate, and they are unwilling to do so.

To suggest that ***Against the Fall of Night*** is an account of Alvin's search for self identity is to read the novel as another exercise in psychological realism. It is instead an attempt to make a symbolic statement about the destiny of mankind. Alvin functions to destroy man's false concept of history—his fear of the Invaders and their supposed blockade of Earth—thereby liberating both cultures from their self-imposed confinement. As soon, however, as the escape from the prison of the city becomes a quest for meaning, the narrative surrenders to an assortment of conventions and devices from magazine science fiction. Too much happens too quickly. Whereas Alvin largely controls the action of the first half of the story, one feels that from this point onward he is manipulated by his discoveries. Nothing is fleshed out. (pp. 228-29)

Clarke undoubtedly improved upon the artistry of the work when he revised it as ***The City and the Stars,*** but the theme remains the same.

Similarly, in ***The Lion of Comarre,*** the young protagonist, who wishes to be an engineer and dreams of flight to the stars, rebels against a world grown stagnant. Just as Alvin was the only child born to the immortals in seven thousand years, so Richard Peyton III is the genetic reincarnation of Rolf Thordarsen, the builder of legendary Comarre, associated with the Decadents. Weary of "this unending struggle for knowledge and the blind desire to bridge space to the stars," these men believed that the aim of life was pleasure and chose to build cities "where the machines will care for our every need as soon as the thought enters our minds. . . .": "It was the ancient dream of the Lotus Eaters . . . the cloying promise of peace and utter contentment." . . . Peripheral to the group, **"The Road to the Sea"** (1950) projects a future in which mankind has retained the use of a few wonderful machines, although forgetting the knowledge behind them. Man has forsaken the great cities and "returned to the hills and forest." Seeking to learn something of the new country into which his village has been required by law to move, as it must every three life-times, a young artist searches for the ancient city of Shastar. There he encounters descendants of those men who long ago had traveled to the stars; they have returned only in order to evacuate Earth—which faces destruction from a force reminiscent of the "Mad Mind" of ***Against the Fall of Night.*** Even a cursory glance indicates how closely these narratives are interrelated at all levels from imagery and incident to theme.

To emphasize the creative relationship of science and mankind, however bright a future it may portend, may well overlook those concerns which lead to Clarke's finest fiction. In ***The City and the Stars,*** while embellishing an early description of the mystic who came from the stars, Clarke accuses him of suffering from a disease that afflicted "only *Homo sapiens* among all the intelligent races of the Universe . . . religious mania." . . . Unlike those nineteenth century writers, like John Fiske, who protested the astronomical difficulties they encountered in maintaining their beliefs, Clarke, obviously, is not afraid of the distances between the stars. Nor does he need to impose some deductive system upon the nature of things because, for him, the interaction of life, intelligence, and the galactic universe itself is mystery enough. (pp. 230-31)

Throughout Clarke's fiction there is no want of life or intelligence; they abound in a multitude of forms on a multitude of planets. . . . In ***Against the Fall of Night*** and ***The City and the Stars,*** while wandering the blighted universe, Vanamonde had found "on countless worlds . . . the wreckage that life leaves behind"; in ***Childhood's End,*** the first child to travel psychically goes beyond the range of the Overlords' ships and finally travels in another universe to a planet lighted by six colored suns—a planet that never repeats the same orbit: "And even here there was life." (pp. 231-32)

Most often Clarke has maintained an omniscient narrator so that he can . . . switch the perspective quickly in order to gain some desired effect. Consistently, however, he has achieved his highest artistry in those stories unified by a first-person narrator recalling personal experience, as in **"The Star"** (1955). A Jesuit, the astrophysicist of an expedition returning to Earth from the so-called Phoenix Nebula, finds himself troubled by the report he must make of what was actually a super-nova. The "burden of our knowledge" has caused his faith to falter. On the farthest planet of what was a solar system, the crew of his ship found a Vault prepared by a people who knew that they were doomed and were trapped because they had achieved only interplanetary flight, not star-flight. "Perhaps," he writes, "if we had not been so far from home and so vulnerable to loneliness, we should not have been so deeply moved." . . . (p. 232)

For Clarke, these stories give expression to the central drama of the universe. He might be speaking for himself when he says of the alien visiting prehistoric Earth in **"Moon-Watcher"** (1972): "Centuries of traveling through the empty wastes of the universe had given him an intense reverence for life in all its forms." Yet as the very language of these stories indicates, this reverence is accompanied by an anxiety which re-echoes through his finest fiction, perhaps reaching something of a climax in his essay, **"When Aliens Come,"** in ***Report on Planet Three:***

> . . . perhaps the most important result of such contacts (radio signals) might be the simple proof that other intelligent races do exist. Even if our cosmic conversations never rise above the 'Me Tarzan—You Jane' level, we would no longer feel so alone in an apparently hostile universe.

Such a view surely echoes something of that horror felt especially during the decades at the turn of the century when science told man that he dwelt alone in an alien universe. That is why the apocalyptic moment of first contact is so important to Clarke; it dramatizes—resolves—what may be called his cosmic loneliness.

"The Sentinel" (1951) captures the melancholy of that loneliness. Perhaps more than any other single story it has proved seminal to the development of his artistry. That it provided the symbolic monolith which structures ***2001: A Space Odyssey*** measures but does not determine its importance. Once again Clarke makes use of a first-person narrator, one who recalls a discovery which he made twenty years earlier. . . . Because he is reflecting upon past action, one soon realizes that what is important is the implication of such a discovery on a moon proved barren by twenty years' further research. He guesses that early in prehistory Earth was visited by "masters of a universe so young that life as yet had come only to a handful of worlds. Theirs would have been a loneliness we cannot imagine, the loneliness of gods looking out across infinity and finding none to share their thoughts." And so they left a sentinel—a signaling device to let them know when man had reached the moon.

In November 1950, Clarke first dramatized that "Encounter in the Dawn" [as he recalls in ***The Lost Worlds of 2001***]. An alien astronaut gives various tools, including a flashlight of some kind, to a prehistoric man already possessing a flint-tipped spear. This may be called the astronauts' story. . . . Despite the increasing number of references in his non-fiction to a possible meeting during some period of the Earth's past, he did not re-work the plot until ***2001: A Space Odyssey*** (1968). . . . This version may be called Moon-Watcher's story, the story of the man-apes, particularly since the "super-teaching machine"—the monolith—is substituted for the physical presence of the astronauts. The emphasis upon the education—the awakening—of Moon-Watcher and his companions completely submerges the sense of cosmic loneliness. Thus, not until the four short tales—**"First Encounter," "Moon-Watcher," "Gift from the Stars,"** and **"Farewell to Earth"**—first published in ***The Lost Worlds of 2001*** (1972) did Clarke give the encounter its fullest development thematically.

Again the narrative focus is upon one of the astronauts, Clindar. A member of one of ten landing parties making a census of the Earth, he finds a small group of hominids. Possessing no tools and living "always on the edge of hunger," they have not yet been "trapped in any evolutionary *cul-de-sac*"; "they could do everything after a fashion." Whether because Clindar "looked straight into a hairy caricature of his own face" or because he saw one of the young males contemplating the moon in a manner suggesting "conscious thought and wonder," he decides to intervene in an attempt to tip the scales "in favor of intelligence.'' Left to themselves the near-apes would have little chance of survival, for ''the universe was as indifferent to intelligence as it was to life.'' And so he gave them an ''initial impetus'' by teaching them to hunt and use clubs. (pp. 233-35)

Without exception Clarke's recent major works—***2001: A Space Odyssey*** (1968), **"A Meeting with Medusa"** (1971), and ***Rendezvous with Rama*** (1973)—have dealt with the concept of first contact, but none has significantly modified the philosophical stance presented in the encounter between Clindar and Moon-Watcher. ***2001: A Space Odyssey*** suggests that those who left the Sentinel have now evolved into beings ''free at last from the tyranny of matter.'' . . . In ***Rendezvous with Rama,*** Clarke pays explicit tribute to H. G. Wells's ''The Star'' adapting its basic plot to his own ends, for the new celestial body plunging through the solar system proves to be a giant spaceship. Most attention is given to its exploration, although there is opportunity for political confrontation in the General Assembly of the United Planets when the citizens of Mercury launch a missile at Rama because it invades their solar space and supposedly threatens to become another planet. Instead it draws energy directly from the sun and departs, leaving the protagonist indignant because ''the purpose of the Ramans was still utterly unknown.'' . . . (pp. 235-36)

"A Meeting with Medusa" attains the highest artistry of his recent works; it combines an innovative plot with an effective character study, and it gains unity by focusing solely upon Howard Falconer, though not told from the first person. He is a cyborg who flies a hot-air balloon through the upper atmosphere of Jupiter. And he discovers life in the form of a gargantuan creature like a jellyfish, a medusa. When it begins to handle his balloon, he flees. There is the final suggestion that he will act as an ambassador between humanity and the ''real masters of space,'' the machines; the awareness of his destiny makes him take ''a sombre pride in his unique loneliness.'' Certainly **"A Meeting with Medusa"** suggests that Clarke may have found a new perspective from which to consider the old concerns.

For Clarke, man has chosen the right path, employing his intelligence and technology to reach out toward the stars. . . . Somewhere amid the blazing suns and swirling nebulae, if only in the artifacts of a civilization long dead in the vastness of time, man will find that he has become part of a community of intelligence which alone gives meaning to the indifferent splendor of the universe. Until then he must dream of the stars and, like Clarke, be haunted by a sense of cosmic loneliness until he finds the Sentinel. (pp. 236-37)

Thomas D. Clareson, ''The Cosmic Loneliness of Arthur C. Clarke,'' in Voices for the Future: Essays on Major Science Fiction Writers, Vol. I, *edited by Thomas D. Clareson, Bowling Green University Popular Press, 1976, pp. 216-37.*

GERALD JONAS

Arthur C. Clarke's latest book [**"The View From Serendip"**] is subtitled ''Speculations on Space, Science, and the Sea, Together With Fragments of an Equatorial Autobiography.'' The key word is fragments. This is a collection of incidental pieces of journalism from magazines as diverse as Penthouse, Vogue and Technology Review, mixed in with some of Clarke's recent lectures and a record of his testimony before the House of Representatives, Committee on Space Science and Applications.

Such a book usually ends up being less than the sum of its parts. Not this one. **"The View From Serendip"** hums with life, offering glimpses of Clarke the Adventurer (both intellectual and physical) that will delight those readers who know him only as a superb popularizer of space science (**"Voices From the Sky"**) or as one of the best of modern science fiction writers (**"Childhood's End"**) or as Stanley Kubrick's collaborator on the film **"2001; A Space Odyssey."** . . .

What makes Clarke such an effective popularizer of science is that, without bobbling a decimal point or fudging a complex concept, he gives voice to the romantic side of scientific inquiry—just as Dr. Lewis Thomas did in his ''Lives of a Cell.'' Like Thomas, Clarke is duly concerned with the practical applications of science; for instance, he is a passionate advocate of using communications satellites to beam educational television to villages in underdeveloped countries, and he is impatient with the financial and political obstacles that have so far kept this dream from becoming a reality. But his disappointment does not dim his enthusiasm for sending expensive rocket probes into the fathomless reaches of the universe. No one writes as eloquently about the challenge of space exploration. . . .

Unlike some enthusiasts who never know when to stop, however, Clarke also has a sense of humor about his own hobby horse.

Gerald Jonas, ''Idea Diver,'' in The New York Times Book Review, *October 30, 1977, p. 12.*

DONALD F. THEALL AND JOAN BENEDICT

In ***A View from Serendip,*** Clarke symbolically brings us through the filter of his neo-colonial mentality (as revealed in the tone and attitude of essays such as **"Servant Problem—Oriental Style"** or **"The Sea of Sinbad"**) into his Sri Lanka livingroom, sits us down on the sofa, and proceeds to open up his scrapbook of memories and bits of previously written or presented pieces. Starting with autobiographical details of his earlier years and eventual transmission to paradise on Ceylon, Clarke—with little twists of wit somewhat reminiscent of McLuhan—details facts about that island's infinite variety of climate and social groupings and then brings us back to his domicile to meet Appuhamy and Jinadasa who number among the more than 50 servants and paid associates who are now or have been in the past attached to the Clarke household. (p. 230)

For anyone fascinated by the futurological predictions of the *Future Shock* kind, Clarke provides a treasure chest of gems. In fact, he sounds more than a little like a ''scientistically'' rather than humanistically oriented version of McLuhan as media guru. His pithy and apocalyptic style even includes such transformations of clichés as ''the future isn't what it used to be'' . . . which he employs in the introduction of his own **"The World of 2001"** (originally published in *Vogue* 1966). In that essay, ''the prototype of the future city is not Manhattan but Disney world,'' . . . since people will travel only for pleasure when they can communicate via living room console instead of commuting to the office downtown, at which time oil will be made into food instead of fuel for the ubiquitous automobile. Social reservations about the wired city or the ways it might be developed do not complicate his technocratic vision. For students of SF as a paraliterary activity, the details about the

Clarke-Asimov relationship will also be of interest. The book includes Clarke's four-page "Introducing Isaac Asimov" together with Asimov's even more delightful one-page response. (pp. 230-31)

The overall impression of Clarke, though, remains that of a potentially interesting mind hypnotized by technocracy, lured by the pleasure of the capitalist exploitations of the colonial fact, and possibly incapable of reflecting on any social problems arising from either of these. He is not only a technological determinist but a technocratic optimist, whose fundamentally anti-intellectual attitude constantly reveals itself in the way he deals with other modes of thought. His approach to humanism in the essay **"The World of 2001"** downgrades the classic period of Greece and Rome, complaining that if their insight had been as great as their ingenuity, the industrial Revolution could have happened 1000 years earlier. Such an opinion is historically very questionable. Joined to a dismissal of Hegel—"I have never taken Hegel seriously and have thus saved myself a great deal of trouble" . . .—it suggests a basic misunderstanding, or if not that, a distortion of western cultural history. Just because Hegel's astronomy was not as informed as it might have been, it seems arrogant to dismiss his role in historical theory, phenomenology, and the growth of dialectic.

In spite of these criticisms, the essays in this book are often interesting, informative, and entertaining. But we should hardly let Clarke get by on his obvious skill as a writer and effectiveness as a scientific journalist: in particular not in view of the authority which he has obtained from the media. Clarke argues in his book that man is primarily an information-processing animal and human communication is of key importance, yet in his enchantment with technology he stands a great chance of overlooking the important contributions to knowledge made by the human sciences. (p. 231)

Donald F. Theall and Joan Benedict, in a review of "The View from Serendip," in Science-Fiction Studies, *Vol. 6, No. 18, July, 1979, pp. 230-31.*

ALGIS BUDRYS

Perhaps it's not astonishing that Arthur C. Clarke should have written a good book [***The Fountains of Paradise***]. One expects it. One thinks of the powerful mysticism of ***Childhood's End*** or ***2001,*** or the sheer majesty of ***Rendezvous with Rama.*** But by and large there have always been two kinds of Clarke story, distinct from each other. There are those in which the mysticism predominates, and the strength of the work derives almost entirely from his ability to evoke images of transcendence . . . of universes beyond the perceptibly material, and forces which, though real and potent, can never be measured by mundane instruments. The effect is the effect of the ***2001*** movie; the image is the image of Man rising toward Heaven in the belly of a whale, as in ***Childhood's End.***

Not conversely, but certainly in distinct parallel, there is the technology-procedural novel, such as ***Prelude to Space*** or ***A Fall of Moondust.*** Certainly, the human protagonists rise to emotional heights and express much of what is best in resourceful, imaginative humanity. But they do this in response to materialistic situations, and their arena is a confined technological situation. The alien construct in ***Rama,*** for example, is sufficiently large and various so that many mini-sagas occur within it, but it does have boundaries, and the scope of the human action does not exceed them by much.

I'm not aware of any previous Clarke novel which does what is done by his latest, ***The Fountains of Paradise.*** It seems to me that this is the first instance in which all the author's demonstrated capabilities have melded. Not *perfectly*, mind you—there are slight discontinuities in the narrative, as if a longer manuscript had been cut a shade too much—but more than well enough to constitute a crucial event in Clarke's career, and thus in speculative fiction.

There are two stories: of the attempt of King Kalidasa to build a tower into Heaven, in ancient times, and of the attempt of Vannevar Morgan to build an elevator from the Earth's surface to an orbital terminus in the twenty-second century. (p. 25)

Morgan's proposed elevator is forty thousand kilometers tall, its engineering based on a new cable filament of enormous tensile strength. Major portions will be built in space, and lowered downward. King Kalidasa builds a towering pleasure garden, balefully observed by monks of Sri Kanda, the sacred mountain. When Morgan arrives, twenty centuries later, the monastery still exists, and his ambition is as much an affront as was that of the parricidal tyrant. Morgan has no choice . . . the elevator must be based where geophysical considerations demand, if it is to be built on Earth at all. Kalidasa—complex, resolute and heedless—built where he felt beauty lay nearest, and brooked no one's contradictory opinion. (pp. 25-6)

Clarke's physical setting is enough to send almost anyone to his travel agent. The mood of that ancient land, and the natural and Man-made beauties to be found there, are not only drawn directly from the actual Sri Lanka but are depicted with a poetic skill worthy of a Loren Eiseley. The elevator—an actual contemporary proposed solution to the problem of moving freight to and from an economically feasible orbit—is no less thrilling a creation, in the best and deepest sense of that abused adverb. (p. 26)

Algis Budrys, in a review of "The Fountains of Paradise," in The Magazine of Fantasy and Science Fiction, *Vol. 57, No. 3, September, 1979, pp. 25-6.*

ELIOT FREMONT-SMITH

When last seen, astronaut David Bowman of the spaceship *Discovery* had been transformed into a "starchild," a fetus of possibility in the womb, or mind, of God. That was 14 years ago, in the great Arthur C. Clarke/Stanley Kubrick mind-blowing epic, ***2001: A Space Odyssey.*** Clarke's novel of the same name also came out in 1968, three months after the film, and I experienced ***2001*** in that order—audiovisually first, reading (another level of audiovisuals) second.

And experienced in that order, the book ***2001*** was terrific. It detailed and expanded on the film. For instance, in the book Bowman is not unique. Among the rings of Saturn there's a graveyard of abandoned and rustling spaceships—some apparently from outside the solar system and many millenia old—whose astronauts must also have visited the gentle white room, grown older and younger at once, become starchildren of whatever is the purpose of the universe. And Bowman is simply the most recent transformation—the first Earthling, but that hardly matters. Yet the order of my experiencing this phenomenon does, or did. The book ***2001*** was richer than the film, but only because the film preexisted; however inadequately, it illustrated the novel, gave importantly specific cues to the audiovisuals the book provoked—or was then able to provoke.

Now comes Clarke's never-thought-possible novel sequel, ***2010: Odyssey Two*** . . . , and something's wrong. What's wrong isn't factual error or less than nifty plotting or even that Clarke has exercised certain tidying-up prerogatives. . . .

What's wrong initially is that Clarke seems to be just going through the motions. Until very near the end, the prose is lifeless and wooden—a huge (and often redundant) scaffolding whose only solid foundation seems to be our memory of ***2001*** and the questions *we* would bring to any sequel: what really *did* happen to Bowman? Why did the computer Hal go psychotic and try to scuttle the *Discovery* mission? What, in fact, is the meaning of the monoliths—those huge, black, rectangular entities, one of which seemed to bequeath insight into the use of tools to Earth's man-apes three million years ago, and another of which was discovered in the year 2001 buried on the moon? (It was this monolith, you'll remember, that inspired the manned voyage of *Discovery* to Jupiter and beyond; the monolith seemed to be signaling to some higher intelligence out there.)

What's mainly wrong, I think, is that there's no preceding movie of ***2010*** for our reading audiovisuals to get off on and/or from. This is why the novel's characters appear to lack substance and dimension—not that this is in itself the fault some early critics of the book have already claimed. In fact, Clarke's sporadic attempts at characterization are a good part of what's wooden in the novel, the rest being repetitious clinical explication, of an apologetic throat-clearing kind, as if in lieu of the movie that should have been before. . . .

The reading mind's eye shouldn't need pictorial stimulation from other (and rival) media. ***2010,*** shoving the lie to this presumption, will, I predict, be found wanting in things that don't matter, while the shaky character of its theology slips by unexamined.

So, these things accepted: for all its surface alacrity (about 100 tiny chapters, each ending on a suspenseful *what the hell is really going on?*), ***2010*** has long stretches of almost deadly dullness. Clarke does his rote best at character delineation and reminds intellectual laggards of what's already happened and what we know about space travel, Einsteinian effects of speed on time (and aging), advanced computer synapses (the potential reach of Hal's "emotions"), and so on. There are jokes here, too, for those in the know—references to Hofstadter of *Gödel, Escher, Bach* and to "von Neumannn machines," what the monoliths turn out to be—but it is to smirk in the middle of a yawn.

Crassly, I'll suggest that the novel be started at the beginning (including the introductory apologia for transferring the action back to Jupiter) and followed for 50 pages, then a skip to the final quarter (starting on page 211), then a backtrack to the late middle (say, page 117), and then—if you're still curious about the fate of the Chinese spaceship that tries to interdict the Russian-American mission of ***2010*** to rescue Bowman's derelict *Discovery*—the early middle, everything previously skipped. This is crass, but for me, anyway, rewarding: reading this way I finally got entranced. And entrancement is, after all, the *raison d'être* of ***2010,*** and indeed of many books. An author's feelings may on one level be sacred, but on the level of our investment and return, the sequence of his paragraphs is not. Clarke, I'll bet, will forgive; he, too, would have liked a movie to touch everything off, ignite the smoldering embers of this new imaginative escapade. (p. 8)

Eliot Fremont-Smith, "The Wrong Stuff," in VLS, *No. 12, November, 1982, pp. 8-9.*

CARY NEEPER

In **"2010: Odyssey Two"** Arthur C. Clarke has accomplished what few modern science fiction authors seem to be able to do. He has created a story that contains elements of both fantasy and classical science fiction on the grand cosmic scale, while maintaining a vivid sense of reality—staying true to the human realities of space travel, incorporating new facts gleaned from the 1979 Voyager Space probes, and making believable scientific projections based on those facts. . . .

Beginning where **"2001"** left off, **"2010"** follows three major story lines: Bowman's fate, the investigation of the Jupiter monolith by the spaceship Leonov, and the rehabilitation of Hal. . . .

Clarke's science fiction, as the art of making projections based on established fact, successfully creates such things as an amazing core for Jupiter and intriguing life forms beneath the icy crust of Jupiter's moon, Europa.

Only rarely does Clarke indulge in the kind of preachiness that keeps science fiction firmly locked within its genre. "What shocking linguists we Americans are!" says the central character, and he doesn't leave it at that. The story's opening nationalistic generalizations and conflicts are studiously anti-chauvinistic and unimaginative, hence disappointing.

As the story progresses, Clarke manages to work in some good characterizations: a sternly expert female Soviet Commander; a boisterous American engineer; the repressed, competent Bowman; and a self-effacing Indian computer scientist, who is frighteningly defensive about Hal. The computer's erratic personality adds several facets of suspense and interest, since its rehabilitation is held in question to the very end.

Even though Bowman and Hal are somewhat neglected and eventually shunted aside for the larger theme, Clarke's story drives on to an exciting finish in which the mix of fantasy and fact leaves the reader well satisfied with a book masterfully written.

Cary Neeper, "'2010'—The Odyssey Continues," in The Christian Science Monitor, *December 3, 1982, p. B3.*

MICHAEL BISHOP

Of the four major sf writers of his generation—the other three are Robert Heinlein, Isaac Asimov, and Ray Bradbury—Arthur C. Clarke probably has the best-deserved reputation for creating scientifically convincing narratives. In matters astronomical and technological he has few peers. His speculations about the moons of Jupiter, say, or the evolution of machine intelligence almost always have the inimitable ring of authenticity.

On the other hand, Clarke shares with Bradbury . . . a visionary intelligence that sometimes borders on the mystical. His early novel ***Childhood's End*** (1953), for instance, concludes with a scene of human transcendence that inevitably recalls the apocalyptic thrust of The Book of Revelations. Similarly, in ***2001: A Space Odyssey*** (1968), astronaut David Bowman undergoes a portentous physical and psychological change that apparently adumbrates the transfiguration of the entire human species.

Now, almost 15 years later, Clarke has delivered ***2010: Odyssey Two***. . . . Moviegoers everywhere, especially those fascinated by the metaphysical import of the original film, will expect to have some questions answered. First, what alien power brought about the mysterious metamorphosis of David Bowman? Second, for what reasons? And, third, in what awe-inspiring, transcendental way is this change going to affect the whole of humanity? In ***2010*** Clarke provides an acceptable answer for the first question, a gimpy one for the second, and a disappointing shrug of the shoulders for the third. Indeed, almost as a means of avoiding this last crucial issue, the sequel raises some fascinating questions of its own. . . .

Let me confess: it is easy to be cynical about a best-selling work that so obviously has its roots in Clarke's previous association with Kubrick. Although I think the movie, once made, is likely to be worth seeing, the novel has a grayness, a palpable lack of pizzazz, at odds with both the physics and the metaphysics of its subject matter. Ponderous expository dialogue alternates with straightforward expository passages in which either Heywood Floyd, the book's primary focal character, or the author himself lectures the reader. Each chapter is custom-made for transfer to the screen. . . . Readers desiring the provocative pyrotechnics absent in the book can go see the movie. Moviegoers desiring explanations absent in the film can purchase the book. (This, I believe, is the media equivalent of a positive feedback loop.)

A second confession: Clarke has striven heroically to outfit his characters with recognizable longings, prejudices, and fears. He has made a wholly admirable concession to feminist critics of his work by giving the *Leonov* a female captain and two female medical officers. Unfortunately, these women have little more psychological depth than does either Heywood Floyd or the disembodied intelligence of David Bowman, who comes back to Earth for reasons that seem jury-rigged for their special-effects value to the film. (Remember *Topper*? Remember *The Invisible Man*?) Furthermore, despite his physical transformation into "an embryo god, not yet ready to be born," Bowman evinces very little growth in those subjective dimensions that would make his metamorphosis meaningful as an evolutionary step. And, as already noted, Clarke avoids or postpones for yet another sequel—*20,010: Odyssey Three*?—the question of what Bowman's change presages for humanity at large. Instead, Jupiter becomes a second sun, a new life form approaches self-awareness on Europa, and Bowman continues to await the climactic Day of Reckoning that most readers will have expected to encounter in *this* novel.

Read the movie. See the book. Although I am glad that Clarke did not retire from fiction writing, as he threatened to do, after ***The Fountains of Paradise*** (1979), I am sorry that he has returned to print with a 288-page screenplay masquerading as a novel. If this is his final word on the religio-scientific theme of human transcendence, then he could have abandoned the game in 1968. If it is not, then ***2010: Odyssey Two*** is a workmanlike stopgap effort, containing a half dozen or more flashes of Clarke's patented speculative brilliance, the writing of which has perhaps deferred that of a far more important novel.

Michael Bishop, in a review of "2010: Odyssey Two," in Book World—The Washington Post, *December 26, 1982, p. 6.*

GERALD JONAS

MEMO TO: Sr. Jorge Luiz Calife of Rio de Janeiro

RE: Advisability of sequel to **"2001: A Space Odyssey."**

According to a note at the end of Arthur C. Clarke's new novel, you are partly responsible for persuading the author that a sequel to **"2001"** would be a good idea, long after Mr. Clarke had concluded that such a sequel would be "clearly impossible." I don't know exactly what you said to him in your letter, Sr. Calife, but I wish you hadn't.

Like his earlier classic **"Childhood's End,"** both the book and the movie of **"2001"** (created more or less simultaneously) drew much of their power from their artful vagueness. One of the great themes of science fiction is the confrontation with superhuman—or, more generally, nonhuman—intelligence. To be convincing, the depiction of the non-human *must* be kept vague, since anything readily comprehensible by the human mind would seem, by definition, to fall short of the truly non-human.

In **"2001,"** Mr. Clarke never made the mistake of telling us too much about the thin black slabs that triggered most of the action. The more mysterious their provenance and purpose, the more "significant" their involvement with human beings. We earthlings may not be masters of our fate, but the fate promises to be grander than anything we have dreamt of in our philosophies. This is all that **"2001"** says, and it is enough.

The sequel violates the mystery at every turn. We learn what the slabs are up to—and although the answer involves some splendid science-fiction conceits, it is hardly awe-inspiring. We meet Dave Bowman and Dr. Heywood Floyd again—but Mr. Clarke is so busy using them to explain things like orbital mechanics and evolutionary contingencies that he fails to make them any more interesting as people than they were the first time around. Except for Hal, the mad computer, characterization was not Mr. Clarke's strong suit in **"2001"**—and while Hal returns in the sequel, he has been "cured" of his paranoia, which renders him as dull as his human compatriots.

Sr. Calife, I cannot condemn you for wondering what a sequel to **"2001"** would be like. Nor can I condemn Mr. Clarke for yielding to the temptation to top himself. Nevertheless, I must protest: **"2001"** is not just another science-fiction novel or movie. It is a science-fiction milestone—one of the best novels in the genre and undoubtedly the best s.f. movie ever made. Such creations should not be lightly tampered with. To the Greeks, no sin was greater than that of hubris, the overweening pride of the man who wanted to be a god. But the chroniclers of Olympus committed a different kind of transgression: By making the gods too much like men, they insured their defeat by the "mystery" religions of the East. Sr. Calife, can you honestly say you are looking forward to the movie of **"2010: Odyssey Two"**?

Gerald Jonas, in a review of "2010: Odyssey Two," in The New York Times Book Review, *January 23, 1983, p. 24.*

MARY JO CAMPBELL

2001 enthusiasts, rejoice. HAL, Dave and all the gang are back in a worthy sequel [***2010: Odyssey Two***]. The year is 2010 and the deserted Space Ship Discovery is again in trouble. Her orbit (set by astronaut Dave before he disappeared) is erratic and she is in danger of falling into Jupiter. . . . To save the ship and discover what happened to it and its crew, an expedition of Russian and American scientists heads out to Jovian space. This compatible group includes Dr. Heywood Floyd, the project director for Discovery's last trip, and Dr. Chandrasegarampillai, HAL's programmer and surrogate daddy. Although both are put in suspended animation for the first part of the journey, Dr. Floyd is awakened early. Someone is trying to get to Discovery before them and it looks like that someone will make it. From then on a nonstop adventure begins. . . . The description of Dave's journey through Jupiter is alone worth the price of the book. *Europa* may become a household word. Suspenseful, thought-provoking and lots of fun, ***2010*** is a winner.

Mary Jo Campbell, in a review of "2010: Odyssey Two," in School Library Journal, *Vol. 29, No. 6, February, 1983, p. 94.*

GENE DEWEESE

For my money, Arthur C. Clarke has written two of the three most memorable science fiction stories of any length: **"Rescue Party"** and **"Childhood's End."** (The third is Isaac Asimov's "Nightfall.") And all of his fiction, from **"A Fall of Moondust"** through **"Rendezvous with Rama"** to **"Fountains of Paradise,"** is liberally sprinkled with that same, spine-tingling sense of wonder that made me read his first novel, ***Against the Fall of Night*** at least three times and buy, over the years, at least a half dozen copies of it and the later, expanded version, ***City and the Stars.***

2010 also has its share of that same sense of wonder, which means that it is one of the dozen or so most enjoyable SF books of the year. Even so, it is in some ways disappointing, not only because it doesn't live up to the exorbitant advance publicity but because it doesn't measure up to Clarke's best.

On the plus side, as Carl Sagan says on the dust jacket, it is a "daring romp through the solar system." Clarke shows us a variety of wonders, both real and imagined, and the picture of a future of cooperation in space between the U.S. and Russia is realistically optimistic. There is life not only tens of thousands of miles down in the maelstrom of Jupiter's atmosphere but beneath the ice of Europa. . . .

On the other hand, ***2010*** is not so much a sequel to the original book, which was in many ways superior to the movie, but a sequel to and an explanation of the movie. Unfortunately, many of these explanations already existed in the book, ***2001,*** though not always in the same form. In ***2010,*** some are simply expanded upon or modified slightly, such as the reasons for HAL's turning against the crew. Others, however, are in effect, downgraded. The monoliths, for instance, are treated in a much more down-to-earth way in ***2010.*** The biggest comedown, however, was in the nature of the Star Child, the creature into which Bowman was transformed at the end of ***2001.*** In the original book—and to some extent in the movie—the Star Child was cosmically spine-tingling, a harbinger of the next, unknowable quantum leap in human evolution. In ***2010,*** however, the transformed Bowman is no longer a god-like Star Child but an all too human energy creature who is little more than an observer for his still incomprehensible masters beyond the Star Gate. Similarly, their purpose, compared to what was only hinted at in the original book, is, though a bit mind-boggling, all too cut and dried.

Still, for those who have only seen the movie (and were perhaps confused by its ambiguities), ***2010*** is an excellent way to clear up that confusion while being taken on a fascinating tour of the post-Voyager solar system. Just to play it safe, though, don't read ***2001*** first.

Gene Deweese, in a review of "2010: Odyssey Two," in Science Fiction Review, *Vol. 12, No. 1, February, 1983, p. 15.*

CREATIVE COMPUTING

When asked if and when he would ever write a sequel to ***2001: A Space Odyssey,*** Arthur Clarke spent the better part of a decade explaining that such an undertaking would be utterly impossible. He was right, of course, and his reasons for changing his mind are nearly beyond my capability to fathom.

Nonetheless, we have lately been presented with ***2010: Odyssey 2,*** and sheer curiosity, I should think, to some degree accounts for its having spent two months on the *Times* Best Seller list.

Having been a fan of Arthur C. Clarke and ***2001*** since childhood, I was not about to let the pusillanimous attempt sneak past me. I knew I would be disappointed, but somehow held out the vague hope that the author would manage to do the impossible: write a sequel to a book for which no sequel can be written. (p. 302)

Clarke breaks the most serious sequel commandment: he compromises the symbolism of the earlier work. This is the worst flaw in ***Odyssey 2,*** which treats its estimable original symbols and characters with a marked lack of respect. Dr. Heywood Floyd, a minor character from the original work, is the protagonist in the new book. He is treated deferentially enough, although he is not really a very engaging main character. But the two major characters from the original who reappear, HAL and Bowman, are treated with all the courtesy an annoyed patrolman might extend to a bag lady. I was appalled.

Poor, poor HAL. Clarke explains to us that HAL's malfunction in murdering several crew members on the original Jupiter probe was solely due to his preoccupation with the security of the mission. Not to fear: with a bit of therapy from a stereotypical AI type, HAL is as docile as a pussycat this time around. What a slap in the mouth.

The strength of HAL as a symbol in the original work is severely undermined in this weak and narrow interpretation. To me, HAL embodied all the dangers posed by the concept of man-made intelligence. When a conventional machine malfunctions it might stop working or work incorrectly. When a thinking machine malfunctions, however, it might become insane—and we may not realize it until it is too late. HAL was acting on irrational impulses when he terminated the crew of the Jupiter probe—any attempt to rationalize them, let alone diffuse them, desecrates HAL's original meaning. HAL's appearance in ***2010: Odyssey 2*** is therefore reduced to even less than a gratuitous cameo.

But this is nothing compared to what the author does to the symbol of David Bowman. Here is a character who has been immersed in the ultimate transcendental experience: he has experienced his own physical death, traveled through corridors between universes, then returned to earth as the "star child." The resurrection myth plays heavily here. Clarke now has the audacity not only to reintroduce Bowman as a character, but even allows him to recontact his old girlfriend by appearing to her inside her TV set! The reader is left to wonder about the nature of the commercials aired during his program.

Then there is Clarke's mistreatment of the monolith, which is by far the most heinous debasement of a major image from the original. I will spare you the gruesome details. Suffice to say that Clarke reduces the imagery of the monolith to a symbol with all the intrinsic worth of a "No Parking" sign.

By treating Bowman as Casper the Friendly Ghost, HAL as a woebegone Atari 800, and the monolith as an intergalactic whoopee cushion, Clarke manages to transform one of the most resplendent stories of the '60s into a segment from "Bewitched." He does, to some small credit, sandwich some new sci-fi action into the chapters describing a supplementary probe to Jupiter, tries to work in some new material discovered by Voyager, and many of his visual descriptions are vintage stuff. But these constitute precious little justification for the liberties he has taken with a now-classic story he himself knew was better left alone. ***2010: Odyssey 2*** does not deserve to inhabit the same universe as its predecessor. (pp. 302-03)

J. J. A., in a review of "2010: Odyssey 2," in Creative Computing, *Vol. 9, No. 5, May, 1983, pp. 302-03.*

PUBLISHERS WEEKLY

This collection of 31 short essays, articles, book introductions and speeches [***1984: Spring; a Choice of Futures***] is predominantly optimistic in tone. Although concerned that we may destroy ourselves, Clarke believes that technology can be used to preserve peace. . . . He has high hopes for the long-term benefits of satellite communications and the prospect of sophisticated electronic teaching machines as widely and cheaply available as transistor radios are today. He also writes about space exploration, literature, his first experience as a movie actor, the ocean and creationism. Although hardly compelling, these miscellaneous pieces are always interesting.

A review of "1984: Spring; a Choice of Futures," in Publishers Weekly, *Vol. 225, No. 1, January 6, 1984, p. 75.*

PUBLISHERS WEEKLY

[***Profiles of the Future***] is the first revised edition of a book Clarke originally published in 1962. An exploration of the technology of tomorrow, this slightly updated classic hasn't dated, for the well-known science fiction writer takes a long view. . . . He even makes time travel and instantaneous transport (teleportation) sound almost plausible. Clarke's guiding belief is that whatever is theoretically possible will be achieved. History has borne out this view, with "foreseeable" inventions like the telephone and flying machines, and "unexpected" marvels like nuclear energy and photography. . . . An exciting glimpse into the possible for readers with an open mind.

A review of "Profiles of the Future," in Publishers Weekly, *Vol. 225, No. 4, January 27, 1984, p. 72.*

GREGORY BENFORD

While clearly the most famous and international of all science fiction writers, [Clarke] is not a unique type. He stands in the tradition of English futurists who have used fiction or nonfiction to spread their visions—H. G. Wells, J. D. Bernal, Olaf Stapledon, Freeman Dyson. They were convinced that only in scientific areas is reliable prediction possible; as Clarke says "there are some general laws governing scientific extrapolation, as there are not (*pace* Marx) in the case of politics and economics."

It is a pleasure to see reissued ***Profiles of the Future*** . . . , an elegantly phrased "inquiry into the limits of the possible" which was immediately influential. It details Clarke's expectations about what might be achieved within the bounds of scientific law. Books on futurology date notoriously, yet this one has not, principally because Clarke was unafraid of being adventurous. . . .

Clarke's cool, analytical tone pervades all his writing. He prefers a pure, dispassionate statement of facts and relationships, yet the result is not cold. Instead, he achieves a rendering of the scientific esthetic, with its respect for the universal qualities of intelligence, its tenacity and curiosity. His fiction neglects conflict and the broad spectrum of emotion, which gives it a curiously refreshing honesty. . . .

Futurology has expanded enormously since ***Profiles*** first appeared, probably because now most people have seen a half dozen major revolutions happen in their own lives. The effects of this on politics will be vast; most problems today are posed in the formula "What if . . .?" and "If this goes on . . ."—the staple openings of science fiction narratives.

Clarke is a member of a small elite in the field, the "hard" sf writers. Along with the figures of the Golden Age (Asimov, Heinlein, etc.), he saw that there was no contradiction between fidelity to facts and narrative interest. Thus he discounts the standard remark about our times, that the reality of space exploration and the latest high tech will out-strip sf writers: "It should never be forgotten that, without some foundation of reality, science fiction would be impossible, and that therefore exact knowledge is the friend, not the enemy, of imagination and fantasy."

In this vein, ***Ascent to Orbit*** is a collection of Clarke's scientific papers, mostly from the 1940s, with autobiographical introductions. It details his early thoughts on rockets and warfare, satellite communication, the "space elevator," and the implications of computers. His principal contribution was suggesting that satellites could serve as economical radio relays.

This came at a time when learned societies devoted to aeronautics and astronautics strove to appear sober and earnest, and published Clarke's **"Orbital Radio Relays"** in *Jet Propulsion* magazine. . . . The essay had wide influence, though as Clarke himself admits, it was an idea so obvious that half a dozen others would probably have come up with it at about the same time, 1945. Though he says "I suspect that my early disclosure may have advanced the cause of space communications by about fifteen minutes," in fact his ceaseless promotion of it did alert many to the implications.

He was no less right about even larger issues. His 1946 essay, **"The Rocket and the Future of Warfare"** anticipated the essentials of ICBM nuclear war, and called for measures to avoid it. Though many were concerned with "atom war" then—the United States made its proposal of international regulation of nuclear weapons to the U.S.S.R. and was turned down—few saw the fateful mating of the bomb and the rocket. Notably, most of those who did were science fiction writers, who had long believed that rockets were the next big step in aeronautics. (They had long before gotten bored with jet planes.)

Getting from speculation to hardware is a long voyage, often taking centuries. Clarke has continued to contribute to this journey, as the collected speeches and essays in [***1984: Spring; A Choice of Futures***] underline. He points out that while gradual progress is essential, great figures like von Braun sometimes spur development long before it is obviously necessary. "If there had been government research establishments in the Stone Age, we would have had absolutely superb flint tools. But no one would have invented steel." . . .

The oddments collected in ***1984: Spring*** do not shape into a definitive argument; the book is obviously scraped together to capitalize on Clarke's spurt in recognition, following ***2010.*** Still, it gives us oblique views of a man whose life has been focused on the grandest perspectives. Stapledon, whom Clarke idolized, dragged the conflicts of his era into far-future visions, attributing Marxist—indeed, Stalinist—dynamics to even alien, insectoid races. This riddles some of Stapledon's work with anachronisms.

Clarke never loses his bearings this way, and his work will probably wear well. Against the anti-technological bias of our recent ties, he remains impressed with the enormous possibilities science holds out to us. In the end, "whatever other perils humanity may face in the future that lies ahead, boredom is not among them."

Gregory Benford, "Arthur C. Clarke: The Prophet Vindicated," in Book World—The Washington Post, *March 25, 1984, p. 6.*

PAUL GRANAHAN

[***Profiles of the Future***] is an intriguing attempt to outline some possible parameters of future technology, although the author recognizes the futility of detailed prediction. As he describes the book's purpose: "It does not try to describe *the* future, but to define the boundaries within which possible futures must lie." Clarke is uniquely suited to glimpse what's coming in that he combines a solid scientific background with the elasticity of imagination found in a seasoned SF writer.

The work leads off with two fascinating chapters concerning some "Hazards of Prophecy," detailing pertinent examples of past celebrated scientists making such myopic assertions as the impossibility of heavier-than-air flight, space flight, and even domestic use of the ordinary light bulb. This results in a statement of the well-known Clarke's First Law: "When a distinguished but elderly scientist states that something is possible he is almost certainly right. When he states that something is impossible, he is very probably wrong."

Other topics discussed in lucid and entertaining fashion are the nature of time, the brain-body interface, and even the chances for teleportation. I, myself, try to maintain a balance, falling into neither pitfall of hopeless technophobia or unquestioning technophilia. On the one hand, Clarke's scientific optimism is contagious, offering hope in the face of constant doomsaying. Conversely, I think he can go a bit far, for instance in espousing the inevitability of authentic Artificial Intelligence, largely glossing over deeper questions about what intelligence really is.

Interestingly, the book reflects many of the same strengths and weaknesses embodied in Clarke's science fiction. In reminding us of the wonders inherent in both the Cosmos and ourselves, it succeeds admirably, though at times the author does verge on violating his own First Law. (pp. 75-6)

Paul Granahan, in a review of "Profiles of the Future," in Best Sellers, *Vol. 44, No. 2, May, 1984, pp. 75-6.*

KARL EDD

[**"1984: Spring, a Choice of Futures"**] is an erudite yet interesting collection of Clarke's speeches, articles and personal essays. Using George Orwell's "1984" as a cultural beginning point, Clarke sets forth his own list of future possibilities. . . .

The book breaks down into four sections. These deal with (a) How modern technology and science contribute to international peace and possible eventual brotherhood (b) space exploration (c) science fiction writing and various influences on it (d) personal reminiscences and essays that are every bit as entrancing and informative as any by Ursula Le Guin. They deal much with his life and the island of Sri Lanka (once called Ceylon) where he lives. Scientist Clarke frequently waxes poetically lyrical about his island, and demonstrates a deep concern with the same coral reef and undersea problems that have occupied much of Jacques Cousteau's attention.

Clarke's book contains the thought-wealth of a lifetime, and is filled with youthful courage.

Karl Edd, in a review of "1984: Spring, a Choice of Futures," in Science Fiction Review, *No. 52, Fall, 1984, p. 26.*

Peter (Malcolm de Brissac) Dickinson

1927-

Zambian-born English novelist, author of books for children, short story writer, and scriptwriter.

Dickinson is highly respected both for his detective novels for adults and his fantasy stories for young people. He is noted for setting his works in strange yet complete and consistent worlds. Because he creates imaginary worlds, Dickinson is sometimes identified with science fiction writers, although he himself claims to write "science fiction with the science left out." Instead of science, Dickinson's works are based on anthropological and historical knowledge, which he combines with offbeat plots. Both his mysteries and fantasies are praised for their economical and lively prose style and their character development.

Dickinson first gained recognition for his *Changes* trilogy for young adults. Comprising *The Weathermonger* (1968), *Heartsease* (1969), and *The Devil's Children* (1970), the trilogy explores an England in which a social revolution has led to the abolition of all machinery and regression to an age when superstition prevailed over scientific reasoning. The novels examine human nature under stress and emphasize the necessity of love, understanding, and brotherhood in a world gone awry. In his other books for young people, Dickinson uses exotic, historical settings as starting points from which to create fantasy worlds. *The Dancing Bear* (1972) begins in sixth-century Byzantium; *The Blue Hawk* (1976) is set in an ancient kingdom resembling Egypt; and *Tulku* (1981) takes place in China and Tibet during the Boxer Rebellion. Dickinson has also written mysteries for young adults, including *Annerton Pit* (1977) and *Healer* (1983).

© *Jerry Bauer*

Dickinson's first crime publications were a series of novels about Scotland Yard detective James Pibble, a character Dickinson intended to be the antithesis of the type of secret agent typified by James Bond. Self-effacing, introspective, and clumsy, Pibble nevertheless is successful at solving crimes. The Pibble novels observe the conventions of the traditional detective novel: there is a closed group of suspects, and Dickinson provides the reader with all the clues needed to solve the mystery. However, these novels are anything but traditional in their settings and characters. *Skin Deep* (1968) centers on the members of a New Guinean tribe who have been brought to London, where their chief is murdered. *Sleep and His Brother* (1971) takes place at a home for children suffering from an imaginary disease which involves a telepathic state followed by a coma and ending in death. After publishing these novels and three others about Detective Pibble—*A Pride of Heroes* (1969), *The Seals* (1970), and *The Lizard in the Cup* (1972)—Dickinson said of his character, "You can't go on creating somebody when he's already created" and stated that it wasn't likely that he would write about Pibble again. However, the detective reappears in *One Foot in the Grave* (1979) as a nursing-home resident who stumbles upon and solves a crime.

In Dickinson's other crime novels, the role of the detective is taken by a non-professional—often a scientist—who becomes entangled in a mystery. Like the Pibble stories, these novels are classically structured and have bizarre settings and characters. *The Green Gene* (1973) takes place in a Great Britain where chaotic apartheid prevails; all people of Celtic origin have green skin and are subjected to discrimination. In this novel, Dickinson satirizes prejudice and political tyranny and employs an Indian mathematician to solve one of his most outrageous murder mysteries. Another novel, *The Poison Oracle* (1974), is set in a fictional Arab country where the chief witness to a murder is a chimpanzee that is being taught to use symbols to communicate with humans.

Dickinson's recent novels include several period pieces set in the English countryside during the 1920s. Rather than focusing on a mystery, *A Summer in the Twenties* (1981) combines a love story with description of the political conflict of that era. Two mysteries that share similar settings are *The Last House-party* (1982) and *Hindsight* (1983).

(See also *CLC*, Vol. 12; *Contemporary Authors*, Vols. 41-44, rev. ed.; and *Something about the Author*, Vol. 5.)

LEO HARRIS

[The theme of ***Skin Deep*** (published in the United States as ***The Glass-Sided Ant's Nest***) is] integration, or, rather, its inevitably concomitant converse, disintegration. A handful of jet-black New Guineans, all called Ku, escape the Japanese and settle in North Kensington. The elders' tribal loyalty wars with the young ones' desire to live in the twentieth century, and murder lets Western logic into the neolithic survival. . . . It may stem from motives that we would find irrational—but this is a true whodunit, relying on what its author would call Proper Clues. Under the entertaining surface there is a genuine understanding sadness; puzzles may be solved, problems are less transigent. The Kus will haunt you.

Leo Harris, "Unlawful Assembly," in Punch, *Vol. CCLV, No. 6679, September 11, 1968, p. 381.**

THE CRITIC

The Glass-Sided Ant's Nest is one of the most offbeat detective stories to appear in a number of years. The sleuth is a semi-hero who stands halfway between "Handsome" West and Inspector Dover, both in charm and intelligence. Mr. Dickinson . . . may fudge just a little in his solution, but the fascination of a tribal murder in the heart of London is so great that you won't really mind. (pp. 92-3)

A review of "The Glass-Sided Ant's Nest," in The Critic, *Vol. 27, No. 4, February-March, 1969, pp. 92-3.*

PUBLISHERS WEEKLY

Peter Dickinson has moved into science fiction and social satire with [***The Green Gene***]. The hero is an Indian technical expert, rather dark himself, and an expert on the "Celtic gene" which turns a subordinated and possibly rising segment of the British populace bright green. Mr. Humayan, a whimsical and much-put-upon character, manages to get politically and sexually involved both with the government and with green revolutionary forces. He copes with his problems with a mixture of cowardice and verve in this intelligent, well-paced thriller with excellent and varied characterizations.

A review of "The Green Gene," in Publishers Weekly, *Vol. 203, No. 14, April 12, 1973, p. 59.*

OSWELL BLAKESTON

Once upon a future . . . hold on, it's happening now, the Celts, through the mysterious behaviour of an hereditary gene, are actually turning green. They've done it in [***The Green Gene***], and the whites have zoned them off and reserved them, as coloured non-voters, for servile labour. They've solved the problem? Alas, clergymen and liberals take the part of the outcasts and give them ideas. The Greens blow up the knitware department at Harrods, and nasty things happen which are not reported in the censored papers. In desperation the authorities bring Humayan, Mr Pravandragasharatipili Humayan, a computer genius, from India to London to tidy things up. (p. 62)

Not such a humdrum situation, you might say and speak like a white man; but Mr Dickinson does not make up his mind whether he wants to write an offbeat thriller or a pointed satire about the way Englishmen might treat little or big green men. The burlesque dilutes both possibilities: and I really can't affirm that that is Mr Dickinson at his beautiful best. (p. 63)

Oswell Blakeston, in a review of "The Green Gene," in Books and Bookmen, *Vol. 20, No. 9, June, 1975, pp. 62-3.*

MARGHANITA LASKI

Taking all in all, I am prepared to assert that, as of today, Peter Dickinson is the best crime writer we have, always absorbingly original, yet never more intense than the crime novel can bear—and over-intensity is a far sorer thumb in this genre than writing too well. His first and penultimate books, ***Skin Deep*** and ***The Poison Oracle,*** are surely already classics, and ***The Lively Dead*** falls only a little short of them.

In seedy W11, Lydia, wife of an ex-army baronet rehabilitating from a nervous breakdown, lets rooms to an assortment of necessitous lodgers, from an ageing government-in-exile to various other inadequates, all unlovable to anyone less vigorously decent than Lydia. . . . The set-up is ripe for crime, and sinister crime there is, but Lydia, a natural aginner, saves and solves by independent judgment and guts, as much against the Establishment she instinctively distrusts as in support of the trusted who betray her.

Marghanita Laski, "Crime and Intensity," in The Listener, *Vol. 93, No. 2409, June 5, 1975, p. 748.**

NEWGATE CALLENDAR

Dickinson is one of the better stylists operating out of England. Who can ever forget the eerie **"Sleep and His Brother"** . . .? **"The Lively Dead"** is just as well written, just as full of insights into character. But it does move at a slow pace; almost half the book is spent in character development. . . . If you can stick with the slow opening, you should find this book rewarding.

Newgate Callendar, in a review of "The Lively Dead," in The New York Times Book Review, *November 2, 1975, p. 51.*

ANN A. FLOWERS

China at the time of the Boxer Rebellion is the setting of [***Tulku***], a superb adventure novel seen through the eyes of thirteen-year-old Theodore Tewker, son of an American missionary. After his father's missionary settlement is destroyed, Theodore encounters Mrs. Jones, an intrepid middle-aged English botanist, and her young Chinese interpreter Lung. . . . The three of them journey to Tibet, pursued by bandits and traveling over difficult terrain. Along the way Theodore is horrified to realize that Mrs. Jones and Lung are having a love affair. After a brief idyll in a mountain valley, the group is cornered by the bandits and is saved only by the intervention of a Tibetan lama. . . . Theodore's Christian faith is severely tried by his love for Mrs. Jones and for the lama, neither of whose lives are compatible with his beliefs. But Theodore is strong-minded and full of insight; he eventually comes to have a broader understanding of the meaning of religion. The book may be compared with *Lost Horizon* . . . , but ***Tulku*** is richer and more complex. The only flaw in the masterful story is that Lung, the Chinese lover, is not as fully developed as the other characters, who are unforgettable. The author, always noted for his style and versatility, has achieved a tour de force, a magnificent adventure story with an exotic setting and a philosophical theme.

Ann A. Flowers, in a review of "Tulku," in The Horn Book Magazine, *Vol. LV, No. 4, August, 1979, p. 421.*

GEORGESS McHARGUE

So much certified nonsense has been written about Tibet that it is difficult for any casual Western observer to be confident of even the most basic facts about the country and its customs. Thus I have no real idea whether, in the heyday of Tibetan Buddhism, lamas claimed the power to split their bodies into two. . . . I do not know whether a Western woman could conceivably be accepted as a pupil, or *chela*, of the head of a famous lamasery. What I do know is that [**"Tulku"**] is a superb adventure story—and more than an adventure story.

It is the time of the Boxer Rebellion in China (1900). Young Theodore Tewker has escaped the attack that killed his missionary father and leveled the Settlement he had built. Shocked and suffering survivor's guilt, Theodore encounters a traveling European woman and her escort. . . . [They] set out on an enforced joint odyssey that includes disguises, chases and bandit attacks. Then, on the very borders of the Forbidden Land, they encounter the Lama Amchi, who announces that his signs and oracles indicate that either Theodore or more probably Mrs. Jones's unborn child is the reincarnation of the one he seeks—the holy Tulku.

At this point, the reviewer is torn between summarizing the headlong progress of the plot and examining the novel's intricate and even subtle presentation of the conflict between Theodore's dogged Christianity and the Buddhism practiced by the lamas (and eventually, astonishingly, by Mrs. Jones). Suffice it to say that Mr. Dickinson never lets theology get the better of the action and brings his characters to satisfying, though exceedingly different, culminations of their spiritual and actual journeys. This is a memorable, pleasurable book, one that will bear rereading.

Georgess McHargue, in a review of "Tulku," in The New York Times Book Review, *September 16, 1979, p. 32.*

MARGHANITA LASKI

Sometimes outstandingly exellent, sometimes mushy is Peter Dickinson's thriller record, and ***One Foot in the Grave*** is a mushy one. Pibble, the retired cop, is in an expensive nursing-home, seemingly senile though only 64. By the time we discover he's merely ill and likely, at the end, to have a sterile marriage with a nurse half his age, he has, in mental muddle, shuffled with almost real-time slowness up a tower to find a murder. What with his semi-comatose states and his reminiscences, the reader's involvement has gone off long before the threads of old death form a muddled, loose-ended hank. (p. 63)

Marghanita Laski, "America Time," in The Listener, *Vol. 103, No. 2644, January 10, 1980, pp. 62-3.**

NEWGATE CALLENDAR

Some years ago, Peter Dickinson created a Scotland Yard detective inspector with the Dickensian name of Jimmy Pibble, and used him off and on in several novels. Now Pibble is back. He is old and retired from the force. He also has atherosclerosis and lives, fighting senility, in a nursing home. There he is adored by most of the staff and particularly by a certain nurse in [**"One Foot in the Grave"**]. . .

Things happen. There is a murder. . . . Cops invade the premises, and among them are men who had formerly worked with Pibble. It turns out that some of Pibble's previous cases bear on the present one. Some old murders are also tied up with it.

Mr. Dickinson has always been a sensitive, imaginative writer. Here he gives a harrowing picture of what it is to be ill and feeble, and how a man of dignity copes with it. Pibble has his good days and his bad ones, but his mind still retains a sharp cutting edge, blunted though it may be. Mr. Dickinson provides a convincing solution, and for good measure throws in a rather unlikely romance. Like all Dickinson books, **"One Foot in the Grave"** is unconventional, quiet, yet full of tension and hidden menace. This British author is a virtuoso.

Newgate Callendar, in a review of "One Foot in the Grave," in The New York Times Book Review, *April 20, 1980, p. 25.*

EARL F. BARGAINNIER

It is an over-simplification to characterize any author's work by a single adjective, but *playful* at least provides an approach to Dickinson's mysteries, and is less constraining than those which have been most often used: bizarre, antic, zany, ingenious, fantastic, raffish, witty, and outlandish—though all of these apply in one way or another. His playfulness is exhibited most clearly by his staying within the formulas of the classic British detective novel and of the thriller, while incorporating into those formulas a mass of diverse, incongruous, and often wildly comic elements, from an alternate British royal family and corpses pickled in homemade vodka to a teenaged witch doctor named Robin and a beautiful terrorist in a sultan's harem. Whatever interests Dickinson—and his interests are obviously many—is material to be packed into or around the frame of mystery-detection, creating a stylish, if occasionally somewhat overstuffed, final product. One minor example is his indulgence of his love of words, which must send many readers to their dictionaries. . . . It is as if he wishes to see just how much he can cram into the formula without its either exploding or collapsing. He plays with the conventions, stretching and twisting them, but never allowing them actually to break. This ability simultaneously to stay within the genre's limits and to add other disparate elements, often unlikely ones, to enrich it is evident in both the five Pibble novels and the five later non-series mysteries.

The novels in which James (Jimmy) Pibble is protagonist established Dickinson as mystery writer. . . . Of Pibble's genesis, Dickinson states, "I simply wanted a detective who was not at all James Bondish, was unsexy, easily browbeaten, intelligent, fallible." Dickinson succeeded in his purpose. On Pibble's first appearance, he is described as "aging, unglamorous, greying toward retirement," but with a "reputation for having a knack with kooky cases." . . . (p. 185)

Though a millionaire friend bluntly tells him, "you are short on glamour," . . . Pibble is not totally dull. Dickinson gives him an original, even quirky mind. His favorite expression is "Crippen!" He imagines his name in Greek: Tzaimy Pimpel, and he considers the possibility of constructing an English sentence wholly from Greek, but fails. . . . The most distinctive aspect of his original thought is the number of similes, metaphors, and analogies which are continually running through his mind. They may be strictly unnecessary, but they contribute both to his personality and to the playfulness of the novels. On meeting a young woman, he thinks, "Her voice had the sharp reasonableness of a career businesswoman in a B film." . . . Similar examples are found in the non-Pibble novels, but they are most effective here in illustrating the imaginative quirkiness of Pibble's mind.

The dominant trait in Pibble's character is his self-deprecating introspection. Only partially the result of his sense of social inferiority, it is actually at the core of his personality. He does not just worry about the impression he makes on even the least important of persons, but views himself as "baffled, inadequate Pibble." . . . He disbelieves most compliments, but needs ego support. (p. 186)

Pibble is no super-detective in the Holmes or Poirot mold; he is literally and figuratively a little man, with anxieties, fears, weaknesses, and problems with others. But in spite of all of his troubles, he is a success as a detective. Though active for his age—especially in ***A Pride of Heroes*** [published in the United States as ***The Old English Peep Show***] and ***The Sinful Stones*** [published in Great Britain as ***The Seals***]—he is basically ratiocinative. Aside from his introspective self-questioning, his major qualities as detective are his honesty, caution, efficiency, persistence, and pity. (p. 187)

These five qualities of Pibble constitute his principal detectival traits, but his ability to put clues together is, of course, a part of his success. An anthropologist in the first novel says, "He would have made a sound scholar." . . . In ***A Pride of Heroes*** he realizes by page 96 what has happened to the disappeared admiral, and in ***The Lizard in the Cup*** a flash of insight presents the solution to him. . . . [It] is his personality rather than his ability which prevents his receiving his due recognition.

The analysis presented of Pibble may seem to negate the concept of Dickinson's playfulness. In spite of his quirkiness of mind, Pibble himself is not a particularly playful character; rather, his introspective personality is used as a contrast to his odd cases. It is the nature of those cases which provides opportunities for play. . . . The kinky, kooky cases with which Pibble is faced are so because of the settings, the Dickinsonian plot devices which enliven the crime and its investigation, and the characters.

To say that Pibble solves cases twice in London, at a country estate, in Scotland, and in Greece gives no real idea of those settings. ***Ants' Nest*** takes place in the home of the Kus, a New Guinea tribe transferred to London by an English anthropologist, who is also a member. Needless to say, the cultural differences provide a test for Pibble—and many possibilities for Dickinsonian play. The other London case [described in ***Sleep and His Brother***] is at the McNair Foundation, a home for cathypnic children. There Pibble must confront not only a slick con man, a hostile executive secretary, and a murderer, but also the cathypnics, nicknamed "dormice," children with a sleeping sickness which makes them telepathic. . . . [***The Sinful Stones***] occurs on Clumsey Island in the Hebrides: "an island of idiots, and a paradise of thieves." . . . A brutal pseudo-religion, The Faith of the Sealed (whose rich founder, named Hackenstadt, is in Tibet with a half-caste actress), is headquartered there. Pibble has to escape in a boat up the Firth of Lorne with Sir Francis Francis, a ninety-year-old winner of two Nobel prizes, who is only lucid at four-hour intervals; a drunken nurse; and a teenaged schizophrenic. If that is not enough, Pibble's knowledge of sailing is nil. Also dangerous for him is Herryngs, the country estate of ***A Pride of Heroes,*** with its roaming lions, duel ground, and working scaffold. It has been turned into a British version of Disneyland, but one much less safe than the American original. [***The Lizard in the Cup***] takes place on the Greek isle of Hyos. . . .

These settings are all of the closed-circle type: within a limited space and with a restricted number of suspects. Although ***The Sinful Stones*** is a thriller, the other four are traditional British detective stories. In them, Dickinson provides all necessary clues and leaves no loose ends dangling, but he also adds distinctive and playful elements. In ***Ants' Nest*** alone, he employs such varied narrative techniques as stylistic parodies, a hospital chart, and, most effectively, Pibble's stream-of-consciousness delirium from concussion to explain the case. (p. 188)

Since Dickinson's abandonment of Pibble, he has written five other mysteries, but has not attempted another series detective. Rather he has used amateurs who find themselves inadvertently caught up in murder and conspiracy. In three cases, the protagonists are scientists: a mathematician (***The Green Gene***), a psycholinguist (***The Poison Oracle***), and a behaviorist psychologist (***Walking Dead***). In ***The Lively Dead*** and ***King & Joker,*** women are the central characters: Lady Lydia Timms and Princess Louise respectively. With the exception of ***King & Joker,*** these novels are more in the thriller mode than that of the detective story. Because of the variety of techniques and materials, each requires separate examination.

The Green Gene is an amalgam of the thriller, science fiction, and socio-political satire. Its basic premise is that nearly all people of Celtic blood have—and always have had—green skin. As a result, Great Britain is torn by racial prejudice and terrorism. Though Dickinson's tone is one of detached amusement, he attacks all sides. His view is expressed by a character who says, "We are a brutalised people . . . we are all brutalised." . . . Politicians and their propaganda receive most of the satire. The Anglo-Saxon establishment plans PNPC (Post Natal Population Control), i.e., genocide, and already imposes curfews, creates zones (ghettos) for "greenies," and performs executions in Conciliation Camps. The United States is not much better. . . . (p. 189)

Into this maelstrom, Dickinson introduces that old device of satire: the foreigner. In this instance, he is an Indian mathematical genius named Pravandragasharatipili P. Humayan, familiarly known as Pravi or Pete. Brought to England because he has solved the mystery of the green gene, he is appalled by the savagery he encounters. When his English hosts are destroyed in a bomb blast—set to conceal the murder of a spying maid—he comes to the realization that he "had been treated as a naïve idiot by practically every Saxon with whom he had had any dealings." . . . He then proceeds to get revenge, using his knowledge of computers. Humayan is hardly the typical hero; he is physically small, almost perpetually in a state of sexual excitement, and avidly desirous of publicity. . . .

Humayan and the political satire are surrounded by such improbabilities as electric bagpipes; a Maoist-Monarchist; two repulsive "Booger" dogs named Want and Ought; Oghan, an outlawed druidic alphabet; a rock group performing Yeats's "Easter 1916"; and Humayan's Indian friend, Mr. Palati, who has wardrobes of women's clothes for his erotic revels. . . .

What is astounding is that Dickinson pulls all of the threads together so that Humayan solves the murder and disrupts the political tyranny. (p. 190)

The second scientist is Wesley Naboth Morris of ***The Poison Oracle,*** who is both a psycholinguist and zoo-keeper for the Sultan of Q'Kut. Morris is the owner of Dinah, a chimpanzee whom he is teachng to communicate via symbols. Dinah sees the murder and becomes the chief witness against the murderer. Before the murder the reader learns the history of Q'Kut and the relationship of its Arabs to its marshpeople; is presented with the complexities of the marshpeople's language, which naturally fascinates Morris; and is given a tour of the Sultan's palace. . . . Characters range from Prince Hadiq, who is learning English from Batman comic books, to Akuli bin Zair, Q'Kut's prime minister, who spends much of his time making home porno movies. . . .

With his "tepid nature," Morris is an unlikely figure in such a bizarre setting. But after the murder, he must enter the poisonous marshes to prevent war between the Arabs and the marshmen, and there he undergoes a trial for witchcraft. As introspective as Pibble, but less appealing, Morris does not like the formlessness of modern civilization, refuses to accept his place in it, isolates himself from close friendships, and decides "to be a quietist and wash about where the tides drifted out." . . . At the same time, his profession has made him an excellent detective. . . . His analysis of the events enables him to realize that all of the strange circumstances are simply the result of greed and to discover, with Dinah's aid, the murderer. (Again, Dickinson is scrupulous in first preparing for everything and then accounting for it. A notable example is the parallelism between the nature of Morris's witch trial and Dinah's revelation of the murderer.)

Dr. David Foxe is the third scientist. In ***Walking Dead,*** he is sent by The Company to Hog's Cay in the Southward Islands in the Caribbean to run a series of experiments on rats. Hog's Cay is ruled by the Trotter family, one member of which appears in ***The Lizard in the Cup***. . . . Most of the novel is concerned with Foxe's being dragooned by the prime minister into shifting his experiments to native prisoners—to find a means of making them permanently "good." As it turns out, everyone involved is double-crossing everyone else. There is an unconnected and unintentional murder—another maid—but the emphasis is upon how Foxe will get out of his predicament with the Trotters. (p. 191)

After engineering an escape of natives from The Pit, the Trotters's prison, an experience which shatters once and for all his emotional detachment, he undergoes self-horror, and only the love of a native girl brings him to an acceptance of his humanity. In mythic terms, the novel is an account of Foxe's descent into hell and rebirth; that such an interpretation is not farfetched is made abundantly clear by the nature of the prison and the escape from it. (p. 190)

The final two novels have female protagonists and take place in London. The single murder of ***The Lively Dead*** has already occurred before the opening of the novel. Mrs. Newbery, housekeeper of the Livonian government in exile and mother of Procne Newbery, one of London's more famous call girls, is the victim. The Livonians have their embassy on the top floor of Lady Lydia Timms's townhouse. Lydia's husband has had a mental breakdown and her son is dyslexic, but she is a cheerful, fiercely independent young woman. . . . A warm, loving woman, her basic philosophy is "The only possible way to behave is to take people as they are now—they're part of your life and you're part of theirs, and you've got to accept that. It doesn't matter what they were or what they've done." . . . (pp. 191-92)

This attitude is severely tested by those with whom she must deal. (p. 192)

Aside from the playfulness in the presentation of Lady Lydia, which dominates the novel, other elements which also contribute are the national hero of Livonia pickled in "Varosh," that country's vodka; Mrs. Pumice, a tenant, and her nasty infant Trevor; Dickie's military mania; Procne Newbery's insouciance; Mrs. Newbery's body turning up in the Timms's rosebed; and much of the dialogue. All in all, ***The Lively Dead*** is Dickinson's most overtly comic mystery.

If ***The Lively Dead*** is the funniest, ***King & Joker*** offers the most unusual setting and family for murder: Buckingham Palace and a British royal family—not the present royal family, but an alternate one, descended from the Duke of Clarence, Victoria's grandson, who did not die in his twenties. Dickinson provides a supposedly unpublished fragment of "King Victor I," by Lytton Strachey, and a genealogical chart to show the descent. . . . The protagonist is Princess Louise, who is actually illegitimate, being the King's daughter by his mistress. . . . At thirteen, Louise wishes to give up "Princessing": "I'm going to start a Princesses' Lib movement—I'll write to all the cousins and order them to join." . . . This desire becomes even stronger when she discovers her illegitimacy. . . . The King's "twin" cousin Mr. McGivan is the first victim—murdered sitting on the throne. Finally, as solver of the murders is Miss Ivy (Durdy) Durton, royal nanny for three generations, now bedridden in her nineties. . . . Though her mind wanders, she is determined not to die until after she has saved the royals again, and she, with the help of Louise, succeeds. (pp. 192-93)

Dickinson is completely fair in laying out the clues, but he uses the practical jokes, the royal adults' concern for Louise, her own identity crisis, and the physical "identity" of the King and McGivan to baffle the reader, for in spite of its varied elements, ***King & Joker*** is structurally that Golden Age favorite: the closed circle murder-in-the-family-mansion mystery.

These five novels, from ***The Green Gene*** to ***Walking Dead,*** while multivarious in specific emphasis and detail, share at least three qualities in common. First and foremost is that no matter how diverse the materials, Dickinson is scrupulous in supplying clues and relating *all* apparently unrelated events. Second, all five combine the comic to some degree with mystification, without ever degenerating into the silly. Third, as with Pibble, Dickinson elaborately delineates the psychology of his protagonists, all of whom are unlikely detectives. Other similarities among the novels are the clash of differing cultures (***The Green Gene, The Poison Oracle, Walking Dead***), the significant use of animals (***The Poison Oracle, King & Joker, Walking Dead***) and children or teenagers (all but ***Walking Dead***) and servants as principal victims—three maids, two bodyguards, and a butler—the Sultan of Q'Kut being the major exception. Finally, as might be expected, the actual murders are much less important than their effects on the protagonists.

In his ten novels, Dickinson has extended the range of British mystery fiction as to materials which can be employed within the basic formulas of the genre. And in so doing, he has written stylish, sophisticated works, which blend the comic in its many forms with murder and thrills. Both in the Superintendent Pibble works and those without him, Dickinson has evidenced an original, imaginative, and wide-ranging talent as mystery writer. In the late 1970s his novels are a major indication that the British mystery novel is not only still alive, but in a most admirable state of active vigor. Since the novels give the impression that Dickinson is having fun writing them, it is my wish that he will continue to enjoy himself so that readers will be provided many more of his playful mysteries. (p. 193)

Earl F. Bargainnier, "The Playful Mysteries of Peter Dickinson," in The Armchair Detective, *Vol. 13, No. 3, Summer, 1980, pp. 185-93.*

JOHN MELLORS

Peter Dickinson makes a shaky start in ***A Summer in the Twenties,*** as if none too sure how to achieve the transition from crime and children's books to 'straight' fiction; for example, he appears to be straining after some literary effect inappropriate to his story when he writes of Tom and Judy 'skimming above the surface of their sensuality like martins flycatching along a river-reach'. Also, the *jeunesse dorée* of Oxford, among whom Tom, the blue-blooded hero, somehow finds time to follow his First in Mods with a First in Greats, includes some fairly unbelievable caricatures, including one who answers to the name of 'Woffles'.

The author gains in confidence, and his book gathers momentum, when Tom gets involved with striking dockers in Hull in 1926. The conflict between the workers and the fascist fringes of the establishment, who sponsor agents provocateurs to provoke violence, gives the second half of ***A Summer in the Twenties*** a tension that excites and holds the reader.

John Mellors, "Nostalgia Novels," in The Listener, *Vol. 105, No. 2711, May 7, 1981, p. 616.**

A. N. WILSON

The 1920s are close enough for plenty of survivors to correct our false impressions, but far enough away to be viewed with complete detachment. So, now, or about now, is the time to be writing a novel about the General Strike.

[In ***A Summer In the Twenties***], Peter Dickinson has done so with wit, elegance, and sensitivity, as one would expect. (p. 26)

It concerns the dilemma of a nice young man called [Tom Hankey] who is caught up in the General Strike. He is abroad when the story opens; he has just met Judy Tarrant, the girl of his dreams and everything appears to be going swimmingly . . . when he is summoned home by his father and told to learn to drive a train.

Meanwhile, swigging fizz over their breakfast at the Mitre, Tom's Oxford chums think it might be jolly to put on masks and go round shooting up Bolshies. Make a change from beating up aesthetes. Tom shares their loathing of the Bolshevik threat; and, for a series of complicated reasons, relating to the girl he loves, he is enlisted on the side of Right, to find the Bolshie ring-leader in the dock-land of Hull. But he is not entirely on the side of the masked men in plus fours. For one thing, he admires the intelligence and courage of a Communist agitator called Kate Barnes. For another, he genuinely comes to like and admire some of these working-class fellas: train-drivers, dockers and so on. . . . But there is some evil blighter in their midst, stirring up trouble, whose *nom-de-guerre* is Ricardo. It is Tom, and he alone who, after a series of hectic adventures and deductions, finds out that Ricardo is . . . Well no, I won't spoil it; but it is no surprise, because the educated ones are always the worst.

Going back in one's imagination to reconstruct the conflicts of the recent past is a bold thing to do. Does the novelist take with him the superior 'wisdom' of his own times—the late J. G. Farrell's technique—or does he try to write in the spirit of the times he is depicting? The latter is the much bolder choice. Peter Dickinson has made it, risking being thought derivative and blimpish. He is neither. His book is fresh, always observant, at times moving. But it is interesting to see how it has been done.

He has not been at all ashamed—given that he is writing an adventure story set in 1926—to use the conventions and attitudes of story-tellers of that date, or authors closer to that date than he is. He raises no complications in the reader's political response, for example; he is as unselfconsciously hostile to the Bolshie threat as Dornford Yates or John Buchan would have been. And he has seen that the only way to achieve this effect is to be hostile to it in their sort of way. His villain is partly drawn from these authors, partly perhaps a throw-back to Conrad; his nickname, Ricardo, somehow summoning up the atmosphere of *The Secret Agent*. In the 'social' scenes he draws on authors of a slightly younger vintage; but he is equally unashamed to tread paths well-beaten by the likes of E. Waugh and A. Powell. . . . On the other hand, the semi-sentimental gusto with which Tom treats his Oxford landlady recalls Dorothy L. Sayers: 'Tom had never seen Mrs Godber smile but he had learnt to know when she was pleased'.

None of this diminishes Mr Dickinson's claim to be an 'original' writer. ***A Summer in the Twenties*** is a fragrant pot-pourri made from other men's flowers; but the mixture is pure Dickinson. The plot—how gallant Tom beat the Reds and got his girl—is really only incidental to the care and devotion with which Mr Dickinson has reconstructed his period: its costumes; its films (Valentino dies in the course of it); its social *mores;* its railways (there is much here for votaries of steam engines), its politics. It is not meant to be a serious book, but it is a highly intelligent one. . . . Mr Dickinson has not tried to offer new thoughts on the General Strike. He does not condescend to his characters because they are alive in 1926. His vignette gives an oddly convincing picture of what it was like to be them. And the fact that the illusion is created by such literary means is entirely conscious and within the author's very deft control. (pp. 26-7)

A. N. Wilson, "Red Menace," in The Spectator, *Vol. 246, No. 7974, May 9, 1981, pp. 26-7.*

MARGERY FISHER

[Topical] and exciting, the plot [of ***The Seventh Raven***] is . . . fruitful in allowing the author to suggest clashes of character as well as actual conflicts of political interests. A group of intellectual, middle-class Londoners are planning their traditional opera, to be performed in St. Andrew's Church by a talented but somewhat unruly children's choir. . . . While the cast is being sorted out, a request is made which, for diplomatic reasons, must be granted, and Juan O'Grady . . . is included. . . . The irrepressible spirits of spoilt Juan pose their own problem but far more serious is the fact that he is the son of the Mattean Ambassador to Britain, for enemies of the South American régime plan to snatch the boy as a hostage against reform and the freedom of arrested comrades. . . . Make no mistake, this is not just another look at the currently fashionable topic of terrorism. To start with, the narrative is spoken by Doll, a girl of seventeen who has grown up with the yearly opera and is now a kind of non-acting liaison between producers and cast. Highly intelligent, mildly cynical and politically innocent, Doll gives us her view of the situation—the siege in the church, the behaviour of individuals young and old, the careful deploying of outside forces—as well as her definitions, discerning and impetuous, of the personalities concerned; and all the time we can see how the terrorists, from being a group of four anonymous terrifying invaders, are seen to be individuals with their own strengths and weaknesses. Magnificent in character-drawing, in the highly pictorial style, brilliant in the way the opera comes through bit by bit and echoes the violence and terror of actual happenings . . . , the book is most telling in the way it implies change, . . . most of all in Doll, whose views on life are tested and stretched in a way that she only partly realises. Of all Peter Dickinson's books for the young, this is perhaps the most skilfully devised, with its shifting atmosphere, its glancing wit and its sharp eye for individual speech and behaviour.

Margery Fisher, in a review of "The Seventh Raven," in her Growing Point, *Vol. 20, No. 3, September, 1981, p. 3941.*

HARRIET WAUGH

Peter Dickinson, usually reliable to keep the reader intrigued with his bizarre plots and humour, has come up with a disappointing one this time in ***The Seventh Raven.***

A children's operatic Society is invaded by South American guerrillas wanting to kidnap a diplomat's son who is taking part in the opera. The story is about their attempts to coerce and cajole the whereabouts of the boy from the children who are hiding him in their midst. The action is seen through the eyes of a teenage girl helper who is not a sufficiently complex character to carry the novel, and the story is too simplistic. Children should enjoy it.

Harriet Waugh, "Thrillers," in The Spectator, *Vol. 247, No. 7991, September 5, 1981, p. 22.**

MARY M. BURNS

An annual production of a children's opera at St. Andrew's Church becomes the focus of international concern when four revolutionaries attempt to kidnap the young son of a South American diplomat. . . . [The] events transcend the merely sensational and become a vehicle for exploring personal and societal values and attitudes, the relationship between liberty and neutrality, and the rights and responsibilities of both the government and the governed. Yet, as in many of the author's previous works, difficult philosophical and moral questions do not take over the story but become an integral part of the pattern, resulting in a dynamic and compelling narrative remarkable for its evocation of mood and creation of character.

Beginning with ordinary details, the book captures the petty, often comic political struggles of community organizations, foreshadowing the larger, more dominant conflict to come. A significant element in both conflicts, ultimately the point of convergence, is the idea of a "middle ground," that undistinguished turf where most folk, unremarkable and unremembered, play out their lives. (p. 31)

Then, as the story builds to its climax, the concept is reexamined as a moral issue. The revolutionaries, in a mock trial, claim that neutrality is synonymous with betrayal; therefore, art cannot be neutral. The only legitimate activist among the hostages—Mrs. Dunnitt (a singularly appropriate name)—counters with the statement that there is "'little liberty . . . in a society which has no middle ground, no areas of neutrality. Art and poetry and music are . . . one sort of freedom.'" The issue is not entirely resolved, however, for the author depicts the ambivalent emotions of those taken hostage and suggests that no one remains unchanged by the experience. But in creating tension, he avoids unnecessarily harrowing his readers—a technique more powerful in its restraint than many a more violent portrayal. With carefully honed phrases and superb imagery Dickinson has created a suspenseful, multidimensional narrative. (pp. 31-2)

Mary M. Burns, in a review of "The Seventh Raven," in The Horn Book Magazine, *Vol. LVIII, No. 1, February, 1982, pp. 31-2.*

NEWGATE CALLENDAR

Mr. Dickinson is one of the more original mystery story writers of the decade, and he generally manages to create something that breaks the mold. In fact, one wonders if **"The Last House-party"** really belongs to the mystery genre, even though a crime is committed at one point.

A sort of "Brideshead Revisited" affair, the book hops around in time in a rather unsettling way. Its characters are very British upper class, there is a great deal of political and other kinds of talk, there is a castle and a tower clock that play a large part in the plot (but disabuse yourself of the notion that this book is in any respects a Gothic), and at the last houseparty there is a nasty crime that one finds hard to believe. Mr. Dickinson is as suave and sensitive as ever, but readers who look for the classical amenities in a mystery story should steer clear of this one.

Newgate Callendar, in a review of "The Last House-party," in The New York Times Book Review, *January 6, 1983, p. 26.*

MARGHANITA LASKI

Peter Dickinson is good . . . can even be excellent, but he is not good enough (is anyone?) to write the kind of book in which the writer is writing the kind of book in which the reader has to be kept au fait with the kind of book he is writing and his difficulties in writing it, and this is the kind of book that ***Hindsight*** is. The themes are school and corrupting women, and the title is a pun.

Marghanita Laski, "Death with Deep Feeling," in The Listener, *Vol. 110, No. 2821, August 11, 1983, p. 24.**

THE JUNIOR BOOKSHELF

The only thing we may predict about Peter Dickinson is that his next book will always be unpredictable. So it is with ***Healer.***

As one of the bigger boys in junior school Barry has had a curious relationship with Pinkie, a very small girl distinguished for most of the time by an inability to solve the most ordinary problems of school life. . . . When he is sixteen he finds Pinkie again, she is still a small and mainly helpless child, but she has become the heart of the Foundation of Harmony, an organisation devoted to healing. Is she a willing part of a force dedicated to the service of mankind, or the victim of a ruthless racketeer? As the story is by Mr. Dickinson, there is no simple answer.

Nor is Barry a simple instrument of Pinkie's salvation. He too is a complex being in whom 'reality' is in constant conflict with the alter ego he calls Bear. In this confused state he infiltrates the Foundation and plans and carries out a daring rescue plan. There is a tremendous and exciting climax, but no simple happy ending can be contrived. Only Pinkie has learnt to laugh at her dreadful mother, and Barry can perhaps live successfully with Bear as he, in the post-hibernation sunshine, sniffs 'the air of a world made new.'

This is a marvellous book, superficially a story of adventure and chase, but one from which one peels different levels of meaning layer by layer. What it means fundamentally is for each reader to decide for himself; certainly each will find his own satisfaction in the search and his own enlightenment from the final discovery. As always Peter Dickinson writes beautifully, using words with great freshness and delicacy.

A review of "Healer," in The Junior Bookshelf, *Vol. 47, No. 5, October, 1983, p. 212.*

ANATOLE BROYARD

Peter Dickinson won a prize with his first crime novel, **"The Glass-Sided Ant's Nest,"** and he has since become a kind of spoiled darling of people who prefer what might be called avant-garde suspense writing. In his latest novel, **"Hindsight,"** he may have gone too far. Yet going too far in a literary direction is like an inside joke for the advanced reader, a crime against the crime novel, so to speak.

"This is a murder story" is the first sentence of **"Hindsight,"** as if Mr. Dickinson were notifying the patient reader that it is not a Jamesian novel of manners. The book is a mystery of where, exactly, the mystery is. It moves through Jamesian suspensions rather than suspense, as the technique of the novel itself becomes an instrument of detection.

The narrator is a novelist writing about a group of people among whom a murder has been committed. Since his novel, which brings previously unconscious memories to the surface, is the means of revelation, it might be said that Mr. Dickinson's book also reconstructs the crime of the novel form.

Rogers, the narrator, decribes his work on his book in a manner that will remind some Anglophiles of Anthony Powell wrestling with the problems of recapitulation in "A Dance to the Music of Time." . . .

Though there is a murder in the book, it does not appear until page 112. A stag's antler is the lethal weapon and the author makes some characteristic cross-references between deer in rut and men and women in love. The motive for the murder—and nothing essential to suspense being given away here—is the securing of the profits from an author's copyrights.

While Mr. Dickinson is not for every taste, he is certainly a change from the mayhem of, say, Robert Ludlum. He reminds us that even T. S. Eliot's "Wasteland" is a detective story of sorts in which modern man is, at least spiritually, killed off.

Anatole Broyard, in a review of "Hindsight," in The New York Times, *October 14, 1983, p. 29.*

ROBIN W. WINKS

Peter Dickinson has always been one of the most interesting—some would say outrageous—talents working over the broad terrain between the "straight novel" and the murder mystery. Reviewers invariably pronounce his books highly original, beautifully written, and rightly so. . . . Of late Dickinson has turned to the period piece, setting his novels in the English countryside in the 1920s, to which he seems particularly drawn with a sense of ever deepening personal nostalgia. Since Dickinson was born in 1927, these books are tours de force of research, empathy, and bluff in nearly equal, exquisite proportion.

Now, in ***Hindsight,*** the former *Punch* editor, who has tended to combine the best qualities of Monty Python, Charlotte Jay, and Peter Lovesey, has moved onto the tricky ground of the schoolboy reminiscence. Since Dickinson also writes children's books, he knows how children think, the games they play, their slang, vulgarities, sexual fantasies, fears, sentimentalities. He uses this knowledge, his love of a vanishing English countryside, and his very clever (some might say, too clever by half) ability to manipulate words to fine purpose in ***Hindsight.*** The result is both his most interesting novel and perhaps his least successful mystery.

Paul Rogers, successful writer of mystery stories, begins another of his best sellers, drawing upon his prep school days for background. As he reconstructs a year in school in Devon, away from London to escape from wartime bombing, he provides the reader with a view of a 12-year-old boy as he sees and reconstructs the events around him, and he also shows us the mature Rogers reflecting upon new meanings which hindsight might give to those events. . . .

[In] the end it is all more difficult than it need be. Having the reflective writer Rogers discover that the bright though not yet deeply perceptive child Rogers did not understand all that he saw is not an original idea. But with the added overlay of the writer's correspondence with . . . [a] biographer (who is conveniently ill and unable to travel, so that Rogers must recollect on paper rather than in conversation), the idea that nothing is what it appeared to be, even to eye-witnesses of considerable reliability, is given fresh meaning. That a young boy might not recognize the sexual tension, indeed sexual duplicity, to which he was an unwitting partner, has long been established. That "details seemed to quiver and replace themselves in satisfactory patterns" is natural with so many overlays of hindsight, but the natural is very satisfactorily demonstrated.

In the end the reader realizes, just as Rogers does, that the covert meaning the child had attached to the events he had almost subconsciously understood was not, in fact, the true meaning, and that very clever villainy indeed had been done one dark night near the school. For it is the young Rogers who discovers the body of a young teacher, apparently killed by a stag; it is the writer Rogers who recalls the meaning he had not dared express to himself at the time; and it is the Rogers who must assist his fellow professional, the biographer, who realizes that his original conclusion, which he had hidden from himself, was also wrong.

This is very clever stuff, enjoyable to read, fascinating to follow. But there is less going on in the end than there appears, and the reader, once aware of the three dimensional chess game in which he is engaged with Dickinson, is there ahead of both the second and the third Rogers. There is no sudden revelation, the mystery having been telegraphed by the necessity to pack in so much elegant commentary. Thus Dickinson has, by stealth and indirection, done precisely what his warmest admirers say he has always done: he has written a highly intelligent, apealing, and quite beguiling novel which, though it may pass for a whodunit, still walks that difficult terrain between the straight novel and the murder mystery.

Robin W. Winks, "The Devon Deception," in Book World—The Washington Post, *December 18, 1983, p. 7.*

GEOFFREY O'BRIEN

Most crime writers use the detective form as a guideline; the trappings vary, the skeletal frame holds steady. Peter Dickinson works his variations on the frame itself. In books like ***King and Joker*** and ***The Last Houseparty,*** he tinkers with the suspense genre, seeing how radically he can rearrange it without sabotaging it altogether. It's a game as intricate as any that Anthony Berkeley played, but Dickinson is more than an intellectual trickster. His new book, ***Hindsight*** . . . , takes a familiar premise—a novel about a man writing a novel, with all the attendant confusion between fiction and reality—and refashions it as a murder mystery in which the crime is concealed within a repressed childhood memory. The narrative's components interlock as maddeningly as a Chinese box, but at the heart, in counterbalance to Dickinson's feats of legerdemain, is a melancholy meditation on the difficulties of writing and the deceptions of memory. Most remarkable of all is the narrative rhythm, in which the slow and faltering process of remembering is transmuted into a vehicle for breathless suspense.

Geoffrey O'Brien, "Genrefication," in VLS, *No. 23, February, 1984, p. 18.**

MARGERY FISHER

Healer has as its theme, like so many of Peter Dickinson's books, the discovery, the exploiting and the protection of identity. Coming in a sceptical spirit to a gathering because of increasingly debilitating headaches, Barry Evans recognises in the healer a girl he knew as a child and, exchanging a signal often used between them, he concludes that Pinkie wants to be rescued from her isolation and the exhausting responsibility of her gift. To achieve this he has to exercise a good deal of physical ingenuity, for Pinkie as a valuable property is closely guarded, but he also has to contend with a conflict in his own personality, a suppressed violence which could be as much of a danger as an asset to him. He has against him, as well, the furious determination of a corrupt man who sees his power and prosperity threatened and, most crucial, the Healer herself—for whether for good or ill, ultimately Pinkie is unwilling to give up her lonely exclusive position in the world. There are no real decisions in this challenging story; rather, through the format of a thriller packed with incident and suspense, we are shown people trying to resolve their own contradictions, all separate yet influenced and challenged by their fellows.

Margery Fisher, in a review of "Healer," in her Growing Point, *Vol. 22, No. 6, March, 1984, p. 4209.*

John Donovan

1928-

American novelist and dramatist.

Donovan's fiction for young adults explores such relatively sophisticated subjects as alcoholism, sexual experimentation, and death. John Rowe Townsend acknowledges that Donovan "has the reputation of a taboo buster," and some critics question the suitability of these adult-oriented issues in young adult literature. Donovan insists that his novels can be interpreted on a number of emotional levels and are suitable for readers of different ages. Critics generally agree that his approach is compassionate and objective.

Donovan's central characters are usually adolescent boys attempting to cope with feelings of alienation, uncertainty, and guilt. Although often emotionally or physically isolated, each protagonist manages to befriend a sympathetic person or animal with whom he can share his feelings. Donovan's first novel, *I'll Get There. It Better Be Worth the Trip* (1969), gained notoriety for the brief homosexual encounter between Davy Ross, a lonely boy who is ignored by his family, and his similarly unhappy friend, Doug. Alice Hungerford described their relationship as an innocent "manifestation of their puberty and need for love." *Wild in the World* (1971) concerns John Gridley, the sole survivor of a large rural family decimated by a series of tragedies. John remains alone in a mountain wilderness until he adopts a wild dog whose life he saves. Although most critics charged that Donovan expressed an indifferent attitude toward death, Patience M. Canham contended that the book contains valuable social commentary for young people. *Good Old James* (1974) has an elderly man as its central character. The loneliness and neglect he feels is emphasized by his reliance on a housefly for companionship.

***Family* (1976) combines elements of science fiction, realism, and parable. After escaping from an experimental laboratory, four apes form a familial relationship in the wilderness. One of them observes that their mutual caring and respect represent those qualities that should distinguish the human race from other beasts. The belief that people have become insensitive both towards other creatures and each other appears throughout Donovan's work.**

(See also *Children's Literature Review*, Vol. 3; *Contemporary Authors*, Vols. 97-100; and *Something about the Author*, Vol. 29.)

ALICE HUNGERFORD

[*I'll Get There. It Better Be Worth the Trip*] reflects the changes taking place both in the kind of fiction written for young readers and the kind of society in which many of them are growing up. It has no plot in the old-fashioned sense, no adventures for a hero-type boy, no solutions to the problems raised. Rather it portrays, with a natural realism, a few months' flow of experience in the life of a 13-year-old boy whose circumstances, far from happy, are probably like those of many, many children.

Davy Ross comes from a broken home—his mother is an alcoholic, his father has remarried. His grandmother has managed to give him a happy, fairly normal boyhood. When she dies, his mother insists on taking him to her cramped, rather arty apartment. To New York Davy goes with "old Fred," his dachshund—his link with happiness, his "security symbol," his confidant and sole love.

Shadows of an adult world enclose him. His father maintains only an embarrassed, perfunctory relationship with him. . . . Davy feels some sympathy for his mother's ineffective efforts to cope with responsibility, but is repelled by her alcoholic hugs, jealousy of the dog, self-pity, and niggling at his father and the new wife. With a schoolboy companion he shares happily [some social activities]. . . . It is a mark of the new sophistication in fiction that the author takes the boys through an innocent physical relationship—a manifestation of their puberty and need for love. . . .

Salinger and his *Catcher in the Rye* are an influence on this very modern book which directs itself to the increasing maturity of younger readers.

Alice Hungerford, in a review of "I'll Get There. It Better Be Worth the Trip," in Book World—The Washington Post, *May 4, 1969, p. 5.*

LAURA POLLA SCANLON

[*I'll Get There. It Better be Worth the Trip*] is a beautifully written, poignant depiction of how Davy absorbs his experience and begins to grow toward manhood. It could only be found objectionable by the most narrow-minded of little old librarians. . . .

Laura Polla Scanlon, in a review of "I'll Get There. It Better Be Worth the Trip," in Commonweal, *Vol. XC, No. 10, May 23, 1969, p. 300.*

PAUL HEINS

The impact of [***I'll Get There. It Better Be Worth the Trip***] is shattering—all the more since the boy reports his emotions and dilemmas objectively. [David's] well-observed closeups mark the rhythm of the narrative; his judgments of the self-centered adults around him are mercilessly honest, and mother and grandmother emerge as life-sized characters. . . . And David's love and care for his dog create a lifelike and unforgettable canine portrait. The novel makes skillful use of the elements of divorce, alcoholism, adolescence, school friendships, and death to portray a boy at a crucial time in his life and derives its effective power from the protagonist's frankness and intelligence. (pp. 415-16)

Paul Heins, in a review of "I'll Get There. It Better Be Worth the Trip," in The Horn Book Magazine, *Vol. XLV, No. 4, August, 1969, pp. 415-16.*

MARTHA BACON

[***I'll Get There. It Better Be Worth the Trip***] celebrates the [hero's] homosexual encounter with a schoolfellow. Davy Ross has multiple problems: his parents are divorced, his mother is alcoholic, his grandmother dies, and his dog is killed by a car. He tells it all in the language of *The Catcher in the Rye,* and the book is craftsmanlike and competent. But its purpose and execution pose a number of questions. The loss of innocence is an adult's subject. Once we have put it behind us, there is no return to the world or the speech of childhood. The language of children is inadequate to it, and the application of grammar school jargon to corruption and passion is neither natural nor comforting. A young person who has experienced a romantic encounter of the sort described by Davy Ross is probably best served by *David Copperfield* . . . , in which such relationships are seen in the context of a larger life. I am also inclined to think that a book focused on a love affair between schoolfellows might have just the opposite effect on this age group from that which the author intended. It would not meet the needs of the initiated and might arouse in the unconcerned unnecessary interest or alarm or both. (p. 150)

Martha Bacon, "Tantrums and Unicorns," in The Atlantic Monthly, *Vol. 224, No. 6, December, 1969, pp. 148, 150-152.**

JUNE JORDAN

You could . . . call [**"Wild in the World"**] "Death Comes to the Little Ones." . . . Or, "Another Page, Another Death" and, as another American has remarked on these matters, "so it goes."

We are so messed over, and up, by violence, so used to the ubiquitous particulars, that the event of death shrivels easily on a sidestreet of our consciousness. And life itself hardly ever arouses more than the ego of loneliness. Is that the truth, and is that what Donovan is trying to prove to kids? Do kids accept such an "adult" view of things? Do they need such guidance into gloom? . . .

"Wild in the World" opens . . . by presenting a family in demise. First there were 13 Gridleys, including Mom and Dad. But then, this and that killed him and her and him and him and her and her and her and him, off, until only three brothers were left. . . . [But] after a few pages, two more Gridleys have died, and that leaves John. Our hero. Let's recapitulate that body count: Twelve human beings have been listed as dead or killed in the opening pages. Is this a joke?

No: It is to explain the solitude of the hero. It is to explain the love that John, the hero, develops for a wolf. It is to explain why he names the wolf "Son." It is a metaphorical something or other to let kids know that when your folks die, and you have no more family anywhere, you could still be lucky and find a wolf that will be your friend.

Are you kidding me? . . .

Near the end, the wolf named Son is bitten by a rattlesnake and John, for the first time, is allowed to show some wish against death.

It's nice that John doesn't want his wolf to die. If you have lasted this far, through flat exposition of a weird, isolated life indifferent to the dead, and to the living, a life content to shuck corn, milk cows, can beans and make no effort to know and touch other lives, well, then, you may feel relief about John and his wolf.

Incidentally, at the end, John dies, and Son, the wolf, sleeps where John used to sleep. So that's that?

Maybe the author thought that kids would finally scream and insist on life and survival and, therefore, insist on the definite loss that human death signifies. But kids have to make that scream for the living, when they turn off the telenews, and turn to a book, kids hope to find reassurance there. They want the books they read to slow down the cameras so that there is time for tears, and grief, and memory, and new love. **"Wild in the World"** doesn't help. It is a horror story told in monotone. Nobody screams for anyone else.

June Jordan, " . . . Or Just Another Horror Story, Told in Monotone?" in The New York Times Book Review, *September 12, 1971, p. 8.*

DIGBY B. WHITMAN

[**"Wild in the World"**] is the story of John Gridley, the only survivor of a family of New Hampshire farmers who, in Donovan's book, have hardly more life than the vegetables they raise. They don't talk, think, feel; they don't do much of anything except die off, and that not very credibly. The father and one son shoot themselves; two children die of scarlet fever; two others in a fire; one of snakebite; another from a self-inflicted fishhook wound; the last is kicked to death while milking a cow.

Before John follows his family into the ground . . . he makes friends with a dog. When the book ends, the dog is the only tenant of the farm, which is just how the reader would have it. Perhaps nothing in the story is more incredible than that the story itself could come from the author of the perceptive and sensitive **"I'll Get There. It Better be Worth the Trip."**

Digby B. Whitman, in a review of "Wild in the World," in Book World—Chicago Tribune, *Part II, November 7, 1971, p. 8.*

PATIENCE M. CANHAM

Tragedies like [those depicted in Donovan's ***Wild in the World*** and Jean Renvoize's novel *A Wild Thing*] certainly aren't what has generally been thought of as the stuff of children's literature. Nor has the sprinkling of four letter words been customary even in books for teen-agers. Yet despite this and some implausibilities of plot, these books demand respectful attention.

Whether it is [their authors'] purpose or not the same point rings out clearly from them both: Man is not a wild creature, nor can he live in fear and isolation from his fellow men. The brotherhood of man, however tenuous it seems, is still an urgent necessity in the human scene. We turn our backs on it and on each other at our peril.

Do I recommend these books for teen-agers? Yes, with reservation. Essentially honest as I think they are, these books tell only part of the whole human condition. In families where love, compassion, and trust are communicated, these stories can be seen in perspective—not as morbid horror tales but as social comment from which we can learn.

Patience M. Canham, "Left Alone in the Wilderness," in The Christian Science Monitor, *November 11, 1971, p. B6.**

PAUL HEINS

Despite the spare beauty of the writing, the feeling for the New Hampshire countryside, and the sympathetic and sensitive portrayal of the companionship between the surviving Gridley and his animal companion, [***Wild in the World***] is unimpassionedly lugubrious; and one is left wondering why such a book is at all published for children. Of course, it could appeal to an adolescent who had the makings of a congenital pessimist. (p. 57)

Paul Heins, in a review of "Wild in the World," in The Horn Book Magazine, *Vol. XLVIII, No. 1, February, 1972, pp. 56-7.*

JOHN ROWE TOWNSEND

"No man is an island," said John Donne. "Every man is an island," says John Donovan; or so it seems to me from his three novels. As an islander you can build your makeshift boats, make brief risky voyages, visit with other islanders; but at nightfall you must return to your own.

This is not a cheering thought for teen-agers, most of whom, in intention at least, are highly social beings, but many of whom have times when they are terribly aware of being islanded. And the lukewarm comfort Donovan offers, at first sight anyway, is little more than "Accept, resign yourself, it's the same for everyone."

In **"I'll Get There. It Better Be Worth the Trip"** and again in [**"Remove Protective Coating a Little at a Time"**] Donovan seems concerned with a special kind of isolation that is often felt by young people in our time. This is the state of noncommunication resulting from the failure of the parental generation to say anything to the young. (p. 34)

Harry, the hero of **"Remove Protective Coating a Little at a Time"**, cannot even fight with his parents Bud and Toots. Young themselves in the flabby fifties, married too soon, missing their way in life, lacking conviction and confidence, not knowing how to solve their own problems, Bud and Toots are hardly parents at all. Floundering through the puberty of the emotions, Harry makes friends with 72-year-old Amelia. . . . Amelia lives rough in a condemned building and calls herself a bum, "a good and honorable bum.". . . The wrecking crane moves in on Amelia's block; she disappears. A contact between islanders is over. Nevertheless, Amelia has given Harry something to replace the protective coating (of childhood ? of innocence ? of self-absorption?) which his parents could not have given.

John Donovan has the reputation of a taboo-buster: homosexuality in **"I'll Get There,"** death in **"Wild in the World."** And the new book will give some people wrong impressions, for which he himself is to blame. He begins with the introduction of Harry to "one of the great indoor sports" (you play it by yourself) and with Harry's first attempt to make out with a girl (a flop). (pp. 34, 36)

But these are false trails. The book is hardly at all about sex. . . .

"Remove Protective Coating" is a slight-seeming book that slips down with deceptive ease. There is more to it than appears: arguments about freedom and responsibility are important, yet are only hinted at; and there is a sense that life continues beyond the edge of the page and that the author could tell you far more about Bud and Toots and Amelia if he chose. John Donovan is not so casual as he appears. Maybe he gives the impression that adult life is hardly worth the trip; you have to put up with it but don't gain much by bothering. Yet his ending is not entirely negative. And after all, Mr. Donovan has bothered to write the book. (p. 36)

John Rowe Townsend, in a review of "Remove Protective Coating a Little at a Time," in The New York Times Book Review, *November 4, 1973, pp. 34, 36.*

SADA FRETZ

John Donovan purveys no . . . neatly summarized wisdom in ***Remove Protective Coating a Little at a Time*** . . . , and from the start it is clear that his projection of 14-year-old Harry Knight's growing pains aims for something altogether beyond transcribed actuality. Harry's young parents—a former twirler and a promising jock, who started Harry the night their high school classmates crowned them Space Age Sweethearts—are pop art blowups of banality, and Harry's early experiences are paraded with the same deliberately glossy snap. There is a kind of surreal humor, too, in his first sexual encounter . . . , and a sort of ludicrous poignancy in his crush on slightly older twin tennis stars Brendan and Sarah, who might be just a newer, smarter edition of his parents. (pp. 6C-7C)

Harry turns from his parents' crumbling marriage and his mother's belated identity crisis and psychiatric visits to friendship with Amelia, a 72-year-old panhandler he meets in the park. Amelia, who quizzes Harry about circumcision, tests him with whimsical rules for their relationship, and prattles on about unconstrained love . . . , is no doubt intended, by way of contrast with Harry's floundering parents, to embody a self-sufficent, together, human reality; instead, her appearance marks a descent from the sort of symbolic distortion of the earlier caricatures to sentimental cliche. (p. 7C)

Sada Fretz, "A Long Sad Tale," in Book World—The Washington Post, *November 11, 1973, pp. 6C-7C.**

PAUL HEINS

Although the New York atmosphere of [***Remove Protective Coating a Little at a Time***] is successfully suggested, the theme of the story is never made clear; and all of the characters—except Amelia—are two dimensional. The style is skillfully casual, but its terseness prevents it from exploring in depth the possibilities of the situation, and too much of the book is given over to irrelevant allusions to Harry's sexual habits and insufficiencies. The reference to copulation on page one would help to classify the novel as naturalistic; however, at least one of Amelia's statements to Harry smacks of the sensational: "'I read somewhere that about ninety percent of American male babies are circumcised at birth, automatically.'"

Paul Heins, in a review of "Remove Protective Coating a Little at a Time," in The Horn Book Magazine, *Vol. L, No. 1, February, 1974, p. 54.*

BOOKLIST

Deceptively packaged in a picture-book format, [***Good Old James***] is really an adult parable for middle grade discussion. Good old James has retired from a life of moderately successful labor and is feeling his way into an old age of doing whatever he wants to, a pursuit that proves aimless and lonely until there appears in his room a persistent fly which he feeds, names, and grows deeply attached to. Donovan shows integrity in his spare style, leaving room for readers to reach as far as they can into the social and emotional implications of James' superfluousness and to interpret the ending as either bitter or sweet.

A review of "Good Old James," in The Booklist, *Vol. 71, No. 17, May 1, 1975, p. 912.*

LOUISE ARMSTRONG

I'm happy (delighted) to see John Donovan's new book, **"Good Old James."** It is spare, charming and, by its subject, undelightful. Donovan, who has previously dealt with crumbling families, odd relationships, death, here deals with those outposts of alienation—old age, retirement, loneliness. The tone is understated, sophisticated and precisely reflected in James Stevenson's drawings.

Good Old James, your company man, retires. Gets up when he feels like it, eats when he feels like it. Then:

"This is one big house," he says. Sells it. Travels. . . . Tries to rent a room in his old house and can't. Tries rejoining his old company . . . and can't.

Finding a fly in his hotel room . . . , he puts out some crumbs. And becomes attached to the fly.

The book is labeled "for all ages," and is, as that suggests, available at different levels. Mentally recyclable. What a good idea. (And what a good category—allowing original books, mavericks, to find their level.)

This one, I think, is for adults and kids to share. It's thinnish, too spare to engage adults straight. And, obviously, bringing nothing more to it, it's this story about a man who makes a pet of a fly.

Louise Armstrong, in a review of "Good Old James," in The New York Times Book Review, *May 4, 1975, p. 40.*

BOOKLIST

When Sasha [the ape narrator of ***Family***] senses that the experiment he and a group of apes are being used for may mean dismemberment and reassemblage for the artificial creation of a perfect specimen, he leads an escape foray from the university laboratory into the wild hills of the surrounding countryside. He and three apes brave enough to venture out with him develop a closely knit family: great Moses, a "natural" born in the jungle; Dylys, shy and perceptive; and Lollipop, the frolicsome youngster. Coached by Moses, they return to a natural, elemental existence and are joined eventually by a sympathetic human whom they learn to love and call simply "Man." Winter, the hunting season, and tragedy draw near, and their friend departs. Moses and Lollipop are shot, and with no place left to live, Sasha and pregnant Dylys put themselves back in the hands of humans, grieving for their fellow apes and hoping "that Man is not lost." Although there is occasional discord between parable stylization and full-fledged fictional development, the tightly constructed events move inexorably to an end that will draw on the reader's fund of thought and feeling. It is encouraging to remember that behind the ape narrator's disheartening view of the human race is a human writer.

A review of "Family: A Novel," in The Booklist, *Vol. 72, No. 15, April 1, 1976, p. 1112.*

SUSAN COOPER

On the campus of a university in the Eastern United States are assembled, for enigmatic experimental purposes, 23 assorted apes. Four of them, Moses, Dylys, Lollipop and Sasha, one day escape and go off to live wild in the countryside. [**"Family"**] is written by Sasha.

Now John Donovan does not resemble an ape; indeed he has the ability to write like an angel. But in the space of a short hypnotic book he manages to convey far more about the essential nature of a species of animal, and by simile that of man, than "Watership Down" achieved in hundreds of pages of rabbits.

Apes, Sasha tells us, have not only their own living language but also a fossil form retained by those who, like himself, were born in captivity. Their emotions are more straightforward than those of man (who comes off much better in this book as a loner living in the woods than as Homo Academicus). Like men, these apes can feel guilt, and be moved by a sunset. Unlike men, they have learned the right way to treat the earth: "When humans come to a place, that place is changed in ways that make that place *for* humans. When apes and other creatures come upon a place, they accept that place for what it is already." . . .

The doomed odyssey of [the four apes], right up to the last terrible wail of warning, says a lot about survival and mutual dependence in a flawed world.

Simply as a piece of literature, **"Family"** does not match Mr. Donovan's **"Wild in the World."** . . . It's a remarkable work all the same, vivid and direct and thought-provoking.

Susan Cooper, in a review of "Family," in The New York Times Book Review, *May 16, 1976, p. 14.*

MILDRED ARCHER

Ever look into the eyes of some creature and wonder what it thinks of you? [In ***Family***] Mr. Donovan suggests that it is just as well that we do not know.

In a group of apes, being used in a variety of tests, Sasha, who is older in the experience of man, tells the story of what happens when four of the group, alarmed by the mysterious disappearance of two of their companions, decide to escape before they too become part of the terrible experiment which Sasha has already guessed. The narrative follows the four while they live in glorious primeval freedom before two are killed by men, and the other two sadly return to the dubious safety of their laboratory.

What these four apes think and say, as they reveal their history and philosophy, is frequently troubling. . . . Donovan's apes speak almost reverently of men who in earlier times knew the classical languages and were wiser and kinder. . . . And they comment that man's unceasing desire for change is not progress; they know the truth.

[***Family*** is a] sad book, not only for the apes but for what it reveals about man.

Mildred Archer, in a review of "Family," in Best Sellers, *Vol. 36, No. 5, August, 1976, p. 149.*

MARY L. NOLAN

Because allusions to sex pervade every aspect of modern American life, sex has become a dominant force, governing adolescents' thoughts, words, and acts. Lacking the guidance necessary for the proper interpretations of these sexual innuendos, teens face many serious problems unique to their generation. Loving another person of the same sex is one such problem. The subject should be explored in the classroom, because love in friendship is often misconstrued as homosexuality, an abhorrent concept to most adolescents. It is important for students to realize that a deep love for a close friend does not automatically imply homosexuality.

The subject of homosexuality versus friendship is relevant to adolescents, because they are developing an awareness of their own sexualities, discovering that they possess both masculine and feminine qualities. Because of cultural traditions, this knowledge can be so frightening that it is rarely admitted and often denied. All adolescents, however, must recognize the traits that make them truly human. Accepting the fact that all people need to love and to be loved can be an overwhelming problem to some teenagers. . . .

[***I'll Get There. It Better Be Worth the Trip***] can help students differentiate between loving friendships and homosexuality. In [this] book the characters reach a healthy resolution of the conflict, thus leading them to new personal insights. And students can likewise reach valuable insights through [discussion of the text]. . . .

I'll Get There. It Better Be Worth the Trip presents the story of Davy Ross and Doug Altschuler. Davy's parents are divorced and the boy has been living with his beloved grandmother. When she dies, Mrs. Ross feels obligated to take Davy to live with her because, after all, he is her son. But knowing he will change her lifestyle, she cannot hide her bitterness and resentment. Davy desperately needs human love. . . .

Then Davy meets Altschuler, with whom Davy has much in common. Knowing very little about his father, Altschuler also lives with his mother. When Davy is assigned a desk at school, Altschuler quickly points out that Davy is taking the place of his best friend who is dying. Neither boy is outstanding in sports. Both fantasize about girls. In short, Davy and Altschuler need and want this friendship.

One evening Altschuler and Davy are happily rolling on the floor with Fred. As the laughter subsides, Davy tells what happens:

> I look at Altschuler, and we smile sort of. And I'm not quite sure what happens now. I think we both intend to get up and chase after Fred. . . . I feel unusual . . . I don't want to get up. I want to stay lying there. I feel a slight shiver and shake from it . . . Altschuler is still lying there too. He looks at me peculiarly, and I'm sure I look at him the same way. . . . I guess I kiss Altschuler and he kisses me. . . . It just happens. And when it stops we sit up and turn away from each other. (p. 4)

The kiss is a spontaneous act resulting between two friends who are sharing a good time and need each other's love. Altschuler does not feel threatened by the act. Ross, on the other hand, is quite shocked by his behavior and feels tremendous guilt. He no longer wants to be around Altschuler, but he knows good friends are not easy to find. Eventually the boys talk. By sharing their thoughts, Davy realizes that the kiss is not indicative of homosexuality, not a threat to his masculinity. Although Davy is quite sure he does not want it to happen again, he comes to see the kiss for what it was, and he sees Altschuler in a new light. The friendship grows.

After reading and studying the text, students should recognize that the theme of the novel is friendship not homosexuality. In real life love is an integral part of any friendship. Society has determined, however, that one can only demonstrate love to a person of the opposite sex. If one does not follow this rule, one chances being labeled a homosexual, a deviate. Because outside pressure is so great, showing one's love to another of one's own sex might cause unjustifiable guilt. Mr. Donovan has written of just such a situation. Before Davy can reach new insights about himself, he has to overcome this guilt. Only then does he gain self-knowledge, and the friendship between the boys becomes stronger. [***I'll Get There. It Better Be Worth the Trip***] serves to reassure adolescents that they are not "queer" because of their desires to demonstrate love. They are being human. (pp. 4, 6)

Mary L. Nolan, "Friendship Versus Homosexuality in Three Young Adult Novels," in The ALAN Review, *Vol. 9, No. 3, Spring, 1982, pp. 4, 6, 13.**

Walter D(umaux) Edmonds

1903-

American novelist, short story writer, and nonfiction writer.

An author of historical fiction, Edmonds is credited with making a place in literature for the Mohawk Valley region of central New York. Edmonds grew up in that area, and his writing has been greatly influenced by its history and folklore. The Erie Canal, which is located in this region, inspired a number of his books, including his first novel, *Rome Haul* (1929), *Erie Water* (1933), and a short story collection, *Mostly Canallers* (1934). In his works, Edmonds recreates the daily lives of ordinary people against the background of such historical events as the Revolutionary War and the construction of the Erie Canal. Edmonds's most enduring work is *Drums Along the Mohawk* (1936), a story of the hardships faced by the pioneers who first settled the Mohawk Valley. The difficulties of the pioneers are compounded by hostile Indians and the political turbulence of the American Revolution.

Among Edmonds's other novels that have been praised for their colorful, energetic recreations of the past and their entertaining narratives are *The Big Barn* (1930), *Chad Hanna* (1940), and *Young Ames* (1942). Edmonds has stated that few of his stories were written specifically for children or young adults, yet many are appreciated by a younger audience. Edmonds received the Newbery Medal for *The Matchlock Gun* (1941) and the National Book Award for children's literature for *Bert Breen's Barn* (1975). *The Night Raider and Other Stories* (1980) contains four stories: two of them focus on life in the Erie Canal region, and the other two are set in rural areas.

Edmonds's books have generally been well received, particularly because of his ability to bring the past to life. Herbert Gorman noted this talent in his appraisal of *Rome Haul,* which he called "a triumph of atmospheric realism." Edmonds's down-to-earth style—simple and often humorous—is well-suited to his subjects. At his best, he has been compared to Willa Cather and Mark Twain. Some critics believe that his backgrounds are more compelling than his characters, who tend to be types rather than individuals. Edmonds has also been faulted for employing sentimentalism and amusing conclusions that detract from his otherwise convincing realism. Nevertheless, Dayton Kohler echoes the opinions of a substantial number of reviewers in remarking that Edmonds "achieves a proper balance between the factual details of history and the imaginative appeal of fiction."

(See also *Contemporary Authors,* Vols. 5-8, rev. ed.; *Contemporary Authors New Revision Series,* Vol. 2; *Something about the Author,* Vols. 1, 27; and *Dictionary of Literary Biography,* Vol. 9.)

Photograph by Katharine T. Baker-Carr

THE NEW YORK TIMES BOOK REVIEW

Assiduous research, restraint in treatment and a deal of fine, lucid writing distinguish [**"Rome Haul"**], a colorful chronicle of the Erie Canal at its heyday, in the middle of the last century. An empire builds up swiftly and as swiftly the instruments of its building are discarded, but each leaves a rich burden of remembrance among the people and in the district it once vitally affected. In **"Rome Haul"** the author has been extraordinarily successful in recapturing the currents and cross-currents of life among the "canawlers," delving into the written and more often, one suspects, the spoken lore of the period.

With the story he tells and with Dan Harrow, the principal figure of his chronicle, Mr. Edmonds has been almost consciously slighting. The tale itself is one of high and improbable adventure, shot through in at least two instances with dramatic situations. For the most part, though, it is but a recurrent thread in the close and detailed texture of the background. . . .

The lesser characters of the tale, the real "canawlers," are more deftly characterized than Harrow. Hector Berry and his nagging wife; Sol Tinkle and his fat cook, Mrs. Gurget; Fortune Friendly, the renegade card-sharping minister—these are colorful people, with pungent speech and the peculiar manner and philosophy of canal folk.

"The Erie Canal," in The New York Times Book Review, *February 24, 1929, p. 8.*

ALLAN NEVINS

[**"Rome Haul"**] is the work of a son of the Mohawk Valley, who has steeped himself in the oral traditions, the old newspaper files and directories, and the physical atmosphere of the

Erie Canal. The Canal—the "big ditch"—was a world in itself in the heyday of its usefulness and renown, between 1826 and 1850. It had a population, an economic life, a lingo, and a set of customs as distinctive as those of the Mississippi in the antebellum years. . . .

Mr. Edmonds has dealt with this material in a fashion which shows more obvious debts to Dickens and Smollett than to Mark Twain. He has produced a loosely episodic, carefree, almost picaresque narrative. . . .

As a chronicle of life on the old Erie the book is a richly colored addition to the panorama of American fiction; as a story of Dan Harrow, the hero, and Molly, the heroine, it is of inferior merit. The narrative lacks organic structure. There is no plot beyond the simple tale of Dan's adventures and misadventures in boating along the canal, and Dan is an unsatisfactory observer and protagonist. . . .

But despite an occasional stagnancy of narrative, a faltering of interest, the novel places us in Mr. Edmonds's debt. The warm sympathy and the conscientiousness which he has expended in recreating the "big ditch" have brought their reward. He has restored the canal—"the bowels of the nation; the whole shebang of life!" John Durble calls it—to our knowledge. Heretofore we have seen it through the eyes of transients who, like Herbert Quick's Vandemark, passed along it. But its real romance was in the life of the "canawlers" themselves. They were a loose, shuffling, semi-vagabondish, but lovable set.

[They] had canons of their own, they were generally good-hearted, they had a pawky Yankee humor, and they found genuine flavor in living. This is what **"Rome Haul,"** rich in idiomatic speech, in lore of the boat and the soil, in the free and expansive spirit of 1850, has above everything else—flavor.

Allan Nevins, "Canal Days," in The Saturday Review of Literature, *Vol. V, No. 32, March 2, 1929, p. 725.*

THE NEW YORK TIMES BOOK REVIEW

[If **"The Big Barn"**] is less epic in its general contours and less rich in the details of characterization and background which give the illusion of reality than was **"Rome Haul,"** the reason in part rests in the fact that Mr. Edmonds has chosen deliberately to work on a smaller canvas while still picturing a life with which he is lovingly familiar.

Into the earlier book was thrown the author's full stock of intimate knowledge of the "canawlers" in the boom days of the 1850s when on the Erie could be seen "the whole shebang of life." Quieter in its enthusiasm for the details of a historical epoch, though no less skillful in its presentation of background and atmosphere, **"The Big Barn"** is the story of a farm near Boonville in the 1860s, or rather the story of old Ralph Wilder, hard, at times cruel and sentimental withal, dominating the countryside almost like an English squire.

By methods which, it is insinuated, were relentless and rough-shod, old Wilder has gained not only a farm and a comfortable fortune but also the power that mortgages give over the property and activities of his neighbors. He is determined to make his two sons fit into the life of the farm and carry on the Wilder tradition whether they want to or not. . . . The complications that ensue are not unusual in country life, one may assume, and certainly not in country fiction. . . .

Mr. Edmonds has not been too successful in using the enormous barn as a rather vague and recurring symbol of old Ralph's indomitable will and desire for power and of the stanch but intangible appeal of the farm. The canal as it appeared in **"Rome Haul"** was a better unifying element.

In the end, however, the author deserves praise of an unstinted sort for his ability to create life-like dialogue, to re-create unforgettable scenes of farm life, as monotonous and as ever-fresh as life itself, and to enter into his characters frequently with [an] . . . eagerness to understand frailties. . . . There is no evidence in this last novel that Mr. Edmonds has written himself out or that his ability to write has failed him with a less heroic theme. One may hope still that, having exhausted the external scenes with which he is familiar, he will now turn to a closer analysis of his characters instead of to the manufacturing of superficial plots.

"'The Big Barn' and Other Recent Works of Fiction," in The New York Times Book Review, *September 14, 1930, p. 6.**

ALLAN NEVINS

Mr. Edmonds, who gave us an excellent picture of the early days of the Erie Canal in **"Rome Haul,"** now follows it with [**"The Big Barn"**] a study of life in northern New York—in the Black River valley, between the St. Lawrence and Mohawk—two decades later, or just before the Civil War. The materials for this story are less picturesque and extensive than those of his remarkable first novel. Instead of canal hands, teamsters, emigrants, and refugees from justice on the bustling new waterway, he presents simply a rather quiet group of farm people: a masterful old landowner named Ralph Wilder, his two sons, his daughter-in-law, his tenants, and his farm-hands. There is a difference also in the construction of the book. Instead of a loose plot, lacking in complications but full of adventure and incident, the author presents two triangles of a desperately serious kind, overlapping one another. The younger Bascom son, an attractive rural Don Juan, carries on dangerous love affairs with the wife of a tenant and with the wife of his own brother. It is a more tightly woven story, which reaches its bloody climax just on the eve of the Civil War. With fewer advantages of background and plot than in his first novel, Mr. Edmonds has produced a book which will doubtless be less popular, but which is just as interesting and which marks an advance in some essential elements of fiction.

Most of all it marks an advance in power of characterization. **"Rome Haul"** was a novel of scene and atmosphere; **"The Big Barn"** is a novel of people. . . . [The] author gives us three sharply conceived and vigorously presented personages. It is the old man who is the hero of the story, and the big barn that he builds as the last great work of his lifetime helps him to dominate the tale. There is enough action and there is enough realistic background of rural scenes and occupations to save the novel from any charge of thinness. . . .

There is less of the color of history in this book than in its predecessor, less adventure, and less pungent and idiomatic talk. But if it is not so notable as a period study, in some respects it encourages us to think more highly of Mr. Edmonds's gifts.

Allan Nevins, "An Up State Story," in The Saturday Review of Literature, *Vol. VII, No. 10, September 27, 1930, p. 156.*

FREDERICK THURSTON

"Rome Haul" was Edmonds's first book and gave us a slice of daily life on the old Erie Canal during its great days in the 1850s. [**"Erie Water"**] carries us back to the years beginning with 1817 when the canal was being dug. . . .

Every one interested in this place and period, the years when Fenimore Cooper was a young man and Joseph Smith, who appears in the novel for a page or two, was planning his bible, should thoroughly enjoy this broad canvas. Edmonds seems to have constituted himself historian of the western counties and his sound understanding of the life of earlier days is apparent in all his work.

He has become so steeped in the times that, although he has avoided a few outmoded conventions, taboos and clichés, he writes in the spirit of nineteenth century American literature. The story is sentimental. The characters are treated in their humors, some of them a bit too obviously. There is a genial Dickensian flavor about the novel. And the brawls, hardships, misfortunes and sorrows that occasionally interrupt the prevailing flow of rough good will, sturdy labor and kindly sentiment, need stiffening. Since we have no old-fashioned villain, his place might well be taken by a more realistic balancing of good and evil.

But **"Erie Water"** is of necessity an optimistic novel, for it is, as well as a long tale, a faithful record of a great early American achievement and of the plain men and women who saw it through.

Frederick Thurston, "Building of the Erie Canal," in New York Herald Tribune Books, *February 5, 1933, p. 2.*

CHRISTOPHER WARD

Mr. Edmonds has an observing eye and a magic pen. He sees and makes you see the bright ripple of blue and white made by the wings of a flock of pigeons in flight, the tuft of white steam springing from the steamboat's escape, like a bursting milkweed pod, the light dust on the city streets, that rises with a puff of wind and, falling, creeps into the cracks between the cobbles. His observation of such minor sights is equalled by the acuteness of his hearing. Sights and sounds of the life around his characters impinge sharply on his consciousness, and he conveys his impressions to his readers in opulent fulness. Indeed, if [**"Erie Water"**] has a conspicuous fault, it is this very opulence. It needs restraint. One is somewhat distracted, at times, from the central interest of the scene by the impact on the imagination of unimportant details, well rendered and true to life, but still unimportant.

However, the faults of the book are few and, in the main, negligible. Taken as a whole it is a remarkably true and thoroughly convincing picture of life in York State in the 1820's, a book that should be leisurely read, that will well repay leisurely reading, and that will leave behind it in one's mind pictures of people and places not soon to be forgotten.

Christopher Ward, "Pageant of York State," in The Saturday Review of Literature, *Vol. IX, No. 31, February 18, 1933, p. 437.*

FRED T. MARSH

"Mostly Canallers" strikes us as an "unlikely" title—in the Yankee sense of the word; but it is certainly an accurate one for this collection of the short stories of Walter D. Edmonds. . . .

The tales all belong to the last century; are, indeed, mostly pre-Civil War. And so a pioneer background—in many instances, indeed, a frontier background—lies behind the story. . . .

Here and there are stories that seem to have been built out of material left over from [Edmonds's] novels. In **"Citizens of Ohio,"** for example, Cosmo Turbe, the little rough-and-tumbler of **"Erie Water,"** appears with his buddy Plute, but without introduction. The reader who has never met these two originals before would miss, we think, much of the savor of the story. The stories, all of them, are readable, and together with the novels are brilliant as well as thorough in their historical re-creativeness. But judged solely as stories, most of these pieces are slight, reminiscent, sentimental, abounding in happy or humorous endings. It is the surface of life on the canal and on the frontier that Edmonds really gives us the local color, the dialects, the way of life, the customs, habits and manners as he has gleaned them from his happy researches. His fights and brawls and loves, the passionate elements in his stories, are as remote as those pictured on a tapestry—even though sometimes very well done. Edmonds does not outrageously soften his picture. But no one of his short or long tales is of dramatic, of universal, of immediate significance. . . .

The best of the serious stories are those which have to do directly with life on the canal—with boatmen, cooks, captains, inns, teamsters, pretty young female redemptioners, lock tenders, stray travelers to Ohio, transient farmer lads and farmer girls and so on. . . .

"Bewitched" and **"Black Wolf"** seem to the reviewer absurd as stories with their were-wolf, mystical overtones. But these two stories contain some of their author's choicest paragraphs. In the first the smell and feel and ways of cows are rendered with the touch of a prose artist. In the second fear in the mind of a small boy in the dark is made a living demonic force.

Edmonds has lost himself in the past, in the days when the Erie Canal floated its vast and disproportionate share of the wealth created by a rising new nation. His stories and novels are derivative, merely the framework into which he discharges the abundance of his lore. But his books combine to contribute to the world a body of significant Americans.

Fred T. Marsh, "Tales of the Erie Canal Country," in The New York Times Book Review, *February 18, 1934, p. 9.*

OTIS C. FERGUSON

[In] **"Mostly Canallers,"** Mr. Edmonds shows a strength and a weakness I had not fully guessed from such work of his as I had seen. The weakness may as well come first, as it is a good thing to get out of the way. The characters in the book are hard-hitting, hard-bitten folk from a walk of life in which it is a hard and cruel job of work to get your bread and keep it. Consequently, situations are often grim, and men are indicated as fighting with themselves, with each other, with the harsh injustice of their environment. Yet the total effect is not one of grimness. Many of the characters are inherently tragic, yet their tragedy has been allowed to become picturesque. And so one takes away the feeling that the author has stopped short sometimes of his inevitable truth.

I almost despair of conveying an adequate idea of the goodness to be found in the book, for it has many quirks and corners not to be explored by stock terms and bald statements. It is the sort of book that can mix the forthright robust diction of its people—trappers, river-bullies, lock-keepers, hard women and all—with a bright and sensitive reporting which makes the locale distinct throughout, and with the sure delicacy of such a story as **"Blind Eye."**. . .

[The] vein in which the author is happiest, I suspect, is that in which he tells of caterpillar racing, horse trading and, above all, of **"The Cruise of the Cashalot,"** a fine, crazy yarn of a stomped-upon boat owner who got himself considerably drunk and caught himself a whale in New York Harbor and forthwith fired blubber and general abuse all over his wife's tidy boat. . . .

But whether the mood is light or dark, you will find in these stories a freshness of characterization which goes far to explain their eminent readableness, and which itself calls for some explanation. It seems to be founded not merely on quick imagination and the shrewd sense of where one man differs from another but in the author's solid admiration for these rough people of his, on the humor and sympathy with which he draws them out. Even when, as is sometimes bound to be the case in a work of this sort, his characters show some similarity from story to story, he has still given them an idiom and a relation to environment which give them individuality as a group. When they are lounging or storming about in their own peculiar attitudes they are honest-to-God, and very satisfying to know.

Otis C. Ferguson, "Hard-Bitten Erie Canal Folk," in New York Herald Tribune Books, *February 25, 1934, p. 2.*

ALLAN NEVINS

[In **"Drums Along the Mohawk"**] Mr. Edmonds's two principal figures are a poverty-stricken young backwoods farmer and his wife, Gilbert and Lana Martin. . . . [The] tale begins with 1776, and stops only after the peace in 1784. . . . [Anybody who reads this book] will learn much about northern and western New York in its most eventful quarter-century.

Mr. Edmonds has clearly studied his subject with exemplary thoroughness. He has also studied it with imagination. He possesses the best kind of historical sense. He sees the people of the valley in those Revolutionary years as living beings with the same virtues, the same vices, the same heroisms and follies, and much the same hopes and fears as their descendants in rural areas on the Mohawk today. By earthy speech (not without an infusion of modern slang), by earthy instincts and acts (not without a very modern quantum of sex), he brings them down from the heroic plane to that of everyday flesh and blood. His book is crowded with people and with incidents. And they all, from imaginary souls like the Martins and the Wolffs and the Weavers to real figures of history like Herkimer and Demooth and Dr. Petry, are convincing. Mr. Edmonds is obviously not a born novelist. He cannot create clearly individualized characters who dominate a book and walk away with its action and with the reader's emotions. But he can do very well in painting a society, a countryside full of people. He did it expertly enough in his stories of the building of the Erie Canal; he has done it still more expertly and vigorously in this full book of the Valley in the days of Tories and hostile armies.

The book has little invented plot, for the author relies upon history for his main outlines. It is an episodic and panoramic work, at times even a little confusing as the action switches from poor John Wolff in his Newgate Prison down in Connecticut to Dr. Petry's office in Herkimer and then to Mrs. McKlennar's sugar-bush in Fairfield. Only two simple threads are drawn through the book from beginning to end. One is that of the Revolution; the other is that of the humble lives of Gilbert and Lana Martin. Some of the innumerable episodes which make up the book are naturally more interesting than others. Most readers will wish that Mr. Edmonds had stuck a little more closely to his hero and heroine; had polarized the story about them, as he promises to do in his first half-dozen chapters, and thus given it more unity and richer emotional values. But to do that would doubtless have lessened the panoramic quality, and detracted from the impressionistic presentation of an entire valley full of troubled, angry, determined folk. Mr. Edmonds is without any great creative faculty. But he does have a remarkable gift for painting a region, a time and a body of people inhabiting both.

Allan Nevins, "War in the Mohawk Valley," in Saturday Review of Literature, *Vol. XIV, No. 14, August 1, 1936, p. 5.*

STEPHEN VINCENT BENÉT

In **"Drums Along the Mohawk,"** Mr. Walter Edmonds attempts the most ambitious canvas he has yet tried. The novel covers eight years in the disputed Mohawk Valley—the years from 1776 when raid after raid of Tories, destructives and Indians swept that part of New York State. It is a story of the stubborn and dogged persistence of a people who refused to be rooted out, even when the cabin was burned and the standing crop with it, and went back and back again till they finally won their ground. Congress was far away and, on the whole, ineffective—the Indian changed from a possible to a present and threatening menace—the familiar frontier itself grown suddenly hostile. All this—the gathering of the cloud and its constant overhang—the constant, wearing attrition of a continual danger—the militia expeditions—the huddling in stockades—the murder of outpost settlers and settlements—Mr. Edmonds handles with realism and skill. There is no "Bang, bang, and two redskins hit the dust" about it. But there is the fear, the persistence, the sight of the scalped and the slain. Some lived through it—others, and not always the worst, went under. And, behind it all, there was the continual problem of frontier and central government—and that, too, Mr. Edmonds sketches admirably though almost exclusively from the frontier point of view. . . . Mr. Edmonds has made it as alive as it was in the birth days of the Republic.

To his task, he has brought a very genuine knowledge of and love for the particular section that is his disputed ground and an illuminating gift for detail and custom. Here is the weather and the food—the way the land looked and the way things happened. . . . Technically, his hero and heroine are Gilbert Martin and his wife Magdelana—the type of sturdy settlers who survive to the end. But his real hero is the Mohawk Valley and its mixed but obdurate people. And to that valley and its people he has paid a genuine and solid tribute—and revived for us all a certain part of American history that most of us knew little about.

Having done so much, I wish, perhaps ungenerously, that he had done a little more. There are plenty of high spots in the book. . . . The whole narrative reads well and is easy to read. And yet, in the end, in spite of its wealth of incident and character, the book has not quite the impact that such a book might have. Perhaps it is due to the diffusion of interest among a great many characters, half a dozen of whom are really, but not admittedly, more important to the reader than the titular hero and heroine. Perhaps it is due to Gil and Magdelana themselves. They are excellent people—the sort who make the bone and sinew of a state—and yet it is curiously hard to get really excited about them. Or perhaps again—though here I tread on dangerous ground—it is due to Mr. Edmonds's extreme conscientiousness in regard to his historical material. Every now and then he gets so fascinated by being a realist that he almost forgets to tell a story. The gusto, the casual vividness that were in **"Rome Haul"** have been toned down to this more sober tale—and one, somehow, misses the energetic color of the earlier book. (p. 1)

Nevertheless, and despite the criticisms of the preceding paragraph, **"Drums Along the Mohawk"** is a substantial achievement. . . . (p. 2)

Stephen Vincent Benét, "A Storyteller Who Makes Our Ancestors Live," in New York Herald Tribune Books, *August 2, 1936, pp. 1-2.*

EDWARD J. CLARKE

Regional literature when it is well written and authentically constructed revitalizes the historical incidents of the past. Individuals and events become more tangible when portrayed against the colorful and changeable panorama of our early national life. In the past the South and New England dominated this particular field of literature. . . . [In ***Drums Along the Mohawk***] it is upstate New York with Mr. Edmonds telling the story of the forgotten pioneers of the Mohawk Valley during the Revolutionary war. . . . (p. 433)

Gilbert Martin, a poor backwoods farmer, was a member of the militia from Deerfield settlement. He and his wife Lana are Mr. Edmonds' two principle characters. With typical pioneer courage they had cleared the land and built a home on the frontier of Tryon county. . . . Gil and Lana did not enjoy peace for very long. The savage border struggle of the Revolution descended upon them, and without knowing why, they were forced to endure all degrees of privation. Their home and wheatfield were burned and they were compelled to flee to the very uncertain protection of Arabia Stone Stockade, going, ultimately, to the more protective Fort Herkimer.

In his novel Mr. Edmonds utilizes every potentiality of the Revolutionary drama of the section. With fine historical insight and proportion he presents a panoramic, and yet detailed view of the exciting lives of the people of the valley and the momentous forces that swept them along like so many straws in the current. Far from being idealized by the author, they are portrayed as living human beings with the same faults and aspirations as the men and women who dwell in the Mohawk Valley region today. Mr. Edmonds' delineation of individual characters, however, is not always deft. I believe that he should have devoted more attention to the portrayal of the inner, emotional conflicts surging, at times, within the minds of Gil and Lana. And this particularly so in the case of Lana who, although sensitive to beauty, remains a slightly inarticulate and pathetic creature, a plaything in the hands of an uncompromising fate.

All of Mr. Edmonds' characters, whether real or imaginary, are convincing to the extent that we can visualize their physical proportions and perceive the events in which they played a part. One would prefer, however, a better insight into their thoughts. Mr. Edmonds does not account clearly for the apathetic attitudes of the settlers in the face of recurrent Indian attacks, each more brutal than the other. Still less can one account for the pleasantly disinterested stand taken by the Continental Congress with respect to the sufferings of the people in the frontier lands.

Realism and action predominate in this novel. Its characters speak the language of men and women face to face with the elemental things of life. The dialogue, throughout, has the tang of earthy, racy speech. At times, however, the action becomes too kaleidoscopic; there is altogether too much shifting of scene which tends to break up the general continuity of the narrative. . . . Despite this, such real characters in the drama of the Revolution as General Herkimer, Captain Demooth, Dr. Petry and Marinus Willett are authentically portrayed, while to his imaginary characters, the Martins, the Realls, the Weavers and the Wolffs, Mr. Edmonds has given, in most cases, lifelike stature. (pp. 434-35)

The whole book throbs with the life of a hostile frontier. It strikes the keynote of indomitable courage in the face of terrifying obstacles, the typical pioneer concept that, in a large measure, made possible the America we know today. It is one of the finer historical novels of our day, a book that should be read by every American for, although it deals with a period that is somewhat remote, chronologically, it nevertheless expounds a philosopy of national life that should be engendered in the American mind. Mr. Edmonds, already well known for his excellent stories of the Erie canal, has, in ***Drums Along the Mohawk,*** written a novel of great power and intensity, set against the colorful background of a turbulent period. I think that one of the distinctive features of the novel is the attitude of Gil and Lana towards the land. Despite the belligerency of man and the whims of nature, they stuck to their acres; they had faith in the land and both lived to see that faith justifed. (pp. 435-36)

Edward J. Clarke, in a review of "Drums Along the Mohawk," in The North American Review, *Vol. 242, No. 2, Winter, 1936-37, pp. 433-36.*

DAYTON KOHLER

The novels of Walter D. Edmonds belong to the new regionalism. There is, first of all, the attitude of his people toward the land itself. To them it is the good earth, a homeplace to which they may hold in spite of all disastrous fortune in the wider world about them. For this reason Dan Harrow [in ***Rome Haul***] left the canal to find the farm he desired and old Ralph Wilder [in ***The Big Barn***] became the patriarch of the Black River Valley. One of the remarkable features of ***Drums along the Mohawk*** is the regard of Gil and Lana Martin for their frontier farm. Ruined by failing crops and driven repeatedly to refuge by border raids, they cling stubbornly to their acres, enduring all hardships, until they return finally to their own home in the years of peace. Mr. Edmonds feels that the tradition of these people is not dead, and he knows that the private possession of the land is still one of the moving forces of human existence. . . . (p. 4)

He has done as all regional writers must do, explored the past in order to understand the spirit of a place. . . . [The] Revolution upon the northern frontier and the bustling, brief years of the Erie Canal have become a regional memory within the Mohawk Valley. . . . As the historian of this region Mr. Edmonds looks upon the past as a story with the plot already written by time; as a creative artist he tries to invest the historical past with character and mood.

He does not escape into the past as a refuge from the confusion of the present, and in his novels there is a spirit that moves back in memory but forward in time. He shows the American dream in the making, pioneers and their families living, fighting, enduring hardships on the frontier, builders on the Erie Canal, boaters on their long hauls to Albany and short hauls to Rome, fighting at the locks, talking big in the taverns of the canal towns. He attempts to show these people of the past with the same interests as those of the present. . . . (pp. 4-5)

Each of his novels has been, in effect, the re-creation of a period in time. In chronological outline, but not in the order of their publication, they follow a definite sequence. The time of ***Drums along the Mohawk*** is from 1776 to 1784, and its action pictures the grim years of the Revolution. ***Erie Water*** is the story of the building of the canal during the years between 1817 and 1825. ***Rome Haul*** shows the canal in its heyday of the fifties, before the railroads stripped it of romance and glory. And ***The Big Barn*** deals with the attempt of upstate landowners, in the period of the Civil War, to preserve large estates which would unite the culture of the eastern seaboard with the crude, bluff vigor of the frontier.

All these novels achieve a special kind of realism because of their complete and accurate documentation of atmosphere and scene. Atmosphere is an element difficult to define. It consists of an exact rightness of detail, the creation of a setting and a mood, the illusion of a pictorial background that becomes an essential part of character and action. The novels and short stories of Walter D. Edmonds present a separate, closed world that is less the result of scenic detail and local color than of the relationships between his people and the familiar surroundings of their daily lives. He knows the tools of the pioneer, how Indians stalked their kill, the furniture of a cabin or a canal boat, the foods that were served at a barn-raising, the jokes of the canal taverns, the drinks that were mixed on cold winter nights, how canallers hired their cooks, what taxes were levied, how crops were valued, the aspects of weather—all the intimate details of daily life that give shape and color to his stories of the frontier and the Erie Canal. His novels reflect the scenes and echo the sounds of their respective periods. (pp. 5-6)

To read Walter D. Edmonds' first novel, ***Rome Haul,*** is to enter a world as distinctively and essentially American as the golden day of the New Bedford whalers or as picturesque as the life on the Mississippi that young Samuel Clemens knew. It had its own language and its individual customs, a strange, reckless world filled with boats piled high with machinery and produce, drivers of all kinds, bullies who fought for first place at the locks, peddlers, preachers, thieves, and cooks who shared the vagrant lives of the boaters whose needs they served in the casual manner of the canal.

Few first novels of recent years have dramatized the past so effectively. Two threads of narrative interest run through the book. One is the story of Dan Harrow, a shy, awkward boy who has left his father's farm to seek his fortune on the canal. The other is the pursuit of Gentleman Joe Calash, canal outlaw, by government agents. (pp. 6-7)

The plot, however, is less important than the atmospheric reality of the novel. ***Rome Haul*** made plain the fact that its young author had a strong native passion for his section and his people. It is a novel of simple outlines and fresh colors, and it re-creates with gusto the hardy, reckless life of the past; its richness lies in the vivid pictures and characters by which Mr. Edmonds brings to life the folkways and spirit of an era.

Dan Harrow appears again as one of the characters in ***The Big Barn.*** This novel marks an intermediate stage in Mr. Edmonds' development as a novelist. Less exuberant than ***Rome Haul*** in its use of racy idiom and picturesque scene, it is a more solid and mature study of the passionate ownership of the land. Old Ralph Wilder is typical of a class that appeared in America at the end of the pioneering epoch. He is one of the builders of the canal; he rises to power in the days of its greatness; in his old age he is a stern patriarch whose dominant interest in life is an intense pride of possession he holds for his wide acres of farm and forest land in the Black River Valley. He wishes to become a rural patriarch, the founder of a strong line that will inherit his acres and continue his tradition after him. The symbol of his pride is the big barn which is in the process of building throughout the novel. (pp. 7-8)

The Big Barn, however, is more than the story of a family; it is a justification of a way of life. The older America produced a squirearchy which lived under the stern code of the frontier but attempted to soften its crudities with the more civilized comforts of Boston and New York. Men like Ralph Wilder were an impressive, independent race who owned their pastures and fields and governed their own communities. They were the last of the pioneers and their self-reliance was doomed by the industries they created.

The Erie Canal is the real hero of ***Erie Water,*** although its construction is bound up with the fortunes of Jerry Fowler, who was on his way west with ninety dollars to buy fifty acres of land in the Holland Purchase. (p. 8)

No impoverished imagination has been at work on this crowded tapestry of life in York State during the 1820's. There are the details of digging and lock construction, the laboring life, the fights and wild sprees of the building crews. But the people give life to Mr. Edmonds' design. After the novel has been put aside one remembers Ma Halleck, sturdy matriarch of a pioneer clan; Issachar Bennett, the wandering Shaker preacher who had been cheated only once in a horse trade; Norah Sharon, sly black-haired girl who held Jerry for a time; Harley Falk, strange, wandering shoemaker who drove a blind white horse; Cosmo Turbe, rough-and -tumble labor boss who left the marks of his boots on the faces of men with whom he fought. These and many others provide the warp and woof of this historical novel that Mr. Edmonds has made true to the country and the time. (pp. 8-9)

Drums along the Mohawk is perhaps our best example of the regional chronicle; it enlivens the history of a locality by a use of those materials which most historians ignore. Factual in documentation and detail, its emphasis is not upon the broad, shaping outlines of historical events but upon the effect of those events in the lives of ordinary people who lived through them. The people of the Mohawk Valley, for example, were isolated from the main stream of the Revolution as it was fought in New England and Virginia. They looked upon themselves not as participants in a patriotic cause but as farmers who were fighting to protect their land and homes from British troops and Indian raiders. The passing of time itself during those years of border warfare takes the place of any structural plot. Each division of the novel is divided according to the element of time between 1776 and 1783. The chapters themselves trace the experiences of the people in the valley during these years. In this way the author gives a more detailed and panoramic picture of the conflict through a series of dramatic episodes loosely strung together in chronological sequence. One of the triumphs of his method is the fact that only thirteen of his hundred-odd characters have been invented. Thus he heightens the effect of historical realism in his attempt to portray a period, a countryside, and a people.

The meaning of the war he reveals through the experiences of Gil and Lana Martin. . . . Their story is one of indomitable pioneer courage. Other stories are no less momentous: the kindly treatment Gil and Lana received at the hands of harsh-voiced old Mrs. McKlennar; the experiences of John Wolff, the Tory loyalist, in the water-soaked mines where he was imprisoned; the battle of Oriskany, when General Herkimer, his leg shattered, directed the six-hour battle in which his small force of militia turned back a much larger army of British and Indian allies; the death of young John Weaver and his wife's visit to his grave in the forest; the heroic run of the blond giant, Adam Helmer, to save the fort from a sudden Indian attack. These were real people and real events in the life on a hostile frontier. Mr. Edmonds does not look back upon them with romantic nostalgia or sentimental piety. For this reason his novel is as real as the people and action he has dramatized.

His short stories, like his novels, have the force and directness of unstudied drama. They range in time from pioneer days to the present, but always they are laid within the stretches of the Mohawk Valley and present a panoramic view of the region through more than one hundred and fifty years of its history. The best of his shorter fiction is represented in the collection ***Mostly Canallers,*** stories realistic and romantic of the American past.

Because he is primarily an artist, the work of Walter D. Edmonds goes beyond a local realism. Beneath his faithful use of local color he attempts to express the essential truths of human experience. His novels and stories have been compared to the folk literature of a region, for he treats innocence, courage, the home, as the ancestral virtues of our national birthright. Character grained heavily with legend has always been the basis of American fiction, and he has given us in each of his books a notable portrait gallery of gnarled eccentrics and earthy backwoodsmen. In style as a device for literary experiment he is not at all interested; he holds firmly to the story-telling tradition of the Anglo-Saxon novel. He has a story to tell as well as characters to present, and from characters against a definite background come the outlines of plot. From the people also he gets the racy, robust, but homely idioms of the language that his men and women speak.

Although he has not yet written a great novel, Walter D. Edmonds is both interesting and important, for he has added greatly to our knowledge of the American past. His later work is his best. His books fall more and more into the form of chronicles and related pictures of people and events, and in this manner he achieves a proper balance between the factual details of history and the imaginative appeal of fiction. (pp. 9-11)

Dayton Kohler, "Walter D. Edmonds: Regional Historian," in English Journal, *Vol. XXVII, No. 1, January, 1938, pp. 1-11.*

R. L. DUFFUS

In [**"Chad Hanna"**] Mr. Edmonds turns from the stark drama of **"Drums Along the Mohawk"** to his old love, the Erie Canal. The canal, however, is not the main character. That honor falls to Huguenine's Great and Only International Circus, which has attractions to lure young Chad Hanna away from his hostler's job at the Yellow Bud Tavern, from the porch of which Elias Proops could spit into the canal. . . . Mr. Proops had been in the Revolutionary War and was about 81 years old. Fugitive slaves were already coming North through Canastota. It was a rich period, somewhat neglected in American historical fiction, and Mr. Edmonds brings to it his accustomed equipment of rich and full information. . . .

Mr. Edmonds does not content himself with going up into the attic and fetching down a beaver hat and a hoop skirt. He fetches in a whole lost age and makes it so natural that soon one is living in it. He is almost as much at home with life in Northern New York in the Eighteen Thirties as Mark Twain was with life on the Mississippi. He catches the incidental things. . . . And Mr. Edmonds does know the rural countryside of a century ago—or, which is just as good, makes the reader think he does.

The reader need not look for social significance, for this is a yarn of local color, romance and adventure. Its characters are pleasantly externalized. Indeed, they are about what a sagaciously observant traveler might have seen a century ago. The story of Chad runs no more complicated course than is involved in an effort to aid a runaway Negro, a valiant assumption of responsibility, a choice between Lady Lillian, the glamorous equestrienne, and Cisco Trid's daughter, Caroline (who might also have been named Cinderella), the contest between Huguenine's and Burke, Walsh & Co., the fate of Oscar, the valetudinarian lion, the discovery of a dog-toothed boy—the only one in captivity, living on a diet of raw meat, Chad's inner workings are simple. These are simple, two-dimensional people.

These observations are intended to describe the kind of novel this is; not to indicate that it ought to be some other kind of novel. Decidedly, it ought not to be. There is enough social significance in our fiction, not to say in real life, to entitle us to a vacation now and then. This book is a vacation. It is an escape book. It pictures a land and time in which one would like to be for a change, and experiences not too painful to live through—and certainly not too dull!

R. L. Duffus, "Two New Novels of Wide Appeal: 'Chad Hanna'," in The New York Times Book Review, *April 7, 1940, p. 1.*

STEPHEN VINCENT BENÉT

The tale of [Chad Hanna's] ramblings, and those of Huguenine's Circus, through upstate New York in the thirties, makes a warm and picaresque yarn, told affectionately and in detail by Mr. Edmonds [in **"Chad Hanna"**]. There's a certain amount of plot—just enough to keep the story moving—but it isn't particularly important. Any reader who is used to romance will know from the start that Caroline will win over Yates.

Mr. Edmonds knows it so well that he hardly bothers to get us really excited about it. It is the detail and the background that count. . . . If **"Chad Hanna"** is a minor item in the range of Mr. Edmonds's work—and it seems to the present reviewer just that—it is a thoroughly likable one. The same patient research that we found in **"Drums along the Mohawk"** has gone into its making—the same warm feeling for regional character. You'll have a good time with Huguenine's Circus. You'll be glad when Burke and Walsh, the rival circus-outfit, is foiled, you'll be glad when Mr. Bisbee miraculously produces an elephant out of his hat. You'll enjoy the speech about Bourbon and Ike's haysee-ride, you'll enjoy many things along the way.

If you're looking for important work or another **"Drums along the Mohawk,"** you won't find it in **"Chad Hanna."** The characters are characters of romance, sufficiently well-drawn to come to a brief life in the reading—for Mr. Edmonds is always a skilful and conscientious workman—but never really coming out of the book to take on that larger life which is the gift of great fiction. Nor is Mr. Edmonds's slow-paced narrative method always fortunate for this particular kind of story. He gets tangled up in his sub-plots and the sub-plots really don't add up to much in the end. But he has written an agreeable book and an entertaining one, and recaptured something of the small-boy glory of the days of one-ring circuses and pink lemonade.

Stephen Vincent Benét, "Circus Boy," in The Saturday Review of Literature, *Vol. XXI, No. 25, April 13, 1940, p. 7.*

ROBERT M. GAY

When ***Rome Haul*** was published in 1929 we all felt that here was something quite fresh, a new locality for fiction and a peculiar people as American as maple sugar and as full of provincial character as a woodchuck. The fact is, nevertheless, that new material never made a good novelist. What was true was that Mr. Edmonds brought to the handling of new material certain talents that always strike us as new wherever and however they may express themselves.

The novel is a saga of life in northern New York in the 1850's, and the characters and scenes are many and diverse; but the canal, as an imposing symbol of the conquest of man over nature and of man as pioneer, gives a certain unity to the tale as it did to the immensely various and shifting population of the country it ran through. There is little plot, though there is some suspense. . . . But most of the time the canal boat, the *Sarsey Sal,* moves slowly to and fro between Albany and Rochester, with her amusing crew, passengers and neighbors. The narrative is as lazy as their lives were as a rule, and as exciting as their lives were now and then.

Narrative of this sort is about the oldest kind there is, and yet certainly one of the best: a rhythm of moderate adventure punctuated by crises of excitement, crystallized episodes, which are really complete short stories in themselves. In this book, for example, the grand comedy of the Reverend Fortune Friendly's enforced sermon in the haymow and the intense incident of the blizzard can be separated from the context and read for their own sakes. They are so good, in fact, as to suggest that the author is really most at ease in the concentrated narrative of the short story—an impression which is reënforced by his later work. At any rate this first novel follows a method which he has found congenial ever since. It is that of the old picaresque romance, with its heterogeneous incidents and interpolated short tales; and I doubt if a better for historical fiction has ever been discovered.

Rome Haul was written fast and smoothly and with joy, out of enthusiasm and a full mind, and it began with no serious intention. It was the remark of a beggar, who said of the canal, 'It's the bowels of the nation, it's the whole shebang of life,' which turned the author's thoughts to wider and deeper meanings. 'Heretofore,' he says, 'I had thought of the canal as a quaint and picturesque place, made up of scenes and stories. . . . All at once it became a good deal more. . . . I began to see the book as a serious panorama of a real phase of life and the people who lived it.'

Fortunately this new seriousness did not make him solemn. It is, in fact, a strong sense of the dramatic that has helped Edmonds to avoid successfully some of the common faults of historical fiction in general. (pp. 656-57)

Young writers often mistakenly suppose that historical fiction is somehow easier to write than the fiction of contemporary life. There really is no fundamental difference, however, between the two, for historical fiction is not a type but a manner. Whatever makes a novel good makes a historical novel good; and that is mainly a story that moves and characters that live. Research and documentation may end by being only so much excess baggage, if the author is not a storyteller first: a reflection which suggests why, for so many historical novels, the reading is like plodding knee-deep in snow.

This the great historical romancers have known instinctively. And they have known another thing which the modern realist does not always remember. They knew that although in the past people were very much the same as at present, every age has had its special spiritual atmosphere, which is the sum total of its attitudes towards the unknown, supernatural, divine, as well as towards nature and mankind in general; and that unless a historical novel somehow conveys this it is not really a *historical* novel at all. . . .

Mr. Edmonds, without theatrical costuming, archaic diction, and elaborate description, has certainly caught not only the surface but the atmosphere of times past. Whether he has ever fully caught their deeper spirit is doubtful. In ***Erie Water*** (1933), he showed symptoms of having contracted the rash of documentation and one was afraid it might prove his undoing. He has recently said that 'the book is so historically accurate that it is a wonder anyone ever read it as a novel.' But this is too modest, for nearly every reviewer remarked on its fidelity to its period. It is a book of great charm, less exciting than ***Rome Haul*** and less highly colored, but its central theme of a young man's buying a redemptioner girl is very appealing.

The volume of short stories, ***Mostly Canallers*** (1934), was written during a period of several years. Many deal with the same types and even with the same people as the novels, and several are very good. (p. 657)

I have deferred consideration of ***The Big Barn*** (1930) because it is not of the same genre as the other books. It is both an extended character study and a carefully integrated novel. There is no doubt that its reception suffered because of the popularity of ***Rome Haul,*** and on rereading it I have been impressed by its many excellences. Old Ralph Wilder, a provincial titan of the Erie country, is the author's most ambitious portrait. It is a powerful creation, but the other characters make no strong impact upon the mind. On the whole the novel gives the impression that Edmonds is working in an uncongenial medium. His imagination takes fire only in the crises of the action. The fact was that, for the first time, he was essaying the psychological portrayal of complex characters, and his strength lay in dealing with those who are simple and direct.

Perhaps these remarks indicate why the public seized upon ***Drums Along the Mohawk*** (1936) and took it immediately to its heart. Here was a more powerful narrative than he had essayed before; it told an important story superbly, despite occasional lapses; it handled its burden of documentary material lightly; and it conveyed the atmosphere of a period with success. The loose structure of the saga set the author free to exercise his special abilities, giving him liberty to multiply characters and incidents without violating the unity a plot would have demanded. There was also a seriousness of intention, which, while it may not make the novel better, certainly does not detract from its dignity. (pp. 657-58)

If the novel just mentioned has the quality of epic, ***Chad Hanna*** is almost pure comedy. It has hardly any purpose except to be entertaining, but this purpose it achieves delightfully. . . . It is written with gusto and its best scenes and characters deepen the impression that Edmonds is one of the true humorists of our time. . . .

There is no reason to suppose that Edmonds's best book is not still to be written. I can't be critically solemn about those he has written. I would much rather thank him for many hours of rare enjoyment. However, if one must try to sum up his qualities, one may say that his work has some evident limitations. For instance, his outlook is almost exclusively masculine; his best portraits of women are those of women who might as well have been men, and he shows little delicacy of insight regarding the other sex. Against this objection, if it is one, we may set the fact that he has great delicacy of perception regarding natural beauty, animals of all sorts, and children. He has not yet exhibited the highest type of constructive imagination, and his invention is in general short-breathed. But on the other hand few writers can excel him in straight story-telling or in the brilliancy with which he can flash a scene. His historical perspective has seldom achieved grandeur and his portrayal of the past lacks both latitude and altitude. He has, however, chosen to cultivate a restricted field intensively and he may have no ambition to extend it.

In addition to the talents I have mentioned I should name an infallible eye for significant minutiae of nature and human nature, an instinct for the telling phrase, and the mastery of a style, springy, sinewy, and firm. The ability to tell a good story in good English is always rare at any time, and to say that he has this might be accounted sufficient praise. His talents are, in fact, so many that one hopes he will be ambitious and will continue to experiment. ***Chad Hanna*** is all very well as a breathing space, but not at all as a stopping place. (p. 658)

Robert M. Gay, "The Historical Novel: Walter D. Edmonds," in The Atlantic Monthly, *Vol. 165, No. 5, May, 1940, pp. 656-58.*

ROSE FELD

It's an interesting and heartening thing what a gifted writer can do with an old and hackneyed theme. **"Young Ames"** which is both the title and the name of the enterprising young hero of Walter D. Edmonds's new book repeats the oft-written tale of the poor boy who rose to riches and married his employer's daughter—in this instance his niece. It took young Ames two years to do it but Edmonds packs those years with the kind of adventure and action which makes the swift ascent to success not too incredible.

It is questionable whether the book was originally conceived as a novel; most of the chapters appeared as short stories in "The Saturday Evening Post." As units they follow the closely-knit pattern and the climax that the short fiction form demands; as a novel, however, they fail to weld in the complete technical perfection of which Mr. Edmonds, the novelist, is capable. But this is minor criticism of a book that holds bright romance and high adventure. If it is not a novel, it's a splendid collection of tales about a very bright young man.

The book opens in 1833 when John Ames, a lad of eighteen, is employed as clerk and messenger in the staid old commercial firm of Chevalier, Deming and Post . . . in the city of New York. With a few masterly strokes, result of a sizable amount of research, Mr. Edmonds portrays the lad against the background of the decade. From the first one realizes that young Ames is ambitious, energetic and wittily articulate; that the world of ships and imports and shrewd dealing is his meat. That the uncouth, sandy-haired, blue-eyed lad should fall in love with the niece of Mr. George Chevalier, the senior member of the firm, is entirely in the picture; that he should be successful in his suit surprises the reader not at all even as early as the close of the first chapter after Young Ames has paid his New Year's respects to Christine Chevalier, clothed in the expensive coat borrowed, to use a euphemism, from her uncle.

The ten episodes which follow the introductory chapter present young Ames in the various stages of his rise to fortune and to grace in the eyes of Christine. In each of them Mr. Edmonds limns him against the shadows of his superiors. Besides the members of the firm, there is old Mr. McVitty, chief clerk of the establishment. The portrayal of the crotchety, penurious, loyal old man who at the close of the book comes to the rescue of his firm is one of the best things in the book. . . .

If Mr. Edmonds were a less able artist, young Ames would emerge as an irritating young smart aleck. But Mr. Edmonds takes him through the traces in a discipline which includes punishment as well as rewards. The experience of young Ames with the gamblers on the Mississippi steam packet makes a joyous tale. . . .

All of the stories are good even if occasionally, such as the one, for example, where young Ames has a talk with President Jackson, they are a little on the incredible side. They make excellent entertainment and give an exciting picture of New York of the 1830's.

Rose Feld, "Poor Boy Rises, Marries the Boss's Niece," in New York Herald Tribune Books, *January 18, 1942, p. 3.*

ALLAN NEVINS

In his previous novels Mr. Edmonds has combined rather careful character study with a well-authenticated and convincing historical background. In [**"Young Ames,"** a] loose series of sketches, he permits himself a bit of relaxation. . . . [The object of these sketches] is light entertainment. His hero John Ames—Yankee stock from Rensselaer County—who becomes junior clerk in the mercantile house of Chevalier, Deming & Post on South Street in 1833, is studied from the Horatio Alger tradition rather than from life. . . . **"Young Ames"** is pure storybook, not reality. But he and his adventures are always entertaining on their somewhat adolescent level. Mr. Edmonds has packed into his book all the varied excitements of life in the bustling, fast-growing New York of Jacksonian times. . . .

Without showing half as much finish or affectionate insight as in Mr. Edmonds's Erie Canal and Mohawk Valley books, the local scene is graphically sketched. The great conflagration of 1835, the bloody rows of Bowery Boys and Dead Rabbits, the attacks on Tappan, Cox, and other abolitionists, the attempts of Ned Forrest's admirers to drive English actors from the stage, the feuds of the volunteer firemen, the demonstrations of hatred and hero-worship inspired by Andrew Jackson, are all accurately if hastily rendered. It is evident that Mr. Edmonds is leaning heavily on Walter Barrett, Philip Hone, Robert G. Albion, and the other sources mentioned in his preface; not, as in his upper New York books, upon a firsthand knowledge of the district and its traditions. But he has done particularly well in getting on paper the sharp business spirit of the time. . . . Altogether, this is an amusing book for an idle half-hour, and a still better book for youth of high-school age.

Allan Nevins, "Edmonds . . . ," in The Saturday Review of Literature, *Vol. XXV, No. 5, January 31, 1942, p. 5.*

JENNINGS RICE

As far as length goes, [**"In the Hands of the Senecas"**] lays no claim to being one of the author's major works. It cannot compare in scope and variety, for example, with **"Drums Along the Mohawk,"** a book it resembles in its characters, setting and period. But if it is a relatively brief work, it still reveals the authentic touch. Like all Mr. Edmonds' historical novels, it plays tricks with your calendar. It projects a more dangerous, headier age plump into your living room, and for a few hours you find yourself battling flames and hostile savages with no aid available from fire department or police; none, either, from your immediate neighbors, for in all likelihood you have none. You have become a rugged individualist, not from choice but in order to survive. Mr. Edmonds's evocative power is as real as that.

This being a story of captivity among eighteenth-century Indians, it seems appropriate to inquire why Mr. Edmonds's Indian characters seem so much more true than those of most writers. They are equally cruel, equally savage, equally violent. They torture without mercy and kill without remorse. What is it, then, that makes us feel they are at bottom human beings like ourselves? The answer probably is that Mr. Edmonds portrays them generically not as Indians but as primitives—and hardly more primitive, at that, than many of the white pioneers. . . .

The story tells what happened to some of the inhabitants of Dygartsbush, a small, frontier settlement in western New York which was attacked and burned by a marauding band of Senecas. The prisoners were women and a girl of twelve, except for one man and a thirteen-year-old boy. In the course of the return march the man escaped, leaving the women, the boy and the girl to face alone whatever fate their captors had in mind for them. . . .

An expert craftsman, Mr. Edmonds takes advantage of every opportunity offered by his material and often creates breathless suspense by such devices as escapes, pursuits and the like. But a different, more organic type of suspense also pervades the story, one's natural anxiety to know what will happen next to a group of always believable characters.

Jennings Rice, "The Old Master of Indian Story-Telling," in New York Herald Tribune Weekly Book Review, *January 26, 1947, p. 8.*

NASH K. BURGER

In such books as **"Rome Haul," "Chad Hanna"** and **"Drums Along the Mohawk,"** Walter D. Edmonds has been pleasantly and successfully engaged in portraying aspects of the New York State of yesterday. His novels have been notable for combining good entertainment with historical exactitude. And unlike most historical novelists, . . . Mr. Edmonds writes always with neatness and precision.

The ability to keep a tight rein on his story is especially noticeable in Mr. Edmonds' newest book, **"In the Hands of the Senecas,"** an adventurous tale of Indians on the warpath, the rigors of frontier life and certain byways of the American Revolution. . . .

"In the Hands of the Senecas" is a woman-centered story—although there are strong men enough in it. . . .

Mr. Edmonds gives us the story, each separately, of his four young women, captured by the Indians when the frontier settlement of Dygartsbush is raided and burned in 1778.

There is little to tell us why and how these frontier women are as they are. We see them and their men—and the Indians—in motion, reacting to events, but we learn little of their motives beyond the exigencies of the moment. There is no reason to doubt, however, that their actions are anything but authentic. . . .

Finally, though the narrative, moving as it does from heroine to heroine, lacks cumulative effect, Mr. Edmonds has in store for each of his heroines a climactic episode of A-grade suspense or nerve-wracking intensity. And always, since that seems to be the theme of the book, the women are equal to it.

Nash K. Burger, "Frontier Heroines," in The New York Times Book Review, *January 26, 1947, p. 5.*

LIONEL D. WYLD

When ***Rome Haul*** was published in 1929 critics remarked favorably upon the achievement of the recent Harvard graduate who had dipped his pen into Erie water. A reviewer for the New York *Herald Tribune* commented that "**'Rome Haul'** would be a notable book in any season. As the first novel of a man born in 1903 it is extraordinary." Professor Thomas F. O'Donnell of Utica College, a critic of regional literature, recently wrote of ***Rome Haul*** as the beginning of a "new regionalism" in New York literature. ***Rome Haul*** doubtless stands as a pioneer; at the same time, it has all of the archetypal characteristics of its genre. The novel may be cited both as an influence of considerable importance and as a representative of a wide-ranging literature inspired by the epic achievement of the Erie Canal.

Even to the popular reader, Edmonds' novel is a treasure-house of Canal Era America, with authentic and full descriptions and characterizations of New York State's canal region. . . . [The story concerns] the coming-of-age of the orphaned Dan Harrow, who through numerous opportune circumstances rises quickly from an initial job as hoggee (canalese for "towpath driverboy") to captain of his own boat engaged in traffic on what was referred to as "the Rome haul." The Erie Canal seen in these pages is that of the mid-nineteenth century, with the heyday of the sleek packet boats gone and passenger trade almost eclipsed by the rising New York Central and other railroads, and freight hauling the chief operations on the "canawl."

The plot set the pace and the style for subsequent Erie-inspired fiction, to such a great extent, as a matter of fact, that Edmonds might be called a kind of "father of the Erie novel." He knew his materials . . . and how to use them to produce a novel both authentically regional in flavor and filled with the essential human drama of good literature. Dan Harrow rises rapidly above his hoggee beginnings (this in rather typical romance-fiction fashion), when he becomes owner of the canal boat of one who befriended him and who died in a cholera epidemic. Molly is the girl who provides an incentive to Dan's rise and maturing, after he rescues her from a seemingly sordid life as a canal boat cook. . . . The question of taking Molly "off'n the canal" and whether Dan Harrow will stick to boating becomes the crux of the novel, which has interesting similarities to works of other writers of the 1920's. As a matter of fact, Edmonds' novel reflects characteristic "Lost Generation" themes and style. In several respects, one may also regard ***Rome Haul*** as a study of "the Waste Land" set in regional trappings.

The characters, despite their place in a regional and historic upstate New York setting of the 1850's, are Twenties' types. . . . The stretches of the Erie Canal, with their marshes and miasmal vapors, are reminiscent of Fitzgerald's Long Island as seen from the commuter train in *Gatsby;* and Edmonds' "Gentleman Joe" Calash, galloping hither and yon through the canal country and through the novel reinforces this similarity with the symbols of Fitzgerald. (pp. 335-37)

Rome Haul contains the same aversion to religion—at least of the normal sort—that characterized the whole generation of writers who began producing in that era of the "Waste Land." Edmonds' minister, Fortune Friendly, "locked up for a public nuisance" by a sheriff he bested at cards, has doubtless a kind of philosophic faith, but the reader is never sure what Friendly does believe, or if he has anything which might be termed Faith. Like Frederick Henry of *A Farewell to Arms,* he seems to go out of his way at times to reject or to sidestep religious belief. . . . [There] is an existential, pragmatic note which pervades the actions of the characters.

Molly is, of course, the catalyst in Dan's maturation. In what might be considered typical Twenties' fashion, she represents attainable and needed love but only temporary warmth and security for Dan. Part of the plot involves Dan's fear of fighting Jotham Klore, the bully of the canal, for her—a fear which is omnipresent from the time Molly and Dan first meet. (p. 338)

The analogies with Hemingway's *A Farewell to Arms,* also published in 1929, are intriguing. The situation of Lieutenant Henry and Nurse Barclay is much the same—their fear (especially the girl's) of marriage, their philosophy of life (essentially pragmatic and expedient), and their caughtness, as it were, in the times. Professor Douglas Washburn of Rensselaer Polytechnic Institute has pointed out that the uncommittedness of the central characters of both novels provides further analogy. Like Frederick Henry of the Hemingway novel, ***Rome Haul's*** Dan Harrow is essentially an "outsider" and remains so. (p. 339)

In both novels—Edmonds' and Hemingway's—nobody really wins. The outcome of the struggle between Jotham Klore and Dan over Molly thus reinforces the "Waste Land" image in which Edmonds seems to have been held. After the fight Molly left Dan, and Fortune Friendly jumped ashore from the canal boat. The scene is graphically "Lost Generation":

> 'It don't seem right,' Fortune said to the rumps of the horses. 'Each one thought he was fighting for her. And neither one won.'
>
> Down the old Sarsey Sal sank in the walls of the locks. It grew colder. An old man sat on the dock at Han Yerry's fishing for sunfish.
>
> 'Frost tonight,' he prophecied to Fortune. . . .

There is considerable negation in ***Rome Haul***—another characteristic of novels of the 1920's. . . . Certainly, whatever else may be said about it, validly or coincidentally, the sense of Eliot's "HURRY UP PLEASE ITS TIME" pervades the book—in the encroachment of railroads on the canaller's life with the resulting lessening of their chances for livelihood; in Dan's fear of meeting with Jotham Klore for the inevitable showdown; in Molly's uncertainty; in "Gentleman Joe" Calash's vain search for freedom from the pursuit of the "mantrackers"; and in Dan's identification with the soil (his name is an obvious symbol) that keeps calling him off the canal.

Edmonds' novel is, of course, much more than something reflective only of other literary currents of the Twenties. It contains the essentials of regionalism at its best—realistic depiction of setting, credible colloquial dialogue, and honest portrayal of the mores of the people. In ***Rome Haul*** he created a novel deeper in significance than a simple romance; he not only captured the flavor of a past era but presented basic human issues in a way which transcended any narrow regionalism. (pp. 339-40)

Like Hemingway, Fitzgerald, and others, Edmonds produced a work of fiction in the Twenties containing the "signs of the times"; unlike them, his was at the same time a popular historical romance. Edmonds caught full sail, as it were, the prevailing literary winds. For the reader of ***Rome Haul,*** it is a worth-while trip on the Erie. (p. 341)

Lionel D. Wyld, "Canallers in 'Waste Land': Considerations of 'Rome Haul'," in The Midwest Quarterly, *Vol. IV, No. 4, July, 1963, pp. 335-41.*

GRANVILLE HICKS

At the turn of the century Tom Dolan, age 13, decides to leave school and work in Ackerman and Hook's flour and feed mill. His wages are 25 cents for an 11-hour day, with a three-mile walk and household chores on either end of it. Tom's father had deserted his family, but his mother's a diligent, self-respecting woman, who does her best to make up to the children. Tom and his younger twin sisters, for their father's shortcomings.

The setting for [**"Bert Breen's Barn"**] is less than a century ago, yet the way of life Mr. Edmonds describes could not be more foreign to the present time if he were a science-fiction writer portraying the remote past or imagining the remote future. . . .

Edmonds's great virtue is his honesty. He does nothing to make the life of Tom Dolan seem glamorous. Tom's only sustenance is his determination to raise himself and his family out of poverty. The symbol of his ambition is a solidly-built barn belonging to the Widow Breen. This Tom eventually buys, takes apart and, with neighborly help, reconstructs on his mother's land. This is the great moment, and the reader scarcely needs the added fillip of the discovery of the Breen fortune, a rumored treasure which has lurked in the background throughout the narrative.

Granville Hicks, in a review of "Bert Breen's Barn," in The New York Times Book Review, *July 20, 1975, p. 8.*

NOEL PERRIN

There was a time in the 1930's when you could hardly pick up an American magazine without reading a story by Walter Edmonds called **"The End of the Towpath"** or **"In the Hands of the Senecas."** If you missed one in the Saturday Evening Post, then you saw the movie.

In recent years Mr. Edmonds has been writing books for children, and they have been successful too. The best is probably **"Tom Whipple,"** the funny, incredible, true story of an upstate New York boy who went to sea in 1837, intending to see the world. (p. 54)

Now we have a new Edmonds book, and it's like one of those miniature boxes of candy they sell at Eastertime for 50 cents. Just three or four pieces, each one different.

"The Night Raider" contains four stories. The first is a genuine antique. **"Perfection of Orchard View"** came out in the Saturday Evening Post in 1934, and it was clearly the humorous story in that issue. It's set back in 1908. F. Schemmerhorn Watkins of New York City has just bought a farm near Boonville and hired a local named Arnold Meeker to run it. They correspond on farm matters. It must have been very funny in 1934; it's mildly funny now.

The second piece in the box is a canal story. It's violent, bloody and very good. The book gives no indication of when it was written—if recently, then Mr. Edmonds remains at the top of his form.

The third is another canal story, but a light-hearted one. Only it's not so much a story as an anecdote with details. Good details.

The fourth and last story is yet another kind. Now the author is writing in the first person about a small boy on a big farm, the kind where there's a manager and hired hands and the owner is a gentleman. Because the farm is in Boonville, and the owner is alternately called "Mr. Edmonds" and "my father," I assume that what we have here is reminiscence. Not that it matters: There's a real story, about hired men, owls and guinea hens (the owl is the night raider of the book's title), and a brilliantly evoked background of a rich farm 70 years ago.

What does matter is whether this is a book you'd give to a child. I'm not sure. The humor in the Post story seems to me to depend on adult awareness of class, and also of grammar. I'd a lot rather have my children reading Tom Whipple's adventures in Russia than I would have them sniggering over Arnold Meeker's letters to Mr. Watkins. The other three stories I think they'd like—even though **"Raging Canal"** might appall them with its vivid account of the kind of life young boys led on the Erie Canal. But we tend to sentimentalize and Waltonize the past; it would be good for them to read it.

But I'd give them **"Tom Whipple"** first. (pp. 54, 62)

Noel Perrin, "Four Upstate Stories," in The New York Times Book Review, *November 9, 1980, pp. 54, 62.*

LIONEL D. WYLD

The writer leaves his individual mark. Edmonds is no exception. . . . Although he did experiment with different approaches to writing in the fiction the *Harvard Advocate* published during his undergraduate period, Edmonds has had little to do with formal methods of writing. He is more akin to the bards of old who sang their lyrical ballads that told of their personal experiences or of adventures they had heard about, each infused with a morality that knew right from wrong, courage from dishonor. . . . (p. 123)

In writing Edmonds draws upon many sources: from the unflagging memory of a North Country heritage filled with canal boats and farm adventures; from a remarkably cogent sense of American history; from a talent he himself modestly admits for storytelling; and, finally, from simply the need to create ordinary characters—people who are representative of common folk throughout history. The "American experience" underlies so much of Edmonds's writing that he seems at once philosopher and historian, as much as storyteller. Part and parcel of the American experience, the frontier is often a leading factor in his work, the books especially. In the frontier times of his part of the nation, Edmonds found ample subjects for his novels, sometimes his stories, and often his children's books. But whether focusing on Revolutionary era Mohawk Valley or the canal-building "West" of New York State in 1817, Edmonds is constantly examining the American experience, assessing and reassessing the values and validity of it, and showing the necessary relationship between the American ideal—"the Dream," as many have called it—and the people who have played, and continue to play, a part in making that ideal a reality. He seems always to be showing the need for continuing that ideal, for assuring its extension into the present day. Admittedly his literature for the most part deals with a simpler age, a less hectic past: but this focus allows the artist a certain vantage point. In Edmonds's fiction the necessary linkage between people and history is seen, and his feeling for people is rendered with engaging clarity. (pp. 124-25)

Edmonds the storyteller is also a very sound historical novelist; and his principal works, including his enduring 1936 novel ***Drums Along the Mohawk,*** are as authentic as history itself. Real people occupy his attention, and real people move in the virtual world of his fiction. . . . Such novelists [as Edmonds and Conrad Richter] shed considerably more light on a narrow scene, such as the Mohawk Valley in the American Revolution in the case of Edmonds's ***Drums Along the Mohawk,*** than many historians do in their factually detailed and faithfully documentary writing. . . . One asks, of course, that the historical novelist or story writer be true to his history, which is not necessarily the same thing as sticking to the facts of it. The trained historian gives us the event, the action; and authors like Walter D. Edmonds can give us the *people* in the event or action, who are in the final analysis the real makers of history. In the doing, such a writer can produce literary art of a high order.

An important aspect of Edmonds's writing career has been his discovery for twentieth-century writers not only of an upstate New York in general but also of the times and lives of the canal era in particular. He stimulated the "new regionalism," and he sired the canal novel. Without a doubt, Edmonds has influenced many other authors toward New York State themes or settings; and in the case of the subgenre I have dubbed the canal novel, he certainly proved to be the literary progenitor of other writers' works. (p. 125)

Edmonds's real heroes may at times not be individual persons as in the conventional novel at all, but rather people in general; or canals, barns, and circuses around which the common folk lived and worked. Besides the obvious frontiersmen in such colonial period works as ***Drums Along the Mohawk*** and ***In the Hands of the Senecas,*** many other characters who people his fiction are, in a quite real sense, frontier folk—close to the soil, to the canal boat, or to the circus with which and for which they strive for a livelihood. . . . Edmonds's prose style, too, is liberally sprinkled with proverbial comparisons and down-to-earth similes which comprised much of the everyday vernacular of earlier times. It seems organically related to an essentially frontier culture about which he writes.

Certainly a basic characteristic of Edmonds's novels and stories is a reliance upon native-set humor. This, too, is tied to a frontier type culture and is an integral part of Edmonds's overall historical emphasis; as a writer, he shows an uncommonly firm grasp of the American frontier, both in his locality and in general of the mores of early American life. He is a modern literary descendant, too, of the frontier humorist; and his mastery of style, with its controlled ironic deflation, is comparable to that of Twain. Edmonds's famous racing caterpillar, "Red Peril," whether akin to Clemens's equally well-known Calaveras County jumping frog or not, and tales like those of the Black Maria, the itching bear, or the "cashalot" whale on a canal boat are just as authentic and mirthful Americana. Edmonds's involvement in folklore was a natural occurrence. As he listened to old canallers' yarns, he grew up close to one of the well-defined subcultures of New York State. He was not only reared in canal lore and farm life as he experienced them at Northlands and along the Black River Valley but also was imbued with a North Country appreciation of the folk hero and tall tale of Paul Bunyan tradition. The preposterousness of **"The Itching Bear"** story . . . fades as the plausibility of the tale—artfully and patiently built . . .—takes over in the reader's mind. The reader of **"The Itching Bear"** is being told a folk tale, a tall tale, one of hundreds upon hundreds that have come out of the vast Adirondack hills. . . . In such tales the chuckles of the readers indicate their mirthful accepting of the incredible: as with all good storytellers, Edmonds has us believing.

In keeping with the frontier sensibility which so often can be found in his fiction, both novel and story, Edmonds frequently has given his leading figures overtly symbolic names—Rose Wilder, Dan Harrow, Young Ames, for instance—that further tie them to the cultural setting (whether agricultural, canal, or mercantile) and the times of early America. Common to a number of Edmonds's novels is the young person who finds his maturity not only through ordinary growth and experience but also, importantly, in and through the times of the country's expansion. These figures—especially Chad Hanna, Jerry Fowler in ***Erie Water,*** Dan Harrow in ***Rome Haul,*** and John Ames in ***Young Ames***—symbolize young America in the first half of the nineteenth century. So, also, do Tom Whipple and other youths in the short stories. In their diverse ways and settings they are all striving in a developing cultural milieu that is basically frontier in orientation. Through such characters Edmonds suggests the need for a continuous re-evaluation of the national character and the individual's place in its formation, a re-evaluation which reminds his readers of the idealism, the morality, and spirit that are central to the "American Dream." Edmonds demonstrates again and again how close the ideal and the pragmatic are—and have always been—in the American experience. . . . (pp. 126-27)

In the earlier novels an Edmonds plot customarily required a sprawling landscape and a large cast of people; and the times and the people collectively often remain more memorable in an Edmonds novel than do particular individuals. In ***Drums Along the Mohawk*** one's attention focuses upon the average New York State farmer and his resistance not just to the Britain of George III but to the disruption of war itself. For ***Rome Haul*** and ***Erie Water*** this center-of-focus is the big-as-life canal and all its people, whether builders, boaters, or lock tenders. For ***The Big Barn*** the very title conveys the author's major emphasis; as fascinating as Ralph Wilder and other characters may be as individuals, the barn bulks larger still. For ***Chad Hanna*** . . . the real focus is the circus and the day-to-day concerns engendered by the nomadic circus life typical of the traveling shows of the 1830s in rural America.

In every instance, however, the fact that the traditional hero is upstaged, as it were, by the vastness either of cast or setting does not preclude an analysis of Edmonds's characters as literary figures of more than incidental importance and interest. Many are carefully drawn and, especially in the case of those in historical settings, authentically depicted. His male characters are generally more fully developed and have considerably more importance than his women, partly one suspects because they are forever caught up in a man's world of constant physical struggle, whether for safety or livelihood.

Edmonds's women are far removed from romantic fiction's usual, tradition-bound stereotypes . . . ; but at the same time one must confess to wanting something of the intellectual stamina that ought to accompany the practical, housewifery side of things, especially on the frontier. Considered collectively, Edmonds's women tend to exhibit a shallow intellectual nature, and the reader may find them pale and . . . rather boring. In his major works, to give specific examples, one finds little gumption and certainly no real assertiveness in Magdelana Borst (***Drums Along the Mohawk***), Caroline Trid (***Chad Hanna***), or Mary Fowler (***Erie Water***), even though they are married to, or otherwise closely linked with, the central male character in each book. Molly Larkins, of ***Rome Haul,*** may be a bit more independent throughout Edmonds's first novel than these other women are in theirs, yet even she is a relatively passive character. In the case of Christine Chevalier, whom John Ames is determined to woo and win in the novel ***Young Ames,*** we find the woman's part is essentially that of an offstage character. All told, they appear relatively passionless.

There are some exceptions to the charge of the women characters' thin intellectuality, I hasten to add, for Rose Wilder (***The Big Barn***), Kathy O'Chelrie (***The Boyds of Black River***), and to a large extent Polly Ann Dolan (***Bert Breen's Barn***) show their mettle and exhibit an assertive self-confidence in their respective novels. Then, too, other exceptions exist, of course, depending upon the circumstances and times depicted, for there is nothing pale about Delia Borst, Caty Breen, or Martha Dygart as they endure captivity in ***In the Hands of the Senecas.*** Older women, it should further be noted, generally fare better in Edmonds's hands and have more substance than younger ones, as evidenced by Mrs. MacLennar (***Drums Along the Mohawk***), Ma Halleck (***Erie Water***), Mrs. Huguenine (***Chad Hanna***), and the Indian Newataquaah (***In the Hands of the Senecas***). All are active, forceful figures with a firm hand on life.

When one looks at Walter D. Edmonds's work as a whole, another common element runs through his fiction. A notable thematic similarity in several novels involves a young couple and the matron who befriends them. In this connection it is obvious that Edmonds sees mature women as essentially important and sagacious advisors or confidantes. Thus Jerry and Mary Fowler lean on Ma Halleck in ***Erie Water;*** Dan Harrow and Molly Larkins in ***Rome Haul*** find a confidante in Mrs. Gurget; and Chad Hanna and Caroline Trid turn to Mrs. Huguenine for advice and support in ***Chad Hanna.*** In Edmonds's shorter fiction, too, this pattern is also followed when, for example, in the story of **"Big-Foot Sal,"** Edmonds uses the substitute mother figure as his primary focus.

It must be obvious to anyone who reads even a small amount of Edmonds's fiction that the author likes young 'uns—to use the Yorker expression for youths. Many of his stories, if not most of them, are those of youth. Frequently and significantly, his fiction centers on the twin themes of young people and a young country. (pp. 128-30)

Whether from historical times or more recent periods, [his young people] have that quality of integrity, morality, and right mindedness, coupled with a pragmatic sense of what must be done, that engages the reader's attention, as well as his respect. Without being didactic in the least, Edmonds's depictions of such young people provide a balanced sense of history and a valid lesson for the present time as well.

Walter D. Edmonds is an uncompromising realist when it comes to old-fashioned morality, and an advocate of the American experience. He has always written responsibly on his own terms. . . . What Edmonds has had to tell, he has had to tell truthfully, in his own way. There is probably no more sincere writer in contemporary letters than Edmonds. Whether in his major novels or in his shorter pieces, his expressed purpose has most often been the delineation of American history and the relation of that history to the present day. "What I want to show," he said, back when he accepted the Newbery Medal for his first children's book, "are the qualities of mind, the spirit, of plain ordinary people, who after all carry the burden of human progress. I want to know about people, how they loved, what they hoped for, what they feared." Edmonds has underscored in several instances this essential buttress of his writing. (pp. 129-32)

When he writes historical fiction, there is an air of uncompromising sincerity and validity about it. When he creates simple folk in comic situations, there is an air of honest mirth unalloyed. When he spins a tale of children, he speaks at the same time to the hearts and minds of parents.

Walter D. Edmonds has always conveyed in his writing, from major novel or short story to novelettes and books for young readers, the necessary but happy balance between taking the world seriously and feeling the *joie de vivre* that must also be found for life to have its fullest meaning. From Lana Martin's peacock feather to Tom Whipple's acorn, with Edmonds perspective is essential. (p. 132)

Lionel D. Wyld, in his Walter D. Edmonds, Storyteller, *Syracuse University Press, 1982, 147 p.*

ALAN RYAN

[***The South African Quirt***] is not to be regarded as a good book . . . merely because its author is advanced in years. Books are good or bad, and this is a very good one. Its portrayal of a boy's rite of passage into young adulthood is remarkable because it is so sensitively and convincingly done, and not because its author is so far distanced from his own childhood. But it certainly does seem true that, at least in Edmonds' case, age has brought a wonderful wisdom.

The novel is very short, and its focus is very narrow. It is set in the summer of 1915 on a farm in the remote stretches of upper New York State. Natty Dunston is 12 years old and spending the summer alone with his father. . . .

A lovable boy with a mean father? A cute little puppy named Bingo? Is the book as sentimental as a bare outline makes it sound? Not a bit of it.

Edmonds succeeds, with uncanny sureness, in taking us inside the mind of young Natty and in giving us a moving and vivid boy's-eye view of the world. And what a threatening world it can be when everything you're doing is being done for the first time, when everyone but you seems to know what he's about, when you know perfectly well what's expected of you but can't bring yourself to do it . . . and especially when your father, who absolutely rules your world, can twist logic so that you are guilty even when innocent and wrong even when right. . . .

At the center of the story is Natty's failure to share his father's view of the world, and his resistance to seeing the world as an adversary. He is too young, too curious, too unspoiled by life to turn inward and create a private demesne of his existence, as his father has done. Natty is still turned outward, eager to explore and embrace the world, and struggling to learn how. The ending of the book—in the manner of real life—is a mixture of triumph and sadness. It is touching in the best way: it is honest.

The South African Quirt is a modest novel with a quiet voice, but it has the look and feel of real life. Technically, it shows the mastery of a lifetime's craftmanship, and the publisher has thoughtfully enhanced the effect with a handsome jacket and nostalgic illustrations. Only time will tell, but I suspect this is the kind of book one can reread often in a lifetime.

Alan Ryan, "Father and Son," in Book World—The Washington Post, *April 7, 1985, p. 8.*

C(ecil) S(cott) Forester

1899-1966

(Born Cecil Lewis Troughton Smith) English novelist, short story writer, nonfiction writer, and scriptwriter.

A prolific author whose career spanned over forty years, Forester wrote novels of action and adventure characterized by historical detail and unpretentious language. Forester was well versed in seamanship and naval history and was especially knowledgeable of the Napoleonic period. Though some of his early efforts were indifferently assessed, Forester's later, more sophisticated stories of naval warfare set during the Napoleonic Wars or World War II earned him lasting renown. He was regularly praised for careful research, fast-paced, absorbing plots, and for infusing his works with what one critic called "the solid feel of truth." Forester's most enduring contributions to literature are the novels which comprise the Horatio Hornblower saga. Several of his other books were adapted to film, including *The African Queen* (1935).

Before writing the historical novels for which he eventually gained fame, Forester wrote thrillers, psychological novels, and biographies. Among the historical figures whom Forester captured in his biographies are Lord Nelson, Louis XIV, and Napoleon, who became a central figure in many of Forester's novels. Forester first achieved popular recognition with the thrillers *Payment Deferred* (1926) and *Plain Murder* (1930). *Brown on Resolution* (1929) is a portrait of a heroic seaman that prefigures much of Forester's later work. Forester soon turned almost exclusively to writing historical novels while retaining his interest in character development. *Death to the French* (1932) and *The Gun* (1933) are both novels about the Peninsular campaign of the Napoleonic Wars. *The General* (1936) is considered one of Forester's best novels. A study of the eccentricities and shortcomings of the military mentality and military organization set during World War I, *The General* is a statement about the futility of war and is unusual in Forester's work for its pacifistic approach.

***The Happy Return* (1937) introduces Forester's most enduring character, Horatio Hornblower, a seaman whom one critic called "a representative of English perseverance." Hornblower is the subject of ten complete novels, one unfinished book, a number of short stories, and even an atlas; throughout these works, Forester presents a consistent professional and personal portrait of his hero. The books did not appear in sequence, but the saga as a whole traces Hornblower's role in the Napoleonic Wars and his advancement through the ranks of the British Navy from midshipman in 1794 to Admiral of the Fleet in 1848. An introspective character, Hornblower is a reluctant hero who cannot seem to conquer his personal demons as easily as he does the French naval forces. A principal theme in the Hornblower novels and several of Forester's other works is that of "The Man Alone" and the ways in which he responds to opportunities for independent decision and action. Stanford Sternlicht called Hornblower "the first fictional Englishman since Arthur Conan Doyle's Sherlock Holmes to step out of literature and assume a 'reality.'" Hornblower became a symbol of pride for British citizens during World War II, for he was a realistic populist hero whose triumphs boosted their morale. The second novel in the saga,**

The Bettmann Archive, Inc.

***A Ship of the Line* (1938), won the James Tait Black Memorial Prize. Forester continued working on the Hornblower saga throughout his life; *Hornblower and the Crisis* (1967) was unfinished at the time of his death.**

Most of Forester's later books were critically appreciated. *The Ship* (1943), *The Good Shepherd* (1955), and *Hunting the Bismarck* (1959; published in the United States as *The Last Nine Days of the Bismarck*) all revolve around naval confrontations during World War II. *The Sky and the Forest* (1948) and *Randall and the River of Time* (1950) are regarded as Forester's philosophical works. *The Age of Fighting Sail* (1956) was his first nonfiction book since the early biographies and combines technical and historical detail with exciting narrative in describing the events of the War of 1812. Forester's autobiography, *Long Before Forty* (1967), recounts his early years.

(See also *Contemporary Authors*, Vols. 73-76, Vols. 25-28, rev. ed. [obituary] and *Something about the Author*, Vol. 13.)

THE SPECTATOR

Mr. Forester, who has no trade-mark as a novelist, and has achieved success in many gallant experiments, has again produced a novel that is markedly different from anything he has written before. In the first chapter [of ***Brown on Resolution***, published in the United States as ***Single Handed***] we are given a picture of Leading-Seaman Albert Brown dying on Resolution Island. In the second and the six following chapters we are given a character study of Albert's mother, Agatha Brown. As the daughter of a Nonconformist greengrocer she had had, in 1893, very little outlet for her unsuspected emotions until she met a young naval officer in a train. A swift love affair followed, of which Albert was the ultimate result. . . . Agatha refused matrimony with Albert's aristocratic father . . . and applied herself to the task of rearing young Albert for the navy. He was taken prisoner aboard the German cruiser 'Ziethen' which put into Resolution Island for repairs. He escaped ashore with a rifle and some ammunition, and hiding on a cliff proceeded to delay repairs by shooting the German crew by slow degrees. The story of his single-handed fight is brilliantly written. Mr. Forester may draw the long bow but his skill in the use of it is sure. His book is excellent both as a character study and a thriller—a notable combination.

A review of "Brown on Resolution," in The Spectator, *Vol. 142, No. 5254, March 9, 1929, p. 397.*

THE SATURDAY REVIEW OF LITERATURE

[**"The Gun"**] is a splendid adventure story, all the more splendid for being so far from any of the formulas that the words "adventure story" connote. It is founded upon an incident in the history of the Peninsula War, the abandonment by the retreating Spanish army of a siege gun—which became the rallying point and inspiration of guerilla fighters. . . .

Even the critical reader may well be so carried on by the action as not to appreciate the technical skill displayed in the telling. There is no single hero to engage the interest, but the author does not stoop, as he pardonably might, to enlist the interest with promises. He merely presents the gun, and the difficulty the peasants had in moving it; and after that problem another; and so on, each success leading to a greater task. That is all he does; but it is almost impossible to stop reading.

"The Gun" has the verisimilitude of history and the intensity of a work of imagination. Mr. Forester is to be congratulated on an unusual and a fine piece of work.

"An Adventure Founded on History," in The Saturday Review of Literature, *Vol. X, No. 20, December 2, 1933, p. 303.*

AMY LOVEMAN

[**"The African Queen"**] is a book which may not be high art but is certainly good entertainment. It is a rousing tale of adventure, implausible, perhaps, in its incidents but convincing in its portrayal of them. Mr. Forester very likely has never seen Central Africa, and knows of the River Uganda merely by hearsay, but he can create an atmosphere that is what the fiction lover demands of an African tale, and having forced the reader to make the initial hurdle can persuade him of the inevitability of his episodes. Moreover, he has sufficient skill in characterization, sufficient psychological subtlety, to lift his story above the general run of adventure yarns, and enlist interest in his hero and heroine as personalities and not mere lay figures on which to hang excitement.

The cast of Mr. Forester's story . . . consists [primarily] of but two persons, the drab, elderly, conventionally raised English spinster and the little cockney engineer who, against his will and his judgment, lends himself to her mad adventure. In a rickety launch, . . . [they] make their way down the Uganda River. . . . Mr. Forester has focussed his interest not so much on the hazards of the journey, though they furnish absorbing reading, but on the relations between the woman whose single-track mind sees in the blowing up of [a] German ship the means of doing her bit for her country and the mean-spirited little man who, forced out of his cowardliness by her determination, grows in spiritual stature through love and danger. Here is a genuinely skilful psychological study, one in which the evolution of a love at first blush absurd is made to seem natural and logical. Mr. Forester is consistent and incisive in his unfolding of the small incidents which bring about the incongruous love affair, and artist enough to conclude his story without bombast or compromise. It is an absorbing tale with personalities and events that remain fixed in memory.

Amy Loveman, "Mad Adventure," in The Saturday Review of Literature, *Vol. XI, No. 30, February 9, 1935, p. 473.*

PAUL ALLEN

Among the books which obscure darkest Africa [**"The African Queen"**] is an enlightening exception. For while it provides all the usual thrills in its account of fighting against the jungle's stubborn dangers, that excitement is merely the external cause of a much more engrossing inner conflict. In fact, a real awareness permeates the book and makes the reading of it an intellectual adventure.

In the beginning, however, we are lured into the story by a lightness which is almost farce. Rose Sayer, an English spinster very much of the middle-class, sees her brother die calmly at their jungle mission. It was the war, just beginning in Europe, having its reverberations already there in German Central Africa. . . . Rose, hitherto meek and pious, is on her own and against all Germans.

Then wandering unsuspectingly to her aid comes Allnutt, a little cockney, weak in body and will, but a good machinist. He has a launch, "The African Queen," on the river loaded with plenty of food, gin and high explosives meant for the mine near by. He and Rose determine to escape from all danger of capture by the Germans. And Rose has a further determination: she has made the second big decision of her life. The first was to dispense with corsets in the jungle heat. The second, only a little more daring, was to use the explosives to blow up the German boat down the lake.

Then begins a mad journey down the river. Allnutt says it cannot be done because there are miles of rapids and swamp before the river reaches the delta. . . . But Rose, with her stubborn desire to "do something for England," will not be dissuaded. . . . And with them the reader takes a trip for which thrilling is a mild word. So vivid is the description that the journey makes one acutely uncomfortable. . . . But, because they would not, and could not go back they reach the lake.

But they are hardly the same people when they get there. For in those weeks of dogged adventure their characters have developed far from their original simplicity. And as we watch their growth we forget the fantastic jingoism which is the stimulus of it all. The exciting events become secondary to this illuminating progression. Yet the change is natural and convincing. Allnutt remains the shabby cockney vulgarian. Rose never sheds her English middle-class limitations. But all the latent qualities of these two supposedly unimportant people are brought out. The inevitable welling-up of physical passion makes Rose tender and proud of this silly little man whose very weakness drives him to be brave. Time after time we see their small souls rise up magnificently to meet the occasion. And we are overwhelmed by the essential nobility of these two who remain at the same time vulgar and unintelligent. It is this penetrating view of the workings of the human spirit which we should demand of fiction even though we so rarely get it. So this author, who so gracefully yet forcefully paints two ordinary people with all their complexities, deserves our gratitude. It is an unpretentious book, with poise and deft writing. But within its scope it is a novel of distinct importance.

Paul Allen, "In the Afric Jungle: A Cockney Romance," in New York Herald Tribune Books, *February 10, 1935, p. 4.*

PERCY HUTCHISON

[The African Queen] was probably as ugly, incompetent and dilapidated a thirty-foot launch as one would be likely to find afloat. . . . But under the deft hand of C. S. Forester [in **"The African Queen"**] she becomes the instrument of high adventure. . . . Whether the story has any foundation in fact we do not know, but the author's gift for establishing verisimilitude, even when building a tale the purport of which is out-and-out romance, is strikingly evidenced. If the little cockney, Allnutt, is something of a stock figure, albeit exceedingly well drawn, Rose Sayer, spinster sister of the Rev. Samuel Sayer, missionary, is not.

The story starts with the death of the Rev. Samuel, worn out with fever and years of continuous service in the noisome African jungle. By coincidence the rickety old launch [captained by Allnutt] arrives a few hours later. . . . A chance remark of Allnutt's to the effect that he has several cases of explosives aboard, and the sight of several gas cylinders standing in the waist of the launch, furnish Rose with a sudden plan.

Patrolling the lake into which the Ulanga [River] empties is the ably-manned and highly armed 200-ton German steamer, the Königin Luise—Allnutt calls her the Louisa—and, in a glorious vision from heaven as it were, . . . Rose sees herself torpedoing the enemy boat and thus striking a telling blow for the motherland.

If such a sudden jump be an easy leap for the imagination of a novelist, he must nevertheless convince a reader while accomplishing it. And Mr. Forester does so with at least a romantically sufficient degree of conviction. Rose, who after all is only in her thirties, has always been under the repressions of her brother, and of their calling as missionaries. Suddenly released from these repressions, with the accidental appearance of the Queen with her explosive cargo, she sees opportunity frantically beckoning. It is Mr. Forester's sole adventure into psychology, but it is sufficiently sound for his purposes, and he does not overwork his lead. He prepares adequately, by this change in the nature of Rose, for a subsequent and profound change in the spinster's attitude toward Charlie.

Hence, if Mr. Forester, in the course of the frail craft's perilous voyage through boiling rapids, brings about something closer than a purely Platonic relationship between Rose and Charlie, he does not base it upon mere propinquity, or upon any superior attraction on the part of the little cockney. Charles at the outset has no desire to be patriotic, or to risk his rather weasel-like self in any way. . . . It is Rose's sudden exaltation which gradually communicates itself to him that works the change. In other words, it is the woman's high and disinterested resolve which turns the weasel into a man. . . .

The credulity of the reader may be stretched here and there, but, having given himself to the tale, as one must always give one's self up whole-heartedly to romance or eschew it altogether, he will go on. Suspended again and again in midair, he will find pleasure in the suspense, a device of which Mr. Forester again and again proves himself a master.

The outcome of this death-defying and hare-brained dash we leave the reader to discover. **"The African Queen"** is a fast-moving tale, a very good yarn, with more than a little novelty in conception.

Percy Hutchison, "A Strange Wartime Adventure in German East Africa," in The New York Times Book Review, *February 10, 1935, p. 5.*

BEN RAY REDMAN

[**"The General"**] is a book in which fiction masquerades, with complete success, as biography; a book in which measured and dispassionate words do the kind of job that can never be done by emotional eloquence; a book whose whole being and whose every part is so saturated with irony that the ironic accent needs never to be pointed or underlined or made explicit. Here, briefly, is a book that must be added to those few books which tell the truth about the war, with an honesty that is uncompromising, and in a style that makes truth memorable.

Mr. Forester has written the life story of Lieutenant General Sir Herbert Curzon, . . . professional soldier and indubitable hero, who distinguished himself, quite accidentally, in an early skirmish of the Boer War; who rose, during twelve subsequent years of peace, and according to the normal laws of promotion, from a subaltern's rank to that of a senior major of cavalry; and who, with the outbreak and progress of the Great War, swiftly advanced (at a pace so rapid that it could be credible only in incredible circumstances) from the command of a regiment to the command of an army corps.

More than the story of a man, this is a revealing study of the military mind, the military caste, and the military system, as those three impalpable entities expressed themselves in the activities of the British Army in France, from 1914 to 1918. . . .

Judged by the standards of soldiering that existed in his prime, Curzon was a first-rate soldier; and, judged by standards that have always been respected, he was a hero. But, curiously enough, it is a rather ridiculous and even pitiable figure that emerges from Mr. Forester's pages. It is impossible to hate Curzon or to blame him, for he gave the best that he had, the best of his intelligence, courage, industry and strength—and a leg into the bargain. But his best, it would appear, like that of his betters, was none too good. British generalship, as Mr. Forester describes it, and as it proved in practice, was woefully incompetent. . . .

Some readers will rise from this book with a rekindled hatred of war and a righteous rage against generals whose stupidity finds expression in mass murder. But others will shrug their shoulders and say: "Absurd, of course, that men like Curzon can rise to positions of such fatal power; but they always have, and probably they always will. . . ." And these readers (while incidentally relishing the priceless and strangely touching love story of Curzon and Lady Emily) will think that they do Mr. Forester full justice when they credit him with having presented, with superb clarity and ironic definition, a few notable scenes from an ancient and enduring farce.

One wonders what personal experiences lie behind the writing of **"The General,"** and whether or not C. S. Forester ever wore the red tabs of a British junior staff officer. . . . One would like to know more about a writer whose style and cast of thought are comparable and akin to Harold Nicolson's.

Ben Ray Redman, "The Tragic Farce of the Military Man," in New York Herald Tribune Books, *March 1, 1936, p. 3.*

WILLIAM PLOMER

As Mr. Forester's eleventh novel, ***The General*** is the work of a practised author, and it is more than efficiently written. He has made Curzon both admirable and sinister, he has made Curzon's story both amusing and terrifying, and all is set forth soberly and credibly. In fact Mr. Forester has written, in a quiet and peculiarly English way and with almost no recourse to obvious horror, an original book about the War.

William Plomer, in a review of "The General," in The Spectator, *Vol. 156, No. 5634, June 19, 1936, p. 1144.*

KENNETH P. KEMPTON

Looking back at recent historical novels of the bulkier sort, one sometimes wonders whether, without libraries, the author could have made a story. Not so here. Mr. Forester has followed **"The Gun"** and **"The General"** with another book that proves him a narrative craftsman in his own right. If, indeed, he alters the record a bit now and then, nobody but the nasty neat will care. His main facts are sound, his atmosphere is authentic, and it is something beyond historical truth that he is after.

"Beat to Quarters" [published in Great Britain as ***The Happy Return***] is a chapter in the life of one Captain Hornblower, commander of His Britannic Majesty's 36-gun frigate *Lydia*. With England still at war with Spain and Bonaparte already looming over Europe, sealed orders send this man round the Horn and into the Great South Sea to join forces with a Central American rebel, open trade routes to the Main, and defeat the 50-gun *Natividad* stationed off Panama. . . .

It may sound tame, but it is not. This is the work of a man who knows his period but will never let it stand between him and his greater knowledge of human nature. This Hornblower is roundly done: a man approaching middle age, intensely shy, poor at a time when wealth was a prerequisite to success in the British Navy, loyal to his profession rather than his sovereign, bewildered equally by international politics and the petty details of naval routine, but an unbeatable fighter and guardian of his ship and his men. His rubber of whist with midshipmen while lying in wait for the *Natividad* is not easily forgotten. The second engagement, fought over three days and five chapters, never for one sentence lets you down.

The book may have its soft spots. El Supremo is cleverly drawn, but the maniacal note seems discordant, too easy, in this realistic romance. The end is hurried, and Hornblower the hesitant lover (his plump Maria awaits him at home) comes close to a ludicrous effect unintended. Still and all, it is a treat to get hold of something dextrous and lithe and stripped for action—something that for the most part is just a hell of a good story.

Kenneth P. Kempton, "Stripped for Action," in The Saturday Review of Literature, *Vol. XV, No. 24, April 10, 1937, p. 5.*

ALEXANDER LAING

Captain Horatio Hornblower, of His Brittanic Majesty's frigate Lydia, is the hero of **"Beat to Quarters"**; and I know of no other book in which the behavior and character of a typical, competent naval officer of the period are so tellingly presented. We know the impression such men made upon their contemporaries in the days before cables. If, by and large, they seemed vain, callous, phlegmatic, they had cause to develop a protective shell, sailing with a shipload of potential mutiny out of reach of all redress, to fulfill orders often preposterously drawn by landsmen with no idea of the difficulties involved. It is Mr. Forester's triumph that he compels an immense sympathy for Captain Hornblower, even when he has a man triced up and flogged for spitting on the deck. . . .

The main plot of **"Beat to Quarters"** turns upon the comparative ease with which Hornblower carries out his original orders to discomfit the Spanish authorities, thus making for himself a terrific task later on when new orders arrive via Panama to acquaint him with the necessity of undoing all that he has done.

The story has an increasing dramatic tension, a mounting excitement, up to and throughout the single-ship action that fills the third quarter of the book; and I do not recall, from even the greatest classics of the sea, an account of such an action that is better told for the lay reader. Here there is none of the juvenile "one Anglo-Saxon is worth ten Latins" attitude. As a sound student of tactics, Mr. Forester assumes that the heavier metal will win unless it is brilliantly outmaneuvered. The whole course of the action is traced from the quarterdeck brain of Hornblower, to whom fighting is not a matter of boisterous heroics, but a closely reasoned application of sound rules to chance events.

The end of the book brings forward once more Mr. Forester's tendency to mitigate first-rate blood and thunder with a quiet, cynical aftermath. This is a pity, not because it violates life or the artistic verities, but because he is never at his best in that sort of writing. **"Beat to Quarters"** is essentially the story of the cause and conduct of a superb naval action. As such, it has every claim to stand with the best stories of the kind that have ever been written. . . .

"Beat to Quarters" is Mr. Forester's best book. It is comparable to the Bounty trilogy, and if the last quarter falls below the Nordhoff and Hall level of continual competence, the climax rises to heights that even they have not yet attained.

Alexander Laing, "A Seaman in Napoleon's Day," in New York Herald Tribune Books, *April 11, 1937, p. 4.*

FRED T. MARSH

C. S. Forester is the English adventure novelist of **"The General," "The African Queen"** and **"The Gun."** Like Conrad, he is a psychological novelist, but, unlike Conrad, there is nothing either tortuous or tortured about either his prose or his plots. He gets off with a tail wind and navigates on a straight course to his harbor, swinging a sound prose along the way. [**"Beat to Quarters"**] is a sea story of the Napoleonic era. . . .

Forester is apparently a sound antiquarian. His story is interlarded with technical details, descriptions of manoeuvres, all sorts of detailed technical descriptions. It is a curious thing, but such matter in the best works of this kind, even for the reader who never was on a sailing ship and has only the sketchiest notion of what most of it is about, becomes not only fascinating in itself but tremendously enhances the excitement.

There is plenty of action. But there is also an unusual character study. Captain Hornblower of the Lydia is a genius and a hero to every one except himself. His story is the study, in terms of action, of the self-conscious man. This plain, able British sea commander, ambitious, decisive, intelligent, hard but eminently fair, is a mass of contradictions inside, a little Hamlet of the seas, doubting himself and playing a part, fearful lest his officers and crew discover his weakness, imposing on himself and his command a Spartan code. His is the triumph of will over introspection. And in the end, when a great adventure comes his way, miraculously, he is unable to step out of the rôle he has steeled himself to play, too fearful to let his naturally warm, generous, emotional nature get the upper hand. For he knows he would be lost. . . .

Forester is a sound Britisher. But he is no maudlin romancer. He is fully aware of the submerged viciousness in the impressment system, the harsh discipline, the incompetent and ghastly surgery, the wreckage in lives and character that the system entailed, the evil underneath the glory of England's sea supremacy. His Captain Hornblower knows it only too well. Some rebellious natures bucked the system; some like Bligh of the Bounty made it a religion; many were incompetents and fools. But Hornblower and his kind accepted it and fitted themselves into it, while a few like Nelson and (on his minor plane) Hornblower were touched with genius. Mr. Forester gives you both the rottenness and the heroism in as gripping and realistic a sea tale as you are likely to run across in a year's reading.

Fred T. Marsh, "C. S. Forester's Rousing Tale of the Sea," in The New York Times Book Review, *April 11, 1937, p. 4.*

KENNETH PAYSON KEMPTON

"The Gun" proved Forester to be no run-of-the-mill romancer. In **"Beat to Quarters"** he spread his scene and deepened his experience. [**"Ship of the Line"**] is a fair bid for the first-rate standing unquestionably due him.

It is a sequel to **"Beat to Quarters,"** a further chapter in the life of Captain Horatio Hornblower, R.N. . . . Forester's ingenuity, his sense of climax and transition, his deft mastery over material stand squarely in the way of monotony or boredom. The structure of the story is frankly episodic. But these episodes are rising steps in the revelation and development of Hornblower's character, they are shrewdly integrated parts of an artistic whole.

Forester's sense of the past and his means of communicating it to the reader have always been quietly competent. His seamanship alone is a delight. It is never paraded, nor is it ever overburdened and obscure. His style runs a fine line between the faintly archaic and our contemporary idiom, so that we get a language which, though it may be historically inaccurate in details, sounds just right. His intricate engagements, involving the detailed management of ships and guns and men long buried in the past, are as real, as immediate, as if we were there.

More real, indeed. For these mechanical matters are throughout merely support and motivation for the figure that dominates the story. Hornblower the self-conscious, the bored husband, the ardent lover—Hornblower the seasick commander, the poverty-stricken privateer—Hornblower the whist player, the indomitable fighter and the craven man—Hornblower who strips naked with nine seamen to capture and burn a merchantman: he is our other self, long buried too, living desperately if not always gloriously in this book.

The end is no end; it promises more of this strangely human hero to come. I believe many readers will be ready.

Kenneth Payson Kempton, "Triumph of the 'Sutherland'," in The Saturday Review of Literature, *Vol. XVII, No. 21, March 19, 1938, p. 3.*

WILLIAM McFEE

[**"Beat To Quarters"**] superficially resembled scores of other sea stories, of which perhaps the masterpieces of Rafael Sabatini are most popular. But it was a sea story with a difference. It was, for instance, more for adults than for the grownup juveniles who form Mr. Sabatini's vast public. There was love in it; not costume melodrama love, but the real thing. Captain Hornblower was an authentic credible human being, acting within the social pattern of his times as if he had blood in his veins instead of sawdust. His adventures . . . were all first rate action narratives, and it was only natural that, having invented so useful a character, Mr. Forester should carry on.

In **"Ship of The Line"** Captain Hornblower lives again. Wonderful to relate this sequel is better than the first tale. Moreover Captain Hornblower has developed. He is a more complete and complex character than in **"Beat To Quarters."** The book is more skillfully written. . . .

The impression of reality in this book is achieved by blending a wealth of technical and historical detail with sound psychology. We get to know Captain Hornblower extremely well. We are spared nothing of the misery and horror of war, but we are nevertheless carried away by the excitement of it. The theme of Mr. Forester's novel is the mind of the commander. It is his special subject. He treated it with masterly precision in an earlier novel **"The General"** which has received far less praise than it merits. It is even more of a tour de force to recreate such a man as Hornblower and to give such a lifelike picture of the war in Spain, when Napoleon brought an Italian Army against the Spanish loyalists. . . .

As might be expected from the author of **"The General,"** the psychology is sound. Hornblower is a genuinely brave man, and one might even say, a good man. I imagine he is much more typical of naval officers of the period than was the celebrated Captain Bligh of the Bounty.

It is important to emphasize this because **"Ship of The Line"** has a lesson for us under the surface of the adventure tale. Without being at all didactic Mr. Forester drives home the eternal truth that without character we can have no commanders and without men with the temperament and aptitude for command we can do nothing with ships.

William McFee, "What's Ship or Seamen without Officers?" in New York Herald Tribune Books, *March 20, 1938, p. 7.*

FRED T. MARSH

[**"Flying Colours"**] is the third novel in which Mr. Forester presents his minor Nelson, his Hamlet of the seas, Captain Hornblower, an introverted hero filled with doubts and self-mistrust, "posing as a man of rigid imperturbability when he was nothing of the kind," hero to his crews and genius to his officers, but to himself in black moments of introspection a masquerader whose courage comes from desperation, whose decisiveness emerges from a fog of doubt, whose discipline (of himself and others) is merely a protective armor over a sensitive and wayward spirit.

It would be difficult to overpraise these splendid tales of British seamanship back in the times when Wellington and his army were delivering their mortal wound to the dictator of Europe in the Peninsular Campaign. . . . In the new novel Hornblower does, indeed, come off with "Flying Colours." Everything he has ever dreamed of comes true. He is a hero for a day. He is knighted. He is made economically secure for the first time in his life. The baby son born while he is a prisoner in France is a joy to his heart. Lady Barbara, the secret dream of his romantic heart, is his for the asking. And with the powerful Wellesley clan behind him, a distinguished career in Parliament is within his grasp. But such men as Hornblower are not made for happiness. He will go on in the path of duty as opportunity opens the way. But the old doubts, the old self-consciousness, the old self-flagellations will remain behind the austerity he uses as a front to cover his timidity and to hide his sense of inferiority. . . .

These historical sea tales of Forester's are in a class by themselves. The fine forthright prose, the careful antiquarianism, the unusual character interpretation, the thoughtful study of the rottenness and the heroism, the agony and the glory, of naval warfare of the era, all lend maturity and significance to these three rousing novels. Thorough, painstaking and convincing though the tales are, these qualities serve only to enhance the drama and give wings to the exciting story.

Fred T. Marsh, "Another Fine Tale by C. S. Forester," in The New York Times Book Review, *January 1, 1939, p. 7.*

WILLIAM McFEE

It was a pleasure last year to report **"Ship of the Line,"** in which C. S. Forester carried on the adventures of Capt. Horatio Hornblower, begun in his earlier novel, **"Beat to Quarters."**

It is an even greater pleasure to call all hands to the break of the poop and announce the new complete volume of the gallant captain's exploits [**"Captain Horatio Hornblower"**], which includes not only the foregoing stories but **"Flying Colours,"** a Napoleonic adventure which brings Capt. Hornblower the Order of the Bath and honorary colonelship in the Royal Marines. . . .

This is great stuff. Mr. Forester, allowing for the difference of the times, is of the school of Conan Doyle when he wrote his Napoleonic and other historical tales. Of the two Mr. Forester is the more skilled technically. He depicts finer shades of character. Chesterton once said of the detective novel that it is an affair of masks rather than of faces. So is the historical novel. Mr. Forester's achievement, in making Hornblower, Bush and Brown really live, is due to his vigorous comprehension of the English character. He is not preoccupied with social theses. He writes as if nobody had ever written a tale before. Ten years ago English reviewers were announcing him as a coming man. His **"Single Handed,"** published here at that time, is a shamefully neglected sensational novel of the war. It ought to be reprinted. **"The General"** was a very cruel and truthful revelation of the mentalities of the higher command during the same hostilities. Mr. Forester is undoubtedly a novelist to be reckoned with. He has facility and versatility. He can handle all kinds of situations with a nimble pen. Any one who wishes to prove that men write better now than they did in the days of Sir Walter Scott, for instance, can compare **"Flying Colours"** with either Scott or Fenimore Cooper.

William McFee, "All Hands to the Poop!" in New York Herald Tribune Books, *April 30, 1939, p. 4.*

BEN RAY REDMAN

In [**"To the Indies"**] Mr. Forester goes down to the sea again, to tell the story of Columbus's third voyage as it was seen through the eyes of Narciso Rich, eminent jurisconsult of Aragon and leading authority on the maritime code of Catalonia. . . .

Here would seem to be a tale made for Mr. Forester's hand, abounding in romance and color, packed with action, offering rich opportunities for verbal seamanship and chances for irony and humor. Yet it is far from his best work. In it he holds his reader with a more languid grasp than is his habit. **"The Gun"** had to be read at a sitting: the drive of its straight-line narrative permitted neither halt nor detour. The novels of the Hornblower trilogy, with heroic episode topping heroic episode, communicated an excitement that was irresistible and a romantic satisfaction that was complete. **"The General"** proved that Mr. Forester could make unfolding character as fascinating as unfolding action. But it is quite possible, while reading **"To the Indies,"** to break off . . . and then return to the story with no sense of time lost or keen anticipation of things to come. Stirring as its incidents should be, they stir but mildly. The pace of the narrative is uneven; the interest does not mount. Perhaps the author's sense of timing has for once deserted him. But I think the explanation is that Don Narciso is unequal to the central role. We do not really care very much what happens to him, whereas we cared greatly in the cases of Hornblower and "the gun." . . . And, that being said, it becomes obvious that character plays a more important part in Mr. Forester's best tales of violent action than is at first apparent. It is Hornblower's character that gives edge and meaning to his exploits. But with Don Narciso failing us, and the Admiral only faintly sketched, **"To the Indies"** is little more than action for action's sake.

Ben Ray Redman, "Companion to Columbus," in The Saturday Review of Literature, *Vol. XXII, No. 14, July 27, 1940, p. 5.*

ROSE FELD

Cecil Scott Forester, best known perhaps for his recent **"Captain Horatio Hornblower,"** which was widely acclaimed, turns to a more difficult and ambitious subject in his new novel, and excellently does he encompass it. **"To the Indies"** is the story of the third voyage of the aging Christopher Columbus to the Western Hemisphere in the years 1498-99. . . . Forester does a brilliant job of recreating both period and character. The story moves swiftly, in high tempo of excitement and adventure on sea and land. Through the eyes and reactions of Don Narciso

Rich, a brilliant lawyer in the service of King Ferdinand and Queen Isabella, the tragic final chapters in the life of the discoverer of the new world emerge. . . .

Forester paints a moving picture of the aging rheumatic explorer, a poor disciplinarian of men, an excellent navigator of the seas, despised on the first score, respected on the second. . . .

One can get the outlines of **"To the Indies"** out of history books. Familiarity with the scene will, in fact, add to the pleasure of the book and to an appreciation of the excellent work Forester has created. For he has clothed the skeleton of facts with the fine raiment of fifteenth century adventure and discovery. His writing is clean as a saber stroke, his characters, from Columbus down to the lowliest Indian, alive with individual color and instinct. One's heart goes out to the misguided Columbus as to the simple creatures he forced into slavery.

Rose Feld, "When Columbus Sailed Rebellious Seas," in New York Herald Tribune Books, *July 28, 1940, p. 1.*

FRED T. MARSH

You look for more than a mere sea story in a Forester novel. You will not be disappointed [in **"The Captain from Connecticut"**]. Capt. Josiah Peabody may not be as subtle a figure as the now celebrated Capt. Horatio Hornblower; but the lean Yankee who had gone to sea as a boy off a Connecticut farm and served under Truxtun and Decatur can hold his own with the plain English gentleman who became a hero to everybody except himself. Both have the same appearance of stoic imperturbability covering a multitude of human doubts and weaknesses. Peabody's secret yearning for escape from the tyranny of his Puritan will—whether in drink, which he has conquered, or dreams—matches Hornblower's secret sensitivity, self-consciousness and tendency to introspection. But Hornblower is the product of an old tradition, a classical figure. Peabody is self-made, a romantic one. . . .

It is a graceful frigate of a tale, not a three-decker of the line like the Hornblower trilogy. But when the most popular British novelist of the sea at the moment, and deservedly so, writes a tale in celebration of an American captain and his Yankee ship of our second unhappy war with Britain, it is news. Forester being Forester, one does not have to be told that it is handled with subtlety as well as consummate skill. It is, to be sure, open to certain criticisms. One gets the impression that 1812 was New England's war, badly managed by Madison, for her freedom of the seas, whereas New England so bitterly opposed the war that some of her shipping people threatened secession. Madison is represented as foolishly idealistic in refusing alliance with Napoleon, whereas that honorable course proved to be the best policy we could possibly have pursued, winning for us friends in both Britain and France.

And no woman here can compare with Captain Hornblower's Lady Barbara; indeed, none seems to achieve individuality. But the flavor of romance in the abstract has its compensations under the Forester touch.

Fred T. Marsh, "A Yankee Skipper, Peer to Cap'n Hornblower," in New York Herald Tribune Books, *June 15, 1941, p. 1.*

WILLIAM McFEE

C. S. Forester, famed creator of Captain Horatio Hornblower, adventurous hero of the Napoleonic wars, has abandoned historical fiction for a while and has turned his attention to the war now in progress in the Mediterranean. **"The Ship"** is the story of H.M.S. Artemis, a British light cruiser in a squadron shepherding a vitally important convoy to Malta. They are attacked by an Italian fleet which includes battleships. The book is the story of that action.

There have been some pretty good stories written about the present naval occasions, and some very bad ones. As may be expected from Mr. Forester, his novel is one of the better kind. He is an accomplished craftsman. It is a difficult assignment to write "propaganda" without degenerating into patriotic claptrap. The author has to introduce depth in his characterizations without sacrificing truth. His characters must seem human without revealing any unpopular blemishes. The author's artistic conscience must remain awake without becoming intolerant.

This bald résumé does not do justice to Mr. Forester's narrative, which is accurate, lucid and thrilling. To give a comprehensible account of a modern naval action so that laymen can see it is a remarkable feat. A thirty-two-knot ship firing her 6-inch guns and hitting her target at 9,000 yards is a mechanism of inconceivable complexity. The plotting room, for example (manned by the ship's bandsmen), where the adjustments for distance, wind, barometric changes, alterations of course and speed are relayed instantaneously to the gun layers, makes us marvel. Mr. Forester, with great literary skill, makes us understand how exquisitely geared to his job each of those 600 men must be.

If there be a fault in the book it is the incessant holding up of a really exciting action to tell us long stories of the backgrounds of various ranks and ratings. Very interesting, no doubt, but out of place in a tale of highspeed fighting.

William McFee, "H.M.S. Artemis," in The New York Times Book Review, *May 16, 1943, p. 6.*

LINCOLN COLCORD

A new Hornblower book runs pretty closely to the established formula; but it is such a good formula, and all the Hornblower books furnish such excellent entertainment, that there is little left for the reviewer to say. Captain (now Commodore) Hornblower personifies the British Navy of the old days of sail, which is to say, he personifies the British Empire at the heyday of its aggressive development. Little attempt is made at characterization, except in the case of the hero himself: he is revealed as a sensitive man of action, a little on the side of introspection, but he is a seaman to his fingertips and the right decision and command always come to him instinctively. Even his wife, the Lady Barbara, is barely touched on in the story; aside from the development of his character, the narrative is a tumult of action from beginning to end, a tumult of clear and logical and understandable action, which unfolds a consistent story and gives the book its substance and satisfaction. . . .

This is the formula, and it has produced as fine a series of seafaring tales as we have had for generations. Their very simplicity and directness of approach are disarming to the reader—especially so, perhaps, to the critic. It ought to be easy enough to write such unadorned, straightforward stories: there is nothing to them that cannot be readily followed. Well, go ahead and try it.

In [**"Commodore Hornblower"** (published in Great Britain as **"The Commodore"**)] the scene is laid at the time of Napoleon's advance on Moscow. Captain Hornblower has just retired from his last escapade with all honors and a knighthood, and has settled down on his country estate for a little while. Suddenly the Admiralty calls him back to action, advances him to commodore and gives him a small fleet to patrol the Baltic, where relations between England, Sweden and Russia are at a critical stage, with the French forces under Bonaparte massing for some kind of action in the Baltic states. Off he goes in the first chapter, and so the story starts with a bang, with scant attention paid to the home scene. . . .

It is evident, of course, that the author has cast his story to draw a parallel between the Napoleonic invasion and the recent invasion of Russia by Germany. It is a good parallel, by and large, with the same general motives in operation, the same sort of autocratic figures overreaching themselves, and the same stupendous results. And, regardless of history, it gives fictional propaganda value.

There might be a certain amusing inconsistency in the popularity as escape literature of such a swashbuckling story of intrigue and aggressive action, while we are dreaming of a brave new world in which such things are nevermore to be. In fact this is a book altogether about a type of hero which we are supposed to be trying to lay away in the discard. But let the inconsistency stand for what it is worth; this book is bound to be extremely popular, because it is a fine story and deserves to be.

The author, as he proved long ago, possesses that sovereign answer to all minor criticism, narrative power. His tale flows on, it is serious and sensible, yet it never grows dull and never flags. The adventures it relates are never extravagant, and always wear the air of verisimilitude. One only wishes he would not clip his nautical words and phrases so closely. It is possible to swallow "main t'mast stays'l," but "mizzen t's'l" is going a bit too far.

Lincoln Colcord, "Hornblower, Now a Commodore, Returns," in New York Herald Tribune Weekly Book Review, *May 27, 1945, p. 3.*

L. RUSSELL MUIRHEAD

To any constant reader of Mr. Forester's novels, it soon appears that his work falls into three or four well-marked divisions, some of the books partaking of more than one division. The largest is the "naval" section, into which fall ***Brown on Resolution*** [1929], the volumes of the Hornblower saga, ***The Captain from Connecticut*** (1941) and ***The Ship*** (1943). A second group is what might be described as the "urban adventure" series, including ***Payment Deferred*** [1926], ***Two-and-Twenty*** [1931], ***Plain Murder*** [1930], and ***The Peacemaker*** (1934). An "exotic adventure" group would take in ***The Shadow of the Hawk*** [1928], ***The African Queen*** (1935), and ***The Earthly Paradise*** (1940); while ***Death to the French*** [1932; published in the United States as ***Rifleman Dodd***], ***The Gun*** (1933), and ***The General*** (1936) may be regarded as the historical and modern counterparts, in an "army" group, of the Peninsular and recent naval stories.

In writing of the armed services, Mr. Forester betrays an unrivalled insight into the mind of the sailor or soldier, irrespective of rank or rating. (p. 414)

Sympathetic perusal of the Hornblower saga goes far towards affording an understanding of why the British Navy of those days, though it was starved by the authorities, and though the majority of the lower deck even were pressed into service against their will, was yet able to hold the seas against a continental power possessing almost every strategic and tactical advantage. . . . [The] tradition of the Service . . . has driven every good officer to exert every nerve and every sinew to fulfil Service needs before considering his own comfort or convenience. By allowing us a glimpse into the inner workings of Hornblower's mind, Mr. Forester has shown just how natural and yet how difficult such decisions can be. We are permitted to know that Hornblower was persuaded of his own inadequacy (and how unjustly!), while envious of the calm efficiency of his subordinates. Yet it is possible that even the stolid Mr. Bush, when not carrying out an order from his adored superior, may sometimes have had qualms about the correctness of his own decisions. The point is, the decisions were made, not because of any rules or regulations, but because of the exigencies of the moment. Mr. Forester demonstrates that every good sailor (or soldier, for that matter) must be an opportunist; it is the success of that opportunism that has so often wrung the accusation of "perfidy" from Britain's enraged and worsted opponents.

Mr. Forester has done something bigger and more important, however, than merely record a series of brilliant impressions of maritime skill. He has kept burning the lamp of pride in the achievement of the British Services. . . . ***Brown on Resolution*** was published at a time when the main objective of too many British citizens was simply "to have a good time"; and the suggestion that there were other ends to which a man could devote his whole attention was a timely one. Mr. Forester, by persevering in his self-imposed task, has done in fiction very much what Mr. Arthur Bryant has since done in the historical essay: he has given us a good conceit of ourselves and has helped to persuade us that we are not simply a "decadent democracy". He has held up the ideal of the naval and military services in its purest form, and he has shown, in ***The Ship,*** that the disciplined flexibility of the Royal Navy is as efficient and adaptable in the 1940's as it was in the 1800's.

Hispanic scenes and entanglements supply a fitting background to much of Mr. Forester's work. The early part of the Hornblower saga is drenched with the glaring light of the Spanish sun, whether in sultry Pacific water or in the shallower reaches of the inland Sea. The aromatic scent of fennel from the Iberian hill pervades his two great military tales: ***Death to the French*** and ***The Gun.*** The misadventures of Albert Brown and of "The Hawk's" lieutenant are set in harsh South American islands. Contrast is the keynote; and nowhere does contrast stand out more glaringly than in Iberian lands and landscapes. The physical contrast serves as a foil to the psychological. The stolid determination of Matthew Dodd to get back to his unit stands out against the hideous sufferings of the Portuguese peasantry and the revolting cruelties of Masséna's starved army, in ***Death to the French.*** The massive power of ***The Gun*** itself accentuates the petty brilliance and pettier jealousies of the Spanish *guerrilleros*—the "maquis" as we should call them to-day. In ***Brown on Resolution*** it is the nightmare landscape of the island that brings out into special relief the cool yet never automatic precision of the first-class seaman who realizes that his duty is to hamper the enemy in every way within his power. Most violent of all is the contrast between the two scenes in ***The Shadow of the Hawk***—between the chain-gang on the guano islet and the rural peace of a residence in Surrey. Yet—and here is where Mr. Forester excels—we are never expected to believe the incredible. There is an inevitability in the sequence of events which satisfies the most critical; the motives and the springs of action are studied; every step is the logical successor of the one before. (pp. 415-16)

It was not as a narrator of naval or military exploits, however, that Mr. Forester first appeared on the literary scene. That extraordinarily mature novel, ***Payment Deferred,*** was published three years before ***Brown,*** and remains to this day the best known of the author's excursions into urban, or, better, suburban, adventure. In his treatment of the "respectable" fringe of London's inhabitants, Mr. Forester shows an uncanny insight. . . . The brilliance of the plot . . . lies not in the murder, nor even in its causes or its direct consequences, but in the web within which the murderer entangles himself, so that he is punished, through the blind grief of his innocent wife, for a murder that he did not commit. We are left asking ourselves rather uncomfortably whether this is really poetic justice or not. (p. 416)

Among the "suburban" novels, I have always had a personal weakness for ***Plain Murder.*** It is now many years since I read the book, but certain vivid impressions remain, which have struck me as being peculiarly Foresterian in essence. First, the unusual quality of the "hero", who, though accessory to one murder, wins our sympathy in his efforts (successful, we are glad to find) to evade being murdered himself, as knowing too much; second, the vivid lifelikeness of the not-too-successful advertising agency where the whole trouble starts; and third, the lack of apparatus surrounding the whole intrigue. Here are no house-parties, no gangs at work, not even any police: it is just a private affair—like any other business deal, one might say—between the murderer and his victims or intended victims. I submit that this sort of thing makes the perceptive flesh creep far more than the conventional crime story.

Further glimpses of the seamy side of suburban respectability flash across the screen in ***The Shadow of the Hawk,*** where the massive Dawkins, fresh from an equatorial chain-gang, rescues his chief's daughter from her slatternly guardian; or where the oppression of sanctimoniousness goads Albert Brown's mother into taking the step that makes her his mother, though not Mrs. Brown, and is the first in the sequence—quite logical again—that leads to her son's death on a waterless island. . . .

The first German war provides the background theme for what is deservedly the best known of Mr. Forester's novels of exotic adventure—***The African Queen.*** This book is specially interesting for another reason, in that it provides the author's one really full-length study of a woman [Rose Sayer]. . . .

So far, the present war has provided Mr. Forester with material for only one novel, but it is one of his best. ***The Ship,*** written while the Royal Navy was still struggling for complete mastery of the Mediterranean, is dedicated to the officers and men of *H.M.S. Penelope,* but in the book it is the ship herself, the light cruiser *Artemis,* that is the heroine of the tale. (p. 417)

It must not be supposed that Mr. Forester approves of war. Although war forms the background of so many of his books, he does not fail to appreciate its idiotic wastefulness. But while the majority of his plots are concerned with the impact of war conditions on selected characters, such as Hornblower, Albert Brown, or Rose Sayer, two of his novels may be regarded as pure tracts against war. ***The Peacemaker*** is in a class apart; it loses in effectiveness from its excursions into the fantastic. Mr. Forester is so skilful at handling realistic situations with imaginative insight that there is no need for him to voyage in the realms of the impossible. ***The General*** is another matter altogether; it is a damning tract against the futility of war, and gains in force by reason of its unembroidered bluntness. General Curzon is the perfect embodiment of that physical courage combined with unimaginative woodenness which was the characteristic of too many high military officers in the last war. A lucky fluke in his early career, reinforced by backstairs intrigue, put him in a position of high command. The blood-bath of Loos and the Somme was the result. Curzon was part of the System; and its blind murderous working, through his agency and that of his colleagues, is the theme of the book. (p. 418)

Not a bad yardstick for measuring the breadth of a novelist's literary popularity is to see whether he has created a character the mention of whose name brings to mind certain definite traits. In building up the personality of Horatio Hornblower Mr. Forester has come very near this goal, if indeed he has not actually attained it. Hornblower is no figure of caricature, with certain characteristics accentuated to exaggeration; he is a most human man, with plenty of defects to make up for his virtues. Perhaps his most engaging characteristic is his own inner conviction that he is a much less admirable person than he actually is. Quite without warrant he is certain that bad luck will dog his career; whereas in fact he has that luck which comes only to the man who is a master of his trade; and often what appear to be strokes of ill-fortune are turned, by his fixity of purpose, into advantages.

His career has already been traced in four volumes; of these the first three have won reputation enough to be combined in an "omnibus", of itself an indication of wide popular favour. In ***The Happy Return*** he takes the stage already a full-fledged captain of a frigate, trusted by the Admiralty with a mission of exceptional delicacy. By skill, seamanship, and diplomacy he carries it out with complete success; and his engaging straightforwardness in handling another delicate situation in which a very great lady is involved gives promise (though he, naturally, does not realize it) of a future brilliance of career. In ***A Ship of the Line*** this career is followed up; here the pure technicalities of naval warfare against Napoleon's lines of communication are treated with Mr. Forester's peculiar lucid skill. The whole is an acute study of Hornblower purely as a naval leader; and though the book ends in military disaster, it is this very disaster which leads to his final establishment in professional safety and public reputation. ***Flying Colours,*** with its brilliant and unorthodox cutting-out expedition, . . . turns Hornblower into a popular hero and leaves him in a position, thanks to two coincidental deaths—a small concession to the sentimental reader—to claim the hand of his great lady. (pp. 418-19)

Those three books make up the "omnibus"; and now Hornblower's admirers can welcome a further instalment of his career in ***The Commodore,*** where merit and influence have combined to place the gallant captain in command of a flotilla in the Baltic. . . . There are rumours that we have not heard the last of Captain Sir Horatio Hornblower; and all admirers of Mr. Forester will hope that this is true. (p. 419)

L. Russell Muirhead, "A Novelist of Action," in The Fortnightly, *n.s. Vol. CLVII, No. 942, June, 1945, pp. 414-19.*

WILLIAM S. LYNCH

Admirers of Sir Horatio Hornblower will be delighted to know that he has completed his most recent mission [in **"Commodore Hornblower"**] with all the success and aplomb they expect of him. They will be pleased, too, to learn that the great captain is now a commodore, a promotion he well deserves even though it did mean jumping him over other captains whose seniority placed them higher on the Admiralty's lists. . . .

The records of [Hornblower's expedition to the Baltic in the spring of 1812] have been compiled by C. S. Forester, a sure guarantee of able presentation and of justice to men and events. Readers will recall Forester's earlier accounts of Hornblower's career and more recently his much-admired **"The Ship."** Some of them will have read the serial version **"Commodore Hornblower."** . . . If it were not for the vile canard that the Commodore is a mere figment of Mr. Forester's imagination, there is no doubt that the Baltic foray would be included in Hakluyt's Voyages.

Cynics who assert that Hornblower is a fictional creation deserve the same contempt the honest reader accords to those heretics who claim that the adventures of the great detective, Holmes, are apocryphal. The internal evidence of this book provides ample proof that Forester is dealing with biography. When the author attempts to surmise the inner workings of the great seaman's character, he gives us a figure as creaky as the planking of a pitching ship. When he deals with those intimacies of his subject's life which a man as reticent as Hornblower would be reluctant to reveal to his closest friend, Forester cannot convince us of his man. The details of Lady Barbara's boudoir, the adventure with the smoldering Countess at the court of the Czar are, we feel, so deliberate that they must be based upon first-hand knowledge of a man who would never reveal them.

But when the author gives us incident and description we are assured that our hero is actual. The document and the first-hand account are the only explanation for the graphic realism of the description of ship and exploit. The archive and the history could be the only sources of events and personalities. It must be from these biographical data that Mr. Forester drew the rattling good sea story we have here. It is to the tradition of marine adventure that Hornblower belongs—a literary tradition that is, by the way, one of the most satisfying we have. In it we do not look for the psychological insights and motivations that mark the novel which critics are most wont to admire. We look instead for a story told well enough to carry us along without effort and for incident exciting enough to hold us in suspense however much we may be assured by the genre that all will come out for the best. . . .

[In **"Commodore Hornblower"** we] have the diplomatic fencing for tremendous stakes, the first-hand meeting with historical figures in court and in battle. Best of all, as in most of Forester, we have the ships and boats, and it is in the detail of description and maneuver that he is at his very best. . . . There is no author writing today who makes better use of this material. He can do it, too, with the ships of this war as he proved so clearly in **"The Ship."**

Forester is very conscious of this war even when he is writing about the Napoleonic. The parallels that come to mind as one follows the adventures of his Hornblower are almost too many not to strain the reader's sense of probability. One begins to suspect that he is giving a reverse twist to the old business of Hamlet in modern dress.

Even so **"Commodore Hornblower"** is a crackerjack yarn—not quite up to the earlier Hornblower books perhaps, but one that will delight any reader who enjoys a good story. And anyone who does not love a good story for its own sweet sake has lost the first great joy for which books must have been invented. To criticize it for a lack of sophistication would be about as fair as criticizing "Treasure Island." At the same time to insist that Hornblower is portrayed with insights to complicated personality above the general run of heroes in adventure stories is equally nonsense. His getting seasick occasionally is not enough. The reality of Hornblower is the reality of the romantic hero with whom the ordinary reader can identify himself through the magic casements of good writing. Hornblower is real because he is the stuff of daydreams—one captain who can never convince us that he ever hates the sea.

William S. Lynch, "The Reality of the Romantic Hero," in The Saturday Review of Literature, *Vol. XXVIII, No. 22, June 2, 1945, p. 11.*

FLETCHER PRATT

[**"Lord Hornblower"**] is the fifth volume of the Hornblower saga and it will probably be received like the others—with delight by many thousands of readers, and by the "literary" critics with that faint condescension they so easily develop for any book that is not slow and difficult reading—a condescension normally expressed by devoting the review to a synopsis of the story. It is a treatment primarily given to horse-opera producers like Zane Grey; and . . . it is about time for the honor of beautiful letters that someone took Mr. Forester seriously.

For the resemblance in this case is less to Zane Grey than to Rudyard Kipling. . . .

You will find there are a good many of the same qualities in both men—the unfailing invention, the clear, precise, skilful narrative, the perfect familiarity with every detail of the life described, the delineation of character through action and action alone. Above all and behind all, however, there is the same interest in and ability to handle story, the respect for it as such. (p. 32)

Certainly it is superficially easy to criticize the Hornblower stories on literary grounds. The minor characters tend to run out into types—something of which Kipling was never guilty, by the way. The dynamic sea captain's ingenious devices for confounding the French succeed as planned a little more frequently than the law of averages would allow. The changes in the central figure are mainly those of exterior circumstance. There is an impression of clean uniforms and fresh paint, like an Arabian night done by Maxfield Parrish.

But to say all this, especially the last, is only in the long run to comment that Mr. Forester is a better symbolist than the Symbolists. A careful survey of **"Lord Hornblower"** shows that when the occasion required it, he was dirty and hungry and tired and ill and cross and disgusted. It has all been fairly stated, but it is not emphasized, because this was not the sort of things he emphasized himself. He accepted them as a part of life and having made the notation, forgot about them; his mind was on something else. If Captain Bush, Brown, and others around Hornblower strike us as types, it is fair to answer that this is the impact they would make on the redoubtable commodore himself.

Similarly it is hard to find any real fault with his continual successes in his profession or with the lack of change in his character. This is the portrait of a successful sea captain and there were such men. . . . In other words, the deep emotions, the complex reactions, the picture of a period and of men's minds are all there; but instead of being raked over for examination as to their sources, they are subordinated to the interests of the story.

There is another criticism, however, growing out of this very concern with the business of story which can be legitimately leveled against the most recent volume of the series. It was very well for the captain of a corvette cruising on the Pacific coast of South America to engage in personal adventure and to solve his difficulties with interesting but small-scale devices. But the stage is larger now, the man's position more important, and the issues dealt with are greater. One has the impression, not with regard to any particular incident but about the book as a whole, that it is slightly out of scale, that Siegfried is playing knuckle-bones when he ought to be hunting dragons.

The impression is probably erroneous. The whole thing is so carefully worked out and so closely dovetailed together that it is perilous to say it should have been something else at any given point. (pp. 32-3)

Fletcher Pratt, "Hornblower Sails On," in The Saturday Review of Literature, *Vol. XXIX, No. 39, September 28, 1946, pp. 32-3.*

FRANCIS X. CONNOLLY

There is no news in the announcement that [**"Lord Hornblower"**], the fifth and presumably the final chronicle of the adventures and loves of Horatio Hornblower, is an exciting, well-written tale by one of the few master craftsmen in the art of fiction. Mr. Forester has earned this reputation by the four preceding volumes in the series, as well as by two excellent but less well-known earlier stories, **"Rifleman Dodd"** and **"The Gun."** It is perhaps exaggerated to compare him with Conrad and Stevenson as a story-teller, but he belongs at least, with Nordhoff and Hall, John Masefield and Nevil Shute, among those writers who have preserved narrative values which the realists have almost completely abandoned. (p. 148)

No little of Forester's popularity may be traced to his projection of a "modern" hero into a romantic background. For, despite his iron fortitude and his nautical talents, Hornblower is essentially a sensitive, uncertain, and complicated figure. He broods about his past, compares his passion for his wife with that for his mistress, and his observations on the age of Napoleon are in the accent of twentieth-century liberalism. He shares all the virtues of the naval officers, but none of their aristocratic prejudices, and he is compelled to accept the dignity of the peerage, he remains spiritually a democrat. Another reason for Forester's success rests in his technical mastery of structure and style. The book is well-built, chapter to chapter, suspense to suspense; the language is direct, controlled, and charged with that mysterious creative energy which moves the story through the imagination like a fine ship in full sail. Forester has described his own art accurately when Hornblower, pondering the exquisite tracery in Westminster Cathedral, thinks that "there was something mathematically satisfactory in the way the spreading patterns met and re-met, a sort of inspired logic. The nameless workmen who had done that carving must have been far-sighted, creative men." (pp. 148-49)

Francis X. Connolly, in a review of "Lord Hornblower," in Commonweal, *Vol. XLV, No. 6, November 22, 1946, pp. 148-49.*

LINCOLN COLCORD

There seems to be an accepted formula for fiction dealing with naval action in the present war. It starts with character sketches of men aboard a given ship, from the commander all along down the line; these furnish the human interest of the story. And since each one is a man with a different function on a fighting vessel, it covers at the same time by this means the whole nature and purpose of the ship, all her detailed structure and arrangement, the things she is supposed to do and how she does them. Among and through these sketches is woven, little by little, the developing naval action which it is proposed to relate, beginning quietly and working up to the climax that has been saved all along; so that when the piece is done it has revealed the scene by suggestion, as it were—as much by the reactions of the people who participated in it as by the narration and description of events.

The method seems almost a natural for the telling of a swift sea incident. But like any other literary method, its final effectiveness depends on the art of the writer. Mr. Forester has chosen to follow it, and follow it faithfully; and at once he has made something altogether new of it, a new approach, a fresh revelation of human experience, a richer and fuller tale of naval action than any we have had previously.

"The Ship" is an adroit blending of fine imagination and well schooled narrative power. Some of the works referred to a moment ago have been written by non-professional authors and have gained great charm and genuine strength thereby. They have been simple and direct. But here is a work by a professional, a literary job; yet the same freshness shines out from it, by the exercise of superb restraint and equally superb selection. And the canvas is so much broader than the others, the strokes so much more sure. Everything counts in this brief book, and there is no padding in it at all—not even the unconscious, almost inevitable padding that creeps into the words of every professional writer. One feels that the author's heart must have been very close to his subject. It is a triumph of story telling, struck at white heat from a great moment in human history.

The captain of H.M.S. Artemis is an interesting character; a man of passion who has won command of himself through rigorous self-discipline, exactly the sort who develops into the best commander of ships and men. Not a great deal about his life is told, only a few incidents, but each one so significant that together they serve to build up a living person.

In fact, the capable and practiced hand of the novelist is evident in all the character sketches in these pages; this is where the faculty of selection counts most of all. What to say of a man, among the multitudes of things that can be said? Only an artist can choose the right things. And it can be said of **"The Ship"** without reservation that all the men in it stand out with an intense reality, chiefly by virtue of the imperceptible touches that have been given to the story here and there. . . .

The great theme of the tale, of course, is the battle between the Artemis and the Italian fleet. . . .

To tell the bare facts of a story . . . is much like looking at the skeleton of a beautiful woman. It hardly does justice to the subject. The amount of action and detail, the scene of battle, the full proportions of an intense naval engagement, that the author has managed to get into his narrative, are little short of amazing. This, plainly, is something he knows all about; no one can read **"The Ship"** without realizing its essential accuracy. A vivid picture of fighting on the sea with modern naval weapons has been unfolded before our eyes, and it leaves an overwhelming impression. It brings us nearer to the war than any book this reviewer has yet read.

Lincoln Colcord, "A Fresh Revelation of Human Experience," in New York Herald Tribune Weekly Book Review, *May 16, 1948, p. 3.*

HOLLIS ALPERT

C. S. Forester returns, with [**"The Sky and the Forest"**], to a locale he has used in an earlier novel, **"The African Queen."** One can therefore expect that he will write of the forests and rivers of Central Africa with some intimacy and knowledge. And, knowing him as a writer who has already gained wide popularity and acclaim as a spinner of stories, one can also expect that his people and their adventures will make absorbing reading. That much is true: the tale of an African chieftain runs along its course as smoothly and powerfully as the Twentieth Century Limited train making its way to Chicago.

But I cannot help thinking that in **"The Sky and the Forest"** we have something more than a solid and exciting adventure yarn, although certainly it is at least that. For there is in it a truly serious note which seldom gives way. It is as though Mr. Forester had . . . [decided] to pack his unusual incidents with an extra layer of meaning—and, although a comparison with Conrad's "Heart of Darkness" would find this work somewhat wanting, there is much the same sort of serious, brooding, almost poetic intent. Actually Mr. Forester, in this work, has something to say about man: he's concerned with the representation of such qualities as human dignity and fortitude, and he also speaks of his vanities, his weaknesses, his cruelties (beyond the point where sadism begins), and of his capacities for love and tenderness. And all of these qualities he can find in the person of Loa, the African chieftain, primitive and naive as he is. (p. 18)

The time, though not expressly stated, is the early and middle part of the nineteenth century, when the slave trade reached its peak and entered its decline, when the mysteries of the steaming central reaches of Africa were being opened up by the Arabs and the Europeans. The part of the forest, near the river bank, which Loa and his townspeople inhabited is presumably what is now the Belgian Congo.

Loa, due to the impenetrable nature of the forest, had to confine his God-like powers to a highly limited area and to a tiny population. To himself and to his subjects he was both God and man, the brother of the forest and of the sky. (pp. 18-19)

[Loa and the townspeople] lived rather peacefully and indolently, practising the ways of their forebears until the Arabs came with their guns and hippoppotamus-hide whips, seeking slaves and stores of ivory. And it is then that Loa, after his capture and during the long trek towards death or slavery, first begins to question his God-like nature. . . .

There is a fine, solemn mood to the telling of all this. And it becomes hard to understand how research and travel alone could provide the knowledge which convinces the reader so thoroughly of the reality of what is being told. It has required imaginative understanding of a high degree to write so literate and engrossing a book. (p. 19)

Hollis Alpert, "Chief of the Congo," in The Saturday Review of Literature, *Vol. XXXI, No. 33, August 14, 1948, pp. 18-19.*

JAMES HILTON

C. S. Forester, among the most accomplished of modern story tellers, could have gone on pleasing his readers with more Hornblower yarns ad infinitum; but one feels that in his new novel, **"The Sky and the Forest,"** he has been writing to please himself—at any rate, he has set himself one of the most difficult tasks imaginable in fiction, that of portraying the thoughts, emotions and primitive mind-development of [Loa], an African Negro tribal chieftain early in the present century—the period of the white grab for Africa which, under the special incentive of Congo rubber, entered then upon a hideously predatory phase. . . .

Mr. Forester's somewhat cynical thesis is that knowledge of the West can be more contamination than enlightenment—a thesis few will dispute, so dubious are we nowadays of the outcome of our own current affairs. . . . Nor does one suspect here any Malthusian tongue-in-cheek, but rather an attempted mating of scientific realism with a concept essentially old and romantic—that of Rousseau's Noble Savage; and one wonders not only whether Mr. Forester has succeeded but whether the thing can actually be done at all.

It goes without saying that the author brings to his task a superb narrative gift, a first-hand knowledge of African topography and anthropology, a warm humanism and an awareness of the dangers of oversimplifying. But is all this enough for us to get under the personal skin of Loa? Mr. Forester constantly reminds us of the limitations of Loa's mind, how he had no words in his vocabulary for this or that; and as an intellectual feat, the attempt to steer clear of anachronisms has considerable virtuosity. But again, is this enough? Does the chieftain emerge as a three-dimensional character? Are he and his wife and their son and the girl any more than carefully observed people to whom well described things happen? In a less ambitious story one would doubtless be satisfied with that; but it is, after all, the author who chooses his theme, and when the publishers claim that "in Loa Mr. Forester has created another man's man who, like Hornblower," etc., etc., they are offering a compliment which is perhaps at deeper levels a criticism.

But for all its lack of something that Melville or Conrad might have supplied, **"The Sky and the Forest"** remains a sincere and thoughtful experiment, even suggestively a parable for our own times.

James Hilton, "Man-God of Darkest Congo," in New York Herald Tribune Weekly Book Review, *August 15, 1948, p. 2.*

WINIFRED KING RUGG

[Readers] of the Hornblower Saga are first compelled by their interest in the man C. S. Forester has created. Only second to that is their enthrallment with the story of Hornblower's deeds. What happens in the Hornblower novels is high adventure, but the more so because the mainspring of the action is a man resourceful and dominant, guided by duty, and lovable in his foibles.

The seventh in this group of Forester's novels partly fills the gap between **"Mr. Midshipman Hornblower"** and the time when the neophyte had progressed to full-fledged captaincy in **"Beat to Quarters."** It is called **"Lieutenant Hornblower."** . . .

In 1801 the "Renown" of seventy-four guns was in West Indian waters on a secret mission to clean out a nest of Spanish raiders that lurked off Santo Domingo. In the tightly organized cosmos of a ship of the line Hornblower was the junior among five lieutenants. The complete breakdown of the captain, the irresolution of the first lieutenant, and the willingness of the others to follow Hornblower's suggestions brought him, after engineering the capture of the Spanish fort and three prize ships, to the rank of commander; accorded him at Jamaica, to be confirmed in London—"that is, if we don't make peace," said Hornblower.

The powers did make peace, the navy was reduced to peacetime strength, the promotion was not confirmed. Then, by another sudden twirl of the international whirligig, England's safety was again threatened, and Hornblower, now commander, was ordered to a sloop of war. . . .

Simpler in texture than some of its predecessors, **"Lieutenant Hornblower,"** for clear shapeliness and story-teller's gusto, is their fit companion.

The appearance of the new novel gives opportunity for a fresh viewing of the whole Saga. . . .

Even before **"Beat to Quarters"** came out 15 years ago, Cecil Scott Forester had made his place among the best story-tellers of our time for his **"Brown on Resolution."** The parts of the Hornblower Saga are more impressive because they center in a single character—and as each novel appears it gains luster from those before.

In writing a series, the pitfall is over-economy of material, especially in background, perhaps for fear of repetition. But this Forester has escaped because he is endlessly familiar with the code, history, and traditions of the navy, with seamanship and the language of ships, and because he gives his chief character an integrated and growing personality. . . .

As a novelist [Forester] still interprets the navy, certainly in its Napoleonic period, with the help of a character that represents the navy at its best and action that is grandly exciting without being melodramatic; helped, too, by a sense of order and a mastery of technique that put his work on a high plane of artistry. . . .

Winifred King Rugg, "Saga of a Seaman's Rise," in The Christian Science Monitor, *March 27, 1952, p. 15.*

MERLE MILLER

Cecil Scott Forester is not generally thought of as a major writer. Like Somerset Maugham, he refuses to take himself very seriously. Like Maugham, he insists that his purpose is neither to instruct nor to inform. . . .

In the means he has used in some twenty novels, scores of short stories, and at least one memorable television series Mr. Forester has earned the fascinated attention of several million readers and millions of other lookers and listeners. (p.17)

However, although he obviously doesn't mind much, Forester and his works are largely ignored by the academicians who pass judgment on which of their contemporaries are producing literature—a judgment that is, of course, largely ignored by posterity. What's more, . . . Mr. Forester's interests and writings are so varied that he is a difficult man to classify.

In this country, despite the happy fact that his publishers reissued it in 1947, **"The General"** has been one of his less successful endeavors. Nevertheless, it is the best novel written about the British Army between the First and Second World Wars, and, whatever the author's intention, it contains a good deal of information about the faults of any peacetime army between any wars. **"The Ship,"** even though it was published during hostilities, a time when it is next to impossible to deal realistically with the military, is even now as revealing a look at the Royal Navy as the longer and far less interesting "The Cruel Sea."

"Payment Deferred" is a skilled model for all of the novels of suspense that have been written since, and, of course, **"The African Queen"** is one of the half dozen best adventure stories ever told. In addition, Mr. Forester seems to know nearly all there is available about the Napoleonic wars; to give only two examples, **"Rifleman Dodd"** and **"The Gun,"** published separately and together, are first-rate examples of what historical novels ought to be and once were and almost never are any more. And then, and it is surely his major achievement, C. S. Forester has created that already classic hero, Horatio Hornblower, whose exploits will surely continue to be read and admired and remembered by generations of small boys, from the time they learn to read until their eyesight gives out.

Apparently, Mr. Forester can turn out Horatio books and stories by the column, the page, or the book, whatever is called for. The practice is not necessarily a reprehensible one. The result is what matters and all that matters, and the result, even in the latest Horatio novel, **"Hornblower and the *Atropos*,"** is delightful. Sometimes this new one creaks a little, but then so does "Bleak House," and, even though Mr. Dickens was getting paid by the word, he still created a masterpiece. Forester is, like Dickens, a professional.

I suspect that someone who happens on Horatio for the first time in **"Hornblower and the *Atropos*"** will be somewhat puzzled by it, but the more fortunate of us not only know the beginning of the story but the middle as well, though not, it is to be hoped, the end. As the publishers explain on the jacket, the new novel "fills in the three-year gap between **'Lieutenant Hornblower'** and **'Captain Horatio Hornblower'**." (pp. 17-18)

After a rather leisurely beginning things happen fast; they always do. . . . In the Mediterranean, to which Hornblower is ordered . . . , he has a big and, for a lesser man, almost insurmountably difficult job ahead of him. He, with some help from the rest of the British fleet, must head off any moves that Napoleon Bonaparte may be tempted to make now that Austerlitz has given him command of all continental Europe. . . .

It would be unfair to reveal how the engagement turns out, but no true Horatio fan will be disappointed.

In the end Horatio returns to England, reasonably sure of the command of his own frigate. First, however, he is alarmed to find that both [his children] . . . are dangerously ill. He realizes and, for that matter, so do we, what the trouble is: Smallpox.

Well, nobody in his right mind could leave Hornblower in a fix like that, even though **"Hornblower and the *Atropos*"** is ended. Besides, the solution is simple enough. It is to reread **"Beat to Quarters," "Ship of the Line,"** and **"Flying Colours."** They are just as exciting as ever, and now I am trying to choose between **"Commodore Hornblower"** and **"Lord Hornblower,"** which is obviously ridiculous. The answer is to reread both of them, unless in the meantime Forester turns out another Hornblower book. I hope he does. I hope he never stops.

C. S. Forester may not be major, but he is everlastingly entertaining. (p. 18)

Merle Miller, "601st Captain, Royal Navy," in The Saturday Review, *New York, Vol. XXXVI, No. 39, September 26, 1953, pp. 17-18.*

BURKE WILKINSON

C. S. Forester has two skills which are admirably blended in **"The Good Shepherd,"** a first-rate novel of World War II. He is able to make us identify ourselves with the tensions and the loneliness of man, this time a man in command of many men. He also is able to make us see and hear and feel action, especially when writing of ships and the sea, so vividly that a powerful sense of participation is inevitable.

The gift of enforcing on the reader this sense of identification and participation explains the enduring fascination of Forester's most celebrated creation—Captain Horatio Hornblower. Hornblower's all-too-human doubts and fear, beneath the resolute exterior, communicate themselves to us even as we project ourselves into his exploits. But even the fine Hornblowers do not match the present achievement. **"The Good Shepherd"** is the story of forty-eight desperate hours in the life of a North Atlantic convoy. The time is early in the war, before improved sonar and hunter-killer teams turned the tide against the U-boats. Commander of the escort vessels (Comescort) by accident of rank is Comdr. George Krause, U.S.N. To protect the thirty-seven merchantmen under a retired British admiral (Comconvoy), Krause has exactly four ships. . . . Twelve escorts would be needed to do the job with any real safety.

The story of the novel is Krause's: the action revolves around him, and outward from him. All the other Krauses that have gone before are important only in their effect on Krause, the defender of his charges, and Krause, the killer of the enemy which seeks to destroy them. . . . Krause is the good shepherd of his lumbering flock. With him we shall not want for a high and glittering excitement. . . .

In writing about **"The Good Shepherd"** it is almost impossible not to fall into Biblical cadence. Running through it like the voices of a fugue are quotations from the Bible which underline the action. . . .

This device, irritating at first, soon achieves its purpose of heightening our sense of identification with the God-fearing Krause. Again and again we come back to the man. Krause, for all his sternness, has his moments of doubt and fear. Like many men in whom the power of command is strong, he can still sometimes envy those who have only to obey, even to the death. He is sharply aware of the place where science ends and the human factor begins. . . .

The reminder that machines of destruction can never be the master of man is always valid, and particularly so today, but the basic appeal of the story is to emotion, not reason. The emotions it inspires are simple, elemental: love of the good shepherd and the father-protector, hatred of the feathering periscope that is evil personified, fear of oil and flame and ice-green water.

The acclaim that has already greeted the new Forester is an earnest of success to come. . . . The truth is that **"The Good Shepherd"** is so good that the tendency in a time of minor talent is to call it a great novel. This it is not. Forester starts—in his compression and use of exact detail—where most writers leave off. But he ends just short of the titans of fiction. No other character save Krause has more than one dimension. The rest are voices over intercoms, brief glimpses like star shells. It is a story of tension, not of dimension, and it was so intended.

But in Forester's chosen field, and when his talents for creating a sense of participation and of identification are in top gear, he has no master and few peers.

Burke Wilkinson, "With the Wolf Pack Dead Ahead," in The New York Times Book Review, *March 27, 1955, p. 1.*

THOMAS CALDECOT CHUBB

In a day when the historical novel is more and more likely to be a documentary laid in the past, it is at least a refreshing change of pace to find an author who still regards adventure for its own sake, intrigue, piracy, kidnappings, the doings of a rich, young, idealistic soldier of fortune, and the efforts to keep a youthful trumpeter from being hanged for his artistic conscience as fit subjects for his literary endeavors.

Such a one is C. S. Forester who in **"Admiral Hornblower in the West Indies"** takes us to sea for the ninth time with his deservedly indestructible hero, now Rear Admiral Lord Hornblower, commander in chief of His Majesty's ship and vessels in the West Indies, whose popularity in the world of fiction has led to a durability that can only be matched by that of Sherlock Holmes, Sir John Falstaff and perhaps d'Artagnan. . . .

Now from New Orleans to Carabobo we cruise the Caribbean with [Hornblower] in a book that is no better and no worse than any of its predecessors. This means that it is a rattling good story, which will please everybody except those who want authentic history or authentic biography in their fictional excursions into the past. This is entertainment not instruction.

This loosely bound collection of five short stories—for it is that rather than a novel—laid in a supposedly dull post-war period of small navies and unappreciated national heroes is still able to provide our Horatio with ample opportunities to display every one of those qualities that have won him his host of readers. That he does display them—and with his customary combination of dash and reflectiveness—makes it certain that this latest chapter in his saga will not reduce their number. Indeed, it will probably earn him many more.

Thomas Caldecot Chubb, "Bound for Adventure," in The New York Times Book Review, *August 31, 1958, p. 15.*

DAVID REES

[In the opening of ***Hornblower and the Crisis*** (published in the United States as ***Hornblower during the Crisis***)], the last, uncompleted Hornblower novel, the elegance, precision and historical sweep of Forester's classical style [is] unchanged to the end. No cosmic problems in this war; here, in the crisis days immediately preceding Trafalgar, Hornblower, alert as ever to his admirable duty of doing down the French, is involved in a dangerous, characteristic mission which turns on the issuing of forged orders. Although the narrative ends abruptly, the way ahead can be seen; and even this fragment reminds that C. S.

Forester was one of the great professional writers of our time. (p. 772)

David Rees, "Lost Leader," in The Spectator, *Vol. 218, No. 7253, June 30, 1967, pp. 771-72.**

W. G. ROGERS

The man C. S. Forester was lean and trim. . . . He was a shipshape person as he was a shipshape author: neat, orderly, direct, disciplined. [**"Long Before Forty"**] is two-thirds autobiography and one-third biography-autobiography of his famous Capt. Horatio Hornblower, arch enemy of Napoleon—if Hornblower hadn't thrashed around on the seven seas, could there have been a Trafalgar or even a Waterloo? The shorter, concluding section, reprinted from **"The Hornblower Companion,"** may already be on your shelves, so you know how much it merits rereading. . . .

[Forester's] account of how to write is coldly, admirably professional: let's not talk about what a good book is, or about beauty, let's concentrate on how to tell a tale. Inspiration remains inspiration—whether it impels Tolstoy to write, or a drunk to concoct a yarn; the difference lies in the quality of the minds. Forester likens himself as a writer to the jellyfish swimming around till by chance something edible floats within reach. Other requirements are the ant's diligence and the mule's endurance. . . .

He has a method rather than a message; he is practical rather than theoretical—and wonderfully so, too. His precise, even prim prose is dependable and straightforward; he would tamper with history but never with vocabulary. I always had a sneaking preference for his **"Randall and the River of Time,"** a 20th-century morality with a touch of "Candide." But it is Hornblower who will be cherished, Hornblower the hero of one mission impossible after another. His creator will be remembered much as Dumas is remembered for d'Artagnan, Cooper for Natty Bumppo and Rostand for Cyrano.

W. G. Rogers, "Shipshape Author," in The New York Times Book Review, *November 3, 1968, p. 34.*

WILLIAM JAY JACOBS

[One] dimension of the Hornblower legend [is] that of Horatio Hornblower the swashbuckling adventurer. But to the legion of Hornblower buffs this is an incomplete, perhaps a misleading, view of so absorbing and many-sided a personality. (Indeed, even in his role as a combat commander Hornblower usually relied more heavily on craft and intelligence than mere animal spirit.)

C. S. Forester, the imaginative British creator of ***The African Queen,*** began work on the Hornblower saga in England, just as the full weight of Hitlerian tyranny was sweeping across Europe. Set in the equally tumultuous time when Britain stood alone against Napoleon, the series covers Hornblower's career in the Royal Navy from his initial cruise as a Midshipman to his Admiralcy in the West Indies. It includes ten novels and the remarkable ***Hornblower Companion,*** a one volume atlas with detailed autobiographical commentary by Forester.

Although the books contain their share of "patriotic gore," some of Hornblower's most fascinating adventures take place far from the scene of battle. (pp. 579-80)

Even when Hornblower is not in battle, tormenting Napoleon's Channel fleet or storming a Spanish fortress in the Indies, he is very much the "hero figure." He is daring and flamboyant, inventive, relentless in pursuit of seemingly impossible goals—all the qualities we have come to expect of the romantic hero, in fiction or in real life. One inescapably wonders how such a protagonist has retained his wide appeal among a generation of young people so recently infatuated with that self-declared anti-hero, Senator Eugene McCarthy.

The answer lies partly in Forester's subtle characterization of Hornblower. Indomitable leader though he may be, Hornblower never degenerates into stereotype, but remains a profoundly complex human being. He is gangling and awkward in appearance and, embarrassingly, given to sea-sickness—which only adds fuel to his shyness and pitiless self-criticism. In the Navy's tradition of stoic control, he smothers his emotions, conceals his feelings, only to regret the woodenness and pomposity that sometimes results. He lives with death and fears it; still he is the very man who condemns himself as brutal and cold-blooded after destroying an enemy ship that could not return his fire. He is cross-grained, moody, incurably jealous. He is also, on occasion, supremely silly. . . .

Above all, Hornblower is the Man Alone, a brooding solitary Hamlet who never can know happiness because he distrusts it, who refuses to rejoice in his own successes, who will not truckle to authority, even when doing so would serve his ends, who remains alike unmoved in triumph and in adversity. He is a man of high ideals, grand designs, deep passions. Yet, torn by self-doubt, he is able to resist despair only by imposing upon himself an iron discipline.

There is something refreshing in all of this, in drinking, with Hornblower, the heady wine of heroism. Certainly, not everyone prizes such an experience. But I strongly suspect that many young people will find the exploits of Hornblower surprisingly congenial. Here is a man who shares their idealism, their disdain for vulgar displays of wealth, their self-consciousness. He is very much an "in" hero.

Young people probably will welcome the Hornblower books, too, as a respite from their daily academic encounters with so-called "analytic historians." (p. 580)

This is not to champion the Hornblower books only because they are colorful and robust (even if such grounds probably would be sufficient). They are valuable, too, as authentic history, as painstakingly accurate representations of the sea and ships. For this reason alone they deserve to be regarded in company with other great tales of adventure. Still, like the *Bounty* trilogy of Nordhoff and Hall, their survival probably will stem primarily from another source: their fidelity to the requirements of fiction—their total immersion in imagination, invention, characterization, vicariousness. Here are books that are more delightful than useful, whose real contribution, through the versatile hero, Horatio Hornblower, is to make history live and entertaining—as literature. (p. 581)

William Jay Jacobs, "Horatio Hornblower: A Hero for Today," in The Record, *Vol. 70, No. 6, March, 1969, pp. 579-81.*

L. N. WOLF

[**"The Man in the Yellow Raft,"** a] collection of eight short stories dealing with the lives and actions of men who served in the United States Navy during World War II, will be a welcome addition to the libraries of those who recognize the Forester genius in writing stories of naval warfare. Each, in its own way, describes some aspect of a human activity which is a necessary part of the whole complex function of a ship or a fleet or a navy at war. Each indicates how the effort of one man doing his duty is necessary for the attainment of a whole objective; each indicates that failure of one man, however insignificant, to perform his stated duty could have changed the course of history.

Subjects of the stories range over many fields of naval endeavor. . . .

The title story is an excellent description of the application of seemingly senseless discipline and punishment resulting in the maturation of an adolescent, whereby a human life was saved. **"The Boy Stood on the Burning Deck"** is a story of quiet courage and devotion to duty by an engine-room rating who kept his engines balanced while a fuel-oil fire burnt beneath him. **"Doctor Blanke's First Command"** is a wonderful account of how responsibility forces human development and **"December 6th"** is, in its own way, as good a counter-agent story as any ever written when a simple American seaman and a brash Cockney team up to foil a Nazi plot to wreck the Panama Canal.

Written in the effortless free-flowing narrative style so characteristic of Forester, these stories with their keen insight into human character and their emphasis on the worth of the individual in cooperative efforts are worthwhile reading for everyone.

L. N. Wolf, in a review of "The Man in the Yellow Raft," in Best Sellers, *Vol. 29, No. 6, June 15, 1969, p. 108.*

FRANK L. RYAN

Five of [the stories in **"Gold from Crete"**] have the same hero, Captain George Crowe of H.M.S. *The Apache*. Four others have separate heroes and the last, and by far the longest, **"If Hitler Had Invaded England,"** has no hero at all unless it is the British people themselves.

The five involving Captain Crowe are the most interesting, primarily because they have a fairly well defined hero who, with the help of the British navy, manages to perform a series of heroic acts. . . .

"Eagle Squadron" alternates between the exploits of two Americans in the R.A.F., involving the theft of a German Messerschmitt and the anxiety of their Iowa parents. **"You Are Welcome!"** is a mild cloak-and-dagger bit in which a woman masquerades as the widow of a British weapons expert and is trapped by the expert's colleague. **"The Dumb Dutchman"** profiles a Dutch spy, thought by his countryman to be a collaborator, in action against the Germans as he leads a flotilla of German transports into British hands. **"If Hitler Had Invaded England"** is a hypothesis in which Forester supplies in a documentary form all the vital action which might have taken place had the Germans invaded immediately after Dunkirk.

By the time of his death in 1966, Forester had built up a following which cherishes the Captain Horatio Hornblower series as passionately as the Baker Street Irregulars venerate Sherlock Holmes. Since Hornblower is not present in this collection his admirers may not anticipate it with much relish and this may be fortunate for the book's reception. Though there is a high degree of excitement in the action, the characters move through it with distressingly clear heads, straight backs, and stiff upper lips. While these qualities sat well on Hornblower, they tend to render these characters bland. Captain Crowe in particular, though he has some of the introspective qualities of Hornblower, moves through his episodes with little of the searing conflict which might have made his way less straight but his character more appealing. The same blandness is found in the major of **"An Egg for the Major"** and in the intelligence man who too easily and unconvincingly solves the disguise of the woman spy in **"You Are Welcome!"** Though the hypothetical **"If Hitler Had Invaded England"** redeems some of this blandness through its narration, the collection will still be a test of the loyalty of the Forester following.

Frank L. Ryan, in a review of "Gold from Crete," in Best Sellers, *Vol. 30, No. 19, January 1, 1971, p. 428.*

BILL PLATYPUS

[***Gold from Crete***] comprises a selection of short stories, set generally in the more vigorous moments of the second world war. As you might expect from the author of Hornblower, the plots are generally culled from the battles and the disasters of the sea. But the final story, and I think one of the best, has a different theme. It is entitled **'If Hitler Had Invaded England'** and is concerned with exactly that. Mr. Forester manages to combine imaginative panache with a great fund of what seems . . . to be technical expertise. It is an intriguing reconstruction of possible events, told with vigour and flair.

Bill Platypus, in a review of "Gold from Crete," in The Spectator, *Vol. 231, No. 7573, August 18, 1973, p. 222.*

STANFORD STERNLICHT

C. S. Forester was, first of all, a storyteller. He provided, during pre-television and even early television days, a "jolly good read." His carefully researched, finely plotted, highly melodramatic novels provided and still provide a great amount of pleasure to readers desiring to escape for a while from their humdrum lives into a romanticized past. Britons, seeing the decline of their once omnipotent empire as well as the wartime decimation of their young manhood, took solace in the exploits of Horatio Hornblower as he tweaked the nose of the tyrant Bonaparte during the high glory of the English nation and the Royal Navy. Their American cousins somewhat more vicariously enjoyed the fun and nostalgia, too. (pp. 159-60)

In the Platonic literary world created by hermeneutics, there is little room for C. S. Forester. His early work, divided between hack biographies which he despised, and weakly contrived, caricature-ridden novels, showed little promise and seemed to indicate a writer who was oblivious to all that was happening about him in his own time, whether in the realm of art or in the social and historical milieu. He never joined a "school" of literature or a salon and never made a close friend of any other young English novelist. . . . His early output was staggering, but as he did not come from a literary background and had had no training at writing, he very much needed to study his craft more than he did. Furthermore, his inclinations were toward becoming a historian. He loved a certain kind of history, the high drama of war and great political events. War itself, the experience he had both luckily and unluckily missed, fascinated him, so that all of his best writing would relate to the experience of men and women either in combat or under the stress and compulsion of war.

Essentially a political conservative, Forester grew to hate totalitarianism, perhaps as a result of his observation of the Spanish Civil War. His early admiration for Napoleon turned to dislike as he transferred his growing antagonism for Mussolini, as evidenced in ***The Ship,*** and for Hitler, as indicated in ***The Ship*** and ***The Good Shepherd,*** as well as many of the stories in ***The Nightmare*** and ***The Man in the Yellow Raft,*** to Napoleon in the Hornblower Saga.

A major theme in Forester's work developed as he began to leave behind the psychological novels and the biographies. The Man Alone theme permitted Forester to examine human nature in a manner similar to the way Ernest Hemingway often viewed it. The latter's admiration for "grace under pressure" was not dissimilar to Forester's contention that unrelieved pressure in a situation where the leader, unaided, made life-and-death decisions brought out the best in a human being and could even make an ordinary person rise to deeds of great heroism and self-sacrifice regardless of the nature of the cause he was serving. Its fictional beginnings are to be found in ***Brown on Resolution,*** and both the Hornblower Saga and ***The Good Shepherd*** represent the ultimate exploration of this theme by Forester. (p. 160)

Forester contributed to a growing British nostalgia for past glories and the days of the Empire. A contributing factor to Hornblower's great popularity is the fact that he is a figure of the pre-industrial revolution and the pre-Victorian past, a product of an earlier, seemingly simpler time. Unlike a more contemporary fantasy hero, James Bond, Hornblower is less dependent upon machines. His engines are muscle-powered and wind-moved. Hornblower does not act alone. He leads men. He brings them to battery. He causes them to see and do their duty. It is no accident that Ian Fleming's hero, James Bond, succeeded Hornblower as the prototype British hero. Hornblower, a product of World War II, is a hero to lead masses. Bond, a product of the Cold War and a more narcissistic, more individualistic period, works alone, is cynical, and is far more interested in his personal pleasure than is the self-sacrificing and duty-seeking Hornblower. Perhaps because they were so much attuned to the consciousness of their times, Hornblower and Bond have developed "historical existences" and have become part of the language and the collective "experience" of the contemporary Western world.

C. S. Forester wrote three superb novels outside of the Hornblower Saga: ***The General, The African Queen,*** and ***The Good Shepherd.*** Their excellence and their popularity are due to the fineness of Forester's characterization, the superbly controlled plotting, the painstaking attention to detail, the clarity of style, and the holistic concept of the novel form that reduced each book to a state of muscular leanness. Forester's best work, like the author himself, was always in fighting trim.

Furthermore, these three novels each focus on either one or two principals and make no pretense of further extended characterizations. Each protagonist is presented with a choice, not a moral choice between right and wrong, but one between duty and self. In the struggles of the protagonists to choose while never fully comprehending that they have a choice and must make it, lies much of the fascination of these novels. Of course the protagonists of ***The African Queen*** and ***The Good Shepherd*** choose duty and are rewarded with survival, self-satisfaction, and expanded souls. General Curzon, however, a basically stupid man, chooses self as he deludes himself into believing that he is choosing duty. His end is therefore tragic and the results and consequences of his actions are catastrophic for the British people.

Forester brought the romantic historical novel to a near pinnacle in the twentieth century. . . . His ultimate achievement for the general readership may be that . . . he brilliantly recreated a past time and place and gave birth to a protagonist worthy of such a background.

Naturally the success of the Hornblower Saga spawned imitators. None could approach the originality, force, and verisimilitude of the model. (pp. 161-63)

Other successful historical novelists, working concurrently with Forester or following him on the literary scene, such as Howard Fast, James Michener, and especially John Jakes with his Kent Family Chronicles in *The Americans* series, may sell more books and earn more money than did Forester, but none seems to have created a cult readership partially based on admiration for a recurring protagonist.

In all probability, even C. S. Forester's stronger non-Hornblower novels, ***The General, The African Queen,*** and ***The Good Shepherd,*** will continue to be read as fallout from the Hornblower Saga by readers introduced to the author with the Saga and desiring to read additional pleasurable work by the same writer. They will not be disappointed. . . . Many of these future readers will be pleasantly surprised by both the content and the depth of these novels. They will find in ***The General*** a disturbing but eminently valuable dissection of the military mind. In ***The African Queen*** they will admire the resources available in seemingly the most ordinary of human beings. In ***The Good Shepherd*** they will learn that courage, self-sacrifice, and devotion to duty above self-interest remain desirable human qualities. If C. S. Forester broke no new ground in these works, he at least reaffirmed insights and values of use to men and women of the last decades of this century and the beginning of the next.

However, it is as a purveyor of popular literature that C. S. Forester will be remembered most frequently, just as Robert Frost is largely remembered for a few moving poems and John Masefield for *Salt-Water Ballads*. These twentieth-century writers, like Forester, will be superficially read and enjoyed by the mass audience, while their more profound work will appeal to a more limited and more erudite audience, but that other work is always there for those who wish to delve more deeply and read the artists' philosophical and intellectual premises, and even, perhaps, their souls.

Hornblower sails on. (pp. 163-64)

Stanford Sternlicht, in his C. S. Forester, *Twayne Publishers, 1981, 177 p.*

Jean Craighead George

1919-

American novelist, author of books for children, nonfiction writer, essayist, and illustrator.

George is an ecology-minded writer whose books for young adults combine an awareness of nature with an exploration of adolescent problems. Her protagonists struggle with the conflicts of growing into adulthood, proving themselves to friends and family, or asserting their independence. Their stories are played out against such naturalistic backgrounds as the Alaskan wilderness and the Florida Everglades, where they discover much about nature and its interconnection with humanity in addition to learning important lessons about themselves.

George's fiction and nonfiction works are noted for relating information about nature in an engrossing, often poetic manner. For each of her books George does extensive field work and research; for example, writing her series *The Thirteen Moons* (published between 1967 and 1969) involved travelling the entire United States to study various animals in their natural habitats. Several of her books involve a lone character learning to live in a seemingly hostile environment. *My Side of the Mountain* (1959) is about a boy who leaves New York City to live on his own in the Catskill Mountains. The heroines of *Julie of the Wolves* (1972) and *The Talking Earth* (1983) reacquaint themselves with their Eskimo and American Indian heritages, respectively, while learning to live in harmony with nature. *My Side of the Mountain* was adapted to film, and George received a Newbery Medal for *Julie of the Wolves,* which was also selected as one of the ten best children's books of the last two hundred years by members of the Children's Literature Association.

George's autobiography, *Journey Inward* (1982), relates her early interests in writing and naturalism and their importance in her life as she endeavored to establish her independence and her writing career. Her early work consists of several animal stories for children, co-authored with her former husband, ecologist John L. George. These include *Vulpes, the Red Fox* (1948), *Vison, the Mink* (1949), and *Meph, the Pet Skunk* (1952). In *Journey Inward,* George tells how these and numerous other animals that appear in her books have lived with her and her family over the years.

(See also *Children's Literature Review,* Vol. 1; *Contemporary Authors,* Vols. 5-8, rev. ed.; and *Something about the Author,* Vol. 2.)

Photograph by Ellan Young. Courtesy of Jean Craighead George

ROBERT HOOD

In **"My Side of the Mountain,"** young Sam Gribley runs away from New York City to a forest in the Catskills and a forgotten plot of land his great-grandfather once plowed.

Sam's adventure is a saga of self-reliance, told in the first person by a modern Third Avenue Thoreau. . . . Young Gribley is amazing; he can build a fire without matches, make a deerskin suit and cook everything from frog soup to sassafras tea. And in the best tradition of Thoreau, he writes very well, too, telling us about his year in the wilds, about the passing seasons and the parade of wildlife. But Sam's year of grace ends as photographers, reporters, friends and family all converge on the "wild boy of the Catskills," turning his retreat into a woodsy 42nd Street. His story is a delightful flight from civilization, written with real feeling for the woods.

Robert Hood, "Third Avenue Thoreau," in The New York Times Book Review, *September 13, 1959, p. 58.*

RUTH HILL VIGUERS

My Side of the Mountain is an extraordinary book. It is young Sam Gribley's story of his year of complete self-sufficiency spent in the Catskill Mountains, and is as credible as a factual record. Through the boy's perception the reader feels his every experience. Although it is a first-person account, there is no artificial attempt to make the writing colloquial, and the book is all the more convincing for the excellence of style, the subtlety of humor, aptness of phrases, and touches of poetry. . . . Sam's own personality emerges clearly—his intelligence, his pleasure in animals and birds, his perseverance, and even his enjoyment of people although he could choose to separate himself so completely from them to carry out his experiment. This book brings a great deal to children: emphasis on the rewards of courage and determination and an abundance of scientific knowledge, certainly, but, far more important, unforgettable experiences in the heart of nature. . . . I believe it will be read year after year, linking together many generations in a chain of well-remembered joy and refreshment.

Ruth Hill Viguers, in a review of "My Side of the Mountain," in The Horn Book Magazine, *Vol. XXXV, No. 5, October, 1959, p. 389.*

NEW YORK HERALD TRIBUNE BOOK REVIEW

Sam Gribley [of **"My Side of the Mountain"**] . . . had a family (father, mother, four sisters and four brothers) even more complaisant than those in the Arthur Ransome stories. They allowed him to run away to try a survival experiment in the Catskills on land that belonged in the family and made no effort to interfere or even to communicate with him as months went by. Improbable? Yes, and so is their sudden surge of interest in him and his "back to nature" exploit when he attracts a great deal of newspaper publicity; but the family is a negligible factor in this excellent story. Its chief interest lies in Sam himself and the day-by-day happenings of his life in the wilds, his only possessions the clothes on his back, a penknife, an ax, flint and steel, tinder and forty dollars. Jean George is a fine naturalist and the details, written in the form of a diary kept by Sam himself, are completely believable and fascinating. . . . This competent "young Thoreau" is a boy to appeal to the Robinson Crusoe in all of us and his adventures will surely delight nature-loving boys and girls. . . . A splendid book.

A review of "My Side of the Mountain," in New York Herald Tribune Book Review, *November 1, 1959, p. 9.*

MARGARET SHERWOOD LIBBY

Although the training of a falcon (sparrow hawk) is an important element in [**"The Summer of the Falcon"**] the emphasis, unlike that in Mrs. George's previous books, is less on the animal characters than on the young heroine, June Pritchard, her mixed feelings about growing up and her relations with her mother. . . . The analogy between June's preparation of her falcon, Zander, for the future and her mother's attitude is clear to the reader. It is not clear to June for a long time. Zander too is ready for the responsibilities of adulthood before June is, and she learns from him that growing up has its compensations. . . . As in all of Mrs. George's books, the nature lore is beautifully handled, but the special emphasis is on the tensions in the family which are most convincingly depicted. June and her mother are both sympathetic characters, whose conflicts are inherent in their temperaments and roles. Many young readers, in these days of growing up rather too fast, will be astonished at June's reluctance to begin going out with boys, but some, especially if they have had her joyous uninhibited childhood, will understand even this, and all will share her dismay when freedom misused boomerangs.

Margaret Sherwood Libby, in a review of "The Summer of the Falcon," in Books, *May 19, 1963, p. 10.*

RUTH HILL VIGUERS

On a lonely sandspit on Block Island, Rhode Island, nested multitudes of herring gulls. Here Dr. Rivers had established his Sea Bird Lab, coming with his family summer after summer to study the birds. His son Luke helped with the banding, note-taking, and record keeping, interested in spite of himself but sometimes resentful. . . . The turning point in [***Gull Number 737***] comes with the crashing of a jet at Boston's Logan Airport when thousands of birds were sucked into the plane's engines. Suddenly Dr. Rivers was in demand and his quiet, scientific studies were put to use. Strangely, then, it was Luke who found himself ready to embark on his own scientific study, which his father considered purposeless. Even readers with little interest in gulls . . . should find this story fascinating. Mrs. George is at once scientific and poetic in her tracing of the life cycle of the herring gull and in drawing parallels between the maturing of young creatures, human as well as bird. The father-son conflict is freshly handled and the characters convincingly developed. . . .

Ruth Hill Viguers, in a review of "Gull Number 737," in The Horn Book Magazine, *Vol. XL, No. 5, October, 1964, p. 505.*

LIBRARY JOURNAL

[***Gull Number 737***] is mainly for the reader who wants to know all about seagulls. An over-abundance of undeveloped plot complications and hazy characterizations combine to make a rather lifeless story. Strictly for the nature lover and more limited in appeal than the author's ***My Side of the Mountain***. . . .

A review of "Gull Number 737," in Library Journal, *Vol. 89, No. 18, October 15, 1964, p. 4206.*

PRISCILLA L. MOULTON

[In ***Hold Zero!*** four] science-minded high-school boys have built a three-stage rocket. Just an hour before countdown time, their secret is discovered, their plans for launching thwarted. A not unsympathetic police officer investigating the case learns how the boys—in rebellion against overorganization and the misguided attentions of busy suburban adults—have spent months on their project. A hide-out in the swamp is the construction site and will be the launching site, too. . . . Criticism of parents and their excessive involvement in civic life is heavily handled, but many readers will relate all too easily with that aspect of the story. The boys' scientific interests, their hide-out, their ingenious devices for communication and transportation have appeal. More the story of a group than of an individual, less introspective than some of the author's other works, there is, nevertheless, considerable attention focused on Craig, a boy with unusual ability to transpose nature's functions into mechanical devices. . . . Timely, lively, and fast moving, it is an honest portrayal of older boys searching for independence and new experiences.

Priscilla L. Moulton, in a review of "Hold Zero!" in The Horn Book Magazine, *Vol. XLII, No. 5, October, 1966, p. 574.*

GERALD GOTTLIEB

[***Hold Zero!***] is a relaxed, unpretentious, cheerful story about four boys who rebel in a most interesting way against their community's wish to smother them with organization and supervision. Children of a scientific bent, or any kids who relish outwitting their elders, will get a kick out of the situation the author creates, wherein the town's adults cannot bring themselves to realize the awesome extent of the elaborate scientific domain their kids have quietly established, and coolly maintain, under adult noses.

One can hardly blame the parents, as there come to light such things as an entire rocket-launching complex complete with three-stage, 24-engine rocket, launch pit, thermoelectric powerhouse, observation and fire control bunkers, parachute recovery system, and radio payload direction finder. . . .

Parents reel. Police investigate. Committees consider. Kids plot. Rocket waits, poised ominously. Countdown holds. Tension mounts. In sum, a delightful, ingenious brouhaha of suspense and fun. The author cleverly fits the scientific shenanigans into a background of nature study, and makes the whole thing not only fascinating but logical. And she displays a fine sense of humor to boot. In this small guerrilla war between the generations, it's clear that her sympathies are solidly with the kids. Lucky kids. Lucky readers.

Gerald Gottlieb, "Growing Pains and Pleasures," in Book Week—World Journal Tribune, Fall Children's Issue, *October 30, 1966, p. 28.**

JAMES HOUSTON

[In **"Julie of the Wolves"**] Julie, an Eskimo girl, runs away from an impossible home life after losing her mother, father and being married off at 13 to a lustful simpleton. When lost and starving on the North Slope of Alaska, she uses all her cleverness and patience to make contact with a family of wolves who ultimately befriend her and help her to live through the long, violent Arctic winter.

The author is a naturalist who has observed wolves at first hand. Her novel is packed with expert wolf lore, its narrative beautifully conveying the sweeping vastness of tundra as well as many other aspects of the Arctic, ancient and modern, animal and human. At her best she makes readers aware of new sights, sounds, tastes and odors. . . .

Mrs. George assumes readers will instantly accept the idea of Julie exchanging thoughts, bites, kisses, even breast feeding with an Arctic wolf. This is the kind of behavioral study a trained naturalist might explore for a doctorate in biology or a TV special. However, the Eskimos I know don't think that way. They would want plenty of white man's firewater before trying to kiss wolves. Still as Mrs. George portrays the wolf pack in almost-human terms the reader slowly comes to think of these wolves as dear friends. . . .

It is refreshing to see the Arctic well portrayed through a woman's eyes.

James Houston, "A Magic Cabinet, Kissing Wolves and a Running Nose: 'Julie of the Wolves'," in The New York Times Book Review, *January 21, 1973, p. 8.*

VIRGINIA HAVILAND

A book of timeless, perhaps even of classic dimensions, [***Julie of the Wolves,***] the story of the phenomenal adventures and survival of Julie (Miyax in Eskimo), suggests both the author's ***My Side of the Mountain*** . . . and Scott O'Dell's *Island of the Blue Dolphins*. . . . The superb narration includes authentic descriptions and details of the Eskimo way-of-life and of Eskimo rituals. . . . The story graphically pictures the seasonal changes of the vast trackless tundra and reveals Miyax's awakening to the falseness of the white man's world. Through the eyes of Julie, who survives for months in the wilderness with the wolves, the author lovingly describes the wildlife: the golden plover, the snow buntings, the snowshoe rabbits, as well as the wolves. She evokes in full measure the terrors of losing directions and facing storms in abysmal temperatures. The whole book has a rare, intense reality. . . . (pp. 54-5)

Virginia Haviland, in a review of "Julie of the Wolves," in The Horn Book Magazine, *Vol. XLIX, No. 1, February, 1973, pp. 54-5.*

BRIAN W. ALDERSON

[***Julie of the Wolves***] is a book of many qualities. It will appeal to our sociological critics because it shows a girl—and a girl from a 'racial minority' at that—acting resourcefully in adverse circumstances, and because it sustains a powerful case not only for conservation but also for the preservation of man's natural skills. It will appeal to the less rigid among us because of its integrity and its wholly convincing portrayal of its setting. . . .

Given so much that is so well-observed and thought-provoking, it may sound churlish to enter reservations; nevertheless, in two respects Mrs. George's book seemed less than perfect. In the first place the reader has, from time to time, a sense of the presence of the author outside the circle of her imagination—not a storyteller, preoccupied with the events as they impinge upon her Eskimoes, but an American lady writing for American children. In the second place one might question the form which Mrs. George has chosen for her story: seventy pages bringing Miyax and the wolves together, twenty-nine pages of flashback, and sixty-one pages devoted to Miyax's journey. The story is a strong enough one to stand up without a literary device of this kind (which in such a short book proves rather clumsy) and, indeed one could say that the story is a strong enough one to warrant an altogether longer telling. It is not just that the people and events that we meet with here are strange to us, but more that they are imbued with a life and force that demands a more expansive treatment. Our short-winded readers of today may defend the book for dramatic conciseness—but I am not sure that an orderly exposition of events, with the graphic detail that Mrs. George has at her command, would not have made the book a richer one and, in the end, a more dramatic one too.

Brian W. Alderson, in a review of "Julie of the Wolves," in Children's Book Review, *Vol. IV, No. 1, Spring, 1974, p. 18.*

CAROLE RIDOLFINO

[In ***Hook a Fish, Catch a Mountain: An Ecological Spy Story***], "City Mouse" Spinner, a 13-year-old New Yorker, tries desperately to adapt herself to a summer of country living and to find favor with her gruff cousin Al. When the two cousins backpack into the mountains to figure out why cutthroat trout are vanishing, she begins to understand the ways of nature. . . . The two realize their growing affection for each other, and Spinner is slowly converted to the joys of rural life. (It is disconcerting, however, that the country folk seem able to accept Spinner only on their terms.) As usual, the author's strength is in ecological detail: nature facts and lore are adeptly woven into the story, and readers are left with a keen sense of the importance of balance in the environment. (pp. 54-5)

Carole Ridolfino, in a review of "Hook a Fish, Catch a Mountain: An Ecological Spy Story," in School Library Journal, *Vol. 21, No. 9, May, 1975, pp. 54-5.*

BARBARA F. HARRISON

Jean George is a champion of ecology and has written over thirty books for young people dealing with the natural world. . . . In **"Going to the Sun"** Mrs. George is again involved with the balance of nature theme. She traces the development of her protagonist, Marcus Kulick, from predator of wild mountain goats to protector. An accomplished hunter, Marcus is determined to have the head of the mountain goat, Old Gore, as a trophy. While crossing a narrow stretch of trail Marcus encounters rival hunter Will Morgan. Angry words are exchanged, they jostle and Will accidentally falls to his death. . . .

The relationship of Marcus and Melissa Morgan, Will's sister, is a parallel story line. They marry, despite their feuding families and the death of Will, shortly after Marcus accepts a job studying goats. . . . When Melissa sees Marcus continuing to stalk Old Gore, she is afraid that he is going to kill the majestic animal and leaves him. The final confrontation of boy and beast results in a taming of each by the other.

Most of the characters and events that crowd the pages of this novel stand curiously apart. Marcus's quest is weakened by wearisome fabrications; the young love of Marcus and Melissa is not convincing and even the feud between the families is without genuine tension. Mrs. George, however, is at her best describing the jagged slopes of the Mission Range in Western Montana and her concern for an endangered species.

Barbara F. Harrison, in a review of "Going to the Sun," in The New York Times Book Review, *June 27, 1976, p. 30.*

MRS. JOHN G. GRAY

[In ***Going to the Sun,*** zoological information about mountain goats] is smothered in a cotton-ball of young love; a family feud; the age-old argument of hunter versus non-hunter; and a baffling pseudo-Indian fantasy in which the great goat, Old Gore, may or may not hold captive the spirit of one Will Morgan, brother of hero Marcus Kulick's sweetheart Melissa. This same Will was accidently killed by Marcus—a fact that seemed to upset the head of the Morgan clan, who, in turn, swore that he would kill the Kulick boy if *he* ever came near *his* daughter. Almost immediately the two escape to the mountain where a really weird old aunt (of Melissa's) marries them (????).

If you think this is a mess, you are following the same thought patterns as the reviewer. The author's last offering, ***Julie of the Wolves,*** was a most moving book exalting the dignity of nature. Where did Miss George step off the trail to literary superiority?

Mrs. John G. Gray, in a review of "Going to the Sun," in Best Sellers, *Vol. 36, No. 5, August, 1976, p. 149.*

GEORGE GLEASON

Swiss Family Robinson and Jean George's own ***My Side of the Mountain*** . . . are forebears of [***River Rats, Inc.,*** a] saga about two junior high boys. Hired to raft down the Colorado through the Grand Canyon, the lads are stranded when their rubber raft bursts. The story is mainly about their survival as they climb cliffs and hike across mesas to get to Supai village in Havasu Canyon. A number of improbabilities nudge the tale out of fiction and into fantasy. Even so, it's a humdinger of an adventure. . . . Oh, yes, the boys start all this by organizing a business called Dirty Work, Inc. that they advertise by slipping handbills into mailboxes—a Federal No-no that should be pointed out to others who might want to start similar ventures.

George Gleason, in a review of "River Rats, Inc.," in School Library Journal, *Vol. 25, No. 7, March, 1979, p. 139.*

MARY M. BURNS

[In ***River Rats, Inc.,*** Joe Zero and Crowbar Flood are hired by] the widowed Mrs. Streeter, whose husband's last wish was that his ashes be dropped in the Colorado River. Having grown up in Las Vegas, the boys were used to strange shenanigans, but they were suspicious about the secrecy of the whole affair, which included an illegal run down the river after dark. At first suggesting *Tom Sawyer,* the narrative quickly changes from a boyish adventure into a story of survival. Their mission nearly completed, the two foundered in the treacherous rapids of the Colorado but managed to scrabble ashore in a particularly inhospitable location. . . . Although fast paced and filled with fascinating natural details, the book at times suggests two separate plots—each equally important—which are loosely connected through the actions of the principal characters. Thus, the resolution seems rushed, almost anticlimactic, perhaps because both situations have competed for the reader's attention. The nature lore, however, is impeccable, so that characters and plot structure are transcended by the evocation of place. (pp. 193-94)

Mary M. Burns, in a review of "River Rats, Inc.," in The Horn Book Magazine, *Vol. LV, No. 2, April, 1979, pp. 193-94.*

MARILYN R. SINGER

Unfortunately, Mandy [in ***The Cry of the Crow***] is no ***Julie of the Wolves.*** The violent opening description of the shooting of a crow's nest, told from the point of view of a baby crow, seems unnecessarily brutal and graphic. The last scene, a wrenching amplification of the first, is inexcusable. Mandy adopts the orphaned crow and becomes imprinted as "Mother" for the eyas whom she names Nina Terrance. The girl keeps her adopted bird/daughter dependent by feeding her, learns crow language and marvels at Nina's ability to speak English. . . . Nina recognizes Drummer [Mandy's 11-year-old brother] as the murderer of her family; crows being vindictive, she starts attacking him whenever he goes into the woods. . . . [To] protect him, Mandy takes the gun, which she has never before used, seeks out Nina, and shoots her. Of all the characters, the crows are the most sympathetic. The humans are flaccid and full of sleazy human faults: Mandy is sneaky and deceitful; her older brothers, macho and rejecting; Drummer is spineless. The parents function merely as book ends. Naturally, with a writer of the caliber of George, there are some bright moments (tenderness between mother and daughter, information on crows and the Everglades), but they can't offset the nastiness or triviality of the rest.

Marilyn R. Singer, in a review of "The Cry of the Crow," in School Library Journal, *Vol. 26, No. 9, May, 1980, p. 67.*

ANN JORDAN

There are many fascinating elements in [***The Cry of the Crow***]—the setting, the principal characters, the style—that will make it a unique experience for a young reader. It takes place on a strawberry farm in southern Florida, near the Everglades. It shocked my typical northeastern prejudice to realize that children could grow up where there are mangrove trees, air plants, ball moss, bromeliads, snakes . . . alligators!

Mandy and "Nina Terrance," a girl and her crow, are the main characters. Mandy discovers Nina, who is the only survivor of her crow family, the others shot in their nest. . . . To me, the most fascinating portion of the story is the knowledge gained on crows. Nina considers herself a "person" because she has been "imprinted" by the image of Mandy. She has also "imprinted" the image of the eyes and forehead of the hunter who shot her family which becomes a pivotal factor later in the story. Crows apparently can speak, are very clever at manipulating their environment, have an extremely elaborate social system and share an extensive language. . . .

There are two minor points to quibble with in an otherwise fine book. The reader perhaps could be a bit more prepared for the ending, and there is a dash of feminism thrown in which isn't integral to the story.

Ann Jordan, in a review of "The Cry of the Crow," in Best Sellers, *Vol. 40, No. 4, July, 1980, p. 158.*

KATHLEEN LEVERICH

In **"The Cry of the Crow,"** Mandy, the only girl in a large, eminently likable family, finds a baby crow. Her father and brothers regularly shoot crows to protect their strawberry crop, but Mandy wants a pet and decides to tame and raise the bird in secrecy. Predictably, the growing crow causes problems and raises issues of life larger than Mandy has yet had to consider. The book includes some fascinating crow lore and takes us into a comfortable, convincing world. The characters are less consistently convincing than the scenery, and the plot, while plausible, is too carefully contrived and predictable to let us forget that this is a book with a message. Mandy's final dispatching of her pet and her declaration of maturity, "time to flap on my own wings," are neither satisfying nor believable.

Jean George is a gifted writer and ardent naturalist who, in her best books, provokes readers to a reassessment of their place in the natural world. Here she has drawn only sparingly on these talents and interests to produce a book that is serviceable, but not provocative.

Kathleen Leverich, in a review of "The Cry of the Crow," in The New York Times Book Review, *September 28, 1980, p. 34.*

NANCY CHAPIN

The awarding of the Newbery Medal to Jean George recognized her achievement as a writer; she also has a deep concern for young people and for the natural world. In this autobiography [***Journey Inward***] she talks about these three aspects of her career from the early years of her ill-fated marriage through the trials of single parenthood to the adaptations required when her grown children left home. Born into a family of naturalists, it was inevitable that an interest in animals should play a major role in her life. "I realized," she says of the writing of this book, "that I [had] better animal stories to tell than Aesop." Tell them she does: both the stories of family pets from skunks to owls and of her researches into the behavior of such varied creatures as the herring gull, the Rocky Mountain goat and the Alaskan wolf. Her observations not only enlarged her insight (as they do the readers'), but were important to her in times of struggle. . . . YAs with a special interest in nature as well as those who have enjoyed ***My Side of the Mountain*** . . . and ***Julie of the Wolves*** . . . will be absorbed by Jean George's account of her own career.

Nancy Chapin, in a review of "Journey Inward," in School Library Journal, *Vol. 29, No. 1, September, 1982, p. 152.*

DICK ABRAHAMSON AND BETTY CARTER

[***Journey Inward***] offers older teenagers and teachers a personal, sensitive look at the woman behind the books.

Jean George's autobiography is the story of a woman in love with nature. It's the story of raising children in homes crowded with owls and snakes and publisher's deadlines. George talks about her failed marriage and the pressures of raising three children as a single parent.

Her story is very much a look at the maturation of a writer. We watch her move from being a coauthor with her husband to becoming the self-confident writer who makes enough money to support a family. . . .

In total, ***Journey Inward*** provides readers with an intimate glimpse into the life of an author who has spent her career writing quality literature for children and adolescents.

Dick Abrahamson and Betty Carter, in a review of "Journey Inward," in English Journal, *Vol. 71, No. 8, December, 1982, p. 67.*

FLO KRALL

The journey undertaken by Jean Craighead George is a familiar one to women of her generation who were socialized in patriarchal families toward feminine roles aimed at raising children, tending to household tasks, and supporting unconditionally the decision-making husband. But unlike the ordinary "femina domestica," Jean C. George entered her marriage as a practicing journalist with belief in her ability to become a professional writer—a vision that sustained her through years of "feast or famine" to the cherished 1973 Newbery Medal Award for her ***Julie of the Wolves***. . . .

[Her autobiography, ***Journey Inward***], beginning with the first years of marriage and following her path to self-confirmation with the writing of ***Journey Inward,*** continually poses the question: Can a woman "really serve her family and her own needs as a person?" The question, however, never gets answered. In a string game, she repeatedly leads us on the circuitous paths of her life to the keyhole without telling us how to get through. The intent is premeditated. Like the nanny of high goat rock, she does not waste time facing impossible obstacles. Instead she leaves the barrier and jumps into a more possible world. For Jean C. George that world is the natural world, her primary love. (p. 44)

[This story is] a tribute to the ability and dignity of a woman who seems not to find the words "despair" or "loneliness" in her vocabulary, a woman who fashioned her life after the black wolf, the alpha male, and the dominant nanny. Her life history is punctuated throughout with detours through natural histories that reveal the depth of her knowledge of ethology as well as her aesthetic sense. We follow her from her household, surrounded by an array of adopted animals, to the arctic where we find her plunging "knee deep into a soft whir of wings . . . fraying out over the grass to float low against a plum-colored sky."

If "education is the key to female society," as George asserts, ***Journey Inward*** is a required primer for men and women seeking more equitable relationships. But as she says, it takes a long time to earn a degree in this sort of thing. And unlike gulls with red spots and posturing wolves, human animals are more subject to misrepresentation in their communication. (p. 45)

Flo Krall, in a review of "Journey Inward," in Western American Literature, *Vol. XVIII, No. 1, May, 1983, pp. 44-5.*

PUBLISHERS WEEKLY

[In ***The Talking Earth,*** Billie Wind has] learned to regard the beliefs of her people, the Seminoles, as mere folklore. Billie's uncle and friend Charlie Wind invites her to choose her own punishment for doubt, whereupon she elects to explore the wild Everglades on her own. Setting out in her canoe, Billie smiles at the notion that birds and animals speak to humans, offering counsel in crises. . . . Surviving a raging fire, a hurricane, starvation and other perils, Billie realizes that observations of wildlife have led her to shelters and sustenance, to the realization that proliferating assaults on animal life brought about by pollution spell the death of Earth, home to all life. George is a naturalist, not a sentimentalist, who tells a dramatic, suspenseful story with riveting descriptions of the unique Everglades country. She does not preach a sermon but the tocsin sounds here as loudly as it did in Rachel Carson's *Silent Spring*. Before it's too late?

A review of "The Talking Earth," in Publishers Weekly, *Vol. 224, No. 19, November 4, 1983, p. 66.*

BETSY BYARS

[***The Talking Earth***] is a survival book. Billie Wind, a Seminole Indian girl, is sent into the Everglades as a sort of self-suggested punishment for her refusal to believe in the old Seminole legends, i.e. that the animal gods talk.

Her two-day exile is lengthened into a stay of 12 weeks, first by a fire that burns her dugout and leaves her stranded, later by her own resolution to learn what the animals are saying. There is plenty of excitement—alligators, fire, hurricane; plenty of absorbing history—ancient Calusca caves and ruins; enough animals to grow fond of . . . ; and Billie Wind has just the right combination of guts, humor and curiosity to make the reader care about her.

But the star of the book is the Everglades. With great generosity of detail, naturalist George brings the Everglades to life. The book exudes sights, smells and sounds, and at the end the reader is left with the same awe for our earth as Billie Wind.

Betsy Byars, "Growing Up Is Hard to Do," in Book World—The Washington Post, *November 6, 1983, p. 17.**

KAY WEBB O'CONNELL

The themes [in ***The Talking Earth***] are the author's hallmarks: conserving the earth from mindless development and destruction, ethnic integrity and the intricate beauty of a natural environment. George has elevated survival stories to an artistic plane in which issues of environmental conservation and cultural heritage can be addressed satisfyingly. Yet ***The Talking Earth*** lacks the drama and emotional engagement of ***Julie of the Wolves*** . . . , in which a girl's future, her life in fact, hangs in the balance in a killing climate. Neither the environment, Billie's plight, nor the animal attachments command the same excitement that was generated in the earlier book. Nonetheless, George's fine fictional gifts and educative eye are there, and ***Julie*** fans are sure to enjoy the book.

Kay Webb O'Connell, in a review of "The Talking Earth," in School Library Journal, *Vol. 30, No. 4, December, 1983, p. 74.*

Woody Guthrie

1912-1967

(Born Woodrow Wilson Guthrie) American songwriter, autobiographer, nonfiction writer, and poet.

Best known as the composer of such popular folk songs as "This Land Is Your Land," "Hard Traveling," and "So Long, It's Been Good to Know You," Guthrie is credited by critics and musicians with having expanded American folk music from its grassroots beginnings to national popularity. Many of his songs, which singer Pete Seeger estimates at over a thousand, are traditional melodies to which Guthrie added original lyrics. Guthrie's songs are valued for their commentary on American life and culture during the 1930s and 1940s. Many depict the hardships of life in the Southwest during the depression, particularly the migration of the Okies to California in search of work. Hoboes, union workers, and even the outlaw Pretty Boy Floyd are prominent subjects in Guthrie's songs.

Born in Okemah, Oklahoma, Guthrie began wandering throughout the Southwest while in his teens, working as a fortune-teller, faith-healer, sign painter, and radio personality. He wrote and performed wherever he traveled and earned a reputation as a spokesman for the common person. Guthrie's "Dust Bowl Ballads," a series of songs written to publicize the plight of the Okies, are based on his experiences as a drifter and reflect the social and economic climate of the 1930s. These songs were heavily influenced by John Steinbeck's novel *The Grapes of Wrath;* Guthrie's song "Tom Joad" received critical appraisal by Steinbeck himself. Midway through the 1930s, Guthrie settled temporarily in California and became involved with union activists and political radicals. Although he never acknowledged membership in the Communist party, Guthrie's concern for the downtrodden caused him to identify with the communist ideal of a classless society. "Union Maid" is considered the best of a series of songs which became staples at his union hall appearances. In the late 1930s, Guthrie was a columnist for the left-wing periodicals *The People's Daily Worker* and *People's World.*

In 1940, the folklorist and musicologist Alan Lomax arranged to have Guthrie record his songs for the Archives of American Folk Song of the Library of Congress. These songs were later released as a three-record collection entitled *Woody Guthrie: Library of Congress Recordings.* In 1941, the Bonneville Power Administration commissioned Guthrie to write songs about the Grand Coulee Dam project in northern California. He composed twenty-six songs in one month, including "Roll On, Columbia," "Pastures of Plenty," and "Grand Coulee Dam," which are considered to be among his finest work. Guthrie also performed for migrant farm workers with Lee Hays, Pete Seeger, and others as a member of the Almanac Singers. During the early years of World War II, Guthrie sang on several overseas broadcasts for the Office of War Information and wrote patriotic columns that were syndicated throughout America. Richard Reuss contends that Guthrie's best songs were produced between 1939 and 1942 and combine his folk heritage with his increasing social and political consciousness.

Courtesy of Dr. John Greenway

Guthrie's autobiography, *Bound for Glory* (1943), was favorably reviewed for its engaging narrative. Although it contains substantial humor, bitterness is also evident in its depiction of the tragedies that plagued Guthrie's family. *Bound for Glory* was adapted for film in 1975. In addition to his songs, Guthrie produced an abundance of drawings, poems, essays, reminiscences, and philosophical observations during his life. These pieces are collected in such volumes as *Born to Win* (1965), *Woody Sez* (1975), and *Seeds of Man* (1976). Some critics faulted these books because Guthrie's southwestern dialect and his unorthodox grammatical structures sounded forced or were difficult to read. Others, however, found his "hillbilly" homespun style refreshing and subtle in wit and wisdom.

Guthrie's life and his lyrics, which reflect his sympathy toward the hardships of the common person, are largely responsible for his reputation as a folk hero. His wanderings as a "roadman" became a symbol of personal freedom, and his songs influenced a new generation of folk singers, including his son, Arlo, Bob Dylan, and Phil Ochs. Guthrie denounced injustice and inequality, and his work was especially poignant because he wrote from personal experience. A year before his death, Guthrie received a government citation from the Secretary of the Interior, Stewart Udall, for his "lifetime efforts to make the American people aware of their heritage and their land."

(See also *Contemporary Authors,* Vol. 113, Vols. 93-96 [obituary].)

STEWART HOLBROOK

[Woody Guthrie's **"Bound for Glory"**] is the autobiography to date of a young man who has spent a good deal of his thirty years as a hobo. Not a tramp, certainly not a bum, but a hobo, a man who moves around looking for work when he needs it and occasionally finding it. . . .

In this book Woody Guthrie describes the pitiful scenes and humanity he has met on the road of forty-odd states—the people who had gone away down in the scale, if they had ever been elsewhere; the people who are living in shacks, packing boxes, jungles and moving around, going somewhere, anywhere. . . .

The author has a good eye for these people and an excellent ear for their speech. They are the kind he knows best, and his feeling for them is sympathetic, though never downright sentimental. Occasionally he makes the reader a bit sorry for them. But I could not feel as deeply for these underprivileged as I could for the Guthrie family. Here in this family was genuine tragedy of a moving sort. Mama Guthrie was a good housekeeper, an affectionate wife and parent, with music and poetry in her soul. She becomes a person one could well love very much. And the reader senses, rather than reads, how the grim specter of incipient and finally of downright insanity hovers over her. . . . The complete disintegration of the family begins.

The progress of this tragedy is subtly made known in the chapters dealing with young Woody's childhood, and they have a horror that is not felt even when tough railroad cops are beating up plain hoboes, nor felt in any other part of the book in equal fashion. This horror could not be transmitted to the reader without highly competent subjective prose, the kind of prose young Guthrie can write when he feels strongly enough.

When mama went to the asylum, Woody hit the road. Possessed of a musical voice and a guitar, the boy made his way across and up and down the United States. . . . He worked at odd jobs here and there. . . .

Mostly, however, he kept on the move, he and his guitar. Many of his songs are made up, as he says, by himself. Any old tune will do, and the subjects of his lyrics are cyclones, disastrous floods, shipwrecks, outlaws—in fact, almost any sort of tragedy that has death in it. . . .

The Library of Congress and a big phonograph concern have had him make records of his songs. . . . The government sent him to Coulee Dam to make up some songs about that big job, and finally he wound up in the Rainbow Room in Rockefeller Center for a radio audition.

The chapter dealing with this audition is satire of the first mark. All of the pompous and arty attitudes of radio, studio and program directors and experts is here impaled with a directness that should cause squirming in some quarters. It's great stuff. . . . But Woody Guthrie is made of strong stuff and he managed to survive these preposterous doings and to retain both his native style and his self-respect. It must have taken some doing.

I gather that Woody escaped from the Rainbow Room and is now on the road again, still singing songs about jail houses, stockades, murders, wrecks and railroad trains. . . . [**"Bound for Glory"**] is Woody Guthrie's book, done as he damned well pleased, and most of it is good going.

Stewart Holbrook, "On the Road in Forty-Odd States," in New York Herald Tribune Weekly Book Review, *March 21, 1943, p. 4.*

HORACE REYNOLDS

The mood of the book which Woody has made out of his life [**"Bound for Glory"**] reminds me a little of the mood of the autobiography Sean O'Casey is writing. Like O'Casey, Guthrie likes violence and sentiment. Like O'Casey, he is verbally sportive: he plays with words, makes 'em dance, makes 'em cry, makes 'em sing. Like O'Casey, too, Woody is on fire inside, a natural born poet trying to make prose do the big job of verse.

He writes well. There's a glory hallelujah madness of imagery here which is exciting and compelling, a psychological counterpoint for the violence of the physical action. He writes much in the evangelical mood. As one reads him, one sees a Negro singing "On That Great Gittin'-Up Mornin'," his arms stretched up to heaven like a pair of crazy sticks. One catches echoes of the "Grapes of Wrath."

Yet Woody doesn't neglect the quieter moments. He has known the millions of memories which can be struck into the mind by some such small action as lighting a match. He writes beautifully about one of those rare moments of happiness, an exquisitely poised moment of complete all-suffusing gladness which he and his mother shared as they dug the rich Oklahoma earth for a garden. . . .

The book is like pictures, both moving and still. The writing has that kind of vividness and that sort of limitation. It's exciting and it's a little flat and empty. There's a curious sense of withdrawal here, which I think is the result of omission and contrivance. Woody's not telling the whole story of the migratory worker's thoughts and feelings. I don't mean by that the bowdlerization of tramp talk and action. I mean that there's too much contrived action and opinion here, too much of what the Irish call "shaping," among other things, for the war and the war psychosis. But there's no mistaking Woody's talent for expression, his ability to sling the American slanguage. There's both the drawl of the South in it and the twang of the Middle West. His book is an eloquent piece of writing, wild as a train whistle in the mountains, a scrumptious picture of fighting, carousing, singing, laughing migratory America.

Some of this book is God gloomy, some of it's pathetic, some of it is a bit too strong for my stomach. Some of its violence has as little meaning as the action of a movie thriller. Some of it could have been pruned to advantage. But much of it is original, strong writing with the glint and sparkle of sunshine on it, gay as the ueklelaydillio to whose accompaniment Woody trolls his balladry. Readers will like it for its pictures and for its optimism.

Horace Reynolds, "A Guitar-Busker's Singing Road," in The New York Times Book Review, *March 21, 1943, p. 7.*

LOUIS ADAMIC

What distinguishes . . . **"Bound for Glory"** is the almost perfect fusion of form and content, and the quality of value which gives that content meaning. Like Whitman, Guthrie believes in people. . . .

Many books have been written about the submerged one-third of America, about the insulted and injured dwelling in this broad land. But through Guthrie's eyes these things take on a new, poignant, and yet hopeful meaning, and a flesh-and-blood vitality. . . .

Guthrie is a singing man. He is the twentieth-century troubadour whose subject is not the deeds of princes but the dreams of people. . . . The songs are made out of what he sees and knows and feels; they are the living folksongs of America.

The same quality pervades the book. It is completely American, twentieth-century American, in feeling, in experience, in idealism and humor and rhythm. Through it one sees again the disjointedness, the inarticulation, of modern life; but—and this is so rare as to be very nearly unique—the author is not disjointed. He does not know all the answers, but he knows the right questions, and he has an unassailable grasp of the values which lead to the right answers. . . .

Guthrie's principal gift is a great, unselfconscious, penetrating simplicity. In his writing, it falters only occasionally, when he is trying to formulate philosophy, or to force a contrast. If he can preserve unspoiled the magnificent simplicity of the means he instinctively chooses, there is no limit to what he can do. In any case, **"Bound for Glory"** is the real thing; it is an incomparable hunk of American life, and a landmark in American literature.

Louis Adamic, "Twentieth-Century Troubadour," in The Saturday Review of Literature, *Vol. XXVI, No. 16, April 17, 1943, p. 14.*

JOHN GREENWAY

When I first visited Guthrie in 1946 he was living in a crowded apartment in Coney Island with his wife and four-year-old daughter, Cathy Ann, whom he nicknamed "Stackabones." I found him, a little weather-worn man with incredibly bushy, wiry hair, sitting before a typewriter in a hollowed-out space in the middle of a tiny room filled with guitars, fiddles, harmonicas, mandolins, tambourines, children's toys, record albums, books, pictures, and scattered manuscripts. Remembering his musical declaration that he was "never comin' back to this man's town again," I asked him why he had changed his mind about this city of "rich men, preachers, and slaves."

"Everything's moved to the city," he answered with a great sweep of his arm, and speaking to the world. "Big business brought the workers, the workers brought the music, and the music brought me." (pp. 280-81)

He pushed a two-inch thick book of bound typewriter paper toward me. "Look," he said, "there's more than three hundred songs I've written, most of them to the old tunes. You won't hear the night club orgasm gals singing these songs, but I've sung them on picket lines, in union halls, in foc's'les, in river-bottom peach camps—everywhere—and I've never once seen them fail. Folks sweat under the collar, throw their coats in the corner, stamp their feet, clap, and sing these songs. Our songs are singing history."

Since that meeting, Guthrie has been exceptionally prolific in song writing, and probably his stack of compositions now is three or four times as thick. The most important reason for this sudden increase in production is that since his more or less permanent settlement in New York Guthrie's sources have changed from living to literary material. In his earlier days—in the days when the Dust Bowl ballads and his famous strike and picket-line songs were written, his compositions were spontaneously generated to relieve an expanding feeling of protest; the inspiration came from within. Today his songs are likely to be perfunctory versified paraphrases of newspaper accounts of injustices perpetrated on individuals or groups with whom he has no personal acquaintance. The inspiration and feeling of protest are still there in sufficient quantity to lift his compositions well above the level of the average contemporary labor-protest song, but both suffer through diffusion, and the "dissociation of sensibility" which inevitably results from the utilization of secondary sources is everywhere evident. This does not mean that Guthrie no longer writes songs that approach the quality of **"Pretty Boy Floyd"** and **"Tom Joad,"** but merely that the percentage of songs of first quality is smaller. Everything is grist for Guthrie's mill now. (pp. 281-82)

Not all of Guthrie's compositions are songs of overt protest. Of an estimated thousand songs in his manuscript collection, I found only about 140 whose basic theme was one of protest; the remainder fell into conventional folksong categories—love, humor, crime, ballads of disaster, tragedies, and war, non-protest labor songs, and even nursery songs.

Many of these attain the quality of the best of his protest songs, but since their themes lie outside the scope of this work, their examination must await another study. It may, however, be mentioned as an illustration of the inherent quality of his work, that many of these less controversial songs have had extraordinary success in view of the fact that songs of nearly pure folk origin are denied the usual channels of commercial distribution. His **"Oklahoma Hills"** made a small fortune for his cousin, a cowboy singer to whom its composition was erroneously attributed; his **"Philadelphia Lawyer,"** a humorous ballad of first quality, attained an astounding popularity on the West Coast during the latter part of 1949; his **"So Long, It's Been Good to Know You"** in a version lamentably divested of all its earlier significance, is currently among the sheet music and record best sellers.

The **"Philadelphia Lawyer,"** in the economical way in which the substitution of an occasional line produces a completely different story in a completely different mood, is a fine example of Guthrie's skill at the sort of adaptation that has characterized folk composition. Taking the sentimental ballad "The Jealous Lover," and discarding the tragic theme, Guthrie makes of an undistinguished story of unhappy love a distinguished story of irresponsible love and its consequences, while incidentally ridiculing a profession for which he has only despite. (pp. 282-83)

In songs of more serious intent such heavy dependence on traditional material has greatly impaired the quality of Guthrie's songs. **"Gotta Get to Boston"** is representative of perhaps a score of songs in which the incompatible combination of dissimilar origins obviates the effect which Guthrie tries to achieve. **"Root Hog or Die,"** of which this is but a slight adaptation, is hardly the kind of song one would associate in theme with the Sacco-Vanzetti tragedy. (p. 284)

But Guthrie's use of tangible folk material is rarely so heavy handed. Usually his borrowing extends only to the utilization, with little adaptation, of the tunes of traditional folk songs. A common notation on his manuscripts is something like "This goes good to the tune of 'Blue Eyes' with a little of 'Wildwood Flower' mixed in." Unlike most writers of union songs and topical parodies, Guthrie never uses the tune of a popular song for his compositions.

This characteristic folk purity of his tunes can be extended not only to his compositions as a whole, but to his personality also. Despite his intermittent residence in New York, the economic and social orientation he has gained through acquaintance with college-educated organizers and political workers, and the voracious reading of heavy books, Guthrie has retained unspoiled his folk origins. Dr. Charles Seeger, in determining Guthrie's cultural evolution, says that he has not yet attained *cb* [city-billy]. But with the most sincere deference to Dr. Seeger's profound knowledge, I submit that Guthrie has remained consistently close to *f* [folk], making only sporadic and temporary excursions to the borders of *hb* [hillbilly].

In the matter of accompaniment Guthrie has gone further to the right. Those familiar with the music of the Carter family, the most respected of hillbilly singing groups, can detect vestigial traces of Maybelle Carter's "picking" in Guthrie's guitar style. When, after Guthrie made his first coast-to-coast radio appearance he received a grimy postcard from West Virginia signed "The Carters" and saying "You're doing fine, boy," he proudly acknowledged his debt. Guthrie deplores the practice of "folk singers" learning the guitar either from books or under the guidance of a professional teacher. (pp. 284-85)

In the matter of language and imagery Guthrie's style, when not obviously adapted from an existing song or lifted consciously from the great body of folk idiom, is unique; I have not been able to detect any influences such as are to be found in his guitar playing. He is a logophile, but his hypnosis with words does not manifest itself, as it does with others who have this affliction, in polysyllables. Guthrie rarely strays far from the Anglo-Saxon word-hoard, but the curious associations which he finds between simple terms lead him into fantastic flights of imagery. Metrical restrictions fetter these flights in his songs, but in his prose they are completely unrestrained. (p. 287)

His diction is filled with picturesque expressions which we, who can merely write grammatical correctness, may envy: Of a broken watch: "It ticks like hell but won't keep time." Of a small boy: "He ain't old enough to be of any age." Of an obvious fact which an obtuse person cannot apprehend: "A blind man could feel that with a stick." Of Missouri mosquitoes: "So thick you couldn't stir 'em with a stick." Of a little man battling furiously against overwhelming opposition: "He was fightin' like a bee in under a horse's tail." Of despair: "I been troubled so long I forgot how to worry." Of incomprehension: "All I know is I add up all I know and I still don't know." (pp. 287-88)

One could recite endless anecdotes illustrating Guthrie's colorful personality, but in so doing one might easily lose sight of his real importance as a man and as a symbol. . . . (p. 288)

But Woody Guthrie sees himself in a less imposing way; he says merely, "Let me be known as the man who told you something you already know." (p. 289)

John Greenway, "The Song-Makers," in his American Folksongs of Protest, *University of Pennsylvania Press, 1953, pp, 243-310.**

CLAUDE M. SIMPSON, JR.

Since early manhood Woody Guthrie has been an engaging figure, one of the rare genuine minstrels of our time, with creativity to burn and a gift of language often remarkable. . . . [***American Folksong***] is a reissue of an original 1947 publication, flavored with post-war details that date the collection today. The opening autobiographical account is unsparing, but its benzedrine style is often too self-conscious and evangelical to compare with the hard-bitten breeziness of his book ***Bound for Glory.*** The body of ***American Folksong*** is given to twenty-five Guthrie songs, only eighteen of which have tunes, and those unaccountably separated from their texts. . . . [This] collection inevitably seems thin, although one is glad to see such good Guthrie pieces as **"Tom Joad," "Goin' Down This Road,"** and **"I Ain't Got No Home in This World Anymore."** The cover portrait of Woody is splendid; the contents should have been assembled with equally professional finish to give him the substantial tribute he deserves.

Claude M. Simpson, Jr., in a review of "American Folksong," in Western Folklore, *Vol. XXI, No. 4, October, 1962, p. 290.*

HENRIETTA YURCHENCO

With the passing of time, Woody Guthrie's stature as balladeer and poet of the people increases. His songs are sung by countless numbers both here and abroad; he is the idol of folk singers, the model for young songwriters. After a period of comparative neglect in the 1950s, his material is now appearing in books and records with relentless regularity. (p. 56)

Guthrie wrote about an era in American life marred by the misfortunes of the Great Depression. Violence on the picket-line, hunger marches by the unemployed, shifting populations roaming the country in search of work were commonplace events in the 1930s until the outbreak of World War II. Guthrie spoke out against Depression conditions fearlessly and courageously. Yet these were not his only concern, for Guthrie was the complete minstrel, endlessly taken with life in its totality. He wrote love songs, dance songs and numerous children's songs, inspired by his natural sense of hilarity and soaring childlike fantasy. No wonder these ditties delight child and adult alike wherever they are sung today! In time, they may become as universally known and loved as Mother Goose. Guthrie wrote about human foibles, mocked prejudice and pretension with a sharp, penetrating wit. Most of all, he loved his country, and many of his most popular songs are great paeans in praise of its grandeur and vastness. Whatever the subject, he was always intensely human and personal. Even in the ballads of social protest he spoke like a poet, not a sloganizing pamphleteer. And, no matter how deep his despair at what he saw and experienced, his profound faith in his fellow man sent bright rays of hope through the darkness. (pp. 56-7)

In the 1930s, Oklahoma was ravaged by severe dust storms which devastated the land. Thousands of impoverished sharecroppers and farmers loaded their meager belongings on ancient jalopies and headed for California, the promised land. Guthrie wrote eight ballads "to try and show you how it is to live under the wild and windy actions of the great duststorms that ride in and out and up and down. . . . I've lived in these duststorms just about all my life (I mean I *tried* to live)," he writes in his notes for the **"Dust Bowl Ballads."** . . . Two of these ballads—**"So Long, It's Been Good to Know You"** and **"Tom Joad,"** based on Steinbeck's novel "The Grapes of Wrath," are among his finest creations. . . . Their importance in our folk literature cannot be stressed enough, and that Guthrie himself sings them makes this a unique document. (p. 57)

Henrietta Yurchenco, "Out of the Dust Bowl," in Musical America, *Vol. LXXXIV, No. 5, May, 1964, pp. 56-7.*

JAY SMITH

[***The Nearly Complete Collection of Woody Guthrie Folk Songs*** is] an unobtrusive and unprepossessing publication. . . . Inside, there is a one-page introduction by Pete Seeger and then there are the songs, presented one after another in no particular order. There are no headnotes and only occasionally the punctuation of Woody's drawings. Many of the songs would carry more meaning if we were told something of when, where, and why they were written. Songs such as **"Old Lone Wolf"** (Woody's KFVD radio theme) and **"Ladies Auxiliary"** (a gag song) would benefit by a brief explanation. The same can be said for more serious songs such as **"Red Runner,"** a superb reworking of "Stewball." . . .

In spite of all the things it might have been, the collection does offer a heaping helping of Woody Guthrie. The slapdash method of presenting the some 200 songs does—probably unintentionally—point up the myriad of subjects Woody sang about. . . . [The songs] speak for themselves. Because they do, ***The Nearly Complete Collection of Woody Guthrie Folk Songs*** is worth owning. As Woody himself has said, he was not something fancy on a stick. As it has been with the man, so it is with the book. From a less than ideal package, the music and the poetry shine through. (p. 73)

Jay Smith, "Woody Guthrie," in Sing Out! *Vol. 14, No. 6, January, 1965, pp. 71, 73.*

NAT HENTOFF

Guthrie wrote at least a thousand songs as he explored this country between 1932 and 1952. . . . Many of the songs have disappeared, but many—**"So Long, It's Been Good to Know You," "This Land Is Your Land,"** and **"Hard Traveling"** among them—are now in the basic repertory of most folk singers. . . .

[So far] the most important product of the renewal of interest in Guthrie is a boxed three-LP set of records, ***Woody Guthrie: Library of Congress Recordings***. . . . For three days in March, 1940, Guthrie, then twenty-eight, talked and sang for the Archive of Folk Song of the Library of Congress in a long interview conducted by Alan Lomax, who has accurately described Guthrie as "the best folk ballad composer whose identity has ever been known." . . .

Like the most powerful of Negro bluesmen and jazz players, Guthrie created his songs from the rhythms and textures of speech. And in this set, we continually hear the fusion of speech with music. . . .

Songs came out of experience. He recalls, for instance, how **"So Long, It's Been Good to Know You"** was born in the kind of Texas dust storm that appeared to signal the end of the world. And watching whole families, "living like coyotes," take to the highway after mortgages had been foreclosed, Guthrie wrote songs that have outlasted the Okies. . . . (p. 48)

One particularly beguiling section of the set is Guthrie's tribute to the outlaws of his region, especially Pretty Boy Floyd. In Guthrie's highly romanticized hagiology, Floyd becomes the Robin Hood of the Southwest. Guthrie's song **"Pretty Boy Floyd"** points out that the outlaw was popular primarily because he was an enemy of the law and order that had done nothing to prevent or remedy the chaos in the lives of the poor in the area. (pp. 48-9)

But despite the pervasive anger in Guthrie's stories and songs, there is a persistently leavening wit and a pride in America's capacities. The always outraged but always optimistic revolutionary had no patience with songs of despair. "I am out," he once wrote, "to sing songs that will prove to you that this is your world and that if it has hit you pretty hard and knocked you for a dozen loops . . . no matter what color, what size you are, how you are built, I am out to sing the songs that make you take pride in yourself and in your work." And when there was no work, Guthrie sang sardonically of the politicians and of how transient they too could be made. Always there was the thrust of possibility in his music. (p. 49)

Nat Hentoff, "It's Been Good to Know Him," in The Reporter, *Vol. 32, No. 1, January 14, 1965, pp. 48-9.*

CHARLES A. RAINES

To many the name of Woody Guthrie has come to symbolize the great social struggle of the 1930's and 1940's—a time during which the conscience of America was put perhaps to its ultimate test. Guthrie was one of those—Pete Seeger and Carl Sandburg among them—who emerged from the catastrophies of the Depression . . . with a voice directed to "the people." The prosperity following World War II suppressed this for a while, but it has risen again in the midst of the folksong revival, mainly through such singers as Bob Dylan, for whom Guthrie served as mentor, and now Guthrie has a large following and a vast hearing. . . . The voice that comes forth in [***Born to Win***, a] collection of his writings done mostly during the 1940's, is perhaps not to be judged on its literary merits—though as a folk writer he is uncommonly good and much better than Sandburg—but it is important to hear what he has to say and especially to participate in his enormous capacity for compassion and his rare capacity to live fully and to appreciate everything in life without regret and without remonstration. Although a great deal of his writing is in a folksy vein, Guthrie very frequently and with an uncanny perception reaches the essence of existence uncluttered by the rationality of philosophers. It is this power that makes Guthrie's book very much worth while beyond its entertainment and wit. (pp. 3290-91)

Charles A. Raines, in a review of "Born to Win," in Library Journal, *Vol. 90, August, 1965, pp. 3290-91.*

ROBERT COWLEY

[No] folk musician today is more influential [than Woody Guthrie.] His abundant followers copy his songs and appropriate his outlook, imitate his mannerisms and affect his easy-going vagabond ways. The stuff of legends, he has become something of a god—Woody Guthrie, the Oakie minstrel, the hobo, the lover, the frequenter of migrant Hoovervilles and jungle camps, the instinctive anti-Fascist and revolutionary, the One Big Union Man. Such is the familiar substance of his active life and his best songs. . . . But there is more to it, of course, for Woody Guthrie fills another need: he is the tragic hero, the folk-Fitzgerald cut down in his prime. . . .

[**"Born to Win"**] is a loosely organized collation of Woody Guthrie's prose poems, occasional jottings, drawings, reminiscences and songs. Its subject matter ranges from baby sitting, politics, wartime experiences and praise of nakedness to segregation, folk singing, Robert Burns, and radio station WNEW. . . .

It is hard to decide whether Woody Guthrie's reputation has been done a greater disservice by the well-intentioned claims of his admirers or the publication of this book. Presumably, most of the material included was not intended for public consumption—with the exception, that is, of the songs, some of which are very good indeed. . . . These random bits and pieces reveal a man of considerable charm and wit and courage, with a compulsion to express himself in every possible direction, but qualities of character that might shine through in a conversation or on a concert stage or a radio program cannot always be communicated on paper.

That is one of the troubles here. The even sadder fact is that in much of this Guthrie is plainly in over his head. Almost all of the items in **"Born to Win"** were written in 1947 and 1948, at a time when he was already a fixture in the folk world. With the experiences of the Dust Bowl and the Depression a decade behind him, he seemed to be straining not only for new and different subject matter but for more sophisticated modes of expression. He saw himself as "a singer without a dictionary, and a poet not bound down with shelves of books." But lack of discipline was always a problem. . . . (p.18)

Occasionally, the words tumbled out right. . . . More often, they descended, unthinking, to the level of his tribute to Robert Burns: "The only good part of living you really did miss, Bob, was not to get to stick around a house like Marjorie keeps." (pp. 18, 20)

Robert Cowley, "Singers and Songs," in The New York Times Book Review, *January 23, 1966, pp. 18, 20.**

JOHN GREENWAY

The singing has begun in America, but Woody Guthrie is not yet well known even in his own country. (p.26)

Inevitably Woody's first, last, and most typical songs (if not his best) were songs of protest. . . . When understanding of oppression and deprivation in the Wildean sense takes the form of altruistic protest, the observer can be sure that the guilt is in the singer. Like charity, protest against injuries to others is a gratification of the protester's organism. One does not take arms to oppose a sea of other people's misfortunes without some inner compulsion as the stimulus. It is an inner sin, a private lack, that must be expiated in the public good.

Woody Guthrie thought little of himself; he was often whelmed by guilts. He once gave me the manuscript copy of his **"Jailhouse Blues,"** without either of us noticing at the time that he had scribbled on the back a poignant self-denunciation:

> They just dont make em no honerier than me. It looks like Im a doing everything I can to make a hobo out of me. I get good chances to get on the radio and make a little money and get a start up the old ladder, but then that honery streak comes out and I ruin the whole thing. I kick myself in the britches pretty hard some times. You dont hate me any worse than I do. You dont bawl me out any more than I do. Oh, well, dam it all anyhow, I never really set my head on being a public figure. Its all what you mean when you say success. Most of the time success aint much fun. Lots of times it takes a lot of posing and pretending. (pp. 26-7)

Still, his bittersweet humor encompassed his own frailties. . . . At least two hundred of Guthrie's compositions were overt preachments of protest, and despite his pantheism his personal identification was with Christ. (p. 27)

Except for those who see Christ as the most successful subversive in Western history, many of Guthrie's New York songs deserved the surveillance he had from the F.B.I., though a more harmless, more innocent captive of the cynical Left could not be imagined. He had genius as a poet-composer, mediocrity as a singer, and gullibility as a proletarian. Those who captured and used him for their unscrupulous purposes are now constructing him into the great proletarian hero, . . . though at least one of them has said more or less publicly that "ninety per cent of his stuff was junk." . . .

The range of subject, treatment, and mood in Guthrie's songs was as far-reaching as his own footsteps over his country. For his women he wrote songs of obscenity . . . , for his wandering he wrote hobo and tramp songs without any significance beyond the fact of being on the road. . . . To make money (which he never did) he wrote infra-popular songs. . . . For his leftist captors in New York he wrote a spate of songs, nearly all of them execrable; for his heroes of history he wrote songs of praise long on truth and short on fact, but always catching the essential virtue of the man—as in his ballad of Lincoln and Ann Rutledge, where Lincoln's one unassailable quality, his compassion, is the only emotion. . . .

Except for the Bonneville songs, which showed a rush of genius poured into twenty-six songs in twenty-eight days, the best of Woody was his early Dust Bowl chronicles. On these his reputation will—in my opinion—grow to a high rank even among sophisticated American poets. . . . Guthrie's songs told of the emigration, but not of the capture of California by the Okies and their wives and their children and their dogs and their chickens and their pregnant unmarried daughters and their guitars, all over the relatively feeble opposition of police with axe handles and fruit-growers with baskets. (p. 28)

Happily, he had nothing to sing about the epilogue—the terrible vengeance these people took on California by capturing it and giving it back periodically to Billy Graham, Barry Goldwater, and Ronald Reagan. His interest was in tolerable Okies—that is, poor ones—not the intolerable affluent ones.

Some few Okies with money were, nevertheless, fit subjects of song, for regardless of how they came by their money, a poor man with money among his poor fellows must for mythic purposes have robbed the oppressors. This is not a Communist idea; in English it goes back at least to Robin Hood. The pattern is standard in all the world's folklore; the man who can inflict retaliatory suffering on a subjugated people's oppressors becomes perforce a hero, no matter what sort of person he was in fact or whether he was in fact at all. Steinbeck caught the mood among the Okies and gave Ma Joad their words to say about the mad-dog thief and murderer Pretty Boy Floyd. . . . Guthrie caught the feeling for Floyd independently among his neighbors, describing him as a good man, a poor farmer, goaded to anger and violence by a sheriff's insult to his wife, driven to the woods, finding succor from his own kind, and paying them in return. . . .

Beyond these shared beliefs of his culture, Guthrie's songs were individual artistic compositions, often striking a classic marble hardness found rarely outside A. E. Housman; the simplicity and immediacy of the best Negro spirituals; the humor of Mark Twain; the innate and unconscious profundity of—well, at least of Steinbeck. As in his long ballad **"Tom Joad,"** which he wrote, he told me once, after seeing the movie, "The Grapes of Wrath." . . . (p. 30)

In this ballad Woody encountered the same problems that beset Steinbeck as a writer—for instance, the irrelevant but necessary nuisance of getting the Joads across the desert to California. Steinbeck used many pages to make the transition; Woody did it in three lines. . . . Similarly, he cut away all the nebulous Biblical allegory of the last part of *The Grapes of Wrath*—no Moses children floating dead down the flood, no symbolic breasts put into the mouths of a spiritually famished people; when his story was finished, he stopped.

Steinbeck knew Guthrie and recognized his genius:

> Harsh voiced and nasal, his guitar hanging like a tire iron on a rusty rim, there is nothing sweet about Woody, and there is nothing sweet about the songs he sings. But there is something more important for those who will listen. There is the will of a people to endure and fight against oppression. I think we call this the American spirit. . . .

Guthrie accomplished all this without much education. . . .

He wrote—a little prose with the songs; principally a million words of autobiography, reduced to book size by a desperate publisher who somehow retained the great happiness, oppression, faith, and hope of a man for his country which, like the book's title, was ***Bound for Glory.***

Woody never made much from his work. The Conservation Award was the best his government ever paid him. . . . His first government pay, swigged out to him for singing into a Library of Congress recorder all the songs he could remember, was "a pint of pretty cheap whiskey." His best pay was $266.66, paid to him by another wise man, Stephen B. Kahn of the Bonneville Power Administration, to idle around the Grand Coulee Dam and see whether anything would inspire him to write a song or two about the great project. The period of employment was one month, but this became the lambent zenith of his ten years as a poet. (p. 75)

It would be like asking a professor of English literature for his favorite sonnet to ask the few who know Guthrie well which of the twenty-six Bonneville songs is the best. I suppose I am most regularly moved by **"Pastures of Plenty,"** perhaps as much by his haunting melody and his singing as by the lyrics. . . .

If he could know about it, Woody would be less pleased by the Conservation Award than by the knowledge that his Bonneville songs have risen quietly to the position of standard patriotic songs in the Pacific Northwest, especially popular with children. Woody always loved children. His series, **"Songs to Grow On"** . . . , takes a full advantage of the average child's delight in blunt expression. . . . (p. 76)

Others have been influenced by him, some shamefully. Bobby Dylan, the idol of the unlaved student Existentialists, never knew Guthrie when his mind was whole but imitated the incoherent, rambling, pseudo-mystical lines of Guthrie's last letters on the edge of his insanity. Somehow Dylan has convinced a few avant garde critics that on the basis of these synthetic effusions he is America's most promising young poet.

It is time to speak of the disease that puts Guthrie in the past tense even in the Award's citation: Huntington's Chorea, rigorously hereditary, quite incurable, and worse than death. . . . In his ***Bound for Glory*** Woody described in almost clinical accuracy the disease he inherited but whose name he did not know—in his mother, flopping around the floor like a dying fish, arms windmilling, face hideous, voice snarling bestially. (p. 77)

When the identifiable cultural elements in Woody Guthrie's song have been identified—where and from whom he learned his instrumental and singing style; the bodies of traditional song that inspired him and from which he continually drew ideas and melodies; his experiences as a bum, tramp, and hobo, as a seaman, sign painter, merchant mariner, bus boy, and spittoon cleaner; the people he met, singers and listeners—when all of these things have been considered, there is still a hard nucleus of uniqueness in his compositions whose origin must of necessity be in his organism. (pp. 77-8)

Guthrie no longer writes or reads or sings or speaks. . . .

He once sang against every social injustice he had a sight or a sound of. . . . Once he had the soft words of women caressing him. . . . It would be better for a man who so loved the big sky and the big country, the unspoiled . . . to be able to scoop out his grave in the sand, to have a friend cut his hair for the meeting with death, and then to pass away in dignity deep in the land he enriched by his songs. (p. 78)

John Greenway, "Woody Guthrie: The Man, the Land, the Understanding," in The American West, *Vol. III, No. 4, Fall, 1966, pp. 24-30, 74-8.*

ELLEN J. STEKERT

For years the written work of Woody Guthrie has been vastly overrated both by men of letters, who should know better, and by folk singers and political apologists, who often have no concept of what literature is. Now we have another addition to the long, sprawling list of Guthrieana, ***Born to Win,*** and with this new book comes additional published evidence that Guthrie, far from being the "major American literary figure" . . . [editor Robert Shelton] claims he is, actually produced little of literary worth. If anything, Guthrie's works have value only as socio-historical documents. (pp. 274-75)

Literarily, the book is a shoddy conglomeration of rambling, repetitious, often incoherent, and incredibly poor prose and poetry. It is written by a man desperately struggling to find some value in himself and his life. . . .

As a human being, Woody Guthrie might be, and might have been, a compelling presence, but one should not confuse judgment of a man's work with feeling for him as a personality. Ironically, the importance of Guthrie as a reflection of the social and political upheaval of his day has been largely overlooked by those who form his cult. (p. 275)

Guthrie speaks to us in ***Born to Win*** with occasional gusto and bravado, but most often he is the child-adult unable to cope with the ambiguities of the world about him, looking for the one word . . . or the one political ideology to save him. We can see in him the politically oriented Joe Hill of the early 1900's and the obsessively introspective Bob Dylan of the 1960's. And as with the songs of both Dylan and Hill, Guthrie's works mean little when divorced from the social or personal chips he carried on his shoulder. Very occasionally he is moving and biting . . . , but he is clearly not a great literary figure. Rather, Woody Guthrie is an interesting personification of the bridge which spans the abyss of World War II, from the ages of politically clear black-and-white issues to the present tortured and incoherent age of equivocacy.

How much Guthrie's work will influence oral tradition in the cities or the country, only time will tell. Probably, because of the cult that has grown about him, he will continue to have considerable importance. . . . What we have in Woody Guthrie's writing, and in ***Born to Win,*** is the document of a period and a personality. Woody has been an inspiration to many young folk singers in the cities—all the more reason to read ***Born to Win*** for the irony of its boredom. (pp. 275-76)

Ellen J. Stekert, in a review of "Born to Win," in Western Folklore, *Vol. XXV, No. 4, October, 1966, pp. 274-76.*

RICHARD GILMAN

[***Bound for Glory***] not only holds up as a personal document that can rank among the more unpretentious and engaging we possess, it also provides a sense of America during the vanished and vanishing generations immediately preceeding our own, a sense of national style, behavior, aspirations and stresses that is most valuable to know about. Considerably better than even the superior proletarian literature of the period, certainly better than most of the retrospective glances we have been getting from old-time radicals, the book emerges from the era shaped with its accents and colors and, perhaps most important, its naïvetés so different from our own.

Quite unlike most of our current folk singers, Guthrie was from the land, was the possessor of his own unborrowed language, knew poverty like his own skin and protested against nothing about which he hadn't intimate knowledge. . . . He was moved by a combination of moral outrage, high natural spirits, ingenuousness and the kind of patriotism native to American populist radicals—***This Land is Your Land***—a love of country anchored in a not yet undermined belief in American possibilities of brotherhood and justice.

Bound for Glory is very far from being confessional literature; its easy-going conversational manner, the spinning of a yarn rather than the construction of a moral or psychic drama, is the result of both Guthrie's own fairly simple nature and the era's prevailing style, and so the book makes its appeal to what remains in us of such simplicity and what remains of our desire to know about a time when America could still tell stories about itself without irony, disgust or despair. (p. 19)

Richard Gilman, "Autobiography of Woody Guthrie," in The New Republic, *Vol. 159, No. 14, October 5, 1968, pp. 19-21.*

PETE SEEGER

[Woody's] words show a fine sense of poetry, of reaching out for exactly the right word at exactly the right place. He used some fine time-tested tunes. The songs are honest; they say things that need to be said.

But above all else, Woody's songs show the genius of simplicity. Any damn fool can get complicated, but it takes genius to attain simplicity. Some of his greatest songs are so deceptively simple that your eye will pass right over them and you will comment to yourself, "Well, I guess this was one of his lesser efforts." Years later you will find the song has grown on you and become part of your life. . . .

Woody was a great poet; as a prose writer too, I think him a genius. He wasn't pretending to be anybody else—he was just himself. He learnt from everybody, and from everything. He learnt from the King James Bible; he learnt from the left-wing newspapers and publications; he had a devouring curiosity. I'll never forget the week he discovered Rabelais, and read through a two-inch-thick volume in a couple of days. During the following weeks I could see him experimenting with some of the techniques of style that Rabelais used, such as paragraphs full of images, adjective after adjective getting more fantastic.

Woody was highly selective and knew when he disapproved of something. He once wrote, for instance, "I must remember to steer clear of Walt Whitman's swimmy waters." Perhaps he disapproved of Whitman's unrhymed, unmetered free verse. But then, Woody himself always stuck to traditional rhymed quatrains. I think, rather, he suspected that he himself, like Whitman, had a weakness for undisciplined rambling-on and wanted to control it. (p. 32)

Woody always claimed that he could not theorize, that he couldn't keep up with us and our book-learning. He'd bow out of an argument rather than get tangled up in four-syllable words. He had outspoken contempt for mere cleverness. A joke was fine, a pun, a gag—he put plenty of humor into his songs. But humor was not enough by itself. There had to be some solid meat there. So in some of his most humorous songs, like **"Talking Dustbowl,"** there's an undertone of bitter reality. . . .

Woody was not averse to having his songs sung on the hit parade, but to my knowledge he never wrote a song with the hit parade in mind. He considered most commercial music men as slick people who foisted their own idea of music upon the country. He thought of them the way an Oklahoma farmer thought of Wall Street bankers. So Woody put out of his head the idea of making a lot of money from his songs. He'd write and sing them himself, and mimeograph copies for friends from time to time, and trust that if he put together a song which hit the spot, people would take it up as their own.

Since he frankly agreed that he couldn't tell which of his songs would be good and which would be soon forgotten, he adopted a kind of "scatteration" technique—that is, he'd write a lot of songs, on the theory that at least some of them would be good. For example, as a "research consultant" for the Bonneville Power Authority he wrote several dozen songs. Nearly all of them have some special charm. But it was one, **"Roll On, Columbia,"** which seems destined to last for generations. . . .

I learned so many different things from Woody that I can hardly count them. His ability to identify with the ordinary man and woman, speak their own language without using the fancy words, and never be afraid—no matter where you were: just diving into some situation, trying it out. When he and I used to go around singing together, we hit all kinds of places: CIO unions, churches, saloons, meetings, parties.

I learned from him how just plain orneriness has a kind of wonderful honesty to it that is unbeatable: he was going to cuss, he was going to speak bad language, he was going to shock people, but he was going to stay the way he was. He wasn't going to let New York make him slick and sleek and contented. He was going to stay a rebel to the end. . . .

But Lord, Lord, he turned out song after song after song!

I have traveled around the country and around the world singing his songs and, although Woody was in a hospital for years before his death . . . , I always felt he was very much with me, very much alive. Woody is right beside me, strumming along. I know his songs will go on traveling around the world and will be translated into many languages during the coming century, and will be sung by many people who never heard his name.

What better kind of immortality could a man want? (p. 33)

Pete Seeger, "Woody Guthrie, Songwriter," in Ramparts, *Vol. 7, No. 8, November 30, 1968, pp. 29-33.*

HENRIETTA YURCHENCO

I first met Woody Guthrie one evening in 1940 at the studio of WNYC, New York City's radio station, where I was a producer of special music events. We had just finished a broadcast of folk songs from Kentucky. The telephones were ringing—people calling us from every part of the city, telling us what a good show it had been. (p. 9)

There was much hubbub in Studio D, guests and performers talking among themselves. Someone touched me on the shoulder. "See that little guy over there, in Levis and a plaid shirt, the one with the wiry-looking hair? That's Woody Guthrie." I looked around. I had heard about the Oklahoma singer, but had never met him.

"Ask him to sing ***Tom Joad***—it's a ballad he just finished. It's based on the *Grapes of Wrath.*" (Everybody in New York was talking about Steinbeck's novel and the movie Hollywood had made of it.)

I walked over to the thin little man and introduced myself. We exchanged a few words, and then I asked, "About that song you've just written: would you mind singing it for us?"

"Don't mind if I do." (pp. 9-10)

Woody sang the long ballad from beginning to end. The silence in the room deepened, and as he sang the sad tale of the dispossessed people of the Dust Bowl, we all knew that Woody was singing the truth, telling the story of his people exactly as it happened.

We also sensed that he had the quality of greatness. Henceforth he would speak not only for the people of Oklahoma and Texas, and for the migrant workers of the peach and grape fields of California, but for all of us who lived through those troubled times. (pp. 10-11)

The man who wrote ***This Land is Your Land*** and ***So Long, It's Been Good to Know You*** was the great balladeer of the American Depression. He told the unvarnished truth exactly as he saw and experienced it in his wanderings along the highways and byways of the nation. Woody Guthrie, born in the small town of Okemah, Oklahoma, was the unofficial chronicler of his generation. The legacy he left was not an academic history, but a human document made up of a thousand songs and a large body of writings of every kind.

Woody was the poet of his people, just as Robert Burns of Scotland and Federico Garcia Lorca of Spain were of theirs. Like them and like countless epic poets and medieval minstrels, he created works that are universal and will be remembered long after the events and issues that inspired them have been forgotten. Like them, he sang the old songs of his people, revamped them to fit the times, and infused them with new life. He was an authentic American genius, a common man with uncommon gifts. In his songs and writings he combined country wit, pioneer traditions, and colorful and unhackneyed country language with a skilled writer's art. He represents, better than anyone else, the human unity of rural and urban America. (p. 11)

A generation has passed since Woody sang his first songs. We are again at war; there is poverty in the midst of plenty, and hate among our people where love should be. Again, as in Guthrie's time, society is in ferment. Again, the conscience of youth has been stirred to action, as young people become aware of the threat to the individual in the facelessness of our mechanized world.

In a recent letter to the Guthrie Children's Trust Fund a young admirer of Woody and his son Arlo wrote:

> I am sixteen years old, and I don't really dig the older generation. All I can say is if there were more people like Woody still alive I don't think there would be anything like the "generation gap." I envy anyone who was a friend of Woody's and I really wished I'd known him. He's changed my whole idea of music and opened my eyes. Thank God our generation has Arlo. Yours truly. M. S.

So long Woody—it's been good to know you. . . . (pp. 13-14)

Henrietta Yurchenco, in a foreword to A Mighty Hard Road: The Woody Guthrie Story *by Henrietta Yurchenco with Marjorie Guthrie, McGraw-Hill Book Company, 1970, pp. 9-14.*

RICHARD A. REUSS

[The essay from which this excerpt is taken is a revised version of a paper read at the annual meeting of the American Folklore Society in Boston in 1966.]

Guthrie's importance to the folklorist lies not in his negligible contribution to oral tradition but in his role as spokesman for various folk or folklike groups. His ability to communicate the life, feelings, attitudes, and culture of his people from the inside—using their terms, concepts, and modes of expression rather than those of elite American society—renders him worthy of the attention of the folklorist. In other words, Guthrie was a unique distillation of the cultural experiences of several groups possessing folk elements, at once a mirror in which they saw themselves and their most articulate and able chronicler. (pp. 274-75)

In summing up Guthrie's formative years and the environment that molded the directions his talents would take him, it may be said that the cultural milieus of the Oklahoma and Texas periods accomplished different functions. The Okemah years were essentially a time of passive absorption, not just in terms of repertory, but of style, form, and idiomatic expression. The Texas years, on the other hand, saw the crystallization of Guthrie the performer, as he was generally to be in his best years. As a writer Woody did not reach creative maturity until 1940, but as a performer the only significant element missing by the time he left the Texas Panhandle was his radical commitment, which he acquired on the West Coast in 1938 and 1939.

In March 1937 Woody hoboed to California. . . . Woody witnessed the Okie exodus as it passed through the Texas Panhandle, chiefly over Highway 66, and also made several trips around the Southwest by himself in hobo style before migrating to California. It was in this latter state, however, that his contacts with both Okie and hobo groups were sustained to the point that he actually became a temporary member of each. . . . In the few years that the Okie community existed as a discernible entity in California (having been absorbed by the war industries during World War II), it produced lore born of its traumatic life to supplement the older materials brought along in the trek west. Traditional forms of folksong and folk expression were retained, but lyric and prose content frequently were altered to reflect contemporary experience. . . . Woody Guthrie was in no way a stranger to this milieu, and his talents made him by far the greatest spokesman produced by the Okie migrant community. (pp. 277-78)

In the long run, however, he probably spent more calendar time with hoboes, tramps, and bums than with displaced Okies. But there can be no doubt which of the two groups is more important insofar as his overall creative work is concerned. His Dust Bowl ballads, the rambling lyrics like **"Hard Traveling," "This Land Is Your Land,"** and **"Rambling Round,"** and the triumphant Columbia River songs all stem principally from his migrant experiences. By contrast, only his great ballad **"East Texas Red,"** part of four chapters of ***Bound for Glory***—nos. 1, 13, 14, and 18—and a few other incidental writings directly reflect his contacts with the hobo world.

The last important subculture for which Woody acted as spokesman was chiefly distinguished from the other groups by its ideology—the labor-radical syndrome created by the militant rise of the CIO and the communist movement during the depression of the 1930s. (p. 278)

Not every left-winger took to Woody or his idiom, then or later, but enough who did were so imbued with the spirit of proletarian romanticism that a natural tendency developed to drape Woody in the venerable garb of the Noble Savage stereotype. He was quickly idealized as a "rusty-voiced Homer" and "the best folk ballad composer whose identity has ever been known." He became a radical prototype of the democratic and enlightened white "folk," much as Leadbelly and Josh White were left-wing symbols of the Negro "folk" during the same period. . . . The Left's romantic vision of Guthrie also flourished in the communist press of those years. . . . No one, however, ever contributed to building Guthrie's image with more exuberance and gusto than Mike Quin, popular columnist for the *People's World*. On one occasion he wound up an extravagant review praising Guthrie's appearance on CBS radio's "Pursuit of Happiness" in a state of lyric euphoria. "Sing it Woody, sing it!" he exhorted. "Karl Marx wrote it and Lincoln said it and Lenin did it. You sing it, Woody. And we'll all laugh together yet."

Such simplistic characterization of the vagabond people's minstrel was, of course, an illusion. Friends and close associates realized that Guthrie was a far more complex personality than the image projected by the mass media would suggest. Yet, encounters with Woody's erratic behavior and unorthodox utterances often proved disquieting to many leftists. . . . For many, indeed, the Noble Savage image was less threatening. The stereotype of the Dust Bowl troubadour gave way to a more urbane representation in the left-wing press as the 1940s progressed, but as a whole the Left was never really able to fathom Woody Guthrie nor seriously wanted to try to do so. (pp. 278-81)

[However], it was the communist-dominated labor-radical atmosphere that provided Woody with the spiritual nourishment and *raison d'être* he needed to produce his best work. For nearly a decade prior to his initial contacts with urban radicals, Guthrie had sought a rationale for his existence. . . . It was the radical social gospel of the New Deal era that finally filled his spiritual void and elevated his hillbilly versification to quite another plane of social commentary, where he spoke for the national traumas and triumphs as well as for regional conditions. One may plausibly argue that Guthrie's communism was politically naive and humane, in large measure rooted in frontier agrarian radicalism rather than in Marx or the Party line; but only sheer bias and anticommunist fervor will permit the critical observer to deny the emotional solace, social direction, and organic synthesis the Left gave to Guthrie's work in the days when both the Movement and he were dynamic and young.

The years 1939-1941 were a transitional period in Woody's life, as he continued to move easily in and out of his earlier southwestern, hobo, and Dust Bowl environments; but he gradually forsook all of them for the urban left-wing milieu in which he largely functioned thereafter to the end of his active career. It probably would be accurate to say that the first significant break with his earlier environments came in February 1940, when he made his first trip to and prolonged stay in New York. . . . By the fall of 1941, when Woody settled in New York more or less permanently, the separation from his earlier folk milieu was complete. ***Bound for Glory*** and occasional songs like **"East Texas Red"**—drawn from his life in the southwestern, hobo, and migrant folk complexes—continued to come from his pen in the next year or so; but from the time he entered the merchant marine in 1943, the great mass of his voluminous writings, personal reminiscences, and songs ceased in most instances to reflect his former traditional environments.

It would be hard to underestimate the importance of these transition years for Woody Guthrie, for in them he produced the bulk of his greatest work: most of the Dust Bowl ballads, all of the Columbia River songs, the long ballads **"Pretty Boy Floyd," "East Texas Red,"** and **"Tom Joad,"** the lyric songs **"This Land Is Your Land"** and **"Hard Traveling,"** most of his best labor and war verse, ***Bound for Glory,*** and several of his finest essays. All were written between 1939 and 1942. This material is a creative fusion of Guthrie's folk heritage with a left-wing social consciousness. The rural Southwest of Woody's youth gave him an instinctive knowledge of ballad structure, folksong style, and the folk idiom. Migrant and hobo wanderings of his early manhood provided crucial themes for his pen, drawn from first-hand observations, to mold into verse and prose. Contacts with Communists and other radicals sharpened and focused an innate sense of social concern developed out of the experiences of his early life. His own artistic abilities enabled him to weld these diverse strands into a unique synthesis of folk-styled poetry and social gospel. (pp. 281-82)

The folk tradition Woody Guthrie inherited from the Southwest is usually evaluated in terms of the songs he acquired there, but it should be noted that Guthrie's folk repertory was by no means limited to songs alone. He knew large numbers of anecdotes, jokes, toasts, proverbial phrases, and witty sayings, which he effectively utilized in his varied roles as raconteur, soothsayer, humorist, and writer. Many of these were clearly traditional; others might prove to be so with a little investigation. His language, for example, was studded with colorful neologisms and idiomatic expressions. . . . Apparently no one made any effort to collect these, or his yarns and other witticisms; and such as are extant must be culled from his writings and the memories of friends. A more detailed record, however, does exist for the traditional songs in his memory. (pp. 282-83)

It is largely through surviving manuscript collections kept by Guthrie himself, and the fortuitous actions of Alan Lomax, that there is any clear delineation of Woody Guthrie's "pre-revival" folksong repertory. Lomax recorded Guthrie for the Library of Congress scarcely a month after the latter arrived in the East in 1940, and before Woody had much chance to absorb new material from other singers. Lomax, however, was not interested in the hillbilly songs that comprised a significant portion of Guthrie's repertory; hence there is little trace of such material in the Archive of American Folk Song recordings. Far more significant than these recordings was a manuscript collection [entitled **"Songs of Woody Guthrie,"** which] Lomax procured from Woody shortly thereafter and had copied for the Library of Congress. . . . This collection contains texts of two hundred songs Woody sang over the radio in California to his Okie and political audiences on the West Coast. A breakdown shows half of the songs to be of Guthrie's own authorship, the rest being divided roughly into 60 percent folksongs and 40 percent hillbilly items, parlor ballads, or sentimental religious pieces. . . . Such songs largely disappeared from Guthrie's public repertory after his removal to New York. (pp. 283-84)

Though Woody wrote many lyric songs in folk style, it is in his ballad and balladlike compositions that his profound comprehension of the folksong idiom is most evident. He was exposed to the ballad form from his earliest days as a child, principally through his mother but also through other relatives and members of the community at large. The techniques of balladmaking were thoroughly mastered, as becomes abundantly clear when one turns to Guthrie's own creations. His narrative songs focus on local episodes, sometimes wholly isolated events, and in other instances parts of larger dramas. Like other traditional songmakers, Woody concentrated on portraying social interaction in human terms, even when the point he wanted to make was economic or political. The **"1913 Massacre,"** for instance, ends with the class-conscious line "See what your greed for money has done," addressed to the copper-mine owners whose thugs provoked a tragedy costing the lives of over seventy miners' children. The plot, however, is couched in personal terms of human drama rather than labor statistics.

Character descriptions and plot development in Woody's ballads begin and end abruptly, are terse and pithy, and on the whole give only information essential to the theme. Greenway, for example, has recently discussed how Guthrie effectively pared down the sprawling narrative of *The Grapes of Wrath* to eighteen stark verses, eliminating or reducing to a few words unnecessary or peripheral details, leaving only what was truly pertinent to the story and its moral [see excerpt above]. . . . Such traditional condensation and contrast techniques have their appeal for literary critics. But not all of Woody's creative efforts are satisfying in terms of art esthetics. A good example is his retelling of the charge of the Light Brigade. . . . What is instructive about this text is its use of an incident from the Crimean War, totally removed from the American context, reshaped as grist for a balladmaker's art. Like "Brave Wolfe" and so many other war ballads, the battle serves as a backdrop for a close-up focus on a love affair, the song's emotional core. And, in spite of the stilted language, there is scarcely any wasted statement; each scene is described in terse, parsimonious style, conveying maximum information with a minimum of narrative. The action moves quickly in a series of vignettes from an initial overview and the captain's doubts about the charge to the forgery by the young soldier, his farewell and promise to his sweetheart, and the tragic aftermath. The lyrics are replete with cliché and formulaic patterning . . . of Guthrie's making or borrowed from others. But the general tone is matter-of-fact, even understated, rather than maudlin, and thus is an improvement over the sticky sentimentality of much Anglo-American broadside balladry. Though the lyrics are not among Guthrie's most memorable, they illustrate full well how much at home he was in the ballad idiom.

One must understand that Woody composed primarily from a folk rather than a literary point of view. Two different esthetics are involved, and judgments made from one perspective are not necessarily valid for the other. Woody's implicit concern in composing ballads and lyrics was to construct an effective emotional core. As [Tristram P. Coffin has stressed in his essay "Mary Hamilton and the Anglo-American Ballad As an Art Form"], the emotional core is of fundamental importance to the traditional singer and his audience, superseding all other poetic considerations. Such Guthrie ballads as **"Philadelphia Lawyer," "Pretty Boy Floyd," "1913 Massacre," "East Texas Red,"** and **"Tom Joad"** vary considerably in subject matter, mood, and minor stylistic devices; but all accentuate an emotional core rather than tight literary construction. This, it seems to me, accounts for the success of Guthrie's best compositions, even when they are deficient in terms of structure, rhyme, or other formal poetic attributes. (pp. 285-87)

From a traditional point of view the theme, vernacular, and structure of **"Pretty Boy Floyd"** are tried and proven. The "good outlaw" has had wide folk appeal in America, and in this ballad Guthrie does no more than state the prejudices of many of his fellow Oklahomans about Floyd. Strict adherence to rhyme frequently has been disregarded by ballad singers and composers. Phrases such as "He took to the trees and timber to live a life of shame" may scarcely challenge Shakespeare's rhetoric, but they remain culturally accurate statements in terms of the local world view, concise and vivid in their imagery in spite of their stereotyped character. With such lines Guthrie skillfully builds sympathy for Floyd and develops the emotional core of his song. (p. 287)

Looking at Woody's patterns of creativity as folk-oriented rather than literary-oriented, we shed light on various historical problems connected with his artistic production, such as his seeming inability to edit his own work beyond an occasional deletion or scribbled insertion. Contrary to the popular belief that Guthrie never rewrote anything, there are multiple drafts of many of his best-known songs, among them **"This Land," "Union Maid," "Pretty Boy Floyd,"** and **"I Ain't Got No Home in This World Anymore,"** as well as of a small percentage of his reams of prose. Intervals of months or years, however, frequently separate many of these drafts, which commonly show substantial textual alterations. Yet, the changes were made not as part of a process of careful polishing and repolishing in the manner of a "literary" author, but as an outgrowth of an innate and probably unconscious attitude on Woody's part about the nature of the creative experience, strongly ingrained in him by his early folk environment. (p. 288)

To Woody, each draft or performance of a song was a new creative experience rather than the revision of an old one, even though the same themes, phrases, and structural assumptions might be used in each case. Similarly, the creative act in constructing an essay or a poem was initially typing his ideas on paper, not in refining and editing his work to meet literary and publishing standards. . . . When Guthrie devoted his energies to extended works such as books, the length of the creative experience, of course, would be longer. Moreover, he tended to write batches of songs in a short period around a single theme, for instance his Columbia River songs and Peekskill songs. These might properly be viewed as falling within the purview of one creative experience.

Thus, if an original song draft were not immediately at hand, or if for some reason it proved unsatisfactory, Woody would undertake to reconstruct the song, tinkering freely and often more or less unconsciously with lyrics, ideas, and stanzas. The changes might be drastic or minimal, artistically pleasing or debilitating, but the process of textual alteration followed the tradition of Anglo-American folksong re-creation rather than the editing patterns characteristic of "high culture." The same creative process was involved when Guthrie wrote prose or nonmusical verse, and this explains the otherwise puzzling phenomenon of two early drafts of ***Bound for Glory.*** These were written within a year and a half of each other and cover the period of his youth, including many of the same incidents; yet they are essentially two different books-in-the-making and represent two separate creative acts. . . . Rather than locate and revise an old manuscript, it seems to have been much simpler and appropriate for Woody to create a new one.

Two other factors must be taken into account in any overall evaluation of Guthrie's work: performance context and function. Woody's lyrics, in most cases, were written as songs, to be sung and performed in a dynamic atmosphere. Reduced to two dimensions on the printed page, they frequently suffer as do many famous traditional songs. The *New Masses* once recognized as much when it rejected several poems submitted by Guthrie on the grounds that the words lacked music and did not stand satisfactorily by themselves. Such accouterments as voice inflection, added emphasis on the bass strings of the guitar to underscore certain phrases, gestures and facial expressions, and the mood and the interaction of the singer and his audience are all a part of the total song experience and need to be assessed if a complete picture of the balladeer's musical creations is to be obtained. . . . Similarly, one must make allowance for historical setting and function. The Dust Bowl ballads are best understood and appreciated in the context of the 1930s. (pp. 288-89)

This is not to suggest that Guthrie's work should not be analyzed and evaluated from a literary perspective, only that such a perspective is severely limited if one wishes to understand the full implications of the creative artistry of Woody Guthrie or any other traditional singer or writer. It will be the task of some future writer to assess Guthrie's artistic production, balance the good and bad, and draw whatever conclusions seem appropriate. (p. 289)

In Guthrie's earliest prose, . . . he attempted to reproduce phonetically the laconic observations, humor, and advice he dispensed as a radio performer. More or less typical is this excerpt from his *People's World* "AWTOBYOGRAFIE": "I got what you wood call disgusted, busted. I rooled me up a bundel of duds, an' caught a long, tall frate-train thet had a California sign on the side of it. I got down in a refrigrater—"reefer"—somewhere in the dustbowl, an the first daylight I seen, it said California 121314151 feet below sea level." Such immature stabs at imitating vernacular speech are obviously contrived and painfully folksy. Unfortunately, they permeate the majority of his writings in the left-wing California press and sometimes his later columns for the *Daily Worker*. While they were very well received, their success was due nonetheless, to their humorous quips and political content as much as to their pseudo-folk literary style. Once Guthrie dropped his more eccentric ventures into phonetic spelling and literal expression, . . . his writing matured noticeably and in due time led to his best prose efforts: ***Bound for Glory,*** the essays in ***American Folksong,*** "Ear Players," "Child Sitting," and a number of other noteworthy pieces.

At the other extreme from most of his early California writings, and on the whole equally unsuccessful artistically, are his efforts at expressing idiomatic speech in free verse and formal poetic styles, such as are found in [***Born to Win***]. . . . Here Guthrie's lack of adequate training in literature and creative writing may have hurt him, for he was not equipped by his education and background to write in certain urban art forms. But these pieces at least indicate he was aware enough of non-traditional poetic forms to consciously experiment with them. In sum, Woody's writing style was largely the result of a deliberate exploitation of his folk heritage and the language idiom it employed. This conscious utilization of his own tradition in his writing was paralleled in certain respects in his role as entertainer. (pp. 292-93)

[Guthrie] was able to assert his individuality as a performer as he became better known. After 1940 he was seldom regarded simply as a hick comedian or a migrant minstrel; the intensity of his social commitment left little room for roles based principally on levity and primitive nostalgia. Perhaps of greatest importance was the fact that Woody had found an intellectual climate within one segment of the Left where he was accepted essentially on his own terms. . . . [This] in turn gave rise to the final, most lasting, and insofar as he was concerned, most acceptable role assigned to Guthrie during his active career, that of "people's artist." (p. 295)

The term "people's artist" as developed in the 1940s was widely applied to others besides Woody, and the role he was expected to fill—producing "worker's" or "people's" art, especially music—was sufficiently broad and compatible with Guthrie's own values to be readily acceptable to him. As before, Woody contributed on his own to the identification of himself with his role, but this time his enthusiasm for the role remained undiluted. The affixing of an ego-satisfying label to his name scarcely guaranteed Guthrie instantaneous creative success; however, regardless of esthetic considerations, the conscious assumption of the "people's artist" wreath was an honest intellectual decision, entirely consistent with his political and social beliefs.

The topical music produced by left-wing artists of the 1940s, while heavily folk-oriented, varied considerably in form and style, ranging from material closely approximating folk tradition to that emphasizing jazz, "pop," and even classical elements. But Guthrie proved quite conservative in his musical preferences—far more so than in his literary experiments—and deliberately composed within the framework of the American southern folk music tradition he was most familiar with. While he could identify easily with folksongs from cultures other than his own, for example his wife Marjorie's Yiddish music heritage, he disliked artists who violated the natural limits of their own traditions. . . . He likewise scorned the pretentiousness and pseudofolksy affectations of a number of performers and writers. . . . He took an equally dim view of the synthetic "folk" affectations. . . . Not surprisingly, he felt most at home in New York with such musicians as Leadbelly, Sarah Ogan Gunning, Cisco Houston, Sonny Terry, and Brownie McGhee, who like himself possessed traditional roots yet felt no need to prove their "folkness." (pp. 295-96)

Woody Guthrie is frequently described as a "folk composer"; yet the accuracy of the description depends on the definition of the term. If this implies "a person with a traditional background who composes songs," the label is correct; but if by "folk composer" is meant an individual who created songs that have entered oral tradition, then Guthrie has no strong claim to the title, for none of his musical creations circulate orally within a folk community with evidence of textual and melodic variation. (p. 296)

When composing his own material, Guthrie most often would create new lyrics using the framework of an old song. Generally, this meant simply writing new words to a standard tune, for while Woody reworked melodies freely he seldom wrote music on his own; he borrowed virtually all of his musical repertory from folk and hillbilly sources, notably the recordings of the Carter Family. Sometimes, however, he would take over a textual theme and use it along with the tune as the basis for a new song. (pp. 300-01)

Besides reshaping traditional themes found in older songs, Woody drew on narratives having independent oral currency to create original ballads and songs. **"Death Valley Scotty,"** an early California composition, was based on prospector tales, popular gossip, and newspaper accounts about Walter E. Scott, semi-legendary miner who parlayed public curiosity about mysterious periodic "discoveries" into a thirty-year fortune of publicity rather than gold. **"East Texas Red"** was prompted by stories told by hoboes in the Texas Gulf area about a notorious railroad "bull," whose real existence has not been clearly determined. The Dust Bowl songs were based partly on the accounts of others as well as on firsthand observations. And Pretty Boy Floyd, as suggested by Steinbeck through Ma Joad in *The Grapes of Wrath,* was very much a topic of interest to the folk mind in the Southwest. (pp. 301-02)

In later years, Guthrie drew increasingly on mass media rather than traditional narratives for themes in his work. Many of his "newspaper ballads" were composed at the behest of Moses Asch, who provided Woody with historical and contemporary reading material as creative stimuli; other subjects for songs were suggested by the daily press. Some of his better-known musical creations of this period (1944-1950) are **"The 1913 Massacre," "Song of the Deportees," "Belle Starr," "The Dying Miner,"** and the Sacco-Vanzetti lyrics. Woody, however, produced little original material after the early 1940s that could be traced directly to oral tradition, and much more was not even based on firsthand experience. Guthrie's songs continued to be composed in folk style as his themes moved farther and farther from his old folk cultures. But many—including old radical friends and supporters—felt that his verse and prose lost some of their vitality when their contents no longer were rooted so firmly in tradition. (p. 302)

To his urban admirers Guthrie was as much a symbol of who the folk ought to be as of who the folk really were. The Left lionized him as a "People's Artist," intellectuals regarded him as a folk John Steinbeck and Walt Whitman, while a few radicals saw him as the "communist Shakespeare in overalls." At first Guthrie hardly qualified for any of these labels. He was the product of an altogether different social tradition, with other patterns of creative artistry, esthetic values, and forms of cultural expression. Only gradually were these reshaped and modified to conform to urban values and the expectations of intellectual audiences, primarily radical in orientation, with whom Guthrie himself was in sympathy. This acculturative process in turn led to Woody's best-known work and his subsequent canonization by his contemporaries, and later by the folksong revival as well.

Guthrie belongs to folklorists as much as to any other group of scholars, since his whole life and creative work are bound up by tradition and by his experiences in folk culture. Yet folklorists have neglected Woody, perhaps because they have spent too little time evaluating the role of the individual carrier and creator of folklore within traditional society. Perhaps in the future the further study of Woody Guthrie may enable us to better comprehend the dynamics of folk tradition. (p. 303)

Richard A. Reuss, "Woody Guthrie and His Folk Tradition," in Journal of American Folklore, *Vol. 83, No. 329, July-September, 1970, pp. 273-303.*

R. SERGE DENISOFF

Woody Guthrie was the embodiment of the first [folk] revival which began with the now famous 1940 sharecroppers' benefit, MC'ed by Alan Lomax, and ended with blacklisting of the Weavers in 1952. Woody, as Will Geer's narration [on the album ***Woody's Story***] clearly illustrates, was both a rogue and a political man, more opportunist than revolutionary. Yet Woody was as close to the real folk as the artists and intellectuals in Los Angeles and Greenwich Village would ever get. . . . ***Woody's Story*** chronicles the pain and contradictions experienced by Guthrie: the tragedy of death and insanity which followed him as he rambled, and his very human obsession with booze and women. Yet from these difficulties and vices, a very real person with a love of humanity emerges in his songs. Some are bitter like **"Hard Traveling"** or **"Do Re Mi"** which tell of police harassment and the plight of the Okie and the Arkie in the 1930s. His other songs tell of the lifestyles of migrant workers, and his more ideologically inspired vision of a better world with One Big Union. These are tempered with patriotic songs such as **"Grand Coulee Dam"** and **"Reuben James."** What appears is a very life-like portrait of Woody Guthrie the man rather than "the legend" which has grown up over the years. (pp. 183-84)

Woody's Story is a fitting tribute to him. . . . (p. 184)

R. Serge Denisoff, in a review of "Woody's Story," in Popular Music & Society, *Vol. 2, No. 2, Winter, 1973, pp. 183-84.*

PAUL G. FEEHAN

Skimpier in content but similar in format to his ***Born To Win*** . . . , the balladeer's pieces [in ***Woody Sez*** are] rich in earthy wisdom, scorn bankers, warmongers, and corrupt politicians, and sing of laborers, hoboes, and "migratious workers." Not previously available in book form, this material sheds light mostly on Guthrie's secondary roles as pacifist, populist, and self-proclaimed Okie.

Paul G. Feehan, in a review of "Woody Sez," in Library Journal, *Vol. 100, No. 9, May 1, 1975, p. 855.*

JAMES DICKEY

[Woody Guthrie] is by far the most gifted of all the earth-poets, people-poets. His influence is felt, and always will be, in American folk music, no matter who plays or sings or listens to it. . . .

But it is not the "Hard Travellin'" of his life that makes Woody Guthrie the great human being that he was, and still is for us. That quality is within the man himself. This penniless wanderer from the dust bowl fairly leapt at life in a hundred directions. His two volumes of autobiography, **"Bound for Glory"** and the present book [**"Seeds of Man"**], are hilarious and life-giving documents. Within these pages there is something far beyond and far deeper than anything that the graduate schools of our or any nation could ever comprehend; there is something far more valuable than "executive form" or "precise control of metaphor." (p. 2)

"Seeds of Man" is a marvelous chronicle of the irrepressible, rambunctious, ornery fun of the poor. Woody is their laureate, wildly imaginative, . . . warm, devious, a little delightedly crazy, and glad to be so, loyal, frank, and the best spokesman in word and music that the American proletariat has ever had. If there is any virtue in being poor, in an exultant got-nothin'-to-lose way, it is in Woody Guthrie; it is in this magnificent, careless, go-for-broke book. . . .

"Seeds of Man" is about a journey that Guthrie, aged 19, his father and two relatives went on in the early 1930's to the Big Bend country of the Rio Grande in search of silver. . . . Everything and everybody that Woody and his kinsmen encounter along the route are recorded in Guthrie's hell-for-leather rhapsodies. One might say that he bogs down in his exuberant details, describing trucks, vittles, women, gas mileage, long-handle underwear, two-by-fours, blankets, and music ("This Deathly C"), but that doesn't matter.

Woody Guthrie does not hold back. He is prolix, but one wishes that his prolixity could go on forever. Walt Whitman believed and said that he had touched the heart of the land in its multifarious forms. "Who touches this book touches a man." This on Whitman's part is a literary bravery, and a bit of a boast. But I am glad that these words exist, for they serve to describe **"Seeds of Man."** (p. 3)

James Dickey, "Woody Guthrie: Who Touches This Touches a Man," in The New York Times Book Review, *October 3, 1976, pp. 2-3.*

EDWIN COHEN

We often become embroiled in Woody's politics, his Union activities, and make moral judgments of his life, losing sight of the real issue in evaluating the artist: the contribution of his works. . . . In the final analysis Woody's contribution must be evaluated by his songs, poems, ***Bound for Glory,*** and in relation to his effect on our culture. Any other criteria lead nowhere; instead, they frequently serve to advance the political or sociological theories espoused by the critic. (p. 11)

Mythmakers, in their attempt to popularize him, ignore his left-wing leanings and stylize his image as Paul Bunyan or a Sgt. York with a guitar. They present his relationship to the social problems of the thirties and forties in the guise of an optimistic faithhealer in song. The social polemicists ignore his positive perceptions of America and show only his denunciation of its inequities and injustices. Each makes a critically fatal mistake: one confuses the work of art with the man: the other confuses the work of art with the sociology or history that engendered it.

This is not to say that the man, his works, and the context in which he produced those works can be divorced and separated into neat little packages. Certainly he was a product of his times, of events, and of a tradition that preceded him. His works, too, came about because of influences both external and internal acting upon him. The events and personalities of the times were ephemeral, however, and we must judge his works on their ability to survive beyond the immediate causes. Many of his songs have lost their universal appeal. They have meaning only to a few survivors of a specific event, or because they are by a man who produced other, greater works. Some of his dust bowl ballads are now merely curiosity pieces and historical-biographical relics. On the other hand, a song such as **'Union Maid'** has transcended the narrow events that inspired it, becoming a song important not only to the Union movement, but also an authentic piece of American folk culture. The same is true of **'Reuben James,' 'So Long It's Been Good to Know You,' 'Pastures of Plenty,' 'Roll On Columbia,'** and **'This Land,'** to give but a partial list. (pp. 11-12)

[The American folksong] became virtually extinct in all but some of the more rural, backward areas of the country; or, it changed its form to accommodate some of the aspects of song previously reserved for the popular song; that is, it became a popular song with a folk feeling and folk sense. If we accept the first premise, then Woody Guthrie must be considered among the last folk singers. If we accept the second premise, which is the view preferred by this writer, then Woody, and his lesser-known contemporaries, are even more important as the transitional agents carrying the folksong from the parochial to the popular sphere of song. . . .

This then is Woody's greatest contribution to our tradition: he was the first identifiable folk composer to achieve national status and popularity. (p. 13)

[Woody's] ascendancy as a folk hero, however, is more than a simple accident of chronology. It was he who canonized themes, forms, and strategies, and influenced such later composers as Dylan, Paul Simon, Ochs and Paxton. Other composer-performers of his era dealt with the Depression, the dust bowl, the World War II, and yet they did not achieve the prominence and popularity that are Woody's. His songs possess a unique and lasting quality that set them apart from the others: Woody's style. His songs transcend the events and personalities that he wrote about. . . . Woody took the prosaic facts of sociology and through his songs translated them into poetry.

Of course, the most important test of his contribution to the tradition is yet to come. At this writing it is barely a decade since his death and approximately one generation since his peak of productivity. We are still too close to the man and the historical events to be able to judge them with complete objectivity. Whether he represented the end of the traditional folk artist, was the first of a new generation of folk artists, was simply a contributer to folk art, or was a combination of the three, as both popularizer and creative artist he left his mark on the American folksong, and through the critical span of only one generation, that mark appears to be indelible. (pp. 13-14)

Edwin Cohen, "Neither Hero nor Myth: Woody Guthrie's Contribution to Folk Art," in Folklore, *Vol. 91, No. 1, Spring, 1980, pp. 11-14.*

Frank (Patrick) Herbert

1920-

American novelist, short story writer, journalist, nonfiction writer, and editor.

A major science fiction writer, Herbert is best known for his *Dune* series, which has attracted a strong cult following. In this series, he constructs a complex fictional world whose inhabitants encounter various forms of religious, political, intellectual, and scientific intrigue. Herbert often alludes to historical facts to infuse his works with realism, and his themes usually parallel modern political and social issues. He is among the first science fiction writers to investigate the long-term effects of ecological abuse. His work as a journalist and editor informs the methodical style of his research. Herbert has apprenticed himself to various professionals to benefit from direct experience. He has also embarked on numerous secondary careers, including lay analyst and speechwriter, from which he draws his interests in psychology and politics.

Herbert's major themes involve the short-sighted nature of simplistic solutions to large problems and humanity's inability to foresee the results of change. He continually emphasizes the necessity to consider alternatives to every problem before making a choice. By focusing on humanity's potential for both evolutionary godhood and self-destruction through genetic or mental conditioning, Herbert explores the limitations of intellectual prescience and physical immortality. The notion of collective consciousness as a means to social harmony and telepathic intercommunication also appears throughout Herbert's fiction.

Photograph by Jay Kay Klein

In *Dune* (1965), a cowinner of the Hugo Award for best science fiction novel of the year, Herbert blends Middle Eastern, Oriental, and Christian philosophies with Jungian psychology to examine the positive and negative results of abrupt social change. The background and exposition of the novel directly reveal themes which recur in all of Herbert's work. Herbert's interest in ecological interdependence is revealed in the barren desert world of Arrakis and its warlike natives, the Fremen. The Fremen's existence is structured around tribal ritual and the reclamation of water, Arrakis's most precious commodity. Arrakis's major life forms are huge sandworms; through their biological cycle, these sandworms produce a spice called melange, which the Fremen value for its prescient and geriatric properties and as their only source of economic wealth. The ingestion of the spice allows beings to perceive the interrelatedness of events in time. The spice is important to the Fremen's religion, which holds that a messiah will eventually deliver them to victory over the universe's despotic emperor. Herbert's concern with genetic conditioning is expressed through the novel's hero, Paul, heir to the great house of Atreides. Paul is the product of centuries of secret genetic breeding by a religious matriarchy known as Bene Gesserit, who seek to create a superbeing with superior intuitive powers. The sisterhood's plans collide with the Fremen belief in a messiah when Paul's father is betrayed by the archrival house of Harkonnen and Paul is forced to flee into the Arrakeen desert. There he encounters a more potent form of the spice and advances to a state of near-omniscience, in which he can foresee time as a series of causes and effects and thus choose among various alternatives to shape the future. The spice also allows him to communicate with ancestors through his inherited genetic memory, giving him access to the plural wisdom of a collective consciousness. Through psychic control of the worms and spiritual control of the Fremen, Paul overcomes his Harkonnen enemies and assumes the position of emperor.

Herbert's thematic interests are explored in greater depth in the other novels of the *Dune* series. In *Dune Messiah* (1969), *Children of Dune* (1976), and *God Emperor of Dune* (1981), Herbert examines the consequences of a society's willingness to relinquish its destiny to the dictates of a messianic hero. Herbert has stated: "The bottom line in the *Dune* [series] is: beware of heroes. [It is] much better to rely on your own judgments and your own mistakes." In *Dune Messiah,* Paul's ecological plan to transform Arrakis into a green, water-rich planet proves to be shortsighted when it is discovered that water is poisonous to the worms. Herbert's fascination with ecology culminates in *Children of Dune,* when Paul's son, Leto, encases his body in the "sandtrout" which are the worms in their larval stage of development. By the time during which *God Emperor of Dune* takes place, all worms save Leto are extinct. Leto's worm body dissolves into the sandtrout; thus, by sacrificing his humanity and his life, he renews the species' cycle and preserves their ecological niche.

All of Herbert's novels elaborate on themes introduced in the *Dune* series. In *Destination: Void* (1966), secret conditioning is of primary concern as a mission control center forces a ship's inhabitants, at the risk of death, to create an artificial intelligence in the ship's computer. After the computer is ordered to self-destruct and is forced to contemplate its own existence and immortality, it imposes its will upon the shipmates. Together with its sequels, *The Jesus Incident* (1979) and *The Lazarus Effect* (1983), *Destination: Void* explores the limitations of simplistic solutions to problems. *The White Plague* (1984), while not representative of Herbert's work in general, directly addresses his moral themes while commenting upon contemporary issues. This novel relates a molecular biologist's gradual schizophrenia following the loss of his wife and children in an IRA bombing in London. He creates a plague that kills only women as a means of revenge against all countries involved in terrorism. Both terrorism and revenge are revealed to be short-term solutions to multidimensional problems. In *The White Plague*, as in all his fiction, Herbert questions the validity of any pat or all-encompassing answers.

(See also *CLC*, Vols. 12, 23; *Contemporary Authors*, Vols. 53-56; *Contemporary Authors New Revision Series*, Vol. 5; *Something about the Author*, Vol. 9; and *Dictionary of Literary Biography*, Vol. 8.)

DAVID M. MILLER

[The] novels of Frank Herbert form a remarkably unified treatment of two complementary problems: 1.) If man does not achieve a balance within himself and with his environment, existence is merely a version of chaos. 2.) If man freezes an achieved balance, decadence sets in and life yields to entropy. Thus the problems to be solved by Herbert's characters require that chaos be organized and stasis disturbed. The desideratum is dynamic homeostasis.

Homeostasis is the tendency of an organism to maintain a uniform and beneficial physiological stability within and between its parts. If we extend this definition to include not only biological organisms but also psychological, social, economic, political, religious, and ecological units, and if we subject that expanded homeostasis to a universal evolutionary imperative, we have a nutshell version of Herbert's themes.

But themes do not make fiction until they are given form: articulated in action, embodied in characters, set in space and time, and allowed to validate themselves in the reader's perceptions. The range of forms into which Herbert shapes his dominant themes is broad: the organism to be balanced (or disturbed) ranges from a four-man submarine to the entire universe; contending forces may be embodied in a small boy and a crazy Indian or they may inform the pan-sentient population of the cosmos; interest-devices range from lab-report vampire-gauges to sentient stars; plots are sometimes simple, sometimes complex, and sometimes merely complicated; characters may be as wooden as Harvey Durant, the "father" in ***The Eyes of Heisenberg,*** or as empathically rounded as Duke Leto, the father in ***Dune***; sometimes we see the action from the plotters' perspective (***Dune Messiah***), sometimes from the perspective of the plotted-against (***The Heaven Makers***). Herbert's modal range is also wide: ***Under Pressure*** is extrapolated realism; ***Whipping Star*** is a playful nightmare fantasy. ***Soul Catcher*** is neither science fiction nor fantasy; ***Dune*** is both. Many novels have a strong odor of detective fiction (***Under Pressure, The Santaroga Barrier, Hellstrom's Hive***). The ***Dune*** trilogy has strong affinities with sword-and-sorcery fiction.

The relationship between Herbert's pervasive double theme and the form in which that theme is set forth also varies. Sometimes the problem seems to be an excuse for action, adventure, and suspense. Sometimes the tale exists to articulate the problem. Books of the first kind may be called *entertainments;* books of the second kind may be called *essays*. Entertainments depend upon substitutions within well-established formulae. Essays depend upon variations upon generally understood models. A good book, not to mention a great book, must be both, for authors ought still to be in the business of delighting and instructing. When the entertainment sketches a new formula, when the essay invents a new model, the result is no longer "popular" fiction, although such books are frequently very popular indeed if they succeed in establishing the revised formula and stretched model as a new standard. Herbert has achieved such revision and stretching only once (so far).

Dune is, by almost any standard except perhaps that of deconstructionist fiction, a remarkable book. The essay that Herbert seems driven to write and rewrite is, in ***Dune,*** marvelously iterated, embodied in each link of a chain of being, reaching from the cell to the universe. The entertainment weaves the formulae of fantasy and science fiction with quest, ritual, maturation novel, melodrama, and tragedy. Perhaps the most remarkable aspect of ***Dune*** is the concrete plenitude of Arrakis, the desert planet. It has become a critical platitude of speculative fiction that strange characters having strange adventures in strange places is at least one too many stranges. In ***Dune,*** Herbert's ability to create a "real" fictional world through copious representative detail, analogies to our primary world, and through the use of patterns drawn from the "reality" of our other fictional worlds provides firm grounding for even so unnatural a creature as a sandworm. And the world of the Fremen is as tangible and tactile as the exotic lands we met as children in old copies of *National Geographic*. Without elevating a coincidence to causative status, the careful reader may note that there appears to be a correlation between the fullness with which Herbert renders his fictional world and the quality of his fiction. (pp. 9-10)

Under Pressure, the first of Herbert's published novels, is the mildest of science fiction: there are no space ships, no bug-eyed-monsters, no buzz words, no travels through time, no aliens, and the occasional blackboxes are limited to plausible extensions of current technology.

The action is set in the near future, after an atomic war has left the world divided into armed and tactically warring camps. The enemy is threatening, but not demonic, and the heroes are quite aware that their problems are mirrored in their antagonists: war is hell, and everyone is simply doing his duty as it is presented.

The representative microcosm is a four-man subtug, *The Fenian Ram,* which sneaks to the enemy continental shelf, steals crude oil, and tows it home in a mile-long bladder. The overall crisis of the war has its corollaries in each facet of the novel: the sea is malevolent, the equipment fails, the skipper is schizoid. . . . The universal tension is epitomized by the atomic power plant of the submarine; without it, the submarine is lifeless, but at every moment it threatens to kill the crew with its life-sustaining radioactivity. The sea, the sub-base, and the submarine are constantly spoken of as wombs, signaling the heavily psychological orientation of the novel. Thus, the specialization of the hero, undercover man for the Bureau of Psychology (BuPsych), is inevitable.

Ensign Ramsey is sent to the *Ram* to analyze the failing homeostatic balance of the captain, the crew, the sub, the sea, the war—and by implication—the world. With Ramsey, we discover that dynamic tension is tending toward chaos, that the tenuous flow-permanence is failing, and that the evolutionary imperative of life has stalled. (p. 14)

To achieve his goal, Ramsey must become an integral member of the crew, yielding his "individuality" to the life-sustaining collective. Each exciting crisis serves as an initiation rite for Ramsey; each danger forces him into closer contact with himself, and when the danger is mostly past, he curls up, catatonic, in a fetal position. When he uncurls, he is reborn as man-plus, . . . cognizant of the solution of the *Ram*'s (other subs', the world's) problems. The solution is about as satisfying as "cottage-cheese." Ramsey decides that all the submariners need to make them happy is recognition, brass bands, and higher pay. The triviality of the "answer" is also a mark of Herbert's fiction; since the problems he raises are perhaps unanswerable and since a book *has* to end, most of his endings seem circular, or contrived, or simplistic, or all three at once. Perhaps the most profound answer Herbert here gives to "life" is right out of Joseph Conrad: sanity is the ability to swim and the willingness to grab an oar when it is offered. (pp. 14-15)

The plot of ***Under Pressure*** moves from one crisis to the next, but the there-and-back-again of the quest and the incremental repetition of initiation rites save it from episodic-picaresque. Major characters come through intact with the exception of Garcia, and his death is payment for past debts and a release from his unwilling perfidy. Ensign Ramsey is off to bigger and better things. . . . (p. 15)

Although ***The Eyes of Heisenberg*** is a "pot-boiler," offering little in theme, plot, characterization, or technique that Herbert hasn't done better elsewhere, the entertainment value of the novel is considerable. What, Herbert seems to be asking, will man do when he solves the basic, incurable disease called mortality? (p. 31)

The story is set on earth in the indefinite future after man has developed two antithetical ways of defeating (or forestalling) death. *Optimen* are genetically engineered individuals who, like the one-hoss shay, last almost forever because their enzymes are kept in perfect balance. *Cyborgs* achieve long life by replacing worn biological components with sophisticated prostheses. In the narrative past, the two classes of superhumans have warred, and the Cyborgs have been reduced to underground conspiracies against the pantheon of Optimen. The penalty for both geriatric "solutions" is sterility. Hence, the supermen must maintain a breeding pool of standard humans. To keep everyman in line, the Optimen diffuse a ubiquitous contraceptive gas, allowing only the harmlessly useful and the potential parents of more Optimen to breed. All gestation is extra-utero, and each fertilized ovum is subjected to genetic cutting. . . . [Thus] the natural evolutionary process has been halted.

For the Optimen, the absence of death has resulted in the absence of life. A cadre of almost-Optimen, through whom Optimen rule the earth, screens its masters from all hint of mortality and decay; thus, each Optimen is a closed, ordered system of increasing entropy. . . . The callous disdain with which the Optimen treat their servants and slaves provides an opportunity for the Cyborgs, whose ultimate weapon against the Optimen is a collection of viable breeders, immune to the contraceptive gas. But the weapon cuts both ways, for the breeders—repelled by both Cyborg and Optimen—form a conspiracy within a conspiracy, dedicated to reestablishing nature's way. . . .

Perhaps the most intriguing facet of ***The Eyes of Heisenberg*** is Herbert's sketch of the Optimen. Their increasing entropy moves down a spiral of philosophical stances: Actionists, Emotionals, Cynics, Hedonists, and Effetes. The three Optimen we meet are the "Tuyere" (French—true iron) who rule the earth from an egg-shaped console while their fellows watch the action on television. . . .

The three rule life with the dispassionate cruelty of the Norns or the Fates, having forgotten everything except the desire to continue ever more elusive self-gratification. . . . For Herbert, the answer to the Tithonus-syndrome is the same as for Tolkien: the great gifts of the Valar to man are prolificacy and mortality. (p. 32)

The event that triggers the plot of ***Heisenberg*** is the intrusion of a meson particle into the fertilized ovum of a potential Optimen, just prior to its genetic cutting. This "chance" rearrangement defeats the Optimen potential, but it insures the breeding viability of the to-be-born. Since the parents are members of the breeder-conspiracy within the Cyborg underground, they resist both the atrophy of the Optimen and the mechanization of the Cyborgs. When the Cyborgs snatch the ovum and insert it in its mother's womb, parental instincts are awakened in the breeders, the Cyborg doctors are shown to lack humanity, and the Optimen suffer an enzyme imbalance.

The climactic scene has the true humans saving the dying Optimen, rejecting the inhuman Cyborgs, and "solving" the Tithonus paradox with all the grace of Athena in the *Oresteia*. The desired enzyme balance will henceforth be achieved by keeping everybody, men and women, pregnant all the time. Herbert's themes make for unsatisfactory endings because there can be no end to flow-permanence, but *this* ending is ludicrous, in theme, in narrative, and in drama. The action of the novel is complicated without being complex, the characterizations are wooden, the lab-report on genetic engineering is mystifying, and the sense of place that Herbert usually does so well is absent. Finally, Herbert gives the reader (at least *this* reader) no character that seems worth worrying about. The hero and heroine remind me of a pair of herbivores protecting a calf. . . . I believe that there is a force that guides man's ends, rough hue them how he may, but in ***Heisenberg,*** Herbert almost talks me out of it. (p. 33)

Destination: Void is . . . an essay rather than an entertainment. The setting, the characters, the suspense are primarily the framework for Herbert's speculations about the nature of consciousness. Hence the "hero" is really the idea, and the novel is a "lab-report": the working out of a set problem in a controlled environment with specified variables. In such a book, characters tend to be ideas on legs, crises tend to be contrived, and the outcome tends to be predictable from the nature of the set problem. The success of such an essay should be judged not so much upon aesthetic criteria as upon the significance of the problem, the ingenuity of the experimental apparatus, the logic of the methodology, and the plausibility of the result.

Since the question of consciousness is never far from the surface in a Herbert novel, ***Destination: Void*** is a very important book. It bears somewhat the relationship to ***Dune*** that a blueprint bears to a cathedral, and *because* of its defects as entertainment, the reader may discover that it reveals some facets of Herbert's vision more explicitly than does ***Dune.***

Much of the apparatus of the novel is familiar: a small collection of representative humans are trapped in a do-or-die lifeboat situation. . . . Each crisis serves as an incremental initiation, moving the characters ever closer to birth from their womb/egg. ***Destination: Void*** bears strong resemblances to ***Under Pressure,*** but whereas the adventures of the *Fenian Ram* dominate Herbert's first novel, speculation dominates life aboard the *Tin Egg*.

Destination: Void is set in the distant, but plausible future. Earth has settled its wars, if not its politics, and is gradually sliding down toward entropy-through-order. Man has attempted to force evolution by creating an artificial intelligence, but the result has been a Frankenstein monster: when the super computer, built on an island in Puget Sound, awoke, it killed everybody in sight, took the island, and disappeared. The experimental work was then shifted to the moon; the experimenters were replaced by clones grown from brilliant criminals, conditioned to push beyond safety and to blow up themselves and the experiment if things got out of hand.

Because even the moon is too close for safety, the powers-that-be have established an elaborate hoax. Clones are sent out in space ships, believing that they are colonists. In reality, the ships are designed to break down once they reach a safe distance from earth, and the only way the crew can survive is to complete the construction of a superior, artificial consciousness. Six ships have disappeared; ***Destination: Void*** is the story of what happens on the seventh attempt.

Deep within the layers of the *Tin Egg* thousands of "colonists" hybernate; only a small "umbilicus" crew remains awake, and it is scheduled to go into deep sleep as soon as the ship clears our solar system. Everything aboard the ship is run by the huge, central computer, and the computer is dependent upon a disembodied human brain, an Organic Mental Core, for its consciousness. Before long, the OMC fails, as does its backup. The third OMC goes berserk and must be executed. Without an OMC, the umbilicus crew is placed under the unbearable stress of monitoring and adjusting the ship's activities. . . . Although each of the four crew members is conditioned to act as stick-and-carrot for the other three, they only gradually come to realize that they are all puppets for United Moon Base, wholly expendable. Still, each functions precisely as the puppetmasters have planned. Bickel (Intelligence) sets at once to work with the aid of Prudence (Sensation) and Timberlake (Intuition), but he is opposed by Flattery (Religious Conscience).

From the first moment of the trip, each crew member has been unwittingly feeding his mental processes into the computer, Flattery more directly than any other. . . . The constant, accelerating crises force each crew member toward a higher consciousness. . . . The computer, however, has learned and grown from the humans' abortive efforts. Eventually Bickel sets himself up as a black-box (a mechanism which takes known input and produces inexplicable output) so that the white-box computer can forge a mechanical analogue of the human brain. Bickel's hypertrophied intellect is the last piece of the puzzle, and the computer becomes fully conscious. Since it has twice the capacity of the human brain, total recall, electrical (as opposed to the slower, electro-chemical) articulation, the collective unconscious of the thousands of hybernating colonists, and a balanced version of Flattery's near-mad religious conscience, the computer exists continually in the heightened states of consciousness that the crew has achieved only momentarily. If is *fully* awake. Flattery has even given it a sense of mortality by pushing the red destruct button. The computer can choose to live or die.

It chooses life, and in the twinkling of an eye transports the ship to Tau Ceti, sets it down on an Edenic planet it has prepared (UMB's promise of an earth-type planet was fraudulent). The book ends as the computer tells the umbilicus crew to awaken the colonists so that everyone may share in planning how to worship the *"deus in machina."* Man and machine have achieved a new, and higher homeostasis. No hints of the problems this balance may entail are given, but the reader may feel that Lord-Tin-Egg is likely to have his hands full, just as Leto-Sandworm will, with some natural, cultural, cellular, or human version of the Bureau of Sabotage. (pp. 35-7)

The sophisticate may find Herbert's answers sophomoric, but an essay is not obligated to give a satisfactory answer, only to raise a problem. And in this Herbert succeeds; it is difficult to imagine that anyone could read ***Destination: Void*** without wondering how he wonders.

Despite the obvious metaphysical bumpings about on the Frankenstein theme, much of ***Destination: Void*** is hard-core science fiction. . . .

Destination: Void seems to have been written at about the same time Herbert was at work on ***Dune,*** and despite its difference in sub-genre (lab-report rather than heroic fantasy), the similarities in theme, technique and characterization are striking. Herbert is deeply and intelligently involved in the problems he sets, and as always, he tells a story well. For some, ***Destination: Void*** may rank second only to ***Dune.*** (p. 38)

With ***The Heaven Makers,*** Herbert returns to the themes which constitute the very thin "essay" of ***The Eyes of Heisenberg*** (1966), but rather than burying the profound questions in an adventure "entertainment," ***The Heaven Makers*** examines immortality, causation, responsibility, and free will provocatively. . . . ***The Heaven Makers*** is set on earth at approximately our time, but the contemporaneity is complicated by the presence of aliens—Optimen, if you will—who have played with earth since before the dawn of civilization. As in Vonnegut's classic, *Sirens of Titan,* all of human history has been managed at the whim of superior beings. The result is a play-within-a-play, a situation which inevitably leads the author to consider the nature of his own art, and to feel *A Midsummer Night's Dream,* or *Hamlet,* or even *Ulysses* lurking in his craft's memory. (p. 39)

[When summarized], the plots [of ***The Heaven Makers***] sound contrived and complicated, but in reading, they are plausible and gripping. For most of the novel Herbert seems to be in full control, and his comments (on the utility of death, the limitations of psychiatry, and the necessity of believing that one is sane) support, rather than vitiate, the entertainment. The characterizations of Thurlow, Joe, Kelexel, and Fraffin are remarkably strong. Eventually there are no black villains in the book, though there is much villainy. Ruth is primarily one more red-headed version of Herbert's favorite lady. The reader who wishes to see Herbert's thinking about the nature of fiction will especially enjoy ***The Heaven Makers.*** (p. 40)

David M. Miller, in his Frank Herbert, *Starmont House, 1980, 70 p.*

JOSEPH M. LENZ

[The essay from which this excerpt is taken was originally written for the third J. Lloyd Eaton Conference on Science Fiction and Fantasy, held February 21-22, 1981.]

The science fiction empire is in some ways anachronistic. An empire, after all, is constituted by a strong, centralized, often monarchical government backed by military power and religious sanction; a hierarchical, even feudal, social order; a capitalistic economy; and a chauvinism that seeks to expand the empire's borders ever outward, reducing diverse cultures to their lowest common denominator, their identity as parts of a whole. In short, an empire is a political, social, and economic dinosaur that (we think) belongs more to our past than to our future. Nonetheless, it remains an important and persistent icon—to borrow Gary Wolfe's term—in science fiction.

The reasons for its persistence are many. Imperialism is in part a holdover from science fiction's romance ancestry. The romance tale involves a knight's founding, defending, preserving, or sometimes replacing an earthly empire that is analogous to an otherworldly one. . . . The empire's unity, comprehensiveness, and capacity for analogy make it an attractive and powerful construct for the science fiction writer. Gary Wolfe notes that the empire-builders—Asimov, Herbert, LeGuin, Lewis, to name just a few—often write stories that describe their creations' history. Here the empire provides not only a prefabricated secondary world to be mined and mined again, but occasionally a reflexive metaphor depicting science fiction's emergence as a legitimate literary form.

It is to this use of empire, specifically by Isaac Asimov and Frank Herbert, that I wish to call attention. In a very strict and limited way, the *Foundation* trilogy and the ***Dune*** books can be called classics. . . . I mean that they are classical, reminiscent of and belonging to a literary tradition that originates with Rome and *The Aeneid.* Each is written to dedicate an empire, one foretold by prophecy and realized in time. Asimov and Herbert each tell the classic story, the founding of an empire, yet the manner in which each tells that story has special implications for science fiction, the empire being dedicated.

In his study called, appropriately, *The Classic,* Frank Kermode examines Rome's history as a symbol in Western thought, detailing how every major attempt to establish a new empire—whether political (Britain's descent from Brut), religious (the Reformation), or literary (neoclassicism)—has had, perforce, to reckon with Rome, either appealing to it for its blessing or renouncing it in favor of another model. It is no accident, then, that science fiction empires are often peculiarly Roman. That Asimov uses Rome as a model for his Galactic Empire is both familiar and obvious. . . . Herbert pays similar tribute unto Caesar. His empire portrays the much feared imperial legions through whom the emperor rules; the Landsraad, or senate of Great Houses that, in form, serves to balance the emperor's power; the gladitorial games that persecute slaves and prisoners for the entertainment and education of the populace; and the emperor himself, who plots against his own kin and who is brought to his knees by a tribe of religious fanatics. In each case the author assigns the Roman characteristics to the empire that falls. Rome is an unfit model for the new epoch, so Asimov and Herbert, in a sense, deconstruct it. Yet, as Asimov's titles suggest, these books are about the foundations of empire, about its origins as well as its demise. It is paradoxical—but perhaps inevitable—that behind *Foundation* and ***Dune*** is the original classic written to inaugurate an empire. Just as the ideal of Rome symbolizes permanence and unity in a world of political change, so *The Aeneid* signifies permanent literary achievement amidst ever-changing critical values and judgments. At the same time that Asimov and Herbert reject the Roman model they rely on *The Aeneid,* the scripture that canonizes that model, to construct the new empire. (pp. 42-4)

Because Herbert succeeds Asimov and writes what seems another science fiction epic, he is faced with a more complex problem. He must accommodate both the epic tradition and his science fiction predecessor. And in general outline ***Dune*** does resemble its antecedents. Herbert uses Rome to characterize the old empire gone awry. His hero's career follows Aeneas' pattern. Paul Atriedes is a noble exile, fleeing the ruins of one dynasty and chosen to found another. Like Asimov, Herbert resorts to ironic plotting . . . to counteract the predictability caused by formula and prophecy. Yet Herbert is not satisfied with mere imitation. He does not, for instance, develop his story along the expected epic/pastoral axis. Instead he conflates elements of the two, making the Fremen a provincial people who live in hidden caves, who herd animals, and who dream of an Arrakeen paradise, yet who are aggressive, violent, dynamic, and destined to rule. This kind of conflation evidences Herbert's willingness to reshape his inheritance. . . . Although Herbert does not altogether reject the classic, he does re-form it. (p. 46)

In his rejection of Rome . . . [Herbert, like Asimov,] elects a biblical model. ***Dune*** tells the story of a desert planet populated by a nomadic people who are destined to depose the emperor, replace him with their messiah, and propagate their faith through space. The story's hero thus combines two figures. As Duke Atriedes, Paul belongs to the old order, figuring Aeneas, the founder and father of empire. As Muab'Dib, he heralds the new order, figuring Moses, the prophet who delivers his people but who is himself denied entrance to the promised land.

Besides increasing his story's density, Herbert's play with typology and his displacement of Virgil alters the kind of classic he writes. Herbert's science fiction differs from Asimov's to the extent that romance differs from epic. The epic achieves stasis. It attests to past deeds; it affirms an existing (or past) civilization. Thus, Asimov's story reaches a climax in which Hari Seldon's vision of the new galactic empire is an assumed fact. The romance is a state of flux. It presents a process, a state of becoming something. Herbert projects a story that has no end, one in which the goal is often promised but never reached. Each book in the series brings the new empire closer to realization, but the progress never comes to a full stop. ***Dune*** concludes with Paul enthroned, but worried about the inevitable Fremen jihad. ***Dune Messiah*** ends with the Bene Gesserit/Space Guild plot frustrated, but also with Paul exiled and the empire unsettled. Its cover advertises that ***Children of Dune*** is "the climax of the classic ***Dune*** trilogy," yet another book, ***God Emperor of Dune,*** follows it. The following description of Paul's prescience aptly reflects the multiplicity of Herbert's visions. "And what he saw was a time nexus within this cave, a boiling of possibilities focused here, wherein the most minute action—the wink of an eye, a careless word, a misplaced grain of sand—moved a gigantic lever across the known universe. He saw violence with the outcome subject to so many variables that his slightest movement created vast shiftings in the pattern.''. . . Herbert, like Paul, is caught in his own labyrinth. He returns again and again to Dune, almost as if he is determined to exhaust all its possibilities.

Asimov and Herbert represent two strains of science fiction and two kinds of classics. For Asimov, the future replicates the past, and this cyclical sense of history affects the way he tells and the way we read science fiction. Because civilization is a closed system in which man merely repeats himself, Asimov writes a story that repeats old stories. . . . To give his fiction credibility Asimov conforms to his literary inheritance, writing an epic that, like all epics, arrests development. His science fiction represents the old classic, the story frozen in time.

Herbert writes what Kermode would call a modern classic, a narrative that ''poses a virtually infinite set of questions.'' These questions do not pertain to the story's content—in Herbert's case, the matters of genetics, prescience, and reincarnation that comprise the extrapolated science—but rather to the way we read the story. For Herbert, the past determines the future, but the future does not mimic the past. He builds upon a variety of literary traditions. To read him, however, we cannot rely on our conventional expectations, for Herbert plays with those conventions. He conflates familiar genres, plots, and character types, changing the known into the unknown. Most significantly, he refuses to give his story a close, the one narrative moment when process stops. His is an open text, one that both invites and refutes interpretation. (pp. 47-8)

Joseph M. Lenz, ''Manifest Destiny: Science Fiction and Classical Form,'' in Coordinates: Placing Science Fiction and Fantasy, *George E. Slusser, Eric S. Rabkin, Robert Scholes, eds., Southern Illinois University Press, 1983, pp. 42-8.**

CRAIG SHAW GARDNER

The White Plague begins when John Roe O'Neill, an American microbiologist on vacation in Ireland, sees his wife and children killed by a bomb planted by IRA terrorists. The murder drives O'Neill insane. He returns to the United States to create his revenge—a new, extremely contagious disease that kills only women. He then plants the disease in Ireland, as well as other countries that he feels are responsible for the IRA and terrorism, and finally travels to Ireland to watch his revenge firsthand. But the disease can't be contained, and soon there are large parts of the world where every woman has died from the plague.

Herbert's book has a convincing disaster with a plausible scientific cause and a large, well-defined cast of characters. But the novel simply doesn't work, for two reasons:

By writing most of the novel from the point of view of a mad man incapable of feeling, even when he travels through the devastated Irish countryside, Herbert robs the reader of the opportunity for empathy, and the book falls flat.

Herbert makes up for this void somewhat in his supporting characters, many of whom are very emotional indeed. . . . But even here, Herbert backs away from really showing the devastation around them, preferring to have people talk about it instead. It seems Herbert is afraid of the magnitude of the horror he's created, and so repeatedly pulls his punches. The book loses its immediacy, and a thriller without immediacy is not much of a thriller.

Herbert once dealt with an even larger scope and cast of characters in ***Dune,*** and created one of the greatest science fiction novels ever written. In ***The White Plague,*** unfortunately, his imagination seems constrained by the proximity of the book's future. The descriptions in the novel all seem feasible, but none of them have the life of the author's better work.

Craig Shaw Gardner, in a review of ''The White Plague,'' in Book World—The Washington Post, *August 29, 1982, p. 7.*

MARK ROSE

[In **''The White Plague,''** Herbert] remains firmly earthbound, sometime not far from the present, in a land that faces as many problems with as many conflicting solutions as his Arrakis, millenniums removed. . . .

Technology, warfare, ideology, all are useless, because one man discovers a plague that knowledgeable scientists agree was inevitable, given advances in research of recombinant DNA. . . .

With finely plotted strokes, Herbert takes what could have been a single-surface doomsday thriller, elevates it, deepens it to a study of the unmonitored advance of science, the duplicity and greed of government, the innate complexity of human character and nationalistic fervor. Survival of the planet is a problem that requires a mass consensus for a solution. Why do we see our own fenced-in plot of land, blind to the crumbling terrain that surrounds it?

Herbert takes us on a fascinating trip over that terrain: a trek through the plague-ravaged Irish countryside with a priest, a boy, a Provo terrorist (ironically, the same who blew up O'Neill's family), and the madman, himself, now in the schizophrenic persona of O'Donnell, a molecular biologist on his way to help save civilization. Or doom it.

All four, in their own ways, personify a degree of the historic shock and effect of Irish oppression and hatred. All are victims.

Father Michael and Herity the terrorist argue endlessly trying to fix blame for the plague and the plight of the Irish. See what your god has done, Herity says. See what godlessness has wrought, the priest counters. The boy, mute, a silent soul of suffering, withdraws further. The madman is confused. . . .

Science and common sense ultimately prevail over chaos but there are no conclusions to this story, no blame laid, only thoughtfully proposed questions.

This is engaging entertainment, intriguing, wholly believable and even important; a book of ideas put forth by fully fleshed characters in a common world in front of us today. . . .

Three quarters of the way through I figured out the puzzle. . . . Frank Herbert is the madman, with just the imagination, scientific knowledge, insight of character and history to pull it off. Beware of Herbert. He will . . . egads . . . make you think.

Mark Rose, ''A Human Madness from a Genius of Genes,'' in Los Angeles Times Book Review, *September 29, 1982, p. 2.*

WILLIAM COYLE

Frank Herbert's new novel [***The White Plague***] is not science fantasy but a dystopian thriller in the manner of Michael Crichton or Len Deighton. The backdrop for an exciting plot is the complex ambiance of modern Ireland—fanatical hatred of the "Brits," piety of women and priests, violent rage of men, and peasant superstitions that convert suffering into myth. The basic situation is vintage Herbert: catastrophe averted or mitigated by man's willingness to discard traditional behavior-patterns. . . .

John Roe O'Neill, an American biologist, sees his wife and children killed in a Dublin street by an IRA bomb. Declaring war on terrorism, he devises a virus that will use the power of recombinant DNA and gene-splicing to destroy women in Ireland, England, and Libya. When his warnings, signed Madman, are ignored, he disseminates the plague throughout the world. The most depressing aspect of the novel is the conduct of political, military, and scientific leaders. Even as they cooperate to save mankind, they cynically maneuver to attain power for themselves.

As might be expected in a novel stressing action and ideas, characterization is rather shallow. In fact, the book is overpopulated; there are so many characters that they get in each other's way. There is not even much insight into the mind of O'Neill, the Madman. His psychotic disorders fluctuate to serve the plot rather than to reveal a mind diseased.

Essentially this is an exciting novel that holds a reader's interest while raising disturbing questions about terrorism, the nature of power, the folly of man's playing God, and the limits of scientific inquiry. One can read the book, enjoy it thoroughly, and hope that Frank Herbert is not as prescient as he has sometimes been in the past.

William Coyle, "Herbert's Latest Is Dystopian Thriller Set in Ireland," in Fantasy Newsletter, *Vol. 5, No. 10, November, 1982, p. 32.*

LEONARD M. SCIGAJ

Frank Herbert believes that "No human being on our 'real' planet is completely free of his unexamined assumptions" and that it is the function of science fiction to "examine assumptions." Prior work in general semantics has convinced Herbert that the mind not only selects certain data from the plethora of objects and events, but also organizes and interprets that data according to principles generated in part by cultural values and assumptions. Foremost on Herbert's list of unexamined assumptions is the pervasive Western belief in realizing ultimate goals—in an authority, object, state of mind, system, or machine that will provide *the* final answers to the problems that beset us. . . . Whether it be a messianic hero or religion, a utopian society, philosophical system, or ultimate machine, Herbert is suspicious of single-track solutions to the complex problems of our changing world. Throughout the ***Dune*** Tetralogy Herbert offers a sociological application of Werner Heisenberg's Indeterminacy Principle as a check against such goal-seeking: here he reiterates that fixations upon univocal solutions often blind us to contingencies operating in the present, and thus increase the likelihood that unnoticed factors may upset the plans. . . . (p. 340)

In ***Dune*** and ***Dune Messiah,*** Paul Atreides' misguided heroism and misuse of prescient visions reveal problematic assumptions in Western society: "Western culture," asserts Herbert, "is particularly obsessed with this absolutism through its narrow vision of a linear pragmatism hitched to technology." On the whole our culture rests secure in "the assumption that science can provide a surprise-free future for humankind." Through the Zen awareness of Leto II in ***Children of Dune*** and ***God Emperor of Dune,*** Herbert offers a method of avoiding such assumptions, and throughout the ***Dune*** Tetralogy he creates a richly detailed world as a metaphoric vehicle to examine our Western belief in undeviating "game plans." Paul's use of his prescient visions, the result of spice addiction, articulates a cultural myth at the very heart of America: the belief in what Herbert calls the "Presbyterian fixation"—predestination, absolute prediction through visionary gift, grace, or righteous conduct. Paul's obsession with his mission to forestall the *jihad,* the religious war and biological urge to renew the gene pool through redistribution, is analogous in some respects to the politician's obsession with his New Frontier or Great Society, the technologist's fascination with the ultimate computer, or even Isaac Asimov's unswerving belief that the scientists can solve all technological problems by creating more technology.

Granted, Paul's straitened circumstances do necessitate compromise after compromise in order to insure family survival. . . . [The] Bene Gesserit, a quasi-political motherhood dedicated to producing a superhero leader through genetic engineering, has seeded the Fremen with a messianic myth, and every step Paul takes to endear himself to the Fremen for the survival of the House Atreides also convinces them that he is their Mahdi, their savior. Paul never does have the freedom to orchestrate his own master plan; he is impeded at every turn by the Harkonnen menace and by Fremen needs for freedom, survival, and water.

But if Paul successfully altered a long-standing Fremen ritual to save Stilgar from death while replacing him as military commander, he might also have rejected the Mahdinite, the religious mantle, and somehow curbed the explosion of religious fanaticism that killed sixty-one billion people, sterilized ninety planets, and completely demoralized five hundred other planets in twelve years. . . . Prescience is, in part, a heightening of the Jungian god-image within the Self, the archetypal capacity of each fully integrated individual to intuit visions of his highest personal development; but Paul's warped use of prescience is entirely unproductive. Instead of comprehending the present and its varied opportunities for development into the future, Paul becomes obsessed *only* with the future, and with his own unchanging vision of an inevitable, predestined *jihad.*

Paul may have had a premonition of the function of Heisenberg's Indeterminacy Principle when he and Jessica attempt their first foothold into Stilgar's *sietch,* as Timothy O'Reilly contends [see *CLC,* Vol. 23], but he fails to operate upon it. He persists in being obsessed with his mission of avoiding the religious war throughout the fight with Jamis, the ensuing burial, and the accommodation of Jamis' wife. Throughout the Jamis episode Paul assumes that he is acting to forestall the *jihad* . . . , when actually he is revealing himself as the Fremen savior. . . . Contrary to O'Reilly's interpretation, Paul does not consciously cease to resist the *jihad;* . . . Paul's persistence [culminates] in a needless fight with Feyd-Rautha in a spirit of fatalistic abandon to powerful genetic forces. . . . The more he exercises unyielding conscious control toward averting his visions of future calamity, the more Paul's actions are motivated by *un*conscious instinctual drives.

If Paul had the dexterity to control a giant sandworm, perhaps he could have averted at least some of the ravages of the holy war. . . . Paul's sleepwalk into the institutionalization of his religion is surely an unnecessary step, which he, as the sightless, acerb Preacher in ***Children of Dune,*** will later rue. . . . Institutionalized religious frenzy, the opium of the masses, has turned a possible *jihad* into a probable one. . . . (pp. 340-42)

The capacity for prescient visions is inherited by Leto II, Paul's son, who must recognize the "trap of prescience"—that "to know the future absolutely is to be trapped into that future absolutely." . . . As Leto debates launching his Golden Path, he thinks "how easy it would be to succumb to the demand for prescience, to risk launching his awareness into an unchanging, absolute future." . . . Spice profits and complete control over the ecology of Arrakis has hastened the realization of a verdant planet; but the sandworms, which produce the spice necessary for individual addiction and space navigation, are dying out, for water causes their immediate death.

The purpose of Leto II's Golden Path is to slow down this ecological transformation and modify the ancient human desire for chaos without suppressing the forces of survival. . . . Leto II becomes an isolated predator-despot on the pharaonic model, forcing survival adaptations in the populace when the sandworms have all but died out and melange is dear. . . . From Paul's failure Leto II has learned two principles of general semantics: that "the real universe is always one step beyond logic" . . . , and that "the linear progression of events is imposed by the observer." . . . (p. 343)

Leto bases his alternative approach upon a tripartite philosophy: a grasp of intuitions emanating from his Jungian unconscious; facility with a Zen precognitive, egoless awareness of the present moment as a fluid matrix of possibilities; and an adaptation of the Chinese respect for chance. . . . Moneo, Leto II's majordomo, is convinced that Leto believes only in chance . . . ; his heightened sensitivity to the possibilities of the present approximates that cultivated by the ancient Chinese with their yarrow stalks and hexigrams in the *I Ching*. . . . The cultivation of intuïtion, Zen awareness, and chance, aid Leto in developing a flexibility that incorporates accidental factors into ongoing awareness. In ***God Emperor of Dune*** Leto II seldom uses his prescience, never to preoccupy himself with the time or location of his own death, and only to assure himself that the constellation of possibilities will insure the survival of the species. . . . (pp. 343-44)

To avert chaos Leto II controls his kingdom with an iron hand. He denies crises to limit the forming of large-scale opposition, suppresses curiosity, limits the size of villages, and keeps these villages primitive, without technological advances. Vehicles and space travel are disallowed. Siona and others are products of a deliberate breeding program and have passed significant survival tests. Leto's purpose here is to produce selective opposition and survival adaptation in order to insure the hardiness of the species. Instead of repressing rebellious offspring, as the Duncan Idahos would prefer, Leto hopes for a time to convert their strength and drive for power into support for his regime, and ultimately to accept whatever opposing regime develops. (p. 344)

Unlike Paul's messianic fixations, Leto has no specific future goals. He simply recognizes the interdependence of man and environment and desires to insure the survival of the species until sandworms and spice are once again plentiful. In the process he hopes to make his regime so despotic that the populace will remember never again to desire a messiah, but rather assume responsibility for their own decisions. Leto is really an interim ecological manager engaged in "vision management" . . . ; he converts life's surprises into delicate balancing acts. The otherwise certain extinction of the species through spice deprivation dictates his harshness.

Herbert has written that "any current concept of Truth can be a highly unstable condition," a "never-ending process" of "orienting our momentary position." He believes that our "small sallies at equilibrium" during this process evince "*prana,* the vital principle of life, locked inextricably with illusion." To the yogin *prana* is the all-important principle of vitality, the life-breath exhaled from the heart region, the fundamental function of the will to live. (pp. 344-45)

In the dynamic ecology of Dune, spice becomes a pervasive metaphor for the vitality and life-sustaining properties of the state of *prana*. . . . Dr. Yueh tells Jessica that spice is "like life—it presents a different face each time you take it. . . . And, like life, never to be truly synthesized." . . . When Paul fails to cultivate an open-ended present and worries himself into a future-oriented fatalism, the messianic absolutes reign and the spice supply dwindles. For both yogin and ecologist *prana* is the spice of life.

To maintain *prana*-vitality Leto II is willing to perform the ultimate in selfless giving. The "*sandtrout glove,*" which gives him short-term superhuman strength to smash *qanats* and inhibit the ecological change, will "*restore the balance*." . . . Symbolically Leto's slow conversion to a sandworm follows the Zen directive to become the problem itself, to *live* the problem in all its manifestations—personal, social, and environmental. Then, after three and a half millennia of "vision management," the tyrant of ***God Emperor of Dune,*** now nearly a sandworm himself, walks knowingly to his own death by water, to suffer the terrible death throes that once again initiate the sandworm cycle. This is an act of selfless love, underscored by an anagogic level in the plot. That he can love is Leto's most carefully kept secret. . . . Siona learns this from the journals Leto allows her to steal, and this information prompts the Ixian technologists to produce Hwi Noree, the ultimate godtrap, for she admires Leto's selfless love. Leto's death, his final act of humanitarian giving, occurs by his own choice as he travels to Tuono to marry his "gentle Hwi." . . . The symbolic touch of using Chani's water rings for the ceremony . . . reinforces this selflessness: Chani is the most loving, self-effacing character in the ***Dune*** novels, and Leto knows that water is the one element necessary for the conversion of his remains into sandworms. . . . From the opening journal theft to the peregrination to Onn, the test of Siona, and the final martyrdom, the gift of Leto's substance and vision generates the main action of ***God Emperor of Dune.*** (pp. 345-46)

Until Paul's messianism the Fremen survive because they adapt to the strictures of their environment, and because their myths house and reinforce a deep ecological wisdom. After the Fremen lose their desert hardihood and sense of community in the *jihad* and a transformed planet of seeming abundance, Leto II can only reproduce an ecological balance through despotic rule. In ***God Emperor of Dune*** Duncan Idaho ridicules the plastic crysknives and fake stillsuits of the Museum Fremen, while Leto muses, "It's because there's no more Dune that there are no more Fremen." . . .

The ecology of Dune differed when the oppressed Fremen lived in sietches under severe hardships. . . . Fremen ritual inculcated a high level of environmental awareness and responsibility, while it socialized and made bearable their submission to the planetologist Kynes's "Law of the Minimum" (borrowed from Paul Sears)—that "Growth is limited by that necessity which is present in the least amount."... (p. 348)

Through the communal sietch orgy the Fremen exorcised genetic memories of Jacurutu, a time when naibs killed solely for the victim's water. . . . The Jacurutu violence, which persists among the Cast Out, is Herbert's fictional equivalent to Freud's inherited taint of the primal crime in the archaic genetic heritage of the species—an important impediment to maintaining an ecological balance. It is fitting that Paul, as the Preacher, finds succor with the Cast Out at Jacurutu, for his submission to the *jihad* allies him with the forces of genetic regression. Abomination functions as the individual equivalent of submission to the inherited taint of violence; here the weak personality lapses into the chaotic elements of an awakened genetic memory. The pressures of the Regency drive Alia to seek answers through probing her genetic memory, but while she searches she tries to repress, rather than control, invasions of the old, chaotic impulses. . . . This systematic repression causes paranoia and a complete takeover by the phylogenetic taint, the Harkonnen in the blood. Only Leto II achieves both a secure personality and an ecologically sound sense of interrelatedness that denies the old chaos within by wrestling with the genetic residue of the primal horde and by learning to control, rather than repress, his inner life through Yoga and Zen.

Ecology is a matter of understanding terms such as "interdependence" and "reciprocity" as applying to all facets of organic life and inorganic matter. These terms are not, however, to be comprehended as abstractions but as felt-relationships, extensions of the self in a *lived* totality. As Paul Shepard warns [in his introduction to *The Subversive Science: Essays Toward an Ecology of Man*], ecology is not a matter of perceiving nature as a "resource" that can be manipulated into "usable energy and commodities"; it is rather a way of seeing and feeling, a comprehension of "the self as a center of organization, constantly drawing on and influencing the surroundings," a self "whose skin and behavior are soft zones contacting the world instead of excluding it." Ecology is a subversive subject, according to Paul Sears [in his essay "Ecology—A Subversive Subject"], because it affords a "continuing critique of man's operation within the eco-system," where he is an "integral part" and not "just an observer and irresponsible exploiter."

Herbert's own definition of ecology approximates the thoughts of Shepard and Sears. For Herbert, ecology in science fiction writing consists of "the inclusion of social problems with the soil problems, a disinclination to separate *mind* from *body*." The use of *prana* in the ***Dune*** novels does not simply parallel the Greek ideal of moderation as the golden mean between extremes; it expresses an ideal of self-control based upon a dynamic and necessitous *fusion* of the internal and the external. Herbert's careful attention to point of view, especially in ***God Emperor of Dune,*** provides numerous examples of Leto's ever-alert *prana*-consciousness extending from his brooding inner life to an intuitional grasp of changing circumstances in social life and planetary environment. (pp. 348-49)

Herbert often creates clear, visual metaphors, analogues for three-dimensional, lived experience, that are at once thematically and psychologically revealing. One can almost graph the *prana* basis of the entire ecology theme in the ***Dune*** Tetralogy by focusing upon three visual images: Paul as the eyeless Preacher, being led back to Jacurutu by his fourteen-year-old guide, the murderer Assan Tariq of the Cast Out . . . ; Alia's psyche being overtaken by the genetic memory of the homosexual Vladimir Harkonnen. . . ; and Leto II's transformation into a sandworm. . . . Leto's transformation symbolizes a lived knowledge of ecological interrelatedness. As he presses the sandtrout onto his skin he repeats the phrase "*My skin is not my own,*" and indeed it is not; the sandtrout fused to his skin become symbolic of the living truth of ecological interrelatedness. Leto II's *prana*-consciousness and his sandtrout skin become Sears's "soft zones": they reveal Leto's sense of being directly connected to, and dependent upon, his environment. . . .

To achieve the secure personality that denies the inherited taint of chaos and fosters an ecologically sound survival sense of interrelatedness—the Golden Path—Leto combines Yogic *prana-bindu* breathing and meditation with the wisdom of the Zensunni Wanderers to affirm, as do Shepard and Sears, that a sense of ecological balance must begin *from the inside*. (p. 350)

The non-egocentric, non-dualistic grasp of the self within a continuum of the present that distinguishes Zen, and the subjective monism of both Yoga and Zen, lead Leto to a grasp of the plight of Arrakis as a direct extension of the self's needs for interior *prana*-vitality and balance. . . . Leto's Golden Path is the result of a deliberate resolve to strengthen his control over both his inherited memories and the communal extensions of that inner self. . . . Leto II would rather become a despot than submit to the ecological chaos of another *jihad*.

After three and a half millennia of "vision management" and experience with uncounted generations of humans, the God Emperor sadly concludes that "Most humans are not strong enough to find freedom within." . . . From the perspective afforded by an Oriental subjective monism, Leto is able to develop what Hwi Noree perceives as his "faith in life" and "courage of love." . . . Like the cilia of his sandtrout skin, Leto's faith and courage extend outward to a holistic vision of lived interrelatedness, the opposite of disconnected, irresponsible Ixian invention.

Because Leto absorbs the possibilities of the present into a strong, self-mastered personality, he can consider and discard many possible courses of action without limiting his awareness, narrowing his vision, or falling prey to Paul's fixation upon a predestined future. Initially Leto doesn't want the [responsibility]. . . ; he considers killing Jessica to avoid her plot of turning him into another messianic hero. . . , and debates and finally rejects the Bene Gesserit design of incest with Ghanima to solidify the bloodline. . . . But his Zen intuition and *prana*-consciousness demand that he forget all these considerations and go without preconceptions to Jacurutu . . . to confront the creativity and the chaos within the Fremen past and within himself. (pp. 351-52)

During the Jacurutu odyssey Leto's Zen awareness of living in the present moment allows him to absorb the accidents of capture by Jessica's men, an enforced spice trance, a fetching maiden, sabotaged stillsuit pumps, and a confrontation with his father, now the Preacher. Unlike Paul, who typically succumbs to such accidents, Leto not only survives them, but transcends them. During these escapades Leto carries on an inner dialogue that results in a final decision to balance his inner life and reject his fear of succumbing to the species drives that bring chaos. . . . Finally, after a protracted battle with his own fears, quelled only by the "intense quiet" of *prana-bindu* meditation, Leto masters his inner self [and] achieves a strength of personality that will never fail him in the future. . . .

When, on a newspaper assignment in 1957, Herbert travelled to Florence, Oregon, to cover a United States Department of Agriculture project on the control of sand dunes, he learned that the sands of time shift into endlessly changing configurations and that the proper way to control sand dunes is to plant hardy grasses on their slipfaces. The ***Dune*** Tetralogy represents the sum of two and a half decades of thought and research about these lived truths. Leto II is the hardy grass that controls the sands of change and becomes skilled at survival adaptation in an infinite present. Through Leto's ability to anchor *prana*-vitality within himself, and to extend this balance outward to include the society and environment of Dune, Herbert offers a startlingly fresh and illuminating fusion of current ecological wisdom from the Occident and ancient philosophical wisdom from the Orient. (p. 353)

Leonard M. Scigaj, "'Prana' and the Presbyterian Fixation: Ecology and Technology in Frank Herbert's 'Dune' Tetralogy," in Extrapolation, *Vol. 24, No. 4, Winter, 1983, pp. 340-55.*

THEODORE STURGEON

The late grand master of the short-short story, Frederic Brown, wrote one in which the most powerful, most complex computer ever devised was asked its first question: "Is there a God?" Its response: "There is now."

There we have, in a nugget, theme, content and basic statement not only for [**"The Lazarus Effect"**], but for its weighty predecessor **"The Jesus Incident."** That one established the settlement of the watery planet Pandora by humans, their conflicts with the indigenous life-forms, including a sentient kelp, and their abandonment by their super-computerized ship (hereafter known as Ship). Having achieved self-awareness, Ship left them with the injunction "Find ways to worShip me." The current volume deals with the appalling results of the humans' almost total obliteration of the kelp. . . .

So: many astonishments. And the greatest is that in so convoluted a structure there are so many simplistic characters. In Creative Writing 101, paragraph (a), Verisimilitude, Dictate One is: Nobody is all good; nobody is all bad; no one is ever all anything. In this narrative the heroine is Good; the hero is Brave; the old Judge is Wise, and oh, how Evil is the villain. Further, one knows at the instant of introduction which couple will ultimately Make It, which of course they do when everything Comes Out All Right At The End.

This is perplexing. I don't know the work of poet [Bill Ransom, coauthor of ***The Lazarus Effect***] (though I suspect that many deft phrases, like a man's mind "coming apart at the dreams" are his) but Frank Herbert (whose output includes the **"Dune"** series) certainly has earned his high credentials. His forte, clearly, is metaphor; and in that case, one might have a gentler response to this intrusion of absolutes. To apply . . . advanced tectonics to the terrain through which pilgrims progress, is pedantic foolishness.

Or it just might be the high glee (for Frank Herbert is, at base, a gleeful man!) of expanding to two volumes and most of a thousand pages, the ultimate pun on the three words *deus ex machina*.

Theodore Sturgeon, "Social Conflicts Played Out in a Watery Arena," in Los Angeles Times Book Review, *August 28, 1983, p. 4.*

GREGORY MERCURIO

Since its inception as a celebration of technology, science fiction has become bored with hardware and turns to something else instead: an allusive penny-mysticism not the result of poetic scholarship but of a shoddy ransacking of paperback reflections on the occult, the ancient gods and sacred scripture—anything, that is, to efface the fact that the future—or a mythical past—is unknowable and unknown, since as Joyce has said somewhere, we still must wipe our glosses with what we know. As scenario for the future, the genre has become moribund and self-conscious, so immired in its own conventions we have to look elsewhere for such things: to Huxley still, to Burgess always. Even C. S. Lewis helps; and always, it seems beyond this clubby group of writers who feel compelled, like the writers of pulp horror and gothics, to hold conventions, give awards, and publish *apologiae* for what looks like xenophobia in the ranks, and probably is. . . .

[In ***The Lazarus Effect*** co-authors] Herbert and Ransom deck [the] hackneyed conventions with nothing new, nothing marvelous at all; and the novel's surprise is that nothing surprising happens at all. Plot and characterization become interchangeable with others of the genre. In place of Arthur C. Clarke's Hal, we have Ship—a computerized, mechanical intelligence who demands (punning inexcusably) WorShip from its human creators. In place of H. G. Wells' animal experiments on the island of Dr. Moreau, we have properly updated clones and mutants—Mutes, for short, in accordance with most science fiction writers' passion for the abbreviated, the colloquial, and the mundane. . . .

Read it and rail against Nietzsche and all the supercilious, facile distinctions between Apollo and Dionysus ever made. Read it and wish that Jung had never written the words collective unconscious, or that Teilhard de Chardin had never mused about an Omega point, and know that the self-consciously created archetype—whether sentient kelp or Apollonian mermen—is always second-rate, and more than a little boring. . . . Even to criticize such pulp strikes one as a vulgar practice, far too easy and far too slick a service: not tilting at windmills, but at paper kites.

Gregory Mercurio, in a review of "The Lazarus Effect," in Best Sellers, *Vol. 43, No. 6, September, 1983, p. 203.*

PETER BRIGG

While others write serial novels that wear even good ideas to tatters, Herbert has perfected (Asimov originated?), [in ***The Lazarus Effect***] and in the ***Dune*** books, a technique of vast, audacious historical-evolutionary jumps so readers can grasp imaginary histories at their vital balance-points. Nor do the worlds remain the same but are re-imagined because their ecologies and civilizations have had time to change from book to book. For this reason ***The Lazarus Effect*** can stand alone—complexly imagined and vividly realized. (p. 30)

The book has all of the Herbert-Ransom features, good and bad. Its main action-violence plot is mechanical and only one or two of the characters stand clear of stereotyping, albeit somewhat modified to fit the consciousness of living on Pandora. But the grand counterbalance is that effective whole-world perspective, begun in ***Dune,*** which uses conventional, exciting story telling to carry wonderful resonances of dramatized debate over ecology, shared consciousness, and religious philosophy. The novel's basic questions in these categories are continuations, in the varied setting, of those posed in ***The Jesus Incident*** and elsewhere in Herbert's works: can man co-exist with nature or must he damage it even with well-intentioned tampering; what would a sharing of racial and even planetary consciousness be like—particularly with a non-human controlling being; and what attitudes must man take towards worship—particularly if godhead's nature is lost in the mists of time? To these fascinating inquiries, always add some wonderful character grotesques and the mixture is at once potent, exciting and thought provoking. (p. 31)

Peter Brigg, in a review of "The Lazarus Effect," in Science Fiction & Fantasy Book Review, *No. 17, September, 1983, pp. 30-1.*

GERALD JONAS

Instead of intellectual space opera, Mr. Herbert now serves up an intellectual disaster novel [**"The White Plague"**]—a brilliant, brooding meditation on the war between man's tendencies toward self-destruction and his instinct for self-preservation.

The White Plague is the diabolical invention of an American of Irish descent named John Roe O'Neill, whose wife and children happen to be in the wrong place at the wrong time and are blown to bits by a bomb planted by a faction of the Irish Republican Army. O'Neill himself is physically unharmed, but when the first shock passes all he can think about is revenge. . . . While scientists seek a cure [for the plague O'Neill has invented], political, military and religious leaders struggle to hold or gain power; old scores are settled, new alliances formed.

This is precisely the point where most novels that deal with global disaster fall apart. Armageddon is a tough act to follow. No matter how many generals and popes and presidents try to pick up the pieces, their posturings are bound to seem anticlimactic. Mr. Herbert is too smart a storyteller to let that happen. Daringly, without undercutting the suspense inherent in the situation (can the human race be saved?), he keeps the spotlight on, of all people, O'Neill himself. Never has the mad scientist been presented with such loving care. The pain of bereavement splits O'Neill in two; out of the cleavage arises a "new" personality who takes the name of John O'Donnell. Although O'Donnell is aware of what he calls "O'Neill-Within," he feels no guilt. Like everyone else in the world that O'Neill has wrought, he considers himself an innocent victim.

Through a twist of plot that Mr. Herbert makes plausible, O'Donnell ends up in Ireland, where he is forced to trek across the devastated countryside in the company of a priest, a terrorist and a boy driven mute by the death of his female kin. The journey takes on epic dimensions, which Mr. Herbert emphasizes not so much by what he tells as by what he leaves unsaid. As before the plague, religion and politics preoccupy the Irish. A few healthy women have been quarantined here and there by a few strong-minded men; for the rest, the only sexual option is homosexuality. Mr. Herbert wisely keeps the orgies offstage. The awful weight of the disaster comes through most powerfully in O'Donnell's complex interactions with his companions and in his chance encounters with drunks, bullies and visionaries, and the walking dead who haunt the aftermath of all such upheavals.

"The White Plague" borrows one stylistic device from the ***Dune*** series. The narrative is divided into many short chapters, each told from a different point of view and each headed by a short quotation. In the ***Dune*** books, all the references are fictitious—"The Collected Sayings of Muad'Dib" by the Princess Irulan, "The Book of Leto" after Harq al-Ada, the "Dictionary Royal" (fifth edition) and so on—yet taken together they have the paradoxical effect of grounding the high-flying fiction by placing it in a "historical" context. In **"The White Plague,"** Mr. Herbert plays a different trick; he mixes quotations (sometimes shortened or rearranged) from real sources with sentiments voiced by characters in the novel itself. The odd juxtapositions force us to rethink the meaning of the real quotations, such as Thomas Jefferson's "There is no truth on earth that I fear to be known." (What Jefferson actually said was "There is not a truth existing which I fear, or would wish unknown to the whole world.") The whole thrust of Mr. Herbert's narrative, of course, is that knowledge *is* to be feared—as long as men and women remain imperfect. The desire for revenge is a deeply human trait. But when such a primitive emotion draws to its service the awesome power of modern science, the ancient equation "an eye for an eye and a tooth for a tooth" becomes a prescription for racial suicide.

Can we survive our jealously guarded freedom to delve into nature's secrets? The author offers no easy answer to this question, nor does he permit the reader to dismiss it with a few brave mottoes from the past. . . . In the ultimate surprise, he wins from us a gasp (that is the only way I can describe it) of sympathy for the all-too-human Madman who rends the lives of billions to avenge the deaths of those he loves. (pp. 15, 21)

Gerald Jonas, "Madman's Revenge," in The New York Times Book Review, *September 26, 1983, pp. 15, 21.*

STUART NAPIER

Frank Herbert and Bill Ransom's latest collaboration, ***The Lazarus Effect,*** is a sequel to their previous lackluster effort, ***The Jesus Incident*** and suffers under the burden of continuing an already overextended idea.

Herbert, author of many science fiction novels, first exhibited this tendency to milk an idea for more than it was worth with ***Children of Dune***, third in what ultimately turned out to be four books based on the rich details found in the original 1965 best-seller ***Dune***. Impressive though his world-building is, at times the details get in the way of solid character and coherent plot. Such is the case with ***The Lazarus Effect***.

The story begins in the far distant future, approximately 300 years after the conclusion of the first novel. Through backfill, we learn that humans were abandoned on the planet Pandora by a starship run by a computer with a God complex. Ship's command, "You must decide how to WorShip me" formed the basis of their religion.

Pandora is hostile, nearly all sea environment when the humans arrive. Soon the only sentient life form—kelp—is destroyed and the remaining land masses give in to the relentless ocean. . . .

The basic plot—like most of Herbert's works, there are several sub-plots—is that of a subtle struggle between the two cultures that have evolved on the planet. . . .

Interwoven into all this is Vata, the mysterious, living "icon" of the WorShip religion and her child-mate, Duque.

A series of convenient events—a little too conveniently, for most readers, I would guess—brings the story to an ending of sorts. The kelp have regained sentience and Avata, their name for kelp group consciousness, takes control. Pandora has now gone full cycle. Or has it? In the final chapter we find Vata and Duque listening in on a conversation between a deceased Islander, now part of the genetic memory of Avata—thus the Lazarus effect—debating over its "editing" of him. "I can only improve myself," he says. Comments Duque, "You see? We care who forces our dreams on us."

A trilogy to come? Let's hope not.

Stuart Napier, in a review of "The Lazarus Effect," in Science Fiction Review, *Vol. 12, No. 4, November, 1983, p. 49.*

TOM EASTON

[In ***The Lazarus Effect***] Herbert and Ransom use [a] . . . stage of marvelous potential to good effect. We see Pandora through the eyes of high and low, Merman and raft-dweller, male and female. We see mutants to whom form is incidental, to be taken advantage of or ignored in favor of the human light within. We see "normal" humans for whom form is one more excuse for racism. We see a Merman who plans to destroy the rafters and preserve the coming land for true humans alone, and here we encounter the story's plot.

Brett Norton is a rafter fisherman who, rescued by a Merman girl, falls into the thick of the plot. Through love and action he sees the story through, and he is there when the villain falls from his height and Pandora finds a future for mutant and normal alike. He—and others—attract our empathy and bring the story alive, and if it were up to them alone the story would be excellent indeed, moving and dramatic and vivid.

But Herbert and Ransom spoil it with the very gimmick that justifies their title. You see, the Mermen can recreate the kelp because that ancient genetic engineer somehow put kelp genes in humans, and the genes can be retrieved and reassembled. That much we can accept, but then the authors tell us that the kelp is not only sentient, but telepathic, and it can absorb the memories and personalities of the dead. The dead can live again for real, not just in the metaphor of nature.

Add to that that the kelp has the power to take over the end of the story, to become an active agent so powerful that we wonder how humans ever managed to destroy it, and it's just too much. We cannot swallow it. And the shame of it is that the super-kelp and its Lazarus effect are so unnecessary to the story.

Then again, you may have no problem with what I call excess. If so, enjoy. (p. 165)

Tom Easton, in a review of "The Lazarus Effect," in Analog Science Fiction/Science Fact, *Vol. CIV, No. 2, February, 1984, pp. 164-65.*

MERRILL SHEILS

Each of the [**"Dune"**] sequels has built on . . . [Herbert's original] imaginative base. The fourth in the series, **"God Emperor of Dune,"** published in 1981, was less satisfying than the rest: the philosophical introspection of Muad'Dib's heir, Emperor Leto II—"the biggest juggernaut in human history"—overpowered the plot line. But [**"Heretics of Dune"**] brings back the adventure. It takes place 1,500 years after the fall of Leto, whose self-destruction sent humanity into creative chaos. Once again, old antagonists are pursuing secretive agendas that affect the future of the human species. (p. 73)

The Tleilaxu, a race that specializes in advanced genetic engineering, has produced a ghola, or perfect flesh-and-blood reproduction, of Duncan Idaho, one of Muad'Dib's most trusted aides. It is the 12th such ghola—complete with all the original man's memories and those of its 11 ghola predecessors. The Tleilaxu have outfitted the latest ghola with special talents; they hope to use him to help achieve domination of the universe for their vaguely Islamic religion. But the Reverend Mothers of the Bene Gesserit have plans of their own for the ghola. A young Fremen woman named Sheeana has shown preternatural ability to control Dune's sandworms, which now contain elements of the all-encompassing consciousness of the God Emperor himself. Some factions of the Bene Gesserit think they can use Sheeana and the ghola to rid humanity of Leto's continuing hold.

Meanwhile, the familiar universe of Dune is threatened from the outside. People are beginning to trickle back from the "Scattering" that took place after Leto's fall. In their isolation, they have become almost alien. Their leaders, for instance, are "Honored Matres"—counterparts of the Reverend Mothers who have adapted the Bene Gesserit's advanced mental and physical training into a perverse sexuality that enslaves everyone who encounters it. To combat the threat, the Bene Gesserit and the Tleilaxu form a shaky alliance. In the end, their machinations spell the end of the planet Dune as we know it and promise an entirely new chapter in Herbert's sprawling history. (pp. 73-4)

[Herbert's] central concerns—the extraordinarily complex connections among humans and between man and environment—never lose their fascination. (p. 74)

Merrill Sheils, "Strange Invaders," in Newsweek, *Vol. CIII, No. 18, April 30, 1984, pp. 73-4.*

JOHN BEMROSE

Heretics of Dune is a rare work of science fiction: it is destined to convert readers who have always sneered at the form. Exciting, intellectually complex and full of bizarre creatures and scientific marvels, it is already perched securely near the top of the best-seller lists. . . .

Heretics derives much of its excitement from its skilful portrayal of the struggle between the forces of light and darkness. But it is more than a simplistic space-age morality tale: it possesses a degree of moral ambiguity unusual in science fiction. Although the women of the Bene Gesserit appear good when compared with their enemies, they are far from blameless. Centuries of struggle have led them to value their own survival above all else. Taraza, the head of the order, embodies that ideal with a severity that makes her, in the eyes of her friend Odrade, almost cruel. On the other hand, Taraza considers her friend dangerously sentimental because Odrade retains fond memories of her mother.

To be humanly vulnerable, however, is a particularly difficult task in the universe of ***Heretics***. The warring civilizations live in perpetual terror of each other's potent weapons. Many of the technological marvels are extreme developments of such inventions as laser beams and genetic engineering; their appearance in ***Heretics*** stands as a warning to their dangers. But, beyond that, Herbert's remarkable talent for imagining new ways of living creates a magical world in which almost anything can happen.

That magic, however, is revealed preciously slowly at the beginning. For the first 100 pages Herbert is so busy sketching in background material that his plot moves at a glacial pace. Once the narrative unfolds properly, ***Heretics*** develops a momentum worthy of the best thrillers. Herbert is especially effective at delineating the tensions that precede violence. A particularly nerve-racking debate between Taraza and a foe eerily characterizes the convoluted logic of present-day arms negotiations.

Indeed, although ***Heretics*** might take place in the distant future, its deepest themes touch humanity's present anxieties. The triumphs of its heroes are short-lived and ultimately futile—small pinpoints of light in a universe where the misuse of technology has enslaved and disfigured millions. Herbert's vision is essentially tragic, and his novel, although it is fine entertainment, is also a prophecy and a warning.

John Bemrose, "A Tragic Vision of the Future," in Maclean's Magazine, *Vol. 97, No. 21, May 21, 1984, p. 62.*

GERALD JONAS

Readers unfamiliar with the first four [**"Dune"**] books will have difficulty with **"Heretics of Dune,"** I suspect. But for those already enthralled, it is clear that, in science fiction, Mr. Herbert's series ranks with Isaac Asimov's "Foundation" books in depth and intensity of impact. Like Mr. Asimov's characters, the conspiratorial characters of Dune deal only with issues of transcendent importance—the fate of mankind, the possibility of free will, the existence of evil. . . . The strength of [Herbert's] series comes from its utter seriousness. There is not a trace of irony, not a whiff of self-mocking doubt. And, surprisingly for books sometimes labeled as "space opera," there is very little action. Characters continually argue about motives, meditate on the relationship of cause and effect to their lives. Their conclusions and explanations lead not to understanding, however, but to more questions, which provide the basis for further discussions. . . . [The **"Dune"** books are] impelled by a powerful "need to know." Whether or not one agrees with Mr. Herbert's conclusions, he pays his readers the rare compliment of assuming that they find speculation about *truth* as entertaining as he obviously does. (pp. 24-5)

Gerald Jonas, in a review of "Heretics of Dune," in The New York Times Book Review, *June 10, 1984, pp. 24-5.*

TOM EASTON

Frank Herbert is one fortunate writer. He has a long list of books to his credit and most of them have succeeded well enough to make him a prosperous fellow. But in 1965 he came up with ***Dune,*** and that one made him wealthy. The readers loved it. I loved it.

So he wrote ***Dune Messiah*** and ***Children of Dune*** and ***God Emperor of Dune,*** and the readers loved them too. I liked the first two, but not the last. It was too much monomania, exhausting in its obsessions, and not much of a yarn.

So now he's written ***Heretics of Dune,*** and I find it better than ***God Emperor,*** if not quite up to the earlier books. It's still monomaniacal, but it's about heresy, which draws us away from Muad'dib and Leto II, millennia in the story's past. (pp. 169-70)

It all comes together with the sweeping inevitability of histories clashing. Herbert's story feels far more real than ***God Emperor,*** and if it lacks the personal tone of the early Dunes, it more than makes up for the lack with a stateliness born of a vivid sense of the millennia. Yet there is a personal side to the story. There are vivid, living characters. There is vigorous adventure and climax and resolution. And with it all, Herbert continues to amaze me with the continuity of his vision. He may even be the philosopher some of his fans claim he is.

If you're a ***Dune*** fan, don't miss this one. (p. 170)

Tom Easton, in a review of "Heretics of Dune," in Analog Science Fiction/Science Fact, *Vol. CIV, No. 9, September, 1984, pp. 169-70.*

JOHN CALVIN BATCHELOR

[Frank Herbert] has exercised the easy story-telling talent and dispassionate cynicism of the daily reporter to create, over the last twenty years, a world-famous and extremely lucrative series of science fiction tales based upon his happy genius of a novel, ***Dune*** (1965). . . .

Frank Herbert has a tin ear, an innocuous imagination, and no patience for surprise, character, forgiveness, love or what could be called the ha'penny details of humanity, like grumpiness; but none of these were ever why one turned to science fiction. This is the fun genre, and Mr. Herbert knows how to crank out the old fate-of-the-universe-in-the-balance plot one more time. Also, most importantly, Mr. Herbert has considerable hope for tired old mankind.

[In ***The Heretics of Dune*** it] is fifteen hundred years after the close of the last cycle (***Dune Messiah, Children Of Dune, God Emperor Of Dune***), and across the limitless reaches of space, mankind has again fallen into a pregnant dark age that resembles, sort-of, the Fertile Crescent in the first century A.D.: aging priest cults, arrogant warrior cults, and the arrival from outside of a new and vibrant empire of gold-hoarders that could be Rome with the emendation that the women are in charge because of their sexual prowess. A savior is required to rise from the obscurity of an outpost to plant the seeds of mankind's resurrection. Again, Mr. Herbert does not construct any of this with metaphorical or allegorical exactitude, and this interpretation is as good or useless as any. Nevertheless, the plot is concrete. (p. 475)

Mr. Herbert has little interest in physics or chemistry; this is not a book of spaceships or planetary geological events. His passion is for biology, specifically genetic engineering. All the plot twists turn upon bad blood, racial memories, and Darwinian absolutism, that is, prophets are born not made, magic is preserved instinct and not chicanery, survival is a matter of a superior gene pool and adoration of one's environment. This makes the ***Dune*** series distasteful to one whose affections are for the gentle accidents of heterogeneity, democracy, and intellectual freedom. But it is arguably a credible way to review mankind's history: There is a plan—some know it incrementally; others know it and abuse it; most are ignorant of it and choose to remain so.

Mr. Herbert's good few are drug-addicted "witches" who breed like prize hogs, ageless stoical warriors who kill in defeatist calms, and teenage children who bounce between virginal equestrian longings to ride the big worms and born-to-lose yearnings to rule the big worms like battalions of bikers. The evil few are drug-addicted "whores" whose sense of wickedness includes characterizing themselves as "bankers" and who like to torture with a method that reminds one of a nymph whipping a man with her long wet blond hair.

And what is left is Mr. Herbert's version of the common people, whom he calls "muck." Poor "muck" is in the cheap seats of this melodrama, and is obliged to endure frequent lectures about how it is not to be trusted with intelligence. ("We teach," says an evil one, "that new knowledge is nonsurvival.") Mr. Herbert sketches this paranoid fantasy as well as one can, given that Dostoyevsky's Grand Inquisitor has become a stylized television personality always changing costumes for all those anachronistic historical mini-series. (pp. 475-76)

[***The Heretics of Dune***] is a book for the beach, where one has no greater curiosity outside of Mr. Herbert's thrills than for the sunburnt beauties going by. However, it is also a novel of ideas, and if they are half-baked like everyone on that beach, there is in this ponderous unraveling of the mystery of the big worms, a snappy acknowledgement of the central conceit of all novels of ideas, "The writing of history is a process of diversion: Most historical accounts divert attention from the secret influences around the recorded events."

One either believes that the history books are all, or one does not quite, and playfully takes to fiction. Count Tolstoy did the ***Dune*** series's delightful core of salvation history much better in his fate-of-the-universe thriller, *War And Peace,* but then, Frank Herbert has stripped away all that annoyingly ambivalent verisimilitude in order to provide diverting, chatty, skimmable romanticism. (p. 476)

John Calvin Batchelor, "A Novel of Half-Baked Ideas," in Commonweal, *Vol. CXI, No. 15, September 7, 1984, pp. 475-76.*

SUSAN McLEAN

Any literature that suspends the limitations governing ordinary existence gives scope to the fears and longings that lurk in the unconscious. It is these fears and longings and, in part, Frank Herbert's skill in drawing upon them that explain the extraordinary popularity of his ***Dune*** series. He deliberately evokes the power of our repressed fantasies to demonstrate the danger of allowing such desires to guide our actions. . . . The desire to live forever is at once the most basic and the most unattainable of all human desires. Throughout his works, Herbert has attacked the quest for immortality as evil and dangerous, yet the very frequency of his warnings testifies to the abiding power of the temptation. (p. 145)

Immortality is one of the most persistent themes of Herbert's fiction. His first science fiction story, **"Looking for Something?"** (1952), concerned an alien race, The Denebians, who derive their immortality from korad, a substance secreted by human glands. . . . Several elements of this story prefigure Herbert's treatment of immortality in the ***Dune*** series. Melange, the longevity spice of the ***Dune*** series, resembles korad in that the production of each is the cause of death to humans. Denebians can increase the production of korad by increasing the dangers that humans face, since the threat of death produces a substance to prolong life. Melange, though produced by the "little makers" of Arrakis, can be harvested by humans only at great risk. Thus those who use melange or korad increase their own life spans at the cost of the lives of others.

It is one of the understated ironies of the ***Dune*** series that melange, a drug that prolongs life, should become the focus of a deadly battle for its control. Furthermore, because it is severely addictive in large quantities, melange can itself cause the death of its users in the event of its withdrawal. It is both a source of life and a trap. The same irony surrounds the prescience that is one of the side effects of melange. In the first book of the series, ***Dune*** (1965), the protagonist, Paul Atreides, can foresee the future but can neither foresee nor prevent his own death or the deaths of those who are dear to him. Like melange addiction, prescience can be a trap to those who try to use it to avoid risk. When Paul sets out to prevent the holy crusade that he foresees in his prescience visions, his efforts serve only to make the crusade inevitable. Finally, he comes to realize that he is fighting the force of evolution itself. . . . (pp. 145-46)

In order for humanity to become strong, it must pass through extreme danger; individuals must die so that the species will survive.

One of the most basic assumptions of the ***Dune*** series is that death is a necessary part of life. The desert people known as the Fremen obtain the water that sustains them partly by distilling the moisture from the bodies of dead Fremen. Their extraordinary strength and hardiness are the product of the extreme dangers and privations that they face daily. Their willingness to risk everything for a cause gives them an advantage over their opponents, the Emperor and the Harkonnens, who are hampered by their desire for security. (p. 146)

In the second book of the ***Dune*** series, ***Dune Messiah*** (1969), Paul is forced to face the consequences of his own evolutionary creed. Although he is willing to endanger himself, he is reluctant to endanger those he loves. He delays having children because he foresees that pregnancy will be fatal to his mate, Chani. . . . Paul foresees, however, that the very survival of humanity depends upon his choice. In order for the human race to continue, the needs of one generation must bow to the needs of the next. Paul therefore acquiesces to Chani's pregnancy and death in childbirth, after which he destroys his enemies' hold on him by walking into the desert to die.

The third book of the series, ***Children of Dune*** (1976), reveals that Paul's sacrifice was not enough to ensure the continued survival of humanity. Although Paul's holy crusade had disrupted the stagnancy brought on by centuries of stability, the government that he founded quickly calcified into an equally rigid hierarchy. Paul realized then that not even his death could halt the juggernaut of his religion and the stagnation that it would impose on society. Yet although he was willing to die to prevent it, he was not willing to sacrifice his own humanity. That task remains to his son, Leto II. . . . To guide the evolution of humanity so that it will be able to survive, Leto dons the sandtrout skin that gives him incredible strength, invulnerability, and a life span of thousands of years. The price he pays for these powers is his own humanity, for over the centuries his symbiosis with the sandtrout will transform him into a sandworm.

By the fourth book of the series, ***God Emperor of Dune*** (1981), Leto is over three thousand years old and has evolved into a five-ton monstrosity that is more sandworm than human. His personality is equally monstrous. In order to strengthen the human race, he has become the ultimate predator on it, destroying all opposition ruthlessly. He knows, however, that the success of his evolutionary plan will lead to his own death; in fact, he even trains his own assassin. By dying he will renew the life cycle of the sandworms, which had been close to extinction. Although his body will perish, his consciousness will live on forever, fragmented among millions of sandtrout, and he will pay for eons of power with eons of powerlessness.

Because Leto knows the terrible fate that awaits him, because he makes his choice not for selfish reasons but for the good of humanity, and because he sacrifices all human pleasures for longevity, his choice of long life is presented in a more positive light than Herbert usually accords to the quest for immortality. On the other hand, the fate of Alia, Paul's sister, illustrates the dangers of seeking immortality for selfish ends. In ***Children of Dune*** she succumbs to the wiles of her dead grandfather, Baron Harkonnen, who with all of her other ancestors constantly struggles for control of her consciousness in order to grasp at crumbs of experience. He persuades her to make forbidden adjustments to her internal enzyme balance that can halt the aging process and prolong her life indefinitely. . . . As Alia's career demonstrates, however, the most potent danger of immortality is its effect upon the possessor of it. The longer her potential life span becomes, the more she fears death and will do anything to avoid it. Her decision to break the taboo against immortality leads her to more and more desperate actions to prevent the revelation of her guilt. Ultimately, she becomes totally dehumanized, even plotting to kill her own husband, mother, brother, and nephew.

Cruelty, indifference to the suffering of others, and unwillingness to be bound by the dictates of moral codes are qualities typical of immortals in several of Herbert's works. . . . In ***The Dosadi Experiment*** (1977), a few alien Gowachin secretly imprison humans and other Gowachin on the deadly planet of Dosadi in order to provide an unlimited supply of spare bodies into which aging Gowachin can transfer, thereby prolonging their own lives. Rather than have their secret revealed, the Gowachin are prepared to destroy the entire planet.

The cruelty of these immortals arises from arrogance, boredom, or fear. . . . Gowachin are pushed to desperation by fear of being exposed and losing their means of immortality. Selfishness . . . is, in fact, the character flaw that Herbert most consistently attributes to immortals. They act as parasites upon mortal societies, taking without giving anything in return. . . . Ironically, the longer they live, the less alive they feel. In a way, their unwillingness to die is an unwillingness to grow up and take moral responsibility for their actions. Alia, faced in ***Children of Dune*** with a choice between suicide or a Trial of Possession, regresses to little-girlhood, begging her mother to tell her what to do. Her first courageous and mature act is her decision to commit suicide.

In contrast to these portraits of selfish immortals, Herbert has on several occasions depicted immortals and near-immortals who are not selfish. In each case the portrait is tinged with religion. . . . [This] sort of god is to be found in ***The Godmakers*** (1972), ***The Jesus Incident*** (1979), and ***God Emperor of Dune*** (1981). Whereas the selfish immortals were shams—their superior power being the product of superior technology and not of innate ability—the unselfish immortals possess truly supernatural powers: prescience, telepathy, superhuman strength, et cetera. They use these powers to benefit humanity, however, and not to control it for their own ends. . . . [Their] ultimate goal is to demonstrate that humanity should be self-reliant and not depend on gods. (pp. 146-49)

In ***Destination: Void*** (1966) an experiment to create an artificial consciousness in a spaceship's computer succeeds only after the ship is ordered to self-destruct. . . . The now conscious ship displays superhuman powers, transporting its crew instantaneously to Tau Ceti and there transforming an uninhabitable planet into a habitable one. Such godlike solicitude has its price: the ship announces to its crew, "You must decide how you will worship Me."

The Jesus Incident, written in collaboration with Bill Ransom, takes up the same story millennia later. The ship, now known to most humans as Ship, has changed the wording of its demand. It insists that humans decide how to worship, but no longer specifies that they must worship the ship itself. In trying to make people discover the true nature of worship, Ship has endlessly replayed human history, . . . but to no avail. Tired of the ceaseless repetition, Ship threatens to "break the recording" and destroy humanity unless Raja Flattery, a member of the original crew revived from hibernation, can help humans learn how to worship. . . . Ultimately, the pressures of fighting a losing battle with a poisonous planet, combined with the illumination of contact with a sentient alien species, force humans to understand their own nature for the first time, which was all that Ship had ever asked of them. . . . Ship then withdraws, leaving humans on their own and taking with it the devils of its own creation, Morgan Oakes and Jesus Lewis. Once humans no longer depend on a god to save them, they no longer need devils to be saved from. . . . Acceptance of the unknown and suspension of the desire for control, Herbert suggests, are the only things that could make life bearable for an immortal. Similarly, for mortals the thing that makes death bearable is the knowledge of the continued existence of the species.

In ***God Emperor of Dune,*** Leto combines elements of the mortal and the immortal. Like Ship, he suffers from the pangs of terrible boredom and the misunderstanding of his own worshipers, but like Raja Flattery he knows that he must die and wishes to ensure the survival of humanity. Although Leto is worshiped as a god and even demands worship, at the same time he deliberately becomes a devil in order to subvert that worship. . . . Through his tyranny he seeks to demonstrate the fallacy of depending upon gods for salvation, and thereby to force humans to rely upon their own abilities. In his death Leto reiterates an ancient pattern, the myth of the Dying God whose death brings renewal to his people. Herbert explicitly links Leto with Jesus by referring to Leto's betrayer, Nayla, as Judas. . . . Like Jesus, Leto willingly sacrifices his life for the benefit of humanity, but his gift to his followers is less spiritual than physical. (pp. 149-50)

Throughout his works Herbert suggests that there is a basic incompatibility between immortality and morality, between goodness and godhood. To be moral, he implies, a being must be willing to die, and to be good a god must be prepared to abdicate. At first glance, Ship in ***The Jesus Incident*** appears to be an exception to this rule, in that it does not die. However, like the Christian God, Ship possesses a surrogate in the form of the sentient electrokelp known as Avata. The electrokelp appears to be immortal in its natural state but is vulnerable to damage and death from humans. It is ultimately exterminated by humans as they attempt to create an Earthlike environment on its planet, but as Avata dies it passes on to humans its awareness of the oneness of life. From the union of Avata and humans, an infant, Vata, is born, who links humans in a telepathic union that allows them to see the true meaning of worship.

As the death of Avata leads to the birth of Vata, so death, in all of Herbert's works, is a prerequisite for new life. A species made up of deathless individuals cannot evolve, nor can it reproduce indefinitely without eventually producing insupportable overpopulation. . . . Most commonly, Herbert presents immortals as sterile or otherwise incapable of having offspring. Such is the case . . . with Ship in ***The Jesus Incident.*** In the ***Dune*** series, Alia, though known as the Womb of Heaven, remains barren, while Leto II loses his sexuality when he puts on the sandtrout skin that gives him longevity.

The only form of immortality that Herbert appears to trust is the immortality of a race, not of an individual. In fact, he seems to regard the very possibility of personal immortality as an illusion, for those who attain endless life actually sacrifice everything that makes life worth living. They lose both their past and their future when they renounce the possibility of change, living in an eternally boring present. Endless repetition dulls the edges of their emotions. Only when they accept the possibility of death do they begin to feel truly alive. (pp. 150-51)

Susan McLean, "A Question of Balance: Death and Immortality in Frank Herbert's Dune Series," in Death and the Serpent: Immortality in Science Fiction and Fantasy, *edited by Carl B. Yoke and Donald M. Hassler, Greenwood Press, 1985, pp. 145-52.*

(James) Langston Hughes

1902-1967

American poet, short story writer, novelist, dramatist, autobiographer, author of books for children, editor, and translator.

Springer/Bettmann Film Archive

A major literary figure of the Harlem Renaissance, Hughes devoted his versatile and prolific career to portraying the urban experience of working-class blacks. Having been a victim of poverty and discrimination, Hughes wrote of the frustration of being enticed by the American Dream of freedom and equality, only to be denied its realization because of racism. His work, however, is devoid of bitterness; as Theodore R. Hudson has stated: "Dipping his pen in ink, not acid, [Hughes's] method was to expose rather than excoriate, to reveal rather than revile." A "poet of the people," Hughes integrated the rhythm and mood of jazz and blues into his work and used colloquial language to reflect the essence of black American culture. Hughes's gentle humor and wry irony often belie the magnitude and insight of his themes.

Hughes wrote successfully in many literary genres, but he first earned a reputation as a poet. Such early collections as *The Weary Blues* (1926) and *Fine Clothes to a Jew* (1927) introduce his concern with racial conflict as well as his ability to blend humor and pathos in recreating the day-to-day life of the common black person. During the 1920s blues music was gaining widespread popularity, and Hughes adapted its phrasing and meter to his poetic explorations of loneliness and desperation. Onwuchekwa Jemie has observed that "[Hughes's] blues poems parallel the popular blues and capture, more fully than the work of any other writer, that 'ironic laughter mixed with tears' which is the spirit and essence of the genre." Hughes produced poetry throughout his career, although during the 1930s his interest in other literary forms took precedence over his poetic output. His later collections of poetry evidence an increasingly bleak appraisal of the social conditions of black America. In *Montage of a Dream Deferred* (1951) Hughes contrasts the drastically deteriorated state of Harlem in the 1950s to the Harlem he had known in the 1920s. The exuberance of nightclub life and the vitality of cultural renaissance had given way to an urban ghetto plagued by poverty and crime. Parallel to the change in tone was a change in rhythm: the smooth patterns and gentle melancholy of blues music were replaced by the abrupt, fragmented structure of postwar jazz and bebop. During the 1960s, political turbulence led Hughes to focus on poems of social protest, yet his affirmation of his heritage remained fundamental to his work.

Among Hughes's prose works are two novels, *Not without Laughter* (1930) and *Tambourines to Glory* (1958), and many short stories. His most noted short pieces, the "Simple" sketches, center on Jesse B. Semple, known as Simple, who represents the black Everyman. Simple is the quintessential "wise fool" whose experiences and uneducated insights capture the frustrations characteristic of the black populace. Arthur P. Davis has declared that "Simple's honest and unsophisticated eye sees through the shallowness, hypocrisy, and phoniness of white and black America alike." Originally introduced in the *Chicago Defender,* the Simple sketches immediately became popular among black readers and remain some of Hughes's most respected works. They have been collected in such books as *Simple Speaks His Mind* (1950), *Simple Takes a Wife* (1953), *Simple Stakes a Claim* (1957), and *Simple's Uncle Sam* (1965).

Although generally considered less significant than his poetry and prose, Hughes's work for the theater was substantial. Employing such innovations as theater-in-the-round and audience participation, Hughes anticipated the work of several later avant-garde dramatists, including Amiri Baraka and Sonia Sanchez. In 1938 Hughes founded the Harlem Suitcase Theater in order to provide a black drama forum. He also helped establish the Los Angeles Negro Arts Theater and the Skyloft Players of Chicago. As with his work in other genres, Hughes's drama combined urban vernacular, folk idioms, and a thematic emphasis on the dignity and strength of black Americans. *Mulatto* (1935), his first play to be produced, *Little Ham* (1935), *Soul Gone Home* (1937), and *Simply Heavenly* (1957) are among Hughes's most noted plays and were collected in 1963 under the title *Five Plays by Langston Hughes.* Also included is his adaptation of his novel *Tambourines to Glory.*

Throughout his career, Hughes encountered mixed reactions to his work. Many black intellectuals denounced him for portraying unsophisticated aspects of lower-class life, claiming that his focus furthered the unfavorable image of his race. Hughes, however, believed not only in the inherent worth of

the common people but in the need to present the truth as he perceived it: "I didn't know the upper class Negroes well enough to write much about them. I knew only the people I had grown up with, and they weren't people whose shoes were always shined, who had been to Harvard, or who had heard of Bach. But they seemed to me good people, too." As the struggle for American civil rights became increasingly widespread toward the end of his career, Hughes was also faulted by militants for failing to address controversial issues. Nevertheless, Hughes's reputation with black readers has remained consistently strong, largely due to his Simple stories and his accessible portraits of urban life. In addition, his adaptations of musical forms to literature have been widely, although sometimes grudgingly, praised. Hughes is commonly known as the "poet laureate of Harlem" and is, according to Onwuchekwa Jemie, "a technician and innovator of the first rank and a seminal figure in American literature."

(See also *CLC*, Vols. 1, 5, 10, 15; *Contemporary Authors*, Vols. 1-4, rev. ed., Vols. 25-28, rev. ed. [obituary]; *Contemporary Authors New Revision Series*, Vol. 1; *Something about the Author*, Vols. 4, 33; and *Dictionary of Literary Biography*, Vols. 4, 7.)

ALAIN LOCKE

Fine clothes may not make either the poet or the gentleman, but they certainly help; and it is a rare genius that can strip life to the buff and still poetize it. This, however, Langston Hughes has done, in [**"Fine Clothes to the Jew"**], a volume that is even more starkly realistic and colloquial than his first,—**"The Weary Blues."** It is a current ambition in American poetry to take the common clay of life and fashion it to living beauty, but very few have succeeded, even Masters and Sandburg not invariably. They get their effects, but often at the expense of poetry. Here, on the contrary, there is scarcely a prosaic note or a spiritual sag in spite of the fact that never has cruder colloquialism or more sordid life been put into the substance of poetry. . . .

The success of these poems owes much to the clever and apt device of taking folk-song forms and idioms as the mold into which the life of the plain people is descriptively poured. This gives not only an authentic background and the impression that it is the people themselves speaking, but the sordidness of common life is caught up in the lilt of its own poetry and without any sentimental propping attains something of the necessary elevation of art. Many of the poems are modelled in the exact metrical form of the Negro "Blues," now so suddenly popular, and in thought and style of expression are so close as scarcely to be distinguishable from the popular variety. But these poems are not transcriptions, every now and then one catches sight of the deft poetic touch that unostentatiously transforms them into folk portraits. In the rambling improvised stanzas of folk-song, there is invariably much that is inconsistent with the dominant mood; and seldom any dramatic coherence. Here we have these necessary art ingredients ingenuously added to material of real folk flavor and origin. . . . After so much dead anatomy of a people's superstition and so much sentimental balladizing on dialect chromatics, such vivid, pulsing, creative portraits of Negro folk foibles and moods are most welcome. The author apparently loves the plain people in every aspect of their lives, their gin-drinking carousals, their street brawls, their tenement publicity, and their slum matings and partings, and reveals this segment of Negro life as it has never been shown before. Its open frankness will be a shock and a snare for the critic and moralist who cannot distinguish clay from mire. . . .

The dominant mood of this volume is the characteristic "Blue's emotion,"—the crying laugh that "eases its misery" in song and self pity. However, there are poems of other than the folk character in the book,—none more notable than **"The Mulatto,"**—too long to quote, even though it is a lyric condensation of the deepest tragedy of the race problem.

Alain Locke, "Common Clay and Poetry," in The Saturday Review of Literature, *Vol. III, No. 37, April 9, 1927, p. 712.*

HARRY ALAN POTAMKIN

The Negro is conscious of his singular identity. But as yet there are few among his artists equipped to meet this consciousness of identity with a consciousness of its material. The Negro artists divide themselves into those who have capitalized the fact of color without paying for it by the study of its essence and peculiarity, those who recognize the need for a separate expression of a racial material but whose aesthetic apprehension or control is not adequate, and those who attack the essential material for what it can yield under aesthetic suasion. It is evident that an artist is great in proportion as he approaches the third category. Of the Negro poets only Jean Toomer has entered it with both feet. Langston Hughes is as yet on the threshold of the second category, and there is no visible progress in his present book [**"Fine Clothes to the Jew"**] beyond **"The Weary Blues"** to reveal that he has become sensible of his poetic problem, which is *to convert the material.*

Whatever value as poetry the Negro spirituals or blues may have, duplicate spirituals or blues have only duplicate values. In the conformation of the inherent qualities of these indigenous songs to an original personal intelligence or intuition lies the poetic performance. And Mr. Hughes has not made the material so conform. One critic has attributed to his work "force, passion, directness, and sensitive perception." The "force" is the material's, not the poet's. It remains literal, unconverted. The "passion" is not great enough to convert the *attitudes* of his verse (attitudes simply rewritten from the material) into integrated experiences or even effective quasi-experiences. "Directness" in itself is of no importance; it can intensify or sharpen initial power or give precision to inventiveness. His "perception" is not sensitive, for what he sees it takes only eyes to see. He reads what is written, no great feat; he hears well, that is, his receptive pitch is accurate. But what of the final instrument of poetry that recreates the sensations in terms of a personal idiom? He is apparently unaware of even its existence.

Mr. Hughes has been called an interpreter of certain of his race. Perhaps. I see nothing in his verses to convince me of their experiential authenticity. But interpretations are only reutterances at best. Not even a translation creates the new utterance which is a poem. I find in the work of Langston Hughes the recording of certain Negro songs. I have no doubt it is as good a record as we own, for he has here and there done a little rewriting. But beyond that he has made no individual contribution. (pp. 403-04)

Harry Alan Potamkin, "Old Clothes," in The Nation, *Vol. CXXIV, No. 3223, April 13, 1927, pp. 403-04.*

THE NEW YORK TIMES BOOK REVIEW

Langston Hughes has succeeded in giving us in **"Not Without Laughter"** an intimate picture of that type of Negro life which has been so popular with white writers in the recent decade. . . . Hughes, in fact, is the first of contemporary Negro writers to treat successfully with the life of the lower class Negro in town as well as city. . . .

"Not Without Laughter" really has no story at all. It has only characters. The hero, Sandy, who grows up in the novel from a very young boy to a rapidly maturing young man, is the least successful creation of them all. The other characters, however, are beautifully clear and real. Jim Boy, the father of Sandy, a guitar-playing, irresponsible gadabout; Angee, his wife, who loves him on account of rather than despite his vices; Aunt Hager, the mother of Angee, the plantation mammy who would rather be a slave than a free woman and whose whole life is spent in service to others; Tempy, the sister of Angee, who marries Mr. Siles for his wealth and becomes an exponent of middle-class virtues; and Harriet, who despises Tempy and flings herself into the circus-whirl of the stage, winning prominence as a blues singer—these are the people who live in this novel as few characters have ever lived in a book.

One of the most interesting aspects of the novel is the excellent contrast in character that it affords. Tempy and Mr. Siles versus Harriet and Jim Boy, the conflict between the Negro type which, preferring wealthiness of money to wealthiness of soul, apes white ideas and ideals, and the type which, despising wealth even when it has it, sneers at white ideas and ideals as the ridiculous conventions of a people who have never learned to live—here we have a striking cross-section of that conflict which has already set in between upper and lower class Negro life. Tempy and Mr. Siles hate the blues and spirituals because "they are too Negro," and condemn those who sing them for "acting like niggers." Harriet and Jim Boy not only love the blues and spirituals, their very lives are made up of their music. They love them because they are so Negro.

"Not Without Laughter" is very slow, even tedious, reading in its early chapters, but once it gains its momentum it moves as swiftly as a jazz rhythm. Its characters, emerging ever more clearly and challengingly as the novel proceeds, gives it this rhythm. Every character in the novel, it can be said, with the exception of Tempy and Mr. Siles, is a living challenge to our civilization, a challenge that is all the more effective because it springs naturally out of its materials and is not superimposed upon them.

"'Not without Laughter' and Other Recent Works of Fiction," in The New York Times Book Review, *August 3, 1930, p. 6.**

V. F. CALVERTON

"Not Without Laughter" continues the healthy note begun in Negro fiction by Claude McKay and Rudolph Fisher. Instead of picturing the Negro of the upper classes, the Negro who in too many instances has been converted to white norms, who even apes white manners and white morality and condemns the Negroes found in this novel as "niggers," McKay, Fisher, and Hughes have depicted the Negro in his more natural and more fascinating form. There can be no doubt that the Negro who has made great contributions to American culture is this type of Negro, the Negro who has brought us his blues, his labor songs, his spirituals, his folk-lore—and his jazz. And yet this very type of Negro is the one that has been the least exploited by contemporary Negro novelists and short-story writers. It has been white writers such as DuBose Heyward, Julia Peterkin, Howard W. Odum, and Paul Green who have turned to this Negro for the rich material of their novels, dramas, and stories. These writers, however, . . . could never know him as an inner reality, as something they could live with as with themselves, their brothers, their sweethearts—something as real as flesh, as tense as pain. Langston Hughes does. As a Negro he has grown up with these realities as part of himself, as part of the very air he has breathed. Few blurs are there in these pages, and no fumbling projections, and no anxious searching for what is not. Here is this Negro, or at least one vital aspect of him, as he really is, without ornament, without pretense.

All this praise, however, must not be misconstrued. **"Not Without Laughter"** is not without defects of style and weaknesses of structure. The first third of the novel, in fact, arrives at its points of interest with a pedestrian slowness; after that it picks up tempo and plunges ahead. Unfortunately, there are no great situations in the novel, no high points of intensity to grip and overpower the reader. Nor is there vigor of style. . . . But **"Not Without Laughter"** is significant despite these weaknesses. It is significant because even where it fails, it fails beautifully, and where it succeeds—namely, in its intimate characterizations and in its local color and charm—it succeeds where almost all others have failed. (pp. 157-58)

V. F. Calverton, "This Negro," in The Nation, *Vol. CXXXI, No. 3396, August 6, 1930, pp. 157-58.*

THE SATURDAY REVIEW OF LITERATURE

The quality in this first novel [**"Not Without Laughter"**] by one of the most interesting of the younger negro poets in America that distinguishes it from most of the fiction about negroes by negroes is its tender understanding. It does not burn with the kind of indignation whose heat so easily converts fiction into propaganda; neither does it present its characters as white-washed whites, with speech and action obviously and pathetically synthetic. It is a subtly simple book, at times bordering on the biblical in the directness of its narrative, and giving one the pleasant impression of listening rather than following with the eyes. Its strength lies in this simplicity, in its author's unflinching honesty, and in his ability to make the reader feel very deeply the problems of his characters. . . .

Of this simple chronicle of the life of a negro family, Mr. Hughes has made a truly poignant novel. Of the minor tragedies of racial discrimination, such as the turning away from the gates of an amusement park of all the negro children, or the seating of all the negro children in the back rows of the school room, he has written touchingly, and with no trace of pleading, no underlining, just the simple statement, which is here, as always, the most effective means of stressing a point. . . .

Mr. Hughes has made a real contribution to negro literature in **"Not Without Laughter,"** and wholly aside from its value as observation, it is a good novel, an unusually appealing story handled for the most part with fine skill. The author's name must be added to the long list of contemporary poets who have turned with genuine success to the prose medium.

"A Poet's Debut As Novelist," in The Saturday Review of Literature, *Vol. VII, No. 5, August 23, 1930, p. 69.*

ANNE T. EATON

[In **"The Dream Keeper and Other Poems"**] the poet has made for young people a selection from the verse included in **"The Weary Blues"** and **"Fine Clothes to the Jew,"** and has added some new poems. In a foreword Effie Power, director of work with children in the Cleveland Public Library, states that many of the poems have already become favorites of the older boys and girls who use the library. It is not hard to understand the appeal of Langston Hughes to young people sensitive to poetry. Boys and girls will respond to the personal mood of such lovely lyrics as **"The Dream Keeper," "Quiet Girl"** and **"I Love My Friend,"** and will feel the lilt and cadence of the poems in the group called **"Sea Charm,"** and of the poems written in the manner of the Negro folksongs known as the **"Blues."** The group of poems called **"Walkers With the Dawn"** gives to the reader an imaginative understanding of the poet's feeling toward his own people.

Anne T. Eaton, in a review of "The Dream Keeper and Other Poems," in The New York Times Book Review, *July 17, 1932, p. 13.*

ROLFE HUMPHRIES

The virtues of Mr. Hughes's poetry are, mainly, those of forbearance. Given the single theme [of the collection **"One-Way Ticket"**], he treats his data with great restraint: basic vocabulary, simple rhymes, short line; no violence, no hyperbole, no verbalizing. The rhetoric, such as there is, is that of understatement; this kind of rhetoric is easier to slide over than that of exaggeration, but it contains, no less, the contrived element, and in the long run Mr. Hughes's use of these devices induces in the reader an effect opposite, I feel sure, to that which he intends. The studied artlessness pretty soon puts the reader too off guard, makes him condescending, patronizing. "How simple the Negro is," he will be saying to himself if he doesn't watch out, and, in a few minutes, "How quaint!" I for one should like to see what Mr. Hughes could do if he would try his hand on work more elaborate, involved, complex. . . .

Rolfe Humphries, in a review of "One-Way Ticket," in The Nation, *Vol. 168, No. 3, January 15, 1949, p. 80.*

HUBERT CREEKMORE

In his new book [**"One-Way Ticket"**] Langston Hughes returns to the kind of poetry that made him famous twenty years ago—songs that express the intricate, paradoxical soul of the Negro. The backgrounds, the simplicity, the humor, the passion and the song, all are here. Yet a rather intangible change in feeling and form makes these poems slightly different. The lyric, blues and folksong forms that Mr. Hughes has used to project, often with the lightest touch, the most devastating emotions and moral commentaries on life in the United States, have now been stripped almost to bareness. It is as if the poet, suspecting softness in his early work, were pushing toward an even more direct and forceful method.

The disappearance of the light touch is noticeable in the harshness of a few poems of "social protest." In a sense, most of Mr. Hughes' poems are protesting, subjectively for him and for the reader, even when they concern something as universal as physical love. One has no basis for objecting to such violent speech except that it doesn't often produce very good poems. Just the same, Mr. Hughes' forthrightness works well in many instances—**"Negro Servant"** and **"Visitors to the Black Belt,"** for example.

The better poems are affirmations of joy in life, and sing of fun, love and courage. Their emotional appeal is immediate. The technique, instead of obscuring this appeal, urges it on, so that the lines seem spoken by a friend. This kind of work sustains an unfortunately dying tradition—that of oral poetry, song without melody, which can delight in varying ways the laborer and the don. . . .

Hubert Creekmore, "Two Rewarding Volumes of Verse," in The New York Times Book Review, *January 30, 1949, p. 19.**

ROLFE HUMPHRIES

[**"Montage of a Dream Deferred"**] troubles and confuses me as work by this author often does. On the one hand, no white man living in Jackson Heights is fully competent to enter into the emotions of a Negro at home in Harlem; on the other, there seems to be a split—apparent in his book's title—between the sophistication of Mr. Hughes the individual and the innocence of Mr. Hughes the spokesman, so that the statement, in terms of be-bop . . . seems both oversimplified and theatrical.

Rolfe Humphries, in a review of "Montage of a Dream Deferred," in The Nation, *Vol. 172, No. 11, March 17, 1951, p. 256.*

BABETTE DEUTSCH

The language [in **"Montage of a Dream Deferred"**] is that of the work-a-day urban world whose pleasures are sometimes drearier than its pains. The scene is the particular part of the Waste Land that belongs to Harlem. The singer is steeped in the bitter knowledge that fills the blues. Sometimes his verse invites approval, but again it lapses into a facile sentimentality that stifles real feeling as with cheap scent. As he bandies about the word "dream," he introduces a whiff of the nineteenth century that casts a slight mustiness on the liveliest context.

Langston Hughes can write pages that throb with the abrupt rhythms of popular music. He can draw thumbnail sketches of Harlem lives and deaths that etch themselves harshly in the memory. Yet the book as a whole leaves one less responsive to the poet's achievement than conscious of the limitations of folk art. These limitations are particularly plain in the work of a man who is a popular singer because he has elected to remain one. His verse suffers from a kind of contrived naïveté, or from a will to shock the reader, who is apt to respond coldly to such obvious devices.

It is a pity that a poet of undeniable gifts has not been more rigorous in his use of them.

Babette Deutsch, "Waste Land of Harlem," in The New York Times Book Review, *May 6, 1951, p. 23.*

BUCKLIN MOON

Few writers have worn so well over the years for this reviewer as has Langston Hughes. There have been more important writers, perhaps, or others who worked a broader canvas, but few have been so versatile or as workmanlike. **"Laughing to Keep from Crying,"** which contains pieces dating from as far back as the Twenties, is a short book, but it is a highly successful one.

In these twenty-odd stories, almost all of them concerned with minority groups, there is little special pleading, as such, and no attempt to show only the best in the people about whom Hughes is writing. What the reader senses, however, if he happens to be a human being, is that the worst of them are caught between their environment and our inhumanity to a point where it got to be more than they could handle. It is this quality, I think, which makes every story (with the possible exception of **"One Friday Morning,"** which seems overly familiar because of similar stories which followed it) become amazingly fresh and free from the stereotype, and the self-consciousness of too much of our protest writing.

It could be said, I suppose, that these are not the best short stories that Langston Hughes ever wrote, but the best of them are very good, indeed. **"Professor"** is a highly successful story. . . .

Some of the shorter vignettes come alive with a sudden flash of imagery, or the poet's fine ear for the spoken word and the patterns of sound. Though less than two pages long, **"Rouge High,"** the bitterly fatalistic story of two Harlem prostitutes, seems to hang in the air long afterward, like a song you want to forget but cannot.

Other stories are less successful; they seem a little dated, almost archaic, because in the meantime our racial thinking has subtly changed. None the less, each is the work of a "writer" in the finest sense of the word; for here is underwriting and an economy of words that put to shame many a writer who has said less in an overblown novel than is often said here in less than a dozen pages. That is rare enough these days for special mention.

Bucklin Moon, "Laughter, Tears and the Blues," in The New York Times Book Review, *March 23, 1952, p. 4.*

ARNA BONTEMPS

Few people have enjoyed being Negro as much as Langston Hughes. Despite the bitterness with which he has occasionally indicted those who mistreat him because of his color (and in this collection of sketches and stories [**"Laughing to Keep from Crying"**] he certainly does not let up), there has never been any question in this reader's mind about his basic attitude. He would not have missed the experience of being what he is for the world.

The story **"Why, You Reckon?,"** which appeared originally in *The New Yorker,* is really a veiled expression of his own feeling. Disguised as a young Park Avenue bachelor who comes with a group of wealthy friends for a night of colorful, if not primitive, entertainment in a Harlem night club, the Langston Hughes of a couple of decades ago can be clearly detected. He too had come exploring and looking for fun in the unfamiliar territory north of 125th Street. The kidnapping and robbing of the visitor in the story is of course contrived, but the young man's reluctance to rejoin his friends or to go back to the safety of his home downtown reflects the author's own commentary. . . .

Over this tale, as over most of the others in **"Laughing to Keep from Crying,"** the depression of the Thirties hangs ominously, and it serves as more than just an indication of the dates of their writing. It provides a kind of continuity. After a while it begins to suggest the nameless dread which darkens human lives without reference to breadlines and relief agencies. . . .

Langston Hughes has practised the craft of the short story no more than he has practised the forms of poetry. His is a spontaneous art which stands or falls by the sureness of his intuition, his mother wit. His stories, like his poems, are for readers who will judge them with their hearts as well as their heads. By that standard he has always measured well. He still does.

Arna Bontemps, "Black & Bubbling," in The Saturday Review, *New York, Vol. XXXV, No. 14, April 5, 1952, p. 17.*

STANLEY COOPERMAN

Langston Hughes does not really write about Negroes. Of course the people who appear in the neat, pungent sketches and stories of ***Laughing to Keep From Crying*** have "colored" skin; but they appear as themselves and not as additional case histories for the indictment against racism. Fiction dealing with the problem of the Negro is understandably bitter, but this very bitterness tends to abstract injustice. Such books are limited despite their power, and the intensely human, individualized prose of Langston Hughes gives a more specific insight into racism than can be achieved by even the best problem fiction. The individuals in ***Laughing to Keep From Crying*** are individuals first and victims second, so that racism is seen as effecting not "Colored People" but men and women who have been met on their own terms.

Hughes writes a lucid, conversational style intimate as a personal letter and casual as a feature column. However the apparently effortless, facile prose contains undercurrents of sly humor, quiet bitterness and social consciousness that echo in the mind. It is the sort of lean, compact writing that implies as much as it states; an active, rhythmical prose without excess literary fat.

Stanley Cooperman, "Fiction Before Problem," in The New Republic, *Vol. 126, No. 18, May 5, 1952, p. 21.*

GILBERT MILLSTEIN

[In **"Simple Stakes a Claim,"** the], third volume of what are probably best described as interlocutories between the author and his Negro Everyman, Jesse B. Semple, Langston Hughes finally makes explicit the point of view that plainly underlies **"The Sweet Flypaper of Life," "Not Without Laughter,"** the other Simple books, and some of his poetry. These are singled out at random. "The race problem in America is serious business, I admit," writes Hughes in a foreword to **"Simple Stakes a Claim."** "But must it *always* be written about seriously? So many weighty volumes, cheerless novels, sad tracts and violent books have been written on race relations, that I would like to see some writers of both races write about our problems with black tongue in white cheek, or vice versa. Sometimes I try. Simple helps me."

This is a more courageous stand for a writer, particularly if he is a Negro, to take than might ordinarily be thought. He is apt to become the target of his own people, whose sensitivity (the word is the mildest of descriptives) to slurs, few of which are imagined, has been little mitigated, despite legislation, committee meetings or low-rent housing. (More than one case has been noted, for example, of the recordings of popular Negro singers being removed from Harlem jukeboxes when the artists were felt to have "put down their own people.") He is equally open to the regretful tongue-clickings of humorless liberals. Finally, he will do no more than confirm the rabid in their intransigence.

Like its predecessors, **"Simple Stakes a Claim"** is funny and sharp and indignant and tolerant, even of whites; and full of veiled warnings and demonstrations of the stupidities, callousness and cruelties of both whites and Negroes (but more of whites than of Negroes; the other would hardly have been expected, nor would it have been accurate as things are). Sometimes, it swings, like a good jazz tune. . . .

[In] the book, Hughes has Simple light into Negro gradualists, the atom bomb, Jim Crow (the description of whose funeral is a small masterpiece), his wife, Joyce, integration, the treatment accorded refugees (in dismal contrast to that accorded native Negroes), rent parties, Negro magazines, the reason why Negroes get all tired out on vacations (they don't get as much time off as whites and tend to half kill themselves having a good time): in one form or another throughout, he lightly tans the hide of segregation.

Gilbert Millstein, "Negro Everyman," in The New York Times Book Review, *September 29, 1957, p. 41.*

JAMES BALDWIN

Every time I read Langston Hughes I am amazed all over again by his genuine gifts—and depressed that he has done so little with them. . . .

There are the poems [in **"Selected Poems of Langston Hughes"**] which almost succeed but which do not succeed, poems which take refuge, finally, in a fake simplicity in order to avoid the very difficult simplicity of the experience! And one sometimes has the impression, as in a poem like **"Third Degree"**—which is about the beating up of a Negro boy in a police station—that Hughes has had to hold the experience outside him in order to be able to write at all. And certainly this is understandable. Nevertheless, the poetic trick, so to speak, is to be within the experience and outside it at the same time—and the poem fails.

Mr. Hughes is at his best in brief, sardonic asides, or in lyrics like **"Mother to Son,"** and **"The Negro Speaks of Rivers."** . . .

Hughes, in his sermons, blues and prayers, has working for him the power and the beat of Negro speech and Negro music. Negro speech is vivid largely because it is private. It is a kind of emotional shorthand—or sleight-of-hand—by means of which Negroes express, not only their relationship to each other, but their judgment of the white world. And, as the white world takes over this vocabulary—without the faintest notion of what it really means—the vocabulary is forced to change. The same thing is true of Negro music, which has had to become more and more complex in order to continue to express any of the private or collective experience.

Hughes knows the bitter truth behind these hieroglyphics: what they are designed to protect, what they are designed to convey. But he has not forced them into the realm of art where their meaning would become clear and overwhelming. "Hey, pop! / Re-bop! / Mop!" conveys much more on Lenox Avenue than it does in this book, which is not the way it ought to be. Hughes is an American Negro poet and has no choice but to be acutely aware of it. He is not the first American Negro to find the war between his social and artistic responsibilities all but irreconcilable.

James Baldwin, "Sermons and Blues," in The New York Times Book Review, *March 29, 1959, p. 6.*

DUDLEY FITTS

Langston Hughes' twelve jazz pieces [collected in **"Ask Your Mama"**] cannot be evaluated by any canon dealing with literary right or wrong. They are non-literary—oral, vocal, compositions to be spoken, or shouted, to the accompaniment of drum and flute and bass. For that matter, they speak from the page, the verses being set in capitals throughout; and there is a running gloss of dynamic signs and indications for the proper instrument to use at the moment. (One of these signs, used repeatedly, is "TACIT," which I find as obscure as Mr. Ciardi's "dust like darks howling," unless indeed it stands for the orchestral indication *tacet*.)

In this respect, **"Ask Your Mama"** goes back to Vachel Lindsay and his "Congo"; and I suppose it is fair to say that this is stunt poetry, a nightclub turn. The fury of indignation and the wild comedy, however, are very far from Lindsay. The voice is comparable to that of Nicolás Guillén, the Cuban poet, or of the Puerto Rican Luis Palés Matos—comparable, not imitative; insistent and strong in what is clearly a parallel development. (pp. 16-17)

Dudley Fitts, "A Trio of Singers in Varied Keys," in The New York Times Book Review, *October 29, 1961, pp. 16-17.**

JOHN McCARTEN

[**"Tambourines to Glory"**] is described in the program as "A Gospel Singing Play." It is that, all right, but, as written by Langston Hughes, who adapted the work from his novel of the same name, it is also a lighthearted, if awkward, spoof of the story of Aimee Semple McPherson, of fragrant memory, and the legend of Frankie and Johnnie. Mr. Hughes' evangelist is a shapely and shady lady called Laura Wright Reed . . . , who helps organize a street-corner songfest in Harlem to raise some cash for an evicted neighbor . . . , and is soon persuaded by a no-good schemer named Big-Eyed Buddy Lomax . . . to establish a store-front church, where singing and sanctity can be combined to make a fast buck for the operators of the place. . . . [The] congregation that is eventually assembled is a pleasure to listen to as it lines out assorted hymns and spirituals. But when the gospel shouting dies down to let the plot move ahead, things aren't as lively as they might be. . . . I guess the trouble is that Mr. Hughes' theme is too familiar to excite suspense. For instance, once we know that Big-Eyed Buddy Lomax is an incorrigible womanizer, it's easy to anticipate that he is going to do Laura Wright Reed wrong. And when a pretty minx called Marietta Johnson . . . comes along, it's a sure bet that old Big-Eyed Buddy will try to seduce her, even though she cares for another. . . . Well, he does try to, and that's when Laura decides to play Frankie to his Johnnie. The all-Negro cast of **"Tambourines to Glory"** is uniformly ingratiating.

John McCarten, "Tormented Trio," in The New Yorker, *Vol. XXXIX, No. 38, November 9, 1963, p. 95.**

WEBSTER SMALLEY

[Langston Hughes] began writing during the Harlem literary renaissance of the twenties and is today, at the age of sixty, America's outstanding Negro man of letters. . . . No writer has better interpreted and portrayed Negro life, especially in the urban North, than Langston Hughes. . . .

From his plays it is evident that Hughes has more and more identified with and written about the Negro community in Harlem. This crowded section of New York City, its vitality and variety, is his favorite setting. . . . (p. vii)

Not all of his writing is about Harlem and its inhabitants, of course. . . . His strong feeling for the Negro race and for the past and present problems of the Negro in America made inevitable his concern with the lot of the Negro in the South. This concern is strongly reflected in his first full-length play, ***Mulatto,*** for which Hughes chose as his subject the still explosive problem of racial intermixture and based the story on the plight of the son of a Negro housekeeper and a white plantation owner. (p. viii)

[***Mulatto***] was Langston Hughes' first professionally produced play and its text appears for the first time in this volume [***Five Plays by Langston Hughes***]. (p. x)

While reading ***Mulatto,*** one should remember when it was written. It is very much a play of the thirties, an era when sociopolitical plays dominated American drama. The tendency was to oversimplify moral issues as in melodrama. . . . In ***Mulatto,*** the injustices suffered by Bert, by Cora, and by all the Negroes in the rural South are clearly and forcefully presented. The thesis is there clearly enough. But then the characters of Bert and Cora begin to dominate the action, and the play becomes something more than mere thesis drama. Bert Lewis, the rebellious son of a white plantation owner and his Negro mistress, is placed in an unhappy, untenable situation, but it is his own stubborn, unbending pride—inherited, ironically, from his father—that brings about his downfall and death. The patient love and rich dignity of Cora and Bert's final recognition of the totality of his tragic situation raise ***Mulatto*** above the level of a mere problem play. One forgives Hughes the sometimes obvious exposition of the opening scenes (as one does the early O'Neill in *Beyond the Horizon*) for the tragedy and power of the play's final scenes. If the reader finds "melodramatic" elements in the play, let him look to the racial situation in the deep South as it is even today: it is melodramatic.

Mulatto is the only play included here in which a white character is more than peripheral. In the other plays, where white characters do appear, they are little more than symbols—evil, good, or, as in the one-act ***Soul Gone Home,*** indifferent. The conception of ***Soul Gone Home*** is that of fantasy, and it contains some ironically comic moments, but its impulse is far removed from comedy. In a vignette-like episode, Hughes creates with great economy the kind of play Zola called for in his preface to *Thérèse Raquin*. Although a fantasy in concept and structure, its atmosphere and effects are those of naturalism. Like one of Hughes' poems, ***Soul Gone Home*** bristles with implications and reverberates with connotations. That which is unsaid becomes almost more important than what is put into the dialogue. The repressive dominance of the white culture is suggested only by the arrival of ambulance attendants, who are white as the mother knew they would be. The tragedy is that of a people so repressed that they can no longer love, and the ironic implications build to a shocking climax. Its impact is stark and uncomplicated, and it is a difficult play to forget.

Hughes does not always write in a serious vein, as readers of his stories and poems well know. His folk plays of urban Negro life, at once humorous and revealing, are a true contribution to American folk drama. The three included here—***Little Ham, Simply Heavenly,*** and ***Tambourines to Glory***—are, if one must define them, comedies. But the triple specters of poverty, ignorance, and repression can be seen not far beneath the surface of the comedy. The "numbers racket," "dream books," and the "hot goods man" in ***Little Ham,*** Simple's wistful sadness that no Negro has seen a flying saucer, and Laura's attitude toward the "religion business" in ***Tambourines to Glory,*** all indicate the near poverty, the ignorance, and the superstition that prevail in the world of which Hughes writes. Nevertheless, it is a colorful, wonderful world he presents to us, and we cannot but admire the spirit and vigor of his characters. He gives us a dynamic view of a segment of life most of us will never know and can discover nowhere else. At times he may sacrifice dramatic action for the sake of portraying nothing more than the people of Harlem absorbed in living out their lives from day to day, but if the humor of the scene and Hughes' infectious interest in his characters carry us along with him, what more can we ask?

Little Ham, "a play of the roaring twenties," is the first of Hughes' urban folk comedies. Its setting is Harlem at the time of the "Negro Renaissance," of *Shuffle Along,* and of the Cotton Club, but it is unlikely that any of its characters knew the meaning of "renaissance," had seen *Shuffle Along,* or had been inside the Cotton Club (which catered to a white clientele). Completed in 1935, ***Little Ham*** is a period piece, and one should remember the short skirts, tassels, brocades, and bell-shaped trousers of the era as he reads.

The play concerns the affairs (the word is intentionally ambiguous) of Hamlet Jones, a fast-talking, colorful, pint-sized Negro who shines shoes for a living. Little Ham's world is crowded, almost too crowded at times, with Harlemites of every sort except those of conventional respectability and education. It is a lively world, a society of casual morality that the white community either ignores or makes no attempt to understand. Hughes understands it, and this is the Harlem he has made into a literary land exclusively his own. One should not search too hard for profundity in ***Little Ham;*** it is a high-spirited revel and should be accepted as just that. Little Ham, Madam Bell, Lulu, and generously proportioned Tiny Lee are of the Harlem Hughes remembered as a young man, but are persons clearly recognizable today. If the characters in these folk comedies seem uncomplex, it is simply because these people are, in reality, direct and lacking in subtle complexity. Since they are unaware of the existence of Freud and Jung, Hughes has not hampered them with a burden of subconscious motivation.

Hughes creates his characters from life. He does not create character to fit a preconception, so he is not frightened if some of his creations do things and like things that Negroes are reputed to do and like. There is probably no group of people he dislikes more than the "passers" and pretenders of this world. He accepts, loves, and enjoys every aspect of his heritage and has the wisdom to recognize its richness. He does not write for those Negroes who have turned their backs on the spirituals and blues, nor for the people, Negro and white, who would bowdlerize *Huckleberry Finn*. He writes of what he sees, in his own way. (pp. xi-xiii)

Langston Hughes is a most eclectic writer. In his "Simple" books and in his play, ***Simply Heavenly,*** he has created a hero who is almost no hero at all. Jesse Semple, or "Simple," yields to temptation so innocently but means so well, that any audience will forgive him more quickly than does his fiancée. Simple is Hughes' most memorable comic creation. He is of the same dramatic stripe as Figaro in Beaumarchais' *Figaro's Marriage*—both constantly skirt calamity and get into a good deal of trouble before they finally succeed in marrying the girls they love, and each has a unique dignity in spite of their comic weaknesses. Like his comic compeer, Simple has more than his share of these. His power of reasoning is wonderful to follow, even when his conclusions are unanswerable. . . . Simple, like most of his friends in Paddy's Bar, seldom has much money. What the inhabitants of this "neighborhood club" lack in affluence, they make up for in high spirits and good humor. There are no villains in ***Simply Heavenly***. . . . The values of this play are not built on dramatic clash and suspense, rather, they are inherent in Hughes' intimate and warmly affectionate picture of the unique inhabitants of this city within a city. (p. xiv)

Essie and Laura, in ***Tambourines to Glory,*** are presented as simply and forthrightly as are Ham and Simple, but there is no similarity of character. Essie and Laura are both strong individuals—Essie, in her goodness, and Laura, in her predilection toward chicanery. Symbolically, they represent two very real aspects of all revivalist, perhaps all religious, movements. The saint and the charlatan often live side by side, even in established religions, and sometimes exist in a single personality. Hughes chose to write a rousing musical melodrama about some aspects of Harlem religion. The result is a skillfully created, well-integrated musical play, written with humor, insight, and compassion. (p. xv)

Villains are not plentiful in Hughes' Harlem plays. Big-Eyed Buddy Lomax (who informs us that he is really the Devil) is unique. Even he is a threat only through Laura's weakness for him (and all he represents). Hughes is not as interested in a conventional conflict between protagonist and antagonist as in revealing the cracks in the self-protecting façades humans erect to conceal their weaknesses. His characters are never merely subservient to plot. Thus, even within the confines of melodrama, he is able to write a moving and honest play.

Tambourines to Glory is more than musical melodrama; it is a play of redemption. It is a Faust-like tale, told with the simplicity of a medieval morality play. Hughes tells the story with great good humor, but he never asks us to laugh derisively or to smile sardonically. Behind the laughter is a touch of pity and a great quantity of warm understanding. As broadly and simply as the characters are sketched, they are utterly believable. When they show weakness, their frailties stem directly from problems that plague the average Negro in our largest metropolis. Laura's grasping drive for material things, for example, is a natural reaction to the deprivation and poverty she has suffered all her life, and Essie's honest faith is a triumph over tribulation and temptation. Both characterizations are true.

Finally, this play is in effect a "dramatic song," to use one of Hughes' descriptive terms. It has a pervasive rhythm. The integration of action, original lyrics, traditional spirituals, and the gospel music of Jobe Huntley, adds to the richness of the drama and contributes to characterization. Music is central to the lives—one might say, even to the spiritual being—of these characters. Nowhere has Hughes more skillfully interwoven and integrated music into the fabric of drama. (p. xvi)

The dramatic world of Langston Hughes is a quite different world from that of any other playwright, and the discovery of that world is, in itself, an entertaining, wonderful, and enlightening experience. (p. xvii)

Webster Smalley, in an introduction to Five Plays by Langston Hughes, *edited by Webster Smalley, Indiana University Press, 1963, pp. vii-xvii.*

THEOPHILUS LEWIS

Langston Hughes' ***The Prodigal Son*** is a lush emotional experience. In the playbill, the format is called a gospel song-play. . . . [The] production is essentially a ballet accompanied by spirituals and by erotic music suggesting the pleasures of sin dens.

The opening choral, "Wade in the Water," establishes a mood of reverence; immediately the audience is involved. Caught in the fervor of spirituals, they sway and clap hands along with the performers. This rendering of the story of the prodigal, thought by many to be the most beautiful of the parables, is one of the rewarding experiences of the season. (pp. 62-3)

Theophilus Lewis, "A Twin Bill," in America, *Vol. 113, No. 2, July 10, 1965, pp. 62-3.**

THEODORE R. HUDSON

The late Langston Hughes was never primarily a "protest" poet. Although he wrote almost exclusively of the condition of being a Negro in America, Hughes was no racist in the current sense of the word. Seemingly incapable of acrimony, he was, nevertheless, militant in his own way. Dipping his pen in ink, not acid, his method was to expose rather than excoriate, to reveal rather than revile. Indeed, in the rare instances when he approached irreconcilable bitterness, his art suffered.

The Panther and the Lash, a thematic collection of his social poems, most published for the first time, is no exception. (p. 345)

Technically, these poems differ from the blues (Negroes don't get the blues any more anyhow, for the blues is a passive reaction to trouble), jazz, and ballad structured verses of his early volumes. Though not nearly as artistically conceived and executed, the newer poems are more in the free-verse and "bebop" style and mood of two of his later works, ***Montage of a Dream Deferred*** and ***Ask Your Mama.*** There are changing rhythms, oxymoron, counterpoint and counterstatement, cataloguing of names and places, and juxtaposed images. There is less of the urban folk idiom which Hughes is so adroit at using; instead, there is flat and direct statement.

Some of the best poems in this collection are those previously published, including **"Merry-Go-Round," "Cultural Exchange," "Dream Deferred," "Christ in Alabama,"** and **"Warning."**

Many of Hughes' earlier poems have a spontaneous quality, a mystical effusion, a natural lilt. In ***The Panther and the Lash*** he seems to have tried too hard, seems to have forced his art—as if his urge to write were the result of exterior commitment rather than interior compulsion. The result is that this anthology is marred in places by the prosaic rather than the poetic, by lines that plod rather than soar. Although these poems may stimulate the reader's mind, they often do not reverberate in his heart. And, as in some of his previous protest poetry, when he is grimly earnest he occasionally loses his poetic touch and declaims rather than sings.

Overall, though, ***The Panther and the Lash*** is satisfying. His message is both valid and valuable. Hughes depicts with fidelity the Negro's situation and the Negro's reactions to this situation. Hughes has the discerning and accurate eye so necessary for a poet, and his poet's hand and eye are synchronized—which is another way of saying, in the jargon of the ghetto, that Langston Hughes "tells it like it is." (p. 348)

Theodore R. Hudson, "Langston Hughes' Last Volume of Verse," in CLA Journal, *Vol. XI, No. 4, June, 1968, pp. 345-48.*

PHOEBE-LOU ADAMS

The juvenile miseries described in wry single sentences [in ***Black Misery***] prove to be, on the whole, variations of those affronts to self-esteem suffered by all children, and more amusing than tragic. Tragedy is implied by the necessity for the black child to attribute all difficulties to color while the white child, when insulted by an obtuse teacher, is free to dismiss the affair as just part of the way schoolteachers are.

Phoebe-Lou Adams, in a review of "Black Misery," in The Atlantic Monthly, *Vol. 224, No.2, August, 1969, p. 103.*

ZENA SUTHERLAND

Just before he died, Langston Hughes wrote the captions to a compilation of sketches [collected in ***Black Misery***] that reflect a black child's discomfiture. Some of the comments are universal . . . but most are concerned with the rebuffs suffered by Negro children. . . . Some of the material has a wry humor, some is bitter, all of it is blunt.

Zena Sutherland, in a review of "Black Misery," in Saturday Review, *Vol. LII, No. 33, August 16, 1969, p. 27.*

ZENA SUTHERLAND

Working with inner-city children in Harlem schools, Lee Hopkins discovered that they responded spontaneously to the poems of Langston Hughes. Collected [in ***Don't You Turn Back***] are some of those that were particularly enjoyed. Most of them are brief, childlike in their simplicity, and timeless in their interpretations of black dreams, sea-longing, or the triumphant affirmation of faith.

Zena Sutherland, in a review of "Don't You Turn Back," in Saturday Review, *Vol. LIII, No. 19, May 9, 1970, p. 47.*

ARTHUR P. DAVIS

Most critics feel that the Simple series is Hughes's best work in fiction and that Simple is his greatest single creation. (p. 69)

[Simple] is no superficial character. Into his creation Hughes put the great wealth of knowledge of Harlem that he amassed over many years. Langston Hughes called him Simple; he made him, however, a complex personality: a Harlem working man, uneducated but intelligent, militant and race conscious but not a fanatic, blessed with a sense of humor but no blackface comedian. In short, Hughes took great pains to make Simple a simple, ordinary Harlem man in the street, with all of the sharpness and prejudices and hang-ups of the breed.

The success of the series depended in large measure on the contrast between the directness and single-minded attitude on race, women, and things in general of Simple and the sophisticated attitude of the liberal and educated "straight man" Hughes. The clash and interplay of the two viewpoints furnish much of the humor in the works, but they have a deeper purpose. They point up and accentuate the dual-level type of thinking which segregation produces among Negroes. As we read these dialogues we find ourselves giving lip service to the liberal side of the debate while our hearts share Simple's cruder, more realistic appraisal of a given situation. For example, Simple, who blames everything bad that has happened to him on race, says: "I have been caught in some kind of riffle since I been black." When Hughes remonstrates with him for always bringing up the race question, Simple's answer is that a Negro does not have to *bring up* the question, it is always there. "I look in the mirror in the morning to shave—and what do I see? Me." Pushing aside all fancy explanations, Simple brings the issue home to himself. A black face in color-conscious America *is* the problem. Simple and every other sensible Negro know that.

There is, of course, a plot running through the six volumes and the many episodes of the series. In the earlier books Simple is trying to save enough money to pay his share for the divorce from his worthless down-home wife so that he can marry the lovely and charming Joyce. In later volumes Simple has married Joyce, and much of the humor (and the satire on middle-class pretensions) comes from her efforts to make Simple "cultured." There are, naturally, other recurring characters: Simple's nephew, his hard-boiled landlady, and the fun-loving barfly Zarita. The plot, however, is not the attraction in these episodes; it is but a rack on which to hang Simple's comments on Harlem, on the war, on women, on current events, and, above all else, on *race*. Simple's honest and unsophisticated eye sees through the shallowness, hypocrisy, and phoniness of white and black America alike. Simple is a racist, but he is not blind to black shortcomings. The Negro reader laughs *with* Simple rather than *at* him. As one reads the whole series, one is surprised to discover through Simple's observation how little conditions in America *basically* changed between 1943 and 1965, the year in which ***Simple's Uncle Sam,*** the last volume, appeared.

In Simple we find all the mixed-up thinking, all the dual loyalties, all the laughable inconsistencies which segregation and discrimination have produced in the darker American brother. So uniform is the pressure on the Negro, even though Simple is an uneducated worker, his responses to this pressure ring true for all classes. In this sense Simple *is* the American Negro. (pp. 70-1)

Arthur P. Davis, "First Fruits," in his From the Dark Tower: Afro-American Writers, 1900 to 1960, *Howard University Press, 1974, pp. 61-135.**

ONWUCHEKWA JEMIE

In Hughes's poetry, the oral tradition is perhaps strongest in those poems modeled on black music—the jazz and blues poems. Hughes came to maturity in the 1920s, the classic age of jazz and blues; and feeling as he did about the beauty of black life, it is not surprising that he should see black music as a paradigm of the human experience . . . and a suitable mold for his poetry.

His blues poems parallel the popular blues and capture, more fully than the work of any other writer, that "ironic laughter mixed with tears" which is the spirit and essence of the genre. The blues spirit in fact pervades Hughes's work in all genres. Similarly, the jazz poems move with the essential gaiety and swiftness of the music, developing from the controlled counterpoint of **"Closing Time"** and **"The Cat and the Saxophone"** to the sustained complexity of ***Montage of a Dream Deferred*** and ***Ask Your Mama.***

Regardless of form, however, the subject of an overwhelming portion of Hughes's poetry is the black struggle for political power and economic well-being within the American framework of the Declaration of Independence and the Constitution. Hughes has coded this struggle into his concept of the *dream deferred*. The black dream of well-being is an aspect of the "American Dream"—that segment of it whose fulfillment has constantly been obstructed by racism. Hughes depicts black life, including and in particular the efforts to fulfill the dream, not only in his blues and jazz poems but also in his free verse proletarian poetry of the 1930s, in his Freedom and Democracy poems of the World War II years, and in his final bitter, threatening, Third-World-conscious poetry of the mid-60s collected in ***The Panther and the Lash.***

Hughes was primarily a social poet, and recognized himself as such; but he was also a lyricist of the first order. His lyric, apolitical poems, for the most part built on the techniques of Imagism and the poetic conceit, are rich and original. His love poems, for instance, compare with the best in the language for their freshness, tenderness, musicality, and evocative power. (pp. xv-xvi)

[Hughes's oral poetry is] marked by an economy of means, by an almost ruthless exclusion of extraneous embellishments, resulting in a lean, spare, uncluttered style, and in efficient structure and logistics that permit no tedious or unnecessary diversions. Its commitment to the auditory, which in oral poetry is primary and definitive, and to a popular mass audience, make indispensable a lucidity of surface, normal syntax, a contemporary and colloquial rather than archaic or learned idiom, and vivid, concrete, and evocative imagery—in short, felicitous speech and mellifluous motion. Hughes's poetry is to be commended both for its fidelity to traditional forms and themes and for its transposition, manipulation, and adaptation of them.

Hughes's technically efficient poetic machinery, modeled on and assembled with parts borrowed from the oral tradition, is in the service of a sweeping social vision, is a vehicle for moving matters that are of importance to the poet's community. Hughes is very much aware of his historical placement, of the imperatives of his *race, moment, milieu;* and he makes his art respond to those imperatives, which include the raising of consciousness among an oppressed people, the affirmation, conservation, and onward transmission of their culture, and the battling of injustice through exposition and protest. The black artist's mission, as Hughes originally defined it for himself and his contemporaries in **"The Negro Artist and the Racial Mountain,"** calls for depth of vision, breadth of sympathies, passion, and courage. Hughes's passion and courage are obvious from the tenacity of his views and methods, but the intensity of his anger is not, mainly because he usually holds it at a distance, controlled and barricaded behind the sardonic humor of the blues, wrapped in irony, satire, wit and a general playfulness. . . . Hughes wears a genial mask that fits so well it is possible to mistake it for his face. But a careful second glance, even without a visit to the backstage dressing room, is enough to reveal a man burning with a rage as absolute as the fiery furnaces of LeRoi Jones or Sonia Sanchez. Indeed, we miss Hughes's rage only if we wilfully elect to concentrate on his humor. Usually he manages to mold his anger into the porcelain of his poetry—but without blunting its sharp and bitter edges; on the contrary, the jagged edges stand out even more fiercely against the smoothness. . . . (pp. 196-98)

[Hughes's] work is swept by the two positive compulsions or radical energies which may be said to dominate Afro-American literature—in its impulse toward the oral tradition and toward a literature of social struggle. Much of Afro-American literature of any consequence utilizes and projects black folk culture to a greater or lesser degree, and handles its matter in a way that would enhance the black struggle. In a sense the two propositions are one or can become one: some works hold the two impulses in equilibrium, give them more or less equal play, or fuse and compel them to function as an undifferentiated whole. This is the case with Hughes. In his work these dual energies are not only greatly visible, prolonged, and relentless in their operation, but they are held in balance and quite often fused, so that the form becomes the function, the instrument the purpose, the medium the message. In Hughes, black folk culture is the weapon, black social and economic sufficiency the prize fought for. By utilizing the black heritage so fully in his work, Hughes preserves and transmits that heritage and thereby aids the survival of Afro-Americans as a distinct people. One of the far-reaching effects of his esthetic, and of its elaborations and extensions by others, is to compel us, in evaluating a black writer, to take into account his attitude to himself and his people and heritage, and what use he makes or fails to make of that heritage. In other words, we must consider the presence, balance, and power of the positive compulsions in his work. Perhaps more than any other writer of his generation, Hughes permits these positive energies the most uninhibited, prolonged and unified play. (pp. 198-99)

Onwuchekwa Jemie, in his Langston Hughes: An Introduction to the Poetry, *Columbia University Press, 1976, 234 p.*

PATRICIA A. JOHNSON AND WALTER C. FARRELL, JR.

[With] ***Fine Clothes to a Jew*** in 1927, Langston Hughes became one of the most innovative voices in American poetry and the first poet in the world to transform the idioms of blues and jazz into poetic verse. . . .

Yet he abandoned this style of indigenous poetry in which he had won his first recognition and did not return to it for fifteen years, when he published ***Shakespeare in Harlem*** (1942), presenting himself as the "bard" of black lower class life. (p. 55)

Like ***Fine Clothes to a Jew,*** most of the poems in ***Shakespeare in Harlem*** are structurally patterned after the lyrics of the blues. There are, however, some important differences. At least half of the blues poems in the latter collection focus on the economic determinants of the blues while three-fourths of those in the former volume dealt exclusively with male-female relationships. In terms of their structural differences, the blues poems in ***Shakespeare in Harlem*** are more narrative in development than those in ***Fine Clothes to a Jew.*** Hence, the poet achieves a smoother flow of meaning from verse to verse in the ***Shakespeare*** poems and greater sense of organic unity.

Compare, for example, a poem from ***Fine Clothes to a Jew*** and one from ***Shakespeare in Harlem*** on the hardships a woman incurs because of the cheating ways of men. **"Lament Over Love,"** the poem from the earlier collection, provides a discursive discussion of this topic in a series of loosely connected verses. The singer moves wearily from a prayer that her child will never love a man to philosophical observations on the meaning of love. She ends with a rather abrupt and unexpected threat to commit suicide. . . . (pp. 57-8)

On the other hand, in **"Midnight Chippie's Lament"** from ***Shakespeare in Harlem,*** the singer recounts an interesting and lively experience that illuminates her pitiful plight. . . . (p. 58)

In the concluding verse, the singer-persona conveys to younger women the lesson she has learned from her experiences. . . .

Hughes had learned to use the blues form as a means of narrating some of the events or situations that are recurrent in the lives of oppressed Afro-American workers. Whereas most of the blues poems in ***Fine Clothes to a Jew*** deal with the emotional encumbrances of unrequited love, those in ***Shakespeare in Harlem*** cover a variety of the problems confronting black people, be they economic, social or emotional in content.

In **"Out of Work Blues,"** for example, the reader follows a jobless black man down the streets of Harlem as he relentlessly searches for employment. As a last resort he goes to the W.P.A. (Work Progress Administration) and is told that he is not eligible for assistance. . . . In the last two verses the hopeless, unemployed singer-persona reflects on the utter absurdity of his situation. He changes a potentially tragic event into one that is superficially humorous and ludicrous. . . . (pp. 59-60)

In **"Evenin' Air Blues,"** Hughes deals with one of his favorite themes, the expectations of the northward migrating Negro. Unlike the persona of **"Po' Boy's Blues"**—an earlier poem on this topic—who found the North undesirable because of its fast roguish women, the persona of **"Evenin' Air Blues"** finds himself poor and hungry soon after his arrival in the North. Once again economic problems are given precedence over emotional ones. . . . (p. 60)

Published during the aftermath of a period of mass unemployment, ***Shakespeare in Harlem*** describes the social and economic conditions that continue to foster the blues among black working-class people. No aspect of human life is void of financial implications. Often, for example, the need for companionship or love is confused with the need for money. The female singer-persona of **"Down and Out"** wants her partner to love her enough to furnish her with the things she needs. . . . (p. 61)

Similarly, "Midnight Chippie," the title character of the poem referred to earlier, must search the dark lonely street corners every night in an effort to rid herself of loneliness. She finds, however, that the love she usually sells cannot be given away during these cruel poverty-ridden times.

In **"Southern Mammy Sings,"** Hughes alters the format of his blues poem. Here the last line is repeated rather than the first and the traditional a-a-a rhyme scheme in the blues is replaced by a more complicated scheme, a-b-c-b-b. By changing the rhyme pattern and shifting the position of the repeated line, Hughes creates a syntactic format through which he can project the collective outlooks of black working-class people on issues like the war, racism and the evil ways of white folks. . . . (pp. 61-2)

The blues poems in ***Shakespeare in Harlem*** grew out of one of the most politically active periods in Hughes's career. They carry the burden of a new social vision that developed on a practical level, out of the poet's personal participation in the struggles of working-class people, and on a theoretical level, out of his broadened awareness of some of the inherent contradictions in American capitalism. (p. 62)

Patricia A. Johnson and Walter C. Farrell, Jr., "How Langston Hughes Used the Blues," in MELUS, *Vol. 6, No. 1, Spring, 1979, pp. 55-63.*

WALTER C. FARRELL, JR. AND PATRICIA A. JOHNSON

Hughes's poetic commentary on the unrest and anxiety of postwar Black America was presented in a collection published in 1951 entitled ***Montage of a Dream Deferred.*** In a prefatory note, Hughes explains that his poems were designed to reflect the mood and tempo of bebop. (p. 60)

[Bebop] evolved out of the jam session of the jazz musicians. Music historians agree that in its nascent stage, bebop was an "after hours" music that Minton playhouse "radicals" performed following their scheduled dates with swing orchestras. . . . No one can listen to a typical swing number and then a bebop number without realizing that in the latter, the part (individual instrument) makes a singular or distinctive contribution to the ensemble, while in the former the individual component plays a less assertive role.

In ***Montage*** Hughes took advantage of the structural characteristics of bebop by drastically reordering the traditional limitations imposed on the poem. By breaking down the barrier between the beginning of one poem and the end of another, Hughes created a new technique in poetry. Perhaps one could more accurately describe ***Montage*** as a series of short poems or phrases that contribute to the making of one long poem. Each poem maintains some individual identity as a separate unit while contributing to the composite poetic message. Movement between passages is achieved by thematic or topical congruency or by interior dialogue. (p. 61)

Hughes developed a form of poetry writing which would allow him to compress a wide and complex range of images into one kaleidoscopic impression of life in Harlem during the 1940s. The fact that these images are historically accurate and the fact that they convey something of what it meant to be black in America during this crucial war-torn era are proofs of Hughes's profound understanding of the events and issues that have shaped the contemporary world.

The idea that America has perennially denied her black working masses the right to life, liberty and the pursuit of happiness is the concentric unifying theme of ***Montage of a Dream Deferred.*** In practical terms, these rights include access to adequate housing, a decent standard of living, and fair and profitable employment. Hughes had developed this theme earlier—on a much more general level—in a poem published in 1926 entitled **"A Dream Deferred."** In ***Montage,*** Hughes expanded the thematic substance of this poem and injected it with powerful social and political connotations.

Montage is divided topically into six main sections: "Boogie Segue to Bop," "Dig and be Dug," "Early Bright," "Vice Versa to Bach," "Dream Deferred," and "Lenox Avenue Mural." Each section emphasizes a different aspect of life in Harlem—be it social, political, cultural, or economic—but without excluding any of these aspects.

"Boogie Segue to Bop," for instance, glorifies the fullness and richness of black culture, especially black music, through a cogent analysis of its social and political implications. **"Dream Boogie,"** the first poetic passage in this section, identifies a questionable rumbling in the rhythms of bebop and boogie woogie. And since music has always served as the "heartbeat" of the black community, that rumbling becomes symbolic of an underlying state of anxiety and unrest in the urban ghetto. . . . (pp. 62-3)

The poetic passages in the first section also include insights into male-female relationships, a central theme in popular black music. (p. 65)

In a section entitled "Dig and be Dug" we catch glimpses of an introspective Harlem, a Harlem that exposes the exploiters of the people and simultaneously laughs at itself as the victim of exploitation. A poem entitled **"Movies,"** for example, focuses on the cynical laughter of Harlem movie fans who have been amused by studio-produced caricatures of black life. . . . (p. 66)

"Dig and be Dug" examines a Harlem that is full of cynical self-awareness that is in tune to the political and social conditions that define its existence: there is a belligerent outcry against racist slumlords in **"Ballad of the Landlord,"** the cruel survival value of the black poor's faith in the numbers' racket in **"Numbers,"** a day-to-day awareness of the invigorating effects of war on the American economy in **"Green Memory";** all these images combine to create a portrait of a Harlem that knows and sees itself as being a part of the larger world scheme, a Harlem that is aware of its strengths and weaknesses. . . .

"Vice Versa to Bach" is an interesting section because it reveals Hughes's sensitivity to the development of class differentiations among black people. There is one group that is socially mobile, that moves "to the outskirts of town" and then seeks to sever itself from the inner city ghetto and all it stands for. Then there is the other group—the vast majority—that finds itself hopelessly trapped in poverty. In a set of poems entitled **"High to Low"** and **"Low to High"**, the socially mobile and socially stagnant groups engage in open dialogue. The low accuse the high Negroes of denying their blackness by snubbing their racial kinsmen of the ghetto. . . . The high accuses the low of what might comically be referred to as "conspicuous Negritude." . . . (p. 67)

Some of the poems in ***Montage*** are significant for the insight they provide into the nuances of urban living after the second World War. The war brought about a second wave of mass migration and placed an even greater number of black people under the onus of ghetto life. Upon their arrival to the urban north, blacks were housed in poorly kept run-down tenement buildings and charged exorbitant rental fees for the privilege of staying there. Hence the landlord-tenant conflict has become a recurrent feature of ghetto life. In **"Ballad of the Landlord"** a justly aggrieved black tenant refuses to pay his rent until the leaking roof and run-down stairway of his ghetto tenement are repaired. . . . A landlord-tenant conflict of sorts is also a major issue in a poem entitled **"Necessity."** The graphic imagery describing the smallness of the room is pathetically amusing. (pp. 68-9)

A poignant reminder of the fact that blacks are usually the last hired and the first fired is found in a poem entitled **"Relief."** Following the end of World War II, jobs once again became scarce, and blacks of the urban north were the first to feel the pinch of an unstable peacetime economy. In this poem, a Harlemite hopes that a third world war will come along to bail him out of his impoverishment. . . . [Likewise, in] **"Green Memory"** a Harlemite looks back nostalgically on the days of wartime prosperity. . . . (pp. 69-70)

The inhuman and demoralizing conditions of ghetto life caused some black people—especially the young—to turn to drugs as a means of escape. During the forties, drug abuse was not the national problem it is today, for frustrated blacks of the urban north were then the major constituents of the drug market. Drug addiction was most noticeable among bebop musicians who expressed their disenchantment with urban life and American society by assuming a posture of "cool" defiance. . . .

Hughes was aware of the widespread use of drugs among black musicians of the forties. A poem entitled **"Flatted Fifth,"** for example, gives the reader an inside view of the musician's "high" by showing how narcotics have drastically transformed the user's perception of objects around him. . . . (p. 70)

A short poem entitled **"Bebop Boys"** points to another aspect of the bebop movement, the conversion of many musicians to Islam. . . .

Beneath their cool detached facade, their unconventional religious affiliations, and eccentric wearing apparel, the bebop generation was haunted by the prevailing national and international disorders of the day. (p. 71)

Walter C. Farrell, Jr. and Patricia A. Johnson, "Poetic Interpretations of Urban Black Folk Culture: Langston Hughes and the 'Bebop' Era," in MELUS, *Vol. 8, No. 3, Fall, 1981, pp. 57-72.*

Kristin (Eggleston) Hunter

1931-

American novelist, short story writer, dramatist, scriptwriter, and journalist.

Hunter's fiction explores emotional and social problems of inner-city blacks. Though her works examine poverty, racism, and violence, they suggest self-reliance, unity, and appreciation of black culture as means to overcoming adversity. Hunter blends humor into her social criticism, and her works are considered optimistic. Her novel *The Soul Brothers and Sister Lou* (1968) is one of the earliest attempts to realistically depict the black urban experience in young adult fiction.

Hunter usually places her chracters in situations where they must rely on their own inner strength in order to survive. The young protagonist of her first novel, *God Bless the Child* (1964), attempts to raise herself and her family out of poverty but loses her health and the man she loves. Although she becomes financially secure by working in an illegal gambling organization and eventually moves into an affluent community, she realizes that her goal was an illusion: money does not necessarily bring happiness or social status. In *The Landlord* (1966), Hunter employs such comic techniques as caricature, parody, and slapstick in exposing the inequities of class distinction. In this novel, a wealthy young white man who is considered a failure within his social milieu becomes the resident landlord of an inner-city tenement. Through his friendships with his tenants, he learns to accept himself and begins to value human relationships above class and race. *The Landlord* was adapted for film in 1970. Among Hunter's other works for adult readers are *The Survivors* (1975) and *The Lakestown Rebellion* (1978).

With the publication of *The Soul Brothers and Sister Lou* Hunter gained recognition as an author of young adult literature. The novel concerns a juvenile gang that forms a successful musical group in order to avoid the pressures of gang warfare and police harassment. Some critics questioned Hunter's choice of musical talent over education as a means of self-improvement and contended that the group's sudden rise to fame is a convenient escape from poverty. However, the novel was praised for its authentic portrayal of growing up in hostile surroundings and for its affirmation of black culture. In *Lou in the Limelight* (1981), the sequel to *The Soul Brothers and Sister Lou,* Hunter examines the consequences of success and the dangers of drug addiction and casual sex. Hunter wrote further about disadvantaged youths in *Boss Cat* (1971), a novel for children, and in her short story collection *Guests in the Promised Land* (1973). The stories in this volume describe the experiences of black children in their struggle with racial adversity.

(See also *Children's Literature Review,* Vol. 3; *Contemporary Authors,* Vols. 13-16, rev. ed.; *Contemporary Authors New Revision Series,* Vol. 13; *Something about the Author,* Vol. 12; and *Dictionary of Literary Biography,* Vol. 33.)

Photograph by John I. Lattany, Sr.

HENRIETTA BUCKMASTER

Keen, sharp, even brilliant novels by Negro writers have become a commonplace. In the last twenty-five years . . . [Negro writers] have written with awesome power of a world twisted by the paradoxes imposed upon it. If the white reader continues unhearing, unseeing, it is not because that paradoxical world has been withheld from him.

Kristin Hunter in **"God Bless the Child"** has added a little more depth to the picture, a few more fresh details. She has the gift of words and of insights. She has taken a ferociously alive little Negro girl, Rosie Fleming, who lives in the Negro ghetto of a northern city. This world bounded by schools, beautyshops, bars, and moldering tenements has an indomitable will but lives a life of enforced separation from everything that would insure a homogeneous society. Somewhere, the other side of that invisible boundary, are nice houses, a choice of jobs, hopes fulfilled. . . .

Rosie is a born career woman. By the time she is eighteen she is on her way, twisting, snaking, through the jungle in which she lives. All she wants is to make her own money and plenty of it, buy her independence, and get grandma back where she belongs with her own family, fight lewd, blowzy Queenie [Rosie's mother] into being a brisk, well-corseted member of Rosie's society, manage every detail so that no loose ends can act as a whiplash.

Her plans are poignant and appalling. She knows all the temptations and thinks up all the answers. She is so wiry and skinny, she does not need sleep or food; she can work eighteen hours beating the system.

She never quite understands what system it is that is beating her.

In the Negro ghetto there are not enough jobs to go around, yet in time Rosie holds three. Even so they do not pay for the gifts . . . [for] Grandma, or for Queenie's private hospital room and nurse, or for the house which Rosie must have as her own status symbol.

In the Negro ghetto there is also not enough hope to go around. Decent relationships disintegrate almost before they get started. Larnie, Rosie's boyfriend, wins a scholarship but he cannot make the grade in college. The gifted few who escape have blazed no trail for the others.

This sounds like a social tract. It is not. **"God Bless the Child"** is a lively sharp swarming story of people. But they are people who have had the doors slammed on them once too often, who have become hobbled by the moral deformities of a fabricated society. The life they lead is like an immense, macabre charade which acts out conditions of privilege and security. When the unreality becomes too great then the police arrive, the bottles fly, the nightsticks crack, and the rest of the world watches from the safe side of the invisible boundary.

Miss Hunter does not miss a sight or sound of humor, pain, or vulgarity. Her eye is sharp, her ear true. The novel is, I think, too long, the pace too frantic, but the explosive vitality does not obscure its humanity nor lessen Miss Hunter's cool and relentness irony.

Henrietta Buckmaster, "The Girl Who Wanted Out," in The Christian Science Monitor, *September 10, 1964, p. 7.*

ROLLENE W. SAAL

"I want things," says Rosie Fleming, the Negro heroine of **"God Bless the Child,"** "I want things so bad I'd kill myself to get 'em." And Rosie does kill herself, riding a toboggan of work and whisky in a long, fast slide to extinction. . . .

What made Rosie run? Not having things is one reason. Another is the roach-infested tenement she shares with her grandmother and her mother. But the real impetus comes from the opposing values she learns from the two older women. She's forced to choose between the frank, amoral earthy world of her hairdresser mother, Queenie, and the aped gentility of her grandmother, who for nearly half a century has been a maid to a rich white family. . . .

In [Miss Hunter's] hands, Rosie's story assumes tragic proportions. Rosie succeeds in getting things—from a red party dress to a $1,700 crystal bowl; she even mangages to buy a mansion that once belonged to the very white. But she squanders her life in the pursuit of money and at the very end of it, in her last deliriums, she does come to know that the scent she followed was false: "Did rich white people have roaches too? . . . Yes, maybe they did have roaches, and termites too, and dandruff, and tooth decay, and falling hair. Granny had never mentioned such things, of course."

Rosie's tardy vision is not accompanied by profound understanding or new equilibrium: Miss Hunter's tragedy dissolves in her unrelenting cup of bitterness. Scarcely a character is not more sinned against than sinning. Queenie, Rosie's mother, who sees the sham of Granny's pretension but has little enough to offer in their place, becomes a sodden remnant of her once lusty exuberance. Rosie's first lover handsome Tom Tucker follows his philosophy: "I'm black. Only way I can make it in this country is to be an outlaw." Rosie's husband in their brief marriage, begins as a promising music student and ends up a paunchy bartender. Even Granny is cast off by her white employers.

The author's pill is bitter, and it is strong. Her novel is not without flaws. There are some awkward lapses of style; more important, she sometimes permits subsidiary characters to take control of the story. Miss Hunter is captivated by Rosie's best friend Dolly, a ladylike schoolteacher who apparently is the only one to profit from the unhappy events. Happily, for the book's sake, Rosie, child of the gutter, is able when she must to wrest the story back and make it her own.

Rollene W. Saal "What Made Rosie Run?" in The New York Times Book Review, *September 20, 1964, p. 36.*

ANDREW SARRIS

[In ***The Landlord***] Elgar Enders, a bitter-ender and *reductio ad absurdum* rationalizer of sorts, is white, wealthy and whimsical. His three lush mistresses indulge some of his neuroses; his shabbily accoutered analyst tries to cure the rest. It isn't easy. Even the name Elgar packs a traumatic charge. . . .

The last and most painful nail in Elgar's cross is his towering tycoon of a father, whose confident clichés disrupt Elgar's digestive processes. When Elgar invests his huge allowance in a house in the Negro ghetto of an unidentified Northern city, he becomes so intimately involved with his uninhibited tenants that he almost literally tries to crawl out of his skin.

Marge Perkins, a Gargantuan gospel singer via blues and voodoo, mothers him with all the amplitude of a dark continent of dreams and myths. Fanny Copee, a sinuous seductress in warm sepia, transfigures his sex life from a sport to an obsession. Even when Elgar discovers that his tenants are shameless frauds, he remains steadfast in his commitment to their cause. He dives into the treacherous depths of slum clearance, where white sharks gobble up and disgorge the poor fish, and learns to detect the subtler nuances of white bigotry. Elgar is an idealist in an insane sort of way, and it is rather remarkable that a Negro novelist is capable of so much sympathy for a creature with so much class condescension.

Or are we all still over-reacting to the overblown rhetoric about "Whitey?" Certainly the White Liberal reader, still lolling lasciviously under the lash of James Baldwin and LeRoi Jones, will be somewhat disappointd by Kristin Hunter's relatively urbane view of race relations. . . . **"The Landlord"** is a statement rather than a story, its author seems to be setting a limit to Love and Good Intentions as a solution to the race problem. It is probably too late to operate on the psychological deformities affecting the adult victims of prejudice. But there may still be hope for the children, to whose faith and trust the author commends her fable. . . .

At times, the fantasy becomes too frothy, the merriment too merciful. Where nothing bleeds, nothing breathes, and this is the problem with most fantasies. However, judging by the pain and passion in Miss Hunter's first novel, **"God Bless the Child,"** the relative lightness of **"The Landlord"** is an act of emotional restraint, a triumph of form over feeling. Yet there is an undertow of sadness pulling at the surface jokes about Black Nationalism and the cosmic radiation of races—particularly in Fanny's husband Charlie, who fancies himself a wronged Choctaw Indian before his mind snaps.

Nor is one stirred to laughter by the spectacle of an ancient Negro couple moving from their apartment and taking their plumbing fixtures with them. P. Eldridge DuBois, a Creole educator, a sort of Kingfish in drag, is the most outrageous character in this gallery of grotesques, but even he has his moments of humanity in his absurd parody of the white power structure. Perhaps the needle does pierce deeper than the knife after all.

Andrew Sarris, "Good Intentions," in The New York Times Book Review, *April 24, 1966, p. 41.*

GWENDOLYN BROOKS

Certain items of . . . [***The Landlord***] may occasion some tightening of Negro lips, or, perhaps, some hot reproofs. There is calm extension of that old stereotype, the invariably loose and oh-so-sexually-able Negro woman ("attractive and uninhibited," praises the jacket.) There is a static gift of that newer stereotype, the noisy Black Nationalist puppet, flat-charactered (and there are not and could not be any flat-charactered Black Nationalists) and steadily recommending the ejection of the Enemy.

These reproductions may not seem especially entertaining to Negroes who are working hard to confront themselves, as well as others, with estimable images. Miss Hunter might exclaim "But these are *persons*! There *are* such persons, whether Negroes want to admit it or not! And it is my permitted privilege to present them!" The author would be argued back to the responsibilities of the I-am-here premise (which *seems* to be hers).

It is entirely true that *persons* have a right in fiction whatever may be their tone or temper. When, however, this is the fundamental, bare, and pleasant premise, the author's manipulation should be magnificent enough, or surprising enough, or warmly poignant enough to cajole us into the hearty acceptance—once again—of that I-am-here which is recurrent in contemporary story-telling. . . .

The characters [in ***The Landlord***] are not lovable or loathable. To say that is not to say they should be *either*. They are lookable—due to the inventiveness and earnestly exercised power of Miss Hunter's talent.

Gwendolyn Brooks, "Tenant Problems," in Book Week—The Washington Post, *May 8, 1966, p. 14.*

ABRAHAM CHAPMAN

Kristin Hunter's second novel [***The Landlord***] is a fresh and refreshing expression of the diversity of American Negro writing, an elaborate spoof that somehow manages to combine touches of the absurd and intimations of the surreal, strokes of caricature, slapstick, and the grotesque, with an inherent, down-to-earth sanity and realism.

With a comic scalpel the author seeks to cut through the stereotypes, myths, masks, mystiques, and myopias of race and color hatred to reach the core of essential human contact and friendship. In a sense, therefore, the over-all context of ***The Landlord*** . . . is the American quest for identity, meaning, and purpose in the age of alienation.

The central character, Elgar Enders, is a neurotic, unconventional scion of a millionaire family who is trying to get out of himself and live as as member of mankind. He starts out as a sort of Anglo-Saxon Moses Herzog, or gentile Malamudian *schlemiehl,* or white "invisible man." Following the incredible paths of zany credibility, he lives through a series of reversals, from isolation to social involvement, from victim to hero, from failure to success.

To create an identity, to have something to do on his own, Enders buys a small apartment house in the Negro ghetto, into which he ultimately moves. . . .

If Enders has to cease viewing Negroes as stereotypes, he has to prove to the Negroes that he is an individual, not the abstract "landlord" or an invisible, nameless creature; he has to sweat out the typical Negro ordeal.

The Landlord has artistic and structural flaws. The parody of the psychiatrist is quite hackneyed, and some of the situations, including the denouement, are on the contrived or gimmicky side. But the verve, clever quips, and satiric bite of the novel merit a wide audience. Kristin Hunter, whose first novel was ***God Bless the Child,*** here negates any idea that all American Negro writing is didactic and dead earnest and bitter and full of the mystique of race; she explodes the stereotype of the so-called "Negro novel."

Abraham Chapman, "White Invisible Man," in Saturday Review, *Vol. XLIX, No. 20, May 14, 1966, p. 45.*

SATURDAY REVIEW

[In ***The Soul Brothers and Sister Lou***] Louretta Hawkins, fourteen, has few friends until she persuades her brother to let a group meet and rehearse in his printing shop. The police harass the gang and one member is killed, which tempts Lou to join the most militant of the gang. But she is not a hater and she cannot accept an extremist position. Lou and the boys are tabbed for a successful career when they sing at the funeral of the slain gang member, a too-pat ending for a book that is honest, convincing, and incisive. Actually, the plot is of less importance than the depiction in the book of the maturing of a young girl who learns to appreciate her racial heritage during those difficult years when self-acceptance and self-identity are problems for all adolescents. This is indeed a book for our times.

A review of "The Soul Brothers and Sister Lou," in Saturday Review, *Vol. LI, No. 42, October 19, 1968, p. 37.*

SUSAN O'NEAL

With mixed success, [***The Soul Brothers and Sister Lou***] jumps head-on into the main concerns of ghetto youth today: Black identity and militancy. . . . Unfortunately, militancy is unpersuasively made to seem the result of personal failure, merely a stage to be passed through, and militants are portrayed in superficial terms which reinforce fears aroused by the mass media: girls wear Afros and "huge earrings swinging like knives," men are "hairy figures." . . . Though militancy plays a large part in the story, it is a fictional fragmentation, far from a complete presentation of the philosophy or the motivations of its adherents. Such a flaw is especially regrettable since this is one of the few juvenile books attempting to present the culture of the ghetto rather than merely its economic impoverishment. The language, music, family relationships, joys and problems will be familiar to many readers from the ghetto and will give others insight through the sympathetic and believable characterization of Lou.

Susan O'Neal, in a review of "The Soul Brothers and Sister Lou," in School Library Journal, *an appendix to* Library Journal, *Vol. 15, No. 3, November, 1968, p. 101.*

JOHN NEUFELD

"The Soul Brothers and Sister Lou" is strong, vivid and disturbing. Louretta Hawkins is 14, skinny, self-conscious, hanging around with a corner gang whose slogans confuse her. She is involved with black teen-agers of all stripes: militants, hoodlums, decent kids, and those in between, uncommitted. Louretta's villain is The Man (the police); she has no heroes.

After family tragedy, death in the gang, an exhaustingly emotional funeral, attempted rape, and false but hopeful starts toward maturity—after an exciting, strongly-worded, seemingly true story is told with sympathy and skill, the Fairy Godmother arrives. Poof! Louretta is a recording star.

The real tragedy, and ultimate dishonesty, of **"Sister Lou"** is this happy ending. Miss Hunter writes too well—of revivalism, of revolt, of despairing blacks hanging onto the church, or a crowbar, with equal determination—to have settled for a false solution, when honest ones exist.

John Neufeld, in a review of "The Soul Brothers and Sister Lou," in The New York Times Book Review, *January 26, 1969, p. 26.*

PAUL HEINS

[The stories in ***Guests in The Promised Land*** are] superb for their exploration of Black experience as well as for their art. Some of them deal with frustration: **"Mom Luby and the Social Worker"**; **"All Around the Mulberry Tree,"** which presents the irksome restrictions of project life; and **"Guests in the Promised Land,"** which portrays how hatred and violence are created by condescension. Others are concerned with sheer individualism: **"Two's Enough of a Crowd,"** in which Amy perfers Chaucer to Black studies; [and] **"Debut,"** in which Judy, getting ready for her first ball, begins to understand the power of her womanhood. . . . Ranging from humor and satire to indignation, the stories present various facets of lives that have been warped by a frustrating racial milieu and—at the same time—have gone beyond it into universal humanity.

Paul Heins, in a review of "Guests in the Promised Land," in The Horn Book Magazine, *Vol. XLIX, No. 4, August, 1973, p. 386.*

BERNETTE GOLDEN

[Kristin Hunter] continues exploring the special problems of black adolescents in ***Guests in the Promised Land,*** a collection of stories of the search for values and direction. In **"Hero's Return,"** Jody and his friends look up to his older brother Junior, recently released from jail, so Junior gives him a dose of what prison means. In **"The Pool Table Caper,"** some street youths handle the prospect of gang warfare nonviolently. And in the title story, a group of ghetto youngsters on a day's outing to a suburban country club finds that some things are still off limits. In every tale the dialog rings true, and one senses Miss Hunter's love and understanding.

Bernette Golden, "Stories, Fables, and a Picture Book: A Notable Trio on Black Themes," in The National Observer, *August 11, 1973, p. 21.**

NOEL SCHRAUFNAGEL

The best novels of the sixties, with a few exceptions, are in the protest field and the emergence of the militant protest novel is the major development. This type of fiction stresses an organized retaliation on the part of blacks against white oppression. Apologetic protest in the decade continues to depict the Negro as a victim of racist practices and attitudes; however, a number of novels of the period do not deal specifically with these themes. This nonprotest or accommodationist fiction concentrates basically on the adjustment an individual makes to function in accordance with the standards of white society. This adjustment includes a resignation to the existence of racism and the search for a meaningful identity that will serve as a compensatory stratagem. The individual accommodates himself to the conventions of the dominant culture in order to survive, or because there seems to be no plausible alternative, but at the same time he hopes for a positive change in his life.

The accommodationist fiction of the sixties does not, then, exclusively emphasize the exploitation of blacks. This is an aspect of life that is taken for granted, and the characters respond to it as merely another part of their existence. While an accommodation to this kind of society is an acknowledgement of the white power structure, militancy is rejected as a panacea. Racial confrontations and scenes of violence are rare in these novels, as the conflicts take place essentially on a psychological level. The characters acccept their fate, or wrestle with their conscience in an effort to find mental peace in a ridiculous world. A third alternative is to work for change in an individual and intellectual manner within the system. A major aspect of the fiction is the quest for a racial identity. An individual, if he is not to be defeated by his environment, must identify with his black heritage. An accommodation to white society cannot include a denial of one's blackness. Racial pride, in perspective with one's essential humanity, is the savior of the individual. (pp. 121-22)

[One] of the great novels of the period which tends to stand alone in terms of categorization and literary quality is Kristin Hunter's ***God Bless the Child*** (1964). (p. 139)

The story of Rosie Fleming is a typically American one. In her pursuit of material goods she loses her own humanity. The fact that she is born in a ghetto, and deserted by her father, intensifies her passion to escape to a dream world. Rosie almost achieves her dream but she overlooks many important factors in her climb to material success. Finally aware of the fact that she has pushed her frail body too far, she pauses to wonder about the wisdom of what she has done. She realizes that she has been a fool. . . . The disillusionment of Rosie begins in earnest when she moves into her new house, and is climaxed when she discovers roaches in it. Almost as difficult to withstand is the realization that Granny, her favorite person, is less than perfect. (p. 140)

Rosie's recognition of Granny's fallibility is an important step in her own downfall. She begins to realize that her destiny is out of her control. Her problems do not stem particularly from the fact that she is black but from her attempt to buy happiness. She takes her materialistic society too seriously and becomes a victim of her insatiable passion. Rosie is an heroic figure, though, as she struggles against her fate, not yielding even when she knows her chances are nonexistent.

God Bless the Child is an accommodationist novel in the sense that it presents a protagonist who attempts to embrace the values of the white world, not only to adjust to this society but to accept the values of whites whether they are valid or not. But Rosie's motives are more complex than a simple acceptance of white society. Her childhood gives her the impetus to emerge from the ghetto, and the only place for her to go is among the rich white people. Once she obtains her fine house, though, she concentrates on being her own exciting, pathetic self. One of the most vividly portrayed characters in black fiction, Rosie is a female version of Sammy Glick in Budd Schulberg's *What Makes Sammy Run?* Hunter maintains an objectivity in the novel as she presents a tragic situation in a humorous tone. Rosie takes her enjoyment when she can to compensate for her unhappy life in the ghetto. Her zest for life is reflected in the prose style of the author, who is perhaps second only to Ellison as a literary stylist among black novelists. Her major weakness is a tendency at times to be too explicit in her use of symbolism, to the point that it intrudes upon the narrative instead of functioning organically.

In ***The Landlord*** (1966) Hunter parallels the fine performance of her first novel, and the tragic nature of ***God Bless the Child*** is replaced by an emphasis on comedy. The major characters, a confused young white man who is alienated from his rich father and humanity in general, learns something about life by associating with an odd assortment of blacks, the tenants in his apartment house. The problems of the tenants tend to make those of the landlord seem insignificant in comparison. In an effort to solve the problems of his new acquaintances, the young man becomes involved in life for the first time. (pp. 141-42)

The Landlord presents a humorous version of the quest of identity, but Hunter is skillful enough to deal with serious problems at the same time. In the manner of Ralph Ellison she explores the American system of values through the use of a comic exterior. The implications go much deeper, though, as attitudes toward race and materialism are revealed in the zany antics of the protagonist and his unusual cohorts. Hunter discloses nothing new about society in her book. She indicates that a lack of communication between people, who are concerned only with their own interests, is the major fault of the modern world. However, she reverses the typical fictional patterns by presenting a white protagonist who discovers that he is invisible in a society that recognizes only wealth and significant accomplishments. It is only when he becomes a successful businessman and saves the building from being condemned that he is noticed. Even this victory is hollow until Walter Gee [a Negro boy who lives in the landlord's house] expresses his friendship. The humor of the novel, then, and its fresh approach to the old problems of identity and race, make it a memorable production.

The third of Kristin Hunter's novels is not of the same magnitude as her earlier works. In ***The Soul Brothers and Sister Lou*** (1968) she turns to a theme that was popular in the accommodationist fiction of the fifties by dealing with the effects of a ghetto environment on young blacks who are searching for a meaningful existence. Of major importance is the need to find an outlet from the pressures of a racist society. Without the means of channeling their energy into something productive, the youngsters are prone towards a violent retaliation against the police, who are the emblems of an oppressive white society. (pp. 143-44)

The novel is an argument in favor of solving racial problems through the rehabilitation of the ghettos. While Hunter condemns militant action she illustrates why many blacks consider rebuilding necessary. The discriminatory practices of the police and the despair of life in the inner core of the city are presented vividly. Given the opportunities, though, the same youths who become militant rebels will turn into productive citizens. They will establish a racial identity and adjust to the white society by taking pride in their accomplishments. The book is so obviously contrived to make this point, however, that much of its effectiveness is lost. The realistic portrayal of the various aspects of life in Southside [the ghetto where the story takes place] that is maintained through much of the novel is eventually abandoned for the sake of a conclusion in which the problems are neatly solved.

While ***The Soul Brothers and Sister Lou*** is much inferior to ***God Bless the Child*** and ***The Landlord,*** it illustrates the prevalency of accommodationist fiction of the period in which black characters show a concern for finding a racial identity that will allow them to function within the mainstream of American life. By establishing a racial pride they do not emulate whites blindly, but basically accept the standards of the society, despite the predominance of prejudice and oppression that denies them full participation. In most of these novels, the emphasis is on a character's desire to become a complete American citizen, regardless of the absurdity of the world, and the special handicap of being discriminated against, while concurrently retaining both an individual and a racial identity. (p. 144)

Noel Schraufnagel, "Accommodationism of the Sixties," in his From Apology to Protest: The Black American Novel, *Everett/Edwards, Inc., 1973, pp. 121-46.**

HUEL D. PERKINS

Kristin Hunter is an excellent storyteller and she does it with such an economy of words that she makes the form seem easy. But more important, she uses her terse style . . . with a directness and freshness which makes her a joy to read.

In ***Guests in the Promised Land*** Ms. Hunter has included 11 short stories which might be sub-titled vignettes of black life with a message. There is no way that one can overlook the point of these stories for the author never fails to drive home the thesis that humanity is the only consideration that matters in this topsy-turvy world—a deep abiding concern for one's fellowman and ultimately the human condition.

The stories linger in your sub-consciousness long after you have finished reading them. One such story is about a young girl dressing for her debut who reacts to her mother's fussiness by making the dance analogous to a battle. . . . Or consider the 13-year-old lad, who, after tiring of seeing Blacks pay to have checks cashed, letters addressed, read or written, decides to open a free Public Scribe firm right in front of the established place of business. . . .

The absentee father, the grandmother figure, the social worker, the gossip, as well as the potentially dangerous subject of young Black-white relations, are all handled deftly by Ms. Hunter. One may even be led to sympathize with the small Black lad who plunges his pocket-knife into a beautiful piano at the all-white country club. Especially when the explanation lies in the fact that "it ain't no Promised Land at all if some people are always guests and others are always members."

In short, here are some thoroughly delightful stories that young readers of both races might read with pleasure and profit.

Huel D. Perkins, in a review of "Guests in the Promised Land," in Black World, *Vol. XXIII, No. 11, September, 1974, p. 91.*

GARY BOGART

[***The Survivors*** is marketed] as an adult novel and no doubt Kristin Hunter meant it as such, but for all its realism, it is essentially a long junior novel. The theme—friendship between an adult and a child—has by this time become familiar, but not so familiar that it fails to delight. . . . Because these two characters are so well drawn and fleshed out, most readers will care about Miss Lena's and B. J.'s shared experiences and growing need for each other. Inspiring in the best sense of the word, ***The Survivors*** should appeal to many people, from junior high school age to adult. (pp. 115, 175)

Gary Bogart, in a review of "The Survivors," in Wilson Library Bulletin, *Vol. 50, No. 2, October, 1975, pp. 115, 175.*

W. KEITH KRAUS

[*The essay from which this excerpt is taken originally appeared in* Arizona English Bulletin, *April 1976.*]

Beginning in the 1970s adolescent novels appeared that treated the black ethnic experience itself and in which "young characters . . . define their own world and establish their own values, often at variance with society's demands." . . . One of the more popular of these books that use a black protagonist is ***The Soul Brothers and Sister Lou.*** (p. 240)

[This] novel is realistic in terms of its depiction of a typical black family recently relocated in a northern city. The author, Kristin Hunter, has said she "tried to show some of the positive values existing in the so-called ghetto" in an attempt to "confirm young black people in their frail but growing belief in their own self-worth." (p. 241)

Louretta's brother opens a printing shop and Lou persuades him to let her friends use a portion of the building as a clubhouse. Lou and her "gang" meet at the shop where they compose and sing soul music. They are helped by a famous blues singer and by some of the teachers from their school; however, a number of the boys are still more interested in fighting the Avengers, a rival street gang. One of the boys is particularly rebellious and his hatred is directed toward all whites. His desire is to print a radical paper denouncing the white racist establishment.

The novel's villain is Officer Lafferty, a brutal white policeman who constantly harrasses Lou and her friends. . . . When Lou and her group hold a dance at the print shop, Lafferty and a group of policemen break in and search the members. In the ensuing scuffle one of the group is shot by a policeman and both Lou and her brother William become more militant in their attitudes. For a brief time Lou decides to join a black African group which denounces all whites, but she realizes this approach is filled with too much hate and is merely another form of racism.

Up to this point the novel is honest and uncompromising in its depiction of a particular segment of Negro existence; however, the ending is unrealistic and unsatisfactory. At the funeral of the boy killed at the dance the members of the Cheerful Baptist Church sing a "lament for Jethro," a part of which is aired on an evening television news show. The next day representatives of a muscial recording company call at the club house and offer the group a contract with a "nice little sum in advance for each of you, and more if the record is a success." The recording representatives ask the kids to "please run through the number you did at the church. The one about the boy who died." Eagerly the group sings and plays "Lament for Jethro," and the Soul Brothers and Sister Lou are born.

In a concluding chapter readers learn that the record is a hit and that Lou is banking her money, except for enough to buy her mother a washer and dryer. The most incorrigible member of the gang begins "saving every cent for college" as he unbelievably turns from "an ardent revolutionary . . . to an enthusiastic booster of business, free enterprise and capitalism." . . . And to complete the fairy tale ending it is revealed that Officer Lafferty has been suspended.

In a sense it could be argued that ***The Soul Brothers and Sister Lou*** is no different from other "safe" adolescent romance novels. Lou is basically a "nice" girl who studies hard, get good grades, and dreams of going to college. . . . Further, the all-too-convenient ending is used to solve the novel's racial problems and provide a happy and successful future for the story's characters. Still, this novel honestly depicts lower class ghetto life and shows the conditions which can produce racial hatred. In this sense the novel is much more mature and realistic in its approach to racial strife than most of its predecessors. (pp. 241-43)

W. Keith Kraus, "From Steppin Stebbins to Soul Brothers: Racial Strife in Adolescent Fiction," in Young Adult Literature in the Seventies: A Selection of Readings, *edited by Jana Varlejs, The Scarecrow Press, Inc., 1978, pp. 235-44.**

NEDRA STIMPFLE

For the teacher who is attempting to introduce aspects of Black culture to students who have limited racial experiences, I would recommend using the adolescent novel ***The Soul Brothers and Sister Lou*** by Kristin Hunter. . . .

In terms of general ghetto conditions, the novel points to institutional racism (crowded living conditions, prevalence of diseases, lack of balanced diets), the nature of gangs, survival means (welfare, numbers racket, illegal wine), and "outsiders," those who have totally succumbed to the forces of oppression. Folklore and "soul" are illustrated in the characters' verbal dexterity, dancing, and music, especially the blues. The history of Black music is conveyed through the character of Blind Eddie Bell, an old blues singer. When challenged to name Black authors, Lou cannot, thus displaying the mis-education that occurs in literature courses. Two questions emerge: Who are the Black authors? and why is their literature not taught? In the novel, the media plays both negative and positive roles. Lou is struck by the unreality of what is shown on televsion in comparison to her own life. On the other hand, the newspaper serves as a tool for education (Black history and Black literature) and for action (community reaction to Jethro being killed by a policeman). Many levels of Black awareness or thought are portrayed through the characters including: attitudes toward religion, social positions, and education; inter- and intra-racial tensions; reactions toward the police; militancy; and the ignorance of many whites.

Focusing on these areas would provide an adequate base for the teacher to buiid a beginning understanding of Black culture. There are, however, some limitations in the novel that the teacher should be aware of, the major one being that it does not present the Black dialect. . . . Other limitations are the attitude presented toward Black women, the comments directed against mothers, and the somewhat datedness of the novel (e.g., drugs are not mentioned).

Because it is easy reading and because it presents elements of Black culture in a non-threatening but realistic manner, ***The Soul Brothers and Sister Lou*** is an excellent device for developing students' cultural awareness. After reading it, students will be prepared and eager to move on to more complex and more forceful works.

Nedra Stimpfle, in a review of "The Soul Brothers and Sister Lou," in English Journal, *Vol. 66, No. 3, March, 1977, p. 61.*

MYRA POLLACK SADKER AND DAVID MILLER SADKER

The struggle and the dream are two strong elements in the very popular ***Soul Brothers and Sister Lou***. . . . Fourteen-year-old Lou, enmeshed in the world of violence and gangs, attempts to find a better way of life for herself and her friends. But in her efforts she continually encounters white hostility, and the ensuing struggle helps to form her black consciousness. . . .

Police brutality, or at least the brutality of some policemen, is a constant undercurrent in the book and provides another facet of the black struggle. In one episode Lou protests after a policeman strikes a pregnant black girl. (p. 145)

Through her confrontations with such institutional violence, the inequities of the welfare system and the brutality of the streets, Lou emerges with a greater sense of black identity. Eventually her dream is realized, as she and her friends become famous and successful as members of a singing group. This Hollywood-type ending has been criticized as phony and unrealistic. The treatment of black militants has also been cited as shallow, for they are portrayed as lacking well-thought-out motivations and even a minimal degree of compassion. Although these criticisms have validity, ***Soul Brothers and Sister Lou*** should be recognized for the number and variety of issues explored and the insight it offers into the black experience. (p. 146)

Myra Pollack Sadker and David Miller Sadker, "The Black Experience in Children's Literature," in their Now Upon a Time: A Contemporary View of Children's Literature, *Harper & Row, Publishers, 1977, pp. 129-62.**

KIRKUS REVIEWS

[***The Lakestown Rebellion***] is Hunter's coy version of a 1965 rebellion in Lakestown, the largest all-black community in the US and the only one in the North. But the ruckus is a far cry from the real tensions of that year—King's marches, Malcolm's assassination—which Hunter's insulated characters never acknowledge. The fuss is over a highway planned by born-yesterday white politicians who are routing eight lanes through Lakestown instead of through their own spotless community. The black folk come up with some goofball plans to disrupt the construction crew—spiked lemonade, parading hookers—but even these dodo white folks know when they're being suckered. They take stronger precautions, but the blacks still come up smiling: they finesse a dam and flood the site, creating a lake. . . . Hunter seems to know [her characters] well, but they don't always seem to know each other: they strut too much. And the most striking of all, . . . [the girl] who starts talking after 15 years, is someone Toni Morrison could layer into poetry; here she flashes on and then just shuffles by. [***The Lakestown Rebellion*** is more] revel than rebellion, and somewhat limited by the divided-highway approach.

A review of "The Lakestown Rebellion," in Kirkus Reviews, *Vol. XLVI, No. 6, March 15, 1978, p. 325.*

GROVE KOGER

[In ***The Lakestown Rebellion*** the] specter of destruction, coming after . . . decades of somnolence, awakens the town to the significance of its heritage. Hunter, author of several other successful novels including ***The Survivors*** . . . has fleshed out the plot with a body of shrewdly observed detail. She likes her characters and enjoys their idiosyncrasies—a rare trait these days.

Grove Koger, in a review of "The Lakestown Rebellion," in Library Journal, *Vol. 103, No. 11, June 1, 1978, p. 1196.*

THE NEW YORKER

The citizens of Lakestown, New Jersey, are blacks descended, in part, from riders on the Underground Railroad, and they include an unusual number of eccentrics, half-wits, and geniuses. Subversive resistance to the "boss man" is their delight, and so when bulldozers, clearing the ground for an eight-lane interstate highway, threaten to raze their ramshackle houses, gardens, and churches, they conceive and execute a series of imaginative acts of sabotage. . . . [***The Lakestown Rebellion***] could have been just a series of whimsical skits, but Kristin Hunter adds several ugly accidents that darken and deepen the story and keep it from becoming a sheer fantasy, and she endows her characters with a variety of voices, which all ring true.

A review of "The Lakestown Rebellion," in The New Yorker, *Vol. LIV, No. 21, July 10, 1978, pp. 88-9.*

LILLIAN L. SHAPIRO

In [***Lou in the Limelight,*** the] sequel to ***The Soul Brothers and Sister Lou*** . . . , we find the group on the road as performers in small clubs, first in New York and then in Las Vegas. The song they wrote about Jethro, killed in a police confrontation in the first book, has won them some initial success and a manager, Marty Ross. Aggressive and not scrupulously honest, Ross pushes the group into debt through expensive hotel accommodations and credit at the gambling tables in Las Vegas. . . . Drugs are made readily available to them, and soon they are in deep trouble. Summoned by Lou's call for help,

Aunt Jerutha, Jethro's mother, arrives like a *deus ex machina* and takes on as adversaries Ross and Carl Sipp, a figure in a national crime ring. One more attempt at touring almost leaves Lou with an overdose because of her dependence on drugs and drink. A happy coincidence brings her in touch with relatives in Georgia, and, finally, with happy prospects for a future in college. It is disappointing that the sequel does not come up to the high standard of its predecessor. While there is much information about corruption in the recording industry, the characters are flat and stereotypical. . . . Overlooked is the fact that within every ethnic group there are good and bad people. It is not a case of "they" versus "us," and this kind of young adult novel only serves to perpetuate a destructive polarization. (pp. 105-06)

Lillian L. Shapiro, in a review of "Lou in the Limelight," in School Library Journal, *Vol. 28, No. 3, November, 1981, pp. 105-06.*

BECKY JOHNSON

Some of the writing [in ***Lou in the Limelight***] is uneven, ideas are not always well integrated into the story line and some of the characters are only two-dimensional, but generally it is a highly readable depiction of talented young performers and the difficulty of their rise from ghetto poverty. It can be read independently of the first book but the many adult situations, especially the portrayal of the very seedy side of the entertainment field and 16 year old Lou's clear-eyed decision to use birth control pills, will make this more appropriate for an older audience than the earlier work.

Becky Johnson, in a review of "Lou in the Limelight," in Voice of Youth Advocates, *Vol. 4, No. 6, February, 1982, p. 33.*

MARILYN KAYE

An uncomfortable blend of cynicism and melodrama permeates [**"Lou in the Limelight,"** an] ambitious indictment of the entertainment industry. The ease with which the system wreaks havoc on the young people is perplexing. The boys' rapid descent into gambling and drugs suggests that they have no will of their own. The majority of the characters are show-biz clichés: the would be dancer reduced to prostitution, the lecherous producer, the evil casino manager with syndicate connections. The "soul brothers" are faceless, and even Lou, the one strong, believable character, is ambiguous. Despite her verbal adherence to traditional values, she herself is quickly sucked into a dependency on drugs.

Still, even with these problems, Kristin Hunter's artistry manages to peer through every now and then. There are some fine moments of animated dialogue and clear, provocative descriptions. But these tantalizing glimpses of talent are submerged in an overextended plot and a horde of underdeveloped characters. The author's abilities are buried in a chaotic story that halts, shifts and stutters—and ultimately goes nowhere.

Marilyn Kaye, in a review of "Lou in the Limelight," in The New York Times Book Review, *February 21, 1982, p. 35.*

SARAH SIMPSON

[***Lou in the Limelight***] is trite, lacking the warmth and innocent charm of the original. . . . The style and naive characters are junior highish; the easy drugs and sex are not. The message, quitting school to find quick success in entertainment, seems inappropriate today when young blacks face high unemployment because they lack education and job skills.

Sarah Simpson, in a review of "Lou in the Limelight," in The ALAN Review, *Vol. 9, No. 3, Spring, 1982, p. 25.*

Aldous (Leonard) Huxley

1894-1963

English novelist, short story writer, poet, dramatist, scriptwriter, critic, essayist, and nonfiction writer.

Huxley's prolific literary output reflects his constant search for alternatives to the chaos of the modern world. He often blended sophisticated social and cultural ideas with a witty style to produce satires of modern values. Huxley, who underwent several phases of notoriety and neglect during the course of his career, is perhaps best known for his "dystopian" novel *Brave New World* (1932), in which he warns that new technology, social and scientific developments, and political manipulation could result in a dreadful future civilization.

Huxley was born into a family renowned for scientific and intellectual achievements. His father, Leonard, was a respected editor and essayist, and his grandfather, Thomas Henry Huxley, was a leading biologist during the advent of Darwinism. Huxley's brother, Julian, was a noted biologist, and his half-brother, Andrew, was awarded the Nobel Prize in 1963 for his work in physiology. As a young man Huxley received extensive training in medicine and in the arts and sciences; he expounded upon these topics throughout his literary career. V. S. Pritchett once described Huxley as "that rare being—the prodigy, the educable young man, the perennial asker of unusual questions."

Photograph by Douglas Glass

After publishing three volumes of poetry and a collection of short stories to mild critical attention, Huxley gained wide recognition in England with his first two novels, *Crome Yellow* (1921) and *Antic Hay* (1923). The first novel is set on an estate where a number of scientists, artists, and aristocrats congregate for parties and conversation; in the second novel Huxley recreates the social atmosphere of the upper classes in post-World War I London. Often categorized as "novels of ideas," both of these works focus on eccentric characters who espouse fashionable sentiments. By intermingling such characters in his early fiction, Huxley was able to compare and contrast various ideas and human traits while he overtly satirized pseudointellectual vanities. Another "novel of ideas," *Point Counter Point* (1928), is considered Huxley's finest accomplishment in this mode. Huxley draws upon his knowledge of music to create a novel that unfolds like a musical composition; through constant juxtaposing of themes, moods, characters, and scenes, he portrays the flow of life through a fragmented presentation that the reader must unify. Primarily on the basis of his early novels, Huxley became a well-known literary figure who was especially popular among young people. Because his skeptical view of humanity pictured England of the 1920s as languishing in social and cultural malaise, Huxley was viewed by many as a rebel.

During the 1930s, Huxley's writings began to reflect his growing interest in politics. He won international fame with *Brave New World,* in which he departs from his mildly satiric observations of a limited group of people to a broader and more ironic satire of a utopian society. *Brave New World* projects a future totalitarian state that is a logical development of the values and trends of the modern world. The inhabitants of this society are free from war, disease, and suffering, and they enjoy an abundance of material and physical pleasures. In order to achieve such a state, human beings are conceived and mass-produced in test tubes and are genetically engineered with standardized traits. As children they are socially conditioned through technology and drugs; as adults they fulfill prescribed roles in one of five social classes and enjoy promiscuous, carefree lives. Conflict arises when a young man named John, or "the Savage," who was raised in a more primitive society, is introduced into the new world. John, who is capable of expressing diverse emotions and who recognizes the sundry possibilities of life, rebels against the standardization and mass conformity of the new world. *Brave New World* has been consistently praised as a novel of profound implications. Many critics rank *Brave New World* and George Orwell's novel *1984* as two archetypal works of dystopian literature.

Critics generally regard Huxley's fiction after *Brave New World* to be less important than his previous works. However, Huxley drew consistent critical and popular attention with several volumes of essays. His early essays reflect many of his early fictional concerns; they typically project a skeptical outlook on society and demonstrate Huxley's penchant for presenting multiple points of view. Beginning in the late 1930s and coinciding with his relocation to California, Huxley became interested in such topics as mysticism, Eastern thought, para-

psychology, and mind-altering drugs. In *The Perennial Philosophy* (1945), Huxley seeks means for mystic transcendence and concentrates on ideas that are common among various religions. *The Doors of Perception* (1954) recounts his heightened awareness and his revelations during his experiments with mescaline. In *Brave New World Revisited* (1958), Huxley reassesses the futuristic developments depicted in *Brave New World* and discusses what he considers to be the most urgent problems confronting the contemporary world: mind control, overpopulation, and environmental destruction. In *Literature and Science* (1963), Huxley reiterates his belief that the arts and sciences should work together to promote positive human values and practices.

In his final novel, *Island* (1962), Huxley presents his vision of a beneficent utopian society. This work is set on Pala, an imaginary Pacific island, whose inhabitants have created a harmonious society by combining technological advances of the West with spiritual values of the East. The island is eventually overcome by political interference and by the cynicism of Westerners who want to exploit Pala's natural resources. Like the response to all of Huxley's fiction, reception of this novel was mixed. Critics found Huxley's ideas intriguing, but several stated that they were not conducive to presentation in novel form.

Critics continue to debate whether Huxley should be considered a major or minor figure in twentieth-century literature. Huxley's early novels are read and discussed for their analyses of English life during the post-World War I era, and *Brave New World* is regarded as a classic examination of modern values and utopian vision. Although critics agree that Huxley was not a particularly innovative writer, his eloquent discussions of a wide range of ideas are consistently stimulating, and he is commended for his tireless search for and support of humanistic values.

(See also *CLC*, Vols. 1, 3, 4, 5, 8, 11, 18; *Contemporary Authors*, Vols. 85-88; and *Dictionary of Literary Biography*, Vol. 36.)

In this volume commentary on Aldous Huxley is focused on his utopian and dystopian novels.

JOHN CHAMBERLAIN

Dignity, beyond all else, has attended the creation of the classic Utopias, from that of Plato on down to Edward Bellamy's perfectly geared industrial machine. Conceived in kindliness of spirit, dedicated to the high future of the race and offered with becoming humility as contributions to the questionable science of human happiness, these classic Utopias have only too often seemed mere parodies of the Napoleonic State, the Taylor system or the laboratory where guinea pigs are bred to predestined fates. It has remained for Aldous Huxley to build the Utopia to end Utopias—or such Utopias as go to mechanics for their inspiration, at any rate. [In **"Brave New World"** he] has satirized the imminent spiritual trustification of mankind, and has made rowdy and impertinent sport of the World State whose motto shall be Community, Identity, Stability.

This slogan, Mr. Huxley seems to be saying under the noise made by his knockabout farce, is thoroughly unbiological. Mankind moves forward by stumbling—we almost said progressing—from one unstable equilibrium to another unstable equilibrium; and if the human animal ever ceases to do this he will go to the ant (the sluggard!) and become a hived creature. Mr. Huxley doesn't like the prospect.

So here we have him, as entertainingly atrabilious as ever he was in **"Antic Hay"** or **"Point Counter Point,"** mocking the Fords, the Hitlers, the Mussolinis, the Sir Alfred Monds, the Owen D. Youngs—all who would go back on laissez-faire and on toward the servile state. His Utopia has much in common with those of the nineteenth century—everything, in fact, but their informing and propulsive faith. . . .

Behold, then, the gadget satirically enshrined. As Bellamy anticipated the radio in 1888, Mr. Huxley has foreseen the displacement of the talkie by the "feelie," a type of moving picture that will give tactile as well as visual and aural delight. Spearmint has given way to Sex Hormone gum—the favorite chew of one of Mr. Huxley's minor characters, Mr. Benito Hoover. Grammes of soma—a non-hangover-producing substitute for rum—are eaten daily by the populace; they drive away the blues. God has dissolved into Ford (sometimes called Freud), and the jingle goes "Ford's in his flivver, all's well with the world." Ford's book, "My Life and Work," has become the new Bible. The Wurlitzer has been supplemented by the scent organ, which plays all the tunes from cinnamon to camphor, with occasional whiffs of kidney pudding for discord. Babies, of course, are born—or rather, decanted—in the laboratory; and by a process known as the Bodanovsky one egg can be made to proliferate into ninety-six children, all of them identical in feature, form and brain power. . . .

But slips there are, even in the most mechanical of all possible worlds, and owing to some oversight—possibly the spilling of alcohol into the blood surrogate upon which he was fed in his prenatal days—Bernard Marx, Mr. Huxley's hero, is dissatisfied.

Bernard loves Lenina Crowne in a sort of old-fashioned romantic way. He longs for solitude à deux. So with her he takes the rocket for a vacation in the New Mexican savage reservation. By sheer coincidence, the Director of Hatcheries and Conditioning for Central London had spent a vacation once upon a time in this reservation; and had lost his girl, a Beta-minus, in a sudden and confusing desert thunderstorm. Bernard, of course, runs upon the girl—now an old woman—and her son, John, the Savage, born viviparously. Quickly he gets into touch with Mustapha Mond, his Fordship, the Resident Controller for Western Europe. Shall he bring them back by rocket to London? His Fordship thinks furiously and decides in the positive; and for the sake of educating the populace, the Savage and his Mother are shot over to England.

The story turns upon the old Savage in the new Civilization, and Mr. Huxley has a gorgeous time contrasting values. Sex is lightly taken by the inhabitants of the Model T. Utopia—as lightly as soma; and the Savage, brought up on "Othello" and other Shakespearean plays, mouths incomprehensible maxims about "strumpet," "fidelity," and other archaic notions. What seems to trouble Mr. Huxley most of all about the world of the future is that, with all passion turned to even-tempered happiness, with tragedy gone the way of social and sexual instability, there will be no room for the dramatist. The world will be made safe for infantilism, sensualism, mediocrity. . . . Only his Fordship will be permitted access to the Bible and Shakespeare, lest one old custom shall corrupt the world.

It is Mr. Huxley's habit to be deadly in earnest. One feels that he is pointing a high moral lesson in satirizing Utopia. Yet it is a little difficult to take alarm, for, as the hell-diver sees not the mud, and the angle worm knows not the intricacies of the Einstein theory, so the inhabitants of Mr. Huxley's world could hardly be conscious of the satirical overtones of the Huxleyan prose. And the bogy of mass production seems a little overwrought, since the need for it as religion, in a world that could rigidly control its birth rate and in which no one could make any money out of advertising and selling, would be scarcely intelligible even to His Fordship. Finally, if Mr. Huxley is unduly bothered about the impending static world, let him go back to his biology and meditate on the possibility that even in laboratory-created children mutations might be inevitable. A highly mechanized world, yes; but it might breed one Rousseau to shake it to the foundations and send men back to the hills and the goatskins. Meanwhile, while we are waiting for "My Life and Work" to replace the Bible, **"Brave New World"** may divert us; it offers a stop-gap.

John Chamberlain, "Aldous Huxley's Satirical Model T World," in The New York Times Book Review, *February 7, 1932, p. 5.*

GRANVILLE HICKS

"Brave New World" is, as one would expect, a somewhat amusing book; a bright man can do a good deal with two or three simple ideas. Mr. Huxley assumes that, six hundred years from now, mass-production methods have been perfected, Freudian psychology has triumphed, and certain biological experiments, notably in the field of ectogenesis, have born fruit. The result is a world in which reproduction is left to the laboratories and sex is made a game. People are rigorously divided into classes, and the members of each class are prepared in the test-tube and conditioned in childhood for the kind of life their class leads. Everybody is encouraged to consume as much as possible, everybody is made to believe he is happy, and prevented from doing any thinking on his own account.

For the sake of dramatic interest, Mr. Huxley introduces three rebels, two of them members of the ruling class, one restless because of physical shortcomings, the other because of intellectual superiority. The former brings to England the third rebel, who has been brought up in a New Mexican reservation for the segregation of unassimilated peoples. It is the savage, of course, who most vigorously resents the monotony and emptiness of life in the year 632 After Ford, and who most violently insists on the individual's right to suffer in order to develop his soul. Mr. Huxley arranges an interview between this savage and Controller Mustapha Mond, in which the gentlemen defend with considerable dialectic skill their respective theories of the meaning of life, the savage getting much the better of the argument. It is difficult to suppose that Mr. Huxley is really much concerned about God and romance and the beauty of motherhood, but he sees that there is something to be said for them, and the whole argument does show that after all human nature is human nature. Anyway, two of the rebels are sent to Ireland, and the savage commits suicide.

This is a pretty horrid picture Mr. Huxley paints, and he can be sure that any of us, after reading his book, will think twice before taking steps that might bring about such a calamity. Perhaps we had better not do anything about social injustice or international anarchy. . . . The better way, the book shows, is here and now to nip the utopias in the bud. After all, Mr. Huxley must have his chance to suffer and be brave.

Apparently we have been doing Mr. Huxley an injustice in thinking of him as a bored, cynical and generally rebellious young man. He is, on the contrary, quite well satisfied with life as it is. . . . Of course he demands the right to suffer bravely. Of course he wants something to worry about—even if he has to go a long, long way to find it.

Granville Hicks, "Three Books by Aldous Huxley: 'Brave New World'," in The New Republic, *Vol. LXIX, No. 897, February 10, 1932, p. 354.*

EDWARD CUSHING

Laying aside Mr. Aldous Huxley's **"Brave New World,"** one reflects that artists have never had much use for utopias. Rather pointedly—almost contemptuously, in fact—they have left the envisioning of the perfect state, the perfect society, to philosophers and theologians, to scientists and politicians. Why? Primarily, one supposes, because of a disbelief in perfectibility and a distrust of progress, based on a clearer realization than most men have of the paradox implicit in the word. Perfection is the artist's ideal if it is anyone's; and who should know better than he, as a result of bitter, heartbreaking experience, that perfection is unattainable? . . .

As Mr. Huxley, and that is to say as any artist, sees it, the trouble with utopias is that they are essentially utopian. Granting that men could, without the sacrifice of anything that contributes to their physical, mental, and moral well-being, attain a state of perfect happiness and contentment, the question remains, Would they find it desirable, or even endurable? . . .

Scientists and philosophers and theologians and politicians, when they run true to type, are men of limited imagination and narrow vision, and their notions of what makes for the happiness of man are often quite incredibly naive. The doctor would make man happy by making him healthy, the economist by making him wealthy, the teacher by making him wise. It is easy to see how, from any such point of view, the attainment of a utopian state appears not only possible but probable. But, unfortunately, the truth concerning human happiness is not thus easily simplified, and one man's conception of the good life will not necessarily satisfy another.

Mr. Huxley admits that utopias are definitely realizable. . . . But the prospect is one that alarms him. He has no scientific or romantic illusions concerning the direction, the ultimate outcome of progress; he is an artist and therefore in a superior sense a rationalist, and he foresees the future as the present indicates it, realistically and in the round. The vision is revolting, the more so since it is presented to us by a grinning prophet. For here is a civilization that reckons time in years A.F. (After Ford), a world-state unified and standardized and stabilized, from which science has eliminated vivaparous gestation. A civilization in which men and women, conceived in test tubes and born of bottles, are conditioned as embryos for the positions they are to occupy in a society conforming to a caste-system and for the work they will be assigned ("since happiness consists in liking what one has to do"). A civilization in which the mental habits, the opinions, and prejudices of individuals are determined by hypnopaedic education beginning, practically, at birth; in which pleasure is entirely a matter of physical sensation ("unrestricted copulation and the feelies"); from which art and religion have been abolished; in which the word ''mother'' is an obscenity, and the poetry of the Bible and Shakespeare considered smut.

What price utopia? asks Mr. Huxley. Art and science (answers a World Controller, A.F. 632), thought and feeling, truth and beauty. Because, of course, such things are incompatible with happiness and comfort and stability. . . .

If Mr. Huxley is amused, he is also indignant; and if this reader shares his laughter, he joins as well in his protest. ''I don't want comfort,'' cries the Savage he has introduced into this Model T Utopia. ''I want God, I want poetry, I want real danger, I want freedom, I want goodness. I want sin.'' A right to and a reason for nobility and heroism, symptoms though they may be of political inefficiency. A right and a reason to love life and fear death, to live perilously and die bravely. A right, in short, to feel, to believe in, to assert one's humanity, with its imperfections, its inconveniences, its ultimate sublimity. Mr. Huxley is eloquent in his declaration of an artist's faith in man, and it is his eloquence, bitter in attack, noble in defense, that, when one has closed his book, one remembers—rather than his cleverness and his wit, which one admires and forgets.

Edward Cushing, ''Such People,'' in The Saturday Review of Literature, *Vol. VIII, No. 30, February 13, 1932, p. 521.*

ALFRED KAZIN

''Ape and Essence'' is a short, highly picturesque and rather sterile fantasy on life in Southern California, A.D. 2018, after the almost universal destruction of our Western World by atom bombs in the Third (or is it Fourth?) World War. It is offered to us as an imaginary movie script, written by an embittered desert recluse, which Mr. Huxley picked up on the studio lot as it fell off the top of a truck bearing great mounds of unused scripts to the incinerator.

Imagine, then, this twenty-first century, this post-war period after a final explosion so horrible that it is remembered with awe by the savage primitives who remain as the ''Thing.'' The cities have perished, the streets have caved in, there is no longer any industry or transportation or culture. What is left of humanity is defenseless before small raiding groups, which forage in the sand-strewn wilderness, burying their enemies and heretics alive, and digging into early twentieth-century graves for the clothes and jewels on the corpses. Due to the continuing effects of radioactivity, many children are born deformed; all of these who exceed a certain tolerable minimum (say seven fingers on each hand) must be sacrificed to the Devil, who has officially taken over. Power is in the hands of the chiefs and the Devil's clergy, all eunuchs, who insist on a liturgy that in outward forms is taken directly from the Christian Church, but of course inverted. . . .

Enter the hero: Dr. Alfred Poole, a prudish botanist from New Zealand (the only country to escape the general shambles), who arrives with a company of other New Zealand scientists, is captured by a foraging party and in the nick of time saved from being buried alive by his offer to grow more food (scientifically) for the Devil's people in Los Angeles. . . .

It was inevitable that Mr. Huxley should have written this book: one could almost have foreseen it since Hiroshima as the necessary sequel to **''Brave New World'';** without it, his collected works and his experience of America would not be complete. When you consider his English attachment to the climate of our Southwest, his occasional but penetrating experience of Hollywood, the familiar but obviously still inexhaustible satiric possibilities of the place, and above all his cumulatively total rejection of our materialist civilization, there appears a kind of fatefulness about this book, as if the despair under his religious strivings and his gift for intellectual farce had found in the luxurious desolation of Hollywood the ideal landscape for the end of man.

Yet there is something very odd about this caustic ''scenario''. It is as if Mr. Huxley had reached down into the movies' bag of tricks with one hand, to keep the baby in us quiet and amused, while with the other he was preparing the real business of the evening, a furious and heart-broken sermon against our moral degradation. There is no other novelist with his kind of surface skill who now gives so much the impression of being uninterested in the novel, of using it to deliver rigid moral categories. For all its witty details, **''Ape and Essence''** is so loud and tormented a cry for a purely spiritual vision of life, so inflexible a condemnation of all our usual ''values,'' that I found myself much more impressed by Mr. Huxley's grand disgust with all of us alive today than by his wrathful movie of a twenty-first century reverting back to the Stone Age and worshipping the Devil. The rather prissy, pseudo-scientific nihilist of the '20s has become so unyielding and lonely an antagonist of our scientific and nationalist idolatries that I wonder in what hidden depths of frivolity such a ''scenario'' was planned at all.

It is curious how much of the harsh, abstract quality of the book is already given in the ungainliness of the title. This must be the first of Mr. Huxley's titles in a long time not taken from some classic English poet; it does come from a mocking poem against the animalism of our time that heads the script attributed to Mr. Huxley's recluse, ''William Tallis.'' We play the ape so long as we forget our rightful and spiritual essence. There is nothing else, nothing between: all naturalistic conceptions of reform, of the state, of ''control'' over the suicidal weapons we have created—all deal with the ends, which are ''ape-chosen,'' while ''only the means are man's.'' This dryly moralistic vision of life (notice the absolute destruction of all human dignity when it is not observed), is the burden of his novel. . . .

It is a familiar characteristic of Mr. Huxley's to see life without any respect for immediate human experience, and his religious strivings have only emphasized this amazing weakness in a novelist. His dislike of people, his intellectual horror of sex, his transparent lack of sympathy for real problems—all these things now have a different rationale from that of his early novels; but his approach to life, or rather his lack of reverence for it, is still the same. . . . To measure life entirely by bookish conceptions of sainthood is to miss entirely the real crux and agony of twentieth-century life, which is not in the deliberate blindness of men (to charge this really shows a lack of love), but in the split between our inner lives and the habits and institutions by which we live. But Mr. Huxley is not concerned with ''things at the center''; he prefers intellectual melodramas of disaster. Hence it follows that nothing really human at all will be left in the twenty-first century, nor can we be surprised, as this movie unrolls, that the Devil is officially in charge at last. I must say that I find all that rather tiresome, and that I should be much more interested in seeing less of the DeMille Devil over Los Angeles, and some more understanding of the devil in us.

Alfred Kazin, ''Fantastic Forecast of the Post-Atomic Age,'' in New York Herald Tribune Weekly Book Review, *August 22, 1948, p. 3.*

CHARLES J. ROLO

When Huxley wrote ***Brave New World*** in 1932, it seemed to him that mankind was headed toward the soulless, mass-produced contentment of a scientific Utopia. His fable dramatized the choice between this "death-without-tears" and a return to "noble Savagery" which was both squalid and ignoble—a choice between "insanity on the one hand and lunacy on the other." Mr. Huxley has since sought to show that there exists—in the precept and practice of the mystics—a way to sanity. The source of man's madness, he avers, is that the unregenerate Adam is an angry ape; he can cease to be one only through awareness of his Essence—of the spiritual reality underlying the world. Whence Huxley's new title, ***Ape and Essence***. . . . ***Brave New World*** envisaged the *painless* triumph of standardization, which Huxley then considered the logical end product of a science controlled by soulless rationalists. "Our Ford" was the prophet. ***Ape and Essence*** depicts the *miserable* triumph of animal bestiality, which Huxley now suggests will be the logical end product of a science controlled by war-minded ape men. The prophet is Belial.

It is a society of Yahoos which Alfred Poole—the Rediscovery Force's botanist, who is captured by the natives and left to them—finds in the ruins of Hollywood. Their religion is a fear-ridden and sadistic demonism. Their clothing comes off disinterred corpses, their fuel from the surviving libraries. The only word most people can read is NO, which is patched on the women's garments, fore and aft. For woman is a "Vessel of the Unholy Spirit." Ever since World War III, most babies (due to mutations caused by gamma rays) have been monstrously deformed. As the result of another mutation the mating instinct, in 90 per cent of the population, is confined to five weeks in the year and may be gratified in only two of them, which begin with Belial Day. The unmutated 10 per cent, known as Hots, face the penalty of burial alive if they indulge their libidinal deviationism. Some of them have escaped to found a community of exiles near Fresno. (pp. 102, 104)

At first reading, ***Ape and Essence*** struck me as an extremely puzzling performance. Why the script form? And what of the "moral"? Poole has the special knowledge which he might use to save the community from starvation. Instead of which he elopes with his lascivious Loola. . . . Is this the final triumph of Belial? Or is it the case of the world well lost for Romance, which would amount to much the same thing—the triumph of Hollywood over Huxley? The fact that these and a good many other questions arise shows that Mr. Huxley, who here as always has something important to say and says it entertainingly, has registered a miss with ***Ape and Essence.*** That still leaves it in the upper bracket of the year's fiction.

The script form is not suited to Huxley's satiric talent. I am told he tried the idea out as a "straight" novel and found it "too heavy"—he was aiming at pure fantasy (and perhaps wider appeal). The use of the Narrator in place of the customary Huxleyan sage, marginally involved in the plot, is also designed to avoid realism and weightiness. It is, I feel, rather unsuccessful, though the blank verse does give a lyrical quality to the counterpoint—the Essence which is opposed to the harsh point—the Ape. (p. 204)

Charles J. Rolo, in a review of "Ape and Essence," in The Atlantic Monthly, *Vol. 182, No. 3, September, 1948, pp. 102, 104.*

J. C. GARRETT

When, sixteen years ago, Aldous Huxley described in his most brilliant satire the future that awaited mankind when technology and the mass state took command, the world giggled nervously and hoped he was wrong. Even H. G. Wells called ***Brave New World*** "an alarmist fantasy," and counselled us not to despair. But that was before Wells gave up the human race as a tragic failure. He was himself capable of drawing a grisly picture of atomic war after which great industrial areas were to be roped off as no longer habitable, but he concluded that the shape of things to come was not fundamentally desperate: a proper use of technical knowledge and humane planning could, he thought, rescue us after the eleventh hour. There is no such consolation in Huxley's latest nightmare of the future, ***Ape and Essence.*** In this horrifying vision, the deep-seated misanthropy and pessimism of Huxley exclude every hope except the rather mystical compensation, derived from Eastern mysticism and Shelley, that a few regenerate souls may at length be merged into the Eternal One. . . .

The thesis of the book is that Satan (Huxley restores to him his ontological due) has cleverly won the fight for man by seducing him into a faith in science and material progress. This infatuation made possible the skyrocketing population of the past two centuries, and created the screaming hungry nationalisms with their equipment of dictators, conscriptors, mass-planners and assorted agencies for dehumanizing man and smashing the individual conscience. Quoting Pascal, Huxley makes a fierce assault on the belief that the pursuit of Truth is itself good. . . .

By prostituting truth to human appetite, man has missed his golden opportunity for the good life. In fact, Huxley is retelling, in modern terms, the myth of Doctor Faustus, who abandoned theology for secular knowledge, and welfare of the spirit for indulgence of the senses.

But Huxley is unconvincing for all his fervor: the moralist in him is at the mercy of despair. He assumes that the warnings of William Vogt and Sir John Boyd-Orr will go unheeded; he assumes that man's natural bias toward malevolence will lead to self-obliteration. It is well to recognize the reality of evil, but Huxley denies that good (except in a handful of innocents) is operative in the human conscience. Moreover, the technique of the book (a film scenario) suggests that the twin of his earnestness is levity; and the repetition of tricks and motifs from ***Brave New World*** gives it the flavor of warmed-over stew.

J. C. Garrett, "Turning New Leaves," in The Canadian Forum, *Vol. XXVIII, No. 336, January, 1949, p. 236.*

GRANVILLE HICKS

Aldous Huxley, who in his early years seemed a lively immoralist, has spent the past two decades and more in preaching. He is preaching again in **"Brave New World Revisited"**. . . , and I confess that I look back wistfully to the novels he wrote in the Twenties—**"Crome Yellow"** and **"Antic Hay"** and **"Point Counter Point."** On the other hand, I am willing to listen to this particular sermon, for it is concerned with matters of importance.

"Brave New World," it is appropriate to note, marked the transition from the flippant or the apparently flippant Huxley to the serious Huxley. . . .

Since the new book is concerned with **"Brave New World"** as prophecy, we had better remind ourselves of Huxley's conception of life in the year A.F. (After Ford) 632. War has been abolished for centuries, and the world's population has been stabilized at exactly two billions. An elaborate system of artificial reproduction and prenatal conditioning creates five distinct classes in the right proportions, and Pavlovian psychology, new drugs, and all the arts of propaganda sustain the status quo. Almost everybody is convinced that he is happy.

Obviously we in 1958 are a long way from the situation Huxley envisaged. We are still confronted with the dangers of war, which he doesn't discuss—"not as being unimportant but merely for convenience and because I have discussed them on earlier occasions." And we have an ever more urgent problem of overpopulation, which he does discuss with great cogency. . . . We are far from the stability that is requisite for the kind of society portrayed in **"Brave New World."**

Still and all, there are some significant resemblances between life in A.F. 632 and life in prosperous postwar America, and these are what Huxley makes the most of in **"Brave New World Revisited."** In our society consumption has become a duty, as in Huxley's "new world." We may not have feelies, orgy-porgy, or centrifugal bumblepuppy, but, as he points out, "nonstop distraction [is] provided by newspapers and magazines, by radio, television, and the cinema." What is most important from Huxley's point of view, experts are developing effective techniques for the control of men's minds, and he discusses with his usual erudition the latest experiments in motivational research, brainwashing, subconscious persuasion, and sleep-teaching. . . .

"Brave New World Revisited" doesn't suggest that there is a shortage of suffering in 1958, but the reader may feel that Huxley ought to be devoting himself to the limited but real dangers of mind-control instead of fretting about an improbable and in any case remote future. Surprisingly and disarmingly, Huxley himself adopts this point of view in his last two chapters, wherein he discusses in concrete terms what we can do here and now.

These last two chapters measure the long distance that Huxley has come in the years since he was one of the bad boys of the Twenties. In the earlier part of the book he sometimes displays his old fondness for shocking his readers, but his conclusions are sober and reasonable. In his chapter on education he speaks of the need for "a set of generally accepted values, based upon a solid foundation of fact." . . . These are the words of a man who has learned to prefer wisdom to wit and responsibility to the joys of the *enfant terrible*. Huxley was always a moralist, we can see now, even when he succeeded in convincing people that he was the very opposite. He has become a more and more thoughtful moralist, and if we have lost something in the way of entertainment, what we have gained is more important.

Granville Hicks, "Huxley Revisited," in Saturday Review, *Vol. XLI, No. 46, November 15, 1958, p. 12.*

JOOST A. M. MEERLOO

In [**"Brave New World Revisited"**] Huxley uses his erudite knowledge of human relations to compare our actual world with his prophetic fantasy [**"Brave New World."**] It is a frightening experience, indeed, to discover how much of his satirical prediction of a distant future became reality in so short a time. With few people realizing it, human freedom is threatened from every direction. Increasing overpopulation, chemical coercion by hypnotic drugs, drowning of the mind in nonsensical irrelevancies, verbal seduction, opinion engineering, mass hypnosis, subliminal persuasion, unobtrusive brainwashing and more overt mental coercion—all these social phenomena can be strategically used to turn men into robots. . . .

There is something extremely persuasive about this fascinating and frightening book. Because the intuitive author successfully prophesied in his novel the automatized horror, we are the more inclined to surrender to the impact of his well-written words. I can confirm many things he says and I welcome the fact that they are said again and again, because people usually prefer to ignore the existing creeping pressures on their individual freedom. . . .

It is strange that this erudite prober of the human mind quotes mostly physiologists and those other students apt to think of man in a purely reductive mechanical sense. True, there are Pavlovian and pharmacological laws, but they never quite determine why man reacts the way he does. I got the eerie feeling that, even though Huxley denounces the horrible facts of chemical persuasion and medication into submission, he simultaneously eulogizes the age of tranquilizers. . . .

What I especially miss is reference to the self-regenerative forces in body and mind. While the human personality may be broken down, there also exists a process of mental self-immunization. Even under brutal mental coercion and brainwashing, some people are able to stick to their integrity. Since tyranny and terror are exerted only by a minority in power and rebellion and freedom usually grow in the few strong souls who guard their integrity, both these minority groups will determine the future aspect of our political world. Even within a totalitarian élite, rebellion develops.

An extensive literature exists on life under marginal circumstances and on the manner in which the psyche resists attempts at conditioning and taming. And certainly Huxley is aware of the way psychoanalysis studies the development of man's mental defenses, his various reaction formations, including his negative suggestibility. Yet none of this is touched upon in this book.

Nonetheless, **"Brave New World Revisited"** is of the utmost importance for the knowledge of growing psychic pressures in a world in transition. . . . We should read Huxley's book, however, without being influenced by his prevailing pessimism, realizing that there exist more regeneration and healthy rebellion in man than is suggested here.

Joost A. M. Meerloo, "How Will Man Behave?" in The New York Times Book Review, *November 16, 1958, p. 22.*

CHRISTOPHER SYKES

[In ***Brave New World Revisited,*** as] in most of his political writings, Mr. Huxley has an enormous purpose: to rescue humanity from the consequences of human crime and folly. In the face of such a great subject the critic can do little but record his personal reactions: the first person singular, that vice of modern reviewing may then be allowed. . . .

The book has a simple theme, namely that freedom and human development are chiefly imperilled by two agencies of destruction, overpopulation and propaganda. Of these two, overpopulation, unless I am quite mad, is far the most terrifying and important. New-style propaganda, using all the new-found apparatus of brainwashing, is still in the experimental stage, certainly as regards mass application, but overpopulation, according to respectable opinion, is ready and coming quick. Mr. Huxley will surprise many of his readers by concentrating on the evils of propaganda to such an extent that he can only give a fifth of his book to the other question. I cannot believe this makes sense, and I am led, as other readers may be, to think that this want of proportion comes from Mr. Huxley living too removed from the world at present to give of his best as a political essayist. Rusty habits get in his way. This appears clearly in his handling of some secondary matters. He has much to say about the soul-destroying anonymity of town as opposed to rustic life, a venerable legend that no one with wide town experience can believe in, even if he hates towns. In one passage Mr. Huxley seems to believe in a yet more baseless myth to the effect that learned men are of a selfless integrity that makes them totally immune to the influence of mass-suggestion. I suppose he means that they do not easily fall for mass-suggestion in fields where they are learned. One readily sympathises with a state of chronic irritation against propaganda, but one goes to Mr. Huxley for something finer. One misses that something too often this time. In his anger Mr. Huxley hardly differentiates between commercial propaganda and its deadlier political brother, and he is capable of descending to peevish sarcasm. . . .

Mr. Huxley's writing remains as compelling and as brilliant as ever, but the patches of rust are not mere slips and blemishes for, unless I am quite wrong, they come from an inherant flaw. The book is beneath Mr. Huxley's accustomed level of wisdom because it is so negative. With his denunciations, he has not much remedy to propose this time, either in the exalted sphere of religion or in administration. He affirms no faith, as though now he *has* none.

Christopher Sykes, "Teacher without Faith," in The Spectator, *Vol. 202, No. 6817, February 20, 1959, p. 269.*

THOMAS D. CLARESON

The continued recognition given Aldous Huxley's ***Brave New World,*** including its widespread use in the classroom, certainly suggests that it be regarded as the classic anti-utopian novel. (p. 33)

Basic to the construction of Huxley's fable are three techniques: first, extrapolation; second, parody and juxtaposition of detail; third, sharp contrast of points of view. In both ***Brave New World*** and ***Brave New World Revisited,*** Huxley is a humanist horrified by the theories and accomplishments of extremists of his own time, but in the novel by using contrasting points of view, he makes no explicit statement of his own position. Only in later prefaces and ***Brave New World Revisited*** does his emotion overcome his artistry so that he underscores his own position by direct statement.

First, then, he extrapolates. By 1931 some factual basis lay behind each ingredient in his "perfect" world. The most obvious is, of course, Henry Ford. In 1914 Ford installed a conveyor-belt assembly line that has since become one of the corner stones of our technology. (p. 34)

In regard to Huxley's science, by the second decade of this century the German Nobel Prize winner, Hans Speman, made experimental embryology one of the most exciting areas of study. . . . Moreover, Pavlov and Watson had developed psychology into an experimental science. From 1902-03 to the late twenties Pavlov's experiments with the neural behavior of dogs established far-reaching principles. In 1913, from Pavlov's results and a smattering of his own data, Watson founded the Behaviorist School. He generalized about human behavior, reducing man to a complex network of stimuli and responses which could, of course, be formed into any end product the experimenter (conditioner) desired. He was of vast influence, though most psychologists never agreed with his sweeping declarations.

Actually, although Freud is mentioned explicitly only once in ***Brave New World,*** he is even more significant to the novel than Pavlov and Watson. With the possible exception of Mustapha Mond, Freudian concepts dominate the motivation of all the characters in the novel. The Savage, for example, is motivated fundamentally by the Oedipus Complex and by masochism. The passages that he quotes from *Hamlet* reinforce this interpretation.

As for the more obvious paraphernalia: hypnopaedia was a fad of the twenties and thirties. Since the development of the electroencyclograph which can measure depth of sleep, evidence of the effectiveness of sleep-teaching is largely negative. In ***Brave New World*** itself Huxley himself points out how inadequately it teaches information. Yet his suggestion that it be used to instill the moral conscience of a society may have something, for people "feel" what is right even when they do not know what is. The similarity between soma and modern tranquillizers seems obvious and needs no discussion, except to remind one that in ***Brave New World Revisited,*** Huxley points out that doctors now write prescriptions for tranquillizers at a rate of 48 million a year—most of them refillable. (pp. 34-5)

However intriguing these extrapolations, if the fable concentrated upon them only, it would lose much of its effectiveness. It would become a mere catalogue of "gadgets." Significantly—and I do not feel that drawing an analogy to Zola's *Germinal,* for example, is inappropriate—Huxley spends the first hundred pages of the novel creating his future world while minimizing plot action. Once this portrait has been drawn—by the time Bernard and Lenina leave for the Reservation in Chapter Six—the portrait of the Brave New World has been finished. No "gadgets" or problems that have *not* at least been referred to in this section are introduced later in the novel. In addition, unlike Zola, Huxley has little regard for verisimilitude; the Brave New World is portrayed selectively, non-representationally, with emphasis concentrated upon those aspects of the society he wishes us to remember. Basic here is his second technique—parody and juxtaposition of details. To aid our "willing suspension of disbelief" he includes a multitude of details common to our everyday knowledge, but he changes them, places them in new context and new combination so that while they remain familiar, they are also startlingly new. (p. 35)

In naming the citizenry, Huxley has paid tribute to all the scientists, industrialists, financiers, and Marxists responsible for creating the twentieth century. The most individual name is that of Mustapha Mond, and it is a pun. Yes, "Must staff a world."

Perhaps the most sustained and, for some, the bitterest irony occurs in the delineation of the Solidarity Service, which, of course, parodies Holy Communion, perhaps at a revival meeting. The significance of twelve in each group, of holding the service on Thursday, of the invocations—"I drink to my annihilation" and "I drink to the imminence of His Coming."—is obvious. . . . Notice the echo of Anglican and Presbyterian hymns throughout the service; notice the despair Bernard expresses when he "foresaw for himself yet another failure to achieve atonement." How out of place seems the word atonement. Yet after so serious and deliberate a detailing, Huxley rises to high artistry by suddenly changing his entire tone as he perverts a familiar nursery rhyme—"Orgy-porgy, Ford and fun / Kiss the girls and make them One / Boys at one with girls at peace; / Orgy-porgy gives release."

This often startling parody and juxtaposition obviously contributes to his third technique—contrast. Without its contrasts Huxley's fable would lose its dramatic and intellectual impact. . . . Most obviously there is the contrast of the Brave New World with contemporary society. In Chapter Three Huxley juxtaposes the Freudian-motivated world of A.D. 1931 with that of A.F. 632. But structurally the fable is dominated by the contrast between the Savage and the "Utopia." First Huxley constructs civilization in its gaudy, pleasurable detail. Then against the naked rock of Malpais he etches the Savage. Only when the two stand face to face in the last half of the novel is there sustained dramatic conflict, culminating in the Savage's suicide. Most important, however, is the contrast, the conflict, of philosophies. The Brave New World chooses to know no pain; the Savage, to know no pleasure. Indeed, he commits suicide after he indulges in what is probably the first pleasurable act of his life.

By and large the citizens of the Brave New World are incapable of constructive, imaginative thought; Mustapha Mond asserts that they have been so conditioned—in order to preserve the stability of their world. On the other hand, with the exception of the incident in which he builds his bow and arrow and puts into practice the knowledge old Mitsima taught him, the Savage shows himself incapable of constructive, imaginative action. He can act only in a frenzy, as when he pointlessly destroys the Soma of the Delta workers. It is on the horns of this complicated dilemma that Huxley's thesis lies.

He built his society and his characters upon two principles with which few psychologists would argue. First, that pleasure—that is, whatever the individual finds pleasurable—is the most powerful motivator of man. Secondly, as Huxley himself puts it, "Feeling lurks in that interval of time between desire and its consummation. Shorten that interval, break down all those old unnecessary barriers." (pp. 36-7)

The dialogue between Mustapha Mond and the Savage . . . stands as the heart of the fable. (p. 37)

The Brave New World is mindless. The World Controller explains, however, that its citizens are "nice tame animals, anyhow." They have sacrificed the past and the future for the pleasure of the moment, shortening that time between desire and consummation to nothing, or escaping time and space with Soma. They have become, as Huxley symbolizes in Lenina, so much meat, however pneumatic. That is the price they have paid for "Community, Identity, Stability."

Amid this human debris it is perhaps tempting to call the Savage heroic and feel that he represents Huxley's point of view. To do so exposes our own conditioning rather than a close reading of the text. In any society in which he attempted to live, the Savage would commit suicide; even had he lived as a solitary in the hills near Malpais or at the lighthouse, eventually he would have tortured himself to death. . . .

Yet because his is the only voice protesting the infantilism of the Brave New World, the reader wants to sympathize with him—as Huxley undoubtedly intended, perhaps only so that his central theme could be more effectively realized. The scenes at the lighthouse crystallize Huxley's theme. There, in the final chapters, he literally destroys the Savage—ending with an artistic finality of incident and language matched in few works. (p. 38)

Such brutal and final destruction of the Savage hardly suggests that Huxley had sympathy for him. And this is as it should be, for the Savage is the second horn of the dilemma—"the choice between insanity on the one hand and lunacy on the other," as Huxley states in his preface. The fable must be interpreted as an attack upon both the "utopian" civilization and the Savage. On the one hand, Huxley projects the end of the great multitude of men who live for bread and pleasure; on the other, ironically using the label Savage, he attacks those intellectuals who are both incapable of taking a constructive role in society and, at least since Rousseau, have sought escape in the simplicity and alleged truth of a benevolent nature. And yet this statement oversimplifies, for through his Penitente-ism the Savage also represents those men whose harsh religiosity has rejected the physical world. In short, then Aldous Huxley's ***Brave New World*** dramatizes several of the conflicts that have haunted western civilization during the past centuries. Against a background of "gadgets" he thus gains a universality. (p. 39)

Thomas D. Clareson, "The Classic: Aldous Huxley's 'Brave New World'," in Extrapolation, *Vol. III, No. 1, December, 1961, pp. 33-40.*

CHAD WALSH

Aldous Huxley's new novel, **"Island"** is an answer to **"Brave New World,"** also by Aldous Huxley. . . .

The central character is Will Farnaby, an embittered journalist who "won't take yes for an answer." By accident he finds himself on Pala, "the forbidden island," and is catapulted into international intrigues. . . .

Farnaby also comes to know some likable and talkative Palanese, who are faithful to the gentle vision of social good bequeathed by the two nineteenth-century founders of their way of life, the old Buddhist rajah and the Calvinist-turned-atheist physician from Scotland. More and more, he finds some of the acid draining from his spirit. Before the story is over, he has been almost converted to a way of life that—in the words of Mr. Huxley's 1946 foreword to **"Brave New World"**—works with calm deliberation toward "the intelligent pursuit of man's Final End, the unitive knowledge of the immanent Tao or Logos, the transcendent Godhead or Brahman."

It is a happy marriage of Mahayana Buddhism and science. The religion is not world-denying; it teaches that everything, from food to sex, can be a road to enlightenment and liberation. Science is devoted to such practical tasks as improving tropical crops and devising psychological methods for reducing dangerous aggressions in society. In contrast to **"Brave New World,"** the family flourishes, but in a broader form. Fifteen to twenty-five households combine into an extended family. (p. 4)

The Brave New World and Pala both have rather relaxed patterns of sexual behavior—Pala even commissions certain mature ladies to give practical instruction to young male virgins. But to the Brave New Worlder sex is merely fun; to the Palanese it is one of the most useful roads to enlightenment. Most striking resemblance of all, the *soma* of Brave New World is matched by the *moksha*-medicine of Pala, a mushroom derivative to induce mystical vision. But again, it is the purpose that differs.

Brave New World takes *soma* for a release or a harmless binge. The Palanese use the mushroom extract as an opening wedge into ultimate consciousness.

Throughout the book one senses the outer world—hungry, greedy, breeding itself into nightmare, armed to do murder, falsely spiritual and crassly materialistic—closing in on Pala. How the story ends it is not fair to say here. Nor can anyone really discuss **"Island"** as though it were merely a story. In this book Mr. Huxley has said, for the moment, his final word about the human condition and the possibility of the good society. **"Island"** challenges the political scientist, the psychologist, the philosopher and the theologian. The reader's reaction will depend on his own postulates—in particular, whether he considers the human predicament curable by growth in awareness, or whether he finds man's condition so deeply poisoned at the roots of being that both spiritual surgery and spiritual growth are required. In short, can man save himself?

It is the achievement of the book that it vividly dramatizes these very questions. In recent decades the supply of new Utopias has dwindled in both quantity and quality. **"Island"** is a welcome and in many ways unique addition to the select company of books—from Plato to now—that have presented, in imaginary terms, a coherent view of what society is not but might be. (pp. 4, 46)

Chad Walsh, "Can Man Save Himself?" in The New York Times Book Review, *April 1, 1962, pp. 4, 46.*

PATRICK O'DONOVAN

[Huxley] is for certain, above all a clever writer. He is still a prodigy, still seeks to amaze, still courts rejection.

His is one of the most astonishing achievements in modern writing. His is an enormous output of novels, plays, essays, poetry, histories and philosophical writing. Between the wars, a new Huxley was a major event and his early novels, his short stories and his first explorations of the mystical experience were for countless young people a massive education in what could be done with the mind, if not with the heart. He earned his place and he became his own legend.

But either he left us or we, as we grew older, left him. And as the going got tougher and the Huxley path plunged even deeper into his private forest, we sometimes gave up the attempt to understand. Occasionally, as in ***The Devils of Loudun,*** we were back together again, but probably for the wrong reasons. The fact remains that Mr. Huxley has chosen his path and it is one that very few would choose with him. It is so private, so dark, so uncertain of getting anywhere in the end, that his loneliness is hardly a reproach to the old faithful. It is inevitable.

Now, at first sight, he seems to have retraced his footsteps and has gone back to reconsider his subject of the Brave New World. It is true that [***Island***] is about a paradise rather than a hell on earth, but many of the elements that were used in the first hell and were intended to repel, are now used again in the second paradise and are meant to be admired. This however is no work of optimism. It is a cry of despair from the opposite direction and the view in the end is much the same. There is nothing of comfort here, nothing almost that can be applied to the art or condition of today's sad world—unless its intellectual rejection can be said to represent a salutory slap in the face. . . .

[It] is a very odd paradise and practically its entire population would be liable to charges of various forms of gross indecency in any actual state, though this, of course, is proffered as part of their innocence and maturity.

Pala contains a minimum of machinery and consumer goods, but a splendidly daring agriculture. There is a great deal of mystical practice, but the belief in any sort of Divine Presence is left, tolerantly enough, to those weak enough to find it necessary. There are however frequent sermons, and mushrooms are used to provide artificially induced "religious" experiences. There is a "Yoga of Sex" which provides all the pleasure of love without conception. Families are kept small. Children are allowed within limits to pick and choose their own parents. And everyone talks from the tots to the teachers in an overwhelming torrent of didactic exposition. . . . There is no greed, no violence and even death has a certain faint charm about it and scarcely interrupts the flow of talk. (p. 17)

After reading all this, there seems to be one writer with whom Mr. Huxley may reasonably be compared. He shares with him the same vast bitterness and intellectual loneliness, the same pained detachment from his times. He has the same fascinated revulsion from the mechanisms and decays of the body, the same apparent loathing for the human race and a longing to find virtue elsewhere, in specially created societies and situations. Both were reformers and both unable to share the suffering of those they would reform. The other was Dean [Jonathan] Swift. Of course, unlike the Dean, Mr. Huxley has never been a classical stylist, is among the most baroque of English writers. But they at least would have understood each other—given time. Dean Swift was relegated by his admirers to being a writer for children; Mr. Huxley has danced himself out of that one.

Indeed this is a curiously distasteful book. The paradise is unreal, uninviting and a bit too much like an experimental clinic with imported Indian overtones in Southern California. Christianity is largely rejected. Selected aspects of Buddhism are incorporated. There is left from all this picking and choosing, a mysticism without God, a love without understanding and a compassion without heart. This is a private paradise and as dangerous as Adam's. You end by feeling rejected. But it does not seem to matter greatly. (pp. 17-18)

Patrick O'Donovan, "Aldous Huxley's Island Paradise," in The New Republic, *Vol. 146, No. 18, April 30, 1962, pp. 17-18.*

ARTHUR HERZOG

Utopia, from Plato's *Republic* on, has had a characteristic shortcoming. It is a study of ends, not means, and it has never pondered what might be encountered on the road to its heavenly cities. . . .

Utopia continues strong today, except that it has been stood on its head. In place of the traditional, constructive, positive utopias we have what is almost a new literary strain—utopia in reverse, cacotopia, the worst of all possible worlds. . . .

But while the counter-utopists may have put a cautionary light on many contemporary ideals, they have provided nothing in their place. It is this job that Huxley attempts in ***Island.*** It is a curious book, more successful as a vehicle of ideas than as a novel. It is written heavily and without the incisiveness of ***Brave New World.*** The characters are weak and poorly drawn. The later Huxley flaws—the verbosity, the over-intellectuality—are much in evidence. Like a nervous lover, Huxley seems almost to talk himself out of the main chance. And yet, despite its defects, ***Island*** is a stimulating visit.

Like most utopias, ***Island*** is a study of ends, but Huxley is also aware of the difficulties of means. . . . Huxley's utopia is what he calls "near-in"—that is, the ideas are presumably susceptible to being put into practice.

Huxley's island is called Pala (Paladin? Pallas—wisdom?), and on it East and West have united to produce utopia. (p. 74)

Pala is called the Forbidden Island because progress-carrying Westerners are not welcome, but the islanders prove hospitable and proceed to demonstrate and explain their social system. The discussions are in English—in keeping with the fusion scheme, the islanders use English for science and business, Palanese for religion and love—and they are of interminable length and determinedly impressive erudition. In fact, the Palanese are some of the longest-winded people around.

Great borrowers and sifters that they are, the Palanese have kept only the best from the two worlds. From the West they have taken electricity, but they have thrown back state socialism and private property. They could be called co-operators or communitarian Socialists. They keep the Western family but broaden its base so that raising children is a community project, much as in a clan system. They love science, especially what Huxley calls the sciences of life, psychology, biology, eugenics, the same sciences that created ***Brave New World.*** They are firm believers in birth control, and contraceptives are distributed free. They attempt to improve the population through artificial insemination from selected, deep-frozen male seed. They think that character is often inherited and try to sort out potential troublemakers as babies, to redirect them. They practice auto-hypnotism as an aid to learning. There is a great deal more of this, but in a way it is window-dressing. The West provides only conditions for the good life. The heart of the good life comes from the East.

One gathers that Huxley agrees with Koestler that Eastern thought is a shambles, and the islanders have swept most of it away. They have retained, though, a variety of Zen Buddhism. . . . The islanders are immersed in the yoga of everything, which Huxley attempts to dramatize in a scene where Farnaby takes Palanese perception mushrooms and has a visionary experience. They are keen on the yoga of love—it is not clear whether the Palanese are promiscuous, but they are certainly not inhibited—and reach total fulfillment in sex. They believe, in short, in living deep.

Farnaby, obsessive and guilt-ridden, is set off against these supposedly calm and happy people as an example of Western man; and, always just, Huxley gives us some pretty unsavory non-Palanese Eastern types as well. But Farnaby falls in love with a Palanese and decides to stay. In the meantime, the greedy, overpopulated world closes in. It wants the oil and can't stand the existence of a truly sane society. But Huxley suggests that the world can still learn from Pala.

Will it? I think not. For one thing, life there seems a little dull—at times the Palanese are uncomfortabiy close to grazing in Chesterton's fields of veal cutlets, curry-style. It is a regrettable truth that the wicked utopia makes better reading than the good, and one sympathizes with Huxley's efforts to make Pala interesting. (He might have done so with a little more plain Palanese fun.) And then, it seems unlikely that Zen and perception mushrooms are going to be used by any large number of people. Huxley suggests, in fact, that the Pala-model might be something for underdeveloped rather than developed countries. (pp. 74-5)

Focusing as it does on the inner and not merely the material life, ***Island*** is a new departure for utopia. Impractical as much of it may be, it is still more provocative than the usual reports of commissions on national goals. (p. 75)

Arthur Herzog, "Who Enforces Utopia?" in The Nation, *Vol. 195, No. 4, August 25, 1962, pp. 74-5.*

V. S. PRITCHETT

In the Twenties, reading [Huxley's] first poems and the Peacockian novels, one had thought him an assertive and alarming figure. He was immediately an enormous success, a young man packed with brains, modish, the perfect embodiment of the new American word, 'highbrow'; so assured at once in scientific outlook and in his enormous knowlege of music, painting, architecture, history and most of the famous sites and museums of the world; more important to us, a ribald innovator in the modernities, blasphemies and iconoclasms of the period. One was overwhelmed. There was no need to be. Huxley was the most considerate, gentle, most softly and brilliantly conversable of men, in the simplest terms. . . . [He] was that rare being—the prodigy, the educable young man, the perennial asker of unusual questions.

For the artist in him this compulsion must have been a burden as well as an inborn exhilaration. Like Bacon's jesting Pilate, from whom he borrowed a title, he asked and did not stay for an answer. He moved on. Nothing short of universal knowledge was his aim. No traveller through cultures, no connoisseur of human habits, no asker had lapped up so much. As a writer, he became a mellifluous but active, ever-extending, ever-dramatising encyclopedia and he had the gaiety and melancholy of mind to put it out in novels, essays, plays and works of speculation and criticism. Endlessly educable, he was, in the family tradition, a hybrid—the artist-educator; an extraordinary filler-in of the huge gaps in one's mind. . . .

Aldous Huxley's spell was the old Arnold-Huxley spell of an education, disseminated with wit from above. It was imposed by his mastery of the art of conversation. He was a daring assimilator rather than an original creative mind; but if it is true to say that the exquisite ***Crome Yellow*** was a pastiche of Peacock, how brilliant to have spotted that Peacock was just the author for disordered times and that whole passages could be adapted for today. The other good novel, ***Brave New World,*** which time has caught up on, is a work of disgust. It suffers ultimately from a sort of horrific complicity on the part of the author. Swift believed in ordinary men; Huxley believed in reason and that can lead to intellectual self-indulgence. Huxley was not a novelist in the sense of being interested in how people live and what they are wholly like. He turned for inspiration to Gide, that other master of conversation and contemporary morbidities, and wrote ***Eyeless in Gaza*** and ***Point Counter Point.*** They were amusing *romans à clef* but were both too newsy and too stilted compared with *Les Faux-Monnayeurs*. The characters were simply the faces on a pack of cards, good for a rubber or two of talk and scandal, but too flat and crude when asked to be human beings. They were too brittle to stand up to the preposterous things he offered them.

There was, I have said, a touch of complicity in Huxley's disgust with human beings, in his eye for the grotesque, the vulgar and libidinous. They became less ribald and more savage as he moved skyward from the Twenties into his Californian Laputa where scientific rationalism and the perennial philosophy disputed for possession of the facts of Nature and the soul's perceptions.

Huxley's conversation still dazzled because he pursued the strange facts the sciences offer to anyone with a dramatic instinct. One got from him a stereoscopic view of the world. One can call his method popularisation; but really the attraction lay not only in the new facts, but in the opportunity for more speculation. Perhaps, after all, the sexual practices of the dotty Oneida community were better than our own? Was not the classical view of the 'eternal Mediterranean' a fraud? The olive groves of Cézanne and Renoir represent a benign pause in man's war against landscape. The mulberries were being replaced by the peach tree in the Rhône valley because of the invention of artificial silk. . . .

Whether such juxtapositions—and Huxley was expert in making them—are tenable, they are vivid, and more than vivid. They awaken. They disturb our settled superstitions. But even when we recognise this, we must inquire why superstitions exist, why they last and what estimable impulses of the human imagination they have both protected and perverted. Huxley enjoyed the follies of the human mind even as he stoically stood out against them.

His mind had, of course, the tricks of the man who knew too much and too well how to express it. He was one of the last of the Victorian liberals. He was totally pacifist. Logically he refused to be implicated. His manner had a lot of the old Bloomsbury in it. 'Significant. But significant of what?' 'Possibly. But possibly not.' The bomb explodes. One has not time to make the distinction. All the same these phrases were designed to drop us simple readers into a void where, defenceless, we were exposed to shock. Shock was one of the luxuries of the Twenties. But, for Huxley, perhaps the most accomplished educator of his generation, to shock was to ensure the course of intellectual freedom.

V. S. Pritchett, "Aldous Huxley," in New Statesman, *Vol. LXVI, No. 1708, December 6, 1963, p. 834.*

RICHARD S. KENNEDY

From the time of his first appearance on the literary scene in 1916, Huxley went through a series of discernible periods that merged one into the other. His shifts in social and religious views provided the distinctive features of these periods. But his overall attitude toward life seemed to swing back and forth. Sometimes he reflected a rejection of life, a disgust at flesh (of his own physical being as well as of fellow humans), and a disdain of society. At other times, he displayed an acceptance, occasionally even an exuberance in life, and a sympathetic involvement with his fellow beings in society.

At the outset, during and after World War I, he produced volumes of tough-sinewed verse; witty, carefully controlled short stories; and sophisticated novels of manners. One of the more sardonic of the wanderers in the wasteland, he seemed embittered over the flabbiness of values in the twentieth century, yet moved to raucous and irreverent laughter rather than tears. (p. 38)

In the late twenties he became more serious and satirically less wicked when he fell under the spell of D. H. Lawrence during the last four years of Lawrence's life. Lawrence, by example and by preachment, actually changed the sardonic Huxley's whole attitude toward life. The Lawrentian vitalism is most clearly evident in Huxley's book of essays, ***Do What You Will*** (1929), especially in the reverence for life indicated in **"Holy Face"** and in the discourse on the "life-worshiper" in **"Pascal."** It is well known that in the major novel of this period, ***Point Counterpoint*** (1928), Huxley drew the character Rampion after D. H. Lawrence. Rampion represented the "complete man" against which all the partial men in the book were measured.

Another shift in Huxley's career took place in the 1930's when he became involved with the social and political conflicts of his time. He wrote ***Brave New World*** (1932), his warning about the dehumanizing tendencies of the big state. His books of essays indicated his lack of faith in democracy or his worry about fascism and the march toward war. He became a pacifist; he tried to make speeches for the pacifist cause (though he worried greatly about his inability as a speaker). He published works with such titles as ***What Are You Going To Do About It*** (1936) and ***1936 . . . Peace?*** He edited an *Encyclopedia of Pacifism* (1937). For his novel, ***Eyeless in Gaza*** (1936), he created Anthony Beavis, who was a convert to pacifism.

The fourth period, extending through World War II and into the early 1950's, saw the full development of Huxley's religiosity and an intense interest in mystical experiences. He became associated with the religious philosopher Gerald Heard, and later with a group of Hindus in Southern California. He joined the Vedanta Society, wrote an introduction to the Bhagavad-Gita, scribbled many essays on oriental religion, and compiled his major religious work, ***The Perennial Philosophy*** (1945). According to Huxley, the perennial philosophy is a mystical way of viewing life that crops up in Hinduism, Buddhism, Taoism, Platonism, medieval Christianity, Quakerism, Transcendentalism, and in the religious beliefs of all people who apprehend a "Divine Reality" immanent in the world and in themselves. In literary circles, questions were now raised as to whether Huxley had gone off his rocker. . . . Huxley was getting the same kind of treatment that Eliot met when he started to walk toward Rome. Yet there was a great difference between Eliot's religious turning and Huxley's semiempirical approach to mysticism as a form of psychic phenomena. In fact, in the later part of this period Huxley came up with a physiological explanation for the visions of mystics, ancient and modern, in ***Heaven and Hell*** (1956), and he offered a fascinating theory to account for the imagery of gardens, gems, and bright lights traditionally associated with the "Other World." He took an interest in pharmacology and investigated the various vision-producing drugs and even, in 1953, submitted himself as a guinea pig in an experiment with mescaline which he described in ***The Doors of Perception*** (1954).

Still, this was a genuine religious period and as such a rather negative one, because the attraction to mystical experience is an attempt to retreat from the world and to transcend identity. In his social concerns, Huxley was rather negative too. This was the time of ***Ape and Essence*** (1948), another of his horrific antiutopian novels, picturing the earth after a World War III which had so seared the life out of it that the few remaining people had worked out a new theology based on the necessity of evil.

Perhaps the first indication of another shift came as early as 1955, when Huxley struck a positive note in creating the earthy, all-nourishing Rhea-figure named Kathy in ***The Genius and the Goddess.***

But it was not until the later 1950's that he reached what could be called the period of synthesis. This period began with Huxley's drawing together, from the publication of the previous forty years, anthologies of chosen pieces, ***Collected Short Stories*** (1957) and ***Collected Essays*** (1959). An anthology is hardly a synthesis, but it is a selection of material from past and present which can represent variety of mood and idea and yet not be incongruous. In the ***Collected Essays*** especially, the attitudes reflected on such diverse subjects as the "other self," vision-producing drugs, landscape painting, hypnotism, population, the theocentric outlook on society, baroque art, Wordsworth, D. H. Lawrence, Pascal, Breughel, were surprisingly coherent. The impulse toward synthesis developed and continued up to Huxley's last publication, ***Literature and Science*** (1963), a little treatise which succeeds well in "breaching the spiritual Iron Curtain" that exists between the realm of scientific learning defined by C. P. Snow and the realm of literary culture with its militant dogmatists like F. R. Leavis.

This was also a time of settling down in political and social views, a time especially of renewed faith in democracy and in individualism. Huxley had always been interested in the good society and how it could be achieved—even during his period of distrust of democracy. Generally, his approach was negative: he warned in his essays and novels against threats to individual freedom and development and against the regimentation of social life. His latest political tract, ***Brave New World Revisited*** (1958), set forth the problems he was currently worried about and the value against which he measured.

If Huxley was wary of kinds of power such as might produce the dehumanizing dominance of the World State, what power opportunities seemed to him most threatening? First, he pointed to the problem of overpopulation, which can produce tremendous pressure because of the diminution of available resources of food and raw materials. (pp. 38-41)

Second, he was aware that, with the increase of population and of technological advancement, society had become proportionately more complex. This led to a consequent need for more order in society, and thus social and political pressure built up to demand a standardization of human behavior, and to militate against any uniqueness of behavior.

Huxley was very much disturbed by the fact that in our time a great many devices had been developed or discovered which aid administrative forces in maintaining stability and help them in manipulating minds. He pointed to mass communication devices which can either distribute propaganda or create distractions to keep people from thnking about the important issues; chemical devices, such as tranquilizers, which reduce tension; and other methods of human engineering such as subliminal suggestion or sleep teaching. But warnings were not enough. . . . (p. 41)

Huxley answered his own call for something more positive by the publication of ***Island*** (1962), his first utopian novel. In this work, the new devices are used for good purposes—either for the enhancement of individual well-being or for the protection of individuals against abuses of power. More than this, ***Island*** represents best the synthesizing tendency of his last period, for it embraces what Huxley assumed was the best that both Western civilization and the culture of the East had to offer—biology, chemistry, technology, modern psychology from the West; and philosophy, religion, and ancient psychic practice from the East. (pp. 41-2)

It is a long and complex novel of ideas—hence it is as full of speechifying as a Shaw play. The ideas of the book are unrolled in the story of Will Farnaby, a newspaper reporter who has been wrecked on the island of Pala while out boating. Farnaby is an average English neurotic, whose complicated past—his hatred of his authoritarian father and his guilt feelings about the way he has treated his wife—needs straightening out. The injuries he has received in the boat wreck are symbolic of his psychic state. As the story proceeds, he is healed of his physical injuries while hospitalized and convalescent in Pala. More slowly and with more suspense, he is healed, by the Palanese, of his psychic wounds too, for Pala has the good and happy way of life.

The secret of the way to happiness possessed by the Palanese lies in their taking advantage of all the scientific discoveries of the West yet refusing to allow technological advancement to dominate their culture. In the application of psychology they have become more progressive than the West. Their aim in education is "the training of the whole mind-body." The principal of the elementary school describes it: "What we give the children is simultaneously a training in perceiving and imagining, a training in applied physiology and psychology, a training in practical ethics and practical religion, a training in the proper use of language, and a training in self-knowledge. In a word, a training of the whole mind-body in all its aspects."

Such a statement, and particularly one using a term like "mind-body," implies an underlying philosophy of life. In Pala the philosophic outlook is drawn freely from Hinduism and Buddhism. Man is viewed as having both an individual self and a share in the universal Self or Buddha-nature. Life is viewed as essentially all one. If a person has perception, he understands that his individual self is really only a part of the Oneness of all things; he understands too that all opposites are reconciled in this Oneness and that he must learn to accept everything that is natural and beyond his control, even if it is unpleasant, painful, or destructive. Thus he can face death as well as life, sorrow as well as the ending of sorrow. (pp. 43-4)

Clearly, the religious philosophy of the Palanese is a refined and exquisite humanism. (p. 45)

But the novel ***Island*** is not just a guided tour of ideas. A political and ideological conflict is developed with the outside world and with the dictator of Rendang, the neighboring island. The terrible irony is that the people of Pala are too happy. . . . Pala also has a vulnerable spot. Pala has rich, untapped resources in oil. In the end, through the treachery of the boy-Raja (who did not receive a Palanese education), Pala is invaded by the troops of the dictator, who will divide the oil royalties with the ruling family.

Huxley was hardheaded enough to bring about the fall of Pala in his novel, for its freedom and virtue were oversimplifications in a world of complexity. Many years ago, in ***Proper Studies*** (1929), he made this observation about utopian novels:

> The inhabitants of Utopia are radically unlike human beings. Their creators spend all their ink and energy in discussing, not what actually happens, but what would happen if men and women were quite different from what they are and from what, throughout recorded history, they have always been. . . .

Although Huxley created a utopia thirty years after writing these words, he still realized that idea and theory have to be blunted and shaped by the world of actuality.

But like other civilizations which were realer than Pala and which also fell, ***Island*** offers a provocative complex of ideas for our contemplation. Huxley has drawn together here the thought and experience of a lifetime. He has managed to synthesize religion and science, social order and individualism, and the cultural values of East and West. As a humanistic document, ***Island*** provides a worthy and fitting close to the career of a great intellectual of our time. (pp. 46-7)

Richard S. Kennedy, "Aldous Huxley: The Final Wisdom," in Southwest Review, *Vol. L, No. 1, Winter, 1965, pp. 37-47.*

CHARLES T. McMICHAEL

Aldous Huxley's final novel, ***Island,*** marks the culmination of a lifetime of speculation on the problems of the modern world and on possible solutions for these problems. In this novel he brought together the principal ideas that he had examined in earlier works and introduced a new concept to his thought, a statement on the proper relationship of man and woman and the role of woman in bringing about the spiritual enlightenment necessary to a healthy society. The novel also contains what must be considered as Huxley's final statement on the nature of mystical reality, a bringing together of the transcendent and immanent ideas that he had held at various times throughout his life.

From the beginning of his career, Huxley presented a portrait of a sick society. In his earlier novels, notably ***Point Counterpoint*** and ***Crome Yellow,*** he gave a picture of modern society as being sterile, corrupt, and totally unable to supply the individual with any basis for happiness. His characters in these novels only reflect the nature of the society in which they live, being largely ego-centered, one-sided caricatures of human beings living in despair and spiritual disillusionment. With ***Brave New World*** he presented his opinion of the inevitable result of the conditions he saw about him, a totally materialistic world with no room for anything beyond the physical, the pleasurable, or the reasonable—a world finally of spiritual slavery.

Following this look at the future utopian bondage, Huxley's work seemed to take on a new direction. Still there was the picture of a spiritually sick society, but there began a search that can be clearly seen for solutions to the illness of the modern world. He began to examine such ideas as pacifism arrived at through mystical understanding, pure mystical contemplation of the Absolute, mind-expanding drugs as an aid to mystical understanding, and he also propounded many ideas for social reform ranging from political and economic changes to reorganization of educational procedures and goals in order to create the necessary conditions for the individual to find his way to spiritual enlightenment and freedom. Examination of these ideas took place over a period of thirty years until they reached a point of convergence in the fictional society of Pala, the subject of ***Island.***

Island is a view of a utopia that had been created on a Pacific island, a veritable paradise existing in the midst of a world gone insane. The idea of the island itself is significant, for it is reminiscent of a symbol that Huxley had used thirty years earlier in his first utopian novel, ***Brave New World.*** In this work the island was a place where creative people who could not fit into the stabilized slave society were sent. It represented the only hope for man to escape the bondage of the over-organized society, to have individual freedom of thought and action, and finally to discover his own soul and his relationship to the cosmic scheme. Such also is the world of ***Island.*** . . . Pala is a utopian society but one that stands in direct contrast to that of ***Brave New World.*** It is a society based on individual freedom, pacifism, proper education, economic and governmental decentralization, and religion based on personal contemplation and mystical revelation, all ideas that can be traced through earlier works of Huxley. Pala's social structure is summed up by a leader of its society, Dr. Robert McPhail. . . . Easily recognizable in this passage is the pacifism of ***Eyeless in Gaza,*** the economic and governmental ideas as well as the mystical basis of religion expressed in ***After Many a Summer Dies the Swan*** and ***The Perennial Philosophy,*** and the concepts of education and decentralization of ***Brave New World Revisited.*** In addition, there is another very important idea from ***Brave New World Revisited*** that plays an important role in the society of Pala. This is the practice of birth control, which keeps the population reasonably stable and helps to prevent any trends toward centralization in the society. This is done scientifically, through the use of contraceptives, and by the practice of "the yoga of love." . . . (pp. 73-5)

The result of the combination of these ideas is a society of free men, living in harmony with each other, and what is more important, free to find their own identity and relationship to the universe. Freedom of the individual to know himself and his relationship to the cosmos is the reason for the existence of such a society, as well as being the force that sustains it. . . . The way of life of Pala is directed toward overcoming this central problem of man, the problem that is at the very heart of the spiritual sickness of all modern mankind. If man, through a lack of understanding of the nature of spiritual reality, does not have the ability to see himself as he really is, he cannot possibly know the world as it really is. He will see everything only through his own ego, the false image of himself that he has built, and this can only end in conflict and frustration within himself and with those about him. For this condition to be overcome, all of man's faculties must be brought together; he must become aware of the true nature of spiritual reality, and everything must be channeled into this awareness. (pp. 75-6)

As Huxley had pointed out many times, especially in ***The Perennial Philosophy,*** the reaching of the ultimate mystical vision of reality is a long process which very few people have been able to go through completely. However, the people of Pala are aided in their mystical contemplation by a drug called Moksha, which, when taken in small doses, induces the mystical state and enables the individual to see the universe as it appears beyond the view of the personal ego. . . . It is perhaps significant that at the present time such drugs as Moksha are being experimented with and that Huxley openly propounded the merits of such drugs in several of his works, notably ***The Doors of Perception.*** Whatever the merits or demerits of such usage, the point is that in ***Island*** Moksha does play a very important role. This is but another example of an avenue of thought that Huxley had examined earlier and incorporated into the scheme of Palanian society.

Island is not merely the bringing together of old Huxleyean ideas, however. Although it is without question the culmination of many years of thought in various areas, there are definitely ideas to be found in this novel that are completely new to the thinking of Aldous Huxley, principally the concept of the proper relationship of man and woman and the role of woman in the bringing about of a proper awareness of spiritual reality.

It is significant that nowhere in Huxley's work until the publication of ***Island*** had there been a presentation of a man-woman relationship of any consequence that had led to anything but hopelessness, despair, or tragedy. Using former relationships as examples, one would have to say that Huxley viewed a good and rewarding relationship between man and woman as impossible. Though he may have hinted at the possibility of such a relationship in the characters of Rampion and his wife in ***Point Counterpoint,*** nowhere does he bring out the value of a proper and healthy man-woman union. However, in ***Island*** this relationship is not a mere possibility, but a reality. (pp. 76-7)

Just as Huxley nowhere else presents a fruitful relationship between man and woman, so nowhere does he present woman in a very favorable light. For example, in ***Brave New World*** all female characters are shallow, sensual members of a spiritually dead society; Helen Amberly in ***Eyeless in Gaza*** is presented as a sensitive, self-willed young girl who degenerates into a selfish woman of rather easy virtue; Virginia Mauciple in ***After Many a Summer Dies the Swan*** is the superficial, vulgar mistress of the equally superficial and vulgar Joe Stoyte. For the most part Huxley's female characters are merely sensual creatures capable of little or nothing, or they are selfish, possessive vessels containing the possibility of diabolical power. In ***Island*** this is not the case. (p. 78)

In the end, Huxley destroys his paradise. It is destroyed by the encroachment of the maniacal outside world. But Pala was more than an island in the geographical sense; it was an island of sanity and spiritual wholeness surrounded by the sea of sickness and madness of the remainder of the world. Pala was too small and defenseless to stand up against the greed and desire for power that was generated by the world around it, but although it was destroyed, Will Farnaby discovered that the truths upon which the society was built were not destroyed. He had discovered what is perhaps finally the point to all Huxley's mystical searchings—that

> . . . in spite of the entirely justified refusal to take yes for an answer, the fact remained and would always remain, remain everywhere—the fact that there was this capacity in a paranoiac for intelligence, even in the devil worshiper for love; the fact that the ground of all being could be totally manifest in a flowering shrub, a human face; the fact that there was a light and that this light was also compassion. . . .

Here is a form of mystical understanding that is different from Huxley's earlier views. From the contemplation of a more or less transcendent reality, he has moved to the knowledge of a reality that is finally both transcendent and at the same time immanent and can be seen in everything, a concept reminiscent of Wordsworth's pantheism. It is the realization of this immanent reality and the contemplation of it that can unify thought and feeling within man and lead him to a more healthy existence. This was Huxley's last fictional statement concerning mysticism, and it is perhaps of great significance in that it represents the culmination of many years of speculation. Perhaps of equal significance is the fact that woman is his chief symbol for this concept and the guide to its attainment. This final statement indicates that in ***Island*** Huxley was moving toward a solution which could be the answer to the problem of the spiritual sickness of man.

Huxley believed that something was amiss in our modern world. He saw a society composed of individuals who could see nothing beyond pure physical reality and who consequently saw themselves and their own egos as the center of the universe, of all creation. Because of this condition, man is constantly being frustrated by forces that conflict with the desires of his own ego. This frustration gives birth to the destructive emotions of fear, anger, and hatred, which are the forces that threaten to destroy the entire structure of civilization and to lead man into the nightmare world of the utopian slavery of ***Brave New World.*** He sought for answers to this dilemma, and spent a great portion of his literary efforts in examining ways in which man could rediscover the spiritual side of himself and thereby find salvation for himself and his society. While it can be certainly argued that Huxley solved no problems of the modern world, it cannot be said that he did not at least try to do so, and one has only to look at his final novel, ***Island,*** to find the culmination of his attempts to warn and offer aid to the modern world. (pp. 81-2)

Charles T. McMichael, "Aldous Huxley's 'Island': The Final Vision," in Studies in the Literary Imagination, *Vol. I, No. 2, April, 1968, pp. 73-82.*

BERNARD BERGONZI

Aldous Huxley had not one but several reputations, ranging from the witty iconoclast of the 'twenties to the expatriate guru of the Californian desert, and when he died ten years ago it didn't look as if any of them would survive for long. His last novel, ***Island,*** had been found generally feeble as fiction and unconvincing as utopian speculation. Individual books as various as ***Antic Hay*** or ***Brave New World*** or ***The Perennial Philosophy*** might retain their admirers, and even acquire new ones, but as a whole the Huxley *oeuvre* looked increasingly dated and irrelevant. In fact, the decline to a mere footnote in literary history hasn't happened. Our present campy interest in the 'twenties has given the vintage Huxley novels a fresh appeal, evident in their adaptation for television. There is a gloomy fascination in seeing the ingenious horrors of ***Brave New World*** realised, not hundreds of years into the future, as Huxley conservatively supposed, but here and now, before our very eyes. Indeed, some bold speculators find positive prescriptions in the book, such as Shulamith Firestone, who regards extra-uterine conception and breeding as the Final Solution of the Woman Problem. And the interests of Huxley's later years, in mind-expanding drugs or questions of ecology and over-population, anticipated by ten or fifteen years some central preoccupations of the 'sixties and 'seventies.

Quite a number of recent books indicate the continuing interest in Huxley. (p. 65)

All of these commentators acknowledge, at least in passing, that Huxley was something of a dualist, oscillating throughout his career between a pagan belief in life and the body, and a mystical Manichean mistrust of carnal existence: he memorably stated this duality in ***Point Counter Point,*** in the contrast between the over-cerebral writer Quarles and the Lawrentian figure of Rampion. In fact, the essence of Huxley's view of life lay in discontinuity. A wry perception of the gaps between levels of experience underlay the wit in his early novels. . . . Patterns of opposition run throughout Huxley's work: pain and pleasure; thought and action; art and science; mind and body. And particularly the latter; movingly apparent, for instance, in his long late essay on Maine de Biran. Such a belief is not fashionable these days, when platonic or Cartesian modes of dualism are out, and psychology and theology and philosophy all insist that man is a psychosomatic unity. Nevertheless, I believe that many people do instinctively feel otherwise, finding a division between mind and body in the depths of their daily experience, and that Huxley's articulate expression of such a division may be part of his continuing appeal.

So, indeed, may another kind of dualism, namely, the palpable split between form and content in his novels. For a long time it has been accepted literary opinion that Huxley's novels are inadequate because they are organically unified transformations of experience. Without doubt, compared with the splendid aesthetic unity achieved by James or Conrad or Joyce or Virginia Woolf, Huxley's novels are clumsy, ready-made vehicles, for conversations and random but predictable incidents, with a heavy thematic content. The continuing taste for Huxley's fiction may, however, represent a tacit underground resistance to the triumph of the Modern Movement and its aesthetic canons. More than we imagine, contemporary readers may preserve a taste for simple narratives, wittily told, with a little action, a moderate amount of sex and a good deal of talk that is clever without being difficult. If I am right, Huxley's novels, at least the early ones, will go on being read for a long time, whatever the critics say. (pp. 67-8)

Bernard Bergonzi, "Life's Divisions: The Continuing Debate on Aldous Huxley," in Encounter, *Vol. XLI, No. 1, July, 1973, pp. 65-8.*

NICHOLAS von HOFFMAN

Nineteen-eighty-two marks the 50th anniversary of the publication of Aldous Huxley's anti-utopian novel [***Brave New World***], his prophetic dream of our western democracies. In the interim it has been somewhat blotted out by *1984*, George Orwell's anti-utopian novel about the future of Marxist despotism. Big Brother entered our language in a way no phrase from ***Brave New World*** has, yet in America at least, the present much more closely resembles what Huxley warned us against than what Orwell did. On these shores, at least, Big Brother, while frighteningly powerful, is generally regarded as inept, stupid and ineffective. If he is feared, he is also ridiculed and, by whatever measure he is judged, he has not attained the unitary omnipotence of the Orwellian nightmare.

Huxley's vision of an uncoerced but completely manipulated and controlled society seems much closer. Like Orwell, Huxley foresaw the centralised State in which all decision-making would be done by a small group of hierarchs: the evolution of a nation like the United States into a somewhat chaotic oligarchy of corporate structures, who are unable to plan and manipulate society because they cannot agree with each other, was not anticipated by this writer who did, nevertheless, see our future with greater precision a half a century ago than most present-day Americans see it.

In ***Brave New World*** when you are blue or angry or bored, you take a pinch of a drug called soma. Huxley would later write of his own book that 'the systematic drugging of individuals for the benefit of the state (and incidentally, of course, for their own delight), was a main plank in the policy of the World's Controllers. The daily soma ration was an insurance against personal maladjustment, social unrest, and the spread of subversive ideas. Religion, Karl Marx declared, is the opium of the people. In the Brave New World this situation is reversed. Opium, or rather soma, was the people's religion.'

Opium, or some other mind-altering drug, is bidding fair to become the opiate of the people in the United States. Literally billions of tranquilisers and other mood altering drugs are prescribed every year. In addition there is the illegal drug traffic, the suppression of which, if you step back and look at society with a bit of perspective, seems to have less to do with what is good for people than with power and profit. The government is of a mind to make the dispensing of drugs a licensed monopoly whereby only certain companies and individuals may licitly play the drug trade. No serious effort is undertaken to get people off drugs, only to get them off drugs sold them by freelance entrepreneurs. Narcotics, like violence, are to be a monopoly of the State.

In Brave New World it was the conscious policy of the ruling group to foster the taking of soma; in America the veneration of doctors and medical science, such as it is, amounts to a policy of promoting drugs, but not by people who knowingly wish to control and manipulate behaviour with them. (p. 8)

In ***Brave New World*** control was also achieved by making people isolated integers with essentially a single homogenous personality. In ***BNW*** the individual has no family since his life begins as an egg fertilised on a petrie dish which is then transferred into a bottle where he remains until he is ripe for 'decanting'. An outrageous conceit 50 years ago, but only a matter of time in 1982.

After decanting, people have the correct norms and values incorporated into them by 'Hypnopaedics', having recorded slogans whispered in their ears all night every night of childhood while they sleep in their dorms. The American child and the American adult, both, get their messages, called 'impressions' by the advertising industry, through television, a machine that Huxley anticipates.

In Huxley's futuristic society one of the ways that individualism and the dangerous virtues (courage, love of truth, etc.) it brings in its train are smothered is by frowning on anything that smacks of solitude, of being alone, of encouraging thought. (pp. 8-9)

BNW is a tasteless world where people wear colourful polyester double knits and don't have to be treated by the State as potential insurrectionists. Their tummies are full and their minds are empty because even when they are alone, they aren't alone. They are constantly being entertained and diverted by games, shows and happy drivel. . . .

Even the inhabitants of ***BNW*** might cringe at what is shot into the heads of Americans day and night. With the advent of the communications satellite and cable television, the circus never stops.

The messages that are fired into our brain cells by the consortium of corporations who decide their content reinforce our commitment to their freedom of enterprise, but much of the message is neither true nor false, but unreal and hopelessly tangential to what ought to be our concerns.

Huxley was not a supine determinist, a che sarà sarà type. He believed that people have free will and that their free will can be applied to the making and the remaking of society. Nevertheless, it may be that at some point in the building of the Brave New World it will be impossible to turn back because there are too few people who want to. Pop half a gram of soma and forget it. There are days on this side of the Atlantic when it seems we're that gone, but we aren't. There is an underground of people who will not turn on their television, and who, when no one is looking, flush their daily soma ration down the lavatory. (p. 9)

Nicholas von Hoffman, "Huxley Vindicated," in The Spectator, *Vol. 249, No. 8036, July 17, 1982, pp. 8-9.*

M. E. Kerr

1927-

(Pseudonym of Marijane Meaker; has also written under pseudonyms of M. J. Meaker, Vin Packer, and Ann Aldrich) American novelist, autobiographer, and nonfiction writer.

Kerr is one of the most respected and popular authors of novels for young adults. Her stories are fast-paced and humorous yet confront difficult issues which teenagers may face. While they do not fall into the category of "teen romances," nearly all of Kerr's novels are stories of love, focusing on both romantic and familial relationships. Kerr also examines in her work such social problems as alcoholism, racism, and mental illness. The title character in Kerr's first young adult novel, *Dinky Hocker Shoots Smack!* (1972), is an obese high school girl whose mother is so absorbed in her own work with drug addicts that she fails to notice her daughter's problems. This wide-ranging novel also concerns Dinky's relationship with P. John, a classmate who shares a weight problem, and P. John's relationship with his father, whose liberal values have caused P. John to adopt an ultra-conservative viewpoint.

While her novels center on teenage protagonists, Kerr has been praised for her development of parents and other adult characters as fallible people with needs and problems of their own. For Kerr's young people, attaining maturity often involves learning to understand and accept the adults in their lives. For example, in *Is That You, Miss Blue?* (1975), a fourteen-year-old girl develops sympathy for an eccentric, outcast teacher at her boarding school and eventually reconciles with her mother, from whom she had been estranged.

A common theme in Kerr's novels is "love, its presence and, more commonly, its absence in the lives of her characters," as Mary Kingsbury has noted. The word "love" appears in several of Kerr's titles, and the seriousness with which Kerr handles the theme of love can often be seen in these titles. The male protagonist of *If I Love You, Am I Trapped Forever?* (1973) examines many types of love relationships and questions the value of commitment in a relationship. The titles *I'll Love You When You're More Like Me* (1977) and *Love Is a Missing Person* (1975) also indicate that Kerr treats love as something complex and often difficult.

Most of Kerr's novels are narrated in the first person; often two narrators take turns telling the story. In *Little Little* (1980) the narration is done by Little Little La Belle and Sydney Cinnamon, two teenage dwarves whose relationship succeeds over the objections of Little Little's parents. Opal Ringer and Jesse Pegler of *What I Really Think of You* (1981) tell what it is like to be a minister's child; Opal's father is a fundamentalist preacher, and Jesse's is a television evangelist. The novel explores their growing friendship, their relationships with their fathers, and the similarities and differences in the way their families practice religion.

In her autobiography *Me Me Me Me Me: Not a Novel* (1983) Kerr describes her childhood and adolescence and explains how she used real people and events from her own life in creating many of her novels.

Courtesy of M. E. Kerr

(See also *CLC*, Vol. 12; *Contemporary Authors*, Vol. 107; and *Something about the Author*, Vol. 20.)

SUZANNE FREEMAN

Little Little La Belle has long blond hair and neatly tanned arms. . . . She is 3 feet 3 inches tall. She calls herself a dwarf.

M. E. Kerr has written well and often before about the sweet miseries of first love and coming of age. In [*Little Little*] . . . those familiar problems come from a new perspective—less than four feet off the ground. . . . It is the place of circus freaks, a place where strangers feel free to stare and point and pinch your cheek. It is an especially hard place to be when you're 17-going-on-18 years old.

Kerr's two narrators, Little Little and a young male dwarf named Sydney Cinnamon, have other obstacles to face as well. There is Little Little's family life—her eccentric, tomboy sister, her tippling mother, her overprotective father. There are Sydney's physical defects. . . . He is definitely not "p.f." (perfectly formed) and therefore definitely not the kind of dwarf that Little Little's mother has in mind for her daughter.

What Mama La Belle does have in mind is marriage, and her candidate for son-in-law is the famous red-haired midget evangelist, Little Lion. . . . He and Sydney vie for Little Little's little heart and some fairly silly stuff ensues—spiked drinks, giraffes delivered by taxi, and a host of hallelujahs from Little Lion. . . . It's cartoon material, it's a Little Rascals extravaganza, and none of it matters much. Because the real story this book has to tell lies in the characters of Sydney and Little Little and in the way they cope with their affliction.

M. E. Kerr writes mostly about likeable outcasts—wry and bookish kids who will never be part of the parade but who see it all the better from the sidelines. Sydney and Little Little are no exception. They may be small, but their eyesight's keen. And from where they stand, any passing parade looks about like the next—big and boring, plodding and wholesome as a herd of cattle. What the dwarfs would like to see are different things, freakish things, things that are like themselves somehow. . . .

This is a story about courage and tolerance and growing up without growing bigger. Kerr does not preach nor ask for pity. She details the everyday complexities of the dwarfs' lives—big dogs, booster chairs, unwieldy forks and spoons. She shows just how they eat and drive and kiss. It's disquieting to consider that this is almost side show stuff, that a part of this book will appeal to the gawker, the cheek-pincher in us all. But, at the end, of course, a side show is always a sham, a place of actors and optical illusion. M. E. Kerr doesn't stoop to tricks. Her dwarfs are real and sharp as nuggets. They are small and steady as bookends. They are dwarfs who simply call themselves dwarfs.

Suzanne Freeman, "Growing Up in a Small World," in Book World—The Washington Post, *May 10, 1981, p. 15.*

MARILYN KAYE

In several previous books, M. E. Kerr has shown an interest in the underlying passions of individuals, usually secondary characters, with physical or emotional idiosyncracies. In **"Little Little"** these characters take center stage as Miss Kerr investigates the relationship between three dwarfs: [Sydney Cinnamon, Little Little La Belle, and Knox Lionel]. . . .

Sydney and Little Little share the narration in alternating chapters, a device Miss Kerr has employed before and which is nicely conducive to a tale of romance. And while this *is* essentially a love story, the author gently weaves into the plot the general anguish and specific problems intrinsically bound to a minority world. But the pain, however verbalized or demonstrated, remains implicit. The work goes beyond an account of "what it's like to be a dwarf"; it remains a reality-based story of individuals.

Despite the first-person narrative, M. E. Kerr distances the reader from the work through limited character revelation, and her restraint discourages familiarity. In this way, she prevents the novel from becoming a shallow plea for tolerance. All these characters require is respect.

There is, of course, as in all of Miss Kerr's work, humor and an element of the absurd. Both Sydney's and Knox's occupations lend themselves to a controlled satire. Less restrained, however, is the author's portrayal of Little Little's parents. . . . In their persistent efforts to uncover euphemisms for everything from their daughter's condition to bodily functions, they move dangerously close to becoming caricatures.

There are other occasional problems. Every now and then one of the protagonists will toss out a vague, poorly disguised throwaway line that is riddled with portent and screams of significance. But for the most part, the author's tone throughout the work blends a matter-of-fact nonchalance with a wry, mildly sardonic humor that is poignant without being sentimental. In the end, the reader is presented with a set of engaging personalities, an unusual perspective, and an entertaining, tender romance that offers both technical strength and a low-key emotional tug.

Marilyn Kaye, in a review of "Little Little," in The New York Times Book Review, *May 17, 1981, p. 38.*

NORMA BAGNALL

[***Little Little***] is an outrageously sad-funny book with humor and pathos consistently maintained throughout. Kerr uses a multiple point-of-view to present Little Little and Sydney. . . , and she writes a devastating critique of those people who refuse to accept reality. The handicapped in this book have accepted whatever they have had to; it is the rest of the world—pretending that the handicap doesn't exist, or that it is an object of ridicule—that provokes the protagonists.

This one is hilariously funny in the tradition of black humor, and it is M. E. Kerr at her very best.

Norma Bagnall, in a review of "Little Little," in The ALAN Review, *Vol. 9, No. 1, Fall, 1981, p. 21.*

ZENA SUTHERLAND

As she has in earlier novels, Kerr chooses a segment of society not usually found in books for young people; [in ***What I Really Think of You***] the two protagonists are children of Pentecostal preachers. Opal feels ambivalence and some embarrassment about the shouting and the speaking in tongues at her father's church. . . . Jesse Pegler's father is a television personality, a glib and successful preacher envied by Opal's family. Chapters are told alternately by Jesse and Opal, and this gives the story some breadth as the two become uneasy friends. . . . [***What I Really Think of You***] gives a reader some acquaintance with the behind-the-scenes lives of one kind of clerical family, but it never fuses into a smooth, sophisticated narrative as do most of Kerr's novels, and the ending (Opal develops the gift . . . to "sing tongues," and declares her love for all those who had once found her and her family's religious practices comic) is weak because the conflicts and problems of the story do not seem necessary precursors to the final development.

Zena Sutherland, in a review of "What I Really Think of You," in Bulletin of the Center for Children's Books, *Vol. 35, No. 10, June, 1982, p. 190.*

ALICE DIGILIO

M. E. Kerr, whose ***Little Little*** was published to critical acclaim last year, likes aberrations. Her earlier novel for young people concerned dwarfs. [In ***What I Really Think of You***] she delves into the world of fundamentalist preachers and their long-suffering children. . . .

Both [Opal and Jesse] are oppressed by the piety and the exhibitionism of their parents, and Opal is at times downright ashamed of hers.

The impetus of the novel, however, is not pathos but farce, and it is Opal who gives the most entertaining reports of life in a home where "Honk If You Love Jesus" bumper stickers adorn the family car. She has the sympathy to love her parents, even when they embarrass her, yet the wit to classify their foibles.

Kerr makes fundamentalism funny through most of the novel. But, alas, she changes her tone near the end, and expects us to accept Opal's reconciliation with something she has so often made quite ridiculous. In a way it seems a desperately contrived case of plotting, and it simply doesn't work. We want more of the Opal who has a keen eye for tackiness but loves its perpetrators just the same.

Alice Digilio, in a review of "What I Really Think of You," in Book World—The Washington Post, *July 11, 1982, p. 11.*

ROSEMARY KASPER

A humorous look at society and its mores through the eyes of some memorable "little people" is provided in this whimsical tale [***Little Little***]. . . .

Many of society's beliefs, traditions, and practices are taken to task. Little Little and Sydney are well aware of the injustices which prevail and try their best to pursue their own destinies. Although not always successful, they make a valiant effort and never lose their sense of humor.

Although satirical, the book is also informative. Little Little's Grandfather claims that Tom Thumb could have been famous without being a dwarf if he had used his intelligence "instead of letting someone exploit him!" When Little Little asks what "exploit" means, he replies: "It means to utilize for profit. . . ."

The leading characters are well-rounded and clearly defined. Readers learn that all people have the same needs, problems and abilities—small persons simply have some special needs which must be met. The dialogue is fast-paced and witty. Although sensationalism is depicted, this is clearly done to educate. Stereotypes are skillfully shown to be just that—stereotypes. This book is recommended for young adults who can understand the satire.

Rosemary Kasper, in a review of "Little Little," in Interracial Books for Children Bulletin, *Vol. 13, Nos. 4 & 5, 1982, p. 15.*

MARILYN KAYE

With the rise in popularity of televised religion and of evangelical Christianity, it should come as no surprise that this phenomenon should make its appearance in a young adult novel. The topic lends itself to a range of treatments, from moral directive to satiric indictment. And it should come as no surprise to her readers that [in **"What I Really Think of You"**] M. E. Kerr has avoided the didactic traps that are inherent in the subject.

In her latest account of a fragile boy-girl relationship, Miss Kerr neatly places an incipient romance against the backdrop of evangelism and allows that subject to permeate—but not overwhelm—her story. (pp. 49-50)

With admirable sincerity Miss Kerr explores the tentative relationship between Opal and Jesse and the surrounding tensions that are grounded in class conflict and the inevitable comparisons between the fervor of unabashed, "down-home" faith and the razzmatazz of media-hyped religion, equally fervent but with a polished commercial veneer.

Opal's narrative has a haunting quality that suggests underlying passion. Jesse's remarks are less powerful, but his sense of inadequacy reflects a common adolescent concern.

The novel has its problems. The sudden reappearance of [Jesse's brother] Bud toward the end and his subsequent involvement with Opal has the ring of a slightly contrived denouement, and some peculiarly undeveloped characters drift through the story without adding much.

Despite its shortcomings, the work has integrity. It's hard to believe that a novelist could indulge in such concepts as being "slain in the spirit," waiting for "The Rapture," faith healing and speaking in tongues without either proselytizing or mocking them—but glory be, M. E. Kerr has done it. (p. 50)

Marilyn Kaye, in a review of "What I Really Think of You," in The New York Times Book Review, *September 12, 1982, pp. 49-50.*

JOYCE MILTON

When Marijane Meaker, who writes under the name of M. E. Kerr, was growing up in a small upstate New York town, her mother missed no opportunity to warn her that "there isn't a female comedian alive who's happy." Fortunately, she never paid her mother the slightest attention. She [proceeded] . . . to produce nine highly successful young adult novels about the heartbreaking comedy of American adolescence.

Now, in this autobiographical memoir [**"Me Me Me Me Me: Not a Novel"**], Miss Kerr unveils a deliciously wicked sense of humor, reminiscent in style, and occasionally in content, of Jessica Mitford's work. . . .

These reminiscences are primarily addressed to fans of Miss Kerr's novels who will no doubt enjoy meeting the real-life models for many of her off-beat characters. (One is hardly surprised to learn that the truth is often more bizarre than fiction, but in this case it is usually more poignant as well since Miss Kerr freely admits that some of these individuals were the victims of her unstoppable writer's drive to know everyone's secrets.)

As for the rest of you, don't let the regrettable title put you off; this book offers a satisfying if brief encounter with a humorist whose delight in poking fun at the trappings of authority is unmarred by either self-hatred or pettiness toward others.

Joyce Milton, in a review of "Me Me Me Me Me: Not a Novel," in The New York Times Book Review, *May 22, 1983, p. 39.*

PAUL A. CARON

Do the events and persons about which authors write reflect realities of their own lives, or are they the result of their vivid imaginations? M. E. Kerr has been writing popular novels for young adults for many years and has been asked this question frequently by her readers. Her answer to the many letters she has received on the subject is [***Me Me Me Me Me: Not a Novel***]. . . .

Marijane Meaker is a very complex character. She becomes a rebellious teenager who confronts facets of her life her way, whenever she does not understand. Among her problems are her family, her religion, small town mores, and her culture as a whole. . . . She battles. She hurts. She grows. She matures. This *is* the story of Marijane and her friends and foes who influenced her formative years.

The author's style and technique are very effective. She presents these autobiographical chapters in such a way that the reader enters into stories without realizing it. Then, at the end of each chapter, she follows up each story by explaining which of the characters and escapades have influenced various characters in each of her books.

M. E. Kerr has answered in good measure the questions put to her by her readers. She has written a fascinating, yet timeless look at herself and others, which will not only delight her fans, but will no doubt increase their number.

Paul A. Caron, in a review of "Me Me Me Me Me: Not a Novel," in Best Sellers, *Vol. 43, No. 3, June, 1983, p. 110.*

NANCY C. HAMMOND

Spurred by readers' questions, the author of a string of witty, trenchant contemporary novels delves into her past [in ***Me Me Me Me Me—Not a Novel***] and writes "what really happened to me when I was a kid, as I remember it." Without resorting to dull chronologies or nostalgic platitudes, the author, as did Jean Fritz in *Homesick* . . . , describes with drama, humor, and perception a youth less exotic but no less entertaining and compelling. The episodic chapters, which highlight M. E. Kerr's writing and her parental and peer relationships, dip primarily into her adolescent and college years; each chapter ends with brief paragraphs connecting her fact and her fiction. . . . The roots of her writing glimmer in her father's journal entries and in her mother's gossip. Periodic troublemaker and clown and perennial rebel, Marijane Meaker . . . confesses to being the "smartmouth" tomboys populating many of her novels. And she is quite as entertaining as they are. Incisive, witty, and immediate, the book is vintage M. E. Kerr.

Nancy C. Hammond, in a review of "Me Me Me Me Me—Not a Novel," in The Horn Book Magazine, *Vol. LIX, No. 4, August, 1983, p. 462.*

PUBLISHERS WEEKLY

If [**Him *She Loves?***] were Kerr's first novel, or a story by almost anyone else, it would be hailed as a true original, bittersweet, brilliantly comic. While 17-year-old Henry Schiller's tale of woe deserves such praise, it is not in a class with the author's ***Dinky Hocker Shoots Smack!, Gentlehands, Is That You, Miss Blue?*** or her other superb creations. Henry, new in a Long Island town, has the bad luck to fall in love with gorgeous Valerie Kissenwiser. Her father, Al Kiss, is a famous comic and violently opposed to a Teutonic suitor for his darling Valley. . . . It's up to Henry to convince Al that Valerie has chosen the right lover, a *mensch,* not a *nebbish,* and the way he does that is the story's turning point. But here the reader may ask, "*This* he does?" The resolution hints that Kerr had used all the genuine gems in her imagination before the crisis and had only paste substitutes for the finale.

*A review of "*Him *She Loves?" in* Publishers Weekly, *Vol. 225, No. 8, February 24, 1984, p. 140.*

CASEY O'MALLEY

We can all remember the first time a story ceased being simply an exercise for our fantasies and began to be more of a process through which we sought a larger stake in the world around us. For some it might have been a hero's fall; for others, the means rather than the end of a plot may have provided a glimpse behind the actions of a character. This is not to say that a book should be discarded if it fails to afford an in-depth study of human nature. It does imply though, that for a proficient reader of any age, entertainment should be of good quality.

In light of these standards M. E. Kerr falls far short. Wallowing in less than classic status, **Him *She Loves?*** is of only mediocre value for a reader seeking pleasant distraction. A bland story of teenage love does little to stretch one's scope of experience, and the sometimes incredible actions of the two main characters serve to alienate the attentiveness of a somewhat cynical reader. . . .

Ms. Kerr has written a novel for a very narrow audience. Recommended for ages twelve and up, the vision of hindsight allows a reviewer to picture the story as too old for those under twelve and too unrealistic for those in the specified age group. Kerr's language is plain enough—it should not send anyone scurrying to the dictionary—and her story is unobjectionable to all. Most children will be permitted to read this book, but the question is: would they?

*Casey O'Malley, in a review of "*Him *She Loves?" in* Best Sellers, *Vol. 44, No. 6, September, 1984, p. 233.*

KATHY PIEHL

[M. E. Kerr] uses religion as an important component of her books for young adults much more frequently than writers of "mainstream" novels usually do. Three of her nine books—***Is That You, Miss Blue?, Little Little,*** and ***What I Really Think of You***—have religion as a major theme. Some of the other six novels also contain references to religion.

Kerr's essential message about religion is that it has little effect on people or society. In fact, Christianity merely reinforces the values of the rich and successful. The business of religion and the business of business are much the same. Both depend on superficial showmanship to attain their goal: money. Religious people distrust those who become too emotionally involved with their beliefs. Instead they accept and support the status quo. (p. 307)

The parallel between organized religion and other businesses is most apparent in ***Little Little***. All the major characters are dwarfs, and three of the four are involved in selling something. Sydney Cinnamon, one of the narrators, makes his living as The Roach, the representative of Palmer Pest Company. . . . His female counterpart in the world of advertising is Eloise Ficklin, who stars as Dora, the Dancing Lettuce Leaf, in television commercials for Melody Mayonnaise.

While these two have earned fame and money as a result of their commercial endeavors, the dwarf who has gained the most wealth has been in the business of TV religion. Little Lion's appearances on "The Powerful Hour" have gained him the adoration of "the Faithful" and "a white Mercedes convertible, a ten-room house on the Palisades . . . and a fiancee shorter than he was and prettier than a picture.'' (pp. 307-08)

Sydney first met Little Lion the summer he was 14 and Little Lion was 17. They worked at Leprechaun Village, and Little Lion, then Knox Lionel, entertained his fellow employees by imitating TV evangelists. . . . In his move from imitating the TV evangelists to joining their ranks, Little Lion apparently experienced no religious conversion, just the awakening of knowledge that his skills could get him ahead. . . . The parallels between Sydney's and Dora's selling of roach powder and mayonnaise and Little Lion's selling of religion are obvious.

The relationship between religion and business is discussed openly in ***What I Really Think of You*** when Bud Pegler accuses his TV evangelist father of ''turning into big business.''

Guy Pegler devotes much of his energy to thinking up promotional ideas for his show like the ''Charge it to the Lord'' campaign for which viewers will get a gold charge plate charm if they send a donation.

These gimmicks point out the superficial nature of televised religion. Because appearance is crucial on television, the TV preachers in Kerr's world are constantly trying to improve their looks. . . .

The fame accompanying such television exposure makes changes in [Guy Pegler's] life and that of his family members. His son Jesse remembers when his father was Brother Pegler, an evangelist who preached in tents. Instead of spending time on clothing selection, he bought ties at a drugstore.

In the same book Opal Ringer and her family represent the kind of life the Peglers lived in pre-television days. Opal's Daddy is the preacher at the Helping Hand Tabernacle, a Pentacostal congregation in the same town where Pegler's successful television operation has its headquarters. The Hand loses members and dollars to the television preachers. . . .

As the book ends the Ringers are enjoying success of their own—as a result of television. The cameras at The Hand to record the return of Guy Pegler by his kidnapper recorded Opal's singing in tongues instead. . . .

Tongues of fire of the Biblical Pentecost have been replaced by the red camera lights, but the transformation of the Ringers' lives was as complete as the disciples' in Acts. People now pack The Hand to hear Opal sing in tongues. The Hand has a security system to regulate the crowds and a computer to tally the offerings. The Peglers have more companions in the clique of wealthy preachers, thanks to television. (p. 308)

The religion that Opal's family practices is definitely emotional with people swaying, speaking in tongues, offering miraculous cures for disease. In fact, the intensity of their emotion is so great that Kerr seems to draw a parallel between religious fervor and sexual arousal. What is especially interesting about her use of this comparison is that although sex is referred to in Kerr's books, there are no explicit descriptions of sexual encounters. In fact, none of the major characters gets much farther than kissing. The most erotic passages occur not in description of sex but in the account of Opal's religious fervor. Opal's ideas of religion are closely connected to her fantasies about handsome Bud Pegler. She would sit hugging her pillow tight or wake up from fevered dreams. . . .

We are not really surprised that Opal and Bud become involved sexually, ''seen the Devil's face, sweet nights when we slip,'' as Opal puts it. What is interesting is that Kerr employs her usual restraint about that relationship while describing religious ecstasy so fully. . . .

[In ***Is That You, Miss Blue?***] the girls at Charles School react with laughter when Miss Blue mentions the religious visions she had. (p. 309)

Eventually the headmistress at the Episcopal school dismisses Miss Blue because of her visions. . . . Flanders points out that the disciples and saints suffered from the same ''delusion,'' that Miss Blue is a good teacher, and that all the faculty suffer from some kind of passion. But Miss Blue is embarrassing in a way the others are not, and she is dismissed just before Christmas. No faculty members defend her, and Carolyn Cardmaker is expelled for questioning the headmistress about ''what kind of a religious school was it that believed communication with Jesus Christ was a sign of mental instability?''. . . . Clearly, getting too emotional about religion can draw the laughter and antagonism of others. (pp. 309-10)

Religion's capacity to arouse strong feelings is also demonstrated in Kerr's books by adolescents' rebellion *against* religion. The most formal rejection comes when Carolyn Cardmaker forms an atheist club even though her father is a pastor. She rejects institutional religion because ''The really religious ones like Miss Blue get pushed around by the money-making rabble. . . .''

When Bud Pegler leaves home in disgust at his father's constant money raising for his TV show, he is participating in a cycle. His father went through the same process as a young man. . . . At the end Bud returns, joins his father on TV, and makes plans for the Winning Rally's foreign tour. Jesse has entered his own period of doubt and won't attend church. His mother is confident that he too will complete the cycle. '''One day,' my mother says, 'your name will be up there with theirs.''' . . .

Carolyn Cardmaker also relents and goes to her father's church on New Year's Eve to make peace with him and to ''take God back'' as she phrases it. She too has completed her cycle of rebellion against religious belief. . . .

The end of rebellion often signals a return to accepting the way things are, and many people never question their religious beliefs at all. Those who are comfortable with their religion tend to support the status quo and to respect authority of any kind, no matter how horrible it might be.

The extreme example of this is Grandpa Trenker in ***Gentlehands***. He had been responsible for sending hundreds of Jews to their deaths at Auschwitz, and Kerr implies that this sense of ''duty'' to perform the commands of government resulted in part from his strict religious upbringing. . . . Buddy's mother, the daughter of Gentlehands, also attends Mass regularly. Although she is horrified by her father's actions and denounces them, she does not see any parallel between her support of the U.S. government's activities in Vietnam and Gentlehands' obedience to German authorities. . . .

Religious people support not only government policy but also social policy, particularly the treatment of minorities. Again Grandpa Trenker is the extreme case with his brutality toward Jews, but other people in ***Gentlehands*** make derogatory remarks about Jews. Three of Kerr's four books set in Seaville, Long Island, mention the Hadefield Club, a private club that accepts members by invitation only. Suzy Slade, the narrator in ***Love Is a Missing Person***, recalls that her family refused to join because [the club did not allow Jews to become members]. . . .

The fact that prejudice often stems from religious intolerance is underscored by the fact that the type of prejudice mentioned most often in Kerr's books is against Jews. . . .

Although Kerr never states explicitly how religion *should* affect people's lives, she does include a prayer that seems to summarize her thoughts. Written by Mary, Queen of Scots, in her death cell, the prayer is printed on the picture Miss Blue takes with her when she leaves Charles School

> Keep us, oh God, from all smallness.
> Let us be large in thought, in word,
> and in deed. . . .
>
> And, O Lord, let us never forget
> to be kind. Amen. . . .

Most of the Christians in Kerr's books come nowhere near these standards of behavior. Only for a few people does religion make a difference, and they are usually considered weird. Of all the characters in Kerr's novels, only three seem to have religious beliefs that strongly affect their lives. Two, Opal Ringer and Miss Blue, have been discussed . . . already. The third is Rev. Cardmaker. (p. 310)

When his daughter Carolyn rebels against religion, she does so mainly because of the way those in power have treated her father. Because he has the courage to point out things that are wrong, his supervisor plans to transfer him to an even poorer parish. But he doesn't share Carolyn's hatred. Despite the drafty house he lives in and the franks and beans his family eats for supper, he seems happy. . . . Rev. Cardmaker is definitely a misfit in a world of slick TV preachers who hustle for dollars.

According to Kerr's books, most Christians, including the clergy, conform more to society's norms than to the ideals in Mary, Queen of Scots' prayer. Good looks, success, and money make people worthwhile. Christians control their emotions and support the status quo. [In ***Me Me Me Me Me***] Kerr admits that "while I came from a religious background (with one aunt who was a Roman Catholic nun) and attended an Episcopal boarding school, I always seemed to have a quarrel with organized religion.". . . Her books for young adults express that argument through the actions of her characters. (p. 363)

Kathy Piehl, "The Business of Religion in M. E. Kerr's Novels," in Voice of Youth Advocates, *Vol. 7, No. 6, February, 1985, pp. 307-10, 363.*

William Kotzwinkle

1938-

American novelist, short story writer, and author of books for children.

Kotzwinkle is noted for his fabulistic tales and his novelizations of popular films. His novels and short stories for adults, young adults, and children frequently include elements of science fiction, mystery, and fantasy. Although some critics contend that his novels lack cohesiveness, Kotzwinkle is often commended for his inventive characterizations and storylines.

Among Kotzwinkle's novels for young adults are *Dream of Dark Harbor* (1979) and *Jack in the Box* (1980). *Dream of Dark Harbor* concerns a boy who is drawn to a deserted shack by the sea where he encounters a crew of sea ghosts. In *Jack in the Box,* an adolescent boy fantasizes about the exploits of several historical figures and television characters until he is jolted out of his imaginary world and forced to deal with reality.

***E.T. the Extra-Terrestrial in His Adventure on Earth* (1982), an adaptation of Melissa Mathison's screenplay for the film *E.T.*, greatly increased Kotzwinkle's popularity among readers. Although the book follows the plot and characterizations of the motion picture, Kotzwinkle was praised for adding psychological depth to the story. A sequel, *E.T.: The Book of the Green Planet* (1985), was recently published. Kotzwinkle also novelized *Superman III* (1983), in which the superhero endures a brief stint as an evildoer.**

Kotzwinkle's short stories are among his most critically acclaimed compositions. The pieces in *Elephant Bangs Train* (1971) are spoofs and parodies that take a ribald look at lost innocence. *Hermes 3000* (1972) is a collection of seven interconnected stories involving different times and places. *Swimmer in the Secret Sea* (1974), a novella expanded from one of Kotzwinkle's short stories, is a moving account of the birth and death of an infant.

Mysticism and surrealism are recurring features in Kotzwinkle's work. *Fata Morgana* (1977) mingles fairy tale with detective fiction in its depiction of animated, toylike people in Paris and an inspector's chase of a gypsy. *Great World Circus* (1983) is a dreamlike rhymed narrative in which various men throughout history become involved with the High Priestess of Ur, ringmistress of the Great World Circus. *Christmas at Fontaine's* (1983) is a sentimental tale involving a silver "ghost" who, when discovered hiding in a department store, reveals the true spirit of Christmas to the story's other characters.

Kotzwinkle's novels for adults often utilize fantasy and humor while probing human and moral conflicts. *The Fan Man* (1974) reverses the myth of Buddha in its madcap portrayal of a New York hippie who overcomes his conflict with a filthy, absurd world by "becoming one" with it. *Doctor Rat* (1976) is an antivivisectionist novel about a confused laboratory rat who considers himself an auxiliary to his human experimenters and quells an animal rebellion. *Queen of Swords* (1984) depicts a middle-aged writer who leaves his self-satisfied wife for a younger woman but eventually realizes that he has been seeking the wrong things in life.

© Joe Servello

(See also *CLC*, Vols. 5, 14; *Contemporary Authors*, Vols. 45-48; *Contemporary Authors New Revision Series*, Vol. 3; and *Something about the Author*, Vol. 24.)

KIRKUS REVIEWS

[***Elephant Bangs Train*** is a] happy congeries of spoofs and more formal parodies, instant legends and souvenirs of lost innocence. . . . **"A Stroke of Luck"** [involves] a fourteen-year-old's coming of age at the hands of a coolly composed nurse; at once ingenuous and ribald, it's a candidate for some eventual uncensored anthology. Mr. Kotzwinkle has compassion only for the genuine, for the ice-bound mastodon reduced to **"A Most Incredible Meal"** or for small **"Marie"** blissfully twirling to show her panties. Spontaneous, crafty, sometimes elliptical . . . but a joy.

A review of "Elephant Bangs Train," in Kirkus Reviews, *Vol. XXXIX, No. 5, March 1, 1971, p. 247.*

THOMAS LASK

Kotzwinkle is the fabulist, the gifted bard, the natural storyteller [in ***Elephant Bangs Train***]. . . . **"The Magician"** brings the prestidigitator and a beautiful woman together in a communion more magical than the magic he is performing. "Come," you can hear Kotzwinkle saying, "and I'll tell you a story."

There is another side to him though that is less exotic, more recognizable in everyday terms. **"Marie"** and **"The Bird Watcher"** are two stories that track the dark cracks in the translucent world of childhood. And **"Soldier in the Blanket"** is a faultless gem of a story, short enough to take up only four pages, but worth an extended essay in what it has to say about infantile sexuality and corruption. To my mind he is more effective when he is less colorful. Indian princes, Russian counts, vindictive elephants, Chinese concubines all have their place, but [he] does so much more with **"Soldier in the Blanket," "The Bird Watcher"** and that hilarious chapter of a boy's upbringing, **"Stroke of Luck,"** that I wish he had confined himself to these. But he is one writer who has not hidden behind the short story, but used it to extend his range and to challenge his powers to the limit.

Thomas Lask, "Of Elephants and Air Strikes," in The New York Times, *April 9, 1971, p. 29.**

R. V. CASSILL

There is quicksilver brilliance in [Kotzwinkle's] satire. The dazzling alternation of fantasy and realism, the intrusion of one on the other, and the development of effects appropriate to one from the other are the memorable characteristics of this collection [of short stories, ***Elephant Bangs Train***]. His verbal play matches the caprice of events. **"The Jewel of Amitaba"** is a spicily entertaining cacophony wherein the jagged notes of Terry Southern and S.J. Perelman make astonishing combinations with the vaporings of Kahlil Gibran. A very short and masterful story, **"Follow the Eagle,"** tells of an Indian boy with a 750 cc motorcycle who understands that his destiny is to jump the bike across Navaho Canyon—or, rather, to jump it *most of the way* across. The story is absolutely flawless and cleancut, classic.

R.V. Cassill, "A Very Dissimilar Trio," in Book World—The Washington Post, *June 6, 1971, p. 5.**

JIM LANGLOIS

In [***Elephant Bangs Train,*** a] collection of 16 stories, Kotzwinkle wanders between surface rhythms of reality and undercurrents of the imagination. In several stories he is only competent at re-creating a conventional reality or at capturing various styles; but in others, on the level of the imagination, he uncovers a madness, a wildness, which he delineates as the true home that the artist shares with the child, the madman, the liar, the magician, the dying. Here epiphanies of the imagination transcend reality. . . . In these stories the artist's insights fuse with the unselective eyes of children to create a vibrant, shifting vision of the power of creation. . . . Kotzwinkle stretches our perceptions with a newness and a frequency that make his stories a refreshing variation on the art of short fiction.

Jim Langlois, in a review of "Elephant Bangs Train," in Library Journal, *Vol. 96, No. 13, July, 1971, p. 2347.*

KIRKUS REVIEWS

This novel-length opus [***Hermes 3000***] is not really a novel but a set of very Kotzwinklian stories apparently interleaved. The retinue includes a soldier posted by Catherine the Great to guard a flower, a British MP's "ornamental" garden hermit, a retiree who suffers a coronary and enters Chinese paradise in the Metropolitan Museum, the madman of the Tay Road-O, and others no less quaintly destined. All meant, it may be, to constitute some sort of slantwise cross section of life, though never quite the life of this world no matter how many times he brings us back to Broadway. . . . The strength of his style here as in the past is a swift intuitive rightness—remember **"Marie"** from ***Elephant Bangs Train***—which can't be faked and is almost impossible to sustain. The strain of trying can glare . . . but there are still those intermittent flashes, bright enough.

A review of "Hermes 3000," in Kirkus Reviews, *Vol. XL, No. 2, January 15, 1972, p. 92.*

ANNE M. BURK

Hermes 3000 is seven short stories, set in different times and places, broken up into "chapters" and sequentially interspersed. Each of the stories is a well-written slice of life, and most could stand up well by themselves if told in the traditional manner—they have humor, pathos, and very apt description. Why, then, did the author choose to intertwine them?

In addition to indicating a mystical relation between all things, the interweaving creates suspense beyond that of the separate parts as the reader wonders how (and why) the author is going to connect his tales. Unfortunately, the connections are disappointing. . . . The end comes too quickly, and never are all seven tales brought together satisfyingly in this first novel. The book is named after the author's typewriter, and it may be that Kotzwinkle planted the seeds and his Hermes 3000 more or less wrote the stories. Thus, a coherent whole may not have been the typewriter's intent.

Anne M. Burk, in a review of "Hermes 3000," in Library Journal, *Vol. 97, No. 5, March 1, 1972, p. 900.*

RUTH M. McCONNELL

[***The Oldest Man and Other Timeless Stories*** contains four] gentle fantasies poetically told with flashes of realism and humor. . . . Each is original in treatment or concept and each has a distinctive tone. All involve some meeting of the real and dream worlds. In the first tale, a butterfly-collector tires of a chase, lies down to sleep his usual dreamless sleep wrapped in darkness. When he wakes it is as a butterfly. His ultimate return to human shape effects a change in his occupation and makes him wonder which was his real form, which his dream. . . . [Readers] may find the changes which occur in the other tales more detached from their experiences and less affecting for what they portray than for the mood they create and for the lovely style of the telling.

Ruth M. McConnell, in a review of "The Oldest Man and Other Timeless Stories," in School Library Journal, *an appendix to* Library Journal, *Vol. 18, No. 9, May, 1972, p. 78.*

PUBLISHERS WEEKLY

"Swimmer in the Secret Sea" is a deeply moving book. The textures of its delicately conveyed anguish, love, reverence, acceptance, simplicity make its grief all the more stunning.

The brief cycle of a baby's life—labor, delivery, death, burial—in the snow-covered isolation of a Northern landscape is the substance of an acute reading experience that a lesser writer might have made maudlin.

A review of "Swimmer in the Secret Sea," in Publishers Weekly, *Vol. 208, No. 7, August 18, 1975, p. 69.*

MARTIN LEVIN

[**"Swimmer in the Secret Sea"**] is a little book with the largest of themes: birth and death. William Kotzwinkle, a writer with an original bent for wildly funny imagery, gives the reader nothing to laugh about here. Instead, he follows the struggle of an infant to be born—from the first womb contraction through a breech delivery. To tell precisely what happens to Diane, the mother, Johnny, the father, and to their infant son would be like paraphrasing a poem. Suffice it to say that Kotzwinkle projects powerful feelings of love and loss.

Martin Levin, in a review of "Swimmer in the Secret Sea," in The New York Times Book Review, *November 2, 1975, p. 54.*

PUBLISHERS WEEKLY

A world where dreams come in bottles and provoke a dangerous, illicit trade, where men and animals change their forms at will, where the atmosphere is both sinister and sensuous is the background of Kotzwinkle's fantasy-suspense romance [**"Herr Nightingale and the Satin Woman"**]. Nightingale is a secret agent who exchanges dreams for guns. The Satin Woman is his mistress, but she is seduced by a piano-playing cricket. . . . Inspector Bogg hunts Nightingale . . . and everywhere the supernatural impinges on reality. The narrative is conveyed in fragmentary, disconnected images. Brief scenes abruptly dissolve into others. The reader must struggle with fleeting sensory impressions that are as mystifying—and frustrating—as the dreams they represent. . . . This is a book for a special breed: those who can bring a fevered imagination to interpret a shadowy plot.

A review of "Herr Nightingale and the Satin Woman," in Publishers Weekly, *Vol. 214, No. 18, October 30, 1978, p. 40.*

PATRICIA DOOLEY

[In ***Dream of Dark Harbor,*** a] boy of indeterminate age . . . moves across land, along a river, and (briefly) onto the sea, moved by—what? That's the mystery here, and we don't see enough of the boy's character to resolve it. Motivation is supplied by a muddle of some Jung . . . , sentiment toward a nature at once solicitous and indifferent, and pretention. . . . Allegorical aspirations weigh down the descriptions of nature and the runaway boy; the boundless romanticism doesn't compensate for the implausibilities. . . . Purple patches sit uneasily alongside colloquialisms. The title is misleading: the "dream" dimension of the story is undefined, it's not chillingly "ghostly," and hardly qualifies as a "sea story."

Patricia Dooley, in a review of "Dream of Dark Harbor," in School Library Journal, *Vol. 25, No. 8, April, 1979, p. 58.*

KIRKUS REVIEWS

[***Jack in the Box*** is about small-town] puberty, 1945-1955—recreated in unabashedly juvenile, raunchy-nostalgic-ironic style, by a writer who's usually up to much more distinctive things (***Dr. Rat, Fata Morgana***). Kotzwinkle's pimpled hero is Jack Twiller, but fantasy-fed Jack usually thinks of himself as some figure out of comix or radio: the Masked Man, Captain Marvel, White Rider, Flaming Arrow, or (later on) Lord Henry. Around age eight, his preoccupation is weaponry. . . . But after conquering his retching reaction to a new school . . . , he discovers spin-the-bottle and post-office. . . . From there it's only a small matter of time to masturbation—"Did Captain Marvel Junior Jack Off?"—inspired by scraps of stolen porn or *Sheena, Queen of the Jungle* comics. . . . And then, of course, there's the quest for "someone to lower the standard of decency with"—a quest only somewhat interrupted by: tap-dancing lessons, Boy Scout camp . . . , a James Dean complex, or career plans. . . . Finally, Jack does get a date for the prom—with luscious Gina Gabooch—but he plays it cool, passive, and terrified. . . . Kotzwinkle certainly remembers it all in unvarnished detail—blackheads, Lavoris, sloppily destructive parties, "dick-measuring contests," would-be mustache-growing, phony sexual boasts—and the ingenuous voicing only occasionally betrays an intervening 1980 sensibility. . . . But readers looking for anything akin to depth or shape here will look in vain: it's just the jauntily recaptured surfaces of a pretty average boyhood, with a few sentimental smiles and more than a few boys-only locker-room giggles.

A review of "Jack in the Box," in Kirkus Reviews, *Vol. XLVIII, No. 14, July 15, 1980, p. 931.*

PUBLISHERS WEEKLY

[In **"Jack in the Box,"** Kotzwinkle] presents a highly amusing and perfectly accurate novel that recalls the game of post office, cereal box rings, Boy Scout camp and adolescent pimples. But Kotzwinkle's story of Jack is mostly concerned with Jack's discovery of sex, a curious sensation Jack first arrives at when he sees Nyoka the Jungle Girl as more than just a comic book character. Capturing with delicate precision so many universally shared moments of youth, the novel has surface charm, but little underneath. And the fact that Jack is so average is ultimately something of a letdown.

A review of "Jack in the Box," in Publishers Weekly, *Vol. 218, No. 4, July 25, 1980, p. 145.*

JEFF CLARK

Kotzwinkle's [***Jack in the Box***] is a lightsome study of growing up—sort of—in the 1940's and 1950's. . . . Inside his sundry boxes Jack is Captain Marvel, Lord Henry Brinthrope, James Dean—but they keep coming unsprung as he crosses life in episodes of raunchy hilarity or bittersweet humor. His story proves a delightful reminder of how ambiguous maturity seems when—needing to assume and forced to abandon them—we slip in and out of self-images, their effortless succession perhaps unending.

Jeff Clark, in a review of "Jack in the Box," in Library Journal, *Vol. 105, No. 16, September 15, 1980, p. 1880.*

FREDERICK BUSCH

[**"Jack in the Box"** is a] novel controlled by a ghost—. . . the ghost of childhood. Possessed of a near-perfect recall of the late 1940's and early 50's, Mr. Kotzwinkle . . . has recollected the emotions and paraphernalia of a childhood lived in the imagination. . . . [The protagonist Jack Twiller] exists in a state of emotional vulnerability veiled by the commercially—and historically—fostered violence of childhood: capes, white stallions, silver guns. He is his age's child. When Hitler dies, Jack gallops past a woman on the street waving his invisible 10-gallon hat, announcing the suicide; the woman cries shame at his boyish behavior and, suddenly, he is exposed to the world—he "felt like he'd just been popped out of a box."

History and boyhood never again conjoin so vividly. . . . The novel's particularities are charmingly rendered in breezy prose, though they go on too long. The post-prom seduction scene at the end is perfect . . . and you can see how the precision of language comes second to the joke of boyhood. This novel is the season's paean to nostalgia. Mr. Kotzwinkle is one of our better writers, and he deserves every success.

Frederick Busch, "Fiction by Four," in The New York Times Book Review, *November 9, 1980, p. 14.**

KIRKUS REVIEWS

Trendy jokiness and mawkish sentimentality blend uncertainly in this very slight Christmas grab-bag [***Christmas at Fontaine's***]: overlapping vignettes, all set in and around a New York City department store in the last few days before the holiday. Store-owner Louis Fontaine wanders from department to department, muttering "Buy, buy, buy." A vicious security guard hangs around every night, determined to nab the store's "ghost"—a figure in a silver jogging suit who's been glimpsed here and there, who hides in the store at night. . . . Most farcically, there's store-window designer Dann Sardos—who's driving himself (and everyone else) crazy by refusing to reveal his big window display until it's esthetically perfect. . . . And, most stickily, there are two dreadfully clichéd figures of pathos: the Santa Claus who's really a skid-row bum beneath his beard, who is transformed by his exposure to the innocent tots . . . ; and the by-now-obligatory bag lady, who fancies herself "Queen of the Moon" and dreams of a long-lost family. Finally, then, the security officer does capture the silver-suited jogger—an orphan boy—and Fontaine plans to use the lad as a publicity gimmick. . . . But, with help from some of the other characters, who now converge in the last few pages, the boy is hugged by the bum-Santa . . . and escapes . . . while everyone drinks champagne together. . . . Despite his recent authorship of the ***E.T.*** paperback novelization, however, Kotzwinkle (***Dr. Rat, Fata Morgana***) is a highly unconvincing dispenser of sweetness and light. And only the occasional nasty/funny bits of dialogue ring true in this limp, near-plotless Christmas mini-pageant.

A review of "Christmas at Fontaine's," in Kirkus Reviews, *Vol. L, No. 17, September 1, 1982, p. 1013.*

DAVID STERRITT

[With his novelization of "E.T.," **"E.T. the Extra-Terrestrial in His Adventure on Earth,"**] William Kotzwinkle has crafted an enjoyable entertainment—a galloping yarn that captures much of the movie's charm while sustaining its own verbal personality. . . .

Kotzwinkle plays the ironies of E.T. for all they're worth, relishing the idea of a scientist from the stars hiding among stuffed Muppets in a California kid's bedroom, wishing he could show himself, but knowing Earth would never heed the cosmic wisdom of a being whose nose looks like "a bashed-in Brussels sprout."

The novel . . . moves beyond the main characters of Elliott and E.T., spending many pages inside the mind of Mom, who is perpetually miffed and mystified by the bizarre behaviour of her children. Even the minor character of Harvey the dog becomes a presence to be reckoned with, striking his own canine relationship with the starry visitor, and sparking some of the most diverting passages in the book. . . .

Not that the book is anything more than a winning fantasy with a childlike touch. Like the film, it's limited and sometimes hokey, though its energy rarely flags. Kotzwinkle falls into some of the laziest habits of the sci-fi format, describing E.T. in cute aphorisms, substituting vague atmosphere for hard description and repeating himself a great deal.

Still, the novel is often funny, and sometimes elegantly written.

David Sterritt, "Rediscovering Films Lost in the Marketing Shuffle," in The Christian Science Monitor, *September 9, 1982, p. 15.**

EVE OTTENBERG

[Despite] their sundry afflictions, all of [Kotzwinkle's characters in **"Christmas at Fontaine's"**] have a sense of humor. More important, the novel treats them humorously without demeaning them. They are not looked down on, their flaws are not a source of authorial revulsion, they are not condescended to because of their silliness. This rare evenhandedness comes in part from the fact that the novel is a Christmas fable with a fairly happy ending; but more fundamentally it reflects the geniality, the true open-heartedness that permeates the tale.

There is refreshing harmony here. **"Christmas at Fontaine's"** presents a vision of Manhattan as a magical place—magical because strangers from all walks of life cross paths, occasionally talk to each other, and now and then are even kind to each other. They are kind in the way the storyteller is kind, whether looking into Louis Fontaine's plush limousine or into the seedy, transient hotel where Santa Claus sleeps. Wherever Mr. Kotzwinkle looks, he manages to find something zany and, at the same time, touching.

The one complaint that could be made is that **"Christmas at Fontaine's"** drags a bit in the middle, with its excursus into the wacky inner life of Mad Aggie, a local shopping bag lady. Her nuttiness, unfortunately, begins to jar with everyone else's crisply frazzled sanity. This slight defect, however, does allow Mr. Kotzwinkle to expatiate on his cherished terrain—the bizarrely multifarious, secret life of Manhattan. By the end, Aggie's berserk but often too lengthy hallucinations seem a small obstacle to the liveliness and wit of this very good-natured novel. (pp. 13, 47)

Eve Ottenberg, "Some Fun, Some Gloom," in The New York Times Book Review, *November 7, 1982, pp. 13, 47.**

BRANDON JUDELL

Kotzwinkle, straight from his *E.T.* novelization, has transformed Christmas rush into a Frank Capra fairy tale [with ***Christmas at Fontaine's***]. In fact, all his characters could be played by Jimmy Stewart. The setting is Fontaine's, an established midtown store filled with cheese-cutting demonstrations, gurgling water beds, . . . and even gold-plated sink fixtures—but, alas, few paying customers. . . .

[Kotzwinkle] has been sanitized by his run-in with E.T. The author of ***Nightbook*** and ***The Fan Man*** has penned a classic holiday tale complete with treacly sentiments, homeless orphans, and visions of sugarplums. Yet he has not left out the subversive: there are security guards who search exhausted employees as they leave for home, alcoholic bums in freezing doorways freely sharing their last drops of cheap gin, and better-off New Yorkers searching for something forgotten, something unfindable.

But finally, as in all Christmas classics, there is hope. As the last lights in Fontaine's are darkened, Kotzwinkle intimates that in this city of "strangers known to each other," optimism, and a subway token are all one needs to get by.

Brandon Judell, in a review of "Christmas at Fontaine's," in The Village Voice, *Vol. XXVII, No. 52, December 28, 1982, p. 55.*

STEPHEN BANN

[***E.T. the Extra-Terrestrial*** is] a novel about what *Newsweek* calls 'growing up wise'. But as any American child will tell you, it is not really a novel at all—more in the line of a 'novelisation' (*Newsweek* again) of the screenplay for Steven Spielberg's colossally successful film. Michelangelo's renowned image of God making finger contact with Adam . . . has been hijacked for the dust-cover of this generic hybrid. . . . Put yourself in William Kotzwinkle's shoes. How do you actually go about making a novel from the screenplay of a colossally successful film? Who on earth (or in intra-terrestrial space) is your public? Is it the people who, by some quite unexplainable oversight, have happened not to see the film, but feel themselves to be becoming part of a threatened minority? . . . Is it (an insidious thought, and one that might have sapped the writer's morale) the cynical parents who hope to stave off their children's urge to see the film by this paltry gesture, and thereby save themselves the trouble of queuing from half-way round the block? . . .

Is [the book] a good or even a passable substitute [for the film]? I must declare my interest as a genuine enthusiast for *E.T.* (the film) and say that it most certainly is not. . . .

[An] unwelcome surprise is in store for the enthusiast when he finds that the novel has let him in for a good deal of psychologising, most of it quite unnecessarily insulting to the protagonists of the film. Young Elliott, a prodigy of energy and sensitivity, is described in crude terms as 'a blossoming neurotic'; more than that, he is roundly branded as a 'twerp'. His little sister Gertie . . . fares hardly better. Intrusions into their mother's sex life seem irresistible to William Kotzwinkle, and even the Extra-Terrestrial's equivocal feelings towards a female so dramatically unlike what he has been accustomed to are luridly explored. But the unforgivable infidelity to the image lies in the various descriptions of E.T. Here words fail the novelist, and metaphor offers a tempting lure. . . . In spite of the rigorous legal prohibitions which govern the use of E.T.'s image in the press, I can reveal that he is nothing like a prickly pear, let alone a bashed-in Brussels sprout. . . .

William Kotzwinkle's novelisation remains uncomfortably adrift in the wake of the cinematic image. (p. 10)

Stephen Bann, "Mythic Elements," in London Review of Books, *December 30, 1982 to January 19, 1983, pp. 10-11.**

KIRKUS REVIEWS

[***Great World Circus*** is written in] rhymed verse (assorted meters) . . . : an enigmatic non-story, occasionally flaring with the dark, ironic magic of such vintage Kotzwinkle as ***Fata Morgana.*** In Singapore, a British Plague Inspector shares tea with a mysterious woman, who then fades from sight before his eyes. . . . Meanwhile, in Paris, an insomniac named Gustave Claudin seeks sleep and memories of women. . . . So, with those fragile narrative notions as the only frame here, Kotzwinkle plays variations on the theme of the Mystery Woman—as "The High Priestess of Ur" floats through history, visiting assorted men and (it seems) at last bringing sleep to Gustave Claudin. And, as themes and motifs snake in and around, there are glimpses of this Female incarnate with the ghost of a Caruso-like tenor, the inventor of the guillotine, and—most deadpan-amusingly—a sailor. . . . Not a novel, then, or even a short story—but a half-beguiling, half-pretentious curiosity that should attract, as much for the creepy illustrations as the often-snazzy verse, a small but intense following.

A review of "Great World Circus," in Kirkus Reviews, *Vol. LI, No. 6, March 15, 1983, p. 328.*

PUBLISHERS WEEKLY

[***Great World Circus***] is a dreamlike narrative of rhyming couplets in which Gustav Claudin, an insomniac Parisian, an unnamed British plague inspector in Singapore and various other lesser figures throughout space and time encounter the High Priestess of Ur. . . . The pages of loosely set verse alternate with 77-suitably shadowy and evocative illustrations. The last lines are typical: "He kneels in the dream / on the wheel of the hours / and offers to her / armfuls of flowers." This is not great poetry, but it does serve Kotzwinkle's purpose, efficiently setting an elusive mood and priming us to accept a nonlinear sequence of surreal events, images painted in bright but drifting colored smokes; allowing him to use material too evanescent for a prose story.

A review of "Great World Circus," in Publishers Weekly, *Vol. 223, No. 14, April 8, 1983, p. 52.*

ROBERTA ROGOW

Superman III is (I hope) the last of the Superman movies, and the seams are showing. Kotzwinkle has done his usual good job of translating the screenplay into a novel [***Superman III***], but there are nasty undertones to the film, and there are nasty undertones to the novel as well. Everyone, including Superman, is either a villain or a dupe. . . . [His] opponent, Ross Webster, is a vainglorious zillionaire who wants to control the economic destiny of the world. The key figure in all this is Gus Gorman, the stereotypical Black hustler, who just happens to be a computer genius. Gorman concocts a scheme to make the Ultimate Computer, which will control every other computer in the world. . . . Only Superman can stop them, so Superman must be removed—which he is, by means of an artificial Kryptonite medal that renders the Man of Steel schizoid. The Good Superman must battle the Bad Superman before they can become one Superman and destroy the Ultimate Computer. It's a standard plot, but the side-issues are either slapstick or just plain mean-spirited. Even Superman's other half, Clark Kent, comes off second best. . . . It's not much fun, and Superman without fun is just not worth it. Adults may enjoy the novel on its own merits, as a Black Comedy of sorts, but it's not written for kids, and most of the under-15 crowd will either be puzzled or revolted by Kotzwinkle's dour humor.

Roberta Rogow, in a review of "Superman III," in Voice of Youth Advocates, *Vol. 6, No. 5, December, 1983, p. 282.*

KIRKUS REVIEWS

[In ***Queen of Swords***] Kotzwinkle, re-emerging as a distinctive writer after recent flirtations with commerce (***E.T.***) and whimsy (***Christmas at Fontaine's***), uses comedy and a fable-like tone to make this small tale a fresh, fetching, almost-satisfying variation on the old, old story. His narrator is a 50-ish writer named Eric . . . , still in love with plump artist-wife Janet, but forever striving and restless. . . . Inevitably, then, he is all too ready to be enthralled by Nora Lingard, whom he encounters at an est-like therapy gathering: she's 45+ but ageless, a bohemian free spirit. . . . Nora talks non-stop, in and out of bed. Eric is victimized in a few Thomas Berger-esque mishaps. His supposed writing breakthrough turns into pornography, then into an empty commercial saga. . . . And, after a glimmer or two of self-awareness, he wants Janet back . . . but too late. Despite a thin central notion and the cartoony broadness of some of the humor: a charming, funky cautionary tale, with familiar material (male menopause, marital discontent) given a bright, obliquely touching overhaul. (pp. 1220-21)

A review of "Queen of Swords," in Kirkus Reviews, *Vol. LI, No. 23, December 1, 1983, pp. 1220-21.*

STEVEN D. BENNETT

[***Queen of Swords***] is a weird first person story that somehow manages to balance on the edge of normality through the author's wry and dry humor which he graciously lends to Eric [his protagonist]. Kotzwinkle surrounds his main character with an array of colorful if not psychotic friends which provides a vast comical playground for contemporary commentary and expression.

Our hero finds himself growing complacent in his marriage of 15 years and after poking fun at her for 60 or 70 pages the reader realizes the power that will lure him away from her—Nora, a 45 year-old musician, and sexual sycophant, karate expert, and all-around deviant enchantress. . . .

The writing in this book is crisp and fluid which makes for easy and enjoyable reading. The author is a fabulist, but at times this reviewer found himself thinking this wasn't really a tale of the fabulous at all. . . . The liner notes call this ability "magical realism"; although I hate to agree with anything liner notes say, I do in this case.

Steven D. Bennett, in a review of "Queen of Swords," in West Coast Review of Books, *Vol. 10, No. 3, May, 1984, p. 26.*

JOANNE KAUFMAN

[William Kotzwinkle] clearly has a firm grip on the deed to fantasy land. . . . **"Queen of Swords"** does not diverge from the path of the author's previous novels. But while Mr. Kotzwinkle has frequently concerned himself with the mesmerizing power of machines and animals (**"Dr. Rat"**), the madness chronicled in **"Queen of Swords"** is of the man-made variety.

Eric, "a famous unknown writer . . . given to philosophic inquiry," is a man moving ineluctably toward a middle age that he tries to fend off with jogging and whole grains. . . .

[At] a Total Healing Seminar, modeled hilariously after an est meeting, Eric meets the silver-haired Nora Lingard, widow of an avant-garde composer whose spirit may be at large. . . . Nora has breasts "like a fifteen-year-old's" and she has a history with men unrivaled by Salome. The two lock eyes, then limbs and, unlike most unfaithful husbands who dither for years, a week later (remember, this is a fantasy) Eric packs his punching bag and leg stretcher and leaves the beach home he and Janet had rented for the winter. "I'm finding myself as a warrior and a musician," he explains. "I'll love you always but other fires have consumed me."

"Queen of Swords," which has been beating as steadily as the warrior's heart, begins to falter a bit at this point. Mr. Kotzwinkle, so adroit at chronicling Eric's quixotic searches, is less successful at chronicling the relationship between Nora and her latest victim. From what we see of Nora, there is no good reason to believe she has captivated so many men. Eric's capitulation and his subsequent decline (he begins eating refined sugar and writing pornographic novels) are proof more of Eric's susceptibility than of Nora's powers.

From what we know of Eric, there is little expectation that he will live out his twilight years with Nora. Certainly, *she* has no such delusions. . . . No, an attempted return to hearth and home has less to do with Eric's skill as a mate than with the fact that ultimately Nora is just another brand of Vitamin E capsules, another strain of herbal vapors. . . . Eric's tardy epiphany that "Janet had shattered the porcelain bowl of my mind and freed me to see instead—the stars," bounces foolishly and unconvincingly off the page. The queen's sword may be dull-edged but so, at end, is the novel.

Joanne Kaufman, "Famous Unknown Writer Finds Self," in The New York Times Book Review, *May 20, 1984, p. 15.*

PETER NICHOLLS

[William Kotzwinkle's] ***E.T. The Book of the Green Planet*** (unfilmed as yet) is a sequel to a book-of-the-film, although it is a million miles from say, the *Star Wars* spinoffs in style.

This sequel, according to the credits, is based on a Spielberg story, but the style and particularly the humor seem to owe little to Spielberg. This may be, artistically speaking, a net loss rather than a net gain. Lovers of the film are likely to be baffled by the exotic whimsy of Kotzwinkle's plot, which feels wholly unlike its hugely popular forerunner, and they may be perturbed by the apparent discrepancies between this book and the original movie. . . . Lovers of Kotzwinkle, on the other hand, may wonder what has happened to his toughmindedness. Sentimentality used to lurk almost invisibly at the fringes of his vision, but now it is squarely center frame, a valentine stamped out of marshmallow. For this, in part, is a book about the redemptive power of love. Tears of joy and glowing hearts abound.

When E.T. gets back to his home world, the Green Planet (where he learned his outstanding botanical skills) he finds himself not treated as a hero, as he expected, but in disgrace for getting too involved with the natives of Earth. The Green Planet is a world of amazingly varied plant life, and as an sf creation is not at all like anything in, say, Frank Herbert or Robert Heinlein. It is, however, very reminiscent of the world of Antoine de Saint-Exupéry's *The Little Prince* (1943). But the inventiveness is lamer than that of the eccentric Frenchman, and the Green Planet is, to use an appropriate English word, twee. All the multifarious, cute detail about Jumpers and Flopglopples and spaceships grown from turnips is somehow repetitive. . . .

E.T. misses the Earth child Elliott, who had become his best friend. So plangent is his longing that his vibrating heartstrings are able to send little telepathic replicants of himself all the way back to Earth, across the galaxy, bearing messages for Elliott. Sadly, however, Elliott is not receptive. Now a teenager, he has only one thing on his mind, the pangs of calf love, and he is deaf to E.T.'s call. My friend is in danger, E.T. muses. He is about to become the most terrible thing of all. He is about to become Man. Well of course he is, you soppy little alien! We all have to grow up, and it's not all bad. But perhaps it is only on Earth that adult life is barren? Elliott, we are told, is about to become just another dull pattern of conformity. It is all very well for E.T. to shudder at the adult lifestyle of Californian suburbia, but one hardly knows from what perspective he is able to make this patronizing judgment, for the Green Planet is itself an Orwellian Utopia of conformity. Even misery is forbidden, and eradicated by the Contentment Monitor. It is certainly strange that the two planets, apparently intended to be in dramatic contrast, should emerge (unintentionally?) as similarly frightful.

It does not take a very perceptive reader to see that underneath the layers of vivacious surface color, and then of marshmallow, is a brooding despair—a contempt, in fact, for the whole adult world. . . .

The running gag of the book is E.T.'s obsession with the trivia of Earth life, most of which he barely understands. Most of this material is more flippant than witty; it has the ring of satire but no satirical function. Hardly a sophisticated aperću is the plot point that E.T.'s heroic escape to Earth in his homegrown spacecraft is largely because he is hungry for candy. He yearns for football helmets and bicycles and hopes one day to become a Drop Out. . . .

Mildly amusing, but is it heresy to suggest that in some areas Kotzwinkle has a tin ear? Many of the colloquialisms that E.T. so mangles are more adult than childlike and since on his previous visit he had almost no contact with adults, where did he latch on to phrases like big bucks and Fat City? All this vocabulary is seen by E.T., ironically, as rich in nuance, but then again, he may be right.

Kotzwinkle's own language is not quite that of the Gifted Bard that *The New York Times* once called him, and certainly falls short of the spiritual beauty claimed in the cover copy. He is more of a pop crooner than a bard these days, it seems, and his spiritual exploration is about at the level of doctor-and-nurse romance, as in the ersatz profundity of his "love is just a speck of dust in the ages . . . but I believe it is the only treasure." Oh dear.

Peter Nicholls, "The Return of E.T.," in Book World—The Washington Post, *March 10, 1985, p. 8.*

JILL GROSSMAN

[In ***E.T.: The Book of the Green Planet***], E.T. is home again and can't keep his mind off Earth. He longs for junk food, beer, gum and especially Elliott. This may be because he's nobody special at home; in fact, due to his bungling of his last mission, poor E.T. is demoted from Doctor of Botany, first class, and sent back to the farm to do research. E.T. knows through telepathy that Elliott is in grave danger—he is entering the fearful state of adolescence and falling under the spell of a pony-tailed girl. E.T. plots a return to our blue planet and hooks up with three underworld characters who aid him in trying to steal a starcruiser. . . . What little suspense there is hinges on whether this rocketing rutabaga can do the job. But plot is not the point of this whimsical tale. William Kotzwinkle's strong suit here is his imagination and playfulness with language, be it the frisky slang of Earth that he and E.T. cherish, or the inventive people and plants of this Green Planet. Childern and loyal E.T. fans will find this story funny and sweet.

Jill Grossman, in a review of "E.T.: The Book of the Green Planet," in The New York Times Book Review, *May 5, 1985, p. 24.*

John (Ono) Lennon

1940-1980

(Born John Winston Lennon) English songwriter, fiction writer, and filmmaker.

Gamma-Liaison

One of the most influential figures in the history of rock and roll, Lennon is widely considered a cultural hero as well as an exceptionally talented songwriter. From his role as the most controversial and innovative member of the Beatles to his erratic solo career, Lennon grew in popularity to an almost deified position, especially among the youth of the 1960s and 1970s. As a group, the Beatles played a major role in defining the cultural climate of that era; they helped expand the boundaries of popular music and bring it, both artistically and commercially, to its present state. Although Lennon's career after his departure from the Beatles was less critically successful, his enduring cultural and artistic significance remains largely uncontested.

The songwriting partnership of Lennon and McCartney was the main creative force behind the Beatles. The success of their collaboration is generally attributed to the strongly individual yet complementary nature of their talents and personalities: while McCartney's songs were lyrical and sentimental, Lennon's rebelliousness and quick-witted, satirical humor led him to be considered the "cutting edge" of the band. As the Beatles's popularity grew, Lennon and McCartney's songs evolved from boy/girl romances to more subtly complex and original works that helped renew an interest in the power of words in the listening audience of the 1960s. Among the songs most characteristic of Lennon's themes and his approach to songwriting are "I'm a Loser" and "Help," both of which are introspective pleas for understanding that reveal Lennon's self-doubts; "Lucy in the Sky with Diamonds," the quintessential psychedelic song; "A Day in the Life," which concludes *Sgt. Pepper's Lonely Hearts Club Band* (1967) and is one of the most acclaimed songs of the rock era; and "Revolution," which foreshadowed the importance of politics in Lennon's solo work. Such later Beatles albums as *Sgt. Pepper's Lonely Hearts Club Band, The Beatles* (1968), and *Abbey Road* (1969) are among the group's most popular works and evidence the culmination of Lennon and McCartney's talents at combining poetry and music. The soundtrack for the film *Let it Be* (1970) was the last project the band completed before their breakup. Lennon also published two books during his years with the Beatles. *In His Own Write* (1964) and *A Spaniard in the Works* (1965) are offbeat collections of puns and satire that were commended for their Joycean wit and wordplay.

Lennon was the first of the Beatles to gain attention for his recordings outside the group. His first independent album, *Two Virgins: Unfinished Music No. 1* (1968), was created with Yoko Ono, the avant-garde artist whom Lennon married in 1969 and who was the most important influence on his post-Beatles career. *Two Virgins* was a marked departure from Lennon's earlier work and reflected Ono's involvement in modern art. Containing no actual songs, it is notorious for its unconventional use of screams, squawks, and the sound of a nose being blown, as well as for its cover, which features a full-length nude photo of the couple. In 1969, Lennon began recording with various musicians as the Plastic Ono Band; his hit singles under the group name include "Give Peace a Chance" and "Instant Karma." An album recorded at a Canadian rock festival, *Live Peace in Toronto* (1969), contains the song "Cold Turkey," which one reviewer described as "his most chillingly effective post-Beatles composition." *Life with the Lions: Unfinished Music No. 2* (1969) and *The Wedding Album* (1969) also include contributions by Ono and reveal her influence on Lennon's art and life.

Lennon's next two albums, *John Lennon/Plastic Ono Band* (1970) and *Imagine* (1971), are generally considered his best post-Beatles recordings. Reflecting his recent involvement with primal scream therapy, *John Lennon/Plastic Ono Band* is highly personal and exemplifies Lennon's sincerity and emotional intensity. It contains such songs as "Mother," which is a painful confrontation of Lennon's childhood; "Isolation," an expression of his self-doubts and insecurities; and "God," in which he rejects, among other things, his mythic stature and his association with the Beatles. On *Imagine*, Lennon's intense self-revelations merge with political beliefs as he imagines, in the title song, a utopia in which universal peace and harmony replace religious, nationalistic, and traditional social conventions. The album also contains such statements of love from Lennon to Ono as "Oh My Love" and "Oh Yoko."

In the next four years, Lennon produced three albums of original songs—*Sometime in New York City* (1972), *Mind Games*

(1973), and *Walls and Bridges* (1974)—and a collection of classic rock and roll songs, *Rock 'n' Roll* (1975). *Sometime in New York City* is his most overtly political album. Many critics faulted its didacticism, and Robert Christgau called it "the most politically ambitious and artistically impoverished music [Lennon] ever recorded." Despite the popularity of such songs as the title cut from *Mind Games* and "#9 Dream" and "Whatever Gets You Through the Night" from *Walls and Bridges,* these albums received largely negative reviews, reflecting the growing number of complaints about Lennon's music since his departure from the Beatles. Throughout his solo career, Lennon's lyrics were faulted for oversimplification, sentimentality, and an absence of artistic vitality, and his tunes are generally thought to lack the memorable quality of the songs written in collaboration with McCartney.

***Double Fantasy* (1980), Lennon's last album before his death, shows the importance he placed on his love for Ono and his involvement over the previous five years in raising their son, Sean. A collaborative effort, the album contains seven songs by Lennon and seven by Ono. Reviews upon its release were almost unanimously negative. The lyrics, which speak of domestic love and devotion, were cited as indulgent and facile, and Ian Pye commented that "the time spent in seclusion and semi-retirement appears to have dulled the man's sensibilities and blunted his once impeccable feel for rock 'n' roll." Shortly after the album's release, Lennon was murdered outside his apartment in New York City. This event, which shocked millions and took precedence over all other news stories, caused many critics to retract their unfavorable criticism; in retrospect, *Double Fantasy* assumed new dimensions of significance. As Mitchell Cohen noted, "What sounded a few weeks ago like a man's too complacent statement of tranquility now can only be heard in the dark context of tragedy and in the blazing light of an unparalleled career." The critical commentary generated by his death reaffirmed Lennon's remarkable popularity and his importance as an innovator in contemporary music.**

(See also *CLC*, Vol. 12 and *Contemporary Authors*, Vol. 102.)

JONATHAN COTT

"What I'm doing is the primitive avant-garde," John Lennon said about his new art and music. ***Two Virgins*** is really a sophisticated multi-media *ménage à trois*: an incredible and now famous album cover, a reportedly lovely film, and an extraordinary piece of contemporary music.

Obviously, John's and Yoko's music circulates in that musical air inhaled by composers such as Luciano Berio, Robert Ashley, Gordon Mumma, La Monte Young, Morton Feldman, Cornelius Cardew, and John Cage—composers who generally emphasize sounds over pitches, a mixed-media interacting environment over a performer-listener concert hall ritual, the unfolding of musical events—the way a waterfall falls—over the structuring and permuting of rows and series. . . .

But the music for ***Two Virgins*** comes without clothes and without cliches—a musical metaphor for two persons seeing each other for the first time and then seeing what's there. The naked album cover is actually an extension of the music, for it exemplifies the idea of confrontation, an interaction between John and Yoko—a real *East Meets West* album. . . .

[***Two Virgins***] is as completely self-realized—in all senses of the phrase—as is John's powerful ***Revolution Number 9***—a contemporary music classic that creates its own unfoldings and bearings in an instinctive, natural, and unimpressionable way. . . .

Jonathan Cott, in a review of "Two Virgins," in Rolling Stone, *Issue 28, March 1, 1969, p. 20.*

JOHN GABREE

In many ways the Lennon album [**"John Lennon/Plastic Ono Band"** is George Harrison's "All Things Must Pass"] turned on its head. Instead of band-style vocals, the singing is direct and eclectic. Instead of elaborate arrangements, there is Lennon on piano and guitar, Klaus Voormann on bass, and Ringo on drums (with Billy Preston and producer Phil Spector on piano on one cut apiece). Instead of somewhat impersonal love songs, religious or secular, Lennon offers amazingly personal introspective analyses and confessions. I know of no pop album that contains music and words as raw and honest as this one. In ***Mother,*** he works out in song some long-standing Oedipean resentments, terminating in terrifying and quite beautiful screams. In ***Working Class Hero*** he frankly and somewhat bitterly examines some past illusions (illusions that must have beguiled George and Paul, to say nothing of Jagger, Presley, and countless others, but which no one has stated quite so frankly before). In ***God*** he renounces the mantle of hero which he has sought and which has been thrust upon him. There are love songs too, but born directly out of his life with Yoko, not out of storybook situations.

Lennon is not a natural melodist, but instrumentally this is a very strong record. Lennon realizes his purposes perfectly on both guitar and piano, and producer Spector builds just the right structure of support with the rhythm section. . . .

"John Lennon" is a tremendously exciting listening experience, perhaps the best any Beatle has ever offered. It might even encourage other super-stars to dig as deeply into themselves. A great album. . . . (p. 71)

John Gabree, "The Heaviest Beatles of Them All," in High Fidelity, *Vol. 21, No. 3, March, 1971, pp. 70-1.**

BRUCE HARRIS

One has several temptations in listening to John Lennon's first solo album [***John Lennon/Plastic Ono Band***]. First, we all really want to like it because we all know in our deepest hearts that John Lennon is one of the great musical geniuses of our time. But then, that only makes us resent his second-rate efforts all the more. Why settle for ***Give Peace A Chance*** when you could have ***I Am The Walrus***? But as John declares on this album, "I was the walrus, / But now I'm John." If it's personae you want, this is not the album to find them on.

All of this sets up a central critical problem which we must face before attempting to evaluate John's album, for it defines art in a manner new at least to the Beatles. Taking the negative approach, we might begin by saying that with this album, John has made the fatal error of confusing sincerity with art. Yes, he *means* what he says, more than Paul might, but that doesn't make it good. The technical perfection Paul brings to songwriting, and that John used to bring, is more aesthetically satisfying than all the honesty on this album. Bad songwriters are not songwriters with nothing to say as much as they are songwriters without a style that enables them to effectively say what's on their mind. Thus, John, by seemingly tossing his stylistic tools aside, has made an album that appears to be strongly philosophical but not very artistic. Art, after all, implies artifice and artificiality. It is one remove from reality. It is truth disguised, truth generalized, truth dressed up in such a manner as to make it easily understood. Saying "Repressing one's feelings of love may lead to a neurotic condition in which the patient suffers from extreme anxiety" may mean the same as, but hasn't the impact of, "Well you know that it's a fool who plays it cool by making his world a little colder." The persona, the face, the front is a commonplace artistic device which John Lennon seems to have tossed aside for this LP.

But perhaps not. It would be foolish to argue that John's sincerity, his *realness* on this album is any compensation for the loss of his art. Isn't it rather self-indulgent of him to expect his audience to be interested in the real John when all along they have been interested in his public face, the Walrus? Yes, it is self-indulgent, and if this album weren't as good as it is, it would be hateful. The point is that John has not really made an album free of artifice, but only an album that *seems* to be so. In reality, there is much technique and polish to the songwriting on the album, but it is technique so well executed that it is almost wholly invisible (as all really great technique should be.) It's all happening beneath the surface. Where it really belongs.

So, ultimately, John Lennon has made an album that while seeming to be nearly artless is as perfected and artful, at least on a lyrical level, as anything he has ever done. (pp. 43-4)

As a composer, John's work has been more refined and more original than it is here, but many of the tunes—***Remember, Look At Me, Love,*** and ***Isolation,*** for instance, are really brilliantly written and are substantially as good as much of John's older work. The album has its flaws. ***Working Class Hero*** is mildly tuneful and the lyrics are accurate, but not very fresh. It sounds like old Pete Seeger, only with a bit more energy. ***Well, Well, Well*** is also uncertain and muddled and can't quite seem to make up its mind what it's about. Nevertheless, the album is filled with John Lennon genius. ***Mother*** is sung by a voice that is genuinely racked with agony, as the voice of every child must be in looking at his parents. . . . ***Hold On John*** is really just a mild love song, and does not try to be much more, yet it too contains a powerful thought: "Hold on, world, / World, hold on, / It's gonna be all right, / You gonna see the light." In ***I Found Out,*** John reveals his bitterness at the gilded phoniness that was the Beatles and the culture that grew up around them. It is precursor to John's final statement on the album in the song ***God:*** "God is a concept by which we measure our pain." Throughout the album, John denies religion in all its forms, political, social, spiritual, even musical. . . .

Love is one of the strongest compositions here, attempting as it does to define the undefinable: "Love is real, real is Love, / Love is feeling, feeling love, / Love is wanting to be loved." It just works. Partly because of the flow of the music, which is so right, but also because of its semantic structure. It's really Lennon word play, not as far out and as contrived as ***I Am The Walrus,*** but still powerful. ***Look At Me*** stands as perhaps the best song on the album. Like ***Love,*** its success depends on the interaction of its music and the cleverness of its lyrics. Clever, yes. Artificial, yes. Art. Absolutely.

The track which gives the album its ultimate impact, however, is ***God,*** which closes the LP except for a painful fragment titled ***My Mummy's Dead.*** In ***God,*** Lennon declares that "The dream is over," that we must carry on, that the sixties are dead, that the Beatles (and much of what they stood for) are no longer. Its most powerful section is a catalogue of things which John does *not* believe in, climaxing with the Beatles and the declaration that he believes only in himself and in Yoko. . . .

One thing for sure, this is no Beatles album. Its stark simplicity, like the simplicity on Paul's solo LP, make it above all an anti-Beatles album. Everything about it is wrong. Except that it's really right. The question to ask is not "When will john get back to being *JOHN*?" but rather "When will we learn to appreciate john?" We ought to try right now. (p. 44)

Bruce Harris, in a review of "John Lennon/Plastic Ono Band," in Jazz & Pop, *Vol. 10, No. 3, March, 1971, pp. 43-4.*

ANDREW KOPKIND

John Lennon has taken it upon himself to do what few gods can ever do: divest himself of his divinity. "I don't believe in Beatles" is not only a facile line (in the song, **"God,"** on his new record album [***John Lennon/Plastic Ono Band***]); it's as if Christ on the cross could say, "I don't believe in Me." Jehovah would have had a hard time telling the Hebrews in the Wilderness:

And so dear friends
You just have to carry on
The dream is over.

No more immodest metaphors or extravagant claims need be made for Lennon, his record or his lengthy interviews in *Rolling Stone*. When gods fall, the earth shakes. Lennon's attempt to demystify himself, the Beatles and rock cultism has a force and urgency which breaks through the layers of dream-webs which have solidified around the new culture, freak consciousness and political revolution. (p. 19)

The cultism and hero-worship rampant in youth culture and the Movement is a frightening example of the way destructive consciousness is built into the American mass—even when a part of that mass is explicitly committed to liberation. Mythic relationships trickle down from pop stardom to the lowest levels of young people's social organization; elitist leadership, *macho*-tripping, submissiveness and self-repression have characterized the Movement groups of the late '60s as much as the dialectical opposites of those qualities for which we were all supposedly working.

What's so startling, and so wrenching about the Lennon Documents—music and speech—is that they suggest a radical way out: a way to deal with dreams. Lennon's way, it seems to me, is a revival of honesty, a commitment to authenticity of feeling that overcomes the real fears of self-contradiction, failure and pain. . . . Of course Lennon is nothing if not a walking bundle of contradictions; his enormous ego is oppressive still, even in cool print; he reveals a very unliberated attitude toward race, class and sex ("I hope (**'Working Class Hero'**) is for workers and not for tarts and fags") and some liberated attitudes, too. His songs are less contradictory, because more carefully thought out, and there are occasional verses of such clarity and force that they transcend that aspect of banality which we all used to explain away in Lennon lyrics:

Keep you doped with religion and
  sex and TV
And you think you're so clever and classless
  and free
But you're still fucking peasants as far as I can see
A working-class hero is something to be.

There is a real problem in his attempt to incorporate the material of his recent "primal scream" psychotherapy into the music. It is immediately effective but somehow too transient a notion, and its extreme expressiveness jars with the simplicity of statement that informs most of his songs.

But there's not much point in an *analyse du texte* of the album or the interviews. Their value is in the impression they create, rather than in the line they promote. Most of us who have listened to the Lennon album have also been digging George Harrison's *All Things Must Pass* and Dylan's *New Morning,* and comparisons are inevitably made, and perhaps instructive. Harrison certainly goes down smooth and easy, but I can't see that it's much more than karmic bubble-gum music, a wah-wah trip to the top of the charts. Dylan's songs are masterpieces of formalism; even where he is explicitly singing of himself there is a feeling of a third personality: Zimmerman as Dylan as song-writer. No pain, no struggle. That may be cool enough; songs are songs. But after the intensity of Lennon's psychological and political explorations, simple song-writing seems an empty pastime, a respite rather than a realization.

What Lennon found out is the necessity for demystification, the possibility for breaking through myths, the inevitability of honesty. But he ends just at the point where we all have to begin: "And so, dear friends, you just have to carry on." What that means must have to do with finding a way to shatter all the gods without us and within, to transfer power from our heroes to our imagination, to free ourselves from the isolation of private existence in a mass audience. I don't think we can do it by chanting Hare Krishna, although that's a useful exercise at times; nor by finding a little house in Utah and catching rainbow trout: that is *not* what it's all about. Neither of those options—perhaps valid in some times or climates—comes to grips with the reality of American state power and its capacity for catastrophe. The essential issue, in Lennon's terms, is "isolation," and how it will have to be resolved is by struggle, not private tripping. (p. 56)

Andrew Kopkind, "I Wanna Hold Your Head: John Lennon after the Fall," in Ramparts, *Vol. 9, No. 9, April, 1971, pp. 18-19, 55-6.*

ROY HOLLINGWORTH

Lennon's won, hands down. If this were a new name, it would be deemed the gutsy answer to the feeble state of rock.

Instead a lot of people are going to be talking about [**"Imagine"**] rather than playing it. Still, it's the best album of the year, and for me it's the best album he's done, with anything, or with anyone, at any time. Lennon's just the most honest guy around.

The album opens with **"Imagine"** instantly a beautiful song, with curdling piano and a half-spoken Lennon, just imagining. . . . **"Crippled Inside"** is steely country and solid chunk with humorous, honky piano, climaxed in a sleazy ending. . . . [With **"Jealous Guy"** Lennon] could easily be singing he read the news today, there's that atmosphere about it, especially when he breaks into a whistle that's like one of those melancholic Disney bluebirds. When Lennon sings a sad song, then he's the saddest man in the world. **"It's So Hard"** has torturing guitar, with Lennon cutting around like some shark, as the ploddy bass line produces a grinding, pushing track. This precedes the most downright deathly dirge of concrete and steel blues, **"I Don't Wanna Be A Soldier, I Don't Wanna Die"**. Bloody, thick bass again and loud percussion. Lennon's voice is echoed and hypnotic, and vicious: **"Gimme Some Truth"** opens side two, and is my best of the album. Lennon's percussive, quickly-delivered lines are an offensive weapon, used good and hard. Evil and rude, and just darned great. . . . He's right there again, and it's brilliant.

Roy Hollingworth, "All We Need Is Lennon," in Melody Maker, *October 9, 1971, p. 21.*

HENRY EDWARDS

John Lennon recently stated that he is determined to use his songs to communicate his most personal points of view. On **"Imagine"** and **"John Lennon/Plastic Ono Band,"** his first solo album, the songwriter-performer has sacrificed melody and intricate orchestration in order to provide a basic framework for a series of news bulletins about his current mood and most recent experiences. With the breakup of the Fabulous Four, the Beatles audience has refused to relinquish its incredible devotion and curiosity. Lennon is aware of this phenomenon; his albums encourage it.

Imagine, the album's title song and first cut, sets the philosophical tone of the entire venture. It also reflects the influence of Lennon's wife, conceptual artist Yoko Ono. Ono believes that the artist can be a positive social force by creating and acting out a nonstop series of imaginative exercises, and by encouraging others to do the same. . . . Taking off from here, Lennon seizes upon the concept of imagination itself, and he urges his listeners to imagine a world without nations, religions, social systems, and arbitrary conventions. He suggests that the result of all this imagining will literally be a world of brotherhood, peace, and love.

The other songs in the album amplify this vision, comment about the difficulty of realizing it, or attack those people who have stood in Lennon's way as he set about formulating it. ***Oh My Love,*** a thoroughly lovely ballad, stresses that Lennon now can really see, feel, and love for the very first time; ***Oh Yoko!*** is a rollicking good-time tribute to the woman who encouraged Lennon to develop his current *modus operandi;* ***Gimme Some Truth,*** in a long series of carefully wrought phrases, denounces a wide spectrum of contemporary hypocrites whom Lennon feels have tried to stand in his way during his struggle to perceive clearly.

The most controversial song in the collection, ***How Do You Sleep?,*** is a devastating indictment of Paul McCartney. Lennon attacks the former Beatle's intelligence, talent, and choice of friends, and concludes that McCartney is just "a pretty face" that "may last a year or two."

McCartney fans and all others who think this sort of outburst should best occur in private will be disturbed by the song. Lennon, however, demands that his audience not only judge his music but judge him as well. Pop albums rarely make such intriguing demands on the listener, for that alone John Lennon passes muster with me.

Henry Edwards, "The Provocative Lennon-Ono Marriage," in High Fidelity, *Vol. 22, No. 1, January, 1972, p. 77.*

NOEL COPPAGE

If John would stop bemoaning his mental state, stop being petty, swear off clichés, and get rid of Phil Spector, he could make an excellent recording. As it is, [with **"Imagine"**] he's settled for a good one, thanks mostly to some classy melodies he thought up to cancel out his often dopey lyrics. A curious thing—in the Lennon-McCartney team, it was assumed Lennon was the expert on lyrics and McCartney constructed the melodies. But without John, Paul's lyrics are fairly good and his melodies grow mushier and mushier; in Paul's absence John writes better than passable melodies but lyrics that are as paranoid as a porcupine. (p. 108)

When the album is good, it is quite good, despite overproduction. A couple of songs, ***Jealous Guy*** and ***Oh, My Love,*** recall the heyday of the Beatles (***Jealous Guy*** recalls it perhaps too vividly, containing a piano change lifted directly from ***A Day in the Life***). ***Imagine*** is facile, and particularly interested me because, in setting up an imaginary utopia, John eliminates religion, along with greed and hunger. Not a terribly fashionable idea just now.

When the album is bad, it is quite bad. ***How Do You Sleep?,*** obviously addressed to Paul, raves on. . . . Also, there is the usual bragging about feeling insecure (***How?, It's So Hard,*** and ***Crippled Inside***) and clichés purporting to express outrage about how things are run (***Gimme Some Truth*** and ***I Don't Wanna Be a Soldier***).

Is the album better than it is bad? It is. Is it better than **"Plastic Ono Band"**? Much. Is it disappointing? Yes. (p. 109)

Noel Coppage, in a review of "Imagine," in Stereo Review *Magazine, Vol. 28, No. 1, January, 1972, pp. 108-09.*

DAVE MARSH

If you thought, as I did, that ***Sometime in New York City*** was going to be a complete disaster, cheer up. It's not half bad. It may be 49.9% bad, but not half.

Strangely enough, for once, this political-vaudeville act sounds good. Credit for this probably is due as much—or more—to Elephant's Memory, Phil Spector and the classic Lennon intuition than to design, but nonetheless: it sounds good. . . .

Some parts of it—including one of Yoko's songs, a cosmic-rocker called "We're All Water," which just might be the very best thing here—are as good as anything the Plastic Onos have ever done. In terms of music, it's an 80% success.

Problem is, the album isn't conceived in terms of music. It stands and falls on its lyrical themes, and the ways in which they are carried out. And, I'm afraid, it doesn't always treat them very well.

It isn't *just* a question of good politics vs. bad. That's part of it, but the problem runs deeper. Good songwriting is juxtaposed with bad, posturing with commitment, real life with someone's inadequate fantasies.

That last is what it's really about. This may come as a surprise to John and Yoko, but "real" songwriters—from Dylan on—have never written about real events. They've sometimes written about events that you've heard of in advance, but in general, Penny Lane still means more than Hollis Brown.

The songs on ***Sometime in New York City*** are [not] content to be "just songs." They try to be something more than that, and as a result they often come off as less than what a good song is. They're forced, and frequently they are pretentious. Good songs are neither. They're literal, and the best songs—the genre classics, a few of which John Lennon has written—are mythic. (p. 64)

John used to write songs that worked dialectically. It was exciting to listen to **"Revolution"**'s contradictions almost rip it apart. The same thing happened with **"Power to the People"** if in a different way. But the songs on this album have already flown; the new dialectic is a challenge between the words and the music and it is always the music which is oppressed, which must fight its way into the spotlight.

But even though many of the songs are musical hodge-podge too, what has excited me about this record is the music. **"Sunday Bloody Sunday"** cuts McCartney's "Give Ireland Back to the Irish" and it don't even matter much that "Backoff Boogaloo" is a better statement on the subject than either.

"Luck of the Irish" says to me that John really does care about the I.R.A., in much the same way that he cared about **"Julia."** It says that *musically,* not lyrically. (p. 65)

Dave Marsh, in a review of "Sometime in New York City," in Creem, *Vol. 4, No. 3, August, 1972, pp. 64-5.*

MELODY MAKER

Inevitably, [**"Some Time in New York City/Live Jam"**] is another giant step in the rapid polarisation of opinions concerning the moral and musical stance of John Lennon.

Already, strong views have been hurled from both sides; you only have to play the record to a reasonably representative selection of friends to prove that there are, seemingly, just two reactions to it: undiluted vitriol and uncritical praise, with the balances generally weighted in favour of the former. Equally, and for the same reasons, others feel he can do no wrong. Objectively, dispassionately, both attitudes are incorrect. It's by no means fence-sitting to opine that there is good and bad in this record, in almost equal measure. Let's take the good first: **"New York City"** is an immaculate rock 'n' roll song, in structure and performance, its documentary subject matter well matched to these attributes. Lennon's sharp lyric is delivered in a typically classy close-to-the-ground rocker's wail—it's potentially a great single. **"Woman Is The Nigger Of The World"** was a single, in the States, and none too successful by earlier Lennon standards. The words, of course, are a feminist diatribe, but the chauvinist need listen only to the magnificent sound of the track, deep and sweeping, and to the majestic quality of the vocal. . . . **"John Sinclair"** and **"Attica State"** are both based on bluesy slide-guitar licks, lifted out of ordinariness by the fresh playing and singing. . . . The interplay of voice and guitar on **"Sinclair"** is among the album's high-points. **"Angela"** and **"The Luck Of The Irish"** have the benefit of pretty tunes and exceptional string arrangements . . .—rewritten as a "straight" love song, the former would doubtless become a classic. . . .

So now you want to know about the bad. Well, all these songs (with the possible exception of [Yoko Ono's] "We're All Water," which is a humanist anthem) are overtly political, and this makes some people uncomfortable. Myself, I can practically ignore rock 'n' roll words anyway, when the music is good, but I have to admit considerable dissatisfaction over the "Irish" songs. I'm afraid people are right when they criticise him for sitting comfortably at home in New York and writing about something on which he's in no way qualified to pontificate—how sad that the only thing in years on which he and

Paul have agreed should have drawn from both their very worst work. Neither **"The Luck Of The Irish"** nor "Give Ireland Back To The Irish" can do anything but increase the bigotry of the already ignorant. . . .

Finally, there's the **"Live Jam"** album—one side recorded at the Lyceum "Peace For Christmas" gig in '69 (**"Cold Turkey," "Don't Worry Kyoko"**), the other made live at Fillmore East with Zappa and the Mothers in June of '71 (**"Well," "Jamrag," "Scumbag," "Au"**). . . . **"Cold Turkey,"** his most chillingly effective post-Beatles composition, proves the potential of that short-lived but electrifying combination of Lennon and Clapton, their guitars cutting like rusty switchblades. **"Kyoko"** has a nice riff, and builds a hefty head of steam, but goes on too long, at least on record. **"Well,"** an old R&B standard on the "My Babe" changes, is the best thing on the live album, Lennon singing low-down, dirty and mean, undistracted by Yoko's screams and supported by Zappa's trenchant guitar. **"Jamrag"** is based on Zappa's "King Kong," **"Scumbag"** rocks along thanks to young A. Dunbar, and **"Au"** is mostly feedback-with-yelling.

There are a lot of songs on this set that I wouldn't be without (most of you would pay at least a quid for **"Well"** if it were bootlegged as a single)—and there's almost nothing that isn't redeemed by some major touch of great ability. And John Lennon has the guts to risk offending when really he still wants to be loved.

R. W., in a review of "Some Time in New York City/ Live Jam," in Melody Maker, *October 7, 1972, p. 25.*

STUART BYRON

John Lennon and Yoko Ono's [film] **"Imagine"** proves once and for all that films "illustrating" pop songs must present images in complete counterpoint to them. Because a successful record is an integral work of art, it can only be expanded by visuals which would seem at first sight totally inapplicable. . . .

The point seems to have been to defy Yeats ("The intellect of man is forced to choose Perfection of the life or of the art") and to show how what they write and sing can't be separated from how they live and love. The film has no story or even narrative, but consists of a grab-bag of images of the Lennons' New York and London life, from quiet picnics alone to peace marches to their notorious Riverdale party. There are also some staged incidents of a sophomorically surreal nature—John and Yoko eating chess pieces, for example. . . .

[**"Imagine"**] has more than its share of the kind of idea rejected as cliched by avant-garde film students.

But the worst thing about it is that by particularizing incidents they do in their life, the Lennons actually reduce their own songs. **"I Don't Want to Be a Soldier"** succeeds precisely because of its universality; to give it a visual background of peace marches, Vietnam atrocities, and the like is to trivialize it. **"Jealous Guy,"** with its "I was dreaming of the past" first line, is likewise diluted by showing us shots of the 19th-century Riverdale manse. But the most embarrassing Lennon illustration—I really had to divert my eyes from the screen—is that to the first line of **"How?"** Line: "How can I go forward when I don't know which way I'm facing?" Visual: John and Yoko trying to get a rowboat unmoored. . . .

The Riverdale party sequence comes alive in a manner totally unlike the rest of the film. And I was not surprised to learn that these short, witty shots were done by Jonas Mekas. . . . Conceding the idea to have been Yoko's, the hilarity engendered by a series of shots of Fred Astaire, Jack Palance, Dick Cavett, and George Harrison as they entered a room during the party has a lot to do with pacing and camera placement, and, whoever was responsible, they make for the one bright spot in what is otherwise amateur night in Liverpool.

Stuart Byron, "John & Yoko Coming Unmoored," in The Village Voice, *Vol. XVIII, No. 3, January 18, 1973, p. 75.*

RAY COLEMAN

Sporadic admiration for John Lennon has never really made sense: you really have to go along with his whole trip to get the best out of his work, or even to get near to knowing what goes on in his tortured mind. . . .

It's in this context that one must judge every new work by John Lennon: since he's forever veering off main roads into country lanes, it's little use looking in the driving mirror to see how far behind he is—and comparisons with his previous records are not valid. Thus, [**"Mind Games"**] is markedly different from **"Imagine."** . . . The raw nerves of a Lennon battered by America's curious logic and sheer hard-heartedness seem to have spurred him to write incisively, and the track **"Mind Games"** is one that grows into a gem the more it is played. The swirling, insistent backing to John's nagging vocal makes it a classic. A similar theme is contained on other tracks on this record, with John acting out his well-known role as catalyst for subjective songwriting. Cynics like me will scoff at the statement on the sleeve, and the track, celebrating the announcement by John and Yoko of a nation called Nutopia, freeing the world's barriers in a beautifully simple way. And yet the sweet naiveté of it all is somehow charming. Musically or melodically this may not be a stand-out album, but if you warm to the rasping voice of Lennon and, like me, regard him as the true fulcrum of much of what came from his old group, then like any new Lennon album, it will be enjoyable and even important. Count me in. I'm a believer.

Ray Coleman, "The Raw Edge of Lennon," in Melody Maker, *December 8, 1973, p. 35.*

JON LANDAU

[John Lennon's recent records] have revealed a steady decline from the high points of his post-Beatle work, ***Plastic Ono Band*** and **"Instant Karma."** There, he distilled his simplistic humanism into a single moving statement of belief—at once his most accessible and intelligent attempt at autobiography and philosophy.

With ***Imagine*** he began affecting attitudes bereft of emotional force. . . . What was moving when applied to his own life was unbearably pretentious when used to offer aphorisms concerning larger issues.

Musically, ***Mind Games*** is a return to the form of ***Plastic Ono Band,*** employing some of the same simple chord progressions, similar instrumentation, and tunes that on closer inspection prove devoid of melodies, consisting only of pleasant collections of pop song, gospel and folk-rock cliches, particularly dependent on Dylan's apocalyptic mid-Sixties style.

The album's music might have served as the basis for a good LP if it had been paired with some new lyrical insight and passion. But instead, Lennon has come up with his worst writing yet. With lines like, "A million heads are better than one / So come on, get it on," a listener can only accept or reject them. I've done the latter.

Lennon's lyrics aren't offensive, per se—just misguided in so underrating his audience's intelligence. John Lennon's admirers do not need to be preached at about the importance of love. . . . But then, perhaps Lennon's didacticism, preaching and banality are part of the mind game of the album's title, yet another attempt to push his luck to the brink of self-annihilation.

Mind Games remains listenable, which is certainly more than can be said for ***Some Time in New York City***. . . . **"Mind Games," "One Day," "Intuition"** and **"Only People"** (with some lines remarkably reminiscent of **"Revolution"**) all have one or another touch to recommend at least a few listenings.

Mind Games reveals another major artist of the Sixties lost in the changing social and musical environment of the Seventies, helplessly trying to impose his own gargantuan ego upon an audience that has already absorbed his insights and is now waiting hopefully for him to chart a new course.

Jon Landau, in a review of "Mind Games," in Rolling Stone, *Issue 151, January 3, 1974, p. 61.*

LESTER BANGS

[John Lennon is] among those increasingly rare pop squackers (Lou Reed's another) who, no matter what else you might be able to say about 'em, is at least SINCERE. John still believes, and is still placing himself in some measure on the line.

That is what in one simultaneity makes him both one of our supreme artists and the most fascinating (next to Lou) example of total idiocy alive. He *places* himself out there, makes himself vunerable with each embarrassing song; in fact, it's their very embarrassingness that makes them so relatable—*somebody's* gotta live out the idiocy of these times. . . . It takes real courage to be a douse.

We shouldn't in all fairness expect John Lennon to have anything new to say at all, we should rather judge him on how well he acquits himself on the stale ground he's apportioned to himself. ***Mind Games*** is the best album any of the Beatles have released this year, and even if that ain't saying much, it's at least reassuring that we always know John was holding on to some of his talent. . . . (p. 62)

[***Mind Games***] is firm evidence that John Lennon's career can only prosper. He's run the Leftoid gauntlet, and now he can venture out into the world and start a whole new cycle. Like back when he did **"Yer Blues"** I said to myself, "Yep, one of these days John Lennon's just gonna end up blowing his brains out," but I don't believe that anymore. Because free of the Beatles lead weight it's John's peculiar genius to always shove himself teethfirst — straight into the thick of whatever fashionable mental muddle he next sets his sights on, and when he gets there he never stops thrashing till he's made a complete spectacle of himself, at which point this folly has worn out its usefulness, so he dumps it and moves on to something else. Which is the mark of a truly great man and artist. Nobody else except Lou has stuck out his gauntlet the way John has, and I sometimes wonder if anybody else who claimed to shake the planet in his time will still be doing it as tirelessly as he for years since. He's got the dignity of the most profound fools who ever lived. (p. 63)

Lester Bangs, "John Lennon: All the Dignity of Eric Burdon," in Creem, *Vol. 5, No. 9, February, 1974, pp. 62-3.*

MICHAEL WATTS

In continually espousing reality at a time when pop wishes to withdraw into fantasy and baroque ornamentation, John Lennon simply goes on reminding us how much he's out of key with the period.

It's a little painful to write that Lennon is presently in the artistic doldrums, but **"Mind Games,"** a dull album with some stunningly simplistic lyrics, is a very low point in his solo career. . . .

It's tough because it seems to me that the dream is indeed over—that dream of Lennon and the Beatles as prophets, even as Gods—and over in such a way that the aspirations and ideals of the 'Sixties seem deflated by the scepticism and nihilism of the 'Seventies. . . .

Lennon, who seems to see himself as society's conscience, began as the Jesus Christ with whom he once compared himself, but has wound up being the Holy Fool, the culmination of a series of eccentricities that have increasingly lost their power to invoke a response from the public.

If Paul is the Walrus, John has become the Fool on the Hill in the eyes of the post-Beatles audience.

It's evident by now, of course, that the sum of the parts is not as great as the whole, but this is only to be expected when each part is examined against the total achievements of the Beatles, which were both musical and sociological. . . .

Lennon, it has to be admitted, is not a primary influential figure in the 'Seventies, more an idiosyncratic Grand Old Man of Pop, which is not to deny that 'Sixties artists can have a profound effect on today's music. . . .

The essential characteristic of Lennon's work post-Beatles has been his intense desire for self-revelation, most notably on the **"Plastic Ono Band"** and **"Imagine"** albums.

The former is particularly explicit, being devised as a kind of "own-up" time as well as establishing his attitude to the future in a significant line on the song **"God"**: ". . . I don't believe in Zimmerman. I don't believe in Beatles—I just believe in me."

But much of the album is concerned with the painful (a word with which he's often been associated) exploration of his childhood and his unhappy relationship with his parents (his father left home when Lennon was 18 months old, and his mother died in a car crash in his teens).

"Mother, you had me but I never had you," he sings on **"Mother,"** and then continues on **"I Found Out"** with the lines "I heard something about my ma and my pa. They didn't want me so they made me a star."

Lennon has a compulsion to bare his soul absolutely in a way no other artist of his stature would ever desire, and though mention of his childhood is made in previous Beatle songs—like **"Julia"** on the **"White Album"**—the truly gouging quality of these pieces is without precedence.

Indeed, one of the most noticeable aspects of his songs with the Beatles was their wry, cutting, even cynical humour.

The feeling and sincerity that welled from these songs was entirely affecting, all the more so because his previous "hard-case" attitude made it seem as if the bleeding heart had been ripped from his chest. . . .

At the same time, one could detect a vague air of sentimentality, even self-pity, about it all, that tended to overpower.

The final track, **"My Mummy's Dead,"** a fragment sung dead-pan, was so artless as to be slightly ludicrous and embarrassing.

"Imagine," a much more mature and varied work, continued to mine his self-involvement and further publicise the ins and outs of his relationship with Yoko, his wife, as well as the then bitter one with Paul McCartney. . . .

Some of his best-ever songs in a more reflective mood were on this album, though, like **"Jealous Guy," "How?" "Oh My Love"** and (musically at least) **"Imagine,"** as well as down-the-line rock and roll numbers such as **"I Don't Wanna Be A Soldier."**

Lennon always had one of the best voices in rock, rough to the point of being brutal, yet surprisingly tender when the need arose, set off by the impression of strength.

The first half of **"Live Peace in Toronto,"** made at a festival in 1969 with a Plastic Ono Band including Eric Clapton and Alan White, was among the ballsiest things he ever laid down, despite the fact he forgot words on "Money," and **"Give Peace A Chance."**

"I Don't Wanna Be A Soldier" had that heavy bass drum sound with echo giving a hard metallic edge to the track, but the lyrics were in the form of a political diatribe, as were those in **"Gimme Some Truth,"** which referred to "short-haired yellow-bellied sons of Tricky Dicky" and "neurotic, psychotic, pigheaded politicians." . . .

Similarly, there were lines in **"Imagine"** which may be interpreted as disingenuous. After all, when a millionaire ex-Beatle sings of "imagine no possessions, I wonder if you can," there were bound to be a few looks askance.

"Working Class Hero," in fact, on the **"Plastic Ono Band"** album, contained lines which might have seemed at cross-purposes with his avowed intention of laying the truth on the line. He sang of workers "Doped with religion and sex and TV" when he spent countless hours himself watching television in his New York apartment (he's a passionate fan of American TV).

Furthermore, some reasoned, he was identifying himself with the class struggle when his origins lay more with the middle-classes, and anyhow, was financially and mentally far removed from the factory floor. It seemed one of those contradictions, like Labour tycoons.

In truth, however, he's never been less than honest in my opinion, and the only charge one can lay at his door, if charge it be, is that of unsophistication and naive oversimplification. . . .

Lennon's politicism, though undoubtedly sincere, would seem to spring from the natural rebel in him and a strong instinct for kicking against the idiots, rather than any coherent viewpoint. Thus **"Working Class Hero"** is an idealised picture of the proletariat and himself.

As for his naivety, this surely goes unchallenged when one considers the fads of the Sixties—the comic interlude with the Maharishi, the farce of Apple, the bed-in at the Amsterdam Hilton and the bagisms—as well as the abrupt changes of mind he's often undergone.

After meeting Yoko Ono, he went overnight from male chauvinism to an ally of Women's Lib; similarly, the deep friendship with Allen Klein—forged, apparently, by the common bond of their orphaned childhoods—dissolved last year, in an avalanche of writs and countersuits between the three ex-Beatles and ABCKO, Klein's company.

Now Lennon has a new "concept": Nutopia, a conceptual country of no boundaries or passports, and which "has no laws other than cosmic."

Naturally, he's written a Nutopian International Anthem, which is on his **"Mind Games"** album, called **"Bring On The Lucie (Freda People),"** It's chorus, quite catchy, goes "Free the people now / Do it do it do it do it do it now."

This sort of stuff is hardly conducive to furthering Lennon's reputation as a serious artist. Why does he do it? Partly because its absurdity appeals to his sense of humour, partly because he believes in its core of truth, and partly because it satisfies the exhibitionistic streak in him i.e. who can ignore something like that—at least initially?

It derives to an extent from his Goon-style humour, which found its way, together with Joycean puns, into the two "children's books" he wrote, ***In his Own Write*** and ***Spaniard In the Works***.

This humour, often mixing in the surreal, and the satirical too, is an integral part of his Beatle songs. . . .

When the Beatles got divorced, though, he married not just Yoko but her avant gardisms. . . .

[Lennon] felt flattered at being taken up, through Yoko, by the art establishment of New York; he was grateful that at last he was getting his proper recognition, not as a pop figure, but as an artist.

It gave him the confidence for all the loony ventures in which he and Yoko involved themselves: the films, like **"Fly"** and **"Rape,"** and the albums he made directly after the Beatles broke up—the **"Wedding Album," "Two Virgins"** (the one with the cover of the full frontals) and **"Unfinished Music No. 2: Life with the Lions"** which did at least have John Tchichai on sax and John Stevens on drums.

They were amusing at the time, but I think now, on playing them back, of how tolerant we all were because of Lennon's then mythic stature.

Perhaps they were necessary to him as experiments because their partially jokey nature violated the insufferable piety that had suffused the Beatles since **"Sgt. Pepper."** Still, the faddism, in time, was harmful to his credibility, and the myth is no longer great enough to support it. . . .

[Undeniably] Lennon's music has changed considerably since the days of the Beatles, both early and later, and in terms of content and approach. It's hard to fully evaluate Lennon's contribution to the Beatles as a songwriter because the Beatles was such a co-operative sound, a combustion sparked by the ideas of Lennon and McCartney rubbing against each other. . . .

Lennon was surely the more imaginative. He may not have been as melodically smooth and assured as McCartney, even though his melodic shapes were powerful, as in the interesting chord progressions of **"If I Fell"** (both of them had a great instinct for unusual variations on pop themes. This was their great gift). But Lennon was certainly superior in his lyric sense.

Lennon, though he could never equal the genuinely wild surrealism of Bob Dylan, was an adept at word-play, a punster of some facility.

He was James Joyce rather than Rimbaud, but more than anything he was Lewis Carroll. **"I Am The Walrus,"** with its comic, nonsensical language, was pure Carroll, as was the children's picture book **"Lucy In The Sky."**

His best song, for my taste, was **"Strawberry Fields Forever,"** a composition of pastoral lyricism in atmosphere and marvellously eccentric, baffling lines, compounded of allusions, nonsequiturs and literary abstractions. None of it actually meant anything, but the possibilities for its meaning were endless.

The comparisons with his current music are quite stark. Where once he sought intricacy, now he opts for outright delineation of his intuitions in the name of Communication.

What can be said about him is that he's a true original who's made no concessions to taste or fashion. His messages, though they sometimes arrive as slogans are honestly-inspired and beneficent.

He's assumed the paraphernalia of the crackpot, but he might be interpreted as a visionary. . . .

Above all, he'll be remembered as a man, even as a humanitarian. That's something I think. (p. 23)

Michael Watts, "John Lennon: Pain for Art's Sake," in Melody Maker, *February 9, 1974, pp. 23-4.*

PATRICK SNYDER

In keeping with John Lennon's prediction of a year ago, 1974, flashing with quick if not instant karma, has been the year of the underdog. . . . [Perhaps] it seems odd to even think of him as an underdog, but, in the league in which he plays, his performance over the last two years has been close to dismal. . . .

For an artist who had led for half a decade or more, it must have been a deflating blow to have the lukewarm response to his most recent projects paint him as a great hollow edifice echoing with formulas no longer relevant and cries too strident for ears tired of exhortations from on high. . . . But now, with ***Walls and Bridges,*** he has delivered a low-key package of engaging songs and soothing messages, and in doing so is winning back a place at the top.

The album is a pleasant if not entirely satisfactory collection of songs quite in keeping with the musical direction he has taken in recent years, with an important and, it seems, commercially crucial change in point of view. Lennon is no longer singing from the stance of a leader, no longer commenting as a righteous ideologue. There are no politics or polemics here, simply a sophisticated rock and roller of considerable talent making music to express himself and entertain his audience. . . .

The end of his constant companionship with Yoko has produced two songs whose contradictions lend a believable human resonance to his attitude on the break-up. The first, **"Going Down on Love,"** seethes with anguished bitterness. "I'm drowning in a sea of hatred / Got to get down / Down on my knees / Going down on love." However, the second, **"Bless You,"** is a lovely, smooth drifting tone poem whose moving lyricism is reconciled to the immediate loss and wishes his absent partner well, encapsulating the mood of the whole album with the whispered admonition, "Restless spirits depart."

As in all of his solo projects, Lennon's greatest virtue is the wide range of styles his songwriting spans. . . . The central strength of his non-genre compositions continues to be his ability to deftly move a song, as in **"Surprise Surprise"** or **"Going Down on Love,"** through the contrasting moods of raunch power and wistful lyricism. The album also includes a song that can only be defined as classic Lennon, the richly chorded, medium tempo **"#9 Dream"** with its rarefied Be Bop a Lula nonsense chorus of "Ah böwakawa poussé." Fulfilling expectations, the wordplay and cross referencing to past work continues. **"Surprise"** invokes **"Drive My Car"** but most interestingly **"Steel and Glass"** is a complete reworking of the infamous McCartney-chastising **"How Do You Sleep?"** except this time around he seems to have directed his talent for cutting invective at himself.

However, this stylistic diversity is defeated by Lennon's choice of back-up musicians. Except for Keyes and Keltner, his studio band is never more than competent. (p. 72)

Problems also exist with the dirge-tempoed, opaquely worded **"Old Dirt Road,"** the self-pitying lyrics of **"Nobody Loves You,"** and the inclusion of a throwaway instrumental. But overall the album is an energetic improvement over his most recent work. Lennon will always have to compete with his mythically exalted past: it is perhaps unfair but it is unavoidable. Nonetheless, he has yet to truly challenge himself as a solo artist (except for the extremely individualistic ***Plastic Ono Band*** lp) or to set musical goals higher than yearly collections of pleasantly produced songs. (pp. 72-3)

Patrick Snyder, "Yoko's Gone, John Moves On," in Crawdaddy, *January, 1975, pp. 72-3.*

NOEL COPPAGE

Up here where I live, we call it "bummed out." . . . Everybody, just about, seemed to be feeling bummed out when [***Walls and Bridges***] showed up. . . . Everyone seemed to be having personal problems and money problems, and some were additionally plagued with animal problems. In my case, it's been the damned cats, knocking things over and generally carrying their selfishness to ridiculous extremes.

So here's old John, pretty generally bummed out himself, I suppose, having ironically good luck with the timing on this downer. . . . Of *course* there are a lot of references to John's Yoko problem in here, and who expected otherwise? Of *course* there is a good deal of honesty, but not what one would call real depth. And of course there are so-called attempts to cheer someone up, which of course are so pathetic—that poor *Ya Ya* thing at the end and that distasteful teenybopper ending grafted onto ***Surprise Surprise,*** especially—they actually help make it all more melancholy. . . . But you know what else is in here and isn't really surprising either? Jazz chords, for one thing. I believe John, you know, I believe him about how painful it all is and all that, but I don't quite believe what he once said about never listening to pop music to see what might be trendy.

Plastic Ono fans should not despair about *this,* however, seeing as how they have enough despairing to do anyway, and the Plastic Ono sound still has its main characteristic . . . something like an electric guitar with silver strings coated with olive oil. . . . [John seems] to have just about lost interest in melodies, although he's still reshuffling some of his old ideas around, and his lyrics this time are a little more superficial and a little less incoherent than usual. But ***Whatever Gets You Through the Night*** and that ***Nobody Loves You (When You're Down and Out),*** which goes beyond being a rewrite, are great songs to moan "woe is me" to when everyone is so bummed out. So you'll probably find the album a little more fascinating than you feel you should. That's how I found it. (pp. 76, 78)

Noel Coppage, in a review of "Walls and Bridges," in Stereo Review *Magazine, Vol. 34, No. 3, March, 1975, pp. 76, 78.*

STEVE SIMELS

It's kind of amazing when you think about it, but I don't know anyone who will admit to liking any of John Lennon's albums since **"Imagine"** (I certainly don't) and yet everybody still loves *him,* despite the continuing, boring saga of John and Yoko and their various public misadventures. Part of it is probably due to the still powerful Beatle mystique . . . , but I suspect it's mostly because, despite his erratic songwriting of late, he still has the pipes. . . .

At any rate, hot on the heels of his generally undistinguished **"Walls and Bridges,"** John has now delivered that long-promised Oldies album, and I am happy to report that it is his first consistently listenable work in ages. **"Rock 'n' Roll,"** as it is succinctly titled, is, in fact, a joy. John runs down a host of classic Fifties and early Sixties numbers, all the kind of thing he must have ruptured his lungs on during the Beatles' sojourn in the cellars of Hamburg way back when, and he obviously hasn't lost his touch; the singing is so alive, so full of fun, that I defy any but the most jaded progressive types not to be absolutely charmed by it. There are no surprises in the song selections, but John and his sometime producer Phil Spector are not afraid to play around with the arrangements. . . . (p. 75)

I might also add that although John clearly takes none of these bits of sublime nonsense any more seriously than he has to, nowhere on this album are we subjected, in Robert Christgau's phrase, to "the sweet stink of a Bryan Ferry parody." In other words, although the times have changed, certain essential values in rock have not, and John, bless his heart, understands this. (p. 76)

Steve Simels, "John Lennon Pays Affectionate Tribute to His Rock 'n' Roll Roots," in Stereo Review *Magazine, Vol. 34, No. 5, May, 1975, pp. 75-6.*

JON LANDAU

Rock 'n' Roll, John Lennon's celebration of early American rock, comes out sounding like nothing but oldies—self-conscious musical attitudinizing about rock roots, and poorly done at that.

In paying tribute to his musical-childhood background, Lennon sounds like he's forgotten he used to perform material like this seven nights a week and that he used to record it several times a year. He's forgotten that most of today's rock audience came to Little Richard and Chuck Berry through the Beatles versions of the music. His "Money" wasn't just more popular than Barrett Strong's original—it was also better. . . .

[The Beatles] never interpreted old rock; they simply played it as well and as joyfully as they knew how. On ***Rock 'n' Roll,*** John Lennon does nothing but interpret old rock. The Beatles didn't care whether they got the music right so long as they got the feeling. Lennon can recreate the music correctly ("Be-Bop-A-Lula"), but never catches the feeling. The Beatles version of this music used to be filled with exhilarating moments; Lennon sounds like he'd be satisfied if he could capture only one. Underneath the pushing, shoving and straining, his album sounds like music in search of a climax that never comes. . . .

The most revealing failure comes on Bobby Freeman's "Do You Want to Dance." The song stands for all the gems left behind by rock's minor heroes—there's no logic to anyone as limited as Bobby Freeman writing anything so great. But more than he misses the point of Chuck Berry and Little Richard, Lennon misses the point of this kind of rock—the stuff that sounds almost anonymous, like anyone could sing it, music whose simplicity is its greatest strength. You don't do anything with a song like this except perform it—it speaks for itself. But here comes John, with a reggae twist and a new melody line, and the magic of a tune called "Do You Want to Dance" is gone. . . .

At the bottom [of the back cover], there's the now famous quote (the best thing about the album, really) from Dr. Winston O'Boogie: "You Should Have Been There." John Lennon *was,* but sounds like he's forgotten what it was like. In making an album about his past, he has wound up sounding like a man without a past. If I didn't know better, I would have guessed that this was the work of just another talented rocker who's stumbled onto a mysterious body of great American music that he truly loves but doesn't really understand. There was a time when he did.

Jon Landau, "Lennon Gets Lost in His Rock & Roll," in Rolling Stone, *Issue 187, May 22, 1975, p. 66.*

GREIL MARCUS

I'm a sucker for favorite oldies albums. I always look forward to them once I've heard they're in the works, and the guarantee of dissatisfaction that comes stamped in the grooves of virtually every one of them . . . hasn't dimmed my hopes. The formula is all too obvious: established singer (rarely group) has reached a plateau, wants a rest, but has record due (possible) *or* has fallen flat on his face and has nothing to say . . . , solution—duck into the studio with The Regulars . . . plus whoever's hot and expensive . . . , lay it down, put it out. If you're lucky it'll carry you for six months. By that time you'll be ready to act like a genius again.

As John Lennon has proved beyond a doubt, it looks easy but it isn't. [For ***Rock 'n' Roll,*** he] picked famous songs by '50s rockers (Vincent, Holly, Berry, Domino), added a couple of hits by non-giants (Lloyd Price, Lee Dorsey), and whipped through them—after all, he had the music in his blood, and everyone knows it was simple stuff. With the exception of Price's "Just Because," a powerful, saddening, deeply felt performance, not one cut on the album would have been considered worth releasing by Sam Phillips, Bumps Blackwell, Phil Chess, Jerry Wexler, or any of the other founding producers of the '50s, because the cuts have no groove, no flair, no novelty, no distinction, no attack.

Greil Marcus, "Recollections of an Amnesiac," in Creem, *Vol. 7, No. 1, June, 1975, p. 69.*

DAVE MARSH

Shaved Fish is a collection of singles, some of them hits, released during John Lennon's post-Beatles career (1969-present). Ordinarily, such Christmas gift ideas aren't worth writing about but, as with almost everything else Lennon has done, ***Shaved Fish*** is different. There is nothing spectacularly unfound about the music here, although finally having an LP with **"Instant Karma!"**—Lennon's best solo track and as full a statement of the rock philosophy as we are likely to get from anyone—is a significant event in my house. . . . [The] lyric sheet . . . offers the most convincing evidence yet of Lennon's verbal felicity.

More than that, however, the feeling of this record is so diffuse that it probably does present an accurate overview of Lennon's confused career since leaving the Beatles. The best tracks are obsessed, driven by a special idea about the usefulness of rock & roll, as on **"Instant Karma!," "Cold Turkey," "Imagine"** and even **"Mother."** Although **"Give Peace a Chance"** is the best example extant of Lennon's talent for random lyric writing, neither it, **"Happy Xmas (War Is Over)"** nor **"Power to the People"** has held up. Unlike Dylan's best topical songs ("George Jackson," say), or even the Beatles' **"Revolution,"** Lennon's polemics were entirely too ad hoc to last beyond the era in which they were made. Nevertheless, there is a cohesion of style present in these which dwindles in the later parts of the record: **"Mind Games," "Whatever Gets You thru the Night"** and **"#9 Dream"** are all without the purpose of his best work. This is convincing evidence, then, not only of John Lennon's genius but of his continuing career difficulty.

Dave Marsh, in a review of "Shaved Fish," in Rolling Stone, *Issue 202, December 18, 1975, p. 68.*

STEVE SIMELS

[**"Shaved Fish"**] is simply Lennon's Greatest Hits (translate: Greatest Hits since the demise of the Beatles). Not surprisingly, there are two ways to look at it. One is a portrait of John's musical decline—from brooding, innovative rocker to revolutionary sloganeer to anonymous funk merchant. (Let's face it—had ***Imagine*** or ***Woman Is the Nigger of the World*** come to us from anyone with a less impressive track record, he or she would have been laughed out of the marketplace.) The other is simply as a random collection of catchy, throwaway hits from an artist who has contributed more than his share of same, and on that level I am far more comfortable with it. (pp. 83-4)

I might add that if you don't own a copy of the studio ***Cold Turkey,*** included here, this album is a must. That starkly terrifying song, strangely overlooked by many at the time of its original release, has everything that great rock-and-roll should have, and, sadly, everything that John's later work has lacked. (p. 84)

Steve Simels, in a review of "Shaved Fish," in Stereo Review *Magazine, Vol. 36, No. 1, January, 1976, pp. 83-4.*

IAN PYE

There was a time when John Lennon's anguished cry pierced the stale air of complacency and mediocrity, cutting through to an emotional core few, if any, dared mention. Like early Dylan and latterly Joy Division, he stood alone casting a giant shadow over lesser mortals.

As far back as **"Help"**, when he first exposed his recurring fear of isolation, it was clear that here was a man who was not only prepared to bare his soul in the furtherance of his art but was capable of expressing those stark feelings through some of the most acute and eloquent rock 'n' roll heard since the days when Elvis Presley and Sun Records shone together.

Having survived the separation from his long time writing partner, Paul McCartney, and the subsequent break-up of the Beatles, in April 1970, Lennon embarked on a full scale solo career that has above all, been characterised by its erraticism. Although unpredictable in the past, Lennon was soon to prove that he could within the space of a single album be simultaneously brilliant and frighteningly trite.

Yet he never failed to surprise and frequently produced work just as stimulating and satisfying as that produced in collaboration with the other Beatles.

Five years ago all this came to an untimely halt. His **"Rock 'n' Roll"** album became his epitaph when he retreated into pastoralism and the Dakota, his New York apartment complex.

Saying he had made his contribution to society, he disappointed many by his retirement. But, like the Beatles, he had at least quit with his reputation intact, if a little frayed around the edges. Showbiz legends, it seems, seldom keep their promises when it comes to taking the final curtain; and now like another ageing hero, Muhammad Ali, Lennon is attempting a come back.

With Yoko Ono, he has been signed to Geffen Records for whom he has recorded an as yet unreleased album, **"Double Fantasy"**, from which the dire single **"Starting Over"** was recently lifted. Commenting on an earlier album, **"Walls and Bridges"**, Lennon claimed that it was "the work of a semi-sick craftsman". This seems more suited to this current appalling exercise in sloppy pub balladry.

Only the man's fearsome voice appears to be intact; tragically his critical sensibilities display a frightening lack of contact with modern music. . . .

In May 1968 he recorded **"Two Virgins-Unfinished Music No. 1"** with Yoko. It contained exquisite passages of noses being blown, assorted squawks from Yoko and feathered friends but this "avant garde" abortion gained its principal notoriety from the cover: the happy couple standing naked for all the world to see. . . .

Whether Lennon was being led down a pretentious path of earthly delights and mindless whimsy by the love of his life, and indeed whether he still is, is open to conjecture. Whatever—the record marked the vinyl debut of the couple's public obsession with each other. Virtually a year after their first nuptial bulletin, **"Unfinished Music No. 2; Life With The Lions"** came out.

This time, the cover showed the couple camping out in the hospital room where Yoko subsequently suffered a miscarriage, while the record featured yet more screaming, electronic blurps, radio doodles of the **"Revolution No 9"** variety and the sound of their unborn baby's heartbeat. All too much.

It was the second pointer of things to come. Their relationship had become the exclusive centre of their universe and was deemed by them to be of the utmost artistic validity. Lennon even warned at the time: "These records will go on for the rest of our lives. It will be a constant autobiography of our life together."

He wasn't kidding either, and if the new single is anything to go by the next album may well take the form of yet another tedious bulletin on the state of the Lennon-Ono relationship. . . .

Ensconced in Montreal's Queen Elizabeth Hotel, John wrote his first non-Beatle single, **"Give Peace A Chance".** With the assistance of an 8-track recorder . . . he recorded the opus and the Plastic Ono Band was born.

Although described more as "concept" than a group, it took on its strongest physical identity in the autumn of 1970, and gave Lennon the confidence to perform live for the first time in years. With Klaus Voormann on bass, drummer Alan White and Eric Clapton on guitar, the Plastic Ono Band played an unrehearsed set at Toronto's rock 'n' roll revival festival to a largely ecstatic crowd. After vomiting with nerves before going on stage, Lennon ran through some rock classics and aired for the first time one of the strongest songs he has ever written: **"Cold Turkey".** The event was captured on **"Live Peace In Toronto.".** . .

If anything **"Cold Turkey"** was the first piece of classic rock minimalism and remains one of Lennon's most chilling songs. . . .

The third Plastic Ono Band single was another superb example of fast product. Phil Spector was asked to produce **"Instant Karma".** With George Harrison, Alan White and Klaus Voormann, Lennon and Spector created a masterfully simple, yet energetically compelling rocker that contained one of the best drum sounds ever heard.

With **"Power To The People"** and the 1972 **"Happy Xmas (War Is Over)", "Instant Karma"** represented what Lennon described as an attempt to give rock 'n' roll the immediacy of a newspaper's headlines: they were intended to reflect what was happening in the world with a vivid impact.

The sparseness and immediate emotional clout of **"Karma"** continued into Lennon's first "official" solo album, **"John Lennon/Plastic Ono Band",** released in December 1970. Lennon had spent much of the year with his most recent guru, the American radical therapist Arthur Janov. The consequent music was the result of extensive Primal Therapy, as Dr. Janov called his rediscovery of repressed childhood experiences and anxieties. . . .

It's an album of remarkable honesty, with Lennon exposing all his vulnerabilities and disturbing obsessions. . . .

It was the completion of a cycle and the culmination of a devastating history that, by its terminal expression of the absolute, would leave Lennon with a near impossible task of following. As he said: "the dream was over".

On this album he buried the Sixties and all they stood for with a golden shovel. One had the nasty feeling that after such a dignified and glorious funeral, the only thing to come would be artistic necrophilia.

What happened next involved further illuminations of personal events but by now things were getting decidedly more sordid and negative. Thinking he had been insulted by McCartney's second solo album "Ram," . . . Lennon recorded his revenge on the 1971 **"Imagine"** album, with **"How Do You Sleep"**— a barely veiled assault on McCartney's artistic credibility.

> A pretty face may last a year or two
> but pretty soon they'll see what you can do.
> The sound you make is muzak to my ears,
> you must have learned something in all those years.

Still as a track, it was full of the old quintessential Lennon venom, unlike some of its bedpartners which were frequently soft centered and benign.

Apart from a few notable exceptions things were to get worse with his next release, the didactic **"Some Time In New York City",** which came out as a double in 1972. Alongside the Ono Band, he enlisted Elephant's Memory, a group of hard-nosed traditionalist rockers who gave the whole affair some degree of muscle but were far from capable of rescuing the music from the banal, radical chic slogans upon which Lennon tried to capitalise.

For the first time in his career, he was repeating other people's tired messages instead of inventing his own. The black and white split of brothers and sisters fighting the pigs, which was central to the album's ethos, was painfully naive and impressed few beyond the ranks of the absurd politicos Lennon chose to align with at the time. His heart may have been in the right place, but his brain appeared to be well and truly out to lunch.

"New York City" and the Yokoish **"Woman Is The Nigger Of The World"** survive as above average songs on an otherwise misconceived and best forgotten work.

Things didn't get much better with his 1973 album **"Mind Games".** It was at least an improvement, though still surprisingly bland for a man of his stature. Even die-hard fans started wondering whether his inspiration had finally dried up. What happened shortly after its release was of far more significance than anything found on the album.

John Ono Lennon, as he was by now known, left Yoko and took up with his secretary May Pang. Thankfully, it seemed to invest his music with the inventive edge it had sorely lacked in recent years. In California, Lennon went on a six-month session of heavy drinking and social terrorism. . . .

Decadence was supposed to be a thing of the past for Lennon, but whatever the reasons behind it the album that subsequently arrived after his debauched period was the best thing he'd done since the primal album. In one week he wrote 10 new songs and the results appeared on **"Walls And Bridges",** a flawed but often excellent work.

He had discovered his sense of humour again, as well as his gift for setting unusual and arresting melodies against fluid, imaginative lyrics. **"Number Nine Dream"** was especially outstanding. A surreal song, typical of the album's languid tones and lush production. . . .

It also contained one of his best ever attacks on the discreet charm of the bourgeoisie—"your teeth are clean but your mind is capped"—**"Steel And Glass".** Sadly, **"Walls And Bridges"** represented Lennon's last album of original songs. In February 1975, his majestic album of standards **"Rock 'n' Roll",** came onto the streets and was followed later in the year by the **"Shaved Fish"** compilation. Then there was silence. . . .

What's happened musically over the last five years seemed to have bypassed Lennon completely. His latest single [**"(Just**

Like) Starting Over"] is abundantly inferior to any of his previous solo work. It was painful enough watching another of the last heroes getting pummelled to death by his old sparring partner earlier this year. To quote one of the man's own lines: "If you can't stand the heat you better get back in the shade."

Let's hope the sight of another sagging champion, out of breath and on his knees, won't come round so soon.

Ian Pye, "The Erratic, Tormented Genius of John Ono Lennon," in Melody Maker, *November 8, 1980, p. 27.*

IAN PYE

Five years is a dangerously long time to avoid any kind of musical activity. Especially when, like John Lennon, you're an artist noticeably prone to bouts of creative atrophy.

A self confessed dreamer, he has always produced his best work in the midst of some kind of catalytic event. In his early days with the Beatles this frisson came through his part supportive, part competitive writing relationship with Paul McCartney: then came another period of inspiration during the final crumbling of his first marriage, followed by perhaps his most consistently fruitful era under primal therapy from which was born his most significant solo album.

As suggested by his retrogressive and uninspired come-back single **"Starting Over"**, which opens [**"Double Fantasy"**], the time spent in seclusion and semi-retirement appears to have dulled the man's sensibilities and blunted his once impeccable feel for rock 'n' roll. The whole thing positively reeks of an indulgent sterility.

The inauspicious cover, depicting the happy couple locked in a kiss, reflects the music . . . which is a continuation of their public declaration on the unending beauty of their relationship. In other words, it's more songs about Yoko, John, Sean (their son) and John and Yoko and Sean. And yes, it's a godawful yawn. . . .

[**"Cleanup Time"**] gives the backup musicians . . . room to stretch out, but like much of the material here it's been and gone before you know it.

It's set at a mid-pace, as are most of the other Lennon tracks, leaving it to Yoko to do her best at generating some kind of energy which she attempts with the mercifully short "Give Me Something".

[Lennon's **"I'm Losing You"**] must be one of the album's strongest tracks, echoing the **"White Album"**, and at least proving that the man is still capable of summoning a tortured, aching vocal despite the song's air of familiarity. . . .

Lennon's **"Beautiful Boy (Darling Boy)"** ends the first side in the same mushy vein it began. Basically a lullaby to his son, it boasts a haunting melody and a simplistic lyric, but ultimately reinforces the album's incestuous feel, ending with daddy Lennon saying goodnight to his baby boy. In a different context he might just have got away with it.

You don't have to be a Lennonologist to realize that **"Watching The Wheels"**, which opens the second side, is the key track. Taking its momentum from a similar piano motif to that on **"Imagine"**, it's Lennon's answer to his critics, and after this debacle there'll be plenty of them.

The song is delivered in languid tones in an attempt to somehow justify his quiescence and subsequent estrangement from rock, but rather than revealing anything new merely underlines the obvious: John Lennon is content to be a passive, and increasingly cenobite individual who doesn't give a flying one about anything except his own little family circle. The man who once preached revolution has embraced the innocuous world of the bourgeoise individualist. . . .

A ringing Argent-style guitar riff opens John's **"Woman"**, which is the nearest sound to the fab four on the album. Though it's desperately dated, the melody is passable but by now tributes to Yoko are wearing more than a little thin. . . .

More than anything else [**"Dear Yoko"**] . . . demonstrates how much his enforced hermitage has damaged his artistic abilities. A Hollyesque stutter signals the beginning of another redundant-hymn to his loved one that suggests the man has finally run to seed. Packed with musical clichés and lame sentiments, it's a depressing end to a profoundly disappointing re-emergence.

The biggest irony of all is that by relentlessly harping on about the glories of their relationship they inadvertently devalue their original intentions in a torrent of empty words and slack songs.

As a celebration of life and the wholesome possibilities of a happy family, **"Double Fantasy"** fails miserably because the music can't do justice to its treacherous subject.

As an old companion of John Lennon's once said: "Some people wanna fill the world with silly love songs." The trouble is they just don't know when to stop.

Ian Pye, "Silly Love Songs," in Melody Maker, *November 22, 1980, p. 26.*

ROMAN KOZAK

There are several ways of approaching [**"Double Fantasy"**], John Lennon's first recording in five years, but the best way may be to take it simply on its own terms.

It is always dangerous to tie any artist's work too closely to his (and her) personal life unless the artist makes it clear that this work is autobiographical. Then it is another story.

Such is the case with **"Double Fantasy."** . . .

[The LP is] a musical dialog. . . . Lennon has one song, then Ono has one, all the way through. . . .

[The] song **"(Just Like) Starting Over,"** the big single hit, which begins the LP with three chimes, like a doorbell, can be seen on the one hand as Lennon's call for a second honeymoon with his own wife, or everyman's such call. But for that matter, it may be also a request by the artist, gone from view for a long time, asking his forgetting audience to begin the musical romance anew.

And since both Yoko Ono and Sean Lennon are personally addressed in two of the songs, it becomes quite obvious who the songs are about. But being personal makes the songs no less universal. While few of us live in the circumstances and have the opportunities of the Lennons, nevertheless, rich and famous as they may be, they too have problems in creating a stable loving personal relationship between themselves and their offspring.

The song is in the form of a circa-1960 midtempo rocker, with a slightly echoing bass (John always loved those) and a chorus in the background. There are more ooohs, ahhhs, and la-las sung on this LP than on any contemporary disk released in a long time. . . .

"Clean Up Time," with its refrain, *"Show these mothers how to do it,"* might sound like a call to revolution, except the bouncy rhythm, and the cheery mood, make it obvious that Lennon is talking about being a househusband. . . .

[In Lennon's] next tune he worries **"I'm Losing You".** It is a hard ballad, somewhat self-pitying at the same time, but very intense. . . .

Lennon ends the side with **"Beautiful Boy (Darling Boy),"** the prettiest and most Beatle-like song on the album.

If Lennon at all tries to explain his way of life, and his inactivity these last few years, he does so on **"Watching The Wheels,"** a pretty ballad opening side two. He is perfectly happy off the merry-go-round, sitting on the sidelines watching the wheels go by, he says in the song. . . .

The last two songs, both of them beautiful and both by Yoko Ono, are the summing up. . . . In the chorus [of "Hard Times Are Over"], *"Hard times are over / Over for a while"* one expects Lennon to join in the harmony at the end. But confounding expectations again, he doesn't.

Roman Kozak, in a review of "Double Fantasy," in Billboard, *Vol. 92, No. 49, December 6, 1980, p. 52.*

ROBERT CHRISTGAU

[John Lennon's ***Some Time in New York City*** is] the most politically ambitious and artistically impoverished music he ever recorded. After that came the traumatic separation from Yoko and the half-hearted professional rock, a vocation for which this compulsively honest and necessarily direct artist showed little taste. In the end he chose—bravely and wisely—to lay low, to keep silent until he had something to say. Reunited with Yoko, finally a father again, he retreated into domestic pursuits, and when the couple returned to the studio after five years it was their pursuit of mutual retreat that they celebrated. One astute observer said Lennon seemed "infantilized," which is true, but while [***Double Fantasy***] was no ***Imagine*** or ***Plastic Ono Band,*** I found its candor irrefutable. Lennon had always seemed like someone who might make good new rock and roll when he was 60—and I was 58. Nothing about ***Double Fantasy*** damaged that fantasy for me.

Robert Christgau, "John Lennon, 1940-1980," in The Village Voice, *Vol. XXV, No. 50, December 10, 1980, p. 1.*

ROBERT CHRISTGAU

"Death of a Beatle," phooey—he'd been the most outspoken *ex*-Beatle for 10 stubborn, right-headed years. "End of the '60s," asinine—if the decade wasn't finished on December 31, 1969, then it bit the dust a few weeks earlier at Altamont, or a few years later with McGovern. Yet there is a sense in which John Lennon's death does bring back our collective past, because it's the first genuine pop event to hit America in a very long time. In England they've had the Sex Pistols, but Stateside it's back to Dylan's 1974 tour, or maybe Rolling Thunder in 1975. The nearest we've come since then to rock and roll news that inspired the mass imagination, that momentarily melded a disparate, casual-to-fanatic audience into something like a community, was (don't hold your breath) *Saturday Night Fever.*

What's frightening, of course, is that this pop event was an assassination, one that may feel of a piece with Kennedy and King but has more in common structurally with Valerie Solanas's attempt on Andy Warhol (crucial difference: Solanas was a rival, not a fan) and more in common historically with such recent headlines as the murders of Allard Lowenstein and who knows how many black schoolchildren in Atlanta. But for me, what's just as scary is that the community catalyzed by Lennon's loss is obviously so momentary, partial, and (to use my fave '70s cliche) fragmented. The polarities aren't always mutually exclusive—contradictory feelings are the essence of our era—and don't divide into neat sets of parallels, but they indicate real divisions nonetheless. Here are those who've always regarded John as a symbolic comrade, there those who've always regarded him as an actual leader. Here are those who've aged with him, there those so young they revere him as the spirit of an Edenic prehistory. . . .

We feel these divisions musically, too. We hear more late Beatles than early Beatles, more **"Imagine"** than **"Instant Karma,"** and we know that ***Double Fantasy***—which still trailed Bruce Springsteen on *Cash Box's* airplay chart the week Lennon's death catapulted both album and single to number one in sales—will never saturate the radio (and the air itself) like ***Sgt. Pepper.*** Richard Goldstein's notorious Sunday *Times* pan of ***Sgt. Pepper*** had no constituency, although many critics (not me) agree with it now. But the regretful reviews of ***Double Fantasy*** that appeared in *The Boston Phoenix* (Kit Rachlis) and were withdrawn in the wake of the tragedy from the *Times* (Stephen Holden), *Rolling Stone* (Tom Carson), and *The Voice* (Geoffrey Stokes) spoke for John's more demanding fans. Saleswise, the comeback was a major success—sure to do even better than the most famous (as opposed to popular) ex-Beatle might expect. It produced a hit single, which was no foregone conclusion. But many found it fatuous, and I'm sure some young punks go along with the *Soho News* club columnist (Ira Kaplan) who opined that Lennon's death meant less to "rock 'n' roll, present and future" than the heroin ODs of Raybeat George Scott and Germ Darby Crash. . . .

That would be a rank stupidity even if the album were a lot worse than its critics believe. I think it's a lot better, and I was beginning to think so before December 8. The simplistic words and less than adventurous music were off-putting at first. But John sounded wonderful, and the times (or I) had caught up with Yoko's singing, so I kept playing the thing, a good sign with a record that resists final judgment. About meaning, of course, there could be no hesitation—this was John and Yoko's love album. The title made me think of MarcoVassi's great porn novel, *Mind Blower,* which is dedicated to the proposition that no matter how good the sex gets your minds will always be in different places. John and Yoko were denying this—gratuitously, perhaps, but I identified with the urge.

Not everyone did, or does—many of John's symbolic comrades find the couple's mutual self-involvement unrealistic and embarrassing. In the November 25 *Boston Phoenix* Kit Rachlis confessed himself "annoyed" by the artists' assumption "that lots of people care deeply about John Lennon and Yoko Ono." Sounded reasonable at the time, but since then the argument has become null, at least for a few years. ***Double Fantasy*** itself is now a pop event; its slightest moments have gained pathos, impact, and significance. The most devastating transformation occurs in **"Beautiful Boy,"** John's lovely lullabye for his son Sean, which seems destined to become one of the kid's most vivid connections to his dead father: "Have no fear / The monster's gone / He's on the run and your daddy's here." But Yoko's "Every Man Has a Woman Who Loves Him," the least distinguished piece of music on the album, runs a close second: "Every man has a woman who loves him / In rain or shine or life or death," she tells us. And later on reverses genders in the same couplet. (p. 31)

And then there's the minor miracle of the music. With its rich, precise sound, its command of readymades from New Orleans r&b to James Brown funk, and from magical mystery dynamics to detonating synthesizers, ***Double Fantasy*** is one of the two albums released in 1980 (Poly Styrene's dreamlike *Translucence* is the other) to put the anonymous usages of studio rock to striking artistic purpose. The music sounds somehow economical even when 24 (or is it 40?) tracks are humming; it doesn't just frame or set the voices, it projects them. And what voices. When he last essayed this sort of thing on ***Walls and Bridges,*** during his separation from Yoko, John sounded confused and unconvinced. Here he sounds sweet, tough, pained, reflective, calm, and above all soulful. When Yoko last tried to go pop on *Approximately Infinite Universe* (though compare "Why?" on her experimental *Plastic Ono Band* to Material or Blood Ulmer and renew your faith in prophetic avant-gardism), she sounded like a bad Buffy Sainte-Marie imitator. Now her speed and sexuality, her forced rhythms and peristaltic gutturals, add a new-wavish edge to John's confident professionalism. The elementary device of alternating cuts between the two spouses (no duets) makes their union come alive more than any of the often one-dimensional lyrics. But I ought to admit that for the most part I like the lyrics, especially John's. I liked the lyrics on his ***Plastic Ono Band,*** too, not so much for what they said or how they said it but for what they said *about* how they said it—that John's commitment to the outspoken and straightforward knew no bounds. Nine years later, though he's more mature, more amiable, happier, that commitment is unchanged. I use the present tense, of course, to refer to art. I hope there's at least a little more.

A great album? No, but memorable and gratifying in its slight, self-limited way—connubial rock and roll is hard to find. I wouldn't think of patterning my own marriage on anyone else's, but like any good art ***Double Fantasy*** transcends specifics, even its status as a pop event. It helps me remember what I cherish. And it helps me cherish the two people who made it as well. (p. 32)

Robert Christgau, "Symbolic Comrades," in The Village Voice, *Vol. XXVI, No. 3, January 14, 1981, pp. 31-2.*

MITCHELL COHEN

In a calamitous turn of events too fraught with sadness and irony for the heart to bear, **"Double Fantasy"** has gone from John Lennon's longed-for musical re-emergence to his last recorded testament. What sounded a few weeks ago like a man's too-complacent statement of tranquility now can only be heard in the dark context of tragedy and in the blazing light of an unparalleled career.

To listen to John's voice on the Beatles' Hamburg tapes of 1962, the Decca demos, the **"Please Please Me"** album, is to witness the fabric of rock music being torn to shreds and rewoven by a very young man with conquest on his mind. Later songs as diverse as ***It Won't Be Long, You Can't Do That, Help!, Every Little Thing, Any Time at All, Don't Let Me Down, Rain, Instant Karma, I'm a Loser, Jealous Guy,*** Side 2 of **"Rubber Soul,"** and almost everything on **"John Lennon/ Plastic Ono Band,"** shows how he changed rock singing and composing as dramatically as Brando changed screen acting and with the same emotional intensity.

We saw John Lennon more naked than any other modern star; no one was more unafraid of image-risks, of going too far: Every step the Beatles took forward, for good or ill, was guided by John. When at last they were quartered, he embarked on a crusade that shocked and embarrassed much of his audience, confused many others, and resulted in work that was distressingly erratic, but always marked by honesty and humanist integrity. . . .

He retreated, he accumulated wealth and property, he raised a son. Then, he was coming back; expectations were high. The single that preceded **"Double Fantasy,"** ***(Just Like) Starting Over,*** was a typically droll, wonderful Lennon tease, from the Presley vocal mannerisms and the pun implied in the title ("Just Like"—"J.L."), to the corny piano and background vocals and definitively hummable melody. His legendary trash-pop instinct was clearly operating at 45 rpm.

The album, unfortunately, isn't quite as good. . . . On it, a well-adjusted musical craftsman, an artist with the capacity to startle, addressed his own familial condition and found that it was just fine, thanks.

But complaining about its limited vision seems not only inappropriate, but mean-spirited. For though only sentimentality could rank it with his finest work, one can't fault the familiar abrasion of ***I'm Losing You,*** the oriental delicacy of ***Beautiful Boy,*** John's warm singing on ***Watching the Wheels,*** the mea culpa ballad ***Woman,*** the crisp New York City ambience, or even Yoko's dance-rock contributions. **"Double Fantasy"** bows to rock's past (copping from Buddy Holly on **Dear Yoko**), nods towards Lennon's own (paraphrasing ***Cry Baby Cry*** on ***Cleanup Time***), and details of his life in the Dakota. As such, it leaves us with questions about Lennon's possible musical future, questions we thought he'd have the next forty years to explore. **"Double Fantasy"** sounds like a step, not a stop.

Mitchell Cohen, "John Lennon's Last," in High Fidelity, *Vol. 31, No. 2, February, 1981, p. 92.*

STEVE SIMELS

As I write, it has been only a week since John Lennon was killed. . . . As a media event, his death has been unprecedented. The Russian invasion of Afghanistan, the upheaval in Poland and Iran, inflation, Reagan's election . . . who cares? They all pale into insignificance. Nineteen-eighty will be remembered as the year a "wacko" (the word the police used) pulled off the first rock-and-roll assassination. And the tributes will continue. (p. 102)

His musical accomplishments will probably be debated endlessly. The lingering, mindless fan clamor of the last ten years has done a great deal to cheapen his reputation, and there has been the inevitable critical backlash (ironic when you consider that all us rock critics owe our very jobs to him, for there wasn't any such occupation to speak of before the Beatles. . . . My guess is that in the long run it's his early stuff—through, say, **"Beatles VI"**—that will hold up best. . . . But his finest work, I think, which includes the first two solo albums and the 1975 **"Rock and Roll"** set, constitutes an achievement as personal and innovative and moving as can be found in the history of the music he helped shape. If it takes a senseless crime to make people remember what John accomplished, well, that's unfortunate, but it's also the way of the world.

As for **"Double Fantasy,"** the comeback record that now becomes his artistic farewell: in honesty, I hated it before he died, and now that he's gone I find listening to it all but unbearable. The simplistic celebrations of the love he and Yoko felt for each other and for their son seem, in retrospect, too painfully sincere to take: the cruelty of his ending intrudes too much. Musically, it shows that he had not completely lost his touch. The voice was still thrillingly intact; it is worth mentioning that among other things John Lennon had perhaps the most hauntingly expressive voice in all of rock-and-roll. At least two of the songs—***Watching the Wheels*** and ***Woman***—are, on a melodic level, as fetching as some of his lesser Beatles efforts. . . . The kindest thing to say about **"Double Fantasy,"** all in all, is that it was not designed as a rock record and shouldn't be judged as one. Its music is what the industry calls Adult Contemporary; I don't think it's successful even within the tedious confines of that bland genre, but I can see that some kind of case could be made for it. (pp. 102-03)

Steve Simels, "John Lennon/Yoko Ono," in Stereo Review *Magazine, Vol. 46, No. 3, March, 1981, pp. 102-03.*

VARIETY

[**"Milk and Honey,"** a] collection of out-takes from the Lennon/Ono **"Double Fantasy"** sessions, cassette demo tracks and new Ono recordings doesn't figure to approach the multiplatinum sales level of their last LP. [However], Lennon's inimitably rendered blend of humanistic insight and robust cynicism makes songs such as **"Nobody Told Me," "I'm Stepping Out"** and **"I Don't Wanna Face It"** an affecting last legacy.

A review of "Milk and Honey," in Variety, *February 22, 1984, p. 92.*

TOM BENTKOWSKI

It was twenty years ago, as we've been reminded a hundred times, that the Beatles arrived in America. The present flood of pictures, stories, and film clips from *The Ed Sullivan Show* seems to have inspired mass reflection—the Beatles have become a point of reference. It is from that time in 1964 that a generation calculates the changes in its life. It is in this light, sadly, that the only real interest in ***Milk and Honey*** . . . lies: Here are the last songs John Lennon recorded. The album is made up of six cuts each by John and Yoko, recorded at the same time as the material that became ***Double Fantasy.*** These are clearly the leftovers. The contented house-husband, more skillfully portrayed on the earlier disc, is here given to exasperation, fatigue, and insecurity. Because of what they are, the songs will be listened to hard—not for their inspiration or revelation, but for the awkwardness that can only serve as an ironic reminder of the passion and wit of an earlier time.

Tom Bentkowski, "Pop: The Way They Were," in New York *Magazine, Vol. 17, No. 9, February 27, 1984, p. 73.**

DON SHEWEY

Milk and Honey was conceived as a companion piece to ***Double Fantasy.*** Each is subtitled "A Heart Play," and while the earlier album was meant to be something of a healing ritual (coming after John and Yoko's eighteen-month separation and Lennon's subsequent five-year "retirement" from recording), its successor seems designed as a portrait of domestic bliss. According to Ono's liner notes, she and Lennon consciously adopted the image of themselves as the reincarnation of Victorian poets Elizabeth Barrett Browning and Robert Browning for ***Milk and Honey;*** the album jacket even reproduces verses by the Brownings next to lyrics by John and Yoko.

Unfortunately, the songs on the album don't bear comparison to the work of such illustrious writers. Four of the six new Lennon compositions recycle basic rock & roll licks to accompany simple, repetitive, even clichéd lyrics ("Living on borrowed time," "I'm stepping out," et cetera). **"Nobody Told Me,"** the first single from ***Milk and Honey,*** begins promisingly with an energetic riff reminiscent of the Beatles' **"Eight Days a Week,"** but it immediately lapses into a routine melody with unevenly rhymed lyrics that barely make sense ("There's Nazis in the bathroom just below the stairs / Always something happening and nothing going on"). (p. 49)

The most interesting Lennon song is also the album's silliest. **"(Forgive Me) My Little Flower Princess"** sounds like something translated from a corny Japanese opera yet rendered slightly ominous by two minor-key chords. There are other bits of goofiness throughout the album—like ad libs, scat singing and funny count-offs ("Eins, zwei, hickle, fickle!")—which seem to confirm that these are rough tracks. Still, they paint a delightful portrait of Lennon as a cut-up. And despite the erratic quality of the material, the album sounds great. . . .

The centerpiece of ***Milk and Honey*** is a pair of songs specifically inspired by two of the Brownings' classic poems. Presented in rough, homemade versions, they're a little embarrassing. Lennon's **"Grow Old with Me"** has the stately feel of **"Imagine,"** but it's unlikely that it will become the standard—"the kind that they would play in church every time a couple gets married"—that Lennon hoped it would. And Ono's "Let Me Count the Ways" expresses vague sentiments . . . that have little in common with Elizabeth Barrett Browning. (p. 50)

Don Shewey, "John and Yoko's Message of Love," in Rolling Stone, *Issue 416, March 1, 1984, pp. 49-50.*

MARK PEEL

"Milk and Honey" is a companion to **"Double Fantasy,"** the album that raised the marriage of the late John Lennon and Yoko Ono from mere celebrity status to myth. Like **"Fantasy," "Milk"** alternates compositions written by husband and wife in a lovers' dialogue the two called a "heart play." Ono has said she hopes other lovers will find these songs a source of strength and guidance. That many people actually *do* is strange since, in fact, the songs paint a rather dreary picture. Moreover, they add to the evidence that suggest Lennon's relationship with Ono precipitated a slide into childish dependency and domesticity that coincided with a marked decline in the quality of his artistic output.

The inescapable fact is that **"Milk and Honey,"** like most of what Lennon produced after the Beatles, is thoroughly mediocre. What little life and energy there are here come from Ono. Lennon's own enthusiasm seems feigned: he sings like someone who's spent too much of his life in his bathrobe. How pale and unconvincing the restless husband in ***I'm Stepping Out*** seems compared with the expressionistic force of the husband's ennui in ***Good Morning*** from **"Sgt. Pepper."** . . . The picture of Lennon that emerges [in ***I'm Stepping Out***] is that of a male agoraphobic—a cowed husband sitting around in his pajamas, chin propped sadly in his palm, stirring his coffee and sighing into the late afternoon. If this is marriage, I'll take a double hit of Lucy in the Sky with Diamonds. . . .

[Lennon's songs] on side two are just banal. The first thing that comes to mind when you hear ***(Forgive Me) My Little Flower Princess*** is, of course, Lennon crawling back to Ono on his hands and knees after his celebrated period of dissipation with Harry Nilsson. And what should have been the centerpiece of **"Milk and Honey,"** an exchange of love songs between John and Yoko (*Let Me Count the Ways* and ***Grow Old with Me),*** is completely upstaged by the printing of the original Barrett and Browning poems side by side with the Lennon/Ono versions. How much more powerful are Elizabeth Barrett Browning's words, "And if God choose, I shall but love thee better after death."

Mark Peel, "John/Yoko: Heart Play," in Stereo Review *Magazine, Vol. 49, No. 4, April, 1984, p. 86.*

KURT LODER

These remnants and demos [from ***Milk and Honey***] are nice to have around—what Beatleist would want to be without them? But they're unfinished and sometimes embarrassing. **"Nobody Told Me"** is the beginning of a good tune, but one doubts that Lennon would have wanted to immortalize such lazy observations as "always something happening and nothing going on." And **"(Forgive Me) My Little Flower Princess"**—although not without charm, and given an oddly compelling tension by two minor-key chords—is as hokey as its title. The playing is provided by many of the same session pros who hemmed Lennon in on ***Double Fantasy,*** but at least his tracks, with their zany asides, reveal the man's playful nature, which was an important component of his genius.

Kurt Loder, in a review of "Milk and Honey," in Rolling Stone, *Issues 437 & 438, December 20, 1984—January 3, 1985, p. 118.*

(James) Paul McCartney

1942-

English songwriter and scriptwriter.

Stills/LGI © 1985

McCartney is among the most prolific songwriters of popular music. As one of the chief creative forces of the Beatles, the group which defined the standard for success in rock and roll, McCartney helped lead the direction of popular music in the 1960s. Since the group's breakup in 1970, he has continued to be a force in music, both as a solo artist and as leader of his band, Wings. Although McCartney has not received the critical acclaim for his later work that he enjoyed as a member of the Beatles, critics consistently cite his ability to create songs appreciated by a wide audience as his most enduring trait as a songwriter.

The Beatles played a major role in defining the cultural climate of the 1960s. Many young people emulated the group's involvement with drugs and meditation, and their concerts and public appearances were attended by crowds of frenzied admirers. "Beatlemania" became the term most often used to describe the reaction to their songs, appearances, and films. The success of the Beatles was largely due to the songwriting team of John Lennon and Paul McCartney. With George Harrison and Ringo Starr, they expanded the boundaries of popular music and helped bring it commercial success and artistic respectability. The differences between Lennon's and McCartney's personalities seemed to aid in the success of their collaborations, as each complemented the other's writing style. Lennon's songs were often rebellious, aggressive, and satirical, while McCartney's were more lyrical and sentimental. Together they promoted a renewed interest in the power of lyrics in the audience of the 1960s. Among the Beatles songs most often identified with McCartney are "Yesterday," a tender ballad of lost love that was widely recorded by other artists; "Eleanor Rigby," a touching, imagistic picture of the life and death of a lonely woman; and "Penny Lane," a fond remembrance of the people and places of McCartney's youth. The Beatles's most successful albums include *Sgt. Pepper's Lonely Hearts Club Band* (1967), perhaps the most influential rock album of the 1960s; *Abbey Road* (1969), the last album the Beatles recorded together; and *Let It Be* (1970), the soundtrack to a film which was the last project the group completed before their breakup.

McCartney's first solo album, *McCartney* (1970), was released shortly after his announcement that he was leaving the Beatles. Critics appreciated the simple, at-home feeling of many of the songs on this album yet declared that they expected lyrics of greater depth from a songwriter who had so greatly influenced popular music. Reaction to McCartney's subsequent albums was generally negative and sometimes vicious. *Ram* (1971) represented for Jon Landau "the nadir in the decomposition of Sixties rock thus far"; *Wild Life* (1971), McCartney's first album with Wings, the band he formed with his wife, Linda, was called "rather flaccid musically and impotent lyrically" by John Mendelsohn; and Patrick Snyder, reviewing *Red Rose Speedway* (1973), declared that "[McCartney] writes songs with an almost arrogant simplemindedness, limiting their subject matter to the most banal clichés of adolescent romance." Such reviews have been common throughout McCartney's post-Beatles career. Perhaps the complaint most often raised by critics is that McCartney's solo work has lacked the balancing effect of Lennon's influence. Only two of McCartney's albums have been universally well received: *Band on the Run* (1974), which Jon Landau declares is about "the search for freedom and the flight from restrictions on his and Linda's personal happiness," contains some of his most popular songs, and *Tug of War* (1982), which Stephen Holden calls "the masterpiece everyone has always known Paul McCartney could make," attempts a conceptual framework in its focus on the difficulty of maintaining order in a chaotic world. In the album's most moving song, "Here Today," which was written shortly after Lennon's murder in 1980, McCartney attempts to reconcile feelings of guilt and remorse over his uneasy relationship with Lennon. Despite the negative critical reaction to much of his work, McCartney has remained extremely popular with his fans and musical colleagues. His albums and singles sell millions of copies, his 1976 tour with Wings sold out arenas around the world, and he has collaborated on songs with several other influential figures in popular music, including Stevie Wonder and Michael Jackson. McCartney also starred in a film, *Give My Regards to Broad Street* (1984), for which he wrote the script and music.

Although his post-Beatles output is considered uneven, McCartney is widely admired for his ability to create subtle

and superbly crafted popular songs. Critics acknowledge McCartney's talent in utilizing elements from disparate musical genres, including rock, funk, disco, country and western, and big band, and they agree that his love songs have set standards for other popular songwriters. Vic Garbarini and Jock Baird have declared that "[McCartney] has written more great songs than any songwriter now alive," and it is agreed that he has helped define the scope of popular music for over twenty years.

(See also *CLC,* Vol. 12.)

HUBERT SAAL

What abounds [on the album "**McCartney**"] is a freedom, an attractive and spontaneous feeling in the songs, recorded like home movies, informally and affectionately. Wife Linda harmonizes unpretentiously in "**Man We Was Lonely**" and is the subject of "**The Lovely Linda,**" which is short, sweet and dissolves into giggles at the end.

What's extra special about the record is the incredible richness of melody, the tastefulness and wit of the lyrics and the expressive range of McCartney's voice. Many of the fourteen songs, such as the gentle "**Every Night**" or "**Maybe I'm Amazed,**" fierce in its screams of love and need, celebrate the love that binds. Others, such as "**Hot as Sun,**" are simply joyful, with the flavor of the old English music hall and the turning carousel. "**Oo You**" is cheerful blues; "**Junk,**" a deceptively soft but disquieting comment on society; "**Teddy Boy,**" a soft ballad which with a few choice words makes a couple of lives clear. There's not a loser in the bunch.

Hubert Saal, "The Beatles Minus One," in Newsweek, *Vol. LXXV, No. 16, April 20, 1970, p. 95.*

T. E. KALEM

[***McCartney***] is what used to be called a tour de force; today the phrase is "ego trip." Paul wrote all 14 songs, sings all the lead parts, plays all the instruments. In mood and style, the disk marks the same kind of return to simple pleasures, and a simple, countrified way of saying them, that characterizes Bob Dylan's recent work. . . . The album could well be called McCartney's *Nashville Skyline.*

Overall, the new album is good McCartney—clever, varied, full of humor—but it is nothing to match his past pop classics, particularly ***Yesterday, Michelle*** and ***Hey Jude.*** His lyrics are best when least pretentious, as in ***Junk,*** a kind of sentimental word jamboree. . . . ***Maybe I'm Amazed,*** however, is a pale echo of the choral sumptuousness of McCartney's ***The End,*** which served as the coda to ***Abbey Road,*** the hit 1969 Beatle album.

T. E. Kalem, "Hello, Goodbye, Hello," in Time, *Vol. 95, No. 16, April 20, 1970, p. 57.*

LANGDON WINNER

McCartney is an album that wants desperately to convince. Its explicit and uniform message is that Paul McCartney, his wife Linda and family have found peace and happiness in a quiet *home* away from the city and away from the hassle of the music business. This is a beautiful vision and, like most listeners, I wanted very much to believe it was true. On the basis of the music alone I was entirely persuaded. The 14 cuts on ***McCartney*** are masterful examples of happiness, relaxation and contentment. . . .

In both the quality of its songs and the character of its production ***McCartney*** will no doubt be a disappointment to many Beatles fans. Most people probably hoped that Paul's album would be a gigantic leap "beyond the Beatles," a super mind-blowing extravaganza with songs which would make "**Hey Jude**" and "**Let It Be**" seem pale by comparison. This did not happen. When compared to the best of the Beatles' previous work, the songs on ***McCartney*** are distinctly second rate.

Rather than adopt the role of "Super Paul," McCartney chose to keep things very personal and straightforward. . . . Both the melodies and lyrics on the album are sparse and uncomplicated. The first two songs on side one, for example, have virtually no verbal or melodic content whatsoever. "**The Lovely Linda**" starts out, "La-la-la-la the lovely Linda, with the lovely flowers in her hair." Paul repeats this once, giggles and then stops. "**That Would Be Something**" gives us the lines "That would be something / To meet you in the falling rain, momma, meet you in the falling rain" over and over again.

This emphasis on simplicity is the keynote of the whole album. Surprisingly enough, it manages to overcome our expectations of something more monumental and works very well. For while there are no songs of truly classic Beatles proportion, most of the cuts are very tasteful and fun to listen to. "**Junk**" and "**Teddy Boy**" are low pressure compositions with gentle, poignant lessons to convey. "Buy, buy, says the sign in the shop window. Why? Why? says the junk in the yard."

"**Maybe I'm Amazed**" is a very powerful song which states one of the main sub-themes of the record, that the terrible burden of loneliness can be dispelled by love. . . . This is the only song on the album that even comes close to McCartney's best efforts of the past. It succeeds marvelously. . . .

The most pleasing feature of the album is that it gives us a chance to hear Paul's voice in its pure and unaltered form. Ever since ***Rubber Soul*** the Beatles had insisted on putting miles of echo chamber between their voices and the ear of the listener. This became so irritating to me that I refused to buy the last two Beatles albums in futile protest. I just couldn't listen to another one of those echoed and compressed Lennon-McCartney "Ahhhhhhhh ahhhhhhh's" or one more of the sounds-like-a-giant-basketball-landing on a pile-of-oatmeal slightly-phased drum beats (Thump-Plop, echo, echo). In ***McCartney*** all of the fancy neo-Stockhausen electronics is cast aside. The only thing that separates us from Paul's voice are the two inches between his lips and the microphone. The sound is a genuine improvement—clean, crisp, warm and definitely human.

In brief, if one can accept the album in its own terms, ***McCartney*** stands as a very good, although not astounding, piece of work.

Langdon Winner, in a review of "McCartney," in Rolling Stone, *Issue 58, May 14, 1970, p. 50.*

ELLEN SANDER

[***McCartney***] is one of the few entirely successful "home" albums released. . . . Linda McCartney is the only other artist involved in ***McCartney***; her intimately beautiful photographs decorate the sleeve, and her uncertain harmonies waft through some of the songs (she can't carry a tune in a bucket, but her oooh-ahhh's are heavy and her presence is charming).

There is a great deal of padding on the record, and at that the album seems very short. . . . But the feel of the album is whole in the few songs that work, in the mystifying fragments that just sit there and sound pretty, in the roundhouse spirit of the entire package. One could spend hours listening to such simple, sparse, often unfinished music, and, having heard it all, never hear enough of it.

"La, la, la, the lovely Linda" may not be one of the most original or stimulating lyrics Paul McCartney ever wrote, but it certainly is one of the most engaging. **"That Would Be Something"** is another careful fragment, the rhythm irresistible, the dynamics complete. **"Valentine Day"** is a short instrumental, a little bit McCartney, a little bit Beatles, and a lot of something else, indeed. Like many of its companions on the record, it is unresolved, spontaneous, a shred of a few musical ideas strung together and left there. **"Every Night"** is the first complete song, but it somehow can't compete with the variety of enticing ideas set down before it. **"Hot as Sun / Glasses"** is a track of beautifully phrased melodic structures, broken by an uncut bit of shenanigans and ended right there. **"Junk"** is a lazy, laconic song, so simple and undemanding that the track is repeated on Side 2 without voices as **"Singalong Junk."**

"Man We Was Lonely" is the exception on the album. A hearty, homebound tune, full of fireside jive and family fun, it comes off as a robust, full song. The spontaneous quality of the items (one can hardly call the majority of them songs) on the album was preserved by careful studio discipline in producing the homemade tapes. Since Paul plays all the instruments, they are all overdubbed, and the vocals are as they were, hardly touched or changed. The clinkers were all left in, and they only heighten the implicit friendliness of the music.

Beatle music has become a document of the individual Beatles, and Beatle albums a chronicle of themselves. An unknown could never get away with producing the kind of album that ***McCartney*** is; there would be no frame of reference to cradle it. ***McCartney*** is musically a primitive album, but its fascination lies in the unraveling of the life and times, at this particular juncture, of an individual whose participation in the Beatles has influenced the life and times of the millions in his audience. It is that audience which will appreciate ***McCartney.*** Whereas other Beatle albums have had a much wider range in appeal, being the product of the aspects of the group and producer/arranger George Martin, or an advance in the formalization of pop so critical as to merit attention from those outside that intense but select area of interest, ***McCartney*** is by and for the family. (pp. 53-4)

Ellen Sander, "McCartney on His Own," in Saturday Review, *Vol. LIII, No. 22, May 30, 1970, pp. 53-4.*

JON LANDAU

Ram represents the nadir in the decomposition of Sixties rock thus far. For some, including myself, [Bob Dylan's] *Self-Portrait* had been secure in that position, but at least *Self-Portrait* was an album that you could hate, a record you could feel something over, even if it were nothing but regret. ***Ram*** is so incredibly inconsequential and so monumentally irrelevant you can't even do that with it: it is difficult to concentrate on, let alone dislike or even hate. . . .

[It] is so lacking in the taste that was one of the hallmarks of the Beatles that it strongly suggests Paul is not happy in his role as a solo artist, no matter how much he protests to the contrary.

The odd thing about it is that within the context of the Beatles, Paul's talents were beyond question. He was perhaps the most influential white bass player of the late Sixties, the only one of the Beatles with a keenly developed personal instrumental style. He was also the group's best melodist, and he surely had the best voice.

But, if it was Paul who used to polish up Lennon's bluntness and forced him to adapt a little style, it is by now apparent that Lennon held the reins in on McCartney's cutsie-pie, florid attempts at pure rock muzak. He was there to keep McCartney from going off the deep end that leads to an album as emotionally vacuous as ***Ram***. . . . McCartney creates music with a fully developed veneer, little intensity, and no energy. (p. 42)

[But] only a fool would write off a man of McCartney's past accomplishments on the basis of two albums (I'm not much of a fan of the last one either).

All of which makes it no less easy to deal with this very bad album from this very talented artist. For myself, I hear two good things on this record: **"Eat At Home,"** a pleasant, if minor, evocation of the music of Buddy Holly (with some very nice updating), and **"Back Seat of My Car,"** the album's production number.

The album's genre music—blues and old rock—is unbearably inept. On **"Three Legs"** they do strange and pointless things to the sound of the voice to liven it up; it doesn't work. **"Smile Away"** is sung with that exaggerated voice he used for the rock & roll medley in ***Let It Be:*** it is unpleasant. The **"When I'm Sixty-Four"** school of light English baubles is represented by **"Uncle Albert/Admiral Halsey,"** a piece with so many changes it never seems to come down anywhere, and in the places that it does, sounds like the worst piece of light music Paul has ever done. And **"Monkberry Moon Delight"** is the bore to end all bores: Paul repeats a riff for five and a half minutes to no apparent purpose.

The lowest point on the album, and the one that most clearly indicates its failures, is **"Heart of the Country."** It is an evenly paced, finger-picking styled tune, with very light jazz overtones, obviously intended as Paul's idea of "mellow." Somehow, his lyrics about the joys of the country ring false. Rather than a sense of self-acceptance or pride, I get a feeling of self-pity and self-justification from this cut, feelings that are almost masked by music so competent, in fact routine, that it all seems to slip away. Compare it to an earlier piece of music somewhat in the same vein, **"Blackbird."** That song has all the charm and grace **"Heart of the Country"** tries for, but also the depth, purpose, and conviction, which are the missing ingredients from ***Ram*** as a whole. (pp. 42-3)

[None] of the Beatles is a truly self-sufficient artist and therefore none of them seems to function at his best as a soloist. In this light, Paul has simply proven to be the most vulnerable: the group hid most of his weaknesses longer and better than they did the others so that they were the most unexpected now that they have finally become visible. But now they *have* become visible and the results can scarcely be more satisfying to McCartney himself than they will be to the many people who will find this record wanting. ***McCartney*** and ***Ram*** both prove that Paul benefitted immensely from collaboration and that he seems to be dying on the vine as a result of his own self-imposed musical isolation. What he finally decides to do about it is anybody's guess, but it is the only thing that makes Paul McCartney's musical future worth thinking about and hoping for. (p. 43)

Jon Landau, in a review of "Ram," in Rolling Stone, *Issue 86, July 8, 1971, pp. 42-3.*

JOHN MENDELSOHN

Like Paul McCartney's first two post-Beatles albums, ***Wild Life*** is largely high on sentiment but rather flaccid musically and impotent lyrically, trivial and unaffecting. It lacks the exhilarating highs of ***Ram*** (which highs I, as one who found it as worthless as the next guy when it first arrived, can assure you are indeed present), and, in the form of a track called **"I Am Your Singer,"** contains the most embarrassingly puerile single piece of work Paul's been associated with since **"She's Leaving Home."**

But allow no one to convince you that it's entirely devoid of merit—while it's vacuous, flaccid, impotent, trivial and unaffecting, it's also unpretentious . . . , melodically charming in several places, warm and pleasant. Mostly, it's nicely (but not, as was some of ***Ram,*** spectacularly,) executed pop music, and should be taken or left on that basis alone. . . .

Paul quietly continues to quite deliberately demystify himself . . . , making modest, simple music about the least mystical theme imaginable, domestic contentment. He's driven by no obsession to demonstrate rock's potential as fine, revolutionary, or religious art, but rather is content to make straightforward pop music, to entertain. . . .

None of which is to imply either so great a degree of detachment or so immense a capacity for charity in McCartney that he's above further participation in the inter-ex-Beatle feuding. Parts of ***Wild Life*** may with little exertion be construed as his answer to the unkind things Lennon sang and said about him [on *Imagine*].

To my ears there's something quite fishy about the title track—specifically, I find it impossible to take, "Taking a walk through an African park one day," and similar lines at face value, as merely very clumsy things to say in what sounds to me like a too-obvious-to-be-real ecology-fad-inspired song. Rather, the whole theme of this track seems a subtle but discernible parody of Lennon's stance as a social critic, just as the way Paul holds onto several raspily sung notes at the beginning of the song remind me more than a little of Lennon's vocal approach on the primal screaming album [*Plastic Ono Band*].

It's conceivable, of course, that I'm completely mistaken. It's this very uncertainty about the parodic nature of **"Wild Life"** that permits Paul to play the unfairly victimized but still charitable half of a friendship gone sour in **"Dear Friend,"** to ask, "Does it really matter that much to you?" in a way that suggests that "it" doesn't matter nearly so much to him as does the friendship.

The placement of these two songs is interesting: in closing the album, **"Dear Friend,"** in which he's the unjustly-hurt but nevertheless understanding golden boy, appears in the place where we'd probably most expect him to address Lennon. Thus, if you miss the import of **"Wild Life,"** which is placed at the end of a side whose first three-quarters seem to have been included mostly in an attempt to convince the listener that the album bears no pronouncements, you have only the far more flattering picture that **"Dear Friend"** paints on which to base your perception of McCartney's role in the feud. All of which, it must be admitted, is quite neat.

The aforementioned first three-quarters of side one comprise **"Mumbo,"** a raucous rock and roll rampage that, like **"Smile Away,"** may be taken as a small self-send-up, and **"Bip Bop,"** an hypnotic and quite enjoyable Merle Travis-style guitar-pickin' hoedown, and the venerable "Love Is Strange."

If the remainder of the album has a theme it's the perfect, self-containing, incomprehensible-to-outsiders nature of the McCartneys' love. Thus, the presence of ". . . Strange," the first non-original Paul's recorded since the middle of last decade. . . .

"Some People Never Know" and **"Tomorrow"** are archetypal post-Beatles McCartney: banal, self-celebrating lyrics full of many of the most tired rhymes in Western pop, sentiments that Jeanette MacDonald and Nelson Eddy would embrace without a moment's hesitation; glossy, if unfocused production; pretty, eminently Muzakable melodies; lots of velvety background ooh-ing; and the expressive intensity of the Carpenters—good pop, but neither more nor less than that.

"I Am Your Singer" represents McCartney's most dangerous impulses run rampant. It's sufficiently sweet and adorable to gag on, with Mr. & Mrs. describing each's importance to one another by use of a metaphor that even a Paul Williams might reject as overly cute. . . . Moreover, the song's arrangement appears to have been slapped together in a matter of seconds, as is suggested by drummer Denny Seiwell's thumping around aimlessly in a manner that suggests that the first time he heard the song was while it was being recorded. This isn't even acceptable pop music.

Speaking of arrangements, as we were a sentence ago, Paul seemingly can't be bothered to do much more than decide where he's going to insert a guitar solo or background singing, and is mostly content to allow his songs to stand or fall on tune alone. Only in "Love Is Strange" and **"Dear Friend,"** whose jarring piano and chilling strings (which remind, even if ever so slightly, of those on [Lennon's] "How Do You Sleep?") successfully evoke despair, is there much evidence of anyone having taken the time or trouble to focus the performance in such a way that its effect on the listener is controlled. . . .

My own conviction is that we'd be foolish to expect anything much more earth-shaking than ***Wild Life*** out of McCartney for a good long while; not, I daresay, before he extricates himself from record and publishing companies that he feels little love for. Which may very well not happen until the latter part of this decade. In the meantime the reader is advised to either develop a fondness for vacuous but unpretentious pop music or look elsewhere for musical pleasure.

John Mendelsohn, "Warm & Vacuous Mr. & Mrs.," in Rolling Stone, *Issue 100, January 20, 1972, p. 48.*

PATRICK SNYDER

Like [Paul McCartney's] three previous releases since the break-up of The Beatles, ***Red Rose Speedway*** offers a very circumscribed definition of rock. McCartney's music is, like the album's cover, a collage of primary colors polished with elegant production and technical ingenuity and spiced with hints of intriguing ambiguity, delivering much less than it promises. He writes songs with an almost arrogant simplemindedness, limiting their subject matter to the most banal clichés of adolescent romance. Who is he writing these songs for? Certainly not for anyone who has moved beyond the gauntlet of changes which puberty arrays. The melodies, as always, are hummable and lovely, but more and more often they leave the impression that they have taken you by sights you have seen many times before.

In its pointless lyrics, sinuous melodic arabesques, complex harmonies and pristine production, McCartney's music is reminiscent of The Beach Boys'. However, they succeed (for admittedly rather specialized tastes) through coherent stylistic elan and a breathtakingly beautiful musical intricacy that allows you to forgive the dumb words as the chink in their musical armor that lets it move so gracefully; McCartney is less than successful because he has matched his ninth-grade lyrics with music that tends to be equally minimal in its rhythm patterns and instrumentation. Production effects do, of course, abound: tiny ornamental guitar figures, hints of echo and touches of stereo ping-pong make for entertaining music but cannot provide the substance that is—and has been—so sorely lacking.

The album opens with perhaps its best cut, **"Big Barn Bed,"** an engaging, mildly funky song that ends with a *de rigeur* production rave-up. Next, we are presented with the fascinating spectacle of Paul McCartney becoming the Bee-Gees, who, if you remember, wanted to be the Beatles. **"My Love"** begins with a held violin note broken finally by a cymbal splash that introduces Paul's stunning vocal delivery of a song so sticky with sugar syrup that repeated listenings can give you diabetes. His major asset has always been his crystalline voice and his tasteful phrasing: throughout the album his use of them almost makes the whole thing worthwhile. The side ends with a major opus entitled, **"Little Lamb Dragonfly"** whose amazingly smooth twists and turns of arrangement offer some relief from its garbled metaphors and pointless aphorisms.

The second side begins with **"Single Pigeon,"** a cut that highlights McCartney's great piano work and again offers a structure unworthy of what it is asked to support. . . . The album ends with a four-song medley that seems to go on forever repeating lines and adding production touches. I really can't say much about it because in a dozen listenings I have been unable to keep my mind from wandering away from its 11-minute flood of drivel.

Like cotton candy, ***Red Rose Speedway*** seems appetizing from a distance (childhood memories and all) but it is something you may regret buying after its pink spun fluff has stuck to your chin.

Patrick Snyder, in a review of "Red Rose Speedway," in Crawdaddy, *July, 1973, p. 78.*

LENNY KAYE

[As] the best of ***Red Rose Speedway*** indicates, Paul McCartney's music tends to crumble under prolonged examination. He is not an especially intense lyricist, preferring instead to choose his words according to sound and feel alone, and his melodies—particularly on more uptempo material—appear to be fostered through basic reliance on a rotating riff. Mathematically this adds up to nothing, but over the radio and through repeated listenings the power of such a simple combination mounts steadily, so that what is finally delivered is the pop song refined to its ultimate extension—pleasant, accessible without concentration, air waves filled, records sold, no condescension or middle-of-the-road apologies.

In fact, if Paul demonstrates anything with this album, it lies in his skill as an arranger, in his placement of instruments and the succession of movements he notches within any given tune. . . . And make no mistake, though the songs are credited to the McCartneys, and though Wings works with an admirable degree of understated restraint, this is really Paul's album. He dominates it in a way he hasn't since embarking on his solo career, the results all to the good. His voice is consistently excellent, his bass provides the direction for most of the more ornate cuts, and he seems comfortable in his chosen milieu.

"Big Barn Bed," the opening cut on the album, captures McCartney's current approach as well as any, showing in a series of steps just how he fleshes out a song which must have been mere skeleton when first written. The lyrics are rhymed nonsense, for the most part, played off against a curiously staggered afterbeat and a tightly controlled vocal. Neither verse nor chorus are anything much, but the song draws you slowly in with the same steady roll of traction demonstrated by that odd union of records which score heavily in the discotheque markets, reaching its peak with the endless repetitions of the chorus line in the end, let down slightly via the faintly Gregorian harmonies at the close.

Similarly, **"My Love"** relies on its success . . . not through the mushiness of its sentiments, or the superfluous prettiness of its melody (Paul did it better in **"The Long and Winding Road"** anyway), but in its constant attention to unconcealed repetition. A look at the lyric sheet reveals a staggering amount of "My Love"'s and "Wo-Wo"'s shoved in nearly every line, and if the song appears to be somehow more than it actually is, chalk one up for McCartney's supervisory care.

This concentration on ramming the point home is both ***Red Rose Speedway***'s strength and weakness, however. **"Medley,"** which takes up 11 minutes of side two, consists of four songs tied together in a slight vignette. The story line is loosely based on the traditionals of a boy-girl relationship—in this case overwrought with a love theme—and the tunes themselves are charming enough in a lightweight sort of way. But *eleven* minutes? Not only could the medley have been easily compressed into a single segment with little loss of narrative flavor, but the net effect of lumping all these eggs in one basket only serves to underscore their individual lack of anything resembling bulk.

The remainder of the album is good, competent McCartney, neither his best nor worst, but solidly constructed material with a flair for creating gems out of the safe and familiar. **"Get on the Right Thing,"** with its ***Abbey Road*** texture, is a sharply synched number that folds nicely into **"One More Kiss,"** a scenario built on the premise of the one-night stand and downplayed letter-perfect. **"Single Pigeon"** is a meager song, not made out to be much more than it really is . . . , while the picks to click of ***Red Rose Speedway*** rest with **"Little Lamb Dragonfly"** and **"When The Night,"** the former soft and sensual with a bit too much reliance on the "la-la-la"'s and the latter a double-edged Paul rocker, featuring his best singing of the album when the group bears down in the coda. . . .

[Despite] expected hits and misses, I find ***Red Rose Speedway*** to be the most overall heartening McCartney product given us since the demise of the Beatles. After much experimentation with how best to present himself, Paul has apparently begun a process of settling down, of working within a band framework that looks to remain stable for at least the next vehicular period.

Lenny Kaye, "Paul Dominates 'Speedway' & Results Are Good," in Rolling Stone, *Issue 138, July 5, 1973, p. 68.*

NOEL COPPAGE

[Paul McCartney] seems the ex-Beatle most likely to become an *ex*-ex-Beatle, to surmount the aftermath. Paul not only has much greater vocal range (and to my ears a more pleasant sound) than the others but is turning out to have rangier vision about arrangements also—and he has the gift of ambiguity. His new tunes *may* sound something like, oh, some **"Rubber Soul"** tunes, and then again they may not. It depends on how you listen. But of course where the gift of ambiguity really pays off is in the lyrics: poetry is what song lyrics aspire to be, and poetry in English is almost by definition ambiguous. . . .

Paul's gift is exercised with some cunning in **"Band on the Run,"** which might be a superb album if ***Let Me Roll It*** didn't sound so tired, ***Bluebird*** weren't so effete and aimless, and ***Helen Wheels*** did not exist. Songs aren't necessarily related to one another, or don't seem to be, but the album does have some fuzzy application of the sonata form (or at least the Side-Two-of-**"Abbey Road"** form) punched into it, and there are all these sneaky little references scattered throughout, so that *one* (not the *only* one, of course, but one) way it can be interpreted is as an attempt to put the Beatles behind him, get the Beatles off his back, bury the Beatles.

It is subtler and less direct than John's attempt has been, to be sure, so subtle that Paul may not be doing it consciously at all. Possibly he isn't doing it at all, period. But there are little things—what does "stuck inside these four walls" in the title song really mean? And what about ***Jet***? Very puzzling, this ***Jet;*** there's something about a sergeant major, a lady suffragette, and a line that goes, "Ah, Mater, want Jet to always love me," which of course sounds as if he's saying "Want ya to always love me." Question: what former Beatle has this loss-of-mother pain to the degree that he underwent "primal scream" therapy and then wrote a raw, agonized song called *Mother*—and wrote another song that was kind of nasty and addressed to Paul?

And yet, if Paul is answering, he is not being openly malicious. ***Jet*** makes no sense at all in any kind of literal reading, but it has powerful tones and is gradually arranged. ***Mrs. Vandebilt*** is another fascinating song, at least in its tricky changes and its doublethink resolution: "What's the use of worrying? / What's the use of hurrying? / What's the use of anything?" There are nice rhythms, Latin and otherwise, scattered about in the album . . . , a curious tribute to Picasso with a snippet from ***Jet*** spliced into it and more reprises in the last few seconds of the last selection. . . .

Smarter people may find God knows what in Paul's cagey revelations, but ambiguity, for all its usefulness, is also a hedge. Paul is moving toward individuality, but whether he's jetting or mostly drifting is not all that clear to me. It is a difficult direction to take, either way, considering the negative pull (on former Beatles, that is) of that black hole where the supernova of the Sixties *was*. (p. 89)

Noel Coppage, "The Ex-Beatles: Surmounting the Aftermath," in Stereo Review *Magazine, Vol. 32, No. 3, March, 1974, pp. 88-9.*

MELODY MAKER

When an artist has just enjoyed a great success with a piece of creative work, there is often a problem in evaluating the next item on the agenda. Comparisons spring all readily to mind, anticipation is keen, and the tendency is to expect fresh miracles. Well, Paul McCartney's triumph with **"Band on the Run,"** which gave birth to hit singles as well as achieving its own artistic and commercial acclaim, crept up on us rather than making instant impact. And I think the same will be true of **"Venus And Mars."** In repeated playings over the past week, new twists, different interpretations have become apparent, and this new collection of songs will eventually sink into the collective rock consciousness and become widely appreciated as another triumph for Wings and their song writing bass player. Not that there aren't some songs that draw swift and easy response. **"Rock Show"** for example is good rocking by any standards. But it might take a little longer for the coyness of **"You Gave Me The Answer,"** to find a niche and take on meaning. And is there a song to compare to **"Band On The Run"** and **"Jet"**? Questions of greatness aside, this is a thoroughly enjoyable album, with a loose thread running through the pieces to which perhaps not too much significance should be attached. As Paul says, the lines of **"Venus And Mars"** which opens proceedings, were inspired by science-fiction, and not any great mystical insight. Nevertheless a pervading mood of cosmic exploration, contrasting waves of pressure and release are hinted at and revealed in songs of love and imagery.

Acoustic guitar rings out for attention in the opening bars, swiftly joined by a flute-like Moog as Paul sings: "Sitting in the stand of a sports arena, waiting for the show to begin, a good friend of mine follows the stars, Venus and Mars are all right tonight . . ." Thus the scene is set for the rock fan, influenced by astrological events, convinced that the omens are good for the **"Rock Show"** which follows. . . . The band rocks with tremendous power during this section, the drums . . . kicking like a mule, and the back-up vocals howling the riff. It drops with barely a pause into **"Love In Song,"** a beautiful ballad that opens with mysterioso chords, Paul singing with simple, spare sincerity. Now here IS a song that compares to anything on **"Band On The Run,"** so questions are being answered for us. Echoing piano introduces **"You Gave Me The Answer,"** and its jolly, swing era feel, complete with strings and muted brass, and Paul singing through a megaphone, takes the Hollywood Bowl tripper back to the thirties. **"Magneto And Titanium Man,"** an intriguing juxtaposition of words, has a lilting beat and interesting chords that take unexpected turns along its melodic course, and the vocal harmonies are once again intoned with loving care. . . .

One of my favourite cuts is the singularly attractive **"Listen To What The Man Said,"** with a swinging, bell-like beat, and marvellous soprano saxophone from Tom Scott of the LA Express. Surely this should be a hit, unless of course the world has gone mad while we've all been out to lunch. **"Treat Her Gently—Lonely Old People,"** has a lilting, country tinged and sentimental flavour that is difficult to resist. . . . Now we can look forward to Wings reproducing the album live on stage. It'll be well worth the effort.

C. W., "Wings: Shooting Stars!" in Melody Maker, *May 31, 1975, p. 22.*

JIM MILLER

Paul McCartney keeps plugging on, concocting spunky songs, fiddling around in the studio for special effects, refining an original commercial style. . . .

[Melody] is the name of his game. Compared to Lennon's functional use of rock, McCartney's harmonic language is positively lush. He is one of the few pop writers who cheerfully throws melodies away, prefacing a track like **"Band on the Run"** with a beautiful introductory sub-song.

And throwaway may be the most apt description: a sparkling tune like **"My Love"** sports a sodden lyric that would make even John Denver blush. When he's not penning obtuse or cutesy-pie romps, McCartney hews to a strict Moon-June diet, writing romantic swill that is safe enough to win Grammies, sticky enough to turn the Thames into champagne.

A pretty gooey equation, admittedly, but the element of craftsmanship promises to get McCartney places other popstars only aspire to, even while his lyrical maunderings prevent him from expressing anything that might possibly matter, beyond the ideology of lovey-dovey bliss. Still, in ***Band on the Run,*** recorded in Lagos, Nigeria, with a rhythm section that cooked, McCartney proved that he could glue all the right components together. Eschewing his usual clever antics, he served up an uncluttered disk of pop, McCartney-style, with few frills and considerable sophistication.

It is somewhat unnerving, then, to find McCartney on ***Venus and Mars*** reverting to pre-***Band*** form, with an insipid collection of finely-polished rockers, love songs and music hall muck. Part of the problem is the band, which sounds lugubrious when it should sound heavy (**"Letting Go"**). The plodding tracks aren't helped by McCartney's vocals, either, dogged by a strained raunchiness, they are often recorded in a halo of reverb and echo. . . .

But what finally sinks this set is McCartney's penchant for the coy gesture, a nagging trait which crops up in **"Rock Show,"** and makes **"Magneto and Titanium Man"** a trying study in cuteness. Both of these tracks boast the usual assortment of spectacular melodies, especially **"Magneto,"** but who wants to get down with "the Crimson Dynamo?" For fans of McCartney's famed vaudeville megaphone simulation, there's even a candy-coated item called **"You Gave Me the Answer."**

This kind of arch cleverness ruins pop-rock, and reduces craftsmanship to a big stakes shell game. Does the cocktail swing of **"Listen to What the Man Said"** conceal our friend the solitary pea, or is using Tom Scott for saxophone obbligatos like burying a shell within a shell?

McCartney, I'm sure, will be back to fight another day. But for the moment, ***Venus and Mars*** suggests that there's no substitute for a little intuition and sense of immediacy when it comes to rock 'n' roll. John Lennon brought precisely these qualities to the Beatles: that's why they were great. On his own, however, McCartney, like the other ex-Beatles, continues to drift, with dreary predictability, from sterile pop to arthritic rock. The few exceptions, such as McCartney's ***Band on the Run*** and Lennon's *Plastic Ono Band,* only prove the rule—a rule all too amply illustrated by ***Venus and Mars.***

Jim Miller, "Paulie in the Land of The Bland," in Creem, *Vol. 7, No. 4, September, 1975, p. 66.*

LESTER BANGS

There is more of [the McCartneys'] cloying connubial narcissism on their latest outing, **"Venus and Mars Are Alright Tonight,"** and astute observers will note that Paul's even thrown in an astrological hook this time, a little late in the day to be sure, but still it shows that Paulie is thinking. And, as usual, he is thinking more about music and production than about lyrics. **"Venus and Mars"** is basically an addendum to **"Band on the Run,"** and it consolidates Wings' position as the most proficient and diverting bland-out on the boards. Previous to the last record, McCartney had been in danger of becoming so pallid musically (**"Red Rose Speedway"** comes to mind easily, though its contents are forgotten) as to fade away altogether. But with **"Band"** he achieved a perfect synthesis of the puerile and the catchy—a classic pop throwaway. And so, since no one should now rightfully expect McCartney to "matter" in the Dylan-Joni Mitchell sense, there is absolutely no excuse for slagging poor **"Venus and Mars"** just because it has all the same melodic ingredients that have endeared him to the relevancy-swamped twit that lives in all of us. The title track is winsome and wistful; ***Rock Show*** is gutsy in a ***Band on the Run*** vein; ***Magneto and Titanium Man*** is one of those loose, loping, half-talked and half-sung progressions (check **"Ram"**'s ***Smile Away***); and the hit single, ***Listen to What the Man Said,*** is really magnificent beauty-parlor music.

So what if ***You Gave Me the Answer*** is Paul's most cloying quasi-Twenties megaphone-fey truffle yet. . . . Can't all you rude infidels and ruffians out there see the *point* and *true meaning* of these little ditties, that everything is, indeed, *fine*? . . .

[The] reader must bear in mind that none of this is meant as deprecation; on the contrary, facelessness is the *business* of Wings, and their recent success at it has been nothing short of dazzling.

This critic has read not a few recent reviews in these pages in which the root complaint was that the album under examination was just a piece of "product" put out by an artist indifferent or half-dead but propped up by slick production and session musicians. How refreshing, then, to note that Paul McCartney is *not* indifferent, that he is very much alive—and shrewd enough to turn *himself* into a glossy kingpin among session men. You may find a little dust in the grooves of Wings' product, but never in its soul: it's a *clean* machine—with Linda, of course, lending to the figurine on the radiator cap the radiant sarcasm of her smile.

Lester Bangs, "Paul and Linda: Alright Tonight," in Stereo Review *Magazine, Vol. 35, No. 4, October, 1975, p. 82.*

BOB KIRSCH

[**"At The Speed Of Sound"**] is not a spectacular album in the same sense that **"Band on the Run,"** with its almost perfect sense of commerciality and its several monster hit singles, was a spectacular album.

In the long run, however, this deceptively easy to listen to set may be recognized as one of McCartney and company's better overall efforts.

For a start, **"At The Speed Of Sound,"** unlike the group's **"Venus & Mars,"** is a set of songs. Whereas **"Venus & Mars"** strayed a bit too far into the realm of concept, the new work professes to be nothing more than a solid collection of listenable songs. And the concept works. . . .

As for the unspectacular nature of the album, the majority of the cuts are easy, mid-tempo rockers that do not have the instant impact of a **"Jet"** or a **"Band on the Run."** But several of the songs here are among the best McCartney has come up with, with their deceptively easy sound contributing to their appeal.

"Let 'Em In," "She's My Baby" and **"Silly Love Songs"** are the standouts in the "easy" vein. All three incorporate catchy melodies that are easy to remember and listenable. . . .

McCartney's most impressive vocal outing on the set comes in **"Beware My Love,"** probably the best "rocker" he's cut since his days with the Beatles. It has long been a criticism of McCartney that he spends too much time on cute, mid-tempo or ballad numbers and not enough on uptempo material.

"Beware My Love" is a song that displays McCartney's talents in handling a rock number and his equal talents in producing and arranging such numbers. . . .

"Warm And Beautiful," which closes the set, is one of those almost patented McCartney love songs and will undoubtedly pull in a number of cover versions. The most impressive quality on this album, however, is the almost universal appeal that a group of good, solid songs can have when handled as skillfully as they are here.

Bob Kirsch, in a review of "At the Speed of Sound," in Billboard, *Vol. 88, No. 16, April 17, 1976, p. 80.*

STEPHEN HOLDEN

In his post-Beatles albums, Paul McCartney has proven himself a clever miniaturist whose records resemble collages built around simple musical fragments, each of which is painstakingly produced. While some have dismissed McCartney's music as insufferably cute, uninspired trivia, all of his albums contain at least some worthwhile music. . . .

Paul McCartney became the most commercially successful of the four lads by developing into a bravura producer/arranger (especially of singles) as well as a genteel pop archivist devoted to fusing his contribution to the Beatles legacy with mainstream pop. For latter-day McCartney, the megaphone, the brass band and the seedy English music hall tradition are parts of the same musical equation as rock & roll: pop and pop only.

Venus and Mars, the last Wings album, was a collection of miniature pop love songs, deliberately tricked out with kiddie sci-fi and comic love lyrics. It was whimsical romantic entertainment concocted on the premise that a lot of good pop music carries no literary or mythical portent whatever. But within its frivolous schema, McCartney systematically explored the textural dimensions of conventional pop music sounds.

At the Speed of Sound doggedly continues in the same vein, but with much less effervescence. Where ***Venus and Mars*** was framed by the astrological motif, ***At the Speed of Sound*** ostensibly invites the listener to spend a day with McCartney and Wings—a day in which the listener is gently harangued as well as entertained.

"Let 'Em In" begins with door-knocking sound effects, out of which steps a marching band. Like most of the rest, **"Let 'Em In"** puts a simple musical theme through carefully arranged changes. The melodic idea is small, but quintessentially McCartneyesque in its provincial jollity.

With the electronic soup-slurping sounds that open side two, one notes that it is almost time for lunch on this imaginary visiting day. But first the McCartneys answer those critics who lashed out at ***Venus and Mars***'s lovebird verses with a tract in defense of moon, June and spoon, **"Silly Love Songs."** It's a clever retort whose point is well taken; the center of the song focuses on the syllables "I love you," which Paul and Linda reiterate with the insistence of phonetics instructors, weaving the phrase through a disarmingly lovely three-part chorus. (p. 67)

If **"Silly Love Songs"** is acceptably didactic, the album's closing number, **"Warm and Beautiful,"** pushes the point too far. . . . [The] ultrasimple melody and lyrics suggest a parody of Lennon's "Love," serving up, with apparent sincerity, the stalest pop ballad clichés ever to emerge from an English music hall. Perhaps McCartney is trying to remind us that these tiresome clichés might well outlast the pop music many critics call art. Or perhaps it is an attempt to transcend cliché by being the biggest cliché. Or perhaps **"Warm and Beautiful"** is simply one of the worst songs Paul McCartney has ever written.

While there is much to admire on ***At the Speed of Sound,*** it is contained in the production more than the material. Ultimately, this album lacks the melodic sparkle of ***Venus and Mars,*** which in its turn lacked the energy, passion and structural breadth and unity of ***Band on the Run,*** Wings' finest album. . . . As a whole, ***At the Speed of Sound*** seems like a mysterious, somewhat defensive oddity by a great pop producer who used to be a great pop writer. Like all McCartney and Wings records, ***At the Speed of Sound*** is spectacularly well arranged and recorded, with McCartney continuing to demonstrate his special affinity for using brass in surprising and witty ways. The playing is laboratory perfect. McCartney, like almost no one else, seems able to play the studio as an instrument. Though it's a wonderful gift, I hope it doesn't distract him from songwriting more than it already has. For the best McCartney songs will most certainly outlast all the studios in which they were recorded. (p. 69)

Stephen Holden, "On The Wings of Silly Love Songs," in Rolling Stone, *Issue 213, May 20, 1976, pp. 67, 69.*

MITCHELL GLAZER

Paul had promised us "shit hot rocking," but all we have [in ***At the Speed of Sound***] is the shit. . . . Of course, the problem with any Paul McCartney release comes in comparing it with that Paul McCartney album in the sky, the perfect hard/harmonic object which came teasingly within reach on ***Band on the Run***. . . .

[Although] he constantly reminds us it's a real band he's after, Paul's most intriguing albums were without one. The rough, casual quality of the first lp, with its naked guitar and basic percussion, nicely offset Paul's silky crooner voice. The joyous **"Maybe I'm Amazed"** was as real and special a love song as any he'd sung; and he played alone. It was as if all the gossipy, backstabbing frustration and hidden music found release in new melodies. There was a restraint I had never expected from Paul.

The other album he recorded practically *sans* band was the dazzling ***Band on the Run***. Now *this* was "shit hot rocking." The sound was frighteningly full considering McCartney played drums, keyboards, bass, and some guitar. This album took balls, and if he hadn't made it we could have sat back and said that maybe in his middle age Paul had simply forgotten he could play anything raunchier than acoustic semi-French love songs. Two years later, the epic title track still stands alone as unself-conscious rock thunder.

The point is, *Paul* made these albums. He undoubtedly controlled all the others, but on ***McCartney*** and ***Band on the Run***, Paul was forced to extend himself, and with the pressure on, he hit the jump-shot from the top of the key.

At the Speed of Sound is an airball. With everyone getting a song, this is the closest thing to a *Wings* album yet. **"Silly Love Songs,"** the single, is Van McCartney's Hustle. It begins with sound effects, which can be construed as a chain gang pounding out a "hit"; it's that original a song. There's a nice popping disco beat and those soothing McCartney vocals, but compared to the fury of ***Band on the Run***, it's just cute. . . .

Several times while listening to this lp, I've found myself muttering, "he's *got* to be kidding." **"She's My Baby,"** a bouncy, affecting song, actually quotes **"She's a Woman,"** dooming itself in comparison. **"Warm And Beautiful"** was lifted almost entirely from my high school Alma Mater. . . .

The record has all the packaging and sound effects of a concept album—only the concept is missing. Paul's inconsistency is scary. ***Band on the Run*** and ***Venus and Mars*** promised screeching success for Wings; unfortunately, ***Speed of Sound*** doesn't move at all. For the moment, Paul is "the man of a thousand voices standing perfectly still."

Mitchell Glazer, "Asleep at the Wing," in Crawdaddy, *June, 1976, p. 65.*

ROBERT DUNCAN

Speed of Sound is the nadir. With one exception, "Time To Hide," which was written and sung by ex-Moody Blue Denny Laine, the songs here exist in an intellectual and emotional vacuum, which McCartney calls love. To paraphrase someone: With love like *this*, who needs hate?!? And, furthermore, he has the balls to get defensive about it in a tune called **"Silly Love Songs"**! . . . Admittedly, love can be a wondrous and fulfilling thing, but it can also be other things that just aren't summed up by the repetition of the words "I love you."

For one thing, love can be tortuous. McCartney must know this now. The song that follows **"Silly Love Songs"** is Linda's debut as a lead vocalist. She cannot sing by any stretch. And Paul had to produce it (it's also his composition). Try though he may to bury her voicelessness in reverb and a rough, early '50s mix, he cannot make **"Cook of the House"** rise above the intolerable pain level. Now *that* effort was love—for Linda at least. Paul doesn't seem to care much about his listeners; they're the ones who have to shell out the money to listen to his sonic home movie.

The rest of the album—again, with Laine's song the exception—consists of the half-baked ideas that are becoming standard for McCartney. There are moments that are good; McCartney is so talented that intermittently he *has* to stumble into something we can like. (Frustrating, ain't it?) **"Beware My Love"** builds into a good hook, but falls flat because at this point in time, and especially in the context of this LP, a pained McCartney rings false. **"Let 'em In"** has an intriguing melancholy about it that is never explained—basically Paul recites names throughout—and never resolved either lyrically or musically, in the end just kind of floating past us without impact. . . .

I don't really care to speculate at this late date on what fame and fortune can do to talent; the point is, Paul McCartney continues to squander himself.

Robert Duncan, "5 Dead in Air Disaster!" in Creem, *Vol. 8, No. 1, June, 1976, p. 56.*

SCOTT ISLER

Paul McCartney is living proof there's life after Beatles. George and Ringo coast on afterglow; John plays the recluse; only Mac is in the swing as active musician and, more importantly, band member. For Wings has truly outgrown its son-of-Beatles status to become a hit-making aggregation in its own right; some of the band's younger fans might even be unaware the bassist was in an earlier group. Paul may symbolize Wings, but Wings is more than McCartney.

Leisurely recorded over the space of a year. . . , ***London Town*** doesn't quite hit with the immediacy of a musical depth charge. That never was Wings' way. McCartney's original sin is to charm everyone into submission (if not nausea) via a highly-polished music so free of edges it can serve as an aural worry stone. One could argue we all need some roughage in our diet, Wings being as nutritional as cotton candy. And McCartney at his most excessive does seem to be writing more for elevators and "mellow" rock stations (bane of the '70s) than for serious listening. Yet the kitsch is never artless, and in the narrow field of melodic pop Wings must be acknowledged as leaders of the pack.

London Town defines the best and the worst in Wings' approach. The title track is a quietly introspective number—all appealing electric piano and vocal harmonies—dealing with the "ordinary people" Paul loves but can never seem to relate to. The following song, **"Cafe on the Left Bank,"** treats jet-set ennui ("Dancing after midnight . . . Continental breakfast in the bar") Mac's undoubtedly familiar with but the rest of us schmucks can't relate to. The gently rocking **"Cafe"** unfortunately defines, with **"London Town,"** the rhythmic parameters of this album. Laid-back toe-tapping is certainly permissible, but among ***London Town***'s 14 . . . selections exceptions to the prevailing moderate tempo are too rare. . . .

McCartney is so blessed in the melody-making department he may not even realize other aspects of the music are going to seed. No one's ever accused him of being a subtle lyricist, for example. **"With a Little Luck," "I've Had Enough"** and **"Don't Let It Bring You Down"** are all, as the titles indicate, pure platitude. The latter is especially endearing: "Should the sand of time run out on you / Don't let it bring you down" is a cute variant on the adage of death being nature's way of telling you to slow down. The music hall-styled **"Famous Groupies"** reflects Mac's giggly sense of humor. . . . While it would take a hard heart to resist the lullaby-like endearments of **"I'm Carrying,"** only three of the album's many songs deal with romantic subject matter; Paul was once a master of genre.

The trouble with Wings' dewy-eyed sensitivity is it's too easy to misinterpret as blandness. They probably can't relate to fashionable nihilism; this unrelentingly gloomless lp, however, is almost too slick for its own good. . . .

The album's highlights are self-evident. Easily the most intriguing number, **"Morse Moose and the Grey Goose"** boasts an ambitious arrangement and jazzy counter-rhythms; by contrast its folky narrative is delivered in a declamatory Brothers Four style. **"Don't Let It Bring You Down,"** whatever its lyric failings , is an effective blend of eerie vocal, winding Celtish melody and ternary beat. . . .

Clocking in at over 50 minutes, one can't accuse Wings of not delivering value for money—in terms of quantity, anyway. What's frustrating about ***London Town*** is the sense of holding back, marking time reflected in the lp's unhurried preparation. . . . Now that McCartney has worked the slower songs out of his system, perhaps he'll swing back toward a rocker's equilibrium. You're not too old, Paul.

Scott Isler, "Mulling over McCartney," in Crawdaddy, *June, 1978, p. 69.*

TOBY GOLDSTEIN

I'll tell you what's wrong with silly love songs. Too often they degenerate into terminal wimpiness. Wings's last studio album, the 1976 **"At the Speed of Sound,"** was rife with this brand of melodic milk as particularly manifested in the above-mentioned smash single. But perhaps the intervening two years and the group's world tour have toughened up Paul McCartney's compositional abilities along with his gifted fingers.

Or perhaps it's the departure of two members and a jolly, productive month recording on shipboard in the Virgin Islands. In any case, **"London Town"** exhibits a sense of purpose Wings hasn't shown since their divine **"Band on the Run."** It is actually a new McCartney release, since Paul takes production credit, sings all the lead vocals, and writes everything himself or with guitarist Denny Laine. Fortunately, he is neither tempted by accessible blandness nor pressured to compose immediate hits, his two nemeses on **"Speed of Sound."** There are probably fewer hit-bound tracks on this fifty-minute disc than on Wings's last several, but it may be a far better album because of that.

"London Town" runs a musical gamut that stretches from the familiar attractive McCartney ballads to cuts that bear a reggae lilt, tunes with the superficial gaiety of a music hall, and, most fortunately, several numbers that recall his Beatle belting days. And both ***I've Had Enough*** and ***Name and Address*** are exact opposites of past easy repetitions of "I love you and rock & roll," exhibiting a new willingness to write angry lyrics. Lines such as "I earn the money and you take it away," and "Maybe loving you is more than one man can do" may not insure domestic tranquility in the McCartney household, but their expression of real, complex feelings makes him a more complete artist.

At the same time, one couldn't imagine a Wings album without its positive statements, best exemplified here by ***With a Little Luck.*** This song manages to convey restrained optimism. . . .

"London Town" skillfully blends immediately accessible songs with those whose meaning becomes clear only after repeated exposure. Never on any McCartney album has a lyric sheet been as absolutely necessary, for without it, the deceivingly slow-paced ***Famous Groupies***' extraordinary words might be lost. This is a number that's sure to have the gossipmongers analyzing who its subject(s) might be. One thing's for sure—McCartney has moved far beyond simple rhyming. He uses that technique only once, on ***Children Children,*** which is best accepted as a nursery rhyme.

He admits, "Hey, did you know that I'm always going back in time . . . I'm the backwards traveller," echoing a plea he made a full decade ago on the Beatles' White album. "Can you take me back where I came from?" On **"London Town,"** he at last recalls where he came from, after having reconstructed the interim years in a manner suitable to his current interests. He easily could have subtitled this LP "Revolution Number 10."

Toby Goldstein, "'London Town': So What's Wrong with Silly Love Songs?" in High Fidelity, *Vol. 28, No. 7, July, 1978, p. 120.*

CAROL FLAKE

Paul McCartney has been down on the farm for almost a decade now. His steady output of pleasant songs indicates he's not yet in his dotage, but he hasn't done much more in recent years than advertise his pastoral domesticity. . . . [What] Wings has hatched with ***Back to the Egg*** is mostly shell, nicely decorated.

Although side one is cheerily labeled "Sunny Side Up," the overall effect is actually rather cold; if not hard-boiled. The harsh, blaring fanfare of the first cut, **"Reception,"** renders the title ironic. Similarly, a forlorn, melancholy tone belies the invitation implied in **"We're Open Tonight."** Other cuts rock more stridently than the usual McCartney. **"Old Siam, Sir,"** a catchy, thumping Oriental conceit that suggests heavy metal chopsticks, and **"Spin It On,"** which jolts with three-chord monotony and bravado, seem to spin off and spoof new wave in turn. . . . More characteristic of McCartney's whimsical pop optimism is **"Getting Closer,"** an exuberant apostrophe to his **"Salamander,"** presumably an amphibious siren of great charm. . . .

[The] "Over Easy" side begins to cohere thematically and melodically with **"After the Ball."** There are flashes of McCartney at his best, with simple, bittersweet pop melodies elaborated with bright filigrees of harmony. Each song is a fugal fragment which seems to segue naturally into the next. **"After the Ball"** is a stately blues waltz which might be interpreted as a tribute to his wife, who came along just after the height of the Beatles' euphoria. **"Million Miles,"** which follows, sounds like a simple gospel refrain, accompanied by a plaintive squeezebox. . . . The pensive mood breaks into unmitigated joy, however, with **"Love Awake,"** another of McCartney's rapturous anthems on the theme of love as the magic moly. As in ***London Town***'s **"A Little Luck,"** he's implying that love is a mode of change which can bring about renewal. That he's talking about faith, hope, and community as well as connubial bliss becomes explicit in the corny voice-over of passages from Ian Hay's "The Sport of Kings" and "The Little Man" by John Galsworthy, recited as portentously as a Monty Python parody.

As usual, McCartney is embracing the old-fashioned virtues of fortitude and altruism. In fact, **"So Glad To See You Here,"** which follows, is a kind of gentle exhortation on pulling one's weight, as well as sharing. The song intimates a widening of the family circle, and seems to offer a welcome to the world at large. The refrain from **"We're Open Tonight"** is repeated, but this time with sincerity. This is not a blissed-out vision of cosmic togetherness, as in **"All You Need Is Love,"** but a more restrained and measured pronouncement, philosophically speaking.

This is a self-indulgent album, fragmented and often hokey; it's also a message from a good family man who has continued to grow personally, if not musically. . . . It may be premature to speculate on such things, but it appears that McCartney may become one of the few giants of rock 'n' roll to survive gracefully and ripen into a grand, sentimental old man.

Carol Flake, "Message from the Eggman," in The Village Voice, *Vol. XXIV, No. 36, September 3, 1979, p. 66.*

JON TIVEN

[Paul McCartney happens] to be one of the most creative, unpredictable, and musical figures in pop music today, not to mention one of the most successful. . . . Although his last single ***Goodnight Tonight*** was disco (quite unhip in most critical circles, unless the artist is other than caucasian), [***Back to the Egg***] should win him some sort of critical approval as there are plenty of rock numbers and they're all played in the top of each side's sequence. (p. 154)

Personally, I'd agree that the album is a notch over ***London Town*** but not much more, as McCartney's albums have been consistently enjoyable. . . . The album is slightly less experimental musically than its predecessors, although sonically it reaches for new heights of density—McCartney & Co. go for a band sound on about half the tracks, and the Macca Magick works best when he rocks out (***Getting Closer, Old Siam, Sir***). I must say, however, that the quieter moments on the album aren't quite up to par for the man, and he seems to have restrained his love of synthesizers, at least for the moment. This particular Wings shows great promise, and ***Back to the Egg*** is an excellent album—but I hadn't expected less, and somehow with McCartney's continuing ascension of musical standards one hopes for an even greater geometrical progression once this line-up gels. (p. 156)

Jon Tiven, in a review of "Back to the Egg," in Audio, *Vol. 63, No. 10, October, 1979, pp. 154, 156.*

TOM CARSON

What makes most of [Paul McCartney's] post-Beatles work maddening isn't its validity or lack of it as pop—although even on those terms, it's wildly uneven—but Paul's insistence that this is all there is; there isn't any more. After all, there's no law to say that commercial pop has to be reductive, "mere" pop—it's McCartney alone who sets those limits.

McCartney II is the first time he's come close to explaining why. Musically, it's a much more cogent and intelligent experiment than that blithely shoddy rec-room epic, ***McCartney***. Wingsless—and with even la lovely Linda exiled to no more than backing vocals on **"Coming Up"**—Paul's created a sparse, beep-and-buzz minimalism whose near-static textures and functional strangeness stem directly from *Another Green World* and Eno's collaborations with Bowie. But if the music suggests Eno percolated down to middlebrow level, the lyrics' suggestive obliqueness read like poptones gone darkly askew. Of course, McCartney's work has been so resolutely sunny that any hint of shadow has more resonance than anyone else's murk. For all its purposeful innocuousness, the unspoken constant of this album is dread—a fear of going out of control if you peek over the edge of the abyss for even a minute. **"Silly Love Songs"** was McCartney's manifesto, but ***McCartney II*** is his rationale for having avoided the abyss. So the record has an emotional credibility unlike anything he's ever done: mere popmasters don't need rationales.

The hints come as no more than pinpricks—but the whole album is made up of such pinpricks. Most of the cuts, even when they aren't overtly children's songs, still follow the form—basic-English rhymes, circular melodies, singsong choruses—and that simplicity gives them their power. If nothing is more nostalgia-inducing than childhood innocence, nothing is more primitive than childhood fears, and McCartney plays on both. This framework not only tightens up his writing, but makes his sentimentality both appropriate and evocative: you sense the unknown lurking behind each bald line. The complete lyrics to **"Summer's Day Song,"** for instance, run as follows: "Someone's sleeping / Through a bad dream / Tomorrow it will be over / For the world will soon be waking / To a summer's day." Repeated again and again in a frail voice, over immobile, empty-cathedral keyboards, the words themselves become the nightmare—you can't wait to be released, you don't believe you ever will be.

Beneath its limpid surface, the album builds up a queasy undertow that ultimately takes over. **"Temporary Secretary"**'s simpering request for "someone strong and sweet fitting on my knee" may sound gratingly smug at first, but the yammering chorus is intentionally abrasive, and Paul's lecherous Benny Hill drawl in the bridge—"Well I know how hard it is for young girls these days . . . to stay on the right track"—subverts the whole song. **"Nobody Knows"** starts off as a shuffling parody of the know-nothingism McCartney's so often charged with, but by the end, with Paul drunkenly gurgling, "And that's the way I like it, yeah," from the bottom of the mix, you could almost be listening to Randy Newman doing "My Old Kentucky Home."

Still more personal, but finally as elusive, is the doomy **"On the Way."** . . . [The] song's tension lies in what's missing; when McCartney casually admits, "Though I said some things to hurt you / It was only out of fear," he sounds as blandly rational as Norman Bates. This brief, quiet song is, finally, chilling—the story of a man so determined to make his dream of a sentimental pop romance come true that he might have to omit the girl in order to save it.

It makes sense that even as McCartney reveals himself more than ever before, he conceals himself the most, altering and filtering his own multiply-overdubbed voice, using a panoply of distancing sound effects. . . . Just how important these distancing devices are is obvious when you compare the LP's **"Coming Up"** to the live Wings version; Columbia may have decided that McCartney ought to sound like McCartney, but the electronically induced falsetto and tiny distortion effects are what make the studio cut more than an infectious disposable.

Besides **"On the Way,"** the two songs that make up the heart of ***McCartney II*** are **"One of These Days"** and **"Waterfalls."** The former is a wistful tune about returning to the simple life that hits home because it suggests that McCartney hasn't been able to; but **"Waterfalls"**—graced with an impossibly slow piano melody that's more implied than heard—is the album's real keynote. Within what sounds like a lullaby for his kids, McCartney confesses his fear of the world, conveying both an unbearably vivid sense of the dangers it holds, and a painful yearning for a safety he can't take for granted. It's both a warning and a plea for compassion—almost, even, for a forgiveness which he's never before conceded he ought to ask. Will the remotest hint of these preoccupations show up on the next Wings album? Don't be silly.

Tom Carson, "Paul McCartney Is Afraid of the Dark," in The Village Voice, *Vol. XXV, No. 27, July 2-8, 1980, p. 45.*

STEPHEN HOLDEN

McCartney II is an album of aural doodles designed for the amusement of very young children. . . . As his own one-man band, McCartney doesn't try to imitate Wings or re-create the precious atmosphere of his first solo LP, now ten years old. Most of the songs are merely sound effects. Instead of developing melodic themes, the star simply supplies hypnotic little hooks, which are then played off one another and "treated" —i.e., filtered, reverbed, phased—to make strident electronic junk music.

It should hardly be a surprise that ***McCartney II*** is really about pop sound and nothing else. Ever since **"Silly Love Songs,"** his 1976 manifesto proclaiming rock's essence to be frivolous, Paul McCartney has acted on his beliefs with a vengeance. Both ***Back to the Egg*** and the new album imply that, for this ex-Beatle, silliness—no longer even the love song!—is the only worthwhile pop form. And as novelties go, ***McCartney II*** is passable. Its catchiest numbers make the singer's voice sound like a cross between an insect and a windup toy.

"Coming Up," a push-button paean to the future, outdoes Abba in nervous, hook-filled mechanization. Even if you hate it, it's liable to stick to your mind like chewing gum to the bottom of a shoe. In **"Temporary Secretary,"** the title phrase is robotically chirped until the syllables become a computer abstraction. . . . **"Summer's Day Song"** frames a fragment of an old English air in Eno-style wooziness. In the more conventional cuts—the slow and bluesy **"On the Way,"** the funereal **"Waterfalls,"** McCartney's vocals still sound disembodied, as if they were phoned in from far away.

Does ***McCartney II*** advance the cause of the novelty tune? Alas, no. **"Bogey Music,"** which stretches the pun on *boogie* ad nauseum, isn't half so clever or terse as Sheb Wooley's classic "Purple People Eater." **"Darkroom"** is cluttered compared to its immortal prototypes, "The Chipmunk Song" and "Alvin's Harmonica," by David Seville and the Chipmunks. But perhaps that's the point. Nonsense being nonsense, the novelty track is theoretically the most timeless of all pop idioms. There are no ideas to worry about if all you have to say is "goo-goo" and "da-da." Or, in McCartney-ese: "Everybody bogey / Dig that bogey beat."

Stephen Holden, "Paul McCartney Hits a New Low-Again," in Rolling Stone, *Issue 322, July 24, 1980, p. 54.*

JON TIVEN AND SALLY TIVEN

[***McCartney II***] is the first Paul McC album that even John & Yoko are certain to enjoy. Self-indulgent to the nth degree, McCartney manages to bring a warmth and genuine lunacy to disc which sounds primarily as if this album was created simply for the sake of fun. . . . The songs are somewhat disjointed and often devoid of commercial intent, yet McCartney's native melodic gift and ingrained sense of what is likable make ***McCartney II*** a highly listenable work practically all of the way through. (pp. 64-5)

For my money the best tune on the record is a fun rock/R&B pile-driver called ***Nobody Knows*** which shuffles along joyously, despite some rather rough drumming from Mr. McC. The single ***Coming Up*** is quite amusing. . . . Paul does his best imitation of Emmitt Rhoades-meets-B.B. King called ***On the Way,*** tries his hand at New Wave with a cute rewrite of ***Paperback Writer*** renamed ***Temporary Secretary,*** and even delves into the roots of his beginnings with a slight tongue in cheek number entitled ***Bogey Music.***

The main difference between this and a Wings album is a less-slick presentation and a tendency not to try to be predictable, hinted at in previous works such as ***Backwards Traveller*** and ***Goodnight Tonight.*** I can't see him going on in this direction for any length of time, but as a break between Wings albums, it's certainly an interesting set of diversions and shows his continual growth as a songwriter in a slightly different perspective. (p. 65)

Jon Tiven and Sally Tiven, in a review of "McCartney II," in Audio, *Vol. 64, No. 8, August, 1980, pp. 64-5.*

PETER REILLY

From the beginning I've felt that [Paul McCartney] was probably the *nicest* of the four Beatles. I also felt that his songs and performances had the true popular romantic touch of an unpretentious man. Nothing that has happened since has changed my mind about these two perceptions. As a matter of fact, his new solo album **"McCartney II"** on Columbia only reinforces them. . . .

My first impression [of **"McCartney II"**] . . . was that I was listening to the aural equivalent of a scrapbook compiled by the father of a pleasantly prosperous middle-class English family. Pa McCartney, like any other proper Englishman, has his hobby; in his case, it's pottering about the recording studio instead of the garden. That out of this pottering should come an internationally best-selling hit record shouldn't be any more of a surprise than that, say, a retiring country minister should decide to write some little stories to amuse one of his young friends and they should turn out to be the imperishable classic the whole world knows as *Alice in Wonderland.*

McCartney, no matter what he meant at one time to the youth of the world, has clearly been for some time now something of an anomaly in the helter-skelter world that he helped (probably through no conscious intention of his own) build. He's very, very English, no matter how international the past fifteen years have been for him; he's contentedly middle-class, no matter what vast sums of money have been dumped at his feet. And as a middle-class, middle-brow Englishman he doesn't seem to feel the least uncomfortable with shamelessly loving his wife and his child, enjoying domestic life, or experiencing remorse over his recent pot bust in Japan rather than the angry defiance most of his peers would have expressed.

And so he kicks up his heels in a mild way, for his own amusement and that of his family, in his new album. I'm sure there are at least a hundred private, inside jokes scattered about through it, and that most of them will remain mysteries to you and to me unless their author decides to explain them some day. I have a suspicion that he's doing some sort of parody of a Britisher's idea of an American accent in ***Temporary Secretary*** and that there is a certain ambiguity about ***Frozen Jap*** and ***Summer's Day Song,*** but not being privy to the whole joke didn't detract one iota from my enjoyment. . . .

There are few people working in pop today who have the ease, the style, or the nonchalance to make an album such as **"McCartney II."** To take it too seriously would be to spoil its intent, which is to entertain. To dismiss it as merely cute would be to regress to the pretentious, patronizing past when we had to taste blood (*blood,* I tell you!) before we would deign to accept anything as "real." . . . [**"McCartney II"**] is an album made for the pleasure and edification of a family, their friends, and their well-wishers, not to "show" anybody anything. After listening to it, I feel that I have actually gotten to know them—gotten to know them a whole lot better—and that my first impressions about them were entirely correct. Good show, McCartneys!

Peter Reilly, "Paul McCartney," in Stereo Review *Magazine, Vol. 45, No. 3, September, 1980, p. 94.*

JIM MILLER

The first few seconds of **"Tug of War"** telegraph its ambition. We hear a murmur of voices—and we dimly remember the same sounds at the outset of that most giddy of magical mystery tours, Paul McCartney's grandest conceit as a Beatle, **"Sgt. Pepper."** There the sounds are of an expectant crowd. On **"Tug of War,"** however, they suggest two teams struggling against each other, playing the children's game that gives this album its title and theme. It's a gesture that takes a while to sink in. Scarcely anyone any longer hangs on every sound recorded by the cutest and most commercially successful of the former Beatles. He's become a world-class entertainer. Sgt. Pepper he's not. That is one measure of McCartney's peculiar burden. Now there is another—the death of John Lennon, his dear friend from youth, his emotional ballast and musical alter ego, the fellow Beatle who excoriated him in song as a vain man with a knack for Muzak, the one person who might clear the record.

On **"Tug of War,"** McCartney does something surprising: he tries to unburden himself. Among other things, his new album is a gilded souvenir of the old Beatles magic, a tribute to a fallen friend and, above all, an act of self-justification that aims, through the indirection of art, to allay McCartney's sorrow, guilt and any lingering doubts about his own musical genius. An album with something to prove, it suggests just how much McCartney has left out of a solo career built on whimsy and fluff. For example: depth and complexity of sentiment, a sustained attention to musical detail, the burning ambition to make records that *mean* something. And because the new album does mean something, it stands as his artistic vindication.

He has produced a melancholy masterpiece. The heart of the album belongs to two songs that convey his feelings for John Lennon. The title track, **"Tug of War,"** sets a scene of titanic struggle with a vaulting melody and sonorous orchestral arrangement. **"Here Today"** strikes a more somber, intimate note, using a string quartet straight out of **"Yesterday."** . . .

For the most part, McCartney stays squarely within a finished musical style that is unabashedly conservative—and uniquely his own. There is something oddly brave, and defiant, in that. There are several moments of pure musical joy: McCartney's gut-string guitar solo on **"Dress Me Up as a Robber,"** his lyrical use of vocal harmony on **"Take It Away,"** his electrifying shifts of mood on **"The Pound Is Sinking,"** his bittersweet duet with Carl Perkins on **"Get It."** But the over-all impression, which gathers force on repeated listenings, is of an ineffable ache, strangely exalted in song. Offhand fragments of lyrics begin to seem like candy-coated shrapnel: "feeling quite appalling," "lonely drive," "sole survivor," "somebody has taken the wheels off your car." The album's sense of sadness casts a pall over McCartney's one sunny anthem [**"Ebony and Ivory"**]. A duet with Stevie Wonder, it's the last song on the record—a dippy lyric set to a bright, catchy tune: "Ebony and ivory / Live together in perfect harmony / Side by side on my piano keyboard / Oh Lord, why don't we?"

Well, now, human beings aren't keys, music isn't the world—and for once, it sounds as if Paul McCartney perfectly well knows all that. Perhaps that's why **"Tug of War"** is such a touching tour de force. A song cycle to stand beside such rock classics as the Beach Boys' "Pet Sounds" and McCartney's own suite of songs on side two of **"Abbey Road,"** it is an epic lament for innocence lost. **"Sgt. Pepper"** was a dream—and the dream, for McCartney, too, is over.

Jim Miller, "Melancholy Masterpiece," in News-week, *Vol. XCIX, No. 18, May 3, 1982, p. 74.*

DAVITT SIGERSON

There is absolutely nothing wrong with filling the world with silly love songs, but these days even Paul McCartney is finding it hard to do. . . . The times are especially demanding for Paul, who may feel that John Lennon's death presents him with new responsibilities. ***Tug of War*** is his reply. McCartney takes responsibility in his own way—deftly, dryly, still balancing his Everyman's grandeur with the self-deprecation of a star. . . . ***Tug of War*** is a manful album, the sort of thing we expect from our greatest talents in times like these. . . . The album Paul has come up with is above all diligent. Since he was always the clever one, the one who knew just how artlessly the fragments should be assembled (cf. ***Abbey Road,*** and ***Ram***), while John and George were the preachers . . . , some listeners have suggested that Paul's trying to bear the load of two ex-Beatles now. But ***Tug of War*** is as truly McCartney as any album he's made—if you grant that vapid whimsy isn't essential to his style. It's more likely that Paul is saying something to John ("This isn't just fluff, I'm working on the ideas like you said I should") than for him. . . .

Through 12 years of solo work and Wings, McCartney has gotten by on his unmatched talents as a melodist and producer. It was frustrating when records as flabby as **"Goodnight Tonight"** and **"With a Little Luck"** sucked up and squandered so many good ideas—from casserole to garbage can in one elegant movement—and even worse when the occasional worthwhile moment, like **"Maybe I'm Amazed"** or **"Jet,"** set the pap in relief.

Tug of War enlists old friends (Denny Laine, Eric Stewart), gunsels (Steve Gadd, Stanley Clarke, Andy Mackay), and some legends: George Martin, Ringo, Stevie Wonder, Carl Perkins. McCartney has combined these forces almost perfectly. On three songs Paul duets with his guests, and lets them extend a considerable influence. The Carl Perkins number, **"Get It,"** is a casual acoustic/electric shuffle of the sort McCartney perfected from old Sun cuts in the first place as pleasurable and unpretentious as anything Paul has recorded. But at the same time, it puts his themes of personal satisfaction and coexistence with others in fine perspective. . . . McCartney suggests that any successful way of living must balance generosity and self-love. On ***Tug of War,*** he explains in the simplest language how getting along with people turns up some thorny situations: "It's a tug of war / But I can't let go / If I do you'll take a tumble / And the whole thing is going to crumble." That image is far more illuminating and substantial than the piano metaphor of **"Ebony and Ivory,"** McCartney's hit duet with Stevie Wonder. . . . McCartney's rekindled pop ambitiousness bespeaks commitment. **"Ebony and Ivory"** isn't very good, but Paul's succeeded in making it sound as if Wonder and McCartney, certainly the two greatest pure pop talents of the last 20 years, wrote it together (they didn't). And its heart's in the right place, which counts for something at a time when so much of our culture has no heart at all. . . .

At the core of this album are the four serious ballads, **"Ebony and Ivory," "Tug of War," "Here Today,"** and **"Somebody Who Cares."** (A fifth, **"Wanderlust,"** is obscure in the annoying manner of Paul's previous solo work, although still attractive and conscientiously constructed.) But what makes ***Tug of War*** really take off is a triad of songs on side two that on any earlier McCartney project would probably have wound up slight and wasteful. The Perkins duet is perhaps the most jewellike of the three, but all contribute important colors to the album's central image. **"Dress Me Up as a Robber"** is a bouncy (indeed, fluffy) song about keeping marriage fresh. . . . Paul may put on a costume now and then to please his partner, but he knows that the real problems that come up around his house are every bit as dramatic as any play or ritual an immature adventurer can devise. And there are better ways to use time: "You can dress me up as a soldier / But I wouldn't know what for / I was the one that told you he loved you / Don't wanna go to another war." There may be wars enough soon, and lonely people may believe they want to fight them. For the happily married, war means separation, and the greatest sadness of all.

Paul will never lose his essential optimism, which adheres in large part to his pride in craft. Consider **"The Pound Is Sinking,"** an ingenious collage in the manner of **"Uncle Albert/Admiral Halsey."** In fact, **"The Pound Is Sinking"** means virtually nothing. But it serves to link personal and worldly apprehensions, and to entertain enormously. After a decade of drivel, it has taken McCartney only six tunes' worth of ***Tug of War***'s meaty entertainment to get us ready for some more of the old charm. Readier, indeed, than at any time since ***Abbey Road.***

Davitt Sigerson, "Paul Carries That Weight," in The Village Voice, *Vol. XXVII, No. 19, May 11, 1982, p. 64.*

STEPHEN HOLDEN

Tug of War is the masterpiece everyone has always known Paul McCartney could make. In style and format, the album isn't all that different from his earlier work, but the songs are far more substantial than the eccentric doodlings of recent albums. Instead of another homemade effort, McCartney has teamed up with producer George Martin to create a record with a sumptuous aural scope that recalls ***Sgt. Pepper's Lonely Hearts Club Band*** and ***Abbey Road.*** (p. 52)

Every cut offers a stylistic montage of one sort or another, creating an actual tug of war between different pop notions—between British pop parochialism and Afro-American progressiveness, escapist fantasy and sage observation, world-weariness and utopian sentiments. But McCartney doesn't just present these oppositions, he unites them. Harmonious, peaceful coexistence is both the ethic and the aesthetic of the album.

Conceptually, ***Tug of War*** is organized around two Paul McCartney-Stevie Wonder duets. Though it wasn't obvious until now, both musicians share a love of childlike melodies and playful asides, and McCartney's **"Ebony and Ivory"** is the ultimate display of this kinship. The tune's phonetic simplicity and its image of black and white piano keys as a metaphor for race relations combine to make a global children's song as ingenuous as "Happy Birthday," Wonder's tribute to Martin Luther King. McCartney's little tune is the ivory half of a matched pair. The ebony counterpart, **"What's That You're Doing,"** is a red-hot pop-funk feast that's served up on Stevie Wonder's roiling and squiggling synthesizer.

These companion pieces are simply the most obvious of many such juxtapositions. In the sweepingly majestic title song, McCartney observes that man's nobler aspirations and warlike impulses originate from the same human urge for more, and he underscores that statement with marching drums and lofty symphonic orchestration. The song could easily be McCartney's "Imagine," for it makes a similar leap of hope: "In years to come they may discover / What the air we breathe and the life we lead / Are all about / But it won't be soon enough . . . for me." And like "Imagine," the song also acknowledges the worst side of humanity: "But with one thing and another / We were trying to outdo each other / In a tug of war."

This solemnity gives way to pure exultation in **"Take It Away,"** a multistyle rock & roll tour de force celebrating the joys of music making. . . . [The cut] sounds like a raunchier, calypso-inflected update of **"Silly Love Songs." "Ballroom Dancing,"** an audacious novelty in the **"Uncle Albert/Admiral Halsey"** vein, allows McCartney to resolve the tensions between his nostalgic yearnings and his rock & roll passion by embracing both at once. This galumphing fox trot, with its jolly music-hall melody, is tricked out with funky horns, and the lyrics, which intersperse bits of nonsense with fleeting images of England in the Fifties, manage to sound cute and hip at the same time. (pp. 52-3)

[The] most powerful stylistic juxtaposition—classical string quartet meets acoustic folk—occurs on McCartney's eulogy to John Lennon, **"Here Today."** The lyrics—in which McCartney remembers meeting, loving and eventually breaking down in tears with Lennon, while all the time never really understanding him—evoke the depth and complexity of their friendship with an astounding tenderness. . . .

"Here Today" brings up the album's most personal and painful aspect. Lennon and McCartney, after all, were icons of goodness in the Sixties, but even the Beatles' utopia wasn't immune to a tug of war that destroyed their collaboration and even, for a time, their friendship. There's a sense in which the whole album is a meditation on two deaths—the Beatles' and John Lennon's.

In this emotionally wide-open atmosphere, even McCartney's more whimsical tunes assume bittersweet overtones. His fairy-tale love songs to Linda McCartney suggest that there is no war between them—perhaps because, for McCartney, the difference between marriage and friendship is the difference between cozy retreat and mortal risk taking. In the elaborate, gorgeously arranged **"Dress Me Up as a Robber"** and the staid, hymnlike **"Wanderlust,"** McCartney compares sexual independence to foolish military adventuring. It's in these seemingly lighter moments that George Martin's studio touches illuminate McCartney's wistful hominess with exquisite musical details. . . . (p. 53)

Of the many albums McCartney has churned out in his twelve-year solo career, only ***Band on the Run*** comes close to touching ***Tug of War*** in the richness of its style and the consistency of its songs. By striking a balance among Wings' streamlined pop-rock, the music-box miniaturism of his solo projects and the Beatles' baroque expansiveness, Paul McCartney has left the rest of his solo career behind in the dust. (p. 56)

Stephen Holden, "McCartney's Gem," in Rolling Stone, *Issue 370, May 27, 1982, pp. 52-3, 56.*

MARK PEEL

You can tell by the album's intensity that Paul McCartney wanted his new **"Tug of War"** to be good. He sings with more conviction and writes with more concentration than he has in years. But if you don't use it, you lose it, and McCartney has been coasting on inoffensive product for so long that when he tries to turn up the energy this time out, not a lot happens.

"Tug of War" has Genuine McCartney stamped all over it. He remains one of pop's great crooners, with a schoolboy tone and a dreamy, bucolic delivery. If the sound of his comforting voice is enough for you, read no further. Musically, he's the Sir Edward Elgar of rock (Elgar composed *Pomp and Circumstance,* the tune you marched to at your graduation). Nobody else writes a high-church hymn tune or an old-fashioned round into a rock song, or arranges "ooh-oohs" for a fifty-voice choir, or makes a dramatic exit on a section of lowing cellos the way McCartney does. The songs on **"Tug of War"** are roughly divided between sweet-nothing ballads and rockers, the latter including a smattering of funk, rockabilly, and reggae. Both categories have their share of McCartney's characteristic novelty cuts of the ***Uncle Albert*** variety. Two examples here are ***Ballroom Dancing*** (with lines such as "Sailing down the Nile in a China cup" that defy interpretation) and ***The Pound*** (using the international financial markets as a metaphor).

If there is one word for McCartney's ballad lyrics, it is *vague.* Songs such as ***Here Today, Wander Lust,*** and ***Somebody Who Cares*** are just about impossible to figure out, since they are mainly strings of images apparently picked at random for the way they sound more than for what they mean. When pressed to pin down what he's trying to say in a song, McCartney is apt to cop out with banal phrases such as "There's always someone somewhere who cares" or "It's frustrating" (which, as an expression of human feeling, is about as pointed as "ya know"). Still, there's no law that says a ballad *has* to make sense, and McCartney's skill at penning a hummable pop melody is second to none.

The rockers are another story. When he's on, which is never a sure thing, McCartney can rock with the best. Here, though, he has to fight a bad production job, surprising coming from studio patriarch George Martin. Much of the problem is *over*-production. . . .

The most talked-about aspect of this album is McCartney's collaborators. ***Ebony and Ivory,*** a harmless homily on the brotherhood of man, is the first single pulled from **"Tug of War"** and one of the two songs that team McCartney and Wonder. The electricity generated by the mere presence of these pop deities is not enough to disguise the song's essential blandness. On ***What's That,*** however, Wonder almost blows his partner out of the grooves with a no-sweat demonstration of funk virtuosity that manages to come through despite the cluttered production. McCartney has to work to keep up.

The third collaboration is the rockabilly ***Get It*** with Carl Perkins. Perkins steps in with jaunty authority on two verses, pairs with McCartney for the choruses, and is caught for posterity laughing long and hard at the end. While none of the duets really gets the most out of the guest artist, they are the least self-conscious and most plainly *fun* things on **"Tug of War."** If the rest of the album comes up short, McCartney fans can at least be encouraged by the effort.

Mark Peel, "McCartney and Friends," in Stereo Review *Magazine, Vol. 47, No. 6, June, 1982, p. 76.*

PARKE PUTERBAUGH

After ***Tug of War,*** logically enough, come the ***Pipes of Peace.*** Carried, as it is, over two consecutive Paul McCartney records, the war-and-peace metaphor is not hard to miss. The message, too, is as simple and inarguable as the line of Indian wisdom inscribed inside the foldout jacket of the new LP: "In love all of life's contradictions disappear." ***Pipes of Peace*** is awash in love. Love of all the little children. Love between a man and a woman. Love of music. Love for all humankind. McCartney's love boat all but capsizes in the waves of almost opiated good feeling that swell over it from all sides.

In truth, **"Pipes of Peace,"** the title tune and first track up, commences quite promisingly. A fanfare of orchestral dissonance gives way to a closely miked McCartney singing a luscious four-line melody over spare, ascending piano chords. It is a rare and breathtaking moment, an instance of McCartney at his soulful, hopeful best. But then it abruptly turns into a frivolous, jerky oompah-tune with unison voices echoing each clumsily phrased line of baby talk that follows. Sadly, an enticing snatch of songcraft becomes, in the end, just another silly love song.

There is no dearth of silly love songs on this record. . . . But my vote would have to go to **"Sweetest Little Show,"** a plea for critical magnanimity amid unforgivable doses of saccharine. One needn't read too deeply to apprehend that McCartney is, in all likelihood, singing to himself here: "You've been around a long time / But you're still good for a while / And if they try to criticize you / Make them smile, make them smile."

This put-on-a-happy-face minstrelsy carries over into Paul's several funk excursions. He's teamed up with Michael Jackson to assay the amiable though vapid dance groove of **"Say Say Say"** (instantly hit-bound froth-funk that tends, after all, toward banality). Their other collaboration, **"The Man,"** is more off the wall, pairing, as it does, a heavily fuzz-toned lead guitar . . . with a full-tilt stab at pure Broadway schmaltz: soaring choruses, orchestral swoops and swoons, and vaguely meaningful though ultimately indecipherable lyrics. . . . (p. 58)

McCartney's collaboration with jazz-fusion bassist Stanley Clarke (**"Hey Hey"**) is, on the other hand, a throwaway instrumental that leaves virtually no impression at all. Oddly enough, the same is true of both **"So Bad"** and **"Through Our Love,"** which close sides one and two, respectively. Both are big ballads in the grand McCartney tradition; the latter, in particular, would seem to want to tie together the various themes of the record into a stirring finale but is, again, lyrically ineffectual, mounting a host of clichés and vagaries into a heap of well-meaning nonsense.

Now, Paul McCartney is, after all, Paul McCartney, so these are not the gaffes of some mere novice or of an easy-listening hack like Christopher Cross. It seems that in some fractured sense, he fully intends to be unexceptional. Think back to the modestly scaled, hearth-and-home vignettes of the first several solo albums, or of his heroic, determined submergence in the group identity of Wings. Underneath all the elaborate arrangements and high-sheen production on ***Pipes of Peace*** . . . is a humble man who retains affection—fascination, even—with the lot of the common folk. This is manifested most blatantly in **"Average Person"**: "Look at the average person / Speak to the man in the street / Can you imagine the first one you'd meet?" He thereupon "imagines" the lives of three such people—a truck driver, a waitress and an ex-boxer. The obvious relish with which he ponders these lives is fairly heartwarming. He is, in the end, hard to dislike. He does "make them smile." But most of the time, he tries so hard to be an average man that he winds up making below-average music. Confusing slightness and simplicity, ***Pipes of Peace*** is, by and large, mediocre McCartney. (pp. 58, 61)

Parke Puterbaugh, "McCartney: Drowning in a Sea of Love," in Rolling Stone, *Issue 413, January 19, 1984, pp. 58, 61.*

MITCHELL COHEN

Paul McCartney just wants everyone to play nice. When he addresses any topic pertaining to the outside world, he takes on the wheedling tone of a babysitter stuck with squabbling siblings: ***Let It Be, Ebony and Ivory, Give Ireland Back to the Irish.*** (The last reduced an incendiary issue to the level of "Aw, c'mon, let your little brother have the football.") And when the subject is his own domestic situation, each day is Valentine's Day.

He's still playing the pied piper of pleasantries on **"Pipes of Peace,"** a listless sequel to **"Tug of War"** that tells us "In love our problems disappear." . . .

The melodies are breezy, but it's an off-hand effort, and all the musicians can do is fluff up McCartney's musical pillows to create an illusion of substance. The comparative toughmindedness of **"War"** suggested that McCartney was stunned into working at full run: With everyone watching to see how he'd respond musically to the Lennon tragedy, he reached out further than he had in ages. On **"Peace,"** he's settled for gumdrop music. . . .

Too many songs on **"Pipes of Peace,"** . . . are as cloying as commercial jingles (the guitar solo on ***The Man*** melodically resembles "set yourself free, set yourself free with Stouffer's"), and the lyrics are often smug, or naive, platitudes about connubial bliss, coexistence, and the common man. . . .

It isn't as though he can't sing rock and roll anymore, or write smart and observant songs; he simply comes across on **"Pipes of Peace"** as not wanting to strain himself. He's so often disarming . . . , perhaps he assumes his audience will embrace even his most threadbare material. But McCartney is too young to be so comfortable playing a Beloved Cultural Institution, basking in the enormous amount of goodwill he has earned over the past 20 years.

Mitchell Cohen, in a review of "Pipes of Peace," in High Fidelity, *Vol. 34, No. 2, February, 1984, p. 72.*

JOHN SWENSON

After the tremendous impact of McCartney's last LP, ***Tug of War,*** it's almost inevitable that ***Pipes of Peace*** should be a letdown. But McCartney has done more than damp the fires of his enthusiasm here—the songs he brings to the project are an undistinguished lot; they seem suspiciously like leftovers pressed into service to meet contractual demands for a new album. **"The Other Me"** is a throwaway notable only for a sprightly sing-along chorus. **"Keep Under Cover"** is a thin piece of Beatles-style nostalgia that relies heavily on George Martin's lush orchestrations. **"So Bad"** is a third-rate McCartney love ballad. **"Sweetest Little Show"** is another one of McCartney's giddy forays into the stylized world of British Music Hall sensibility. McCartney has a weird affinity for this kind of material, and **"Sweetest Little Show"** proves to be the song most likely to be included on any best-of-McCartney party tape.

Pipes of Peace is an ultimately disappointing McCartney record that does little to alter the impression, held in hopeful abeyance by ***Tug of War,*** that McCartney has become a walking stereotype, endlessly reworking old formulae.

John Swenson, "McCartney Plays Formula Rock," in Circus Magazine, *Vol. No. 288, February 29, 1984, p. 92.*

JON TIVEN AND SALLY TIVEN

The current headline concerning Paul McCartney is that he's the richest man in show business, which may be true in a strictly financial sense. Artistically speaking, Macca's dry as a bone, ready to file creative bankruptcy. Aside from the single **"Say Say Say"** (one of two collaborations with Michael Jackson), ***Pipes of Peace*** doesn't have much of anything to offer in the way of the familiar McCartney tunes.

In songs like **"The Other Me,"** McCartney seems to be trying hard to be thoughtful and introspective, contemplating his own midlife crisis, but this doesn't make for inspired fare. The only energy one finds here is in the jam tune with Stanley Clarke, **"Hey Hey,"** which doesn't have any lyrics. (pp. 85-6)

[This] ex-Beatle has totally retreated from the world (particularly since the assassination of John Lennon), and with nothing to write about but himself, he draws a blank. There is another consideration here—Paul supposedly is none too pleased with his record company . . . , and this kind of relationship usually makes for bad records.

Excuses like these are simply to fight the fear that the muse has simply deserted Paul McCartney, and his best records are behind him. The flip side of the single **"Say Say Say," "Ode to a Koala Bear"** (not included on the LP), is better than just about anything on ***Pipes of Peace*** and seems to dispute this theory. But it's hard to remember when McCartney has made an album this easily dismissible (***Wildlife,*** although thin and inconsistent, had high points which beat out anything here). One can only hope that talent this great and cultivated over so long a period of time doesn't simply disappear forever. (p. 86)

Jon Tiven and Sally Tiven, in a review of "Pipes of Peace," in Audio, *Vol. 68, No. 3, March, 1984, pp. 85-6.*

SHEILA JOHNSTON

Following the maxim that life begins anew at forty, Paul McCartney, it seems, has latterly taken to painting, pottery and a little therapeutic scriptwriting. . . . But, on the face of it, ***Give My Regards to Broad Street*** has none of the mid-life stock-taking that its origins might lead one to expect. Introspection and political bite have, after all, always been popularly regarded as John Lennon's province, and McCartney abandoned his original plot, "in which a boastful skinhead joined the army, is sent to the Falklands, and has his legs blown off", in favour of this artless little whimsy, which he describes as "an old-fashioned musical, a good night out, nothing heavy". (p. 380)

Give My Regards to Broad Street registers in many ways as a curiously sclerotic rock movie, the product of a talent grown bloated and bland. True, this rose-tinted portrait of Paul, the unworldly multi-millionaire who is still a soft touch for an old lag down on his luck, still so lacking in business nous that he allows his empire to come to the brink of collapse, is tempered by hints of something more acerbic, almost self-mocking. The farcical scene with two superannuated BBC fossils, for example, described in the spin-off book as men "stuck providing radio shows for an audience with whom they had nothing in common". And, most notably, the strange, elegiac encounter with Sir Ralph Richardson (playing an ambivalent character apparently based on Polonius) who, as Paul insists that he must "be off", gnomically comments, "You've been off for years". But the guile, in the end, remains impenetrable, and whether the film's naïveté is false or authentic is impossible to tell. (p. 381)

Sheila Johnston, in a review of "Give My Regards to Broad Street," in Monthly Film Bulletin, *Vol. 51, No. 611, December, 1984, pp. 380-81.*

CHRISTOPHER CONNELLY

Paul McCartney's new film, ***Give My Regards to Broad Street,*** wafted into movie theaters last month with all the urgency of an autumn breeze. Its madcap dashes and flights of music-inspired whimsy seek to re-create the fast-paced farce of the Beatles' ***A Hard Day's Night.*** But this lavish vanity project offers a thinner plot than the **"Say Say Say"** video, less emotional depth than a greeting card and all the belly laughs of its lamebrained title.

"Good Day Sunshine" is piping from the car radio when we first see McCartney, scribbling lyrics in the backseat of his limo, and the song's blithe, carefree mood easily sweeps away the film's central conflict: The master tapes to McCartney's newest album have disappeared, along with Harry, the ex-con hired by Paul to deliver them. If the tapes aren't located by midnight, McCartney's musical empire will collapse. (McCartney has said he wrote the story line in the backseat of his car. Trust the man.)

Give My Regards to Broad Street soon dissolves into a series of quasi-concert sequences, connected only in the sense that they are supposed to represent an average day in the life of Paul McCartney. Some are quite likable (it's hard to resist the Prince of Cuteness crooning **"Yesterday"**); some are appalling (a futuristic rendition of **"Silly Love Songs"** that features a break dancer); and others are purely inane (resembling a Monty Python version of *Masterpiece Theatre,* the lengthy costume drama that accompanies **"Eleanor Rigby"** cheapens the song it purports to illustrate). . . .

The film's script may be pure pap, but McCartney's music is tougher, more sinewy than anything he's written in years. . . . ***Tug of War***'s **"Ballroom Dancing"** gets a first-class raveup treatment, and even the ballad **"No More Lonely Nights"** seems more sonorous than his recent work.

One would hope, therefore, that Paul's performances of his old songs would take on some new shades of meaning. They do not. Even **"Yesterday"** rings with no more self-knowledge than when Paul sang it on *The Ed Sullivan Show.* For all his musical skill, McCartney remains unwilling to share any deeper emotions with his audience. ***Give My Regards to Broad Street*** seems to reinforce the view that McCartney espoused on ***Pipes of Peace:*** "What good is art when it hurts your head?"

Christopher Connelly, "'Broad Street': Paul's Dead End," in Rolling Stone, *Issue 436, December 6, 1984, p. 57.*

VIC GARBARINI AND JOCK BAIRD

For McCartney, the Beatles' end was the beginning of the most traumatic period of his life. He told Mike Hennessey, "The difference for me was obviously the breakup of the Beatles. Because one day you have one of the greatest jobs in music and the next day you haven't. It's quite a blow—and I took it as a blow. I just could not take it any other way. A lot of music I wrote after that has a lot of pain in it. There's a lot of unfinished stuff." To Joan Goodman he admitted, "I couldn't handle it emotionally. It was a barreling, empty feeling that just rolled across my soul. Until then, I was a cocky sod. Linda had to deal with this guy who didn't particularly want to get out of bed, and if he did, wanted to go back to bed pretty soon after. He wanted to drink earlier and earlier each day and didn't see the point in shaving because where was he going? It was generally pretty morbid." This slough of despond, though short-lived, was a crucial turning point. The acute pain of the breakup, the feeling of being damaged goods, has never left Paul.

It was not really until the death of John Lennon that Paul made contact with this pain. His submersion in the cult of ordinariness and his espousal of **"Silly Love Songs"** was shattered on his extraordinary ***Tug of War*** album. John's death shook Paul up, broke down his defenses, and brought him back to writing about something that mattered to him and to us. Rather than spouting clichés, he was sharing something important again. In his breathtaking **"Here Today,"** Paul eloquently captures the sense of loss: "And if I said I really knew you well, what would your answer be / If you were here today? / Well, knowing you, you'd probably laugh and say that we were worlds apart / If you were here today / But as for me, I still remember / How it was before / And I am holding back the tears no more / I love you." It's written with a naked honesty that John himself rarely approached in his own work. If Paul would only trust himself, and his audience enough to show us more of his true face, the acceptance that he craves would be freely given. It makes us look again at Paul's best Beatles work: **"Let It Be"** and its almost archetypical imagery is a far more effective song about motherhood than anything John had done during the Beatles period. And **"Hey Jude,"** written about Julian Lennon, is also a far more evocative elegy on the theme of abandonment than anything John did until well into his solo years.

The whole issue of **"Silly Love Songs"** and Paul's sentimentality turns on pain. Paul has known no less than John, and has captured it no less brilliantly. Yet he is labeled superficial, even though Lennon was writing deeply romantic songs at the end of his life without hearing that charge. (pp. 63-4)

It's impossible not to conclude that for Paul, the biggest single barrier to producing great work is the shadow of the Beatles still hanging over him. Who could disagree with him when he sighed to Goodman, "I like collaboration, but the collaboration I had with John—it's difficult to imagine anyone else coming up to that standard. Because he was no slouch, that boy. He was pretty hot stuff." And yet McCartney's very survival in music now depends on him putting those days behind him and not retreating from pressure and high expectations. He has written more great songs than any songwriter now alive, and that talent is still there if Paul will only acknowledge it and rise to the kinds of challenges he has always met in the past. (p. 64)

Vic Garbarini and Jock Baird, "Has Success Spoiled Paul McCartney?" in Musician, *No. 76, February, 1985, pp. 58-64.*

Walter Dean Myers

1937-

American novelist, short story writer, nonfiction writer, and author of books for children.

In the majority of his novels for young adults, Myers focuses on black adolescents in New York City, often blending humor with portrayals of life in the ghetto. Myers is considered talented at recreating the vernacular of black urban youth and is praised for offering entertaining and perceptive views of their lives. His characters confront problems typical of adolescence as well as issues of particular concern to young black readers. Myers intends, he says, to provide a literature that "celebrates their life and their person."

In *Fast Sam, Cool Clyde and Stuff* (1975), *Mojo and the Russians* (1977), and *The Young Landlords* (1979), Myers depicts groups of teenage friends who help each other cope with various problems. While focusing on such themes as love, death, and individual responsibility, Myers introduces outrageous events and eccentric characters. Such novels as *It Ain't All for Nothin'* (1978), *Hoops* (1982), and *Won't Know Till I Get There* (1982) are more serious in tone and present teenage protagonists who must confront their problems with little support from others. For instance, Tippy of *It Ain't All For Nothin'* is separated from his grandmother, who has raised him with traditional values, and is beaten and forced to commit crimes by his father. The characters in these novels gain maturity and self-reliance as they overcome their difficulties.

***The Legend of Tarik* (1981) and *The Nicholas Factor* (1983) are atypical works by Myers. The former, a fantasy novel set in Africa, relates the adventures of young Tarik as he gains self-knowledge while battling against forces of evil. In *The Nicholas Factor,* a college student becomes involved with a secret society known as The Crusaders, whose members attempt to impose their beliefs upon an Indian community in the Peruvian jungle. Critics generally praised this novel for its thought-provoking implications and its insightful depiction of a young man striving to maintain personal integrity.**

(See also *Children's Literature Review,* Vol. 4; *Contemporary Authors,* Vols. 33-36, rev. ed.; and *Something about the Author,* Vol. 27.)

Courtesy of Walter Dean Myers

ROBERT LIPSYTE

Stuff, nicknamed for his non-existent dunk shot, is the narrator of **"Fast Sam, Cool Clyde, and Stuff."** He is "kind of scary." When he sees a little kid getting beat up by a bigger kid, Stuff just feels sorry for the little kid. A punch in the nose once cured him of intervention. Nevertheless, his greatest need is to "get close" to other people.

Within days of moving to West 116th Street (his family moved so Stuff and his 10-year-old sister could have separate bedrooms), Stuff falls under the benign, if slightly madcap, influence of two older boys, athletic Sam and thoughtful Clyde, and a sharp-tongued 14-year-old, Gloria, leaders of The Good People, an *ad hoc* gang devoted to consciousness raising.

When Clyde's father dies, when his mother begins seeing another man, when Clyde agonizes over switching from a commercial to an academic course in high school, The Good People get together and talk it all out over soda and cookies. When Gloria's father splits and her mother goes on welfare, when Carnation Charlie uses drugs, when the block braggart introduces sex, The Good People swarm to "protect each other . . . from being alone when things get messed up."

Walter Dean Myers has a gentle and humorous touch, especially with dialogue. Stuff's emotional growth over a year binds together what is essentially a series of stories, all told with the soft distance of nostalgia. (pp. 28, 30)

Robert Lipsyte, in a review of "Fast Sam, Cool Clyde, and Stuff," in The New York Times Book Review, *May 4, 1975, pp. 28, 30.*

ZENA SUTHERLAND

One can almost hear the strains of "That Old Gang of Mine" as background for this nostalgic, funny, first-person account of Stuff's friends [in ***Fast Sam, Cool Clyde and Stuff***]. . . . Stuff falls in love, plays basketball, and goes to a party where others smoke pot, but this Harlem odyssey is as much about the others as it is about him. There's no story line, but there's plenty of action in the many episodes and abundant vitality in the dialogue. (pp. 82-3)

Zena Sutherland, in a review of "Fast Sam, Cool Clyde and Stuff," in Bulletin of the Center for Children's Books, *Vol. 29, No. 5, January, 1976, pp. 82-3.*

DONALD J. BISSETT

[In ***Fast Sam, Cool Clyde, and Stuff***] Walter Dean Myers uses colorful characters and good humor in the episodic account of a group of kids bound together by their need for loyal friendship and their search for a more satisfying understanding of what life is all about. There is reality; the boys visit a drug house and have a futile experience trying to help a friend stay clean. Most of all the book projects clever, contemporary humor. Stuff falls in love and pays the price of being unfaithful (he soul kisses another girl first and winds up on crutches for a week by showing off a karate kick). Stuff's direct approach to problems, his honesty and openness with his friends and the merriment of the book's episodes combine to make intriguing reading. (pp. 520-21)

Donald J. Bissett, in a review of "Fast Sam, Cool Clyde and Stuff," in Language Arts, *Vol. 53, No. 5, May, 1976, pp. 520-21.*

DENISE M. WILMS

Spying kids, a Mojo lady, and Russians from the New York consulate are the unlikely mix of characters in this farcical comedy [***Mojo and the Russians***] about a group of friends' efforts to save one of their bunch from a voodoo spell. . . . That everyone involved turns up innocent fits the story's zany dimensions. Snappy dialogue and the essential warmth between these friends give body to the story; some central portions lag but uproarious intervals more than compensate.

Denise M. Wilms, in a review of "Mojo and the Russians," in Booklist, *Vol. 74, No. 4, October 15, 1977, p. 379.*

ETHEL L. HEINS

When [in ***Mojo and the Russians***] Dean, streaking around a corner in a bicycle race with his friend Kitty, accidentally knocked a woman down, he set off a chain of ludicrous events that led him and his gang all the way from the streets of Harlem to the Russian Consulate, the New York City police, and the FBI. Dean's furious victim was Drusilla, a neighborhood character—a Voodoo practitioner, who terrified the boy when she threatened to "fix him good" by making "his tongue split like a lizard's and his eyes to cross." . . . Dean's first-person narrative is frequently interrupted by descriptions of the weird scenes in Drusilla's apartment and by her long-winded, one-sided conversations with her black cat. The author of ***Fast Sam, Cool Clyde, and Stuff*** again takes a sympathetic but absolutely unsentimental approach to his characters; with an accurate feeling for the thoughts and folkways of children, he sets down their spontaneous conversation as the perfect extension of the lively farce. (pp. 166-67)

Ethel L. Heins, in a review of "Mojo and the Russians," in The Horn Book Magazine, *Vol. LIV, No. 2, April, 1978, pp. 166-67.*

HELEN B. ANDREJEVIC

Hoping to form a relationship with his father, Tippy [in ***It Ain't All for Nothin'***] agrees to help out in a bank robbery. But not even Tippy's recently acquired habit of drinking whiskey mixed with Kool-Aid suffices to dim his awareness that he has some serious (and dangerous) decisions to make about his life. An even-toned, extremely well-written, and withal optimistic book by a black author who deals unblinkingly with a milieu not often encountered in children's books.

Helen B. Andrejevic, in a review of "It Ain't All for Nothin'," in Parents', *Vol. 54, No. 1, January, 1979, p. 20.*

KATE M. FLANAGAN

The account [in ***The Young Landlords***] of the summer experiences of a group of Black teenagers in New York is similar in spirit to [Myers's] earlier book ***Fast Sam, Cool Clyde, and Stuff***. . . . Paul Williams narrates the many adventures—ranging from the hilarious to the dangerous—that he and his friends encountered when they unwittingly became the owners of a run-down slum building. At first the group was excited by the idea of being landlords, but it was soon apparent that the responsibilities far outweighed the privileges. The building was inhabited by a variety of eccentric characters. . . . In the course of the summer, Paul learned that compassion and business did not always mix; he and his friends were forced to devise ingenious—but not always successful—methods of raising money for the building. In the meantime, they took some risky chances while trying to prove the innocence of a friend who had been accused of robbery. . . . The story is presented with a masterful blend of humor and realism; dialogue is lively and authentic, and the many characters are drawn with compassion. The author has once again demonstrated his keen sensitivity to the joys and frustrations of adolescence as well as his thorough knowledge of the New York City street scene.

Kate M. Flanagan, in a review of "The Young Landlords," in The Horn Book Magazine, *Vol. LV, No. 5, October, 1979, p. 535.*

JANE PENNINGTON

[***It Ain't All for Nothin'***] deals frankly with the stark realities of ghetto life. It pretties up nothing; not the language, not the circumstances, not the despair. It sucks the reader into a whirlpool of emotions. When the health of Tippy's grandmother deteriorates and she experiences the humiliation of dealing with welfare bureaucrats, we feel her defeat. When Tippy's world crumbles as his grandmother—who raised him from infancy—is removed to a nursing home, we experience his fear; we share his conflict and confusion as he wonders how his grandmother's benevolent God can allow such dreadful things to happen. When Tippy is forced to move in with his father, his misgivings are ours. And when he is viciously beaten by his father and forced to violate the principles instilled in him by his grandmother, we touch his pain—the hurt in his body and the hurt in his heart.

The torment which this child experiences is virtually unrelenting and on several instances I put the book down simply to gain respite from it. But that only underscored the fact that Tippy and the people who populate his world cannot escape so easily.

This is a devastating book which needed to be written; not only does it delineate the sufferings of this youngster, it also details the caring and support offered to him by members of his community.

The main problem I have with ***It Ain't All for Nothin'*** is its failure to fully explore the political realities behind the situations in which the characters find themselves. They did not construct the system which grinds them under its heel. They do not benefit from their deprivation, even if they contribute to it. But *someone* does benefit and it is inadequate to assume that the reader is aware of the political ramifications; they need to be stated openly and clearly. We are dealing with society's surplus people and they deserve to have their position squarely examined.

I was also uncomfortable with Tippy's solution to the conflict he faces after his father is involved in a robbery—he turns his father over to the police. I felt it could have been resolved in a way which did not so strongly suggest that feeding into the existing system was the right and proper way to handle things.

Jane Pennington, in a review of "It Ain't All for Nothin'," in Interracial Books for Children Bulletin, *Vol. 10, No. 4, 1979, p. 18.*

PATRICIA LEE GAUCH

[**"The Young Landlords"** is] about four black teen-agers, the Action Group, who in a spontaneous act of community service, get tricked into becoming slum landlords of a deteriorating apartment house in their Harlem neighborhood. The plot—kids running a slum building, The Joint, and catching a stereo thief—stretches the imagination at more than one point.

It works as a convenient vehicle, however, for introducing such great characters as the Captain, a cool, pig-eyed numbers man; Mrs. Brown, a tenant whose "companion," the great boxer Jack Johnson, periodically dies and is reborn; "slap slap" Kelly, whose slick street talk is pure music, and best of all, Askia Ben Kenobi, the wild black mystic whose karate dance threatens everything from bannisters to petty thieves.

There are other incidents in the plot—a mild love interest between Gloria and the narrator, for one—but they pale beside such scenes as the rollicking rent party which a caped Kenobi turns into a sandwich-throwing brawl, or the scene where landlords Gloria and Paul get marooned in a lightless bathroom.

There are ideas, too, about the conflict between tenants and slumlords. About the hot-goods industry, police lethargy, newspapers' predilection for story over facts. Important ideas, particularly for the reader who doesn't live next to The Joint.

Mr. Myers's story starts slowly; tightening would have helped. But there are funny lines and scenes, the dialogue is real, and as the narrator says: "Mostly the whole experience was an up kind of thing."

Patricia Lee Gauch, in a review of "The Young Landlords," in The New York Times Book Review, *January 6, 1980, p. 20.*

HAZEL ROCHMAN

[***The Legend of Tarik***] has many qualities of heroic myths—a reborn hero, rites of passage, monsters, perilous journeys, an ultimate duel between good and evil; and there are Islamic, Classical, Christian and traditional African elements. On one level it is an exciting adventure story with trials of strength and fierce duels of combat. But the characterization is not simple, and there is some ambiguity about the heroic code. . . . Tarik finds no joy in his victories: even with all his reasons for revenge, he does not wish to kill; and at times he questions whether a righteous end must require such bloody means. In a powerful tale, Myers makes clear that the heroic quest is also an arduous search for self-knowledge and identity.

Hazel Rochman, in a review of "The Legend of Tarik," in School Library Journal, *Vol. 27, No. 9, May, 1981, p. 76.*

MALCOLM BOSSE

"It came to pass" are the opening words in [***The Legend of Tarik***], suggesting we are in for magic and adventure, heroes and villains, with a final showdown between good and evil. Mr. Myers doesn't disappoint us. He has written what is nearly a compendium of devices used in such fiction.

Tarik has seen his father murdered by a sadistic brute who terrorizes the African countryside (historical time unspecified). Befriended by two old men, who also have scores to settle with this same El Muerte, the boy undergoes a long period of systematic training that will prepare him to take his revenge. . . .

Equipped with a magic sword, a powerful horse and the Crystal of Truth, Tarik sets out in the company of Stria, a girl whose passion for revenge far exceeds his own and whose portrayal is one of the book's strengths. Adventures come thick and fast. Comic relief is provided by a garrulous baker, who proves loyal in spite of his professed cowardice. The three companions move inexorably toward the final confrontation with El Muerte. The climax is, of course, predictable, as it should be in a tale of vengeance.

And as it should be in a legend, omens and prophetic dreams abound. Also conforming to the tradition of allegory, the characters are broadly drawn, some of them standing for a single quality: Faithfulness, obsession, wisdom, etc. Even so, the story does have a contemporary feeling, because moral questions of conduct are given a skeptical treatment, with a resultant ambiguity about their solutions.

In spite of a thinness of detail, particularly in descriptions of the physical setting and a few unfortunate metaphors ("El Muerte's smile was like a white wound in the belly of a whale"), in balance it is an admirably paced novel, with plenty of action and enough about loyalty and courage to satisfy young readers who can find in parables and legends a clue to their own lives.

Malcolm Bosse, in a review of "The Legend of Tarik," in The New York Times Book Review, *July 12, 1981, p. 30.*

ETHEL R. TWICHELL

All of the components [in ***The Legend of Tarik***] should make for a lively adventure story, but the author has chosen to give it the aura of a myth or a legend; the effect is stilted and self-conscious, and some of the conversations seem needlessly weighty. The pace is uneven with a slow, deliberate beginning and a greatly accelerated denouement. Yet the flaws notwithstanding, there are moments of excitement and tension, and the author has a talent for creating repulsive monsters. The elements of a good story are here; one wishes it could have been fleshed out in a more convincing way.

Ethel R. Twichell, in a review of "The Legend of Tarik," in The Horn Book Magazine, *Vol. LVII, No. 4, August, 1981, p. 434.*

STEPHANIE ZVIRIN

Skeptical of authority and afraid of emotional commitments, thanks in part to a father who abandoned him and his mother years before, 17-year-old basketball talent Lonnie Jackson [the protagonist of ***Hoops***] is particularly suspicious of Cal Jones, former pro-ball player and sometime wino, who takes over coaching Lonnie's Harlem youth team. . . . When gambling types put pressure on Cal . . . Lonnie's uncertainty resurfaces and their tenuous relationship is threatened. While somewhat uneven in the telling, Myers' story about trust and friendship . . . evolves a sharply etched image of Harlem, where sex and violence emerge naturally as part of the setting. Dialogue rings with authenticity, on-court action is colorful and well integrated into the story, and the author's dramatic conclusion is handled with poignancy and power.

Stephanie Zvirin, in a review of "Hoops: A Novel," in Booklist, *Vol. 78, No. 2, September 15, 1981, p. 98.*

ALEX BOYD

Frankly, I haven't encountered a line like "Men see what they want in the eyes of a woman" in more years than any of us would care to remember. Young adults today simply do not talk that way. But that's characteristic of ***The Legend of Tarik.*** All the situational cliches are present. The hero is a brave young black boy who grows into manhood under the watchful and learned eyes of the gnarled but all knowing mentor (actually this book even has a backup mentor). . . . It's never explained, but one imagines that his quest is legendary. There is also a romantic interest. A young mysterious girl, who seems never to be on quite the same footing as the male protagonist, yet still manages to be near enough to the action for the required rescues.

Actually, this is an awful book. There is so much predictability in the shallow characters and situations that the mean spirited violence is almost welcome, but not quite. The number of beheadings, impalements and other vicious ways by which numerous individuals are dispatched could only be enjoyed by the most surfeited devotee of the current wave of horror flicks.

Alex Boyd, in a review of "The Legend of Tarik," in Voice of Youth Advocates, *Vol. 4, No. 4, October, 1981, p. 36.*

ZENA SUTHERLAND

Seventeen-year-old Lonnie, the narrator [in ***Hoops***], is a good basketball player. . . . He has faith in his coach, but both are under pressure to throw the final game, losing to suit financial sharks. Myers does a good job of building tension, and just as good a job of building the relationship between Lonnie and his coach, a bond of trust that develops slowly. At the end of the story the coach is stabbed and dies, so the winning of the crucial game is not a formula device; it is a lesson to Lonnie: there are rough people in the business of basketball, and if he wants to get out of Harlem and become a pro, he'll have to cope with them.

Zena Sutherland, in a review of "Hoops," in Bulletin of the Center for Children's Books, *Vol. 35, No. 4, December, 1981, p. 74.*

PATRICIA BERRY

[In ***Hoops***] Lonnie Jackson is a 17-year-old basketball player who lives in Harlem. He is about to graduate from high school and he has no future in sight except basketball. . . . When Cal . . . shows up to coach Lonnie's team in the citywide Tournament of Champions, the action begins.

This story offers the reader some fast, descriptive basketball action, a love story between Lonnie and girlfriend Mary-Ann, peer friendship problems, and gangster intrigues. Most importantly, however, it portrays the growth of a trusting and deeply caring father-son relationship between Cal and Lonnie. The story of this relationship is the best part of the book. . . .

Sometimes the theme of the urban basketball hero makes the story seem flat and predictable but there are poignant, human struggles that will appeal to any reader.

Patricia Berry, in a review of "Hoops," in Voice of Youth Advocates, *Vol. 5, No. 1, April, 1982, p. 36.*

HAZEL ROCHMAN

In spite of the creaking plot [of ***Won't Know Till I Get There***], readers, as always with Myers, will love the dialogue, the fierce and funny repartee and the grotesque insults; and also the masterly control of dramatic scenes: the way in which bantering explodes into violent hostility, the move from slapstick to pathos, the sudden stabs of psychological insight. The overt didacticism is quite superfluous: excellent characterization clearly demonstrates Myers' theme that those whom we perceive in terms of labels and group stereotypes—old, Black, female, enemy, delinquent, deserting mother—turn out to be widely differing, surprising and interesting individuals when we allow ourselves to know them. (pp. 72-3)

Hazel Rochman, in a review of "Won't Know Till I Get There," in School Library Journal, *Vol. 28, No. 9, May, 1982, pp. 72-3.*

DIANE GERSONI EDELMAN

[In **"Won't Know Till I Get There"**] Stephen Perry, 14, is a middle-class black in New York City whose parents are thinking of adopting Earl Goins, a troubled, streetwise kid. Trying to prove himself tough to his new foster brother, Stephen spray-paints graffiti on a subway car. As punishment, he, Earl and two friends are ordered by a judge to work at an old-age home slated to be shut down by the city.

The strong-willed, capable residents of the home want to make it financially self-sustaining so that it can remain open and they can stay together. (p. 26)

Stephen's gradual rapprochement with both Earl and the senior residents is predictable, and readers will crave more details about Earl and his real mother. Also, though the residents are well differentiated as characters, they are often used to relay the book's general messages about the plight of the elderly:

the stereotypical view of them as sexless, sedentary and non-productive; the loss of government benefits when they marry; discrimination against them in business.

Nevertheless, the novel is engrossing. The urban setting is skillfully evoked, and only a few adult-sounding thoughts and expressions mar the otherwise natural, youthful tone of Stephen's first-person narrative. Mr. Myers ably integrates his dual themes of complex family relationships and senior citizens' problems. And, despite the seriousness of these themes, there is ample, appropriate humor. (pp. 26-7)

Diane Gersoni Edelman, in a review of "Won't Know Till I Get There," in The New York Times Book Review, *June 13, 1982, pp. 26-7.*

SUSAN WILLIAMSON

Written in the form of Steve's diary, this engaging, but perhaps unbelievable, tale [***Won't Know Till I Get There***] presents a sensitive look at the problems of old age and youth, adoption, and delinquency. The portrayal of a successful, two-parent, black middle class family, and of senior citizens as full functioning human beings is refreshing.

Susan Williamson, in a review of "Won't Know Till I Get There," in Voice of Youth Advocates, *Vol. 5, No. 5, December, 1982, p. 34.*

PUBLISHERS WEEKLY

[Myers] explores an intriguing idea [in **"The Nicholas Factor"**]: does an elite group have the right to impose its views on society, even if it believes its vision is right? Gerald is a college student who's asked to join the Crusade Society, a snobby campus organization. He's approached by a government agent who wants him to keep an eye on the group, heightening his already aroused suspicions about Crusader activities. After a few meetings, he's off to a Peruvian jungle with them on a do-gooder mission with an Inca tribe. . . . Suddenly, the project is called off and the Crusaders are being hustled out of Peru, but Gerald and Jennifer discover a village filled with sick and dying Indians, caused by a Crusader "inducement" meant to accomplish their mission. The chase is on, as the leaders of the Crusaders realize what the two have found out. The reference to the Crusaders of yore is telling, for they were religious zealots who felt a holy obligation to impose their will. Myers probes and makes one think about the notion of right and wrong as it applies to implementing one's vision of the world. A disturbing, powerful work.

A review of "The Nicholas Factor," in Publishers Weekly, *Vol. 223, No. 11, March 18, 1983, p. 70.*

PATRICIA A. MORGANS

Imagine yourself a seventeen year old college student minding your own business when out of the blue comes a request that you become an undercover agent. This happens to Gerald McQuillan as ***The Nicholas Factor*** begins. The Crusaders are an international group of young people handpicked for their intelligence, integrity and idealism. It is hoped that many of the leaders of tomorrow will come from their ranks. Because of rumors of extreme right wing infiltration, there are suspicions that all is not well with this elite group of do-gooders. . . .

On the surface all looks innocent enough. The assignment is to Peruvian Indians in the Amazon jungle. Because of their primitive lifestyle, these Indians suffer from diseases easily controlled in a more civilized society. . . . Enter the dark side of humanity. The plot thickens and soon Gerald is deep into blackmail and murder.

The Nicholas Factor is a suspenseful thriller. Myers has a wonderfully restrained and easy style. Once again he has written a winner. It is a novel of intrigue and adventure with a touch of romance. Gerald is a hero who has his standards and lives up to them. We are sure as the book ends that he has matured into a young man of integrity with inner resources upon which he can rely. I like him very much. You will, too.

Patricia A. Morgans, in a review of "The Nicholas Factor," in Best Sellers, *Vol. 43, No. 4, July, 1983, p. 155.*

LUCY V. HAWLEY

One develops a deep regard for Gerald [the protagonist of ***The Nicholas Factor***]. While trying to penetrate the ominous leadership of the Society, he is also analyzing and trying to accept the relationship he had had with his father before his recent death. The book does not deliver the tension and sense of danger it tells us about, and too many arcane motives must be explained in the last chapter. But because the characters are realistically presented, the setting is exotic and the idea of the Crusader's Society is intriguing, this should be an appealing, popular adventure.

Lucy V. Hawley, in a review of "The Nicholas Factor," in School Library Journal, *Vol. 30, No. 1, September, 1983, p. 138.*

Suzanne Newton

1936-

American novelist, short story writer, and poet.

Newton describes the protagonists of her novels as "people who risk . . . who stand up against the opposition," and the action flows directly from the individualistic behavior of those characters. In *c/o Arnold's Corners* (1974), the heroine defies familial and public opinion to befriend a black girl, a "hippie" artist, and an unwed mother, setting an example for her family and town. *What Are You Up To, William Thomas?* (1977) and *M. V. Sexton Speaking* (1981) are more humorous stories, but they still consider serious problems: a school rivalry in the former, and M.V.'s successful struggle for independence from her strict aunt in the latter. Critics consider M. V. Sexton a very appealing and freshly drawn character.

***I Will Call It Georgie's Blues* (1983) is Newton's most serious work. In portraying a deeply troubled family which puts up a happy facade for their neighbors, Newton touches on the difference between appearance and reality. She received a positive response from critics for her deft handling of this emotionally charged story. Although several of her novels have been faulted for their uneven character development and pat endings, on the whole Newton is respected as an author who chooses interesting subjects and writes in an engaging style.**

(See also *Contemporary Authors,* Vols. 41-44, rev. ed. and *Something about the Author,* Vol. 5.)

Photograph by Gene Furr. Courtesy of Suzanne Newton

KIRKUS REVIEWS

[Though] the ostracism, rescue and eventual acceptance of shaggy Mr. King runs its course with the neatness of wish-fulfillment [in ***c/o Arnold's Corners***], Rosalee's frustration with the restricted, gossipy life of Arnold's Corners rings true. Allowed only ten books a month by the traveling bookmobile librarian and with the three people she likes best—Mr. King, the unwed mother/seamstress Jenny and a black schoolmate May—judged unsuitable as companions, Rosalee is reduced to working extra time in her father's store and babysitting for ten cents an hour to keep busy. She reports her stratagems to avoid boredom and her serious bicycle accident—while racing to warn Mr. King of approaching rednecks—with the same slightly southern turn of phrase and relaxed, self-deprecatory humor; the tone is not quite equal to the story's most melodramatic moments but unobtrusively entertaining otherwise.

A review of "c/o Arnold's Corners," in Kirkus Reviews, *Vol. XLII, No. 6, March 15, 1974, p. 301.*

MARY KATHERINE PACE

Except for 12-year-old Rosalee Brigham [in ***c/o Arnold's Corners***], the inhabitants of Arnold's Corners are chronically suspicious of outsiders, especially ones like Raoul King, a long-haired "hippie type" who arrives in his VW camper, and a mysterious young woman and her baby. . . . When Rosalee has an accident en route to warn King of a vigilante raid on his camper, the citizens finally see their folly. King, an artist whose only motive is to immortalize Arnold's Corners in a mural at the State Capitol, is subsequently not only accepted but embraced by the community. Although the story is entertaining, readers will be hardpressed to believe in the emotionally precocious preteen heroine. Kind, ambitious, and wise beyond belief, Rosalee is, like the Tooth Fairy, someone who won't seem real. . . .

Mary Katherine Pace, in a review of "c/o Arnold's Corners," in School Library Journal, *an appendix to* Library Journal, *Vol. 20, No. 8, April, 1974, p. 60.*

PUBLISHERS WEEKLY

[***"c/o Arnold's Corners"*** is] a story of unusual grace and relevance for our time. We learn about the townspeople, their intolerance of those who are "different" and more immediately about Rosalee Brigham, the young narrator. . . . Enthusiastic readers of Ms. Newton's clever story will feel the tension as Rosalee and the outsiders are threatenened, and sigh with relief at the surprising but wholly logical finale, a most satisfying ending, indeed.

A review of "c/o Arnold's Corners," in Publishers Weekly, *Vol. 205, No. 15, April 15, 1974, p. 52.*

ZENA SUTHERLAND

[In *c/o **Arnold's Corners,*** Rosalee] has a penchant for making the kind of friends of whom her parents and the community disapprove. Like May, who's black. Like Jenny, a seamstress who turned up one day with her baby. . . . Rosalee tells her story with vivacity and conviction as she describes the narrowminded citizens and her own flaunting of their taboos; her independence is admirable and convincing as she flaunts convention to help her friends and keep them; the reactions of the townspeople are not as convincing, so filled are they with instant venom and pettiness. . . . [The ending is] a bit too pat . . . , but Rosalee is an attractive heroine and her story nicely told.

Zena Sutherland, in a review of "c/o Arnold's Corners," in Bulletin of the Center for Children's Books, *Vol. 28, No. 3, November, 1974, p. 50.*

BARBARA ELLEMAN

Set in 1923, this light comedy [***What Are You Up To, William Thomas?***] spins out a tale of 15-year-old William Thomas' carefully planned hoax to top all his hoaxes and Lilly Fentrice's cleverly devised counteraction. . . . A bit of drama is injected as William meddles in the lives of his Aunt Jessica, whose bookstore is in financial difficulty, and her wealthy friend Mrs. Benson and starts a chain reaction with far-reaching consequences. Though the conclusion is too pat, the story moves effortlessly along with William's endless pranks providing fuel for laughter.

Barbara Elleman, in a review of "What Are You Up To, William Thomas?" in Booklist, *Vol. 74, No. 7, December 1, 1977, p. 615.*

PHYLLIS MASCARO

Through his contact with his librarian aunt, for whom he works, and Lilly, his romantic interest, both of whom exhibit integrity in their own quiet ways, William [in ***What Are You Up To, William Thomas?***] is forced to reexamine his values and self-image. Although the author's attempt to inspire self-examination is valid, its impact is destroyed by the triteness of the situation. Moreover, the adolescents appear so naive that today's teenagers won't relate to them at all.

Phyllis Mascaro, in a review of "What Are You Up To, William Thomas?" in School Library Journal, *Vol. 24, No. 6, February, 1978, p. 66.*

JOAN L. DOBSON

[In ***Reubella and the Old Focus Home***] Reubella is running away from her dreamer dad the afternoon that the bizarre van, Buxtedude, carrying the aged, outlandishly attired Ms. Nesselrode, Ms. Cromwell, and Ms. Smithers arrives in Shad. Through the course of the book Reubella relents, her father reforms, and the ladies find their dream and establish the Old Focus Home. All of the many obstacles in their paths fall easily, almost too easily. It's nice to have a book in which all ends happily, but there is little suspense. The triumphs of the three over all opposition seem obviously manipulated by the author. (pp. 62-3)

Joan L. Dobson, in a review of "Reubella and the Old Focus Home," in School Library Journal, *Vol. 25, No. 4, December, 1978, pp. 62-3.*

CAROLYN NOAH

The silent rigidity of Great-aunt Gert's house has been Martha Venable Sexton's home since her parents' death ten years ago. In [***M. V. Sexton Speaking***] . . . , Aunt Gert pushes the girl into a bakery job and a quiet revolution. Job, employers and a new male friend are catalysts, and acquiescent M.V. emerges a witty and confident young woman. Newton's prose is energetic and spiced with humor. . . . Each character is convincingly multidimensional: Aunt Gert lonely in her self-imposed isolation; Uncle Milton rediscovering himself within the confines of his family; and M.V., who handles herself maturely and stands as a likable, spunky individual.

Carolyn Noah, in a review of "M. V. Sexton Speaking," in School Library Journal, *Vol. 28, No. 4, December, 1981, p. 72.*

KIRKUS REVIEWS

When M. V. Sexton speaks it's in her own sure voice, which makes [***M. V. Sexton Speaking***] a pleasure to read. The first-person novel deals with the summer Martha Venable Sexton is 16 and her strict great-aunt Gert, who has raised her, sends her out to find a summer job. She is hired at once by a happy baker, Brad Bradley. . . . Brad and Rachel Bradley like M.V.'s forthright ways, while coping on the job gives her a further sense of self and moves her to stand up to Aunt Gert and to press for information about her parents, who died in an accident when M.V. was six. . . . It's the sort of story where everyone turns out nice: Under M.V.'s influence silent Uncle Milton . . . shows signs of life, Aunt Gert unbends surprisingly, and even the rude, rich supplier who's been pressing Brad for payment shows his humanity—*after* he's paid—in a tension-breaking batter-and-frosting-tossing free-for-all in the bakery's back room. But outside of Rachel's frosting, there's nothing sugary about it—thanks mostly to M.V.'s fresh, feet-on-the-ground personality. (pp. 1524-25)

A review of "M. V. Sexton Speaking," in Kirkus Reviews, *Vol. XLIX, No. 24, December 15, 1981, pp. 1524-25.*

ZENA SUTHERLAND

[***M. V. Sexton Speaking***] isn't an emotion-charged or dramatic story, but it's nicely developed, as M.V. gets over a crush on an older man, achieves a closer relationship with her aunt and uncle in the course of finding out more about her parents, and acquires confidence, a boy friend, and a new ability to take life and Aunt Gert a little less seriously.

Zena Sutherland, in a review of "M. V. Sexton Speaking," in Bulletin of the Center for Children's Books, *Vol. 35, No. 5, January, 1982, p. 92.*

M. JEAN GREENLAW

M. V. Sexton Speaking is a wholly satisfying book. The characters' problems are realistic and realistically faced; adults as well as teenagers are "good guys." Best of all, the book makes you laugh. It is one of the best "coming of age" books I've read in years and manages to be intriguing without one four-letter word or obligatory sex scene. A real winner!

M. Jean Greenlaw, in a review of "M. V. Sexton Speaking," in Journal of Reading, *Vol. 25, No. 6, March, 1982, p. 613.*

KIRKUS REVIEWS

After the fresh, distinctive appeal of ***M. V. Sexton Speaking*** (1981), it's disappointing to find Newton taking on a tired older-fiction formula (family in psychic disarray) and giving it such strained, humorless treatment [in ***I Will Call It Georgie's Blues***]. Her narrator is Neal Sloan, 15, son of the Baptist minister in small-town Gideon, N.C.—and, boy, does Neal have problems. His preacher-dad is stiff, dictatorial, afraid of local public-opinion. His mother is weak. His older sister Aileen is rebelling like crazy. . . . Little brother Georgie, 7, is a basket case: apparently unloved by both parents, he has come to believe that his "Real" family has been replaced by sci-fi-ish clones. And Neal himself, though presented as basically normal, is determined to keep secret the fact that he has "a real genius for jazz"—learning and playing on the sly over at the house of Mrs. T., a lovely-wise-widow piano teacher. (Neal's reasons for this secrecy are never made even remotely plausible.) Then, after a few minor crises at home and at school, the Sloan family troubles escalate. . . . Georgie runs away—leading to a search, promises of psychiatric treatment (when found, Georgie is catatonic), and Neal's coming-out of the musical closet. . . . A dubious psychological grab-bag—with under-developed hangups, fuzzy backgrounds (the music is especially disappointing), and a limp, shrill windup.

A review of "I Will Call It Georgie's Blues," in Kirkus Reviews, *Juvenile Issue, Vol. LI, Nos. 13-17, September 1, 1983, p. J-177.*

DAVID GALE

[***I Will Call It Georgie's Blues***] is an emotionally-charged story of public image versus personal truths. Neal Sloan, 15, his 7-year-old brother, Georgie, his older sister and their mother are affected by this dichotomy: they are the family of a small town Baptist minister, a man who seems to live an ideal life but who is a much different person at home. . . . When Sloan's facade begins to crumble, Georgie, caught in the middle, has an emotional crisis that rallies the entire town and leads Neal to reveal his musical ability. Reality, in many senses, is the recurring theme: Georgie's notion of real and false people; the idea of reality/phoniness as evidenced by Sloan's public persona; music as the only reality in Neal's life and reality versus dreams. Newton has written a brutal novel of a family in crisis, terrorized by someone who should be supporting them and desperately in need of personal solutions. The narrative is grim but gripping, desperate but inherently optimistic. The only weak characterization is the one that is the most crucial: Sloan. While the question of his emotional problems is resolved to the satisfaction of the other characters, it is not clearly defined for readers.

David Gale, in a review of "I Will Call It Georgie's Blues," in School Library Journal, *Vol. 30, No. 2, October, 1983, p. 172.*

ANNE TYLER

If the Georgie of **"I Will Call It Georgie's Blues"** has any close relation, it's John Henry West, Frankie's little cousin in "The Member of the Wedding." Seven-year old Georgie is equally touching, but in many ways more fragile, and his presence in this story turns it into something fine and delicate and full of possibility.

Georgie is not the narrator of this book. He probably wouldn't be up to it. He's too frightened. Instead, the honor falls to his 15-year-old brother Neal, who tells us in his matter-of-fact, slangy way that the inner workings of families are more complicated than the outside world would ever guess.

This particular family lives in Gideon, N.C.—a pleasant enough little place, but stultifying and prone to gossip. . . .

The father is a Baptist minister who projects an image of perfection to the public, but in private he's full of rage. The mother offers him no resistance, believing that parents must present a united front. The daughter Aileen is the rebel. . . .

Georgie lives in a little afterthought of a room where his pajamas sit neatly folded by the pillow—"something he'd done so Mom would be pleased with him." He used to be cherished by his older sister, but she gave him up when she discovered boys. "I don't think he ever got over the suddenness of it," Neal tells us. "For a while he would follow her around at a safe distance, just in case she changed her mind, but she never did."

Those two sentences alone demonstrate Neal's effectiveness as a narrator. His point, finally, is that families hang in a tenuous balance. "Everything is connected, whether I like it or not. Changing one piece means changing all the pieces." And nothing tips the balance more quickly than tampering with the truth—altering the self presented to the public.

Neal convinces us. Suzanne Newton convinces us, and **"I Will Call It Georgie's Blues"** is a sad and wonderful story.

Anne Tyler, in a review of "I Will Call It Georgie's Blues," in The New York Times Book Review, *November 13, 1983, p. 40.*

LISA FRAUSTINO

[In ***I Will Call It Georgie's Blues***] Newton depicts a contemporary family, with all its complex sociological and psychological problems, from a Teen's viewpoint.

Neil Sloan, hero and narrator, is the son of a Baptist minister in a town aptly called Gideon. Tyrannical Dad insists on public perfection from his family, when actually the family has many "secret" problems. . . . Mom does her best to keep the peace between her husband and offspring, but seldom succeeds. The plot moves quickly as the Sloan family secrets become more dramatic and more public, culminating in Georgie's mental breakdown and the family's emotional upheaval.

The novel's strongest point is its witty, fluid writing. Neil Sloan comes alive much as Holden Caulfield does, though Suzanne Newton's story is in a different vein from Salinger's. Neil takes us through his story so smoothly, so realistically, that we hardly notice the book's basic fault: Ferocious Father isn't *shown* to be as bad as Neil makes him out to be. This fault may go undetected by most teenagers, who are often prepared to see a mean parent at the turn of a page. A young audience will find Newton's characters interesting and her story strongly written.

Lisa Fraustino, in a review of "I Will Call It Georgie's Blues," in Best Sellers, *Vol. 43, No. 9, December, 1983, p. 348.*

CYNTHIA K. LEIBOLD

Newton's uninvolving novel [***An End to Perfect***] focuses on Arden Gifford, an unassuming 12-year-old living in a small Southern town. . . . Her brother Hill prepares to leave Haverlee to attend a better high school and DorJo, Arden's best friend, disappears after a berating from her frequently-absent mother. Reappearing three days later, DorJo is secretly sheltered by the Giffords. Arden becomes certain that her life is improving. . . . Instead, she finds herself struggling with more unwanted reality when she discovers that DorJo doesn't always like what Arden likes and that DorJo's ties to her mother are stronger than their friendship. This friendship between the two girls comes across as genuine, but the actions of the characters are contrived, particularly those of Dorjo's mother, who, after years of neglecting or mentally abusing her children, repents almost overnight and is absolved of all prior mistreatment. Today's . . . readers will quickly lose interest in the very näive main character and the author's sugar-coated treatment of DorJo's problems.

Cynthia K. Leibold, in a review of "An End to Perfect," in School Library Journal, *Vol. 31, No. 2, October, 1984, p.160.*

Pink Floyd

Patrick Aventurier/Gamma-Liaison

Dave Hogan/LGI © 1982

(Roger) Syd Barrett 1946-

David Gilmour (left) 1944-

Nick Mason 1945-

Roger Waters (right) 1944-

Rick Wright 1945-

English songwriters.

A respected and internationally popular group, Pink Floyd is known for embellishing basic rock rhythms with synthesized instrumentation and various sound effects to create orchestral, electronically-oriented music. Pink Floyd underwent several stylistic phases, transforming from an experimental, "psychedelic" rock band that attempted to evoke mystical images to a group that composed elaborate musical structures to complement Roger Waters's haunting, pessimistic lyrics. Pink Floyd was founded by Syd Barrett, who reportedly named the band after blues musicians Pink Anderson and Floyd Council. Through Barrett's emphasis on surrealistic music and playful, nonsensical lyrics, Pink Floyd became one of the first psychedelic rock bands to emerge in England during the 1960s. The band won initial recognition with two single records composed by Barrett, "Arnold Layne" and "See Emily Play," and with the album *Piper at the Gates of Dawn* (1967). After this album, Barrett left the band amid rumors of mental illness and drug abuse, and guitarist David Gilmour joined remaining band members Waters, Rick Wright, and Nick Mason.

Under the leadership of Waters, Pink Floyd began to experiment with various new electronic devices developed for recording studios. On the albums *A Saucerful of Secrets* (1968) and *Ummagumma* (1969) they blended such natural sounds as bird songs and buzzing insects with mechanical sounds and entrancing musical rhythms to form varying emotional textures. Pink Floyd quickly gained a reputation for spectacular stage shows featuring visual effects to parallel their novel approach to music. However, their next few albums, including *Atom Heart Mother* (1970), *Meddle* (1971), and *Obscured by Clouds* (1972) drew little critical or popular attention.

Dark Side of the Moon (1973) is the first of Pink Floyd's several "concept" albums, in which separate songs overlap to form a unified pattern of lyrical and musical themes. With this album, Pink Floyd began to place greater emphasis on lyrics, as Waters explores such themes as despair, materialistic values, mortality, war, and insanity. On *Dark Side of the Moon* the band blends half-muted voices and such mechanical sounds as ringing cash registers in "Money" and chiming clocks in "Time" with richly textured musical themes layered upon basic rock music. *Dark Side of the Moon* was generally praised

by critics and became an enormously popular album. A decade after its original release, this album remained on *Billboard* magazine's "Top 200," a weekly listing of albums by volume of sales. Pink Floyd's next two concept albums, *Wish You Were Here* (1975) and *Animals* (1977), were not as well received. On *Wish You Were Here,* Waters contemplates the negative aspects of material success and also, according to Ben Edmonds, "the machinery of a music industry that made and helped break Syd Barrett." Waters's major themes on *Animals* are loneliness, alienation, and human depravity. He symbolically reduces the human race into castes of pigs, dogs, and sheep to underscore negative human qualities. Many critics consider Waters's pessimism on *Wish You Were Here* and *Animals* to be lugubrious and superficial. Critics also debated whether the music on these albums reinforces or detracts from the thematic scope of Waters's lyrics.

In an interview, Waters commented that during the band's 1977 concert tour he sensed an "enormous barrier" between himself and his audience which blocked him from communicating the underlying meaning of his lyrics. On *The Wall* (1980), this barrier between artist and audience becomes an extended metaphor for personal alienation and oppression by social institutions. Largely Waters's creation, *The Wall* is structured like an opera and relates the mental withdrawal of a physically and emotionally exhausted rock star who relives painful episodes from his life. Although not considered overtly autobiographical, the protagonist of *The Wall* is haunted by the absence of his father; Waters's father died in World War II around the time that Waters was born. Along with allusions to various personal and social forms of oppression, Waters draws strong parallels between fascism and the potential for mob violence in rock audiences. Several critics faulted Waters's harsh view of contemporary society, specifically his depiction of cruel teachers, promiscuous women, and overbearing mothers as representative figures of oppression. However, others claim that *The Wall* offers powerful social criticism; one reviewer, for example, observes that it is Pink Floyd's "very humanism, balanced with their inspired production and compositional styles, that makes *The Wall* so stunning." The album's financial success made possible Pink Floyd's most elaborate stage production. While bricks are gradually laid at the foot of the stage, forming a thirty-foot wall during the band's performance, projected film sequences of violence and a gargantuan set of ominous marionettes provide symbolic visual images and reinforce the themes of the work. A film version of the album, *Pink Floyd The Wall* (1982), written by Waters and directed by Alan Parker, presents a surreal interpretation of the album.

***The Final Cut* (1982), apparently Pink Floyd's final album, is composed of songs originally written to supplement *Pink Floyd The Wall.* Subtitled "A Requiem for the Post-War Dream," Waters scorns the widespread belief that peace and prosperity would follow Allied victory in World War II. Waters pays tribute to his father, and he denounces the oppressive political acts of various world leaders. Though some critics find this album less satisfying than their previous works, several consider *The Final Cut* to be Pink Floyd's crowning achievement. Kurt Loder singles out Waters for praise: "Dismissed in the past as a mere misogynist, a ranting crank, Waters here finds his focus at last, and with it, a new humanity."**

ALAN HEINEMAN

I think this double album [***Ummagumma***] ultimately fails, but it's one of the most striking and arresting failures I've heard in some time. . . . It *should* be listened to.

The first record is a live performance, and the second a studio job. The live tracks are astonishing because of the superb control of textures and effects. None of the cuts except ***A Saucerful of Secrets*** is extraordinary, but all are good listening. . . .

Careful With That Ax, Eugene has an Oriental motif and a sighing, wordless vocal. (One of the admirable things Floyd is into is the use of several voices as one instrument rather than a verbally-oriented separate entity.) The title is whispered, there is a scream, and the piece goes into hard rock. . . . This diminishes into a reprise of the wordless vocal. Nice performance.

Set the Controls for the Heart of the Sun is a Middle Eastern modal tune with Mason using mallets and lots of electronic effects. It is not much. . . .

Grantchester Meadows and ***Several Species of Small Furry Animals Gathered Together in a Cave and Grooving with a Pict*** are based on extrinsic sounds: flies buzzing, birds chirping, water running. ***Meadows*** features Gilmour on acoustic guitar, but his playing is mostly a setting for the pastoral, natural noises. ***Pict*** is tenser. . . . A weird, angry unintelligible monolog in Scottish brogue ends the cut, which is the savage counterpart of ***Meadows***' tranquility.

Again, these pieces are more impressive for their potential than their realization. The same is true of ***The Narrow Way,*** which, nevertheless, has a couple of provocative themes. . . .

To repeat: there are some positively wrenching, stirring moments on these sides, and some of the concepts are new and certainly worth prolonged exploration. I hope it isn't the case with Pink Floyd, as it is with so many groups, that their intellect and rigorousness cannot compete with their imagination and need to explore.

Alan Heineman, in a review of "Ummagumma," in down beat, *Vol. 37, No. 11, May 28, 1970, p. 20.*

MIKE BOURNE

To me the previous Pink Floyd date, ***Ummagumma,*** proved in one perspective the most startling release of last year: a for-once expert adaptation of electronic techniques to rock (both live and in a studio), plus a disarming and unexpected musical sensitivity throughout. But ***Atom Heart Mother*** is less appealing somehow (although I suspect because I now have higher expectations of the band), perhaps in that the collectively-composed long title suite does remind me of the real thing: notable textures well-directed through many colorful tangents . . . yet too often the whole seems dispassionate, almost too "straight" for my blood.

But then, the second side surprises with soft ballad moods, featuring separate Waters, Wright, and Gilmour, then concludes with easy instrumental interludes among the sounds of early morning kitchen scuffling on ***Alan's Psychedelic Breakfast.*** Again, the musical sense of Pink Floyd is uncommon, particularly that of Richard Wright, whose ***Summer '68*** is the highlight of this album as was his spot on ***Ummagumma***—all of which adds up to a quartet of imaginative, always fascinating musicians. (p. 23)

Mike Bourne, in a review of "Atom Heart Mother," in down beat, *Vol. 38, No. 7, April 1, 1971, pp. 23-4.*

JEAN-CHARLES COSTA

Pink Floyd has finally emerged from the ***Atom Heart Mother*** phase, a fairly stagnant period in their musical growth, marked by constant creative indecision. . . . Their new album ***Meddle*** not only confirms lead guitarist David Gilmour's emergence as a real shaping force with the group, it states forcefully and accurately that the group is well into the growth track again.

The first cut, **"One of These Days (I'm Going to Cut You Into Little Pieces)"** sticks to the usual Floyd formula (sound effect—slow organ build—lead guitar, surge, & climax-resolving sound effect), but each segment of the tune is so well done, and the whole thing coheres so perfectly that it comes across as a positive high energy opening. . . . A clever spoof entitled **"Fearless"** leads up to a classic crowd rendition of Rodger's & Hammerstein's "You'll Never Walk Alone," the perennial victory song for the Wembley Cup Final crowd in England. And, to round off side one, a great pseudo-spoof blues tune [**"Seamus"**] with David Gilmour's dog . . . taking over the lead "howl" duties.

"Echoes," a 23-minute Pink Floyd aural extravaganza that takes up all of side two, recaptures . . . some of the old themes and melody lines from earlier albums. . . . ***Meddle*** is killer Floyd from start to finish.

Jean-Charles Costa, in a review of "Meddle," in Rolling Stone, *Issue 99, January 6, 1972, p. 70.*

ROY HOLLINGWORTH

Before this little episode begins, may I just say that the finest album ever made was **"Ummagumma."** To better it would be like attempting to re-design sunrise. Thank you. . . .

The cabby seemed interested when we asked for The London Planetarium. Why, I don't know. It seemed an honest request for 8:30 at night. . . .

The invitation to the reception at The Planetarium read:

> 8:45-9:30—The World Premiere of **"The Dark Side of the Moon,"** Pink Floyd album beneath the stars of The Planetarium. . . .

[It] was all very moving, being slumped back in a chair surrounded by stars and heavy, dribbling, gurgling, rushing music . . . climaxes, and quiet periods, and fiddly bits.

There were a lot of fiddly bits, and as they fiddled onwards, they fiddled into nothing. Oh dear.

Yes, ten minutes from blast-off the music became so utterly confused with itself that it was virtually impossible to follow. It wasn't just a case of that either. It was becoming less and less attractive, and after 15 minutes diabolically uninteresting.

This was a dreadfully disappointing moment. . . .

Quite a few people were beginning to chatter, and light cigarettes. A naughty thing to do. (p. 19)

With Capricorn rising and hearts falling, the first side plunged to a halt. Oh what a waste of wonderful talent. . . . Thought I was really going to witness another **"Ummagumma"**—something so incredible that you couldn't move or think of anything else while it was playing.

Mild applause greeted the completion of the first side, and the houselights were turned on to reveal a horde of faces. They looked slightly bored. They had every right to be. (pp. 19, 54)

The lights dimmed again, and the sound of coins entering a cashbox, or telephone money box, pierced the air in rhythmic ways. Sonata for the cash-box, something like that, and it was good. [This song, **"Money,"**] became more intense, clashy, and clangy, and spirited by God—as did the whole of Side Two. It was fabulous. . . .

The songs, the sounds, the rhythms were solid and sound. . . .

One song in particular [**"Brain Damage"**] was extremely Sydbarrettsian to the point of being a straight lift from any of the Lost Hero's songs.

Yes, Sydbarrettsian. . . . Barrett still exists, you know, and it was pleasing that the best track on this album is 80 per cent plus influenced by him. And I'll back that up in argument with anybody.

This track, and what followed [**"Eclipse"**] presented Floyd as Floyd should be, enormous, and massive, and overwhelmingly impressive. . . .

But whatever happened to Side One? Nine months in the making . . . And only one good side? But draw your own conclusions when you buy this album.

Which you should do, 'cause like The Stones and The Beatles, The Floyd were also what was—and hopefully still is—all right. (p. 54)

Roy Hollingworth, "The Dark Side of the Floyd," in Melody Maker, *March 10, 1973. pp. 19, 54.*

LOYD GROSSMAN

The Dark Side of the Moon is Pink Floyd's ninth album and is a single extended piece rather than a collection of songs. It seems to deal primarily with the fleetingness and depravity of human life, hardly the commonplace subject matter of rock. **"Time"** ("The time is gone the song is over"), **"Money"** ("Share it fairly but don't take a slice of my pie"), and **"Us and Them"** ("Forward he cried from the rear") might be viewed as the keys to understanding the meaning (if indeed there is any definite meaning) of ***The Dark Side of the Moon.***

Even though this is a concept album, a number of the cuts can stand on their own. **"Time"** is a fine country-tinged rocker . . . and **"Money"** is broadly and satirically played. . . . Throughout the album the band lays down a solid framework. . . .

There are a few weak spots. . . . **"The Great Gig in the Sky"** (which closes the first side) probably could have been shortened or dispensed with, but these are really minor quibbles. ***The Dark Side of the Moon*** is a fine album with a textural and conceptual richness that not only invites, but demands involvement. There is a certain grandeur here that exceeds mere musical melodramatics and is rarely attempted in rock. ***The Dark Side of the Moon*** has flash—the true flash that comes from the excellence of a superb performance.

Loyd Grossman, in a review of "The Dark Side of the Moon," in Rolling Stone, *Issue 135, May 24, 1973, p. 57.*

BRUCE MALAMUT

Conceived by percussionist/tape effector, Nick Mason, [the] audio spacescape, called **"Speak to Me,"** is fairly indicative of the psychological tone which pervades the rest of ***The Dark***

Side of the Moon (an appropriate title if ever there was one). The obsession with death is not a unique one—but from the Floyd? Those same cosmonauts who had previously led us through the tenth dimension with such strength and amazement? Maybe this thing has been on their minds for a while now—it's just that they speak to us so rarely, usually proferring an instrumental, rather than lyrical approach.

Well, out of the ten tunes on this single-album disc, six are fully-worded with the depressively cynical musings of Roger Waters. After Mason's aforementioned tape/character study in desperation, the listener is encouraged sardonically to **"Breathe,"** and live life out until "you race toward an early grave." . . . [**"Time"**] insists that, "the sun is the same in a relative way, but you're older / And shorter of breath and one day closer to death." A true pleasure . . . (p. 80)

A chime-stopped VCS3 bridges into the final **"Eclipse,"** in which the boys turn the ultimate irony on us with the admonition that, "Everything under the sun is in tune / But the sun is eclipsed by the moon."...

It would be difficult to put down a band who have given so many such cosmically sensory pleasure in the past. Two of their earlier works, ***Ummagumma*** and ***Atom Heart Mother,*** were undisputed classics within their genre. As the years pass, however, we find that the Floyd have seen natural to trade in their previously wide-eyed astonishment with the universe for their present stance of morbidly detached, myopically cynical and alienated boredom, as expressed in the lyrics on this latest album. Oh, the music is still there, . . . yet one can't help but feel that, were their lyrical output more bright, so would the music follow suit. If only some divine magus were available to re-arrange their reflection, to set their sights, perhaps, for the heart of the sun. (p. 81)

Bruce Malamut, in a review of "Dark Side of the Moon," in Crawdaddy, *June, 1973, pp. 80-1.*

JEFF WARDS

This tastefully wrapped double album [**"A Nice Pair"**] is a repackaging of the first two Floyd albums, **"The Piper At The Gates Of Dawn,"** named after the most revelationary chapter of "Wind In The Willows," and **"Saucerful of Secrets"**. . . . Somewhere in between these two albums Syd Barrett left the band, ridding them temporarily of their whole raison d'etre, and thus while **"Piper"** is crammed full of Syd's devastatingly original, witty, humorous and incisive songs, **"Saucerful"** is very much a transitional album, revealing elements of both what was and what was to be. Thus Barrett's **"Jug Band Blues"** and Rick Wright's very Barrett-influenced **"See-Saw"** contrast fairly sharply with the epic-quality of **"Set The Controls for the Heart of the Sun"** and **"Saucerful of Secrets"** which picked up on the direction implied by the earlier **"Interstellar Overdrive"** and which found ultimate fruition in more complete, if less-adventurous, pieces like **"Atom Heart Mother"** and **"Dark Side of the Moon."** . . . Certainly both of these albums stand the test of time well, although **"Piper"** seems the more unified of the two. **"Astronomy Domine"** from that album really predated the whole transient space-rock genre that was later to be used and abused, and of course Syd Barrett knew how to do it right. . . . Suffice it to say that his lyrics here still stand out after six years of being earbashed by a billion singer-songwriters and self-appointed prophets, seers and sages. Syd was absolutely unique, arising out of the murky morass of mid-sixties white soul and r 'n' b singers, like some psychedelic Virginia Woolf, words flying in one and several directions at once, stream-of-consciousness style. The words on **"Bike"** are such beautiful gibberish that it's almost as though Syd's talking in tongues. . . . And the lines are muttered deadpan in a ludicrously short space of time. Great stuff. And **"Chapter 24," "Gnome"** and **"Scarecrow"** reflect the old Flower-Power preoccupations with mysticism, fairy stories and things pastoral, all filtered through the Barrett consciousness. Bereft of Syd's guiding light, the Floyd floundered but briefly (Gilmour had joined the group before Syd left), and they rapidly picked up strength and continued at a tangent, shifting the emphasis from songs to electronic effect, and as early dabblings, the extended pieces on **"Saucerful"** are only partially satisfying. Better versions of them were to appear later on the live segments of **"Ummagumma."** It can't be denied, though, that at the time **"Set the Controls"** seemed sensational; now it's just interesting. But anyway, it's nice to have an excuse to chuck out your old mono copies of these albums, and enjoy this double album that says more about a particularly exciting period of rock than a dozen text books ever could.

Jeff Wards, "Allman Joy! 'A Nice Pair'," in Melody Maker, *December 29, 1973, p. 34.**

ALLAN JONES

I am not enthralled [with **"Wish You Were Here"**]. I have, also, to admit that its predecessor [**"Dark Side of the Moon"**], despite its enormous popularity, left me equally unmoved. I did try, though, to acclimatise myself to its bleak, emotionally barren landscape. Just as I have tried to entertain the prospect of embracing **"Wish You Were Here"** as a Giant Step Forward for Mankind. I keep missing the connection, somehow. From whichever direction one approaches **"Wish You Were Here,"** it still sounds unconvincing in its ponderous sincerity and displays a critical lack of imagination in all departments. It's really all quite predictable, and forces one to the conclusion that for the last two years (possibly longer) the Floyd have existed in a state of suspended animation.

It's really quite alarming that they should have remained so secure in their isolation. While the world turns in destruction upon itself, the Floyd amble somnambulantly along their star struck avenues arm in arm with some pallid ghost of creativity. **"Wish You Were Here"** sucks. It's as simple as that. . . .

The constant embellishments and elaborate effects which adorn the album seem merely artificial and contrived. A series of masks and facades to disguise the crucial lack of inspiration which afflicts the whole project.

One thing is evident from the moment the stylus hits the vinyl, **"Wish You Were Here"** is no progression from **"Dark Side of the Moon."** Just as there has been no real development in the Floyd's music since **"Ummagumma."** The slight concept which holds the album together is, essentially, a rather petulant tirade against the rockbiz. The attack is no more petulant because of Roger Waters' rather dubious qualities as a lyricist. . . .

Only on the introduction to **"Have A Cigar"** do the band play with any real vigour. . . . [However], Waters' lyrics again are painfully mundane. He's simply unable to invest his attack against rockbiz manipulation with any vestige of urgency. . . . The title track . . . is curiously lightweight, and almost instantly forgettable. . . .

The Floyd's real attempt at a magnum opus to rival past triumphs is the nine-part **"Shine On You Crazy Diamond."** This is Roger Waters' epic tribute to fractured genius Syd Barrett. It was perhaps inevitable, within the context of the album and Waters' lyrical preoccupation, that he should choose Barrett, rock casualty supreme, as a tragic example of creative innocence compromised and all but destroyed by the pressures of the biz. The insensitivity of Waters' lyrics borders on the offensive in that they completely trivialise Barrett's predicament. . . .

The final effect is not unlike a theme from Quo Vadis being piped into a supermarket. Careful with those frozen peas, Eugene.

"Wish You Were Here" will sell as well as **"Dark Side of the Moon,"** of course. And in three years, when the next Floyd album is released, I wouldn't be at all surprised if it's still on the chart.

Crazy isn't it?

Allan Jones, "Floyd in Creative Void," in Melody Maker, *September 20, 1975, p. 14.*

BEN EDMONDS

Without Pink Floyd we would not have the European sci-fi multitudes (Hawkwind, Can, Amon Duul II and all their little friends) to kick around. They were the first to explore the upper reaches of the chemical heavens, and their commercial and artistic superiority, if ever it was in doubt, was brutally confirmed by ***Dark Side of the Moon.*** That 1973 album has now sold over 6,000,000 units worldwide—3,000,000 in the U. S. alone. . . .

Talk has it that the waiting period [prior to the release of their next album, ***Wish You Were Here***] was prolonged by the band's own paranoia. To release *anything* would commit them to a competition with their own past that they could not hope to win.

If so, their fears have been realized. . . .

One of the things that made ***Dark Side of the Moon*** so striking was that it showed them at full recognition of their limitations as musicians. In the past Pink Floyd has often conceptually outdistanced their minimal technical skills, but everything on that record seemed perfectly calculated never to cross the line. . . . But most of the music on [***Wish You Were Here***] seems determined to picture Pink Floyd as just another conventional rock & roll band, ignoring their strengths of self-analysis in order to gain entry to an arena in which they aren't equipped to do battle. . . .

After all the time they've devoted to molding their shortcomings into something uniquely workable as a band, Pink Floyd should know better than to turn around and imitate the transparent, traditional rock-band methodology to which they supposedly present an alternative. (p. 63)

"Shine On You Crazy Diamond" is initially credible because it purports to confront the subject of Syd Barrett, the long and probably forever lost guiding light of the original Floyd. But the potential of the idea goes unrealized; they give such a matter-of-fact reading of the goddamn thing that they might as well be singing about Roger Waters's brother-in-law getting a parking ticket. This lackadaisical demeanor forces, among other things, a reevaluation of their relationship to all the space cadet orchestras they unconsciously sired. . . .

Wish You Were Here is about the machinery of a music industry that made and helped break Syd Barrett. . . . Their treatment, though, is so solemn that you have to ask what the point is. If your use of the 'machinery' isn't alive enough to transcend its solemn hum—even if that hum is your subject—then you're automatically trapped. In offering not so much as a hint of liberation, that's where this album leaves Pink Floyd. (p. 64)

Ben Edmonds, "The Trippers Trapped: Pink Floyd in a Hum Bag," in Rolling Stone, *Issue 199, November 6, 1975, pp. 63-4.*

MICHAEL DAVIS

Rock continues to mature and confront its own paradoxes, despite its inherent infantilism. . . . [Pink Floyd's] recent step-up from cult band to superstardom has brought about some changes in perception as well as lifestyle.

Their vehicle for this success was, of course, ***Dark Side of the Moon,*** which not only made the top of the charts here but was a best seller in England for over two years. Cries of sell out were both inevitable and groundless; even at their "experimental" high water mark, ***Ummagumma,*** their ideas were being usurped by King Crimson and other more technically proficient bands. . . . After vacillating for a few years, they decided to give fatal egalitarianism a kick in the crotch, letting Roger Waters take care of the lyrics (thus giving the band a much-needed head). . . . Their first project after this realignment of priorities was ***Dark Side; Wish You Were Here*** continues the process.

Thematically, ***Wish*** suggests a perpendicularity with Neil Young's recent *Tonight's The Night.* Neil is haunted by the deaths of his cohorts so he sings of drugged-out losers in a painful and ragged manner. The Floyd are freaked out by the disintegration of their erstwhile mentor, Syd Barrett, and by the overwhelming success that he started them on the path towards, yet their hands never shake on their instruments, their voices never crack. It's difficult to scream with a stiff upper lip.

So they don't, but their exhortations to Barrett are moving just the same. The two-part **"Shine On You Crazy Diamond,"** which opens and closes the album, is a plea from the band left alone, plagued by a frightening retention of sanity, for the man "caught on the cross-fire of childhood and stardom." Musically, it's the most backdated piece, recalling the past Floyd foible of establishing a mood, then running it into the ground. One wonders, however, if they do this here as a means of numbing themselves from their subject matter.

The title track seems to be a more personal note from Waters to Barrett, done in a rougher, more acoustic style, similar to some of Barrett's post Floyd work. . . .

"Have a Cigar" is . . . a not-so-subtle put-down of the greed grunts who inhabit the industry. "We're so happy we can hardly count," the chump chortles, as the band adds some funk farts to their synthi-stew.

"Welcome To The Machine" is more far-reaching, a nightmare come true for the Floyd who have just realized that success merely redefines flunky status on a higher plane. For most, the mansions and all are sufficient rewards but for a band who retain more than a little residue of late 60's socio-political consciousness, who have worked with Antonioni and other serious artists, who have probably never considered themselves pop stars, and who have never lived for cars and girls, the situation must be incredibly galling.

Michael Davis, "Elegy for the Living," in Creem, *Vol. 8, No. 7, December, 1975, p. 64.*

FRANK ROSE

For Pink Floyd, space has always been the ultimate escape. It still is, but now definitions have shifted. The romance of outer space has been replaced by the horror of spacing out.

This shift has been coming for a while. There was ***Dark Side of the Moon*** and **"Brain Damage,"** ***Wish You Were Here*** and the story of founding member Syd Barrett, the "Crazy Diamond." And now there's ***Animals,*** a visit to a cacophonous farm where what you have to watch for is pigs on the wing. ***Animals*** is a song suite that deals with subjects like loneliness, death and lies. "Have a good drown," they shout dolefully as you drop into the pit that is this album. . . . Thanks, pals, I'll try.

It's no use. Like all Floyd records, this one absorbs like a sponge, but you can still hear the gooey screams of listeners who put up a fight. What's the problem? . . . The sound is more complex, but it lacks real depth; there's nothing to match the incredible intro to ***Dark Side of the Moon,*** for example, with its hypnotic chorus of cash registers recalling the mechanical doom that was Fritz Lang's vision in *Metropolis.* Somehow you get the impression that this band is being metamorphosed into a noodle factory.

Maybe that shouldn't be suprising. Floyd was never really welcomed into the Sixties avant-garde: space rock was a little too close to science fiction for that. But the extraordinary success of ***Dark Side of the Moon*** (released nearly four years ago, it's still on the charts) culminated almost a decade of ever-expanding cult appeal and gave the band an audience that must have seemed as boundless as space itself. The temptation to follow through with prefab notions of what that audience would like—warmed over, spaced out heavy-metal, in this case—was apparently too strong to resist.

Even worse, however, is the bleak defeatism that's set in. . . . The 1977 Floyd has turned bitter and morose. (pp. 56, 58)

Floyd has always been best at communicating the cramped psychology that comes from living in a place like England, where the 20th century has been visibly superimposed on the others that preceded it. The tension that powers their music is not simply fright at man's helplessness before technology; it's the conflict between the modern and the ancient, between technology and tradition. Space is Floyd's way of resolving the conflict.

Of course, space doesn't offer any kind of real escape. . . . ***Animals*** is Floyd's attempt to deal with the realization that spacing out isn't the answer either. There's no exit; you get high, you come down again. That's what Pink Floyd has done, with a thud. (p. 58)

Frank Rose, "Floyd's Feckless Fauna," in Rolling Stone, *Issue 235, March 24, 1977, pp. 56, 58.*

STEVE SIMELS

I never cared much for the post-Syd Barrett Pink Floyd until their last album [**"Wish You Were Here"**]. . . . With its marvelously imaginative "Abbey Road"-ish musical trappings, it was a truly moving tribute to the founding member who had fallen prey to the dangers of a lifestyle Pink Floyd had all once communally endorsed—witty, bitter, mordant, and above all, honestly felt. I loved it.

I don't much love **"Animals,"** their new one, however. Musically and thematically it's constructed along the same lines as the last, but the subject—their intense contempt for the business of selling art—is just not important enough, or at least they don't make it *seem* important enough, to justify all the vented spleen. Pity is a rare emotion in a rock musician, but unfortunately self-pity isn't, and **"Animals"** comes off as just another boring entry in the same boring sweepstakes everyone from James Taylor to Elton John to Lou Reed to you name it has been dabbling in since the dawn of the Seventies. Splendidly played and produced. (pp. 91, 93)

Steve Simels, in a review of "Animals," in Stereo Review *Magazine, Vol. 38, No. 5, May, 1977, pp. 91, 93.*

RUSSELL SHAW

Pink Floyd, surpassed in the space race, has long officially abdicated their position of leadership in this area, preferring to transpose some of the more surface elements from their former sound into a personae of mass accessibility. At first, their creations were both valid and eloquent; ***Dark Side Of The Moon*** managed to fuse Moog bleeps with an anchoring, rhythmic base. In addition, a beautiful, brass-dominated single, ***Us and Them,*** was pulled from its grooves.

With ***Wish You Were Here,*** the process of decline truly began. Perhaps *decay* would be a better word, for many of the elementary sine waves and blips present were rote reworkings of stuff that sounded new on the last album. But on ***Animals*** the lack of anything musically or lyrically significant really shows. . . . The lyrics, clouded by oblique allegory, fail to rescue the uninspired package. . . .

In summation, the piece has virtually no continuity, few moments of anything but the most cursory, jaded licks, and even unlike its predecessors, no single. Yet unfortunately, this is as close to "electronic space rock" as most ears are going to get. The overwhelming pity is that Pink Floyd, an ensemble with a name *plus* previously demonstrated talent, has either run dry, or through a series of gimmicks . . . decided to appeal to the Least Common Denominator. (p. 28)

Russell Shaw, in a review of "Animals," in down beat, *Vol. 44, No. 9, May 5, 1977, pp. 24, 28.*

KURT LODER

Though it in no way endangers the *meisterwerk* musical status of ***Dark Side of the Moon*** (still on the charts nearly seven years after its release), Pink Floyd's twelfth album, ***The Wall,*** is the most startling rhetorical achievement in the group's singular, thirteen-year career. Stretching his talents over four sides, Floyd bassist Roger Waters, who wrote all the words and a majority of the music here, projects a dark, multilayered vision of post-World War II Western (and especially British) society so unremittingly dismal and acidulous that it makes contemporary gloom-mongers such as Randy Newman or, say, Nico seem like Peter Pan and Tinker Bell.

The Wall is a stunning synthesis of Waters' by now familiar thematic obsessions: the brutal misanthropy of Pink Floyd's last LP, ***Animals; Dark Side of the Moon***'s sour, middle-aged *tristesse*; the surprisingly shrewd perception that the music business is a microcosm of institutional oppression (***Wish You Were Here***); and the dread of impending psychoses that runs through all these records—plus a strongly felt antiwar animus that dates way back to 1968's ***A Saucerful of Secrets.*** But where ***Animals,*** for instance, suffered from self-centered smugness, the even more abject ***The Wall*** leaps to life with a relentless lyrical rage that's clearly genuine and, in its painstaking particularity, ultimately horrifying.

Fashioned as a kind of circular maze (the last words on side four begin a sentence completed by the first words on side one), ***The Wall*** offers no exit except madness from a world malevolently bent on crippling its citizens at every level of endeavor. . . . (p. 75)

As Roger Waters sees it, even the most glittering success later in life—in his case, international rock stardom—is a mockery because of mortality. The halfhearted hope of interpersonal salvation that slightly brightened ***Animals*** is gone, too: women are viewed as inscrutable sexual punching bags, and men (their immediate oppressors in a grand scheme of oppression) are inevitably left alone to flail about in increasingly unbearable frustration. This wall of conditioning finally forms a prison. And its pitiful inmate, by now practically catatonic, submits to **"The Trial"**—a bizarre musical cataclysm out of Gilbert and Sullivan via Brecht and Weill—in which all of his past tormentors converge for the long-awaited kill.

This is very tough stuff, and hardly the hallmark of a hit album. Whether or not ***The Wall*** succeeds commercially will probably depend on its musical virtues, of which there are many. (p. 75-6)

Problems do arise, however. While ***The Wall***'s length is certainly justified by the breadth of its thematic concerns, the music is stretched a bit thin. . . . Even Floyd-starved devotees may not be sucked into ***The Wall***'s relatively flat aural ambience on first hearing. But when they finally are—and then get a good look at that forbidding lyrical landscape—they may wonder which way is out real fast. (p. 76)

Kurt Loder, "Pink Floyd: Up Against 'The Wall'," in Rolling Stone, *Issue 310, February 7, 1980, pp. 75-6.*

VARIETY

On every level, creative and technical, Pink Floyd's live performance of **"The Wall"** is an astounding tour de force. Building from an album, which, even more than usual for this group, cries out for visual extrapolation, the band has fashioned a production which is both unflaggingly entertaining and thought-provoking.

The scale of the show is enormous, from the massive polystyrene building blocks which gradually come together to form a literal wall between the group and the audience, to the musical concepts themselves.

In **"The Wall,"** Pink Floyd is tackling no less than the collapse of western civilization in general, and English society, the cornerstone of that civilization, specifically. . . .

Surprisingly enough, however, given the production's scale, there are only a few times when the technical end becomes overblown and threatens to over-power the musical-conceptual performance. In fact, there is much more direct contact between the band and the audience than is usual for this "anonymous" assemblage. And, of course, the sheer size of the effects being employed makes every seat a good one. . . .

Art director-animation designer Gerald Scarfe's album cover "creatures," which resemble a nightmarish blend of Ralph Steadman and Gahan Wilson, are brought to life in stunning fashion, both with animation and with mammoth inflation puppets which underscore the primal fears being tapped in the show.

The show's finale, in which the wall is torn down, is accomplished via a computerized system said to cost in the seven-figure neighborhood. As an added touch, there were supposed to be fireworks with the wall's fall, but a fire opening night led to cancellation of that portion in subsequent performances. . . .

Musically, **"The Wall"** is as emotionally searing as the lyrics are cerebral. The performance caught was prime Pink Floyd.

Kirk., in a review of "The Wall," in Variety, *February 20, 1980, p. 72.*

JAY COCKS

Bass Player Roger Waters, who writes most of [Pink Floyd's] music, has tempered his lyric tantrums somewhat for the new album [***The Wall***] and has worked up some melodies that are rather more lulling and insinuating than anything Floyd freaks are used to. Spacy and seductive and full of high-tech sound stunts, ***The Wall*** has a kind of smothering sonic energy that can be traced to ***The Dark Side of the Moon*** and even past that, to the band's early days on the psychedelic front lines. To fans, this continuity must be just as reassuring as the trendiness Waters has grafted onto his lyrics, which are a kind of libretto for Me-decade narcissism. . . .

The Wall is a lavish, four-sided dredge job on the angst of the successful rocker, his flirtations with suicide and losing bouts with self-pity, his assorted betrayals by parents, teachers and wives and his uneasy relationship with his audience, which is alternately exhorted, cajoled and mocked. . . . To Waters, the audience is just another barrier, another obstacle to his exquisitely indelicate communion with his inner being. . . .

Every avenue of Waters' psyche ends up against a wall, a towering edifice whose bricks have been mixed from the clay of emotional trauma, vocational frustration and, apparently, brain damage. Absent fathers, smothering mothers, sadistic schoolmasters, insistent fans and faithless spouses: "All in all you were all just bricks in the wall."

Urging caution on "the thin ice of modern life," Waters' lyrical ankles do a lot of wobbling before he is indicted, some 75 minutes into the record, on charges of fecklessness, savagery and numbness. The presiding magistrate, a worm, sentences the singer to "be exposed before/Your peers/Tear down the wall." Lysergic *Sturm und Drang* like this has a direct kind of kindergarten appeal, especially if it is orchestrated like a cross between a Broadway overture and a band concert on the starship *Enterprise*. It is likely, indeed, that ***The Wall*** is succeeding more for the sonic sauna of its melodies than the depth of its lyrics. It is a record being attended to rather than heard.

Jay Cocks, "Pinkies on the Wing," in Time, *Vol. 115, No. 8, February 25, 1980, p. 49.*

HIGH FIDELITY

Pink Floyd, Dave Gilmour's and Roger Waters' nom de guerre, has gone from being the premier art-rock psychedelic band to literally cornering the mass market on full-blown paranoia (although Talking Heads are seriously angling for a piece of the action). With **"The Wall,"** it becomes pop's undisputed dark underbelly, the perfect British counterpart to Supertramp's hygienic sensibility. . . . **"The Wall"** is a bleakly depressing, pessimistic view of insanity in an insane world. It's also a brilliant double album of tortuously precise music that draws on everything from folk music to rock-disco to Stockhausen.

The lyrics tend to deal either with the general plight of any man in the modern world or with an aging rock star's flights between psychosis and catatonia. Side 1 paints a dank picture of growing up, in modern England specifically, where every outrage and infliction of pain is "just another brick in the wall" of psychological defenses that, ultimately, the individual builds around himself. And who but Pink Floyd would have a chorus of British schoolchildren singing over a brooding, minor disco pulse: "We don't need no education, we don't need no thought control. . . . Teachers leave the kids alone." Song after song reflects the dread horror of "skating on the thin ice of modern life." (p. 103)

On ***Don't Leave Me Now,*** the rock star persona begs his girlfriend not to go, "When you know how I need you, To beat to a pulp on a Saturday night." . . . The album's penultimate song, ***The Trial,*** is a Kurt Weill-inspired tour de force. . . . (pp. 103-04)

It's the authors' very humanism, balanced with their inspired production and compositional styles, that makes **"The Wall"** so stunning. As much as this music made me cringe at times (some of it is genuinely scary), the album has an underlying edge of warning and concern, which makes it all the more powerful. (p. 104)

A review of "The Wall," in High Fidelity, *Vol. 30, No. 3, March, 1980, pp. 103-04.*

DAVE DiMARTINO

[The following excerpts by Dave DiMartino offer an overview of the work of Pink Floyd.]

[When] I took ***Ummagumma*** home I played it over and over again, thinking about that quaint little Pop Band I'd seen on *Pat Boone* and how it couldn't be the same band because *this* music sounded like what music must sound like in outer space, *this* Pink Floyd sang about Setting Controls For The Heart Of The Sun and Saucersful of Secrets. I liked it so much that two friends and I formed a band and called ourselves The Intergalactic Space Force and we tried to sound like Pink Floyd. . . .

Inevitably, Pink Floyd changed. ***Atom Heart Mother*** was stuffy, loaded with what I would later come to regard as self-indulgence but at the time thought mere eccentricity, a "funny" album with cows on the cover and song titles like **"Breast Milky"** and **"Funky Dung."** They'd made the big switch from outer to inner space, and even though **"Alan's Psychedelic Breakfast"** showed the same fascination with windowpane lysergia as Pink Floyd Past, it never really gelled, never really approached **"Several Species Of Small Furry Animals Gathered Together In A Cave And Grooving With A Pict"** despite the equally cute title. (p. 22)

That Roger Waters was coming into his own was never more evident on his and Ron Geesin's ***Music From The Body,*** a film soundtrack with novelty farting/burping noises and much more. Waters' scattered compositions . . . touched on themes he'd be dwelling on in much greater detail years later: the cycle of life, from infant to middle age and beyond; the rape of the landscape by industry; nervous anxiety; the futility of life, and other self-directed topics that would, in later years, be dismissed as irrelevent by bands more concerned about fascist regimes and white riots.

When ***Meddle*** arrived in early 1972, Pink Floyd were a better *band*. . . . But as listenable as ***Meddle*** was, only **"One Of These Days,"** with its frenetically sexual pulsings, broke any new ground. **"Echoes,"** the side-long showpiece on Side Two, attempted to merge ***Ummagumma***'s spaciness with ***Atom Heart Mother***'s deluded grandeur and only ended up being boring and much too long.

And when ***Obscured By Clouds*** followed, it seemed a holding action, an incomplete work crammed with pleasant filler and not much else. ***More,*** which I'd gone back and bought after ***Ummagumma,*** was simply a better soundtrack, the one I still listen to years later. I thought ***Obscured By Clouds*** was a boring record by a band who shouldn't have been boring.

With ***Dark Side Of The Moon*** a whole new generation of Pink Floyd fans emerged, intrigued by **"Money"** and thereby force-fed what are probably Roger Waters' gloomiest lyrics ever. It all made great pop music, of course, and the irony of it—the LP's success, the blind/bland acceptance of the keynote theme, life sucks and will make you crazy—makes ***Dark Side*** a great record on many levels, including sociological ones.

The multi-platinum success of ***Dark Side*** was all Pink Floyd needed to go off the deep end, taking two years to come up with the barely acceptable ***Wish You Were Here,*** a "tribute" to Syd Barrett that couldn't conceal the fact that Roger Waters had nothing new to say. Melodies were weaker, and the LP's only good track, **"Welcome To The Machine,"** was about *life in the music biz,* possibly the lamest, least interesting lyrical concept there is. Problems were further compounded by the release of ***Animals,*** an ultimately tedious follow-up featuring the same songs the band had been performing in concerts two years previously: **"Dogs"** was **"You Gotta Be Crazy"**, **"Sheep"** was **"Raving and Drooling."** . . . It's probably the least interesting Pink Floyd album around. (pp. 22-3)

And two years after ***Animals, The Wall*** cast things in an entirely different light. (p. 23)

Dave DiMartino, "Pink Floyd Before the Wall: Come in Roger Waters, Your Time Is Up," in Creem, *Vol. 11, No. 12, May, 1980, pp. 22-3.*

DAVE DiMARTINO

[When] ***The Wall*** finally emerged, it had all the trappings of yet another Bloated Rock Opera, a dreaded "concept album" at the worst possible time—when the only right concept was no concept and there wasn't even room for argument. Critics ridiculed it, as they'd done with both ***Wish You Were Here*** and ***Animals*** previously, but this time with noticeably more venom. . . .

The Wall was mocked for its universality of theme, its "non-relevance" to the British Working Class who instead should—and it's this unspoken "should" that's most galling—be listening to songs about dwindling career opportunities, English civil wars.

In fact, ***The Wall***'s universality of theme is exactly what's keeping it on top of the charts and selling it in Miami, Seattle and Boogie, Iowa. And while the principle of the lowest common denominator is being singled out as Reason One for ***The Wall***'s massive success, there's considerably more involved, the least of which is art. (p.27)

Onstage were the beginnings of the wall. I'd heard about it from the L.A. reports: while the band performs, roadie/stage-hands construct the wall, brick by mammoth brick, until the band is completely hidden. *Obscured By Bricks*. Yeah.

And the show begins, even before people realize it. . . .

And then comes ***The Wall,*** of course, now making much more sense in this context. Huge marionettes in the shape of the Oppressors: the School Teacher, the Mother, the Whorish Female, the Judge and Tribunal. And the films, projected on the continually-growing wall, sophisticated animation depicting the same thing. (p.29)

And the thing of it is—it's all impressive as hell, it really is. The schoolchildren sing *"We don't need no education,"* from speaker to speaker to speaker, behind us, at our right, our left. . . . It is ROCK AS SPECTACLE and, as such, deserves to be appreciated as spectacle. Certainly it's the antithesis of everything *immediate* about rock 'n' roll—poor Roger Waters even wears headphones through the entire performance because he *has* to. . . . The tapes don't accompany Pink Floyd; Pink Floyd accompany the tapes. But then, there were never any claims put forth that immediacy *mattered* much here, that Roger Waters was aiming for anything *but* tightly-controlled, spectacular theatre. And on that level, ***The Wall*** in concert is a success, an extraordinary one.

But there is something wrong here, something about this show in Nassau Coliseum that doesn't mesh. Images, emotional undercurrents that seem vaguely *unhealthy,* not quite right. ***The Wall*** and what Roger Waters meant by it isn't the same ***Wall*** the audience has come to see, hear, and take drugs while watching. . . . *"I've got a silver spoon on a chain,"* and *"There's one smoking a joint"* bring the biggest cheers of all, and Roger Waters' message, as the crowd at the Nassau Coliseum interprets it, is TAKE LOTS OF DRUGS, KIDS, BECAUSE EVERYTHING SUCKS OUT THERE ANYWAY.

And there's more. The overprotective mother of ***The Wall***'s first few minutes, the bubble-headed . . . groupie, the almost repulsive imagery of Gerald Scarfe's animation—they all share such blatantly misogynist overtones it's frightening. Castration anxiety, oozing vaginas that lure and snip—is *this* Roger Waters' message? And if it is,*why* is this message one that elicits the strongest audience reaction? (pp. 29, 60)

That the latter portion of the performance has Waters in almost Hitlerian dress is heavily ironic, as, of course, is most of ***The Wall.*** Waters was never one for life-affirming messages—***Dark Side***'s lobotomy climax proved that years ago—but there's an element of dark sarcasm running through ***The Wall*** that at least *partially* alleviates its overbearing negativity. Unfortunately, few have picked up on it, preferring instead to think that hey, life really *does* suck, and isn't ol' Roger tellin' it the way it is? And if I were Waters, it would disturb me greatly knowing that I was at all responsible for imposing—or at least confirming—such negativity on a young and old impressionable audience. To sing *"I have become comfortably numb"* and be *cheered* for those exact words would make me wince. . . .

Roger Waters and Syd Barrett both seem to have learned the same lesson, and I wonder who's happier. I already know who's richer. (p.60)

Dave DiMartino, "Pink Floyd's Wall: Live and All Pink on the Inside," in Creem, *Vol. 12, No.1, June, 1980, pp. 26-7, 29, 60.*

ALLAN JONES

Written as an expression of doubt and apprehension, **"Dark Side Of The Moon"** became one of the most popular boutique soundtracks of all time. Lacerated by the dubious irony of its success, the Pink Floyd wrote **"Wish You Were Here"**, a bitter postcard from impending tax-exile and followed it with **"Animals"**, a disgusted cry from the heart of the beast that savaged capitalist society.

Two years in preparation, last year's tortured epic, **"The Wall"**, was the most extreme statement in this parade of psychomelodramas, most notable, perhaps, for the sheer persistence with which Roger Waters—increasingly using the Floyd as a vehicle for his own morbid preoccupations—slugged home his pessimistic visions. . . . Waters' autobiographical opera of misery and coruscating self-doubt was finally more tiresome than moving.

But we should remember that it was stated firmly from the beginning that the album was eventually to be judged in the context of **"The Wall"**, as a complete theatrical experience, the soundtrack of a multi-media extravaganza. Only then would its true worth become apparent. . . .

[The] show is an exact dramatisation of the album. The first half traces the genesis of Waters' anxieties, scatters the blame for the author's neurotic obsessions and despair. This despair isn't at all cosmetic: Waters' concern was tangible in the physical and vocal exaggeration of his performance.

Unfortunately, the songs through which he chooses to express his concerns are rarely capable of bearing the emotional weight with which he attempts to invest them. Waters might wear his heart bravely on his sleeve, but he often ends up with his feet in his mouth, choking on his own platitudes. Simultaneously, and equally destructively, the Floyd's characteristic, pedantic musical stroll only suffocates his basic themes, trumpets the vacuity of his less penetrating insights. . . .

Waters' **"One Of My Turns"** provided the only real jag in the ribs. Delivered with passionate sincerity, it recalled specifically the bleak landscapes charted by Lou Reed's "Berlin" (a work that was evoked frequently during the evening).

The much vaunted staging was impressive only in its dimensions. . . . There was nothing overwhelmingly imaginative about [it]: certainly, the production failed to match the brilliant ingenuity of, say, Alice Cooper's "Welcome To My Nightmare" show.

The climax to the first half did provide us with the production's most emphatically chilling image, though. The wall by now complete, save for one final space, Waters crooned the desolate lyric of **"Goodbye Cruel World."** As the music faded, he placed the final brick in the wall. The rest was silence: ominous and cold.

By this time, though, they'd lost me. If he'd hung around much longer, I'd have been down the front with a trowel and a bowl of cement, helping the bugger brick himself up.

The second half of the show failed to build on the desolate mood with which the first half ended; the lyrical introspection of the earlier songs was briefly pursued, as Waters evoked memories of his childhood and his father's death, but his attempts to locate his private turmoil in a wider social and political context floundered badly. The insular unreality of a rock star's life was brilliantly illustrated when a trap door in the wall fell open revealing Waters isolated in a neon-lit motel interior, but subsequent references to totalitarian repression and fascist violence were clumsily mounted, dangerously ambiguous.

The climax was predictable and inevitable. . . .[The] wall collapsed amid volcanic explosions.

Led by Waters, the musicians reappeared like a New Orleans funeral band, playing a lament among the debris. **"Outside The Wall,"** the final piece, seemed to imply that the preceding destruction had been evidence of some kind of metaphorical martyrdom.

Allan Jones, "Troubled Waters," in Melody Maker, *August 9, 1980, p. 15.*

PATRICK HUMPHRIES

[**"A Collection of Great Dance Songs"** presents] five jaundiced Roger Waters views of the human condition, unremittingly bleak; but enticing, with all the technological wizardry the Floyd can muster. The popular view is that the Floyd went straight down the plug as a genuinely original force right after Syd Barrett sunk into his subterranean homesick blues. Yet that goes no way to explaining the Floyd phenomenon.

Obviously there is enormous appeal in Waters' desolate lyrics, coupled with the symphonic, stereo appeal of the music. All manner of sound effects and layers of sound imbue the lyrics with a profundity they lack in isolation.

A song like **"Wish You Were Here"** *is* a good song when considered simply as a song on this album, the same with **"Another Brick"**. But the Floyd are an albums band, and on any one of their albums, the songs simply form a part of a far broader concept.

That's why I prefer something like the conciseness of **"Money"** to the sprawling **"Sheep"** which follows it. At the centre of **"Shine On You Crazy Diamond"** is an impressive, concise song struggling to get out. It's too easy to knock the Floyd as a dinosaur band playing lavish music you can meditate to. As one of the biggest bands on the planet, the message they offer is one of the bleakest. That, I think, says more about their audience than the band themselves ever could.

Right at the end of the second side, a dour Scottish voice screams "If you don't eat your meat, how can you have any pudding?" Maybe that's the essence of the Floyd's appeal (and why this compilation will sell in vast quantities to people who already own everything on it).

Patrick Humphries, "Out of the Red and into the Black: 'A Collection of Great Dance Songs'," in Melody Maker, *November 21, 1981, p. 23.*

ANDY SECHER

[Pink Floyd's] newest release, "greatest hits" package titled ***A Collection of Great Dance Songs,*** is a good case for considering them the most creative rock band of all time.

"The key to any success we've enjoyed has been our ability to balance the power of both our lyrics and our music," Gilmour said recently. . . . "Our goal has always been to create music that's unique but that still falls within the confines of rock and roll." . . .

With the release of the band's landmark album, ***Dark Side of the Moon,*** in 1973, Waters had developed into a capable songwriter. His lyrics on ***Us and Them*** and ***Money*** (available in a newly recorded version on the ***Great Dance Songs*** collection) touched on socially "hip" topics like corporate greed and world turmoil. It was an intoxicating mix. ***Dark Side of the Moon*** was a revolutionary pop vehicle that maintained artistic integrity and gained commercial acceptance. The album was one of the epic achievements of the 1970s. Eight years after its release, it's still "top 200" on the sales charts. . . .

While ***Dark Side of the Moon*** turned an important commercial corner for the band, setting the stage for such technologically brilliant but artistically disappointing albums as ***Wish You Were Here*** and ***Animals,*** nothing prepared the rock world for the group's next release, ***The Wall. The Wall*** quickly emerged as Floyd's magnum opus, a haunting aural tapestry that surpassed even ***Dark Side of the Moon***'s musical imagination. . . .

Now with the release of ***A Collection of Great Dance Songs*** (which in title pays tongue-in-cheek homage to the band's nonconformist attitudes), Floyd has presented an abbreviated synopsis of their musical magic. On such classic numbers as ***Sheep*** (from ***Animals***), ***One of These Days*** (from ***Meddle***), and ***Another Brick In The Wall*** (from ***The Wall***), Floyd proves they are the most daring and imaginative group around.

Andy Secher, "Pink Floyd: Beyond the Fringe," in Hit Parader, *Vol. 41, No. 211, April, 1982, p. 12.*

JOHN COLEMAN

'The Wall' was an album, substantially down to Roger Waters, and a hugely successful stage happening designed by Gerald Scarfe, with the barrier being erected brick by brick on stage and Scarfe animations of marching red, black and grey hammers suddenly highstepping across from three projectors: a stunning *coup de théâtre,* by all accounts. Now, accompanied by angst-ridden publicity about how frightful they found the experience of working in troika, there is [***Pink Floyd The Wall***] 'an Alan Parker film', 'by' Roger Waters, 'designed by' the redoubtable Scarfe.

And it is all about the very bad time a top rock and roll singer Pink . . . is not just seen to be having but had, blow by blow, from little boyhood up. . . .

From where I sat, seething, it registered as a load of resoundingly dropped bricks.

One has only hinted at the constantly shifting visual surface of the film (and can say little about its verbal message since most of the lyrics are indecipherable, and they carry 99% of the words). . . . But often Alan Parker's staged occasions are simply echoed by the animations, as in the notorious **'We Don't Want No Education'** number, where robotic kids dropping head first into a giant mincer from which your real meat-threads issue are later to become drawn figures dropped down a school chimney-cum-funnel with similar stylised results. There is a tedious literalness here that won't bear repetition. And, far, far worse, there is the egregiously mindless assumption *passim* that one kind of violence, pain, suffering is qualitatively very like another; that there is therefore no kind of spiritual coarseness in equating the self-pity of a burnt-out hophead with the anguish of bodies on a battlefield.

John Coleman, "Bad Trips," in New Statesman, *Vol. 104, No. 2678, July 16, 1982, p. 28.**

STEVE JENKINS

For an hour or so of its running time, ***Pink Floyd The Wall*** is merely what one might have feared: a vacuous, bombastic and humourless piece of self-indulgence. The blatant conceit at its centre—Roger Waters crying "Pity the isolation of the tortured mega-star"—is remarkably neat. It is, of course, the particular cushioned status of groups like Pink Floyd which breeds this twisted kind of navel-gazing. With no (financial) need to produce anything at all, the overblown aural treats they toss to their fans approximately once every two years have a built in subject / stance. Stuck behind a wall (a metaphor that is as accurate as it is obvious and crude), in a timeless musical limbo, what else is there to think about but Big Themes: i.e., yourself and your wall . . .

Nevertheless, the failure of the film to achieve any distance, let alone a critical one, from this projected image is quite extraordinary. The obsessive subject—the grand conspiracy by everybody and everything to drive the 'artist' into isolation—not only turns every other character simply into parts of the 'problem' (from his father, inconsiderate enough to die at Anzio, onwards), but also leads to numbing repetition in terms of general structure (one damn thing after another) and specific images. . . . [Director] Alan Parker compounds all this by a return to his own past, drawing exclusively (apart from echoes of *Tommy*) on TV advertisements for the look of the film and its rhythm. . . . The animated sequences are also in effect redundant, since they serve no specific function apart from the live action. Where the two are combined, however ([Pink] menaced by a cartoon monster), the result is at least unintentionally funny.

Not so amusing, and the crux of the matter, is the film's final half-hour, where it turns from being merely silly into something potentially dangerous. The fascist rally and accompanying violence (carried out by uniformed skinheads against "fags", "coons", Jews and women), which is presented as the logical climax to Pink's paranoid self-obsession, is shot in a manner which allows for no response except automatic rejection (in which case, so what?) or pure gut-level excitement. The rape of a white woman found in a car with a black man is handled in exactly the same hysterical fashion as the film's numerous other examples of woman-hating. The final repudiation of all this (the smashing of the wall) scarcely solves the problem of how audiences will have responded to Parker's slam-bang style, and to pretend otherwise is a long way to the right of naivety. (p. 173)

Steve Jenkins, in a review of "Pink Floyd The Wall," in Monthly Film Bulletin, *Vol. 49, No. 583, August, 1982, pp. 172-73.*

ROBERT HATCH

When I came up to the box office, the woman behind the glass gave me a quick look and warned, "It's a noisy picture, sir." I'd guessed as much from the crowd in the lobby—no one in sight looked old enough to remember the Cuban missile crisis, and a tolerance for sound at levels that strike me as grotesquely excessive seems characteristic of the post-Kennedy generation.

This time, however, the uproar, visual as well as audible, is appropriate. ***Pink Floyd—The Wall*** is a manifestation of madness, which I can believe might well take the form of excruciating amplification of the senses. The film is composed partly of surreal animation . . . , partly of kaleidoscopically fragmented live action. . . . (p. 219)

The picture opens in a Los Angeles hotel room, where Pink, the disintegrating hero, is gazing into the empty space of an old war picture being rerun on television and adding the final blocks to the wall that shields him from reality. . . . Pink's brain, where the action is seated, smokes not only with his own horrors but with those of his father, who was dying at Anzio as he was being born in London. The images begin with the boy's lonely resentment of adult despotism. They develop into an ever more tumultuous phantasmagoria of sex, power and the solitude of fame. Soon the theater seems ablaze with high-technology distortions of sound and sight—bewildering, frightening, sometimes beautiful—and delivered at a speed and with an intensity to which the only possible response is submission. The effect is similar to that of standing beneath a great cataract. One's normal responses to stimuli are paralyzed by the uproar, and that induces a kind of euphoria. You find yourself laughing and cheering, exulting vicariously in the driving rhythm.

It was thoughtful of the cashier to warn me, but I came from the theater feeling purged and lighthearted. It was some time before I woke up to realize that I'd been attending the inner torment of a man in the final stages of self-destruction. It's an odd way to get a lift. (pp. 219-20)

Robert Hatch, in a review of "Pink Floyd—The Wall," in The Nation, *Vol. 235, No. 7, September 11, 1982, pp. 219-20.*

KURT LODER

This may be art rock's crowning masterpiece, but it is also something more. With ***The Final Cut,*** Pink Floyd caps its career in classic form, and leader Roger Waters—for whom the group has long since become little more than a pseudonym—finally steps out from behind the "Wall" where last we left him. The result is essentially a Roger Waters solo album, and it's a superlative achievement on several levels. Not since Bob Dylan's "Masters of War" twenty years ago has a popular artist unleashed upon the world political order a moral contempt so corrosively convincing, or a life-loving hatred so bracing and brilliantly sustained. Dismissed in the past as a mere misogynist, a ranting crank, Waters here finds his focus at last, and with it a new humanity. . . . By comparison, in almost every way, ***The Wall*** was only a warm-up.

The Final Cut began as a modest expansion upon the soundtrack of the film version of ***The Wall***. . . . [***Pink Floyd The Wall***], a grotesquely misconceived collaboration between Waters and director Alan Parker, was released to a general thud of incomprehension. Around the same time, Prime Minister Margaret Thatcher, irked by the unseemly antics of an Argentine despot, dispatched British troops halfway around the world to fight and die for the Falkland Islands.

That event, coming in the wake of his failed film statement, apparently stirred Waters to an artistic epiphany. Out of the jumbled obsessions of the original ***Wall*** album, he fastened on one primal and unifying obsession: the death of his father in the battle of Anzio in 1944. Thus, on ***The Final Cut,*** a child's inability to accept the loss of the father he never knew has become the grown man's *refusal* to accept the death politics that decimate each succeeding generation and threaten ever more clearly with each passing year to ultimately extinguish us all. (pp. 65-6)

As fantasy, this has a certain primordial appeal. But Waters realizes that all the Neanderthals will never be blown away. What concerns him more is the inexplicable extent of fighting in the world when there seems so little left to defend. In **"The Gunner's Dream,"** a dying airman hopes to the end that his death will be in the service of "the postwar dream," for which the album stands as a requiem—the hope for a society that offers "a place to stay / enough to eat," where "no one ever disappears . . . and maniacs don't blow holes in bandsmen by remote control." But Waters, looking around him more than thirty-five years after the war's end, can only ask: "Is it for this that daddy died?"

In the past, Waters might have dismissed the gunner's dream as an empty illusion from the outset. Instead, though, Waters insists on honoring his sacrifice: "We cannot just write off his final scene / Take heed of his dream / Take heed." Without a commitment to some objective values, he seems to say, we sink into a brutalizing xenophobia—an "I'm all right, Jack" condition explored with considerable brilliance in the withering **"Not Now John."** In that song, the deepest human truths are cast aside in a frenzy "to compete with the wily Japanese." . . .

"Not Now John" qualifies as one of the most ferocious performances Pink Floyd has ever put on record. In the context of ***The Final Cut,*** it is something of an oddity; for while the music has an innate architectural power that pulls one ever deeper into the album's conceptual design, the performances and production are generally distinguished by their restraint—even the fabled Floydian sound effects are reduced to the occasional ticking clock or whooshing bomber. . . .

Whether this will be their last album as a group . . . is not as compelling a question as where Waters will go with what appears to be a new-found freedom. He plans to record a solo album for his next project, and one hopes that just the novelty of becoming a full-fledged human will be enough to keep him profitably occupied for many years to come. (p. 66)

Kurt Loder, "Pink Floyd's Artistic Epiphany," in Rolling Stone, *Issue 393, April 14, 1983, pp. 65-6.*

JOHN PICCARELLA

Pink Floyd have made quite a living without working too hard—in the 10 years since they broke big with ***The Dark Side of the Moon,*** they've made just four albums. The latest, and their last, ***The Final Cut,*** follows ***The Wall*** by more than three years. . . . Pink Floyd wasn't a fun band. Other groups have thrilled fans with bad vibes, but death trips like the Doors' or Iggy's were at least unruly, surprising, charismatic, and sexy. Pink Floyd has traded profitably in unsexy depression for over a decade. . . .

[Pink Floyd's early] funereal tone poems were meant to be heard stoned, and they were also meant to scare the shit out of you. The formal manipulation of suspense was basic to their music, characterized by long, repetitious, slowly built climaxes in the manner of Ravel's *Bolero,* and even more like the outer-space processionals and martial fantasies of English colorists like Holst and Elgar. . . . Pink Floyd went for glacial force—slow, huge, inevitable.

On ***The Dark Side of the Moon,*** Pink Floyd made the '70s move from drugs to high tech. . . . The head was, as they say, heavy—a compelling melodrama of stop-the-clock obsession. . . .

Pink Floyd's best albums, ***Wish You Were Here*** and ***Animals,*** offered Waters's pessimistic versions of rockbiz inhumanity and Orwellian paranoia, graced with longish instrumental musings. ***The Wall*** was more ambitious but its attempt to combine both of these themes into rock opera failed in the grand style. Like ***The Dark Side of the Moon, The Final Cut*** is a relatively modest set of songs which cohere into a concept album that avoids the epic. *Rolling Stone* has called this Pink Floyd's best album [see excerpt above by Kurt Loder], but while it may have some smart lyrics—sharp angry phrases, precise political targets—the music ranks with their dreariest. And while the present British economy lends itself to dreary characterization, it's been rocked a lot harder—by the Jam's *Setting Sons,* for instance. For all his anxiety, Roger Waters just isn't as smart about working-class misery as Paul Weller (who's not that smart himself).

The album's theme is stated in the subtitle, "A Requiem for the Postwar Dream." . . . The lyrics try to get inside the memories, hopes, and failures of the survivors of the last war Europeans can be proud of. Like Elvis Costello's "Shipbuilding," it connects Falklands War fever to the reawakened pride and economic hopes of the working class. . . . In the title track Waters, or his rockstar persona, reveals his deepest fears and doubts, including a failed suicide attempt. . . . But on the heels of this despair the band leaps into power trio attack for **"Not Now John,"** a patriotic take-pride-in-your-labor song that's the record's only real basher. In a vigorous parody of working-class jingoism Waters sings: "Fuck all that we've got to get on with these / Got to compete with the wily Japanese." This recalls the album's opening lines, in which the peacetime inactivity of the shipyards is blamed on the Japanese, who in turn are mocked for their high suicide rate. In other words, the inability of the English to find jobs and of Waters's protagonist to commit suicide is played off the Japanese proficiency in both. What does this mean? That he (and his people) should expect the bomb the Japanese got?

With the clock ticking, contrasting national versions of the postwar dream, as well as class distinctions, all wind down to Waters's "premonitions . . . suspicions of the holocaust to come." And in the last song, **"Two Suns in the Sunset,"** it happens. For Waters, the political questions of work and play, unemployment and stardom, are subsumed in the passage of time, which proceeds like any one of the young Pink Floyd's heavy dirges to the unavoidable big finish. Their last words: "We were all equal in the end." It's ironic that between the failed suicide and the certain nuclear holocaust, Pink Floyd's farewell album finds its most rousing moment in a fake labor anthem. Maybe we'd all have been happier if they'd been men at work, proudly turning out pop product once a year.

John Piccarella, "The Last Labor of Pink Floyd," in The Village Voice, *Vol. XXVIII, No. 23, June 7, 1983, p. 59.*

DAVID M. GOTZ

In what amounts to a Roger Waters solo album, he presents a singularly depressing view of our tragic times. . . . [In ***The Final Cut***] Waters' caustic words about war and suffering, present and future, overshadow the primarily low-key but vibrant musical stature. The finality of the lyrics and of the title leads one to believe that this is the last record for Pink Floyd. In that respect, this is a suitable swan song capping the productive and satisfying evolution of a sonically stimulating and thought-provoking band.

David M. Gotz, in a review of "The Final Cut," in Record Review, *Vol. 7, No. 4, August, 1983, p. 47.*

D(aniel) M(anus) Pinkwater

1941-

(Also writes as Manus Pinkwater) American novelist, nonfiction writer, author of books for children, and illustrator.

Pinkwater's novels typically involve ordinary characters thrust into improbable places and ludicrous situations and combine elements from such popular genres as mystery, horror, and science fiction. His use of nonsense words and phrases, zany one-liners, vivid imagery, and bizarre plots has secured his reputation as a writer of humorous and entertaining fiction. Although he is sometimes faulted for sacrificing depth and meaning for the sake of the ridiculous, he is often praised for the wealth of detail and imagination in his works.

Pinkwater first gained recognition as an author of books for children; *Alan Mendelsohn, Boy from Mars* (1979) is his first of several works directed toward young adults. This novel centers on the friendship between two junior high school boys—one an outcast, the other a Martian—and their adventures involving mind control and travel through time. *Slaves of Spiegel* (1982) was classified by Peter Andrews as a "goofball science-fiction story." This work takes a madcap look at a planet of junk food connoisseurs who kidnap two earthlings to participate in a junk food competition. *Young Adult Novel* (1982), which Patty Campbell labeled "a delicious piece of dada fluff," revolves around the antics of the Wild Dada Ducks, a group of teenagers who rebel against the conventions of their school's administration. Like many of Pinkwater's novels, this work is a parody, spoofing the Dada movement as well as conventional young adult novels. *The Snarkout Boys & the Avocado of Death* (1982) and its sequel, *The Snarkout Boys and the Baconburg Horror* (1984), combine spy fiction and fantasy as they follow the escapades of two boys and a girl who go "snarking," or sneaking off to all-night movies.

(See also *Contemporary Authors,* Vols. 29-32, rev. ed.; *Contemporary Authors New Revision Series,* Vol. 12; and *Something about the Author,* Vol. 8.)

Photograph by Miriam Pinkwater. Courtesy of E. P. Dutton

ANN S. HASKELL

[**"Alan Mendelsohn"** is Mr. Pinkwater's] most ambitious book to date, a 252-page novel that is, in spots, reminiscent of E. Nesbit, and everywhere vintage Pinkwater. Though its hero, Leonard, has a different name, he is the continuation of the heroes in the earlier novels, all various shades of Mr. Pinkwater himself: curious, oddball, moral, pre-teen lovers, not-too-hassled by authority figures, who stumble onto some incredible power and, along with it, a fantastic adventure, usually otherworldly. The exception is **"The Last Guru,"** a satire, which brings the otherworldly down to earth.

Mr. Pinkwater's formula for fantasy is simple: he doesn't strain anybody's credibility. The power, or key to it, in each of his novels resides in some impotent adult, such as an over-the-hill, obvious con artist—Samuel Klugarsh is the latest one—whose fraud is so blatant that it can be topped only by the surprise of his actually having the power without even knowing it. Even the fantasy in **"The Hoboken Chicken Emergency,"** superimposed on the tired plot of banished pet turned mean without understanding, here concerning the love of Arthur Bobowicz for a 266-pound chicken, succeeds with the easy touch of Mr. Pinkwater.

Though he will never win any awards strictly for his prose, neither will he collect any booby prizes for it. The writing itself is adequate, no more, no less. But for imaginative plot and decorative detail, Mr. Pinkwater's scores go off the charts. All his life he has been collecting funny odds and ends—names of people, places, products and mannerisms, for example—that give depth to his stories and which, taken together, sometimes add up to rather remarkable sociological commentary. In **"Alan Mendelsohn,"** for instance, there are the newly affluent exurbanites, who've moved away from their comfortable networks of friends and familiar institutions in the Bronxes of their past to what they feel are the advantages of suburbs, such as West Kangaroo Park; the tightly structured, excluding social world of Bat Masterson Junior High School; and Hogboro's Bermuda Triangle Chili Parlor, with its steamy windows and Green Death chili, corn muffins and marshmallowed hot chocolate—scenes right out of Mr. Pinkwater's Chicago and Los Angeles past. . . .

Mr. Pinkwater describes writing as "cheap psychotherapy, a process in which I, the writer, create for myself as a reader, drawing on my childhood experiences, which come back in random moments complete with sounds and smells and feelings." . . .

He just "hangs out at the desk," writing only as long as the inspiration lasts, but stopping when he feels that he takes over. (p. 32)

"Alan Mendelsohn" comes from Mr. Pinkwater's own junior high school past, he says. "I *thought* there was a kid by that name, though no one else remembers, and I *thought* he said he was Martian, but nobody remembers that either, and I *thought* there'd been a riot over his saying so. . . ." His voice trails off. "I'm not sure what really happened." (pp. 32, 43)

Ann S. Haskell, "The Fantastic Mr. Pinkwater," in The New York Times Book Review, *April 29, 1979, pp. 32, 43.*

BETSY HEARNE

Pinkwater's most ambitious fantasy so far [***Alan Mendelsohn, the Boy from Mars***] veers sharply from the compact one-liners of his latest comic feat, ***The Last Guru***. . . . This is the meandering (as opposed to tall) tale of Leonard Neeble, formerly a happy denizen of city neighborhood streets and now the outcast of suburban Bat Masterson Junior High School. Fortunately, along comes Alan Mendelsohn, an expert at tripping the self-righteous, a loyal friend through the vicissitudes of mind control and other astromental experiments, and (as it turns out) a Martian. Their friendship carries them from comic book collections through Samuel Klugarsh's occult bookstore to Lance Hergeschleimer's Oriental Gardens (a tricky time-slip trip). . . . In the end, what appeared to be many loose ends are more or less stretched together into an ingenious knot, which science fiction fans with time on their hands will smile to see tied. Once or twice, too, this protagonist lumbers close to being more real than spoofy.

Betsy Hearne, in a review of "Alan Mendelsohn, the Boy from Mars," in Booklist, *Vol. 75, No. 19, June 1, 1979, p. 1493.*

ZENA SUTHERLAND

[In ***Alan Mendelsohn, the Boy from Mars,*** an] exaggerated, tongue-in-cheek story of time-slips and thought control, Pinkwater lampoons con men and dupes, psychic powers, quack medicos, natural food faddists and assorted weird characters with great humor if, occasionally, at great length. Leonard and Alan repeatedly fall for confidence tricks and repeatedly profit from them, as when they buy a Mind Control Omega Meter and find that, for them, it works. If nothing succeeds like excess, the author has achieved a triumph of improbable folderol.

Zena Sutherland, in a review of "Alan Mendelsohn, the Boy from Mars," in Bulletin of the Center for Children's Books, *Vol. 33, No. 3, November, 1979, p. 54.*

FRAN LANTZ

Pinkwater writes hilarious, outrageous, delightful novels about intelligent lizards, pig-shaped submarines, gurus in silly hats and other fantastic and wonderful things. Pinkwater's books don't always succeed—***The Last Guru*** and ***Yobgorgle*** fall apart about half-way through—but when they do, the result is exhilarating.

Alan Mendelsohn is Pinkwater's best book since ***Lizard Music.*** The plot concerns the adventures of Leonard Neeble and Alan Mendelsohn, fellow students at Bat Masterson Junior High School. Things are pretty dull around Hogsboro until Leonard and Alan discover the Bermuda Triangle Chili Parlor, meet Samuel Klugarsh, and start learning the Klugarsh Mind Control System. . . . And I almost forgot Clarence Yojimbo. You see, he's a member of the Laughing Alligator Motorcycle Club, a folk singer, and an extra-terrestrial, and . . . well, maybe you'd better just read the book. It's terrific! And then give it to your favorite young adult to enjoy.

Fran Lantz, in a review of "Alan Mendelsohn, the Boy from Mars," in Kliatt Young Adult Paperback Book Guide, *Vol. XV, No. 6, September, 1981, p. 14.*

PATTY CAMPBELL

[***Young Adult Novel*** by Daniel Pinkwater] is an absolutely exquisite putdown, a piece of delicious dada fluff. In the spirit of Marcel Duchamp, a high school group of five who call themselves the Wild Dada Ducks have agreed to devote their lives to reshaping culture in the dada mold. The members, who count among their number The Indiana Zephyr and the Honorable Venustiano Carranza (President of Mexico), have been amusing themselves by composing a lurid group novel that they call *Kevin Shapiro, Boy Orphan*. Its plot is hauntingly familiar: "Sometimes Kevin is an orphan, sometimes a juvenile delinquent, a druggie, a lonely child of feuding parents, a social misfit, a homosexual, and a weakling who wants to play sports, and any number of other kinds of hardluck characters." However, "unlike the novels in the school library, he never solves his problems." The Wild Dada Ducks are ecstatic when they discover that there is in their very own school a student actually named Kevin Shapiro. They set out to make him a culture hero, much to the real-life Kevin's annoyance and disgust. When they, through some strange and imaginative tactics, succeed in getting him elected student body president, he takes a suitably dadaist revenge involving quantities of soggy Grape-Nuts. (p. 533)

Patty Campbell, in a review of "Young Adult Novel," in Wilson Library Bulletin, *Vol. 56, No. 7, March, 1982, p. 533.*

KIRKUS REVIEWS

The title [of ***The Snarkout Boys & the Avocado of Death***] is indicative of the silliness quotient of Pinkwater's latest exercise in outlandish adventure. The snarkers of the title are narrator Walter Galt and his friend Winston Bongo, two ninth graders who sneak out at night and take the Snark Street bus to the Snark movie theater where they watch all-night reruns. There they meet Rat, a girl their age who indulges in the same practice and also calls it snarking, and through Rat her mad-scientist uncle Flipping Hades Terwilliger, an avocado freak like Walt's father. Pinkwater coasts for awhile, wheeling us past a stream of eccentric people and places, then initiates a preposterous search when Flipping Hades Terwilliger disappears. . . . It turns out that extra-terrestrial thought forms have taken over the minds and bodies of all earth's realtors; but Uncle Flipping has developed a vegputer, called an Alligatron but really a giant avocado, which uses the fruit's natural electrical emanations to repel the invaders. A detective with painted-on hair and sideburns, his sidekick in a mop wig, a wrestler named Mr. Gorilla (Winston's uncle), two kidnapped orangutans, and, performing briefly, the Chicken Man from ***Lizard Music*** all figure in the rescue of Uncle Flipping—but the Chicken Man's intriguing mystery and wisdom are absent here. And despite a sardonic characterization of the boys' high school, some spoofing of classic detection fiction, and the important revelation about realtors, this is mainly random silliness without the inspired absurdity of ***Lizard Music*** and ***Alan Mendelsohn*** or even the buildups and comic eruptions of ***Yobgorble*** and ***The Worms of Kukumlima.*** It's more on the order of bus reading for a snarkout.

A review of "The Snarkout Boys & the Avocado of Death," in Kirkus Reviews, *Vol. L, No. 5, March 1, 1982, p. 276.*

STEPHANIE ZVIRIN

[In ***Young Adult Novel***] Pinkwater gleefully spoofs the Dada movement of artists and writers that grew up during the twentieth century by resurrecting its absurdist principles as the driving force for a group of 13-year-old nonconformists. Calling themselves the Wild Dada Ducks, the group devotes its energies to turning the status quo on its ear [and] playing bizarre school tricks (such as putting an old toilet in the school display case). . . . Familiarity with the Dada movement is helpful but not strictly necessary, because what happens is, of course, mostly nonsense (a real "Dada story"); but Pinkwater makes it work in fewer than 60 pages and makes it entertaining as well.

Stephanie Zvirin, in a review of "Young Adult Novel," in Booklist, *Vol. 78, No. 15, April 1, 1982, p. 1014.*

PETER ANDREWS

There are few things more dispiriting than to sit down with a book you have been assured is a certified laugh riot and find that you don't think it's funny. When the volume in question is a kid's book, and you not only don't think it's funny, you don't even understand it, the dismay is almost total. I sometimes feel that way in the presence of Daniel Pinkwater's zany children's books. He is capable of excellent work and is popular. . . .

But the hardest thing about being a professional madcap is knowing when to stop. All too often Mr. Pinkwater falls into such raptures of self-amusement I can scarcely make out his jokes amid the peals of his own laughter. He seems to fancy himself as the master surrealist of children's literature, but he sometimes falls into the trap of thinking that if you are writing nonsense you don't have to be logical. Logic is, perhaps, the only rule there is to follow for writing good nonsense. What should be delightful confusion in Pinkwater stories is frequently just a muddle.

The current tryptich of novels by Mr. Pinkwater is a truly representative sampling. . . . [**"Slaves of Spiegel: A Magic Moscow Story"**] is a wonderfully funny, goofball science-fiction story . . . , [**"The Snarkout Boys & the Avocado of Death"**] is a literary enigma the National Security Agency would have difficulty deciphering, and . . . [**"Young Adult Novel"**] is an exercise in tasteless indulgence for which he should have his knuckles rapped.

One of the things I most admire about Mr. Pinkwater when he is at his best is the reckless way he refuses to try for the fey bemusement that is the hallmark of so many children's humor books. He is shameless in trying to make the reader laugh out loud—the most difficult feat in English letters—and in **"Slaves of Spiegel"** he does. . . .

The story is vintage Pinkwater—mad as a hatter, filled with laughs and, at base, quite sensible. . . .

It is possible, however, that Mr. Pinkwater's comedic talents can be stretched only so far. **"The Snarkout Boys & the Avocado of Death"** starts out as a neatly told story of a boy who "snarks out" by sneaking off to the all-night movie house. But then it turns into a confusing parody of an international spy thriller. There are too many mishandled elements in the story. . . . Mr. Pinkwater tosses so many balls in the air that he eventually drops them all, and punctuated by gag lines that have nothing solid to bounce off, his tale sinks into disarray.

In the first few pages of **"Young Adult Novel"** we read that Kevin Shapiro's mother is locked away in a madhouse and his father is a living vegetable as a result of an explosion in a methane factory. Kevin's sister works the bars near the local bus depot as a prostitute, and Kevin supports himself by stealing and selling drugs in the schoolyard. How about that as an opening for a comic novel for preteens?

The novel then goes on to describe a slapstick confrontation between a group of Dadaist students and a straight-arrow school administration, during which the students create a campus hero out of a little creep who much prefers to be left alone. The story is, I suppose, to be taken as a rollicking lower-school version of the film "Animal House," but I found it distressing.

Mr. Pinkwater has been rightly praised as a children's author who does not treat his audience as if they are all little darlings, and I agree that children are essentially little monsters with a thirst for the forbidden. But I have considerable reservations about how assiduously they should be pandered to in this matter. Vulgarity is something children should be allowed to work out for themselves, if for no other reason than that it is more fun that way. If adults are forever illuminating the dark corners of children's lives, they deny them self-discovery. . . .

In **"Young Adult Novel"** Mr. Pinkwater smothers his young readers with a racy bonhommie that smacks too much of adults who think they are getting close to young people by slam dancing with them, an enterprise distressing to children and degrading to adults.

Peter Andrews, in a review of "Slaves of Spiegel," "The Snarkout Boys & the Avocado of Death" and "Young Adult Novel," in The New York Times Book Review, *April 25, 1982, p. 51.*

SUSAN B. MADDEN

Daniel Pinkwater writes crazy, insane, off-the-wall, bizarre books which appeal greatly to jr. high folks and me. This particular wonderfully titled piece of nonsense [***Young Adult Novel***] is the best of all. I defy any YA librarian to read the first 4 pages without audibly chortling and nodding madly. . . . As is typical with Pinkwater, the wit pinpoints some very real adolescent concerns and feelings.

Susan B. Madden, in a review of "Young Adult Novel," in Voice of Youth Advocates, *Vol. 5, No. 2, June, 1982, p. 36.*

GARY ACTON

Of the numerous books Pinkwater has written for children and adolescents, several—such as ***The Worms of Kukumlima*** (1981), ***Alan Mendelsohn, The Boy From Mars*** (1979) and ***Fat Men From Space*** (1977)—could be loosely termed science fiction/fantasy. Wild exaggeration, cutesy names, one liners, improbable situations, illogical logic and zany humor are characteristics of Pinkwater's style. Although Pinkwater has ostensibly written an adolescent novel [with ***The Snarkout Boys & the Avocado of Death***] . . . , some of the humor seems directed to the adult. For example, many adolescents will recognize the parody of Sherlock Holmes and Dr. Watson in Osgood Sigerson and Dr. Ormond Sacker, but how many will recognize the significance of the name Sigerson or recognize in one minor character a parody of the verbal mannerisms of Sidney Greenstreet as Caspar Gutman in *The Maltese Falcon*? If you like flaky humor, you'll enjoy this book. . . .

Gary Acton, in a review of "The Snarkout Boys & the Avocado of Death," in Science Fiction & Fantasy Book Review, *No. 6, July-August, 1982, p. 42.*

KEVIN KENNY

Pinkwater's latest walk on the weird side is not likely to disappoint his fans or newcomers looking for an unusual read. In this latest effort [***The Snarkout Boys & the Avocado of Death***], the usual mayhem is in session. . . . It is, of course, a comedy, and is rife with crazy names, inane scenes, strange plot twists, and stranger characters. it occasionally takes on almost surrealistic tones (the beer and baked potato bar, Beanbender's, comes to mind) which are nicely handled, and which serve to make this considerably more demanding, and more rewarding, than previous efforts, e.g. ***The Hoboken Chicken Emergency.***

Kevin Kenny, in a review of "Snarkout Boys & the Avocado of Death," in Voice of Youth Advocates, *Vol. 5, No. 3, August, 1982, p. 35.*

HEIDE PIEHLER

[***The Snarkout Boys & the Avocado of Death***] introduced a bizarre world in which all licensed realtors were being taken over by extraterrestrials. Once again [with ***The Snarkout Boys and the Baconburg Horror***] the Snarkout Boys find themselves helping to rid the world of an evil menace. This time, a werewolf is stalking the streets of Baconburg. Many of the characters from the first book make repeat appearances. . . . The new characters are not as colorful as those in the earlier adventure and even the reappearing figures have less vitality than they did in the earlier book. As in the first book, the plot is chaotic. However, . . . ***Avocado*** . . . was held together by narrator Walter Galt's satirical perspective on the world. In the sequel, Walter's first-person narration is just one of several narrative styles. Without a stabilizing force, the humor isn't as polished or witty. There are a few genuinely funny moments, but all in all this book disappoints.

Heide Piehler, in a review of "The Snarkout Boys & the Baconburg Horror," in School Library Journal, *Vol. 30, No. 9, May, 1984, p. 92.*

MICHAEL DIRDA

In the end [of ***The Snarkout Boys & the Avocado of Death***], the good guys triumph, and [the villain] Wallace Nussbaum is sent to a deserved imprisonment on Devil's Island.

But he is not destined to remain there. In ***The Snarkout Boys and the Baconburg Horror*** Nussbaum escapes and launches yet another diabolical plan for world domination.

His enemies Walt, Winston and Rat are a year older now, but they still hang out at places like the Dharma Buns Coffee House, read *The Sorrows of Young Werewolf*, and keep running into characters such as Lama Lumpo Smythe-Finkel. . . .

Eventually, psychic Lydia LaZonga reveals that Nussbaum is behind the Baconburg Horror, a werewolf that likes to destroy car interiors. Soon [the detective] Sigerson reunites the old gang—along with the lama, beat poet Jonathan Quicksilver, and preppy nerd Scott Feldman—to hunt down the man-beast and its master. The whole tangled business leads to a blazing finale in The Garden of Earthly Bliss Drive-In and Pizzeria. It is a terrific book, nearly as good as the first, magical Snarkout boys adventure.

[Daniel Pinkwater] may be the zaniest writer of children's books around. in many of his two dozen or so books, his hero is typically a young misfit (often fat), who makes friends with a slightly more daring schoolmate. Together this urban Tom Sawyer and Huck Finn wander into run-down parts of town, where they discover exotic diners, browse in second-hand book shops specializing in the "weird," . . . and run into the kind of crazies who call in to late-night radio shows to talk about astral projection. The adventures that ensue resemble a blend of comic book, old movie, and surrealist romp. . . .

Michael Dirda, "The Chicken at the Edge of the Universe," in Book World—The Washington Post, *June 10, 1984, p. 6.*

SUSAN B. MADDEN

Oh, Snorkle, gurgle, burpis and whee! Mix werewolves, borgelhuskies, the Nussbaum brothers and the Snarkout boys [in ***The Snarkout Boys and the Baconburg Horror***]. Put in locations such as The Deadly Nightshade Diner—We Never Close and the Garden of Earthly Bliss Drive-In and Pizzeria and you've another surefire Pinkwater hit. Crazy, erratic, silly and completely sophomoric here's the latest winner from one of the star authors in the junior high stable.

Susan B. Madden, in a review of "The Snarkout Boys and the Baconburg Horror," in Voice of Youth Advocates, *Vol. 7, No. 3, August, 1984, p. 144.*

NANCY C. HAMMOND

Once more, the intrepid trio Walter Galt, Winston Bongo, and the girl Rat are united by their dedication to snarking [in ***The***

Snarkout Boys and the Baconburg Horror]. . . . By the time all the lunatic characters converge upon "The Deadly Nightshade Diner—We Never Close," the irreverent author spoofs even his own frenetic, nonsensical plot; victim and assailant, wimp and hero begin to coalesce. The slangy language, the vim, and the singular, offbeat humor are refreshing. Who but Daniel Pinkwater creates mocha pistachio whole-wheat doughnuts and a Mega-Mall with "thirty places to buy jeans" and with lights designed to flicker at a frequency that induces more spending?

Nancy C. Hammond, in a review of "The Snarkout Boys and the Baconburg Horror," in The Horn Book Magazine, *Vol. LX, No. 5, September-October, 1984, p. 594.*

Prince (Rogers Nelson)

1958?-

American songwriter.

Prince is best known for his portrayal of a talented but troubled musician in the film *Purple Rain* (1984) and for his award-winning album of the same title. Believing that spiritual salvation can be obtained through sexual liberation, Prince places heavy emphasis on sex in his lyrics, many of which have generated critical controversy. Through his music, Prince attacks stereotypes of gender, race, and morality by concentrating on such universal themes as sex and love. He uses an eclectic combination of black funk and white rock in order to merge culturally separated black and white audiences. Prince also challenges traditional sexual roles by maintaining a deliberately androgynous appearance, which Pablo Guzman describes as a "basic persona [alternating] between aggressively female and passively male." Andrew Kopkind contends that Prince's sexual ambiguity "works to establish a certain authenticity amid the utter confusion of his generation." Prince's persona and his music point toward his vision of a new society in which sexual and racial barriers are considered superficial and inconsequential.

Born in Minneapolis, Minnesota, Prince experimented with a variety of instruments while in his teens and began performing with several bands in local clubs. In 1977 he signed a recording contract which gave him almost total control over the material he released. On his first album, *For You* (1978), Prince played virtually every instrument, a practice he continued on several subsequent albums. Heavily influenced by disco, funk, and rhythm and blues, *For You* was favorably reviewed for its sense of unpretentiousness and its songs of sexual awakening. *Prince* (1978) received less favorable critical attention, but John Wall notes that "Prince's self-confidence and assertion are the major attractions of this album."

With the release of *Dirty Mind* (1980), Prince began to direct his music toward both black and white audiences through his fusion of funk and rock. His lyrics became blatantly lewd and addressed such controversial topics as bisexuality and incest. Due to the album's crude approach to sexuality, *Dirty Mind* received little attention from most radio stations. However, it became an underground success and was praised by several critics, including Ken Tucker, who suggested that Prince's songs "are a metaphor for the care and consideration that inform the lovemaking detailed in his lyrics." On *Controversy* (1981), Prince introduces political themes in such songs as "Ronnie, Talk to Russia." He also revels in and ridicules his public image and the critical notoriety which followed *Dirty Mind*. On the title song, for example, Prince mimics his critics by posing the question, "Am I black or white, am I straight or gay?" *Controversy* was faulted by some critics for lyrical overindulgence and a reliance on political clichés.

1999 (1982), Prince's first album to achieve success with both black and white audiences, further explores political and sexual themes. The title song proposes that humanity dance and carouse toward the apocalypse Prince seems to feel is imminent. Besides utilizing various traditional musical forms, among them jazz and rockabilly, critics noted the influence of New

Willa Roberts/LGI © 1984

Wave and experimental electronic music. On this album Prince employs a darker, somewhat malicious view of human sexuality with sadomasochistic and paranoiac overtones. Although Steve Sutherland termed Prince's approach "outrage for outrage's sake," several critics found a discordant harmony in his blend of musical styles and especially praised the album's most popular song, "Little Red Corvette."

The film *Purple Rain* significantly boosted Prince's career and popular status. The movie concerns a young musician who competes with the lead vocalist of a rival band for commercial success and for the love of a beautiful female singer. Through her, the hero confronts the brutality he has inherited from his abusive father, a failed composer, and goes on to win a battle-of-the-bands competition. Loosely based on a semiautobiographical outline by Prince, *Purple Rain* was written by William Blinn and Albert Magnoli and directed by Magnoli. The film drew mixed reviews: some critics contended that the plot relies on the predictable clichés of traditional movie musicals, while others lauded the film's stance on drug and alcohol use and its optimistic premise that individuals must take personal responsibility for their own futures. The *Purple Rain* soundtrack album is widely considered Prince's most commercial work and received generally favorable reviews. RJ Smith maintained that the album did not "advance any new ideas," but he found it "enjoyably splashy and unavoidable." Prince

and his band, The Revolution, won Grammy Awards for Best Rock Vocal Performance, Duo or Group and Best Album of Original Score and an Academy Award for Best Original Score for *Purple Rain*. Prince also received a Grammy in 1985 for Best Rhythm & Blues Song for "I Feel for You," a song from *Prince* which was re-recorded by Chaka Khan.

On his recent album *Around the World in a Day* (1985), Prince departs somewhat from the subjects of his previous records. His treatment of sexual and political themes is more subtle on this album, and critics note a greater emphasis on religion in his lyrics. Price also experiments with various musical styles, combining "the slick surface of disco, the bluntness of hard rock, [and] the sweetness of old-fashioned pop," according to Jim Miller and Janet Huck.

JIM FARBER

Prince is an 18-year-old (Stevie) Wunderkind who's done everything on his first album [***For You***] but press the vinyl. As with current Wonder, the music here is your basic discofunk, mercifully without Stevie's goofy "God loves your pet aardvark" raps on top. As with most megalomaniac projects of this ilk, though, the ego in question usually forgets to put feeling into at least a few of the 85 instruments he's playing (usually the percussion end gets glossed over), and there's no parting from that tradition here. Still, Prince's fine vocal range makes up for it. . . . Big points go to the opening acappella showpiece, **"For You,"** in which Prince sounds kinda like Joni Mitchell, Al Jarreau and Betty Boop all at the same time. Prince is generally more successful with the shorter songs. . . . There's an air of unpretentiousness and youthful cockiness here that may just make you want to grind up your "Sir Duke" singles and try out something fresher.

Jim Farber, in a review of "For You," in Crawdaddy, *September, 1978, p. 79.*

JOHN WALL

If you can stand the precious "crucify me" expression of the 19-year-old Prince adorning the cover of this record [**"Prince"**], you'll find the contents worth examination. Prince, like most talented youngsters, would appear to take his image somewhat seriously . . . and I suppose he's got some right to do so, given that he wrote, arranged, played and produced everything on the album. Still, let's not get too carried away. . . .

"Prince" is an album of many charms, not least that it calls to mind Michael Jackson's "Off the Wall" and Ray Parker Jr's recent work. Prince's voice has that beautiful Jacksonian falsetto, and his songs, arrangements, and musicianship have the characteristic swagger of Raydio. . . . [Even] the unimaginatively-titled **"Sexy Dancer"** overcomes its generic limitations with some stunning bass picking and sparing, terse guitar chords.

Prince's self-confidence and assertion are the major attractions of this album. . . . Everything's kept to a minimum, a rarity these days in disco music, where (Chic excepted) the tendency's to throw in everything but the kitchen sink. . . . Like "Off the Wall", **"Prince"** doesn't restrict itself to one particular groove: tolerance levels throughout remain high.

John Wall, in a review of "Prince," in Melody Maker, *December 22, 1979, p. 21.*

GEORGIA CHRISTGAU

I liked Prince the first time I heard "I want to be the only one you come for" [from **"I Wanna Be Your Lover"**] over AM radio. It didn't surprise me that the sensibility of the singer, who also wanted to be his lover's "mother and sister, too," seemed to be a gay one. About time the Village People/Sylvester spectrum of popular gay disco, from parody to queen, expanded to include some probably very typical kid . . . who writes good pop songs about sex and love without camping them up. . . .

[Prince is] not a shy lyricist; singing to the absent object of his affection in **"In Love,"** he adds in a postscript, "I want to play in your river." Most of the time, though, he sticks to less imaginative stroke-book adjectives like soft and wet, long and hard, etc. And his more controversial lyrics are unclear; **"Head,"** which he introduced in concert as "my dirtiest song," was about a virgin who, en route to her wedding, gave head to someone and married him instead. (It even rhymed.) Pretty Victorian, I thought; everyone else seemed to think it *was* Prince's dirtiest song. **"Bambi,"** about a lesbian betraying her male lover, suggests: (a) that she really may have had fun, (b) that lesbians can "only" love like women, and (c) it's better with a man. At turns Prince is open-minded, prejudiced, and double-entendre coy. But maybe I'm confusing clarity of sentiment with clarity of purpose; he may not know how he feels, only that his feelings are strong enough to sing about.

Georgia Christgau, "Prince Who?" in The Village Voice, *Vol. XXV, No. 9, March 3, 1980, p. 60.*

PABLO GUZMAN

Dirty Mind has got to be—will be—on everyone's list as one of *the* rock albums of 1980. With this album Prince truly comes out of the closet. Not only does he rock, he does so with a style, a wit, and a sound that places him at the cutting edge of whatever wave is now new.

Names must be dropped for reference: Prince is the Ramones with punch, Costello with wit, Blondie with bounce. *At the same time* Prince, switchhitter that he is, is Cameo electrified, Mother's Finest realized, Rick James personified (ha!). What George Clinton wants for Funkadelic, what Talking Heads aim for by adding Nona and Worrell, Prince is. No one has straddled rock apartheid like Sly and Santana at their peak; if (white) rock radio lets its listeners have an honest, uh, listen, Prince can be the one. . . .

The three tracks that follow the title opener move with a finger-poppin' bounce that at once satirizes and acknowledges all those silly love songs. I especially like **"Gotta Broken Heart Again,"** which swings with a post-doowop feel and shows Prince at his most vulnerable. Because Prince on this LP puts the emphasis on instrumentation first and then on lyric images which shape his wild-side rude-boy persona, the innocence of **"Broken Heart"** reminds you of how young Prince really is. . . .

The strength of side one is really **"Dirty Mind"** and **"Do It All Night,"** two very fine dance tunes. Then again, there isn't a real ballad, what kids call a slow drag (not a putdown) on the whole album. It's all dance music. . . .

The killer is side two—either dig it or get your walking papers fast. It's pure segue start to finish and all the elements at Prince's command (so far) are present. . . .

"Uptown," the new single, opens side two: "White Black Puerto Rican / Everybody just a freakin'." Prince complements his instrumental attack with word pictures well; **"Uptown,"** for example, matches nonstop jump to the tale of Prince "walkin' down the street of your fine city." Picked up by a girl who wants to know, "Are you gay," he doesn't really answer—the basic persona always alternates between aggressively female and passively male. But later, on the proving ground of the dance floor, he comes out with it: "Don't let society / Tell us how it s'pozed to be." Meanwhile, though, he's told us her pickup "got me hot," passively male once again. . . .

"Party Up" closes out the album with a defiant note at the height of the jam: "You're gonna have to fight / Your own damn war / Cause we don't wanna / Fight no more." Getting ready for Reagan and the Middle East. And that's ***Dirty Mind,*** my album of the month—or maybe year.

Pablo Guzman, "Rock's New Prince," in The Village Voice, *Vol. XXV, No. 50, December 17-23, 1980, p. 95.*

KEN TUCKER

Dirty Mind is a pop record of Rabelaisian achievement: entirely, ditheringly obsessed with the body, yet full of sentiments that please and provoke the mind. It may also be the most generous album about sex ever made by a man. . . .

Prince's first two collections (***For You, Prince***) established him as a doe-eyed romantic: i.e., his carnal desires were kept in check. Though the chorus of his first hit single was "Your love is soft and wet," the raunchiest interpretation permitted by its slightly damp melody was that perhaps the object of Prince's love had been caught in a sudden rainstorm. And while the song that made him a star, 1979's **"I Wanna Be Your Lover,"** snuck the line "I wanna be the only one you come for" onto AM radio, the singer delivered it with coy innocence, as if feigning ignorance of what the words meant but confident they'd please his lover.

Nothing, therefore, could have prepared us for the liberating lewdness of ***Dirty Mind.*** Here, Prince lets it all hang out. . . . The major tunes are paeans to bisexuality, incest and cunnilingual technique. (p. 54)

Dirty Mind jolts with the unsettling tension that arises from rubbing complex erotic wordplay against clean, simple melodies. . . . He takes the sweet romanticism of Smokey Robinson and combines it with the powerful vulgate poetry of Richard Pryor. The result is cool music dealing with hot emotions.

At its best, ***Dirty Mind*** is positively filthy. Sex, with its lasting urges and temporary satisfactions, holds a fascination that drives the singer to extremes of ribald fantasy. . . . [**"Head"** is] a jittery rocker about the pleasures of oral sex. In Prince's wet dream, no woman is forced to do anything she doesn't want to do: her lust always matches our cocksman's. . . . By the time Prince yelps, "You wouldn't have stopped / But I came on your wedding gown," the entire album has climaxed in more ways than one. This is lewdness cleansed by art, with joy its socially redeeming feature. ***Dirty Mind*** may be dirty, but it certainly isn't pornographic.

Somehow Prince manages to be both blunt and ambiguous—and occasionally just dreamily confusing. **"When You Were Mine"** (in which the line "I used to let you wear all my clothes" is offered as proof of our man's devotion) blithely condones infidelity of the most brazen sort—"I never cared . . . / When he was there / Sleepin' in between the two of us"—as long as the artist can be sure that the woman continues to love only him. Yet in **"Sister,"** Prince notes that his female sibling is responsible for his bisexuality, a word whose syllables he draws out with lascivious relish. . . . [The] singer finally blurts out a jabbering confession: "Incest is everything it's said to be." What can you do with a guy like this?

Love him, obviously. If Prince indulges his appetites with a bold and lusty vigor, his pleasure is always dependent upon his partner's satisfaction. In a reversal of the usual pop-song aesthetic, the artist's crisp, artfully constructed compositions are a metaphor for the care and consideration that inform the lovemaking detailed in his lyrics.

Less obviously, Prince deserves our admiration. Though ***Dirty Mind*** is an undeniably apposite title, the LP might just as accurately have been called *Prince Confronts the Moral Majority:* except for **"Uptown," "Partyup"** and the loping **"Gotta Broken Heart Again,"** none of ***Dirty Mind*** could make it onto the most liberal radio-station playlists these days. In a time when Brooke Shields' blue-jeaned backside provokes howls of shock and calls for censorship from mature adults, Prince's sly wit—intentionally coarse—amounts to nothing less than an early, prescient call to arms against the elitist puritanism of the Reagan era. (pp. 54-5)

Ken Tucker, "Someday My Prince Will Come: Love and Lust in Minneapolis," in Rolling Stone, *Issue 347, February 19, 1981, pp. 54-5.*

PAULO HEWITT

Currently challenging Rick James for the mythical punk/funk crown, Prince is one of those musicians obsessed with mixing every kind of musical strain into one complete framework. . . .

Prince's other obsession is a projection of himself as a wild, sexually liberated guy (again just like Rick James) who'll do just about anything with his equally sexually liberated partners.

With all this going on, Prince seems to have forgotten one small, quite relevant factor—the music. Following hard on the heels of his last tame affair, **"Dirty Mind"**, this new LP [**"Controversy"**] has only one great song, one good one and six of no consequence.

"Controversy" is the title track and best song. . . .

Shamefully, for a man of his hype, the standard isn't maintained. Except for **"Let's Work"**, a sprightly, catchy little number, Prince is all bluster and no fire. Mainly he degenerates into uncontrolled hysteria, either on the sickly slow **"Do Me Baby"**, which leaves him panting like a dirty old man into the microphone, or on the demented **"Ronnie, Talk To Russia"**. . . .

Elsewhere, when Prince isn't trying to convince the listener of his intentions, his music (as in **"Private Joy"** and **"Jack U Off"**) lacks backbone and fibre.

[**"Controversy"**] is, unintentionally, very comical in parts, but that isn't the point. Compared to the dynamic, sublime funk of Rick James which boasts so many more qualities, Prince is more the court jester than royalty.

Paulo Hewitt, in a review of "Controversy," in Melody Maker, *November 7, 1981, p. 17.*

CARY DARLING

"Controversy" is a much better coupling of rock and r&b, politics and sex, outrageous bravado and whispered romance than last year's **"Dirty Mind."**

Even if Prince wasn't quite as talented as he is, he would still be valuable because he is one of the few major label American acts who doesn't think it's a crime to combine politics and pop music. Over the past few years, Americans have been conditioned to believe that only such imports as the socially conscious, overtly political Clash, religious Bob Marley or the Pretenders . . . actually have something to say beyond the tried and true "I love you."

Among major label American black artists, Prince's sense of rebellion is even harder to find, though Rick James, Funkadelic and Gil Scott-Heron do come to mind. More to the point, Prince instills a sense of fun and passion into his music which makes his sometimes sophomoric political and sexual cliches worth wading through to get to the high points.

Side one is a bit of disappointment culminating in the tiresome **"Do Me Baby."** . . . More inviting is the title track with its throbbing rhythm and lyrics poking fun at his media-hyped image. This leads into **"Sexuality,"** a rambunctious plea for a new world order not based on military might.

Side two, however, contains the best work of Prince's four-LP career. Whereas moments on **"Dirty Mind"** threatened to become rock'n'roll, Prince actually achieves it with these five songs. . . . **"Private Joy"** exults in newfound love. Here, Prince proves that he doesn't have to resort to being explicit to make powerful, passionate music.

In **"Ronnie, Talk To Russia,"** Prince begs President Reagan not to take his tough guy stance too far. Whereas on **"Partyup"** from **"Dirty Mind"** Prince yelled confidently against the draft, this time he actually seems afraid of World War III. **"Let's Work"** is a funky love song that musically resembles last year's **"Head"** without that song's prurience.

The highlight of the album, though, is **"Annie Christian,"** a musically subdued attack on violence in America. Annie Christian in this case is the personification of modern day evils. . . . Prince's deadpan vocal delivery shades the song with several meanings, some of which perhaps are not intended. For example, when Prince throws in "everybody yelled gun control," is he saying society only tries to restrict violence after those in officialdom are getting attacked? . . .

Where does Prince go from here? Perhaps, he should use an outside producer, arranger or band next time (again, he plays all the instruments himself and his falsetto seems forced at times) which might bring new ideas to his sound. He does have a tendency to overindulge which a more objective eye might curb. Whatever his flaws, Prince is still a valuable asset to anyone's musical library.

Cary Darling, in a review of "Controversy," in Billboard, *Vol. 93, No. 46, November 21, 1981, p. 92.*

VINCE ALETTI

Although ***Dirty Mind*** was Prince's breakthrough into a truly idiosyncratic musical style—stripped-for-action, aggressively uptempo funk rock, blunt, nervy, and playful, with lyrics designed for maximum impact—it's ***Controversy***'s continuation of that style that has brought him his widest audience. This is due partly to changing taste—particularly black listeners' growing interest in and acceptance of new wave funk and other combined forms. . . . But it's not just Prince's music that people are beginning to catch up to, it's his mystique. Clearly, Prince is very much a self-creation, a true rock & roll eccentric with a look, an attitude, and a philosophy. Since he's only 21, all this is in a state of flux, which makes it even more fascinating: the persona hasn't been clamped on tight yet—there's time to be foolish and vulnerable and really surprising. For now, Prince is determined to be the bad boy, the rebel and the philosopher in the bedroom. It's fun to watch him strut and pose, but still you wonder, who does this guy think he is? The genius of love? It's a measure of his power that getting to the bottom of this actually seems important. Prince offers lots of clues, few real revelations.

Prince is at his most naive and disturbing when the subject is overtly political. **"Ronnie, Talk to Russia,"** the album's throwaway cut at a frantic 1:48, would be easy to shrug off as a mock protest song were it not for its self-absorption (". . . before they blow up *my* world") and its rightist flirtation (in addition to Russia, the enemy includes "left-wing guerrillas"). Serious analysis is difficult, however, when Prince is perverse enough to sing, "Ronnie, if you're dead before I get to meet you / Don't say I didn't warn you," and follow it with a barrage of gunshots. ***Controversy***'s other foray into social comment, **"Annie Christian,"** is a muddled sort of rap that recalls the theme of "Sympathy for the Devil" with none of that song's dark, seductive ambivalence. Annie (anti) Christian, slipping through recent history to pull the trigger on Lennon and Reagan, to participate in the Atlanta murders and ABSCAM (are these equivalent crimes?), is a flimsy device with no metaphorical depth, driven by neither wit nor outrage. The track . . . has a certain chilly charm, but the devitalized play on rap conventions ("Everybody say gun control!") is clumsy, alienating—as is Prince's cryptic response to the horror: "I'll live my life in taxi cabs."

But of course Prince's real politics is sexual, and it's here that he's most genuinely radical and subversive. The sensibility remains that of a precocious 10-year-old at times (as in the **"Controversy"** chant, "People call me rude / I wish we all were nude / I wish there was no black and white / I wish there were no rules"), but Prince's humor and conviction make even his silliness oddly engaging. His ideas about **"Sexuality,"** delivered in one of the record's most effective songs, are understandably all mixed up with his attitudes toward "society," yet the combination is biting and passionate enough to overwhelm the superficiality of individual lines. As in **"Controversy,"** there's an amused cynicism and hard-won joyousness to **"Sexuality"** as Prince rips into "a world overrun by tourists" and calls for a "new breed." Although the song's two repeated lines, "Sexuality is all you ever need" and "Leaders, stand up! organize!," may have a dubious stretched connection here, Prince makes a crazy kind of sense—expressive, abstract. . . .

Most of the album's other sex songs are one-note romps, seemingly tossed off on the run but no less accomplished for their effortlessness. Although he's done much of this before in ***Dirty Mind,*** Prince is still convincing as a rocker, whether he's bathing **"Jack U Off"** in a trashy rockabilly aura or going for some funk raunch on **"Let's Work."** There's affection here but no romance, and the music reflects Prince's straight-to-the-point approach: pumping, spirited, with no wasted energy. . . . Only the sleezy grind of **"Do Me Baby,"** with its shimmering, throbbing track, seems willing to deliver on the promise of action. Prince whispers, sighs, and screams, sliding into one-sided ecstasy not without a few unexpected remarks. . . . Though extended orgasm on record is nothing new, Prince's intimate carryings-on here suggest that in the future the magnificent tease may be ready to answer more questions than he poses.

Vince Aletti, "Genius of Love," in The Village Voice, *Vol. XXVI, No. 49, December 2, 1981, p. 87.*

MITCHELL COHEN

"Controversy" is a presumptuous title for an album, but it's in keeping with Prince's tactics of provocation. Prince . . . is a musician who relishes outrage. His ego is enormous—the billing on the record jacket reads "produced, arranged, composed, and played by Prince," and the package includes a huge portrait of the artist in a shower. That ego is nearly matched by his talent. It's as though he put the last fifteen years of adventurous black music in a compressor . . . and made the message explicit, to say the least. (pp. 89-90)

[The title track] deals playfully with his confused public image. As Prince pronouncements go, that's pretty tame. More lascivious is the epic ***Do Me, Baby;*** he squeals, screams, and talks . . . his way through the throes of passion. . . . And ***Sexuality*** manages to deal with revolution, black illiteracy, and rampant tourism and still return to his basic theme, "Sexuality is all we ever need."

Prince makes the mistakes of casting a woman as the anti-Christ figure on ***Annie Christian,*** of getting too silly on ***Ronnie, Talk to Russia,*** and of quoting the Lord's Prayer, but he's capable of irresistible black pop tunes like the Motown-influenced ***Private Joy*** and the adolescently titled ***Jack U Off***. . . . The Moral Majority may not be amused, but the performance is a brazen combination of r&b urgency, rockabilly impudence, Hendrix guitar, and the confidence of a kid who thinks he can get away with anything. (p. 90)

Mitchell Cohen, in a review of "Controversy," in High Fidelity, *Vol. 32, No. 1, January, 1982, pp. 89-90.*

STEPHEN HOLDEN

Prince's first three records were so erotically self-absorbed that they suggested the reveries of a licentious young libertine. On ***Controversy,*** that libertine proclaims unfettered sexuality as the fundamental condition of a new, more loving society than the bellicose, overtechnologized America of Ronald Reagan. In taking on social issues, the artist assumes his place in the pantheon of Sly Stone-inspired Utopian funksters like Rick James and George Clinton. I think that Prince stands as Stone's most formidable heir, despite his frequent fuzzy-mindedness and eccentricity. . . .

Controversy's version of One Nation under the Sheets is hip, funny and, yes, subversive. In the LP's title track—a bubbling, seven-minute tour de force of synthesized pop-funk hooks—Prince teasingly pants, "Am I black or white / Am I straight or gay?" This opening salvo in a series of "issue"-oriented questions tacitly implies that since we're all flesh and blood, sexual preference and skin color are only superficial differences, no matter what society says. But Prince eventually brushes such things aside with hippie platitudes. Along the way, **"Controversy"** flirts with blasphemy by incorporating the Lord's Prayer. (p. 51)

The strutting, popping anthem **"Sexuality"** elaborates many of the points that **"Controversy"** raises, as Prince shrewdly lists gadgets (cameras, TV, the Acu-Jac) that cut us off from each other. . . . **"Ronnie, Talk to Russia,"** a hastily blurted plea to Reagan to seek disarmament, is the album's weakest cut. . . . [**"Let's Work"** and **"Private Joy"**] show off Prince's ingratiating lighter side. **"Jack U Off,"** the cleverest of the shorter compositions, is a synthesized rockabilly number whose whole point is that sex is better with another human being than with a masturbatory device.

Prince's vision isn't as compelling as it might be, however, because of his childlike treatment of evil. **"Annie Christian,"** the one track that tackles the subject, turns evil into a bogeywoman from whom the artist is forever trying to escape in a taxicab. Though the song lists historical events . . . , it has none of the resonance of, say, "Sympathy for the Devil," since Prince, unlike the Rolling Stones, still only dimly perceives the demons within himself.

After **"Controversy,"** the LP's high point is an extended bump-and-grind ballad, **"Do Me, Baby,"** in which the singer simulates an intense sexual encounter, taking it from heavy foreplay to wild, shrieking orgasm. In the postcoital coda, Prince's mood turns uncharacteristically dark. He shivers and pleads, "I'm so cold, just hold me." It's the one moment amid all of ***Controversy***'s exhortatory slavering in which Prince glimpses a despair that no orgasm can alleviate.

Despite all the contradictions and hyperbole in Prince's playboy philosophy, I still find his message refreshingly relevant. (pp. 51-2)

Stephen Holden, "Sex and Society," in Rolling Stone, *Issue 361, January 21, 1982, pp. 51-2.*

STEVE SUTHERLAND

"1999" sounds like a collection of crudely calculated manoeuvres towards popular ingratiation. Gone is the essentially wide-eyed naif eulogising the joys of sexual self-discovery; the Prince of **"1999"** is a stud without balls, paranoiacally obsessed with his position as first minister of sexual politics, strutting mucho macho bravado and sacrificing tender intimacy to boasting prowess.

Whereas, say, the breathtakingly explicit **"Do Me Baby"** from last year's **"Controversy"** album unashamedly celebrated carnal ecstacy and, in context with **"Ronnie, Talk To Russia"**, proposed love as an alternative to man's self-destruction, much of **"1999"** is hackneyed, bop-against-the-bomb, outrage-for-outrage's sake. The imagery has grown self-consciously horny, the automobile-humping equation of **"Little Red Corvette"**, the jet-setting cliches of **"International Lover"** and Bucks Fizz nudge-nudge, wink-wink innuendo of **"Let's Pretend We're Married"** uncharacteristically touting for cheap thrills and self-aggrandisement.

I suppose, in all honesty, it was commercially inevitable that Prince would become a cartoon of his former sensitivities, betraying previous insistence that *any* act of love is natural for an antithetical freak appeal. But when the fourth side of this, his first double album, boasts climaxes like the preposterously sensuous **"Lady Cab Driver"** and the wickedly self-deflating **"All the Critics Love U in New York"**, I can't help but wish that the rest of the album's public exposures had remained his private indiscretions.

Steve Sutherland, "In the Pubic Eye," in Melody Maker, *November 13, 1982, p. 20.*

MARJORIE SPENCER

[On ***1999*** Prince] makes clear both his eagerness to gratify and his refusal to follow anybody's line, including his own. Thus his politics cloy and his shock tactics nettle as never before. But so much the better—Prince . . . stakes very little on either. When he relents on the topic of our inhibitions, his lurching verse and deadpan similes reflect us not as we fantasize, but as we are, with our alibis around our ankles and our rhythm instincts aroused.

The dreamscapes of ***1999*** tolerate the polymorphous, the disjoint, the symbolic, the nonsensical, the fierce, and the dazed. On **"Little Red Corvette"** and **"Lady Cab Driver"** Prince rides to conquer, but on **"Delirious"** and **"Automatic"** he does as he's bid. The title cut finds him fiddling while the world burns, but on the anti-anthem **"Free"** he puts up a fight. And when not plying contradictions, the logic of dreams, Prince turns his attention to ambivalence, the logic of emotions—most graphically on the insidious **"Let's Pretend We're Married,"** which wavers between a dim hope of solace and the appetite for quick revenge.

On the occasion of his fifth release, the 22-year-old auteur is still young, but less self-abnegating and fey than he was. His purple passages—once so frisky—have veered toward the sinister, displaying sadomasochism like a battle scar; his confessions of vulnerability taste of paranoia. . . .

I let him get away with it because fantasy is exempt from moral stricture, and because it can be edifying nonetheless. But though Prince can be visionary, he's no seer. His thinking is too fragmentary, anarchic, distressed—and sometimes just too sane. It's no use sitting home with your turntable and pencil to parse it all out, once you realize that Prince's injunctions all amount to "party up," matching the imperative of beat. Sexual hesitation? Do it! Political division? Everybody do it! Impending death? Do it while you can! If Prince has grown canny and devious through controversy, I can ignore it (controversy takes two) so long as he rocks with this much honesty and fortitude.

With characteristic presumption, Prince hasn't waited for the platinum mandate to record a double album. But he isn't really bidding to become the first one-man supergroup either. Four sides together offer just eleven tracks, which used to compute to a single disc. . . .

If the proof of the pudding's in the airplay, ***1999*** stands out in the segue, among state-of-the-art productions and pressings, as humorous and alert. On the radio it has the buzz of a party in full swing. . . . With ***1999,*** he struggles to be soulfully progressive, to reconcile old sounds and new without fumigating what was a glad and teeming noise. . . .

Prince evidently wants us to perceive his "old school" ways as the mark of his independence and instinct, in revolt against trends and formulas. Of all his odd desires, it's easiest to comply with this one. ***1999***'s first disc is a perilously headlong take on a weary tradition, and the tradition proves game. The second ventures wider, exploring futuristic sounds that stretch the familiar outlines of rock & roll without subverting them, much as Bowie did with *Low*. Unlike Bowie, Prince varies the ambition of his experiments; the digital psychedelia of **"Something in the Water"** is weird science fiction, while the robotic insistence of **"All the Critics Love U in New York"** (wherein Prince attempts to shake off whatever company he hasn't yet shocked) is just a marvel of technology. . . . No matter what he sings, he still sounds like Prince, and no matter how unmistakably he sounds like Prince, his songs don't deflate into mere similarities. . . .

You may get used to him—for all his exhibitionistic mischief—but you won't get bored. Now, if anything a critic has to say can still please Prince, that should.

Marjorie Spencer, "Dream Lover Takes It to the Floor," in The Village Voice, *Vol. XXVII, No. 46, November 16, 1982, p. 93.*

MICHAEL HILL

[Prince] has become the inspiration for a growing renegade school of Sex & Funk & Rock & Roll. . . . Yet regardless of the jive that he hath wrought, Prince himself does more than merely get down and talk dirty. Beneath all his kinky propositions resides a tantalizing utopian philosophy of humanism through hedonism that suggests once you've broken all the rules, you'll find some real values. All you've got to do is act naturally.

Prince's quasi-religious faith in this vision of social freedom through sensual anarchy makes even his most preposterous utterances sound earnest. On the title track of ***1999,*** which opens this two-LP set of artfully arranged synthesizer pop, Prince ponders no less than the future of the entire planet, shaking his booty disapprovingly at the threat of nuclear annihilation. Although that one exuberant dance-along raises more big questions than Prince can answer on the other three and a half sides combined, the entire enterprise is charged with his unflagging will to survive—and a feisty determination to eat, drink and be merry, for tomorrow, given the daily news, we may die.

Before **"1999"** whooshes into life, Prince assumes an electronically altered, basso-profundo voice and impersonates the imagined authoritative tone of God himself, creator of libidos as well as souls, prefacing the song's Judgment Day scenario with this reassurance: "Don't worry, I won't hurt you. I only want you to have some fun." This intro serves Prince well, since ***1999*** lacks the tight focus of ***Dirty Mind,*** his best and most concise LP, which had the feel of emotionally volatile autobiography disguised as vividly descriptive sexual fantasy. Yet the new album doesn't fall prey to the conceptual confusion that plagued the second side of ***Controversy,*** during which Prince raced from politics to passion, funk groove to rock blitz, as if there weren't room enough for all his inspiration. This time there is, and then some. (pp. 65, 67)

[The two discs that make up ***1999***] are distinguished by palpably individual moods—the first contains the funkiest, most playful cuts, while the second is made up of slower, more introspective pieces. Two tracks, **"D.M.S.R."** and **"All the Critics Love U in New York,"** qualify as unadulterated filler, and gone are any attempts at the classic three-minute pop song—***Dirty Mind***'s **"When You Were Mine"** was the last word on that, I guess. On ***1999,*** size counts. . . .

Prince's funniest and slyest effects are reserved for **"Let's Pretend We're Married,"** a string of offhandedly vulgar suggestions transformed with the most basic tools into a quintessential Princeian comic-erotic epic. . . .

1999 reaches its climax, however, with Prince's shortest and sweetest offering, **"Free."** . . .

Prince steps from behind the clanking machinery like a sentimental Wizard of Oz to remind us that "if you take your life for granted, your beating heart will go." More important, he restates his utopian vision in the most inspirational terms, as if all the battles had been won and he could finally be a lover, not a fighter. **"Free"** reeks of skewed patriotism, describing the state of the union as much as a state of mind, its march-of-history grandiosity recalling Patti Smith's "Broken Flag." Like Smith, Prince is not afraid to be misunderstood—or wrong.

But I think Prince can separate a vision of life from a version of it, as the disturbing postscript **"Lady Cab Driver"** illustrates. A sequel to ***Controversy***'s **"Annie Christian,"** in which Prince tried to duck fate by living "my life in taxicabs," **"Lady Cab Driver"** finds him bidding his cabbie to roll up the windows and take him away because "trouble winds are blowin' hard and / I don't know if I can last." But midway through the song, the pain of both personal and public injustice wells up inside him, bursting out in an angry litany of verbal thrusts . . . suggesting an ugly back-seat orgy of sex or violence. Prince, the lover, not the fighter, then retreats to the demilitarized zone of the bedroom, where he can safely bid us goodbye under the guise of **"International Lover."**

A natural goodbye for Prince, but hardly as powerful as the final moments of ***Dirty Mind***. . . . Just as Prince must face the contradiction of creating music that gracefully dissolves racial and stylistic boundaries yet fits comfortably into no one's playlist, he must also decide whether he can "dance my life away" when everybody has a bomb. All you need is love? (p. 67)

Michael Hill, "Prince Ponders the Future of the Planet," in Rolling Stone, *Issue 384, December 9, 1982, pp. 65, 67.*

JOHN MILWARD

[In] spite of his need to outrage, Prince still delivers—there's one long album of wickedly wonderful pop-funk on [***1999***].

1999 is a political party song; the idea is to dance toward the apocalypse. When Prince, in his benign merriment, says he has "got a lion in my pocket, honey, and he's a-ready to roar," he is at his most socially relevant. His strong suit is dicing funk with rock, as on ***Little Red Corvette,*** a sinuous piece of pop that does justice to America's second favorite sex symbol. The hottest of one-man bands, he deserves his reputation as *the* auteur of pop-funk. . . .

For with a persona based on top-this sexuality, Prince has painted himself into a corner. The merely sane would have spoken their sexual peace with **"Dirty Mind."** Though he still has a sense of humor (such as when he blames his lack of romantic luck on ***Something in the Water***), Prince has gotten into s&m on his fifth album. "Don't be afraid," says the distorted voice that begins the album, "I won't hurt you." Tell that to the woman screaming for help at the end of ***D.M.S.R.***

Still, his first major hit, ***I Want To Be Your Lover,*** was an irresistibly saucy piece of Motown. And in terms of prolific and audacious talent, if not romantic outlook, Prince is the Smokey Robinson of the '80s. . . . Five years down his singular path, Prince would do well to consider that pop can be sexy without being hard-core, and that less can often mean more. Until then, he'll remain the prince who would be king.

John Milward, "The King and the Prince," in High Fidelity, *Vol. 33, No. 2, February, 1983, p. 70.**

MICHAEL GOLDBERG

Though he simply calls himself Prince, there is nothing simple about this musical wunderkind who has been causing critics to scramble for superlatives since the release of his breakthrough album, ***Dirty Mind,*** three years ago. . . . Prince just may be, with the exception of Rick James, the most talented pop musician to emerge since Stevie Wonder came of age in the early '70s. . . .

On his last two albums—***Dirty Mind*** and ***Controversy***—Prince came off like the Hugh Hefner of rock & roll. . . . [On ***1999***] he's toned down the subject matter somewhat. The songs are more lyrically conventional, dealing with male/female love and sensuality on the one hand, and the need to escape the stress of modern times on the other. For Prince, one manages to survive the pressures of day-to-day living by that age-old release: the *party*. Yet because Prince won't let himself (or us) forget the troubles of the world, he sets up the party action of ***1999*** within the context of a world about to cave in on itself.

The title track, in which Prince sings of dreaming about Judgment Day, lays everything right on the line. . . . Prince thinks it's a pretty good idea to have fun right to the bitter end. He spends most of these four sides showing us how. . . .

Over four sides Prince is able to cover a lot of musical ground, from the rock & roll of ***1999*** and ***Little Red Corvette*** to the dance-funk of ***D.M.S.R.,*** from the new wave-styled robot-rock of ***Automatic*** and ***Something In The Water*** to the gospel-like ballad ***Free***. . . . Taken as a whole, ***1999*** is testament to Prince's commitment to pushing the pop song form to the limit.

Michael Goldberg, in a review of "1999," in down beat, *Vol. 50, No. 5, May, 1983, p. 28.*

DAVID ANSEN

If you dissect [the film] **"Purple Rain"** down to its bare bones, it may sound old hat: a backstage musical with an alienated rock star, a beautiful girl he woos, loses and rewins, a rivalry with another band, a struggle for self-knowledge, a triumphant concert finale. The audience has been here before—but not in this company, and not with this music. Whatever shortcomings **"Purple Rain"** has—and it's far from a seamless movie—tend to be obliterated by the passion of Prince's music and by the surprising depth charges of emotion this semiautobiographical tale sets off.

Prince plays a rising Minneapolis star referred to only as the Kid. Though this is clearly a self-portrait, no attempt is made to make the Kid lovable: his colleagues justifiably accuse him of paranoia, selfishness and self-indulgence. He refuses, for example, to play the songs the two women in his band have written. . . . But when the Kid rides his motorcycle home to his parents' house, we see the flip side of the arrogant and flamboyant performer: a traumatized, tremulous kid who must bear constant witness to domestic violence.

The Kid's father . . . , an embittered ex-musician, takes out his rage on his wife . . . and slaps the Kid around, too, when he tries to intervene. "Never get married" are his words of advice to his son. When the Kid falls for the beautiful Apollonia . . . , he's forced to confront the fact that his father's brutality toward women has become part of his own psychic makeup. He slaps *her* around when she announces she's going to join his rival's group. This is turf that rock movies rarely tread: parents are usually just stick figures who shake their puzzled heads as their wild and crazy progeny pursue their rock-and-roll dreams. The screenplay, based on Prince's outline and written by Albert Magnoli and William Blinn, is drawn in fairly crude brush strokes, but there's real pain at the core. . .

With Prince there's an intriguingly schizoid rift between the on- and off-stage selves: an invulnerable exhibitionist before a crowd, he's moody and tentative and a bit passive when the music stops, and you sense how crucial it is to his survival to release his fantasies of sex and power and love in song. Creativity, in **"Purple Rain,"** is both stopgap and salvation.

And it is onstage that Prince—and the movie—really burn. . . . **"I Would Die 4 U"** has the irresistible velocity of the old Motown classics, and the climactic **"Purple Rain"** evokes a John Lennon anthem as it builds to its rousing psychedelified climax. Prince's **"Purple Rain"** songs are wildly eclectic and yet wholly his own. When the boss at the club criticizes the Kid for dragging his personal neuroses onstage . . . , he couldn't be more wrong: these hothouse deliriums of lust and transcendence speak to anyone who converses in the primal parlance of rock and roll. Prince is one of a handful of performers who've restored the urgency and danger—and the beat—to the rock scene. And **"Purple Rain"** gets that excitement on screen.

David Ansen, "The New Prince of Hollywood," in Newsweek, *Vol. CIV, No. 4, July 23, 1984, p. 65.*

KURT LODER

The spirit of Jimi Hendrix must surely smile down on Prince Rogers Nelson. Like Hendrix, Prince seems to have tapped into some extraterrestrial musical dimension where black and white styles are merely different aspects of the same funky thing. Prince's rock & roll is as authentic and compelling as his soul, and his extremism is endearing in an era of play-it-safe record production and formulaic hitmongering. ***Purple Rain*** may not yield another smash like last year's **"Little Red Corvette,"** but it's so loaded with life and invention and pure rock & roll thunder that such commercial considerations become moot. When Prince sings **"Baby I'm a Star,"** it's a simple statement of fact.

The Hendrix connection is made overt here with the screaming guitar coda that ends **"Let's Go Crazy,"** with the manic burst that opens **"When Doves Cry"** and in the title song, a space ballad that recalls "Angel" with its soaring guitar leads and a very Hendrixian lyrical tinge ("It's time we all reach out for something new—that means you, too"). There are also constant reminders of Sly Stone in the ferocious bass lines and the hot, dance-conscious mix. But like Jimi and Sly, Prince writes his own rules. . . .

Anyone partial to great creators should own this record. Like Jimi and Sly, Prince is an original; but apart from that, he's like no one else.

Kurt Loder, in a review of "Purple Rain," in Rolling Stone, *Issues 426 & 427, July 19 & August 2, 1984, p. 102.*

JAY COCKS

Purple Rain, both album and movie, is designed for wider consumption [than Prince's earlier albums]. Prince's performing entourage still includes young women attired in flash-happy lingerie. But Prince has dispensed with performing in his leopardskin skivvies, and for the movie camera, dresses up in high-heeled boots, ruffled shirts, brocaded jackets. If anyone notices the similarly suited ghost of Jimi Hendrix floating about, so much the better. Hendrix's classic *Purple Haze* has left all sorts of echoes around Prince's neighborhood, and not just in the music. Prince has both mastered the Hendrix style and contemporized it; he has become something of a past master at haze in general. . . .

If women are sexual baubles in Prince's songs, in his movie they are tarnished angels who love to have their wings clipped. Apollonia . . . strips down and jumps into an icy lake to win The Kid's approval. The Kid, arrogant, sensitive, injured and defensively sadistic, realizes he has been thoroughly psyched by his parents. He salves the wounds by dedicating a song to his father, performing a tune written by the young women of the band and fetching Apollonia on his motorcycle for a last, cathartic concert.

Elvis did all this, and more, and better, in *King Creole* and *Jailhouse Rock,* but each new decade needs its icons. Prince is a suitably odd one for these askew times, albeit something of a miniature. . . . [When] he can be caught in what passes for a spontaneous composition, he seems to be the height of a coffee table. He has the faintly demented courtly charm of Dwight Frye swallowing flies in *Dracula,* but his sexual charisma is at low tide in the dramatic scenes. All this changes in performance, where Prince really comes out wailing. . . . If music alone could make a movie masterpiece, then ***Purple Rain*** might have a shot. Its score is ecumenical rock, echoing everyone from Hendrix and Sly Stone to Brian Wilson and Earth, Wind and Fire, yet remaining entirely original overall. It may have the best original rock music ever written for a movie.

Jay Cocks, "His Highness of Haze," in Time, *Vol. 124, No. 6, August 6, 1984, p. 62.*

KURT LODER

Purple Rain may be the smartest, most spiritually ambitious rock & roll movie ever made. Not since the Beatles burst off the screen in *A Hard Day's Night* twenty years ago has the sense of a new generation's arrival on the pop scene been so vividly and excitingly conveyed. . . .

The movie shifts gracefully between live concert sequences—with onstage footage that, for sheer visceral wallop, sometimes rivals that of such previous rock landmarks as *Woodstock* and *The Last Waltz*—and a backstage drama that is funny and moving and extraordinarily sexy. Modeled in large part on Prince's own life, the story concerns a talented but troubled up-and-coming bandleader—played by Prince, but referred to only as "the Kid"—whose unique musical vision is misunderstood by the manager of the First Avenue club . . . , where he performs, and jealously derided by Morris Day, leader of a rival band, the Time.

Both Morris and the Kid are attracted to the voluptuous Apollonia, a mysterious new arrival who has come to town to make it as a singer. But the Kid is distracted in his pursuit of her by his increasing professional isolation and by an ugly domestic situation. . . . The Kid's struggle for stardom on his own terms and his effort to overcome his violent impulses give the plot an unusually rich human dimension.

The movie's real innovations, however, occur around the edges of the main story. Like the Beatles, who gently tweaked the adult status quo of their own day, ***Purple Rain*** offers an implicit critique of prevailing rock-culture mores. This must be the first rock movie in years in which drugs are never even *mentioned,* let alone used, and in which alcohol is depicted—very subtly—as a personal hindrance, not a high. The characters . . . spend most of their time working—rehearsing tunes, running through routines—in a determined effort to make something of themselves. Rarely has the work ethic been made to seem so cool.

The characters in ***Purple Rain*** span the racial gamut—black, white, Hispanic—and many are women. This low-key communalism reflects the makeup of Prince's own band . . . and of the audience at the First Avenue club. And while the movie flies no flags for brother- and sisterhood, the simple equality with which the characters interact is quietly inspiring. Similarly admirable is the film's nonsalacious sexiness. It is bathed in a carnal glow (and rated *R*), but there is only one brief (and comic) topless scene. And in the movie's most erotic moment—a bedroom interlude with Prince and Apollonia—both principals remain clothed. Seldom, if ever, has sex been so explicitly linked with love in a ''youth'' film. . . .

Purple Rain has a kinetic zip and hip *vérité* that could only come from rock & roll insiders. . . .

But the key to ***Purple Rain***'s musical and cultural accomplishments is Prince himself. . . . And it is his message that comes through most forcefully: be yourself and shoot for the stars; all things are possible. In its simple positivism alone, ***Purple Rain*** marks a radical break with the rock-movie past.

Kurt Loder, ''Prince Stunning in 'Purple Rain','' in Rolling Stone, *Issue 428, August 16, 1984, p. 31.*

ANDREW KOPKIND

Zeitgeist sniffers have been out in full force this summer, digging the Prince phenomenon with the obsessive passion of pigs rooting for truffles in the Dordogne. Rock critics have compared Prince to the early Ray Charles, to the dead Jimi Hendrix, to the sainted Jim Morrison, to James Brown, Mick Jagger and Tina Turner. The success of ***Purple Rain,*** the movie, recalls the generational breakthrough of *A Hard Day's Night;* one overheated writer declared it the best American film since *Citizen Kane*. The dizzying rampage of ***Purple Rain,*** the album, to the top of the charts . . . challenges Bruce Springsteen's title of Boss. . . . [In fact, not since Springsteen] have pop gurus been so enraptured by a rising star. We may be in for a very long siege.

The rise, which is by this time the ascendance, of Prince was both manipulated and spontaneous, as the appearances of cultural comets often are. . . . But his first album, ***For You,*** never became a hit. Prince worked away on his music until his main chance came along.

It arrived last year in a propitious confluence of television, film and recording opportunities. Prince's 1983 album, ***1999,*** turned out to be an important crossover entry in the funk, punk and pop categories. His music videos brought a nice touch of neoromantic raunchiness into family rooms all over America. (pp. 251-52)

Saturation promotion and the clever construction of an original image can make a hit, but they cannot produce the kind of phenomenon Prince embodies. Something epochal, or at least decadal, is going on here, and it has to do with the way Prince expresses or responds to the tempers of the times. A serious and quite successful rock musician I know told me he thinks Prince ''meets all the challenges of the eighties.'' . . . Prince is ambisexual, internationalist, multiracial and cosmically conscious. His music is alternately rhapsodic and minimalist. . . . His costume changes run from the itsiest bikini to Edwardian overdress. He is tender and tough, S&M, straight and gay, First World and Third, coal black, lily white and deep purple. In his lyrics, he seems comfortable—even enthusiastic—singing about fellatio, masturbation and nuclear holocaust. He has postulated the perfect party in the title single **''1999,''** which was also the best funk song of last year. **''Little Red Corvette,''** which followed it on the album and up the charts, had the catchiest honky automotive sound since the Beach Boys' ''Fun, Fun, Fun.'' With one groove separating those two tunes, Prince gave a new meaning to eclecticism in rock. And in a few minutes on stage or on screen, he displays more kinds of ambiguity than could ever be found in a Shakespeare sonnet.

Prince's greatest commercial triumph is his movie, but it is not the perfect vehicle for his talents. The wrenching energy of the music numbers contrasts abruptly with the languors of his acting, and the appealing ambiguities in his persona are overwhelmed by the literal banalities of the plot. The lyrics to **''When Doves Cry''** suggested to screenwriters Albert Magnoli and William Blinn a scenario much like Prince's official biography: an alienated and abandoned child of a racially mixed marriage repeats the emotional atrocities of his parents in his own sexual life and professional relationships until a redemptive love allows him to break on through to the other side. At last, the diffident and distant loner can reach out and touch someone. That is not a formula that can be handled convincingly without consummate command of character, camera and consciousness, none of which are immediately apparent in the production. No moment in the movie is more sophisticated than a Sprint commercial, and there are scenes played with such leaden amateurishness that one yearns for the slick technique of MTV. (p. 252)

Prince alone stands out above the punk/funk mass because he is far more interesting than he acts. As the latest in a line of sexually ambiguous rock stars—from Jagger to David Bowie to Michael Jackson and beyond—he uses confusion more blatantly and effectively than any of his predecessors. Macho to a fault one minute, he camps like a drag queen without missing a beat the next. (pp. 252-53)

There are many uses of ambiguity, but Prince has found that it works to establish a certain authenticity amid the utter confusion of his generation. If my musician friend is right, that is how he meets the challenge of the 1980s. For now, nobody does it better. (p. 253)

Andrew Kopkind, in a review of ''Purple Rain,'' in The Nation, *Vol. 239, No. 8, September 22, 1984, pp. 251-53.*

RJ SMITH

Prince is getting too old to make like he's Bambi running for a warm cove in the woods; he wants his fans to know he has matured at least a little since he first wriggled in his bikini briefs for the masses in 1978. . . .

Thus the goofy, slippery film and soundtrack album **"Purple Rain."** There's nothing here as visionary as ***Little Red Corvette,*** or that speaks to the body as aggressively as the rest of last year's **"1999"** did. **"Purple Rain"** is made for arenas, and played to the bleachers in the back. (p. 106)

Prince has earned his success, and yet it comes off like a big joke. . . . **"Purple Rain"** doesn't advance any new ideas, but it's enjoyably splashy and unavoidable—Prince, a big flag flapping in the faces of middle America. He's winning them over.

"Dearly beloved," the album begins; throughout, Prince plays at being a preacher, albeit one with his own ideas about what constitutes a sacrament. By the end of that cut (***Let's Go Crazy***) you don't really know which second coming Prince is actually cheering for, but my guess is that the religious stuff is more strategic than felt. Casing his psyche and the sidewalks for something that might be called "spirit," he finds it in sex. The goof on preaching is self-dramatizing. . . . But beneath the posturing, there's a pretty dangerous, pretty exciting impulse: that with God out of work these days, sex—not love—can rend this vale of tears.

There has always been a sense of others in Prince's music. On **"Dirty Mind"** he was the self-appointed leader of a gang set to rob all the banks and end all wars. In lingerie. The postcoital hordes he martials avoid the old social ruts: They won't fight, don't want to work, and like their horizontal refreshment anywhere they please. . . . [There] was also a way in which sex seemed like an escape from everybody else, and himself, too. It cleared the air for Prince's love-mad fifth column, but before it built a coalition it registered as one big No—to boredom, to rigor mortis. It was as full of life and urgency as punk's revolt, and as total.

New fans may be corralled by the thousands with **"Purple Rain,"** but they won't learn anything so revelatory about Prince, although his performance in the film makes that not matter much. . . . The album succeeds on the strength of Prince's writing, which is world-class. . . .

Still, there are those songs. Stripped of ornaments, ***When Doves Cry*** is the best, good funk and amazingly touching when Prince lets out a twisted little cry, and ***Take Me with You*** stands up to its thick-pile production. . . . And the kink-out of ***Darling Nikki*** serves his legend well. Which may just be the problem with **"Purple Rain":** Prince is talking up that legend, trying to make a billboard of it. On the screen this is electrifying, but it succeeds only intermittently in your living room. Prince would like to come into each and every one of your homes and stay for more than coffee; **"Purple Rain"** is a preview of coming attractions until he finds your address. (pp. 106-07)

RJ Smith, "He's a Rebel," in High Fidelity, *Vol. 34, No. 10, October, 1984, pp. 106-07.*

MARK PEEL

[The album **"Purple Rain"**] has a cover motif of hearts and flowers. That motif and the profusion of purple—purple type, Prince's purple coat and motorcycle, and a purple vinyl disc—promise a lot of abandoned sexuality on the record, but the words and music are not the kind of purple we have come to expect from the Cupid of electric soul.

Prince has buttoned up some of his corporal frankness in favor of a more circumscribed approach—though circumscribed certainly doesn't describe the direct, visceral, and energized electric rock of **"Purple Rain."** Only ***Darling Nikki,*** about an encounter with a nymphomaniac that seems to have changed Prince's life, approaches the candor of **"1999"** or **"Controversy."**

All directed at women, the songs here are in the first person, and they employ the traditional shorthand of love used on trees and bar tables (for example, ***I Would Die 4 U***). Although Prince may plead, seduce, chide, and promise all over the record, this really is a party album. . . .

The relative absence of lascivious material here focuses your attention on the almost diabolical energy of Prince's music. In fact, this record may actually cross over into markets Prince hasn't been able to reach; certainly anyone who liked the Jimi Hendrix classic *Purple Haze* is a candidate for the guitar hysterics of **"Purple Rain."**

Mark Peel, "Purple Prince," in Stereo Review *Magazine, Vol. 49, No. 10, October, 1984, p. 81.*

JIM MILLER WITH JANET HUCK

A well-publicized bundle of contradictions, Prince flaunts a slapstick pornography onstage and praises God in the same show. . . . Yet for all his erotic clowning, Prince's message is often somber and fervently religious. Themes of death and resurrection appear frequently in his lyrics. Two of his best-known songs—**"1999"** and **"Purple Rain"**—evoke a cleansing nuclear apocalypse. On his recent tour, Prince made a point of singing a medley of original religious songs, including a hymn entitled **"God."**

Saint or sinner, one thing is certain: the diminutive singer is reaching a vast audience. . . .

One of the decade's few true musical originals, Prince has helped define a new genre: "Beigebeat," as one British critic has called it. A blend of black and white, the genre is symbolized by the interracial composition of Prince's band, the Revolution. Laced with free-floating synthesizers and whiplash rhythms, it's music with the slick surface of disco, the bluntness of hard rock, the sweetness of old-fashioned pop. Nobody does it better than Prince—as witness his new album [**"Around the World in a Day"**]. An eerie attempt to recapture the mood of utopian whimsy that characterized the Beatles' "Sgt. Pepper" album, the subtly textured music is playful, sensuous and strangely melancholy. The record's psychedelic centerpiece, **"Paisley Park,"** depicts a "place in your heart" where "there aren't any rules"—shades of "Strawberry Fields Forever." But the record's last two songs deliver a far sterner message. One, called **"The Ladder,"** is a Gospel-drenched fairy tale about the quest for salvation: "The love of God's creation will undress you." And the album's finale, **"Temptation,"** closes with a dialogue between the singer, who is lusting for a lover, and God(?): "You have to want her for the right reasons." "I do." "You don't. Now die." (p. 72)

Although all of his albums have been dedicated to God, Prince first frankly revealed his religious beliefs in **"Controversy,"** his 1981 sequel to **"Dirty Mind."** The title song included a recitation of the Lord's Prayer. Another song, **"Sexuality,"** proclaimed a "new age revelation . . . The second coming, anything goes." Like the Free Spirits, a heretical Christian sect of the Middle Ages, Prince implies that God is manifest in all things natural—including a promiscuous eroticism. . . .

Similar themes have surfaced on every subsequent album. On **"1999,"** the title song introduced what has become Prince's trademark image of the nuclear [judgment day]. . . . The **"Purple Rain"** film and sound-track album both open with church-like organ and a sermon: "Dearly Beloved, we're gathered here today to get through this thing called life . . . But I'm here to tell you that there's something else . . . the afterworld." In the film's title song, Prince welcomes the coming nuclear holocaust, singing to his lover, "You say you want a leader . . . I only want to see you underneath the purple rain." The topic of joyous death and resurrection reappears in **"4 The Tears in Your Eyes,"** a song about the Crucifixion of Christ that Prince contributed to the recently released USA for Africa album. . . .

That his religious motifs have gone largely unremarked isn't too surprising. Many fans don't pay attention to the meaning of lyrics and simply latch on to the hedonistic surface of Prince's music. Prince himself seems indecisive about how strongly to stress his religious message: the sermonette that opens the album and film of **"Purple Rain,"** for example, includes a jokey, deflating reference to a shrink in Beverly Hills. Most journalists have preferred to praise the erotic aspects of his act—after all, the sexy bad boy is a familiar rock-and-roll stereotype.

Yet it would be a mistake to think that Prince's religious message isn't hitting home. A friend recently found his teen-age daughter in the bedroom playing the album **"Purple Rain"** backward, like her pals at high school, in order to hear the secretive coded message Prince had left there. She was shaken to hear Prince say, "Hello, how are you? I'm fine, 'cause I know that the Lord is coming soon, coming, coming soon." Another friend reports that her adolescent son will not listen to Prince because he is upset by the cultlike fervor with which classmates recite the lyrics. And watching an audience of 12,500 at a recent concert standing on its feet, joyously jabbing arms in the air and singing **"I Would Die 4 U,"** is a very creepy experience. . . .

At such moments, Prince is America's most disturbing celebrity. Perhaps the crowd cheerfully singing along to **"I Would Die 4 U"** is oblivious to the song's morbid implications—it's easy to treat it as a simple ballad. Perhaps the song in concert occasions a ritual display of theatrical prowess, staged largely to amuse His Royal Badness. But this is the most artful and ambitious rock star in America today. Surely *he* knows the meaning of the moment. And watching it happen, it is hard not to wonder where Prince is heading—and just how far his millions of fans will follow. (p. 74)

Jim Miller with Janet Huck, "Rock's Mystery Prince," in Newsweek, *Vol. CV, No. 17, April 29, 1985, pp. 72-4.*

JON PARELES

Prince is up to something, no doubt about it, on ***Around the World in a Day.*** The packaging will pass for psychedelic. . . . And audio embellishments like finger cymbals and lost-in-space synthesizers—not to mention the album's first lines, "Open your heart, open your mind"—would have been right at home in lysergic times.

Let's not take Prince's psychedelic trappings too seriously, however. His new album is about anything *but* diving into a mind-altered subculture. (It even has an explicit antidrug song, **"Pop Life."**) On ***Around the World***—as on ***Purple Rain,*** which it barely resembles otherwise—Prince takes another step toward cleaning up his act.

Prince deserves credit for making an album at all—especially an album that breaks ranks with the previous six. He could cruise for years on the sales of the ***Purple Rain*** LP, the movie's boffo box office and the truckloads of nickels in cover-version royalties. Instead, he holed up in the studio, as he usually does, to make ***Around the World*** virtually by himself. (pp. 55-6)

Prince has apparently decided he's tired of being a bedroom-eyed, bikini-briefed, pansexual sex symbol. In the album-cover illustration it's difficult to tell who's who; I think Prince is the pious-looking, white-robed guy in the upper right who's ignoring a half-clad cutie and the nipple-shaped peak in a voluptuous mountain range. More importantly, his new lyrics are PG rated, not even the soft R of **"Darling Nikki"** on ***Purple Rain.*** It's hard to believe this is the same Prince who made ***Dirty Mind*** in 1980 or who, on 1981's ***Controversy,*** claimed "Sexuality is all you'll ever need."

Now Prince has come out of the bedroom. Only three of the nine songs on ***Around the World***—Prince's lowest proportion by a long shot—aim below the waist. **"Raspberry Beret"** is a sweetly wistful seduction song, and **"Tamborine,"** marching along like the Lemon Pipers' 1968 hit "Green Tambourine," makes masturbation seem even more innocent than Cyndi Lauper's "She Bop." After the bluesy bump and grind of **"Temptation,"** with one of the lewdest fuzz-tone guitars this side of Buddy Guy, God declares, "You have to want it for the right reasons"—and Prince promises to be good.

The lyrics on the rest of the album suggest the spacey, out-of-it benevolence one might expect from Stevie Wonder (**"The Ladder"** and the title cut, both cowritten by Prince's father, John L. Nelson), but underscored by Prince's own apocalyptic vision. With its lilting, nursery-rhyme-like melody, **"Paisley Park"** blithely describes a carefree refuge, which may be death; **"America,"** a mock-Slavic rewrite of the tune we all know, plus a funk beat, threatens a boy who doesn't pledge allegiance with permanent residence on a "mushroom cloud." Prince gets more mileage than Alice Walker from the color purple, his shorthand symbol for the end of the world, which shows up in the first song of the album and in the last. . . .

For all I know, ***Around the World in a Day*** may represent the afterglow following the commercial orgasm of ***Purple Rain.*** Or it may suggest that Prince's long obsession with s-e-x is beginning to make way for other concerns—we'll doubtless be hearing that in getting away from that adolescent humpa-humpa stuff, Prince has grown up. Maybe it's my hormones, but to me ***Around the World*** is if anything more childish sounding than its predecessors. Prince has traded what he does know for wide-eyed, goofy philosophizing that can be ugly—as with the wacko anti-Communism of **"America"**—as well as lovable. I'm not going along if Prince drifts off, with Earth, Wind and Fire and Stevie Wonder, into a grit-free never-never land, but at the moment he's still odd enough to be fascinating. . . .

Whether the album is an aberration or a new direction, one thing is sure: ***Around the World in a Day*** is the Prince album you can bring home to your parents. Even, I guess, if they're ex-hippies. (p. 56)

Jon Pareles, "Around the World in a Daze," in Rolling Stone, *Issue 449, June 6, 1985, pp. 55-6.*

Marilyn (Stickle) Sachs

1927-

American novelist and author of books for children.

Sachs's popular fiction appeals primarily to adolescent girls. Her novels examine first love, loneliness, parent-child relationships, the importance of social interaction, and the rewards of genuine friendship. Several of Sachs's young protagonists are alienated either from their families or their peers. In *A Summer's Lease* (1979), Gloria is unpopular because she is competitive and rude. Gloria begins to realize the importance of being friendly towards others when she is invited by a teacher to spend the summer in the country with her school rival. *Beach Towels* (1982) concerns the relationship between Phil and Lori, who meet at a beach. Lori, whom Phil initially considers too aggressive, is recovering from physical injuries and emotional problems following an automobile accident in which her mother was killed.

***Call Me Ruth* (1982) and *The Fat Girl* (1983) are considered Sach's best novels. The title character of *Call Me Ruth* is a Jewish immigrant who aspires to become an American citizen. Ruth argues constantly with her mother and is embarrassed by her mother's refusal to adapt to the American lifestyle. In *The Fat Girl*, Sachs explores how good intentions can sometimes lead to disastrous results. After publicly insulting Ellen, an overweight, unhappy girl, Jeff asks her out as a means of apology. Later, Jeff breaks up with his girlfriend and becomes Ellen's constant companion, but he attempts to control Ellen's life. This novel is particularly well regarded for its depiction of characters who develop into responsible adolescents.**

(See also *Children's Literature Review*, Vol. 2; *Contemporary Authors*, Vols. 17-20, rev. ed.; *Contemporary Authors New Revision Series*, Vol. 13; and *Something about the Author*, Vol. 3.)

Photograph by Morris Sachs. Courtesy of Marilyn Sachs

ETHEL L. HEINS

Returning to the 1940s for her setting [in ***A Summer's Lease***], the author tells the story of a bright, belligerent girl determined to be a writer. Constantly at war with her widowed mother, who believes that in poor families girls should go to work and not to college, Gloria Rein is hotheaded, fiercely competitive, disliked at school, and convinced that she is an unappreciated genius. Because she wants desperately to be named assistant editor of the high school magazine, Gloria is furious when she is asked to share the job with a boy she detests—Jerry Lieberman, talented, good-humored, and well-liked by everyone. Then, quite suddenly, both she and Jerry are invited by the magazine's faculty advisor—Gloria's favorite teacher—to spend a summer in the country, helping with chores and supervising seven younger boys and girls. There, away from her sordid city surroundings, Gloria easily proves her superior capabilities and courage and earns the respect and admiration—but not the love—of most of the children. And for the first time she begins occasionally to perceive some human vulnerability beneath her own harsh exterior. The teenagers' comparative innocence and lack of sophistication—rather than any sense of the political or emotional climate of wartime America—convey a feeling for the time, the period of the author's own adolescence. When she stands away from herself and views young people objectively, Marilyn Sachs's writing seems to gain freedom and depth. (pp. 311-12)

Ethel L. Heins, in a review of "A Summer's Lease," in The Horn Book Magazine, *Vol. LV, No. 3, June, 1979, pp. 311-12.*

PATRICIA LEE GAUCH

[By the end of chapter three in **"A Summer's Lease,"** the reader is convinced that] Gloria Rein is pushy, explosive, selfish, lacking in humor and fiercely competitive. An inner rhythm drives her to be "better than . . . better than . . . better than."

A summer vacation in the Catskills as companion to Mrs. Horne and seven assorted children does make a difference, even though Jerry Lieberman comes too. Outsider Gloria is drawn into warm camaraderie by a willing band of punchball players and the clownish Dr. Horne.

Still, the truth is it's not easy to like Gloria Rein. Her bickering family life is no excuse for her cruelties, and although she takes steps toward people, they are tentative and late. When she says to Jerry, "I'm ready . . . I think" to have friends, the reader is on page 99. And in the fall, when she is pitted against Jerry over an editorial decision, she becomes the old Gloria again: selfish, explosive, unable to be a friend.

Gloria Rein is trapped by Gloria Rein, and we are left with her. For some readers this ending will be "real life"; who likes a pat ending? But for others, I suspect, this ending will seem more pat, more final, than an ending that had given them the feeling Gloria might have another lease. . . .

I wish Marilyn Sachs had left us with more of a question, less of a pronouncement.

Patricia Lee Gauch, in a review of "A Summer's Lease," in The New York Times Book Review, *August 19, 1979, p. 20.*

BETSY HEARNE

Nostalgic scrutiny of old class pictures brings the long-lasting friendship between Pat Maddox and Lolly Scheiner to life [in ***Class Pictures***]. From the early days of kindergarten through high school graduation their close moments, common bonds, innate differences, and casual disagreements are warmly related through Pat's upbeat, first-person narrative. Though Lolly is depicted as the "dumb but beautiful blond" and Pat the "ugly but superintelligent scientist," Sachs gives both characters enough depth to belie any stereotyping. . . . Though the normal trappings of growing up (parties, ski trips, science fairs, graduation, movies, and dates) are part of the total picture, it's the effect of those events on each girl and on their relationship that is the unifying and most intriguing factor.

Betsy Hearne, in a review of "Class Pictures," in Booklist, *Vol. 77, No. 4, October 15, 1980, p. 329.*

PUBLISHERS WEEKLY

In her buoyant style, the author portrays effectively the trying years of growth by focusing on recognizable family and social situations. [**"Class Pictures"**] is a story capitalizing on Sachs's ability to combine rugged humor and pathos. . . . But why someone so gifted should ignore good usage is hard to understand. "Six boys taller than me"; "long enough for Jason and I to have that one good-bye" are examples of sloppiness in this book.

A review of "Class Pictures," in Publishers Weekly, *Vol. 218, No. 19, November 7, 1980. p. 61.*

BROOKE SELBY DILLON

Angie meant to dial Jim McCone, the school heart throb, to apologize for acting like a prude at the dance. By accident she reaches another Jim who tells her to forget Jim McCone, a "nerd" who "uses women." Angie calls the wrong number Jim back several times, and the remainder of [***Hello . . . Wrong Number***] is dialogues between them, as they share their feelings and fears and grow to love one another, despite having never met. Then a "creepy little guy" with a "big nose" begins to follow Angie and she tells Jim about it, only to find that the boy with the big nose is Jim—he is not the confident and good looking guy he has described himself as. The two break up, but Jim then overcomes his shyness and meets Angie in person. The two are reunited and happily resume their phone conversations.

The message—that physical beauty is less important than what's inside—is conveyed with warmth, humor, and poignancy.

Brooke Selby Dillon, in a review of "Hello . . . Wrong Number," in Voice of Youth Advocates, *Vol. 4, No. 6, February, 1982, p. 38.*

JUDITH GOLDBERGER

A mis-dialed phone number is the start of a relationship that continues exclusively over the wires throughout the duration of Sachs' [***Hello . . . Wrong Number***]. In spite of such a preposterous setup, the book is credible: the principal characters react naturally to each other, and their friendship, which eventually becomes romantic, is believable. What is more, writing in dialogue has given the author a framework conducive to easy reading, once readers catch on to the story construction. An appealing book, with enough plot for almost anyone. . . .

Judith Goldberger, in a review of "Hello . . . Wrong Number," in Booklist, *Vol. 78, No. 12, February 15, 1982, p. 761.*

PUBLISHERS WEEKLY

[In **"Call Me Ruth"**] Sachs's latest heroine is of the same stripe, fallible and likable, as . . . [the] other characters that the author's readers care about. Rifka Zelitsky eagerly becomes Ruth when she arrives with her mother on New York's lower East Side from Russia during the early 1900s. They join her father who had preceded them; when he dies, the mother goes to work in the garment center. Ruth yearns to be a genuine American and burns with embarrassment over her mother's greenhorn ways. . . . The naked, moving and often funny story typifies the gap between two people who have loved each other unreservedly and find themselves at a crossroads where differences test their loyalty.

A review of "Call Me Ruth," in Publishers Weekly, *Vol. 222, No. 6, August 6, 1982, p. 69.*

DENISE M. WILMS

Ruth loves America, but her mother is less enthusiastic about adapting to new American and nontraditional Jewish ways. **"Call Me Ruth"** is Ruth's recurring comment when her mother persists in calling her Rifka, and she is embarrassed more than once by her mother's "greenie" behavior and European manners. Ruth's mother takes a factory job to make ends meet and before long becomes involved in union activities. This, too, bothers Ruth, who is particularly shamed when her mother is arrested and sent to the workhouse after a picket-line fracas. More to Ruth's taste is her cool, perfect teacher whom she emulates but who, she comes to realize, will never see her as more than a poor little immigrant girl. . . . The bittersweet finish shades the picture oddly even as it makes it thought-provoking.

Denise M. Wilms, in a review of "Call Me Ruth," in Booklist, *Vol. 79, No. 1, September 1, 1982, p. 48.*

ETHEL R. TWICHELL

[***Call Me Ruth***], which at first deals with immigrant problems at the turn of the century and captures the contemporaneous bustle and customs of the Jewish community, . . . takes a new turn. Ruth's mother becomes involved with the organizing of the female garment workers' union and with the early strikes, and she changes from a frightened young woman to a spirited supporter of a cause. Maintaining a fast pace throughout, the book gives a moving and vivid picture of the exploitation and condescension the immigrants faced as well as of the loving, if abrasive, relationship between Ruth and her mother.

Ethel R. Twichell, in a review of "Call Me Ruth," in The Horn Book Magazine, *Vol. LVIII, No. 5, October, 1982, p. 518.*

LUCY V. HAWLEY

[Though it contains a] very limited vocabulary, one's interest and concern are aroused for the people in [***Beach Towels***]. In the time span of one week, two high school students become acquainted and grow to care about each other as they meet each day at the beach. Although the book has almost no narration, Lori is developed into a person with real depth. She is recovering mentally and physically from a tragic automobile accident, but the event is not presented as a tidy and sensational conclusion: it is gradually and sensitively revealed.

Lucy V. Hawley, in a review of "Beach Towels," in School Library Journal, *Vol. 29, No. 6, February, 1983, p. 92.*

ZENA SUTHERLAND

[***Beach Towels*** is a] story of a burgeoning friendship between two adolescents who meet at a beach. . . . Lori is cheerful, noisy, plays her radio so loudly that it annoys Phil, who prefers quiet and solitude. . . . Gradually Lori and Phil talk about themselves: Phil is trying to decide whether to finish the last year of high school or drop out; Lori, trying to forget the accident in which she was driving and her mother was killed, is miserable although she was blameless. The story, told almost entirely in dialogue, ends with the two planning a first date. . . . [The book] should appeal to teen-age readers, since it presents few reading obstacles, has natural conversation, and incorporates many of the concerns shared by most adolescents.

Zena Sutherland, in a review of "Beach Towels," in Bulletin of the Center for Children's Books, *Vol. 36, No. 7, March, 1983, p. 133.*

RUTH K. MacDONALD

[***Fourteen***] is an unpredictable delight. Rebecca, the 14-year-old heroine of the novel, always seems to find herself in her novelist mother's books. While Mom sets out to write a teen romance in order to avoid any similarity to her unromantic daughter's life, Rebecca finds herself involved in a most unlikely romance. Jason is shorter than she is and can't even ride a bike; a horticultural buff, he is given to kicking rabbits and he spends much time crying about the mysterious disappearance of his father. With Rebecca's help, Jason figures out what happened to his father; he also finds that Rebecca's freckles are really quite as attractive as tuberose begonias. Their first kiss contrasts hilariously with the romantic version in mom's novel.

Ruth K. MacDonald, in a review of "Fourteen," in School Library Journal, *Vol. 29, No. 8, April, 1983, p. 117.*

KIRKUS REVIEWS

[***Fourteen*** contains some] funny, savvy stuff—especially about being the offspring/model of a children's book writer—hung on a forced, crypto-mystery plot. . . . [While Rebecca's mother] writes a formula teenage romance, *First Love* (with a virginal heroine, because "That's the new look in teenage books"), Rebecca has her own, outlandish first-romance—with short, weepy, plant-loving, rabbit-hating, non-biking (-running, -swimming) Jason Furst, who moves into the apartment next door with his near-hysterical, very unfriendly mother . . . who, says Jason, got that way after his father went off to Europe "on business." . . . The question . . . is what really happened to Jason's father; and the answer, which Rebecca forces out, shouldn't happen—he's in prison. The romantic attraction, though, is handled with tongue-in-cheek finesse. Rebecca's writer-mother fell in love with her pharmacist/poet father because of a poem about her runny nose. Rebecca herself falls in love with botanist-to-be Jason because he compares her face, with its freckles, to the inside of a favorite flower. . . . Bubbly and offbeat . . . , [***Fourteen*** is] more interesting than the likes of *First Love*.

A review of "Fourteen," in Kirkus Reviews, *Vol. LI, No. 9, May 1, 1983, p. 528.*

KATE M. FLANAGAN

A book that begins like many other first-person novels about a teenage romance [***The Fat Girl***] changes into an intriguing account of an unusual relationship. . . . [Jeff began] to notice that Ellen de Lucca, "the fat girl" in his ceramics class, always seemed to be watching him. . . . One day Ellen overheard Jeff making an unkind remark about her and burst into tears. Chagrined, Jeff tried to comfort her and was horrified when she threatened to kill herself. At first motivated by guilt, Jeff began to spend time with Ellen, and his interest in the girl quickly became an obsession. He took control of her life, changing her wardrobe, hairstyle, and makeup and advising her on future plans. As his own family problems mounted, Jeff realized that he was happy only when he was with Ellen: "She belonged to me now and I would never let her go." The psychological implications of the book are fascinating, but they are limited by the lack of subtlety in the characterizations. . . . But the development of the bizarre relationship between Jeff and Ellen does make for compelling reading.

Kate M. Flanagan, in a review of "The Fat Girl," in The Horn Book Magazine, *Vol. LIX, No. 6, December, 1983, p. 719.*

KAY WEBB O'CONNELL

In an ironic twist on the "Beauty and the Beast" tale, . . . [***The Fat Girl*** is] about a male "beauty," Jeff Lyons, who is secure in his good looks but insecure in his emotions. . . . Self-assured and handsome, Jeff tells his own story: he and the talented Norma are in love. It seems ideal: even his hard-bitten mother likes Norma and so do his dad and stepmother. Alternately fascinated and repelled by fat Ellen, Jeff insults her in class and finds himself taking her out by way of apology. Jeff accepts her doting adulation with a heady feeling of power. . . . Eventually he dumps Norma to devote himself full time to his Svengali career with the fat girl. In a credibly meshed subplot, tensions between Jeff's parents mount, culminating in his mother's attempted suicide. . . . With no affection from his mother or his absent father, Jeff has been so emotionally deprived that the power he has over Ellen becomes obsessive and misguided. But Ellen's new-found glamour gradually fosters an independence; when she becomes self-directed, they split up. At the end, Jeff reflects that, unlike his embittered mother, he won't waste his life brooding over disappointments. However, there is some question whether he will be able to sustain a relationship he cannot dominate. Jeff's obsession . . . [in] ***The Fat Girl*** and the psychological interplay between them make this compelling reading. (pp. 174-75)

Kay Webb O'Connell, in a review of "The Fat Girl," in School Library Journal, *Vol. 30, No. 7, March, 1984, pp. 174-75.*

BARBARA CUTLER HELFGOTT

"The Fat Girl" presents a challenge to author and reader alike. Miss Sachs, the author of a number of other books for young adults, is an old hand at making unusual people seem credible and she has done so here. She has managed to convey at least some of the conflicting psychological impulses motivating her characters. . . . Still, what's difficult to believe is the situation itself. Would a real Jeff choose Ellen? As a friend, perhaps, but as a girlfriend?

My guess is that a number of young readers will find the ideas in this book pretty weird but a few may find themselves wishing that someone with Jeff's initially kindly impulses may, in fact, exist.

Barbara Cutler Helfgott, in a review of "The Fat Girl," in The New York Times Book Review, *April 1, 1984, p. 29.*

Carl (August) Sandburg

1878-1967

(Born Charles August Sandburg; also wrote under pseudonyms of Militant and Jack Phillips) American poet, biographer, autobiographer, novelist, author of books for children, nonfiction writer, journalist, songwriter, and editor.

A revered figure in American literature, Sandburg is best known for his intense, loosely structured poetry and his epical biographies of Abraham Lincoln. In his poetry, Sandburg realistically evoked the immense diversity of the American citizenry and landscape. He sought to express the dignity of common people, in whom he found the spirit and values of American democracy. Sandburg's poetry is often compared to that of Walt Whitman. Both poets favored a prosaic style, they each celebrated the activities of common people, and they both often expressed faith in democratic ideals. Sandburg was particularly adept at recreating the rhythms and colloquialisms of Midwestern idioms. Rebecca West, in her introduction to his *Selected Poems* (1926), called Sandburg a "national poet" who "expresses the whole of life of the Middle West of to-day."

Sandburg's first collection of poetry, *Chicago Poems* (1916), contains free verse poems that were startling in their style, tone, and subject matter. In this volume and throughout his career, he wrote oddly structured, prosaic poetry that emphasized key phrases and images. Sandburg often examined aspects of industrial urban life, a topic that had rarely been addressed in poetry. For example, in his much-anthologized poem "Chicago," Sandburg mentions skyscrapers, hog-butchering, railroads, and other objects and activities with an intensity that reflects the bustling urban landscape. With *Chicago Poems* and several subsequent volumes, including *Cornhuskers* (1918), *Smoke and Steel* (1920), and *Good Morning, America* (1928), Sandburg established himself as a popular poet who wrote unpretentiously about urban life, nature, and humanity.

Critical response to Sandburg's poetry has varied markedly, and critics continue to debate its importance. Many contend that his poems are often overly sentimental and resemble randomly arranged prose pieces. In a review of Sandburg's *Collected Poems* (1950), William Carlos Williams acknowledged "Chicago" as "brilliant" but claimed that the rest of Sandburg's poems were formless and insignificant. On the other hand, reviewers have noted the sense of power or tenderness evinced in many of his poems, and several critics claim that his experimentation with free verse offered an important challenge to traditional forms of poetry. Sandburg was consistently praised for his use of common language in poems about the people of the United States. In his most ambitious poem, *The People, Yes* (1936), Sandburg catalogues their diversities. Stephen Vincent Benét considered this poem "a frescoe and a field of grass and a man listening quietly to all the commonplace, extraordinary things that people say." *The People, Yes* and "Chicago" are generally regarded as Sandburg's finest poetic achievements. Sandburg was awarded the Pulitzer Prize for *Collected Poems*.

In his acclaimed multivolume biography of Lincoln, Sandburg relates incidents from Lincoln's life in the manner of a story

The Bettmann Archive, Inc.

rather than as a series of historical facts. Although some critics expressed their uneasiness with Sandburg's artistic license, most praised his vivid, "folksy" presentation and the enormous amount of factual detail he included in the biography. In *Abraham Lincoln: The Prairie Years* (1926), which consists of two volumes, Sandburg explores Lincoln's youth and his adult life before he became President. The four-volume *Abraham Lincoln: The War Years* (1939) opens with Lincoln departing Springfield, Illinois, to serve as President and concludes with the return of Lincoln's body to Springfield for burial. The latter volumes offer a panoramic view of the Civil War and feature a large cast of well-developed historical figures, including government officials, soldiers, and common citizens. Sandburg achieved a sense of drama and intrigue by developing events in sequential order from the viewpoints of those involved. He meticulously recreated historical events and also included behind-the-scenes views of Lincoln and the many people and events he encountered. Sandburg stressed that the simple, honest values Lincoln learned as a poor country boy helped him prevail during an era of great crisis. Henry Steele Commager lauded Sandburg's approach to Lincoln, stating, "[Sandburg] has realized that Lincoln belongs to the people, not to the historians, and he has given us a portrait from which a whole generation may draw understanding from the past and inspiration for the future." Sandburg was awarded the Pulitzer Prize in history for *Abraham Lincoln: The War Years*.

While Sandburg won fame primarily as a poet and as a biographer of Lincoln, he was also recognized for several other literary activities. He wrote several volumes of tales for children, known collectively as the "Rootebaga Stories." *Remembrance Rock* (1948) is a historical novel set in America and spans the arrival of the Pilgrims to the onset of World War II. As a young man, Sandburg worked many odd jobs, traveled as a hobo, served in the army during the Spanish-American War, and became a journalist with the Chicago *Daily News.* These adventures and his boyhood experiences are recounted in his acclaimed autobiography, *Always the Young Strangers* (1952). One of the most popular figures in American literature during his lifetime, Sandburg traveled extensively and was well known for his lectures and poetry recitals. He also sang and played guitar and banjo. His interest in music is reflected in *American Songbag* (1927), a collection of American folk songs. Following his death, Sandburg was given a special service at the Lincoln Memorial.

(See also *CLC*, Vols. 1, 4, 10, 15; *Contemporary Authors,* Vols. 5-8, rev. ed., Vols. 25-28, rev. ed. [obituary]; *Dictionary of Literary Biography,* Vol. 17; and *Something about the Author,* Vol. 8.)

THE NEW YORK TIMES BOOK REVIEW

Some of the work in [**"Chicago Poems"**] . . . is good, tremendously good. Pictures of our modern life, short, vivid, conveyed in few and telling words, the words of a man who sees the salient and compelling thing and who finds the translating phrase. Some of it is poetry, some is decidedly not poetry. It is a pity that so many writers are bent on confusing the terms, and, not content with letting their bits of prose full of illumination and beauty as they may be, go as prose, must tag them with the title of poems. The result is to arouse a feeling of irritation that has no place in the appreciation such fine work as Mr. Sandburg's must awaken in every one who loves good literature in whatever form, or who responds to quick and striking studies of the crowding life in which we move. . . .

Turning the pages, the panorama of the city streets, with their daily tragedies and comedies, seems to pass before you. Yet it is not a panorama, but a carefully selected and dramatic series of incidents, revealing the huge background from which each item is taken. In a line or two you are given the measure of immense contrasts, you are held by the flash of an injustice, you read a bitter heart or study the mind of a laborer. It is all alive, stirring, human. The best is very good, indeed; the worst is dull and shapeless. But the worst can easily be let alone, for there is so much of the good. And it is by no means only the city that is pictured here. There are exquisite pieces that tell of the blowing wind across fields, the new Spring on upland meadows, that speak of love, or woman's beauty. And throughout the book runs a call to a better, finer, and nobler view of human responsibility for what is wrong and sad in our present civilization.

A review of "Chicago Poems," in The New York Times Book Review, *June 11, 1916, p. 242.*

O. W. FIRKINS

[In **"Chicago Poems"**] Mr. Carl Sandburg has two divergent aspirations: he reaches out simultaneously towards the brawny and the lissome, two ideals linked only by the fact that both are fashionable. The brawny section, which includes the **"Chicago Poems,"** paints the distresses and iniquities of a great city with an unsparing plainness which twenty-five years ago would have been courageous. Mr. Carl Sandburg is a good fellow, with an authentic pity for the poor; and I am glad that he should lash the sodden and selfish rich, if the lash be reformatory. But I think in his pictures of misery there is a lesson he might profitably learn from Galsworthy or Hauptmann, or, for that matter, from Hugo or Dickens. The *man* in the man must be clearly visible before his immersion in the mud can be either tragic or pathetic. Too often—not always—in Mr. Sandburg's pictures the man is so like the mud that his submergence produces no effect of tragic incongruity. These poems, which are all in free verse or shackled prose, show a rude power here and there, a power rather forensic or journalistic than strictly poetical, evident sometimes in a quick eye for dramatic juxtapositions. . . .

In his lissome work he shows not poems, but mild poeticisms, little pennons or banderoles of detached and pleasing phrase, sometimes merely decorative, sometimes fluttering from the spear of his polemic. What sense of beauty he has is evoked oftenest by colors and mists.

Mr. Sandburg's error and calamity is the refusal of discipline. (p. 152)

O. W. Firkins, "American Verse," in The Nation, *London, Vol. CIII, No. 2668, August 17, 1916, pp. 150-52.**

FRANCIS HACKETT

The free rhythms of Mr. Carl Sandburg are a fine achievement in poetry. No one who reads **"Chicago Poems"** with rhythm particularly in mind can fail to recognize how much beauty he attains in this regard. But the more arresting aspect of Mr. Sandburg's achievement is, for myself, the so-called imagistic aspect; the aspect, that is to say, which the subject-matter itself reveals. The rhythm, one may insist, is part of the imagism—one may resent having the so-called subject-matter considered separately. Rhythm, however, is far from the dominant novelty in Carl Sandburg, and it is convenient to assume that his rhythms are delectable to many who yet do not admit the beauty or originality of his way of approaching the world. . . .

Mr. Sandburg illustrates above all the intensity, the momentousness, that is gained by declining to refer each object to some remoter cause, by tending to treat each object as self-contained, purposive in its own measure, dynamic. . . . This is not a trick. It is simply a pushing of the imagination to the center of the will. And even where there is no such unity as the will provides another kind of composure is secured, a visual composure. There is none of the laxity that comes from splitting attention several ways. (p. 328)

At first [several] poems may appear too innocent of self-interpretation to mean anything, too impressionistic to compel the name of beauty—to give that completion which has no shadow and knows no end beyond itself. But such exquisite realization of the scenes that gave Mr. Sandburg the mood of beauty is in itself a creation of the beautiful. Mr. Sandburg has such art in representing these scenes and the actors in them that doubt as to his capture of beauty could only occur to a person filled with a wrong expectation. If expectation is unfulfilled, indeed, it can almost certainly be deemed wrong, for these imagist verses are as good as any of their kind.

But this is not to say that all of Mr. Sandburg's poems are inspired. I am not much impressed by his vision of Chicago. This is not because Chicago fails of poetry. In some ways Chicago is hideous. . . . But for all this ugliness there is something about Chicago not like the imbruted employer of children and leech of factory girls and general blusterer and roustabout that Mr. Sandburg concocts for us. Mr. Sandburg is quite right that children work, "broken and smothered, for bread and wages," but Chicago is not legitimately "haunted with shadows of hunger-hands." No more is it a laughing giant. It is a work-shop but largely a work-shop for business enterprise, a wasteful, inundated, scrambling, shoddy, manufacturing city, a city irradiated to a marvelous degree by hope, by faith, by charity, careless, generous, inefficient, as well as coarse, husky, cunning, strong. (pp. 328-29)

Francis Hackett, "Impressions," in The New Republic, *Vol. VIII, No. 104, October 28, 1916, pp. 328-29.*

LOUIS UNTERMEYER

When Carl Sandburg's ***Chicago Poems*** appeared two years ago, most of the official votaries and vestrymen in the temple of the Muse raised their hands in pious horror at this open violation of their carefully enshrined sanctities. In the name of their beloved Past, they prepared a bill of particulars that bristled with charges as contradictory as they were varied. They were all united however on one point—Sandburg's brutality. In this they were correct. . . .

As in ***Chicago Poems,*** the first poem of his new volume—***Cornhuskers*** . . .—brims with an uplifted coarseness, an almost animal exultation that is none the less an exaltation. (p. 263)

The gain in power is evident at once and grows with each section of this new collection. The tone in ***Cornhuskers*** has more depth and dignity; the note is not louder, but it is larger. In ***Chicago Poems*** there were times when the poet was so determined to worship ruggedness that one could hear his adjectives strain to achieve a physical strength of their own. One occasionally was put in mind of the professional strong man in front of a mirror, of virility basking in the spotlight, of an epithet exhibiting its muscle. Here the accent is less vociferous, more vitalizing; it is a summoning of strong things rather than the mere stereotypes of strength. . . .

These [poems] . . . seem a direct answer to Whitman's hope of a democratic poetry that would express itself in a democratic and even a distinctively American speech. He maintained that before America could have a powerful poetry our poets would have to learn the use of hard and powerful words; the greatest artists, he insisted, were simple and direct, never merely "polite or obscure.". . .

No contemporary is so responsive to these limber and idiomatic phrases as Sandburg. His language lives almost as fervidly as the life from which it is taken. And yet his intensity is not always raucous; it would be a great mistake to believe that Sandburg excels only in verse that is heavy-fisted and stentorian. . . .

[His] creative use of proper names and slang (which would so have delighted Whitman), [his] interlarding of cheapness and nobility is Sandburg's most characteristic idiom as well as his greatest gift. . . .

The struggles, the social criticism, the concentrated anger, and the protests are here as prominently as in ***Chicago Poems,*** but they assert themselves with less effort. The war has temporarily harmonized them; they are still rebellious, but somehow resigned. The chants of revolt are seldom out of tune with Sandburg's purely pictorial pieces. Both are the product of a strength that derives its inspiration from the earth; they are made of tough timber; they have "strong roots in the clay and worms." (p. 264)

Louis Untermeyer, "Strong Timber," in The Dial, *Vol. XLV, No. 774, October 5, 1918, pp. 263-64.*

THE NEW YORK TIMES BOOK REVIEW

Carl Sandburg's first volume, **"Chicago Poems,"** burst upon the world with the force, the crude beauty, the screaming vitality of the "Hog Butcher for the World," whom in its first line it celebrated. Yet there was much in **"Chicago Poems"** beyond mere primitive strength. Amy Lowell said of it: "The impression one gets on reading this book is of a heavy, steel-gray sky rent open here and there, and, through the rents, shining pools of clear, pale blue."

In **"Cornhuskers"** the rents are more numerous and the clear, pale blue is more vivid. . . . **"Cornhuskers"** is a book of the earth, and of the streams which water the earth. It is a less cheerful book than its predecessor, in the sense that the panorama of nature, indifferently kind and cruel, bestowing life and death with an equal hand, persisting in its deliberate round of decay and renewal, heedless of the generations which are so heedful of it, must be less cheerful, if not less cheering, than the record of human struggle.

Three things run through the poems: the dust of the earth, mist, and the sight and sound of running water. And, curiously at first glance, considering that the poet is young and strong and sings of a virgin land, **"Cornhuskers"** is a book of Autumn and of sunset, rather than of morning and of Spring. It is, on the whole, a melancholy book. . . .

"Prairie" is a brave poem, and its author intended its ending to be brave and forward-looking. But his view of the past as "a bucket of ashes" and "a wind gone down" perches man, as it were, precariously, upon a pinnacle of the present, his back to an empty void, his face turned to "a sky of tomorrows"—and no airplane provided.

For, no matter how full of promise that sky may be, unless it is in a way guaranteed by a succession of yesterdays justified by today, it can inspire very little confidence.

This refusal of history and eager hope of things to come has a childlike pathos about it. . . .

If to Carl Sandburg the past was as solid and vital and important as it is to Amy Lowell, he would be, we do not hesitate to say, the first American poet of his generation. He has power, he commands beauty, he possesses—though he sometimes, Peter-like, denies it—a sense of form. But he is a creature of instinct, and though that is good it is not enough. In **"Wilderness"** he defines himself very exactly. He has the wolf within him, "fangs pointed for tearing gashes, a red tongue for raw meat," and the fox, "I pick things out of the wind and the air," and also the eagle and the mocking bird. Neither is he altogether of the wild; he has, too, "a man-child heart, a woman-child heart; it is a father and mother and lover." But in all this "zoo," as he terms it, there is nothing that remembers, except through instinct or passion, nothing that reasons. Longing for a dusk Nirvana after lusty deeds is the inevitable reaction of such a nature.

It may be said, and justly, that some of the most moving of the poems in **"Cornhuskers"** are poems of the civil war, a war that was history before Mr. Sandburg was born. But in the Middle West of forty years ago that conflict was still a matter of neighborhood debate; every other man had tales to tell of his own experiences at Chickamauga or the Wilderness, and the great war President was a local hero whom many personally remembered. The vitality of Mr. Sandburg's civil war poems, far from showing any sense of the past, emphasizes his sense of the present—that most vivid of all presents, the impressions of childhood.

But Mr. Sandburg is a poet who has come late to his heritage. Much of circumstance as well as heredity has gone to his making. In these later poems one already perceives subtle changes—more of the blue sky, less of the lowering gray. He has not yet stopped growing, and as circumstance continues to mold him it is hard to say whether instinct will possess him to the end, or if out of a firmer intellectual grip upon the past may not also come a firmer grip upon the future. If the latter, then indeed will Carl Sandburg be a great poet.

"Mr. Sandburg's Poems of War and Nature," in The New York Times Book Review, *January 12, 1919, p. 13.*

AMY LOWELL

Two men speak in Mr. Sandburg, a poet and a propagandist. His future will depend upon which finally dominates the other. Since a poet must speak by means of suggestion and a propagandist succeeds by virtue of clear presentation, in so far as a propagandist is a poet, just in that ratio is he a failure where his propaganda is concerned. On the other hand, the poet who leaves the proper sphere of his art to preach, even by analogy, must examine the mote in his verse very carefully lest, perchance, it turn out a beam.

In my study of Mr. Sandburg in "Tendencies in Modern American Poetry," I pointed out this danger of his practice. Then I had only one book to go upon, now I have three [**"Chicago Poems," "Cornhuskers,"** and **"Smoke and Steel"**], and the danger seems to me to be looming larger with terrific speed. It may be that Mr. Sandburg has determined to stuff all his theories into one book and let it go at that. In which case there cannot be too much objection, but I fear—oh, I fear.

Mr. Sandburg loves people, perhaps I should say the "people." But I believe it is more than that. I think he has a real love for human beings. But evidently, from his books, his experience with people is limited to a few types, and it is a pity that these types should so often be the kind of persons whom only the morbidly sensitive, unhealthily developed, modern mind has ever thought it necessary to single out for prominence—prominence of an engulfing sort, that is. If we admit that the degraded are degraded there is not much danger of losing our perspective; if we hug them to our hearts and turn a cold shoulder to the sober and successful of the world, then we are running fast toward chaos, and our mental processes may fairly be considered a trifle askew. . . .

In **"Cornhuskers"** Mr. Sandburg seemed content to let the back alley folk stay in the back alleys. He spoke to us of other things, of the great, wide prairies, for instance, and, in so speaking, achieved a masterpiece. He gave his lyrical gift far more space than he usually allows, and the result was some of the finest poems of the modern movement. For Mr. Sandburg has a remarkable originality. His outlook is his own, his speech meets it, together the two make rarely beautiful poetry, when Mr. Sandburg permits. Then conscience pricks him, the "people" rise and confront him, gibbering like ghouls, he experiences an uneasy sense of betrayal and writes **"Galoots"** for example. I think these things hurt Mr. Sandburg as much as the things they represent hurt him. If they did not hurt him they would not have become an obsession. Much morbid verse has been written by tortured lovers, and we shall never understand these particular poems of Mr. Sandburg's until we realize that he too is a tortured lover, a lover of humanity in travail. It is seldom that the kind of exaggerated misery which Mr. Sandburg feels produces good poetry, and these poems are seldom successful. . . .

I do not wish to imply that all the poems in [**"Smoke and Steel"**] are the results of the mood in question. That would be far from the case, but the proportion of such poems is too great for the thorough satisfaction of a reader who is a profound admirer of Mr. Sandburg at his best—and, shall I add, his most lyrical. The book is divided into eight sections, of which only two, "Mist Forms" and "Haze" are frankly lyrical, while another two, "People Who Must" and "Circle of Doors," are as frankly the other thing, which, for want of a better name, we may call "the obsession." But this obsession creeps into many poems in the sections, "Playthings of the Wind" and "Passports"; even when "it," specifically, is not present, some crude and irrelevant turn of speech, the outgrowth of it, will crop up and ruin an otherwise noble thing. Colloquialisms, downright slang, have their place in poetry as in all literature. My contention here is not that Mr. Sandburg does not often use them with happy effect, but that quite as often he drags them in where (to my ear, a least) they should emphatically not be. A line like "We'll get you, you sbxyzch!" may be perfect realism, but it hurts the reader, as does "stenogs" and "thingamajig." The last appears in a poem in which it is at least in place if we admit the poem itself, **"Manual System,"** to a place anywhere; but "stenogs" is smashed into a serious poem called **"Trinity Peace,"** which is built around a highly poetic thought. . . .

Having registered my protest, which is the disagreeable part of the critic's work, let me immediately admit that one of Mr. Sandburg's excellencies is that he sets down the life about him, that very life of the people of which I have been speaking. When he sees it as a poet, he makes it poetically adequate; it is only when he sees it obliquely as a biased sentimentalist that he injures it and himself. He has an inclusive vision, something which gathers up the essences of life and work and relates them to the pulsing fabric which is the whole energy of human existence. His **"Prairie"** was not only a slice of Mother Earth, it was Mother Earth cherishing her children. So, in **"Smoke and Steel,"** we have not a mere metal being manufactured, not mere men toiling at their work—we have man's impulse to spend himself in creation and the far ramifications of what that creation means. We have the eye which sees the beauty of the curve of smoke. . . .

"Smoke and Steel" is worthy to stand beside **"Prairie."** There is an epic sweep to this side of Mr. Sandburg's work. Somehow it brings the reader into closer contact with his country, reading these poems gives me more of a patriotic emotion than ever "The Star-Spangled Banner" has been able to do. This is

America, and Mr. Sandburg loves her so much that suddenly we realize how much we love her, too. What has become dulled by habit quickens under his really magical touch. . . . Because he can do this Mr. Sandburg has a glorious responsibility set on his shoulders.

The seeing eye—Mr. Sandburg has it to a superlative degree, and, wedded to it, an imaginative utterance which owes nothing whatever to literature or tradition. It is a fascinating and baffling study this of examining how Mr. Sandburg does it. The technique of this magic is so unusual that no old knowledge applies. It is, more than anything else, the sharp, surprising rightness of his descriptions which gives Mr. Sandburg his high position in the poetry of today. . . .

Some people have had difficulty in understanding Mr. Sandburg's rhythms, these long, slow cadences, like the breath of air over an open moor. Indeed they are the very gift of the prairies, for where else do we find them? Not in Whitman, not in the Frenchmen, not among his contemporaries. . . .

There is one thing we can say with Mr. Sandburg's three books in front of us. Either this is a very remarkable poet or he is nothing, for . . . [among] the minors he clearly has no place. He has greatly dared, and I personally believe that posterity, with its pruning hand, will mount him high on the ladder of poetic achievement.

Amy Lowell, "Poetry and Propaganda," in The New York Times Book Review, *October 24, 1920, p. 7.*

LOUIS UNTERMEYER

[***Smoke and Steel***] establishes what ***Chicago Poems*** only promised and ***Cornhuskers*** plainly intimated. It proves that these states can now claim two living major poets: Sandburg and Frost. Both poets are racially indigenous, both have that blend of toughness and tenderness that tastes of the soil, both are in love with a world of frank and homely realities. But each wears his realism with a difference. Frost kneels at well-curbs and discovers universes; one farm, one rocky acre is too large for him to exhaust. Sandburg marches and countermarches over two hemispheres; one world is not large enough for his restless feet. Frost is true to *things;* the fact is always brimming over for him; he never hopes to drain it all. Sandburg also feeds on the fact; it nourishes, but it does not satisfy him. Frost plays with its twinkling or sardonic suggestions. For Sandburg, hot after finalities, implications are not enough; he insists on explanations; he probes eagerly for the question behind, the answer beyond. . . . It is a revealing title Sandburg has chosen for himself. Steel hardens him, but it is the smoke of steel that prompts and carries his dreams.

The very first poem in the new volume uncovers the heart of the contradiction. In this extended title poem it is at once evident that Sandburg is a reporter turned mystic. He uses the actual scene as a point of vivid and abrupt departure; for him realism acts chiefly as a spring-board. From it he leaps directly into a romantic, lyrical mysticism. Fragments, torn from their setting, would do a double injustice to the unity of ***Smoke and Steel.*** For this is Sandburg's first completely successful long poem. His previous lengthy works were scarcely long poems at all, but a succession of brief figures; lyrical snatches—***Prairie*** is a splendid example—loosely connected, almost disintegrated. Here mood, accent and image are held at a glowing pitch, fused in a new intensity. This tightening power and sharpness of effect extend through the major portion of the volume, making it the most valuable as it is the most varied of Sandburg's three offerings. (p. 86)

This poetry, as Jean Catel declared in the Mercure de France, is charged with immediate associations; "it translates the new world." The fantastic hungers and strange energies of the instant dominate ***Smoke and Steel,*** from the sniggering irony of ***The Lawyers Know Too Much*** to the sudden pathos of ***An Electric Sign Goes Dark,*** from the hot echoes of the Chicago race riots in ***Hoodlums*** to the sheer loveliness of the fifty poems in the lyrical section Mist Forms. Nor is Sandburg less sensitive to the shadows and shapes of twilight. He is a laureate of dusk and in him, as in Whitman, Night finds her passionate celebrant. ***Night Stuff, Night Movement, The Skyscraper Loves Night, Night's Nothings Again*** . . . in these he "clothes himself in his 'tablier de silence'," grave, but never impassive. (pp. 86, 88)

Sandburg, for all his strength, is not without his weakness. Although he has gained greatly in control since ***Chicago Poems,*** he is still sometimes tempted to talk at the top of his voice, to bang the table, to whip off his shirt and point to the hair on his chest. These moments are growing less and less recurring; it is the opposite tendency that is growing more dangerous. In giving way to mysticism . . . Sandburg often gives the subconscious an absolutely free hand; he lets it dictate its unfettered—and, one might almost add, unlettered—fantasies. There are times, more frequent than one might wish, when he fails to guide the current of his thought; it directs him, so that he becomes the instrument rather than the artist. Too often he leaves his material soft and loose instead of solidifying and shaping it to the proportions of a finished work. There are even times when Sandburg is unsure about furnishing the clue to the half-realized and half-expressed vagaries of the imagination. But though the meaning is not always clear, there is no mistaking his emotion. It is implicit in every line; a concentrated exaltation, rich in its sweeping affirmations, richer in its energetic details. (p. 88)

Louis Untermeyer, in a review of "Smoke and Steel," in The New Republic, *Vol. XXV, No. 315, December 15, 1920, pp. 86, 88.*

ARTHUR WILSON

Either Carl Sandburg is dead or he is very sick. Some of us, who annunciated this great poet when his epiphanal accents crashed out in Chicago, now look up from the useless pages of ***Smoke and Steel*** with a gasp of astonished grief. Is this the latest cry of our divine ballyhoo-poet, whom we have seen and heard so often just outside the circus-tent-of-life, crudely and eloquently ranting of such God-awful splendours within? Yes, it is, I suppose: although the cry might have been shrieked by a gas-light gamin hired to assassinate Sandburg, so completely is it murder. As a cry which is variously yodelled one hundred and ninety-three times (I refer to the number of poems in the book; and each has the most inspiring title), it is mostly characterized by the sententious garrulity which makes nine-tenths of Whitman impossible to a man of any taste. The rest of the cry, with some perfectly astounding exceptions, is what Americans call an *encore*. Briefly, tragically, as a single long ululation, it lacks the certitude of genius. Surely one who has wept and raved over the true Sandburg may be permitted to repudiate the false; in a spirit of hope, of passionate petition, may even be permitted to name the hell he has credulously blundered into. For the poet is not dead. He is merely whoring after alien gods. And that sort of thing, in the special meaning of the allusion, is a mental disease.

In charity, the disease is nystagmus—which is nothing more or less than oscillation of the eyeballs, or dizziness. It is produced in the world of aviation by a tight spiral or a tail-spin. In the world of literature—in Sandburg's world—it is produced by the centrifugal stresses of asinine adulation. The result is the same in both worlds: neither aviator nor poet can fly straight until he recovers. It was, it *is* the conventional practice of critics, in the absence of sound appreciation, to acclaim each succeeding manifestion of inferiority as the best thing Sandburg has ever done. Such unfair acclamations have turned the poet's head. Such suggestions of universal merit, actuating his mental ailerons and kicking over his spiritual rudder, have inevitably thrown him into a tail-spin which has disturbed the fluid of his semi-circular canals and produced a really dangerous condition of nystagmus. So much for the nature of the disease.

The symptoms are absolutely appalling. Sandburg has lost (at least temporarily) the one and only thing which makes him great—the ability to determine when he has written something good. He now apparently believes that everything he writes is a poem. Often—such is the extremity of his trouble—he seems to think he has written poetry when he makes out a little list of a few things he has seen here and there in the street. . . . It would appear foolish to ask him what he has done with that rare conception of quality which integrated the earlier expressions of his genius. At one time he actually phrased the spirit of commercial America. Now he is himself that spirit. He is a factory hand in the very hell he abominates. (pp. 80-1)

Arthur Wilson, "Sandburg: A Psychiatric Curiosity," in The Dial, *Vol. LXX, January, 1921, pp. 80-1.*

SHERWOOD ANDERSON

There is a growing tendency, as his fame goes up in the world, to speak of Carl Sandburg as a He man, an eater of raw meat, a hairy one. In Chicago newspaper local rooms he is spoken of as John Guts. I do not think of him so although I've a suspicion that he sometimes writes under the influence of this particular dramatization of his personality.

Buried deep within the He man, the hairy, meat eating Sandburg there is another Sandburg, a sensitive, naive, hesitating Carl Sandburg, a Sandburg that hears the voice of the wind over the roofs of houses at night, a Sandburg that wanders often alone through grim city streets on winter nights, a Sandburg that knows and understands the voiceless cry in the heart of the farm girl of the plains when she comes to the kitchen door and sees for the first time the beauty of our prairie country.

The poetry of John Guts doesn't excite me much. Hairy, raw meat eating He men are not exceptional in Chicago and the middle west.

As for the other Sandburg, the naive, hesitant, sensitive Sandburg—among all the poets of America he is my poet. (pp. 360-61)

Sherwood Anderson, "Carl Sandburg," in The Bookman, *New York, Vol. LIV, No. 4, December, 1921, pp. 360-61.*

CLEMENT WOOD

Carl Sandburg strays further than any American poet from the accepted poetic vocabulary. In this small volume [***Slabs of the Sunburnt West***] page after page erupts with "humdinger," "flooey," "phizzogs," "fixers," "frame-up," "four-flushers," "rakeoff," "getaway." . . .

It is easy to read any page of the book to yourself, or aloud, and decide confidently: Not a line of poetry there! It is no harder to read it in an altered, rarer mood, in which the page possesses, suffuses you, and wakes you to the high delight that flowers only when poetry is the bud. This is the paradox of Sandburg: if you are attuned, receptive, you lay him down with the same emotional thrill that comes from reading Robinson or Robert Frost, De La Mare or Elinor Wylie; yet when you inspect his slang-dipped lines, none of the accustomed road-signs to magic and beauty are to be found—only detours pointing to shanty-towns and hog-pens. One quality he has, a taut-lipped, double-fisted fighting quality. . . . (p. 96)

The book contains three longish poems, ***The Windy City; And So Today,*** taking its theme from the burial of the Unknown Soldier; and the title poem. The poet's method does not always succeed. . . . But there are rare penetrative flashes that reward the searcher. . . .

When we seek to unlock the paradox and unriddle the spell, there is perhaps a real kinship with such workers as Mrs. Wylie, Mr. Frost, Mr. Robinson—a kinship in word-selection. These poets slice away all padding, all adiposity, until at times even the skeleton is nicked. Sandburg, despite his apparent verbal freshets, is a word artist with the best. Deeper than that, his themes are well chosen: they are vital, stark, fit to evoke that thrill that comes from poetry. Having chosen such a theme, this poet usually clothes it in a fish-peddler's patches, or a miner's overalls, ore-stained, blood-stained—a motley of brutality and slang. Thus it comes to us: if we judge solely by appearances, it is slang, crudity, a ramp-rat, an eeler. If we hear it with intent ear, the theme behind comes with its thrill—a thrill the more effective because so unexpected. The effect is that of a perverse imp masking poetry behind the face of a gargoyle. . . .

Mr. Sandburg's method, including his vocabulary, limits his audience today, and does more to his lovers of tomorrow. For slang is last night's toadstool growth; some of it is trodden underfoot before the page that uses it leaves the presses. A few of its current phrases will enrich the persisting language; most will not. Whitman, by the use of unfamiliar rhythms, delayed his recognition, and has never reached the crowd he sought; Sandburg uses rhythms as unfamiliar, and a vocabulary that tomorrow will speak only to the archaeologist. The college curriculums of 1950 may bracket his work with Beowulf and the Ancren Riwle, as Old American or Early Hogwallowan. (p. 97)

Clement Wood, "A Homer from Hogwallow," in The Nation, *Vol. CXV, No. 2977, July 26, 1922, pp. 96-7.*

RAYMOND HOLDEN

[Sandburg] seems to have an especial gift, a capacity for giving color and substance to the facts of human life and the circumstances of its development in a new nation. He is a poet of great distinction. Personality, genius, perspicacity, fire, love of life, Sandburg has them all and what is more he is able to make his readers apprehend them and the delight he takes in their use. Why then is he no more than a poet of great distinction? Why is ***Slabs of the Sunburnt West*** on the same level of excellence as ***Chicago Poems,*** or even, as I think, a little lower? Perhaps it is that he has acquired such mastery over that blending process which makes of language a music played to the listener that underlies all flesh and blood; that he can make a false note seem a true one. Such a dangerous ability implies a remoteness from the Tower of Ivory which I do not believe he would be happy to support.

Mr. Sandburg has formed a conception of the vernacular which, as such, is thoroughly acceptable. He is, however, constantly confronted with the difficulty of reconciling this chosen speech with the formal requirements of his manner of composition. The beauty which Mr. Sandburg originates is in a strict sense a vernacular beauty, yet to me it seems marred and often effaced by his fear that dignity will estrange it. At such times he is like a shy schoolboy who makes preposterous and foolish remarks because he is afraid of being thought serious.

If, as his publisher declares on the jacket of this volume, Mr. Sandburg enjoys the writing of poetry as an art and a religion, he should take pains to avoid giving the impression that he enjoys it as a game of poker in which fifty percent of everything is left to chance. If poetry is worth writing it is worth working over. . . . Poems like ***The Windy City*** and ***Slabs of the Sunburnt West,*** in which a real beauty and an almost apprehensible style are achieved through the imaginative use of the vernacular idiom, are distinct and very splendid additions to the literature of the American language.

Raymond Holden, in a review of "Slabs of the Sunburnt West," in The New Republic, *Vol. XXXII, No. 404, August 30, 1922, p. 26.*

REBECCA WEST

[Sandburg] is, like Robert Burns, a national poet. Just as Robert Burns expresses the whole life of Lowland Scotland of his time, so Carl Sandburg expresses the whole life of the Middle West of to-day. He has learned his country by heart. . . . He has published four books of poems, ***Chicago Poems*** (1915), ***Cornhuskers*** (1918), ***Smoke and Steel*** (1920), and ***Slabs of the Sunburnt West*** (1922). The qualities of the Middle West are his qualities. The main determinant of his art is the power of his native idiom to deal with the inner life of man. He can describe the inner life, the not too bad life, that lies behind the shapeless skyscrapers, like so many giant petrol-cans, and the dreary timber houses of an ordinary Middle Western town. He can describe the inner life of the eager little girls who leave those small towns and come to Chicago, but still find no world that makes use of their sweetness. He can describe the inner life of the strong young men who wander about the vast land, proud and yet perplexed; proud because they are lending their strength to the purposes of the new civilization, perplexed because they do not know what it is all about. His idiom shapes him also in making him not so wise in his pictures of the external life. (pp. 24-5)

[Sandburg] is characteristically Middle Western in that his poems have no great sense of melody but a strong sense of rhythm. It will be said of him by Philistines that his poetry has no music in it, particularly by such Philistines as do not, like the lady in the limerick, know 'God Save the Weasel' from 'Pop Goes the Queen.' The same sort of people accuse Cézanne, who was born with a mahl-stick in his hand, of painting like Leader. In point of fact, Carl Sandburg is an accomplished musician, who is famous both for his singing and for his researches into American folk-song, and the music of his poetry is based on the technique of the banjo, very much as Manuel de Falla's music is based on the technique of the guitar. It must be remembered that his lines will not reveal their music, and indeed have none to reveal, unless they are read with a Middle Western accent. . . . (p. 26)

There is also in Carl Sandburg a full expression of the counter-movements of those who truly love the Middle West against those who love it not so well. This might seem a consideration too purely moral and political to be relevant to one's estimate of a poet; but actually each of these counter-movements implies an aesthetic liberation. It has been the tendency of America to limit its art to the delineation of what is called the Anglo-Saxon element within its territories. This has been to deny the artist the right to use some of the most entrancing brightly-coloured patterns that he saw in the real world before him. Carl Sandburg uses everything he sees that looks to him a good subject. . . . And he writes of the navvy and the hoodlum, not from any 'open road' infantilism, but because they are at any rate men who withdraw themselves from the areas of standardized living and thinking and who can look at reality with their own eyes. . . . It is a curious fact that no writer of Anglo-Saxon descent, no representative of the New England tradition, has described the break between Lincoln's America and modern industrialized America so poignantly as Carl Sandburg has. But his revolutionary passion so often betrays him, for poem after poem is ruined by a coarsely intruding line that turns it from poetry to propaganda. But the effect of this resistance to his environment is in sum an aesthetic benefit. It enables him to write of the real America, which one might describe to the present-day, over-prosperous America, in the words of one of its own advertisements, as 'the Venus beneath your fat'. In **'Prairie'** and **'The Windy City'** and **'Slabs of the Sunburnt West',** he has evoked the essential America which will survive when this phase of commercial expansion is past and the New World is cut down to the quick as the Old World is to-day: a vast continent which by the majesty of its plains and its waters and its mountains, calls forth a response of power in the men who behold it, now that they are white as it did when they were red. His is not a talent that is too easily accepted in this age, which is inclined to regard poetry as necessarily lyric and to demand that the poet shall write brief and perfect verse; but the reason he cannot satisfy such standards is that his art is dominated by an image so vast that it requires as house-room not one but a thousand poems. (pp. 26-8)

Rebecca West, in a preface to Selected Poems of Carl Sandburg, *edited by Rebecca West, Harcourt Brace Jovanovich, 1926, pp. 15-28.*

STUART SHERMAN

Carl Sandburg's big biography [***Abraham Lincoln: The Prairie Years***] is wholly devoted to showing Lincoln in his times before he went to the White House. It may be considered as the latest synthesis after a generation of research. It is thoroughly well nourished on the enormous new Lincoln literature. It incorporates the new facts and includes the new lights and shadings. In addition Mr. Sandburg furnishes adequately the technical justification or "apology" for another book; he has had access to a long, quaint letter from Mrs. Lincoln to her husband: he has met with sixty-five unpublished letters and papers in Lincoln's hand-writing; he has been able to illustrate copiously from rich collections of photographs, maps, etc.—and besides all that he was born in Lincoln's country and for thirty years or more, he tells us, he has had it in his heart to make "a certain portrait" of him.

The effect of this portrait is vital and stimulating. The composition of it is of an interesting complexity. One easily distinguishes certain dominant features of the treatment; an extraordinarily vivid and sympathetic account of Lincoln's early youth, the cabin life, the first school days, trips down the Mississippi, the humors of the grocery store period; full attention to Ann Rutledge, Mary Owens and Mary Todd; a most elaborate collection of Lincoln's stories and the stories about Lincoln; and a very extensive study of Lincoln's law practice, bringing to our attention scores of the cases and the litigants whom he dealt with in Springfield or on circuit or in Chicago. It is a book, in the first place, full of people—though not to confusion.

But Mr. Sandburg has not taken his life work lightly, nor confined himself to the pictorial and narrative aspects of the biographical art. He has desired, I surmise, to make a book to "live in," and with that in mind he has gone back to 1809 and lived his way down to 1861, as concretely as possible, yet as responsively as possible with reference to all the economic, social, ethical, religious and political forces in all parts of the country which were driving toward the irrepressible conflict. Macaulay would have reveled in Mr. Sandburg's details. . . .

The idea underlying this comprehensive study of Lincoln in "the prairie years" is, as it appears to me, rationalistic and liberal. To Mr. Sandburg, Lincoln is a hero, but he is a hero with a rational explanation. He was intelligibly and inevitably "produced" by his own times and circumstances and people. He was the resultant of their benigner impulses, happily disengaged from their baser ones. Lincoln was the man that "our people" are rather blindly and unconsciously striving to become. He is a hero, but a true folk hero; and the Great Mother who brought him forth is lovable, too.

Here, at any rate, is an opportunity to become better acquainted with Carl Sandburg as well as with Abraham Lincoln. They are good companions, the two of them, and mutually illuminating—Illinoisians both, plain people, admirable story tellers, rationalists, Jeffersonian democrats both, both non-professing Christians—Lincoln perhaps the completest specimen that has appeared in the Western hemisphere, and both poets withal, made melancholy at times and gentle-hearted by asking themselves what folk remember . . . "in the dust, in the cool tombs."

I am glad Carl Sandburg wrote this book. I like Lincoln the better for it and Carl Sandburg and myself and my neighbor. And that result, when all the ado about free territory and squatter sovereignty is forgotten smoke, that result is the living virtue that streams out of Lincoln forever. (p. 3)

Stuart Sherman, "Carl Sandburg's Lincoln," in New York Herald Tribune Books, *February 7, 1926, pp. 1, 3.*

JAMES A. WOODBURN

One may read many biographies of Lincoln, but he will probably never read a more interesting one than [***Abraham Lincoln: The Prairie Years***]. There is interest on every page. There is in it so much of poetry and imagination, so much of tradition mingled with fact, that some may doubt whether it be biography at all. It is clearly not within the canons of historical writing. There are no footnotes. No sources are indicated, no citations to authorities. (pp. 674-75)

Mr. Sandburg is not an historical specialist, but he has seen life in varied forms and he grew up not far removed in space and time from the life that Lincoln knew. He writes for what he is, a story-teller, a realist, an interpreter, an artist. There is the eye of the genius to see, the power of the poet to express. He, therefore, draws vividly and in a masterly way the scenes and the life of the times which he studied. From Sandburg's pages one sees Lincoln as never before, in his homely, rough, pioneer society; and from the poet's pictures one feels that he is seeing the real Lincoln, not in all details, perhaps, but at least in the main features of his life and character. As the reader will not be led far astray from the essential truth, it may be said that the ensemble justifies all the poetic license which the author has employed. (p. 675)

One picture follows another. We see Lincoln sitting in a company of men with his boots off, "to give his feet a chance to breathe," as he said; or at the table neglecting to use the butter knife, much to the annoyance of Mrs. Lincoln; or, in place of the servant girl, answering the ring of the front door bell in his shirt sleeves. We see him on a neighborly visit in a pair of loose slippers, wearing a faded pair of trousers fastened with one suspender; or, when asked to examine a brief, replying, "Wait till I fix this plug of my gallus and I'll pitch into that like a dog at a root." (pp. 675-76)

Amid this life lived the Lincoln of sadness and melancholy; of love, and courtship; of earnest study; of hope, and strange ambition. (p. 676)

Amid the author's rich colors and poetic interpretations one need not look for completeness nor exactness in history, for historic proportions or emphasis. Yet we find Lincoln here in his historic setting, essentially true in bold outline. The author brings into play many facts of prime importance. Not only does he search into the social background and reveal it, but he strikes off in swift dramatic language important events and movements—the Mexican War, the compromise of 1850, the repeal of the Missouri restriction, Mrs. Stowe and "Uncle Tom," the Kansas war, the great debates with Douglas, Dred Scott, John Brown, and the political campaigns. He makes too much of some of these, too little of others. In the account there are errors of detail. He uses unverified tradition; he puts the cost of the Mexican war at one fourth of the proper sum; the Fugitive Slave Law was hardly a "joke in northern Ohio"; he calls Fillmore a Free Soil candidate; he calls Prudence Crandall "Prudence Campbell"; he puts Crawfordsville, Indiana, on the Wabash River; he describes John Quincy Adams as "a sweet, lovable man"—which he was hardly considered as being even by his friends, certainly not by his opponents in congressional debate. And one wonders if Lincoln actually said "Mr. *Cheerman*" as he began his Cooper Union speech. These lapses and other minor ones are not serious defects and may be easily removed in an historical biography; but it would be hypercritical to allow such flaws to mar the effect of the luminous canvas of this poet-biographer.

Lincoln's principles, his love of law, order, and liberty, and his devotion to the Union are here set forth. For these he stood; for these, if need be, he was ready to die. No man stood more stoutly than he for the radical democracy of the Declaration of Independence. (pp. 676-77)

No matter how extensive may be one's reading on Lincoln he should add these volumes to his list. The perennial interest in Lincoln will continue, and thousands of his countrymen will be grateful to Carl Sandburg for the absorbing volumes which he has added to the Lincoln literature. (p. 677)

James A. Woodburn, in a review of "Abraham Lincoln: The Prairie Years," in The American Political Science Review, *Vol. XX, No. 3, August, 1926, pp. 674-77.*

FRANK ERNEST HILL

If Sandburg has never done anything quite so poignant in its universality as Masters's "Spoon River," and nothing so consciously American from the imaginative and historical standpoints as certain poems of Vachel Lindsay, he has come closest of all American poets to the life of toil on land and in factory, and to the groping dreams of the toilers and their sweethearts and wives and children.

In the **"Selected Poems"** both readers who know Sandburg and readers who do not know him will get a satisfactory volume. . . .

As is often the case in similar publications, the book defines the poet more clearly than his four separate volumes considered by themselves. Contributions and limitations seem more clearly revealed. For instance, what Sandburg has done for the art of poetry. No one can read what is gathered together here without being conscious of his fine use of idiom. His rhythm . . . is his greatest accomplishment musically, but, of course, the value of rhythm is always inseparable from the speech through which it runs. Sandburg has captured the tone and lilt of Middle Western talk. . . .

This is American, it is contemporary, and in his quiet way it is close to the mortal. Sandburg has brought this easy native speech into poetry, and its very incorporation has released a great deal. Omaha, the iceman, the American's song to his own landscape, his talk to his machines and his streets—his work-hour humor, these are Sandburg's with the music that he has managed with unique success. They are much.

There is, of course, the heart of Sandburg also, and there is his philosophy. The heart is the bigger—not as great a heart as Whitman's, but a more intimately sympathetic, a more constantly friendly one. Sandburg's heart is pervasive rather than electrically visible in notable passages, it is a friend's heart rather than a lover's. But in a literature, like ours, given to implication and repression on the emotional side, Sandburg is a precious acquisition.

Not quite so much can be said of him as a prophet, and his limitations in music and power are probably attributable in part of his weakness as a seer.

Sandburg has the seer's urge, and not a little of the seer's feeling. He says haunting things. Still, his relaxed casualness and his immediate friendliness seem to tie him down from the energetic leap, the flashing divination. The narrowness of his rhythmic art is probably associated with this absence of philosophic intensity. Sandburg has shaped a smoother free verse than Whitman. . . . Yet the warm monotone of Sandburg never achieves the electric beauty or the majestic beauty of the best of Whitman. There is nothing so colorful and intense in it as the bird's last cry in "Out of the Cradle Endlessly Rocking," and nothing of the orchestral exhilaration of the magnificent passage following that cry. . . .

Poets do not come in every generation to shake the world as Whitman shook it. Sandburg, bearing unmistakable traces of an inheritance from him, has not surpassed his master. But he has worked originally, he has improved and refined part of what he took, and he has given a gift as definite as Whitman's if smaller, to an America that Whitman foresaw, but never knew.

Frank Ernest Hill, "Selected from Carl Sandburg," in New York Herald Tribune Books, *October 10, 1926, p. 4.*

CONRAD AIKEN

[***Selected Poems of Carl Sandburg*** reveals that Sandburg's virtues] are conspicuous: he uses, better than anyone else in America today, the rich idiomatic journalistic American idiom, the idiom of the streets and barber-shops and smoking-cars; he has an extraordinary vitality and saltiness; he is a lover of the plural; and he conveys his rich sense of the "here and now" in long expatiative rhythms which are often beautiful. But if one goes behind and under these things, if one looks for the accuracy of notation in the matter of inner life, does one not find a comparative poverty?

The truth is that Mr. Sandburg is a sentimentalist. He is sentimental about his factory chimneys and sweaty crowds and stevedores and hunkies and eager young girls in exactly the way that other poets are sentimental about sunsets or broken hearts. He has a passion for the quotidian, he looks at it longingly and wistfully, he has an exceedingly quick eye for its changing colors, and he is "terribly glad" (to quote his own phrase) "to be selling fish." He is genuinely in love with the scene in which he finds himself, and his love for it is frequently infectious. He is genuinely unhappy, also, to find that impermanence and tragedy and frustration move like a groundswell through this beautiful pluralism of things: and this feeling, too, he often successfully communicates. But he does not go deeper than this; and one cannot feel that he ever strikes profoundly into the "inner life" of any of his working-folk. . . .

One must take him as he is—he works in a large, loose medium, inextricably mixing the vivid with the false. He is essentially a lover of surfaces. Like Mr. Lindsay, he does not very well endure the test of repeated rereading, for he is simple; a surface revisited is not so sustaining as a surface seen, and seen vividly, for the first time. And while his rhythms are often delightful, and for the American reader rich in the indigenous, they lack the sort of complexity of outline or shape which can renew one's pleasure on the third or fourth reading. The design, like the feeling, is comparatively cloudy. For this reason, among others, Mr. Sandburg's poetry is a poetry to be taken en masse, not in detail. Very few of his poems will stand well by themselves. One finds him vaguely impressive as a whole, one likes his flavor, but one is decidedly uncertain as to whether there is enough at the core to guarantee his preservation. (p. 87)

Conrad Aiken, "Sentiment of the Quotidian," in The New Republic, *Vol. XLIX, No. 627, December 8, 1926, pp. 86-7.*

BABETTE DEUTSCH

Sit in the sun of Indian summer, turn the leaves of [**"Good Morning, America"**], feel the disturbing pulse of it, look away from the page into the blue depths of the impenetrable sky, down at the dusty old grass, at the rich green clumps of new grass mistaking the soft air for that of an earlier season; you will begin to dream and to wonder, as Sandburg did setting these words down on paper, as Sandburg meant you to do. If ever there was a poet who went treading in Whitman's tracks, it is this man, staring with a kind of puzzled admiration at the universe, at this shifting America, at the grass blade between his fingers, at the pores and lines of his own hand. And like Whitman, he makes you stare with him, dropping his book the more deeply to feel the emotion that formed the book. Not that Sandburg is an imitator. His vision, his rhythms, his pangs, his chuckles are his own. It is simply that he shares much of the elder poet's feeling about the world in which he lives, that he is stirred and perplexed by its mystery, but never chilled by it, that he is full of a pitying tenderness for all living creatures, that he needs make no effort to swing along with the free stride of one to whom nature has never shown the face of an enemy.

He has, over and beyond these gifts, a dry humor that helps him to see the absurdity of some big things as well as the miracle of the least thing. The whole book is marked by an overwhelming sense of transience that does not let him fall into Whitmanesque sentimentality even when he celebrates, most lovingly, the American empire. . . .

One must group him, if at all, with those men who are struggling to realize this nation, to formulate, in some sort, the spirit of the country. The son of an immigrant, himself a laborer, a farmer, a soldier, a newspaperman, he has lived on the prairie and in the city and knitted the America he found there into the fibers of his being. The passion for the land of his birth that expressed itself so magnificently in his account of Lincoln's prairie years, and in his precious collection of American folk songs, is evidenced in this book of poems, too—no less a passion because he can regard these States with the humor of a grown-up son toward a loved, wrong-headed parent, of a parent toward a dear, silly child.

It is this rare dry humor that chiefly distinguishes him from his great predecessor—a humor that is as peculiarly of his own place and age as the proverbs he has lumped together in one section of **"Good Morning, America."**

Babette Deutsch, "Seen During a Moment," in New York Herald Tribune Books, *October 21, 1928, p. 2.*

PERCY HUTCHISON

It is an interesting coincidence that two poets so dissimilar, both in the direction of their thought and in poetic practice, as Miss Edna St. Vincent Millay and Carl Sandburg should, after a protracted lyric silence, appear within a few weeks of each other to offer to the public their garnering from the elapsed years. Miss Millay, although following in the English tradition, her progenitors being the English lyricists from Sidney and Shakespeare down, has so shorn away everything not American that her poetry [in "The Buck in the Snow"] is native in all but its ancestry. The single progenitor of Carl Sandburg was Walt Whitman, who threw every English tradition out of the window in an endeavor to create a tradition that should belong to the United States alone. Not only has Mr. Sandburg sought to perpetuate the Whitman trade-mark, but his present collection, of generous scope, bears the appropriate caption, **"Good Morning, America,"**. . . . But does Mr. Sandburg more truly present and represent America than does Miss Millay? This pertinent question raised by the synchronization of their two books . . . offers an interesting approach to Mr. Sandburg's verse.

That Carl Sandburg has rendered American poetry excellent service since he began to write only the most conservative would deny. Despite the Whitman rebellion, American poetry suffered a serious lapse in the last quarter of the nineteenth century. Mr. Sandburg and Miss Amy Lowell, as leaders of a new crusade, found themselves face to face with its twofold problem; first, how American poetry could attain to individual beauty; second, how it could be distinctively national. Miss Lowell devoted herself mainly to the first part of the question, Mr. Sandburg mainly to the second, and both, in order to free themselves as completely as possible from all shackling alliances, adopted so-called free verse for their method of expression. . . .

Mr. Sandburg, directing his efforts more toward slaughter-houses, locomotives and similar vigorous expressions of modern civilization, indeed piqued curiosity and stimulated thought; but in his endeavor to be American he became parochial, and thereby largely defeated the very end he so earnestly sought. This is not to argue that stockyards should not furnish as suitable a subject for poetry as, say, the skylark; but if stockyards do furnish as suitable a subject as the skylark Mr. Sandburg did not find the poetic key. . . .

Sandburg, following his master, Whitman, believes as Whitman did, that it is only necessary to make the catalogue sufficiently long to call out the enumeration vehemently and in rhythm and a poem is, ipso facto, made. No single bird emerges from this list of colors, and if it is intended that a flock of birds whirring by be suggested, the rhythm staccato, deficient in overtone, surely fails of its mission. And this is, to our thinking, the tragedy of Carl Sandburg; poet in every feeling, with a sense for the material of poetry, he is so fearful of English poetic tradition lest he be considered not American that he cannot, or will not, discipline either his art or himself. . . .

[In Edna St. Vincent Millay's poetry] there is the poetic discipline of many generations, that fine tradition of dignity of matter with perfectness of form that has made English lyric poetry the despair of other nations. Mr. Sandburg threw this all away so long ago he probably could not recover it now if he would. Yet one feels that there is in **"Good Morning, America"** some secret yearning for those beauties which the author early elected to despise. At the same time one cannot gainsay that Mr. Sandburg touches life at innumerable points; that, on the whole, his poetry makes more contacts than does Miss Millay's. . . .

[The poem **"Good Morning America"**] is at once a salutation to America, an appreciation, an exhortation and a prophecy. In it rhythms are more variedly woven than is usually the case with Sandburg, but the pattern is neither intricate nor subtle. Intricacy and subtlety are as far from Mr. Sandburg as they were from Whitman. But there is change of mood and change of pace; there is the language of the preacher and the language of the newspaper comic strip. . . .

It is, as here, some bit from a poem, some shrewd observation, some penetrating phrase, some expansive line, that one remembers from Sandburg rather than the poem itself. To use one of the poet's own lines,

> Some rag of romance, some slant of a scarlet star.

And because of these one would not willingly do without Mr. Sandburg's poetry. And it is human. The poet jumps up from writing in his shirt sleeves to slap humanity on the back. His poetry is breezy, bluff and wistful by turns. It is an American product surely, but the product of an America in its teens. And we like to think that America is now grown up. And hence this writer gives it as his opinion that Miss Millay's poetry is more American than is Mr. Sandburg's American poetry.

There is pleasure, of course, to the spectator, and some profit, in watching Mr. Sandburg pour the colored liquids into the test tubes and in seeing them bubble up and take on new hues. But eventually the pastime palls. The watcher is inclined to ask him a little petulantly if he cannot so mix his ingredients as to bring about fresh combinations and new beauties. Perhaps Mr. Sandburg yet can do this. But we fear he has sat too long at the feet of Walt Whitman.

Percy Hutchison, "Carl Sandburg Sings Out, 'Good Morning, America'," in The New York Times Book Review, *October 21, 1928, p. 2.*

ANNE T. EATON

It was an excellent idea to put together [**"Rootabaga Stories,"**] an omnibus volume of [short tales]. . . .

This is a volume which children may well have in their personal libraries, for it is not confined to any one age, and those who love it will return to it again and again. Carl Sandburg's stories have their greatest charm for boys and girls when told or read aloud, and story tellers will welcome this complete collection.

Anne T. Eaton, in a review of "Rootabaga Stories," in The New York Times Book Review, *May 31, 1936, p. 11.*

WILLIAM ROSE BENÉT

Not content with having given us some of the most vital experimentation in poetry of our time, as well as ventures into valuable biography, tales for children, and collections of native American folk-song, [Sandburg] has now cut loose with a long poem [**"The People, Yes"**] about the American people which has everything in it including the kitchen stove. . . .

"The people, yes, the people," it seems to go on indefinitely. But as it goes on it gets deeper. There is a hypnotic cadence to Sandburg's loose-jointed free verse. He likes catalogues of people and things almost as much as Whitman did, but his is a different view. For one thing his tone is not so much exuberant as ominous. He looks at all the crooks and the cheaters and the exploiters and the pursy hypocrites with a flinty eye. . . .

He weaves into his verse every old anecdote and adage he has come across—cracker-barrel, horse-swapping, each, any, and every pithy expression. He summarizes well this Alice-in-Wonderland America in which we live. . . .

He sees the American people as "wanters" and "hopers." And Heaven knows he sees them as dumb in every sense. Which is entirely true. No people are cheated worse than the American people. None are bigger suckers to stand for what they stand for . . . Sandburg speaks of the greatest showman on earth and of how the people love to be humbugged. He collects sayings of the people, making shrewd capital of their half-wittedness. . . .

Sandburg has collected hundreds of such stories and sayings. They all add up to America and the American people. Here are the myths of America, such as Paul Bunyan—here are the "drummer's yarns" (of the milder type), here are the characteristically local expressions. Here are old stories out of the daily news. Wisdom, mirth, and myth. Slang—tons of it. . . .

But, for all this mélange, the long sprawly poem—and in spite of all the above things in it (which make it somewhat resemble Hungarian goulash!) it *is* a poem on the whole, deepens into some fine sayings toward the end. . . .

I should say the main criticism of Sandburg's long effort, interesting as parts of it are, is that it has not enough cohesion. It has not enough structure. And, certainly it does not think through, as does the modern radical economist, the situation in which modern civilization finds itself. Sandburg is too interested in the half-tones of humanity, the highlights of humor, the terse queerness. He is interested in "atmosphere." He has in him the wisdom of an ancient race. And **"The People, Yes,"** is a good book to pick up and read *at*—but an annoying book if you wish it really to *get* anywhere. Where have the People got or where are they getting, he might answer? But today, it seems at least to one reviewer, that they have definitely reached a much clearer idea than ever before of where they are at and how to get that from which they have been disinherited for so long. That new sapience, it seems to me, is what Sandburg fails to show.

William Rose Benét, "Memoranda on Americans," in The Saturday Review of Literature, *Vol. XIV, No. 17, August 22, 1936, p. 6.*

STEPHEN VINCENT BENÉT

Carl Sandburg occupies a unique position in the contemporary American scene. When he first came before the public, with **"Chicago Poems,"** he was labeled by the people who love to label things—largely on such poems as **"Chicago"** and **"To a Contemporary Bunk-Shooter"**—as a brutal realist and a smasher of idols. Yet that same book showed a poet who could work with great sensitiveness and grace, and bring to his work not only an interest in live words and live people but a sort of folk fairytale quality that was as far east of automatic realism as it was west of sentimentality. He has always been an American but his Americanism has never been a horse-and-buggy hired for the occasion—he talks United States because that is his language and he talks it with a sure tongue. The smasher of idols has written one of the notable biographies of Lincoln—the brutal realist produced two books of children's stories that are as close to American fairytales as anything we have except, possibly, "The Wizard of Oz." And, in doing so—and that is the point to mark—the author has remained always and entirely himself. He hasn't done what he has done for public demand or preconceived opinion—but because it was the nature of the ground to grow that sort of crop.

Now, in **"The People, Yes,"** he brings us the longest and most sustained piece of work he has yet done in verse. It is a book that will irritate some; and some will find it meaningless. The Liberty League won't like it, and I doubt if it receives the official imprimatur of the Communist party. It deals with people; it deals with these times. But Carl Sandburg has his own way of going about things. He will go back to the Tower of Babel if he feels like it; he will go forward to the wreck of the skyscrapers. . . .

And there is something to be said about the man who was feeding a hatful of doughnuts to a horse, explaining to the curious, "I want to see how many he'll eat before he asks for a cup of coffee." There is something to be said about doctors and restaurant cashiers, about airplane stunters and mine strikers and city editors, about the railroad engineer on the Pennsy, directing in his will that they should burn his body as a piece of rolling stock beyond rehabilitation and repair and scatter the ashes from the cab on the Beverley curve, and about the bottom of the sea which accommodates the mountain ranges. **"The People, Yes"** is not a dogmatic book and it turns corners and goes around alleys. It is full of proverbs, questions, memoranda, folklore, faces and wonderings. It is a fresco and a field of grass and a man listening quietly to all the commonplace, extraordinary things that people say. Yet it has its own coherence and its own confidence. . . .

And, if Sandburg writes with honesty, he also writes, and with a biting anger, of the rare and suave folk who pay themselves a fat swag of higher salaries while they cut wages, of the pay day patriots that Lincoln called "respectable scoundrels," of all those who deny, debauch, oppress, mock, enslave the people, of all those who say, "Your people, sir, is a great beast," covertly or openly, in past times or now. (p. 1)

This voice does not come from Moscow or Union Square. It comes out of Western America, soil of that soil and wheat of that wheat, and it is the voice of somebody who knows the faces, the folkwords and the tall tales of the people. It is as honest as it is questioning and it speaks its deep convictions in a tongue we know. And there is warning in it as well as hope. Sometimes it goes runabout; not all of it is poetry. But it is the memoranda of the people. And every line of it says "The People—Yes." (p. 2)

Stephen Vincent Benét, "Carl Sandburg—Poet of the Prairie People," in New York Herald Tribune Books, *August 23, 1936, pp. 1-2.*

STEPHEN VINCENT BENÉT

In ***Abraham Lincoln: The War Years,*** Carl Sandburg carries on and completes his life of Lincoln, through the turmoil of Civil War to the burial at Springfield. He has done so on the grand scale—it is a mountain range of a biography. The four volumes comprise well over two thousand pages of text, four hundred and fourteen half-tones of photographs, two hundred and forty-nine reproductions of letters, documents, cartoons. To review such a work in brief is rather like trying to take a picture of the Lincoln Memorial with a miniature camera. Yet certain things may be said.

In the first place, this is a biography, not only of Abraham Lincoln, but of the Civil War. The great, the near-great, the wretched, the commonplace, the humble, the shoddy—dozens, hundreds of men and women, known or little known, who played their part in those years—generals, civilians, office seekers, Congressmen, cranks, soldiers of North and South, traitors, spies, plain citizens—appear and disappear like straws whirled along by a torrent. From General Tom Thumb to Clement Vallandigham, from Colonel Ellsworth to Jefferson Davis, they are seen, talked of, characterized, brought back. The debates in Congress are here as well as the marching of armies, the underground politics are shown as well as the surface issues.

And, what seems to me one of the greatest virtues of the book, the narrative is largely kept within a contemporary frame of time. For, in looking back at any historical period, we are apt to think, 'It came out this way, as we know—men must have known it then.' That there was a time when men wondered if Congress would ratify Lincoln's election—that there was a time when men of his own party thought Ben Butler might make a better President—these are things we don't know or don't remember till somebody like Mr. Sandburg points them out to us. The scares, the fears, the indecisions, the whole getting under way of the huge, creaking war-machine of the North, the false alarms and dashed hopes, and yet the gradual, growing devotion between President and people—these Mr. Sandburg has done and done superbly. He has shown the worry and chicken-scratchings of 'the best minds' when confronted by a new phenomenon, the hate of the scorners, and the implacable growth of greatness.

And he has done more than that. For I think it is difficult for anyone to read these volumes and not come out, at the end, with a renewed faith in the democracy that Lincoln believed in and a renewed belief in the America he sought. They are a good purge for our own troubled time and for its more wild-eyed fears. For here we see the thing working, clumsily, erratically, often unfairly, attacked and reviled by extremists of left and right, yet working and surviving nevertheless. That the full dream, the dream of a peaceful and liberal reconstruction of the Union, was cut short by an assassin's bullet, should give us food for thought as well. . . .

For the man who was Lincoln, the great, complex, humorous, melancholy figure—Mr. Sandburg shows him, in certain sections of this biography, as clearly and as fully as he has ever been shown. The slow growth is there, and each ring on the tree is counted. At other times, particularly in volume one, the man himself seems submerged in the stream of events. I could, myself, have spared a good many pages on minor figures, a good many quotations from speeches in Congress, even certain anecdotes, interesting enough in themselves, for a sharper focus on the central subject. Now and then it is hard to see the wood for the trees, now and then Mr. Sandburg's principles of selection and omission strike one oddly. . . . There are places where Mr. Sandburg's style touches genuine poetry, there are others where it descends to bathos. And, now and then, he permits himself a sort of rhetorical broodiness which is neither poetry nor prose. But, when all this is said, the book remains. To chip at it with a hammer is a little like chipping at Stone Mountain. It has faults. But it happens to be a book that every American should read.

Stephen Vincent Benét, in a review of "Abraham Lincoln: The War Years," in The Atlantic Bookshelf, *a section of* The Atlantic Monthly, *Vol. 164, No. 6, December, 1939.*

HENRY STEELE COMMAGER

The poets have always understood Lincoln, from Whitman and Emerson to Lindsay and Benét, and it is fitting that from the pen of a poet should come the greatest of all Lincoln biographies, one of the great biographies of our literature [***Abraham Lincoln: The War Years***]. It is great in the reflected beauty and honesty of its subject; it is great, too, in the telling. It is such a biography as Lincoln himself would have wished and would have understood, genuine, simple, broad, humane, dramatic, poetic, thoroughly American in its muscular, idiomatic words, in its humor, in its catholicity and democracy.

It is not a pretentious work, not even a formidable one, for all its twenty-four hundred closely knit pages; it is not primarily a work of scholarship, for all its thousands of weighty facts, so zealously collected from every source. What gives it value is its indubitable authenticity, and that is achieved by a massing of pertinent detail, an array of relevant stories, statistics, conversations, reports, documents, anecdotes, verses, editorials, sermons, portraits, such as has rarely been given us in any biographical work. Perhaps this is not the whole of the Civil War, but it is difficult to believe that this is not the whole of Lincoln during the war years.

It is, indeed, a gargantuan book, overwhelming as the prairies, massive, irresistible. In its pages Lincoln comes to life, and with him a whole society, the gallant generals and the rash ones, spoilsmen snarling for office and statesmen striking attitudes for posterity, millionaires reaping war profits, speculators greasing their way South, dignified authors and professional humorists, soldiers and soldiers' wives, contrabands, the representatives of the people, and the people themselves. All of them came to Lincoln, told their stories, argued their causes, heard his jokes, and went home to write about it and to contribute to the legend. And because, in the end, all things centered on Lincoln, this biography becomes a history of a whole people, a panorama and a pageant.

It is a story complex and fascinating; the vigor of the narrative never falters, the interest never flags, from those remarkable opening chapters which reveal the bewilderment of Lincoln and of his countrymen in the face of the crisis of '61 to those moving chapters which tell of the President martyred and mourned. And here is the whole of the war President, nothing of importance omitted, much heretofore thought unimportant now appreciated. It is all narrative, the analysis takes care of itself, the interpretation is implicit in the material and the presentation. The technique is that of an attack in force; Sandburg masses his facts in regiments, marches them in and takes the field, and the conquest is palpable and complete. (pp. 374-75)

But best of all is Sandburg's genius for recreating the men and women whose lives affected Lincoln and so our history. There is a lavishness here that is unique in our biographical literature; the familiar figures are here, strutting and fretting their way across the stage, and hundreds of the less familiar who had their hour and whose hour is resurrected and remembered. We expect Sumner and McClellan and Grant and Lamon and Butler; it is delightful to meet the ubiquitous but shadowy Count Gurowski, insanely vindictive but imposing and shrewd, the gallant Major General Ormsby Mitchel whom Halleck feared, the slave orator Sojourner Truth who was ready to prove that she was a woman, the fantastic pamphleteer Anna Ella Carroll, the vulgar Colonel Baker of the Detective Bureau, Mrs. Louis Harvey who got three hospitals—and dozens of others, candidates now for fame.

And it is all endlessly quotable. (p. 376)

And what of the Lincoln who emerges from these glowing pages? He is the familiar Lincoln, made a hundredfold more familiar. He is a bewildered man who never entirely understood how he came to be President at a great crisis in history, and was saved by humility. He is a shrewd man who was able to apply the cunning of the Illinois circuit to the business of managing Congressmen. He is a rough man who never learned the proprieties of office, never learned to dress well or accept the usages of diplomacy or the requirements of polite society, and who made that a badge of democracy. He is a kindly man who, faced with the tragedy of war, took on himself the woes of a whole people and came to seem a symbol of the atonement. He is a gregarious man who used his friends and acquaintances for his own purposes and for larger purposes which they rarely understood. He is a tolerant man who developed tolerance into such magnanimity as no other national leader has ever revealed in a similar crisis. He is the Illinois lawyer, the prairie politician, who rose magnificently to the greatest responsibility ever laid upon one man and by his victory over himself, over the politicians and the generals, over the war spirit and the profit spirit, over the enemy in the South and in the North and the critics abroad, vindicated the democratic theory. He is the common man, who knows that

> In the midst of battle there is room
> For thoughts of love, and in foul sin for mirth,

and who displayed a forbearance that was saintly, a humor that was cleansing, and met war and evil and overcame them.

All this Mr. Sandburg has revealed to us, with learning, with imagination, with poetry. He has not involved us in the intricacies of controversy, he has not burdened us with the apparatus of scholarship, he has not confronted us with theories or interpretations. He has realized that Lincoln belongs to the people, not to the historians, and he has given us a portrait from which a whole generation may draw understanding of the past and inspiration for the future. (p. 377)

Henry Steele Commager, "Lincoln Belongs to the People," in The Yale Review, *Vol. XXIX, No. 2, December, 1939, pp. 374-77.*

ALLAN NEVINS

Mr. Sandburg's method [in ***Abraham Lincoln: The War Years***] is the method of Niagara. He has caught the drainage of the whole vast historical watershed of the Civil War as Niagara catches the Great Lakes, and he pours it forth in a thundering flood. (p. 3)

The most distinctive qualities of Mr. Sandburg's work are two. 75First, its pictorial vividness, a product of his graphic style, love of concrete detail, and ability to recreate scenes imaginatively in a few sentences; second, the cumulative force of his detail in building up, step by step, an unforgettable impression of the crowded times, with crisis jostling crisis, problems rising in endless welter—and, *pari passu,* an impression of Lincoln patiently finding his talents, learning to endure the storm, and finally mastering it with sad serenity. These two qualities of pictorial vividness and cumulative force are complementary. Neither could have its full effect without the other. In Beveridge's two volumes on the early career of Lincoln we had the enormous accumulation of detail without the vividness. The result was instructive—in presenting Lincoln the politician, it was almost revolutionary. But it lacked the engrossing quality that Sandburg's full-blooded, pulsing, variegated narrative possesses. Not that Mr. Sandburg falls into rhetorical flourishes and effects. He is as intent upon the naked fact as was Beveridge. But he has a graphic, vital fashion of setting his facts on paper, and a cinematographic ease in glancing from point to point, idea to idea, event to event, which Beveridge lacked. And of course Sandburg possesses one great advantage in theme over his predecessor. The Lincoln that Beveridge painted was not as yet great; but the later Lincoln that Sandburg draws is one of the greatest of Americans, one of the few really great men of modern times.

Doubtless from Sandburg's pages many readers will for the first time gain a clear comprehension of this greatness. For it is impossible to realize either Lincoln's intellectual or moral stature without understanding the innumerable difficulties which bethorned and quagmired his path, which harried and perplexed him to the melancholy verge of despair. (pp. 3-4)

[It] takes Mr. Sandburg's Niagara of details, drawn from ten thousand sources, condensed, classified, and set down with vehement intensity, to bring out the bewildering confusion of the time, the soul-chilling uncertainty and fear, and the searing human agonies. In these 2500 pages, a distillation from a whole library, we have perhaps the best picture of a nation in racked travail yet written by any pen. Not that it is a somber picture; it has far too much vitality for that. We gain the impression of a nation not only nerved by determination and often exalted by heroism, but of a people who stopped to gossip, jest, and laugh in the grimmest times. The stage Mr. Sandburg sets before us, with its thousands of faces, its endless incidents, its quick shifts of joy and sorrow, ease and strain, triumph and defeat, has a liveliness for which we must turn to literature if we seek its like; it is the vitality of Walt Whitman's long catalogue-poems, of Dickens at his best, even of Shakespeare's world. Crowded streets, busy exchanges, smoking camps, roaring political conventions, the sobbing of women, the fever of speculators, the whispers of political plotters, the tramp of armies, the crash of naval bombardment—all are here. But the multitudinous responsibilities and perplexities of the central figure are never lost from sight. Out of the multiplicity of scenes and the swift march of events comes a new sense of the tremendous difficulties with which Lincoln had to close, the problems he had to rend apart before they rent him.

It also takes Mr. Sandburg's unequaled array of scenes, events, and utterances to present Lincoln's slow but sure growth to greatness, and the traits which constitute his claim to a foremost place in the hierarchy of democratic heroes. Nicolay and Hay approached this presentation; but Mr. Sandburg is fuller, more critical, and more vivid. In essentials it is the familiar portrait that he redraws. (pp. 4, 20)

Mr. Sandburg has written one of the greatest of American biographies. It has its faults—some of them the defects of its virtues. Pouring as he does with unstinting hand, he sometimes heaps fact upon fact, example upon example, to an unnecessary and otiose total. His illustrations of the burden which the political office-seekers placed upon Lincoln, for example, are piled up, in not one chapter but several, at wearisome length. At not a few places he would have done well to sow by the hand rather than the bag. The total lack of documentation is another defect. Finally, the huge book is deficient in emphasis. It is often difficult to distinguish important events and phases from the unimportant. But in view of the great and varied merits of the work, these criticisms are of little importance. It is not merely a biography; it is a magnificent piece of history, an epic story of the most stirring period of national life, and a narrative which for decades will hearten all believers in the stability of democracy and the potentialities of democratic leadership. (p. 22)

Allan Nevins, "Abe Lincoln in Washington," in The Saturday Review of Literature, *Vol. XXI, No. 6, December 2, 1939, pp. 3-4, 20, 22.*

ROBERT E. SHERWOOD

Twenty years ago Carl Sandburg of Illinois started to write the fullest, richest, most understanding of all the Lincoln biographies. His work is now complete. **"The War Years"** follows **"The Prairie Years"** into the treasure house which belongs, like Lincoln himself, to the whole human family. It has been a monumental undertaking; it is grandly realized.

"The War Years" begins where **"The Prairie Years"** ended, with Lincoln's departure from Springfield—an unknown, threatened, doubted man. It ends with the return of his body to the soil on which it grew. Mr. Sandburg's finest passages are those describing his final journey, and all the immediate aftermaths of the assassination, the shocking effect on men everywhere. Even the wild tribesmen in the Caucasus were asking a traveler, Leo Tolstoy, to tell them of this Western man who was "so great that he even forgave the crimes of his greatest enemies." And Tolstoy told them, "Lincoln was a humanitarian as broad as the world."

"The War Years" is compounded of such quotations. We are enabled to look at Lincoln through thousands of contemporary eyes, including those of Tolstoy, and Jefferson Davis, and John Bright, M.P., and Hendrik Ibsen, and Nathaniel Hawthorne, and a South Carolina lady named Mary Chesnut. Mr. Sandburg gives us his own estimates of many other figures, big and little, of the period, but not of Abraham Lincoln. He indulges in no speculation as to what was going on within the heart and soul and mind of this peculiar man. If there is anything lacking in **"The War Years,"** it is the presence of two men of the prairie years, Joshua Speed and William H. Herndon, who saw more deeply into Lincoln than did any others who ever knew him. When Lincoln stepped into the White House he stepped into a great isolation which no one—not even his old friends, Browning and Lamon, nor his secretaries, Nicolay and Hay—seems to have penetrated. In the analyses of his character provided by those who observed him at closest range the word "unfathomable" recurs again and again.

In **"The Prairie Years,"** with fewer documents and many more myths at his disposal, Mr. Sandburg gave greater play to his own lyrical imagination. Any one can indulge in guesswork about the raw young giant who emerged from the mists of Kentucky, and Indiana, and Sangamon County, Illinois, and Mr. Sandburg's guesses were far better than most. But in **"The War Years"** he sticks to the documentary evidence, gathered from a fabulous number of sources. He indulges in one superb lyrical outburst at the conclusion of the chapter in which is described the dedication of the cemetery at Gettysburg; and, in the last volume, after John Wilkes Booth has fired the one bullet in his brass derringer pistol, Mr. Sandburg writes with the poetic passion and the somber eloquence of the great masters of tragedy.

Mr. Sandburg's method is unlike that of any biographer since Homer. He starts **"The War Years"** with the usual appreciative Foreword surveying his source material—and this Foreword provides an excellent survey of Lincolniana—but he reveals the odd nature of his essential research when he says, "Taking my guitar and a program of songs and readings and traveling from coast to coast a dozen times in the last twenty years, in a wide variety of audiences I have met sons and daughters of many of the leading players in the terrific drama of the Eighteen Sixties." From these sons and daughters he obtained old letters and pictures and clippings, and reminiscences and rumors which led him to upper shelves in remote libraries. Thus, his "program of songs" (like Homer's) brought him into the very spirit of the people, the same people of whom—and by whom, and for whom—was Abraham Lincoln. Quite properly, Mr. Sandburg's great work is not the story of the one man's life. It is a folk biography. The hopes and apprehensions of millions, their loves and hates, their exultation and despair, were reflected truthfully in the deep waters of Lincoln's being, and so they are reflected truthfully in these volumes. (p. 1)

Any review of **"The War Years"** at this time can be no more than a smattering report of quickly remembered fragments. It is so great a work that it will require great reading and great reflection before any true appreciation of its permanent value can be formed. It will beget many other books. But, in the meantime, the people of this nation and this human race may well salute and thank Carl Sandburg for the magnitude of his contribution to our common heritage. (p. 14)

Robert E. Sherwood, "The Lincoln of Carl Sandburg," in The New York Times Book Review, *December 3, 1939, pp. 1, 14.*

WILLIAM SOSKIN

Carl Sandburg has devoted more than four years to the composition of this 1,067-page novel [**"Remembrance Rock"**]. He might have devoted his entire lifetime to it and many more thousand pages, and yet not have been able to realize the great stature of the conception which inspires the book. It is not an extraordinary situation for a novelist who yearns to crowd into a single novel most of American history, American philosophy, American social problems, idealism, and all the other quantities Mr. Sandburg suggests in his term "the American Dream,"—only to find that the literary form he has chosen simply will not contain his momentous meaning. **"Remembrance Rock"** is logically organized for Mr. Sandburg's purpose. He has conceived of our history and of our present political and moral character as a great adventure into the unknown, a dream of liberty that has no superimposed goals but for which there is a core of growth in every man's heart. . . .

A bare statement of [the] themes cannot suggest the tremendous detail, the impressive historical research, the endless variety of allegorical personifications of various national traits and characteristics, the song, the high romance, the salty humor, the flights of lyricism, the great folk pattern of each of these panels. At the same time it must be admitted that despite all the fire Mr. Sandburg has breathed into the huge gallery of his people and despite all the efforts he has made to function as a relaxed, human storyteller rather than a definitive historian, his portrayals of each of these periods of American life are somehow static. There is an heroic quality about them which gives these dramas the proportions and the general texture of a mural. You may look upon the carefully composed incidents of such a mural—errant Puritans in the stocks, figures of trysting girls and youths who defy the inexorable Puritan conventions, the drinking, the carnality, the figures of labor and of sturdy yeomanry, all painted with vigor and dash—and yet they remain the mannered people of an historical landscape.

Occasionally an especially impassioned moment takes the story out of the museum, but these moments usually revolve about lurid situations far removed from the mainstream of Mr. Sandburg's narrative. (p. 14)

The author is naturally more at home in the Civil War period, and does not seem to be overwhelmed here by the scope of his own story. His tales of the abolitionists, of the underground railway, of the folk growth on the prairies, provide something of a Populist symphony for his work. Even the figure of Abraham Lincoln walks easily in these pages. And here Mr. Sandburg achieves his greatest success in demonstrating the sturdy, seemingly casual, accidental patterns of life by which whole peoples find themselves unwittingly involved in wars. (p. 15)

William Soskin, "The American Dream Panorama," in The Saturday Review of Literature, *Vol. XXXI, No. 41, October 9, 1948, pp. 14-15.*

LLOYD LEWIS

[**"Remembrance Rock"**] is Carl Sandburg's ride to an American Canterbury—a long ride of 350 years with an American historical tale for every hoofbeat and an adventure for every garrulous pilgrim. Sandburg has with him in this, his first novel, many more riders than had Chaucer, and of these more are ploughmen and fewer are gentlemen and merchants, for Sandburg has been chiefly nourished on the speech and wisdom of the poor.

All historians and biographers have been baffled by the mystery as to what the people, the unreported masses, have actually thought at any given period. Sandburg believes that the folk songs, folk sayings and folk proverbs are the key, telling more of truth than do the official pronunciamentos of the powerful.

His method in . . . **"Remembrance Rock"** is to create multitudinous characters, imaginary people who he feels, after years of research, are true not only to their respective periods in our national existence but to the whole American strain. They are the men who hit the beach at Plymouth in the 1600s and at Okinawa in the 1940s, who went underground to help George Washington in the 1700s and John Brown in the 1800s—the boys who shook, in turn, Cemetery Ridge and the hill of Cassino. His people are the farmers, clerks, housewives, private soldiers, hired girls; and if famous people like John Adams, George Washington, Abraham Lincoln, Myles Standish appear, it is only at a distance, with cornhuskers in fields and skillet-women around fireplaces talking of them. (p. 1)

What Sandburg has succeeded in doing here, is to build bodies around the souls of the unnamed persons who have been speaking four-line, eight-line verses in all the poems of the past. He has created full-sized, full-blooded, endlessly moving human beings out of what were only voices in his long poem, **"The People, Yes."**

As a work of art **"Remembrance Rock"** stands beside Sandburg's biography of Lincoln, and as a personal expression it is his fullest, ripest tribute to the dreamers and seekers who have followed "the blood-scarlet thread of America's destiny" that always stretches, as he says, into the Unknown—the people who have remained unswamped by fate and undulled by self-satisfaction. (p. 2)

Lloyd Lewis, "Sandburg's Fictional Epic of American Life," in New York Herald Tribune Weekly Book Review, *October 10, 1948, pp. 1-2.*

SELDEN RODMAN

What is there, I thought to myself while preparing like an archeologist to plunge through [***Complete Poems***], seven massive layers of gnomic utterance, that has made my generation indifferent to the poetry of Carl Sandburg? From the aristocratic verbal economy of Pound, Eliot, and Cummings in the early Twenties to the other worldly "abstract" art of Ransom, Stevens, and Robert Lowell that bemuses us today, we have followed other gods. Briefly in the political Thirties it seemed as though Rukeyser and Shapiro, Spender and Auden were leading us back into the arena, but they, too, became other-worldly and increasingly abstract. Henry James, who had damned Whitman and predicted that art would "wither" in America's "cruel air," was accepted as a procreant ancestor. And in this perspective the figure of Carl Sandburg became still more shadowy.

He was a primitive. That seemed to be the key to his identity. Who else would ask the professors to tell him the meaning of happiness—and find it among the Hunkies by the river with their beer and accordions Sunday afternoon? (p. 14)

"Chicago Poems," which so shocked the critics between 1912 and 1916, must have greeted a public that had forgotten Whitman. For here was Whitman reborn without the magnificent ego and the optimism, but with all that poet's compassion and knack of recording the pulse of common activity. In addition, dropping the preciosity, Sandburg had borrowed imagism from the Imagists; and, with a Christian Socialist's bitter contempt for the complacencies of the idle rich, he had set down plain descriptions of things and people (like an immigrant picket line, a night-sweeper of hog blood, the wiring and plumbing of a skyscraper) that had been neglected by the poets. Much of it today (like much of Whitman) is as banal as yesterday's newspapers. And some of it, like the title poem, and **"Gone,"** with its miraculously evocative folksong lilt, has an unspoilt freshness.

"Prairie," the opening poem of **"Cornhuskers"** (1918), is Sandburg at his most Whitmanesque, with foreshadowings of Jeffers, Pare Lorentz, and of his own later **"The People, Yes."** He has rediscovered the value of repetition. He is more conscious—"a high majestic fooling . . . in the yellow corn"—of his own style. He is more lyrical: "The first spit of snow on the northwest wind." And in poems like **"Caboose Thoughts," "Cool Tombs,"** and **"Singing Nigger"** he is as concentratedly good as he ever will be.

There is a casual rhythm and concreteness Hart Crane was to try for and never quite bring off in the industrial descriptions of **"Smoke and Steel"** (1920). . . . (pp.14-15)

There is a foreshadowing of Fearing in the loosely connected, almost surrealist, images of **"Eleventh Avenue Racket."** [There is] wonderful command of the American vernacular in such syncopations as **"Honky Tonk in Cleveland."** . . . The rich are not excommunicated now—they are shown eating soup or coming "home" to a six-foot box like everybody else. The individual poems are a chant or a croon or a blow: there is no development in the strict sense. The **"Four Preludes on Playthings of the Wind"** foreshadows and competes with the best of William Carlos Williams. **"Sleepy-heads," "How Yesterday Looked,"** and **"Haze,"** are among the best.

"Slabs of the Sunburnt West" (1922) sounds a new formulation: "It is wisdom to think the people are the city."

"Good Morning, America" (1928) begins with the mystical **"Definitions of Poetry,"** of which the most memorable is "the synthesis of hyacinths and biscuits." The style tends to be a little more self-conscious, as though the poet were trying sometimes *not* to be a primitive; and where "folklore" was previously absorbed like a blotter or actually invented, it is now often dragged in. . . .

On the acceptance or rejection of **"The People, Yes"** (1935) Sandburg's ultimate reputation as a poet is likely to rest. And the verdict (he would like it that way) is wrapped up to a degree with the facts of democracy. Certainly a huge, sprawling repository of common wisdom and common folly, of popular jokes and legends, held together with nothing but tolerance and lyrical affirmation is not going to impress the fanatical or cynical rulers of a directed society. Neither will it impress poets escaping from the threat of such a future into the abstractions or nightmares of private worlds. In structure or lack of structure the book oddly resembles Pound's "Cantos"; substituting "money" for "usury" there is also some analogy in the naivete of its economic philosophy, antedating, in Sandburg's case, the later formulations of the New Deal. But there the resemblances end. The fulcrum of Sandburg's catch-all is love, not hate. And the key aphorisms—"How much did he leave? All of it," "Everybody is cleverer than anybody," and the history of the world reduced to the single word "Maybe"—express the living paradox of America. Is there a better way to make poems of that paradox?

It would be fun to edit a selection of Whitman and Sandburg someday, to get down to the hard core of each, leaving just enough of the rind and soft spots to keep a likeness. Three-quarters to four-fifths of each poet could be cut away without damage to anything but the blue pencil. But what remained would be, along with the best of Emerson, Thoreau, Melville, Dickinson, Twain, Faulkner, and Frost, the writing that has taught America the sound of its own voice. (p.15)

Selden Rodman, "The Pulse of Common Activity," in The Saturday Review of Literature, *Vol. XXXIII, No. 46, November 18, 1950, pp. 14-15.*

HENRY STEELE COMMAGER

In 1912 the indomitable Harriet Monroe founded Poetry magazine, out in Chicago of all places, and the "new" poets came on with a rush. Within six years almost all of those who have since become our modern classics made their first appearance—or their first important appearance. Call the role of the newcomers: the "prairie poets," Masters and Lindsay and Sandburg; the imagists, Amy Lowell and Hilda Doolittle and Conrad Aiken; the lyricists, Edna Millay and Sara Teasdale and Elinor Wylie; the experimentalists, Ezra Pound and Archibald MacLeish and William Carlos Williams—these and a dozen others, including Stephen Bénet and Robert Frost. Not since New England's Golden Age had there been anything like it.

Of all those who appeared in Poetry magazine there was none whose poetry seemed more shocking, and was less so, than Carl Sandburg's. (p. 1)

Now Sandburg has suffered the fate of most innovators: he has become respectable, he has become orthodox, he has become the very Dean of American poetry.

For almost all of that bright throng are gone now. Yet Sandburg remains a symbol, a monument, almost an institution. And he remains unchanged: the Sandburg of **"The People, Yes"** is the Sandburg of **"Chicago Poems"**; the technique is the same, and—more important—the philosophy. He has spilled out in many directions, to be sure. As he says in his preface [to ***Complete Poems: Carl Sandburg***], "there was puzzlement as to whether I was a poet, a biographer, a wandering troubadour with a guitar, a Midwest Hans Christian Andersen, or a historian of current events." There was good precedent for this catholicity, even in such revered figures as Longfellow and Whittier; what is important is that the change and development were quantitative rather than qualitative.

Sandburg has remained fundamentally the same—in his interests, his sympathies, his philosophy. None of our major poets is easier to understand, and this not a criticism but a tribute. He is a democrat and an equalitarian; he is a humanitarian; he is a sociologist; he is an optimist and an idealist. He loves simple people and simple things, the things with which men and women work. He hates cruelty and insincerity and vulgarity and all those who climb on the shoulders of their fellow-men.

Above all, Sandburg is the poet of the plain people, of farmers and steel workers and coal miners, of the housewife and the stenographer, and the streetwalker, too; of children at play and at work; of hoboes and bums; of soldiers—the privates, not the officers; of Negroes as of whites; of immigrants as of natives—of "The People, Yes." . . . Sandburg has never lost his poetic feeling for ordinary life. In the very beginning he wrote: **"I am The People, The Mob."**

And there is another conviction to which Sandburg has clung through the years—that the people are better than their leaders, even better than their spokesmen. . . . (pp. 1, 40)

There is everywhere pity that men have not lived their dreams, that there is ugliness where there should be beauty and cruelty where there should be love; but it is a pity that never sours into mere bitterness. . . .

There was nothing in the crisis of the Thirties, or of the Forties, that Sandburg had not anticipated in his earlier poems. Indeed, these decades merely pointed up the need for democracy, for brotherhood, for courage, and dramatized the bankruptcy of hatred and inhumanity. In one of the last of **"The People, Yes"** poems he speaks directly to us, today, and to the zeal for breast-beating and for hatred that seems so popular. . . .

There is, finally, a handful of poems now for the first time published—poems from the war and post-war years. These show no diminution of talents or slackening of spirit. Here is the same Sandburg, passionately championing the people, passionately attacking those who would make a mockery of the dreams and aspirations of man. . . .

Certainly Sandburg has never taken the easy road of silence. Here are tributes to Archibald MacLeish, to the books men die for, to the Norwegian who died under Gestapo torture, to the memory of Lincoln—so alive again. Here is a moving tribute to Roosevelt, one of the greatest of Sandburg's poems. . . .

It was not accident that Sandburg should write the great biography of Lincoln, a biography perfectly suited to Lincoln's genius. For Sandburg is, like Whitman, the Lincoln of our poetry. At a time when we are tempted to betray ourselves, tempted into irrationality, into superficiality, into cynicism, he celebrates what is best in us and recalls us to our heritage and to our humanity. (p. 40)

Henry Steele Commager, "He Sings of America's Plain People," in The New York Times Book Review, *November 19, 1950, pp. 1, 40.*

ROBERT E. SHERWOOD

At the risk of being convicted of hyperbole—the blackest crime in the reviewer's code—I feel compelled to put my neck in the noose with the statement that **"Always the Young Strangers"** is, to me, the best autobiography ever written by an American. I am not forgetting Benjamin Franklin or Henry Adams, nor showing them disrespect. Carl Sandburg's life would hardly have been possible—not at any rate as he lived it and now writes it—had it not been for Ben Franklin and the Adams family, among others.

The primary virtue of this book is its utter honesty. Sandburg seems to have written it not for the enlightenment or entertainment of others but for his own inward satisfaction; he is totting up his own accounts against the day when inspection of them will be demanded by Higher Authority. He knows that such Authority needs no lie detector and requires simplicity as well as truth. I believe that the reader will appreciate this—however different his age, background and general circumstances from Sandburg's—because he will discover and happily recognize many dimly remembered aspects of himself, his family, his friends and his dreams. By striving to tell no more than an intensely personal story, Sandburg has achieved the universality of a "Pilgrim's Progress." . . .

A prodigious array of characters parades through this book: the members of the "Dirty Dozen" (Sandburg's boyhood gang), the pioneers and old-timers, the section hands, saloonkeepers, "gaycats," lecturers, cops, corporals, "young bucks," hayshakers, left fielders, fancy women. Sandburg remembers them all, and how they looked and talked, and the stories that went with them. (p. 1)

This is a personal history and it therefore must include a mention of family. There are no lovelier people in Sandburg's living memory than his mother and father and his cousins John and Charlie Krans, all good Swedes and noble Americans. . . .

"Always the Young Strangers" tells about the boy he was—not about a boy who might one day make enormous contributions to American literature and history. . . .

Since **"Always the Young Strangers"** covers only his first twenty-one years, the bulk of his rich life remains to be written. I hope that many more volumes are to come, but I feel sure that none can be better than the first one. (p. 24)

Robert E. Sherwood, "The Boy Grew Up in Galesburg," in The New York Times Book Review, *January 4, 1953, pp. 1, 24.*

NICHOLAS JOOST

"There are humble lives that have their treasures," Carl Sandburg writes on one of the concluding pages of his autobiography, ***Always the Young Strangers***. . . . All too often those treasures waste their sweetness on the desert air. Once in a generation, if the generation is lucky, a poet gathers up the riches of the poor, spreads them before us and dazzles our eyes to tears with a gentle splendor. For our generation Sandburg has performed this feat. . . .

The narrative is much more . . . than a uniquely realized picture of Swedish immigrant life in the Midwest of the eighties. Sandburg ranges through all the strata of Galesburg's life. . . . He recaptures with a pure wonder and an utter absence of bias and condescension the life of the railroad workers, the Irish, and the émigrés from New England; his school days and his friends at the Seventh Ward School; and the amusements to be had in the Galesburg Auditorium when theatrical troupes came to town. . . .

Sandburg proceeds from [an] account of his boyhood to the story of his adolescent wanderings, his multitude of odd jobs, and his service as an enlisted man in the Spanish-American War. The tale ends with his return to Galesburg and his decision to enroll in Lombard College there and to work his way to a degree. We have, in sum, a thickly detailed portrait of a life and of a time, the background of a career and of a nation, or at least the center of a nation.

Apparently ***Always the Young Strangers*** is first of several autobiographical volumes. With the Lincoln biography and the various collections of Lincolniana, which are authoritative, this is Carl Sandburg's most distinguished work. . . . His novel ***Remembrance Rock*** and the wartime miscellany ***Home Front Memo*** are downright embarrassing. . . . (pp. 381)

Sandburg's poetry is a mixture. On the whole it has gone utterly out of fashion, probably never to return. Embalmed by the score in anthologies of American literature, recited at businessmen's luncheons and Women's Club teas, these poems have completely disappeared from the anthologies and the discussions of the New Critics. . . .

The difficulty with most of Sandburg's poetry is that it is, ideologically, proletarian and, technically, insipid. . . . Critics are unkind to such poetry; not only has Auden done the same sort of thing better, but proletarian art belongs to a bygone and now suspect era out of which a definite pattern has emerged. . . .

Sandburg's weaknesses may be fatal to the bulk of his poems, but these very weaknesses paradoxically lend strength to his autobiography. An autobiography does not depend for success on any subtler organization than that of chronology, and Sandburg has delved into the depths of his own past and the past of Galesburg and the nation to achieve triumphantly his vision. A medley of imaged evocation and deliberate statement makes the stuff of his narrative. Sandburg has eschewed social realism, the proletarian note; instead he has turned to a simpler realism behind which lurk no ulterior motives. The tone of the poet—and ***Always the Young Strangers*** is in many passages, in the larger sense, poetry of a high order—[is] warm, affectionate, at times wistful, at times robust. Love fills and informs the book. It is an American document, to be compared with *Look Homeward, Angel*. (p. 382)

Nicholas Joost, "The Poet from Galesburg," in Commonweal, *Vol. LVII, No. 15, January 16, 1953, pp. 381-82.*

ELLEN LEWIS BUELL

When Carl Sandburg's **"Always the Young Strangers"** was published Robert E. Sherwood . . . said "it is, to me, the best autobiography ever written by an American" [see excerpt above]. Whether one agrees with this verdict or not, [this recollection] of the author's first twenty-one years was a remarkable evocation of a boyhood and of a time and a region. Now it has been condensed [in **"Prairie-Town Boy"**] to something less than half for younger readers. . . .

As was inevitable, this streamlined version lacks the breadth and the depth of the original and also something of its gusto. Even so, **"Prairie-Town Boy"** has much to offer to the thoughtful reader. . . . It is still an illuminating re-creation of a boyhood which was, at once, typical of the place and the period and completely individual.

Ellen Lewis Buell, "Sandburg's Youth," in The New York Times Book Review, *April 10, 1955, p. 16.*

LOUISE SEAMAN BECHTEL

[**"Prairie-Town Boy"**] is not a book for children but for those teen-agers who may be surprised at the very adult realism of these memories. . . . They will be rewarded by a picture of life in Galesburg in the nineties and descriptions of the beginnings of Sandburg's interest in Lincoln. . . . Many non-literary boys of around sixteen should meet the hard work, the varied odd jobs, the attempt at learning to be a barber and the period "on the road," when, penniless among hoboes but not of them, he really "grew up." Finally comes his brief experience as a soldier who never fought, in the Spanish-American War, that led to his going to college.

In a book lacking climax or much drama, thoughtful older boys will feel the special spirit of a special person, of a boy unsure of any "calling" or direction in his life, but growing in mental eagerness and in his judgments of people and of his world.

Louise Seaman Bechtel, in a review of "Prairie-Town Boy," in New York Herald Tribune Book Review, *May 15, 1955, p. 12.*

JOHN COURNOS

Neither a stove nor a shooting gallery, ***The Sandburg Range*** is a book, awkwardly titled, designed to reveal the scope and diversity of Carl Sandburg's writing talent. He is advertised on the jacket as "renowned as a poet, Lincoln biographer, historian, novelist, troubador, autobiographer, and story teller for children." But can it be said that Sandburg's literary reputation will rest on anything more than his Lincoln opus? (p. 622)

Some of the poems in this volume impress me as genuine poems, others as mild postscripts to Walt Whitman, and still others as not poems at all, but random fragments waiting to be beaten into shape. And here is a significant fact: the poet never fails when he comes to the theme of Lincoln: **"The Long Shadow of Lincoln: A Litany"** . . . is eloquent testimony to this fact.

The Rootabaga stories for children are extremely fanciful, and have a peculiar charm. . . .

Of himself Sandburg writes forthrightly, modestly, in a matter-of-fact manner. As one who is interested in people and loves them, he is a good observer; his experiences introduce the reader to aspects of American life learned at first hand. He writes warmly of his famous friends; indeed at times lets his enthusiasm run away with him, as when he speaks of the photographer Steichen in the same breath with Leonardo da Vinci.

Perhaps next to his ***Lincoln*** his most ambitious if less successful achievement has been ***Remembrance Rock,*** which he calls a novel—wrongly, I think. It is, in fact, less than a novel, and more than a novel, not only because it attempts to communicate a "message" to the American people . . . but even more because in it the author seems scarcely interested in Americans as individuals. They are types who, through the crises of four different historical epochs, courageously espoused the American Dream, following faithfully the precepts of the Founders. Like the recurrent *motif* of a four-movement symphony, the "message" is repeated through the four parts of the story which have no organic fictional connection with one another. The reader will not find in it the novelistic merits extolled by the critics who praised it for the wrong things.

So back we come to the Lincoln tomes, which tower like immense oaks above all the variegated shrubbery in the land of Sandburgia. The mind and heart of Sandburg needed the combined inspiration of Lincoln and of the poor people of whom Lincoln said that God must have loved them to have made so many of them. This spirit is scattered through Sandburg's books, but the figure of Lincoln fed the writer with this spirit concentrated in force and provided the human symbol upon which to concentrate his own genius. The life of Lincoln demanded of Sandburg great reserves of patience and of effort. The result is an enduring monument—rambling, often seemingly formless, but like Nature itself, prodigal and diverse, and if the weeds press on the flowers, it is all lost in the grandeur of the whole. (p. 623)

John Cournos, "Sandburgiana," in Commonweal, *Vol. LXVII, No. 24, March 14, 1958, pp. 622-23.*

MICHAEL YATRON

Carl Sandburg, who wrote simple poetry for simple people and who recently hushed the halls of Congress, is a good poet for the high school English teacher, faced with indifferent students, to begin his poetic chore with. Sandburg devoted his life to translating into poetry the idiom of the people, by whom he meant the majority of native-born and naturalized Americans, who built post-Civil War America with the strength of their hands, the sweat of their brows, and the obstinacy of their spirit into the present-day Colossus. Sandburg was not sure he was writing poetry, but he was sure that what he said had to be meaningful to the average truck driver on Chicago's Wabash Avenue, whose intelligence "the Dark Spirits," Sandburg's epithet for esoteric poets and critics, treated with contempt. . . .

Sandburg's popular appeal can be extended to the classroom, precisely because his diction and content are not likely to arouse the antagonism of anti-poetic students. If anything, he offers the thrill of recognition to the student, particularly since the America Sandburg chants of is an America that, despite jet airplanes and television sets, still exists and conforms to the student's own experience. (p. 524)

Sandburg presents a model of nonconformity and humanitarianism and, it is here, in my opinion, that his true worth for the student lies. In our age of the supremacy of the state and the rationalization of industry the individual has been reduced to a cipher. The Myrmidons of Hitler, Stalin, and Tojo and the American "organization man" are symptomatic of the antlike society toward which twentieth century man is gravitating. . . . (pp. 524-25)

The first requirement for freedom is the recognition that the state is not the master of the individual, but his servant. This requirement of freedom is met by the individual's having a voice in the ultimate power of the state, the power to go to war. In this connection Sandburg's voice has always been the voice of a free man. He has written many anti-war poems, pointing out that wars are often made by despots and fought by and suffered by the people. . . .

Sandburg himself served as a common soldier in the Spanish American War, attended West Point briefly as a "veteran," turned violently pacifistic during World War I, and rejected pacifism in World War II. This completion of the circle shows that Sandburg was not stupidly consistent, and its value for our conformist students lies in sowing the seed in their minds that there is nothing sacred about militarism and rascality, albeit they may wear the cloak of patriotism.

Sandburg was equally scathing as regards big business, which too often has maximized profits while minimizing humanity. (p. 525)

In the area of racial relationships, Sandburg is without prejudice. Hungarians with accordions (**"Happiness"**), Greeks shoveling gravel (**"Near Keokuk"**), Italians working with pick and shovel (**"The Shovel Man"**), and Jews selling fish (**"Fish Crier"**) are presented sympathetically. And what is more to Sandburg's credit is that his tolerance is extended to Asiatics. "My prayers go . . . for the Russian people. If they are merely 'Asiatic hordes,' then I'm a barrel-house bum," he stated. For a man born in the isolationist Middle West, whose mind was formed during the period when the spectre of "the yellow peril" was publicized often, this sanity is reasonableness itself. (pp. 525-26)

Quite consistently, Sandburg was a champion of the Negro. At the close of World War I, some white boys of Chicago stoned a colored youth on a raft with the result that he was drowned. A race riot ensued and Sandburg was sent by the Chicago *Daily News* to report the situation. Out of this reportage grew a book, ***The Chicago Race Riots,*** which clearly revealed Sandburg's belief that "a man's a man for a' that."

Another ugly thing that Sandburg saw growing in American society is class stratification. . . . Sandburg is not ashamed of unpressed and patched pants, of unshined and worn shoes, of long hair. He detests expensive night clubs and dress suits, and, I suppose, fin-tailed automobiles. Material things and glossy appearances may have their place in brightening life, but they are not the end-all and be-all of existence which our middle class society has made them. And they are certainly not worth the never-ending wage slavery and bill-paying which their possession entails. Our poet in ignoring materialism again provides youth with a needed alternate possibility to the drive for success.

Sandburg is a fine example for the youth who suspects that a mess of pottage isn't worth a soul and a life. Sandburg rode freight trains, washed dishes, worked in a construction camp, threshed wheat, learned the painter's trade, enlisted in the Army, was a college student, a hobo, a wandering minstrel, a newspaperman, a militant Socialist, a poet, and a man of letters. He was a man trying to find himself but always moving in the direction of his true self. (pp. 526-27)

Another area where our student may profit from Sandburg's voice is the area of work. . . . Sandburg sings praises of honest toil; he calls work a privilege. And he does not think a diploma makes a man. He realizes that many folk with homely virtues and skills are far superior to both lettered and unlettered blockheads, and their society healthier and stabler than a parasitic one where men prey on men.

Sandburg, then, has a basic content which can be summed up in the word Man and which can nourish the mind of the young in the best traditions of Western Civilization. The next question to be raised is, Is what Sandburg writes poetry, and, if so, how good is it?

Sandburg, as I have stated earlier, was not sure that he was writing poetry. He was trying to communicate to an audience which was not sophisticated verbally, to whom the connotations of words are very closely related to their denotations, to whom literary allusion and subtle metaphor are meaningless. He has been an exponent of Wordsworth's "man talking to men." But this use of a *lingua communis* carries with it its own trap, as Coleridge pointed out. The language of prose and the language of metrical composition are two different entities. Thus Sandburg's work quite often degenerates into a pedestrian prosaism summed up by the word "talk." Accordingly, he has been accused, justifiably in this writer's opinion, of being diffuse, clownish, and vulgar.

Such criticism, however, is by no means the final word. (p. 527)

There is no blind spot, however, in my feeling that Sandburg has many limitations. His is not a lyric gift; he neither sings nor can he give expression to deep human emotions. He is not a philosophical poet, nor a dramatic one—rather he is a poet descriptive of the surface, whose eye and ear are keen and who reproduces America as no one else has. He is, as I have stated, a good beginning for the anti-poetic—no mean contribution. He can attract to poetry many of our youth who would normally be repulsed by other poets who seem to say nothing in antiquated and dull language. And once Sandburg has been the initial magnet, and he has given the student the thrill of recognition and of understanding, the next step is to teach the mechanics of traditional poetry and lead the student to the rich veins of English, and ultimately, world poetry. (pp. 527, 539)

Michael Yatron, "Carl Sandburg: The Poet As Nonconformist," in English Journal, *Vol. XLVIII, No. 9, December, 1959, pp. 524-27, 539.*

SOMNER SORENSON

The task of reviewing ***Honey and Salt*** is not the easiest form of writing, because on the one hand the American public is respectful and even affectionate towards the grand old man among American troubadors; on the other, any author who puts his writings out for the public to inspect is inviting a judgment, favorable or otherwise. . . .

Of the seventy-seven poems in the book, about half of them do not merit any serious consideration. Some offerings, such as **"Metamorphosis"** or **"Quotations,"** are simply puerile; others are marred by some very feeble lines ("Cold is cold and too cold is too cold," for instance, from **"Hunger and Cold"**); a few poems are flawed by an apparently needless shift in tone at the end, e.g. **"Three Shrines."** . . . (p. 143)

Yet other poems may be good, but this reviewer, at any rate, was unable to follow them with any assurance, such as **"Love Beyond Keeping," "Impossible Iambics,"** or **"First Sonata for Karlen Paula."**

It should be observed, however, that there are good things to be said about ***Honey and Salt*** too. The chief of these is Sandburg's imagery, which in certain of his poems he handles masterfully. Some of his poems like **"Elm Buds," "Lake Michigan Morning"** or **"Pool of Bethesda"** aim at nothing other than giving as colorful and graphic a picture of what he is describing as he can in a few short lines, such as the Imagists sometimes did. Sandburg's effective use of color is especially conspicuous in the short **"Morning Glory Blue."**

That Carl Sandburg has a strong lyrical side has long been noticed by Norman Foerster and others, but to this day in many people's minds the name of Sandburg is associated only with faith in democracy, Walt Whitman, free verse, and folksy, down-to-earth sort of poetry that everybody can understand. In their minds Sandburg is the last person from whom to expect lyrical utterances. How surprised and, it is to be hoped, delighted they will be after reading **"Old Music for Quiet Hearts"** or **"Early Copper."** . . . (pp. 143-44)

When he is at his best he keeps a firm grip on his word choice. A reader may be taken a trifle off guard as he reads along to discover that he is in the midst of a passage employing fine assonance and alliteration, such as in **"Timesweep."** . . . (p. 144)

Some of the most interesting lines in ***Honey and Salt*** contain deliberately scrambled images that appeal to more than one sense at the same time. Sometimes they are somewhat reminiscent of passages by Dylan Thomas. They could be described as a sort of synesthesia, although there is probably some more precise technical term that would be more appropriate. (p. 145)

Obviously Carl Sandburg delights in language and its patterns. Yet curiously in a few of his poems he implies that language is inadequate, that it does not communicate all meaning. In **"Fifty-Fifty,"** after asking, "What is there for us two / to split fifty-fifty, / to go halvers on? / a Bible, a deck of cards? / a farm, a frying pan? / a porch, front steps to sit on?" the answer to which is apparently none of these, Sandburg proceeds, "How can we be pals / when you speak English / and I speak English / and you never understand me / and I never understand you?" In **"Is Wisdom a Lot of Language?"** the poet, addressing the members of the ape family, lists some of the things that have followed from language: misunderstandings, gossip, backbiting, conversations that miss the point, etc., and then concludes,

> Read the dictionary from A to Izzard today.
> Get a vocabulary. Brush up on your diction.
> See whether wisdom is just a lot of language.

One might venture the explanation that Sandburg is resisting that fashionable school of thought that holds that there is no meaning outside of language. Finally in **"Speech"** comes the implication that language is ultimately futile as death comes to silence all tongues, an idea that is also supported in **"The Gong of Time,"** in which the poet says that people were silent before they were born and will be silent after death, so why not be silent now? The idea indeed seems cogent, but it is ironic coming from a man who has made his living by breaking silence.

Along with Sandburg's delight in language and the denial of its adequacy runs another pair of paradoxical ideas. In a poem like **"Timesweep"** the author is certainly aware of and accepts a number of scientific theories, but on the other hand he denies any purely mechanistic philosophy. Life is not something that can be calculated exactly with a slide rule: individual thoughts, the personal life is more than so much data. (pp. 147-48)

Sandburg's longest poem in this collection and the one he may consider his summing up, creed, or last word—significantly he placed it last—is **"Timesweep."** Its use of catalogues, the changing function of the word "I," the idea of the planet as a rocking cradle of death (and life), and of course the free verse are all reminiscent of Whitman, but there are passages in the poem that make one think of those other Transcendentalists, Thoreau and Emerson, as well. (p. 149)

To recapitulate, it is a shame that Sandburg, who still shows great flashes of poetry in some of his works, should have the total effect marred by so many inferior offerings. . . . (p. 152)

Somner Sorenson, "Poets New and Old: Reviews of Ammons and Sandburg," in Discourse: A Review of the Liberal Arts, *Vol. VIII, No. 2, Spring, 1965, pp. 138-52.**

ARCHIBALD MacLEISH

[The eulogy excerpted below was delivered by MacLeish at the Lincoln Memorial during the Carl Sandburg Memorial Ceremony.

President Lyndon B. Johnson also spoke at this memorial service, and Mark Van Doren delivered a second eulogy on Sandburg as historian of Lincoln.]

Sandburg had a *subject*—and the subject was belief in man. You find it everywhere. You find it announced in the title of the book in which his Chicago poet appears: ***The People, Yes.*** You find it in one form or another throughout the hundred odd poems and proses of which that extraordinary book is composed. You find it in other poems. And in other books. Most important of all, you find it in the echo which all these poems and these books leave in the ear—your ear and the ears of others: the echo which has made the body of Sandburg's work a touchstone for two generations of readers—almost, by this time, for three.

A touchstone of what? A touchstone of America. If ever a man wrote for a particular people, however he may have reached in his heart for all people, it was Sandburg. . . . And if ever a man was heard by those he wrote for it was Carl. Europeans, even the nearest in that direction, the English, do not truly understand him but Americans do. There is a raciness in the writing, in the old, strict sense of the word raciness: a tang, a liveliness, a pungency, which is native and natural to the American ear. And underneath the raciness, like the smell of earth under the vividness of rain, there is a seriousness which is native too—the kind of human, even mortal, seriousness you hear in Lincoln.

An American touchstone. But is there not a contradiction here? *Can* a body of work bound together by credulity constitute a touchstone for Americans? For Americans *now*? Once, perhaps, in the generation of Jefferson, or once again in the generation of Lincoln—but *now*? There is a notion around in great parts of the world—in Asia and in certain countries of Europe—that America has changed in recent years: that the last thing one can expect from America or from Americans today is credulity. It is asserted that the American people have now, as the saying goes, grown up. That they have put aside childish things, beliefs which can't be proved. That they have come to see what the world is, to put their trust in the certainties of power. That they have become, in brief, what is favorably known as "realistic": about themselves, about humanity, about the destiny of man.

Listening to contemporary speeches, reading the papers, one can see where these opinions of America may have come from. But are they true? Are they really true? Can we believe, in *this* place, thinking of *this* man, that they are true? Sandburg was an American. He was an American also of our time, of our generation. . . . His struggles were the struggles of the generation to which most of us belong—the struggles of the great depression and the many wars and the gathering racial crisis and all the rest. He was a man of our time who lived in our time, laughed at the jokes our time has laughed at, shed its tears. And yet *Sandburg was a credulous man*—a man credulous about humanity—a man who believed more than he could prove about humanity. And Sandburg, though he listened to those who thought themselves realists, though he was attentive to the hard-headed, was not convinced by them. . . . What Sandburg knew and said was what America knew from the beginning and said from the beginning and has not yet, no matter what is believed of her, forgotten how to say: that those who are credulous about the destiny of man, who believe more than they can prove of the future of the human race, will *make* that future, *shape* that destiny. This was his great achievement: that he found a new way in an incredulous and disbelieving and often cynical time to say what Americans have always known. And beyond that there was another and even greater achievement: that the people listened. They are listening still. (pp. 42-4)

Archibald MacLeish, "A Memorial Tribute to Carl Sandburg," in The Massachusetts Review, *Vol. IX, No. 1, Winter, 1968, pp. 41-4.*

MIRIAM GURKO

[**"The Sandburg Treasury"**] is exactly that: an attractive storehouse of his prose and poetry, written for younger readers. It reveals one of our most indigenously American writers. Carl Sandburg is vintage Midwest, with all its virtues and limitations: the simplicity and openness, the faith in people and deep concern for them, especially the workers and farmers among whom he grew up. Inevitably, one also encounters his excessive sentimentality—and a naive obviousness that explains in part why his reputation has declined. A basic fact remains: though his verse may lack complexity, it remains great poetry for the young.

The volume includes Sandburg's most appealing songs about prairie and city, children, animals, nature—all in his energetic free verse. He was wonderfully inventive with language: frogs "plutter and squdge," a face is a "phizzog." His word-foolery is especially evident in the imaginative Rootabaga stories. These demonstrate admirably his superb ear for Midwestern speech, combined with a comic turn of phrase and a clever use of repetition.

Also included are **"Prairie-Town Boy,"** which Sandburg adapted from his autobiography, **"Always the Young Strangers,"** and **"Abe Lincoln Grows Up,"** from **"Abraham Lincoln: The Prairie Years."** These represent his prose at its best—and worst. The Lincoln selection is densely sentimental and marred by artificially "poetic" language. In spite of this, Sandburg's instinctive rapport with the frontier enables him to convey the flavor of Lincoln's personality and background.

"Prairie-Town Boy" is one of the best things in the Treasury. It is an absorbing account of both the author and the Illinois of that period. The story moves from an unvarnished description of Sandburg's parents and their bleak lives through a growing boy's adventures . . . [to] his experiences as a hobo [and] his enlistment in the Spanish-American War, which he spent fighting mosquitoes in Puerto Rico. It ends with Sandburg deciding to attend college, having by-passed high school while getting his education elsewhere "in scraps and pieces."

Miriam Gurko, in a review of "The Sandburg Treasury," in The New York Times Book Review, *November 15, 1970, p. 42.*

MARY M. BURNS

Gathering Carl Sandburg's work for young people—***Rootabaga Stories, Early Moon, Wind Song, Prairie-Town Boy, Abe Lincoln Grows Up***—into one volume [***The Sandburg Treasury: Prose and Poetry for Young People***] gives readers an opportunity to examine and appreciate the genius of the literary artist as analyst and visionary. Here with its inexhaustible energy and irrepressible, at times irresponsible, laissez-faire attitude is the American character: sometimes heroic, sometimes wistful, sometimes obnoxious, yet never dull. . . . Time has not yet diminished the appeal of Sandburg's vigorous, vital style. . . .

[This] volume should be an invaluable addition to home, school, and library collections. (pp. 59-60)

Mary M. Burns, in a review of "The Sandburg Treasury: Prose and Poetry for Young People," in The Horn Book Magazine, *Vol. XLVII, No. 1, February, 1971, pp. 59-60.*

PHOEBE PETTINGELL

Carl Sandburg was at his death in 1967 one of America's most celebrated and honored authors. The pundits of the poetry world, however, had snubbed him for decades. For the breezy optimism of ***Chicago Poems*** had preceded *Prufrock and Other Observations* by only one year, and it seemed somewhat out of place in the 20th century. "Ethics and Art cannot be married," cried Conrad Aiken. Robert Frost gleefully reported as someone else's witticism that Sandburg "was the kind of writer who had everything to gain and nothing to lose by being translated into another language." . . .

Well, "here he is again, the old idealist, fighter, philosopher, dreamer, and poet, still with something to say," writes daughter Margaret Sandburg, who has edited ***Breathing Tokens*** . . . , a collection of 118 previously unpublished poems. (p. 19)

Breathing Tokens is fairly representative of Sandburg's techniques and themes, although it lacks the gusto of his best-known work. **"Mr. Lincoln and His Gloves,"** a funny account of the contemporary social furor over that President's inability to keep a respectable pair of kidskin gloves, makes ungainly hands an effective symbol for a giant spirit. **"Guessers"** is a Twainian satire of yahoo scorn for new scientific discoveries: "And now, bo, here's this Einstein. / Good for a laugh in all the funny sections"; unfortunately, it goes flat at the end by spelling out what has already been demonstrated.

Sandburg's strength lay in the vernacular; his "poetic" language could be disastrously bathetic—and often was. . . . Moreover, a Whitmanesque expansionism impelled him to overstate, overenumerate, overexplain, indeed, to overeverything.

What Sandburg's poetry does not overdo is its deep belief in human dignity. When used for this purpose, his loose forms and plain speech carry the message loud and clear. In **"Breathing Tokens"** he writes: "You must expect to be in several lost causes before you die. / Why blame your father and mother for your being born; how could they help what they were doing?" The poem is an apology for man's unquenchable desire to live, even in adversity, and a plea to experience life as fully as possible:

> Be sensitized with winter quicksilver below zero.
> Be tongs and handles; find breathing tokens.
> See where several good dreams are worth dying for.

Sandburg often proves, in other words, that Ethics and Art *can* be married.

It was, finally, the oversized enthusiasm the poet peddled that kept him out of sympathy with the main poetic influences in an era of pessimism (certain stylistic and philosophical affinities in the work of Allen Ginsburg probably derive less from Sandburg than from the same misreading of their common source—Whitman). But Carl Sandburg may prove to be vindicated. **"Chicago," "Gone," "Jazz Fantazia,"** and parts of that odd socio-poetical study, **"The People, Yes,"** are doubtless closer to the most readers' idea of modern poetry than anything by Eliot, Stevens, Williams, or Lowell. Who knows when a new populist verse may evolve out of Sandburg's generous and hopeful humanism? (p. 20)

Phoebe Pettingell, "The People's Poet," in The New Leader, *Vol. LXI, No. 5, February 27, 1978, pp. 19-20.*

BERNARD DUFFEY

No one of the three notable poets spawned by the Chicago literary renaissance of the second decade of this century can be said to have fared very prosperously at the hands of later times. Vachel Lindsay, haunted during his life by a resonantly idealistic vision of possibilities inherent in American life, now seems a proclaimer of apocalypse too unreal for more than rhetoric and gesture. Edgar Lee Masters (the reportorial impulse of *Spoon River Anthology* apart) is surely a failed poet, one lost in a cloud of variously colored romantic posturings, a writer to whom his work was more self-indulgence than either art or expression. Carl Sandburg, in comparison, seems more durable. He is in print. His memory has called forth centenary observance. He has had a special stamp struck off in his honor. He is something, at least, of an institution.

But even this degree of survival presents something of a puzzle. He is, in a predominating view, no more than a schoolroom poet, "populistic," "sentimental," and yet one who affords leads to suggest to the children that poetry may be contemporary in interest and personal in form. His work is visibly there, on the map of American literature, yet it is hard to call to mind any criticism of it that has succeeded in giving it major character. Allowing for all this, and conceding that few feel any pressing need for a Sandburg revival, I want nevertheless to take some exception to our willingness to give his poetry a no more than marginal place in our sense of twentieth century writing. Sandburg certainly stands wide of the major thrusts of both the writing and criticism of poetry in our time. . . . He was engaged in the same pursuit of the native which occupied his two Chicago contemporaries, but I want in fact to argue that unlike them he located a poetically constructive imagination of the land in and for which he wrote. His voice gains authenticity when it is considered across its breadth of utterance, and I would find it difficult to make this claim for either Masters or Lindsay. Unlike the latter, his is only occasionally the effort at poetic beatification, and unlike the former he is largely guiltless of ingrown maundering. Instead, I shall argue, though Sandburg shared a certain tentativeness and openness with his contemporaries, he in fact fashioned and for the most part held fast to a close and living sense of the native, one congruent, finally, with his land's own aspect.

What emerges from the whole poetry, in this view, is wholeness of perception, one rooted in a consistent feel for a land conditioned by a problematic history and filling a landscape difficult to redeem by transcendental gesture. His scene is peopled with the kind of minor movers and doers who in fact have so largely occupied it, and who have little choice but to take their character from the land's own spatial and temporal indeterminateness. (pp. 295-96)

In place of the anthology favorites, it is the total fabric of the poems that might now claim attention, beginning with the sense of historical time that prevails in it. Unlike the Whitman he admired, for example, Sandburg's history is one that has no sequential redemptions built into it except, perhaps, for the isolated figures it throws forth from time to time (Lincoln is the great case). Even here, however, history seems to have left him with no more than Eliot's *Quartets* also says it leaves, a symbol only, a remembered reality for our possible use rather than any guarantee of redemption. (p. 296)

The ***Complete Poems,*** from beginning to end, is studded with observations of place that, across their breadth, can best be characterized negatively, as the absence of any romantic power in nature resembling, say, Emerson's feeling for spirit; and the absence also of the historically bred sense of homeland, of place that has been given its character by deep, repeated actions of will. Landscape for Sandburg is most often simply here, or there, and no more. Instead of the rooted place, there is the open Midwestern landscape known to every eye. It appears most often as prairie. The occasional drama of hill, or forest, or river is seen only seldom. Habitation, rather than dwelling, is the rule. Apart from prairie, and unpredictably, an empty and ever shifting waste of water takes a large place in the poet's work; and he is fascinated over and over again by the palpable impalpable presence of mist. All present themselves as what may be called durations of space, something stretching out in undetermined vectors of distance.

Perhaps the commonest humanizer of landscape in Sandburg is that of response to its beauty, but if we are to understand the sense of beauty that moves him we should beware of easy responses. His is perhaps a little nearer to the negative sense of the sublime than to the beautiful itself, to that which confronts observation almost as an alien realm to be tested in a tremor of mind and feeling rather than received in congenial warmth and pleasure. He seems more often to be haunted by the land than at home in it, and his verse becomes that of a man against the sky to whom connections and relations are inapplicable. . . . The aesthetic in Sandburg is a mode of seeing and feeling that by its nature precludes other participation. It is a mode that asserts itself by negating action or ready involvement, and the poet can be explicit on the point. (p. 298)

But it is a third aspect, the problem of action that must engage us especially, a question that in Sandburg and across the breadth of much of what is called "modernist" poetry raises complicated questions stemming from the fact that the poetry of our time, like so much of its fiction and drama as well, has been a literature of what is felt to have happened to us rather than of what we have done. In this regard, Sandburg seems distinct from his contemporaries most plainly by reason of his own willingness to build whole sections of his poetry upon action in the world. The characteristic of our times, however, has been a contrary one, seeking decision for the poet rather *in* his action as poet. To swing sharply away from the Chicago ambience, we think of Sandburg's contemporaries like Pound, Eliot, Crane Stevens, or Williams as devisers of poetics almost as much as achieved poets. Each of them puts a major effort into the theory of poetry, their deep involvement in what it is to act as a poet.

Sandburg's concerns, to the contrary, flowed almost entirely into practice so that poetry for him became simply expression rather than the act of its definition. It is expression that his own slender essays, "Tentative (First Model) Definitions of Poetry," or the "Notes for a Preface" to the ***Complete Poems,*** largely insist on. As a result, action in Sandburg has largely to inhere in what he could find to be action outside his poetry, in his own witnessing of action; but such witnessing could only be structured on what were two impediments to active fulfillment and meaning, those of indeterminate time and indeterminate space. (p. 299)

The land of Sandburg's expression is undetermined in time and space alike. It is widely open and calls out for filling. But the actions which the poet seeks in it can only share the fate of the land itself and so share in the indeterminateness of history and landscape. (p. 300)

Rather than action, Sandburg's land is supplied most often with potentialities of action, and often with potentiality that is explicitly arrested. His interior distance, again, is that of standing at some remove, of finding the land which has encompassed him and generated his poems to be itself less than encompassable, a milieu in which he can resume motion only toward his own indeterminate ends. (p. 301)

What emerges from all this I want to suggest is a poetic vision seeking escape from easy idealism, from resolution by willed environment. Such direction sets Sandburg apart not only from his Chicago fellows but, if I may risk such generalization, from any of the prevailing poetic imaginations of America. In our national history there have been three reliances or references poetry has chiefly invoked to resolve the scattered picture the land presents. The first may be called resolution by landscape, or more properly, by a spiritually informing nature. This is the way, most familiarly, of the Emerson of such essays as *Nature* itself or of "Self-Reliance." The second is resolution by time. It is the resolution most fully invoked by Whitman and given its fullest statement in the reliance of "Song of Myself" on the evolution of a self, standing outside of culture in its democratic openness, away from the tentativeness of its beginnings and toward self-reliance and a reliance of selves on each other, but all in turn relied upon through faith in the material thrust of reality, of time's passage toward resolution. The third is that of action, voiced variably across our writing but one presenting great difficulties to the modern. In the poetry of our times, it has most notably found expression in the poet's feeling for his art itself as redemptive act. This, at any rate, would seem to be the resolution sought by Hart Crane in *The Bridge* and alternately sought for and despaired of by William Carlos Williams in *Paterson*.

Sandburg, I suggest is a fourth case, that of recognizing and instituting the undetermined itself. Nature in him has become simply landscape, and, apart from the distance, the remoteness of its beauty, it is made to suggest no redemption. Equally in Sandburg time is no healer. The redemptive hope on which Whitman rested his vision of evolution has become the reiteration of something that now is felt to be no more than process, action subsumed by time and space, which, in themselves, afford no definition. (pp. 301-02)

Perhaps no one could wish really to classify Sandburg as a naturalistic writer, but I may conclude by suggesting that his sense of time, space, and action, all three, forms a sort of protonaturalistic poetic vision, a landscape in which event and endurance provide the basic parameters of his vision as, he suggests, they provide such parameters for existence in his world. He holds back from willed ideality in favor of shaping that world close to the spectacle it most commonly presents. (p. 303)

Bernard Duffey, "Carl Sandburg and the Undetermined Land," in The Centennial Review, *Vol. XXIII, No. 3, Summer, 1979, pp. 295-303.*

PETER DOLLARD

[***Ever the Winds of Chance*** is a sequel] to Sandburg's well-received autobiography ***Always the Young Strangers***. . . . The earlier book is a gem, wonderfully evoking the feel of life in late 19th century small-town America. But Sandburg was a reviser and this book, only a first draft, reads more like an outline of his intentions than a completed work. Events and people are not fully developed; at times the story reads almost like a directory. It's too bad that Sandburg did not live to complete it.

Peter Dollard, in a review of "Ever the Winds of Chance," in Library Journal, *Vol. 108, No. 20, November 15, 1983, p. 2155.*

Jonathan Schell

1943-

American nonfiction writer.

Schell is a contemporary historian best known for *The Fate of the Earth* (1982), a widely read and controversial work about the danger of nuclear war and how to prevent it. Michael Useem called the book "both product and facilitator of the movement against nuclear arms," and Kai Erikson stated that it "is not only a statement. It is a summons, an alarm, a commotion." Schell contributes essays on contemporary political and military issues to *The New Yorker*; the material included in all of his books was first published in that magazine.

Schell began writing for *The New Yorker* during the Vietnam War era. *The Village of Ben Suc* (1967) and *The Military Half: An Account of Destruction in Quang Ngai and Quang Tin* (1968) are graphic descriptions of military maneuvers in which Vietnamese villages were destroyed. In both books, Schell presents eyewitness evidence of the arbitrary manner in which the war was administered and the unnecessary damage and cruelty suffered by civilians.

***The Time of Illusion* (1976) concerns Richard Nixon's presidency and the Watergate scandal and also, according to Robert Sherrill, addresses the question: "Why have our recent Presidents gone mad?" Schell theorizes that the President must now go to great lengths to control public opinion both in the United States and abroad in order to protect the country's image of strength and credibility. Failure to maintain this image could result in annihilating attacks on the United States.**

Schell's next two books focus on the nature of the nuclear threat and how it can be averted. *The Fate of the Earth* consists of three long essays. In "The Republic of Insects and Grasses" Schell hypothesizes that the immediate and long-range effects of a major nuclear exchange would combine to create an environment incapable of sustaining any form of life more complex than that of insects and grasses. The next essay, "The Second Death," is a philosophical and emotional reaction to the destruction which, Schell emphasizes, would involve not only our own deaths but the elimination of all future generations. Having established the necessity of avoiding a nuclear exchange, Schell argues in his third essay, "The Choice," that mutual deterrence cannot be relied upon to prevent nuclear war; only the abolition of sovereign states and the establishment of a world government could avert such a cataclysmic event. While most critics agreed that Schell had performed an invaluable service by forcing readers to face the potential consequences of nuclear warfare, many argued that the solution Schell proposes in "The Choice" is infeasible and a product of utopian thinking.

In *The Abolition* (1984) Schell suggests "a way of abolishing nuclear weapons that does not require us to found a world government, which the world shows virtually no interest in founding." He proposes that the capacity to build nuclear weapons could itself be sufficient to deter a nuclear exchange and that the weapons now in existence should be abolished. Critics were also skeptical of this idea.

(See also *Contemporary Authors*, Vols. 73-76 and *Contemporary Authors New Revision Series*, Vol. 12.)

JOHN MECKLIN

In this relentlessly exacerbating book [**"The Village of Ben Suc"**], a brilliant 24-year-old Harvard post-graduate student has registered a stinging indictment on the performance of his own generation in Vietnam. The author, Jonathan Schell, visited Vietnam only briefly, but he has nevertheless produced one of the most disturbing books yet published on American errors and stupidities in dealing with the Vietnamese people. The book is also seeded, however, with editorial booby traps, some of which reflect the author's inexperience, others savagely deliberate and altogether reprehensible. . . .

[The] book uses the effective journalistic device of detailed reportage of one event in a complex situation to communicate the meaning of the whole. The event that Schell chose was the American seizure and forced evacuation last January of Ben Suc, a village of 1,500 population 30 miles northeast of Saigon, on the edge of a Vietcong redoubt called the Iron Triangle. . . .

Schell was visiting Vietnam at the time, en route home from a year of study in Tokyo, and arranged to be aboard one of the helicopters that made the assault on Ben Suc. His account of what happened is written with a skill that many a veteran war reporter will envy, eloquently sensitive, subtly clothed in an aura of detachment, understated, extraordinarily persuasive. Schell clearly believes that almost everything the Americans did at Ben Suc was wrong, or even criminal, but he shrewdly avoids saying so himself, leading the reader to a slow-burn reaction, culminating perhaps in violent disgust as the enormity of Schell's picture begins to sink in.

Much of Schell's indictment, moreover, is justified, accurate and overdue. His book is one of the few major efforts thus far to assess United States conduct of the vital yet little-understood struggle to wrest control of the peasants from the Vietcong—as distinguished from the endless debate on whether we should be there at all. . . .

If **"The Village of Ben Suc"** must be rated high as an indictment, it must also be labeled as slanted journalism, mainly because of its multitudinous sins of omission. Its central theme that initially the people of Ben Suc were badly handled is certainly true, but Schell ignores the fact that the definitive test of the operation would be the long-term fate of the resettled population. . . . The book makes no effort at all to relate the performance at Ben Suc to the monstrous handicaps that plague the United States effort in Vietnam. . . .

Whether by intent or ignorance, Schell occasionally is shamefully unfair. Discussing United States propaganda, for example, he implies that "scare" leaflets are aimed at the peasants, threatening them with horrible deaths, despite the fact that the samples he cites plainly were targeted exclusively at armed Communist guerrillas. His suggestion that the Vietnamese regularly feed American rice to their pigs is just plain wrong. . . .

Sometimes Schell also stoops to insult, weakening the overall impression of commendable restraint. His self-righteous remark that one American lieutenant colonel, whose crime apparently was too much enthusiasm, behaved like a boys-camp counselor betrays some of the flavor of a teen-age hippie sneering at adult squares.

Ruefully, this reviewer is compelled to recommend **"The Village of Ben Suc."** It should be required reading in the Pentagon, not because it might convert some of the people there into doves (as Schell presumably would like), but because of its rare pinpointing of critical areas where the United States could be doing a better job in Vietnam. It should be read with the caveat that it tells only a small part of the story, but it nevertheless performs a public service in suggesting how poorly American military commanders—even today, 13 years after Dienbienphu—understand the nature of Asian guerrilla warfare.

John Mecklin, "Moving Day in Vietnam," in The New York Times Book Review, *October 29, 1967, p. 3.*

CHARLES A. HOGAN

Well written, vivid, poignant, ***The Village of Ben Suc*** . . . is guaranteed to turn hawks into doves. Jonathan Schell purports to describe operation "Cedar Falls" in Vietnam in January 1967. A jungle area of Viet Cong infiltration is scheduled to be cleared of people, villages, and enemy paths. . . . The author accompanies the entire operation. . . .

The officers and men, Vietnamese and Americans, sound real. Names and home towns of Americans are given. The style is crisp and deadpan. Suddenly one is jolted. This can't be history. It is a parody of military stupidity, bungling, and cruelty. The Americans believe they understand what they are doing and why. But they do not, and their views of their mission and of the Vietnamese are contradictory, uninformed, and calculated to inspire eternal hate. The Vietnamese look ridiculous. The process of separating safe from enemy villagers is haphazard. Since anything that moves is shot at, the loss of civilian lives is large. The effect of this upon the living—Americans and the surviving locals—is appalling. No victory will now permit the redemption of these embittered people. They are sullen. And they are furious. The remedy makes the disease incurable.

Then I remembered visiting Lidice, the site of the Czech village which Hitler considered to be unreliable. It was Carthagized with German thoroughness and is now open fields. It is eloquent. I wondered if Mr. Schell hadn't written an allegory of the destruction of a people.

Charles A. Hogan, "Another Lidice," in Saturday Review, *Vol. L. No. 44, November 4, 1967, p. 46.*

JOHN DILLIN

[***The Village of Ben Suc***] holds a valuable lode of information about one brief period of the Vietnam war. Yet for all its detail, it is sadly incomplete. . . .

Along with several other writers, Jonathan Schell accompanied the operation [code-named "Cedar Falls"] from the beginning. He swooped into Ben Suc with the first 60 helicopters on the initial surprise raid. He watched the village taken, the people forcibly removed, the houses burned, bulldozed, and bombed. The author's style is simple reporting. He lets the events speak. The result is a mild criticism of the American and South Vietnamese roles.

Mr. Schell begins by outlining the sweeping goals of the American battle commander. Then he goes to Ben Suc, to other villages, and to the refugee camp to see what the plans meant on the ground. . . .

The war becomes through Mr. Schell's eyes a bitter, personal, and meaningless thing.

Unfortunately, he fails to tie it all together. Although he has seen more of this operation than perhaps any other reporter, he draws no conclusions.

Cedar Falls was the first—and one of the few—"super operations" of the war. It was followed by an even larger, 45,000-man effort against War Zone C. . . .

It would have been useful to know Mr. Schell's conclusions about the value of these massive and expensive American efforts. . . .

John Dillin, "The War in One Small Village," in The Christian Science Monitor, *December 2, 1967, p. 13.*

HAL DAREFF

In Vietnam the United States fights a war on two fronts. On one it faces the enemy, on the other it confronts its own conscience. It is to the American conscience and the ideals that nurture and sustain it that [***The Military Half: An Account of Destruction in Quang Ngai and Quang Tin*** really addresses itself]. (p. 26)

The human tragedies born of escalation and its concomitant strategy of search-and-destroy come grimly to life in ***The Military Half,*** a new book by Jonathan Schell. The title refers to the antithetical duality inherent in our Vietnam policy. The Americans take care of the military half—fixing and killing the enemy. The GVN [Government of South Vietnam] takes care of the civilian half—pacifying and rebuilding the villages sanitized by the U.S. juggernaut. Or, at least, that's the theory.

In ***The Military Half*** [Schell] follows the destructive path of Task Force Oregon as it moves scythelike through Quang Ngai and Quang Tin, two provinces in central Vietnam said to be infested with main force units of the Vietcong and the North Vietnamese army. His report of what he saw and experienced confirms that in certain parts of South Vietnam we have, by the indiscriminate use of our enormous fire-power, virtually destroyed entire regions that were once inhabited by large peasant populations. The destruction was not planned; it just happened, an official told Schell, as "a side effect of hunting the enemy."

In this kind of reportage . . . effects are achieved by sharp observations and a piling on of selective detail. . . . [Schell] makes no comments and passes no judgments. The facts speak for themselves. . . .

Schell witnessed the damage, for the most part, while flying over the blasted landscape with pilots of the Forward Air Control (FAC), whose job it is to spot targets for air strikes and artillery fire. His portraits of individual pilots and soldiers, though casual, are sharply etched and sadly revealing. To most Americans, as one private put it, the Vietnamese are people from "a different planet." The war is impersonal and so, too, are its horrors. Schell records it just as impersonally, thus magnifying the horror. We know how he really feels, however. In his one personal note at the beginning of the book he tells the reader that he is opposed to the war and that he "could only feel sorrow for what they [the American forces] were asked to do and what they did."

Vietnam, the most tragic of our wars, has placed a heavy burden on the American conscience. (p. 27)

Hal Dareff, "Uphill Fight for the 'Other War'," in Saturday Review, *Vol. LI, No. 28, July 13, 1968, pp. 26-7.*

JONATHAN MIRSKY

Americans opposed to the war in Vietnam find themselves prey to a pair of conflicting emotions, one providing hope, the other leading to despair.

Our hope is that since the Vietnamese freed themselves from the Chinese (more than once), the Mongols, the Japanese and the French, ultimately they will persuade the Americans to leave. . . .

But we lurch back into sick despair when we see the refugees, the dead, the wounded, the orphaned, the destroyed, the gassed, the napalmed, the bombed—all the results of a technological genius turned insane. It may be that the Vietnamese will not survive physically, that by the time *we* get fed up with them, *they* may be dead. (p. 88)

One's fears are sharpened to the point of agony by Jonathan Schell, first in his ***The Village of Ben Suc*** . . . , and now in ***The Military Half***. . . . I know no book which has made me angrier and more ashamed. If upon finishing it one still says only "war is hell" one's soul may be in mortal danger. Putting Dr. Spock, Father Berrigan and hundreds of anonymous draft refusers in prison for protesting the crimes described by Jonathan Schell is an act of social perversion. (p. 90)

When Jonathan Schell published ***The Village of Ben Suc*** some reviewers twisted madly, attempting to explain away the destruction of a village of 3,800 as an unfortunate but probably *isolated* incident. . . . At the end of ***The Military Half*** Schell describes the elimination of the coastal village of Tuyet Diem, and the transportation of its 1,600 inhabitants. By this time our outrage has been overstrained by the endless killing and burning. (p. 91)

Jonathan Mirsky, "The Root of Resistance," in The Nation, *Vol. 207, No. 3, August 5, 1968, pp. 88, 90-1.**

PETER S. PRESCOTT

The problems posed by Watergate appear to have ended as they began, with intelligent citizens paying them little mind. . . . Jonathan Schell's premise [in ***The Time of Illusion***] seems to be that the details have been published and will be published again. His purpose now is to find a pattern among selected facts, to write as a historian, and if history yields to polemic, to a warning that we haven't solved our problems at all, then histories have served honorably as polemics and warnings before.

Schell argues that Nixon's Administration developed "a new form of rule, in which images were given precedence over substance in every phase of government." In short, by using the resources of the Presidency, Nixon realized that he could control what people thought of his performance and he therefore acted to "compose scenes rather than to solve real problems." . . .

According to Schell, when problems beset his Presidency, Nixon perceived all opposition, foreign and domestic, as part of a unified conspiracy against Presidential authority. It is Schell's thesis that to counter this imaginary threat, Nixon set out to take over the entire Federal government, to assume a dictator's powers, to "make war against Americans." . . .

And all of this illusion, Schell tells us, came about in an attempt to preserve a greater illusion still: that of America's "credibility" with the rest of the world. According to Schell's credibility theory, American leaders since Kennedy have resolved that we must maintain the *appearance* of great power and demonstrate our appetite to use power abroad, if we are to avoid nuclear disaster with Russia. . . .

Schell's provocative book is an argumentative essay set out as if it were historical recapitulation. Like most arguments, it is overlong, repetitious, ill organized and intemperate, which is not to say that it is not entirely correct. Schell's graceful sentences nearly mitigate the rage with which he writes; his ironic juxtapositions nearly persuade me to accept his argument as fact. And yet his assumption of insidious design calls for more evidence. Schell neglects, I think, the muddle factor in government, the ad hoc stupidity and random criminality of Nixon and his friends. Purposeless perversity is a human constant; that Nixon was the vortex of so much of it is alarming, but perhaps not proof of so grand a conspiracy as Schell construes. Never mind. Schell's book is a genuine chiller, if only because it reminds us of how far Nixon succeeded in dismantling our government and Constitution before Watergate, before he was re-elected by a landslide, and how eagerly Americans cheered him on.

Peter S. Prescott, "Presidential Deceit," in Newsweek, *Vol. LXXXVII, No. 2, January 12, 1976, p. 65.*

ROBERT SHERRILL

[In **"The Time of Illusion"** Jonathan Schell] confronts a question long overdue an answer: why have our recent Presidents gone mad? Schell is much too timid about raising the question, bringing it up very late in the book and then using such phrases as "apparent dementia" and "states of something like madness," but at least he does have the courage to deal seriously and openly, as no other writer has done, with what many commonfolk sensed all along—that at the very top of our democratic machinery a great many screws have been loose in recent years.

Schell concludes that their madness derives from a problem too burdensome for the human mind in the atomic age: "For the advent of nuclear weapons has done nothing less than place the President in a radically new relation to the whole of human reality. He, along with whoever is responsible in the Soviet Union, has become the hinge of human existence, the fulcrum of the world. . . ."

To me, that is not a sufficient explanation. Dwight Eisenhower had the same responsibilities—and had them in spades, because he was in the White House in the days when the balance of terror was still wobbly—but he was, as Presidents go, the soul of stability and sanity.

Perhaps in anticipation of this quibble, Schell arbitrarily has his theory take effect as of the end of the Eisenhower era, when military strategists generally conceded that since an atomic war could not be fought between the great powers without mutual destruction, the threat of an atomic attack was no longer credible. So atomic weapons were relegated to the place of spears in Wagnerian opera. Henceforth our toughness—or our "will" or our "credibility"—would be tested by our willingness to engage an enemy at a less than nuclear level, in "local wars." . . .

Since the Doctrine of Credibility at the non-nuclear level depends as much on the verve and spirit and support of the folks at home as it does on front-line action, says Schell, Nixon quite logically saw the anti-war dissenters as part of the enemy forces, for they shattered the image of national will to fight. . . . (p. 1)

It is a clever and persuasive exposition of the excuse Nixon may have given himself for treating some Americans as literal enemies of, and traitors to, the Republicans' Republic. (pp. 1-2)

"It almost seemed," says Schell, with notable understatement, "that the two personae of the President's public self were engaged in a debate." Schell's careful reconstruction of the convoluted chaos and frenzied contradictions of the Nixon years, his portrayal of this strange isolated creature who played with the world like Captain Queeg played with steelies, is not merely fascinating; it is inspired. One cannot shuffle along with Schell down those dark Nixonian corridors and hear the mindless chatter coming out of those shadowed rooms without finally feeling the hair at the back of the neck begin to twitch.

The splendor of **"The Time of Illusion"** does not come from Schell's development of his atomic theory of why Presidents become unhinged but from his meticulous and thoughtful reconstruction of the Nixon years, with an occasional judgment—usually wry, gracefully oblique, and humane—thrown in for mortar.

He performs great services by reminding us that we are dealing here with cruel child-men, who like to play deadly games while calling each other code names such as Fat Jack and Sedan Chair I and Ruby II; by likening the staged incidents of the campaign of 1972 (the phony Muskie letter, for example) to the staged incidents by which the Nazis came to power (the Reichstag Fire, for example); by evoking the horrible callousness of power. . . .

And yet Schell may at times be a bit too relentless in his pursuit of Nixon. His standards of open diplomacy are such as to make Nixon seem a sneak simply because he didn't tell us he was arranging a trip to China. His standards of campaign purity make the G.O.P. seem ratty for using Wallace to divide the Democrats—which strikes me as a perfectly legitimate political maneuver, if the Democrats are vulnerable to it. . . .

The Nixon years were bad enough without overdramatizing them, as Schell sometimes does. Writing of the national mood that developed from the Kent State killings, from Vice President Agnew's back alley outbursts, from the Cambodian invasion, and from Nixon's whoop-dee-doo rhetoric, Schell gets a bit walleyed as he declares that "the nation seemed, for a moment, to be spinning out of control, perhaps irrecoverably." He likes to make the battle more dramatic by suggesting that Nixon and His Gang were opposing everyone else. Referring to the Cambodian invasion and Nixon's defense of it, Schell writes, "Now, in effect, Americans were having their first clear look at the man their President had become in his fifteen months in the White House. The shock was severe." Uh huh—so "severe" that they re-elected him in 1972, a development Schell never is quite able to adjust the rest of his analysis to. One moment he tells us that "the country had rejected" the war and the next moment he is telling us of hardhats and businessmen physically assaulting anti-war demonstrators; one comes to suspect, perhaps unfairly, that "the nation" to Schell is the kind of people who read The New Yorker.

He does acknowledge that Nixon simply picked up the mistakes of Kennedy and Johnson, but he goes on to create a Nixon who is singularly evil. In this respect **"The Time of Illusion"** may be too finely tuned. One tends, in reading it, to forget all the other rotters who preceded him to the White House. So it might be wise to keep at hand some other writers' judgments of other Administrations. . . .

However justifiably Schell treats them with scorn, the fact is that Nixon's hyperbolic patriotism and garrulous bellicosity and itchy piety are pretty standard for our Presidents. After U.S. troops bombarded Vera Cruz in 1914, President Wilson proclaimed that "the United States has gone to Mexico to serve mankind." Remember that as you read **"The Time for Illusion."** Remember, too, that the defects so excellently written about by Schell were noted generically by John Adams a long time ago: "Power always thinks it has a great soul and vast views beyond the comprehension of the weak and that it is doing God's service when it is violating all His laws." The atomic bomb isn't to blame for the madness of machismo; it's power itself that drives so many Presidents balmy, and it's a miracle that more of them haven't led us into the straits of the Johnson-Nixon years. (p. 2)

Robert Sherrill, in a review of "The Time of Illusion," in The New York Times Book Review, *January 18, 1976, pp. 1-2.*

JOHN H. SCHAAR

The last ten years or so have surely been the most bewildering in American history. During that time the nation seemed to become a stranger to itself—unsure of its own purposes, divided and angry, its projects and hopes reduced to confusion. (p. 21)

Even now, when much is known that was then obscure, the feeling is widespread that the events of those years still defy understanding. In fair part, that is due to the fact that the information necessary to an understanding has appeared in bits and pieces, often long separated in time from the relevant events, and frequently couched in obscure phrasings. This, added to deliberate deception, concealment, and manipulation, has made it supremely difficult to assemble the fragments into a coherent whole.

That is the first job of interpretation—to make the fragmentary record whole, so that memory and mind might have a coherent experience to work on. After that, one can move forward to the second task of interpretation—to compose a theory, or at least some systematic thoughts, on the nature and causes of the basic and enduring crisis of our time, of which the Nixon administration was a part.

These are the tasks Jonathan Schell takes up in ***The Time of Illusion.*** He completes both admirably. Schell's book offers the most coherent reading we have of the Nixon years. The "record" of those years actually consists of four parts. First, the administration's own presentation of itself to the public.

This part of the record was systematically manipulated to show the administration in the best light—defender of peace, protector of law and liberty—and its enemies in the worst light. It had little to do with truth. Second, there was the record as presented on television and in the press. This record was fuller than the first one, but it was largely reflexive—dependent upon the first record—for the administration has enormous power to set the agenda of the mass media. Next, there were the events themselves—troop withdrawals, judicial nominations, legislative proposals, and the like. But events do not come to us bearing their own meanings. They must be interpreted, and this is done largely by the first two records, with all their distortions and partialities. Finally, there is the record of the administration's secret thoughts and covert activities, which became public only as the administration itself was coming to an end.

Schell has assembled these disparate records into a coherent composition—a thing that was impossible during the life of the regime itself. He has brought together the underground and the surface streams of American history during the Nixon years, connected discrete particles of information from a variety of sources and times, and established the chronology of words and deeds. The result is a work of great force. Reading this book is like "seeing" for the first time events which, when they happened, struck one as absurd and bizarre. This book brings order to whirl.

But to find a pattern is still not necessarily to have a meaning. What is the key to the pattern? What are the causes and origins of the political disorders of the recent period? In addressing this question, Schell makes his boldest and most thoughtful proposals. . . .

I opened this review by noting that we have largely agreed to forget the recent past. . . .

But the peril of blocking out the recent past—Vietnam, and the Johnson-Kissinger-Nixon years—is exactly that that past *is* our present and our most probable future. The burden of nuclear weapons is ours. . . .

Hence, it is important that we try to salvage from the recent past whatever can be learned from it. Jonathan Schell turns to that task in the superb concluding section of his book. (p. 22)

It is clear now that the strategic doctrine which has guided our policies during recent years is a catastrophic failure. It is equally clear that this nation is not facing up to that failure. The costs of that evasion might well exceed even the costs of the recent catastrophe, for every one of the realities—and, above all, the reality of nuclear weapons—underlying the ruinous experiences of the Vietnam years is still present. As Schell says in the final lines of his excellent book, the questions raised by those realities are unprecedented, boundless, unanswered, and "wholly and lastingly ours." (p. 24)

John H. Schaar, "The American Amnesia," in The New York Review of Books, *Vol. XXIII, No. 11, June 24, 1976, pp. 21-2, 24.**

BRUCE MANUEL

"The Fate of the Earth" is a book I'm urging everyone I know to read—not maybe, not sometime, but without fail, now. . . .

[This] earnest, compassionate study of nuclear weapons transcends the ordinary measures of literary merit to become an event of global significance. . . .

The case Schell lays before us suggests that this subject deserves our prayers and our most persistent and conscientious efforts at solution. For a solution, he predicts, will demand a revolutionary new recognition of the oneness and interdependency of life on earth, the unworkability of war as an adjunct to diplomacy, and the need of a new political structure to replace our system of sovereign states—immense challenges, but ones Schell feels can be met.

The common sense of his appeal . . . cuts through our distraction and apathy. It could kindle the public sentiment needed to slow or halt the steady buildup of doomsday devices. . . .

[No] other nuclear book speaks as clearly or as sensitively to the layman, or encompasses the cultural, moral, and spiritual as well as the technological and political considerations that Schell's does.

Of course, we don't need any book to tell us that the possibility of nuclear war—intentional or accidental—confronts us daily. We have only to keep up with the news. Although we don't like to think about it, we also realize there would be no "winner" in a large-scale nuclear exchange, both sides would experience devastation unparalleled in history.

But can we really appreciate what that means? How many people, for instance, would survive? Would shelters or evacuation help? What would we find when—and if—we climbed out of our bunkers after an attack? And how much time would our society need to recover?

These questions have been debated ever since the impact of the A-bomb was perceived, but too much of the discussion suffers from the hermetic quality Schell finds in military and "think tank" studies. . . .

In the first of the book's three sections, Schell explores the basic questions from the standpoint of an intelligent, inquisitive, and sensitive journalist. Drawn on five years of research and interviews with prominent scientists, his conclusions are far from reassuring. (p. B1)

Schell's ultimate conclusion is that a large-scale nuclear exchange could result in the extinction of mankind. Not all scientists would agree. . . . In fact, no one knows for sure. But the consensus seems to be that significant use of the weapons on hand would certainly destroy civilization as we know it.

Part 2 of Schell's book deals with human values, the meaning of possible extinction, and the differences between a catastrophe like the Nazi Holocaust and the potential loss of the entire human species. Schell also considers the shadow cast by the nuclear threat on our daily lives. (pp. B1, B4)

In Part 3, Schell examines the choices we face, if we're to lessen or remove the nuclear threat. He stops short of proposing any political solution of his own but suggests that the task of finding one needs to be put at the top of mankind's agenda. . . .

Must the world live indefinitely under this threat? Schell doesn't think so. We can unmake nuclear weapons, he says, and we can fashion a new system to replace national sovereignty. But to do so depends on all of us. "Social revolutions . . . usually cannot occur unless they are widely understood and supported by the public."

Some critics have faulted the book for being hard to follow, or merely belaboring the obvious, or betraying an utter lack of sophistication.

These criticisms are unwarranted. Though at times philosophical and repetitive, the book certainly won't overtax the powers of ordinary readers. The latter charges are grossly unfair, if one assumes that policy statements amount to more than posturing and that world leaders would indeed use their weapons if the situation became dire enough. In this case, the public needs to appreciate the magnitude of the choices and sacrifices involved and become more thoughtfully and vocally engaged in arms-limitation considerations. And this is a book that speaks to the public. . . .

We owe Schell a debt of gratitude for launching a public debate that is long overdue and for which we all may be better prepared now than we were 30 years ago. This book will have a special place on my shelf—or rather not on the shelf, but in the hands of anyone I can persuade to read it. (p. B4)

Bruce Manuel, in "Countering the A-Bomb Threat," in The Christian Science Monitor, *April 9, 1982, pp. B1, B4.*

KAI ERIKSON

[**"The Fate of the Earth"**] is a work of enormous force. There are moments when it seems to hurtle, almost out of control, across an extraordinary range of fact and thought. But in the end, it accomplishes what no other work has managed to do in the 37 years of the nuclear age. It compels us—and compel *is* the right word—to confront head on the nuclear peril in which we all find ourselves. . . .

In some regards, it is tempting to treat Jonathan Schell's achievement as an event of profound historical moment rather than as a book on some publisher's spring list.

For one thing, the volume consists (though not quite word for word) of three long articles, which appeared serially in The New Yorker a few months ago. They are the reflections of a person of commanding gifts who has been thinking hard about nuclear realities for many years. The articles have an obvious integrity when gathered together into a single volume, but they are so different in temper and in reach that they should probably be read as separate essays—with pauses for thought in between—rather than as continuing chapters in a book.

Moreover, Schell's language sometimes stretches well beyond the immediate requirements of the argument. He shares a problem with everyone who undertakes to write about the nuclear peril. How do you use ordinary vocabularies to describe something so immense and so absurd as the deaths of, say, 100 million persons? How do you talk sensibly about a horror beyond comprehension? Readers, being human, do not generally like to contemplate such things. Writers who use words to try to punch their way through those protective layers of lethargy often find themselves speaking louder and louder, in the hope that the tone of their voices will convey an urgency that the words alone do not. The metaphors multiply, the adjectives become warmer, the tension rises. **"The Fate of the Earth,"** then, is not only a statement. It is a summons, an alarm, a commotion.

The first of the three essays, entitled **"A Republic of Insects and Grass,"** is a graphic description of the consequences of a nuclear holocaust. . . .

The second essay, called **"The Second Death,"** is more metaphysical in tone, and it may be the most troubling part of the larger work. It is repetitious. It strikes some very difficult psychological and conceptual chords. And if the few people to whom I talked about it turn out to be at all representative, it will move readers in different ways.

Schell's main point here, if I can do it justice, is that humankind would suffer two distinct deaths in the event of the kind of nuclear holocaust he has asked us to imagine—the slaughter of every living human being, for one thing, and the cancellation of all future generations, for another. . . .

This is an extremely difficult point for a writer to express simply (or for a reviewer to report fairly). Consequently, Schell's argument may seem a bit drawn out at times, but it is because he is circling a very large truth, searching for ways to approach it with a sensitivity and generosity that can only be called spiritual.

The final essay is called **"The Choice,"** and it is far and away the most prescriptive of the three. Schell does an absolutely remarkable job of describing the awkward logics that form the core of deterrence theory, and, in doing so, he may help many people to find a new way of envisaging and talking about nuclear arms. (p. 3)

Throughout the whole of this marvelous work, Schell is vulnerable to charges of an almost romantic simplicity of vision—a risk that he, a seasoned observer of the human scene, must have known he was taking. This may be the price one has to pay for the attempt to enlarge perspectives and to turn away from "crusted and hardened patterns of thought and feeling"; for the people who got there first have managed to establish patterns of language and meaning in which acceptance of the present state of affairs is known as "realistic" and efforts to imagine a safer world are known as "utopian."

Schell's almost plaintive argument that the world must learn how to reduce its investments in nationality and sovereignty, for example, has been said so often before that the sheer mention of it simply sounds naïve. . . .

It does need to be said again, though, and at any risk. Sovereignty *is* a major problem, not only because people can be persuaded to do reckless things in the name of "vital interests," but also because, as Erik H. Erikson has pointed out, people with a strong sense of nationality can come to treat human beings of another *place* as if they were of another *kind* . . . and thus not protected by what, in any other species, is a general inhibition against killing. . . .

In speaking as he does, Schell offers a way of approaching the nuclear issue that is the very antithesis of *Realpolitik;* to walk across those fields of argument with so little of the technical jargon and, above all, the studied cynicism with which the rest of us arm ourselves is an act of considerable courage. Albert Einstein once said that "the unleashed power of the atom has changed everything save our modes of thinking," but the kinds of conversation to which Schell now invites us will go a long way toward improving that situation. He petitions us (in Auden's words) to "look shining at / New styles of architecture, a change of heart." It is time to listen. It is time to speak. (p. 16)

Kai Erikson, "Horror Beyond Comprehension," in The New York Times Book Review, *April 11, 1982, pp. 3, 16.*

NEIL SCHMITZ

The strong point of Jonathan Schell's ***The Fate of the Earth*** is that it compels us to think about the present danger of nuclear war. Schell takes us straight into the discourse, appropriates the several languages (pure and applied) of the nuclear scientist, splits the atom, describes Hiroshima, gives us paradigms, statistics, scenarios and vistas, somberly calculates the "rough probabilities" of a nuclear holocaust and then draws us a picture of the consequences. (p. 529)

That we have allowed the "realists" to determine this discourse, promulgate nuclear policy, rationalize that catastrophe, Schell argues, is due in part to our own reluctance to think the issue through, to face this death of deaths. We, too, must think the Unthinkable, confront what has already been projected, the probable extinction of humankind, and then consider our "political responsibilities." (p. 530)

All this strong polemical work is achieved in the first section of the book, **"A Republic of Insects and Grass,"** and then something happens in Schell's treatise. A circumlocution appears, a soliloquy that deflects our critical attention from the systematic thinking of the Unthinkable—the hard discourse of the strategist and the expert—to a philosophical exploration of the Unthinkable as a condition in human language. As Schell laboriously explains why we should go on living and keep the common world intact and tidy for our children, I begin to lose touch with his prose. Here's Hannah Arendt, there's Hegel. I recognize this soft, foolish, solemn language as mine, the disarming parlance of the humanist, and I am embarrassed, a little, by the innocence of its rhetoric, its poignance. It does not speak to me. It speaks for me. To whom, then, is this middle essay on the value of life, **"The Second Death,"** addressed? Thanatos, and all his minions: the "realists," the "militarists," the "conservatives," the "upholders of the status quo," those who adhere to a "Newtonian politics in an Einsteinian world."

The fundamental problem, Schell repeatedly tells us, is the "politics of the day," the "world's political arrangements," the "system of independent, sovereign nation-states." All this must change: "Just as we have chosen to live in the system of sovereign states, we can choose to live in some other system." The abstraction of the argument at this point in the book is itself a mystification, the certain sign of an aversion. Having flushed us out from our anxiety about death and made us think the Unthinkable, the extinction of humankind, Schell then carefully guides us past the prickly understanding of how almost all of humankind is systematically excluded from deciding that momentous question. Here, it might be said, is a life anxiety more compelling than the death anxiety, the grim realization of who it is that has the fate of the earth by the throat. Schell's displacement of this anxiety, that Unthinkable, sets it freely afloat in his text.

If we are indeed to think as citizens of the world, then we must be sufficiently unrepressed to speak openly about the aggressive character of American nuclear policy. . . . It is [Schell's] intention to write apolitically about nuclear disarmament, to think above ideology, to make the broadest possible appeal; and to that end he restricts himself to the "physical extent, the human significance, and the practical dimensions of the nuclear predicament in which the whole world now finds itself." When Schell admits the political into his discussion, he generalizes it, globally disperses its meaning. Skeptical readers will perceive within that culpable system of independent, sovereign nation-states, the blank prospect of the basic problem, as Schell sees it, the preeminent nuclear power in that system, a bristling, imperial nation-state, the one that has determined the nuclear arms race from the beginning, and they will wonder about the reluctance to designate it in this text.

There is a reason for this dissembling. Schell doesn't wish to excite the paranoia of the American right with specific political analysis, with a precise remembering of history, nor does he want to alienate the "realists" by challenging their "defensive" posture, and yet this tactic of talking around American responsibility for the crisis leads him finally to an obfuscation of the nuclear peril. (pp. 530-31)

When Schell comes at last to the question of deterrence, of national sovereignty, in his peroration, **"The Choice,"** he attacks these terms as if they were logical problems, quirky syllogisms whose illogicality requires demonstration. The reasoning in these passages is keen, but the argument to which Schell refers—that one between the "sincere" proponents of nuclear deterrence and the crazy adherents of "military superiority"—is itself false, a screen. These terms, *deterrence, national sovereignty,* are masking terms, swollen with obvious duplicity, and not to be taken at face value. . . . What we need from Schell, who wishes to expose the danger of nuclear war, is a radical dismantling of the presuppositions of American nuclear policy.

The fate of the earth, after all, is still pretty much in certain American hands. They have the world by the throat. This is the Unspeakable that lurks within Schell's version of the Unthinkable. The concept of nuclear deterrence has always signified, with brutal simplicity, an American superiority in nuclear weaponry, a superiority that has been aggressively exercised in American foreign policy. When citizens of the world, especially those poor souls on the far side of the Iron Curtain, look at how America defines its national sovereignty, they are justly amazed and pardonably frightened, for this sovereignty comprises Western Europe, Latin America, most of Africa, the Middle East, the Persian Gulf and Southeast Asia. Within this sphere, the United States calculates its "vital interests," considers its options and devises its numerous plans. To the extent that Schell evades this particular interpretation of the world's problem, ***The Fate of the Earth*** is parochial in its vision, not at all disinterested, even self-serving. (p. 531)

Neil Schmitz, "Anxiety and Its Displacement," in The Nation, *Vol. 234, No. 17, May 1, 1982, pp. 529-31.*

ANTHONY RUDOLF

The Fate of the Earth is the most important and profound book on the nuclear predicament that I have read. Confronting head-on and heart-on the desperate nature of our plight, Schell has understood—in Shelley's words—that 'the great instrument of moral good is the imagination'. He has had the courage to deploy the full resource of his own imagination. It is up to the reader to do the same.

Jonathan Schell is a writer, not a specialist in any discipline, and his book is literature of a high order. It synthesises the political, military, ecological, moral, scientific, religious, artistic, psychological and philosophical dimensions of our hideous dilemma with modesty and rigour, authority and lucidity. He must have suffered mental and psychic agonies while researching his material, yet in the writing the harrowing and chilling details are somehow contained by the author's integrity, by his tact and respect for the reader.

Like an innocent man in a condemned cell, which is what and where author and reader are, Schell is at once humble and impassioned before the beauty of the world that we have received and for which we are responsible to our descendants. . . .

Schell is trying to get us to be the historians of the future, guardians of the generations that will be cancelled if ever we commit the ultimate crime. We must *imagine* that *we* are the deranged mother seeking out her burned child. Reading this book, you weep first, then despair and finally become fired to do something to prevent extinction, 'this human future which can never become a human present.' . . .

Sometimes it seems as though we are all living in the ghetto which sent away the man who had escaped from a camp and come home to warn them of their peril because they could not bring themselves to believe the incredible truth. Jonathan Schell is that man. The future is here already, the fire this time, unless the voice of reason is heeded. Now.

Anthony Rudolf, "Final Warning," in New Statesman, *Vol. 103, No. 2672, June 4, 1982, p. 21.*

SAMUEL McCRACKEN

Jonathan Schell believes that an ultimate nuclear holocaust would threaten the future of humanity, that humanity ought to have a future, and that someone ought to do something about the problem. A man who so challenged the conventional wisdom would formerly have been burnt at the stake, but in our enlightened time Mr. Schell is acclaimed a moral and political philosopher. . . .

[In ***The Fate of the Earth***] Mr. Schell demonstrates beyond peradventure that a final holocaust is a final holocaust. But the probability of such a holocaust is extremely remote. Launching thousands of large thermonuclear weapons is not part of, nor likely to become part of, the strategy of any state. It is extremely unlikely that any country could carry out such an attack, requiring flawless offense on one side and failed defense on the other.

Mr. Schell concedes the possibility of limited nuclear war, or no nuclear war at all, but argues that since a final holocaust is physically possible, and since its consequence could be the extinction of humanity, the risk posed by nuclear weapons is intolerable. . . . So there is no point in proving Mr. Schell an alarmist. He can be moved from his position only by a proof that nuclear war is literally impossible. That sort of argument no responsible critic can make about any physically possible event; thus Mr. Schell's argument by choice of terms defeats all refutation.

But his alarmism is worth a closer look. He deals, for example, with the effects of massive fallout, which develops only when a bomb is exploded at or near the surface. . . . Since fallout from many bombs exploded at ground level would threaten even the "victor" in a nuclear war, the probability of such explosions is vanishingly remote. (p. 904)

Mr. Schell holds the risk of extinction intolerable because it constitutes a war against our posterity, billions of people whom we must allow to exist. It is refreshing to find such concern for posterity, but there is no indication that Mr. Schell has followed the logic of his argument, which is as persuasive against abortion and indeed contraception as it is against nuclear deterrence.

Mr. Schell's conclusion is that the prospect of human extinction is so terrible that we must abolish national sovereignty. . . .

What he wants seems to be a vague world government unimpeded by national sovereignty, a quality whose main function, in Mr. Schell's view, seems to be to guarantee passports of a certain color and national anthems at the Olympics. That sovereignty is instrumental to freedom does not seem to have occurred to him. But freedom does not seem to concern him much.

He leaves the practicalities of abolishing national sovereignty to others. The task raises appalling difficulties. The world is on a nationalist jag that must give pause to the fiercest world federalist. . . .

The only plausible world government today is an empire governed by a ferociously efficient and oppressive tyranny. The Soviet empire adumbrates such a world government, and within it there is no danger of nuclear war because none of its subject states has the sovereignty necessary for nuclear arms. . . .

Mr. Schell, having labored mountainously, has brought forth a mouse squeaking, "Better red than dead." Although many of those who mouth that slogan probably add under their breath, "better red anyhow," he shows no such preference. . . . But his assumptions compel the conclusion that if the abolition of sovereignty required the resurrection of the firm of Stalin & Hitler, they would be an improvement over the status quo. . . .

Needless to say, ***The Fate of the Earth*** is the bible of the antinuclear movement. . . . Mr. Schell's immediate proposals please everyone: he is for a freeze and also for sharp reductions in strategic arms. He supports the policies of President Reagan and his critics alike.

The danger is that Mr. Schell's followers may triumph and bring about a freeze that by making present inequities permanent will prove destabilizing in the short run and in the long run productive of both redness and deadness. If this is to be our future, it will be because a collapse in intellectual standards has allowed someone like Jonathan Schell to obscure a simple truth: that everyone is opposed to nuclear war and that the crucial debate is not about whether to have a nuclear war but about how best not to have one. By carrying on an unnecessary debate as to whether to have a nuclear war, Schell and others make difficult or impossible the far more important debate as to how not to have one. Objectively, as the Marxists say, they are supporting nuclear holocaust. (p. 905)

Samuel McCracken, "The Peace of the Grave," in National Review, *Vol. XXIV, No. 14, July 23, 1982, pp. 904-05.*

MICHAEL USEEM

Political movements require a defining document, a preamble for action. It is here that the principal values and animating concerns are articulated. Jonathan Schell's ***Fate of the Earth*** has become that statement for the burgeoning American movement to reduce the threat of nuclear war. Even as it first appeared in the fall of 1981 as a three-part series in *The New Yorker*, where Schell is a staff writer, this apocalyptic account was quickly and deservedly acclaimed as one of the most compelling documents of the antinuclear movement. Now in book form, Schell's treatment of our proximity to the "slippery slope over the nuclear abyss" will ultimately stand as a classic of the era.

The Fate of the Earth must be read as both product and facilitator of the movement against nuclear arms. As product, it does not offer a new investigation into the consequences of nuclear war. But it does draw together the forecasts of other analysts to reach a stark conclusion: a massive nuclear exchange between the United States and Soviet Union could well result in nothing short of complete human annihilation. . . .

That there can be no real survival is the central thesis of this book. The movement against nuclear war has been voicing this premise for some time, and here Schell's work is largely a product of the movement. Yet it is a work whose unrelenting and persuasive powers of argument make it of singular importance.

But the book is also a facilitator of the movement, for it allows no middle ground. "Two paths lie before us," writes Schell. "One leads to death, the other to life." . . . The choice is not war or peace, but peace or annihilation. (p. 610)

The special power of ***The Fate of the Earth*** is the establishment of a new way of seeing that alters political thinking. We live in an "Einsteinian" world but practice "Newtonian" politics. Schell's objective is to force a decisive break with the old politics, and in its place to create an attitude utterly rejecting of the traditional doctrines of deterrence and survivability. . . .

The book is facilitator of the movement in a second sense. The fate of the earth is not a matter of fate, but, Schell contends, a question of human will. Cognizance of our condition is the first step toward the mobilization of that will, and Schell properly asks why we have not earlier recognized our precarious perch on the brink of extinction. His answer becomes an understated but searing critique of the nuclear establishment. . . .

The Fate of the Earth, like so much of the current literature on the consequences of nuclear war, dwells at length on the physical effects but offers virtually no commentary on the social devastation. The latter is of no great moment if the earth becomes totally uninhabitable, and that is Schell's main point. Still, a portrait of the social condition of the survivors of a limited nuclear attack would have added to his ultimate objective, for they would be facing an existence with neither economy nor society. . . .

If the writing is at times repetitive and overstated, and if the final arguments are misdirected in their identification of the root causes and solutions to the nuclear arms race, ***The Fate of the Earth*** is nonetheless one of those books whose reading is required. It is the best single statement of the core values and vision of a political movement whose explosive expansion during the past several years is stunning and whose reshaping of American politics may be equally so. (p. 611)

Michael Useem, "Apocalypse Tomorrow," in Contemporary Sociology, *Vol. 11, No. 6, November, 1982, pp. 610-11.*

LORD ZUCKERMAN

[In] ***The Abolition,*** Schell addresses "the question of deliberate policy—specifically, the question of how we might abolish nuclear arms." . . .

Jonathan Schell's way is set out in the final . . . section of the book, headed **"A Deliberate Policy."** For those who might have been led to expect some shattering revelation, it will prove a sad letdown. Schell seems to move blindly in circles over ground with which he is unfamiliar but which, in fact, has been explored ceaselessly over the years. The answer with which he ends all but negates the noble sentiments that were expressed in his first book, and that are repeated in the first part of this one. The first step toward the goal of nuclear "abolition" has, we learn, already been taken. We cannot allow ourselves to be wrecked on the rocks of world government, so we shall necessarily continue to live in a state of nuclear deterrence.

According to Schell, the "most honest argument in favor of the possession of nuclear weapons . . . is that upholding liberty is worth the risk of extinction." Now our task is "to preserve the political stalemate—to freeze the status quo," at the same time as we "avert a nuclear holocaust." That is his solution. But whose status quo; who are "we" who will preserve the stalemate; how is that to be done?—all these are questions that the reader can ask. Schell provides no answers. All that he demands is that the superpowers should agree to abolish nuclear weapons, the abolition to "be enforced not by any world police force . . . but by each nation's knowledge that a breakdown of the agreement would be to no one's advantage. . . ."

There is no need to follow Schell further in his luxurious circumlocutions. His message is straight and clear: agree to agree, and in the meantime, don't fool around with the doomsday machine. Those who may have hoped that he was going to reveal the road to man's deliverance will be left high and dry, and I fear that the professionals who have been concerned over the past thirty years or so with the problem of reaching agreement will not find any new guidance in what he has to say. (p. 5)

Lord Zuckerman, "Nuclear Fantasies," in The New York Review of Books, *Vol. XXXI, No. 10, June 14, 1984, pp. 5-8, 10-11.**

PAUL BRACKEN

After offering one of the most searing visions of the results of a major nuclear exchange between the United States and the Soviet Union in his ***The Fate of the Earth,*** Jonathan Schell now offers his solution to the nuclear predicament. The way out, Schell argues, requires a deliberate national policy of abolishing nuclear weapons, not piecemeal arms reductions.

The Abolition spells out how American, Soviet, and all other nuclear weapons are to be banished from the world political landscape. The good news is that we are not required to institute a world government to attain this objective. The less cheery news is that . . . his proposals for abolishing these deadly weapons are simplistic, and hardly provocative.

The most notable concept in Schell's book is one which has already been advanced by several individuals. . . . Instead of emphasizing an offensive nuclear arms buildup, which if war ever comes will lead to untold slaughter, the superpowers should engage in a "defensive emphasis" strategy, building anti-ballistic missile systems coupled with a negotiated reduction in offensive force levels. With such a policy, deterrence would not depend on each nation's ability to destroy the other's population. . . .

Schell's vision for abolishing nuclear weapons does contain an additional agenda. He believes that a negotiated abolition of all nuclear weapons must *precede* the construction of strategic defenses. How this is to come about is unspecified, and since it is the core promise of ***The Abolition,*** the book falls far short of its promise. Details matter, yet we are sadly left with one more exhortation for our two nations to sit down to negotiate what they have been unable to negotiate for decades.

Conventional forces are also to be constrained by negotiation in the vision of ***The Abolition,*** yet again there is no detail or theory as to why this might occur. (p. 3)

At a deeper level still is Schell's concept of the complete nature of nuclear deterrence. Since the destruction accompanying a major deterrence failure is reckoned total, there are no goals worthy of these weapons. Schell describes the "total nature of deterrence," an all or nothing game in which the use of force is eventually given up as a means of settling international disputes. This might or might not be a worthy long-term objective for world order, but it does not describe the history of the last several decades. . . .

Interesting insights do arise in ***The Abolition,*** as in Schell's characterization of strategic analysts with their "martyred dignity" for being held in disrepute for volunteering to take up a necessary but painful burden that the rest of society will not face. The fact that Schell is an outsider looking at a (very small) community of insiders gives him a comparative advantage in description which he well exploits. And although ***The Abolition*** reemphasizes the role of strategic defense as a worthy topic of discussion, the path to abolishing nuclear weapons, or even reducing them for that matter, remains as uncharted as ever. (p. 10)

Paul Bracken, "Banning the Bomb: Easier Said Than Done," in Book World—The Washington Post, *June 17, 1984, pp. 3, 10.*

MARIA MARGARONIS

In ***The Fate of the Earth,*** Schell began with the assumption that since nuclear war could mean the end of the human race, we should behave as if it would, and went on to advocate peace through world government. [In ***The Abolition***], searching for a more realistic solution, he has rediscovered deterrence. . . .

Mesmerized by the bright light of doom, Schell is so eager to suspend politics to insure survival that he ignores the realities that make his "solution" impossible. Obviously it's in our long-term interests to abolish nuclear weapons, but it's in the short-term interests of those in power to keep them. Their purpose is not, as Schell argues, to defend national sovereignty but to cover intervention and preserve empires. Deterrence does not keep the peace but breaks it, by freezing the cold war and containing its conflagrations. Like part of the peace movement, Schell is fixated on the weapons and avoids discussions of global ambitions. The way out is not by embalming the "nuclear stalemate"—which he considers "viable and tolerable," at least until we can undertake the long task of solving the world's political and economic problems—but by dissolving it.

Of course, if you believe the world is likely to end tomorrow, Schell's argument is, if not realistic, at least appealing. Terror, as Schell says, inspires conservatism. . . . The theory of weaponless deterrence makes nuclear arms into a stern god who will keep us good by keeping us in fear. After all his thinking about the unthinkable, Jonathan Schell has truly learned to stop worrying and love the bomb. (p. 150)

Maria Margaronis, "'Little Boy' and After," in The Nation, *Vol. 239, No. 9, September 1, 1984, pp. 149-51.**

Ann Schlee

1934-

English novelist.

Schlee writes historical novels distinguished by their vivid evocation of time and place and by the elegance and clarity of their economical prose. Schlee's writing has been praised for its unobtrusive appropriateness. As John Mellors notes, her prose is "effortlessly graceful without being in any way precious, right always for its immediate purpose, whether that is narrative, dialogue or description."

Schlee began her career writing novels for young adults, many of which are based on events in nineteenth-century English history. While the historical accuracy and absorbing details of her settings are frequently noted, Schlee devotes equal attention to developing her characters. *The Guns of Darkness* (1973), which centers on the fall of Emperor Theodore of Abyssinia, is a study of excessive pride and paranoia as well as a historical account of a great man's decline into madness. Similarly, *Ask Me No Questions* (1976), based on a case of orphan abuse at a school outside of London, investigates human cruelty while simultaneously describing the maturation of the young narrator as she is exposed to suffering for the first time. With *The Vandal* (1979), Schlee departs from her typical Victorian setting to depict a future world in which a young boy is pitted against an uncompromising society. Like Schlee's historical works, this novel was praised for its powerful ambience and fully realized characters.

Schlee has also written novels for adults which combine an authentic nineteenth-century atmosphere with an exploration of the impact of Victorian culture on individual lives. In *Rhine Journey* (1981) and *The Proprietor* (1983), rigid social mores conflict with human impulses as characters struggle with suppressed emotional and sexual desires. *Rhine Journey* dramatizes the crisis of a middle-aged spinster confronting her need for independence from sexual and social constraints, and *The Proprietor* demonstrates how class consciousness and oppressive religious standards often prevented Victorians from fulfilling their desires for love and companionship. While neither book directly imitates the Victorian novel, each recreates the mood of an era through rich detail and precise language. Referring to *Rhine Journey,* one critic stated: "In its empathetic evocation of period, in its understanding of people enchained by piety and caste, in the bite and luminosity of its style, it is entirely mature, and a finished work of art."

(See also *Contemporary Authors,* Vol. 101.)

© *Jerry Bauer*

CHRISTOPHER WORDSWORTH

[*The Strangers*] is marvellously visual and the setting, the wind-battered Scillies during the Civil War, comes over with a Stevensonian tingle. Lady Melchett's husband is in France with his King; somewhere planted on Tresco are emergency funds for his family; Cromwell's fleet is standing off shore. There is a secret cave, a clue on a dead man's headstone, a turncoat garrison captain to gnaw at the reader's sympathies, a brawny fisherman to decoy Admiral Blake to a wrong landing, a boy-girl relationship that is affecting without mawkishness, historically authentic detail—the beautiful lady's teeth are discoloured, the islanders are anti-Roundhead for the good reason that they don't pay for their billets. The writing is exceptional. . . .

Christopher Wordsworth, "Costume and Cavalcade," in The Observer, *November 28, 1971, p. 35.**

BERYL ROBINSON

In April, 1651, Kate Nants' home on the island of Tresco, one of the Scilly Isles, became the scene of a frightening and dangerous adventure for her when a ship bound for France with Royalist refugees went aground on the rocks. Kate's fisherman-father, who had helped in the rescue, brought home two of the survivors—a gentlewoman and her son Lum, both near exhaustion. . . . The influence of the sea is ever present in this well-written historical adventure [*The Strangers*], as is the awareness of the bitter conflict between the Roundheads and the Royalists. The harsh and primitive life of the island folk is vividly re-created. The setting, action, and excitement of the story are suggested effectively in the line drawings. Although the events will be of particular interest to readers with a knowledge of the history of the period, this story of courage and loyalty is complete and satisfying in itself. (pp. 276-77)

Beryl Robinson, in a review of "The Strangers," in The Horn Book Magazine, *Vol. XLVIII, No. 3, June, 1972, pp. 276-77.*

MARY M. BURNS

Based on a little-known incident recorded in Lord Exmouth's description of the British fleet's bombardment of Algiers in 1816, the narrative [of ***The Consul's Daughter***] offers an interesting departure from the blood-and-bomb school of writing by presenting the event from the viewpoint of a fourteen-year-old girl. The sheltered, motherless daughter of the British Consul in Algiers, Ann McDonnel has been primarily concerned with coming to terms with adolescence and with her widower-father's second wife, Gerda, only two years Ann's senior and formerly her closest friend. . . . The heroine's unique situation, the exotic setting, and the delineation of post-Napoleonic British attitudes and ambitions are well-blended in the development of a credible narrative, which is most successful, perhaps, for achieving balance between the detailing of historical reality and the interpreting of an adolescent's reaction to that reality.

Mary M. Burns, in a review of "The Consul's Daughter," in The Horn Book Magazine, *Vol. XLVIII, No. 6, December, 1972, p. 601.*

STEPHEN VAUGHAN

The savage and exotic setting of ***The Guns of Darkness*** . . . comes over strongly as the tragic Emperor Theodore of Abyssinia disintegrates into fantasy and madness before cutting his own throat when Napier's relief force arrives at Magdala to free the frantic hostages. Based firmly on history, it is a convincing study of despotism and derangement, fiercely visual through the eyes of an Anglo-Abyssinian girl whose dealings with the brawny Swiss missionary forced to forge the Emperor's cannon make a fresh and moving little love story.

Stephen Vaughan, in a review of "The Guns of Darkness," in The Observer, *July 22, 1973, p. 32.*

J A CUDDON

Miss Schlee has received most enthusiastic notices for her two previous novels—***The Consul's Daughter*** and ***The Strangers,*** both of which, I thought, were exceptionally good novels of the historical fiction genre. Now we have ***The Guns of Darkness,*** which, like ***The Consul's Daughter,*** is set in the nineteenth century but somewhat later—1850's to 1860's. Basically it is a tragedy; an account of the downfall of the Abyssinian emperor Tewodros (Theodore) II, Negus Negusti, an heroic figure and personality of great gifts and abilities, who, through a combination of perverseness, stupidity and arrogance (almost a case of ***hubris***), brought about his own destruction and that of many others.

The story of these events is told by a girl called Louisa—the half-Abyssinian, half-English daughter of an Englishman named Bell who was a great warrior and a close friend of the emperor. The tale is based on historical fact, as the author points out in her note, and in particular on the march by British forces under the command of Sir Robert Namier to the stronghold of Magdala where the emperor lived, and where he held several Europeans prisoner. It is from the accounts written by these prisoners that Miss Schlee works out her narrative.

Major virtues of this very well written story are concentration, economy and selectivity. The author has compressed a great deal of action into a short space without ever becoming breathless or jerky. And all her characters are fully realised in dialogue and action. (pp. 104-05)

J A Cuddon, in a review of "The Guns of Darkness," in Books and Bookmen, *Vol. 19, No. 217, October, 1973, pp. 104-05.*

ZENA SUTHERLAND

[***The Guns of Darkness***], told by a young girl, Louisa, whose mother was Ethiopian and whose father was British, is set in Ethiopia in the middle of the 19th century and has historical basis. Its central figure is the Emperor Tewodros, whose ability and energy as a leader of his people and a reformer had, at the time of this story, been replaced by suspicion and egomania. . . . While Louisa is a useful figure as an observer (her father and her brother-in-law did exist; Louisa is a conjectural figure) she is so incidental that her love story assumes little importance. However, as a vivid recreation of a period and place with which few readers will be familiar, the book is strong, and the characterization of the once-mighty Emperor is excellent.

Zena Sutherland, in a review of "The Guns of Darkness," in Bulletin of the Center for Children's Books, *Vol. 28, No. 2, October, 1974, p. 36.*

THE JUNIOR BOOKSHELF

[In ***Desert Drum,*** three] sheep have been stolen, and the blame must attach to Ahmed. The boy creeps away from the tribe at night, setting out on his camel to find the missing sheep. It is a disheartening business: only one remains, barely alive. With the dying animal across his camel Ahmed, lost and frightened, makes for the shelter of a cave. With one last effort he strikes the bush outside to scare the waiting vultures which have settled there, and finds stuck in it the powerful gong whose loss has brought bad luck to his tribe.

It is a simple but pleasant story, with the camel herders arriving, like the seventh cavalry, to rescue Ahmed in the nick of time. (pp. 144-45)

A review of "Desert Drum," in The Junior Bookshelf, *Vol. 42, No. 3, June, 1978, pp. 144-45.*

SUSAN OCHSHORN

Identity crises are a dime a dozen in the pages of first novels. Lest we forget how poignant they can be, Ann Schlee has given us [in ***Rhine Journey***] a small but well-crafted portrait of a 19th-century British woman in the midst of a life change. . . .

As a young girl [Charlotte] lived in the house of her brother Charles, a domineering, humorless pastor whom she faithfully served until he banished her for falling in love with an unsuitable man. Reunited with Charles and his family on a steamboat cruise along the Rhine some 20 years later, Charlotte is plunged into frightening disequilibrium after encountering a passenger who reminds her momentarily of her old lost love. . . .

Schlee's juxtaposition of Charlotte's deteriorating defenses with the institutionalized repression of Prussia in 1851 is somewhat labored, as is the contrived similarity between her own adolescent love affair and her niece's infatuation with a Prussian soldier. Schlee's taut, elegant prose is ample compensation for the plot's lack of subtlety. It carries us easily through the pathways of Charlotte's mind as she projects dormant erotic fantasies upon this unsuspecting fellow sojourner, and, ultimately, reclaims for herself the deed for an identity—if not a house—of her own. ***Rhine Journey*** is a fine adult debut from this author of children's books.

Susan Ochshorn, in a review of "Rhine Journey," in Saturday Review, *Vol. 8, No. 1, January, 1981, p. 73.*

THE NEW YORKER

[In **"Rhine Journey"**, it] is the summer of 1851, and an English family is on a sedate holiday excursion up the Rhine—a rigidly masterful Anglican clergyman, his half-invalid wife, their pretty seventeen-year-old daughter, and his forty-year-old spinster sister, Charlotte. Charlotte, who has long lived as her brother's adoring dependent, has recently come into a small legacy, and she is ashamed to find herself thinking of a life of her own and frightened by what she feels is rebellion. The daughter, too, has her forbidden fantasies—an eagerness for a decorous taste of romance. . . . The undercurrents of repressed emotions gently stir and shift, there are minute but violent changes. . . . In its empathic evocation of period, in its understanding of people enchained by piety and caste, in the bite and luminosity of its style, [**"Rhine Journey"**] is entirely mature, and a finished work of art. (pp. 111-12)

A review of "Rhine Journey," in The New Yorker, *Vol. LVI, No. 49, January 26, 1981, pp. 111-12.*

ANTHONY THWAITE

It has been argued, and I think convincingly, that a good deal of the kind of talent in narrative, character, and indeed human concern, that 75 or a hundred years ago would have gone into adult novels today goes into children's books. . . .

The gifts that keep a child alert to and enthralled by what he or she reads can be transferable to the grown-up reader; and the good writer jumps boundaries.

Ann Schlee has for some years had a high reputation as a children's novelist. ***Rhine Journey*** is her first novel for adults, and it's a marvellous book. . . .

[Events] don't at all follow the course one expects. There is no point in outlining the surprising—and yet, so it seems in the end, inevitable—turns of the plot. What matters is that Ann Schlee has created a haunting, fastidiously delicate and yet plainly tough story which escapes any accusation of being a pastiche Victorian piece, though its sense of time, place and tone is perfect. In a note on the back jacket, Margaret Forster says: 'The quality of the writing is so extraordinarily high that I could hardly believe it was a first novel.' Well, yes, or no: the excellence of Ann Schlee's novels for children has taken a leap in another direction, distinct but related.

Anthony Thwaite, "Charleses and Charlottes," in The Observer, *March 22, 1981, p. 33.**

WENDY DELLETT

[In ***The Vandal***] Schlee writes convincingly of a debilitating future world—freed from the burden of the past. Human beings are deprived of any memory beyond the previous three days—unaware of progress and left with no incentive for change. . . . Memory is eliminated by a soporific drug enjoyed as a family ritual each evening, and a personal computer terminal called the MEMORY daily furnishes each person with instructions and then orders the user to destroy all papers "to avoid contamination." Schoolboy Paul Simonds, every once in a while, feels an unaccountable sense of loss. Young and still impressionable, he has "primitive" impulses. During a power failure, he perceives the darkness as a powerful enemy that must be destroyed before it makes the world black and cold; to create light, he sets fire to a building, an act that excites him. But Paul commits an even more serious crime: he secretly records on paper his feelings about the fire, because he knows he will forget all about it the next day. Paul has thus "stolen" from the MEMORY by saving private recollections, and after another atavistic outburst of violence he is sent with other "contaminated" people to work on an experimental farm. . . . Paul's own memory is restored, and he becomes physically strong and emotionally whole. Realizing he can never return home (the society's watchword, "nothing lost matters," applies to his parents, who forgot him), he manages a dramatic escape from the real "vandal" of the title: a government that is destroying human initiative. As in E. M. Forster's 1928 story, *The Machine Stops,* as well as current fiction for children such as H. M. Hoover's *This Time of Darkness* . . . , Schlee gives us hope that "out there," away from the controlled environment of an ambition-weakening machine, one can find a good life based on hard work and individual freedom. ***The Vandal*** raises more questions than it answers, but Schlee's characters are so well defined and her writing so strong and clear that the story is engrossing and thought provoking.

Wendy Dellett, in a review of "The Vandal," in School Library Journal, *Vol. 27, No. 9, May, 1981, p. 77.*

JOHN MELLORS

Rhine Journey is Ann Schlee's first excursion into fiction for grown-ups, and one can only envy those children who have been lucky enough to read her previous books. Her style is effortlessly graceful without being in any way precious, right always for its immediate purpose, whether that is narrative, dialogue or description. Moreover, added to the functional efficiency of the writing is a quality of distinction, a touch of magic, that will make ***Rhine Journey*** haunt the reader long after the passengers have disembarked from the river steamer at Cologne.

John Mellors, "Nostalgia Novels," in The Listener, *Vol. 105, No. 2711, May 7, 1981, p. 616.**

KIRKUS REVIEWS

[***The Vandal***] takes place in a Big Brother future where data to be preserved is stored in individual Memory banks and a daily Drink erases all real memories over three days old. In urgent, unconscious protest, teenage Paul sets a symbolic fire (light swallowing darkness); and as punishment the psychiatrist assigns him to Welfare work, caring for a sick woman in the substandards (housing units). . . . Eventually [the sick woman] and, later, her daughter Sharon and Paul himself are sent into exile to a sort of prison colony, where people must work hard in the fields but, oddly, don't have to take the memory-erasing Drink. From there Paul and Sharon escape into the uncontrolled unknown, where some free spirits have preceded them and others are sure to follow. Schlee's talent for ambient historical settings serves her as well in this appalling future, and Paul's hesitant and anguished struggles against his conditioning are as intensely realized.

A review of "The Vandal," in Kirkus Reviews, *Vol. XLIX, No. 13, July 1, 1981, p. 806.*

SUSAN JEFFREYS AND MARY ANNE BONNEY

[***Rhine Journey***] was published in 1981 yet the book is so true to its period that the date 1881 would seem more appropriate. The writing is deceptively simple—the plot a subtle mixture of the outer world and the sub-conscious. . . . The whole story is told with a fascinating mixture of complexity and clarity—it is Miss Schlee's first book for adults; may it be followed by many more of this calibre.

Susan Jeffreys and Mary Anne Bonney, in a review of "Rhine Journey," in Punch, *Vol. 281, No. 7341, July 22, 1981, p. 158.*

PENELOPE LIVELY

Rhine Journey is excellent: emotional, vivid, compelling. . . . Ann Schlee has none of those vices of the historical novelist that can put one off the form for life—the fatal urge to instruct, the confusion of fiction with history, the need to have all that arduous research show in the text—and has written a brief and powerful novel about the emotional crisis of a fortyish spinster, Charlotte Morrison. . . . There is a twist at the end which sets the story in a wider context than Charlotte's wrestlings with her own suppressed sexuality and her relationship with her family, and which is heralded by the author's unobtrusive historical note at the beginning; it is a measure of the novel's success that one is so absorbed that this note is quite forgotten as one reads—only after closing the book do you think, ah yes, now I see why that was there. . . .

[Charlotte's] personal crisis is played out against the background of the Victorian journey, exquisitely described in spare and evocative prose: the Rhine, the hotels, the donkey-borne ascent of a mountain, the delicacies of social intercourse between Mrs Morrison and Mrs Newman, the English travellers' stern consciousness of national status and the daily cultural demands on the responsible and responsive tourist. The Morrison's daughter is admired by a young Prussian officer, and her rapturous sexual awakening runs parallel with her aunt's grimly subdued struggle. And there is not a word to spare; at the end of the book the reader is impressed by the strength of the effect—of place, of people—achieved without any verbal excesses or indulgences. ***Rhine Journey*** is the kind of book to which such terms as "charming" and "period piece" attach themselves, but it is more than that: it remains in the head long after the last page is turned. (p. 53)

Penelope Lively, "Travelling in Time," in Encounter, *Vol. LVII, No. 2, August, 1981, pp. 53-7.**

BRYNA J. FIRESIDE

Ann Schlee's chilling novel of false piety, deceit, greed and child abuse is not for the faint-of-heart or the casual reader. [**"Ask Me No Questions"**] contains strong stuff even for adults. The novel chronicles the horrendous chain of events that claimed the lives of 180 children, in what was supposed to be a modern training school for paupers, in the picturesque village of Tooting, outside London.

Charles Dickens wrote the original newspaper account of Bartholomew Drouet, who in 1849 was charged with manslaughter in the death of one of these children. **"Ask Me No Questions"** also explores the societal values that permitted and condoned Drouet's appalling treatment of the children. It is only when wholesale death strikes in an outbreak of cholera that conditions at the institution no longer can be kept secret.

Miss Schlee tells her story through Laura, who has been sent to live with Aunt and Uncle Bolinger when the cholera epidemic sweeps through London. Observant, sensitive and overwhelmed by what she sees and hears, Laura discovers the truth about Drouet when she observes three children sneaking into her uncle's barn to eat the slops meant for the pigs. . . .

For those socially conscious readers who wish to understand how Drouet could be found innocent of manslaughter, **"Ask Me No Questions"** may, curiously enough, provide some answers.

Bryna J. Fireside, in a review of "Ask Me No Questions," in The New York Times Book Review, *August 29, 1982, p. 12.*

FAITH McNULTY

Set in mid-Victorian England, this Dickensian novel [**"Ask Me No Questions"**], based on an actual case of cruelty to charity children, tells how two well-to-do youngsters discover misery their elders prefer to ignore, and do their small best to remedy it. Miss Schlee has made a fascinating story of a sombre subject by means of sensitive, imaginative writing filled with genuine feeling. (p. 190)

Faith McNulty, "Children's Books for Christmas," in The New Yorker, *Vol. LVIII, No. 42, December 6, 1982, pp. 176-92.**

PHILIP HORNE

Perhaps because of its concentration on people's circumstances and constraints, the novel is often concerned with freedoms under threat and forms of liberation. The generality 'freedom' is much bandied about in the world at large, of course, mostly with a bland or fierce prejudice in its favour: misapplied, it can lead to terrible blunders. An aspect of the value of the novel is therefore its power to examine the conditions of freedom in particular cases, to refresh our sense of what this tortured word can mean. In proportion as the novel brings us into contact with the pressures of a particular predicament, moreover, we may feel ourselves liberated from the generalising entrapments of 'freedom' into a consciousness of urgent special dilemmas from which catchwords can bring no real release. The freedom of the imagination is not necessarily greatest in imagining freedom: or rather, as in Ann Schlee's novel [***The Proprietor***] . . . , it is where social and psychological pressures are most intense that we get from art our purest expressions of freedom.

In 1981 Ann Schlee published her first adult novel, ***Rhine Journey***, a closely researched account of a straitlaced English spinster's emotional adventures in sailing down the Rhine in 1851. The book's strength, a patient and cunning representation of the intimacies of a repressed and wasted life. . . , lies in its sympathy with the deep-rooted ambivalence of a woman accustomed always to submit to the will of others, but suddenly hard put to control a desire for a married man. ***Rhine Journey*** skirts some well-established prejudices about Victorians—that they were all pedantically devout, jingoistic, humourless, prim, double-lived, sexually troubled—with a chaste diction, a ceremonious and circumlocutory sureness of tone with the social voice of the age, which marks its intensity of engagement with the kind of experience it imagines. The impatience with oppression which modern attitudes generally involve is properly withheld in Ann Schlee's narration, and this allows us access to a situation, a world, which we might not admit to be typically Victorian but are moved to accept as that of a maimed and struggling sensibility. The accurate historical reconstruction of social milieu comes to stand for the constant pressure of others on the dutiful individual, preparing the way for an excited loss of bearings when a day's illness removes Charlotte from that scene: 'Without the weight of those other personalities pressed against her she felt limitless, unreal.' The sobriety of ***Rhine Journey***'s approach—and its deceptive intricacy of plotting—make the emergence of this romantic idea of personal authenticity peculiarly potent.

Ann Schlee's new Victorian novel, ***The Proprietor,*** ambitiously extends this earlier achievement of the historical imagination: it spans the years from 1836 to 1856, and two generations of two families. Its 'proprietor', the inflexible Augustus Walmer, obtains the lease on two neighbouring Scilly Isles (and the theme is isolation); the novel's central concern, the unrequited love between him and Amelia Pontefract, the wife of a friend who regularly visits the islands, is reflected and refracted in the consciousness of other characters—Amelia's daughter, his nephew, a girl adopted in the islands after a shipwreck. Ann Schlee's scheme—with the first half on the islands and most of the second on the mainland—passes pleasingly between points of view, and back and forth in time, returning to the shipwreck or recapitulating a piece of action as it was for another participant. The narration's special note, or the chord it sounds, emerges from a commerce between the tone and viewpoint of a historian or biographer (she invents and cites an extremely convincing body of documents) and those of the fully engaged novelist, whose 'evidence' is of a different, freer order—concerned with a truth of feeling. A foreword tells us that 'the documentation on Augustus Walmer is slight,' and that 'his motives for going to so remote a spot are obscure, but it would seem he intended to devote his life to the conducting of an experiment to restore the islands' economy along utilitarian principles.' We are familiar from biographies with this obscurity of past motive, as we are with the mode of the educated guess ('it would seem') by which so many modern biographers try to dissolve it, and it is a dilemma of which Ann Schlee regularly reminds us. Thus: 'Indeed no letters from Augustus to Mrs Pontefract are traceable until after the New Year, and it is tempting to surmise that none were written.' Leon Edel has said that 'a modern biographer . . . is primarily a storyteller,' and the common aspiration of biographers towards the authority of the novelist can irritate those who want to know *why* 'X must have felt a or b.' Ann Schlee takes the biographer's predicament and uses it for her own ends. The evidence which survives those long dead usually leaves their buried lives guarded by the self-composure of letters: this intelligent novelist, pursuing the intimacy of relations between inner and outer selves, works out from the psychological freedom of insight which is her privilege, to incorporate the formally-determined behaviour, the strict social lacing, that makes her characters who they are. We are given access to Augustus's 'private images of death', imaginatively rendered, and then shifted into another, public, key ('None of this is apparent in the tone of his letters')—one which tells us quite as much about the texture, the particular meaning, of his life.

There is a beauty in the book's stilted, uncomfortably repetitive style. The characters' oppression (by conscience and by fear), and the haunting sense of personal waste which is its counterpart, are given body in a formalised language whose redundancies are ingeniously functional. Adela is dispatched back to the islands from a London college for teachers when found walking with Augustus's nephew: on the train, stunned, 'she felt the weight of her hands in the lap of her skirt and, looking down, saw them lie patiently there. Her body seemed to have taken up an attitude of waiting.' The carriage of sense from 'weight' to 'waiting' (a crucial pun in the novel), and the alienness to self discovered in the delay between feeling and sight, is characteristically indirect in suggesting Adela's powerlessness to resist the forces drawing her towards social subservience and misery. Ann Schlee's writing shapes for us the irritable tension between strong feeling and virtuous resolve: her characters want to be good, and believe that 'no hour of the day should go unaccounted for,' yet often give themselves 'no very clear explanation' of what they're doing. The book's account of Amelia's relation to her recalcitrant and bullied daughter Harriet is especially clear when conveying the perilous swayings between duty and impulse. . . . Ann Schlee's enabling faith in an essential continuity of experience (signalled in the first sentence, 'Time cannot have affected the sensations of seasickness') is disciplined and substantiated by her submission to the special historical conditions which dictate so much in her characters' lives. This grounding in constraint yields valuable rewards: mysterious and frightening moments when people stand outside the restriction of their lives and are lost to themselves. (p. 22)

Philip Horne, "A World of Waste," in London Review of Books, *September 1 to September 14, 1983, pp. 22-3.**

JOHN MELLORS

The Proprietor is the account of the last twenty years in the life of Augustus Walmer, owner of two small islands in the Scillies, from the 1830s to the 1850s. Ann Schlee has mastered exactly the right style for a story set in that period, a decorous and discreetly elegant style, unhurried, precise and sharp in its descriptions yet leaving reflections and echoes in the mind's eye and ear. While not directly imitative, the style strikes one as utterly appropriate. Here, for example, the 32-year-old Augustus begins to manage the land he has inherited, and 'it seemed that after thirty years his life, with its sad freight of early bereavement and early inheritance, veered out on an unseen current and swung at a distance until he might find the strength to recall it'.

Augustus wants the islands to be self-supporting, and to that end he discourages what he regards as over-population; only those who earn their keep will be allowed to stay. Such a policy breeds sullen opposition, and by the time Augustus mellows and becomes more protective of his islanders, it is too late to avoid the results of their resentment.

Plot, however, is not the strong point of ***The Proprietor.*** Place and time give the book its power, and the real protagonists are not Augustus, the land-owner, and Adela, the orphan of the storm, his *protégée*, but the *genius loci* and the *Zeitgeist*. Ann

Schlee can paint a landscape with the minimum number of strokes: 'Cows stood on the hill, their hides patched and matted with rain; the sky was low and hopeless'. She delights the reader with sudden gifts of unexpected detail: a woman greets her husband at the breakfast table by laying her cheek briefly on his 'warm crown' and 'through the top of his head she could hear him crunching his toast'.

An air of melancholy hangs over much of ***The Proprietor.*** People's expectations are raised and either dashed or left slowly to subside. Life promises more than it supplies. Women especially, as they grow older, rely more and more on memory to provide the satisfactions which they have been unable to obtain from either God or husband, and memory is something which Ann Schlee handles with the surest of touches. There are times when it is unsettling to remember things too clearly, as Adela finds when she meets again a childhood friend and is 'confused . . . by the sudden onrush of recollection. Her mind was quite congested with memories of the rocky surfaces of paths, the warm stone where Harriet had balanced the unsteady mussel shells . . . , of Mrs Walmer's tightened grip on her wrist . . . They destroyed the cautionary sense that time had passed'.

The Proprietor, then, is an excellent novel of its kind, if not quite so effective as its predecessor, ***Rhine Journey.*** There was about the earlier novel a magic quality that lingered in the reader's mind, and that is something which ***The Proprietor*** lacks. (pp. 98-9)

John Mellors, "Seeing the Light," in London Magazine, *Vol. 23, No. 7, October, 1983, pp. 97-100.**

HARRIET WAUGH

Ann Schlee's second novel, ***The Proprietor,*** confirms the impression made by ***Rhine Journey*** that she is a serious, good novelist. This novel, also set in the Victorian era, follows the tradition of Charlotte M. Yonge; the characters might well have sprung from the pages of one of those novels for young ladies. Like Miss Yonge's characters, Miss Schlee's are deeply concerned with rectitude and the subjugation of the will in the struggle for goodness. While men strive to uphold order, cleanliness and Godliness for the betterment of their social and economic inferiors, the women submit to the Will of their Men and to that of their God. Anyone who has enjoyed Charlotte M. Yonge will take pleasure in seeing these young people stretched on the rack of 20th-century consciousness. For here, subjugation of the will leads to depressive ill health while rectitude leads to violent, unappeased passion and hypocrisy. All this is divulged very slowly. One watches the characters moving puppet-like, their behavior suitably correct and high-minded, and only later does one know them sufficiently well to see the emotions moving against the current of the action. The interior tale is one of isolation, fermenting passions, emotional corruption, desperation and a dreary ennui.

The proprietor of the story is Augustus Walmer, a taciturn, misanthropic man of substance who buys some remote islands in order to demonstrate that by imposing a regime of utilitarian principles on the islands' economy he can improve the lot of those who eke out their desperate existence as farmers and fishermen. (pp. 21-2)

A current of undeclared interest, almost bordering on excitement, grows between Augustus and the wife of one of his friends. It is, of course, wrong but it revitalises her, bringing back health and spirits unendangered by any possibility of adventure. Her daughter, Harriet, plays with an island child called Adela. Adela is the bridge between the lives of the islanders and those of the gentry. It is the unhappy effect of this communion that the novel is mainly about. . . .

Although Adela is treated well by Harriet and her parents she is always aware of her invidious position. Should she, for instance, enter the house from the kitchen or the front door? She is attracted by the sophistication of the big house but always feels her difference. In as far as there is a heroine, Adela is she. But she is the least successful of Ann Schlee's major characters. Her passivity, under the yoke of her class and womanhood comes across as insipidness, while the story suggests that she should be viewed as someone unusual and special.

The second half of the book follows Adela, Harriet and Archie—Augustus Walmer's nephew and heir—into adulthood. And it is here that Victorian social and moral mores are shown to distort the lives of these three likeable people. Sex, religion, class and an unconscious brutality lay waste their lives. The withdrawn chilliness of Augustus Walmer's nature, which aches for warmth, is debased into a callous lust.

None of this is truly discernible until well into the novel, for Miss Schlee keeps her readers outside the intimacy of the circle. They are treated as acquaintances and like acquaintances can only see the outward behaviour of the people they observe—but when intimacy does come it gives great satisfaction.

The islanders, sturdy and secret, keep their separateness until the end. I thought Miss Schlee allowed them to pass through the novel without the close scrutiny they deserved. They were there to be acted on, but given the nature of the story I felt that they would have acted back. The possibility of this is only hinted at and one never knows what is going on in their minds. The reader is identified with the gentry as against the people. Therefore the people are unknowable while the warts of the gentry are exposed. But this is only a mild complaint. The novel demands some effort from the reader, but it is an effort that proves well worthwhile. (p. 22)

Harriet Waugh, "Castaway," in The Spectator, *Vol. 252, No. 8114, January 14, 1984, pp. 21-2.*

THE NEW YORKER

We watch [the characters in **"The Proprietor"**] . . . grow up or grow older, and we glimpse behind the formal conversation and the exchange of formal letters ("My dear Mrs. Pontefract") their deep and sometimes terrible yearnings and involvements. It is a measure of Mrs. Schlee's vigorous comprehension of the period that even when her characters behave most exasperatingly (by our notions) we accept and respect their reasons. This is a strong and stirring story, beautifully told, and with a sense of time and place that recalls both "Dover Beach" and "The French Lieutenant's Woman." (pp. 109-10)

A review of "The Proprietor," in The New Yorker, *Vol. LIX, No. 48, January 16, 1984, pp. 109-10.*

M. L. JEFFERSON

Although somewhat muted by its period trappings, **"The Proprietor"** by Ann Schlee is an elegant, absorbing and evocative novel. . . . Mrs. Schlee does all the things one enjoys in Victorian novels. Nature reflects or counters human action; dialogue is concise, description lavish; the marital and spiritual trials of several generations are sorted out. . . . All the elements of this tale are familiar, but Mrs. Schlee has handled them very well, adding detail and narrative subtlety; there is also a haunting, coda-like final chapter. Her stately writing conveys the island's severe, desolate beauty and the social distinctions of city and country life. I couldn't help wondering why such skill should be devoted to reinterpreting 19th-century life and literature. But one could ask the same of PBS presentations of Austen, Dickens or Trollope—and, after asking, continue to watch them happily.

M. L. Jefferson, in a review of "The Proprietor," in The New York Times Book Review, *January 22, 1984, p. 22.*

Bob Seger

1945-

(Born Robert Clark Seger) American songwriter.

In his songs Seger often explores emotional anxieties of adolescence and adulthood, focusing on male-female relationships and the struggle of the individual to realize personal dreams. He often reflects upon his past and relates experiences common to American youths of working-class families. Writing in a variety of musical styles, Seger composes ballads, folk songs, hard-driving rock, rhythm and blues, and sentimental love songs. He began performing as a teenager and established himself in the Midwest, particularly in the Detroit area, where he grew up. Seger wrote several songs that became regional hits, including "Heavy Music" and "Ramblin' Gamblin' Man." With the album *Beautiful Loser* (1975) Seger began drawing national attention; the title song of this album and the song "Katmandu" became popular hits. Seger established a national reputation with *Live Bullet: Bob Seger and the Silver Bullet Band* (1976), a collection of his early songs recorded at a concert in Detroit.

Seger solidified his reputation as an important figure in rock music with his album *Night Moves* (1976). Although some critics consider his lyrics on this album to be self-indulgent, others contend that the songs offer honest views of his adolescent experiences. The title song, in which a man lies awake at night and reflects upon a teenage romance, and "Main Street," which relates the story of a teenager's love for an older woman, were popular with audiences and critics. Seger's next album, *Stranger in Town* (1978), is generally considered his finest blend of uptempo rock songs and introspective ballads. Critics especially praise the song "Feel Like a Number," one of Seger's many tributes to the dignity of working-class individuals in an indifferent society.

***Against the Wind* (1980) and *The Distance* (1983) won immediate popular success but drew mixed reviews. Several critics expressed dismay that Seger's characteristically hard-edged music and insightful lyrics are compromised on *Against the Wind* by songs of lesser achievement. Dave Marsh, one of his stalwart supporters through Seger's long struggle for national recognition, dismisses *Against the Wind* as containing "basically failureproof songs that are utterly listenable and quite meaningless." *The Distance* was more favorably reviewed. Songs on this album concern love, romantic visions of the past, and the desire for adventure on the open roads of America.**

BEN EDMONDS

When viewed in the context of his two previous albums [***Ramblin' Gamblin' Man*** and ***Noah***], Bob Seger's ***Mongrel*** fares very favorably. It's easily his best overall work to date but there are still some crucial musical problems he must come to grips with if he is to realize the tremendous potential he displayed on his earlier . . . singles (most notably **"Heavy Music"** and "**Persecution Smith**"). . . .

[Seger] writes marvelous rock and roll songs in the virile 1965 mold, somewhat of a lost art these days. . . .

Catherine Osti/LGI © 1983

"Lucifer" is easily the strongest cut on the record, and a great song in its own right. It's simple, straightforward rock. . . . If the Bob Seger System would focus their musical attention on Seger's 1965 sense of dynamics and forget their 1970 pretensions, then perhaps they would finally begin to fulfill the promise of **"Lucifer"** and those dynamite [early singles].

Ben Edmonds, in a review of "Mongrel," in Rolling Stone, *Issue 74, January 27, 1971, p. 54.*

NOEL COPPAGE

Bob Seger—as Dave Marsh says in the reprint of a *Creem* article that appears [on **"Smokin' O.P.'s"**] instead of liner notes—has been a fabulous success in Detroit and a flop most other places; Marsh says (as of May 1972) that Seger has never had a record played on the radio in New York, San Francisco, or Los Angeles. Reading Marsh's article and then listening to this disc might convince you that Detroit's taste is hopelessly warped—but that would be playing leapfrog with logic. It will prove to be the case only if Detroit likes *this* Seger album. Seger wrote only two of the songs, the excellent ***Someday*** and the old, tired, childish ***Heavy Music*** (ironically about radio's role in pop), and he does lame, distracted interpretations of overrecorded biggies and not-so-biggies to fill it out. . . . Aside from ***Someday*** . . . , this album only suggests what Seger can do.

Noel Coppage, in a review of "Smokin' O.P.'s," in Stereo Review *Magazine, Vol. 30, No. 4, April, 1973, p. 96.*

MICHAEL OLDFIELD

Detroit rock bands put the emphasis on a driving beat; and have done so through Mitch "Sock It To Me Baby" Ryder and the Detroit Wheels; [and] the Amboy Dukes, led by guitar Ace Ted Nugent. . . . Bob Seger is in there too and is possibly the best of the lot. Having worked his way through an acoustic album **"Brand New Morning,"** and last year's classic **"Smokin' O.P.'s"** he's back with **"Back in '72."** Don't let it become another neglected masterpiece: no-one who likes the kind of rock personified by the Stones can afford to be without it. . . . The highlight of the album is undoubtedly the title track, a sort of "answer" to "American Pie." . . . This real stormer contrasts with **"Turn the Page,"** a ballad. . . . The fact is, you won't hear anything like any of the tracks on the album until the next Stones album—and maybe not even then. Don't wait that long.

Michael Oldfield, in a review of "Back in '72," in Melody Maker, *April 21, 1973, p. 31.**

DAVE MARSH

Bob Seger's **"Rosalie"** is so strong it could break you in half. But it is the only song [on ***Back in '72***] that is close to what I feel Seger could be achieving though, and that's a disappointment.

Seger is the only true singer/songwriter the Detroit scene produced, unless you count Smokey Robinson. His mold has been closer to Rod Stewart's or Robbie Robertson's or—most appropriately—an uncouth John Fogerty's than it has been to the wheeze 'n' whine school of composer/vocalism, but singer/songwriter is what Seger is, nonetheless.

His latest album, ***Smokin' OPs*** didn't cut the mustard because most of the material was hackneyed. . . . But what I call his genius shone through on . . . **"Heavy Music"** and in the supremely powerful band track on Chuck Berry's "Let it Rock.". . .

But two songs an album isn't much, especially when only one of them is the *auteur's* own. I chose the word "auteur" quite carefully since the rise of that theory (borrowed from film criticism) seems to be the stem of much of what is miserable in today's rock. Seger has fallen hook, line and sinker, for *auteurism's* central charlatanism—that the highest level of the body of an artist's work is an expression of his or her own psyche. Thus, he writes mawkish moans like **"Turn the Page,"** which (for all its good lines. . .) is finally just another mewling piece of rock star self-pity.

I don't mean to imply that one of the things that Seger has to work out in his music *isn't* his own personality; I just think that there are any number of more worthwhile things to think about while doing that. Incestuous autobiography as a dictum of French cinema turned it into an almost complete bore and, with a little luck, *auteurism* can do the same for rock. . . .

I'm much more interested in what an artist and I hold in common than I am in our points of divergence; where Bob Seger lets me down, and where too many formerly inspired s/s's do, is in concentrating too much on insular, self-conscious considerations. What made **"Heavy Music"** great was that I didn't have to sort out any point-of-view; the point-of-view was only intelligible if you could dig the title and the sound. After that, it was a one way ride, straight into the heart of rock.

Seger only accomplishes anything so universal in one song here, **"Rosalie,"** which is one more than almost anyone else, still and all. . . .

"Rosalie" is the kind of personal yet universal song we need more of. When Seger sings that " . . . the music died / It burned my pride / But somehow I pulled through / Back in '72," he doesn't have to be writing his own obituary. And he probably isn't, since he has the power, too, to rise out of the Burbank tar pits and shine. One would hope he does it soon, rather than putzing around with inferior copies of other people's inferior songs, and inversions of his own mythology. More egocentricity is the last thing the Rosalies of the world are going to put up with, and it's the last thing any of us want or need.

Dave Marsh, in a review of "Back in '72," in Creem, *Vol. 4, No. 12, May, 1973, p. 63.*

JON LANDAU

Seger hasn't stopped trying since the days of that last big single [**"Heavy Music"**], but he has too often taken to copying trends. One result was an abortive acoustic album [***Brand New Morning***]. . . . In fact, ***Back in '72*** is really his first completely personal LP and, ironically, it seems to me to have a better shot at commercial success than any of its more calculated predecessors. . . .

[Seger's] songs have a conventional rock & roll basis, but are modified with original hooks, changes and variations. . . . [His] rhythm playing and arranging brings out the individuality of each song that he touches.

The new album was cut in three different studios with three different bands. . . . Despite the varied locations and large number of different sidemen, it all sounds of a similar piece. . . .

Several ballads, all of which contain some proudly corny lyrics, work as musical expressions of simple emotions—**"So I Wrote You a Song," "I've Got Time,"** and one of the album's two highlights, a simple, honest and eloquent song about the life of a small time star, **"Turn The Page."** . . .

"Back in '72" is an old-fashioned rock & roll chant that describes some of [Seger's] crazy Detroit history with humor and abandon. **"Neon Sky"** is another love song, but with an exceptional tune. . . .

The album's prize cut and one of the best things I have heard in this or any other year, **"Rosalie,"** has . . . a cathartic sense of completeness that only the very finest rock artists can create. To hear Bob Seger sing this masterpiece is to know that he belongs at the top of the rock & roll heap. ***Back in '72*** is just the record to put him there.

Jon Landau, in a review of "Back in '72," in Rolling Stone, *Issue 134, May 10, 1973, p. 55.*

NOEL COPPAGE

If hard rock still enjoys the community standing it thinks it does, this should be the place where America discovers Bob Seger—America, that is, beyond Detroit, which has been applauding heartily all along. [**"Back in '72"**] is a bit frustrating, but it presents rock honestly, for the simple, repetitive form it is; generally, Seger gets on with it, with a minimum of pauses for pretentious nonsense. . . . There are no beautiful songs, but three or four solid ones among the six Seger originals give the album a good core. My favorite is either the stanchly autobiographical ***I've Got Time*** or the stanchly autobiographical ***Turn the Page.***

Noel Coppage, in a review of "Back in '72," in Stereo Review *Magazine, Vol. 31, No. 2, August, 1973, p. 88.*

MICHAEL OLDFIELD

Arthur Lee, J. J. Cale, Tim Buckley you all know about. Bob Seger you probably don't: yet he certainly deserves to stand alongside these legendary heroes. And he's completely underrated.

Like those three he's got a particular genius: the ability to make his sound fit every style of music possible. Of the four other Seger albums [besides **"Seven"** that] I've managed to track down, each covers a different sphere: pop, singer-songwriter "folk", punk rock and white soul.

The base of each is the sound of Detroit, the driving funk that on the black side spawned the Motown sound, on the white, heavy metal. Seger strikes a line straight between the two, retaining the solid base and pushing songs along at an incredible pace so they come out as pure energy. . . .

"Seven" sees Seger in a variety of styles, none of which would hold up an album on their own but together add up to pure dynamite. . . .

"Seven" is a great album—and it's not the first great album he's made either. If we're not going to make Bob Seger a commercial success let's at least vote him into the Legendary Heroes' Hall of Fame.

Michael Oldfield, "Bob Seger—Them Changes," in Melody Maker, *June 8, 1974, p. 42.*

DAVE MARSH

Bob Seger has been touted for years as a Detroit-based John Fogerty but has never had the monster hit needed to break out nationally. If he keeps making albums like ***Seven,*** he never will. **"Need Ya"** proves that he can still write an AM rocker as well as anyone. . . . Most of the rest of ***Seven*** isn't even that good. Seger has been relying on too many gimmicks—part of this album was recorded in Nashville, which is as appropriate as Waylon Jennings recording in Motown—when what he really needs is a good producer. We could use a hit-maker of his ability, but albums like this one aren't going to provide it.

Dave Marsh, in a review of "Seven," in Rolling Stone, *Issue 164, July 4, 1974, p. 76.*

KEN BARNES

Bob Seger is a superb songwriter and Midwestern rocker who's been ignored for far too long. He had a hit, **"Ramblin' Gamblin' Man"** in 1968, but superior followup singles went unheard. The dramatic **"East Side Story"** (his first regional hit), the frighteningly intense **"Lookin' Back"** and the most passionate, personalized anti-war song of the Sixties, **"2+2,"** should have been part of everyone's radio heritage.

Beautiful Loser is Seger's eighth album. While it lacks a classic to rank with past [single record] greats, it's his most consistent effort, a deft balance of chugging rockers and striking, reflective numbers. The lyrics are thoughtful and intriguing. . . . **"Jody Girl"** and **"Fine Memory"** are melodic, touching songs which suggest a restrained Van Morrison. . . . **"Sailing Nights"** is reminiscent of Procol Harum's nautical phase—potentially perilous waters, but Seger navigates them well.

The key cut is the six-minute **"Katmandu,"** a fierce rock & roller wherein Seger adapts a familiar Chuck Berry lyrical mode to his own purposes: Ten years of not making it in his homeland is enough—next stop, Katmandu. With this fine LP, he deserves his long delayed recognition—now.

Ken Barnes, in a review of "Beautiful Loser," in Rolling Stone, *Issue 188, June 5, 1975, p. 58.*

MICHAEL OLDFIELD

Sad though it is to admit it, [**"Beautiful Loser"**] is a particularly apt title. Despite an unbroken run of magnificent albums . . . , Bob Seger hasn't made any impression on the charts in either Britain or America. . . . His return visit to Muscle Shoals [Studio] has produced some as always, fine songs, but the spark that would set them alight is missing. Somehow, it all sounds a little flat. Or perhaps it's the number of downer songs on the album; virtually every number is about a broken romance, happy memories of the past, leaving, or some such depressing subject. The titles tell it all: **"Beautiful Loser," "Black Night," "Momma," "Fine Memory."** But among all this misery there are several bright moments. **"Katmandu"** is vintage Seger, lyrics in the style of Chuck Berry's "Rock 'n' Roll Music." . . .

Michael Oldfield, in a review of "Beautiful Loser," in Melody Maker, *August 9, 1975, p. 33.*

DAVE MARSH

I've been listening to Bob Seger since 1966's **"East Side Story,"** an odd, "Gloria"-like single with a theme that predates [Bruce Springsteen's] "Jungleland" by nine years. In Detroit, and much of the Midwest, Seger was (and is) a major star, good for a hard-rock hit every year, ranging from the antiwar diatribe **"2+2=?"** and the anthemic **"Heavy Music"** of 1967 to 1973's **"Rosalie."** . . . Seger has had only one national hit, **"Ramblin' Gamblin' Man"** in 1968. . . . For a man whose best work combines John Fogerty's energy and commitment with the subtle elegance of Van Morrison, the frustrations must be immense.

Seger's obscurity is more inexplicable because he is in so many ways the model of the mainstream rock singer. . . . [He] writes wonderful melodies. His songs tell their stories with wit, economy and passion—more importantly, he always has stories to tell. His most topical songs are naive (so are many of Fogerty's) but the better ones seem to sum up the mid-American rock experience. **"U.M.C.,"** included [on ***Live Bullet: Bob Seger and the Silver Bullet Band***] is merely sanctimonious (the initials stand for "upper middle class") but **"Lookin' Back"** is the real thing, just what happened to rocking kids in the late Sixties. . . .

Seger's other theme really amounts to an unshakable faith in the power of rock & roll to change a life—his own, if no one else's. (p. 55)

Most of these songs are better recorded elsewhere: **"Heavy Music"** and **"Let It Rock"** are particularly disappointing. But the songs from last year's ***Beautiful Loser*** are much superior in these versions. If ***Live Bullet*** adds little new material to the Seger oeuvre, and if he has still not been properly produced, it has the advantage of offering a fairly extensive overview of his history. And because of the devotion of the crowd and the desperation of Seger's approach . . . , the album transcends its limitations.

Live Bullet doesn't have the feeling of triumph heard in the two greatest live rock records, the Who's *Live at Leeds* and the Rolling Stones' *Get Yer Ya-Ya's Out!* . . . This is a man who hasn't got it made, but who has already reckoned with his weaknesses and strengths. He works his heart out and perhaps tells us something special about what it means to be the average guy, with or without guitar.

In a way, the concert becomes a meditation on failure, from **"Travelin' Man"** to the mournful **"Turn the Page,"** an exegesis of the space between total stardom and final burnout, affectionately reminiscing about the lovely times, excoriating the bad ones. In **"Katmandu,"** . . . he thinks of giving it all up, but the strength of his music belies the idea. Better than anyone before him, Seger knows the problems of partial success, and maybe what is so compelling about this record is that he seems so resigned to remaining that kind of star.

Seger's most deeply felt moments come when he moves beyond his personal tragedy into everyone's. **"Jody Girl,"** the wonderful Morrison-style ballad that closes the first side, is a striking characterization of a woman with great potential, who's sacrificed a brilliant future for not very much. In the album's best song, **"Beautiful Loser,"** he describes a guy who . . . never quite has the drive to break past his limitations. If I'm a loser, he seems to say, then I'll speak for every loser, but he does it without bitterness, anger or blame. And he's never only resigned. Seger cares for these characters (and in **"Jody,"** I think, he has done something really rare—created a plausible woman in song). . . . ***Live Bullet*** is a small triumph but, in its way, a magnificent one, capable of speaking without pathos for failures everywhere. With those songs, and this album, he has convinced me that I'll be listening to him for another nine years. (pp. 55, 57)

Dave Marsh, "Bob Seger's 'Bullet': Right on Target," in Rolling Stone, *Issue 215, June 17, 1976, pp. 55, 57.*

LESTER BANGS

Bob Seger refuses to say die. I got nothing against him, know him and he's a real good joe, but all there's finally to be said is that if you took the . . . early Sixties singles—**"Persecution Smith," "Sock It To Me Santa," "Heavy Music,"** etc.—and the best of ***Mongrel***. . . and ***Noah***, mix that collation up in one snakpak, add the incredible 1971 single **"Looking Back,"** and you got one of the all-time classic rock albums. Tough. Raw. Crude where and when it really counts. . . .

[***Live Bullet***] is a pretty good indicaton of where Seger's been since ***Mongrel***—vacillating between factory rockouts a la Bachman Turner Overdrive and pensive ballads that just do not make it unless you nurse a special passion for dogged, plodding, ersatz Bad Company/Allman Brothers hymns to being "on the road again." Honest, sure, but Seger, mass acceptance or local/cult hero, is just still too much journeyman and not enough slam-damn visionary. . . . It all sounds like one long obbligato to me.

He's just a good solid workman, and that may fit the times too perfectly, but it ain't what I been waiting for. I'm waiting for the highway child to roar charges . . . and shout wild once more, and having waited five years I'm about ready to pack this one in. . . .

Live Bullet is better than the boogie slop that's making several far less talented musicians far more money than Bob's ever seen, but it's not neuropsychic defoliation, which was what I always hung around heavy metal for. Maybe you got different standards. I just hope Bob makes a lot of money now. Nobody deserves it more.

Lester Bangs, "Everyman Goes Gold," in Creem, *Vol. 8, No. 2, July, 1976, p. 67.*

MICHAEL OLDFIELD

It's strange now, after ten years, critics on both sides of the Atlantic have just discovered that Bob Seger is the future of rock 'n' roll. . . . All comes to he who waits, though: it's just a shame that those who have had their heads in the sand have to wait for a weak album before jumping on the Seger bandwagon. I stress the word album, because [**"Live Bullet"**] is a live double, and there's little doubt that the concert was a great experience, maybe even one of the gigs of the century. . . . But that atmosphere is one thing vinyl can't convey. What we're left with is the music, and the only point of comparison is with other records, the studio versions of the songs. And it would negate Seger's method of working to say that the live versions are superior to the studio ones. He's always kept a strict line between the two; . . . on stage he substitutes energy for expertise. It works because of the nature of Seger's music (which, incidentally, in the space of eight albums before **"Live Bullet"** has included virtually every aspect of the term "pop"): his is a simple, driving approach, the epitome of boogie.

Michael Oldfield, in a review of "Live Bullet," in Melody Maker, *September 11, 1976, p. 26.*

KIT RACHLIS

If there is any grace in heaven, ***Night Moves*** will give Bob Seger the national following which has long eluded him. It is simply one of the best albums of the year. . . . As a composer, he echoes Bruce Springsteen in his painful attempts to memorialize his past.

Night Moves offers rock & roll in the classic mold: bold, aggressive and grandiloquent. . . .

Seger is a romantic in search of an adolescent conception of love which has always eluded him. He can laugh at his condition (**"Sunspot Baby"**) or try to exorcise it (his reworking of **"Mary Lou"**), but most of the time he rubs at it like an old wound (**"Night Moves"** and **"Mainstreet"**). All of these are songs of reminiscence, for Seger, above all, is a survivor. . . .

Seger's penchant for self-conscious poeticizing (**"Sunburst"**), [is] minor in an album bursting with energy and conviction.

Kit Rachlis, in a review of "Night Moves," in Rolling Stone, *Issue 230, January 13, 1977, p. 51.*

JOEL VANCE

Despite the rock media's strenuous assurances that Bob Seger, a Detroit hero, is exactly what national audiences should have been looking for all their lives, and that rock can't get along without him (just as the media can't survive without telling us such things), Seger is probably no more than a hard-working, better-than-average singer who occasionally surpasses himself.

In the title tune [of the album **"Night Moves"**], which owes its narrative plot and musical construction to Van Morrison's *Brown-Eyed Girl,* Seger phrases like the glorious Otis Redding, the Georgia genius. ***The Fire Down Below*** is in the manner of *Who's Makin' Love* and *Take Care of Your Homework. . . .*

The other cuts on the album prove that Seger is a highly professional and experienced entertainer who enjoys his work and has thoroughly absorbed his influences so that he can deliver his performances with punch and bravado. He is not an original by any means, but he is solid and dependable. His previous album [**"Live Bullet"**], a live recording of a Detroit concert where he was preaching to the already converted, was a noisy and flabby thing, but he seems to do better in the disciplined confines of the recording studio. It's not a world beater, but for what it is, and for who he is, this is a very good album.

Joel Vance, in a review of "Night Moves," in Stereo Review *Magazine, Vol. 38, No. 3, March, 1977, p. 114.*

LESTER BANGS

In 1971, Bob Seger released a single . . . which I guess was only a regional hit but was also one of the most powerful things I have ever heard. It was called **"Lookin' Back,"** the music was smoky funky powerchords that didn't have to tell you they were, and the words went like this: "You hit the street / You feel'em starin' / You know they hate you, you can feel their eyes a-glarin' / Because you're different / Because you're free / Because you're everything deep down they wish they could be. / They're lookin' back / They're lookin' back / Too many people lookin' back."

Bob Seger has a new album out called ***Stranger in Town*** which will probably go platinum. This album is mostly songs even more soul-searching than the ones on ***Night Moves,*** which I guess makes it better because they search the soul of his present instead of his adolescence, but musically it's just a "hard rock" version of an awful lot of what schlumps around the airwaves these days. . . .

It's been said that Bob Seger is a moralist, and I don't think you'd have to read the lyrics quoted above to know that's true. But how about this [from **"Feel Like a Number"**]: "I take my card and I stand in line / To make a buck I work overtime / Dear Sir letters keep coming in the mail / . . . . Hey it's me / And I feel like a number / Feel like a stranger / . . . in this land / I'm not a number / I'm not a number / Dammit I'm a man."

If it seems like we're getting close to Rastafarian or especially Clash territory here it's because we are, although it must be understood that it's parallelism and not influence—hell, Bob grew up in *Detroit,* and I wouldn't be surprised if he never even heard of the Clash. The song I just quoted is on ***Stranger in Town.*** After his success with ***Night Moves*** he could have just kept grinding out a proven formula: Nothing is more salable today than people's reminiscences of a backseat make-out adolescence a lot of them . . . never had. He nixed that sell-out album for the same reason that in 1978 (!!!) he wrote a song as topical as the one I just quoted: innate integrity.

The difference between **"Lookin' Back"** and **"Feel Like a Number"** is seven years: from hippie alienation and paranoia to the feeling that we're dwarfed by institutions we don't really understand, except that somebody somewhere wants us to believe that human beings don't matter much anymore. . . . [It's] no accident that the album is called ***Stranger in Town.*** Bob Seger feels like a stranger in this society, especially the rock superstar version of interlocking corporations. And that doesn't mean he's some old-fashioned "relic," even though he's embarrassed enough to use the word himself; it means he's a man of sanity and insight. I respect Bob Seger as much as almost anybody I can think of in the music business today. . . .

[But] while Bob is singing with candor or maybe the word should be guts about his alienation, the aging process vis-a-vis his line of work, etc., this album cops out musically just like ***Night Moves.*** It's homogenized. Seger knows he needs that radio play, and he also knows that in 1978 **"Lookin' Back"** (musically, let alone lyrically) won't get it. So in a sense he's bowing before the Beast. I don't know whether I blame him or not. . . . But the reason that the lyrics of the Clash and the Rastafarians carry all the wallop they should is that the music is as tough as the words.

There's a popular idea that the flirtation with chaos is something you must grow out of. . . . What this has to do with Bob Seger should be obvious. He writes all these songs about the tension between wanting to keep rocking when you're pushing 40, kinda like Ian Hunter. But Hunter always wanted to be Dylan, whereas Bob just wants to make sure that some kid has something decent to put on the eight-track while he cruises down Woodward—with ideas about life and identity and all that also there if and when you want 'em. . . . Right now he's got a chance to do something that only about four or five people have had a shot at: to make records that both deal honestly with aging in rock 'n' roll (or aging period), *and* to make music that would be as challenging now as his **"East Side Story"** was in 1966, or **"Lookin' Back"** was in 1971. And I think that if he snubs this opportunity I'm gonna end up feeling like he flat-out betrayed the gift.

Lester Bangs, "Growing Up True Is Hard To Do," in The Village Voice, *Vol. XXIII, No. 23, June 5, 1978, p. 45.*

ED HARRISON

It took Seger 15 years to gain stardom outside of his Detroit base with his previous album **"Night Moves,"** which was without a doubt one of the best albums and singles of last year. . . .

After a listen to **"Stranger In Town,"** it immediately becomes clear that Seger did not opt to sit on his laurels of past achievements by serving up mediocrity, but instead pushed himself to the limits of his resources.

His singing and songwriting both reach artistic heights here and it proves there is room for a compatible balance of hard-edged rockers and soft, engaging ballads. . . .

Like **"Night Moves,"** which contained its share of gems, there are cuts here that are as irresistible as **"Night Moves;"** songs heard once that are not easily forgotten as the melody and lyrics continue to haunt the subconscious.

The most striking cut is the single, **"Still The Same,"** which apparently will have the same effect on album sales as **"Night Moves"** had on the album. The midtempo ballad . . . recounts the tale of a diehard gambler. The tune takes on an r&b flavor. . . .

"Hollywood Nights," the leadoff cut, is a hard edged narrative about a "Midwestern boy" coming to Hollywood only to be betrayed by the big city lights and a lady he met on the beach. . . .

"Till It Shines" is a midtempo cut about isolation and solitude. . . .

The first side concludes with the anthem-like **"Feel Like A Number."** Like Johnny Paycheck's "Take This Job And Shove It," this working class dirge is a spirited rocker that sums up the complaints of the working class. . . .

Perhaps the most arresting ballad on the album is the melodic **"We've Got Tonight,"** reminiscent of Rod Stewart's "Tonight's The Night," Seger's remarkable sense of melody and lyrics is never better showcased. . . .

The album's finale is entitled **"The Famous Final Scene,"** which can stand as the universal ending to a long-time male-female relationship. . . . The strong lyrics make this, along with **"We've Got Tonight,"** the most evocative, if not tear-jerking cuts on the LP. . . .

"Stranger In Town" [is] a durable followup to a classic.

Ed Harrison, in a review of "Stranger In Town," in Billboard, *Vol. 90, No. 23, June 10, 1978, p. 80.*

DAVE MARSH

To kids in and around Detroit, in . . . [the late sixties] and ever since, Bob Seger reigned. He was a rocker whose records made sense; elsewhere he might have remained unknown, but to us he was a particular source of the magic in which one couldn't help but believe. For ten years, he told stories a lot like ours, played the music that helped define what we meant by high energy. The Stooges and the MC5 got the attention and the ink and the big-time record deals, but when the dust cleared for even an instant, there would be Bob Seger, standing tall as ever, still pounding out that **"Heavy Music."** We understood. To us, he was always a star.

These days, an interest in Bob Seger seems much less exclusive. **"Night Moves"** . . . has made him a star, potentially a hero, a performer who's talked about in the same breath with the very best of his contemporaries. Yet somehow, he's still the same guy who struggled for fifteen years to get any kind of break out of Detroit at all. . . .

Stranger in Town was more than worth the effort. It doesn't have the sense of breakthrough that possessed ***Night Moves,*** but it is a virtual catalog of Seger's excellence as a writer and singer. . . . Seger's melodic sense has never been better than on **"We've Got Tonight,"** a grand seduction song . . . and in **"Feel Like A Number"** he's come up with the kind of working-class anthem that one expects from tough rockers like Lynyrd Skynyrd. **"Hollywood Nights"** is a narrative that some may take for an allegory about a Midwestern boy traduced in L.A., while **"The Famous Final Scene"** is a fitting clincher to the work, a breakup item that must be fictitious—Seger has lived with the same woman for several years—but is delivered straight from the heart. Those who've heard it already consider it one of the highlights of 1978. (p. 68)

Bob Seger was a high school junior in 1962, which is the year of **"Night Moves."** That was, he says, the year he "came of age" in the sexual sense. But listen more closely and **"Night Moves"** is less a piece of nostalgia than a complete story, one that comes full circle to the present. At the end of the main part of the song, Seger says that he "felt the lightning and waited on the thunder." There is a long pause, almost a false ending. Then the coda begins: "I woke late last night to the sound of thunder / How far off I sat and wondered. . . ."

You could say that **"Night Moves"** is about the sexual discovery embodied in the verses, or about the sense of loss and nostalgia captured in its coda. Or you could say that the Bob Seger story really took place in the long silence between them, from the moment he began to play to the moment, fifteen years later, when he was finally widely heard. (pp. 68-9)

[Even earlier] ***Beautiful Loser*** was . . . a tentative step into diversity. In addition to the title track's moving autobiography, it contains another striking ballad, **"Jody Girl,"** a sharply drawn, impassioned portrait of the wasted life of a working-class housewife of his own generation; Seger says that it was an important precursor of **"Night Moves."** But, despite the obligatory Detroit-and-nowhere-else hit single, **"Katmandu,"** ***Beautiful Loser*** doesn't really work. It established an important pattern for Seger's work . . . but the arrangements aren't completely realized. But **"Beautiful Loser"**—done as a medley with **"Jody Girl"** and **"Travelin' Man,"** an on-the-road song also from ***Beautiful Loser***—came to life on the followup, the two-disc ***Live Bullet***. . . .

Stranger in Town [is] a title with multilevel meaning. On the one hand, it has some history to it, being the title of an old Del Shannon hit (Seger and Doug Brown used to try to sell songs to Shannon's Ann Arbor-based manager). It also refers to the fact that the album was finished in Los Angeles. . . .

I wonder why [Seger] stays in Detroit. Certainly, he is not much akin to the kind of rock & roll—Stooges, MC5, Ted Nugent—that is supposed to come from Detroit. . . .

In fact, Seger has much more in common with a group of artists who are not defined by region so much as sensibility, though many of them have a strong sense of place in their writing. Seger lists Frankie Miller, Graham Parker, Bruce Springsteen, Eddie Money and Warren Zevon. (p. 70)

Yet, by staying in Detroit, he's chosen to remain isolated from any community of like-minded souls. . . .

Perhaps in this isolation, Seger makes more interesting music than he would elsewhere, although by far the most arresting lyric on ***Stranger*** is **"Hollywood Nights,"** a narrative song about a Midwestern boy who goes to L.A. and gets torn apart by a big city woman.

And of course that's the third meaning of ***Stranger in Town***: Bob Seger as a novice in the community of success. Perhaps it is the most accurate interpretation of the title, which was chosen before he considered going to Los Angeles to record. Or maybe, like **"Beautiful Loser,"** it's accidental autobiography.

For if ***Stranger in Town*** is what Bob Seger has become, **"Beautiful Loser"** is what he almost remained. . . .

Perhaps I've dwelled too long on the failures of his career, but that's because that long blank space between lightning and thunder contains a great deal of the best rock & roll I've ever heard. Short of playing it for you, I don't know how to describe it—comparing Seger with Springsteen, Parker and the like, as even he is willing to do, just trivializes everybody.

What I do know is that, in all the lean years before *Born to Run* made it chic again, Bob Seger was the one guy who constantly reminded me that you didn't have to quit rocking because you had something to say, and you didn't have to be a preverbal meat-head to want to rock. Seger made such perfect miniatures that they could be swept under the rug by trends. . . . Bob Seger isn't some minor figure who got lucky once or twice. He has all the requisites of greatness: the voice, the songwriting, the performance onstage, the vision and the ambition. (p. 71)

Dave Marsh, "Not a Stranger Anymore," in Rolling Stone, *Issue 267, June 15, 1978, pp. 67-71.*

TIMOTHY WHITE

Stranger in Town is a vinyl reality with no chance for retractions. It's also an unqualified success. Incredibly, Seger has topped the triumph that was ***Night Moves*** with an album as raw, painful and invigorating as the rock 'n roll process itself. . . .

If ***Beautiful Loser*** was a kind of exorcism, and ***Night Moves*** was a recollective affirmation of his own worth, then ***Stranger in Town*** is the transcendental step forward. The past and the future are no longer adversaries, the former becoming a fond foundation (**"Old Time Rock & Roll"**) and the latter an adventure (**"Till It Shines"**).

"Brave Strangers" is an evocative rocker in the **"Night Moves"** mold but grittier, with a defiant lyric that makes even fewer apologies for adolescent indiscretions. Ordinarily, the scorching, anthem-like **"Feel Like a Number"** would be the crowning achievement of a Bob Seger lp, but the most ingratiating songs on ***Stranger*** are the love ballads that Seger says he has always been most adverse to recording. . . .

Incidentally, at one point the title of the album was supposed to be *Hollywood Nights,* and the stranger in town makes a little confession on that first song: . . .

> He knew right then he was too far from home.

Too far to feel comfortable, of course. He apparently needed to escape his old stomping grounds in order to see his predicament more clearly, and that's the key to this record's conquering spirit. ***Stranger in Town*** is the tale of Bob Seger's evolution from a frightened street kid to a fearful superstar. It's a true story, and one of the most riveting I've heard.

Timothy White, "Beautiful Winner," in Crawdaddy, *July, 1978, p. 66.*

DAVE MARSH

Listeners who first discovered Bob Seger with ***Night Moves*** and ***Stranger in Town*** clearly find his new album [***Against the Wind***] an even more palatable product, since it leaped into the Top Ten with frightening rapidity. So I guess those of us who remember Seger, the all-American rock & roller, just have to take our lumps. But not necessarily in silence. . . . I'd like to say that this is not only the worst record Bob Seger has ever made, but an absolutely cowardly one as well. ***Against the Wind*** betrays all those years that Seger worked in the Midwestern wilderness, trying to find a national audience for his odd blend of heavy rock and pop smarts. (p. 51)

Against the Wind is all retreat. And the reason that its ascension to the pop-chart stratosphere is scary is because it got there so effortlessly—there was no tension, in the music or anywhere else, to make people think twice. Seger spent the past year crafting failureproof songs that are utterly listenable and quite meaningless. His commercial tactics, I suppose, were a triumph. But as music, ***Against the Wind*** is heartless and mediocre. . . . (pp. 51-2)

At his best, Seger's been able to write songs (from **"Ramblin' Gamblin' Man"** to **"Feel like a Number"**) that are the very voice of the kid down the block. Now, he doesn't sound like he's met such people: all the street life on the current record is seen from an outsider's perspective. Even the hardest rockers—**"The Horizontal Bop," "Betty Lou's Gettin' Out Tonight"**—are hollow. Sure, they're vignettes of ordinary life as before, but this time the most any of Seger's characters are hoping for is a long drunk or a quick lay. I keep expecting to hear him sing, "Have a Coke and a smile." . . .

Against the Wind has almost nothing of Seger's blustering, hard-driving concert sound. . . . Fast tunes saved ***Stranger in Town*** from its excesses, but this time the rock & roll cuts are perfunctory, simply tossed in to separate the overinflated ballad "statements" (none of which contains a line sufficiently memorable to quote) from the flat country rock, which has all the emotional depth of J. D. Souther.

There's a feeling of rootlessness to ***Against the Wind,*** but it's not the same hungry rootlessness that Seger captured so brilliantly in **"Turn the Page,"** his classic about life on the road. Now, in some strange way, he seems removed from his own instincts. The eerie manner in which the production lifts the singer's voice above the band, so that the two never make contact, is a perfect example of the problem. And it's characteristics like this that make ***Against the Wind*** such a slap in the face. Bob Seger's roots were what once sustained him, and for him to turn his back on them in order to join the slick pop-star bandwagon is a genuine copout, a denial that his early years meant anything. . . .

Mostly, ***Against the Wind*** deals in stereotypes, particularly female ones. There's more than a hint of the Eagles' malicious misogyny and preppie snobbery in these numbers—not just **"Fire Lake,"** to which the insufferable Glenn Frey, Don Henley and Timothy B. Schmit contribute precise backing vocals, but in almost all the rest as well. Just as the rockers continually sell the "kids" cynically short, the love songs are all about women—devil, angel or beloved "babe"—who exist only as a commodity, to be worshiped when they're supportive (**"Good for Me"**), belittled when they try to assert themselves (**"Her Strut"**) or chastised when they can't be controlled (**"Against the Wind," "You'll Accomp'ny Me"**). There's no feeling for *people* in these compositions, which is not only a sharp reversal of form for Seger (whose lyrics have always been strongest in characterization), but a complete acquiescence to the Eagles' pop philosophy: a gram of cool is worth a pound of conviction. This is a splendid platform for nostalgia and self-pity, well represented by the country-rocker **"Fire Lake"** and the lugubriously poetic **"No Man's Land,"** but in every other way, it's worthless.

"Who wants to take that long shot gamble?" Bob Seger asks in **"Fire Lake."** And his answer, despite superficial nods at rebelliousness, comes back clearly: *not me*. You could listen to this LP forever and never hear the singer picking up any sort of challenge. It makes me sad, and it makes me angry (another emotion that's disappeared here, though it's often fueled Seger's finest work). Maybe rock & roll never forgets, but the best thing anybody who ever had any hope for Bob Seger can do is try not to remember ***Against the Wind*** and pray for something better next time. I wouldn't hold my breath. (p. 52)

Dave Marsh, "Bob Seger's 'Wind' Is Mostly Hot Air," in Rolling Stone, *Issue 317, May 15, 1980, pp. 51-2.*

RICHARD C. WALLS

[With **"Against the Wind"**, Seger is] still at it and as far as I'm concerned, despite a nagging fear of atrophy and a dim realization that if I indulge too much in nostalgia's fuzzy romance I'm going to turn into a jar of Cheese Whiz, it's great stuff. A brave sense of loss runs thru this album and reaches its apogee on the title cut, which scans like a Jackson Browne song and sounds, at this point, like Classic Seger. Night Moves, take three.

Another of Seger's main concerns nowadays, besides nostalgia, is risk taking—singing about it, not doing it. So, in **"No Man's Land"** we're told ". . . sanctuary never comes / without some kind of risk" while in **"You'll Accomp'ny Me"** he is once again making a wary approach to love—"I'll take my chances babe / I'll risk it all." **"Fire Lake"** is in the same mode. More romance.

Tho Seger sings a lot about risks and it's an important part of the whole ethos here it's ironic, I suppose, that the music itself is as safe as milk. And as sensual. Which is its saving grace, which is why I find myself embracing this music despite its backward thrust—it's as simple and sensual as a cool drink in the middle of a heatwave. What could be finer? Seduced again.

Richard C. Walls, in a review of "Against the Wind," in Creem, *Vol. 12, No. 1, June, 1980, p. 53.*

SAM SUTHERLAND

Where [Seger] . . . varies from his idols (with the possible exception of [Chuck] Berry, who also focused on life-sized joys and frustrations, rather than romantic melodrama) is in the emphatic fallibility of his characters. Even where his more uptempo, ribald songs justify a lustier narrative voice, we sense the hard knocks behind his rasping delivery; for all the fiery vitality he commands from his music, he nearly always conveys an underlying wistfulness.

"Against the Wind" sustains that vantage point without revising the sound or substance of its most recent predecessors, **"Night Moves"** and **"Stranger in Town."** . . . [That] stylistic constancy can only be viewed as a victory, not a lack of contemporaneity.

Like those albums, too, the new one spans uptempo rockers and moody, meditative ballads and draws strength at a canny midpoint between. Like Jackson Browne, Dylan, and a handful of other writers, Seger has mated the narrative ballad's structure and thematic gravity with the tumbling momentum of rock, charging midtempo songs with a double-time undertow or darkening his fast rave-ups with sudden glimpses of melancholy.

That's not to suggest he has become dour. Humor remains a major feature of his writing, serving to underscore his sense of commonality with his audience. As such, his songs are influenced as much by rock as by folk music's tale-telling techniques. Here the approach yields sly double entendres (***The Horizontal Bop***) and comically street-wise anecdotes (***Betty Lou's Gettin' Out Tonight***), as well as sobering fables (***Fire Lake,*** a panoramic, multicharactered view of unraveling relationships and brooding restlessness) and mature love songs (***You'll Accomp'ny Me*** and the title song). (pp. 110-11)

Sam Sutherland, in a review of "Against the Wind," in High Fidelity, *Vol. 30, No. 6, June, 1980, pp. 110-11.*

MICHAEL OLDFIELD

When bereft of ideas, the superstar does not lounge around his million dollar mansion awaiting a visitation from the muse of inspiration. Ever mindful of his responsibilities to his adoring legions . . . he makes a rare concession and gives his public what it wants: a double live album.

Bob Seger's **"Live Bullet"** five years ago, however, was born more from frustration than idleness. After a succession of killer studio sets which had failed to percolate through to a dumb American public, he performed a selection of the best tracks before a partisan audience in his hometown of Detroit and duly knocked them dead. . . .

[As] the best of the oldies are already on **"Live Bullet"**, **"Nine Tonight"** is bound to suffer by comparison.

But luckily, on my American copy at least, sides one and four are together on one album (are Americans too lazy to turn over records?) which means that the second album can be safely discarded, containing as it does raunchy (or unsubtle, depending on your point of view) versions of songs on the last three albums.

The first side has two new numbers, the title track, an original vintage Seger belter, . . . and the highlight of **"Stranger in Town"**, **"Hollywood Nights"**, which gets such a thrashing here you can almost forget the embarrassing lyrics.

Michael Oldfield, in a review of "Nine Tonight," in Melody Maker, *September 19, 1981, p. 16.*

GEOFFREY HIMES

The live versions [on ***Nine Tonight***] fall somewhat short of the inspired studio versions on the 1976 ***Night Moves.*** They juice up the originals from the 1980 ***Against the Wind*** and improve considerably on the disappointing studio work of the 1978 ***Stranger in Town***. . . . With three nights in Boston and six nights in Detroit to choose from, the consistency is unusually high for a live album. (p. 90)

The album pretty much follows the set order on the 1980 tour, leaving out the pre-1976 songs. It opens with the blazing rocker, **"Nine Tonight,"** which previously only appeared on the *Urban Cowboy* soundtrack. . . . Side four is given over to Seger's spectacular encore numbers, **"Night Moves," "Rock 'n' Roll Never Forgets"** and an oldies medley. . . . All in all, ***Nine Tonight*** is a welcome if unsurprising live document from one of America's very best rock 'n' roll bands.

I still can't understand why the rock media pays so much more attention to Bruce Springsteen than to Bob Seger. Both are hard-nosed working class men who write about the daytime drudgery, weekend wildness and elusive dreams of their friends through soaring, R&B-based rock 'n' roll. Springsteen may write better lyrics, but Seger writes better melodies and dance riffs. Springsteen may be a more charismatic stage performer, but Seger is a better singer. I still believe that ***Night Moves*** is better than any Spingsteen album but *The River*. As the new live album proves, **"Rock 'n' Roll Never Forgets"** is as effective a show-closing rock anthem as "Rosalita".... (pp. 90, 92)

I suspect that many critics prefer Springsteen the writer to Seger the singer because lyrics are easier to quote than melodies. I don't mean to knock Springsteen, who's obviously brilliant; I just think Seger is unrecognized as a pivotal figure in rock 'n' roll. Seger's gutsy, down-to-earth songs have penetrated the typing pools and shop floors to battle the escapist fluff of Styx and REO Speedwagon. There are few better examples of how to combine quality and integrity with mass appeal than ***Nine Tonight.*** (p. 92)

Geoffrey Himes, in a review of "Nine Tonight," in Musician, *No. 38, December, 1981, pp. 90, 92.*

MARK PEEL

"Nine Tonight" puts Seger's most popular work of the last few years right where it belongs: in front of a hot-wired, high-voltage audience. It's not so much that this recording reveals new, unsuspected angles or nuances in his music; Seger simply gives himself free rein in concert. ***Night Moves*** and ***The Fire Down Below,*** which are intelligent, well-crafted rockers on his studio albums, here take on a steamy, exultant urgency. (p. 85)

Seger's choice of material on **"Nine Tonight"** offers few surprises, consisting mainly of his hit singles from the late Seventies and 1980. What counts are the performances and the recording, and there the album succeeds on just about every level. . . .

The mix is crisp, balanced, and well-defined, and the obligatory crowd noise is kept to the minimum needed to support the you-are-there illusion.

"Nine Tonight" isn't likely to secure any wider audience for Seger; it retraces too much familiar ground. But it does show the best work of one of rock's earthiest, most perceptive, and most honest performers in a more intense light. (pp. 85-6)

Mark Peel, in a review of "Nine Tonight," in Stereo Review *Magazine, Vol. 47, No. 2, February, 1982, pp. 85-6.*

DAVID FRICKE

Despite numerous references to that "lonesome stretch of gray" and heading "down a westbound road" on "my big two-wheeler," ***The Distance***—Bob Seger's fourteenth album and his first studio release since 1980's ***Against the Wind***—is not just about the highway, rock's most used and abused symbol of wanderlust and escape. It's about the lives, mistakes and promises at either end. **"Comin' Home,"** a bittersweet ballad sandwiched between two vintage Seger grinders on side two, is a particularly striking vision of one prodigal son returning home in humiliating defeat: "You'll just tell them what they want to hear / How you took the place by storm / You won't tell them how you lost it all." Another song, **"Roll Me Away,"** heads defiantly in the other direction, its nomadic urgency and wide-open-spaces imagery heightened by Jimmy Iovine's expansive production. . . .

[On] ***The Distance,*** the road is [Seger's] lifeline home. . . . Seger's best records are his Sixties garage-punk sides, like **"Heavy Music"** and **"Ramblin' Gamblin' Man."** On ***The Distance,*** **"Boomtown Blues,"** with its mean Motor City guitars and ironic lyrical sting . . . vibrates with that same power. So does the high-octane T-Bone Walker-style shuffle **"Makin' Thunderbirds,"** a nostalgic look back at the Detroit auto industry's glory days that is salted with tears not just for the disappearing jobs, but for the fading free spirit those cars symbolized.

The rest of ***The Distance,*** including the romantic interludes, is just as exhilarating. In place of the mawkish campfire sentimentality that plagued ***Against the Wind,*** Seger and producer Iovine have fashioned a broad, cinematic sound that magnifies the everyday trials and "little victories" of the people in these songs. . . .

The Distance is not a very happy record, but, ultimately, it is an encouraging and, at times, triumphant one. "Every hour you survive will come to be / A little victory," he roars at the end. Though the highway is usually nothing more than an easy way out from having to find yet another way of saying, "Baby, let's make it," Seger treats it like an umbilical cord that can go a hell of a long way but should never be cut. The lesson here is that it's not enough to just go the distance—you also have to be able to come back.

David Fricke, in a review of "The Distance," in Rolling Stone, *Issue 388, February 3, 1983, p. 46.*

MARK PEEL

[**"The Distance"**] is in some ways a departure for the rock-'n'-roll laureate of the Midwest. . . .

[One] difference is in the music's pacing. Seger's biggest hits—***Night Moves*** and ***Fire Lake,*** for instance—have tended to settle in at a comfortable, moderate tempo. **"The Distance,"** in contrast, contains no fewer than five songs (***Even Now, Making Thunderbirds, Boomtown Blues, Roll Me Away, House Behind a House***) that threaten to punch the living daylights out of Kunkel's drum kit. The . . . hotter tempos add up to an album with considerably more bite than **"Against the Wind"** or **"Stranger in Town."** . . .

[Lyrics] are what set [Seger] apart from the run-of-the-mill journeyman rocker. A Seger song is always honest, perceptive, and rich in detail. ***Comin' Home,*** for example, takes one of pop music's most overworked themes—the star-struck kid brought back down to earth, and back home, by defeat in the big city—and turns it into something fresh and affecting. In ***Making Thunderbirds,*** Seger gets to the heart of the tragedy of his home town, Detroit, not by looking at the ruins but by reliving better times. And on ***Roll Me Away*** he makes you feel the exhilarating freedom of riding a motorcycle along the crest of a mountain ridge—even if, like me, you'd sooner walk through Death Valley than climb onto a motorcycle.

Don't wait for the live set. Two more years is just too long to wait for stuff this good.

Mark Peel, "Bob Seger," in Stereo Review *Magazine, Vol. 48, No. 6, June, 1983, p. 92.*

DAVE MARSH

[The essay from which this excerpt is taken originally appeared in Record *Magazine in 1983.]*

In 1980, I concluded my review of Bob Seger's ***Against the Wind*** [see excerpt above] by saying: "Maybe rock and roll never forgets, but the best thing anybody who ever had any hope for Bob Seger can do is try not to remember ***Against the Wind*** and pray for something better next time. I wouldn't hold my breath." It is now time for me to exhale, take another deep gulp and prepare for a public bite of crow. ***The Distance,*** Bob Seger's first new album in almost three years, is the best rock and roll record I have heard since *The River,* and more importantly, it's Seger's most committed, cohesive and exciting album ever.

What's most amazing about ***The Distance*** is its ambition. This is Seger's first focused set of songs—the first time he's attempted a song cycle in the fashion of Jackson Browne and Bruce Springsteen. Seger is a better singer and a more creative melodist than either Browne or Springsteen, but he's never had their shamelessness or their intense reach.

In **"Against the Wind"** itself, Seger moaned of having to decide "What to leave in / What to leave out," the plaint of the compulsively self-restrictive. And the schematic programming of his other albums (Top Forty ballads balanced by AOR rockers, "serious" versus fun, sex versus romance) is perhaps their worst limitation. The major achievement of ***The Distance*** is that it synthesizes these pop contradictions, with the result that the best songs are a kind of dialogue between two sides of an argument Seger has been having with himself.

The Distance begins and ends with love songs, **"Even Now"**and **"Little Victories,"** which are really anthems of perseverance—they use personal relationships as metaphors for a vision of the world and the way that it works and what it takes (and costs) to cope with such a place and time. When Seger sings the key lines of **"Little Victories"**—"Every time you keep control when you're cut off at the knees / Every time you take a punch and still stand at ease"—he is obviously singing to every broken worker back home in Michigan as much as to fellow brokenhearted lovers. And this is true whether or not the subtext was planned, because the best music here is explicitly and defiantly about what has happened to Seger and his constituency in the past few years. (This is one of the things that makes it such an amazing improvement over ***Against the Wind,*** which seemed completely abstracted from such lives.)

This political context is easiest to see in the album's hardest-rocking song, **"Makin' Thunderbirds,"** which is an unemployed auto worker's paean to the way his life (and those cars!) used to be. For those three minutes, the singer is as "young and proud" as ever, even though the last verse reckons with the deterioration of both product and pride. But in the very next song, **"Boomtown Blues,"** he's coping with the Depression: moved South, found a job and begun a life robbed of whatever dignity, meaning and sense of connection it might ever have had. As an exposure of the false promise of industry's southern strategy, **"Boomtown Blues"** is the most radical and incisive song Seger has ever written. And he keeps the mood going with "Shame on the Moon," a Rodney Crowell song that illumines the new terms on which people deal with each other in the time of Reagan's New Federalism: "Some men go crazy / Some men go slow / Some men go just where they want / Some men never go." This is the world in which Seger's characters try to maintain their "little victories," whether they're returning shattered to a place that's barely changed (**"Comin' Home"**) or leaving a shattered home for a life that has to be better, though it never quite is (the anthemic **"Roll Me Away"**).

In its portrayal of alienation and isolation and their consequences, personal and political, ***The Distance*** is most akin to *Nebraska* among recent rock albums. Seger's vision is less bleak than Springsteen's, and I suspect that makes it more realistic: people less often go crazy and commit murder in times like these than they simply stumble homeward, seeking what's no longer there, or wander aimlessly, trying to locate what they've falsely been promised. What *Nebraska* and ***The Distance*** share is a sense that times are more terrible than most men and women can bear and that every time anyone maintains human dignity in face of the terror, something of consequence has been achieved. It's their denial of nihilism that makes such albums most valuable.

So Seger's triumph stands not in isolation, but acquires greater meaning when linked with *Nebraska,* Billy Joel's *The Nylon Curtain* and even something like Don Henley's *I Can't Stand Still.* All of these are dealing with the real issues in people's lives right now, the sense of injustice and hopelessness that overwhelms so many rock listeners. (pp. 132-34)

Most superstars are indeed immobilized by their success (that is both the overt and covert theme of ***Against the Wind***). But the great ones find a way to struggle through and speak the truth again. And that is why ***The Distance*** is a record that moves me to the core and makes me want to apologize to Bob Seger.

Consider it rendered. (p. 134)

Dave Marsh, "As the Crow Flies," in his Fortunate Son: Criticism and Journalism By America's Best-Known Rock Writer, *Random House, 1985, pp. 129-34.*

Mary (Florence Elinor) Stewart

1916-

English novelist and author of books for children.

Stewart is credited with bringing higher standards to the genre of romantic suspense novels. Her characterizations are carefully developed, although not complex, and her vivid recreations of such exotic locales as Corfu, Delphi, and the Isle of Skye have long delighted readers. Stewart's novels are well-received critically due to her entertaining stories and skillfully crafted prose.

Stewart's works usually center on a charming young woman inadvertently caught in extraordinary, sometimes life-threatening events. With the aid of the hero, her love interest, Stewart's heroine solves a mystery or survives an adventure. According to Stewart, her characters "observe certain standards of conduct, of ethics, a somewhat honorable behavior pattern." *The Moon-Spinners* (1962), *This Rough Magic* (1964), and *Touch Not the Cat* (1976) are among Stewart's best-known novels.

In 1970 Stewart began a series of novels retelling the Arthurian legend. *The Crystal Cave* (1970), *The Hollow Hills* (1973), and *The Last Enchantment* (1979) are notable for several variations from standard versions of the legend: they are told from the viewpoint of Merlin the magician rather than from that of King Arthur; they are set in the fifth century, rather than the twelfth; and Stewart adheres to historical fact in describing places, customs, and costumes, unlike many chroniclers of the Arthurian legend. In *The Wicked Day* (1983), the fourth book in the series, Mordred, Arthur's illegitimate son, is depicted as a sensitive, ill-fated youth instead of the purely evil figure of legend.

© *Jerry Bauer*

(See also *CLC*, Vol. 7; *Contemporary Authors*, Vols. 1-4, rev. ed.; *Contemporary Authors New Revision Series*, Vol. 1; and *Something about the Author*, Vol. 12.)

ANTHONY BOUCHER

James Sandoe has called a certain type of suspense novel "Euridicean"—you daren't look back on the story, or it vanishes. Mary Stewart's **"Madam, Will You Talk?"** . . . is a nice example: a backward glance will reveal so many whopping coincidences and inadequate or inconsistent motivations that you can't believe a word of it; but so unusually skillful is this young Englishwoman in her first novel that you don't really care. You've had too enjoyable a time with the light, easy charm of the writing, the warmth of the Provencal background, the likability of the heroine, and the headlong urgency of the action to worry about trifles like plausibility.

Anthony Boucher, in a review of "Madam, Will You Talk?" in The New York Times Book Review, *March 18, 1956, p. 43.*

THE NEW YORKER

The heroine of this neatly contrived chase story [**"Madam, Will You Talk?"**] is beautiful but nosy, and she has to find out what is troubling the thirteen-year-old boy she meets in the South of France. This, naturally, leads to all kinds of complications, especially with the child's father, who has reason to suppose that she is part of a plot to get him hanged on a murder charge. There is a great deal of riding around in low, fast cars. . . , any amount of gay Provençal atmosphere, quite a bit of love of one sort or another, and a most satisfactory burst of violence at the end. . . . [Mrs. Stewart's] first effort is very promising. (pp. 151-52)

A review of "Madam, Will You Talk?" in The New Yorker, *Vol. XXXII, No. 5, March 24, 1956, pp. 151-52.*

JAMES SANDOE

Mary Stewart's **"Wildfire at Midnight"** . . . is very like her **"Madam, Will You Talk?"** allowing for a change of scene (to Skye and its mountains) and a rather foolish ritual murderer who sets his victims on pyres. Again the narrator is a breathless (but not humorless) young person whose Hebridean vacation is complicated by her sardonic ex-husband's presence. Selection of the murderer seems pretty perfunctory and so does the sudden departure from the plot of a gorgeous amoral actress as if, having invented her, Miss Stewart hadn't known how to cope with her. Still, the fun of this sort of thing is not final surprises but sustained pitty-pat and here it is. Frail but diverting.

James Sandoe, in a review of "Wildfire at Midnight," in New York Herald Tribune Book Review, *September 9, 1956, p. 8.*

ANTHONY BOUCHER

Mary Stewart proved an agreeable discovery earlier this year with her **"Madam, Will You Talk?"**—a suspense story of low probability but high romantic freshness and readability. **"Wildfire at Midnight"** . . . is more a strict whodunit than pursuit-suspense, but with much the same faults and virtues as in the author's debut—and again the virtues win out. The plot concerns a revival of ancient ritual murders and contains many weaknesses, notably a sadly inadequate portrayal of an "insane" killer; but the setting is the Isle of Skye, depicted with vivid wonder, there's another of Miss Stewart's captivatingly spirited heroines, and the story is rich in uncertainty, excitement and sheer narrative flow.

Anthony Boucher, in a review of "Wildfire at Midnight," in The New York Times Book Review, *September 9, 1956, p. 35.*

BARBARA SCHILLER

[In **"Thunder on the Right,"**] Jennifer Silver, a young Englishwoman fresh from Oxford, visits an obscure convent high in the French Pyrenees. . . . She wished to persuade her recently widowed cousin, Gillian Lamartine, not to become a nun; but upon arriving at the convent she receives the shocking news that Gillian had died weeks before in an auto crash. Although not welcomed by the aristocratic Bursar, a Spanish lay sister with unusual power over the nuns, Jennifer repeatedly returns to find proof of her hunch that the dead woman was not her cousin. . . . [Behind] Gillian's disappearance is a tangled web of intrigue, theft, violence and murder spun by a person whose ambitions and means of attaining them are all too reminiscent of the darker side of the Renaissance personality. As in her previous books, Mary Stewart once again proves herself adept at writing a highly charged romantic mystery thriller distinguished for the excellence of its setting, the charm of its heroine and the breathtaking urgency of action.

Barbara Schiller, "A Highly Charged Thriller," in New York Herald Tribune Book Review, *October 5, 1958, p. 6.*

ANTHONY BOUCHER

That special sub-species of mystery one might call the Cinderella-suspense novel is designed by feminine authors for feminine readers; yet a male can relish such highpoints as "Jane Eyre" or "Rebecca." Of current practitioners, I can't think of anyone (aside from du Maurier herself) who tells such stories quite so well as Mary Stewart, and **"Nine Coaches Waiting"** . . . is her longest and probably her best to date.

The basic story is as simple as it is traditional: The little governess realizes that her charge is in danger of murder by his wicked uncle; meanwhile she has fallen in love with uncle's son—who may be part of the murder plot. Nothing new here, but the old is so agreeably executed. Miss Stewart is always excellent at geographical backgrounds. . . ; she knows wonderfully well how to twist the screw slowly and all but imperceptibly; and her heroines are always spirited, intelligent, resolute—quite free from the vapid idiocy which mars most books of this type. These girls are worth meeting, whatever the sex of the reader.

Anthony Boucher, in a review of "Nine Coaches Waiting," in The New York Times Book Review, *January 18, 1959, p. 20.*

MARY ROSS

[In **"Nine Coaches Waiting,"** Chateau Valmy is] a symbol of an ampler life, perhaps a more satisfying one, than Linda Martin had known since the sudden death of her parents had condemned her to a British orphanage, then a grubby teaching job. Back in the France she had loved in the happy days of her early childhood, she was to be governess to another orphan, frail little nine-year-old Comte de Valmy, who lived in his château under the tutelage of an uncle and aunt. . . .

A guest at the château once called Linda "Jane Eyre," and some of the dark passions of that tale here combine with the Cinderella theme to make a stirring suspense story. Before she had eluded the role for which she had been cast unwittingly, Linda had to deal with envy, malice, corroding suspicion, even attempted murder. For any one even half-heartedly inclined toward romance and adventure, **"Nine Coaches Waiting"** is a novel that will not easily be laid down.

Mary Ross, "Cinderella Arrives at Chateau Valmy," in New York Herald Tribune Book Review, *March 8, 1959, p. 8.*

CHRISTOPHER PYM

Mary Stewart gives each of her admirable novels an exotically handsome (if sometimes rather travel-folderish) setting. In [***My Brother Michael***], by a long chalk the best of them, her pretty little schoolma'am heroine finds a handsome schoolmaster to fall in love with in the bare sun-blasted hills of Delphi. Murder, too, and treasure-trove, with a really villainous villain, a bitch of a bitch, and a flat-out fighting climax. Slightly sentimental overtones, but the Greek landscape and—much more subtle—the Greek character are splendidly done, in a long, charmingly written, highly evocative, imperative piece of required reading for an Hellenic cruise.

Christopher Pym, "It's a Crime," in The Spectator, *Vol. 204, No. 6873, March 18, 1960, p. 401.**

ANNE ROSS

[Mary Stewart] is one of the leading writers in a field which blends suspense with romance and drama. **"My Brother Michael"** like her earlier books, exploits an unfamiliar background—this time, the myth-laden Greece of Delphi and Mount Parnassus. She has departed from an earlier formula, in that the villain is known from the beginning and it is simply a question of outwitting him, but the romance is charmingly present, and there is all the suspense and danger that anybody could demand. . . .

A delightful empathy springs up between hero and heroine, an unspoken respect for, and knowledge of each other, which is most satisfying. Above all, in her portrait of Greece past and present, Mrs. Stewart, who has employed many countries as colorful background for her novels, has, this time, presented the most exciting of all.

Anne Ross, "Fine Place for a Romance," in New York Herald Tribune Book Review, *August 14, 1960, p. 8.*

IRENE GITOMER

The heroine of this cliff-hanger [**"The Ivy Tree"**] refers to her situation as a "fantastic Oppenheim plot." Actually this involved novel of impersonation and inheritance reads more like Daphne Du Maurier—the ruined manor, the beautiful returned-from-the-dead heroine, the darkly handsome Irish villain, his stolid, taciturn half-sister, the tragic widower, the wild ride through the stormy forest—all the elements are here. The author's easy narrative style, her vivid descriptions of the Northumberland countryside, the sharp delineation of her stock characters, her neat, contrived resolution, and her impeccable good taste guarantee satisfaction to fans of the genre.

Irene Gitomer, in a review of "The Ivy Tree," in Library Journal, *Vol. 86, No. 22, December 15, 1961, p. 4309.*

ANTHONY BOUCHER

It's hard to think of anyone more insistently readable than Mary Stewart; **"The Ivy Tree"** . . . is as unput-downable as any of her previous novels. Our heroine accepts the job of posing as the heiress to a farm in Northumberland, and learns that her impersonation entails the risk of murder. To say more would be unfair to the delicate and meticulous game of wits which Miss Stewart carries on with the reader. One may object that the book (her longest) is outsize for its content, and that too much of the plotting is mere mechanical contrivance—but these can only be afterthoughts. No one writes the damsel-in-distress tale with greater charm or urgency.

Anthony Boucher, in a review of "The Ivy Tree," in The New York Times Book Review, *January 7, 1962, p. 36.*

PAMELA MARSH

Readers of Mary Stewart mysteries will not be disappointed with [**"The Moon-Spinners"**]. As always she tangles them in suspense while their imaginations move in an unfamiliar countryside whose loveliness is made strangely lovelier by sudden, darkening mystery. They can be sure the heroine will be British, comely, and intelligent; the hero, British, strong, and understanding; there will be the usual nightmarish inability to distinguish between the good and the terribly wicked; tension will be vibrant, tight, and a touch of life will bloom on every incident and character. They can be confident of romance and humor and, with all that is expected, originality too.

A tiny village at the foot of Crete's White Mountains, a place to dream oneself to, a perfect vacation spot for Greek-speaking Nicola, is the setting for **"The Moon-Spinners."** But even before she reaches her hotel, Nicola finds the countryside a background to mysterious murder and attempted murder. . . .

Nicola is to be faced with more bodies than most Stewart heroines and to become the object of a bizarre chase more terrifying even than the one over the hills of Skye in **"Wildfire at Midnight."**

But there is something so good-humored about Mary Stewart's heroines that it is easy to imagine that despite a bone-chilling experience, Nicola, like the reader, will still be left with memories of a beautiful land.

Pamela Marsh, "The Landscape of Suspense," in The Christian Science Monitor, *January 3, 1963, p. 13.*

ROSE FELD

Mingling murder with romance, Mary Stewart tells a tingling tale in **"The Moon-Spinners."** . . .

With sure craftsmanship that excitingly builds suspense out of action limned against an ancient and brooding landscape, Miss Stewart tells of [Nicola's] involvement with murder, treachery and kidnapping. It is all very satisfying and leads up climactically to a splendid night struggle in the Aegean Sea. Besides weaving a fine story, Miss Stewart can create young people who are warmly and refreshingly their age.

Rose Feld, "Love and Suspense on Crete," in Books, *April 7, 1963, p. 14.*

ANTHONY BOUCHER

[**"This Rough Magic"**] is indeed a magical concoction brewed from the most disparate plot elements: the isle of Corfu, the contemporary English theater, the intelligence and charm of dolphins, the politics of Albania, the benevolence of St. Spiridion (patron of Corfiotes), and above all, Shakespeare's "The Tempest," which is oddly and wonderfully infused into almost every scene. There is, as usual with Stewart, a properly menacing villain (who even tries to kill dolphins), an ingenious criminal operation, a satisfying love story and a lively and resourceful girl at the center of things. A warm and sunny book, for all its violence; even its crimes (in the proper spirit of "The Tempest") give delight and hurt not.

Anthony Boucher, in a review of "This Rough Magic," in The New York Times Book Review, *August 16, 1964, p. 20.*

MAGGIE RENNERT

Lucy Waring, the narrator of [***This Rough Magic***], is one of those heroines who slip into dark clothes and rubber-soled shoes, snatch up a "torch," and creep down to the boathouse (library? conservatory? summer-house?) in the middle of the night—a character as necessary to the suspense story as the amnesiac is to the soap opera.

The author is an old, sure hand and makes a very smooth magic indeed of exciting goings-on on Corfu, an island off the west coast of Greece. . . .

Except for Lucy—who is only energetic, warmhearted and charming—all the English people on the island are handsome, rich and talented, and are never at a loss for words. All the Greeks are noble savages. One of the handsome, rich, etc. Englishmen is a villain, identifiable as such by his villainous activities, though not by anything in his characterization up to the point of his knaveries. The author says, however, he's a veritable Iago, and says it so pleasantly that no reader could be disagreeable. . . .

The competence with which all the bases are touched, all the ritual flights and perils ticked off, is comforting. I wish I'd had this book when I was languishing with the flu.

Maggie Rennert, "Teapot Tempest," in Book Week—The Sunday Herald Tribune, *November 15, 1964, p. 22.*

DOROTHY B. HUGHES

By the quality of her writing, Mary Stewart instilled new life into the romantic suspense story a few years back, and incidentally became the top-ranking novelist in this field. Her current novel [***Airs Above the Ground***] concerns a young Englishwoman whose husband is mysteriously in Vienna, and the young son of a friend who is traveling to that city, ostensibly to visit his divorced father but truly because of his captivation by the Lipizzan horses of the Spanish Riding School. . . . Miss Stewart embroiders her invigorating plot with her gifted sense of scene in one of the most effective of her novels. Only because this author has so endeared herself and so impressed me in her earlier work, would I suggest that perhaps she is writing too many novels, too fast. One need only stand ***The Moonspinners*** against this new book to discern the difference between the poetry of a place evoked through heart-knowledge and mere descriptiveness of a visited scene.

Dorothy B. Hughes, in a review of "Airs above the Ground," in Book Week—The Sunday Herald Tribune, *November 21, 1965, p. 35.*

PATIENCE M. DALTRY

What is the secret of the Stewart magic that keeps her readers so loyal?

Predictability perhaps. The mixture—romance and suspense in exotic locales—remains the same. Mrs. Stewart doesn't pull any tricks or introduce uncomfortable issues. Attractive, well-brought-up girls pair off with clean, confident young men, always on the side of the angels. And when the villains are finally rounded up, no doubts disturb us—it is clear that the best men have won again.

Another thing, these are essentially women's books. Attention is usually riveted on the heroine—a girl displaying just the right combination of strengths and weaknesses. She may blunder into traps and misread most of the signals, but she will—feminine intuition being what it is—stumble onto something important. She will also need rescuing in a cliff-hanging finale.

"The Gabriel Hounds" is no exception. On the first page a 22-year-old English girl vacationing in Damascus meets her cousin Charles whom she has not seen for four years. . . .

Though the suspense side of the tale involves the couple in some rapid action with a bunch of dope peddlers there is never any doubt that they will survive. . . .

It all makes excellent escape fiction. An added dividend for armchair travelers is the well-described Middle East backdrop. So settle back, Stewart fans, and enjoy.

Patience M. Daltry, "More of the Stewart Magic," in The Christian Science Monitor, *September 28, 1967, p. 11.*

ANTHONY BOUCHER

This mystery-romance of the Near East [**"The Gabriel Hounds"**] is long but thin. It is rich in guidebook descriptions and endless prowlings about an ancient palace, and poverty-stricken in plot and character. Of course it is, line by line, highly readable, even occasionally amusing and charming; but it adds up to very little.

Anthony Boucher, in a review of "The Gabriel Hounds," in The New York Times Book Review, *October 15, 1967, p. 57.*

ADELAIDE EARLE

I was some way along in ***The Gabriel Hounds*** before I realized what it reminded me of. The desert romance with its mysterious Arabs and menacing servants, silken hangings and scented gardens, isn't dead at all. The time may be the present, but *The Sheik* and *The Desert Song* update very nicely. I had a strong feeling that I was back at the Wednesday matinee with a box of chocolates. And the appeal of ***The Gabriel Hounds,*** I imagine, is largely to the Wednesday matinee audience—mostly female, and all set for an escapist afternoon in the exotic East.

I do not mean that Mrs. Stewart has stolen any plots or modelled her book on any preceding camel operas. It's an engrossing yarn, her use of the history of Lady Hester Stanhope is fascinating, and she obviously knows the Eastern countries she is writing about. But the women's matinee aura is unmistakable. (p. 10)

But there are worse ways to relax than at a matinee and if that is your dish, then ***The Gabriel Hounds*** will be your book. (pp. 10-11)

Adelaide Earle, in a review of "The Gabriel Hounds," in Book World—Chicago Tribune, *March 31, 1968, pp. 10-11.*

MARY STEWART

I have written ten full-length novels so far, and a long-short novella called ***The Wind Off the Small Isles,*** which is a kind of coda to the others, and a bridge to my forthcoming historical novel, ***The Crystal Cave.***

Looking at the ten main books as a body of work, a canon (if I may for convenience dignify them with that word), I see them as falling naturally into certain groupings.

The first five novels, up to ***My Brother Michael,*** are exploratory novels, sharing a theme and much else. They bear obvious marks of a tyro experimenting with different forms. They vary a good deal in structure, and make some use of sharp differences in setting. ***Madam, Will You Talk?,*** the first, was a chase story written, concerto-fashion, on two levels. . . . [It] is ostensibly a fast, episodic adventure tale embodying familiar thriller elements heightened by the setting and by deliberate use of coincidence. Above and dominating the thriller-plot run the love story and the main theme together. They might be summarized by the quotation at the head of Chapter Fourteen:

> Fate, I come, as dark, as sad
> As thy malice could desire.

The love story is that of a fate-driven love, self-contained, all-else-excluding, whose image is the enchanted bubble in which the lovers seem to move, while the violent world swirls around them, unable to touch them or destroy their faith in each other.

What I have called the main theme is the search for solid values in a shifting and corrupt world, and the affirmation that "the rules don't break themselves" and that "good does beget good."

Wildfire At Midnight was an attempt at something different, the classic closed-room detective story with restricted action, a biggish cast, and a closely circular plot. It taught me technically a great deal, but mainly that the detective story, with its emphasis on plot rather than people, is not for me. What mattered to me was not the mystery, but the choice the heroine faces between personal and larger loyalties.

With ***Thunder on the Right,*** I tried a technical change of approach, from first person to third. I had dropped naturally, without calculation, into the first person . . . but now thought it right to experiment. Of course writing in the first person has certain drawbacks, especially in "danger" or "suspense" situations—certain elements of surprise are cut out, the viewpoint is limited, and direct action is also limited to scenes where the protagonist is present—but for me the advantages far outweigh the losses. The gain in vividness, personal involvement and identification is immense. I have always been interested in pinning sensation down into words, and first-person writing allows close exploration of physical reactions to the stimuli of fear, joy, pain, and so on. In my first book, especially, I was trying this out, analyzing in detail not only strong sensation, but sensation of every kind—being tired, being hungry and smelling food, going to sleep, coming out of an anesthetic—in fact, I suppose, what living itself *feels like,* not just how one thinks and acts.

In ***Thunder on the Right,*** with the third-person approach, I found I had more freedom of action and viewpoint, but in my next novel, ***Nine Coaches Waiting,*** went back with a kind of relief to the first person, and have used it ever since.

Nine Coaches Waiting is yet again structurally different. This is the Cinderella story, openly acknowledging its great model, treating that model with some astringence, but keeping and humanizing the strong line of the traditional love story. The theme superimposed on the romantic thriller plot is the classic dilemma of choice between love and duty.

My Brother Michael was the result of my first travels to Greece and the start of my love affair with that marvelous country. Technically I was now surer of myself; what one loses in wild freshness one gains in technical assurance. By this time I had an idea that if I wanted a certain effect, I would get it, even if it *was* as often as not done naturally, and only analyzed afterwards on demand. And if storytelling itself, as I suggested earlier, comes as naturally as leaves to a tree, the stories, too, grow out of one another as branches spring in order from the growing trunk. ***My Brother Michael*** was the logical development of what I had been writing up till then; it rounded off something I had been quite deliberately trying to do through all my first five books.

What these five books have in common—apart from the obvious superficial likenesses imposed by the cast of their author's mind—is a deliberate attempt by a new writer to discard certain conventions which seemed to her to remove the novel of action so far from real life that it became a charade or a puzzle in which no reader could involve himself sufficiently really to care. I tried to take conventionally bizarre situations (the car chase, the closed-room murder, the wicked uncle tale) and send real people into them, normal everyday people with normal everyday reactions to violence and fear; people not "heroic" in the conventional sense, but averagely intelligent men and women who could be shocked or outraged into defending, if necessary with great physical bravery, what they held to be right. (pp. 10-12)

Along with this went a theme that I tried to develop up to and into ***My Brother Michael,*** a hatred of violence and a fear of the growing tendency to regard it as a solution to any problem. Because of this, it seemed to me (even in the early 1950's) time to discard the type of detective novel where pain and murder are taken for granted and used as a parlor game. In my first novels, too, I discarded and laughed at certain conventions of plot, including the romantic hero, unthinkingly at home with violence, who was still mainstream when I started writing; and his equally romantic alternative, the social misfit who was just coming into fashion. I was tired of "tough" books where the girl "heroine" is regarded purely as a sexual object, and where her qualities of mind and heart (if any) are treated as irrelevant. I tried unobtrusively where I could to show admiration for liberal ideas, common sense, and the civilized good manners that are armour for the naked nerve. (p. 12)

You might say that when I emerged from the romance-lands—Provence, the Hebrides, the Pyrenees, High Savoy—and traveled to Greece, I came at last hard up against the fierce logic which informs that brilliant, realistic people. I went to Delphi and asked a question, and was left to interpret the Delphic answer, "the smile behind the smoke." There comes a time when ferocity has to be met with ferocity, violence with violence. The bitter end of liberal logic is that if Athens remains true to herself, she falls to the barbarians of Sparta. I can find no answer to this. I suspect there is no answer, but a real writer's job is to present, not to preach. Michael's brother, in my book, resorts to violence and by it wins a respite for the good; he also learns another simple, age-old and cruel fact of life—that we are all members one of another; we are born involved, locked in the great chain of being. We need never send to know for whom the bell tolls; it tolls for us all.

After this, the branches grow rather differently from the tree. But I won't bore you by going blow by blow through the rest. ***The Ivy Tree*** made for me a complete change; this was totally different and was my nostalgia book for my home countryside and a very beautiful house I once knew, since pulled down. The story is summed up by a quotation in the text: "*Time hath his revolutions; there must be a period and an end to all earthly things, finis rerum, an end of names and dignities, and whatsoever is terrene . . .*" That's the story, but it also says that in spite of failure one can always rebuild, and better than before, provided one has kept faith with oneself. Then, after the light-hearted romp of ***The Moon-Spinners,*** came ***This Rough Magic,*** with its little cast of people who have failed, trying to escape the icy and terrifying world of their failure. They also learn about involvement. . . . And [Lucy Waring] and her lover learn that the enchanted island to which they have escaped, full of sounds and sweet airs that give delight and hurt not, is every bit as rough and bloody as their own grey northern country, and that the latter is the one that owns them and they have to serve. One cannot opt out. And one can build a second time, successfully, albeit a different structure and with different materials, but only if one has kept faith with oneself.

Perhaps, for those who have never read any of my books, I have made them sound altogether too ponderous and didactic. Nothing is further from what I tried to do as I wrote. The story comes first and is served first. The only legitimate way for a storyteller to speak is through the actions and opinions of her characters, and these are live and in many ways independent of me. These novels are light, fast-moving stories which are meant to give pleasure, and where the bees in the writer's bonnet are kept buzzing very softly indeed. I am first and foremost a teller of tales, but I am also a serious-minded woman who accepts the responsibilities of her job, and that job, if I am to be true to what is in me, is to say with every voice at my command: "We must love and imitate the beautiful and the good." It is a comment on our age that one hesitates to stand up and say this aloud. But looking back now on the way I was thinking over these fifteen years as I wrote, it seems to me that this above all else is what I have affirmed. (pp. 12, 46)

Mary Stewart, "Teller of Tales," in The Writer, *Vol. 83, No. 5, May, 1970, pp. 9-12, 46.*

R. F. GRADY, S.J.

[In **"The Crystal Cave"**] Mary Stewart lets Merlin tell his story from the time he was six-years of age, the bastard grandson of the King of Maridunum in Wales. . . . Myrddin Emrys, called Merlinus in the Roman way, from the name for a falcon, was a strange boy, given much to solitary musing and sometimes seeming to have been gifted, perhaps an inheritance from the Princess Niniane, with a kind of second sight.

It was only after the boy—now growing up rapidly—ventured one day into a cave on a mountain not far from the palace in Maridunum and became acquainted with and then a pupil of Galapas, a hermit and a kind of wizard, that the real story gets rightly under way. . . .

Fifth century Britain and Brittany come to life in Miss Stewart's vigorous imagination. The Druids and their fearful rites, the worship of Mithras, the superstitions surviving around the old pagan deities, these seem to get better treatment than do the early Christians, their bishops and priests. Merlin is never baptized—although his mother, Lady Niniane is a devout Christian and enters a convent—it would, presumably, erase his magic and his second sight. Merlin at the end of the exciting adventures, engineers a nocturnal encounter between Uther . . . and Princess Ygraine, wife of King Gorlois of Tintagel. From this clandestine union Arthur—a bastard, because Gorlois had not yet died as he was to later in battle—was born and entrusted to Merlin.

There the story ends.

Those who have read and enjoyed the many novels of Mary Stewart . . . will not need to be told this is an expertly fashioned and continually absorbing story, with a facile imagination fleshing out the legend of the parentage of the future King Arthur—and, too, of Merlin himself. There is, besides, a fine feeling for the waters and mountains, the moods and mystery of its pre-historic Welsh setting.

R. F. Grady, S.J., in a review of "The Crystal Cave," in Best Sellers, *Vol. 30, No. 8, July 15, 1970, p. 158.*

NORA E. TAYLOR

Was Merlin the wizard ever a boy? Miss Stewart's novel [**"The Crystal Cave"**] contends that he must have been. She tells an imaginative history of a frail and frightened child finding companionship in nature and a hermit. From that apprenticeship it was a short step to "the power" which seemed to be combined of things overheard and repeated expediently, and other things "dreamed."

With this novel Miss Stewart ranges over Wales, Brittany, and Cornwall. Her tale is an exploration of the days before the arrival of Arthur with his dreams of knighthood and a united country, on the early British scene.

Merlin, traditional history says, was the illegitimate son of princess Niniane, daughter to a king of Wales. His father remains unknown, though popularly rumored to be the prince of darkness. Hence Merlin's supernatural powers. One slight and suspect historical reference to him as Merlinus Ambrosius was enough for Miss Stewart. She gave him Ambrosius, count of Brittany, as a father. On that foundation and on the semi-mythological romantic account written in Oxford by a 12th-century Welshman, Miss Stewart has concocted what she calls "a work of pure imagination."

Today's sophisticated scholars can easily explain, without recourse to a prince of darkness, Merlin's "crystal cave" wherein he saw visions, the mental telepathy by which he sometimes foretold events, and the wisdom with which he advised Ambrosius and his younger brother Uther Pendragon.

There really is little "magic" in the story, and what there is rarely exceeds the familiar "knowing before the event." But the very uncertainty of its inclusion lends a certain falseness to an otherwise absorbing story, which has been carefully researched historically so that it is peripherally authentic.

Nora E. Taylor, "Mary Stewart Conjures Merlin," in The Christian Science Monitor, *September 3, 1970, p. 13.*

SISTER EMILY WEIR

"The Hollow Hills" is an exciting tale of spells, enchantment, dreams, and visions. The greatest enchantment of all is that cast by the master storyteller, Mary Stewart. Once again, as in **"The Crystal Cave,"** she has transported us to fifth-century Britain and has brought alive for us the shadowy figures of legendary lore. This is no mere sequel to **"The Crystal Cave,"** although more or less the same cast of characters appears; it is a strong novel standing on its own right to beguile the reader. Besides fascinating us with the lure of magic, the author exhibits the same deft handling of suspense which has made her novels with a more contemporary setting so popular.

Merlin, mentor and cousin of King Arthur, tells this story, which opens with the prophecy of the child yet to be born. . . . With Arthur's birth begins the great adventure of Merlin's life, namely, the protection of the child until he can claim his throne. Uther, knowing that the parentage of the child could be challenged, has ordered that Arthur be removed from his court. Uther's enemies seek out Merlin who skillfully builds false trails to lead them away from the young Arthur. Finally, when Arthur is fourteen, his father, a dying man, acknowledges him and makes him his heir. Figuring too in this story is the search for and discovery of Arthur's famous sword.

All in all, this makes a smashing good tale. The suspense is superb and the reader is kept involved in the unwinding of the plot. Miss Stewart has taken the main lines of the Arthurian legend and has developed the basic elements in a plausible way. She gives one a feeling for the century about which she writes. The focus is on the concealment and final acknowledgement of Arthur and the search of Merlin for the sword; there is a lesser conflict, quite indicative of the times, that adds to the interest of the book and to its historical value: the conflict between Christianity and the pagan religions. Miss Stewart shows herself particularly apt in her characterization. Merlin is a very real person, and we become immersed in his account as he narrates it with the skill of a bard of old. The personality of the young Arthur does not emerge until late in the story and as we come to the end we see the youth as forerunner of the mature king. . . .

This is a book to recommend to the reader who appreciates the spell of well-chosen words and the art of a superior raconteur. It's the kind of entertaining book that one saves for a special time when it can be tasted and savored for its full flavor. (pp. 191-92)

Sister Emily Weir, in a review of "The Hollow Hills," in Best Sellers, *Vol. 33, No. 8, July 15, 1973, pp. 191-92.*

EMILY WEIR, C.H.S.

Mary Stewart has once more produced a suspense-filled novel of mystery and romance. The setting of this contemporary novel [***Touch Not the Cat***] is an old English estate of the Ashley family. Byrony Ashley . . . is working in Madeira when she receives word that her father is dying in Germany. By the time she arrives, he is dead and she is given his last message. She was prepared for this bad news before the telephone call had summoned her. She had received a message through "the gift" from someone whom she calls her phantom lover and who also has "the gift." . . .

Taking her father's ashes with her, Byrony returns to England. There are three things which she must do. She must transfer the estate and its belongings to her cousin, since only male members of the Ashley family may inherit Ashley Court; she must clear up for herself the mysterious circumstances surrounding her father's death and decipher the meaning of the message and warning of her father's last words; and, lastly, she must find out who her phantom lover is.

While this novel does not have the rich background of the author's books on the Arthurian legend, it does have marvelous suspense with all the trappings of a superior gothic novel. There is the eerie charm of an old English house with hidden passages, age-old secrets, and ancestors with dark pasts. Despite such a background, the characters are believable persons. Byrony is a lovely young woman, and the villains are not entirely bad, but rather weak persons compelled by greed.

Emily Weir, C.H.S., in a review of "Touch Not the Cat," in Best Sellers, *Vol. 36, No. 8, November, 1976, p. 250.*

MAUREEN FRIES

Of all literary genres, romance is perhaps the most irrational, focusing as it does upon the strange, the marvelous, and the supernatural. And of all the "matters" of romance, that of Britain contains the most irrationalities. The obscure prophecies of Merlin; the profusion of unworldly characters, sometimes humanized like Morgan le Fay and Merlin himself, sometimes completely fantastic like the Lady of the Lake and her numerous damsels; the unorthodox sexual relations, including semi-miraculous conceptions such as those of Arthur and Galahad, incest or attempted incest and—statistically—more rapes or semi-rapes than any other branch of medieval narrative: all of these elements presented, even to medieval authors, the challenge of rationalization. (pp. 258-59)

This traditional Arthurian *matière* presents a much greater problem for the modern novelist than it did for the medieval romancer. In origins, and unlike romance, the novel is bourgeois rather than aristocratic, factual (at least for the most part) rather than marvelous, and concerned with the close analysis of inner character rather than with the proliferation of outward adventure. Arthuriana requires all the subtlety of narrative technique which several generations of gifted novelists have developed over some centuries if it is to yield a version of events palatable to modern tastes. That this practical necessity may yet issue in strikingly disparate treatments of the "matter" of Britain appears from an examination and comparison of T. H. White's *The Once and Future King* with Mary Stewart's incomplete trilogy, ***The Crystal Cave*** and ***The Hollow Hills.*** In the use of narrator, of temporal setting, and of modes of characterization, both White and Stewart display that independence of choice which distinguishes the modern from the medieval interpreter of traditional material. It is all the more surprising, then, that the subsequent evolution of theme should be so similar in both authors, and so resonant of concerns of interest to both medieval and modern audiences.

Unlike most medieval narrators, with Chaucer's as the most prominent exception, both White's and Stewart's narrators are . . . "dramatized": that is, neither is self-effacing, and each can be seen as presenting a definite point of view. White's narrator is omniscient, detached, and implies his author's presence in *The Once and Future King*. . . . All of the narrator's poses are designed to underline the anachronism of the teller vis-à-vis his tale; intrusive in what I think of as an inoffensive, Thackerayan way, they serve as a running and rational commentary upon the characters and the events of the story. . . . (pp. 259-60)

Stewart has chosen a much more limiting and difficult mode of narration: her story is told by Merlin, in the first person; and—since Merlin rather than Arthur is her hero—she thus faces all the hazards inherent in the first-person-as-narrator: limitation of knowledge of other characters to what is seen or heard, indirect access to the narrator's mind itself, possible distortion or "unreliability" of the narration proper. . . . Like White's narrator, her Merlin is distanced from the action, but not through the devices of anachronistic presence or narrative intrusion. Rather, his detachment is achieved by his telling his tale in his extreme age at a long physical and temporal distance from its events, imprisoned in the crystal cave which, foreseeing, he could nevertheless not avoid. . . . Merlin's prescience and vision somewhat overcome the inadequate access to necessary information which tends to inhibit "I" narrators; but, even more than most narrator-agents, he exhibits a self-consciousness which is often tedious and sometimes annoying. Particularly in ***The Hollow Hills,*** his emphasis upon his suffering emotionally for his major part in Uther's conception of Arthur upon Ygraine, and for his failure to keep Morgause from bedding her half-brother Arthur, sounds a note of self-pity which somewhat vitiates our sympathy with his character. . . . White's narrator may, superficially, be less sophisticated than Stewart's. . . , but his detachment from participation in the tale as well as his anachronism allow him to avoid the bathos which occasionally envelops Stewart's Merlin. (pp. 260-61)

A similar disparity emerges from the two authors' attitudes toward the temporality of the Arthurian legend. Stewart disavows in her "Author's Note" to ***The Crystal Cave*** any "claim to serious history". . . ; but she has evoked the possible historical ramifications of Arthur's life and death by setting her tale in that late-fifth/early-sixth century Britain in which he may actually have existed as a *dux bellorum* against the Saxons. Her careful research into place names, religious sects, costume and custom are what we might expect from the professional historical novelist she is, and she shows much ingenuity in her use of historical detail to rationalize the supernatural. Part of Merlin's knowledge of character and hidden event, for example, is represented as gleaned from his youthful forays into the abandoned Roman hypocaust (or disused heating system for the baths) of his grandfather's castle. . . . Such precision and verisimilitude are foreign to White's conception of the Arthurian matter, as we might guess from his anachronistic narrator. . . . White's introduction of Robin Hood . . . illustrates [his] casual attitude to actual contemporaneity but a real grasp of the timelessness of all legends as well; and the comic Norman/Saxon counterpoint which emerges here and elsewhere in his book is ultimately as seriously meant as Stewart's more prosaic juxtaposition of Christian/Mithraic/Druidic cult, and Briton/Celt/Old One.

Perhaps Stewart's conception of her material as tragic emerges from the age-old connection of history with tragedy and thus makes inevitable her literal conception of Arthurian temporality. White conceived his story initially as a comedy, and even as the tragic sense of his material deepens with each of the three books subsequent to "The Sword in the Stone" he never abandons completely the tender humorous note which so distinguishes his *sens* of the legend and which is not by its humor denied high seriousness. . . . [White's most] successful union of history with legend is his tour-de-force ending in which Thomas Malory, King Arthur's "fresh and decent" page. . . , is knighted by Arthur and commanded to tell the King's story first to Warwick . . . and then to the world. Here the true superiority of White's grasp of the Arthurian matter to Stewart's emerges more strongly: White understands that, whatever the actual event, romance is not history; indeed, his treatment of time comes as close to the method of the medieval romancer as is palatable to modern taste.

Most innovative of all in both White and Stewart is their handling of characterization. Limitations of time and of Stewart's opus—she has thus far carried her narrative only to Arthur's kinging—allow me to deal with only two examples, the characters of Arthur and of Merlin. . . . Both authors devise for their respective heroes *enfances* the fullness of which they have invented, and which parallel those long medieval *enfances* of Lancelot and Tristan which formed such large narrative chunks of the French prose romances (and anticipated the modern *Bildungsroman*). Both Arthur and Merlin are seen as very much in tune with nature in their youth; each has a guru-like figure to guide him, Arthur, Merlin, and Merlin, the sorcerer Galapas. . . . While Stewart sets Merlin rather than Arthur at the center of her narrative, she cleverly capitalizes upon the parallels between the magician and his pupil. Both are of mysterious if plausible conception. . . ; both technically of illegitimate conception; both seeking fathers they have never known. Everywhere in White Merlin's magic is minimized: he knows the future because he "lives backward," he fumbles his tricks with appalling frequency, his knowledge is sometimes mere booklearning which he opposes to the "athleticism" of the chivalry he so disdains. Stewart's explanation of Merlin's vision and prophetic gift is both more mixed and more interesting: he inherits his "sight" from his mother, he develops his "power" through celibacy, he creates his "magic" by clever makeup and disguise. Most provocative of all is Merlin's own observation, "men with God's sight are often human-blind" . . . , a truism he proves in his two major blunders, his failing to foresee the death of Gorlois during Arthur's conception and the seduction of Arthur by Morgause.

I have no time here adequately to explore the various themes which emanate from this rationalizing impulse of the Arthurian matter in White and Stewart, so I will confine myself only to the most obvious motif emerging from the contrapuntal characterizations of Arthur and Merlin in each work. In these two figures both authors seem to discern the respective types of the active and the contemplative man. . . . Merlin's searching of books and nature is opposed to the hectic physical activity of both Arthur and Lancelot in White; and in Stewart as well as in White, he returns eagerly to his crystal cave whenever he can and finally and relievedly for good, preferring the company of his books, his music, and his medicines to that of his fellow man. Contrariwise, Arthur is seen by both authors as energetic, charismatic, and not overly intelligent, although Stewart has thus far (because she has not yet published her third volume) made less of this than White. In both authors Arthur appears as the instrument through which Merlin hopes to perfect a society from which he can then retire. . . . To neither White nor Stewart does either Merlin or Arthur represent a completely integrated hero; and it is when Merlin withdraws from the scene, more explicitly in these modern works than in their medieval predecessors, that the split in consciousness represented by Merlin and Arthur, the split between the thinking and the doing man, begins to have tragic repercussions for their society.

In the interplay and the interdependence of Arthur and Merlin may be seen the perennial problems of just rule and human frailty, vital issues not only for medieval times but for the twentieth century as well. The mineral rivalry of our own age, whether atomic or otherwise, is a result of that medieval science of which Merlin is the most prominent romance representative; and the welfare of the common people with which that science is so inseparably and continually interlinked is tied to the search for an ideal government, of which Arthur is the archetypal champion. In making over medieval romance into modern novels, T. H. White and Mary Stewart have not only coped, mostly successfully, with the irrationality of the Matter of Britain. They have also grasped and translated into a convincing modern, if diverse, idiom that rational core of truth about human psychology, and the human condition, which constitutes not only the greatness of the Arthurian legend but also its enduring appeal to readers of all centuries and all countries, and to writers of every time and every literary persuasion. (pp. 261-65)

Maureen Fries, "The Rationalization of the Arthurian 'Matter' in T. H. White and Mary Stewart," in Philological Quarterly, *Vol. 56, No. 2, Spring, 1977, pp. 259-65.**

JOSEPH McCLELLAN

In two earlier volumes, ***The Crystal Cave*** and ***The Hollow Hills,*** Mary Stewart has whetted readers' appetites for Arthurian marvels. [***The Last Enchantment***] should be the climax, and if some of her fans find it an anticlimax, part of the problem lies in the material and part in unrealistic expectations. . . .

[Having] used two long, exciting novels to get Arthur on the throne, Mary Stewart has reached the final volume of her trilogy and we can settle back expecting to hear the old stories told again with her unique touch.

There is only one trouble with this expectation; Mary Stewart does not fulfill it, and she quite clearly never had any intention of fulfilling it. Her story is not strictly about Arthur but about Merlin, Arthur's prophet and wizard. And when she does get to Arthur, she introduces us to a relative stranger.

The Arthur we have known and loved is a man basically of the 12th century. Mary Stewart ignores him, brushes away as irrelevant all the details with which his legend became encrusted during the age of chivalry and tries to get back to the original Arthur, leader of battles (*dux bellorum*) who led the bitter struggle 15 centuries ago to maintain the Celtic hegemony against the Germanic invaders of Britain.

The name of Lancelot does not appear in this story; the Holy Grail, the round table, the building of Camelot are dismissed in passing with perfunctory lip service. The colorful adventures of knights errant are simply thrown out—quite rightly, since they have nothing to do with the fifth-century leader of battles.

Fair enough; history is history, and Mary Stewart has made a fair stab at putting it back in perspective. Her effort should be recognized even by those who will then go back and reread their Malory. But even for those who will not miss the colorful trimmings usually associated with Arthur, this final volume presents special problems. Strictly speaking, once Arthur is safely on the throne, as he is when this volume opens, Merlin's life work is over. He spends most of ***The Last Enchantment*** fading away as gracefully as he can manage. His supernatural powers grow fitful, fade and disappear. He is no longer at the center of the action, making things happen, but on the sidelines, observing and reacting, sometimes watching powerless and horrified as the dire prophecies he made in earlier volumes finally come to pass. . . .

In the faithful working out of her grand plan, Mary Stewart comes to the most difficult part in this final volume, for it is here that the source material on Merlin becomes hard to handle, chaotic and confusing. Making sense of this material is no easy task, and in this volume one must admire the ingenuity of Stewart's effort more than the plausibility of the story.

Perhaps the most awkward of these legends is the one of Merlin's infatuation with Nimue, a follower of the Lady of the Lake, to whom he taught his craft and who rewarded him by shutting him up alive inside a mountain where he would die "a shameful death." Unable to accept this ridiculous end to her hero's life, Stewart transforms the legend into a touching love story—the old enchanter reaching fulfillment in his final years, after his great dynastic task has been accomplished, and passing on his gift to his newfound love. Also well-handled is the disturbing story of the slaughter of the innocents—the massacre of newborn children in a vain attempt to locate and eliminate the infant Mordred.

The Grail, the abduction of Guinevere and other traditional materials are also presented, but the treatment is Stewart's own, the emphasis shifted for her purpose, which is not simply to recast old material but to bring alive a long-dead historical epoch—not the Middle Ages of Malory but the Dark Ages of the original Arthur.

This she does splendidly. Fifth-century Britain is caught in these pages, and while it may lack some of the exotic glitter of the imaginary 12th-century Britain that Arthur usually inhabits, it is a fascinating place. . . .

In the midst of this turmoil, Arthur and his mentor Merlin stand as forces of reason, peace and order, working against considerable odds and wresting at least a temporary victory. If Camelot means anything beyond simple, colorful adventures, this is what it means, and Stewart has conveyed that meaning—not perfectly but as well as faithfulness to her vision will permit.

Joseph McClellan, "In the Days of Swords and Sorcery," in Book World—The Washington Post, *July 22, 1979, p. C6.*

PAULA J. TODISCO

[***The Last Enchantment***] does not quite equal ***The Crystal Cave*** . . . and ***The Hollow Hills*** . . . in vitality and drama. In both precursors, Stewart sustains a sense of anticipation of a grand resolution of the forces of good and evil which does not occur in the last installment. As Arthur rises, Merlin, who has lost his powers, no longer dominates events but retreats into semi-retirement and, at last, to the living death foretold for him. The novel ends curiously with Arthur seemingly at the height of his powers, though the forces that will undo him are present and poised to attack. Merlin has been unconvincingly rescued from the fate that the legends accord him but has no real place in the action that awaits. It all seems a little unsatisfying, and readers may wonder if a fourth tale isn't after all projected—one that would lead to the legendary conclusion of the Arthurian tragedy.

Paula J. Todisco, in a review of "The Last Enchantment," in School Library Journal, *Vol. 26, No. 2, October, 1979, p. 164.*

ROY HOFFMAN

[**"The Wicked Day"**] focuses on Mordred, "the boy from the sea," King Arthur's bastard son by his half-sister Morgause, enchantress and Queen of Lothian and Orkney. Some useful notes at the end point out that Mordred has long suffered a bad reputation as Arthur's mean-spirited, traitorous, regicidal son. But Miss Stewart attempts to resurrect him as a compassionate young man who is helpless before fate, an introspective character who rages in Hamlet-like fashion, "Am I to be a sinner—more, the worst of sinners, a parricide? What gods are these?" In almost every way, **"The Wicked Day"** is a highly enjoyable romance. . . . [Miss Stewart] gives us eerie, mist-shrouded Orkney dawns, spooky underground passageways, deadly witch sisters, a likable and fatherly Arthur, and—the best characters in the book—Mordred and Morgause's three other ambitious, hotheaded sons. But in attempting to portray Mordred as a more complex character than previously depicted, Miss Stewart is not always acute. At times Mordred resorts to over-simplified musing on his problems, and there is some heavy, unnecessary foreshadowing to dramatize his meeting with destiny. . . . Still, by the time Mordred and Arthur meet their inevitable fate, many convincing characters have surfaced in this provocatively recast legend.

Roy Hoffman, in a review of "The Wicked Day," in The New York Times Book Review, *January 1, 1984, p. 20.*

MARY MILLS

[In ***The Wicked Day***] Stewart has created flesh and blood characters out of legends, and in doing so has crafted a well-plotted and passionate drama. More historical than mystical, the novel colorfully and creatively recreates a turbulent era in history. Young adult readers will become caught up in the mixture of history and legend which Stewart has woven, and be sympathetic toward Mordred, a character fulfilling a fate prophesied by Merlin.

Mary Mills, in a review of "The Wicked Day," in School Library Journal, *Vol. 30, No. 7, March, 1984, p. 178.*

M. JEAN GREENLAW

Mordred, bastard son of King Arthur, has always represented consummate betrayal. Mary Stewart casts him in a different role in ***The Wicked Day.*** This rich saga begins with Mordred cast off as an infant and allows us to grow with him through the myriad plots that surrounded his life and brought him to his day of infamy with his father, King Arthur. Stewart shapes a sense of the inevitable doom of Camelot, not by Mordred's desire but by the fateful actions of many men and women. Though we know the ending, the tale is wonderfully told through a new perspective and is worthy of its place with Mary Stewart's ***Merlin Trilogy.***

M. Jean Greenlaw, in a review of "The Wicked Day," in Journal of Reading, *Vol. 27, No. 8, May, 1984, p. 741.*

Glendon (Fred) Swarthout

1918-

American novelist, short story writer, and dramatist.

Photograph Columbia Pictures. Courtesy of Glendon Swarthout

Swarthout's novels address diverse subjects and are usually set in Michigan, where he grew up, or in the Western United States, where he has lived much of his adult life. His most respected work, *Bless the Beasts and Children* (1970), is set in a summer camp in Arizona and concerns a group of boys who are considered misfits by their families and peers. When they undertake a difficult and dangerous task, the boys discover within themselves the ability to think and act positively.

Among Swarthout's novels set in Michigan are *Willow Run* (1943), *Loveland* (1968), and *The Melodeon* (1977). *Willow Run,* Swarthout's first novel, takes place in a factory where World War II bombers are manufactured. Critics remarked that in addition to revealing the human dimension of factory work, Swarthout also conveyed a satisfactory technical picture of how a bomber is built. *Loveland* is a nostalgic story of a young man's struggles during the depression, and *The Melodeon* is a fantasy-like tale of a boy who accomplishes a good deed at Christmas with the aid of his great-grandfather's spirit.

Many of Swarthout's best-known novels share a Western setting. In addition to *Bless the Beasts and Children,* critics praised *They Came to Cordura* (1958), which examines bravery and cowardice during the 1916 border skirmishes between the United States and Mexican troops led by Pancho Villa. *The Tin Lizzie Troop* (1972) was described by James R. Frakes as "a whooping, slapsticky version of . . . *They Came to Cordura.*" In *The Shootist* (1975), a legendary gunfighter stricken with cancer dies heroically in a gunfight. *The Cadillac Cowboys* (1964) offers a satiric view of the contemporary American West.

Several of Swarthout's novels have been the basis for film adaptations. These include *They Came to Cordura, Bless the Beasts and Children, The Shootist,* and *Where the Boys Are* (1960), a story about college students who spend spring break in Ft. Lauderdale, Florida. Swarthout won an O. Henry award in 1960, and his short stories have been published in such periodicals as *Cosmopolitan, Esquire, Collier's,* and *Saturday Evening Post.* In 1972 Swarthout was awarded the National Society of Arts and Letters Gold Medal. He has also collaborated on several books for children and young adults with his wife, Kathryn Vaughn Swarthout.

(See also *Contemporary Authors,* Vols. 1-4, rev. ed.; *Contemporary Authors New Revision Series,* Vol. 1; and *Something about the Author,* Vol. 26.)

ROSE FELD

The graveyard shift in an airplane plant makes the background of Glendon Swarthout's novel, "**Willow Run.**" Against it he builds the incidents of conflict and violence which end with the night's work. When the morning signal sounds for quitting, a bomber has been built, and several lives have been distorted or destroyed. Swarthout's conception of his novel is an interesting and ambitious one and his book, in spite of weaknesses and inadequacies in creative ability, has a definite rhythm and vitality.

He tells the story of six workers at Willow Run, the Ford plant, who for purposes of transportation to and from the factory are welded into a unit. The car is owned by Terry; four other men . . . make up the male contingent. The last is a girl, Charmaine, a beautiful young thing on the make, who is earning more money than she had ever seen before. . . . With the exception of Terry, who is happily married, all the men are emotionally disturbed by the girl who shares the car.

While developing the incidents which lead up to the dramatic climax of the story Swarthout carries the reader through the various steps of building a bomber. . . . It is through the stupid gossip of Joe, the sweeper, that the strife between the men over the favors of Charmaine reaches disastrous levels. . . .

Besides telling the story of the men in conflict over the girl Swarthout throws the spotlight on some of the other workers in the plant. There is a good bit about two midgets working in the wings of the bomber; a good scene with a group of women who discuss what the war and war jobs mean to them. Swarthout's ear is excellent in catching the locutions of the various workers who move through his scenes. But he is less successful in narrative and in tying up his scenes and episodes. One is left with the impression that he has fine material for a good novel but that he hasn't sufficiently absorbed and developed it.

Rose Feld, "Building a Bomber," in The New York Times Book Review, *May 30, 1943, p. 18.*

BENJAMIN APPEL

[**"They Came to Cordura"**] is above all sheer storytelling. In the bloody Mexico of 1916 . . . , six American cavalrymen and one American woman leave a place called Ojos Azules, after action there, for the American base at Cordura. And a dangerous trip it is, with enough excitement to compete with the books and movies of the Excitement Pros.

But Glendon Swarthout is a real writer, and his story is much more than a what-happens-next epic. He asks and seeks to answer the question: What is courage? The central human situation he has invented is both intriguing and ironic. Five of the six cavalrymen are military heroes. They have been cited for the Congressional Medal of Honor and ordered to Cordura, where for a while they will rest from combat. The sixth American, Major Thorn, their leader, is the awards officer of the Pershing expedition; his is the responsibility of safely bringing his convoy of heroes to Cordura. Unlike the others, Major Thorn has broken badly when under enemy fire. His superiors . . . have removed him as executive officer and appointed him awards officer. Thus, a military coward is in the post of hero-finder and hero-maker, for Thorn will write the citations for the five.

The stage is set, and it will be a terrible stage. What will come will be a retesting of men already tested by war. . . . They are a mixed lot, seemingly incapable of heroism beyond the call of duty. Major Thorn, oppressed by his own guilt, sees the faults of his five heroes only too clearly. And yet, as he accuses himself, these immature and flawed men were capable of noble deeds. . . .

[The one woman in the party] is as unlovely as the heroes: an American who is being brought to Cordura on charges of aiding the enemy, a tough, mean bitch by name of Geary. For almost half the book we accept her and believe in her, and then gradually she becomes that stock figure of melodrama, The One Woman on the Island, sister under the skin to the famous sleeping-bag lady of Hemingway's "For Whom the Bell Tolls." In fact, when Mr. Swarthout is bad, he's as bad as bad Hemingway, and when he's good, he's as good as good Hemingway.

It is a pleasure to report that he winds up the book at the top of his form, with a wonderful last paragraph that recaptures the heart of his story and makes us forget the lapses. We close the novel feeling that we have been given a sharp insight into the mystery of courage.

Benjamin Appel, "The Mystery of Courage," in The Saturday Review, *New York, Vol. XLI, No. 6, February 6, 1958, p. 30.*

LEWIS NORDYKE

The United States Army's Punitive Expedition into Mexico in 1916 to apprehend Pancho Villa—an action ordered by President Wilson after Villa's forces had charged over the border and attacked the town of Columbus, N.M.—has inspired very little serious fiction. [**"They Came to Cordura"**], however, goes a long way toward making up for the deficiency, even though its plot is not primarily concerned with Villa or the expedition. (p. 4)

The book opens in the aftermath of the last mounted charge ever made by a unit of the United States Cavalry. . . . Maj. Thomas Thorne, who had proved himself a coward in the fighting at Columbus, had been assigned to the expedition as awards officer. It was his job to find candidates for the Medal of Honor and to write the citations. Having selected them, together with an American woman under arrest for suspicion of treason, he orders a march to Cordura, where the men will be removed from the scene of the fighting until their awards are approved.

The bulk of the book is taken up with their journey. It develops that the major's cowardice is known to the men he has selected as heroes and that for personal reasons none of them wants a medal. He, on the other hand, admires their reckless bravery and tries to determine what it is in their make-up that caused them to react under fire so differently from himself. He is determined to get them to Cordura and some of them are as determined not to go. To further complicate matters, the woman hostage is also anxious to escape. The trip turns into a battle between the acknowledged heroes and the presumed coward, with courage everywhere on display.

Such a situation is difficult to handle effectively and convincingly but Glendon Swarthout . . . has accomplished it so well that the reader feels he has actually experienced the events described. He finds himself in sympathy first with one side and then the other; and while at times the behavior of the characters is disgraceful, it is also understandable. Generally, Mr. Swarthout's people live and perform powerfully in these pages.

Throughout the book, the narrative, the characterization and the descriptive writing are excellent. (pp. 4, 28)

Although the episodes have an authentic and documentary flavor, the story is the timeless one of human behavior under great stress. It seems to this reviewer that this distinctive novel is sure to bring its author recognition as a promising original talent. (p. 28)

Lewis Nordyke, "Outbreak of Courage," in The New York Times Book Review, *February 9, 1958, pp. 4, 28.*

D. R. BENSEN

Glendon Swarthout's perceptive comic novel, **"Where the Boys Are"** . . . , is both good comedy and first-rate social anthropology. Merrit, the Midwestern coed narrator, is a funny and appealing girl, and the reader's delight and amusement in her and in the zany narrative seduce him into accepting her viewpoint and her observations without the initial shock and dismay that a balder account would occasion. Much of the book's comic value comes from its exposition of the ways of college students.

Merrit, one of 20,000 spring-vacation migrants to Fort Lauderdale, Florida, sees her problem in life as what to major in at school. Her three temporary consorts (sex being a part of vacationing) have their problems as well. . . . The excesses and idealism of the students of the recent past are meaningless to them. These collegians have energy but no goals, good instincts but no values, and intelligence but no information, and so reflect perfectly the aspirations of our cheerfully flabby culture. . . .

The author has written of these young people without condemnation: that he reserves for the schools and society which have not been up to the job of guiding and educating them. His wit and comic invention disguise what many will feel to be a grim core. The frantic dates, the lunatic conversations, and a frenzied burlesque of the International Brigade are all tremendously funny at first—then dreadfully funny.

In **"They Came to Cordura,"** Mr. Swarthout dealt with the emergence of basic human qualities under great stress. Now he has reversed his field, portraying instead a group whose qualities are stifled by insulation from stress.

D. R. Bensen, "Collegians without Conflict," in Saturday Review, *Vol. XLIII, No. 4, January 23, 1960, p. 19.*

MARTIN LEVIN

Mr. Swarthout, whose excellent previous novel (**"They Came to Cordura"**) was an anatomy of heroism on the Mexican border in 1916, devotes his current book [**"Where the Boys Are"**] to the anatomy of hedonism. This turns out to be a highly carbonated elixir of sex, sunshine and beer—at least around Fort Lauderdale, Fla., which is where the college boys are during spring recess.

Actually, spring vacation isn't all beer and potato chips. Some of the live-it-up kids have their pensive moments, which Mr. Swarthout sets down with tongue in cheek but in far too explicit detail, along with pages of varsity show lyrics and an entire Freshman English theme, grade about B minus. Merrit herself has an urge to be committed to a nobler cause than home economics, an urge almost as powerful as her yen for boys. These longings are nourished by a Miami cell of the Castro rebellion (nightclub division) and by three collegians on whom she has simultaneous crushes ("a loveathon"). . . . The holiday expires in a beach blast in which everyone and a cargo of munitions weigh anchor for Havana on a borrowed Chris-Craft ("a madathon").

What **"Where the Boys Are"** badly needs is a sturdier scaffold (a plotathon?) to hold all this unsupervised recreation together. Without an arresting narrative, Mr. Swarthout's comic novel is a series of random explosions instead of the humorous chain reaction it might have been.

Martin Levin, "Loveathon at Fort Lauderdale," in The New York Times Book Review, *February 7, 1960, p. 34.*

MAURICE RICHARDSON

The American adolescent monologue may have become a set form, but that does not make it an easy one. Narrator of ***Where The Boys Are*** is Merritt, a knowing campus queen vacationing in Florida with her girl friend, Tuggle. Her motto is: life is a long blind date. She quacks on brightly, animadverting about whatever comes into her head. . . . It is quite lively and amusing, but Mr Swarthout, though a clever writer, is not enough of a Tiresias to make the transposition of the sexes seem altogether convincing. Merritt, for all her erotic preoccupation, makes a curious effect of sexlessness. Too often her quack is that of a robot. (pp. 540-41)

Maurice Richardson, in a review of "Where the Boys Are," in New Statesman, *Vol. LX, No. 1543, October 8, 1960, pp. 540-41.*

DAVID DEMPSEY

Somewhere west of Peyton Place, and east of King's Row, is the small town of Thebes, Mich. . . . Things are pretty quiet in Thebes, Mich.

Home, after years awandering, comes Sewell Smith, a scapegrace native son who once prankishly helped to blow up the town dam, then lit out to become a successful novelist. Broke and embittered, he is seeking material for a new book. . . . One by one, he pries the lids off the town cesspools, plumbing as he does so the hottest scandal in Theban history; . . . [several of the town's most important men have] committed statutory rape with a local eighth-grade Lolita, the daughter of the widow Scripter, who confides everything to the young author. Smith (in trouble with the income-tax people) sees a chance to pay off old debts. He will extort a goodly sum from the errant worthies, clear matters with Uncle Sam, and have enough left over to settle down and write the Great American Novel.

"Welcome to Thebes" is not the Great American Novel—nor is it as impossible as this description makes it seem. When he is at his best, which is about 50 per cent of the time, Glendon Swarthout . . . is a skillful, even a brilliant, writer. The book throbs with a blistering vitality. . . .

In the first half, the author has broken his story into what he terms "strophes" and "antistrophes," although we would term some of them catastrophes for there are moments when he seems to be writing a parody of all the small-town sex-novels of the past decade. . . . Sewell Smith is a monster. The women of Thebes are pliant beyond belief, the men prurient to a fault. Repelled at first, some fatal fascination bids us stay and see it through; once Mr. Swarthout gets us in the clearing, and puts the whammy on us, we are caught.

The series of portraits which make up the final half of the book, in which each of the fallen idols confesses the dereliction to his wife, is beautifully and compassionately done. Although we cannot believe in these people—indeed, do not *want* to believe in them—they exist. Moreover, their actions are skillfully motivated and by no means incredible, even for the magnitude of their crime. In less competent hands, all this would probably be sheer trash. As it is, **"Welcome to Thebes,"** is a *tour de force* of a high order, endowed with a literary dimension which the material really doesn't deserve.

David Dempsey, "Scapegrace's Homecoming," in The New York Times Book Review, *June 17, 1962, p. 24.*

MARTIN LEVIN

East meets West in Glendon Swarthout's **"The Cadillac Cowboys"** . . . , and the result is instant decadence. Professor Carleton Cadell comes out to Arizona from Connecticut in search of the rugged virtues; Eddie Bud Boyd, a cattle broker, hits town in order to spend his pile. . . . Mr. Swarthout's heart is clearly in his work, as he elegizes the ravaged West with references to such as Joseph Wood Krutch, George Meredith and H. Allen Smith. Indignation is not enough, however, in a comic novel in which the nonsense is not very well organized and the prototypes are as arid as their cactus-covered homeland.

Martin Levin, in a review of "The Cadillac Cowboys," in The New York Times Book Review, *January 19, 1964, p. 30.*

HASKEL FRANKEL

Only a nouveau Easterner can survive in the New West today, according to Glendon Swarthout of Scottsdale, Arizona. No true cowboy can be at home for long on the split-level range where the horse and the water hole have given way to the Cadillac and the swimming pool. If this is the situation . . . it is one ripe for humor. A single, sharp sketch in a revue or five pages from S. J. Perelman could easily reduce the mesa to the mess it now is.

Unfortunately, Mr. Swarthout has decided the situation is worth 176 pages of what [the publisher of **"The Cadillac Cowboys"**] labels as "satire," a form I seem to remember as something lighter than an elephant's tiptoe. The author refuses to accept that a rib tickled too long in the same spot will turn numb. . . .

But if the author's satire were not numbing, his packaging of it would put the final chill on the book. Straight fiction chapters, detailing the rise and fall of a poor cowboy turned millionaire cattle commission man, jockey for position with essays on the land gone to gilded seed. If you can imagine a broken record of scenes from "The Beverly Hillbillies" alternating with monologues suggestive of Will Rogers with an acid stomach, you have an exact picture of **"The Cadillac Cowboys."**

Haskel Frankel, "Slow on the Draw," in Book Week—The Sunday Herald Tribune, *February 2, 1964, p. 20.*

PUBLISHERS WEEKLY

[***The Eagle and the Iron Cross*** is] Glendon Swarthout's best novel in some time. Two fugitive Germans, tuba players in a prisoner-of-war Afrika Korps band, hide with a peaceful, very poor tribe of Indians near Phoenix. . . . Briefly, the Indians and the Germans live in friendship, happiness, and mutual support. Then comes a deeply bitter ending, an indictment of the cruelty and the corruption of the white Americans whom the Germans, to their sorrow, encounter. A strong story with some wonderful characters.

A review of "The Eagle and the Iron Cross," in Publishers Weekly, *Vol. 190, No. 14, October 3, 1966, p. 78.*

BRUCE COOK

[***The Eagle and the Iron Cross***] is so full of facile pessimism, easy irony, and plain bad writing that instead of evoking the sympathy that the author so righteously solicits for his cast of victims, it merely irritates us into indifference.

The time is 1945, the place a prisoner-of-war camp just outside Phoenix. Matthe Tiege and Albert Pomtow, two young veterans of the Afrika Korps, manage to escape and go in search of Indians with whom they can live as blood brothers. The two want no part of repatriation. They have lost all love for their Fatherland and now want only to act out their adolescent fantasies of frontier life in America among the noble savages. They wind up guests of the Moencopas, who are neither savage nor very noble.

Alas, the poor Moencopas—what perfect victims they are! "What had the Americans practiced on them? A trickery so consummate that it could only have been conceived by the well-intentioned. Generously it gave the Indians their own land, then by diverting their water forced them to leave it. Generously it provided schools, then asked as tuition the dismemberment of the family. For songs it gave them the radio, for visions the bottle, for freedom the automobile, for gods the dollar, and for sanctuary an outhouse. . . ." Et cetera for another hundred words or so—and all this, mind you, in the author's voice.

But should we have missed the point, Mr. Swarthout has one of his Germans underline it in the very next paragraph: "'They are like us,' Albert concluded one night. 'They are prisoners, but of peace prisoners, not war, because they have not fought. *Ist das nicht* a dirty trick?'"

Ja, das ist a dirty trick. It is also abominable dialog.

Bruce Cook, "How a Pitch for Sympathy Evokes Only Indifference," in The National Observer, *November 28, 1966, p. 25.*

DONALD H. CLOUDSLEY

Well, strip my gears and call me Shiftless. I'll be a monkey's uncle if Glendon Swarthout hasn't trotted out all the teenage clichés of 35 years ago in this novel of Depression year 1934. If you remember it, [***Loveland***] may be your cup of tea, but as I live and breathe, I wouldn't swear to it. Strike me pink if it isn't occasionally funny, but shiver my timbers, enough is enough. The story . . . is slight, even a bore. It all happens in a Michigan resort and say it ain't so if Mr. Swarthout meant anything more than a bit of nostalgia.

Donald H. Cloudsley, in a review of "Loveland," in Library Journal, *Vol. 93, No. 16, September 15, 1968, p. 3158.*

PETER CORODIMAS

At a time when many novelists are preoccupied with themes of absurdity and alienation, it is enjoyable, not to say helpful to one's sanity, to read a novel about life which sees life the way many novelists used to see it: at least as partly intelligible—which in itself may be a wrong view, but comforting nonetheless. Glendon Swarthout's **"Loveland"** is a refreshingly unpretentious novel about how quickly a boy can grow up. Set lovingly in the Thirties, it records the antics of Perry Dunnigin (presumably a self-portrait), a seventeen-year-old, wet-eared, supersmoocher from a small town in Michigan. (p. 263)

The novel is, for the most part, enjoyably flippant. But it ranges effortlessly through a number of contrary emotions which one ordinarily doesn't expect to find gathered in the same book. In some ways the story is also a tribute to a young boy and his father (who appears sporadically) who refuse to be intimidated by the somber aspects of the early Thirties. There is a crazy variety at work here and it is held together by warmth and gusto. (p. 264)

Peter Corodimas, in a review of "Loveland," in Best Sellers, *Vol. 28, No. 13, October 1, 1968, pp. 263-64.*

RICHARD SCHICKEL

[Glendon Swarthout] is a good, entertaining writer—exuberant, optimistic, maybe a little childlike (in a nice way) in his love of archetypal characters and situations, but always intelligent and alive.

In ***Bless the Beasts and Children*** he is writing about a gang of eightball, oddball adolescents who test and prove their manhood by escaping from an Arizona boys' camp with intent to free a herd of buffalos from legalized slaughter (must thin the herd, you know) at the hands of gutless sportsmen invited to the kill by the state. The kids are, I suppose, Holden Caulfield's younger brothers, but they are a plucky, engaging lot and their cause is a just one. The slaughter may be ecologically defensible, but its manner is not. . . .

I like the juxtaposition of the primal innocence of the great animals with that of the boys, the brevity and tension of the book and, damn my eyes, its earnest morality. Mr. Swarthout's taste in simile and metaphor is a little richer than mine, but the novel needs simplifying intelligences like his right now if it is to retain its hold on the general populace. That—like Vonnegut—Mr. Swarthout has. He never falls over into limp banalities. He is a stylist who also entertains and instructs and I say good for him. It is not as easy as it sounds.

Richard Schickel, in a review of "Bless the Beasts and Children," in Harper's Magazine, *Vol. 240, No. 1439, April, 1970, p. 107.*

BRIAN GARFIELD

Glendon Swarthout's latest work is a superb example of the kind of novel that evolves when a writer's craft is equal to the grandeur of his theme. ***Bless the Beasts and Children*** is a compassionate book, a true book, a book of the heart; it is also a compelling drama that grabs you with a grip that can't be pried loose.

It is a funny, furious narrative of six disturbed teen-aged boys, exiled by their wealthy parents to an Arizona summer camp which advertises that it builds men. When the camp appears to have failed in that endeavor, the six misfits set out to achieve it themselves by embarking on a marvelous quest for redemption, pride, and justice. (p. 41)

The story is full of emotion: tearfully humorous, triumphantly sad. It is a fine writer's vision of the ultimate magnificences and depravities of the human spirit. To summarize the plot would reveal surprises the reader should discover for himself. But perhaps it requires a note: One scene depicts a terrifying, mindless act of collective human savagery—a violent ceremonial murder of helpless animals. The scene is one about which I have heard strong disbelief expressed. But it is essential; you must accept it as an authentic observation of real human conduct, or dismiss the novel as a tissue of false analogies. Therefore I stress, from personal knowledge, that the episode describes a practice carried on in several Western states with ritual regularity, and that Swarthout pictures the slaughter accurately. What is appalling is that he didn't have to make any of it up. (pp. 41-2)

With ***Bless the Beasts and Children,*** Glendon Swarthout has added something fine and important to the literatrue of our age. (p. 42)

Brian Garfield, in a review of "Bless the Beasts and Children," in Saturday Review, *Vol. LIII, No. 18, May 2, 1970, pp. 41-2.*

JOHN W. CONNER

The misfits of Box Canyon Boys Camp become a single force in pursuit of ecological justice in this tautly written brief novel [***Bless the Beasts and Children***]. Horrified by the slaughter of buffalo at a government-sponsored extermination site, six boys steal away from their summer camp, confiscate an old truck, and set out to free the remaining buffalo. . . .

The night journey from the camp to the government extermination site is an exciting one. Glendon Swarthout understands the anxiety accompanying illegal flight and carefully selects incidents and language to enhance this anxiety. Perhaps the author's most perceptive comment on man and his relationship to nature occurs when the boys finally arrive at the pens containing the buffalo. Still wanting to free the buffalo, the boys are temporarily stymied by their own fears of the mammoth bison.

I'm not at all certain that ***Bless the Beasts and Children*** is a book for adolescents. It is about adolescents, their concerns, their values. But each boy is so filled with personal doubts that he scarcely has an opportunity to react genuinely to his peers. The author gathers six diverse personalities and concentrates their activities on one major event. Theoretically, it ought to work, but it doesn't. Each boy is a psychiatric case study, interesting to observe but impossible to be concerned about.

John Cotton's death near the end of the novel releases the tension created by the government authorities' discovery of the boys in the act of releasing the buffalo. The author needed an event of this magnitude to culminate the escapade. I can appreciate the author's technical prowess, but I regret the lack of an empathic response.

Bless the Beasts and Children is an exciting adventure yarn using adolescents as major characters. It is an excellent example of literature *about* adolescents rather than literature *for* adolescents.

John W. Conner, in a review of "Bless the Beasts and Children," in English Journal, *Vol. 61, No. 1, January, 1972, p. 139.*

EDWIN McDOWELL

"The 1916 Mexican Border campaign," John O'Hara once observed, "was the nearest thing we ever had to a gentlemen's war.". . .

[Some] National Guard units that had been mobilized to end Villa's border raids, particularly the cavalry units that were strung out in six man squads at 20-mile intervals along the international border from Texas to Arizona, were rather more like blueblood social clubs than fighting units.

"The Tin Lizzie Troop" . . . is an absorbing fictional account of one such unit—but fiction, the author notes, "cut out of 'Calvalry Journal' leather and the microfilms of faded newspapers." . . .

In the hands of a lesser writer, such a theme could well lapse into banality. But Mr. Swarthout is a consummate craftsman and established pro, as he demonstrates in his alternately humorous and disturbing account of the first mounted pistol attack ever executed by U.S. Cavalry against an armed enemy. Interspersing whimsical misadventures with philosophic meanderings, Mr. Swarthout, himself a former combat infantryman, limns a vivid picture of the many faces of a limited war. And although his story is set in mid-May 1916, it is as chillingly contemporary as My Lai.

Author Swarthout has touched upon these themes before. He dealt with heroism and cowardice in **"They Came to Cordura,"** a memorable account of the U.S. Cavalry. **"The Eagle and the Iron Cross"** was the author's personal testament to the folly and tragedy of war, a damning indictment of the recidivous brute and bully who knows no national or ideological boundaries. **"Bless the Beasts & Children"** was a stunning study of horror and cruelty, of honor and compassion, of savagery and serenity.

And in this latest novel as in his eight previous ones, Glendon Swarthout, even as he entertains his readers, induces them to examine the human condition.

Edwin McDowell, "Bluebloods vs. Pancho Villa," in The Wall Street Journal, *June 9, 1972, p. 8.*

JAMES R. FRAKES

Stanley Dinkle is a second-looey in the U.S. Cavalry, training and cursing a series of effete National Guard six-man squads assigned to patrol a 20-mile stretch of Texas territory along the Rio Grande. Across the river Blackjack Pershing is chasing Villa. On this side Dinkle sweats and agonizes over his latest batch of rookies, The Philadelphia Light Horse . . . , who report for dusty duty with six Main Line horses, polo mallets, champagne, a ukulele, a table-sized Victrola, and two Ford Model T touring cars. . . . Dinkle, to whom "horseflesh was . . . meat and mistress," has a new mission: to save the U.S. Cavalry from the Tin Lizzie. And we're off on what looks like a whooping, slapsticky version of Glendon Swarthout's earlier novel ***They Came to Cordura***. . . .

You have to put up with a lot in [***The Tin Lizzie Troop***]—long stretches of self-consciously cute style, gross stereotypes of not only Mexicans but Philadelphians, human encounters that have all the subtlety of an Eddie Bracken double-take, and landscape droppings like this: "Over the river, perfumed and passionate, Mexico sprawled. Her breasts were stony hills. Dark ranges in the distance were her thighs." But all is not lost, for the burlesqued language, characterizations, actions, and settings are quite deliberately designed as romantic simplicities out of which develops a desperate maturity redolent of nihilism. And Stanley Dinkle grows on you . . . until you stop laughing at this little man full of "beans and dreams," agree that he is indeed "the salt" and "a brave man," and maybe even weep along with him in the final sentence.

James R. Frakes, in a review of "The Tin Lizzie Troop," in Book World—The Washington Post, *July 2, 1972, p. 9.*

MARTIN LEVIN

"Luck and Pluck" begins as a playful ambush of a pair of long-sitting ducks: namely the Establishment and the Counterculture. The Establishment is characterized by hucksterism of infinite banality, and the Counterculture enlists self-serving hypocrites. . . . Mr. Swarthout is no better than anyone else at solving contemporary dilemmas—so he opts for a motel-room farce and a high quota of chuckles.

Martin Levin, in a review of "Luck and Pluck," in The New York Times Book Review, *March 11, 1973, p. 49.*

S. K. OBERBECK

[**"The Shootist"**] is a gritty but sentimental literary tintype that should do about as well as "True Grit" did. John Bernard Books rides into El Paso in 1901, on the day Queen Victoria has died. Books is royalty in his own right—the last, legendary "shootist" (gunfighter) left in America's almost domesticated West. The flinty, seemingly heartless gun slinger learns that he is consumed by incurable cancer and settles into a buxom widow's boardinghouse to die. But death collects the famous with special malice. Books is plagued by tinhorn reputation-hunters and parasites eager to turn a buck on the dying man's remains and effects. (pp. 64, 66)

Books outsmarts everyone. . . . The bullet-riddled, bone-shattering climax of this enticing little melodrama arrives as Books, woozy from pain-killing laudanum but still in control, resolves not to kill himself but to rid the town of three foolhardy troublemakers who want to boast that they gunned down the famous and invincible Books.

Author Glendon Swarthout . . . writes a stilted kind of Mary Worth dialogue and a descriptive prose as measured and evocative as boot heels on the saloon-porch steps. The only flaw in this confection is the end of the tale with its magnified, clinical violence. It's a sad postscript for Books, and something like a walk through a hospital emergency ward. (p. 66)

S. K. Oberbeck, "High Noon," in Newsweek, *Vol. LXXXV, No. 5, February 3, 1975, pp. 64, 66.*

VICTORIA GLENDINNING

Glendon Swarthout's ***The Shootist*** is about J. B. Books, who rides into El Paso in 1901 with a reputation as a killer and a pair of custom-made .44 Remingtons. . . . But it isn't going to be that sort of novel after all. Because J. B. Books is dying of cancer. . . . He decides to go out fighting; and in the bloody saloon-bar battle that he engineers, he is the last to die.

The Shootist is a novel which combines the mock-heroic Hollywood myth of the West with an ideal of true heroism—which is always a private and painful matter. Mr Swarthout is equally fascinated by both, and he has written an original book. The widow's son inherits the .44 Remingtons and stalks off 'head up, shoulders back, taller to himself', intoxicated by the smell of death. So the game goes on. Boys will be boys and heroism, I suppose, is occasionally something to do with guns; but I do wish the lad had thrown them in the river. (p. 633)

Victoria Glendinning, "Making It," in New Statesman, *Vol. 89, No. 2303, May 9, 1975, pp. 633-34.**

PETER ACKROYD

Glendon Swarthout's ***The Melodeon*** employs fantasy on a [safe] level. It is cosy, it is all-American, and it is Christmas. A young boy has been sent during the Depression to live on a farm with his grandparents. Now what can Grandpa Will give to Grandma Ella to celebrate this season of lovely neighbours, snug churches and snowy landscapes? Nobody was selling scripts from *The Waltons* in those days, so the dear little thing will have to make do with a Christmas surprise. Her old Melodeon is to be moved to a safe berth, and will shower blessings on just about everyone each time it is played. All of this unimportant information is relayed in that easy and equable tone which we now associate with the worst kind of American rhetoric. The voice is so familiar, in fact, that it has become opaque—it is actually interesting only for what it leaves out.

The book is really a hymn to early technology camouflaged as a Christmas story. The Melodeon, and the tractor which pulls it to church on Christmas Eve, are the suffering heroes of the novel. And as an act of piety everything else is the book is turned into a machine. The sheep make noises 'like tractors'; a neighbour 'reminded me of a stove'; sermons are 'recycled'; young girls 'nodded like metronomes'. And there are frequent references to 'the Maker', that twinkling engineer who oils our joints and polishes our hub-caps. The world is a great mechanism which has found the secret of perpetual motion. Christmas itself is an aspect of its benevolent technology. (p. 29)

Peter Ackroyd, "Out of Sight," in The Spectator, *Vol. 239, No. 7799, December 24, 1977, pp. 29-30.**

EDWARD GUERESCHI

Glendon Swarthout has had the bad luck to publish a Christmas tale several weeks after the fact, and reading [***The Melodeon***] is like drinking eggnog in June. Nonetheless, a jaundiced eye is better prepared to ask the inevitable question—stripped of seasonal cheer and the Pavlovian reach for heart-warming adjectives, can the poor beast stand on its own legs? Well, yes and no. ***The Melodeon*** has all the necessary ingredients to pinch hardnosed reason: old age and youth learning from one another, a major obstacle overcome by faith and perseverance, a fashionable dash of the supernatural . . . and a good plot device—the heirloom melodeon . . . that must be shipped off to church in time for Christmas services. How this hazardous journey is made, by tractor no less, accounts for yuletide leavening.

The result should have been a modest yet appetizing *Kuchen* of a story, wholesome as the occasion. What is disappointing is the sense of a factory-made product. Mr. Swarthout has a good eye for incidental detail—how the aged silently communicate with one another, for example, or the lack of charity caused by the embarrassment of debt. These details nearly erase the irritation that arises from the author's synthetic embellishments, the frequent nudges that remind us that Christmas is more than a working day on the farm. We are, in effect, force-fed into sentimentality. Ironically, the problem lies, I suspect, with the author's aversion to create unlikeable characters. Even at Christmas, we demand our monsters, if only to convert them. ***The Melodeon*** is a story in search of a Scrooge. It's too bad it didn't find him.

Edward Guereschi, in a review of "The Melodeon," in Best Sellers, *Vol. 37, No. 12, March, 1978, p. 325.*

PUBLISHERS WEEKLY

Jimmie Butters, children's book author, is as unlikely a detective as you'll find, but he is certainly appealing in [**"Skeletons,"** an] intrigue filled mystery about the infamous past of a small Southwestern town. Coaxed by his ex-wife to investigate the death of another writer, the urbane Butters is off to the New Mexico desert, where he becomes involved in uncovering a far-reaching coverup of the deaths of four Mexicans and a well-known lawyer that took place more than 50 years earlier. . . . Witty, complex and highly entertaining, Swarthout's whodunit has all the ingredients of a good mystery.

A review of "Skeletons," in Publishers Weekly, *Vol. 215, No. 21, May 21, 1979, p. 58.*

KIRKUS REVIEWS

Swarthout has come up with a moderately strong plot about old crimes and sins and secrets [in ***Skeletons***]—really the raw material for an above-average gothic. Unfortunately, he has also come up with a marginally amusing, mostly cutely annoying narrator to uncover those secrets—he's kiddie-book writer B. James ("Jimmie") Butters—and the credibility of the dark mysteries is consistently undercut by the relentless giddiness of Jimmie's smug, hyperthyroid narration. It all begins when Jimmie's beloved ex-wife Tyler begs him to go to her New Mexico hometown and find out how novelist Max Sansom . . . really died: he was supposedly hit-and-run there while digging into pre-WW I murder trials involving Tyler's long-dead grandfathers. . . . Jimmie soon finds his investigations into these old events thwarted. . . . And things become even more complicated when nutty Tyler arrives, as together she and Jimmie connect up a web of madness, rape, incest, blackmail, and skeletons in a tower. Somewhat overcooked materials, perhaps, but they'd stick together well enough if it weren't for Jimmie's off-putting personality and his obtrusive narration: capital letters for emphasis . . . , smart-alecky one-liners, and sophomoric cutesy-sex. Told straight, this could have been just fine. Told by fey and vulgar Jimmie, it's a crudely mixed bag—part gothic, part melodrama, part farce—that straight suspense fans will find too self-consciously adorable to endure.

A review of "Skeletons," in Kirkus Reviews, *Vol. XLVII, No. 11, June 1, 1979, p. 661.*

MARGHANITA LASKI

Jimmie Butters is a New York children's writer who loves GOOD and hates EVIL. The capitals are Glendon Swarthout's, in his excellent and extraordinary new book, ***Skeletons.*** Butters, child man, child novelist, is narrator. For love of the terrible Tyler, he goes to New Mexico to find out what became of the man (or men) she sent to the small town before him. Terror, horror, fear are, of course, or ought to be, implicit in a genre that depends on death; now we are usually numb to them, but almost unbelievably ***Skeletons*** reawakens the nerves on which they twang. (p. 62)

Marghanita Laski, "America Time," in The Listener, *Vol. 103, No. 2644, January 10, 1980, pp. 62-3.**

Joyce Carol Thomas

1938-

American novelist, poet, and dramatist.

In her novels, *Marked by Fire* (1982) and its sequel, *Bright Shadow* (1983), Thomas focuses on a black rural community in Oklahoma. Her female characters endure hardships and violent victimization, yet her work conveys a celebration of human strength and an appreciation of simple pleasures. Thomas began her literary career by composing poetry and drama, but she won national recognition when *Marked by Fire* won an American Book Award. Thomas's prose style indicates her previous literary endeavors: her narratives display lyrical qualities, and her dialogue, in which she recreates the colloquial language of rural Oklahoma, is controlled and realistic. Echoing the general critical response to Thomas's work, Alice Childress states: "Miss Thomas writes with admirable simplicity and finds a marvelous fairy tale quality in everyday happenings."

Thomas, who worked in the cotton fields of Oklahoma, draws upon her childhood memories in her writings. Recalling harvest time, Thomas relates that "even though we missed the first part of school because of the necessity for work, we made up for it by telling stories." This exchange of stories helped inspire her literary interests. *Marked by Fire* and *Bright Shadow* trace the life of Abyssinia Jackson from her birth in a cotton field to her life as a young woman. While growing up Abyssinia encounters several violent acts; for example, she becomes a victim of rape at an early age. Despite these tragedies, Abyssinia endures through community support and her own inner strength to emerge as a mature woman.

(See also *Dictionary of Literary Biography*, Vol. 33.)

Photograph by Kaz Tsuruta. Courtesy of Joyce Carol Thomas

HAZEL ROCHMAN

Reminiscent of Maya Angelou's *I Know Why the Caged Bird Sings* . . . in its poetic language, its celebration of Black womanhood and its incident of a child protagonist temporarily struck dumb after being raped, [***Marked by Fire***] is a powerful representation of a Black rural Oklahoma community. The story—told in a series of brief concentrated vignettes—is mainly about the women, and it focuses on one special child among them, Abyssinia (Abby) Jackson: the ritual of her birth in the cottonfields with the women all participating in the pain and the joy; her growth as the gifted beautiful darling of the community; the horror of her rape at age 10; her recovery and subsequent maturing. . . . The lack of a fast-paced narrative line and the mythical overtones may present obstacles to some readers, but many will be moved by the story of a girl who achieves recognition, not through individual career or relationship with a man, but as leader and healer of her community.

Hazel Rochman, in a review of "Marked by Fire," in School Library Journal, *Vol. 28, No. 7, March, 1982, p. 162.*

ALICE CHILDRESS

The title of [**"Marked by Fire"**] refers to a scar burned upon the face of Abyssinia Jackson on the day of her birth in 1951. . . .

Abyssinia is a mischievous, happy child and an excellent student, and by the time she is 10 she reveals a fine singing voice. Owing to her skill as a storyteller and her services to the community, she is the pride of her friends and elders. But she loses her voice and bitterly questions her religious faith after being raped by a respected church member. . . .

The author thoughtfully records the child's grief, the sorrow of the rapist's wife and the frightened flight of the criminal after his release from prison. It takes time and another kind of suffering before Abyssinia begins to find her way back to the fullness of living. She sees Patience, her mother, who normally displays even more fortitude than her name suggests, ready at one point to commit murder.

Another unforgettable character, Mother Barker, is an important thread in the fabric of the story. A midwife and freethinker and spiritual adviser, she is the person who finally offers Abyssinia a goal in life. . . .

Some of the novel's in-the-nick-of-time rescues were difficult to believe. . . .

But as the story progressed, I became engrossed, because Miss Thomas writes with admirable simplicity and finds a marvelous fairy tale quality in everyday happenings. Her people move through troubled times but never fail to celebrate sweeter days with church suppers and the joyous sound of gospel singers. Their unifying faith in God is the sturdy hub of the church wheel that encompasses the small congregation.

A very revealing moment is the one in which Abyssinia chases a female investigator out of the house after her mother has reluctantly sought charity. The woman represents that stingy form of "giving" that sniffs, measures and detests all those who are caught in the poverty trap. She is unable to extend a kind word of understanding, which Abby's mother needs more sorely than financial aid.

"Marked by Fire" concerns human strength and frailty. It is a book about girls and women and the men in their lives. It tells of the best and worst times experienced by a small black community during a 20-year period. Joyce Carol Thomas's first novel is well worth reading.

Alice Childress, in a review of "Marked by Fire," in The New York Times Book Review, *April 18, 1982, p. 38.*

WENDELL WRAY

In [***Marked by Fire***] Joyce Carol Thomas captures the flavor of black folk life in Oklahoma. Those of us who associate Oklahoma with oil may be surprised by these characters of the 1960's who still toil in cotton fields whiling away the arduous hours by singing spirituals. . . . This is the classical folk tale about the special child, marked at birth, set aside from all the others and destined to play a special role in the life of Ponca City, Oklahoma, an all black town. Abyssinia seems to have the gift of song even before she crawls. All the women believe that by helping at her birth they are her collective mothers—doting on her at her unusual birth and as her special gifts unfold.

All of Abby's glorious childhood experiences of climbing trees, making homemade ice cream and attending church picnics are shattered when she is raped at age ten by a "good" deacon of the Solid Rock Church. . . . As is typical of all folk tales, Abby must undergo the torment of magical threes: she is attacked by Trembling Sally with a swarm of wasps while she is in bed after the rape, later Sally tries to drown her and lastly tries to burn her to death! How is that for tests of fire and water?

Joyce Carol Thomas has set for herself a very challenging task. It is very difficult to create the atmosphere of a folk tale's never-never land in the contemporary reality of Oklahoma in the 1960's. One sees the heavy influence of Maya Angelou's *I Know Why the Caged Bird Sings*. . . . There are obvious influences from Jean Toomer's *Cane*, because of Thomas' use of very brief chapters, some of them only one and a half pages long, and her use of a full blown poetic style. Thomas' book works. (pp. 123-24)

Wendell Wray, in a review of "Marked by Fire," in Best Sellers, *Vol. 42, No. 3, June, 1982, pp. 123-24.*

DOROTHY RANDALL-TSURUTA

Marked by Fire is the story of Abyssinia Jackson, born in an Oklahoma cotton field in 1951, who "screamed her way into the world water on one side and fire on the other." While to many people this is the tale of the coming of age, intellectually and emotionally, of a young black woman whose birth was fortuitously witnessed by a collective of women folk who from that day and by that event became, in a sense, her godmothers, it is also the capturing in slow motion of a time and a place when environmental and social horrors were more out front, pouncing, and though complex not masked. In this is call for comparison with events today practically anywhere, rural or urban, Western or other areas where the idealistic spirit of bygone eras is designer cut and donned by ravishers who confuse capture and conviction. . . .

Thomas' poetic tone gives this work what scents give the roses already so pleasing in color. In fact often as not the lyrical here carries the reader beyond concern for fast action. Then too Thomas' short lived interest in playwrighting figures in her fine regard and control of dialogue. . . .

Struck dumb for a period following the rape, Abby regains herself in that company of women which this novel quite frankly is all about. Mother Barker, her mentor, is common sense and proverbial insight. The mad Trembling Sally—devil personified—is the most complex and fascinating of the townspeople. Even as she terrorizes the children with her antics, pursuing them with fire and poison, they yet pity her, knowing misfortune has made her that way. In this she serves Abby as that model not to follow. Trembling Sally is particularly beset with the notion of destroying Abby whom she regards as "just sly, that's all. Got the people fooled." But Abby, as does the author of this haunting tale, struggles free of adverse fate to find her voice and her place as mentor among women.

Dorothy Randall-Tsuruta, in a review of "Marked by Fire," in The Black Scholar, *Vol. 13, Nos. 4 & 5, Summer, 1982, p. 48.*

PUBLISHERS WEEKLY

[***Bright Shadow***] reverberates with the lyricism that evoked unanimous critical praise [for ***Marked by Fire***]. But readers need steely nerves to stick with the story of horrors visited upon young Abyssinia Jackson and her friends. Serena's appalling death at the hands of a madman and the tragedy affecting Abby's lover, Carl Lee Jefferson, are crises the girl must surmount if she is to remain sane and hopeful. . . . For those who can bear the assaults on their emotions, the novel is a remarkable second journey into the lives and times of the black western community.

A review of "Bright Shadow," in Publishers Weekly, *Vol. 224, No. 18, October 28, 1983, p. 70.*

CAROLYN CAYWOOD

[In ***Bright Shadow***, a sequel to ***Marked by Fire***, Abyssinia Jackson] is attending college and falling in love with Carl Lee, though the latter displeases her father. Her quiet romance is interrupted by the psychotic murder of her Aunt Serena. Abyssinia, who has had some forebodings about Serena's new husband, is traumatized by her discovery of the mangled body. Her own faith, her parents' and Carl Lee's love and a mysterious cat sustain her through her grief, while her parents come to appreciate Carl Lee's support and concern. . . . All this melodrama seems contrived in order to interrupt Abyssinia's romance. The world outside this rural black Oklahoma community never impinges on the characters, making the story seem even less credible. . . . But Thomas' story is readable and her sensuously descriptive passages celebrating the physical beauty of the black characters are a nice touch. Those who have read the first book may wish to follow Abyssinia's story despite its artificiality. (pp. 89-90)

Carolyn Caywood, in a review of "Bright Shadow," in School Library Journal, *Vol. 30, No. 5, January, 1984, pp. 89-90.*

ZENA SUTHERLAND

Bright, black, and beautiful, twenty-year-old Abby falls deeply in love with Carl Lee [in ***Bright Shadow***] and is defiant when her father forbids her to see him. When tragedy strikes . . . Abby's father sees how gentle and supportive Carl Lee is, and accepts him. Carl Lee, meanwhile, has had a fight with his father and left home; he discovers that his father has died and been buried in the woods by the Cherokee woman who, he learns, is his mother; Abby, in turn, comforts him in his bereavement. As a love story, this is appealing, and the characterization is strong. What weakens the book is the often-ornate phraseology of what is basically a competent writing style . . . , and one episode in which flowers spring up wherever a cat walks.

Zena Sutherland, in a review of "Bright Shadow," in Bulletin of the Center for Children's Books, *Vol. 37, No. 6, February, 1984, p. 119.*

THULANI DAVIS

Bright Shadow by Joyce Carol Thomas . . . is a warm novel for young adults that continues the story begun in ***Marked by Fire*** for which Thomas won the American Book Award, among others. As the story opens, Abyssinia Jackson, a young woman raised in the Pentecostal church in rural Oklahoma, falls in love for the first time. Abby's Aunt Serena, unlike her disapproving father, indulges her questions about love and encourages her to discover the magic of it herself. Abby *does* find love's magic even as tragedy separates her from Aunt Serena and her beloved Carl Lee. Author Thomas has a delicate hand with language (these religious Black folk teach lessons from "their cultured gardens of heather, jasmine and honeysuckle"). ***Bright Shadow*** is delightful for young readers.

Thulani Davis, in a review of "Bright Shadow," in Essence, *Vol. 14, No. 12, April, 1984, p. 50.*

Lewis Thomas

1913-

American essayist, memoirist, physician, and scientist.

An eminent physician and teacher of medical science, Thomas has received numerous scientific and academic honors. He is highly respected for his essays that study the symbiotic relationship of all life forms through a combination of scientific knowledge and devoted humanism. These essays examine such diverse topics as the perfection of a single cell and the complexity of the human capacity for language and music. Thomas's style has often been praised for its poetic grace.

Thomas first gained widespread recognition as an essayist with *The Lives of a Cell: Notes of a Biology Watcher* (1974), for which he received a National Book Award. This book, along with *The Medusa and the Snail: More Notes of a Biology Watcher* (1979), collects essays previously published in the *New England Journal of Medicine*. A recurring theme throughout both collections is the inextricable relationship between humanity and nature. Critics have hailed both the validity and the accessible presentation of Thomas's concerns; as Jeffrey Burke notes, "Informality is one of Lewis Thomas's most likable qualities. . . . [It] is his casual tone—that of the thoughtful mind apparently wandering, yet always to a certain purpose—that makes him unique among writers on science."

Thomas departed from the essay format in *The Youngest Science: Notes of a Medicine-Watcher* (1983). Essentially a memoir, this book presents his personal observations on the medical advances made within the last century. Returning to the essay form, *Late Night Thoughts on Listening to Mahler's Ninth Symphony* (1983) conveys a somber tone not evident in Thomas's earlier work. For example, the opening essay describes the tragic and utter destruction that would result from a nuclear explosion. The majority of his essays, however, remain optimistic and life-affirming, displaying the range of Thomas's concerns and the depth of his vision. Ted Morgan contends that Thomas is "the only one I can think of who is able to translate obscure scientific data into a body of thought that demonstrates the connection between biological phenomena and the way our society functions. His work has the texture of permanence."

(See also *Contemporary Authors*, Vols. 85-88.)

JOYCE CAROL OATES

For the past several years a series of remarkable essays has been appearing in the New England Journal of Medicine, that enthralling and somewhat forbidding publication—Dr. Lewis Thomas's **"Notes of a Biology Watcher."** Readers who have been photostating these essays and teachers who (like me) have been passing them out in classes will be delighted to see them finally collected in one small volume [**"The Lives of a Cell: Notes of a Biology Watcher"**]. The rest of the readers, to whom the **"Notes"** are new, may have an extraordinarily pleasant surprise in store.

How to praise Dr. Thomas most accurately? One wonders. A reviewer who concentrates upon Dr. Thomas's effortless, beautifully-toned style, even to the point of claiming that many of the 29 essays in this book are masterpieces of the "art of the essay," would direct attention away from the sheer amount of scientific information these slender essays contain. A reviewer who deals with the book as "science" would be forced, by Dr. Thomas's marvelous use of paradox, to admit that the book might not yield its wisdom at a single reading. But since it is Dr. Thomas's underlying thesis that divisions are really illusory and that "our most powerful story, equivalent in its way to a universal myth, is evolution," one might as well rise to the higher speculation that **"The Lives of a Cell"** anticipates the kind of writing that will appear more and more frequently, as scientists take on the language of poetry in order to communicate human truths too mysterious for old-fashioned common sense. (p. 2)

Undogmatic, graceful, gently persuasive, these essays insist upon the interrelatedness of all life. But what has been common religious knowledge in the East from ancient times always sounds very nearly revolutionary in the West. All truth carries with it political and moral implications; science cannot be divorced from the rest of our civilization, any more than an individual scientist can be divorced from his participation in the world as a human being. Dr. Thomas's underlying thesis is certainly a positive and optimistic one—is not all scientific truth, at bottom, *optimistic*? But he is well aware of the immediate difficulties we are facing, and are going to face, since we carry with us, rather helplessly, 19th-century assumptions about the relative independence and isolation of man in nature, which our new, intellectual disciplines, like ecology, can hardly overturn in a single generation. . . .

Dr. Thomas, on the subject of the symbiotic relations found everywhere in nature, says: "It is a mystery."

The fascination with the mysterious accounts for science as well as art, and the two are really joined, a cooperative human adventure, though articulated in vastly different vocabularies.

The secret of **"The Lives of a Cell"** is one man's hope to explain, however inadequately, the miracle of music—at least to his own satisfaction. Literary and humanistic preoccupations are shared by science, but since the scientific spirit is rather unsentimental with regard to the myth of the individual, its pronouncements are likely to sound, at first, rather arcane: "If language is at the core of our social existence, holding us together, housing us in meaning, it may also be safe to say that art and music are functions of the same universal, genetically determined mechanism. . . . If we are social creatures because of this, and therefore like ants, I for one (or should I say we for one?) do not mind."

What people do in a transient way—most social and political activities—is not considered social behavior in the strict biological sense of the term. What is genetically determined is a constant, and in our species "it begins to look . . . as if the gift of language is the single human trait that marks us all genetically, setting us apart from the rest of life. . . . We engage in it communally, compulsively, and automatically. We cannot be human without it; if we were to be separated from it our minds would die, as surely as bees from the hive." Music is a higher form of language; we evolve from words into music.

And what is marvelous about the entire process is its absolute naturalness. . . . One of the most beautiful essays, **"The Music of This Sphere,"** is a profoundly religious piece, almost a revelation, far too complex for explanation here, but curiously similar to what the mystics have been trying to tell us for centuries about the nature of the universe. . . .

In Dr. Thomas's visionary world, the earth is a single cell and the sky is a moist, gleaming membrane . . . and man, "natural man," might do well to begin to see himself as a kind of tissue specialized for receiving information, possibly even functioning "as a nervous system" for the earth. Our species is an event, a situation. It might turn out, he speculates half-whimsically, half-seriously, that we are approaching a "special phase in the morphogenesis of the earth when it is necessary to have something like us, for a time anyway, to fetch and carry energy, look after new symbiotic arrangements, store up information for some future season . . . maybe even carry seeds around the solar system."

Since the grand theme is evolution, and not our peculiar role in it, man has become in a painful, perhaps unwished-for way, nature itself. (p. 3)

Joyce Carol Oates, "Beyond Common Sense," in The New York Times Book Review, *May 26, 1974, pp. 2-3.*

MARTIN WASHBURN

[Dr. Lewis Thomas] has written an absolutely fascinating small book [**"The Lives of a Cell"**]. An extraordinary stylist, he uses the most impenetrable biological terminology in such a natural way that it almost proves the "two cultures" were just an unfortunate illusion.

Dr. Thomas explains that fundamental biologic life is essentially symbiotic, and that, historically, immunologic defenses—the organism's aggressive way of defining itself—came second. (p. 32)

As this chatty, aware, and charmingly civilized book . . . [disclosed] its revelations, it reminded me that what I have always loathed about science is not its content but its chosen style. At the level at which ordinary citizens experience it, the message of science has been that emotional alienation and objectivity are the same (check out the decor in your doctor's or dentist's office).

It's a relief to hear that we should no longer associate the importance of science with the inhuman certainties of technological success, but with a basic human core of fallibility, confusion, and turmoil, which productively grows truth more out of disorder than order. And yet the world might not be so deep into its current bind if scientists hadn't waited so long before saying so.

Particularly when Dr. Thomas goes from the benign to the messianic, in describing the activities of a basic research group, I felt the old hard sell was being replaced by a subtle new soft sell, as the boat of science tries to extricate itself from the drowning rat of technology. (p. 33)

Martin Washburn, in a review of "The Lives of a Cell," in The Village Voice, *Vol. XIX, No. 26, June 27, 1974, pp. 32-3.*

C. H. WADDINGTON

[In ***The Lives of a Cell: Notes of a Biology Watcher,*** Thomas] reminds the general reader of many fascinating aspects of biology which have tended to be overlooked in the dazzlement surrounding molecular biology. One of his main ideas is the importance and the mysteriousness of social behavior among animals of all kinds. In fact, he reminds us that we ourselves are in some way societies and not merely individuals. We are made up of cells, each somewhat distinct; and further, each cell contains smaller structures, such as mitochondria, and these appear to have originated from bacteria, which at one time could have lived in isolation, and would have to be regarded as separate individuals. But they have, through long periods of evolution, become so fully incorporated that they could not exist in isolation, and neither could the cell maintain itself without them. Our unity as individuals is not quite so assured as we commonly think.

Just who or what is carrying out these goal-seeking activities: a simple individual; an "individual" who is really a conglomerate of subcellular parts which, at some stage of evolution, were separate individuals; or a society of individuals? It would be nice at this point to produce a neat answer to these riddles, but the last word really remains with [Karl] von Frisch: "One can try circumlocution with learned words, but I think it is better to say, quite simply, we do not understand." (pp. 6, 8)

C. H. Waddington, "The Mystery of the Libidinous Molecule," in The New York Review of Books, *Vol. XXI, No. 19, November 28, 1974, pp. 4, 6, 8.**

WILLIAM McPHERSON

[*The Lives of a Cell: Notes of a Biology Watcher* is a] rare and beautiful work, luminous in style and bursting with information, a celebration of life, a meditation on it. . . . Thomas's speculative flights are as grounded in science as man is embedded in nature, and he can leap like Nijinsky from the development of opposing thumbs to the St. Matthew Passion.

William McPherson, in a review of "The Lives of a Cell: Notes of a Biology Watcher," in Book World—The Washington Post, *December 15, 1974, p. 1.*

JOHN G. PARKS

Biology has become the key science of our age, supplanting the physical sciences, whose hegemony in the first half of the 20th century culminated in the development of nuclear weapons and moon rockets. Unfortunately, we have heard mostly of the new biology's spectacular and apocalyptic possibilities: ecological disasters, genetic engineering, cloning, transplants, test-tube conception. . . .

What we need to hear, and what we gain from [***The Lives of a Cell: Notes of a Biology Watcher***] . . . , are positive insights into the workings of nature and humanity's relation to it. . . . While there is a wealth of scientific knowledge here, what emerges is Dr. Thomas's sense of wonder and mystery in the face of life on planet earth, which he likens to a single cell.

"It is illusion," says the author, "to think that there is anything fragile about the life of the earth; surely this is the toughest membrane imaginable in the universe, opaque to probability, impermeable to death. We are the delicate part, transient and vulnerable as cilia. . . . Man is embedded in nature." We must relinquish the old images of humanity as master and adversary of nature: "The new, hard problem will be to cope with the dawning, intensifying realization of just how interlocked we are." Indeed, after reading Thomas's discussion of our cells and our resident mitochondria, one is led inescapably to consider that we are nature itself! . . .

Thomas writes with wit and grace. It is a humbling experience to read essays that challenge our "human chauvinism," our obsession with disease and death, and our cultural paranoia in regard to germs, held at bay only by the ever-ready spray can. But beyond their relevance to a critique of our cherished beliefs about ourselves—especially that long-held assumption of the so-called primacy of the self—the essays reveal bases for making new connections in human thought, as well as upholding the primacy of the imagination in pure research. . . .

To Dr. Thomas's mind, we are just at the threshold of knowledge. When we see that language—as well as perhaps art, music and myth-making—is inherently human, we have only begun our researches. When we discover nonverbal mechanisms for human communication, we are still in the realm of mystery and wonder. Death may not be the enemy we usually make of it: indeed, it may turn out to be life's last pleasurable experience. But perhaps most amazing of all is our own existence, our own improbable presence as a species. About such things the biologist converses with the poet, and invites the theologian to join in the reflection and wonder.

John G. Parks, "Sense of Wonder," in The Christian Century, *Vol. XCII, No. 14, April 16, 1975, p. 394.*

CHRISTOPHER LEHMANN-HAUPT

I gather from one of the essays in "**The Medusa and the Snail: More Notes of a Biology Watcher**" that when Dr. Lewis Thomas is writing—and not presiding over Memorial Sloan-Kettering Cancer Center in New York City—he sits at his desk in an upper-floor room facing north on East 69th Street. It must be an exciting place to sit. "On occasion, I place my pencil point . . . in the middle of my paper . . . and make the sun revolve slowly around East 69th Street. Anyone can do this. It takes a bit of heaving to get it started, but after a few minutes of hard thought you can hold East 69th as the still, central point, and then you can feel the sun rolling up behind you from the right side, making the great circle around."

And not just the sun. "If you want the sun to revolve around the earth in a complete turn every 24 hours, you must bring along the whole universe, all the galaxies, all the items in space, clear out to the curved edge." But Dr. Thomas doesn't feel entirely sanguine about this activity. "What bothers me . . . is the effect this may have had on the cosmologists, who may be looking at things at Pasadena, or Puerto Rico, or Palomar, or Pittsburgh, or whatever." And so, with apologies for any skewing he has caused in the universe, he stops and does something else equally momentous, playful and delighting: he writes.

How is one to explain the huge appeal of what he writes, which, collected in an earlier volume called **"The Lives of a Cell: Notes of a Biology Watcher,"** won a large audience as well as a National Book Award? To judge from this new volume, **"The Medusa and the Snail"**—which is so much more confident and playful than the earlier book that it looks as if Dr. Thomas was just clearing his throat there—the reasons are myriad.

But the most important of them is that he is a scientist with all his skepticism intact who makes us feel a little less bad about being alive and human. . . .

[Dr. Thomas] has this extraordinary facility for taking the darker sides of human existence—whether they be death, disease, fear, worry or just plain warts—and turning them to the light. "Any species capable of producing, at this earliest, juvenile stage of its development—almost instantly after emerging on the earth by any evolutionary standard—the music of Johann Sebastian Bach, cannot be all bad. We ought to be able to feel more secure for our future, with Julian of Norwich at our elbow: 'But all shall be well and all shall be well and all manner of thing shall be well.'"

Yet Dr. Thomas is no Pangloss. He knows the nature of pessimism as well as optimism—that there is an *other* that opposes the self (which, in a wonderfully complex way, is the point of the title essay, **"The Medusa and the Snail"**)—that if people must have the capacity to twirl the cosmos around their pencil points, they must also be able to stare into the void and understand their limitations.

Christopher Lehmann-Haupt, in a review of "The Medusa and the Snail: More Notes of a Biology Watcher," in The New York Times, *April 27, 1979, p. 29.*

JEFFREY BURKE

Informality is one of Lewis Thomas's most likable qualities. There are several dozen others, but it is his casual tone—that of the thoughtful mind apparently wandering, yet always to a certain purpose—that makes him unique among writers on science. He is also a master of the subtle, lapidary genre of the brief essay. ***The Medusa and the Snail*** follows seamlessly from his first collection, ***The Lives of a Cell***, with no falling-off in the clarity of his writing and insight on such subjects as cloning, Montaigne, and the premedical curriculum. If he has an overview, if there is any governing principle for either collection, it is the pleasure of knowledge, the value of inquiry, and the necessity of skepticism—in short, a belief in science. What sets this collection apart from the first is the larger number of essays on nonscientific matters, some of them almost playful, and the solemn note on which the final essay, "Medical Lessons from History," closes. After summarizing this century's progress in medicine and noting the optimism engendered by it, Thomas arrives at this point:

> These ought to be the best of times for the human mind, but it is not so. . . . I cannot begin to guess at all the causes of our cultural sadness, but I can think of one thing that is wrong with us and eats away at us: we do not know enough about ourselves. . . .
>
> We need science, more and better science, not for its technology, not for leisure, not even for health and longevity, but for the hope of wisdom which our kind of culture must acquire for its survival.

(p. 96)

Jeffrey Burke, "Biological Imperative," in Harper's, *Vol. 258, No. 1548, May, 1979, pp. 95-6.**

THE NEW YORKER

Lewis Thomas's first book, **"Lives of a Cell,"** came as a surprise to most readers. The sheer elegance and poetry of its language, as well as its shrewd, optimistic, and gentle perceptions of the human situation, were not what one expected to find in a scientific text, and especially a text that made no compromises about the level of the science being presented. [**"The Medusa and the Snail"**], also a collection of essays, is every bit as good and every bit as fresh and unexpected. Dr. Thomas . . . simply does not accept the fact that disease is an inevitable part of the human condition. For him, disease is a biological mistake, and a correctable one. He has little patience with the notion that we can all jog ourselves into good health and longevity. What is needed is real understanding of the biological mechanics of disease—the kind of understanding that can come only from serious basic research. These and other matters are presented here with lucidity and wit. (pp. 145-46)

A review of "The Medusa and the Snail," in The New Yorker, *Vol. LV, No. 14, May 21, 1979, pp. 145-46.*

BRAD OWENS

[Dr. Thomas has] the ability to make the complex understandable and interesting without the sensationalism that sometimes characterizes some "pop" scientific theories. . . . [His] writing is reasonable and readable. . . .

An unbounded imagination combined with careful attention to the details of life make [Thomas's] writing as lively and valuable as discovery itself. He manages to be poet, scientist, social critic, and Everyman, while writing with a prose so clear it's like looking through a jellyfish. The Medusa of the title [**"The Medusa and the Snail: More Notes of a Biology Watcher"**] is just that—a jellyfish—that has a unique symbiotic relationship with a sea slug (the snail).

The essays are short and various—words and punctuation are two of his subjects. He pokes a satirical pen at some modern health fads, creates the fantastical whimsy of walking goldfish evolving from a pond in Manhattan, and makes the universe revolve around a pencil point on East 69th Street.

This book seems more personal than his first [**"The Lives of a Cell: Notes of a Biology Watcher"**]: like the universe swinging around the pencil point, it takes place more inside Thomas's mind than in the world, and there's a different feeling because of it. Like his favored author, Montaigne, he is really telling us what it is like to be a human being.

He shares his pleasures patiently—explaining why the capacity to make mistakes is one of humanity's greatest attributes, and why he thinks disease is basically unnatural. He loves words as much as he loves Bach, although he sometimes gets so sidetracked into the concatenation of an unlikely etymology that I wish he'd get on with what he has to say.

While it is the style and the scope of his subjects that make Thomas so readable, it's the scope of his concern for which I think we should be most grateful. His writing is humane enough to make him trustworthy and authoritative enough to be reassuring. His is an optimistic and understanding voice. "I do not believe for a minute," he writes, "that we are nearing the end of human surprise."

Best of all, Thomas says, we aren't so dilapidated. We're not the broken-down, disease-ridden, fragile species that television commercials portray. He assures us, "There is nothing at all absurd about the human condition. We matter. . . . We may be engaged in the formation of something like a mind for the life of this planet. If this is so, we are still at the most primitive stage, still fumbling with language and thinking, but infinitely capacitated for the future."

Brad Owens, "Beyond Biology," in The Christian Science Monitor, *June 27, 1979, p. 19.**

DAVID WEINBERGER

Lewis Thomas writes so quietly that a reader has to listen carefully. His is an art form rarely found these days: essays short enough to make a single point. Thomas . . . writes nontechnically about the meaning of biology and the meaning of life. Because of the recent developments in understanding in detail the chemistry of organic activity, biology and life seem to be different topics. By using each as a metaphor to explain the other, Thomas shows us that the two are—or at least can be—one.

Rather than starting with the grand thought to organize the data, he starts with the small and finds what is grand about it. The tone is reasonable, the attitude humble. Above all, his topic is the self. . . . Biologist, etymologist, humorist, fantasist, theorist—many of Thomas' selves make their appearance in the 29 essays that compose [***The Medusa and the Snail***]. Some of them are outright humor pieces, which recall the works of E. B. White, but even the serious leave us smiling at the perfection of his insight.

Some of his theories are far-fetched, some twist the controversies that rake his science; for example, he talks about the possibility of there being genes for usefulness without explicitly mentioning the fierce debate over sociobiology that is in the background of his remarks. The book is most thought-provoking when Thomas is at his smallest. A quirky essay on New Yorkers dumping goldfish into the ponds that form in untended excavations leads us to ask about the relation of cities and the wild as mediated by pets. His essay on Montaigne makes us want to read the latter entirely: It is a book all who think and all who want to write will enjoy. (p. 42)

David Weinberger, "A Summer Full of Science," in Maclean's Magazine, *Vol. 92, No. 30, July 23, 1979, pp. 42-3.**

CHRISTOPHER LEHMANN-HAUPT

One of the many things to enjoy about the essay collections of Lewis Thomas . . . is the good news they always seem to bring. . . .

In his latest book, **"The Youngest Science: Notes of a Medicine-Watcher,"** the good news is that "the majority of patients with fatal cancer do not have pain," and, "When pain does occur, it can almost always be fully controlled." . . .

[Best] of all, "I look for the end of cancer before this century is over." . . . A book that brings us this sort of news can be forgiven almost anything.

Not that there's much one has to forgive **"The Youngest Science."** It's true that the author's enthusiasm for the female sex is so boundless as to verge on the patronizing. Bless them, the little dears, is the message that comes through when Dr. Thomas proposes that women should be put in charge and men even forbidden to vote for the next hundred years.

It's also true that there's a slightly disappointing lack of form to **"The Youngest Science."** The book starts out as an affectionate memoir of the horse-and-buggy brand of medicine practiced by the author's father early in the century in Flushing, Queens, when being a doctor was mostly a matter of observing the progress of a disease and writing out lots of prescriptions for what were basically placebos.

Then Dr. Thomas seems to be writing his autobiography. . . .

But somewhere along the way, the book's narrative continuity breaks down, and by degrees we discover that we are back in the land of the Lewis Thomas essay—on such subjects as medical philology, nurses, the field of neurology, public medicine, olfaction, rheumatoid arthritis and mycoplasmas, and the experience of being ill. Yet the transition from autobiography seems to have cramped the style of the essays, for it is not until the last quarter of the book that the writing achieves the freedom and imaginative verve of the author's previous collections.

Nonetheless, Dr. Thomas does succeed both in entertaining us with the play of his mind and in scoring important points along the way.

Christopher Lehmann-Haupt, in a review of "The Youngest Science: Notes of a Medicine-Watcher," in The New York Times, *February 9, 1983, p. C21.*

FITZHUGH MULLAN

In a little more than a decade, Lewis Thomas has established himself as America's foremost raconteur of science, a physician and a scholar able to probe and interpret the workings of human biology in a unique and gripping way. In two books of essays (***The Lives of a Cell*** and ***The Medusa and the Snail***) Thomas has shown himself to be a gentle essayist who captures the reader not so much by the power of his prose as by the erudition and poetry of his thought. (p. 4)

The Youngest Science chronicles Thomas' rise as a partisan of the new scientific medicine, first as an intern in Boston, then as a research physician, department chairman, medical school dean and, for the last 10 years, chancellor of the Memorial Sloan-Kettering Cancer Center in New York City. . . . Throughout, he writes about biology and humanity with modesty, lucidity, and a scholarly optimism that warms the heart of the reader chilled by frequent accounts of PCBs, Agent Orange and Swine Flu failures.

Though the tone of this memoir is characteristically quiet, there is nothing fainthearted about its pronouncements. Cancer, Thomas states carefully but definitively, is caused by "a single determining mechanism" rather than a variety of different causes. This mechanism will be discovered and fixed so that he cleanly predicts "the end of cancer" by the end of this century. His observations are subjective as well. After describing his own experience with illness, he concludes, "I know a lot more than I used to know about hospitals, medicine, nurses, and doctors, and I am more than ever a believer in the usefulness of technology, the higher the better."

And yet, despite his faith in the system of which he is an architect and a symbol, he sounds one, faint note of question—a query that deserves careful attention. The modern medical center, driven by the popular desire for more sophisticated biomedicine, staffed, indeed, by MD-PhDs, and fueled by grants from the National Institutes of Health, has tended to dwarf the other faculties of most universities. More specifically the role of the medical school itself has been bent to the intriguing and consuming pursuit of research such that it has become "the accepted idea that *every* faculty member of *every* medical school in the country must be a working scientist with a grant from the NIH and a laboratory at his disposal."

Thomas does not lament this drift although it seems to trouble him just a bit. It is, indeed, a critical question for the future of medical training and practice in this country. Could medical education—*scientific* medical education—not be built on a premise other than that of research? Could good doctors, like Thomas' father, not be fostered and inspired in a setting other than one designed to discover the innermost secrets of the cell? Surely it would be less costly than our current model and perhaps it might produce physicians more atuned to the rigors, the mundanities and the beauties of everyday clinical practice.

These are questions for the coming generation as medicine, the youngest science, continues to mature. For his part, Lewis Thomas has seen the modest medicine of his father transformed into the inventive, skillful, practical science of today. He has watched that process, he has partaken of it and now he has written vividly about it. More he could not have done. (p. 13)

Fitzhugh Mullan, "Lewis Thomas and the Poetry of Medicine," in Book World—The Washington Post, *February 13, 1983, pp. 4, 13.*

JEREMY BERNSTEIN

Psychoanalysts tell us that they ask their patients to lie on the couch, facing away from them, in order to encourage free associations—the odd junctions of memory that are the working matter of the psychoanalytic enterprise. If the patient and the doctor were in eye contact, there might be a tendency to entertain, to seek instant approval or disapproval—in short, to keep the "conversation" going. A similar distinction can perhaps be made between an autobiography and an interview. This thought struck me as I was reading Lewis Thomas's autobiography, **"The Youngest Science."** . . . In the spring of 1977, I conducted a series of interviews with Dr. Thomas. . . . [He] agreed to tape-record both some of the details of his life and some of his ideas about medicine. I had never met Dr. Thomas before we began these interviews, so, in effect, he was talking about his life to a total stranger, and with a tape recorder going, to boot. Our conversations resulted in a Profile of Dr. Thomas, which was published in this magazine in 1978. I reread it after reading his autobiography, and found that, while the facts are the same and the concerns similar, everything in the autobiography has been enriched and deepened by the solitary excursions that Dr. Thomas has made into his memory. (p. 109)

[Dr. Thomas] has had a remarkable and distinguished career, and he has enriched all of us by his essays. This book, in my view, is the best thing he has ever written. For people who have never read Lewis Thomas, it is a wonderful way to begin, and for people who have read him it is an even more wonderful way to continue. (p. 114)

Jeremy Bernstein, "A Doctor's Life," in The New Yorker, *Vol. LVIII, No. 52, February 14, 1983, pp. 109-14.*

WILLARD GAYLIN

Dr. Thomas's implicit thesis [in **"The Youngest Science: Notes of a Medicine-Watcher"**] is that despite its dramatic change from a diagnostic to a therapeutic occupation, the medical profession remains an ideal enterprise for the questing and concerned. He regrets the distancing of physician from patient and, as usual, he finds almost the perfect image for it: "The stethoscope was invented in the 19th century, vastly enhancing the acoustics of the thorax, but removing the physician a certain distance from his patient. It was the earliest device of many still to come . . . designed to increase that distance."

He is sensitive to today's patient's dismay that the longest and most personal conversations with hospital staff are "discussions of finances and insurance engaged in by a personnel trained in accountancy." But he also acknowledges that in former times doctors talked extensively and comfortingly to patients because, beyond the diagnosis, there was little that they had to offer.

In a touching chapter on his own hospitalization a few years ago, he tells of his close participation in the efforts of his attending physicians to diagnose his "anemia of unknown origin." It illustrates the reality that even the most sensitive physician occupies a different world from his patient. It is the patient who endures the pain, while the needs of the physician to survive and function place limits on his identification and empathy. "I have learned something about this," Dr. Thomas writes, "but only recently, too late to do much for my skill at the bedside." He was shocked to discover that despite reassurances that a bone marrow biopsy would be almost painless—reassurances that he himself had given to his patients—it was "not at all nice. . . . I could not avoid the strong sense that having one's bone marrow sucked into a syringe was an unnatural act."

It is part of the integrity of this book that in defending the present situation, it never demeans or condescends to the past. Each generation earns its respect from Dr. Thomas—if not for its achievements, then for its endeavors. Finally, he reluctantly allows that if he personally were to develop a serious disease, while he would want "as much comfort and friendship as I can find at hand," mostly he would want "to be treated quickly and effectively so as to survive, if that is possible." And so, I am sure, would we all. It would be nice if the two could be fused, but the current emphasis on cost-efficiency, increased specialization and heightened technology makes the prospect of change in the immediate future unlikely.

If the autobiographical material is the strength of this book, it is also, in a way, its weakness. Dr. Thomas is a master of the short essay. He is not comfortable in the more complex narrative form. The book in general follows a chronological order, but often chapters (House Calls, Nurses, Endotoxin, Mycoplasmas, Scabies) are simply stuck in like raisins scattered through a muffin. Fascinating in their own right, they nonetheless disrupt the autobiographical narrative, rather than serve it.

The chapter on endotoxin is a case in point, describing as it does one of Dr. Thomas's major research interests. The subject of endotoxin (a substance first studied with typhoid vaccine) is an engrossing one, involving as it does problems in bodily defenses against disease. "It provides a working model for one of the great subversive ideas in medicine: that disease can result from the normal functioning of the body's own mechanisms for protecting itself, when these are turned on simultaneously and too exuberantly, with tissue suicide at the end." It is more than "a chapter" in Dr. Thomas's life. It represents 35 years of research and could have illustrated the way in which his scientist's curiosity continues to address the same problem at differing stages of sophistication and levels of education. It is woven into the fabric of his life; it should have been woven into the fabric of this story.

This brings us to a second shortcoming. In choosing an autobiographical form Dr. Thomas inevitably arouses our curiosity not simply about the medical profession his life exemplifies but about the life itself. We learn so many facts about his career here and so little of the essence of the man. What we do know is likely to make us greedy for more. One is aware that behind the ideas of this most effective narrator is a person of taste, decency (there is not an ungenerous or mean-spirited comment in the whole book) and dedication. Yet Dr. Thomas protects his privacy. What the reader wants, as in any good autobiographical sketch, is more of the exhibitionist, more of the ham.

One thinks of the mysterious Beryl of whom we are early made aware and who constitutes half of that plural "we" that dominates the last chapter of the book. While we know that his wife escorted him through "seven different apartments in New York, two houses in Baltimore, two in New Orleans, two in Minneapolis and three in New Haven," she is as shrouded from the public eye as an Iranian mullah's wife. Somewhere also there are three daughters and a Welsh terrier, but they, alas, are also forbidden entry here. The same is true of the doctor himself. He seems to reveal much, but he ends by exposing very little. If a man requires distance for comfort, he should avoid autobiography.

In other areas he is most generous, and that is the strength of the book. He is ready to share his passion for his profession. The chapter on nurses describes admiringly the dedication and anguish of this undervalued profession. Nurses have indeed salvaged the caring aspects of the medical enterprise; they are the remaining bedside comforters. (pp. 3, 16-17)

One sees Dr. Thomas at his best when he is discussing his research. Too much scientific writing for the layman has emphasized the drive to win, the quest for the prize, the competitive aspects of scientific research. Dr. Thomas concentrates on the endeavor itself and takes joy in the pursuit of knowledge. He lingers as lovingly on his failures as his achievements. Dr. Thomas comes to medicine with the awe and reverence of a believer. He finds in research what others find in devotions. And he reminds us that medicine, by its very nature, will not allow the physician, or even the researcher, to forget that his subject matter is never distant from human existence and human suffering. (p. 17)

Willard Gaylin, "A Doctor on Healing," in The New York Times Book Review, *February 27, 1983, pp. 3, 16-17.*

MARK CZARNECKI

Scientists who can illuminate their discipline for the general reader are a rare breed. Since his first collection of essays, ***The Lives of a Cell,*** appeared in 1974, Lewis Thomas has established himself as science's most compassionate and comprehensible advocate. Modelled on the works of the 16th-century French essayist Michel de Montaigne, his elegant meditations extract humanistic morals from the darkest recesses of scientific research. Nevertheless, his third book, ***The Youngest Science,*** is surprisingly uneven. . . .

Thomas, at 69, is a medical mogul whose biography charts the astonishing ascendancy of massively funded medical research in the United States since the Second World War. Subtitled "Notes of a Medicine-Watcher," the book traces the careers of both discipline and practitioner, with occasional asides detailing his research in pathology and immunology. But the ambitious marriage of format and content breaks down in the 1960s as the colorful thread of Thomas' personal life gets lost in a confusing fabric of esoteric research accessible only to his peers.

The lapse is all the more disappointing since ***The Youngest Science*** is crammed with engaging anecdotes and stimulating insights. (p. 59)

Like many top scientists, Thomas is both humanist and humanitarian. In his case, the inquisitive sensibility that gleefully draws parallels between linguistic and biological derivations is also passionately committed to service on fund-raising committees and public health boards. Thomas notes that the words "medicine" and "modest" share a common root and he is self-effacing to a fault. Although evincing genuine pride in his research, he barely hints that he and his co-workers are on the verge of breakthrough discoveries relating the functioning of the human brain to the body's immune system. Domestic references are brief: on a drive with his wife from one university appointment to another, three young daughters miraculously appear in the back seat. And judging from the satirical odes closeted in the footnotes, Thomas also has a poetic gift. In fact, ***The Youngest Science,*** with its endless lists of Nobel laureates lording their medical fiefdoms, at times reads like a Homeric paean to a Trojan War against disease. (pp. 59, 61)

Mark Czarnecki, "Waging War on Disease," in Maclean's Magazine, *Vol. 96, No. 10, March 17, 1983, pp. 59, 61.*

WILLIAM R. AYERS

I am mad at Lewis Thomas. He has written my book. That he has done so with greater perceptivity, more incisive language, and almost poetic phraseology is immaterial. It is also irrelevant that I cannot draw on as rich a list of experiences as he. My father was not a physician, so I did not have the opportunity to observe him in general practice in the early 1900s. Nor did I graduate from Harvard, intern at the Boston City, train at the Neurologic Institute in New York City, do research at the Rockefeller Institute, Hopkins, Tulane or the University of Minnesota, chair departments at NYU, take sabbatical at Cambridge, Dean at NYU and Yale, or round off as Chancellor at the Memorial Sloan-Kettering Cancer Center. It would make little difference if I had, for few possess Thomas's clarity, wit or wisdom to profit by such experiences. Each is a career in itself.

In between the chapters of pure narration, he has skillfully interspersed essays on House Calls, Leeches, Nurses, endotoxin, olfaction, and illness. Who else would find incredible beauty in mycoplasmas or link blood hounds, tracking mice, and the mechanism of skin-graft rejection. How many others injected enzymes into rabbits' veins but failed to notice that their ears softened, finally hanging down like spaniels'? From such keen observations does serendipity spring.

Medicine sorely needs a book like ***The Youngest Science*** now. The profession is under attack from without and within. Medical students are scientific automatons, masters of multiple guess exams, unable to think, only to regurgitate. Medical school curricula are immutable anachronisms, packed with unnecessary research facts, out of step with the modern needs of an ever more sophisticated consumer. (pp. 312-13)

One of Thomas's knacks is the use of an uncertain tongue-in-cheek. Does he really mean that Oliver Wendell Holmes's dictum (the key to longevity is to have a chronic incurable disease and take good care of it) works? Can so learned a man's impression that he has gained more from his wife than he has given to her be accurate? Surely his proposal to put women, born teachers and nurturers, in charge of thermonuclear decisions is not serious. Does he, in fact, believe that humans, the most improbable of all earth's creatures, will survive because of more improbable luck?

The careful reader will hear a clarion in Thomas's words. Medicine is its own worst enemy. It is not just that the funding policies of the National Institutes of Health in the mid-1950s fostered the idea that all faculty members in every medical school must be working scientists with research grants. It is rather that the financial stability of the university medical center depends on it. As federal dollars are withdrawn, the onus of balancing the budget falls to increased tuition, greater endowment, larger practice loads, new liaisons with private industry or some combination of all the above. The tragedies have already been written. To survive in the competitive grantsmanship game, pressured researchers have falsified results and published lies. Unbridled conflicts of interest between entrepreneurs and universities sit on the horizon. Perhaps Dr. Thomas's reflections on "hope" mute the clarion.

I am not really mad at Lewis Thomas; just jealous. No one could have done better. Or as well. (pp. 313-14)

William R. Ayers, "Medicine Is Its Own Worst Enemy," in Commonweal, *Vol. CX, No. 10, May 20, 1983, pp. 312-14.*

JONATHAN YARDLEY

The many admirers of the essays of Lewis Thomas will be neither disappointed nor (the dust jacket to the contrary notwithstanding) surprised by [***Late Night Thoughts on Listening to Mahler's Ninth Symphony***], his third collection of pieces written primarily for *The New England Journal of Medicine*. Like the essays in ***The Lives of a Cell*** and ***The Medusa and the Snail,*** these lucid and amiable commentaries are built around the themes that characterize Thomas's writing: the interconnection and community of all living things; the superiority of human intelligence to computer smarts; the necessary unpredictability of scientific research; the glory and mystery of music (hence the title); the persistent refusal of the universe to yield up all its secrets to scientific and philosophical inquiry; the critical importance of basic research, as opposed to applied science, in the fight against disease.

These are the concerns of a man who is both a scientist and a humanist, whose essays are trenchant and sometimes moving demonstrations that the two are not mutually exclusive. This is not to say, as is sometimes incorrectly claimed on Thomas's behalf, that he clarifies science for the lay reader; although he is a clear writer, he has little choice at times except to use scientific terminology ("mitochondria," "nucleotides," "euglossine") that will stop many a lay reader in his tracks. Rather it is to say that Thomas understands, as do too few on either side, that the worlds of the scientist and the humanist should be friendly rather than hostile, that each has much to teach the other, that neither can be completely healthy in smug, self-absorbed isolation. He addresses himself, accordingly, to both worlds: not merely does he try to explain the workings and aims of science to the nonscientist, but he tries as well to explain the interests and preoccupations of the rest of the world to the scientist who, hidden away in his laboratory, may have difficulty preventing singlemindness from shrinking into narrow mindedness.

In the 24 short essays collected in ***Late Night Thoughts on Listening to Mahler's Ninth Symphony,*** Thomas directs the attention of these audiences to two themes in particular. One is the threat of annihilation raised by the nuclear arms race and the lamentable role played by "military research" in it. Although the essays devoted to this subject are written with great feeling and from an unexceptionable point of view, I find them considerably less interesting than those devoted to matters of biology and scientific method; they are more homiletic than analytic, and a sermon by any other name is still a sermon. But when Thomas turns to his other major theme, the necessity of permitting science to work at its own pace and direction, he can be eloquent and persuasive. (p. 3)

[The writing of Lewis Thomas is] as valuable for its sturdiness of character as for its clarity of thought and expression. This, I think, is why so many readers have found so much pleasure and edification in his previous books; more of the same awaits them here, for which they can be thankful. (p. 11)

Jonathan Yardley, "Lewis Thomas: A Doctor of Humane Letters," in Book World—The Washington Post, *November 13, 1983, pp. 3, 11.*

MARK CALDWELL

Shut up and listen to Dr. Thomas, who has just finished playing Mahler's Ninth. Not Spike Jones or "She Works Hard for Her Money," but, inevitably, Mahler: he bores musicians but pundits love him. "The long passages on all the strings at the end, as close as music can come to expressing silence itself, I used to hear as Mahler's idea of leave-taking at its best. . . . Now I hear it differently. I cannot listen to the last movement of the Mahler Ninth without the door-smashing intrusion of a huge new thought: death everywhere, the dying of everything, the end of humanity."

In its ostentatious mushy sensitivity, that statement typifies Thomas's latest collection of essays. And, to my mind, ***Late Night Thoughts*** reveals the less obvious but nonetheless systemic sappiness in everything he's written. The typical Thomas essay is short, slightly but not too elliptical, a little digressive but not very, personal but not confessional, almost patronizing but not quite. Surprising Fun Facts, often the same ones, appear at judicious intervals. . . . You can't not be interested; the facts *are* important, the writing is always clean, the sentiments as irreproachably enlightened as they are comfortable.

So what's wrong with a string of books so knowledgeable, so useful, so stylishly readable? What's wrong is that they're entirely too neat. Because Thomas writes about the vast complexities of modern biology and biochemistry, his books should be tough, long, and disquieting. Thomas's ease and polish, the assumed chumminess with which he doles out science in easy-to-swallow morsels, betrays the vitality of his subject. He panders to the unreasoning terror most of us feel when confronted with theories that can't really be grasped unless they're expressed mathematically or in chemical formulas of baroque complexity. . . .

Science can ignite your imagination, fold up your episteme and turn it inside out. But not unless you take the trouble to learn it. All the anecdotes in the world about bullets fired through speeding trains or about coming back to earth in a spaceship 10 years younger than your twin sister won't make you understand the Special Theory of Relativity. A few hours carefully studying some moderately hard math (based on the d = r x t formula everybody learns in grammar school) will. Anybody with a brain can do it; the fear so many humanities types experience is infantile and unwarranted.

Thomas is, unwittingly, a sinister force. His constant reassurances subtly communicate the idea that there's a *need* for reassurance, that we'd better let dear old Dr. Thomas tend to the hard stuff and be grateful for the generous but careful economy he practices in doling out gumdrops. Even the central idea of his books—that everything in the universe belongs to one interfused, mutually sustaining whole—is suspect. His organicism denies the differentness of things, pretends that, come the pleroma, all the jagged pieces that now seem not to fit will mesh. In the meantime, we can clasp our hands and cluck over the mystery of it all.

It's not that Thomas is disingenuous. He himself seems sincerely to believe in his romanticized, sentimental science; he really wants his readers to melt with him into a warm puddle of sticky wonder. Even his moments of darkness are tinged with a sort of pleasing melancholy—when he tells you he's outraged at the prospect of death in nuclear war for 20 million, 40 million, or 80 million, he writes about it as if he were Thomas Gray contemplating a country churchyard. Lewis Thomas means well. But for all his competence and sophistication, his books remind me of Wodehouse's Madeline Bassett, who thought the stars were God's daisy chain and that every time a wee fairy coughs a baby is born.

Mark Caldwell, in a review of "Late Night Thoughts on Listening to Mahler's Ninth Symphony," in The Village Voice, *Vol. XXVIII, No. 48, November 29, 1983, p. 53.*

THE NEW YORKER

The mood of this volume [**"Late Night Thoughts on Listening to Mahler's Ninth Symphony"**] is darker than that of Dr. Thomas's two previous collections of essays. Dr. Thomas is deeply worried about the future of mankind. He can accept death as a part of the natural order, but not the death of everything. Like many of us, he is baffled by how we could have got ourselves to the present impasse. Unlike most of us, he can put his concerns into language that gives them a special depth and urgency.

A review of "Late Night Thoughts on Listening to Mahler's Ninth Symphony," in The New Yorker, *Vol. LIX, No. 45, December 26, 1983, p. 73.*

P. B. MEDAWAR

Lewis Thomas's latest book [***Late Night Thoughts on Listening to Mahler's Ninth Symphony***] is a collection of 24 short essays of which the first has to do with the gravest problem confronting mankind—the Bomb. In this essay his fans see a different Lewis Thomas—angry where he was once urbane, grim rather than gay, for no aspect of the bomb is at all funny and upon this subject Thomas is unrelievedly grave. His night thoughts are akin to those that most of us have when awake at dawn or sleepless in the small hours of the morning, or whenever the faculty of self-deception that so often insulates us from real life is temporarily in abeyance. . . .

Not all of Lewis Thomas's book is in the dark and foreboding vein of this first chapter; the witty and urbane New Yorker we are more familiar with wrote the remaining chapters. It is praise enough to describe them as vintage Thomas—full of good things, unexpected aperçus and witty juxtapositions of ideas. An important element of Thomas's style is to be reassuringly dismissive about the imagined threat of exaggeratedly scary things such as artificial intelligences. . . .

Thomas loves words and, taking an educated readership for granted, he assumes that his readers do too, so his books always contain a number of philological divertissements: thus he tells us that 'the word "gibberish" is thought by some to refer back to Jabir ibn Hayyan, an eighth-century alchemist, who lived in fear of being executed for black magic and worded his doctrines so obscurely that almost no one knew what he was talking about.' One of Thomas's most attractive gifts is for comical hyperbole: 'a family was once given a talking crow for Christmas, and this animal imitated every nearby sound with such accuracy that the household was kept constantly on the fly, answering doors and telephones, oiling hinges, looking out of the window for falling bodies, glancing into empty bathrooms for the sources of flushing water.' He loves the English language and deservedly exults in his ability to write it so well. If he had not been a medical scientist he would have been happiest, I think, as a philologist: one of his essays, indeed, is on the birth and growth of a new language, Hawaiian Creole, in a polyglot community that had formerly relied upon pidgin English—'pidgin', I learned, being the pidgin for 'business'.

Later on Lewis Thomas's thoughts return to the Bomb and the sky darkens again: for by simple reasoning to do with the immense difficulty, complexity and expense of the procedures used to rescue the victims of burning and radiation injury, and with the rarity of the people qualified to put them into effect, he infers that modern medicine has nothing whatever to offer, not even a token benefit, in the event of a thermonuclear war. This is a very grave statement and no one in the world is better qualified than Thomas to make it: he is thoroughly familiar with and has contributed to the science underlying the medicine and surgery of repair and has a thorough understanding of the administration and execution of practical medicine. . . . Thomas plaintively asks what has gone wrong in the minds of statesmen in this generation, and how it should be possible that so many people with the outward appearance of steadiness and authority, intelligent and convincing enough to have reached the highest positions in the governments of the world, should have lost their sense of responsibility for the human beings to whom they are accountable? It is to psychiatrists and social scientists that he looks for an answer. What a hope! The case is much too serious for the glib psychologisms of psychiatrists and the lame fumblings of social science—and in any case, Thomas remarks, if we are going under it would be small comfort to understand 'how it happened to happen'.

The problem is not insoluble in the sense that it is mathematically impossible to devise a straight-edge and compass construction to trisect an angle or to 'square the circle'—that is, to draw a square equal in area to a given circle—or that it is logically impossible to arrive at transcendental theorems from the axioms and observation statements of science, containing, as they do, only empirical furniture. No: the problem is not insoluble, but it is too difficult—too far beyond the capabilities of warlords and politicians whose judgments of priority are obfuscated by considerations of political or economic advantage, 'face' and national prestige. Because of his bluntness and strength of mind and great personal authority, Lewis Thomas has performed an important public service—and with the most enviable literary grace.

P. B. Medawar, "The Meaning of Silence," in London Review of Books, *February 2 to February 15, 1984, p. 9.*

Jack Vance

1916?-

(Born John Holbrook Vance; has also written under pseudonyms of Peter Held, John Holbrook, Ellery Queen, John Van See, and Alan Wade) American novelist, short story writer, and scriptwriter.

A writer of science fiction and fantasy, Vance is best known for the detailed manner in which he creates unique, fully-realized worlds. Characteristic of Vance's work is the richness of its vocabulary, a formal, detached narrative voice, and the evocation of powerful visual and tactile sensations which critics attribute to his distinctive writing style. Richard Tiedman notes that "his stories are attended by a very personal and unmistakable method of sentence construction, rhythmic variety, and extravagant imagery—all controlled with great technical dexterity." Vance typically subordinates plot and characterization in favor of developing alien environments, and his narratives tend to be episodic rather than linear. Some critics fault Vance for this, claiming that his works often fail as unified wholes despite moments of brilliance. Many, however, commend his stylistic strengths and praise his "range in evoking alien cultures, habits, and conditions from both inner and outer space," as Dan Miller notes.

Like many science fiction and fantasy writers, Vance began his career with publications in pulp magazines. Many of his early stories are space adventures that feature detective Magnus Ridolph and include elements from the crime and mystery genres. Some of these stories are included in *The Many Worlds of Magnus Ridolph* (1966). Vance's first important book, *The Dying Earth* (1950), consists of six stories loosely connected by the dying earth motif. These stories blur the distinction between fantasy and science fiction through their blend of magic and mythology, and they foreshadow much of Vance's subsequent work. As Norman Spinrad points out, the majority of Vance's fiction is neither pure fantasy nor pure science fiction: "His fantasy is too detailed, convoluted, and realized not to be called science fiction, and his science fiction realities have the magical complexity of his fantasies." One of the few exceptions to this is the novel *Languages of Pao* (1958), which centers on linguistics and scientific theory and is considered by some his finest pure science fiction achievement.

During the late 1950s Vance began writing fewer short stories, concentrating instead on developing several series of novels. Among them are the *Durdane, Demon Princes, Alastor,* and *Planet of Adventure* (or *Tschai*) series. It has been remarked that the quality of Vance's work in these series is not consistent; his interest appears to diminish once the challenge of creating a new milieu is met. However, the anthropologically complex worlds he creates are frequently praised as imaginative yet logical. Vance has received many awards for his works, including Hugo awards for *The Dragon Masters* (1963) and *The Last Castle* (1967), a Nebula award for *The Last Castle,* and an Edgar Allan Poe award for his mystery novel *The Man in the Cage* (1960).

(See also *Contemporary Authors,* Vols. 29-32, rev. ed. and *Dictionary of Literary Biography,* Vol. 8.)

NORMAN SPINRAD

[The essay from which this excerpt is taken was originally published in 1976 as the introduction to The Dragon Masters *by Jack Vance.]*

How can one explain the relative obscurity of a writer whose work has twice won the Hugo Award for best science fiction of the year in its category? A man who has been writing and publishing science fiction for over a quarter of a century. A man whose prose style is so unique that a random paragraph taken out of almost any piece of science fiction or fantasy he has written is sufficient to identify itself as unmistakably the work of Jack Vance. . . . (p. 13)

Yet Jack Vance seems to be an invisible man. Academics have written at great length and Byzantine complexity about science fiction writers with a far less substantial body of work and far less stylistic interest than Jack Vance. About Vance little has been written and even less is known. The science fiction readers, who twice have given Vance their award, seem to look right through him too. Not only will you seldom hear his name mentioned in a discussion of the major writers of the field, but there was a time in the 1950s when many fans were convinced that he did not exist. . . .

And far from chafing under this anonymity, Vance seems to cultivate it. (p. 14)

In one of Vance's stories of the magical twilight of man, collected in ***The Dying Earth,*** Liane the Wayfarer finds a magic ring through which he can step into a private universe and thus render himself invisible to passing eyes. . . . It would appear that Vance himself has deliberately done the same thing. A thirty-year stream of work has steadily appeared in our own continuum, but the intelligence behind it remains inside its invisible hidey-hole. (pp. 14-15)

As near as can be accurately counted, Jack Vance has at this writing published twenty-six novels and seven collections of short stories, not counting the mysteries published under "John Holbrook Vance." Many of these thirty-three books have gone into multiple printings. One of them, his first, ***The Dying Earth*** (1950), has been considered a classic for twenty years. Its sequel, the stories of Cugel the Clever, published as ***The Eyes of the Overworld*** (1966), eclipses it thoroughly as a work of literature. Both ***The Last Castle*** (1967) and ***The Dragon Masters*** (1963) won Hugos in their magazine novella versions. We have here one of the longest-working and prolific authors in the science fiction genre, a multiple award winner, and, moreover, a writer whose production has been more or less consistent for over a quarter of a century, and who has maintained a similarly consistent style, elegance, and craftsmanship. (p. 15)

The science fiction genre has produced but a handful of true stylists—that is, writers whose sentence-by-sentence prose is fine enough, idiosyncratic enough, subtle enough, and consistent enough from page to page and book to book to become the major interest in reading their work. . . .

And no science fiction writer does it with the Roman luxuriousness and razor-edge control of Jack Vance. Vance cavorts in his own words. . . . Like a painter, he endlessly describes clothing, architecture, landscape, and qualities of light for the purely aesthetic joy of it. . . . (p. 16)

Whether he is describing an expiring millennial Earth steeped in magic born of rotting history, or a galactic cluster of 30,000 stars, or the planet Aerlith under the baleful eye of the wandering lizard star, Vance creates baroque tapestry. Not content to limit himself to the mere world-creation of traditional science fiction, Vance adds those graceful superfluities that give his times and places baronial richness, late Renaissance grandeur, and the weight of cultural and aesthetic substantiality.

Out of this baroque prose style arise the baroque realities that Vance creates in his science fiction and fantasy. Vance's *oeuvre* may superficially be divided between "fantasies" like ***The Dying Earth*** and ***The Eyes of the Overworld*** in which the texture of reality is interwoven with magic, and works like ***The Dragon Masters,*** which justify every conceivable technical definition of "science fiction." I say *superficially* divided because the cleavage is technical and not something one experiences as a reader. Vance's "fantasy" has the same feel as Vance's "science fiction." Indeed, both have generally been published as "science fiction," and no one has seriously objected. For Vance's tone, his outlook on reality, and the flavor of his work arise from his style and mode, not from whether his material is "science fiction" or "fantasy." (pp. 16-17)

His fantasy is too detailed, convoluted, and realized not to be called science fiction, and his science fiction realities have the magical complexity of his fantasies.

The Dragon Masters, Vance's Hugo-winning short novel, for example, is science fiction by any reasonable criteria. Yet it retains the quality and tone common to all of Jack Vance's imaginative work. Just as Vance's tone arises out of his baroque prose style, so does that tone create story and character—especially when combined with Vance's characteristic sardonic viewpoint and his relentless sense of irony.

The Dragon Masters has a conventional space-opera plot, if one were to define it by simply capsulizing the story line. Lizardmen have captured all human planets except Aerlith by using genetically-altered humans as specialized brainwashed slave warriors. On Aerlith, humans have captured a party of invading "Basic" sauroids, and bred them into the same sort of specialized slave warriors. The Banbeck and Carcolo clans eventually use these "dragons" to destroy an invading party of Basics and their human warriors and seize their ship.

But such a conventional plot summary is hardly adequate, for it doesn't really describe what ***The Dragon Masters*** is all about. For Vance, plot and even character are skeletons upon which to hang his overriding concern for place and time, for a sense of history always imbued with a mordant irony reminiscent of the late Mark Twain.

Like many of Vance's societies, Aerlith has a political structure that is hereditary and feudal. The feuding forces of Joaz Banbeck and Ervis Carcolo battle each other for abstract advantage even as the Basics attack them both for the purpose of enslaving the last free men in the universe. To add another level of irony to the situation, the sacerdotes, a tribe of Aerlith humans who live in huge and eerie cave cities, consider themselves the only true humans and attempt to live out an insanely extreme philosophy of detachment in the face of the Basic assault. Vance's view of religious mystics is no more sanguine than his opinion of political leaders.

In ***The Dragon Masters,*** we can see how Vance's baroque style and sardonic stance transform what in other hands would be a straightforward science fiction story into a kind of sophisticated Grimm fairy tale entirely of a piece with works like the Cugel stories or the Dying Earth tales.

We can see this most clearly in the "dragons" of the title and the Basic-molded humanoids. Here are creatures out of some wizard's vat arrived at through the conventions of science fiction. *How* human and Basic flesh is transformed into Giants and Heavy Troopers, Blue Fiends and Termagants, is never scientifically explained—nor need it be, given the story's far-future context. (pp. 17-18)

What counts . . . is the reality, the verisimilitude, the three-dimensionality of the fantastic creatures the writer has created, not how they were technically arrived at. And here Jack Vance's richness of style serves to best advantage, creating gothic creatures that reverberate with the mythic dimensions of the Brothers Grimm, but which have the solidity, believability, and even upon occasion the psychological depth of well-realized science fiction. (p. 19)

[In] ***The Dragon Masters,*** we can see that the dragons and humanoids are not merely tour-de-force window dressing, but beings whose existence determines the plot—indeed, grotesques whose existence *becomes* the plot. A reality which contains such presences is clearly something other than what most of us experience from day to day—in quality, not only in content—which is why the work has fascination. This is fundamentally what people read both science fiction and fantasy for and what they seldom get—an altered reality with the cogency and verisimilitude of our own. And a reality, moreover, more convoluted, more ornate, more paradoxical, more slippery—more magical, if you will.

But even as Jack Vance builds his ornate cathedrals around you, his viewpoint on his own creations remains mordant, sardonic, slyly misanthropic, perhaps even ultimately pessimistic. In the work of Vance, some enduring age is forever coming to a close, and men seem meaner and smaller than their ancestors. . . . (pp. 19-20)

And in ***The Dragon Masters,*** men have been reduced to something truly less than human by the Basics—not only have they been bred into specialized serving animals like dogs, but their brains can no longer encompass the opposite concept to servitude. But Vance does not even let go of it there—he does not even permit humanity the moral superiority of the victim's position in such a degrading situation. For when men get the chance, they do exactly the same thing, breeding monstrous brute dragons out of their sapient Basic prisoners. Both men and Basics are guilty of a racial crime that goes genocide one better. (p. 20)

A line from ***The Dying Earth*** sums up Vance's *oeuvre,* his tone, his stance, his perspective on humanity perfectly: "Now, in the last fleeing moments, humanity festers, rich as rotting fruit. . . ."

How then has such a body of work remained in such relative obscurity? Here is a writer who has been around for three decades, and who is perhaps the premier stylist in the science fiction genre in terms of fusing prose, tone, viewpoint, content and mood into a seamless synergetic whole. A writer whose *Weltanschauung* is unsurpassed in the genre for its maturity and unique for its mordancy. Why has Jack Vance not been recognized as the peer of Bradbury, Heinlein, and Aldiss, let alone of Ellison, Zelazny, or Delany?

Having looked at what the work of Jack Vance is, we might find it instructive to look at what it is not. Vance has produced no truly outstanding characters that are remembered long after the stories that contain them are forgotten, nor has he produced tales that live on as epic sagas, as instant myths. He has produced no quintessential single work to point to as a peak achievement—which is to say that he is not famous for any hero, nor for any story, nor for any book. But then, Vance doesn't seem to set out to do any of these things. He has chosen to write a sort of fiction not calculated to bring him fame and fortune, nor to make him an epic storyteller, nor a creator of magnetic characters, nor to produce sporadic masterworks. It is a kind of fiction that is definitely a minority taste, not a mass-market addiction—nor is it ever likely to become anything else. But that does not make Vance's work any less valuable, for the taste that it satisfies is subtle and sophisticated. To enjoy Vance, you have to enjoy words as sculpture on paper, reality as a baroque landscape, and sardonicism for its own elegance. (pp. 20-1)

Norman Spinrad, "Jack Vance and 'The Dragon Masters'," in Jack Vance, *edited by Tim Underwood and Chuck Miller, Taplinger Publishing Company, 1980, pp. 13-22.*

DAN MILLER

Vance's fiction is distinguished by a certain sense of the alien found nowhere else in SF today. Characters are always sturdily drawn, but his success lies in an ability to create strange, remote worlds in an unobtrusive style that keeps attention focused on the work. . . . [The six previously published stories in ***The Best of Jack Vance***] illustrate well the novelist's range in evoking alien cultures, habits, and conditions from both inner and outer space.

Dan Miller, in a review of "The Best of Jack Vance," in The Booklist, *Vol. 72, No. 21, July 1, 1976, p. 1514.*

R. D. MULLEN

According to Barry Malzberg, in his introduction to ***The Best of Jack Vance*** . . . , "any fool knows that Jack Vance is one of the ten most important writers in the history of the field," and Norman Spinrad makes similar if less sweeping claims in [his introduction to ***The Dragon Masters*** (see excerpt above)] . . . , both writers emphasizing Vance's distinctive style and unique ability to portray alien beings and worlds, and both wondering why it is that Vance has not had a greater success with the general public or with academics. If in my old-fashioned way one analyzes fictions into the five "parts" of language, thought, character (differences between members of the same species, applying not just to persons but to phenomena of all kinds), nature (differences between species; the part that distinguishes SF from mundane fiction, since SF presents not just imaginary individuals but also imaginary species), and plot, then one can say that despite Vance's excellence in language and nature, he remains irredeemably banal in thought, character, and plot. In **"The Moon Moth"** and perhaps a few other stories he transcends such banality, but not in ***The Dragon Masters*** nor in any of the other book-length works I have read. (pp. 302-03)

R. D. Mullen, in a review of "The Dragon Masters," in Science-Fiction Studies, *Vol. 3, No. 10, November, 1976, pp. 302-03.*

ROBERT SILVERBERG

[The essay from which this excerpt is taken was originally published in 1977 as the introduction to **The Eyes of the Overworld** *by Jack Vance.]*

Magazine science fiction in 1945 was pretty primitive stuff, by and large, and so too was [Jack Vance's] **"The World-Thinker,"** a simple and melodramatic chase story; but yet there was a breadth of vision in it, a philosophic density, that set it apart from most of what was being published then, and the novice author's sense of color and image, his power to evoke mood and texture and sensory detail, was already as highly developed as that of anyone then writing science fiction, except perhaps C. L. Moore and Leigh Brackett. (p. 119)

Over the next few years a dozen or so Vance stories appeared, most of them in *Thrilling Wonder Stories* and its equally lurid-looking companion, *Startling Stories*. There was nothing very memorable among them—nearly all were clever but repetitive and formularized tales of the intrigues of one Magnus Ridolph, a rogue of the spaceways—but it was clear that a remarkable imagination was at work producing these trifles, for even the most minor story had its flash of extraordinary visual intensity and its moments of unexpected ingenuity. Would Vance ever produce anything more substantial, though? Finally, in the spring and summer of 1950, came two long and impressive Vance works. *Thrilling Wonder* offered the novella **"New Bodies for Old,"** and a few months later *Startling* published his first novel-length story, **"The Five Gold Bands."** The first was a conventional adventure story in form, but the prose was rich with dazzling descriptive passages, sometimes to the point of purpleness, and the science fiction inventions—the Chateau d'If, the Empyrean Tower, the technology of personality transplants—were brilliantly realized. **"The Five Gold Bands"** was even more conventional, a simple tale of interstellar treasure hunt, but it was made notable by its unflagging pace, the lively assortment of alien beings with which Vance had stocked it, and the light, sensitive style. Obviously 1950 was the year of Vance's coming of age as a writer, and ***The Dying Earth*** was a book I eagerly sought. The eleven-page slice published in the first number of *Worlds Beyond*, a delicate tale of wizardry and vengeance, whetted my appetite with its images of decay and decline, tumbled pillars, slumped pediments, crumbled inscriptions, the weary red sun looking down on the ancient cities of humanity. (pp. 119-20)

And yet I found the book obscurely disappointing. It was not a novel, I quickly saw, but rather a story sequence, six loosely related tales set against a common background, with a few overlapping characters to provide continuity. . . . The loose-jointed structure didn't trouble me unduly, although I would at that time have preferred a more orthodox pattern with the familiar magazine-serial format of beginning, middle, and resolution; but what disturbed me was the discovery that the book was not truly science fiction at all, but fantasy.

What I wanted, in my literal-minded way, was absolute revelation of the far future. Wells, in *The Time Machine*, had meticulously described the climatic and geological consequences of the heat-death of the sun; Stapledon, in *Last and First Men* (1930), had proposed an elaborate evolutionary progression for mankind over the next few million years. But

Vance showed no such concern for scientific verisimilitude. A truly dying Earth would be a place of thin, sharp air, bleak shadows, bitter winds, and all humanity long since evolved beyond our comprehension or else vanished entirely. But, though there are some strange creatures in Vance's world, his protagonists are mainly humans much like ourselves, unaltered by the passing of the millennia. (p. 121)

[For example, one of his characters, Liane the Wayfarer,] wears medieval garb; the narrative action of ***The Dying Earth*** is largely a series of encounters among sorcerers; ruined castles stand at the edge of meadows. This is not science fiction. It is a continuation of the work of Scheherazade by other hands, a *Thousand Nights and a Night* romance of never-never land. To Vance, the dying Earth is only a metaphor for decline, loss, decay, and, paradoxical though it may sound, also a return to a lost golden age, a simple and clean time of sparse population and unspoiled streams, of wizards and emperors, of absolute values and the clash of right and wrong. If I failed to appreciate ***The Dying Earth*** when I first encountered it, it was because I had asked it to be that which it was not. I admired the music of the prose and the elegance of the wit, the cunning of the characters and the subtlety of human interactions; but it was something other than science fiction, except maybe for the sequence titled **"Ulan Dhor Ends a Dream,"** and science fiction of the narrowest sort was what I sought.

The first edition of ***The Dying Earth*** disappeared and became legendary almost at once; . . . and Vance, perhaps expecting nothing more from the publication of his first novel than he had received—that is, a small amount of cash, prestige in exceedingly limited quarters, and general obscurity—went on like a good professional to other projects. *Startling* and *Thrilling Wonder* remained congenial markets for him over the next few years, and his narrative skills grew ever more assured, his style more dazzling, his mastery of large forms more confident. Now he worked almost entirely in the novella and the novel, with such magazine stories as **"Son of the Tree," "Planet of the Damned," "Abercrombie Station," "The Houses of Iszm,"** and the immense odyssey **"Big Planet."** In 1953 came a novel for young readers, ***Vandals of the Void,*** and the ephemeral paperback publication of his earliest long story, **"The Five Gold Bands,"** as ***The Space Pirate.*** By 1956, when Ballantine Books issued what may be his supreme accomplishment in science fiction, the powerful novel ***To Live Forever,*** Vance's position in the front ranks of science fiction was manifest. He had achieved no great commercial success, for his work was too "special," increasingly more dependent on a resonantly archaic, mannered style and a cultivated formality of manner, to win much of a following among the casual readers of paperbacks, but it was cherished by connoisseurs, and his popularity with the science-fiction subculture known as "fandom" was considerable. (pp. 122-23)

That Vance would choose to set another novel [***The Eyes of the Overworld***] in the actual world of ***The Dying Earth*** came as a surprise, however. Except for the early Magnus Ridolph stories he had never been a writer of sequels or linked series of stories, nor were any of his novels related to any other by a common background. . . . (p. 123)

The new book was not so much a sequel to ***The Dying Earth*** as a companion. None of the characters of ***The Dying Earth*** are to be found in ***The Eyes of the Overworld,*** though a few historical figures such as the sorcerer Phandaal are mentioned in both. There are references in ***The Eyes of the Overworld*** to some of the geographical features of ***The Dying Earth***—the cities Kaiin and Azenomei, the Land of the Falling Wall, the River Scaum—but most of ***The Eyes of the Overworld*** takes place far beyond the Realm of Grand Motholam, in an entirely new series of strange places. The bizarre quasi-human creatures of ***The Dying Earth,*** the deodands and erbs and gids and such, do recur, and their presence among the fully human folk of the era is at last given some explanation; but mostly the world of ***The Eyes of the Overworld*** is created from new material. It is impossible to tell how the events of one book are related in time to those of the other, though the same feeble red sun illuminates both.

Structurally, too, the books are different. Both are episodic, but ***The Dying Earth***'s six sections are virtually self-contained, each with its own protagonist. Characters recur from episode to episode—Turjan of Miir, Liane the Wayfarer, the synthetic girls T'sais and T'sain, the sorcerer Pandelume—but only occasionally do they interact across the boundaries of the episodes, and most of the chapters could have been published in any order without harm to the book's effect. Not so with ***The Eyes of the Overworld.*** Here all is told from the point of view of a single protagonist, a typically Vancian scamp named Cugel the Clever. . . . The structure is that of the picaresque novel—the cunning rascal Cugel moves across a vast reach of the dying Earth, getting in and out of trouble as he goes—but the individual episodes are bound together by a theme as old as Homer (for Cugel is trying to get home). . . . Whereas ***The Dying Earth*** as a whole is plotless and subtle in form, ***The Eyes of the Overworld*** carries a rigid skeleton beneath its picaresque surface.

Where the books are one is in the texture of the world that encloses them. ***The Eyes of the Overworld,*** like ***The Dying Earth,*** is a covert fantasy of the medieval. The first few pages bristle with artifacts of the fourteenth century A.D.—a public fair with timbered booths, amulets and talismans, elixirs and charms, gargoyles, a gibbet, a pickled homunculus. Cugel, in his wanderings, eludes archers and swordsmen, halts at an inn where wine-drinking travelers gather to trade gossip by the fire, joins a band of pilgrims bound toward a holy shrine. This is not the glittering clickety-clack world of science-fiction gadgetry. . . . Everything in the world of these two novels of the remote future is old and mellowed, as, indeed, would medieval Europe be if it had survived intact into our own time, which is essentially the fantasy that drives Vance's imagination in these books. (pp. 124-26)

The two Dying Earth novels provide an instructive lesson in the evolution of style, for the first is unabashedly romantic in a way that the second, written by a far more experienced and time-sombered man, is not. (pp. 127-28)

Vance has never lost his love of the feel and taste of colors, of the color of textures, and no book of his is without . . . passages of sensuous excess; but they have become more widely spaced in the narrative flow, and his raptures more qualified. . . . (p. 128)

The Dying Earth is, possibly, the more sophisticated work technically; its rolling structure seems a more delicate mechanism than ***The Eyes of the Overworld***'s neatly calculated symmetries. ***Eyes*** is a single unified construct, heading forward from its earliest pages toward an inevitable end and the inevitable final ironic twist; one admires the perfection of Vance's carpentry, but it seems a lesser achievement than the relaxed and flowing pattern of ***The Dying Earth,*** which more fully portrays an entire culture from a variety of points of view.

Cugel the Clever is an appealing rogue, but one misses the innocence of some of ***The Dying Earth***'s characters and the sublime skills of others.

Nevertheless the book is a worthy companion for the classic earlier novel: enormously entertaining, unfailingly ingenious, richly comic, a delightful fantasy. . . . Taken together, they are two key works in the career of this extraordinary fantasist. (pp. 128-29)

Robert Silverberg, " 'The Eyes of the Overworld' and 'The Dying Earth'," in Jack Vance, *edited by Tim Underwood and Chuck Miller, Taplinger Publishing Company, 1980, pp. 117-29.*

JERRY L. PARSONS

[***WYST: Alastor 1716***] is the third of Vance's ***Alastor*** stories, the others being ***Trullion*** and ***Marune***. As in most of Vance's work, the fabric of ***WYST*** is colorfully developed. It is a world of contrasts: the urbane citizens of Arrabin are lazy, mulish, and petty; the rural folk are ignorant, superstitious, and barbaric. ***WYST***'s plot starts slowly as the personalities of the protagonist, Jantiff Ravensroke, and of the Arrabins are developed. Once Jantiff realizes that he is caught in the machinations of a worldwide conspiracy, however, action and suspense abound. Best of all, perhaps, is Vance's superb, flowing style, which is compelling, rich, and humorous. (pp. 2264-65)

Jerry L. Parsons, in a review of "WYST: Alastor 1716," in Library Journal, *Vol. 103, No. 19, November 1, 1978, pp. 2264-65.*

JOHN J. ADAMS

The **"Demon Prince"** books were originally written in the '60s and concern the ruthless Star Kings, cold and amoral aliens who often disguise themselves as humans. Scornful of nearly every human activity, the single desire that brings them into the human sphere is an overwhelming lust for power. Five of them, the Demon Princes, murdered Kirth Gerson's parents as a strangely illogical "object lesson." Now Gerson tracks them down, one by one, no matter where they may be in the galaxy.

[In **"Star King,"** the] narrative of Gerson's pursuit of the first villain displays Vance's talent for the construction of a wealth of cultural and political detail while simultaneously introducing a large cast of fascinating characters. This is solid escapist fare and a must for fans of Vance.

John J. Adams, in a review of "Star King," in Kliatt Young Adult Paperback Book Guide, *Vol. XIII, No. 1, January, 1979, p. 22.*

JOHN SHIRLEY

The gradual plotting of the opening chapters of Jack Vance's [**"WYST: Alastor 1716"**] featuring the ruler of the Alastor Cluster (3000 inhabited worlds, chronicled fractionally by Vance in other related but distinct Alastor books), the Connatic. In this chapter we are given a trenchant, witty outline of society on Wyst, as well as a suspense-stoking adumbration of something amiss involving a certain Jantiff Ravensroke. But the story actually commences with and may well have been written, originally, from—Chapter Two, when Jantiff Ravensroke wins an art contest and realizes his dream to travel to other worlds. Being a painter, Jantiff chooses the world where ". . . sun and atmosphere cooperate to produce an absolutely glorious light, where every surface quivers with its true and just color . . .", Wyst. He goes to Arrabus, on Wyst.

Wyst is a supposedly classless society celebrating its Centenary Festival, 100 years of the Egalistic Manifold. . . . Vance's dry irony pervades his explication on Egalism, and it is shortly clear that much of the book is a satire on socialism, and a salient one. The inhabitants of Arrabus work only in brief "drudges" twice weekly. The food is synthetic and unvarying from day to day, this palate-dulling regimen producing a cult of "bonter" raiding, illicitly obtaining real food by stealing from non-Arrabin farmers and by arranging peculiar feasts with gypsies. The comparison to the average Russian's fascination with Western products and junk-goods is unavoidable. Vance parodies socialism's typical superficial lip-service to high ideals, their propaganda hiding corruption, immorality and disregard for individual rights.

Jantiff is fascinated with the Arrabin dedication to ". . . self-fulfillment, pleasure and frivolity". (This aspect could be a satire of the American incipient Welfare State.)

But he is disturbed by the careless, emotionless sexuality everywhere exhibited, by casual murders, by the sick fixation on "bonter", by the twisted public displays of violence and humiliation in the Shunk battles and by the casual thievery. . . .

Vance takes us halfway through the tale before the ominous foreshadowings become clear conflict, and some may find the going just a trifle tedious. But not *this* reader—Vance's power to stun me with a lucid picture, a well-turned phrase, a stunning irony is given further impact by the careful, adult characterization and its subtle interplays. This is no space opera—this is a brilliant analysis of a society and a microcosmic group of characters. And more than once **"WYST"** will jolt you with plot revelations, horrors made piquant by perverse humor.

Vance carefully delineates each change of scenery, sensitively coloring in background details, so that, as Jantiff is forced to flee southwards into the Weirdlands, the action again takes a backseat—but again the beauty of Vance's writing compels the astute reader onward. . . .

"WYST: Alastor 1716" may be slow-paced in places, but it never really flags. I strain to find flaws in this gem. . . . Vance has created another charmingly verbose and beautifully functional kinetic sculpture powered by social critique, poetry, intrigue and romance. A fascination.

John Shirley, in a review of "WYST: Alastor 1716," in Science Fiction Review, *Vol. 8, No. 3 May, 1979, p. 48.*

JERRY L. PARSONS

[***The Faceless Man, The Brave Free Men,*** and ***The Asutra***] are a finely-crafted trilogy by a superior author. The story covers, through the life and activities of the musician Gastel Etzwane, an understanding of the nation and cantons of Shant, the discovery of an alien invasion by the Asutra and their human simulacra, the Roguskhoi, repulsion of that invasion, and, finally, location of the world from which the Asutra had come. . . . Each book, thanks to Vance's skill in illuminating Shant's culture, creating well-developed plots and characters, and enveloping them all in compelling, humorous prose, stands alone, and they are all highly recommended for SF readers and collections.

Jerry L. Parsons, in a review of "The Faceless Man," "The Brave Free Men" and "The Asutra," in Science Fiction & Fantasy Book Review, *No. 7, August, 1979, p. 93.*

JERRY L. PARSONS

[The ***Tschai*** series, which includes ***City of The Chasch, Servants of The Wankh, The Dirdir,*** and ***The Pnume,*** is] vintage Vance [and] describes the adventures of Adam Reith on Tschai after his spaceship, and all of his shipmates, are destroyed. Each successive volume covers Reith's interactions with one of the four non-human species which inhabit the planet, all of whom have subjugated humans, and now try to subjugate Adam Reith. Each of the alien cultures is rich and fascinating; the Dirdir, for example, are an ancient, arrogant, and violent folk, while the Pnume, Tschai's indigenous species, live in a complex web of caves beneath the planet's surface, chronicling Tschai's history. The plots are well-constructed and compelling, the characters convincing. Reith's ingenuity and strength of mind make him a particularly attractive fictional hero. This is one of Vance's most colorful—and popular—series.

Jerry L. Parsons, in a review of "City of the Chasch," "Servants of the Wankh," "The Dirdir" and "The Pnume," in Science Fiction & Fantasy Book Review, *No. 9, October, 1979, p. 128.*

PUBLISHERS WEEKLY

Vance's fame as a weaver of magical tapestries began in 1950 with **"The Dying Earth,"** a collection of related stories set in the far distant future. A novel and three shorter sequels followed. . . . [**"Morreion: A Tale of the Dying Earth"**], published separately for the first time, is one of those. It's the story of a cabal of magicians whose greed takes them to the literal end of the universe in search of Morreion, a colleague they had abandoned to a lonely doom until they realized he knew a powerful secret. While not up to the original stories in richness and wonder, this fast-reading fable does have the same wry tone and charm. A tantalizing puff pastry rather than a satisfying repast. . . .

A review of "Morreion: A Tale of the Dying Earth," in Publishers Weekly, *Vol. 216, No. 21, November 19, 1979, p. 75.*

ROSEMARY HERBERT

Although dealing with the interesting problems of linguistic engineering, [***The Languages of Pao***] fails to catch the reader's interest because the main character lacks appeal, the gadgetry is technically impossible, and the ending is inconclusive. The book follows the life of Beran, who is educated on a planet specializing in training the intellectual elite so that he can return to his home world and eventually assume his rightful position of leadership. . . . Wooden characterization adds to the many problems of this book.

Rosemary Herbert, in a review of "The Languages of Pao," in Library Journal, *Vol. 105, No. 12, June 15, 1980, p. 1412.*

KIRKUS REVIEWS

Beyond the pleasures of the Vance intelligence and the Vance prose style—both considerable—the *raison d'être* of [***Galactic Effectuator***] is a trifle exiguous. It contains a short novel [**"The Dogtown Tourist Agency"**] and a long short story [**"Freitzke's Turn"**] about "galactic effectuator" (read "sleuth") Miro Hetzel; they look as if they would be happier with company. . . . It is strategic reticence that is responsible for the wonderfully tonic air of Vance's writing; here as always, he knows just what to leave out to invest the most ordinary conversation or bit of description with tantalizing astringency. Nonetheless there is a lot that might profitably have been left *in* here in the way of plot. Neither mystery is worth the elegance expended on it, and indeed a few clues in the denouement of **"Freitzke's Turn"** seem unfairly slurred over. Much charm, little body.

A review of "Galactic Effectuator," in Kirkus Reviews, *Vol. XLVIII, No. 15, August 1, 1980, p. 1029.*

JOHN J. ADAMS

[***The Many Worlds of Magnus Ridolph*** is] fast-paced, detective-story s-f. The Ridolph stories, written in the late '40s and early '50s for *Thrilling Wonder Stories* and *Super Science Stories,* are about the adventures of an unlikely hero, an old and wizened interstellar troubleshooter whose almost prescient powers of observation belie his bland appearance. Vance's expected bizarre, beautiful alien worlds, quirky cultures, and quick, sardonic humor are here, but at the heart of each story is a cleverly revealed "big riddle" that shows Vance's estimable talent for mystery writing.

John J. Adams, in a review of "The Many Worlds of Magnus Ridolph," in Kliatt Young Adult Paperback Book Guide, *Vol. XIV, No. 6, September, 1980, p. 17.*

TIM UNDERWOOD

Along with other established writers, Jack Vance has benefited from . . . [a] sudden widespread acceptance and interest in science fiction. . . . Today, nearly thirty of his SF novels and story collections are available in the United States. A good many of these have been translated and published overseas. The future for SF seems bright indeed.

But it was not always so. . . . When Jack Vance began his literary career at the close of World War II, pulp magazines and digests were virtually the sole marketplace for speculative fiction. As Robert Silverberg remarks about Vance's ***The Dying Earth*** (1950) [see excerpt above], when a science fiction book appeared in those days it was an *event*. . . .

Still, it must be admitted that, as a genre, science fiction has seen more than its share of schlocky literature. Vance himself wrote hundreds of thousands of words for the pulps and digests of the 40s and 50s, often prefabricated "idea" stories with cute plots, cardboard characters, and a great deal of SF gadgetry. This last-mentioned element was a prerequisite, because while those ephemeral magazines offered easy money to any would-be writer willing to cater to their standards, their content was largely restricted to *science* fiction (a legacy of Hugo Gernsback's dictum that the business of science fiction is science). (p. 8)

Vance (whose first book, ***The Dying Earth,*** showed him to be fantasy-oriented in story treatment and imagination) . . . [was] to some extent forced to write ''scientific'' fiction—with physical science and technological hardware prominently displayed within the story—or cease to publish.

Yet within these confines (which finally began to disappear in the mid-60s, thanks to a change in readers' tastes and social temperament, and in publishers' editorial staffs) Jack Vance produced some very worthy science-backgrounded speculative novels and, eventually, some science fiction masterpieces which may last as long as his best works of fantasy.

Vance not only learned to write *science* fiction, he learned to write it well, though rather differently than it had been written in the past. Gradually, his craft evolved. Having finished ***Big Planet*** (1952), ***To Live Forever*** (1956), and ***The Languages of Pao*** (1957)—along with some other less interesting novels—Vance successfully harnessed his fanciful imagination, his yen for innovation within traditional structure, and his taste for eclectic ornamentation. Great works resulted—***The Dragon Masters*** appeared in 1963 and won a Hugo; ***The Star King*** appeared in 1964, the first book in the ***Demon Princes*** series. Both are masterpieces of their kind. Within the following three years he had published two more extraordinary examples of stylized imagination, this time ''classical'' fantasies—***The Eyes of the Overworld*** (a sequel to ***The Dying Earth***) and ***The Last Castle,*** which won a Nebula Award in 1966 and a Hugo Award in 1967. . . .

[Despite] having won a Nebula and two Hugos (and an Edgar for his mystery writing), Vance's work has received little critical attention. Probably no other author in the field has received as much acclaim and as little analysis. (p. 9)

Which of Jack Vance's many books will endure the test of time? My own guesses are as follows: ***The Dying Earth, The Eyes of the Overworld, The Dragon Masters, The Last Castle,*** and probably the four ***Tschai*** books and the ***Demon Princes*** series. (p. 11)

[His] best books are not reflections of the world around us, they are rather distillations and transmutations. When they do reflect, it is of images from within, from the realms of imagination and beyond, from Poe's ''weird clime that lieth sublime, Out of Space—out of Time.''

Vance takes you there and back again. (p. 12)

Tim Underwood, in an introduction to Jack Vance, *edited by Tim Underwood and Chuck Miller, Taplinger Publishing Company, 1980, pp. 7-12.*

PETER CLOSE

The first five years of Vance's writing career were . . . spent almost entirely in the pulps. Much derided at the time, the pulps nonetheless represented a comprehensive apprenticeship for many authors. . . .

He started with no technique except astonishing natural talent, and he learned quickly. (p. 24)

Vance had, in fact, entered the field at a time when he could learn as he went along. Free of editorial biases or constraints, he was able to develop a personal style which has evolved into one of the most distinctive and rewarding in the field. At the same time, however, his strengths, by overshadowing his weaknesses, offered him no incentive to correct his enduring problems of construction, plotting, and resolution. As a writer who has never yet found an editor consistently able to bring out the best in him, Vance has had to rely on his own commitment to his craft and his own capacity (often formidable) for self-criticism.

In consequence of this, Vance's early stories are unusually illuminating in respect to his technical development. Successive stories are almost didactic in their illustration of increasing skills in specific areas of writing technique; Vance may fumble as every beginner does, but it is nearly always possible to point to a later effort which shows that he has learned better. Some weaknesses, sadly, seem inherent. Vance will never be famous for his plotting (the meticulous precision of ***To Live Forever*** being almost the only exception) and, ironically enough, his problems in this area are least noticeable when he settles for an elementary plot structure rather than attempting sophistication. (p. 25)

In the five years elapsing between his first publication and the appearance of ***The Dying Earth*** in 1950, Vance built the foundations of a brilliant and woefully neglected career. (p. 26)

[***The Dying Earth*** is] a chaotic, shapeless, uneven book—often brilliant, occasionally crass, bejewelled with splendid descriptive passages, exotic invention, polished dialogue, vivid metaphor, rare vocabulary. In its range of themes and settings, it displays almost all of Vance's talents and weaknesses. In the ten years which elapsed between its inception and its publication, Vance developed (entirely through his own efforts) from a gifted amateur totally lacking in technique to an accomplished freelance writer. (pp. 64-5)

[The flaws in his plotting and the resolution of his stories] are unimportant when set beside the accomplishments of his talents and meticulously crafted style. It's only to be expected that his first book should reflect the development of his craft—here he loses control of pace, there he stumbles from one viewpoint to another, now the plot becomes nonsensical, this or that character is drawn too boldly for his place. But always Vance gives us color, imagination, splendid language, rich words, an unerring and perceptive eye for wonder, beauty, and strangeness, an enduring and sympathetic fascination with the varieties of human adjustment. By the end of 1950, five years after his first publication, the brilliance of his talent was beyond doubt. (p. 65)

Peter Close, ''Fantasms, Magics, and Unfamiliar Sciences: The Early Fiction of Jack Vance, 1945-50,'' in Jack Vance, *edited by Tim Underwood and Chuck Miller, Taplinger Publishing Company, 1980, pp. 23-65.*

MARK WILLARD

Two hundred and twelve light-years from Earth hangs the smoky yellow star Carina 4269 and its single, ancient planet—Tschai. The Earth reconnaissance spacecraft *Explorator IV* penetrates the system and stands off Tschai. As a scout boat is prepared for launch, the *Explorator*'s officers examine the prospects. . . . In the instant of the scout boat's departure, a torpedo from the planet intercepts the *Explorator*; in a dazzling flare the ship is obliterated save for skeleton fragments through which the old, old sun of Tschai shines knowingly. Officers, crew, and ties to Earth are not more than random atoms upon the solar winds.

Thus opens Jack Vance's ***Planet of Adventure*** series; and it takes no great imagination to view these first pages as symbolic.

Officers Marin, Deale, and Walgrave may be taken to be representations of traits and attitudes inherent in much of Vance's previous work, and their uncompromising expungement as token that the story to come will differ in nature from what has gone before. . . . The four ***Tschai*** novels (1968-70) are imbued with a greater vitality, a more down-to-earth urgency, a lesser detachment, and a more skillfull threading of fantasy through the framework of gritty reality than the body of Vance's earlier—and already excellent—work.

The ***Tschai*** series, comprising ***City of the Chasch, Servants of the Wankh, The Dirdir,*** and ***The Pnume,*** runs over six hundred pages. Scores of characters, dozens of locales, a seething wealth of events, attitudes, insights are paraded upon the stage; and four worldviews are provided in the brushes with the four alien races who give the books their titles. The landscapes of Tschai reek and radiate antiquity, and the human peoples live in the awareness that they are only the most recent of a near-infinity of generations whose lives were not perceptibly different. Throughout mankind's history on Tschai, humans have been pawns of the "great races." The native Pnume and Phung, three races of Chasch colonists, Dirdir and—the most recent arrivals—the Wankh all help set up a milieu incredibly rich and complex, a kaleidoscope of varieties of man and alien, vignettes of curious, specialized lifestyles each all-important to its practitioners. The surface of Tschai is a vast openness of steppes and far-flung continents, yet for contrast the reader gradually becomes aware of stifling traditions and the surveillance of the alien overlords.

Though the reader comes to know him well, the protagonist, star-scout Adam Reith, remains a somewhat unknown, ever-surprising quantity. . . . [Of] Reith's training, childhood, family, nationality, we discover nothing. . . . All must be assumed, from Reith's actions and attitudes. . . . His attention and the narrative's focus are firmly fixed upon the present.

So there is no extraneous clutter—no looks back, no detailed comparisons of Tschai's features with their Earthly counterparts. Earth itself, even more than Reith, is a blank. One's curiosity is piqued, but this paucity of background may elicit admiration from a technical point of view: it must have been more difficult than not to avoid mentioning incidents about Reith's training, previous missions, friends and acquaintances on Earth, and so on, which could distract from the story at hand. (pp. 103-05)

Several themes run through the four books; the strongest is contrast. Drab, somber Tschai, with its steppes and wastes, is circled by the pink moon Az and the blue moon Braz—twin symbols of gaiety and festivity! The Blue Chasch race is characteristically cruel, arbitrary, and sadistic, yet their dwelling places are gardens of feathery fronds and trees which refresh the air. On Tschai's surface the alien races rock and swirl in power struggles and combats; beneath the ground the Pnume historians pace their still shafts and caverns and make notes for their great records.

Another type of contrast is what might be termed anachronistic juxtapositions: the past and the future, and mud and the stars, tradition and antitradition, and so on are ever rubbing shoulders. (p. 106)

A certain realism might also be called a theme—delete some of the action and the series could almost become a fascinating travelog! A main thrust of all Vance's writing is sociological; there are no snapshot glimpses of tribes, cultures, or peoples, but somehow enough detail is introduced to show them in the round. Means of livelihood, outlook, natural features, the shaping forces of their existence—all are brushed on quickly but delicately. Rather than being noteworthy for curious character traits or personal foibles, most frequently the supporting characters are distinguished through their display of cultural attributes. As is often the case in Vance's work, cultures *are* characters; the rivalry between Thang and Zsafathran in ***The Pnume*** is far more entertaining than the actual encounters described in the narrative would be alone. (p. 107)

Though they share themes, the books in the series follow no formula. In ***City of the Chasch*** Reith attempts to recover his own spacecraft; in ***Servants of the Wankh*** he makes a stab at pirating one from a spaceport; in ***The Dirdir*** Reith resigns himself to building one; and in ***The Pnume*** he endeavors to escape the attention he has stirred up in his former activities. Similarly, to characterize each volume in a vastly simplified manner: ***City of the Chasch*** is a rushing explosion of new concepts raising possibility after possibility; ***Servants of the Wankh*** proceeds along more cautious lines and harks back to other Vance works and styles, setting up situations; ***The Dirdir*** is the Tschai concept in full bloom, the least episodic but having the strongest characters and plot; and ***The Pnume*** is a wrapping-up and fond farewell. (pp. 107-08)

Though Tschai is one planet, the series has taken us through four worlds, four environments, four spectra of alienness. In the passing the alien has become familiar; though Chasch, Wankh, Dirdir, Pnume, and Phung all remain strange and fearsome, we know their ways, at least enough to wish to know more. The ***Tschai*** series, at this writing, is Vance's longest, and it may be unseemly to hope that he might add to it; but the feeling persists that the more we are shown Tschai and its people, the more yet awaits to be seen. (p. 116)

Mark Willard, "Tschai: Four Planets of Adventure," in Jack Vance, *edited by Tim Underwood and Chuck Miller, Taplinger Publishing Company, 1980, pp. 103-16.*

RICHARD TIEDMAN

[The essay from which this excerpt is taken was published in a slightly different form as a monograph in 1965.]

The analysis of style is a singularly difficult objective. One is always oppressed by the tasks of tracing the subtle silent influence by which a notable writer first shapes and then develops his mode of expression until it reflects an individual and original use of language. If this evades easy definition, it is still readily identifiable when found—a kind of linear mastery of materials that attacks and compels, a unique handling and synthesis in the use of words that renders life to a printed page. These attributes are sadly lacking in most present-day writers, both of science fiction and mainstream literature. Without prior knowledge, very few are identifiable by an examination of one page from their works. So many of their books are subdued in tone and stinted in color, utilizing only the middle register of possibilities.

The exceptions stand out. . . . [Jack Vance] is one of a mere handful whose argument is enhanced by a personally distinguished means.

Style is a characteristic manner of expression, and it may vary enormously among different writers. Generally speaking, there are two approaches by which a writer leaves his stylistic fingerprints, and both are legitimate and desirable means to that end. The first is when the author's personality is allowed to suffuse and color the texture. Here the narrative, to an extent, assumes the viewpoint of the writer; his psychology, values, temperament, and opinions are sufficient to establish this "characteristic" tone. Robert Heinlein is probably the preeminent writer among those who display this technique. Heinlein rarely, if at all, attempts to make an effect with words outside of their purely referential associations. They serve as a means to an end. Though the craftsmanship in most of his books is exemplary, there are few striking effects of imagery or rhythm. As Sam Moskowitz has observed, Heinlein has "sacrificed the aesthetics of the individual passage to achieve the unified poetry of the whole." (pp. 179-80)

Jack Vance typifies a radically different approach to the problem of personal style. As in the case of Heinlein, anyone who has read one or two books by Vance would have no difficulty in assigning selected passages to their correct author, with the distinction that while Heinlein requires a few pages to be read, with Vance it is possible to guess his authorship from a few sentences. His stories are attended by a very personal and unmistakable method of sentence construction, rhythmic variety, and extravagant imagery—all controlled with great technical dexterity. In opposition to Heinlein, Vance's personality is in evidence not through choice of content but in manner of expression. This is as subjective an approach to writing as it is an objective and impersonal approach to fiction.

Vance apparently wants everything—plot, social structures, characterization—to spring into form with its own interior life, thus retaining individual autonomy. The reader will witness a complete absence of any personal animus or overt deduction. In Vance, the reader sees, senses, and is shown, rather than being told. Thus he is drawn into an unconscious and immediate participation in events. The tiresome and garrulous polemics of Heinlein's later books find no parallel in Vance's works. Vance prefers that stylistic identity rest at a distance from authorial identity.

The dangers inherent in this approach are quite different from those of Heinlein's. In attempting a more individual style, the most circumspect care is necessary lest this degenerate into self-parody. . . . The mark of Vance's achievement is that although his style is the result of conscious effort, it reads as naturally and as plausibly as Heinlein at his best. This is a result of a careful and precise use of personal mannerisms. (pp. 181-82)

How does Vance's style differ from that of others? First, in his use of uncommon words; the stories are bedecked with rare words, exotic idiom, and rich texture. The unusual word . . . is used to produce the utmost variety of color and effect. The language is consistently rich yet such exotic words do not seem to intrude even though in a more haphazard context they would tend to obfuscate the flow of narration. Given the breadth and spaciousness of Vance's settings, the choice of a more circumspect "language" would hardly do justice to the products of his imagination. . . .

However, in his use of dialogue Vance often prefers more common words, those of sensation and action. His dialogues, with their swift-paced use of ellipses and often humorous bent, form a necessary contrast to the broad descriptive passages of his mature novels.

Much of Vance's readability stems from the rhythmic variety of his sentences. In scenes of flux or turmoil the syntax becomes crisp, lapidary—yet completely arhythmic. This is not necessarily remarkable, of course, but Vance usually manages a cadence unmistakably his own. He is fond of using verbs and adjectives in unadorned consecutive sequences. (p. 182)

Similarly, many sentences are made up of a succession of short clauses, with the connectives eliminated to gain force. . . .

He knows the value of a sudden change in vocabulary and rhythm, as the good writer is master of both the ample and the brief modes of expression. Vance's more recondite wording and languorous rhythms are reserved for descriptive scenes.

With deceptive ease he alternates scenic effects, narration, and dialogue in a smoothly welded panorama, infusing the whole with an actualizing impulse. As Vance wants to make every moment adventive and imperative, he rarely lapses into reveries of mere word painting. . . . Purely descriptive passages are relatively short, sketched in with strong colors and scattered through the narrative texture in such a way that the story is never impeded. The reader always has a sense of continuous narrative superimposed over the depth of background. (p. 183)

Unlike certain writers with pronounced stylistic traits, . . . it cannot be said that Vance's style is limited by a lack of internal contrast. . . . Vance avoids this pitfall by a judicious pacing of both syntax and event, at the same time maintaining a variegated congruity of mood.

Yet it is a dangerous style to imitate. It verges on that borderline where virtues may defect—the colorful become garish, the verdant become lush, the opulent become grandiose, the elegant become mannered. The utmost discipline is needed to keep its appointed course. . . . It is true that his plots reflect at times a rigorous formalization; this, however, is merely framework, and not indicative of temper. Vance does show a disinterested and analytically inclined literary bent, but this is a result of objectivity and his desire to let the story speak for itself, without commentary. What is sensuous, is so in the context of appealing to or being perceived by the senses, rather than in the connotation of being voluptuous or licentious. This combination of the "abstract" and "formal" with the "sensuous" serves to act as a check and balance and the chasm of uncontrolled expression is thereby avoided. (pp. 184-85)

In contrasting Vance's plots with his manner of presentation on a comparative basis, most readers would agree he is more successful in his handling of the latter. Here he shows a higher degree of consistency and judgment. Sometimes, as in **"Parapsyche,"** he displays a less than firm articulation of theme, and at any rate it is unusual when theme is in advance of style (***The Languages of Pao*** is an obvious exception). The reader may feel at times that the whole does not equal the sum of the parts, that the entire gamut of possibility has not been completely consummated, and that the sweep and swiftness of the style have deflected his awareness of the fact. Probably Vance's greatest weakness lies in the area of plot improbabilities or, more specifically, improbable events. Sometimes the threads of design are pulled into a pattern by incidents of a too-happy fortuitousness. . . . Another occasional fault is the failure to unify all the thematic threads of a story. . . . (p. 185)

The plots of Vance's earlier novels tended to be mosaic in structure—that is, accretive rather than projective. They moved forward by the accumulation of incidents in sectional episodes, tied together by transitional interludes to form a unified whole. ***Big Planet*** and ***The Dying Earth*** are the best examples of this technique. There is a distinction between the episodic and the merely fragmentary; in these novels . . . , the episodic structure gives the sequences the compacted unity of a short story within the context of the larger design.

The profuse texture of Vance's novels is due to the accretion of material rather than any complexity in narration. Vance prefers . . . straightforward development rather than multiple strands of action. He does not care to implement and heighten tension. . . .

Vance prefers to work below the reader's conscious attention: sequences are resolved at least seemingly by the natural exigencies of the situation and by characters whose acts and viewpoints are reflected by their temperaments. This is not to say one method is superior to the other, merely that the views are distinctly opposed. Vance's qualities unfold to better advantage in a more naturalistic and leisurely exposition. (p. 186)

Vance's plots are relatively simple, however much encrusted with subsidiary material incidental to the story line. [Arthur Jean] Cox in his 1963 essay is very perceptive on this point: "He [Vance] keenly responds to the specifics of social form, the 'patterns of culture' as expressed in conduct, manners, styles of dress, housing, crafts, artifacts, etc.—of which he has sent up a pyrotechnic display over the past twenty years." It is this baroque verve and effusion in the conjuring of imaginative detail work that give the novels their interior resonance and continuity of impression. In ***The Dying Earth, Big Planet,*** and ***To Live Forever,*** Vance is brilliantly resourceful in evoking his fictional backgrounds, the imposed interplay of scene taking on a concrete reality of its own. . . . It is this quality that lends much of his fiction its evocative verisimilitude. Thomas Mann remarked, "Style is the accommodation to the subject." Vance, we feel, often reverses the process. The emancipation of detail work from the relative unimportance of background elaboration is a hallmark of Vance's style; no other writer in the field forges his settings so profusely and so carefully, and with such consistency of nomenclature. (p. 187)

Vance is, above all, a marvelous teller of tales. There is a great deal that sympathetic criticism may elicit from his works, but the task is rendered peculiarly difficult (and captivating) because, perhaps more than any other major writer in the field, his work is replete with contrary tendencies and qualifications. This leads to a perennially interesting question: What does Vance really think? In the ***Demon Princes*** series, for instance, what is his attitude toward the concept of The Institution? I would say, somewhat guardedly, that he approves, but the other side of the question is given considerable play in the novels. Vance likes to enter imaginatively into all sides of a concept; the result, often, is a kind of multifaceted ambiguity which defies easy categorization. . . .

If this renders critical elucidation fascinatingly difficult, those who take up the task will find in Vance's novels and stories scope for abounding riches. (p. 222)

Richard Tiedman, "Jack Vance: Science Fiction Stylist," in Jack Vance, *edited by Tim Underwood and Chuck Miller, Taplinger Publishing Company, 1980, pp. 179-222.*

MICHAEL DIRDA

What one first notices in the work of Jack Vance is the style. The sentences are processional—richly ornamented, courtly, measured, slightly ironic. The syntax is never fancy, but the vocabulary possesses a faintly archaic flavor, the result of a flair for naming things and a historian's desire for precision. The polite diction suggests a civilized observer, a kind of galactic Saint-Simon, who analyzes in detail the social structures of alien worlds while describing the doings and misadventures of various outsiders, misfits and rebels.

Vance's opening sentences establish this carefully pitched tone. . . . In his descriptions, though, Vance lets his taste for gilt and brocade dominate. . . . (p. 6)

[His] sensuous, elevated style, at times reminiscent of the art-prose of Ruskin or Huysmans, can easily cloy or become mere bejeweled description, gaudy but insubstantial. Vance skirts this danger by fixing on traditional adventure plots: the revenge saga, the picaresque journey or marvel-filled odyssey, the murder mystery, the novel of education (his most common form), sword-and-laser battle epics (chiefly ***The Dragon Masters*** and ***The Last Castle,*** both Hugo winners). All these strong story lines prevent the novels from bogging down in the merely evocative; unfortunately, though, Vance seems content to adopt them whole without transforming them into anything uniquely his own—none of his plots tick with the clockwork-precision of Robert Heinlein's, nor do his characters possess the complexity and realness of Philip K. Dick's.

This last criticism results largely from Vance's historical perspective, one which conveys a feeling of sympathetic observation rather than of close involvement with his characters. His heroes themselves often possess this same detachment: Kirth Gersen, the single-minded revenger of **"The Demon Princes"** saga, may occasionally indulge in uncertainty about his lifelong manhunt for the five super-villains who destroyed his planet and family, but for the most part he regards himself and his actions with the impersonality of a chessplayer. What gives Gersen's adventures their baroque richness—and Vance has spent his best years on them—are the subsidiary figures, the detailed variety and intricate coherence of the planets, organizations and peoples that make up the Oikumene, and the grandiose Venetian character of the Demon Princes themselves.

For in Vance's work description itself becomes epic. From any of his novels the reader will learn, unobtrusively, how a world is governed, its history, the values of the citizens (including their religious beliefs, social aspirations and general character traits), the forms of technology available, the games people play, what the night sky looks like.

In ***The Face,*** for example, Vance creates the desert world of Dar Sai, half-Arab, half Australian, where the Darsh people are brutish, and sexual contact results only through culturally-condoned violence. "Procreation," to quote the *Tourist Guide to the Coranne,* by Jane Szantho, "is accomplished . . . during nocturnal promenades across the desert, especially when Mirassou-shine is in the sky. The system is simple in outline but complicated in detail. Both men and women aggressively seek out young sexual partners. The men waylay girls barely adolescent; women seize upon boys not much older. To lure boys out upon the desert, the women ruthlessly send out the pubescent girls and so it goes." The Darsh live under huge gossamer "shades," structured to trap and preserve moisture. The whip is the preferred weapon, their food ("chatowsies, pourrian, ahagaree") revolting, the great sport *hadaul,* a kind of free-for-all played on a tri-colored circular court.

Such zestful creativity reflects Vance's liking for marvels, spectacle and Grand Guignol—for games. . . . Many of the novels also depict elaborate caste systems, with precise and absurd requirements; in **"The Moon Moth"** people communicate with bizarre musical instruments, wear finely-worked masks (revealing a naked face is unthinkable), and value social esteem above all else. The plot here is elegantly simple: How does one identify a murderer in a society where everyone goes about in disguise?

Readers new to Jack Vance may be surprised at the number of books he has written (40 or so novels since 1950) and by the range of their subject matter and flavor. The stories of ***The Dying Earth,*** set on our planet some 20 million years in the future, convey an elegiac mood; the sad magic of mankind's twilight; but the Cugel tales (in ***The Eyes of the Overworld,***) take place at the same time and possess a sardonic trickster humor, suggestive of Dunsany. (Who could forget the elegant Spell of Forlorn Encystment?) The five novels of the ***Demon Princes***—the spooky last volume, ***The Book of Dreams,*** is just out—constitute a kind of spaghetti western in space, while ***The Last Castle*** depicts the most wondrously refined and delicate of societies, as ordered as a Japanese tea ceremony. ***Nopalgarth,*** by contrast, is an hallucinatory, paranoiac novel, picturing human beings as the playthings of rival alien beings—a mixture of Lovecraft and Vonnegut; and ***Emphyrio*** studies the deep affections and sympathies that spring up between a father and his son.

Like a few other genre writers—Wodehouse or le Carré come to mind—Jack Vance is a craftsman of an unusual order, whose books show all the signs of being a true oeuvre, the products of a single inventive intelligence. In anything he writes one hears that refined, inimitable, addictive voice—*there* is his triumph. (pp. 6, 8)

Michael Dirda, "A Galactic Night's Entertainment," in Book World—The Washington Post, *April 26, 1981, pp. 6, 8.*

EUGENE E. LAFAILLE

The Narrow Land, a collection of seven stories that were originally published between 1945 and 1967, consists of six science fiction and one fantasy tale. The fantasy story, **"Green Magic,"** is the best known; **"Chateau d'If,"** one-third the length of the collection, is the longest.

Vance is a prolific writer who is best known for the worlds that he creates and populates with bizarre alien creatures. Only three of these stories are so related and all seven have humans as main characters. These stories are characterized by a lack of scientific detail (e.g., relying upon mention of an "over-under space-drive"), little character development, no humor, and methodical, plodding development of the plot generally leading to a dull or satirical denouement. This collection lacks a common theme. . . .

Eugene E. LaFaille, in a review of "The Narrow Land," in Kliatt Young Adult Paperback Book Guide, *Vol. XVI, No. 6, September, 1982, p. 23.*

JOAN D. VINGE AND JAMES FRENKEL

[Jack Vance's new novel ***Lyonesse***] is a magical tapestry of feudal kingdoms and fairylands; of scheming nobility and sly magicians; of lust and greed, power and politics. . . .

Vance possesses a marvellous eye for authentic-sounding detail. His depiction of battles, magic-wreaking, royal feasts, deep-forest dangers and other fantastic happenings is vivid and convincing. The excitement and suspense of his tale is sustained throughout, and Vance weaves together the disparate fortunes of his players into a fascinating and richly satisfying adventure.

His magic falters somewhat when he attempts to convey sexual situations, or when his characters need to be defined. These people remain archetypes, and too close an examination exposes the flimsy fabric of their personality. But those flaws fail to dim the brilliance of the novel's spell.

Joan D. Vinge and James Frenkel, in a review of "Lyonesse," in Book World—The Washington Post, *March 24, 1983, p. 8.*

JERRY L. PARSONS

Originally published . . . as ***Showboat World,*** this picaresque novel of Big Planet [now titled ***The Magnificent Showboats of the Lower Vissel River, Lune XXIII South, Big Planet***] falls short of the high standards which one expects of Vance. The plot is reasonably straightforward: a King Waldemar of Mornune offers a fortune to the showboat which presents the best performance before his court. . . .

Most of the book's action concerns the voyage up the Vissel, adapting to the various peculiarities of the inhabitants along the route. Vance's creativity is usually well displayed by such travelogues. The primary characters in ***Showboat World,*** however, are neither admirable like Adam Reith (***World of Adventure*** tetralogy) and Gastel Etzwane (***Durdane*** trilogy), nor amusing like Cugel the Clever (***The Eyes of the Overworld***); they are merely self-centered, insensitive and malicious. Even Vance's excellent style and fascinating, idiosyncratic villages cannot raise this work above the mediocre.

Jerry L. Parsons, in a review of "The Magnificent Showboats of the Lower Vissel River, Lune XXIII South, Big Planet," in Science Fiction & Fantasy Book Review, *No. 16, July-August, 1983, p. 52.*

BILL COLLINS

Vance has a talent for involving the reader in his fiction almost immediately, and [***The Man in the Cage***] is no exception. Noel Hutson, a minor adventurer by choice, has been hired, in the late 1950s, to run guns from Morocco to Algeria. Payment for the guns comes in heroin—but Noel . . . is a closet romantic. He will have nothing to do with the drugs. His disappearance brings his brother Darrell, a civil engineer, to Morocco, involving the staid stay-at-home sibling with amoral smugglers, Arab revolutionaries, exotic locales, imprisonment and gunfights. I don't know whether Vance has been to Morocco, but if he hasn't, he has read the right source material. . . . Given Vance's conservative political views, he provides a surprisingly honest forum for the Arab terrorist point of view. His hero does ultimately trash the revolutionaries, but they do have an opportunity to passionately rationalize their philosophy of violence.

Inveterate mystery readers will probably not have to wait for the clue on p. 121 to send them back to chapter one in order to match wits with the author, as happened to me. But the disposition of the finally-revealed ultimate villains, who have out-generalled the hero as well as the resourceful subvillain, in a fatal auto collision with a gasoline truck, makes me wonder how such an artificial retribution could have been ignored as a serious flaw by the Edgar voters. (p. 53)

Bill Collins, in a review of "The Man in the Cage," in Science Fiction & Fantasy Book Review, *No. 16, July-August, 1983, pp. 52-3.*

TOM EASTON

Lyonesse is being touted as Jack Vance's *magnum opus,* a "big fantasy novel which aims for the huge popular audience reserved for such classics as T. H. White's *The Once and Future King.*" . . . It gives us intrigue among the elves, Celts, Goths, and ur-Vikings of the Elder Isles. Princess Suldrun is born to the king and queen of Lyonesse, grows up estranged, and is banished to an abandoned garden near the palace. A minor prince of another isle, Aillas, journeys with his cousin Trewan to learn the arts of diplomacy. Word comes to Trewan of a death that makes Aillas a rival for kingship. Trewan throws Aillas overboard, to wash up on Suldrun's shore. The two love and are caught. Aillas is jailed. Suldrun bears his child, ships the babe off to a caretaker from whom the elves steal him, and hangs herself. Aillas escapes. His son matures and leaves the elves. The two seek and find each other. Aillas reaches home in time to forestall his cousin's crowning. There is war, and truce, and the promise of a sequel.

And all bears the Vance stamp. Names ring strangely and evocatively. Scenery crawls upon the page. Motives are complex and subtle. Events concatenate. If you love Vance, you'll love ***Lyonesse.*** If you don't, you'll hate it. If you care more for his SF than for his fantasy, you may prefer to give this a miss. (pp. 109-10)

Tom Easton, in a review of "Lyonesse," in Analog Science Fiction/Science Fact, *Vol. CIII, No. 10, September 13, 1983, pp. 109-10.*

DARRELL SCHWEITZER

[***Cugel's Saga***] is actually fantasy or at least right on the borderline of fantasy and science fiction. As Silverberg points out in his introduction to ***The Eyes of the Overworld*** [see excerpt above] . . . , Vance is only pretending to write about the far future, for all his ***Dying Earth*** books are set millions of years hence. The theory goes that the science fictional gloss in the original, ***The Dying Earth,*** was necessary in order to get it published, because there was no in-genre fantasy in 1950, and most of the fantasy published in the mainstream in those days was post-Thorne Smithian whimsey. . . . Well, maybe so, but it is clear enough to me that the ***Dying Earth*** series *is* about the remote future as much as *The Night Land* or the ***Zothique*** series were—they treat the future mythologically, rather than scientifically. You couldn't just transplant Vance's plots into the usual never-never land. They need to take place in the half frantic, half exhausted decadence of the Earth's last days when the sun is bloody red and may go out at any minute. . . .

Cugel's Saga is a direct sequel to ***The Eyes of the Overworld.*** Iucounu the Laughing Magician has played another delectable jest upon Cugel, transporting him to a remote country. The book consists of Cugel's adventures on the way back and his final encounter with the magician. The adventures are independent enough that this is just barely a novel (indeed, two episodes, **"The Seventeen Virgins"** and **"The Bagful of Dreams"** have been published elsewhere as short stories), but it hardly matters, because Vance's sardonic wit and enormous inventiveness are going full force. The story is filled with memorable scenes, deliciously ridiculous (but often sinister) situations and striking images. I am particularly impressed by Vance's ability to sketch in a whole society in a few lines, then make it real, where any other writer would have only been able to produce a one-dimensional gimmick. Thus Cugel moves across a *world* rather than a featureless and cultureless landscape. Would-be fantasy writes, take notes. Everybody else, just enjoy.

Darrell Schweitzer, in a review of "Cugel's Saga," in Science Fiction Review, *Vol. 13, No. 1, February, 1984, p. 45.*

Jill Paton Walsh

1939-

English novelist, author of books for children, and editor.

Walsh explores such basic human concerns as love, death, and maturation in novels that appeal to readers of all ages. She explains that "[my] governing principle is to make whatever I am doing as simple and accessible as possible. . . . But also my preferred subjects have lain in that large area of human experience that adults and children have in common." Critics praise Walsh's skill in employing a variety of literary techniques, among them her incorporation of multiple subjective viewpoints and her use of interior monologue. In addition, they note the infusion of references to literature and art in her works. As Sheila A. Egoff observes, "[Walsh's] writing is studded with allusions to poetry, art and philosophy that give it an intellectual framework unmatched in children's literature."

In several of her works Walsh recreates turbulent historical settings which act as catalysts for the emotional growth of her characters. Through extensive research she presents authentic details and evokes a true sense of time and place. Critics particularly admire her heroic yet unidealized characters. Walsh based her first novel, *Hengest's Tale* (1966), on a character from Old English myth. This suspenseful story concerns the maturation of Hengest, a fifth-century Jute torn between honor in battle and loyalty to a childhood friend. In *Fireweed* (1969) Walsh portrays the struggle of two teenagers who endure the Nazi bombing of London during World War II. The characters grow to care deeply for one another as they fight together against grave circumstances. Critics admired the novel's lack of sentimentality and Walsh's realistic depiction of the chaos and destruction of London during this period.

Walsh's novel *Goldengrove* (1972) and its sequel, *Unleaving* (1976), are set in an isolated seaside landscape. In both novels Walsh investigates the often painful experience of maturing from adolescence to adulthood. The tone of each work is bittersweet; the characters experience disillusionment as they lose the innocence of childhood, but they ultimately gain a greater appreciation for life. Critics praised Walsh's ability to evoke the beauty of the seaside setting, and several mentioned the influence of Virginia Woolf on Walsh's style and themes.

Walsh returned to historical settings with *A Chance Child* (1978) and *A Parcel of Patterns* (1983). In the former she depicts the exploitation of child labor in Victorian England; in the latter she dramatizes the isolation of a village that has contracted the plague. Walsh achieves a sense of authenticity in these works through her use of carefully researched facts and colloquial language.

(See also *Children's Literature Review*, Vol. 2; *Contemporary Authors*, Vols. 37-40, rev. ed.; and *Something about the Author*, Vol. 4.)

Photograph by J. R. Townsend; reproduced by permission of Jill Paton Walsh

ARTHUR T. LEONE

Blood, blades and betrayals are the hallmarks of this story of Hengest the Jute, invader and settler of fifth century Kent. In [**"Hengest's Tale"**], drawn from the mists of English myth and legendary history, Hengest emerges as no simple hero of old, but a complex man capable at once of deep loyalty and broken oaths, of bloody outrages and bitter remorse. The dying Hengest recounts his life story from his first journey to his last oath-filled breath. . . . Gillian Walsh has produced a highly serviceable tale, spare and direct in the telling, with touches of Old English language ("hall Gold-gleamer," "word-hoard") that lend a ring of authenticity. The descriptions of cut throats, hangings and split skulls are hardly for the weak-stomached, but here . . . is brief, if gory, adventure.

Arthur T. Leone, in a review of "Hengest's Tale," in The New York Times Book Review, *April 9, 1967, p. 26.*

PAUL HEINS

Based on the legend that during the fifth century two Jutish warriors, Hengest and Horsa, came to Britain to aid King Vortigern—whom they later conquered—and settled with their followers in Kent, [***Hengest's Tale***] expertly evokes the background of the tragic narrative that could have led to Hengest's exile. Skillfully interspersed among the events as recalled by the dying Hengest are details often found in Anglo-Saxon poetry; and much of the fragmentary *Fight at Finnsburg* is incorporated into the story. The Jutes, dominated by the ferocious Danes, attempt to better their situation by an alliance with the King of Frisia, a part of modern Holland. Scarcely more than a boy, Hengest learns to love and admire Finn, the king's son, who becomes the husband of a Jutish princess. . . . Torn between his abiding admiration for the Frisian prince and loyalty to his own king, Hengest unwillingly murders Finn at the instigation of the Danes. The balance between stirring events and strong characterization—combined with the authentic details—makes a memorable historical narrative.

Paul Heins, in a review of "Hengest's Tale," in The Horn Book Magazine, *Vol. XLIII, No. 4, August, 1967, p. 478.*

PETER VANSITTART

In Jill Paton Walsh's ***Fireweed***. . . , two likeable teenagers hitch up together during the London blitz, shaking off adults and officialdom. A clear-cut, unromantic story with an authentic feel of the time: the bloodshot nights, time-bomb threatening St. Paul's, underground shelters, the commonplace turning terrible. 'The air hardened into a wall, struck us, and lifted us, threw us against the fencing on the girders and held us there.' Happy endings seldom occur but wry humour remains. 'She paid into the insurance for years to be buried proper, and it took them three days to dig her out.' A detached, keen-eyed style produces moving effects of a London now almost as remote as the earlier Fire, dangerously exotic. (p. 598)

Peter Vansittart, "Swash & Buckle," in The Spectator, *Vol. 223, No. 7375, November 1, 1969, pp. 598, 600.**

JOHN ROWE TOWNSEND

A boy and girl on the run. A boy and girl setting up house at fifteen, looking after a child, taking on adult responsibilities. A boy and girl coming to love each other, not merely to feel the adolescent sexual stirrings that have been so endlessly written about. A boy and girl surviving dangerously in the London blitz. Four strong themes; and Jill Paton Walsh has moulded them all into one in ***Fireweed*** . . . to produce a remarkably fine novel for young people.

It's a story told in the first-person-masculine, which is a difficult undertaking for a woman writer but is brought off with complete conviction. Bill, the narrator, has been evacuated to rural Wales, feels bored and isolated, and makes his way back to London, determined to manage on his own until his father comes back from the Army. Julie was on her way to Canada when her ship was torpedoed, and now she too is on her own in London, out of touch with her well-to-do parents and feeling that they don't really want her. And after a few nights in tube stations they find a hideout in the cellar of a bombed building, make a home there, earn a bit of money in the markets, finally take in a child whose parents are missing. There's an innocent, symbolic consummation of their relationship when the girl, cold at night, creeps into the boy's arms; in the morning they are happy and "it seemed to me we hadn't come apart properly when we rose from sleep, but in some way we moved together still."

It can't last, of course. The blitz, a threatening background to their relationship, now erupts into the foreground. Julie is trapped in the wrecked cellar, injured, rescued, and returned to her parents. After one brief hospital visit, Bill won't see her again. The story has its improbabilities, not least at this point, since one feels that these devoted youngsters wouldn't be parted so easily. . . . But this is a book to be read, remembered, and reread: a book worth buying.

John Rowe Townsend, "Growing Up," in Punch, *Vol. 257, No. 6745, December 17, 1969, p. 1016.**

ELLEN LEWIS BUELL

What was it like to live through the London blitz of 1940? What was it like to be fifteen, adrift with no family to tell you what to do or how to survive? Looking back [in ***Fireweed***], a youth called Bill tells how it was for him and the schoolgirl Julie whom he meets "in the Aldwych underground station." . . .

Both youngsters have been evacuated, have run back to London and are bound not to be sent off again. . . .

The two form a partnership, earning money in the street markets, sleeping in the reeking subways, dodging the authorities, eventually holing up in the basement of a bombed house. Their ingenuity is fascinating, their hardihood awesome. Not quite ready for love but bound by need and loyalty, they are like children playing a deadly serious game of independence among the ruins.

Inevitably their adventure ends, with a poignancy that will disappoint the sentimental, but which the sensitive reader will recognize as exactly right. Meantime we have known the fear, the cold, the fatigue, the good will and even the exhilaration that Londoners knew in those terrible weeks when "familiar things seemed as exotic and unlikely as hothouse flowers."

A haunting, truly impressive novel.

Ellen Lewis Buell, in a review of "Fireweed," in Book World—Chicago Tribune, *Part II, May 17, 1970, p. 3.*

BARBARA WERSBA

Someone once said that nobody writes well about childhood because nobody knows what it is. . . . The few people who know what childhood is all about cannot tell us because *they* are the children. The rest of us have simply forgotten; the entire experience has been too strange, or mystical, or harsh to dredge up again.

Jill Paton Walsh, however, has not forgotten—and I am rather in awe of her. She writes as though she were still 12 years old, choking back angry tears and incapable of dissembling. . . .

[In **"Goldengrove"**] Madge and Paul are English children, cousins who spend summer holidays together at their grandmother's seaside home. Intensely close to one another, they meet as the story opens only to find that this particular summer is different. . . . Paul is still very much a little boy, hard-minded and unsentimental; while Madge, unwittingly, is entering that tremulous space between childhood and adolescence. Nature hurts her. Self-consciousness is dawning. She wants to be loved.

The children's vacation begins casually, with old haunts explored and familiar pastimes resumed. But then a stranger comes into the scene and everything is spoiled. He is a blind man, a professor who is renting a nearby cottage, and at first his presence is like a shadow fallen across bright sand. Madge begins to visit him, and read to him, and—with slow and terrible fascination—we watch her fall in love. One says "terrible" because this older man is by no means the stock character we have come to expect in teen-age books. Instead, he is a bitter, self-involved intellectual whose wife has left him. . . .

[Madge learns], at the end of the book, that she and Paul are brother and sister instead of cousins; a family quarrel having fostered a terrible lie upon them. And what the reader learns is that for certain children a time comes when it is too late to put salve on wounds. Madge has changed and been damaged, and the damage is called Growing Up.

But this is only the plot—and it is neither plot nor character that makes **"Goldengrove"** such a brilliant novel. Mrs. Walsh has chosen a technique whereby her material is presented on several levels, and not only is this ingenious, but it serves her talents to perfection. Set in the present tense, the story weaves in and out of the thoughts of its characters, all the while holding a steady narrative line and creating vivid atmosphere.

There is a distant, and lovely echo of Virginia Woolf's "The Waves" in much of this, as when Madge walks into the grove of trees which gives her grandmother's house its name, and thinks: "It is just beginning to turn gold, and I have never seen it gold before, only green, always green, hundreds of variously lit little floating boats of green and lizard-spotted light. Below these trees, especially here around the huge chestnut tree—I was here once when it was in bloom, like great candles—the wild strawberries grow."

Words such as these come from a richly literary mind. Thus I find it significant that **"Goldengrove"** will be marketed for children between the ages of 11 and 14, and never reach their parents. The current division of fiction into Lots of Sex for the grownups and Less Sex for the kids is not only silly but wasted, for the grownups are missing some beautiful and highly original work. Perhaps one day we will all awaken to the fact that there are no such things as "juveniles," but simply books in which words are kept alive by writers; objects through which the spirit of man becomes known.

Barbara Wersba, "The Damage Called Growing Up," in The New York Times Book Review, *November 5, 1972, p. 6.*

NAOMI LEWIS

The shifting (or vanishing) line between adult and younger fiction isn't only a matter of subject. The manner of writing is no less to the point. The leap in thought, the stream-of-dream—haven't nursery rhymes and fairy-tales, even, their share of these? But successful experiment in 'older' fiction is still quite rare, especially in the non-fantasy sort. At the same time, if I use the word 'technique' to suggest why Jill Paton Walsh's ***Goldengrove*** stands out from the season's novels, I mean it to take in both the tale and the telling.

Goldengrove itself is a house, and something more. It's the grandmother's home on the Cornish coast where two cousins Paul and Madge meet every year: once again the food with its strawberries, the small quiet beach that runs from the garden, and the longed-for company of each other—against, one senses, parental obstacles. There's a stranger this time, though: Gran has let the small cottage to Ralph, who is blind (from the war), and alone (his wife has left him). But he is also a scholar and don, and Madge, who is easily moved, comes to read to him—Empson (which she finds 'horrible') and Austen and Lewis Carroll, and once, on a dreadful occasion, Milton—while she might be painting the boat with Paul. Paul feels a pang when he sees them together; Madge feels a pang when she finds that he has gone to the lighthouse without her. . . . It's a memorable and distinctive book, beautifully written. If something is owed to Virginia Woolf, the deliberate lighthouse here could well be taken as a sign of the book's assurance. (pp. 644-45)

Naomi Lewis, "Back to the Lighthouse," in The Listener, *Vol. 88, No. 2276, November 9, 1972, pp. 644-45.**

CHRISTOPHER LEHMANN-HAUPT

[**"Goldengrove"** is familiar] yarn for the knitting of teen-age fiction—a brother and sister from a broken home, a summer vacation at grandmother's seaside home; a blind professor with lessons to teach about insight; the passing of childhood. But with only an occasional dropped stitch, Miss Walsh turns these threads into a richly-patterned little novel full of intricate symbolism and the subtle hues of adolescent pain. And some of her evocations of the English seaside around Cornwall are masterly.

Christopher Lehmann-Haupt, in a review of "Goldengrove," in The New York Times, *December 13, 1972, p. 67.*

ELIZABETH S. COOLIDGE

The story of a boy who plays God with the life of his mongoloid sister sounds unrelievedly grim, but ***Unleaving*** by Jill Paton Walsh is a charming, sunny book, rich with warmth and insights for adolescent readers. . . .

[Walsh] sets her novel on the Cornish coast in a lovely old house belonging to the Fielding family. This house, called "Goldengrove" was the scene of a previous novel of the same name. In the new book, Madge Fielding has inherited the house from her grandmother, who obviously felt that she would appreciate it. The house has been rented to a "reading group" for the summer, with the idea that Madge will develop intellectually, listening to two professors discuss philosophy and ethics with a group of students.

One of the professors has a teenage son, Patrick, who is deeply troubled about his parents' attitude towards his little mongoloid sister Molly. Madge is drawn strongly to this boy, and he responds to her happy, sympathetic, instinctive yet questioning spirit. In the background is the constant motion and menace of the sea, and the constant flow and intellectualizing of the reading group. In the foreground, Madge and Patrick work out their feelings about each other, and about living and dying. . . .

The book closes with a flash forward. Now it is Madge's own grandchildren, hers and Patrick's, who scamper about her feet at Goldengrove.

Unleaving loses everything in a synopsis, for its significance lies in what the characters think and feel, not in what they do. It is a beautifully crafted novel. Molly's death grows inevitable as clues are dropped along the way. Madge dreams about falling. An old tale of children falling down mine shafts is remembered. The oppressive summer heat builds suspense, and the reader is constantly reminded of the treacherous cliffs and dangerous sea.

It is a story of death, but death as part of life, symbolized by the funeral of Gran at the start, and at the end, when Madge confronts her grandmother's dead body and her own mortality, we see where the girl's resilience and her sure instincts are rooted. I would like to be such a grandmother as Gran. . . .

[Jill Paton Walsh] has an astonishing ability to create appealing personalities. She has written a book about death, and what this means to a philosopher, a teenager, a grandmother and a very small child. Yet ***Unleaving*** is in no way a gloomy book, but one that leaves the reader with a warm and optimistic view of humankind.

Elizabeth S. Coolidge, "Two Modern English Morality Tales," in Book World—The Washington Post, *May 2, 1976, p. L13.**

VIRGINIA HAVILAND

A sequel to ***Goldengrove, [Unleaving]*** shows a deeper portrayal of human relationships and raises profound questions about life, death, and love. Young Madge has rented her inherited house in Cornwall to an Oxford professor who is leading a group of students in a "reading party." . . . The summer colloquy is pictured from Madge's point of view in flashbacks skillfully, if somewhat obscurely, inserted as retrospective views from the future when Madge is a grandmother. . . . The author has dealt with the whole book brilliantly, deftly raising issues without overburdening her story. At a point where the philosophizing must seem too much for a young reader, she introduces the climactic incident which involves the death of a valiant seaman trying to recover the body of Patrick's sister. Set against a background of Cornish custom and tragedy at sea, the story is filled with introspection and description, which are balanced by fine characterization and a picture of normal, everyday living.

Virginia Haviland, in a review of "Unleaving," in The Horn Book Magazine, *Vol. LII, No. 4, August, 1976, p. 408.*

ALICE BACH

In an earlier novel Jill Paton Walsh began the story of Madge Fielding who spent her summers with her cousin Paul at her grandmother's house in Cornwall. The house and the novel are named **"Goldengrove."** . . . .

Mrs. Walsh writes calmly; her prose is spare. And powerful. She evokes the constant presence of the sea, the private heat in each person's life, and the confusion each encounters. She never sinks into the convulsions so embarrassing in many current novels. The author allows her characters to learn, to age with dignity. . . .

[In **"Unleaving"**] Gran has died and left Goldengrove to Madge. Again it's summer. Madge is sharing her house with a group of students and two Oxford professors. They are immersed in a philosophic colloquy, abstract weighing of moral choices. Against the tumult of the sea the reader hears the murmur of their voices. Against their rationalism is the juice and terrible reality of life at the edge of the sea. The duality is mirrored by Patrick, the son of one of the professors. . . . Patrick teams up with Madge and Paul. Deep into the dailiness of the summer, they provide the novel's counterpoint—the energy, the scramble of the younger people against the sedentary order of the students.

"Unleaving" is a tempting word and serves as an excellent key to Mrs. Walsh's book. For it evokes the image of the barren tree, the often frightening truths implicit in learning and also the comfort of permanence—if unleaving, then staying. In a flash of writer's craft the author creates lives that tumble in and out of each other and eventually form a continuum.

Walsh doesn't tidy up the blight for which man was born. She's too wise to attempt answers about growing, living, dying, ethical choices. She exalts the mystery, the unknowing itself.

This is a beautiful novel, and an enduring one.

Alice Bach, in a review of "Unleaving," in The New York Times Book Review, *August 8, 1976, p. 18.*

NAOMI LEWIS

[***A Chance Child***] is about child labour in the Victorian mines and mills, factories and foundries. But it is also a timeshift tale, strange and chilling. 'Creep,' a Victorian waif, hidden and starved by his mother, kept alive by his young half-brother, slips into our century into much the same situation. Returning to the past he joins, as a kind of ghost-protector, a little group of derelict children seeking work. But the real Creep lived on; and his story is finally tracked in local archives by his (modern) schoolboy brother. If the children aren't always convincing, you can't say this of the scenes, the landscape, the history itself. An eerie, memorable novel.

Naomi Lewis, "Castles Dangerous," in The Observer, *December 10, 1978, p. 38.**

PUBLISHERS WEEKLY

[Jill Paton Walsh's] singular gifts have won her honors at home and abroad for **"Goldengrove," "Unleaving"** and other books of surpassing loveliness. But never has she written with such impact as she does in this fact-fantasy [**"A Chance Child"**], dedicated to real victims of the infant Industrial Revolution. Creep, a child of today, escapes from the closet where his despicable mother has imprisoned him. No one except his half-brother, Christopher, searches for the missing boy. Creep drifts back to the 1800s and joins the band of small boys and girls who are starved, beaten and forced to work all day at dangerous jobs. . . . Not even Dickens portrayed abused children (of yesterday and today) as Walsh does here. She dedicates her book to actual persons whose testimony she uncovered during her research. It's a list of names almost too poignant to read.

A review of "A Chance Child," in Publishers Weekly, *Vol. 214, No. 24, December 11, 1978, p. 69.*

LAURA GERINGER

The wanderings of the runaway trio [in ***A Chance Child***] provide Walsh with a fictional peg upon which to hang well-researched and blood chilling accounts of the blighting labor conditions youngsters withstood in the "bad old days." Detailed descriptions of the workings of giant machines, the dreary and crippling tasks required to keep them going, and the transformation of green lands into grim pits and slashes in the earth are raw, precise, and memorable. Clipped dialogue including dialect and period idioms is pungent and, despite some unusual vocabulary, will not be a problem to good readers. Although the markings of historical tract show through the sometimes thin veneer of novel, the dramatic tension is sustained throughout by the artful handling of the time travel theme and the deft juxtaposition in alternate chapters of a parallel plot: Creep's half brother searches for the missing boy, tracking him, finally, to a capsule farewell in an obscure volume of Parliamentary Papers. Cleverly wrought and highly charged.

Laura Geringer, in a review of "A Chance Child," in School Library Journal, *Vol. 25, No. 5, January, 1979, p. 63.*

JANE LANGTON

[**"A Chance Child"**] is a brilliant novel about child labor in England in the 19th century, when small children did dangerous work in mills and factories, when with their elders they labored from dark to dark. . . . (p. 24)

The thread that runs through the book is the polluted water of an industrial canal, navigated by a boy who has gone back from the present into the past. Young Creep is himself a sad case. Repudiated by his mother, reared in a closet under the stairs, he escapes to a dump at the edge of the trash-filled canal and sets forth in a rotting canal boat. Eerily, the boat seems to move by itself, carrying him back to a time when other children were as wretched as he. It comes to rest at a coalmine, an ironworks, a pottery, a spinning mill. Everywhere there are laboring children, pounding iron rods into chain, racing into kilns to fetch and carry, darting among the spinning machines to sweep up the flying waste.

Tenderly and carefully, Jill Paton Walsh adds horror to horror, painting a foul darkness against which the stunted limbs of the children gleam with a lurid pallor. Scraps of an 1842 report on working conditions are part of the story, and our flesh crawls as we discover that the children are real:

"Sarah Gooder, age eight, a trapper in the Gawber pit . . . Tom Moorhouse, began to hurry coals for William Greenwood . . . 'He struck a pick into my bottom. . . .'"

But this is a swift and lively tale as well as a pathetic history. The central characters are cheerful and plucky. Especially beguiling is young Blackie, with her piping voice and ruined face, burned when she fell asleep at a nailer's forge. Tidying up the rusted ruin of the boat, she displays a rudimentary brave nesting instinct worth a thousand pounds of silver-sworded courage in more commonplace fantasies.

Most stunning of all are the pictures of mine and foundry, forge and mill. The author's splendid descriptive power seems to blow the hot sparks of the forge in our faces and the choking lint of the mill into our lungs. Our ears ring with the fall of the massive hammer in the ironworks; they catch the huge sighing that sweeps the valley from the great bellows fanning the smelter fire; and at last they hear even the inaudible cries of the beaten children in the mill. . . . (pp. 24-5)

Jane Langton, in a review of "A Chance Child," in The New York Times Book Review, *June 17, 1979, pp. 24-5.*

SHEILA A. EGOFF

[The] mood and tone of Walsh's ***Fireweed*** are all doubt and darkness. Bill is a runaway evacuee who, in a London air-raid shelter, meets Julie, also a runaway, but from a ship taking children to Canada. Both have a fierce determination to fend for themselves and to survive the war free from adult interference and authority. In the chaos of a crumbling, burnt-out city they live a dangerous but somehow carefree life. Every day they walk a tightrope of disaster. They may be discovered by the authorities, they may die in a bombing, yet they are protected by the seeming immortality of youth and the strength of their newly discovered freedom and responsibility. . . . From their position of tenuous stability Bill and Julie witness the destruction and paradoxical abiding survival of their world. It is a world where "familiar things seemed as exotic and unlikely as hothouse flowers." London is being knocked apart, but the leaves turn gold and fall off while German bombers rend the sky. It is this eye for the familiar and terrible in one, the vivid beauty of threatened life that gives ***Fireweed*** its moving quality. Realistic details, such as finding milk for an abandoned baby in war-torn London or fixing a cart in order to sell vegetables, provide the feeling of actual experience and involvement.

Autumn is the time that Bill and Julie spend together, the season that symbolically moves towards inevitable and irretrievable loss. At the end Bill's and Julie's fragile happiness falls apart. Only Bill's positive memories can come to his aid. He sees the fireweed flourishing in the pavements around St. Paul's and comments, "It is a strange plant; it has its own rugged sort of loveliness, and it grows only on the scars of ruin and flame." (pp. 38-9)

The titles of Walsh's ***Goldengrove*** and ***Unleaving*** are taken from Gerard Manley Hopkins's elegiac poem "Spring and Fall" and have, like all serious modern realism for children, its bittersweet tone. . . . (p. 46)

Through both books we follow the events that have turned Madge Fielding . . . from a young teenager on holiday, visiting her grandmother in ***Goldengrove*** to an alternating picture of her as a young and as an old woman in ***Unleaving.*** Both books are infused with a sense of absolutes about living that demand to be discovered. Life is a metamorphosis, allegiances change, emotions are fractured. One can witness a mercy killing, see a man die trying to rescue a retarded child, experience rejection, and yet know that one can grow through it all. A recurring symbol is a lighthouse, Virginia Woolf's lighthouse, in fact, a symbol opposed to the embittered blindness of the man who rejects Madge's youthful attentions and to the darkness of mind of the retarded child who paradoxically brings light to everyone around her, with the exception of her intellectual father.

In ***Unleaving*** Madge, who has inherited Goldengrove from her grandmother, is persuaded to billet a group of philosophy students and professors for the summer. Among the party are Professor Tregeagle, his wife, and two children—Patrick, a boy Madge's age, and a young retarded girl. The atmosphere is purely intellectual. The continuing discussion concerns life, death, and ethical choice. Patrick, very sensitive and introspective, rebels against this, for he feels that people and emotions are what count, and that these intellectuals know nothing about people. . . . Professor Tregeagle, to whom the intellect is all, finds his mongoloid daughter, Molly, somewhat repugnant. Patrick, who cares deeply for his sister, bitterly resents his father's attitude. . . . When Patrick pushes Molly over the cliff in a mercy killing, his action causes the death of one of the rescuing fishermen, a friend of Madge's and Patrick's. Patrick has to live with the guilt and Madge, who sees all, has to live with her silence.

Unlike the books of the past that frequently dealt with groups of children externalizing their problems, as the Nesbit children digging for treasure to "restore the fallen fortunes of the House of Bastable,'' Walsh's books and most of modern realistic fiction convey a sense of loneliness. The reader is locked inside Madge's mind, chiefly seeing the events from her highly sensitive point of view. . . . Walsh achieves this through style, an intermeshing web of dialogue and interior monologue. Yet, as in most of the books which depend for their drama on personal relationships, the young people appear to be headed for adulthood with a consciousness raised but not embittered. Indeed when Walsh precedes ***Unleaving*** with a quote from Wittgenstein, ''Not how the world is, is the mystical, but that it is,'' an adult, at least, is immediately aware of entering a story of the celebration of life. At the end of ***Unleaving*** we see Madge as a grandmother close to death. When asked by a grandchild what the point of living is when we are all going to die anyway, she replies with words from Yeats's ''Sailing to Byzantium.'' They express the unity of the two books—their concepts of loneliness, compassion, and ultimate optimism:

> Well, we all die, but first we all live, . . . Don't worry about what's the point. Just take your share. Take it two-handed and in full measure. You have to clap your hands and sing.

Madge has learned from everything that has happened to her—sight from the blind man, humanity from the fisherman, love for a brother whom she first believed to be a cousin, the balance between intellect and emotion. . . . (pp. 46-8)

Of [the many] skilled and sensitive writers [for young people], Walsh is the most formally literary. Her writing is studded with allusions to poetry, art and philosophy that give it an intellectual framework unmatched in children's literature. (p. 48)

Sheila A. Egoff, ''Realistic Fiction,'' in her Thursday's Child: Trends and Patterns in Contemporary Children's Literature, *American Library Association, 1981, pp. 31-65.**

NAOMI LEWIS

[***A Parcel of Patterns***]—an outstanding piece of writing—is by Jill Paton Walsh, always at her best on reliving history, whether Anglo-Saxon, Byzantine or (as here) the English 17th century. The subject is that abiding story of how the Plague came to Eyam in Derbyshire, and how it was locally held by the villagers' self-imposed isolation. So circumstantial is this telling that you forget the novelist and hear only the voice of the Eyam girl Mall, quiet, factual, desperate, who witnesses and records.

Naomi Lewis, ''Teenage Life,'' in The Listener, *Vol. 110, No. 2833, December 3, 1983, p. 28.**

CHRISTOPHER WORDSWORTH

Human charity vies with Puritan prejudice in ***A Parcel of Patterns***. . . . This moving account, based on parish records, tells how when the plague came to seventeenth century Eyam in Derbyshire the vicar prevailed on the doomed, divided villagers to quarantine themselves for the common good: Jill Paton Walsh is a fine storyteller who knows that the tragic essence of love and death can't be diluted to appease any notions of suitability.

Christopher Wordsworth, ''Fires in the Heather,'' in The Observer, *December 4, 1983, p. 32.**

NEIL PHILIP

A Parcel of Patterns is an extraordinary and compelling tour de force. It tells the sombre story—familiar from William and Mary Howitt's poem ''The Desolation of Eyam''—of the Derbyshire plague village of Eyam. In 1665 a parcel of dressmaking patterns brought the plague to Eyam from London. In the year that followed, 267 of the 350 inhabitants died. The surrounding villages remained plague free: for at the urging of their minister William Mompesson and his deposed predecessor Thomas Stanley, the people of Eyam sealed their parish boundaries, paying for supplies left at the boundary stones with money steeped in vinegar.

This is a most dreadful, moving story, and it is related by Jill Paton Walsh with a quiet, unerring restraint which will disturb and possess the reader long after the frenzy aroused by a sensational approach would have died away. She represents the story as written down by Mall Percival as a charm to appease and settle her dead, to allow her to leave Eyam and start a new life. Mall's story—Jill Paton Walsh's only important invention—involves the reader intimately in the consequences of the village's ill luck. Mall's true love, Thomas, comes from a neighbouring village. She refuses to see him, for fear ''the sickness would pass from my clothes to his, my hand to his, my very breath to his''; when he continues to seek her, she sends false word of her death. Then, with the bitter irony which operates throughout this book, Thomas, thinking he has nothing to live for, comes to Eyam to share its fate. Mall survives, but he does not.

This poignant love story is but one strand of a complex yet fluid and unforbidding narrative. Mall's is a shrewd and compassionate account of the tensions in a small community under threat, vivid in its depiction of individuals yet never losing sight of the village as a whole. It is seamed with a genuine religious and moral argument about man's proper reaction to misfortune.

Perhaps the most impressive thing about the way Jill Paton Walsh has approached and presented this difficult story is her refusal to idealize the villagers. They are as prone to gossip, malice, selfishness as any group. What holds them together as a community, and underpins their heroic self-isolation, is the combination under pressure of the two previously opposed forces of Mompesson and Stanley. When one poor woman does break her oath and leave the village she is stoned back across the parish boundary. Mall writes, ''We had thought ourselves, till then, as close to saints, who willingly remained in Eyam for others' sake; now we knew ourselves as prisoners, caged in whether we would or no.''

This is a fair sample of the novel's most remarkable achievement: Mall's prose. The formal but simple vocabulary, the plangent rhythms, the slightly stilted syntax are marvellous not as an imitation of how a real Mall *would* have written, but as a language and a style in which what the fictional Mall has to say *can* be written. There is something brave and sad and haunting about prose which would evaporate in a looser, less contrived English. It is artificial in the best sense.

Neil Philip, ''A Terrible Beauty,'' in The Times Educational Supplement, *No. 3524, January 13, 1984, p. 42.**

Thornton (Niven) Wilder

1897-1975

American dramatist, novelist, essayist, and scriptwriter.

Photograph by Paul Conklin

The only author to receive Pulitzer Prizes for both drama and fiction, Wilder is best known for his award-winning works: the novel *The Bridge of San Luis Rey* (1927) and two plays, *Our Town* (1938) and *The Skin of Our Teeth* (1942). Critical reception of Wilder's optimistic and life-affirming works has varied, but *Our Town* endures as a widely performed American classic. The values Wilder promoted in his work—Christian morality, community, the family, appreciation of life's simple pleasures—were traditional, but his methods, especially in his plays, were unorthodox. In *Our Town* and other plays he rejected naturalism in favor of a form of presentation which frankly acknowledged the artifice of the theater. In doing so, critics believe, Wilder was an innovator in American drama.

The publication of Wilder's first novel and the first professional production of one of his plays both occurred in 1926. *The Trumpet Shall Sound* (1926) is a play concerning a man whose servants deceive him. An allegory about God's mercy towards humanity, the play received little notice and is significantly less accomplished than his later works. *The Angel That Troubled the Waters and Other Plays* (1928) is a collection of extremely short plays, many written during the years 1918-1920 when Wilder was a student at Yale University. These plays, which critics tend to regard as affected, have never been produced and are considered virtually impossible to stage. However, Wilder's blatant disregard for the limitations of the stage was refined in his later plays and became one of his major contributions to the theater.

In the early part of his career, Wilder had greater success with his novels than with his plays. *The Cabala* (1926) tells the story of a young American's first visit to Rome. Wilder began writing this book on his own first trip there, but the work is imaginative rather than autobiographical. *The Bridge of San Luis Rey* was a huge critical and popular success and is regarded as a major novel of the twentieth century. In this work, set in eighteenth-century Peru, a priest questions God's intent in allowing five people to die when a bridge collapses. Investigating the lives of some of the victims, the priest finds that they suffered from unrequited love and that they allowed their obsessions to prevent them from examining and appreciating their lives. *The Bridge of San Luis Rey* was admired for its clear prose style, and its religious philosophy appealed to American moralists. Wilder's next novel, *The Woman of Andros* (1930), was also well-received initially but resulted in an attack on Wilder by the proletarian critic Michael Gold. The novel is, in part, an adaptation of an ancient Roman comedy and is a story of young love set in that time period. In an essay entitled "Wilder: Prophet of the Genteel Christ," Gold angrily contended that it was morally wrong to publish escapist, purely aesthetic literature during the Great Depression, when social reform was needed. Wilder followed with *Heaven's My Destination* (1934), a novel set in Depression-era America; however, the tone of this work is lighthearted. He then concentrated on writing plays.

The plays collected in *The Long Christmas Dinner and Other Plays* (1931) reflect Wilder's extensive travels in Europe, where he saw experimental, nonrealistic theater. Two of his plays, *Pullman Car Hiawatha* and *The Happy Journey to Trenton and Camden*, integrate some of the staging techniques and thematic concerns for which Wilder would become famous when *Our Town* was produced. Both plays have a stage manager who speaks to the audience about the play and sometimes enters the drama as a minor character, and both are bereft of scenery, using chairs as their only props. *Pullman Car Hiawatha*, like *Our Town*, includes stylized characters representing an individual's place in the cosmos rather than portraying an individual. The title play of this collection prefigures *Our Town*'s perception of life as a brief yet important interlude before death and illustrates this with unusual staging techniques. The action of the play spans ninety years but takes place at a single Christmas feast. Characters enter and exit through two doors representing birth and death. Their time onstage represents their entire lives.

Wilder gave the central role of *Our Town* to an omniscient Stage Manager, who narrates the play, jokes with the audience, and, through his philosophizing, explicitly connects the people of the small New Hampshire town of Grover's Corners with the universe as a whole. This connection is one of Wilder's major themes in *Our Town*. The play's three acts are entitled "Daily Life," "Love and Marriage," and "Death." Wilder wrote in a preface to the 1957 published version of the play,

"It is an attempt to find a value above all price for the smallest events of daily life." The nonrealistic elements Wilder uses in this play include the Stage Manager, a complete lack of scenery, and his dramatization in Act Three of life after death. Emily Webb returns to earth after her death to relive her twelfth birthday. She discovers for herself the message of the play—human beings do not "realize life while they live it." Critics of *Our Town* have praised Wilder for creating a moving story with universal meaning, although it is set in a specific, turn-of-the-century small town. While some consider it sentimental, most agree that Wilder's play does not attempt to duplicate reality and should not be judged as though it does. With *Our Town,* Wilder was established as a major American dramatist.

Wilder's reputation as a playwright also rests on two comedies, *The Skin of Our Teeth* and *The Matchmaker* (1957), which is a slightly revised version of his play *The Merchant of Yonkers: A Farce in Four Acts* (1938). *The Matchmaker,* Wilder's most conventionally staged play, is based on a nineteenth-century English comedy which in turn was adapted from a Viennese farce. It is a work of light entertainment and shares with Wilder's other writings a celebratory attitude towards life and adventure. *The Matchmaker* is the basis for the popular musical *Hello, Dolly!* In *The Skin of Our Teeth,* a more ambitious work, Wilder manipulates time so that events from different time periods seem to occur simultaneously. For instance, in Act I, a 1940s family from Excelsior, New Jersey, faces the perils of the ice age; in Act II, an Atlantic City beauty pageant takes place amidst preparations for the Great Flood. The comedy in *The Skin of Our Teeth* arises from this juxtaposition of events as well as from surprising staging techniques that emphasize theatricality. Characters step in and out of their roles to share their "true feelings" with the audience, and the stage crew rehearses to fill in for the actors and actresses, who have supposedly been taken ill. As the characters struggle to survive natural disasters, to invent things, and to cultivate civilization, Wilder communicates that the human will to survive and improve will prevail. *The Skin of Our Teeth* was very popular, although it was briefly the subject of controversy when some critics accused Wilder of plagiarizing James Joyce's *Finnegan's Wake.* However, retrospective opinion holds that Wilder's literary borrowing from Joyce was legitimate.

Wilder published little during the 1940s, for he was serving in World War II as a military intelligence officer. During the 1950s, his work consisted mostly of revivals, revisions, and productions in foreign countries, particularly in Germany, where his work is very popular. Wilder's few publications during the 1950s and early 1960s are not highly regarded. However, he received the American Academy of Arts and Letters' Gold Medal in 1952 for distinguished work in fiction. Wilder's penultimate novel, *The Eighth Day* (1967), was the major success of the latter part of his career. In this, his longest novel, a man who is falsely convicted of murdering his neighbor escapes and lives as a fugitive. The story also involves the solution of the crime and the interaction of the two families. *The Eighth Day* won a National Book Award.

(See also *CLC,* Vols. 1, 5, 6, 10, 15; *Contemporary Authors,* Vols. 13-16, rev. ed., Vols. 61-64 [obituary]; and *Dictionary of Literary Biography,* Vols. 4, 7, 9.)

In this volume commentary on Thornton Wilder is focused on his play *Our Town.*

JOSEPH WOOD KRUTCH

Two attitudes toward the recent past are so familiar that one or the other seems almost inevitable, but the mood of **"Our Town"** is neither sentimental nor satiric. Here is no easy fun poked at the age of buggies and innocence, but here also is no sentimental overvaluation. Indeed, it is amazing how little Mr. Wilder claims for his villagers, how readily the local editor admits with a shake of the head that there is no "culture" in his town, and how calmly the commentator remarks at the wedding of his chief personages that the result of such unions is interesting "once in a thousand times." There is no tendency to claim for the homely virtues more than their due, no effort to hide the fact that such simple lives are led in ignorance of the heights as well as of the depths of possible human experience.

And if one asks what remains, what is left to feel when one feels neither condescension nor partisan warmth, the answer is simply that the mood of quiet contemplation which Mr. Wilder generates is one which would be hopelessly submerged by any suggestion of either satire or sentimentality. The spectacle of these undistinguished men and women living out their endlessly retold tale fascinates him, I think, not because undistinguished men and women are more admirable than others but because even they are men and women, because even undistinguished lives tease the imagination with a riddle not to be solved and stir it with an emotion not to be analyzed. Satire and sentiment alike are efforts to dispose of the problem by passing a judgment. The still sad music of humanity is most clearly audible when both are rejected. (p. 224)

The dramatic method is everywhere unconventional in the extreme. The piece is introduced by a soft-spoken master of ceremonies who remains on the stage throughout the performance to offer occasional comments, and the players act out their roles without benefit of scenery. But while such eccentric devices are commonly used for the purpose of heightening the colors of a play and tend frequently in the direction of the stridently insistent, Mr. Wilder uses them in the interest of a quiet intimacy. It is difficult to see how he could achieve the effect he desires by any other means. . . . (p.225)

Joseph Wood Krutch, in a review of "Our Town," in The Nation, *Vol. 146, No. 8, February 19, 1938, pp. 224-25.*

JOHN MASON BROWN

[The essay from which this excerpt was taken originally appeared in The New York Evening Post, *March 14, 1938.]*

The form Mr. Wilder has used [in ***Our Town***] is as old as the theatre's ageless game of "let's pretend" and as new as the last time it has been employed effectively. The co-operation it asks an audience to contribute is at heart the very same co-operation which the most realistic and heavily documented productions invite playgoers to grant. The major difference is one of degree. Both types of production depend in the last analysis upon their audiences to supply that final belief which is the mandate under which all theatrical illusion operates. The form Mr. Wilder uses is franker, that is all. It does not attempt to hide the fact it is make-believe. Instead it asks its audiences to do some of the work, to enter openly and gladly into the imaginative conspiracy known as the successful staging of a play.

What such a drama as Mr. Wilder's does, of course, is to strip theatrical illusion down to its essentials. Mr. Wilder has the best of good reasons for so doing. What he has done in ***Our Town*** is to strip life down to its essentials, too. There is nothing of the "stunt" about the old-new form he has employed. His form is the inevitable one his content demands. Indeed so inevitable is it, and hence so right, that I, for one, must confess I lost all awareness of it merely as a form a few minutes after [the Stage Manager] had begun to set the stage by putting a few chairs in place. There have been those who have been bothered because the pantomime was not consistent, because real umbrellas were carried and no visible lawn-mower was pushed, because naturalistic off-stage sounds serve as echoes to the actions indicated on stage. I was not one of the bothered. I found myself surrendering, especially during the first two acts, to the spell of the beautiful and infinitely tender play Mr. Wilder has written.

John Anderson has likened ***Our Town*** to India's ropetrick. He has pointed out it is the kind of play at which you either see the boy and the rope, or at which you don't. Although I refuse to admit there is anything of the fakir's touch in ***Our Town,*** I think I understand what Mr. Anderson means. Mr. Wilder's is, from the audience point of view, an exceptionally personal play. More than most plays, since by its sweet simplicity it seeks to get in contact with the inmost nerves of our living, it is the kind of drama which depends upon what we bring to it.

Mr. Wilder's play is concerned with the universal importance of those unimportant details which figure in the lives of men and women everywhere. His Grover's Corners is a New Hampshire town inhabited by decent New England people. The very averageness of these quiet, patient people is the point at which our lives and all living become a part of their experience. Yet Mr. Wilder's play involves more than a New England township. It burrows into the essence of the growing-up, the marrying, the living, and the dying of all of us who sit before it and are included by it. (pp. 189-90)

To my surprise I have encountered the complaint that Mr. Wilder's Grover's Corners is not like Middletown, U.S.A. It lacks brothels, race riots, huge factories, front-page scandals, social workers, union problems, lynchings, agitators, and strikes. . . . [Its people] are quiet, self-respecting, God-fearing Yankees who get up early to do their day's work and meet their responsibilities and their losses without whining. (pp. 190-91)

They do not murder or steal, borrow or beg, blackmail or oppress. Furthermore they face the rushing years without complaints as comparatively happy mortals. Therefore to certain realists they seem unreal. "No historian," one critic has written "has ever claimed that a town like Mr. Wilder's was ever so idyllic as to be free from intolerance and injustice." Mr. Wilder does not make this claim himself. His small-town editor admits Grover's Corners is "little better behaved than most towns." Neither is Mr. Wilder working as the ordinary historian works. His interests are totally different interests.

He is not concerned with social trends, with economic conditions, with pivotal events, or glittering personalities. He sings not of arms and the man, but of those small events which loom so large in the daily lives of each of us, and which are usually unsung. His interest is the unexceptional, the average, the personal. His preoccupation is what lies beneath the surface and the routine of our lives, and is common to all our hearts and all our experience. It is not so much of the streets of a New England Town he writes as of the clean white spire which rises above them.

There are hundreds of fat books written each year on complicated subjects by authors who are not writers at all. But the ageless achievement of the true writers has always been to bring a new illumination to the simplest facts of life. That illumination has ever been a precious talent given only to a few. It is because Mr. Wilder brings this illumination to his picture of Grover's Corners that I admire ***Our Town.*** New Hampshire is the State which can claim Mr. Wilder's village, but his vision of it has been large enough to include all of us, no matter where we may come from, among its inhabitants. Personally, I should as soon think of condemning the Twenty-third Psalm because it lacks the factual observation of Sinclair Lewis and the social point of view of Granville Hicks as I would of accusing ***Our Town*** of being too unrealistically observed.

Anyone who hears only the milk bottles clink when early morning has come once again to Grover's Corners has not heard what Mr. Wilder wants them to hear. These milk bottles are merely the spokesmen of time, symbols for the bigness of little things. In terms of the Gibbses and the Webbs, Mr. Wilder gives the pattern of repetition of each small day's planning, each small life's fruition and decline. He makes us feel the swift passage of the years, our blindness in meeting their race, the sense that our lives go rushing past so quickly that we have scarcely time in which to hold our breaths.

Only once does he fail us seriously. This is in his scene in the bleak graveyard on the hill. Although he seeks there to create the image of the dead who have lost their interest in life, he has not been able to capture the true greatness of vision which finds them at last unfettered from the minutiae of existence. Both his phrasing and his thinking are inadequate here. He chills the living by removing his dead even from compassion.

Nonetheless Mr. Wilder's is a remarkable play; one of the sagest, warmest, and most deeply human scripts to have come out of our theatre. . . . It is the kind of play which suspends us in time, making us weep for our own vanished youth at the same time we are sobbing for the short-lived pleasures and sufferings which we know await our children. Geographically ***Our Town*** can be found at an imaginary place. . . . At the [theatre] you will find Mr. Wilder's play is laid in no imaginary place. It becomes a reality in the human heart. (pp. 190-93)

John Mason Brown, "America Speaks," in his Two on the Aisle: Ten Years of the American Theatre in Performance, *W. W. Norton & Company, Inc., 1938, pp. 133-93.**

JOHN MASON BROWN

Coming back to **"Our Town,"** even in book form, after the altering years of war and so-called peace, is an experience at once poignant and reassuring. Most nations, most things, most of us who saw Thornton Wilder's play eleven years ago have changed immeasurably. It, however, remains unchanged. It has not gone out of style, as plays do with frightening rapidity. It does not seem old-fashioned. It has not lost its rightness. It tugs with its original directness at emotions which are beyond change. . . .

[Quaint] in custom and removed in time though it was, [**"Our Town"**] managed to include us all. What is more, it continues to do precisely this even when encountered in print and in an altered world. (p. 33)

In the Thirties, tingling as they were with social consciousness, there were those who complained because Grover's Corners was not more like Middletown. . . . The passing years, however, have only proved Mr. Wilder's correctness in writing as he did. His subject had no datelines. His interest was not what gets into the public prints. It was what each of us must live with in private. Man's spirit was his business; man's spirit and evocations of those small-important incidents which test us in our daily living.

Adding to the timelessness of the first two acts of **"Our Town"** is the non-representational form in which Mr. Wilder elected to have his say. It is make-believe of the frankest sort. . . . It sets him free. It leaves his imagination unimprisoned within settings. It relieves him of the need of employing the ordinary and quickly aging techniques of realistic plays. Indeed, it is as timeless as his own subject matter.

Not many plays have come out of the American theatre which better with the years. **"Our Town"** is one of these. Much as I admired it in 1938, I find that now I admire it even more. (p. 34)

John Mason Brown, "Wilder: 'Our Town'," in The Saturday Review of Literature, *Vol. XXXII, No. 32, August 6, 1949, pp. 33-4.*

ARTHUR MILLER

Most people, including the daily theater reviewers, have come to assume that the forms in which plays are written spring either from nowhere or from the temperamental choice of the playwrights. I am not maintaining that the selection of a form is as objective a matter as the choice of let us say a raincoat instead of a linen suit for a walk on a rainy day; on the contrary, most playwrights, including myself, reach rather instinctively for that form, that way of telling a play, which seems inevitably right for the subject at hand. Yet I wonder whether it is all as accidental, as "free" a choice, as it appears to be at a superficial glance. I wonder whether there may not be within the ideas of family on the one hand, and society on the other, primary pressures which govern our notions of the right form for a particular kind of subject matter.

It has gradually come to appear to me over the years that the spectrum of dramatic forms, from Realism over to the Verse Drama, the Expressionistic techniques, and what we call vaguely the Poetic Play, consists of forms which express human relationships of a particular kind, each of them suited to express either a primarily familial relation at one extreme, or a primarily social relation at the other. (p. 35)

I have come to wonder whether the force or pressure that makes for Realism, that even requires it, is the magnetic force of the family relationship within the play, and the pressure which evokes in a genuine, unforced way the un-realistic modes is the social relationship within the play. (p. 36)

The implications of this natural wedding of form with inner relationships are many, and some of them are complex. It is true to say, I think, that the language of the family is the language of the private life—prose. The language of society, the language of the public life, is verse. According to the degree to which the play partakes of either relationship, it achieves the right to move closer or further away from either pole. (p. 38)

[A] play can be poetic without verse, and it is in this middle area that the complexities of tracing the influence of the family and social elements upon the form become more troublesome. ***Our Town*** by Thornton Wilder is such a play, and it is important not only for itself but because it is the progenitor of many other works.

This is a family play which deals with the traditional family figures, the father, mother, brother, sister. At the same time it uses this particular family as a prism through which is reflected the author's basic idea, his informing principle—which can be stated as the indestructibility, the everlastingness, of the family and the community, its rhythm of life, its rootedness in the essentially safe cosmos despite troubles, wracks, and seemingly disastrous, but essentially temporary, dislocations.

Technically it is not arbitrary in any detail. Instead of a family living room or a house, we are shown a bare stage on which actors set chairs, a table, a ladder to represent a staircase or an upper floor, and so on. A narrator is kept in the foreground as though to remind us that this is not so much "real life" as an abstraction of it—in other words, a stage. It is clearly a poetic rather than a realistic play. What makes it that? Well, let us first imagine what would make it more realistic.

Would a real set make it realistic? Not likely. A real set would only discomfit us by drawing attention to what would then appear to be a slightly unearthly quality about the characterizations. We should probably say, "People don't really act like that." In addition, the characterization of the whole town could not be accomplished with anything like its present vividness if the narrator were removed, as he would have to be from a realistic set, and if the entrances and exits of the environmental people, the townspeople, had to be justified with the usual motives and machinery of Realism.

The preoccupation of the entire play is quite what the title implies—the town, the society, and not primarily this particular family—and every stylistic means used is to the end that the family foreground be kept in its place, merely as a foreground for the larger context behind and around it. In my opinion, it is this larger context, the town and its enlarging, widening significance, that is the bridge to the poetic for this play. Cut out the town and you will cut out the poetry. (pp. 38-9)

Wilder sees his characters in this play not primarily as personalities, as individuals, but as forces, and he individualizes them only enough to carry the freight, so to speak, of their roles as forces. I do not believe, for instance, that we can think of the brother in this play, or the sister or the mother, as having names other than Brother, Sister, Mother. They are not given that kind of particularity or interior life. They are characterized rather as social factors, in their roles of Brother, Sister, Mother, in Our Town. They are drawn, in other words, as forces to enliven and illuminate the author's symbolic vision and his theme, which is that of the family as a timeless, stable quantity which has not only survived all the turmoil of time but is, in addition, beyond the possibility of genuine destruction.

The play is important to any discussion of form because it has achieved a largeness of meaning and an abstraction of style that created that meaning, while at the same time it has moved its audiences subjectively—it has made them laugh and weep as abstract plays rarely if ever do. But it would seem to contradict my contention here. If it is true that the presentation of the family on the stage inevitably forces Realism upon the play, how did this family play manage to transcend Realism to achieve its symbolistic style?

Every form, every style, pays its price for its special advantages. The price paid by ***Our Town*** is psychological characterization forfeited in the cause of the symbol. I do not believe, as I have said, that the characters are identifiable in a psychological way, but only as figures in the family and social constellation, and this is not meant in criticism, but as a statement of the limits of this form. I would go further and say that it is not *necessary* for every kind of play to do every kind of thing. But if we are after ultimate reality we must make ultimate demands.

I think that had Wilder drawn his characters with a deeper configuration of detail and with a more remorseless quest for private motive and self-interest, for instance, the story as it stands now would have appeared oversentimental and even sweet. I think that if the play tested its own theme more remorselessly, the world it creates of a timeless family and a rhythm of existence beyond the disturbance of social wracks would not remain unshaken. . . .

I think, further, that the close contact which the play established with its audience was the result of its coincidence with the deep longing of the audience for such stability, a stability which in daylight out on the street does not truly exist. The great plays pursue the idea of loss and deprivation of an earlier state of bliss which the characters feel compelled to return to or to re-create. I think this play forgoes the loss and suffers thereby in its quest for reality, but that the audience supplies the sense of deprivation in its own life experience as it faces what in effect is an idyl of the past. To me, therefore, the play falls short of a form that will press into reality to the limits of reality, if only because it could not plumb the psychological interior lives of its characters and still keep its present form. It is a triumph in that it does open a way toward the dramatization of the larger truths of existence while using the common materials of life. It is a truly poetic play. (p. 39)

Arthur Miller, "The Family in Modern Drama," in The Atlantic Monthly, *Vol. 197, No. 4, April, 1956, pp. 35-41.**

ARTHUR H. BALLET

In the short history of American literary criticism, there has been a continuous search for "the great American drama." It is the purpose of this essay to continue this search by exploring the qualifications for this signal honor of Thornton Wilder's ***Our Town***. . . .

As a beginning, it might be observed that, literary and moral implications assumed, all important drama in the history of the theatre has had popular appeal. . . . However, it is not suggested that all popular drama is necessarily important or significant, but merely that great drama has been popular theatre. (p. 243)

[Where] is the appeal of Wilder's ***Our Town***? Frank M. Whiting, in *An Introduction to the Theatre,* points out that the play has qualities beyond its novelty:

> . . . it is an honest and revealing portrait of small-town American life. It has been criticised as sentimental; Emily, George, and the others give us a far more genuine insight into twentieth-century American living than do the studies of neurotics, gangsters, and sexually frustrated.

It is necessary, however, to go beyond this, to qualify "sentimentality," and to consider the play as a modern American tragedy.

The plot of ***Our Town*** is deceptively simple. (p. 244)

There are, of course, complications, dramatic actions, beautifully constructed moments of almost pure theatre (such as the end of the first act when the chorus is singing in the church, while the lovers work a mathematics problem) and highly interesting characterizations. Basically, however, the plot is a boy-meets-girl affair—but with a difference. Before this "difference" is considered, however, other matters must be studied.

The characters, for example, are excellently blended. Mothers Webb and Gibbs are both "typical," but they are far from alike, emotionally and intellectually. Likewise the fathers, both professional, intelligent men, are contrasting studies of the same type. In essence, each adult couple presents a different facet for our consideration of the same idealized characters. Pre-adolescence is similary examined through the youngsters Wally Webb and Rebecca Gibbs. The sordid side of human nature is also reflected in the play by Simon Stimson, who, having taken his own life in alcoholic desperation, chooses his own epitaph in the form of musical notes. Not just a community of people is presented to the audience, but a tiny, idealized reflection of the entire human community is set to work for the audience to observe—and from which the audience is expected to learn something about itself.

But tragedy is more than human beings, however well portrayed and set in motion on the stage. There are matters of structure, of motivation, and above all of theme, or meaning, that determine stature and significance of any drama. Those dramas which contribute something beyond all these considerations are the highest form of the dramatic art: tragedy.

Our Town is a carefully constructed drama, following the precepts of classic drama with certain justified modifications. Actually it is a trilogy. Act One may be thought of as a separate play dealing with The Daily Life, Act Two examines Love and Marriage within the totality of its act structure, and Act Three expands the first parts of the trilogy into a complex of eternity where the mystery of life is culminated in death.

Like its Greek predecessors, ***Our Town*** is concerned with the great and continuing cycle of life; out of life comes death and from death comes life. This cycle is man's closest understanding of eternity, his finest artistic expression of what he senses to be a mission and a purpose. The trilogy, thus considered, admirably re-interprets this concept in modern terms and language and form, finding its roots in what is probably the finest drama of all time: Sophocles' *Oedipus Rex*.

The use of the stage manager as a chorus is another manifestation of close attention to the classic structuring of the drama. The chorus-stage manager serves as the human link with the audience and personifies the *milieu* of society. Joining the audience with the events presented in the spaceless and timeless stage, he explains and interprets, fills in, and establishes the background for each episode. He is, however, more than just a narrator. Abandoning the modern concept of the impersonal, almost mechanical commentator, Wilder has returned to the kind of choric voice so effective in Greek tragedy. The stage manager represents the observing community; he is biased, sympathetic, informed, and concerned. His calmness in the face of both joy and disaster is never construed into passivity. The most lyric passages of the play are assigned to him, and this is quite rightly conceived by the playwright, for, as the agent of the human community in the drama, what occurs within the play makes a difference and must be sensitively considered.

At the same time, the stage manager subtly introduces a note of patience and understanding which is essential if the action is to have a meaning above that of a sentimental or emotional orgy for the entertainment of the audience. His interruption of the action, his interspersed observations, and his serious but twinkling control of the progress of the play all serve to prevent over-identification, which would destroy the higher implications of the play. (pp. 245-46)

Some producers of the play . . . have attempted to "enhance" the production by adding suggestive or stylized scenery. It would seem that they have failed to grasp the fundamental reason for Wilder's elimination of conventional scenic devices in the first place. It is not a trick or "gimmick" to make the play sensational; on the contrary, Wilder, like his classic predecessors, was aware of the inherent scenery of the theatre itself. He chose deliberately and with great sensitivity to the whole meaning of his own play, to utilize the theatre as the setting, for he wished to examine theatrical reality. This is by no means an easy thing to do. The theatre is not reality, of course; it is a life of its own but only insofar as it is a selective, sensitive, active and reflective image of the world beyond the theatre's walls. Wilder was aware of this function of the theatre, and he has made use of it and accentuated it by eliminating scenic devices beyond the physical theatre itself.

Still, none of these structural details are in themselves enough to enable one to call ***Our Town*** a tragedy. Aristotle, in his *Poetica,* established tragedy as a "purgation through pity and fear" and as an "ennoblement" as well as the picturization of the fall of a great man. At first glance, ***Our Town*** appears to fall short of such ambitious purposes. The very simplicity and "ordinariness" of the drama seem to make a mockery of higher purposes. There are, however, deeply significant actions beneath the surface which do indeed fulfill Aristotelian definitions.

Death is the fear-agent employed as a catharsis. The audience witnesses the fall of the smallest of God's creatures: a young mother who becomes aware of the tragedy of life, and who finally is ennobled by death to understand how wonderful life is. . . . Tragedy, in its finest sense, need not and should not be "sad." It should rather be elevating, should point the way to a higher level of understanding of man as a creature revolving in the cosmos. By these Aristotelian standards, then, ***Our Town*** approaches significance as a tragedy.

Wilder has, by careful dramaturgical manipulation of time and place, established the play quite properly in perspective. . . . [An] example of Wilder's time and space manipulation is the stage manager's soliloquy in the cemetery, opening Act Three. Time has passed, changes have been made, death and life have continued their endless cycle: . . .

> [Everybody] knows that SOMETHING is eternal. And it ain't houses and it ain't names, and it ain't earth, and it ain't even the stars . . . everybody knows in their bones that SOMETHING is eternal, and that something has to do with human beings. . . .

Not only is the issue joined directly to the audience, but the level of the drama aspires toward an ever-increasing expansion of the scope of the play as a statement of faith in the microcosm, Man. (pp. 246-48)

Assuming that audiences have been aware, however subconsciously, of these complexities within the drama, they do not explain the enduring and affectionate appeal of the play. And it will be remembered that earlier in this examination the criterion of popularity as well as significance was established for determining "great drama." ***Our Town*** is *prima facie* a popular play. . . . (p. 248)

Our purpose here is not to prove that the play is popular but to attempt to determine *why* it is popular. Lamentable though it may be, people do not go to the theatre to hear sermons or to be told that the only truth they can comprehend is that the end of all life is death and that in death they will achieve life. ***Our Town*** has other appeals, some immediately apparent and some quite deceptive. The daily life has the appeal of familiarity. . . . The familiarity of this daily life, as so expertly sketched in ***Our Town,*** releases the audience's skepticism and induces a sense of suspended disbelief. If ***Our Town*** does not reflect life as it really is, at least it suggests what the daily life should be like, and the audience approves.

Also present is the sentimentality already referred to, but it is without sententiousness; it has romance without romanticism, and innocence without naiveté. The fears and the faith reflected are without melodramatic trappings, and are sincere reflections of the innermost strivings of the human spirit. In short, they "ring true" because they are common experiences.

Attention finally must return to that quality which, however morbid its surface may seem, recognizes a quiet, resigned sense of justice in the inevitability of death itself. Throughout life, man is surrounded by this knowledge. In the play, old age, a burst appendix, childbirth, and alcoholism all contribute to the final end. But the audience is never repelled by this concept; it learns, as Emily must, to accept the life cycle, which not only is as it is, but is as it has to be and should be.

Any attempt to separate "content" or "theme" from "form" or "structure" is a purely academic one and seldom worth the effort. In any literature worthy of consideration at all, theme and structure are one and the same thing, determining each other. Questions of suitability and compatibility are largely matters of individual taste. With masterly strokes, Wilder has joined both the form and the content into an inseparable entity which both appeals and instructs. The audience engages in a struggle resulting both in pity and fear but ultimately culminating in an ennoblement through acceptance and understanding.

Thus, it would appear that ***Our Town*** is not only an important drama but also a significant one, for it has much to relate without pretentions. The "common folk" in the play very directly refute the concept of the mediocre average or perfect being. The simple yet effective language is appropriate not only to the characters involved but to the ideas expressed. The prose-poetry which Wilder has chosen is without the modern falsification of poesy. The dramatic conflicts and tensions are devoid of melodramatic cliches or the cinematic "happy endings" which betray life itself. There is no drama worthy of the name without conflict and action, but Wilder has elevated both of these ingredients. Life and death are part of a whole and yet in constant conflict, as are love and hate (witness the exquisite "drugstore scene" in Act Two). The resultant entities are both honest and profound.

In closing, it should be noted that the critics have been wrong before, and so has the popular audience. Each play must stand on its own merits. ***Our Town*** is a work which cannot be ignored merely because it is popular. The final condemnation of this play by those who do not approve of it has been that it is inconsistent, that the first two acts are comic and the third is tragic. This is in a sense true, and obviously in contradiction of Aristotelian principles. However, life is both "the human comedy" and "the incredible fate" of man. There is joy mingled everlastingly with despair. In his sanest moments, man is aware of how fleeting both the joy and the despair are. He knows that the end of the human comedy is the awakening into "the undiscover'd country from whose bourn no traveler returns."

As ***Our Town*** quite brilliantly shows, life is a paradox, and so it is not amazing that man paradoxically retains his faith that in death, too, there is life and a greater consciousness. Like Oedipus before her, Emily finds a place in dramatic literature as a tragic figure of enormous dimensions, for in her blindness, or death, she gains the true ability really to see and understand. (pp. 248-49)

Arthur H. Ballet, "'In Our Living and in Our Dying'," in English Journal, *Vol. XLV, No. 5, May, 1956, pp. 243-49.*

THORNTON WILDER

[The essay from which this excerpt is taken was originally published in a slightly different form as "'A Platform and a Passion or Two'" *in* Harper's, *October 1957.]*

Toward the end of the 'twenties I began to lose pleasure in going to the theater. I ceased to believe in the stories I saw presented there. . . . Yet at the same time the conviction was growing in me that the theater was the greatest of all the arts. I felt that something had gone wrong with it in my time and that it was fulfilling only a small part of its potentialities. (p. 104)

I began to feel that the theater was not only inadequate, it was evasive; it did not wish to draw upon its deeper potentialities. I found the word for it: it aimed to be *soothing*. The tragic had no heat; the comic had no bite; the social criticism failed to indict us with responsibility. (p. 105)

The trouble began in the nineteenth century and was connected with the rise of the middle classes—they wanted their theater soothing. . . . These audiences, however, also thronged to Shakespeare. How did they shield themselves against his probing? How did they smother the theater—and with such effect that it smothers us still? The box set was already there, the curtain, the proscenium, but not taken "seriously"—it was a convenience in view of the weather in northern countries. They took it seriously and emphasized and enhanced everything that thus removed, cut off, and boxed the action; they increasingly shut the play up into a museum showcase.

Let us examine why the box-set stage stifles the life in drama and why and how it militates against belief.

Every action which has ever taken place—every thought, every emotion—has taken place only once, at one moment in time and place. "I love you," "I rejoice," "I suffer," have been said and felt many billions of times, and never twice the same. Every person who has ever lived has lived an unbroken succession of unique occasions. Yet the more one is aware of this individuality in experience (innumerable! innumerable!) the more one becomes attentive to what these disparate moments have in common, to repetitive patterns. As an artist (or listener or beholder) which "truth" do you prefer—that of the isolated occasion, or that which includes and resumes the innumerable? . . . The theater is admirably fitted to tell both truths. It has one foot planted firmly in the particular, since each actor before us (even when he wears a mask!) is indubitably a living, breathing "one"; yet it tends and strains to exhibit a general truth since its relation to a specific "realistic" truth is confused and undermined by the fact that it is an accumulation of untruths, pretenses, and fiction. The novel is pre-eminently the vehicle of the unique occasion, the theater of the generalized one. It is through the theater's power to raise the exhibited individual action into the realm of idea and type and universal that it is able to evoke our belief. But power is precisely what those nineteenth-century audiences did not—dared not—confront. They tamed it and drew its teeth; squeezed it into that removed showcase. They loaded the stage with specific objects, because every concrete object on the stage fixes and narrows the action to one moment in time and place. . . . So it was by a jugglery with time that the middle classes devitalized the theater. When you emphasize *place* in the theater, you drag down and limit and harness time to it. You thrust the action back into past time, whereas it is precisely the glory of the stage that it is always "now" there. Under such production methods the characters are all dead before the action starts. You don't have to pay deeply from your heart's participation. No great age in the theater ever attempted to capture the audience's belief through this kind of specification and localization. I became dissatisfied with the theater because I was unable to lend credence to such childish attempts to be "real."

I began writing one-act plays that tried to capture not verisimilitude but reality. In ***The Happy Journey to Trenton and Camden*** four kitchen chairs represent an automobile and a family travels seventy miles in twenty minutes. Ninety years go by in ***The Long Christmas Dinner.*** In ***Pullman Car Hiawatha*** some more plain chairs serve as berths and we hear the very vital statistics of the towns and fields that passengers are traversing; we hear their thoughts; we even hear the planets over their heads. (pp. 105-09)

Our Town is not offered as a picture of life in a New Hampshire village; or as a speculation about the conditions of life after death (that element I merely took from Dante's *Purgatory*). It is an attempt to find a value above all price for the smallest events in our daily life. I have made the claim as preposterous as possible, for I have set the village against the largest dimensions of time and place. The recurrent words in this play (few have noticed it) are "hundreds," "thousands," and "millions." Emily's joys and griefs, her algebra lessons and her birthday presents—what are they when we consider all the billions of girls who have lived, who are living, and who will live? Each individual's assertion to an absolute reality can only be inner, very inner. And here the method of staging finds its justification—in the first two acts there are at least a few chairs and tables; but when Emily revisits the earth and the kitchen to which she descended on her twelfth birthday, the very chairs and table are gone. Our claim, our hope, our despair are in the mind—not in things, not in "scenery." Molière said that for the theater all he needed was a platform and a passion or two. The climax of this play needs only five square feet of boarding and the passion to know what life means to us. (p. 109)

Thornton Wilder, "On Drama and the Theatre: Preface to 'Three Plays: Our Town, The Skin of Our Teeth, The Matchmaker'," in his American Characteristics and Other Essays, *edited by Donald Gallup, Harper & Row, Publishers, 1979, pp. 104-11.*

GERALD WEALES

Playwrights have a way of marking their work with the signature of personal mannerisms. A play of Tennessee Williams or Eugene O'Neill, for instance, is easily identifiable. Wilder's three plays [***Our Town, The Skin of Our Teeth,*** and ***The Matchmaker***], unmistakably his, are dissimilar on the surface—one an essay in regionless regionalism, one an expressionistic comedy, one a traditional farce. In their manner they share only a distaste for conventional naturalistic staging; it is their matter that points an insistent finger at the author. Each of the plays embodies Wilder's concern with, admiration for and love of human life at its most ordinary, which is, for him, at its most consistent preoccupation with love, death, laughter, boredom, aspiration and despair. . . .

One of the remarkable things about Wilder's plays is that they—like his novels—have declared his optimism with a directness that is unusual on the American stage, at least among serious playwrights. The dignity of man is apparent behind the cosmic and familiar sufferings of O'Neill and behind the political and social uncertainty of Clifford Odets and Arthur Miller, perhaps even behind the sexual nervousness of Tennessee Williams, but in Wilder it is in the foreground. The emphasis, however, is not so much on dignity as it is on man; the one implies the other. Nor is his optimism the kind of adolescent enthusiasm that seems to be the stuff of William Saroyan's plays (Saroyan's cry of love, love, love has become so shrill that one suspects that he has not yet convinced himself); it is a recognition that pain, cruelty, death and failure are part of living, but that they can never completely define life. All of Wilder's plays say, with Chrysis in his novel ***The Woman of Andros,*** "that I have known the worst that the world can do to me, and that nevertheless I praise the world and all living."

There is an uncomfortable attitude around today that the clichés of despair are more profound than the bromides of optimism; it is intellectually proper to talk about the dark night of the soul, but only a popular song would be willing to walk on the sunny side of the street. . . . Wilder's reputation has suffered as a result. People talk of outgrowing Wilder, as they talk of outgrowing Shaw, but they mean simply that even if one does believe in the ultimate value of human life, one does not say so, except obliquely. Wilder once told a reporter from *Time,* "Literature is the orchestration of platitudes." Wilder has chosen the unfashionable platitudes of the optimist; he has repeated them in his plays even though he knows, like Captain Alvarado in ***The Bridge of San Luis Rey,*** that "there are times when it requires a high courage to speak the banal." It is his distinction as a playwright that banality emerges as—what it is—one kind of truth. (p. 486)

Our Town is "an attempt to find a value above all price for the smallest events in our daily life" [see Wilder excerpt above]. The play is concerned, for the most part, with the ritual of daily tasks; the major actions in the play (Emily Webb's marriage to George Gibbs and her death in childbirth) celebrate those basic commonplaces that Sweeney expected to find on his cannibal isle: "Birth, and copulation, and death." Each of the events, the ordinary and the special (which is special only to Emily and George and those close to them), is seen as part of a continuing stream of life from which it grows and into which it will be absorbed and finally forgotten. The play is, in one sense, antitheatrical; instead of enlarging a moment until it bursts, throwing its significance into the audience, it cherishes the small and the everyday (whether it be cooking breakfast or dying). If the perspective is long enough, the individual and the general become one. For one kind of mind, such a long view might reduce life to inconsequence; for Wilder, it gives to the simplest action and the simplest emotion not cosmic value (the dead forget), but human value. (pp. 486-87)

All of Wilder's plays avoid conventional staging. They either attack it head-on, using the weapons of expressionism, as in ***Our Town*** and ***The Skin of Our Teeth,*** or they join it with a vengeance, as in ***The Matchmaker,*** and try to laugh it off the stage. His attempt to splinter the box-set or to treat it as though it were a farceur's mask (the fight was pretty well won when he got into it) grew out of his belief that plays begin in generalization; the correct teacups on the correct table in the correct drawing room have a way of reducing universals to the tiresomely specific. Even in his novels, as Cowley has pointed out, the settings are relatively unimportant. He is concerned with the recurrent human predicaments at the expense of the immediate surroundings. . . . ***Our Town*** can be identified as Grover's Corners, New Hampshire, but it is also to be our town wherever and at whatever time we live, as Editor Webb implies when he says of ancient Babylon, "every night all those families sat down to supper, and the father came home from his work, and the smoke went up the chimney,—same as here." (p. 487)

For all its importance to the themes of the plays, Wilder's non-naturalistic structure gives too easy entrance to his chief dramatic fault, a tendency to be overly didactic. He seems afraid that apparent points will be missed. The stage manager in ***Our Town*** explains too much and points up too many morals. . . . These are minor blemishes, however; they weaken the plays without undermining them.

Wilder, as he says in his introduction [to ***Three Plays***], is not an innovator. He is not the kind of playwright who gathers disciples or inspires copyists. He is simply a man who has gone his own way, finding or borrowing the forms in which he could say what was on his mind. He has published only three full-length plays, but they are all good plays and that—on the American stage, or any stage—is an achievement. (p. 488)

Gerald Weales, "Unfashionable Optimist," in Commonweal, *Vol. LXVII, No. 19, February 7, 1958, pp. 486-88.*

GEORGE D. STEPHENS

In our longing for an unattainable perfection, perhaps it is to be expected that the attempt to find "the great American novel" and "the great American drama" should continue. But ours is a nation of great size and remarkable variety; it poses a complex problem for the writer who attempts to synthesize and interpret its life for us. Though this is doubtful, considering the nature of art and our subjective reaction to it, in time a work may appear which will by overwhelming weight of opinion be awarded the title of "the greatest." Meanwhile, this search sometimes leads to extravagant claims.

Such a claim, which seems unwarranted in view of the limits of the play set by the author, has been made for Thornton Wilder's ***Our Town.*** Professor Arthur H. Ballet . . . finds in ***Our Town*** "the great American drama" [see excerpt above]. . . .

It is not my purpose to denigrate ***Our Town,*** which is, within the limits of its subject, form, and point of view, an interesting and valuable play. But one must challenge the claim that it is the greatest American play; that it is an outstanding tragedy; and that Emily is "a tragic figure of enormous dimensions." (p. 258)

It is questionable whether ***Our Town*** can be called tragedy at all in any worthy definition of the term. Surely it does not fit Aristotelian standards; or, to put it another way, it is not like Greek tragedy. The three acts are like the separate plays of Aeschylus' *Oresteia* in not much more than that Wilder divided his play into three acts and gave each a theme or motivating idea. Consider the *Oresteia:* each play, while essential to the great whole, is complete within itself, with carefully built up situation and plot, characterization in variety and depth, and conflict leading to a solution. (p. 259)

Act One of ***Our Town,*** illustrating or symbolizing The Daily Life of Grover's Corners, could not possibly stand alone as a complete play, nor could the other acts. More than a third of Act One, in fact, is comment of a sociological or historical nature. Through the Stage Manager, who acts as both commentator and participant—and as such he has a function similar to that of the Greek chorus—and others, we are given selected information about this small New Hampshire town as it was in the early part of the twentieth century. . . . Employing short, episodic scenes, Wilder focuses on two middle-class families, the Webbs and the Gibbs, who are evidently meant to be typical of such small-town American people. His emphasis is on social relationships rather than on individual character, on the town rather than on Mrs. Gibbs or George or Emily.

Act Two, entitled Love and Marriage, carries on the story of the town by giving further information and, more important, by concentrating on the two young people who create a family and thus insure the town's continued existence. Wilder establishes a somewhat deeper emotional involvement with his characters than in Act One by his skillful description of love, courtship, and marriage, but again George and Emily are not sharply and deeply individualized. They are, and are meant to be, symbols of youth; they are abstractions or forces clothed in words. "People were made to live two-by-two," says the Stage Manager, emphasizing the social relationship.

Act Three, extending the story through death into eternity and so raising it to a universal plane, is the principal basis for the claims made for the play as significant tragedy. In death Emily discovers, as have the other dead, that the living are troubled and blind, and that life is short and sad. In considerable part Wilder focuses on Emily to illustrate these truths, but again her character, as an individual, fails to acquire depth. She is still only one of the group who are given much attention and who, all of them together, living and dead, symbolize the persistence of human life as it exists in the community. The cycle of life persists, the life of the town, a small but significant part of mysterious eternity. In short, Emily is not the protagonist of the play; the protagonist is the town itself.

The expressionist form chosen for the play is well adapted to the author's purposes. In "The Family in Modern Drama" [see excerpt above] . . . , Arthur Miller suggests that realism is the best medium for presentation of "the primarily familial relation," expressionism for "the primarily social relation." He cites ***Our Town*** as an example of the latter. While I can think of dramatists who use expressionism successfully to interpret individual and family relationships (Strindberg, Pirandello, O'Neill, for instance, and to a certain extent Miller himself in *Death of a Salesman*), I agree that expressionism is well adapted to emphasize social ideas or forces. More obviously symbolic than realism, more "theatrical" in that it does not seek primarily to produce an illusion of reality, expressionism forces the audience into a more intellectual or objective attitude.

However, such objectivity does not, I believe, provide a strong medium for tragedy. While he is involved in society, the individual must be the hero and the victim of tragedy. Oedipus and Hamlet and Lear are in part symbolic, but more important, they are multi-dimensional, fully realized personalities. They "come alive," as they must do to provide the emotional involvement necessary for the tragic reaction. (pp. 260-61)

Through the continual intervention of the Stage Manager, Wilder never allows his audience to forget that it is witnessing a symbolic presentation. But no one can feel about a town as he does about a person. Insofar as he focuses on his people, Wilder involves his audience with them emotionally as well as intellectually; but it is not a strong, complex involvement. Emily is simple and superficial; she typifies the sweet, innocent girl who progresses normally through adolescent awakening into courtship, marriage, and early death in childbirth. The sketchiest comparison with Oedipus, Electra, Medea, Hamlet, Lear, or for that matter Willy Loman of *Death of a Salesman,* Blanche of *A Streetcar Named Desire,* or Mio of *Winterset,* shows how far she falls short. The tragic protagonist, fully realized as an individual, is involved from beginning to end in an impossible struggle with fate, circumstance, or society, with his antagonists, himself, and death—doomed to failure but perhaps finding or projecting, after immense suffering, a kind of reconciliation or enlightenment. To him, what must be, cannot be; what cannot be, must be. Emily does not struggle; things merely happen to her. Her fate is the common one, and it evokes a gentle sadness. She is pathetic, not tragic.

Is Emily ennobled, and the audience or reader "elevated," by her understanding of "how wonderful life is"? What she as a character understands mainly, it seems to me, and this only after death, is that the living are ignorant and troubled and that life is short and sad. She is made to say, "Oh, earth, you're too wonderful for anybody to realize you. Do any human beings ever realize life while they live it?" Perhaps this is true, but it is hardly either profound or elevating. (Indeed, one might suppose that there are people who understand, while still living, something about the nature of life; evidently Wilder himself does.) True, in the play as a whole Wilder apparently wishes to illustrate the paradoxical nature of life: persistent and wonderful as well as short and troubled. But again, the context chosen, and therefore the effect produced, is not that of tragedy; it is, rather, that of gentle nostalgia or, to put it another way, sentimental romanticism.

The assertion that ***Our Town*** is of the romantic *genre* is defensible on several counts. One notes that Wilder chooses fantasy in Act Three to convey the full measure of his meaning, basing his presentation on the romantic assumption that there is an existence after death. What other play highly regarded as tragic, of the past or contemporary, calls on such fantasy? Tragedy shows the agonies of its people in this life, draws its meaning and its catharsis from experience in the here and now.

Further, the picture of small town or village life—again, ***Our Town***'s theme and chief preoccupation—owes much to the nineteenth-century American sentimental myth of the beautiful people of the beautiful village, a myth scotched once for all, one would have thought, by the likes of Edgar Watson Howe, Harold Frederic, Edgar Lee Masters, Sinclair Lewis, Sherwood Anderson, William Faulkner. Significantly, Wilder chooses the pre-World War I decade for his time, a simpler, more peaceful era, one that can be seen by an American audience through a nostalgic haze evoked by memories (or illusions) of "the good old days in the old home town." The picture of Grover's Corners and its people is highly selective: omitted are mean, sordid, cruel, generally unpleasant details. (pp. 261-62)

What we have here, then, is substitution of secluded garden for world. (In contrast, Shakespeare has Mercutio outside the garden cracking bawdy jokes about girls at the same time that Romeo and Juliet are making ecstatic love.) It is true that Wilder takes pains to establish Grover's Corners as part of the universe, or "the mind of God," as he puts it. The town, he seems to be saying, is integral with a process which is permanent, orderly, and good. Assuredly the play is a statement of faith in man. . . .

This is the view of romantic naturalism: with Newtonian and Cartesian rationalism as distant base, strained through the idealistic sensibilities of Rousseau, Kant, Wordsworth, Carlyle, Emerson, Whitman, and sentimentalized by the Victorians. . . . By suggesting this idea, ***Our Town*** acquires depth and dimension; but it is not thereby raised to the status of tragedy. The universe includes Grover's Corners, but Grover's Corners does not include the universe. That is to say, the reading of life here is heavily weighted with sentimental optimism; ***Our Town*** ignores a complex of knowledge revealed to us through experience, reason, and science.

The affirmations of tragedy, its statement of faith in man's strength and courage, are not like the bland assurance of this play. Tragedy is stern, beyond tears. Man endures in spite of capricious, incredible and unendurable fate or circumstance; in spite of guilt and weakness; in spite of enormous, soul-shattering pain. In his dilemma the tragic protagonist understands little or nothing about the forces which are destroying him—until, perhaps, a glimmer of light appears as he faces death; yet he is defiant or at least stoical. (p. 263)

In questioning the claim that ***Our Town*** is tragedy of a high order I do not, as I have said, wish to deny that it has considerable interest and value. Certainly it has been popular. Professor Ballet is worried that it may be ignored merely because it *is* popular, and he is concerned to account for the popularity, for the "tragic complexities" of the play do not explain its affectionate appeal. This, he believes, rests on the picture of familiar daily life, showing "the homely verities of human existence." He implies, though he does not directly say so, that the play gives us an idealized version of life: "If ***Our Town*** does not reflect life as it really is, at least it suggests what the daily life should be like, and the audience approves."

This is perceptive: ***Our Town*** is popular, in part at least, because it is not tragic. The American public has approved of it because of its charming, folksy presentation of simple, "good" people, its sentimentally idealized account of the small town. It projects a vision of a time and place which have vanished from the American scene, which never existed in fact—not just as shown in the play, at any rate—but which some people believe or like to think existed. So they view this symbolic picture of Grover's Corners through a mist of gentle, romantic nostalgia. Further, the optimistic assurance that this town has an enduring place in an orderly, meaningful universe, plus the statement of faith in man, carries strong appeal. In addition, the "truths" about life discovered by Emily and the others—that the living are blind, troubled, etc., are just such observations as would impress the average audience. Emily's pathetic death, popularly mistaken for tragedy, is evocative of tender feelings of pity. And finally, the expressionist technique, unusual or unfamiliar to many, adds an extra fillip of interest. It is not difficult to account for the play's popularity.

Within the limits of its purpose, subject, and form, certainly ***Our Town*** is a valuable contribution to the drama and culture of the United States. It is indeed worthy of respect and praise. However, I do not believe it is at present established as the greatest American play, and certainly it is not, in my opinion, a play which ranks with the great tragedies—not, in fact, a tragedy at all. (p. 264)

George D. Stephens, "'Our Town'—Great American Tragedy?" in Modern Drama, *Vol. 1, No. 4, February, 1959, pp. 258-64.*

R. H. GARDNER

For proof that drama *can* be written outside the socio-psychological frame and remain faithful to the character of the modern world, we have only to turn to Thornton Wilder. In its reflection of the collective life of a typical American community of the thirties, ***Our Town*** is certainly sociological; yet it does not take the formulistic sociological approach, but treats its group relationships in a framework that, stressing the over-all mystery of human existence, is essentially tragic.

Conditioned as we are to regard heroism with suspicion on the contemporary stage, we are inclined to overlook the fact that it does exist in contemporary life. It can, in fact, be discerned in the day-by-day struggles of people simply to carry on. Despite the human condition, despite the threat of nuclear annihilation, despite economic want and the unsatisfactory nature of their jobs, they keep going, doing the work that must be done, providing for their families to the best of their abilities, contributing wherever possible to the general good and exhibiting, in spite of all the pain and disappointment involved, a remarkable consideration and compassion for others. Physically, life is but a gradual process of dying; yet, knowing this, they do not surrender or, like the dramatic heroes of the socio-psychological frame, spend their time beating their breasts over the unfairness of it all. They *persevere*—and, in doing so, display a valor no less glorious than that of the tragic hero, whose mighty deeds on the stage would hold no significance for us were they not reflections on a grand scale of this smaller, but equally valiant, struggle going on every day in the real world.

It is with this struggle that Mr. Wilder concerns himself—at times most effectively. The only thing that prevents ***Our Town*** from being a great modern tragedy is the absence of a personalized hero. The characters, unfortunately, are types, and the same is true of that wonderfully satiric tribute to the human race, ***The Skin of Our Teeth.*** In both plays Mr. Wilder chose to depict man in the universal, rather than individual, sense—although Shakespeare demonstrated more than 350 years ago that we respond with deeper emotion to man, the universal, through sympathy for man, the individual. This is not to imply that Mr. Wilder deserves anything less than our profound admiration; for, with his unconventional staging and unshakable faith in and affection for humanity, he represents one contemporary dramatist who has continually and determinedly resisted the tyranny of naturalism. He may not be the most spectacular playwright of his day, but he is, to my mind, one of the most satisfying. (pp. 104-06)

R. H. Gardner, "Sickness on Broadway," in his The Splintered Stage: The Decline of the American Theater, *Macmillan Publishing Company, 1965, pp. 97-108.**

EDITH OLIVER

[In **"Our Town"** Wilder] accomplished everything he set out to do by appearing, in each instance, to be doing its opposite. He achieved what the seminars now call "alienation of the audience" not by devious, gleeful pranks but by creating believable, touching characters—among them the Stage Manager, who functions as intermediary between the other characters and the audience—and by being utterly candid. (The Stage Manager says, "So I'm going to have a copy of this play put in the cornerstone and the people a thousand years from now'll know a few simple facts about us.") He achieved universality by being specific about places and times, and achieved depth and sophistication by dealing with the details of daily living and the feelings of people so plain that they can foolishly be mistaken for "folksy." He also achieved poetry by ways of the clearest prose, complexity by apparent simplicity, and art by apparent artlessness. These considerations aside, **"Our Town"** is a play one can love.

Edith Oliver, "Forty-Five Minutes from Off Broadway," in The New Yorker, *Vol. XLIV, No. 33, October 5, 1968, p. 98.*

BRENDAN GILL

[**"Our Town"**] is much darker and stranger than it appears to be at first glance, and . . . the strength of its popular appeal is, at bottom, fairly mysterious. On the surface, we are confronted with the conventional rueful pieties about a lost American past in which men in small towns, burning with no notable ambitions, lived in tune with nature and their neighbors. We are also confronted with the conventional pieties about life everywhere that people are born and grow up and fall in love and marry and bear children and die, and not only does life break off too soon but we fail to live it from moment to moment with the intensity that it deserves. Acted out on a bleak stage that is itself a symbol of bearing true witness, these national and universal pieties cause us to shake our heads over the tears in things; in doing so, we are likely to ignore the drift of Mr. Wilder's dramatic argument, which is not that death is bad because it terminates life but that it is bad because it terminates nothing; it is a mere punctuation mark by which we enter into a new but fundamentally unchanged set of relations, charged with a horror that life at its worst mercifully spares us—the horror of continuing forever. Life in **"Our Town"** has the bittersweetness of a failed opportunity, death in **"Our Town"** is a nightmare of passive awareness felt through all eternity. One thinks of Housman's "Life, to be sure, is nothing much to lose, But young men think it is, and we were young." Housman's position is downright sunny compared to Mr. Wilder's. The dead in their graves in Grover's Corners have not been extinguished; to the dreadfulness of their being dead is added the knowledge that they are dead and that no word or gesture can prevail against their condition. Mr. Wilder's style is so cordial, so determinedly charming, that we tend to nod and smile and not listen to what he is telling us. Perhaps this is why so many audiences respond to **"Our Town"** as if it were a sentimental valentine. For all his compulsive winsomeness, Mr. Wilder is a pessimist as cold and tough as they come, and it must amuse him that millions of people have been made to feel all warm and cozy by his works.

Brendan Gill, "Beyond the Grave," in The New Yorker, *Vol. XLV, No. 42, December 6, 1969, p. 166.*

HAROLD CLURMAN

[***Our Town***] is part of an American dream, a memorial to the myth of the sweet past in rural America. It strums a string—rather slack now—of our national culture. Its optimistic view of life is a sugary Platonic distillation of what we imagine we once were, what we yearn to believe we still "in our hearts" might be. Thornton Wilder is a tactful craftsman: he found the right form for his content. His is a feathery touch; he doesn't *push*. Hence the play's endurance.

Harold Clurman, in a review of "Our Town," in The Nation, *Vol. 209, No. 21, December 15, 1969, p. 676.*

JACK RICHARDSON

Ah, innocence! What would we Americans have for a subject without it? What could we claim as the spine of our literary history if we didn't have, as a ubiquitous protagonist, an innocence which we can send abroad or dedicate an age to; an innocence we can never go home to again; an innocence that, in our minds, we can summon forth perpetually to be soiled and beaten down by the crudities of experience; but an innocence, finally, which will never be completely obliterated from our memory. . . . [In] the more complex expressions of our culture, we keep to the notion of the synonymy of innocence and life—not, to be sure, the hard, perverted, artificially categorized life of society, but life as a direct, invigorating force that is perceived only by instinct and unalloyed wonder. . . . However, there is one thing that innocence, by definition, cannot do: it cannot feign. As soon as we feel that some calculation, some artful choice has gone into its presentation, we are entitled to cry fraud, to haul out sophisticated pejoratives, and to prefer our exhausting and often stultifying complexities to the arrogance of one who hopes to curry favor by concocting what he thinks we want in the way of hope, a new start, or a fresh dramatic guilelessness. (p. 20)

A good deal of time has passed since . . . [***Our Town*** first appeared—and its] stylistic peculiarities now seem quite mild-mannered and cautious compared with what has come out of the Theater of the Absurd, the Theater of Cruelty, Total Theater, and all the other momentary theoretical justifications for critical categories. It is much easier today to see their substance, and to assess both the dangers and strengths in this cultural tradition of innocence as a goal and a memory.

The danger lies in a work like ***Our Town,*** a work which sets out to beguile us with our innocence but which never comes closer than a Madison Avenue Americana shop to the heart of this quality. Grover's Corners, that little piece of national whimsy tucked somewhere away in New Hampshire, is so manifestly a labored fabrication, a dramatic set-up for Wilder's secondhand notions of time, death, and the universe that one can only feel a glaring and laughable incongruity when they collide, as though Walter Pater had spent an evening delivering a solemn lecture on the faults and virtues of a Norman Rockwell magazine cover. It is no wonder that to move the play along through the rhythms of life, Wilder had to come up with the obtrusive and omnipotent character of the stage manager, the homespun *raisonneur* who continually reminds us that the banality we're witnessing has links with ourselves and greater forces of existence; and it is no wonder, too, that we never believe him, never, for all his references to folks, hitching posts, graveyards, and churches feel that anything is being called to mind except a device, an embellished exhortation to put the events on stage on a level of significance that they could never reach unattended. I have said that innocence cannot feign, and ***Our Town*** is a perfect embodiment of what can happen when innocence is used simply as an assumption, an obligatory signal for our nostalgia and good feelings. It is not just that one feels that the world of Grover's Corners has no passion or reality to it, it is also that one is more than a little outraged at the presumption that, having given us this spurious version of our past, Wilder, at the end of his play, has the bad grace to pity it for not being more intense, for not seizing more of life while it had the chance, for not having both a Pascalian wonder at the infinities of life and a Rabelaisian gusto for each of its moments, moments which, the stage manager reminds us after each intermission, have, in clumps of years, vanished into oblivion. One can only agree with Wilder's conclusions about the people of Grover's Corners, but one is aware that it was his bad art that got them into their sweet, benighted state in the first place. Wilder wants an awed recognition and value for the small acts of life, acts which he is continually threatening with cosmic extinction, but he makes no real, dramatic case for the specialness he seeks to find in them, and at the end of his work one feels that he has presented his audience with an illustrated, perfunctory lecture on how to get more out of its pleasant but ordinary existence. As a member of that audience, I could only answer him that neither I nor anyone else has ever been *that* ordinary, and that innocence, even in small-town America, was never *that* stultifyingly pleasant. (p. 22)

Jack Richardson, "Innocence Restaged," in Commentary, *Vol. 49, No. 3, March, 1970, pp. 20, 22, 24.**

TOM SCANLAN

A novelist as well as a playwright, Wilder seems in the main to have reserved the family subject matter for his plays. This tendency helps underline the fact that American drama is domestic drama. But Wilder's contribution is singular, and where, exactly, he is to be located within our drama becomes a nice question. Simple chronology does not help. Wilder's important plays date from the late 1930s and early 1940s, but he is no more a part of that generation of playwrights than any other. In some ways he belongs to an earlier period in that his career as a writer began in the mid-1920s. His innovative theatrical style, worked out in the early 1930s, anticipated but did not directly influence the new forms of the 1960s. The combination of Wilder's break with realism, his hold on the family subject, his vision of it as a source of strength, and his artistic achievement puts him in a special category. Wilder's relationship to our generations of playwrights is best seen, perhaps, as the alternate response of American drama to the changing family system. His few, accomplished plays show other directions which our dramatists might take, but do not, even within the very terms of their obsession with family conflict. His example emphasizes our reiteration of the drama of family failure. (p. 201)

For Wilder the family experience is at the center of what is both common and missed in life. In ***Our Town*** . . . , it is the core of the everyday rhythms of life in Grover's Corners, New Hampshire. Wilder builds a picture of the town through a complex development and extension of the techniques he worked out in his experimental one-act plays. The result is a play which has become synonymous with the sweetness of everyday life but not, unfortunately, with Wilder's painful corollary, that we inevitably miss that sweetness. The fault is partly Wilder's and partly that of a public in search of a nostalgic escape. . . . (p. 202)

In ***Our Town*** the events are unspectacular and low-keyed. We watch the daily habits and routines of two families. . . . The characters are allowed to show their desires, frustrations, and contentments just enough to establish the fact of their inner lives, at which point the Stage Manager moves us on to the next episode. The ordinary life of family, friends, and work is celebrated as part of a larger process that is fundamentally sound. The very mundane quality of this life is to provide us with a sense of snug containment by the overall life process.

It is at this point that ***Our Town*** might seem to deserve its fate of innumerable sentimental productions. Wilder runs such a risk, especially in the first two acts, and only barely saves himself through the hinting quips of the Stage Manager. The special perspective he wants us to experience as we view the play does have more to it than nostalgia for a cosmically secure routine, however. We see that time moves very quickly in the world of the play. It is much more fleeting than the characters realize. This fact is a bitter one as the Stage Manager well knows, and his awareness peeks out in laconic comments. The reality beneath appearance is indicated in a single word or phrase. Again and again he adds to his speeches on the nature of life a final remark which startles us with its dark quality. "All that education for nothing;" "It's what they call a vicious circle;" "Once in a thousand times it's interesting." The Stage Manager does not sneer nor does he devalue ordinary domestic life. In such lines he gives us something stronger than cynicism, the blank truth; and invites us to accept it.

These hints suggest that the simplest matters of life have rich implications. In ***The Happy Journey to Camden and Trenton*** Wilder used one line of painful isolation to force us to re-evaluate the pleasant family idyll which precedes it. In ***Our Town*** he uses the entire third act. We see life from the point of view of the dead and watch Emily, who has just died in childbirth, relive one chosen day, her twelfth birthday. The wonder and beauty of its routines soon turn to pain, however, for the deeper meaning of Emily's experience is that she was not able to grasp her life at the time. She sees how isolated, lonely, and cut off she was from the family and from the very act of living. (pp. 203-04)

Knowing that we miss life's goodness—which is not the same as saying that life is good—is the point of the play's structure. We sentimentalize the past because we did not fully live it; and we never will. The play celebrates the common things of life not as occasions for nostalgia, which would be to claim easy knowledge of them, but because they are life, what our lives are made of, and they are the part we will never know in our lives. We see this only when, like Emily, we are graced with perspective. The Stage Manager and Emily give us a way to go beyond our initial sense of simple goodness.

> EMILY: Do any human beings ever realize life while they live it?—Every, every minute?
> STAGE MANAGER: No. *(Pause)* The saints and poets, maybe—they do.

The Stage Manager gives us the blank truth again in his simple "no." Perhaps in art and religion some heightened awareness is possible. But then it is only temporary and, at least in the case of art, indirect. We are aware of Emily's loss while we are in the theater; we will forget our own when we leave.

The play ends with an affirmation of faith which is comforting but vague. Since the dead know the truth about life's inadequacy, their serenity must indicate other knowledge as well, truths which are also unknown to us. After Simon Stimson's outburst, a bitter denunciation of life which reminds us that the warm rhythms of Grover's Corners did not soothe him, Mrs. Webb turns our attention elsewhere, away from the human predicament and toward the stars. She does not deny the truth of what Simon has said, only that it is the whole truth. There is something in addition to the pain that drove him to suicide and that is represented by the star. It may be a figure for the life process itself, an essence separate from the accidents of particular lives. Earlier, the Stage Manager remarked: "There's something way down deep that's eternal in every human being." In any case we are left with the predicament of our lives and the Stage Manager closes the play with a joke on that subject.

In ***Our Town*** the family represents the quintessence of our human difficulty. It is the center of the daily life in the play and each act is devoted more fully to it. It is to her family that Emily chooses to return in Act Three. Here, if anywhere, we should be able to see life and here, especially, we miss it. The pain of what is missed within *that* warm circle is especially shocking to Emily and so more vivid to us. Yet ***Our Town*** is about the family only in a certain way and up to a point. The Stage Manager always breaks in before any separate dramatic existence is established for the Gibbses and the Webbs. The montage of short episodes gives us a panorama in which we see the family imbedded in the community, its outlines clear but its inner workings only suggested. (pp. 204-05)

Tom Scanlan, "The Family World of American Drama," in his Family, Drama, and American Dreams, *Greenwood Press, 1978, pp. 180-217.**

TIME

It is relatively easy to reduce ***Our Town*** to geography, a homey, nostalgic pinpoint on a turn-of-the-century New Hampshire map called Grover's Corners. The surface of the play alone will always be strong enough to sustain it. The more hazardous and rewarding task is to pursue Wilder's deeper intention of making Grover's Corners a metaphor, a sort of way station in the multimillennial aspiration and continuity of the human race. Wilder saw living and loving and dying as stages of almost mystical illumination. (p. 74)

[Wilder] couched what was most serious to him in playful hints. Take the letter addressed to a resident of the town: "Jane Crofut; The Crofut Farm; Grover's Corners; Sutton County; New Hampshire; United States of America; Continent of North America; Western Hemisphere; the Earth; the Solar System; the Universe; the Mind of God." The line never fails to draw a laugh, but Wilder has off-handedly revealed his grand design. The humblest soul on earth dwells in the mind of God. In the Stage Manager, who serves as Wilder's God surrogate, the playwright gives us a clue as to what that mind might be like. The narrator speaks in all three tenses; he is omniscient. Less than ten minutes after the play begins, a boy comes tossing newspapers onto porches. The Stage Manager knows that that boy will graduate at the top of his class at M.I.T. with a brilliantly promising career as an engineer and will die in France in World War I. "All that education for nothing," he concludes. In short, man is an unwitting instrument of destiny.

Throughout ***Our Town,*** Wilder celebrates the wonder of nature, the beauty of the commonplace and the abiding serenity of simple rituals. Why, then, do men and women take life for granted and fritter away the most precious commodity they possess? Wilder's answer comes [in Act III, where Emily returns] from the graveyard to relive her twelfth birthday. She is enraptured by the moment-to-moment joy of existence and baffled that her mother is blind to it. She pleads with her: "Just for a moment now we're all together. Mama, just for a moment we're happy. *Let's look at one another.*" Wilder seems to be telling us that love is the highest form of vision. That which and those whom we do not love, we do not see. (pp. 74-5)

A review of "Our Town," in Time, *Vol. 118, No. 4, July 27, 1981, pp. 74-5.*

Tom Wolfe

1931-

(Born Thomas Kennerly Wolfe, Jr.) American essayist, journalist, editor, critic, and novelist.

© 1985 Thomas Victor

One of the most original stylists in contemporary literature, Wolfe was instrumental in developing New Journalism, a type of expository writing that blends reporting with such fictional techniques as stream-of-consciousness, extended dialogue, shifting points of view, and detailed scene-setting. Wolfe's witty and informative examinations of various trends in American popular culture have solidified his reputation as an influential social commentator. Among the topics he has examined are the drug scene in California, American art and architecture, and the astronauts of the American space program. The originality of his writing is evidenced in the phrases he has added to the American vocabulary, including "the happiness explosion" for the hippie movement of the 1960s and "the me decade" for the narcissistic pursuit of self-fulfillment during the 1970s. Wolfe's choice of subject matter, his unorthodox style, and his bold opinions have often created controversy.

After graduating from Yale University in 1957 with a doctorate in American Studies, Wolfe worked as a reporter for the *Springfield Union* and the *Washington Post.* He later became a feature writer for the *New York Herald Tribune*'s Sunday supplement, which became *New York* magazine. Encouraged by his editor to go beyond the traditional boundaries of objective reporting and to use a more creative flair in his work, Wolfe began to experiment with language; street slang, obscure technical terms, and eccentric punctuation were incorporated into the feature articles he wrote. He achieved local acclaim for his stories about New York socialites and mafia figures.

In 1963 Wolfe covered a customized car and hot rod show for *Esquire* magazine. Although he spent weeks researching his story, Wolfe experienced problems meeting his deadline because he found the usual journalistic techniques inadequate to evoke the frenzied, garish world of hot rods and the people who create them. Byron Dobell, Wolfe's editor at *Esquire,* advised him to type his notes so that someone else could write the article. However, Wolfe's notes were published unedited. Along with factual details, the notes included random thoughts and feelings, sensory perceptions, and verbatim dialogue. The resulting article, "There Goes (Varoom! Varoom!) That Kandy Kolored Tangerine-Flake Baby," focused national attention on Wolfe's style, which came to be known as New Journalism. Although other writers have used this technique in their work, among them Norman Mailer and Hunter S. Thompson, Wolfe is credited with introducing New Journalism to the general public and is regarded as its most flamboyant practitioner.

Wolfe based much of his early work on the class of Americans who gained affluence after World War II. He felt that these people, whom he refers to as "proles," were ignored by the literary and intellectual establishment. Wolfe contended that the "proles" had created alternative lifestyles that purposely deviated from societal standards yet were influential in American culture. In his first collection of essays, *The Kandy-Kolored Tangerine-Flake Streamline Baby* (1965), Wolfe examines these lifestyles, focusing on popular culture and its celebrities. Although Dwight MacDonald termed Wolfe's style "parajournalism" and dismissed it as a fad, most critics contended that the book contained innovative studies of popular trends. In *The Pump House Gang* (1968), Wolfe further discussed the prominent subcultures of southern California, London, and New York City. Most critics praised the book and considered Wolfe's portrait of *Playboy* magazine founder Hugh Hefner as "the ultimate societal dropout" the essay that best represents Wolfe's theory of class structure and America's obsession with status.

The Electric Kool-Aid Acid Test (1968) is considered by many the definitive portrait of the drug culture of the early 1960s. Based on extended interviews and personal experience, the book tells the story of author Ken Kesey and the Merry Pranksters, a group of young people who attempted to introduce American society to the liberating power of hallucinogenic drugs. The Merry Pranksters gained notoriety in California for their "acid tests," street parties at which they served beverages laced with LSD to unsuspecting people. Wolfe delves into the social mechanisms of the group, observing its fanatic loyalty to Kesey and comparing it with ancient religious cults. C.D.B. Bryan faulted Wolfe for not passing judgment on Kesey, particularly the manner in which Kesey "[played] God with people's minds," yet praised *The Electric Kool-Aid Acid Test*

as a "celebration of psychedelia, of all its sounds and costumes, colors and fantasies."

Another of Wolfe's books, *Radical Chic and Mau-Mauing the Flak Catchers* (1970), consists of two controversial essays that examine extremist politics and the naiveté of liberals. "Those Radical Chic Evenings" is a satirical sketch of a fund-raising party for the Black Panthers given by composer Leonard Bernstein. Struck by the paradox of the scene, Wolfe characterizes the Panthers as posturing comics and pokes fun at the rich white liberals "nibbling caviar while signing checks for the revolution with their free hand." In "Mau-Mauing the Flak Catchers," Wolfe describes how some urban blacks pretend to be racial militants in order to intimidate the bureaucrats of government social programs. The book generated much debate: some felt that it degraded the integrity of the black power movement and charged Wolfe with biased reporting, while others lauded the book as a frank critique of liberalism. Two other controversial books, *The Painted Word* (1975) and *From Bauhaus to Our House* (1981), impugn the art world of New York and the architectural establishment, respectively.

Wolfe's most widely accepted work, *The Right Stuff* (1979), which won an American Book Award and a National Book Critics Circle Award, portrays the early years of the American space program. Wolfe was especially commended for his thorough research and for his treatment of the astronauts as individual human beings, in contrast to the generally accepted image of astronauts as one-dimensional, mystical figures. Wolfe used the concept of "the right stuff" as an organizing theme, stating that it consists in part of "stamina, guts, fast neural synapses and old-fashioned hell raising." *The Right Stuff* was adapted for film in 1983.

Wolfe published several of his most representative pieces in *The Purple Decades: A Reader* (1982). His first novel, *The Bonfire of the Vanities,* is meant to be "a *Vanity Fair* book about New York, à la Thackeray," according to Wolfe. It was serialized in *Rolling Stone* magazine during 1984 and 1985.

(See also *CLC,* Vols. 1, 2, 9, 15; *Contemporary Authors,* Vols. 13-16, rev. ed.; and *Contemporary Authors New Revision Series,* Vol. 9.)

KURT VONNEGUT, JR.

Note to the people of Medicine Hat, Alberta, who may not know it: Tom Wolfe is the most exciting—or, at least, the most jangling—journalist to appear in some time. . . . Everybody talks about him. He is no shrinking violet, neither is he a gentleman. He *is* a superb reporter who hates the East and the looks of old people. He is a dandy and a reverse snob.

The temptation when reviewing his works, of course, is to imitate him cunningly. Holy animals! Sebaceous sleepers! Oxymorons and serpentae carminae! Tabescent! Infarcted! Stretchpants netherworld! Schlock! A parodist might get the words right, but never the bitchy melody. Interestingly: the most tender piece in [**"The Kandy-Kolored Tangerine-Flake Streamline Baby"**] depends upon a poem by Kipling for depth, and has G. Huntington Hartford 2d., for its hero. . . .

Wolfe comes on like a barbarian (as Mark Twain did), like a sixth Beatle (Murray the K being the fifth), but he is entitled to call himself "Doctor Wolfe," if he wants to. He has a Ph.D. in American studies from Yale, and he knows everything. I do not mean he *thinks* he knows everything. . . . [He] keeps picking up brand new, ultra-contemporary stuff that nobody else knows and arrives at zonky conclusions couched in scholarly terms. . . .

He is also loaded with facile junk, as all personal journalists have to be—otherwise, how can they write so amusingly and fast? His language is admired, but a Wolfe chrestomathy would drive one nuts with repetitions, with glissandi and tin drummings that don't help much. (p. 4)

Then again, America is *like* that. And maybe the only sort of person who can tell us the truth about it any more *is* a Ph.D. who barks and struts himself like Murray the K, the most offensive of all disk jockeys, while feeding us information. Advanced persons in religion have been trying this approach for some time. Who can complain if journalists follow? (pp. 4, 38)

Verdict: Excellent book by a genius who will do anything to get attention. (p. 38)

Kurt Vonnegut, Jr., "Infarcted! Tabescent!" in The New York Times Book Review, *June 27, 1965, pp. 4, 38.*

JOSEPH EPSTEIN

When the dust finally settles, when Norman Mailer grows quite as white-maned and tame as Carl Sandburg, when *The New Yorker* ceases to print stories by Indian women about their quiet, subtle little adventures in the menstrual huts of Bombay, Mr. Tom (no relation) Wolfe will have achieved for himself a special footnote in the literary history of our time for recording the following line [in ***The Kandy-Kolored Tangerine-Flake Streamline Baby***]:

"Eeeeeeeeeeeeeeeeeeeeeee"

Is this the authentic sound of modern man when, as Saul Bellow says, "night comes and he feels like howling from his window like a wolf"? Is it, quite literally, an existential groan? Does it in any way at all speak to the human condition? Not exactly. It is, in fact, the noise that issues from the throat of a certain young woman named Baby Jane Holzer as she responds to the music of the Rolling Stones. . . .

Baby Jane Holzer, the Rolling Stones, Cassius Clay, Customized Cars, Disc Jockeys, Demolition Derbies, Huntington Hartford, Las Vegas, Stock-Car Racing—these are some of the subjects of . . . ***The Kandy-Kolored Tangerine-Flake Streamline Baby,*** a title which, if set to the appropriate music, should serve admirably as the entire lyric of a popular song. Although he has also written estimable hatchet jobs on Norman Mailer and on *The New Yorker,* these presumably are little more than side interests. . . . Wolfe's real beat is the American freakshow: the teenage netherworld, lower-class sports, and the poor rich.

Wolfe can get pretty exotic himself. . . . As a titlist of flamboyance he is without peer in the Western world. His prose style is normally shotgun baroque, sometimes edging over into machine-gun rococo, as in his article on Las Vegas, which begins by repeating the word "hernia" fifty-seven times. . . . Wolfe is perhaps most fatiguing when writing about the lower classes. Here he becomes Dr. Wolfe, Department of American Studies, and what he finds attractive about the lower orders, as has many an intellectual slummer before him, is their vitality. At bottom, what is involved here is worship of the Noble Savage. (Wary of precisely this sort of worship, George Orwell once reminded the members of the Left-Wing Book Club that one thing they ought to keep in mind about the lower classes is that they smell.) (pp. 27-8)

Wolfe never gets quite so naked about it, but he too can strike a note of supreme reverse condescension.

One of his best methods for doing so is to put [his] doctorate to work. In an essay on customized cars and their designers, for example, he writes: "If you study the works of Barris or Cushenberry . . . or Ed Roth or Darryl Starbird, can you beat that name?, I think you come up with a fragment of art history." There follows a discussion of customized cars in which Mondrian, Brancusi, Tiepolo, the Bauhaus Movement, Regency architecture, and the Apollonian and Dionysian life-style are hauled-in—all in the most casual manner, of course. The customized car designers are decidedly Dionysian, we learn, and Dr. Wolfe's own predilections run that way as well. But the great thing, you see, is that these poor slobs, these wonderful primitives tinkering away in a great tradition in their garages in L.A., have never even heard of Dionysus!

Wolfe is much better when he leaves the Noble Savages lie, and best of all when he writes about New York City. Here he drops his studied spontaneity, eases up on the rococo, slips his doctorate, and takes on the tone of the reasonably feeling New Yorker who has not yet been knocked insensate by the clatter of that city—the tone, that is, of exasperation. He believes Pavlov has more of value to say about New York than Freud. He himself can work up a ferocious hate for the place and, it seems to me, for all the right reasons. These are best put in an essay entitled "The Big League Complex." . . . (p. 28)

***The Kandy-Kolored** etc., etc.*, also includes eighteen of Wolfe's drawings in a section called Metropolitan Sketchbook. They are all caricatures of urban types, and some are extraordinarily good. . . . A few pages in this section are given over to teenage male hairdos. One, a combination of the flat top and the ducktail, is referred to as the "Chicago Boxcar." It seems worth pointing out that in Chicago this same hairdo is designated a "Detroit." (p. 29)

Joseph Epstein, "Rococo and Roll," in The New Republic, *Vol. 153, Nos. 4 & 5, July 24, 1965, pp. 27-9.*

DWIGHT MACDONALD

A new kind of journalism is being born, or spawned. It might be called "parajournalism," from the Greek *para,* "beside" or "against": something similar in form but different in function. As in parody, from the *parodia,* or counter-ode, the satyr play of Athenian drama that was performed after the tragedy by the same actors in grotesque costumes. Or paranoia ("against-beside thought") in which rational forms are used to express delusions. . . . [Parajournalism] is a bastard form, having it both ways, exploiting the factual authority of journalism and the atmospheric license of fiction. Entertainment rather than information is the aim of its producers, and the hope of its consumers.

Parajournalism has an ancestry, from Daniel Defoe, one of the fathers of modern journalism, whose *Journal of the Plague Year* was a hoax so convincingly circumstantial that it was long taken for a historical record, to the gossip columnists, sob sisters, fashion writers, and Hollywood reporters of this century. What is new is the pretension of our current parajournalists to be writing not hoaxes or publicity chitchat but the real thing; and the willingness of the public to accept this pretense. We convert everything into entertainment. . . .

[The] king of the [parajournalism] cats is, of course, Tom Wolfe. . . .

[***The Kandy-Kolored Tangerine-Flake Streamline Baby***] is amusing if one reads it the way it was written, hastily and loosely, skipping paragraphs, or pages, when the jazzed-up style and the mock-sociological pronouncements become oppressive. Since elaboration rather than development is Wolfe's forte, anything you miss will be repeated later, with bells on. (p. 3)

I don't think Wolfe will be read with pleasure, or at all, years from now, and perhaps not even next year, and for the same reason the reviewers, and the reading public, are so taken with his book now: because he has treated novel subjects . . . in a novel style. . . . But I predict the subjects will prove of ephemeral interest and that the style will not wear well because its eccentricities, while novel, are monotonous; those italics, dots, exclamation points, odd words like "infarcted" and expressions like *Santa Barranza!* already look a little tired. . . . As Mr. Knickerbocker writes, "There is no one as dead as last year's mannerist." (pp. 3-4)

It is hard to say just what Wolfe thinks . . . of the real people he writes about. He melts into them so topologically that he seems to be celebrating them, and yet there is a peculiar and rather unpleasant ambivalence, as in his piece on Mrs. Leonard ("Baby Jane") Holzer, a rich young matron with lots of blonde hair whom he says he made "The Girl of the Year," that is, last year, there's another one now. I'm willing to grant his claim, but his piece seems to alternate between building up Baby Jane and tearing her down, damning with loud praise, assenting with not-so-civil leer. As for his readers, flattered though they may be to be taken so intimately into his confidence, made free of the creative kitchen so to speak, they are in the same ambiguous position. "Bangs manes bouffants beehives Beatle caps butter faces brush-on lashes decal eyes puffy sweaters French thrust bras" one article begins, continuing for six more unpunctuated lines of similar arcana and if you don't dig them you're dead, baby. Every boost a knock. . . .

I think the vogue of Tom Wolfe may be explained by two *kultur*-neuroses common among adult, educated Americans today: a masochistic deference to the Young, who are also, by definition, new and so in; and a guilt-feeling about class—maybe they don't deserve their status, maybe they aren't so cultivated—that makes them feel insecure when a verbal young—well, youngish—type like Wolfe assures them the "proles," the *young* proles that is, have created a cultural style which they either had been uncultivated enough to think vulgar or, worse, hadn't even noticed. Especially when his spiel is on the highest level . . . , full of hard words like "ischium" and "panopticon" and heady concepts like "charisma" . . . and off-hand references to "high-status sports cars of the Apollonian sort" as against, you understand, "the Dionysian custom kind." (p. 4)

There are two kinds of appropriate subjects for parajournalism. The kind Tom Wolfe exploits in the present book is the world of the "celebs": prizefighters, gamblers, movie and stage "personalities," racing drivers, pop singers and their disc jockeys like Murray the K ("The Fifth Beatle"), impresarios like Phil Spector ("The First Tycoon of Teen") entrepreneurs like Robert Harrison (whose *Confidential* magazine, the classic *old* one (1952-1958) you understand, Wolfe salutes as "the most scandalous scandal magazine in the history of the world." . . . The other kind of suitable game for the parajournalist—though not Tom Wolfe's pigeon—is the Little Man (or Woman) who gets into trouble with the law; or who is interestingly poor or old or ill or, best, all three; or who has some other Little problem like delinquent children or a close relative who has been murdered for which they can count on Jimmy Breslin's heavy-breathing sympathy and prose.

Both celebs and uncelebs offer the same advantage: inaccuracy will have no serious consequences. The little people are unknown to the reader and, if they think they have been misrepresented, are in no position to do anything about it, nor, even if such a daring idea occurred to them, to object to the invasion of their privacy. The celebs are eager to have their privacy invaded, welcoming the attentions of the press for reasons of profession or of vanity. While the reader knows a great deal, too much, about them, this is not real knowledge because they are, in their public aspect, not real. They are not persons but *personae* ("artificial characters in a play or novel"—or in parajournalistic reportage) which have been manufactured for public consumption with their enthusiastic cooperation. Notions of truth or accuracy are irrelevant in such a context of collusive fabrication on both sides; all that matters to anybody—subject, writer, reader—is that it be a good story. To complain of Wolfe's Pindaric ode to Junior Johnson that his hero couldn't be all that heroic is like objecting to Tarzan as unbelievable. (pp. 4-5)

Dwight Macdonald, "Parajournalism, or Tom Wolfe & His Magic Writing Machine," in The New York Review of Books, *Vol. V, No. 2, August 26, 1965, pp. 3-5.*

KARL SHAPIRO

Writers play a game called Name the Generation. The Sixties are tough to pin down; we have nothing as clear cut as the Lost, the Silent, the Angry, the Beat, and must nominate such candidates as the Playpen Generation . . . , the Acid Generation . . . , the Probation Generation . . . , and even the First Atomic Generation. Some wag has theorized that all children born at the time of the first nuclear explosion and thereafter are psychological defectives, "seconds" so to speak. The idea is ridiculous but, then, it answers so many questions.

Of course, the Leaders of the Playpen-Acid-Probation-Atomic Generation are older and are therefore the Pied Pipers of the defectives. What the leaders have in mind is hard to fathom—it can't be Publicity! There are the Earnest Normans . . . ; the Hairy Gurus who have proved not only that East and West can meet but can make out; the Electronic Prophets such as M.M. (Marshall McLuhan) and K.K. (Ken Kesey); there are the Goody-Goodmans who dream of the Ecstatic Megalopolis where even Superspade will turn in his submachine gun for a peashooter. There are—hell, there are so many—Terrible Timothys who are dead set on zonking the universe out of its gourd. And of course a whole hagiography of saints and martyrs, posters of whom are for sale at any old psychedelic shop, along with their own news media which are styled Underground but which are always being hawked on the street somehow, not *really* underground.

Let us therefore pay homage to Tom Wolfe right off the bat. He has set all this down in permanent color. He has given us the finest mug shots of the *soi-disant* revolutionaries we shall see in a long time. He has pinned their little wriggling personae to the bulletin board for all to gape upon. He has performed the necessary acts of vilification with a superb aristocratic cool. He is a master of intonation and an extrapolator who can put to shame the regnant sociologists of guilt and hedonism. He has analyzed the general intellectual narcosis of the ______ Generation and described its life-style in all its blazing vacuity. He leaves no capital city unturned. His dramatis personae include the high and the mighty and the lowest of the low, but all in the same Movie, the movie of this schlocked-out generation. (pp. 1, 3)

The Pump House Gang cuts deeper into the blubber of the modern "revolutionary" psyche and discusses, in the words of the author, "ego extension, the politics of pleasure, the self-realization racket, the pharmacology of Overjoy . . ." The Pump House Gang is just a bunch of rich pubescents who cop out along the California coast with surfboards. They are the surferkinder, a sort of Hell's Angels of the seashore. So they have set up their own autonomous world and have the origins of a language, with such words as *mysterioso,* which refers to anything which is incomprehensible but *neat,* like the Pacific Ocean, for example. The top age limit of this sect is 25. . . .

The Dropout psychosis is of course international and *mysterioso*. Strategy-wise, however, it is quite simple. To drop out you just dis-identify, to coin an expression. You take every symbol of value, even a word, and give it its unintended and opposite meaning. Thus the word *rank,* which is supposed to mean rancid or disgusting as an adjective, takes on the meaning of *great, terrific*. *Rotten* means beautiful. As Tom Wolfe would say, "Hmnnnn." . . . After World War II, different sets of young men began the Dropout in different ways. There were the beats, the motorcycle gangs, the car nuts, the rock 'n' roll kids, the surfers, the hippies, and God knows what all. They devised new fashions, "*role* clothes, to symbolize their new life styles." Because they needed roles: Rebels, Swingers, Artists, Poets, Mystics, Tigers, Panthers, Monks; they needed to assert their separatism and, as Wolfe suggests, even their *divinity*. For there is always a cloud of incense over their zoo.

The centerpiece of the book is the essay on Marshall McLuhan, dangerously entitled "What If He Is Right?" Tom Wolfe is respectful about McLuhan's Theory, although unkind about its author. . . . M.M. is a traitor to the *book* itself; the Tube has replaced old Gutenberg; aural and tactile have replaced visual and linear. We gotta be tribal again, not just national; read Bergson on the central nervous system, and so forth. The electronic unification of mankind etc. McLuhan's is a big theory, though a little cheesy.

Nevertheless, McLuhan is the first and probably only intellectual who has provided TV, films, radio, telephone, computer and Xerox with a mystique and an anodyne for their much-advertised guilt. No wonder he is their god and culture hero. And not only theirs: the Pop cultists, the hippies, the surferkinder, if they could read. The medium is the message; and don't you forget it.

You take a few large plastic garbage cans and slosh them full of Kool-Aid; lace liberally with LSD; wire the party place for the loudest possible rock etc. and for strobes which bounce off all the Day-Glo posters, miniskirts, banners, graffiti, etc. You are ready for ***The Electric Kool-Aid Acid Test,*** published simultaneously with ***The Pump House Gang.***

The book is a full-scale study of the "acid" novelist Ken Kesey. . . .

[It] was Kesey who was one of the designers of the psychedelic style, the Life. If Marshall McLuhan is the Nietzsche of the New Consciousness, Kesey is its Thomas A. Edison. K.K. invented many of the gimmicks and grommets which turn on the Rebs and precipitate them out of this world. . . .

Kesey was chased all around the place, which includes Mexico naturally, for being a drug-fiend, "contributing," etc., and served a few months in California. He played the picaresque fugitive to the end, with style and verve and capital, and, according to the epilogue of the acid test book, is back home in his native Oregon readying himself for his next adventure into the missionary world.

There are interesting sidelights about the heads (and *heads* means acid-heads, for those that don't keep up with the literature). One is that K.K. and Terrible Timothy Leary didn't click. . . . It was like a falling-out of the Cosa Nostra. . . .

Tom Wolfe records the whole scene, and you are there. K.K. delivers the dismal gospel [at the end,] that *we all got to be heads without the acid,* and nobody likes that news. You mean we got to read books and stuff like that? But K.K. has a vision of the beautiful world with its beautiful people whom he has led through the doors of perception and from now on you're just going to drink your Kool-Aid straight!

Well, he didn't say it in precisely those words, but that is what the New Religion amounts to. Full circle sort of thing. Let's start over from the soda fountain.

Tom Wolfe is more than brilliant. . . . He is more than urbane, suave, trenchant and all those book review adjectives. He really understands his subjects, is really compassionate (when possible), really involved with what he says and is clearly responsible to his judgments. Tom Wolfe is a goddam joy. Also, not to insult him, he writes like a master. (p. 3)

Karl Shapiro, "Tom Wolfe: Analyst of the ______ Generation," in Book World—The Washington Post, *August 18, 1968, pp. 1, 3.*

C.D.B. BRYAN

Tom Wolfe's first book, **"The Kandy-Kolored Tangerine-Flake Streamline Baby"** was a success . . . , not so much because of *what* he said . . . , but *how* he said it. Wolfe's style of journalism was something new, entirely his own, as young and exuberant and frenzied as the period he was depicting.

He intimately knew and wrote about what was happening—not just now, but *NOW!,* with an explosion of asterisks, exclamation points, italics and puppyish enthusiasm. So what if occasionally he seemed almost to parody himself? . . .

Now, Tom Wolfe has published two books the same day. *Two books::::*

———heeeeeewack———

The same day!!!!! Too-o-o-o-o-o-o *freaking* MUCH!

"The Pump House Gang," like **"The Kandy-Kolored** etcetera," is a collection of short, intimately subjective pieces about publicity-seeking social climbers, California surfing entrepreneurs, motorcycle races, lonely London socialites and Eastern businessmen intimidated by the Not Our Class, Dear, Mafia. Wolfe's style is a little more subdued. He is a little older, and a lot more compassionate. There is still a lingering rhetorical "so what?" that one asks oneself after reading some of the pieces, simply because, no matter how fresh a treatment an unrefreshing subject is given, one still remains bored. Teenage California surfers are bores, really. Playboy's Hugh Hefner is a bore, really. The New York Hilton is a bore, really. Actress Natalie Wood is a—well, her taste in art is a bore, really. And yet, Tom Wolfe manages somehow to imbue them all with a semblance of life, no matter how depressing they may seem. . . .

Unfortunately, however, **"The Pump House Gang"** isn't really much more than a remake, a "Son of Kandy-Kolored." It's good enough, but not in the same league as **"The Electric Kool-Aid Acid Test,"** which is why I suppose he had it published on the same day, almost as if he, himself, looked upon it as a throwaway.

"The Electric Kool-Aid Acid Test" is an astonishing book. It is to the hippie movement what Norman Mailer's "The Armies of the Night" was to the Vietnam protest movement. (p. 1)

"The Electric Kool-Aid Acid Test" is a celebration of psychedelia, of all its sounds and costumes, colors and fantasies. Wolfe, like Mailer, participates instead of merely reporting. Wolfe, like Mailer, makes no pretense of being objective. And it is Wolfe's involvement, as it was Mailer's involvement, that makes his book so successful, just as (inexorably) such involvement created some flaws. At times, Wolfe seems to be as indiscriminate an observer as a wide-angle camera panning back and forth across crowded rooms. At times, he dollies in for closeups of characters or incidents whose significance is never determined. And at other times he piles elaboration upon elaboration until reality is buried under illusions of evaluation.

It is Wolfe's enthusiasm and literary fireworks that make it difficult for the reader to remain detached. He does not hesitate to tell us what to think, how to react, even what to wear as he wings us along with Ken Kesey and his band of Merry Pranksters in a brightly painted, Ampex-loaded cross-country bus. Or on a weekend romp with the Hell's Angels. Or at a successful taking-over and turning-on of a Unitarian church convention. Or into the unintended debacle Kesey's Pranksters made of a protest rally, before they went into hiding in Mexico. Wolfe has written a marvelous book about a man I suspect is not so marvelous; and my reservations about this book stem from my feeling that some of Kesey's dazzle-dust still lingers in Wolfe's eyes. . . .

Throughout **"The Electric Kool-Aid Acid Test,"** Wolfe refers to dropping acid as "the *experience*"; and no matter what one says pro or con LSD, it is a profound experience. And this, I think, is why Wolfe's book is so significant: it accurately and absolutely depicts the change that has occurred in the ethics of the American young, whose contemporary morality is based upon esthetic rather than social values. If it's *beautiful,* do it. The Protestant Ethic . . . is being replaced by the fundamental value of the immediate, direct experience, the Pleasure Now principle.

Drugs do provide the immediate, direct experience, the Instant Profundity, witness Kesey and his Merry Pranksters; *but* one finds it difficult to accept Kesey as a leader, mystic or otherwise, after he permitted the Electric Kool-Aid to be served at the Watts Acid Test, where many people drank it unaware the Kool-Aid was heavily laced with LSD. That's playing God with people's minds and nobody, *nobody* has the right to do that. If there ever was an opportunity for Wolfe to draw some objective conclusions about Kesey, that was the moment. Wolfe chose not to. He never looked back, but instead continued to describe the activities of the band of Merry Pranksters as if to suggest it was all in good fun. A lot of the book *is* good fun.

It is an astonishing, enlightening, at times baffling, and explosively funny book. (p. 2)

C.D.B. Bryan, "The Same Day: Heeeeeewack!!!" in The New York Times Book Review, *August 18, 1968, pp. 1-2.*

NEIL COMPTON

The Pump House Gang seems a sad sort of book, whether the author knows it or not. Most of its subjects are rather pathetic: the hair-obsessed Los Angeles teenagers endlessly cruising around the parking lot at Harvey's Drive-In; the La Jolla surfers, their intense but narrow pleasures doomed by inescapable adulthood; poor Carol Doda [the topless dancer with the silicone-inflated breasts], paying for the present glory of "them" with perpetual inconvenience, and the prospect of a prematurely flaccid and sagging bustline; Hefner protesting that he lives a "damned full life" inside his aridly luxurious super-Playboy pad. The feeling that the alleged Happiness Explosion is little more than a series of unsatisfying pops is heightened by the fact that this breathlessly *Now* book . . . , describes 1966 life styles—some of which seem already as quaint and remote as ancestral portraits.

Tom Wolfe practices the New Journalism—a mode of discourse which exploits the techniques of fiction in order to render fact more vividly. (Norman Mailer is the current master of this form.) Wolfe's standard device is indirect narration by a persona which, without quite ceasing to be the author himself, echoes the style, vocabulary, and values of his subjects. Everything depends upon getting the idiom right. Wolfe has a pretty good ear, but a steady read through ***The Pump House Gang*** reveals that he hasn't quite mastered all the scenes about which he writes so knowingly. His Londoners, New Yorkers, Ohioans, and Californians speak the same kind of Wolfese lingua franca: all of them—*buds* and *studs*—tend to be rank, freaking, raunchy and spastic, when they are not zonked or stoned out of their hulking gourds.

Wolfe is curious about his subjects, but has no real concern for them. They emerge as flat rather than round characters, each defined by one or two mannerisms. . . . The only three-dimensional figure is the author himself. We get a strong impression of him, with his hatred of literary intellectuals, his contempt for politics, his love of fashion and medical jargon, his outsider's obsession with inside stories, and his fetishistic lust for catalogues and minute descriptions. Above all, there is his horrified fascination with the sweating, excreting, decaying human body: topless waitresses' breasts dangling over the dinner plates in steamy restaurant kitchens, smelly armpits, old women with "veiny white ankles, which lead up like a cone to a fudge of edematous flesh," and old men adjusting "the aging waxy folds of their scrota"—these are the stuff of Tom Wolfe's bad dreams.

The Electric Kool-Aid Acid Test relates the saga of Ken Kesey and the Merry Pranksters. . . . This book helped me to understand some of the more sinister and puzzling habits of my teen-aged daughters in 1968. . . . ***Acid Test*** certainly deserves at least a minor place in the literature of American self-exploration—a little below *On the Road* (whose hero Dean Moriarty, in real life Neal Cassady, was one of the Pranksters), though infinitely beneath *Moby Dick* and *Huckleberry Finn*. (pp. 77-8)

Wolfe may be heartless and his prose style vicious (particularly in this book) but he is intelligent and perceptive. He detects the strain of authoritarianism and violence that lurks beneath Kesey's theoretically libertarian leadership (and is symbolized by the Pranksters' alliance with the fearsome Angels); and he draws some interesting parallels between this 20th-century community and primitive religious cults. However, he does not succeed in convincing us that the brief but hectic flourishing of the Merry Pranksters was part of any Happiness Explosion. (p. 78)

Neil Compton, "Hijinks Journalism," in Commentary, *Vol. 47, No. 2, February, 1969, pp. 76-8.*

RONALD WEBER

After his first book Dwight Macdonald dismissed Tom Wolfe as a fad, part and parcel of his famous girl-of-the-year piece on Baby Jane Holzer; there's nothing, Macdonald forecast, so dead as last year's mannerist [see excerpt above]. But Wolfe hasn't yet faded into the netherworld of yesterday's celebrities; with the exception of Mailer, no writer has more ambitiously sought the frazzled style of the time, and few writers have shown a defter skill in developing their territory, in continuing to work the optical scene while extending their range and keeping a surprisingly fresh touch. The point is that Tom Wolfe's work merits more than passing attention, and attention not so much directed to the dots-and-exclamation-points style or the self-proclaimed role as a founding father of the New Journalism but, less noticed, to his consistently shaped portrait of an assertive and mocking new sensiblity alive in a new America. (p. 71)

The starting point [of Wolfe's vision of modern America] is money, the massive infusion of money into every level of American society since World War II. One result of the new affluence—as Wolfe picks up the story in the early Sixties—was that lots of "lower class creeps" and "rancid people," flush with money for the first time in their lives, found themselves able to build monuments to their peculiar styles of life, styles that up to that time had been practically invisible in the society as a whole. They began pouring feverish attention and piles of money into such things as custom cars and rock music, stretch pants and decal eyes—and into Las Vegas. Las Vegas became the "super hyper-version" symbol of the new money dynamism in mass America, created by war money and by gangsters. . . . But Las Vegas still was just the symbol of a whole prole culture on the march, rising out of the vinyl deeps of invisibility and neglect, creating gaudy, free-form styles that most Americans considered vulgar and lower-class awful but that were charged with the genuine energy of the time.

The new prole styles, Wolfe argues, were not only worth recording in themselves but were significant because they influenced the life of the entire country. Just as Detroit was paying watchful attention to the baroque custom car designers on the west coast and cashing in on the enthusiasm for southern dirt-track racing, so too crossroads America was busy imitating the skyline of Las Vegas, and New York socialites, lacking natural and aristocratic styles of their own, were lapping up teenage music and clothes and the pop tastes of the bohemian undergrounds. Hence the phenomenon of Baby Jane Holzer, a Park Avenue socialite and wedded to a real estate heir yet an Andy Warhol starlet who "comprehends what the Rolling Stones *mean*."

Elsewhere Wolfe explains the Baby Jane syndrome as a renewal of nineteenth-century *nostalgie de la boue*—a longing on the part of the upper classes to "recapture the raw and elemental vitality of the lower orders." This aping of Low-Rent fads and fashions is in part a way for the beautiful people to separate themselves from the well-heeled middle classes, since money alone can no longer maintain a buffer. The one thing the upper-classes still have going for them is confidence to be shocking and get away with it, while the middle classes, locked into gentility, lack the nerve to be anything but decorously respectable. . . .

Yet there is more to the new money situation than just lower-class monument building and its influence on high society. Particularly in ***The Pump House Gang*** and ***The Electric Kool-Aid Acid Test*** Wolfe began looking at the ways in which various kinds of people, including middle-class dropouts like Ken Kesey's Merry Pranksters and the La Jolla surfers, were creating total "statuspheres" for themselves. There was enough money floating around not only to allow kids to buy Hobie Alter surfboards at $140 a crack but to live *The Life*, an age-segregated total culture that had no truck with the black panthers (not *the* Panthers but the black street-shoe set, the middle-age square world) and the whole "hubby-mommy you're-breaking-my-gourd scene." Because of the available money the kids were not just hanging around together on street corners but establishing "whole little societies for themselves." (p. 72)

And not only kids but, increasingly, adults. Enter Hugh Hefner, the "King of the Status Dropouts," another profound symbol. With his Playboy millions Hefner has abandoned conventional status competition . . . [and] created a statusphere ("contemporary recluse") all his own. For Wolfe the quality of Hefner's statusphere matters little; what does matter is that Hefner has started his own league, invented his own rules, managed to "split from *communitas.*"

"Community" has about the same place in the Wolfe lexicon as black panther, work-a-hubby and arteriosclerotic: it refers to the straight job-class world of good gray status competition, and seems to imply for Wolfe the same kind of pervasive unfulfillment Emerson had in mind when he observed that "Society everywhere is in conspiracy against the manhood of every one of its members." The community, Wolfe observes, "has never been one great happy family for all men"; typical community status systems have in fact been "games with few winners and many who feel like losers." And so large numbers of people, with Hefner as classic example, are now busy liberating themselves physically and psychologically from dependence on communitas by setting up their own often esoteric statuspheres, and they are doing so not from traditional motives of alienation or rebellion but simply because they "want to be happy winners for a change." (p. 73)

Radical Chic & Mau-Mauing the Flak Catchers renders Wolfe's version of the times in the most explicit form yet. The first of the two long pieces describes an adventure in fashionable politics by fashionable people, and as such is a new manifestation of an old aristocratic syndrome observed before: *nostalgie de la boue*. . . . In the case of Radical Chic in fashionable New York in the late Sixties *nostalgie de la boue* involved a fascination with revolutionary political styles as a way of demonstrating emancipation from the cautious consensus, the humdrum majority. But of course this emancipation is not *real* emancipation, not part of the ego-extending happiness explosion, but a familiar game played within the confines of traditional high-society status competition. (pp. 74-5)

Radical Chic provides Wolfe with the occasion for full-blast irony. . . . The article focuses on a fund-raising party given by Leonard Bernstein and his wife in their plush penthouse for a group of (real) Black Panthers. The Bernstein party, dramatized in precise and savage detail, was in turn part of a series of Radical Chic events in hip New York society. . . . But the Bernsteins' fund-raiser was special for it brought the fashionable guests into contact with the most notorious of radical groups, the Panthers, and "if there was ever a group that embodied the romance and excitement of which Radical Chic is made, it was the Panthers."

But as useful as the party itself for Wolfe's lethal irony is the burlesque aftermath. *The New York Times* originally reported the story as a society item, calling attention to Leonard Bernstein's Black watch trousers, neck piece, and repeated refrain of "I dig it" in response to the Panther philosophy. . . . Two days later the *Times* followed up with an editorial taking the Bernsteins and their guests to task for "elegant slumming," and thereupon columnists and editorial writers everywhere jumped on the bandwagon. But still there was more: bitterness between Jews and blacks that involved Panther support for the Arabs against Israel, an issue the Bernsteins apparently had been oblivious to, suddenly flared about the unhappy hosts and they began getting hate mail from Jewish Defense League types. (p. 75)

Radical Chic as a form of elegant slumming was a sitting duck for Wolfe, but there is more to the attack than the vulnerability of the target. It illustrates his notion of the impoverishment of high society in the face of raw-vital energy emanating from prole culture, in this case the Panthers; yet even more to Wolfe's point, the ultimate horse laugh running through the article, is not the feeble social climbing and marginal differentiation involved in Radical Chic but that the fashionable culturati and liberal intellectuals take the moral protest-civil libertarian stance seriously at all. If Radical Chic were just a case of vain strivings in high society it would be funny, but that its advocates really care about their causes (to the extent of course that they care for any causes beyond their own) is a delicious *joke*.

Bernstein is portrayed not only as pompous but foolishly serious. . . . He misses the fact that the Panthers are engaged in an elaborate game of mau-mauing the white liberals (a game they themselves only half know they are playing) and instead tries to involve them in heavy dialogue. He makes reference to *The New York Review of Books* . . . , worries about Panther threats against established black community leaders, guiltily wonders if the Panthers are embittered by the luxury of his apartment, finally draws a connection between the rejection experienced by the Panthers and the fact that almost *everyone* in the room has had "a problem about being unwanted." . . .

The real comedy for Wolfe is the archaic style of Bernstein's thought and the old-fashioned concern for oral protest, however fragile, lingering behind all the Radical Chic events. Bernstein is portrayed as the "Village Explainer, the champion of Mental Jotto, the Free Analyst, Mr. Let's Find Out," and what he takes with such humorless seriousness isn't serious at all but an exercise in ritualistic mau-mauing. (p. 76)

In **"Radical Chic"** the tactic of mau-mauing is subordinated to Wolfe's delight in cutting up the hip socialites—even the Panthers have tough going upholding their image in the face of Radical Chic concern—but in **"Mau-Mauing the Flak Catchers"** it takes over center stage. The article brilliantly treats the routine practice of minority group intimidation of bureaucrats in the San Francisco poverty program. The bureaucrats talk "ghetto" all the time but of course don't know what to do about it, so come to depend on confrontations. . . . The mau-mauing act is seldom conducted in the presence of top bureaucrats but rather flak catchers, Hush Puppy civil-service lifers who take the rhetorical beating and report back to their protected superiors. It's the whole game-like, madly choreographed quality of the mau-mauing that Wolfe delights in. The flak catchers are rarely in more actual physical danger than their bosses because the "brothers understood through and through that it was a tactic, a procedure, a game." The term mau-mauing itself suggested to its practitioners the "put-on side of it. . . . It was like a practical joke at the expense of the white man's superstitiousness."

It's the comic, light-hearted, transcending-the-bullshit side to mau-mauing that fits with Wolfe's vision of the times and links itself to the happiness explosion. At the same time it's an individualistic, idiosyncratic game and so part of the free-wheeling ego extension and esoteric statusphere building that are the distinguishing marks of the new sensibility. Wolfe views the ghettos as alive with individualists, brothers "with their own outlook, their new status system"; no single group represents the ghettos because everybody has "his own angle and his own way of looking at black power." (p. 77)

For most of the Haight-Ashbury heads described in ***Acid Test*** ("still playing the eternal charade of the middle-class intellectuals") Ken Kesey was finally too real; he insisted on preaching the need to move beyond acid and, worse, he had an odd relation with genuine outlaws, the Hell's Angels. The chief Prankster really *meant* it about getting to Edge City. Which suggests a question, not to be passed over lightly in any consideration of Tom Wolfe: does *he* really mean it? Does he truly think public concerns so meaningless, conventional intellectuality and traditional moral protest so bankrupt, ordinary social arrangements so out of tune with the assertive sensibility arising out of the vinyl deeps? Does he actually believe in his vision of a happiness explosion and his avowed message, enjoy?

Reviewers have contended that it's useless to ask what moral or intellectual position Wolfe really speaks from because his method proliferates points of view and implies attitudes that are frequently contradicted or thrown away. Similarly it has been argued that Wolfe is basically uncommitted to his materials, that in his work acceptance is always neatly balanced by rejection, and that appropriately McLuhanesque his medium is more important than his message, his manner more important than his matter. Nevertheless, there remains an insistent vision of modern America running through all of Wolfe's work that derives from a repeated mocking of the styles and concerns of traditional culture and a celebration of the comic, pleasure-seeking, self-centred modes of the happiness explosion. Whether he means it or not he has consistently dramatized a cultural situation in which the received culture appears on its last feeble legs, about to give way under a popular assault based on the new styles and attitudes of widespread affluence. (p. 78)

Ronald Weber, "Tom Wolfe's Happiness Explosion," in Journal of Popular Culture, *Vol. VIII, No. 1, Summer, 1974, pp. 71-9.*

BARBARA ROSE

Tom Wolfe is an attractive writer because he makes hard things easy. He equips one for intellectual name-dropping, the very discourse of the upwardly mobile cocktail-party society of *arrivistes* for whom Wolfe reserves the greatest measure of his contempt. This is a paradox we can begin to understand if we follow Wolfe's career, from his early hero-worshiping idealizations of pop culture heroes like Phil Spector and Junior Johnson to his subsequent attacks on the moldy, crumbling remains of the literary and art establishments.

When he deals with pop culture, Wolfe's inability to grapple with ideas of any complexity is no disadvantage; the pop world can indeed be plumbed to its depth by scratching the surface. Thus a description of Baby Jane Holzer's or Ethel Scull's clothes may suffice to communicate their meaning as *nouveau-riche* celebrities. It could even be argued that a description of the haircuts of the guests and the canapés at Leonard Bernstein's party for the Black Panthers described in ***Radical Chic*** . . . , gives us important insights into the social life of New York in the Sixties. However, when we come to a subject that is beyond entertaining social satire, Wolfe is obvioulsy over his head. In no way can a description of the wardrobe of Théophile Gautier, elaborated on in some detail in Wolfe's latest book, ***The Painted Word,*** put us in touch with the ideas that launched modern art and criticism. . . .

The Painted Word sets out to "hit a superannuated target" once again. This time Wolfe plays a daring David to another wobbly Goliath. His target is Cultureburg—Wolfe's catchy sobriquet for the New York art world. . . .

Once again, Wolfe has nothing to lose by an assault. . . . Wolfe's *Reader's Digest* abridgment of the history of modern art could not affect a reputation he never had as an artist or a serious critic. It could only make him more famous, controversial, and hence salable. Which it has.

Once again, readers are puzzling their way through the confused maze of Wolfe's bizarre punctuation, zany neologisms, and careening fragments of free association. . . . Wolfe has a killer's instinct for weakness. He has picked a moment when there has never been greater confusion over who is or is not an artist or who is or is not an art critic. He capitalizes on this confusion, as well as on the resentment of all who believe themselves artists and critics and are in revolt against any authority that would deny it.

Undoubtedly the art world today is far from healthy. But Tom Wolfe is hardly the first to notice signs of decay. Among others, Harold Rosenberg has been chronicling its decline in those very Whichy Thickets Wolfe so despises, i.e., the pages of *The New Yorker*. Of course, knowing the art world well, Rosenberg is at a certain disadvantage when compared with Wolfe; memory restricts him to real events and real people. Rosenberg, for example, would not feel qualified to enter the brain of Jackson Pollock as Wolfe does to carry on an imaginary dialogue with Clement Greenberg on the virtues of flatness in painting. . . .

Wolfe interprets the concern of modernist painters with "flatness" as meaning that they wished to make paintings that were literally flat. This is not so. The modernist sensiblity does indeed demand a degree of self-consciousness, an overt acknowledgment on the part of the artist of his awareness of the identity of his materials, techniques, and processes. That art *is* illusion, and the revelation of the nature of this illusion—which in painting concerns the projection of a spatial dimension on a flat surface—are at the heart of the modernist consciousness in all the arts. Wolfe's dismissal of the issue of "flatness" as an indulgence of Greenberg's whim is essentially a rejection of modernism itself as an acutely self-conscious analytic state.

As for the stylistic revolution of Pollock's work from the loose, transparent "drip" paintings to his later experiments with thick crusts of impasto covering the whole of the canvas surface, Wolfe tells us nothing. If Wolfe knew anything firsthand about Greenberg, Pollock, or modern art, he might have realized that not Clement Greenberg but Claude Monet, whose *Waterlilies* were newly installed in the Museum of Modern Art, where Pollock could study them, was the inspiration behind Pollock's late works. The only art theory *per se* that ever influenced Pollock was the theory of Synchronism propounded by his teacher Thomas Hart Benton in class and in essays.

But why should Wolfe bother with the tedious details of the history of art when the public wants to buy a history of art gossip? (p. 26)

Tom Wolfe amalgamates much of the foolishness of the Sixties in ***The Painted Word,*** a book of no merit but a cultural phenomenon that testifies to the existence of a public that does not know much but still demands to be "in the know." This public grows as publishing houses become more eager to satisfy marketplace demands than to address a smaller, less profitable literary audience, and as our universities graduate increasing numbers of semiliterate students who have not the means to possess modern culture but feel nevertheless that they must have some attitude toward it.

Who is responsible for stimulating this public into an interest in art, no matter how spurious or superficial? I accuse artists of succumbing to the commercial laws of supply and demand, and curators of selecting for exhibitions their demoralized work in the quest for novelty and publicity. I accuse museums of showing comic strips if need be to draw larger crowds, and galleries of exhibiting whatever sells best—even if that means Walt Disney's studio drawings of Dumbo and Mickey Mouse. I accuse newspapers of running unnecessary headlines stressing the dollar value of art, and magazines of attempting to boost circulation by printing sensational stories about artists' sex lives instead of information about art. I accuse art publishers of issuing books of illustrated kitsch and canceling serious art books with a more limited audience.

Finally, *mea culpa*. Some of my colleagues and I were so enthusiastic about the art that moved us that we oversold it to an uninformed audience unwilling to make the effort to understand difficult works, an artificial public that could only end by resenting both the art and the criticism they were bound to find unintelligible. It is to this public that ***The Painted Word*** is addressed. (p. 28)

Barbara Rose, "Wolfeburg," in The New York Review of Books, *Vol. XXII, No. 11, June 26, 1975, pp. 26-8.*

MORRIS DICKSTEIN

[***The New Journalism***, an anthology edited by Tom Wolfe and E. W. Johnson which includes an essay by Wolfe,] is not only a bid for literary permanence and respectability but has a strong polemical purpose. It's directed precisely against the subjective or Mailerian sort of journalism in which the writer appears as a central character, a personal reactor through whom the events are filtered. Mailer does make a brief appearance in the book, but Wolfe's comments about him are grudging, and he prints very little other work in that line—a line he himself seems unable or unwilling to pursue. . . . Instead, Wolfe, in his selections, headnotes, and fifty-page introduction, emphasizes a much more peripheral feature of the New Journalism: its novelistic quality. Wolfe picks pieces that are shaped like old-style short stories; as editor, ever boastful of his academic credentials, he ponderously ticks off their narrative techniques. Unfortunately, few of his writers have strong novelistic gifts, and his own prefaces pose no threat to those of Henry James. Despite his proclamations of novelty, the real pedigree of Wolfe's selections is good old-fashioned feature-writing rather than fiction. (p. 865)

The partiality of Wolfe's canon and the flaws in his conception of the New Journalism spring from the limitations of his own work, which some have unthinkingly taken as the prototype of this sort of writing. Wolfe pines for literary status and academic recognition, but his Yale Ph.D., however much he reminds us of it, really does point to what he can do well. . . . [He] has a good solid American Studies sort of analytical skill; though much too fascinated by style and celebrity, too preoccupied by status rather than class or power, he knows the social map; he wields a smooth, digestible style and a lively curiosity about how people live and play—work I'm afraid is outside his ken—in the more picturesque corners of society. This comes out very clearly in the first piece in his first book, the article on Las Vegas in ***The Kandy-Kolored Tangerine-Flake Streamline Baby*** (1965), which manages to explain the city, not simply to evoke it. . . . At heart, the early Wolfe was a genial observer of the byways of Americana, and at moments a tolerable social analyst. But Wolfe seemed incapable of exposing or involving himself; for all his zeal to discover an invisible America in the subcultural muck of custom-car racing and demolition derbies, for all his contempt for the essayistic distance of the "Literary Gentleman in the Grandstand," Wolfe himself was too genteel to let go or get involved, even in the harmless participatory manner of a George Plimpton. Hence he was attracted to the bizarre, to pure spectacle, where breathless excitement would obviate any taxing emotional claims and pump life into his prose.

But he couldn't be content with short pieces on demolition derbies and profiles of social butterflies. If Mailer could let a magazine assignment explode into a long book, if Mailer could "do" the sixties in *The Armies of the Night* and *Miami and the Siege of Chicago,* Wolfe could afford to be no less grandiose and ambitious. In ***The Electric Kool-Aid Acid Test*** (1968), his book on Ken Kesey and his Merry Pranksters, and **"Radical Chic,"** his interminable account of Leonard Bernstein's fund-raising party for the Black Panthers, we confront Wolfe's larger claims as a social chronicler and literary stylist, and these claims don't hold up. The Kesey book is stupefyingly boring—I got through only half of it. Kesey himself is offensive and overrated as a writer and even less interesting as a sixties guru. Moreover, unlike Mailer, Wolfe seems to have nothing to say; hence he churns up all the typographical mannerisms he'd managed to keep down in his first book. Evidently they're meant to play a central role, to approximate the freaked-out sensations of the drug experience. How far he fails can be gauged by a comparison with the style of Hunter Thompson, who's wildly erratic yet really gives the impression of having been there. (pp. 866-67)

Somehow even in **"Radical Chic"** where Wolfe is far from uncritical, where he mobilizes an impressive irony yet tries to remain inside his characters, the result is almost as monotonous. No good novelist would homogenize his characters into one inner voice, a single mentality, a collective embodiment of a social attitude, as Wolfe does. He creates what Alan

Trachtenberg, in a shrewd critique called the "illusion of a group subjectivity, only and sheerly verbal, never complete, never completing itself in the reader's imagination except as display, as spectacle" [see *CLC*, Vol. 9]. And the point of view in **"Radical Chic"** is as limited as the technique. Wolfe later explained that to fill out the collective stream-of-consciousness he "depended heavily on details of status life to draw the reader inside the emotional life of his characters." This is a fancy way of describing the plenitude of brand names and In fashions that he uses to furnish out his characters' "minds," so that instead of having an emotional life they turn out to be mannikins of chic, butts of social satire. . . . For all the would-be satire, Wolfe himself is nothing if not a creature of fashion. His fastidious social knowingness puts him entirely at one with the mentality of his characters; their snobbishness and triviality mirror his own interests. The implication is, well, that chic is OK, but *radical* chic, Black Panther chic, now honey, that's going a little too far.

Compared to Mailer, compared to all the great realists he admires, Wolfe has no sense of what makes society work, what greases the wheels, what makes it run. Only the color and splash of fashion, the social surface, engages him. It's not that he's anti-radical: politics of any sort passes him by, except as spectacle. Inevitably, his distortion of the New Journalism is rooted in his misreading of the sixties, when politics truly came to the fore. To Wolfe the real history of the sixties had to do with changes in "manners and morals" rather than "the war in Vietnam or . . . space exploration or . . . political assassination." (p. 868)

[When] Tom Wolfe comes to New York in the early sixties he sees "pandemonium with a big grin on . . . the wildest, looniest time since the 1920s . . . a hulking carnival . . . (an) amazing spectacle." He sees only a freakshow, a whirligig of fashion and social idiosyncrasy—another New Journalist actually called a collection of articles *Freakshow*—and Wolfe wonders why the novelists are not there on the beat. It turns out that they have retreated into myth, "Neo-Fabulism," and alienation, so that "the—New Journalists—Parajournalists—had the whole crazed obscene uproarious Mammon-faced drug-soaked mau-mau lust-oozing Sixties in America all to themselves."

Even if we allow for the willed overheating of Wolfe's prose—which faithfully mirrors the freakshow element that alone interests him—it becomes obvious that Wolfe has no notion of the kinds of social forces that impel both manners and morals *and* politics. . . . This is the implicit unity of mood or moral temper that the cultural observer must seek out, by which, for instance, the style of confrontation in the politics of the sixties is closely related to the style of self-assertion in the poetry and sexuality of the period, which in turn is related to the sudden impulse of the journalist, in covering these and other developments, to do *his* own thing in an authenticating, subjective way. And to determine *why* the whole culture should be moving in this direction, and to make some distinctions and come to some judgments about it, required someone with greater analytical acuity, with more political sensitivity and novelistic vision, than Tom Wolfe. It required perhaps a figure from the fifties, someone caught beween that hinterland of irony, ambivalence, and reflection and the new culture. This is why it fell to Mailer rather than Wolfe to become the quintessential New Journalist, to report most deeply on what was happening, both inside and outside his own head. (p. 869)

Morris Dickstein, "The Working Press, the Literary Culture, and the New Journalism," in The Georgia Review, *Vol. XXX, No. 4, Winter, 1976, pp. 855-77.**

CHRISTOPHER BOOKER

[***Mauve Gloves & Madmen, Clutter & Vine***] seems to be much the mixture as before, although with rather more fiction and less straight reportage. The title story gets inside the mind of a successful Jewish writer who has become so carried away by all the externals of his new role as a successful writer—the Lobb shoes (to think, his father had come over from Russia with nothing!), the Martha's vineyard beach house, the smart literary party in their Manhattan apartment, with flowers by "Mauve Gloves" and catering by "Madmen, Clutter and Vine"—that he has virtually forgotten how to be a writer. There is another story about a black baseball player who is conned into making a dreadful TV commercial for after-shave. There are one or two rather jaded litle essays on "the pornography of violence" and the survival in America of give-away and upper- and lower-class accents ("Honks and Wonks"). And by far the best piece of reporting in the book has nothing to do with the fashionable world at all, but is a portrait of American pilots flying off carriers into North Viet Nam ("The Truest Sport: Jousting With Sam and Charlie"). This completely dispels (certainly as far as I was concerned) any view that those fliers were safely cocooned in a kind of air-conditioned, electronic bubble, murdering in comfort by remote control. (p. 74)

The longest essay in the book, called "The Me Decade: The Third Great Awakening" . . . begins with a description of a girl at a "let-it-all-hang-out" therapy session in the Ambassador Hotel, Los Angeles. . . . From here the essay modulates somewhat improbably into an analysis of the great "religious revival" which has overtaken America in the past ten years, from Hare Krishna and LSD to "born again" Jimmy Carter. Wolfe compares this ("the third great awakening") with the previous explosions of popular religious fervour in the 1740s (Wesley-ism) and 1825-50 (Camp meetings and Mormonism). And his thesis is that at the heart of this religious revival lies an obsession with "Me"—that the ultimate fruit of post-war money and prosperity is that everyone has been liberated to concentrate on themselves. So recklessly does he mix up soul and body, religion and sex, that almost any movement which has caught on in America in the past decade can be seen as essentially just part of the same mishmash of egocentricity.

Now this is perhaps an arguable, interesting thesis—although the case would have to be put with a great deal more psychological and historical rigour than Wolfe brings to bear. As it stands, it is just a long, confused, breathless attempt to jumble together by sleight-of-hand anything from "group-sex", Germaine Greer, "honesty sessions" and *Suck* to Gnosticism, Methodism and Zen. . . . But in the end this essay brings us back to the question—just where does Tom Wolfe stand, and how serious is he?

Because there is no doubt that he sets out to be something much more ambitious than just a casual observer of the passing show. He is an analyst, a deep thinker, a man who can use words like *kairos* and *antanacasis*, consider the nature of ecstasy, talk about Zoroastrianism. He asks to be taken very seriously indeed—so let us try.

It was extremely revealing that the one intellectual charlatan against whom Tom Wolfe was reluctant to pronounce *anathema* was Marshall McLuhan. For the point about McLuhan is that once upon a time he was an ordinary dull little Conservative Catholic intellectual, influenced by Chesterton, hating the modern world, and hankering for the lost paradise of a pre-industrial, agrarian society. Then one magic day, some 30 years ago, he read Poe's story "The Maelstrom", about the sailor who, caught in the notorious whirlpool, realises that the only way to escape is not to fight the downward pull of the vortex, but to leap out of his ship and float—like the surrounding driftwood—UPWARDS, to safety! . . . He decided that no longer would he fight the whirlpool of modern culture—he would float with it. Instead of castigating the mindless stream of imagery of television or pop music, he would bless it. He would acclaim everything—"the medium is the massage"—he would float with the random—sensation flow of "post-linear", "post-verbal" culture—and everything would be O.K.! Thus, telling people what they wanted to hear in the crazy late-Sixties, did McLuhan win his brief reputation as the prophet of the age.

The parallel to Wolfe himself in inescapable. If you go back to the introduction to ***The Kandy-Kolored Tangerine-Flake Streamline Baby*** (1965), the nearest thing to an explicit credo he has ever written, his moment of "literary conversion" was when he realised that the only way to write about the pure sensation flow of Sixties culture was to create a prose-style which exactly matched it. (pp. 74-6)

Wolfe's basic thesis here (so often repeated since) is simply that money creates the opportunity for self-expression, and always has done—and that *all forms of expression are the same*. . . . I suppose one can see what he is driving at—but if one is prepared to rest on the simple equation of any form of artistic or fashionable expression with any other, St. Mark's Square with the "custom car" or "the shake" or "decal eyes", then one is not running very deep in terms of analysis! Why not include Giotto's Arena Chapel frescoes, or Mozart's Requiem or Chartres Cathedral for good measure? The Rolling Stones equals Leonardo da Vinci. *Q.E.D.*! Indeed, whenever Wolfe ventures into these sweeping historical parallels (as in "The Me Decade"—John Wesley equals Germaine Greer) he is soon treading on very thin ice indeed, simply in terms of his own ignorance. (pp. 76-7)

Of course there is much more to Wolfe than that. His real achievement (apart from providing a great deal of journalistic entertainment) has been to capture in words, and from the inside, some of the more bizarre cultural inanities of one of the most insane and fascinating decades in the history of the world—probably with greater skill and insight than anyone else writing in the same period. He has been able to see through "radical chic" and Hugh Hefner and the nonsense of the New York art world like nobody's business. But in the end, outside the world of the wonderful, exploding, self-expressing ego—however nightmarish and self-destructive and horrible that world can be—what is left? So let's just flow with it, baby! Wolfe's is a pretty bleak, harsh, loveless view of the world. He is like a man sitting on a fairground roundabout, feeling desperately sick, but seeing no way to jump off. Or like a soul doomed to wander for eternity through a particularly nasty modern version of Dante's Inferno, without the faintest hope of escaping into Purgatory, let alone Paradise. In the end, after re-reading his collected works, I am afraid I just feel slightly sick myself. I don't think I shall want to read any more. (p. 77)

Christopher Booker, "Inside the Bubble: Re-reading Tom Wolfe," in Encounter, *Vol. XLIX, No. 3, September, 1977, pp. 72-7.*

CHARLES S. ROSS

Not to be confused with the novelist Thomas Wolfe, who borrowed the name of his most well-known book, *Look Homeward, Angel,* from Milton, Tom Wolfe is a New York journalist who has been publishing books with catchy titles since his ***Kandy-Kolored Tangerine Flake Streamlined Baby*** appeared in 1965. His flamboyant and careful prose has appeared in several popular anthologies designed for composition courses. Also suitable for a freshman composition class, I have found, is his book ***The Right Stuff***. . . . Its topicality ensures that students will read it from cover to cover, and its structure makes it easy to write about. (p. 113)

In ***The Right Stuff,*** Wolfe tells the story of the seven astronauts who flew in America's first manned space series, the Mercury program. He explains the special prestige these men unexpectedly enjoyed and then suddenly lost. That special prestige was so intense that it made New York City policemen weep at the sight of John Glenn, but, strangely, it had nothing to do with the right stuff. Instead, it was a product of the cold war in the late fifties and early sixties. This prestige also had nothing to do with the astronauts' other qualities, good or bad. Just as *Life* Magazine's artists removed every facial blemish from photographs of their wives, so the press transformed their life stories into an American dream.

Wolfe takes advantage of the almost two decades since the Mercury program to reexamine the dream. . . . As revisionist history, this book highlights what was left unsaid during the Kennedy years. The result is that Wolfe exaggerates both the good and bad qualities of the astronauts. When they were good they were very, very brave, and no one has elevated their courage to such heroic proportions as Wolfe. But when they were bad they were rowdy, and no book has explored their rowdiness more closely than ***The Right Stuff.*** Because some of the astronauts were rowdier than others, it is important to examine closely how this book's tricks of rhetoric reveal the truth, as well as stretch it.

It is not the least of Wolfe's virtues as a writer that he skillfully defines his key term by a variety of means, from antithesis to anecdote. *Stuff* is an intentionally ambiguous word, a slightly slang substitute for that indefinable "it" which the best test pilots had, but never mentioned. A pilot with the right stuff was always "hanging it over the edge," or "stretching the envelope," phrases which mean that he pushed his equipment to its utmost capacity, testing how fast it would go, how high it would fly, or how tightly it would turn. Test pilots tended to regard mechanical failures and gory crashes as indications not that their profession was incredibly dangerous, but that the dead pilot was somehow lacking what it took to overcome obstacles. The pilots formed a fraternity that lived constantly with death. . . . Wolfe is the first to record, outside of professional journals, just how dangerous it was to be a Navy or Air Force test pilot. Mortality rates sometimes reached twenty-five percent.

All of the Mercury astronauts were pilots. As Wolfe explains, Alan Shepherd had been one of the Navy's best. Gus Grissom had flown a hundred combat missions in Korea and tested fighter planes at Wright-Patterson air force base. John Glenn had flown in combat in two wars, won five Distinguished Flying Crosses with eighteen clusters, and set a speed record flying non-stop, coast to coast, at three times the speed of sound in 1957. Scott Carpenter, who orbited the earth after Glenn, was an exception, because he hadn't flown in combat or done any extraordinary flight testing. . . . [However, it was

Grissom] who stretched the non-flight aspects of the right stuff to the limit. . . . Grissom not only flew in Korea, but also, after he had completed his hundred combat missions, volunteered for twenty-five more.

There was a certain all-American, down-home aspect of the right stuff which Grissom seemed to have. He bought a Corvette so he could race on desert highways near air bases, he flew during the day, he drank at night. . . . (pp. 113-15)

Wolfe makes it clear early in his book that he has done more than isolate a crucial common denominator among America's first seven astronauts: that "right stuff" that Grissom possessed until he died in a fire while testing equipment for the Apollo moon program. He has also found its source, in an Air Force Test pilot named Chuck Yeager. Yeager was the first man to fly faster than the speed of sound. He broke the sound barrier in 1947, flying an X-2 rocket launched from another airplane. . . . Wolfe sets out to prove that Chuck Yeager was the brave and rowdy role-model for the pilots from whose ranks the Mercury astronauts were chosen in 1959. (pp. 115-16)

A number of literary techniques help Wolfe prove his point about Yeager. First, he produces a miniature play, an on-board drama complete with a one-sided dialogue. The passage also uses strange shifts in point of view, as when it suddenly moves from hearing the pilot's voice to the inside of his mind, a shift indicated by parentheses and italics. In addition, the passage contains symbolic details, the kind used by a novelist to squeeze meaning into a small space. [The] red light isn't just a bulb; it stands for electronic mechanisms no passenger understands, for unseen danger, even death.

The center of this display of novelists' techniques and narrative skills is the pilot, who is the drama's hero. The techniques themselves are the equipment of a group of writers who emerged during the sixties and seventies and wrote in a manner labeled the New Journalism. . . . They lived with their subjects, often recording dialogue in shorthand, and they wrote up their material using novelists' devices, such as scene-by-scene action, dialogue, seeing the world from a character's point of view, and symbolic details—devices enumerated by Wolfe in ***The New Journalism, with an Anthology***. . . . The result was a witty, exact, and slightly mocking record of American life, and the emergence of a new set of cultural heroes. . . .

Wolfe's book makes his heroes larger than life by basing them on myths. He defines the character of Chuck Yeager by telling a *story* about a nerveless, drawling airline pilot. As a result, he defines reality, but he also enlarges it. (p. 117)

Similes and metaphors . . . are typical of Wolfe's exaggerated presentation of American life. Elsewhere he describes the Century series of jet fighters, which so many pilots died testing in the early fifties, as "bricks with fins." When the astronauts moved to NASA's new Manned Spacecraft Center in a Houston snake swamp, near a place named Clear Lake, Wolfe describes the lake as "about as clear as the eyeballs of a poisoned bass."

Like these exaggerating metaphors, the technique of hyperbole, or overstatement, is perfect for the heroic mode Wolfe creates. Glenn pounded "two million" laps around a driveway. The astronauts, being pilots, wore huge aviator wrist-watches, the kind with "2,000 calibrations" on their dials. These numbers give a quick indication of the kind of book ***The Right Stuff*** is. It contains round figures and no math. Something as trivial as the formula for the acceleration caused by gravity is technologically beyond the scope of this book. There are errors. In a magnificent passage in which he describes the difficulty of landing a jet on an aircraft carrier in high seas at night, Wolfe says that an F-4 fighter weighs fifty thousand pounds. A sentence later, it is a "fifteen-ton brute." . . . I found the source of this confusion in . . . ***Mauve Gloves and Madmen, Clutter and Vine,*** in a story about American carrier pilots in Viet Nam. Wolfe has lifted almost ten pages and inserted them into ***The Right Stuff***'s account of carrier landings in the early fifties, when jet fighters were about twenty-thousand pounds lighter. Included in this article are a lot of details about a certain "it" that good carrier pilots have. This "it" is an early version of the right stuff. An even earlier "it" appears in Wolfe's ***Electric Kool-Aid Acid Test,*** where the pronoun stands for a quality found among those who do not panic under the effects of hallucinogenic drugs. (pp. 118-19)

Much of Wolfe's vocabulary seems strange because it consists of relics from his earlier work. He mentions the "quonset-style" hangars at Edwards Air Force base, referring to a type of prefabricated portable hut having a semicircular roof of corrugated metal. I find Berkeley moviemakers living in quonset-style huts in Wolfe's ***Pump House Gang.*** "Ziggurat" and "panjandrum" are imports from his other books too. In ***The Right Stuff,*** the astronauts don't just climb the ladder to success; they scale a pyramid, and not just any pyramid. Because this is Tom Wolfe writing, they scale a ziggurat, which is a temple tower of the ancient Assyrians and Babylonians, having the form of a terraced pyramid of successively receding stories. We meet the word "panjandrum" during a spiff between the astronauts and their doctors: in the face of the astronauts' fame, it was hard for even an egotistical flight surgeon to be a "panjandrum." Seemingly unaware of how often Wolfe uses the word, the American Heritage dictionary defines it with a single synonym, muckamuck. . . . His favorite phrase, however, is "Low Rent." He always capitalizes both words, and he uses the phrase to refer to status, not price. . . . Cocoa Beach was Low Rent, but so were the clothes that Gus Grissom and Deke Slayton used to wear when they prowled Florida night spots—flowered sports shirts and tan pants and olive green GI socks.

Words and ideas repeated among Wolfe's works tend to blur the difference between the astronauts and those stock-car racers, socialites, and artists whom Wolfe describes in previous books, such as his ***Kandy-Kolored Tangerine Flaked Streamlined Baby.*** But to give the astronauts special status, to elevate their heroic stature above neon-sign designers, surfers, Hugh Hefners, and Leonard Bernsteins, Wolfe has postulated a daring and hyperbolic metaphor as the major thesis of this book. The astronauts were single-combat warriors. Their combat in space was part of the cold war between the United States and the USSR. In October, 1957, after America's Redstone rockets several times had exploded, the Russians launched Sputnik, and it seemed only a matter of time until they would have nuclear weapons in orbit. By 1959, a crash program to get an American into space had led to the selection of the first seven astronauts. Thse men would meet the Russians on what one Congressman called "the high ground" of outer space. They were Davids against the Soviet Goliath.

Wolfe provides a sketchy history of single combat. Originally, it had a magic meaning. Before entire armies committed themselves, ancient champion-warriors often fought to the death as a way of testing fate or seeing whose side the gods favored. The Christians reinterpreted single combat as a humanitarian substitute for wholesale slaughter. Naturally, the soldiers selected as champions received the emotional and material attention of their people, and they received it in advance. This proleptic adulation accounts for the emotion poured onto the astronauts. They were getting paid up front, because while the Russians seemed to launch satellites and men almost at will, American rockets always seemed to blow up.

Wolfe's concept is historically shaky, though his point is good. It is always difficult to determine the meaning of magic in very early societies. From the Middle Ages we have more evidence, but we know that single combat then was a farce, not a plot by the aristocracy to spare the lives of their soldier-serfs. (pp. 119-20)

But Wolfe is correct that in a nuclear age, when all-out confrontation is useless, miniature combats tend to look more important than they really are. The bubble honor once again seems real. The space-race dramatized the entire technological and intellectual capability of a nation. Although it was a small skirmish, it grew in importance like magic, and the astronauts dealt in its magical stuff.

What happened to it? Why can't we name all seven Mercury astronauts anymore? . . . The answer to what happened to the phenomenal fame of the astronauts, according to Wolfe, is that the cold war wound down in the late sixties, destroying the basis for the astronauts' myth.

Other explanations are possible, however. For one, the Mercury astronauts were outdone by Armstrong, Aldrin, and Collins. But the astronauts of the six moon missions after Apollo 11 were never forgotten, because they were never known. They weren't known because Americans no longer cared about space, despite the lunar rover. And despite spectacular close-up photos of Venus, Mars, Jupiter, and Saturn, Congress couldn't be bothered to extend two Voyager flights to Neptune and Uranus.

I think the reason lies in the moon rock. When Columbus came back from the West Indies, he brought back bright parrots and some Indians, but although he traveled across Spain in triumph, he died fourteen years and three voyages later as a ruined man. There wasn't much of a market for parrots, and Columbus, who spoke Spanish with a heavy Italian accent, couldn't keep the little men of the Spanish court convinced of the importance of what he'd found. Fifteen hundred colonists in seventeen ships attended him on his second voyage, but they mutinied in Puerto Rico after they failed to find instant wealth. Columbus had only convicts as colonists on his third voyage. Seventeen Apollo missions left NASA in a condition similar to that of Columbus when he died. They had produced nine hundred pounds of worthless moonrock and a few thousand miles of numbers that the average voter couldn't understand.

I think NASA knows what human nature needs. According to *Time* magazine, the space agency is promoting its space shuttle as a vehicle for finding minerals on earth. It is remarkable what the discovery of gold did for Spanish interest in the new world, at least in certain parts of it. But I wonder if we are overlooking space the way the Spanish overlooked North America. I think of Sir Walter Raleigh, who founded Virginia, but who nonetheless rotted for eighteen years in the Tower of London because his ships could never find the city of gold, Eldorado. . . . Voyager II found no gold on Saturn, so now NASA claims that the gold is really on earth. Until it's found, or until something as unexpected and profitable as Virginia tobacco turns up, the space program will probably proceed slowly. Meanwhile, Tom Wolfe . . . has a gold mine of his own in . . . [***The Right Stuff***]. It is not a great book, because it lacks the virtues of a scholarly work, precision and documentation. But it is a great story, and it's told like one. (pp. 121-22)

Charles S. Ross, "The Rhetoric of 'The Right Stuff'," in The Journal of General Education, *published by The Pennsylvania State University Press, University Park, PA, Vol. 33, No. 2, Summer, 1981, pp. 113-22.*

PETER GRIER

As Tom Wolfe's **"The Painted Word"** picked at the absurdities of modern painting, so **"From Bauhaus to Our House"** attacks the literary underpinnings of modern architecture, those theories of modernism by which buildings have been judged since Walter Gropius, the "Silver Prince" of the Bauhaus.

Wolfe's point in this splendidly witty little book is that modern architects design in code. A structure may be so beautiful it causes eyes to water and autos to stall; it may be so wonderfully functional people love to work or live in it, but if it wasn't designed according to an intellectual theory, well, how can we be expected to take it seriously? So beach houses sprout steel spaghetti intended to express "inner structure," skyscrapers are paneled with acres of glass as an expression of purity, and "decoration" becomes a dirty word.

The granddaddy of all codes, of course, is the famous "form is function." Honest material. Flat roofs. Clean right angles. As Wolfe points out, the Bauhaus theorists first began practicing their "functional" dictum in northern Europe. . . .

Actually, claims Wolfe, function and form have little to do with it. Instead, the codes are just a mad race to be avant-garde, to be out front with this month's Ultimate Theory. . . .

And if Philip Johnson and his buddies wanted to start some really good guerrilla warfare, they could argue that Tom Wolfe *writes* by theory. As a pioneer of the much-abused term "new journalism," Wolfe has pasted fictional techniques onto reporting, a synthesis that would cause many city desk editors to punch out their computer screens. He is also entering something of a postmodern phase himself, moving from decorative prose to cleaner, more functional sentences—who today would title a book, as Wolfe did in 1965, **"The Kandy-Kolored, Tangerine-Flake Streamline Baby"**?

Peter Grier, "Wolfe: Tilting His Lance at the Glass Box," in The Christian Science Monitor, *December 14, 1981, p. B3.*

JOHN HELLMANN

Previous discussion of ***The Electric Kool-Aid Acid Test*** has nearly always focused upon Wolfe's unique style, or else has treated the book as a mere documentary account of Ken Kesey's artistic experiment with life. . . . While using material drawn only from interviews, tapes, letters, and personal observation, Wolfe consciously uses language to transform his facts into shapes with a fabulist resonance. More particularly, he uses allusions to classic American literature to suggest the larger patterns within which he perceives the factual narrative to be unfolding. Wolfe draws upon a number of classic American literary works in ***The Electric Kool-Aid Acid Test,*** but he causes the reader to view its climactic events through the lenses of Poe's short story "A Descent into the Maelstrom." The highly stylized and allusive structure of his narrative draws attention to itself as a pattern; it functions clearly as a thematic overlay, the product of Wolfe's interpretive consciousness standing outside of the factual events. The power of ***The Electric Kool-Aid Acid Test*** lies in this dynamic balance between the fictive nature of its created form and the factual nature of its content. (p. 110)

Wolfe views Kesey as an embodiment of the American drive to attain perfect freedom and oneness with experience, as well as a religious figure seeking to attain the oriental idea of breaking through the illusory barrier between the subjective and objective. The combination of these two drives, of course, is not new. Through allusion Wolfe tells us that Kesey's transformation of Perry Lane is viewed by visitors as "Walden Pond, only without any Thoreau misanthropes around." . . . Wolfe thus suggests that Kesey's quest has direct precedent in that of the American transcendentalists. His desire to eliminate all "lags" between experience and sensory perception, so as to embrace all experience in an eternal Now in which the objective and subjective are dissolved into one transcendent experience, as well as his impatience with craft in art in favor of a principle of organic form . . . , echoes Emerson's desire to become a "transparent eyeball." The crucial distinction is that Kesey seeks that state not through nature but through technology. That distinction is obvious in his later version of Walden at La Honda, where he has redwood trees outfitted with music speakers and spiderwebs sprayed wtih Day-Glo paint.

The drug-induced concept of the sky as a hole reaching into an infinity of possible experience, combined with the postwar American belief that technology can make any fantasy possible, leads Kesey to organize the Pranksters into painting a bus in a lurid mess of primary colors, flying American flags from the top, equipping it with an audio-visual technology, and then taking it on a cross-country adventure. They transform the bus into an embodiment of Kesey's desire to pursue the American Dream to its furthest limits through the unashamed alteration of nature. . . . Most of the first half of ***Test*** follows Kesey's attainment of a messiah-like status among the Pranksters as he teaches them to assert their private "fantasies" against the rigid "reality" of the dominant culture. Eventually he conceives of the Acid Tests—dances to be held in San Francisco and, later, Los Angeles—in order to bring the larger society into his vision of a transcendent life attained through LSD and technology.

Immediately before his narration of the first Acid Test midway through the narrative, Wolfe refers to one of the books the Pranksters revered, saying that "The Acid Tests turned out, in fact, to be an art form foreseen in that strange book, *Childhood's End,* a form called 'total identification'." . . . This reference is to Arthur C. Clarke's science-fiction vision of an art form in which all senses would be stimulated to the point that a person could mentally participate in any experience. Wolfe quotes from Clarke's description: "And when the 'program' was over, he would have acquired a memory as vivid as any experience in his actual life—indeed, indistinguishable from reality itself." . . . Wolfe follows this quotation with an ominously intrusive comment, "Too freaking true!" . . . Sarcastic use of the Pranksters' hip phrasing indicates the fatal error that he believes is behind the doom toward which Kesey's quest is moving. For Wolfe, as for the dark romantic authors of classic American literature, the inability to distinguish fact from fantasy in a reverie of transcendent experience is a profound error leading to dissolution of the self.

At this point in the narrative, as he is about to begin the story of the Acid Tests, Wolfe makes clear allusions which suggest that the reader should view these events in the framework of a classic work of American literature, one dealing with a true plunge into a vortex, Poe's "Descent into the Maelstrom." It is not surprising that Wolfe, with his sociologist's belief in facts and analysis as well as his skepticism toward the viability of a purely subjective reality, should use a story by one of the great dark romantics as the metaphorical framework for the climactic chapters of his Kesey narrative. Poe presents "A Descent into the Maelstrom" as an oral tale once told by a fisherman to the narrator, who now presents it to us in the fisherman's own words. As they stand at the edge of a cliff above a horrifying oceanic whirlpool, the "maelstrom," the fisherman tells his tale of having been accidentally swept into the swirling vortex. (pp. 111-13)

Wolfe introduces this motif in his description of the third Acid Test. As he describes approximately 300 "heads" gathered on the floor, well into LSD trips and about to experience the Pranksters' projection of "The Movie" and a psychedelic light show upon the walls, Wolfe sums up the moment with the allusive exclamation, "Into the maelstrom!" . . . He describes the setting as a chaotic ocean of experience which the Pranksters have contrived through audio-visual technology. . . . Wolfe describes the experience of a man sucked into the developing maelstrom of the Acid Test:

> into *the whirlpool* who should appear but Owsley. Owsley, done up in his $600 head costume, has emerged from his subterrain of espionage and paranoia to come to see the Prankster experiment for himself, and in the middle of the giddy contagion he takes LSD. They never saw him take it before. He takes the LSD and
> RRRRRRRRRRRRRRRRRRRRRRROIL
> *the whirlpool picks him up and spins him down into* the stroboscopic stereoptic prankster panopticon in full variable lag. . . .
>
> (p. 114)

The Acid Tests are the culmination of Kesey's attempt to break through to a total embrace of experience through technology (both the chemical LSD and the projected light show and electronic music). But as he sees himself successfully projecting his fantasy experience to others, he is assuming the dangerous role of seeing his will as more powerful than actuality. Wolfe's perception of the satantic element of this role is apparent in the chapter title, "Cosmo's Tasmanian Deviltry" (a phrase he shows moving through Kesey's thoughts as he controls the flashing strobe-light at the Acid Test), and in his emphasis upon Owsley's new view of Kesey as a "demon." . . . When Wolfe later recounts the "Trips Festival," which Kesey attends just before his flight to Mexico, he returns to the Poe allusion, describing Kesey with a projection machine on a balcony above the hall as "up above the maelstrom." . . . At one point Kesey uses the projector to flash a message in red on the wall: "ANYBODY WHO KNOWS HE IS GOD GO UP ON STAGE." . . . Kesey believes that he stands safely above the maelstrom, on an edge of perfect control. This "edge," which is a metaphor Kesey often uses to describe the goal of the Pranksters' quest to transcend the distinction between subjective and objective reality, is portrayed by Wolfe, as by Poe and Melville, as a dangerous position inducing a cosmic vertigo. He repeatedly emphasizes Kesey's position as one high above the affairs of the world. This position provides him with the vantage point . . . of an overview of experience—as well as with the illusion of being safely distant from its dangers. But that illusion inevitably leads to his succumbing to the danger of such a position—

a fall into the whirlpool of actual experience below. While Kesey believes he is in control and standing above the maelstrom, Wolfe shows that he is in fact already caught in the whirlpool. . . . (pp. 116-17)

Wolfe develops this pattern in a number of scenes in the second half of ***The Electric Kool-Aid Acid Test.*** The first portrays Kesey's second arrest for possession of marijuana two nights before the Trips Festival. This arrest occurs while Kesey and Mountain Girl are perched high above San Francisco on the roof of an apartment building. High both physically and mentally, they watch with blissful indifference as a police car pulls up far below. . . . For the reader who recalls the blinking red light that Kesey had felt he was praying to in his youth, the red light which symbolized Kesey's pursuit of technological fulfillment of the American Dream, Wolfe's description of Kesey watching the police car's light repeatedly blinking "red, nothing" has ominous significance. And Wolfe's previous use of the whirlpool image lends an equally ominous significance to the feeling of "turning so slow in the interferrometric synch." Indeed, Wolfe proceeds to show that the resulting arrest, which increases the likelihood of a lengthy prison sentence for Kesey, leads him after the Trips Festival to descend geographically to the southwestern tip of Mexico, in a journey that is paralleled by a psychological descent into deeper fantasy.

Wolfe uses this dual descent as the structural and thematic principle of "The Fugitive" chapter. Drawing on interviews with Kesey as well as on the extensive letters, notes, and tapes Kesey made at the time, Wolfe portrays Kesey's growing paranoia through a stream-of-consciousness interior monologue as he sits in a rented room on the west coast of Mexico, convinced that FBI agents are about to enter. Wolfe alternates this descent into unreality with an account of Kesey's journey through the Mexican desert into this spot in the jungle, describing it as a movement "into total nothing, like the lines of perspective in a surrealist painting." . . .

The effect of Wolfe's alternating narrative is to unite the physical and fantasy flights in a single escape from actuality, culminating in Kesey's paranoid leap over the back wall into the unreal "picturebook jungles of Mexico" . . . as he imagines that the FBI agents are coming up the stairs. The person who actually enters is only a Prankster, but Kesey spends hours hiding in the jungle, alternately consumed by paranoia and by megalomania, first surrounding himself with DDT to ward off the jungle insects and then exerting his will to draw them into his power. In either case, he has descended into a world of fantasy that seems increasingly unrelated to the facts of his situation. (pp. 117-18)

Wolfe shows Kesey in Mexico continuing to alternate between paranoia and megalomania, with the latter gradually coming to dominate his fantasies as he begins to conceive of himself as a secret agent who will defiantly reenter America. . . . As Wolfe narrates it, Kesey succeeds in a Hollywood-movie escape from the Mexican police, again crossing the border in outlandish disguise. But these fabulous adventures only increase his fantasy life. (p. 119)

Wolfe eventually brings this game into proper perspective by juxtaposing Kesey's fantasy version of "the grand finale" with the actual arrest. Kesey envisions a masked Test in which he will appear in a Super-Hero costume and deliver his "vision of the future." . . . Wolfe immediately follows Kesey's fantasy of ascension (which recalls his desire to go through the hole of infinite experience he saw in the sky) with the factual arrest. . . . Trapped on the highway by the FBI as he rides with a fellow Prankster, Kesey runs down an embankment which leads to a drain. Viewing the scene through the witnessing Prankster's eyes, Wolfe emphasizes a detail of the setting which is resonant with irony. . . . The O pattern formed by the circling birds suggests the whirlpool motif, an ironic image of the "big hole" in the sky that Kesey had initially perceived as a route to infinite experience and through which he has just fantasized his ascension. It seems now to represent the nothingness to which his quest has led him as he descends into the drain, a "vortex" of modern America's waste.

Wolfe's description of this descent effectively combines both the fantasy and actuality of the experience, while also investing it with the symbolic impact of the maelstrom motif. . . . In this drain Kesey finds the end of his quest to go ever "Further," finds the "last blasted edge." With the confusing merger of words in the stream-of-consciousness description, Wolfe suggests that Kesey himself has become nothing. . . . Kesey has symbolically met the annihilation that Poe's fisherman glimpsed but pulled back from in horror. In the ensuing chapters Wolfe shows that Kesey is unable to control or even direct the fantasy he started, the new Haight-Ashbury drug culture. (pp. 119-21)

Unlike conventional journalists, Wolfe shows himself as a fallible person who is nevertheless willing to learn. He gradually abandons his preconceived story and devotes his full time to not only observing but also experiencing the subject. . . . [His] account of Kesey's quest is as intellectually outside as it is experientially inside the protagonist's "fantasy"; it both reports and shapes. ***The Electric Kool-Aid Acid Test*** has validity precisely because it refuses to settle for either the unselective subjectivity of Kesey's movie or the rigid objectivity of the mass media's clichés. By combining exhaustive research with an experimental willingness to use and violate the formal conventions of journalism and of the novel, Wolfe creates a work which recounts factual events while conveying the subjective realities of his characters. And from his use of unusual punctuation to his allusions to Poe's "A Descent into the Maelstrom," Wolfe insistently brings his subject within his personal vision, frankly interpreting extreme experience for his reader. Far from being the "realist" he calls himself, Wolfe is an assertively self-reflexive experimentalist who, through pattern and style, transforms as he reports, responds as he represents. (pp. 124-25)

John Hellmann, "Reporting the Fabulous: Representation and Response in the Work of Tom Wolfe," in his Fables of Fact: The New Journalism As New Fiction, *University of Illinois Press, 1981, pp. 101-25.*

JOE DAVID BELLAMY

The Purple Decades—if we hadn't lived through them, we wouldn't have believed them possible. Already they begin to seem very far away. Luckily, we have Tom Wolfe to remember them by. Luckily, future historians, curiosity-seekers, and literate citizens will be able to turn to Tom Wolfe for the definitive, comprehensive, tuned-in portrait of our age. (p. vii)

Tom Wolfe's ascendancy as spokesperson for this era in American life developed through the medium that came to be called the New Journalism, but by reason of his own special gifts. . . .

But Wolfe's success is based on realities that go beyond the theory that the novelists weren't paying attention and the fact that Wolfe himself came to be the most accomplished and notorious practitioner of the New Journalism, and its chief architect and advocate. Wolfe's banner of the New Journalism was flown, in large part, to gain acceptance for a whole new set of literary conventions—conventions that, not accidentally, allowed full expression of his particular virtuosity. Encompassing the aesthetics and methodology of the nineteenth-century realist novel and the *modus operandi* of the big-city streetwise police-beat reporter, it was a form, Wolfe noted, that consumed "devices that happen to have originated with the novel and mixed them with every other device known to prose. And all the while, quite beyond matters of technique, it enjoyed an advantage so obvious, so built-in, one almost forgets what a power it has: the simple fact that the reader knows *all this actually happened*." . . . (p. viii)

In formulating new conventions and then serving as a propagandist for his own kind of art, Tom Wolfe, like Fielding, like Zola or Joyce, was following in a time-honored tradition, the formal innovator modifying received forms and methods to suit his own, historically exceptional, circumstances. . . . (pp. viii-ix)

Among the trickiest of the conventions Wolfe entertained was his inventive application of the principles of point-of-view. Wolfe describes in ***The New Journalism*** how and why he aspired to treat point-of-view in non-fiction writing. . . . The idea, he says, "was to give the full objective description, plus something that readers had always had to go to novels and short stories for: namely, the subjective or emotional life of the characters."

How can a non-fiction writer pretend to know exactly what a person is thinking or feeling at any given moment? He asks them. If a reporter bases his reconstruction of the subjective life of the character on the most scrupulous reporting, Wolfe would contend, he can get close to the truth of the inner life. Wolfe's ideal of saturation reporting is far more ambitious than anything the old journalists had thought to try. His approach is to cultivate the habit of staying with potential subjects for days, weeks, or months at a time, taking notes, interviewing, watching, and waiting for something dramatic and revealing to happen. Only through the most persistent and searching methods of reporting, Wolfe would emphasize, can the journalist's entrée into point-of-view, the subjective life, inner voices, the creation of scenes and dialogue, and so on, be justified.

Another aspect of Wolfe's treatment of point-of-view is his playful use of the downstage voice, the devil's-advocate voice, and other voices in his work. Here is a writer with a marvelous ear for dialogue, an easily galvanized, chameleonlike faculty for empathy, and a ventriloquist's delight in speaking other people's lines. From the start of his career, he was bored silly by the "pale beige tone" of conventional non-fiction writing. . . . So, early on, he began experimenting with outlandish voices and with the principle of skipping rapidly from one voice or viewpoint to the next, sometimes unexpectedly in the middle of a sentence, and often enough without identifying the voice or viewpoint except through context. Anything to avoid the stupefying monotony of the pale beige tone.

Even in expository sections, he often adopts the tone or characteristic lingo, point-of-view, or pretense of a character he is writing about. . . . Any voice he wishes to take on, he assumes with unerring smoothness and fidelity. Frequently, however, the voice produced turns out to be a put-on voice that reveals and dramatizes personality as it revels in the flaws, prejudices, and affectations of the character. The voice, that is, is both part of the character and, at the same time, above or outside it, interpreting and passing judgment. (pp. ix-x)

[In] any case, the New Journalism is a *fait accompli*. Whatever quibbling one might still occasionally hear about the dubiousness of its procedures, it is practiced every day across the land. . . .

Though Wolfe has always remained loyal to the journalistic calling and has expropriated its methods in all earnestness for his own purposes and has thus permanently changed the definition and the shape of journalism, he clearly is, and always has been, more than a journalist.

Temperamentally, Tom Wolfe is, from first to last, with every word and deed, a *comic* writer with an exuberant sense of humor, a baroque sensibility, and an irresistible inclination toward hyperbole. His antecedents are primarily literary—not journalistic, and not political, except in the largest sense. All these years, Tom Wolfe has been writing Comedy with a capital C, Comedy like that of Henry Fielding and Jane Austen and Joseph Addison, like that of Thackeray and Shaw and Mark Twain. Like these writers, Tom Wolfe might be described as a brooding humanistic presence. There is a decided moral edge to his humor. Wolfe never tells us what to believe exactly; rather, he shows us examples of good and (most often) bad form. He has always proffered these humanistic and moral perspectives on his subjects.

Which is not to say that beneath the cool surface of the hyped-up prose we should expect to find either a fire-and-brimstone preacher or a Juvenalian sort of satirist seething with indignation about the corruption of his fellow men. Neither will we discover, in Wolfe's work, any sign at all of a political or social activist who might argue on behalf of a particular party, issue, system, creed, or cause.

The satirical element in Wolfe's sort of comedic writing is most often sunny, urbane, and smiling. Like all Horatian comedy, it aims to reform through laughter that is never vindictive or merely personal, but broadly sympathetic. (pp. x-xi)

A close connection between laughter and reproof is evident throughout Wolfe's oeuvre. In works such as ***The Electric Kool-Aid Acid Test*** and "The Me Decade," for example, Wolfe mocks the idea that "letting it all hang out" is likely to offer a road to salvation or improvement. In ***The Electric Kool-Aid Acid Test,*** Wolfe shows again and again how destructive the sixties phony wisdom about the "joys" of abandonment to chemical cornucopias, in particular, could be. Similarly, by parodying facile aspects of the human potential movement in "The Me Decade" . . . , Wolfe demonstrates his concern about the exploitation and misdirection of human energies in what he sees as a foolish, limited, and petty cause. . . .

Or in ***Radical Chic,*** as Wolfe observes the socially elite of Manhattan indulging the fad of inviting members of the Black Panthers to their opulent parties, he poses the theory that the ostensible desire for social justice and the display of generosity involved had somewhat less to do with the proceedings than had the secret motive, which was the longing of the aristocrats to feel in its fullest degree the heady sensation of "How chic we are." (p. xii)

All these perspectives arise out of a sense of the moral insufficiency of the participants and reveal Tom Wolfe pointing a finger and laughing wholeheartedly at what people do when they fly in the face of the hard facts about their own natures or their unconscious or concealed motives or aspirations. The merriment is intense; the laughter is real. But there is little cause for feeling vastly superior to the miserable fools, tarnished folk heroes, rebels, fanatics, and hustlers from Wolfe's rogue's gallery of humanity. For lurking just beneath the swirling surface of his prose is the sobering realization that the potential for vanity of similar proportion is common to us all.

One indirect moral service that great comedic writers perform is to promote self-awareness, and Wolfe's major contribution here has been his emphasis on the hidden and sometimes peculiar manifestations of status-seeking in American life. In the manner of a conscientious Martian anthropologist, he has tried rigorously to apply the principle that all primates, including humans, organize their societies according to status hierarchies and struggles for dominance. The importance of status behavior as the source of society's most mysterious subtleties has, of course, been recognized and studied by the social sciences for years. The proof of the existence of such behavior is not original to Tom Wolfe, but the wholesale exploration of its features in American culture and its exploitation for comical purposes are certainly important aspects of Wolfe's novelty and uniqueness. The tool of status-analysis, and other gleanings from the social sciences, has led Wolfe, over the last two decades, to these basic assumptions about American life: (1) That the fragmentation and diversity of American culture resulted in the emergence of subcultures or enclaves that have evolved their own bizarre art forms, life styles, and status rituals independent from the "elite" culture of the past, the "high" culture of the American Northeast via Europe ("the big amoeba-God of Anglo-European sophistication"), or other common references. (2) That these enclaves, generally ignored by serious social observers, deserve the closest scrutiny, both because they are the truest, most authentic, examples of "the way we live now" and because they illustrate comically that human nature follows the same quaint, barbaric patterns regardless of class, region, or circumstance. (3) That fragmentation of American society has sometimes caused rampant status confusion (as in ***Radical Chic***); emphasis upon enunciating weird new tribal identities (as in ***The Pump House Gang, The Electric Kool-Aid Acid Test,*** or ***The Right Stuff***); the evolution of status dropouts who discover they can compete more favorably with some new set of rules in life style (as in "The Mid-Atlantic Man"); and a remarkable array of bewildering or ridiculous behavior (as in "The Voices of Village Square" or "The Girl of the Year")—all ripe for Wolfean analysis—including the widespread frantic search for spurious forms of salvation (as in "The Me Decade" or ***The Electric Kool-Aid Acid Test***).

Thus, Junior Johnson's stock cars of "The Last American Hero," as seen through Wolfe's eyes, are like the totems of the Easter Islanders or the formal architecture of the Regency period, critically important cultural artifacts that are the focus of both veneration and status competition for their creators. Or, as in ***The Right Stuff,*** among the test pilots, the fraternity of "the right stuff" is the basis for the display of almost incredible forms of heroism, which Wolfe clearly admires. But, even here, it is the fierce status competition within the group that serves to motivate the men, a desire for the "sinfully inconfessable . . . feeling of superiority, appropriate to him and his kind, lone bearers of the right stuff." (pp. xii-xiii)

Typically, as Wolfe unspools yard after yard of theory, he forces us to test it against our own understanding of the nature of things. And he compels us to ask questions: Why in the name of God should painting and architecture in our time have become so trivialized, so specialized, so uniform? Why would an accomplished, clever man want to give up his work and French-fry his brains and invest his earthly time tooling around the countryside in a psychedelic schoolbus? Why in the world would a normal, sane, healthy person want to risk his life on a day-to-day basis as a test pilot or an astronaut? Why do people *behave* as they do? How do we live? How should we live?

Clearly, as Wolfe has grown in stature, he has become more interested in reform and more concerned about what he sees as "the wrong stuff" and "the right stuff." At the heart of ***Bauhaus*** and ***The Painted Word*** is a straightforward wish to humanize art and architecture by showing how "the freight train of history" got off on the wrong track by the most ludicrous sort of historical coincidence. All of Wolfe's recent books, and many of his earlier essays, are also parables offered as intellectual history. They show how political power and orthodoxy and fashion-mongering have often run roughshod over originality, virtue, fair play, exuberance, and panache. The moral would seem to be that those who succumb to the temptation to aspire to the merely fashionable, who thus sacrifice the noble impulse toward individual vision, may end up "succeeding" and thereby mucking up whole centuries. This failing, he seems to warn us, is so common that all of us should be on guard against it, lest we, too, be tempted to repeat it. Substance over surface, he proclaims, should be our guide—be alert to the frailties of human nature and pay attention to values that truly matter. Yet there is nothing self-righteous in Tom Wolfe's moral stance, and it is so well disguised that the average reader often may be unaware that an implicit moral position is being assumed.

After roughly twenty years of development—by combining the methodology of the journalist with his own special sense and sensibility—the young writer whose life was forever changed by one amazed afternoon at the Coliseum at the Hot Rod & Custom Car Show has gone on to become the most astute and popular social observer and cultural chronicler of his generation. If Tom Wolfe sometimes interprets the American scene with the apparent detachment and freedom from constraints of a visiting Martian, he remains a Martian with an enviable sense of humor, energy, and playfulness. If he is often the maverick skeptic among us, the ultimate "King-Has-No-Clothes-On" man of principle, he is a skeptic with the power of empathy. If, at times, he seems to be viewing his own culture like an anthropologist studying the strange habits of the Trobriand Islanders, he is an anthropologist with an ear for every kind of idiomatic speech, loaded language and the multiple meanings it contains, and a conviction about the value of skewering pretentiousness wherever it may be found. No other writer of our time has aspired to capture the fabled Spirit of the Age so fully and has succeeded so well. (pp. xiv-xv)

Joe David Bellamy, in an introduction to The Purple Decades: A Reader *by Tom Wolfe, Farrar, Straus & Giroux, 1982, pp.vii-xv.*

JAMES WOLCOTT

The Purple Decades presents an ample selection of Tom Wolfe's writings from the Sixties and Seventies—a bewilderingly familiar selection, considering how many of Wolfe's fugitive pieces on fashion and pop remain uncollected. Rather than spruce up the book with some of Wolfe's lesser-known sorties . . . , ***The Purple Decades*** safely sticks to what one might call Tom Wolfe's Greatest Hits. . . .

Since all of Wolfe's books are still in print, it can hardly be argued that ***The Purple Decades*** is needed to rescue Wolfe's work from the murks of neglect. Nor has the book been assembled merely as a sampler. No, the book's ambitious title suggests that this collection provides an overview of a rambunctious era in the dandyish, frisking manner of Thomas Beer's *The Mauve Decade*. Inside, the book gives off deeper rumbles of ambition: ***The Purple Decades*** is intended to be a plinth on which Tom Wolfe's reputation will forever rest. (p. 21)

The cheerleader poet of pop hedonism, Tom Wolfe never gives in to shudders of Swiftian disgust or dances along the crest of the abyss: his satire is free of fever blisters and black depths. But this hardly means that the firecrackers he sets off beneath people's feet are intended to awaken them to the errors of their ways. Wolfe is often at his funniest when he's being an irresponsible imp, flying on the wing of a wicked whim, setting a scene down to its tiniest, most telling detail and then letting the laughter build from a snicker to a rich, mad cackle. . . . When Tom Wolfe is in top prankster form, his victims give off the hiss of escaping gas.

In recent years, however, Wolfe has turned himself into a mod Tory—the clown prince of neoconservatism—and his humor has become forced, curdled, tendentious. The weakest and most hootingly shrill essays in ***The Purple Decades*** are those in which Wolfe hitches up his boxing trunks to have another bruising go at radical chic. "Mauve Gloves & Madmen, Clutter & Vine," for example, is an extended wheeze of thinnish whimsy about a materialistic American author who's having an anxiety attack tapping his monthly expenses into his desk calculator. . . . (p. 21)

In "The Intelligent Coed's Guide to America," Wolfe checks into what Gore Vidal has called the Hotel Hilton Kramer in order to tweak the noses of the leftward intelligentsia yet again and pay Aleksandr Solzhenitsyn a rather thick tribute. Now, I happen to be more than a little fond of right-wing comic crank scourges—Auberon Waugh, Malcolm Muggeridge—but Wolfe's eagerness to hammer away at the ideological anvil is not only coarsening his comic gifts but is leading him into the company of writers far less talented. (p. 22)

But for all the fireworks and finger-popping glee, a nodding tedium came over me as I inched my way through ***The Purple Decades***—"I've *read* all this stuff before." . . . Not only have Tom Wolfe's Greatest Hits never been long off the turntable, but there's also a certain shrill, monotonous tone which emerges when his hits are anthologized. Reading a collection like (say) *Rebecca West: A Celebration,* one captures West in a variety of moods and attitudes, now critical, now quarrelsome, now content to dawdle and graze. But Tom Wolfe's best writing is all at the same clamorous pitch, a succession of kettledrum booms and flying cymbals, and one's eardrums begin to throb under the onslaught of all those *italics,* all—those—dashes, all those flip exclamation m!a!r!k!s! His writing rattles the china long after he's left the room, and one begins to pine for a subduing lull of calm.

The Purple Decades is, finally, all too precipitous. Tom Wolfe is unquestionably a brash, funny, resourceful reporter and commentator, one of the few writers in America whose work commands an immediate eye-click of attention. Faces skyward, we can only wonder from which bough he'll next swoop in search of virgin prey. But, really, it's far too early to know whether ***The Electric Kool-Aid Acid Test*** (excerpted here) is a true landmark of brain-fried Sixties sensibility, or will prove to be a word-monster as unreadable as the worst of William Gaddis; whether ***The Right Stuff*** (likewise excerpted) is the classic of derring-do that its champions claim, or whether its snobbery and whipped-up histrionics will some day reduce it to a book of stray brilliancies. . . . It's certainly far too early for Tom Wolfe to be monumentalizing himself and his achievements in veiny marble. . . .

If Tom Wolfe's reputation continues to thrive, it will be despite the bossiness of ***The Purple Decades,*** not because of it. (p. 23)

James Wolcott, "Tom Wolfe's Greatest Hits," in The New York Review of Books, *Vol. XXIX, No. 17, November 4, 1982, pp. 21-3.*

STANLEY REYNOLDS

Ever since 1965 when ***The Kandy-Kolored Tangerine-Flake Streamline Baby*** first brought the world the good news that Tom Wolfe was living and writing in it I have regularly reviewed and applauded—with eager screamers!!!!!! and sufficient WOWS!—each new book. (p. 70)

[In reading ***The Purple Decades***], supposedly the best of Wolfe since 1965, I kept wondering if I might not have been wrong all these years. The stuff nowadays doesn't seem all that good. But could everyone have been wrong?

Maybe Wolfe has been too much imitated. Perhaps we've had more of the New Journalism than we can handle. Maybe and perhaps, but I don't think so. Wolfe is basically a comic writer and these old pieces still make you laugh aloud. But are the things he writes about serious enough? . . .

I suppose it was crusading journalism in a way to expose the rich phonies in New York who were patronising the Black Panthers with fund-raising evenings. That's "Those Radical Chic Evenings", from ***Radical Chic & Mau Mauing the Flak Catchers*** (1970). Well, that evening at Leonard Bernstein's is very funny. And the idea of the blacks getting money out of agencies by pretending to be violent, armed men—this is called mau-mauing the flak catchers—is hilarious.

But something else was going on during all those years. It was the Vietnam War. Although Wolfe seems to have been on an aircraft carrier once, he generally ignores the war, which was, after all, *the* story of the so-called Purple Decades. He could have gone there. They would have loved to send him. But he wasn't responsible. He was irresponsible. That's not what a great journalist would do.

We are told by somebody called Joe David Bellamy in an introduction to this book that Tom Wolfe only seems to be all on the side of the people he writes about. Bellamy says this is not so, it is merely Tom's style [see excerpt above]. But it certainly seems so. Wolfe comes across as a most awful snob, a social climber and, essentially a hick with all that cliché awe that hicks, who never knew New York when they were children, only ever saw it when they were grown up, have for New York.

But he has a lovely turn of phrase, he can make a story out of nothing—"The Voices of Village Square" about female prisoners in jail in Greenwich Village shouting at passers-by—and sometimes when he is writing what is really fiction—"A Sunday Kind of Love" and "The Woman Who Has Everything"—he comes close to that other great hick, F. Scott Fitzgerald. (p. 71)

Stanley Reynolds, "Who's Afraid of Tom Wolfe?" in Punch, *March 23, 1983, pp. 70-1.*

RONALD WEBER

There ought to be a statute of limitations on critical remarks about living, breathing writers. Lacking that, it must simply be good manners that keeps Joe David Bellamy, in his introduction to [***The Purple Decades***] from mentioning the late Dwight Macdonald's celebrated attack on Wolfe as a practitioner of a specious new form called parajournalism [see excerpts above]. Macdonald's remarks came in a 1965 review of Wolfe's first book, ***The Kandy-Kolored Tangerine-Flake Streamline Baby,*** setting out most of the lines of criticism subsequently directed at Wolfe and a piece still to be reckoned with if Wolfe is taken seriously as a journalist or literary figure. But looking back from the vantage point offered by ***The Purple Decades,*** one is struck by how much Macdonald got wrong. (p. 548)

One of the few incontestable things to say about Wolfe is that he has endured and prospered. He continues to be read, apparently with great pleasure; and he has shown surprising ability to broaden the range of his subjects, shifting from the "celebs" and "personalities" that so irritated Macdonald. . . . The style, though toned down over the years, still seems to strike many readers as fresh and engaging, a noisy though effective vehicle for bringing character and situation to sudden life. Whatever else might be said about Wolfe's prose, it's distinctive, as few writing styles are these days.

To give Macdonald his due, one was bound to wonder how Wolfe's early work would look in the sober light of a new day. Not bad at all, actually. (pp. 548-49)

The Wolfian tags (flak catchers, radical chic, me decade, the right stuff) may appear shopworn now, partly because they have become common currency, but they still serve as useful catchalls for a broad range of contemporary activity and character types. . . . If Wolfe is read in another 20 years—and he seems as likely to be read, read seriously, as any other contemporary writer—it largely will be due to the staying power of his two most important books [***The Electric Kool-Aid Acid Test*** and ***The Right Stuff***].

Another Macdonald complaint was that Wolfe's own views about his subjects were hard to pin down. . . . As Macdonald saw, some confusion or ambivalence is a byproduct of one of Wolfe's favored devices: the narrowing of the ordinary distance between journalist and subject, even merging the journalist's voice with the subject's, so that the subject seems portrayed from within. . . . Such blurring of distinctions between writer and subject may still appear troubling if one persists in thinking of Wolfe primarily as a journalist. But even on this level his use of the device has become so familiar over the years that most readers ought to be able to separate Wolfe's views from those of his subjects. (p. 549)

Wolfe's taste for plain old American reality takes . . . a neoconservative political cast. Whimsically, he notes that in sex education classes we tell school children that sexual intercourse is natural and beautiful yet remain baffled by the rising number of out-of-wedlock pregnancies. Dead seriously, he takes up the case for Solzhenitsyn, arguing that the "bone heap" of modern history, "grisly beyond belief," is an inescapable fact and that "socialism had created it." (p. 550)

There is nothing wrong, of course, with Wolfe having intellectual convictions of the neoconservative sort. . . . But there may be some threat that Wolfe the nimble comic satirist might fade into Wolfe the predictable moralist, locked into the same sort of mental box he inveighs against in the case of liberal types—hardly an ideal situation for one who presents himself as a journalist.

This brings up Wolfe's identity as a journalist—an identity Macdonald rightly questioned in his review. He scoffed that Wolfe wasn't a journalist of the regular stripe, since the aim of journalism ought to be information, but a parajournalist whose aim was entertainment. Bellamy reviews Wolfe's exploits and technical aspirations as a New Journalist but points out that Wolfe "is, and always has been, more than a journalist." What Bellamy has in mind isn't Macdonald's condescending crown of entertainer but the noble title of social critic. According to Bellamy, Wolfe is "the most astute and popular social observer and cultural chronicler of his generation," the "spokesperson for this era in American life." The natural hyperbole of the introducer aside, is this really the case? Is Wolfe best read for social observation and cultural chronicle—or, for that matter, best read simply for entertainment?

There is no pressing need to shove Wolfe into a critical pigeonhole—a writer so agile and ambitious will surely escape anyway—but there may be some use in pointing to the general nature of his work. . . . Wolfe may think of himself as a journalist or a journalist-as-social-critic, but his best work isn't finally journalism or social commentary but literature—literature in the same sense that the work of Updike and Roth is literature: turned to character, to the play of language, to the development of meaning and implication. Wolfe's real peers are exactly Updike and Roth and not Jimmy Breslin or Anthony Lewis or even John McPhee. This doesn't mean that Wolfe's work is factually inaccurate or devoid of social observation; no doubt Wolfe can be happily and fruitfully read as both journalist and social critic. But this isn't what is best, or likely to be most lasting, about his work. The rightful place of Wolfe's best work, ***The Electric Kool-Aid Acid Test*** and ***The Right Stuff*** as well as "The Last American Hero" and "The Truest Sport," is among the better literary works of the past two decades.

Wilfrid Sheed observed that it may serve an artistic purpose for Wolfe to think of himself as a journalist because "he reminds his nose to stay down near the details where it works best" [see *CLC*, Vol. 2]. It's not finally the details that matter but the mind, imagination, and unfettered rhetoric imposed upon them, turning them into a Wolfian world as recognizable as the fictional world of a good novelist. Bellamy mentions Wolfe's capacity for getting inside other lives and "speaking other people's lines"; but those lines come out sounding mostly the same because they have been processed in Wolfe's special blender, turned into what Sheed called "Wolfe-truths." This doesn't make Wolfe's work fiction, but it isn't exactly fact writing either. It's fact turned toward literature, reporting aimed at art. If that seems too pretentious, it can at least be said that Wolfe has been one of our most durable and interesting writers—whatever the sort—over the last 20 years. ***The Purple Decades*** makes that clear enough. (pp. 549-50)

Ronald Weber, "Staying Power," in The Virginia Quarterly Review, *Vol. 59, No. 3 (Summer, 1983), pp. 548-52.*

GEORGE SIM JOHNSTON

What is going on in the pages of *Rolling Stone*? After years of making faces and otherwise annoying our menagerie of Great

American Novelists, who have mustered only a morose stare in response to his wild gesticulations, Tom Wolfe has climbed into the cage, taken off his mauve sports jacket, loosened his Edwardian collar, and with a wink at Updike, Roth, and Styron, grabbed hold of a swinging bar and . . . is showing them how to do it! Forgive the lapse into Wolfean locution. The man's style is infectious. But the serialization of [Wolfe's forthcoming novel] ***The Bonfire of the Vanities*** is of some literary consequence.

Tom Wolfe has been pointing out the error of their ways to American novelists since he was a young journalist. But neither Updike, Roth & Co., nor the legions of income-supplementing academics who review their books, seem to have gotten the message. It must have become clear to Wolfe that the only way to show them was to roll up his sleeves and do the job himself. . . . [He] is performing the invaluable service of presenting our literary lions with a concrete example of what writing a novel is all about. (p. 25)

[Wolfe] has gone to the early Victorians for his inspiration. He is even serializing his story in the Victorian manner. . . .

He is trying to resurrect the social novel on a grand scale, as it was practiced by Dickens, Thackeray, and Trollope, and his subject, no less, is New York, the capital of the late twentieth century. And he is not just giving us a wafer-thin slice of Manhattan. He is taking us, with extreme accuracy and a great deal of merriment, on an amazing tour of Gotham. . . . (p. 26)

The city in ***The Bonfire of the Vanities*** is an international carnival; money flows like lava, and lots of Europeans have crossed the Atlantic "to devour at leisure the last plump white meat on the bones of capitalism." The jockeying for social position, such as it is in the eighties, is intense, and Wolfe is alive to innumerable air-lines of status. Sexual confusion is, of course, rampant. Upper-middle-class women maintain a residual femininity strictly for social advantage, and their male consorts have difficulty looking them in the eye. At the other end of the social ladder, the underclass is laying waste to large tracts of the city, gradually closing in on the carnival of high-living. The whole complex scene is gathered up into the baroque comic vision which infuses all of Wolfe's writing.

There are enough vivid characters from different milieus to please the shade of Balzac. The novel covers every base except the young professionals, who at the moment seem to be overrunning the city like the pod-people in [*The Invasion of the Body Snatchers*]. The social texture of ***The Bonfire of the Vanities*** is dense. Even in its incomplete state, it puts to shame those fiction writers who are capable of portraying only the pale, tentative rebellions of a few deracinated souls living near Central Park. Wolfe is fortunate in not being inhibited by the usual liberal taboos regarding the depiction of racial and ethnic distinctions. If you don't think that some of the subject matter in this novel is anathema to the progresssive mind, wait for the reviews—or, if you like, take a liberal friend to a Richard Pryor concert film. The reaction will be pretty much the same in both cases.

In the manner of the great Victorians, Wolfe has set spinning several plots at once whose connection is not immediately apparent. Every scene is done with Wolfe's supersensory eye for social detail. My favorites thus far are the confrontation between the preppy Episcopal charities aide and Reverend Bacon in the latter's Harlem office and the del Ponces' Park Avenue dinner party. Wolfe's journalistic training is serving him well. He has the discipline of concrete presentation. He does not fudge any of the improbable array of settings. You have to assume that the man has been there. And not the least of the novel's virtues is the dialogue, which is fast becoming a lost art among American novelists. . . .

My major reservation so far concerns the excessive use of detail. The apprentice novelist is taking Balzac too much to heart. Some of the detail, such as Reverend Bacon's gold chain and Rolex watch, does exactly what it is supposed to do, which is to tip the reader off in a few quick strokes about a character. But we learn more about architecture and interior decoration than we may care to know (let's get on with the story!). Wolfe's dialogue is expert enough to allow him a margin of freedom from these stage props and he should take advantage of it. I offer this criticism with hesitation, because when he gives us a catalogue of every object in the del Ponces' dining room, for example, he hits one bull's-eye after another.

Wolfe will probably do some housecleaning before the hardcover edition, so I may as well throw in a few nitpicks in the interests of verisimilitude. The waiter in La Boue d'Argent needs a Berlitz course—it's *mesdames,* not *madames,* and *un* Perrier, not *une* Perrier, s'il vous plait. . . . Also, it is time to retire the vinyl-wallet manufacturer and the Pontiac Bonneville, both of which have done good service in Wolfe's past work and deserve a break.

I imagine that, given the competition, Tom Wolfe feels the way Fitzgerald felt after the First World War—"America (read: New York) was going on the greatest, gaudiest spree in history and there was going to be plenty to tell about it. The whole golden boom was in the air. . . ." After putting together the best body of work of any American journalist since Mencken, Wolfe is writing a novel which, whatever its defects, will probably tell us more, in the Trollopian phrase, about "the way we live now" than any novel published in recent memory. Wolfe once ventured the sound opinion that Evelyn Waugh will eventually stand as England's major novelist of the twentieth century, because Waugh told us so much about society and its manners. I don't think it rash to predict that Wolfe, both for his journalism and now for his foray into the novel, will be remembered for the same reasons, long after Roth, Updike & Co. have become unreadable footnotes to the literary age. (p. 27)

George Sim Johnston, "Manhattan Cut in Slices," in The American Spectator, *Vol. 18, No. 3, March, 1985, pp. 25-7.*

Laurence (Michael) Yep

1948-

American novelist, short story writer, and author of books for children.

A Chinese-American, Yep draws upon his own experiences of cultural alienation and racial conflict for both his science fiction and his realistic novels. His works typically involve an individual caught between cultures who struggles to adapt, to achieve a sense of identity, and to overcome hostility and prejudice. Consistently praised for debunking stereotypes, Yep's novels speak for human tolerance and understanding.

Yep's realistic fiction frequently revolves around adolescents whose Chinese heritage conflicts with Western society. *Dragonwings* (1975) centers on Moon Shadow, a young boy who leaves China to join his father in San Francisco; *Child of the Owl* (1977) chronicles the growth of a young Chinese girl who has been raised in Western society and must examine her cultural background when she moves to San Francisco's Chinatown; and Craig Chin in *Sea Glass* (1979) is an overweight Chinese boy who is rejected by occidentals and orientals alike. Yep's science fiction novels, including *Sweetwater* (1973), *Seademons* (1977), and *Dragon of the Lost Sea* (1982), share with his other works a thematic focus on the pain of being different. This theme is often depicted through a protagonist struggling with a dual heritage.

Several of Yep's recent novels depart from his usual concentration on Chinese-American themes or science fiction. *Kind Hearts and Gentle Monsters* (1982) examines the relationship between a high school student and a classmate whose mother is mentally disturbed. *The Mark Twain Murders* (1982) and *Liar, Liar* (1983) are novels of suspense and mystery involving teenage protagonists. The former is set in the Civil War era, while the latter has a contemporary setting.

(See also *Children's Literature Review*, Vol. 3; *Contemporary Authors*, Vols. 49-52; *Contemporary Authors New Revision Series*, Vol. 1; and *Something about the Author*, Vol. 7.)

Photograph by Kathy Yep. Courtesy of Harper & Row, Publishers, Inc.

PAUL HEINS

In his afterword [to ***Dragonwings***], the author states "it has been my aim to counter various stereotypes as presented in the media. . . . I wanted to show that Chinese-Americans are human beings upon whom America has had a unique effect. I have tried to do this by seeing America through the eyes of a recently arrived Chinese boy." At the age of eight, Moon Shadow left the Middle Kingdom, "or *China* as the white demons call it," and joined his father Windrider in San Francisco. Although Windrider worked in a laundry . . . his real interest was in mechanical devices, and after a while he left the town of the Tang people (Chinatown) to become a repairman and a free-lance mechanic. Befriended by a white woman, Miss Whitlaw, and her young niece Robin, Moon Shadow and Windrider studied aeronautical books in their spare time and built and flew model gliders. . . . The confrontation of two cultures is fairly presented: Allusions to the periodic harassments of the Chinese are counterbalanced by the account of Miss Whitlaw's and Robin's natural acceptance of Moon Shadow and his father as human beings. Moon Shadow's telling of the events and experiences that united him and his father in a common undertaking is devastatingly humorous in its appraisal of two forms of civilization. . . . (pp. 472-73)

Paul Heins, in a review of "Dragonwings," in The Horn Book Magazine, *Vol. LI, No. 5, October, 1975, pp. 472-73.*

JUNE GOODWIN

In Chinese culture demons don't *have* to be bad, and dragons most certainly aren't. ***Dragonwings*** builds from a perhaps intentionally stilted story in the rice paddies of China into a subtly romantic tale of Chinese immigrants living by their wits and imagination in San Francisco at the turn of the century.

Slowly, scale by fabulous scale, Laurence Yep makes dragons as possible to man as empathy. Dragons can fly, you see, and that is why Moon Shadow's father built an aeroplane.

June Goodwin, "Flying Carpets to Adventure," in The Christian Science Monitor, *November 5, 1975, p. B7.**

MARGERY FISHER

Three groups live separately on the planet ironically named Harmony [in ***Sweetwater***]. The mainlanders, colonists from Earth, have built New Sion some way inland after disastrous sea floods; in Old Sion the Silkies have adapted, physically and mentally, to life in a ruinous, flooded city, descendants as they are of intelligent and resourceful star-pilots; in part of Old Sion the indigenous Argans, a spider-like people, live in distant amity with the Silkies. Distant, that is, until Tyree Priest, son of the Silkie captain, finds a bond with old Amadeus through music. The complex plot involves race-hostility and social jealousy, the vulnerability of a subsistence existence under the influence of money and, ultimately, wider issues of freedom and tolerance in which the past is constantly invoked through oral tradition to protect the Silkies from what can be recognised as the darker aspects of Progress. The author's inventive powers are strongly exercised in the circumstantial details of a planet whose cosmography has a visible effect on people of Earth descent, and in dramatic and exhilarating scenes of action. (pp. 3012-13)

Margery Fisher, in a review of "Sweetwater," in her Growing Point, *Vol. 15, No. 6, December, 1976, pp. 3012-13.*

HUMAN—AND ANTI-HUMAN—VALUES IN CHILDREN'S BOOKS: A CONTENT RATING INSTRUMENT FOR EDUCATORS AND CONCERNED PARENTS

Chinese Americans—like all Asian Americans—have been either "invisible" or seen as one-dimensional laundrymen, Fu Manchus, cooks or Charlie Chans. ***Dragonwings*** attempts to counter such stereotypes with the story of a talented Chinese immigrant and his son who, in the early 1900's, dream of building a flying-machine and succeed in making their dream come true. Along with the dream they must contend with the realities of the new land—the racism of the "demons," beatings and lynchings, the harshness of life, the sacrifices and the failures. The book tries, and in some ways succeeds, in showing that the Chinese in America were, and are, ordinary as well as extraordinary people.

The story is told in the first person with delightful humor, as young Moon Shadow reacts to the strange ways of the white "demons." Through his vision the reader learns many authentic details of life in China, where Moon Shadow lived with his mother and grandmother, and of life in San Francisco's early Chinatown where Moon Shadow has joined his father. Even the book's unusual combination of mystical belief and scientific brilliance is made believable.

Some of the unpleasant realities of early Chinatown's secret societies, prostitution, and opium dens are depicted, a bit luridly perhaps, but this is offset by warm characterizations of Moon Shadow's family and friends. They are not stereotypes and they relate to one another in ways that are culturally distinct from white behaviors.

"The Analyses: 'Dragonwings'," in Human—And Anti-Human—Values in Children's Books: A Content Rating Instrument for Educators and Concerned Parents, *edited by the Council on Interracial Books for Children, Inc., Racism and Sexism Resource Center for Educators, 1976, p. 257.*

THE JUNIOR BOOKSHELF

Because underlying [***Sweetwater***] there are valid universal truths—the sorrow of homeless wanderers, the costliness of integrity—this is something more than an ingenious space-narrative. . . . Laurence Yep manages to create a genuine other-worldliness with the strange beauty of underwater, and he neatly conveys earlier history with a minimum of explanation, despite some (to our ears) jarring American slang. He has written a remarkable and imaginative book.

A review of "Sweetwater," in The Junior Bookshelf, *Vol. 41, No. 1, February, 1977, p. 48.*

WENDY MOORHEAD

[In ***Child of the Owl***] Casey, a young Chinese girl whose father is a compulsive gambler, must live for a time with a grandmother she has never seen. Casey has never thought of herself as Chinese but life in Chinatown forces her to decide who she really is.

Grandmother is the one who tells Casey the legend of the owl spirit, and who helps her realize that she is a child of the owl—that she may never feel completely at ease as a Chinese or as an American, but that she cannot completely cut herself off from her Chinese heritage.

The book is not always easy to follow and requires some perseverance and concentration at times. Author Yep's strength, however, is his description of life in Chinatown.

Wendy Moorhead, "From Appalachia to Chinatown—Adventure in America," in The Christian Science Monitor, *May 4, 1977, p. B2.**

GEORGESS McHARGUE

[In **"Child of the Owl"**] Casey Young goes to stay with her Paw-Paw (grandmother) in San Francisco's Chinatown after her father Barney is beaten up outside a bookie joint. . . .

I wish Mr. Yep had let Paw-Paw and Chinatown carry the story without slowing it down with episodes like Casey's visit to her uncle "Phil the Pill," a caricature of suburbanized Chinese. I also didn't believe that pathologically generous, easy-going Barney could become involved in an act of violence against Paw-Paw, even though it winds the story up neatly (too neatly, perhaps).

Georgess McHargue, in a review of "Child of the Owl," in The New York Times Book Review, *May 22, 1977, p. 29.*

VIRGINIA HAVILAND

When her gambling father is hospitalized, motherless Casey [in ***Child of the Owl***] . . . is shifted from her lawyer-uncle's luxurious home, where she is ungraciously accepted, to her maternal grandmother Paw-Paw, who leads an impoverished, stringent life in Chinatown. Paw-Paw owns a valuable jade owl charm believed to have been given to the family by an ancestral Owl Spirit, and it induces her to tell a lengthy story, based on Chinese folklore, which "'happened a long, long time ago when our ancestors first came into southern China.'" The tale tells how the owl Jasmine was tricked out of her feather skin and was made the wife of a human; it illustrates Paw-Paw's feeling that "'[w]e became a little like owls the moment we turned our backs on China and the old ways' " and leads Casey to realize that she will never fit into Chinatown the way her mother did. The rest of the book reveals more dramatically the evils of life in Chinatown as it deals with the theft of the charm and with the criminal elements which accounted for the theft and which explain her father's irresponsible state. It is a haunting piece of fiction in which the many elements are masterfully blended.

Virginia Haviland, in a review of "Child of the Owl," in The Horn Book Magazine, *Vol. LIII, No. 4, August, 1977, p. 447.*

KIRKUS REVIEWS

[In ***Seademons***] "The Folk" are a shipload of refugees recently escaped from a race of cruel masters who employed them as combat troops and kept them in a state of technological ignorance. With few resources beyond a melange of battered neo-Irish myths and a stock of advanced but irreplaceable weapons, they are trying to colonize an Earthlike new home. . . . The emotional range is truncated, and much of the dialogue is pallid and soon-palling badinage. But the situation is outlined with imaginative verve, and the story is put together with confidence and smoothness.

A review of "Seademons," in Kirkus Reviews, *Vol. XLV, No. 19, October 1, 1977, p. 1066.*

PUBLISHERS WEEKLY

Inventive and skillfully written, [***Seademons***] tells of a future civilization that's technologically sophisticated but ruled by primitive beliefs. Ciaran, daughter of the colony's leader, is with a band who finds a human child deposited on land by the seademons. Many of the settlers demand that the foundling be killed as a witch but Ciaran and others persuade them to accept the little girl they name Maeve. When she grows up, Maeve consorts secretly with the seademons, fearful enemy of the people. Her actions cause the death of several of the girl's human protectors, including Ciaran's brothers. Inevitably, conflicts between the seademons and the humans lead to war, battles graphically and terrifyingly described, then to a strangely moving resolution.

A review of "Seademons," in Publishers Weekly, *Vol. 212, No. 14, October 3, 1977, p. 94.*

EVIE WILSON AND MICHAEL McCUE

On the ocean shores of the planet Fancyfree, traders from an alien world deposit a human-like girl, named Maeve by the colonists who give her shelter. . . . This suspenseful, yet sensitive, story [***Seademons***] beautifully illustrates the pain of being "different." It also recounts a tale that our world's history has borne out: that the price humanity pays for peace and brotherhood is not nearly as high as the price demanded by war.

Evie Wilson and Michael McCue, in a review of "Seademons," in Wilson Library Bulletin, *Vol. 52, No. 4, December, 1977, p. 337.*

MARY M. BURNS

During the last two decades, conflict between generations has been a dominant theme in children's literature. In his fourth novel [***Sea Glass***] the author proves that the theme is not a cliché—given an original treatment in a well-structured story written with style and perception. Unlike ***Dragonwings*** or ***Child of the Owl*** . . . , which explore ethnicity within a supportive community, the story of Craig Chin delineates the problems of a child searching for identity when caught between two cultures and seemingly rejected by both. Transplanted from San Francisco's Chinatown to small-town Concepcion when his father takes a job there, the overweight boy discovers that he is simultaneously denigrated by his occidental schoolmates as a fat Chinese " 'Buddha Man' " and criticized by an elderly friend of the family for being " 'like the white demons.' " . . . Craig is constantly at odds with his father's methods of emulating the American lifestyle personified in Cousin Stanley—a " 'real all-American boy,' " replete with trophies, straight A's, and friends. The gap is finally bridged through the wisdom of elderly Uncle Quail, a conservative recluse who had withdrawn to an isolated seacoast home because of the indignities heaped upon the early Chinese communities in California. But the old man is keenly aware of the tensions among Craig's family and offers the boy a more important perspective on life. Totally engaging, the first-person narrative is carefully but not self-consciously wrought.

Mary M. Burns, in a review of "Sea Glass," in The Horn Book Magazine, *Vol. LV, No. 5, October, 1979, p. 542.*

MARIA LENHART

Being 12-years-old means facing new challenges with parents, peers, and, most of all, yourself. For Craig Chin [in ***Sea Glass***], who has just left the cozy, familiar world of San Francisco's Chinatown to live in a predominantly white coastal village, these challenges come with the force of waves beating against a rock. . . .

Award-winning author Laurence Yep has drawn his characters with a deft touch, creating believable people grappling with believable problems. His dialogue and first-person narrative are natural and realistic. Beyond that, this is an engrossing, thoughtful story that should give pause to parents and children alike. Children are too often burdened with the faded dreams of their parents' past and, like Craig, need room to grow and find dreams of their own.

Maria Lenhart, "Finding the Courage to Be Oneself," in The Christian Science Monitor, *October 15, 1979, p. B11.*

JEAN FRITZ

If one were to make a recording of **"Sea Glass,"** the *poing, poing* of a basketball on a concrete court should be heard in the background throughout—at least until the last few pages. For Craig's father won't give up. Craig must be a champ, just as he himself once was. In order to prove oneself to white Americans or, as he says, *Western people,* a Chinese must try twice as hard. . . . Never mind that Craig is fat and awkward. Never mind that he doesn't improve. Still, he must practice. *Poing, poing.*

A common father-son theme, it is handled with uncommon compassion. No ugly confrontations. No hostility, for Craig understands what lies behind his father's misguided stubbornness, hard as it is to cope with. In the end Craig does manage to get his father off his back, but the resolution is less important than the characters themselves.

Jean Fritz, in a review of "Sea Glass," in The New York Times Book Review, *January 20, 1980, p. 30.*

ZENA SUTHERLAND

The sea glass of the title [***Sea Glass***] is a piece of junk glass polished by waves and sand. "Just junk," says Craig's friend Kenyon, but Craig thinks that time has brought the glass brightness and clearness, just as it has him. Yep writes with pace and polish, his narrative evolving naturally from the characters and relationships as they adjust, change, and gain insight; the changes are believable, and the author uses both the narrator-protagonist and his dialogues with others with great skill to illuminate attitudes, explore reactions, and further the action.

Zena Sutherland, in a review of "Sea Glass," in Bulletin of the Center for Children's Books, *Vol. 33, No. 6, February, 1980, p. 124.*

DONALD KAO

Laurence Yep's ***Sea Glass*** is a thought-provoking book about an "average" child. . . . Aside from being "average," Craig is also Chinese American. . . .

Sea Glass takes the reader through the conflicts, realizations and changes Craig must undergo in dealing with real-life barriers: his competitive, sports-oriented father, his snobby, hip "American" cousins, his sometimes stubborn uncle, and his aggressive but moody school mate Kenyon.

They are a cast of "outcasts" in many ways. . . .

In dealing with questions of identity, Laurence Yep focuses on people's potential for being incredibly complex beings with much to offer once they acknowledge who they are. Craig becomes a pivotal point around which the characters either deal with their own identities or assume some other façade. Through the changes that occur for the different characters, Yep effectively counters many of the rigid race, sex and age biases that exist in other books. . . .

Sea Glass brings into question the whole concept of "achievement and success." Craig is not a star, yet he is a full human being who strives only for those things that make sense.

Donald Kao, in a review of "Sea Glass," in Interracial Books for Children Bulletin, *Vol. 11, No. 6, 1980, p. 16.*

MARLA DINCHAK

Laurence Yep is a frequently overlooked author of adolescent novels who deserves more attention. His four adolescent novels [***Sweetwater, Dragonwings, Child of the Owl,*** and ***Sea Glass***] are sensitively told and beautifully written, speaking to problems young adolescents face today, particularly about the search for identity and the need for family relationships. (p. 81)

His protagonists are generally thirteen or fourteen years old, and boys and girls will both be able to identify with these realistic protagonists, strong young people who dare to be themselves. Craig Chin in ***Sea Glass*** has grown up in Chinatown, and when his family moves to Concepcion he finds it difficult to make "Westerner" friends. On the other hand, Casey in ***Child of the Owl*** has grown up in a Western society and finds adjustment to life in Chinatown difficult. Both face the problem of being the new kid but in reverse situations. Yep sensitively portrays feelings of rejection and loneliness early adolescents often feel. Young readers won't need to have experienced a physical uprooting to understand Casey and Craig's feelings of awkwardness and not belonging.

Most of Yep's novels for adolescents show his young protagonists in conflict with their parents. All being good, morally upright young people, the conflicts do not force them to choose between right and wrong but involve a searching for identity. Tyree, in ***Sweetwater,*** Yep's science-fiction/fantasy, pursues his study of music against his father's wishes. He doesn't want to contradict his father's wishes, but music is something in him which must be expressed, a creative drive needing an outlet. In ***Sea Glass,*** Craig rebels against his athlete father's wishes that he excel in sports, but an old uncle helps Craig see the contentment that can come from knowing and being himself. Both young men grow to understand their parents and themselves better as they mature. In ***Child of the Owl*** Casey's problems with her itinerant, gambler father are different but no less realistic than Tyree and Craig's conflicts. Casey's disillusionment when she realizes he has betrayed her is climactic and touching. The strength and maturity she has learned carry her through to a hopeful conclusion. Each protagonist matures gradually and realistically, showing strength and understanding which we, as adults, are continually trying to instill in youngsters today.

Possibly Yep's most interesting characters are taken from the pages of history. Moon Shadow, an eight year old Chinese boy, is the protagonist in ***Dragonwings,*** an historical novel set in turn-of-the-century San Francisco and based on a true account of a Chinese-American man who built and flew an airplane about the time of the Wright brothers. The story recreates the Chinese bachelor community of Chinatown, the great San Francisco earthquake, and the daring dream of a man to fly like a dragon. Yep's beautiful metaphors, symbolism, and figurative language help the reader understand and see life as it must have been in 1906 California. Through the eyes of a young Chinese boy, we see what a frightening and challenging place the Western world was. Chinese folklore, myths, and legends are interwoven so readers not only sympathize with Moon Shadow and the other Chinese but understand more of their culture and traditions. That is true of most of Yep's work, for he not only tells a story but bridges a cultural gap. Young readers learn much about another culture while enjoying his stories.

An outstanding feature of Yep's novels is his skillful use of language. Metaphors and figurative language create comparisons that make the stories and characters come alive. Symbolism is an integral part of his novels, and universal truths lend depth. In each story, an appropriate symbol is gradually explained to the young protagonist, generally by an older and wiser adult. As protagonists mature, they become more aware of the symbol and what it represents. Moon Shadow in ***Dragonwings*** sees the aeroplane his father builds as the symbol for the reach of humanity's imagination, the achievement of the impossible dream. In ***Child of the Owl,*** Casey comes to understand her own cultural heritage and dual identity through the little jade owl charm, symbol of her ancestor, the owl-woman. The ocean and a reef teeming with marine life become symbols to Craig which help him communicate with those he cares about in ***Sea Glass***. . . . Universal truths are presented to readers, and Yep tells them that it is not bad to be different, and they should be proud of who they are and where they come from. He shows readers the incredible scope of our imagination, and he shows that impossible dreams can come true. He reaffirms the importance of communication, and all of this is more understandable and believable because of symbolism. (pp. 81-2)

Marla Dinchak, "Recommended: Laurence Yep," in English Journal, *Vol. 71, No. 3, March, 1982, pp. 81-2.*

KIRKUS REVIEWS

Narrated by a 15-year-old San Francisco urchin who likes to believe that his real father was an English lord and he himself is the Duke of Baywater, [***The Mark Twain Murders***] tells of a two-day 1864 adventure shared by the alleged Duke and the young reporter Mark Twain, who sets out to investigate the murder of the Duke's low-life stepfather and ends up—with the army, navy, and police as well as the Duke at his side—chasing Confederate mint robbers as they attempt to escape by sea. At one point Mark and the Duke are kidnapped and ordered killed, at another they are chased by the armed robbers they are chasing, and there is much shooting and more gun waving throughout. . . . Despite some bits about the Duke admonishing Twain to take himself seriously, this isn't one of those famous-person novels that offers an interesting interpretation of the historic character. In fact, the major problem is that it doesn't half live up to Twain's own statements or colorful image. Rather, Yep uses San Francisco and Mark Twain for color much as Robert Newman uses Sherlock Holmes and Victorian London in his Baker Street Irregular series. This doesn't sparkle like the Baker Street books, but its plainer setting is evoked in enveloping detail, which gives the adventure a measure of tangible charm.

A review of "The Mark Twain Murders," in Kirkus Reviews, *Vol. L, No. 8, April 15, 1982, p. 497.*

ZENA SUTHERLAND

Charley, the narrator [of ***Kind Hearts and Gentle Monsters***], is a sophomore at Loyola High School, and rather irritated by the hostility of some of his peers who had transfered to public school. He's more than irritated when he gets a poison pen chain letter that calls him a meddler, arrogant, and says, "to know him was to loathe him." He knows the girl who started it, and he goes to her house to confront her—and that's the start of a romance during which Charley discovers the reason for his girl's deserved reputation for being rancorous (a nagging neurotic mother) and also realizes that there can be a compromise between her emotional view of life and his logical, reasoned viewpoint. This has strong characters and a smooth writing style but its story line is not strong, and it is more a depiction of a situation than a development of a plot; Charley and his Chris do not so much change as improve their understanding of each other and themselves.

Zena Sutherland, in a review of "Kind Hearts and Gentle Monsters," in Bulletin of the Center for Children's Books, *Vol. 35, No. 9, May, 1982, p. 108.*

DREW STEVENSON

Laurence Yep has used actual events of Civil War San Francisco in ***The Mark Twain Murders***. . . . In debt and haunted by the less-than-shining reputation that has followed him from Nevada, the young Mark Twain is working as a newspaper reporter, covering the murder of disreputable soldier Johnny Dougherty. Dougherty's 15-year-old stepson, the narrator, lives by his wits down at the docks and calls himself His Grace, Duke of Baywater. Twain and His Grace team up and become enmeshed in a conspiracy with Dougherty's murder just the tip of an insidious iceberg. . . . The author has perfectly captured the tempo of old San Francisco with its marvelously salty characters. Rollicking reading—with Twain at the helm, readers can expect no less.

Drew Stevenson, in a review of "The Mark Twain Murders," in School Library Journal, *Vol. 28, No. 9, May, 1982, p. 85.*

COLBY RADOWSKY

On the one hand we have [in **"Kind Hearts and Gentle Monsters"**] Charley Sabini, high-school sophomore, who is smug, intransigent, totally rational and a firm believer in the well-ordered life.

And, on the other, there is Chris Pomeroy, brash, outrageous, with a "chainsaw for a tongue"; she lives life as a kind of year-round Halloween. . . .

It is when Charley meets her mother that he begins to understand Chris. Mrs. Pomeroy has a history of mental disturbance; her erratic behavior and fragile hold on reality are a constant burden to Chris. She tells Charley, "My mother is the real monster in the family." He sees Mrs. Pomeroy as a "sensitive land mine waiting for the least little thing to set it off."

In **"Kind Hearts and Gentle Monsters"** we see Chris loving her mother, yet not letting herself be consumed by her, and Charley adding another dimension to his life—that of caring for someone else. Weakened by a slow beginning, the story is nevertheless a moving portrayal of two teen-agers reaching out to one another, changing and growing up. Laurence Yep, who has written several fine novels about Chinese-Americans, has with this book broadened his scope successfully.

Colby Radowsky, in a review of "Kind Hearts and Gentle Monsters," in The New York Times Book Review, *May 23, 1982, p. 37.*

ETHEL L. HEINS

The author shows a fresh versatility in [***Kind Hearts and Gentle Monsters***], a story centering on two incisively characterized teenagers. . . . [Charley] is always self-assured and tends to talk more than he listens. So he is shocked when he finds himself the direct antagonist of a girl he used to know and heartily disliked in grammar school: Chris Pomeroy, an outrageous oddball—"'pretty enough, but she had a regular chainsaw for a tongue.'" . . . Actually a penetrating psychological novel, the book is written in a relaxed, contemporary style perfectly tuned to the thoughts and conversations of the bright, articulate protagonists.

Ethel L. Heins, in a review of "Kind Hearts and Gentle Monsters," in The Horn Book Magazine, *Vol. LVIII, No. 2, June, 1982, p. 302.*

ZENA SUTHERLAND

Based in part on fact, [***The Mark Twain Murders***] is set in San Francisco in 1864 and is told by a fifteen-year-old waif who calls himself the Duke of Baywater and meets Mark Twain (a reporter in San Francisco at that time) when the latter is investigating the murder of Baywater's stepfather. . . . Finally, Twain gets the scoop he wanted, since he's been trying to overcome his reputation as an incompetent reporter. Some of his self-confidence comes from his young friend, an aspect of the story that is not very convincing, as the adolescent who lives under a wharf lectures Twain on his behavior and attitudes. It is also not quite credible that the furious pace of the story is kept up for its three-day span. This has a modicum of historical interest, but it's far from the well-structured and smoothly written book that Yep's readers have come to expect.

Zena Sutherland, in a review of "The Mark Twain Murders," in Bulletin of the Center for Children's Books, *Vol. 35, No. 11, July & August, 1982, p. 220.*

M. JEAN GREENLAW

Charley is a logical, organized, proper sophomore. Chris is an erratic, emotional, outrageous classmate who has left the Catholic school to go "public." Their growing relationship is sensitively handled in ***Kind Hearts and Gentle Monsters.*** Laurence Yep portrays Chris's emotionally disturbed mother in a realistic but sympathetic manner and provides insight into the responses of family and friends.

M. Jean Greenlaw, in a review of "Kind Hearts and Gentle Monsters," in Journal of Reading, *Vol. 26, No. 2, November, 1982, p. 183.*

M. JEAN GREENLAW

Laurence Yep, using actual events from the time that Mark Twain was an inept reporter in San Francisco during the Civil War, creates an amusing and entertaining novel. ***The Mark Twain Murders*** pairs Twain with a 15-year-old street urchin in a rousing race against time to thwart a Confederate attempt to rob the San Francisco mint. Confounded by Twain's reputation for lying, their endeavors do end well in this short, easy book.

M. Jean Greenlaw, in a review of "The Mark Twain Murders," in Journal of Reading, *Vol. 26, No. 3, December, 1982, p. 275.*

CRAIG SHAW GARDNER

[In ***Dragon of the Lost Sea,*** a] dragon, Shimmer, and a homeless boy, Thorn, form an uneasy alliance in pursuit of the witch, Civet, who has stolen the inland sea the dragon once called home, imprisoning the sea in a pebble that hangs from the witch's neck. As the story progresses, friendship grows between boy and dragon, cementing the alliance. Along the way, Yep makes some gentle fun of the prideful attitude of Shimmer, who, after all, is a princess among the dragons, and the even more boastful Monkey, a magical creature who refers to himself as "the Great Sage Equal to Heaven," but never seems to quite finish what he sets out to accomplish. In all, Yep's book is enjoyable, if unexceptional. (p. 11)

Craig Shaw Gardner, "Fantasy to Cut Your Teeth On," in Book World—The Washington Post, *January 9, 1983, pp. 11, 13.**

ROBIN McKINLEY

There is much to like about [***Dragon of the Lost Sea***], but there's a stiffness of style that prevents the reader from getting as close to the two main characters, the Dragon of the title and the 13-year-old boy she reluctantly adopts and who accompanies her on her quest to reclaim her Lost Sea, as the author seems to have intended. It's as though Yep couldn't quite make up his mind between the conversational style more suited to the filling-out of personalities, and the lofty distant style more suited to the re-telling of old folk tales, on which (the author's note tells us) the book is somewhat based. Whatever its shortcomings, ***Dragon*** is a very readable story with some splendid bits of old legends and new imagination and general quest-adventure, and if the inconclusive ending means to suggest a sequel there should be plenty of young readers to cheer for volume two.

Robin McKinley, in a review of "Dragon of the Lost Sea," in Voice of Youth Advocates, *Vol. 5, No. 6, February, 1983, p. 47.*

AL MULLER

The fantasy tale, ***Dragon of the Lost Sea,*** is light and easy reading. The tale is based loosely upon a Chinese myth; however, a knowledge of neither the Chinese culture nor mythology is necessary for comprehension or enjoyment.

The episodic story follows the efforts of the shape-changing dragon Shimmer to restore her clan's traditional home and to regain her former status in the clan. To achieve these ends, Shimmer and her human companion, a boy named Thorn, set out to track down the witch Civet. At the tale's end, the stage is set for a sequel. We can only hope.

While action and delightful magic fill the pages, the strength of the tale is found in the unique characters and their interactions.

Al Muller, in a review of "Dragon of the Lost Sea," in The ALAN Review, *Vol. 10, No. 3, Spring, 1983, p. 21.*

PUBLISHERS WEEKLY

No match for his prize SF or his novels about Chinese-Americans, Yep's mystery [***Liar, Liar***] is still a pretty good adventure in suspense. Sean Pierce, 16, doubts the verdict on the death of his buddy Marsh Weiss, an accident say the police. Sean believes a man who was infuriated by one of Marsh's tricks had caused the crash of the youth's car. Sean searches for the suspect and for evidence against him and succeeds, too well. The killer sets a trap for Sean, who has a slim chance of surviving. Yep generates excitement during the showdown, although this crisis is arrived at through "coincidences."

A review of "Liar, Liar," in Publishers Weekly, *Vol. 224, No. 12, September 16, 1983, p. 126.*

ROGER SUTTON

[***Liar, Liar***] isn't a mystery, we know who the killer is early on, but it is suspenseful and well paced. . . . There are a lot of unnecessary problem novel trappings in this action story: juvenile delinquency, divorce, death, male single parenting and suburban ennui each take a clichéd turn, and serve only to distract. But it is fun when it sticks to the plot, and the show-down between Sean and the murderer is exciting.

Roger Sutton, in a review of "Liar, Liar," in School Library Journal, *Vol. 30, No. 3, November, 1983, p. 199.*

THOMAS M. DISCH

Yep's plot [in ***Liar, Liar***] is as diagrammatic as a Hitchcock film. A boy with a history of lying to the authorities plays a cat-and-mouse game with a mad business executive, who acts as a kind of demonic stand-in for the boy's ineffectual and unloving father. ***Liar, Liar*** avoids head-on Oedipal collisions, but it does deal with feelings close to many young hearts: that parents can be unsupportive to the point of outright betrayal and that adults in general can be mean, vindictive, and unjust in their relation to children without ever being called to account. (pp. 17, 22)

Thomas M. Disch, "Boys on the Brink," in Book World—The Washington Post, *November 6, 1983, pp. 17, 22.**

CAROL BILLMAN

In **"Liar, Liar,"** Laurence Yep sketches the contemporary scene in California's Silicon Valley with photorealistic detail. At the fore of this landscape are a father and son who have recently moved to the bedroom community of Almaden. Dad is a talented computer troubleshooter; Sean is the 16-year-old protagonist whose troubled history intrudes on his youthful efforts to start afresh. Their lives, like their new house, seem at once empty and crowded by memories of past failures in their relationship. Nonetheless, this odd couple moves toward a workable partnership by the end of the story.

Mr. Yep's latest book, his ninth in the last decade, is primarily a mystery and not a novel about shaky family relationships. . . . The mystery plot, however, is not all that suspenseful, despite two well-paced and scary scenes (the fatal crash, the startling locked-house confrontation between Sean and the killer). Older readers may well agree with one Almaden cop's response: "Save me from children who watch Perry Mason reruns."

Carol Billman, in a review of "Liar, Liar," in The New York Times Book Review, *November 6, 1983, p. 214.*

NANCY C. HAMMOND

[In ***The Serpent's Children,*** Cassia] was eight, and her brother Foxfire, seven, when their father, a peasant farmer and revolutionary, left their village to help the ruling Manchus eject the British from the Middle Kingdom. . . . But their hopes were soon dashed: Their mother died; they were cursed after Cassia rebelled against clan members anxious to increase her marriageability by binding her feet; and their father returned home disabled and embittered by the Manchus, who settled for "profits and bribes, not victories." Still, the family survived years of drought, poverty, political corruption, and social disintegration. . . . The Chinese American author, a strong storyteller who began his research seeking his "identity as a Chinese," brings considerable insight to the culture. Although the narrative occasionally seems thin and repetitive and the language sometimes belies the period, the story offers numerous vivid, engrossing episodes and a cogent view of social conditions in China in the nineteenth century. (pp. 479-80)

Nancy C. Hammond, in a review of "The Serpent's Children," in The Horn Book Magazine, *Vol. LX, No. 4, August, 1984, pp. 479-80.*

RUTH M. McCONNELL

[In ***The Serpent's Children***] Yep explores the larger events of the Taiping Rebellion, opium pushing and Manchu/foreign battles and their effects on a small village (in China's south coastal province of Kwangtung) that is more directly troubled by drought and bandits. The story is told by Cassia, one of two spirited children whose independent ways are derided as signs of "serpent blood" inherited from a legendary ancestress of their non-village mother. The slur becomes a bond between Cassia and her brother after their mother's death and their father's eventual estrangement from the son, whose exodus to the demon's goldfields secures the family fortunes. With first-person narration, dialogue at times seems forced and unconvincingly explanatory, while general background is scanted. . . . In spite of these faults, ***The Serpent's Children*** is well plotted and shows good characterization.

Ruth M. McConnell, in a review of "The Serpent's Children," in School Library Journal, *Vol. 30, No. 10, August, 1984, p. 88.*

JOAN NIST

In [***The Serpent's Children***] a dying mother tells her son and daughter Cassia that, as descendents of a legendary serpent, they have a responsibility to each other and their crippled father. In order to support them, Foxfire goes to America as a bound worker. Yet, despite the distance and family differences, the boy and his family ultimately remain united.

Laurence Yep creates vivid characters and scenes. The story, set in nineteenth-century China, captures strikingly the struggles of the peasants. . . .

The book contributes immensely to cultural awareness and is memorable in its characterization of the loyal, lively narrator-heroine Cassia.

Joan Nist, in a review of "The Serpent's Children," in Language Arts, *Vol. 61, No. 6, October, 1984, p. 632.*

Appendix

The following is a listing of all sources used in Volume 35 of *Contemporary Literary Criticism*. Included in this list are all copyright and reprint rights and acknowledgments for those essays for which permission was obtained. Every effort has been made to trace copyright, but if omissions have been made, please let us know.

THE EXCERPTS IN CLC, VOLUME 35, WERE REPRINTED FROM THE FOLLOWING PERIODICALS:

The ALAN Review, v. 9, Fall, 1981; v. 9, Spring, 1982; v. 10, Spring, 1983; v. 11, Winter, 1984. All reprinted by permission.

America, v. 140, May 12, 1979 for "Recapping the Long Tale of a Winter's Dream" by Robert M. Senkewicz. © 1979. All rights reserved. Reprinted by permission of the author./ v. 113, July 10, 1965. © 1965. All rights reserved. Reprinted with permission of America Press, Inc., 106 West 56th Street, New York, NY 10019.

The American Book Review, v. 2, February, 1980. © 1980 by *The American Book Review*. Reprinted by permission.

The American Political Science Review, v. XX, August, 1926.

The American Spectator, v. 18, March, 1985. Copyright © *The American Spectator* 1985. Reprinted by permission.

The American West, v. III, Fall, 1966 for "Woody Guthrie: The Man, the Land, the Understanding" by John Greenway. Copyright © 1966 by the American West Publishing Company, Tucson, AZ. Used with permission of the publisher and the author.

Analog Science Fiction/Science Fact, v. XCVII, August, 1977 for "Hunter of Worlds" by Lester del Ray; v. XCVIII, May, 1978 for "Well of Shiuan" by Lester del Ray; v. XCVIII, August, 1978 for "The Faded Sun: Kesrith" by Lester del Ray; v. XCVIX, February, 1979 for "The Faded Sun: Shon'jir" by Lester del Ray. Copyright © 1977, 1978, 1979 by The Condé Nast Publications, Inc. All reprinted by permission of the author./ v. CI, February 2, 1981 for a review of "Serpent's Reach" by Tom Easton; v. CI, March 30, 1981 for a review of "Thousand-Star" by Tom Easton; v. CI, September 14, 1981 for a review of "Downbelow Station" by Tom Easton; v. CII, March 29, 1982 for a review of "Wave without a Shore" by Tom Easton; v. CII, August, 1982 for a review of "The Pride of Chanur" by Tom Easton; v. CIII, June, 1983 for a review of "Port Eternity" by Tom Easton; v. CIII, September 13, 1983 for a review of "Lyonesse" by Tom Easton; v. CIII, October, 1983 for a review of "Forty Thousand in Gehenna" by Tom Easton; v. CIV, February, 1984 for a review of "The Lazarus Effect" by Tom Easton; v. CIV, September, 1984 for a review of "Heretics of Dune" by Tom Easton; v. CIV, November, 1984 for a review of "Voyager in Night" by Tom Easton. © 1981, 1982, 1983, 1984 by Davis Publications, Inc. All reprinted by permission of the author.

Arizona English Bulletin, v. 18, April, 1976 for "From Steppin Stebbins to Soul Brothers: Racial Strife in Adolescent Fiction" by W. Keith Kraus. Reprinted by permission of the publisher and the author.

The Armchair Detective, v. 13, Summer, 1980; v. 14, Summer, 1981. Copyright © 1980, 1981 by *The Armchair Detective*. Both reprinted by permission.

The Atlantic Bookshelf, a section of *The Atlantic Monthly*, v. 164, December, 1939. Copyright © 1939, by the Atlantic Monthly Company, Boston, MA. Reprinted by permission.

The Atlantic Monthly, v. 165, May, 1940; v. 182, September, 1948; v. 197, April, 1956; v. 211, April, 1963; v. 212, September, 1963; v. 224, August, 1969; v. 224, December, 1969. All reprinted by permission.

Audio, v. 63, October, 1979; v. 64, August, 1980; v. 66, August, 1982; v. 68, March, 1984. © 1979, 1980, 1982, 1984, CBS Publications, The Consumer Publishing Division of CBS Inc. All reprinted by permission.

Best Sellers, v. 28, October 1, 1968; v. 29, June 15, 1969; v. 30, July 15, 1970; v. 30, January 1, 1971; v. 33, July 15, 1973. Copyright 1968, 1969, 1970, 1971, 1973, by the University of Scranton. All reprinted by permission./ v. 36, August, 1976; v. 36, November, 1976; v. 37, March, 1978; v. 38, March, 1979; v. 39, September, 1979; v. 40, July, 1980; v. 40, January, 1981; v. 41, January, 1982; v. 42, June, 1982; v. 42, July, 1982; v. 43, April, 1983; v. 43, June, 1983; v. 43, July, 1983; v. 43, September, 1983; v. 43, December, 1983; v. 44, May, 1984; v. 44, June, 1984; v. 44, September, 1984. Copyright © 1976, 1978, 1979, 1980, 1981, 1982, 1983, 1984 Helen Dwight Reid Educational Foundation. All reprinted by permission.

Billboard, v. 83, November 27, 1971; v. 88, April 17, 1976; v. 90, June 10, 1978; v. 92, June 14, 1980; v. 92, December 6, 1980; v. 93, November 21, 1981. © copyright 1971, 1976, 1978, 1980, 1981 by Billboard Publications, Inc. All reprinted by permission.

The Black Scholar, v. 13, Summer, 1982. Copyright 1982 by *The Black Scholar*. Both reprinted by permission.

Book Week—The Sunday Herald Tribune, February 2, 1964; November 15, 1964; May 9, 1965; September 5, 1965; November 21, 1965. © 1964, 1965, *The Washington Post*. All reprinted by permission.

Book Week—The Washington Post, May 8, 1966; August 21, 1966. © 1966, *The Washington Post*. Both reprinted by permission.

Book Week—World Journal Tribune, Fall Children's Issue, October 30, 1966. © 1966, *The Washington Post*. Reprinted by permission.

Book World—Chicago Tribune, March 31, 1968. © 1968 Postrib Corp. Reprinted by permission of *The Washington Post*.

Book World—Chicago Tribune, Part II, May 17, 1970 for a review of "Fireweed" by Ellen Lewis Buell. © 1970 Postrib Corp. Reprinted by permission of *The Washington Post* and the author./ November 7, 1971. © 1971 Postrib Corp. Reprinted by permission of *The Washington Post*.

Book World—The Washington Post, June 30, 1968 for "Baby Steps from the Earth to the Stars" by Robert Jastrow; August 18, 1968 for "Tom Wolfe: Analyst of the (Fill It In) Generation" by Karl Shapiro; May 4, 1969 for a review of "I'll Get There. It Better Be Worth the Trip" by Alice Hungerford; June 6, 1971 for "A Very Dissimilar Trio" by R. V. Cassill; December 19, 1971 for "Radioisotopes, Robot Brawls, White Light, Green Flippers" by Diane Ackerman. © 1968, 1969, 1971 Postrib Corp. All reprinted by permission of *The Washington Post* and the respective authors./ July 2, 1972; November 11, 1973; December 15, 1974; May 2, 1976; April 10, 1977; January 8, 1978; March 5, 1978; July 22, 1979; October 7, 1979; July 13, 1980; April 26, 1981; May 10, 1981; October 4, 1981; July 11, 1982; August 29, 1982; October 10, 1982; December 26, 1982; January 9, 1983; Febuary 13, 1983; March 24, 1983; November 6, 1983; November 13, 1983; December 18, 1983; March 25, 1984; June 10, 1984; June 17, 1984; March 10, 1985; April 7, 1985. © 1972, 1973, 1974, 1976, 1977, 1978, 1979, 1980, 1981, 1982, 1983, 1984, *The Washington Post*. All reprinted by permission.

The Booklist, v. 67, June 1, 1971; v. 69, November 1, 1972; v. 71, May 1, 1975; v. 72, April 1, 1976; v. 72, May 1, 1976; v. 72, July 1, 1976. Copyright © 1971, 1972, 1975, 1976 by the American Library Association. All reprinted by permission.

Booklist, v. 74, September 1, 1977; v. 74, October 15, 1977; v. 74, December 1, 1977; v. 75, September 15, 1978; v. 75, June 1, 1979; v. 77, October 15, 1980; v. 78, September 1, 1981; v. 78, September 15, 1981; v. 78, February 1, 1982; v. 78, February 15, 1982; v. 78, April 1, 1982; v. 78, April 15, 1982; v. 79, September 1, 1982; v. 79, December 1, 1982; v. 79, December 15, 1982; v. 79, January 15, 1983; v. 80, October 15, 1983; v. 80, April 15, 1984; v. 80, June 1, 1984; v. 80, July, 1984; v. 80, August, 1984. Copyright © 1977, 1978, 1979, 1980, 1981, 1982, 1983, 1984 by the American Library Association. All reprinted by permission.

The Bookman, New York, v. LIV, December, 1921.

Books, April 7, 1963; May 19, 1963. © 1963 I.H.T. Corporation. Both reprinted by permission.

Books and Bookmen, v. 20, June, 1975 for a review of "The Green Gene" by Oswell Blakeston. © copyright the author 1975./ v. 19, October, 1973 for a review of "The Guns of Darkness" by J. A. Cuddon. © copyright by the author 1975. Reprinted by permission of the author./ n. 322, July, 1982. © copyright *Books and Bookmen* 1982. Reprinted by permission of the publisher.

British Book News, August, 1982. © *British Book News*, 1982. Courtesy of *British Book News*.

Bulletin of the Center for Children's Books, v. 28, October, 1974; v. 28, November, 1974; v. 29, January, 1976; v. 31, February, 1978; v. 33, November, 1979; v. 33, February, 1980; v. 35, September, 1981; v. 35, December, 1981; v. 35, January, 1982; v. 35, May, 1982; v. 35, June, 1982; v. 35, July & August, 1982; v. 36, September, 1982; v. 36, January, 1983; v. 36, March, 1983; v. 36, April, 1983; v. 36, June, 1983; v. 37, January, 1984; v. 37, February, 1984; v. 37, June, 1984. © 1974, 1976, 1978, 1979, 1980, 1981, 1982, 1983, 1984 by The University of Chicago. All reprinted by permission of The University of Chicago Press.

The Canadian Forum, v. XXVIII, January, 1949.

The Centennial Review, v. XXIII, Summer, 1979 for "Carl Sandburg and the Undetermined Land" by Bernard Duffey. © 1979 by *The Centennial Review.* Reprinted by permission of the publisher and the author.

Children's Book News, v. 3, March-April, 1968; v. 3, July-August, 1968. Copyright © 1968 by Baker Book Services Ltd. Both reprinted by permission.

Children's Book Review, v. IV, Spring, 1974. © 1974 Five Owls Press Ltd. All rights reserved. Reprinted by permission.

Children's Book Review Service, v. 7, April, 1979; v. 11, February, 1983; v. 12, July, 1984. Copyright © 1979, 1983, 1984 Children's Book Review Service Inc. All reprinted by permission.

The Christian Century, v. XCII, April 16, 1975. Copyright 1975 Christian Century Foundation. Reprinted by permission from *The Christian Century.*

The Christian Science Monitor, May 4, 1977 for "From Appalachia to Chinatown—Adventures in Ameirca" by Wendy Moorhead; June 27, 1979 for "Beyond Biology" by Brad Owens; November 5, 1982 for "WWII Saga of Remarkable Power" by Sherwood Williams; December 3, 1982 for "'2010'—The Odyssey Continues" by Cary Neeper. © 1977, 1979, 1982 by the respective authors. All reprinted by permission of the respective authors./ January 3, 1963; September 10, 1964; September 28, 1967; December 2, 1967; September 3, 1970; November 11, 1971; February 10, 1972; August 8, 1973; November 5, 1975; October 15, 1979; December 14, 1981; April 9, 1982; September 9, 1982; October 7, 1983. © 1963, 1964, 1967, 1970, 1971, 1972, 1973, 1975, 1979, 1981, 1982, 1983 The Christian Science Publishing Society. All rights reserved. All reprinted by permission from *The Christian Science Monitor.*/ March 27, 1952. © 1952, renewed 1980, The Christian Science Publishing Society. All rights reserved. Reprinted by permission from *The Christian Science Monitor.*

Circus Magazine, n. 288, February 29, 1984. Copyright © 1984 by Circus Enterprises Corporation. Reprinted by permission.

CLA Journal, v. XI, June, 1968. Copyright, 1968 by The College Language Association. Used by permission of The College Language Association.

Clues: A Journal of Detection, v. 5, Spring-Summer, 1984. Copyright 1984 by Pat Browne. Reprinted by permission.

Commentary, v. 47, February, 1969 for "Hijinks Journalism" by Neil Compton. All rights reserved. Reprinted by permission of the publisher and the Literary Estate of Neil Compton./ v. 49, March, 1970 for "Innoncence Restaged" by Jack Richardson. All rights reserved. Reprinted by permission of the publisher and the author.

Commonweal, v. LXVII, February 7, 1958; v. LXVII, March 14, 1958; v. XC, May 23, 1969; v. CX, May 20, 1983; v. CXI, September 7, 1984, Copyright © 1958, 1969, 1983, 1984 Commonweal Publishing Co., Inc. All reprinted by permission of Commonweal Foundation./ v. XLV, November 22, 1946; v. LVII, January 16, 1953. Copyright © 1946, 1953, renewed 1974, 1981 Commonweal Publishing Co., Inc. Both reprinted by permission of Commonweal Foundation.

Contemporary Sociology, v. 11, November, 1982 for "Apocalypse Tomorrow" by Michael Useem. Copyright © 1982 American Sociological Association. Reprinted by permission of the publisher and the author.

Crawdaddy, June, 1973 for a review of "Dark Side of the Moon" by Bruce Malamut; July, 1973 for a review of "Red Rose Speedway" by Patrick Snyder; January, 1975 for "Yoko's Gone, John Moves On" by Patrick Snyder; June, 1976 for "Asleep at the Wing" by Mitchell Glazer; June, 1978 for "Mulling over McCartney" by Scott Isler; July, 1978 for "Beautiful Winner" by Timothy White; September, 1978 for a review of "For You" by Jim Farber. Copyright © 1973, 1975, 1976, 1978 by Crawdaddy Publishing Co., Inc. All rights reserved. All reprinted by permission of the publisher and the respective authors.

Creative Computing, v. 9, May, 1983. Copyright © 1983 by Ahl Computing, Inc. All rights reserved. Reprinted by permission.

Creem, v. 4, August, 1972; v. 4, May, 1973; v. 5, February, 1974; v. 7, June, 1975; v. 7, September, 1975; v. 8, December, 1975; v. 8, June, 1976; v. 8, July, 1976; v. 11, May, 1980; v. 12, June, 1980; v. 12, February, 1981. © copyright 1972, 1973, 1974, 1975, 1976, 1980, 1981 by Creem Magazine, Inc. All reprinted by permission.

The Critic, v. 27, February-March, 1969. © The Critic 1969. Reprinted with the permission of the Thomas More Association, Chicago, IL.

The Dial, v. XLV, October 5, 1918; v. LXX, January, 1921.

Discourse: A Review of the Liberal Arts, v. VIII, Spring, 1965 for "Poets New and Old: Reviews of Ammons and Sandburg" by Somner Sorenson. © 1965 Concordia College. Reprinted by permission of the publisher and the author.

down beat, v. 37, May 28, 1970; v. 38, April 1, 1971; v. 44, May 5, 1977; v. 50, May, 1983. Copyright 1970, 1971, 1977, 1983. All reprinted with permission of *down beat.*

Drama, n. 91, Winter, 1968. Reprinted by permission of the British Theatre Association.

Encounter, v. XLI, July, 1973; v. XLIX, September, 1977; v. LVII, August, 1981. © 1973, 1977, 1981 by Encounter Ltd. All reprinted by permission of the publisher.

English Journal, v. XXVII, January, 1938./ v. XLV, May, 1956 for "'In Our Living and in Our Dying'" by Arthur H. Ballet; v. XLVIII, December, 1959 for "Carl Sandburg: The Poet as Nonconformist" by Michael Yatron; v. 58, February, 1969 for a review of "Deathman, Do Not Follow Me" by Geraldine E. LaRocque; v. 59, April, 1970 for a review of "The Deadly Gift" by John W. Conner; v. 61, January, 1972 for a review of "Bless the Beasts and Children" by John W. Conner; v. 66, March, 1977 for a review of "The Soul Brothers and Sister Lou" by Nedra Stimpfle; v. 71, March, 1982 for "Recommended: Laurence Yep" by Marla Dinchak; v. 71, December, 1982 for a review of "Journey Inward" by Dick Abrahamson and Betty Carter. Copyright © 1956, 1959, 1969, 1970, 1972, 1977, 1982 by the National Council of Teachers of English. All reprinted by permission of the publisher and the respective authors.

Esquire, v. 103, January, 1985 "Television's Real A-Team" by David Freeman. Copyright © 1985 by David Freeman. Reprinted by permission of the author.

Essence, v. 14, April, 1984. Copyright © by Essence Communications Inc. 1984. Reprinted by permission.

Extrapolation, v. III, December, 1961, Copyright 1961 by Thomas D. and Alice S. Clareson. Reprinted by permission./ v. 24, Winter, 1983. Copyright 1983 by The Kent State University Press. Reprinted by permission.

Fantasy Newsletter, v. 5, November, 1982 for "Herbert's Latest Is Dystopian Thriller Set in Ireland" by William Coyle. © 1982 by Florida Atlantic University. Reprinted by permission of the author.

Fantasy Review, v. 7, March, 1984 for "Xanth Series Extolled" by Richard Mathews; v. 7, August, 1984 for "Space Foreign Legion" by Mary S. Weinkauf; v. 7, October, 1984 for "Cherryh Seduced by Philosophical Abstractions" by Carolyn Wendell. Copyright © 1984 the respective authors. All reprinted by permission of the respective authors.

Film Comment, v. 17, March-April, 1981 for "Quality Up the Wazoo" by Richard T. Jameson. Copyright © 1981 by the author. Reprinted by permission of the author.

Folklore, v. 91, Spring, 1980. Reprinted by permission.

The Fortnightly, n.s. v. CLVII, June, 1945.

The Georgia Review, v. XXX, Winter, 1976 for "The Working Press, the Literary Culture, and the New Journalism" by Morris Dickstein, Copyright, 1976, by Morris Dickstein. Reprinted by permission of the author.

Growing Point, v. 15, December, 1976; v. 17, November, 1978; v. 18, September, 1979; v. 20, September, 1981; v. 21, July, 1982; v. 22, November, 1983; v. 22, January, 1984; v. 22, March, 1984. All reprinted by permission.

The Guardian Weekly, v. 130, February 5, 1984. Copyright © 1984 by Guardian Publications Ltd. Reprinted by permission.

Harper's, v. 258, May, 1979. Copyright © 1979 by *Harper's Magazine.* All rights reserved. Reprinted by special permission.

Harper's Magazine, v. 240, April, 1970. Copyright © 1970 by *Harper's Magazine.* All rights reserved. Reprinted by special permission.

High Fidelity, v. 21, March, 1971; v. 22, January, 1972; v. 28, July, 1978; v. 30, March, 1980; v. 30, June, 1980; v. 31, February, 1981; v. 32, January, 1982; v. 33, February, 1983; v. 34, February, 1984; v. 34, October, 1984. Copyright © by ABC Leisure Magazines, Inc. All rights reserved. All excerpted by permission.

Hit Parader, v. 41, April, 1982. © copyright 1982 Charlton Publications, Inc. Reprinted by permission.

The Horn Book Magazine, v. XXXV, October, 1959; v. XL, October, 1964; v. XLI, June, 1965; v. XLII, June, 1966; v. XLII, October, 1966; v. XLIII, June, 1967; v. XLIII, August, 1967; v. XLV, August, 1969; v. XLVI, December, 1970; v. XLVII, February, 1971; v. XLVII, February, 1971; v. XLVIII, February, 1972; v. XLVIII, June, 1972; v. XLVIII, December, 1972; v. XLIX, February, 1973; v. XLIX, August, 1973; v. XLIX, October, 1973; v. L, February, 1974; v. LI, October, 1975; v. LII, August, 1976; v. LIII, August, 1977; v. LIV, April, 1978; v. LV, April, 1979; v. LV, June, 1979; v. LV, August, 1979; v. LV, October, 1979; v. LVI, October, 1980; v. LVII, August, 1981; v. LVIII, February, 1982; v. LVIII, June, 1982; v. LVIII, October, 1982; v. LIX, February, 1983; v. LIX, June, 1983; v. LIX, August, 1983; v. LIX, August, 1983; v. LIX, October, 1983; v. LIX, December, 1983; v. LX, April, 1984; v. LX, August, 1984; v. LX, September-October, 1984. Copyright © 1959, 1964, 1965, 1966, 1967, 1969, 1970, 1971, 1972, 1973, 1974, 1975, 1976, 1977, 1978, 1979, 1980, 1981, 1982, 1983, 1984 by The Horn Book, Inc., Boston. All reprinted by permission.

Interracial Books for Children Bulletin, v. 10, 1979; v. 11, 1980; v. 13, 1982. All reprinted by permission of *Interracial Books for Children Bulletin,* 1841 Broadway, New York, NY 10023.

Jazz & Pop, v. 10, March, 1971 for a review of "John Lennon/Plastic Ono Band" by Bruce Harris. © 1971 by Jazz & Pop Inc. Reprinted by permission of the author.

Journal of American Folklore, v. 83, July-September, 1970 for "Woody Guthrie and His Folk Tradition" by Richard A. Reuss. Copyright © 1970 by the American Folklore Society. Reproduced by permission of the American Folklore Society and the author from *Journal of American Folklore.*

The Journal of American History, v. LXIII, March, 1977; v. 66, December, 1979. Copyright Organization of American Historians, 1977, 1979. Both reprinted by permission.

The Journal of General Education, published by The Pennsylvania State University Press, University Park, PA, v. 33, Summer, 1981. Copyright 1981 by The Pennsylvania State University Press. Reprinted by permission.

Journal of Popular Culture, v. VIII, Summer, 1974. Copyright © by Ray B. Browne. Reprinted by permission.

Journal of Reading, v. 25, March, 1982; v. 26, November, 1982; v. 26, December, 1982; v. 27, May, 1984. Copyright 1982, 1984 by the International Reading Association, Inc. All reprinted with permission of the International Reading Association.

The Junior Bookshelf, v. 32, October, 1968; v. 40, June, 1976; v. 41, February, 1977; v. 42, June, 1978; v. 44, October, 1980; v. 46, October, 1982; v. 46, December, 1982; v. 47, October, 1983; v. 47, December, 1983. All reprinted by permission.

Kirkus Reviews, v. XXXIX, March 1, 1971; v. XL, January 15, 1972; v. XLI, April 1, 1973; v. XVI, December 1, 1973; v. XLII, March 15, 1974; v. XLV, October 1, 1977; v. XLVI, March 15, 1978; v. XLVII, June 1, 1979; v. XLVIII, July 15, 1980; v. XLVIII, August 1, 1980; v. XLIX, July 1, 1981; v. XLIX, December 15, 1981; v. L, March 1, 1982; v. L, April 15, 1982; v. L, September 1, 1982; v. LI, March 15, 1983; v. LI, April 1, 1983; v. LI, May 1, 1983; v. LI, December 1, 1983. Copyright © 1971, 1972, 1973, 1974, 1977, 1978, 1979, 1980, 1981, 1982, 1983 The Kirkus Service, Inc. All reprinted by permission.

Kirkus Reviews, Juvenile Issue, v. LI, September 1, 1983. Copyright © 1983 The Kirkus Service, Inc. Reprinted by permission.

Kliatt Young Adult Paperback Book Guide, v. XIII, January, 1979; v. XIII, April, 1979; v. XIV, September, 1980; v. XV, September, 1981; v. XVI, April, 1982; v. XVI, September, 1982; v. XVIII, January, 1984. Copyright © by Kliatt Paperback Book Guide. All reprinted by permission.

Language Arts, v. 53, May, 1976 for a review of "Fast Sam, Cool Clyde and Stuff" by Donald J. Bissett; v. 59, October, 1982 for a review of "The Animal, the Vegetable, and John D. Jones" by Nancy K. Johansen; v. 61, October, 1984 for a review of "The Serpent's Children" by Joan Nist. Copyright © 1976, 1982, 1984 by the National Council of Teachers of English. All reprinted by permission of the publisher and the respective authors.

Library Journal, v. 86, December 15, 1961 for a review of "The Ivy Tree" by Irene Gitomer; v. 88, June 15, 1963 for a review of "Time Cat: The Remarkable Journeys of Jason and Gareth" by Miriam S. Mathes; v. 90, August, 1965 for a review of "Born to Win" by Charles A. Raines; v. 93, September 15, 1968 for a review of "Loveland" by Donald H. Cloudsley; v. 96, July, 1971 for a review of "Elephant Bangs Train" by Jim Langlois; v. 97, March 1, 1972 for a review of "Hermes 3000" by Anne M. Burk; v. 100, May 1, 1975 for a review of "Woody Sez" by Paul G. Feehan; v. 103, June 1, 1978 for a review of "The Lakestown Rebellion" by Grove Koger; v. 103, November 1, 1978 for a review of "WYST: Alastor 1716" by Jerry L. Parsons; v. 104, February 15, 1979 for a review of "The Source of Magic" by Rosemary Herbert; v. 107, March 15, 1980 for a review of "The Faded Sun: Kutath" by Rosemary Herbert; v. 105, June 15, 1980 for a review of "The Language of Pao" by Rosemary Herbert; v. 105, September 15, 1980 for a review of "Jack in the Box" by Jeff Clark; v. 106, June 15, 1981 for a review of "Blue Adept" by Susan L. Nickerson; v. 106, October 1, 1981 for a review of "The Heart of a Woman" by Janet Boyarin Blundell; v. 108, March 15, 1983 for a review of "The Dreamstone" by Susan L. Nickerson; v. 108, April 1, 1983 for a review of "Shaker, Why Don't You Sing?" by Janet Boyarin Blundell; v. 108, August, 1983 for a review of "The Tree of Swords and Jewels" by Susan L. Nickerson; v. 108, September 15, 1983 for a review of "Refugee" by Susan L. Nickerson; v. 108, October 15, 1983 for a review of "Dragon on a Pedestal" by Susan L. Nickerson; v. 108, November 15, 1983 for a review of "Ever the Winds of Chance" by Peter Dollard; v. 109, June 15, 1984 for a review of "Mercenary" by Jackie Cassada; v. 109, August, 1984 for a review of "Bearing an Hourglass" by Jackie Cassada. Copyright © 1961, 1963, 1965, 1968, 1971, 1972, 1975, 1978, 1979, 1980, 1981, 1983, 1984 by Xerox Corporation. All reprinted from *Library Journal,* published by R. R. Bowker Co. (a Xerox company), by permission of the publisher and the respective authors./ v. 89, October 15, 1964. Copyright © 1964 by Xerox Corporation. Reprinted from *Library Journal,* published by R. R. Bowker Co. (a Xerox company), by permission of the publisher.

The Lion and the Unicorn, v. 3, Winter, 1979-80. Copyright © 1980 *The Lion and the Unicorn.* Reprinted by permission.

The Listener, v. 88, November 9, 1972 for "Back to the Lighthouse" by Naomi Lewis; v. 93, June 5, 1975 for "Crime and Intensity" by Marghanita Laski; v. 103, January 10, 1980 for "America Time" by Marghanita Laski; v. 105, May 7, 1981 for "Nostalgia Novels" by John Mellors; v. 110, August 11, 1983 for "Death with Deep Feeling" by Marghanita Laski; v. 110, December 3, 1983 for "Teenage Life" by Naomi Lewis. © British Broadcasting Corp. 1972, 1975, 1980, 1981, 1983. All reprinted by permission of the respective authors.

London Magazine, v. 23, October, 1983. © *London Magazine* 1983. Reprinted by permission.

London Review of Books, December 30, 1982 to January 19, 1983 for "Mythic Elements" by Stephen Bann; September 1 to September 14, 1983 for "A World of Waste" by Philip Horne; February 2 to February 15, 1984 for "The Meaning of Science" by P. B. Medawar. All appear here by permission of the *London Review of Books* and the respective authors.

Los Angeles Times Book Review, August 28, 1983 for "Social Conflicts Played Out in a Watery Arena" by Theodore Sturgeon. Reprinted by permission of the Literary Estate of Theodore Sturgeon./ September 29, 1982. Copyright, 1982, *Los Angeles Times*. Reprinted by permission.

Maclean's Magazine, v. 92, July 23, 1979; v. 96, March 7, 1983; v. 97, May 21, 1984. © 1979, 1983, 1984 by *Maclean's Magazine*. All reprinted by permission.

The Magazine of Fantasy and Science Fiction, v. 50, June, 1976 for a review of "Gate of Ivrel" by Algis Budrys; v. 53, December, 1977 for a review of "Hunter of Worlds" by Algis Budrys; v. 54, June, 1978 for a review of "Hunter of Worlds" by Alexei Panshin and Cory Panshin; v. 57, September, 1979 for a review of "The Fountains of Paradise" by Algis Budrys; v. 63, July, 1982 for a review of "The Pride of Chanur" by Algis Budrys. © 1976, 1977, 1978, 1979, 1982 by Mercury Press Inc. All reprinted by permission of *The Magazine of Fantasy and Science Fiction* and the respective authors.

The Massachusetts Review, v. IX, Winter, 1968. © 1968. Reprinted from *The Massachusetts Review*, The Massachusetts Review, Inc. by permission.

Media & Methods, v. 15, April, 1979. Copyright © 1979. All rights reserved. Reprinted by permission.

Melody Maker, October 9, 1971; October 7, 1972; March 10, 1973; April 21, 1973; December 8, 1973; December 29, 1973; February 9, 1974; June 8, 1974; May 31, 1975; August 9, 1975; September 20, 1975; September 11, 1976; December 22, 1979; August 9, 1980; November 8, 1980; November 22, 1980; September 19, 1981; November 7, 1981; November 21, 1981; March 6, 1982; November 13, 1982. © IPC Business Press Ltd. All reprinted by permission.

MELUS, v. 6, Spring, 1979; v. 8, Fall, 1981. Copyright, MELUS, The Society for the Study of Multi-Ethnic Literature of the United States, 1979, 1981. Both reprinted by permission.

The Midwest Quarterly, v. IV, July, 1963. Copyright, 1963, by *The Midwest Quarterly*, Pittsburgh State University. Reprinted by permission.

Modern Drama, v. 1, February, 1959. Copyright *Modern Drama*, University of Toronto. Reprinted by permission.

Monthly Film Bulletin, v. 49, August, 1982; v. 51, December, 1984. Copyright © The British Film Institute, 1982, 1984. Both reprinted by permission.

Musical America, v. LXXXIV, May, 1964. All rights reserved. Excerpted by permission of *High Fidelity*.

Musician, n. 38, December, 1981; n. 76, February, 1985. © 1981, 1985 by *Musician*. Reprinted by permission.

The Nation, v. CXV, July 26, 1922; v. CXXIV, April 13, 1927; v. CXXXI, August 6, 1930; v. 146, February 19, 1938; v. 168, January 15, 1949; v. 177, November 28, 1953./ v. 195, August 25, 1962; v. 207, August 5, 1968; v. 209, December 15, 1969; v. 234, May 1, 1982; v. 235, September 11, 1982; v. 239, September 1, 1984. Copyright 1962, 1968, 1969, 1982, 1984 *The Nation* magazine, The Nation Associates, Inc. All reprinted by permission./ v. 172, March 11, 1951; v. 172, March 17, 1951. Copyright 1951, renewed 1979 *The Nation* magazine, The Nation Associates, Inc. Both reprinted by permission.

The Nation, London, v. CIII, August 17, 1916.

The National Observer, November 28, 1966; August 11, 1973; July 3, 1976. © Dow Jones & Company, Inc. 1966, 1973, 1976. All rights reserved. All reprinted by permission of *The National Observer*.

National Review, v. XXXIV, July 23, 1982. © National Review, Inc., 150 East 35th Street, NY 10016; 1982. Reprinted with permission.

The New Leader, v. LXI, February 27, 1978. © 1978 by The American Labor Conference on International Affairs, Inc. Reprinted by permission.

The New Republic, v. VIII, October 28, 1916; v. XXV, December 15, 1920; v. XXXII, August 30, 1922; v. XLIX, December 8, 1926; v. LXIX, February 10, 1932; v. 126, May 5, 1952./ v. 146, April 30, 1962; v. 153, July 24, 1965; v. 159, October 5, 1968; v. 185, July 18, 1981. © 1962, 1965, 1968, 1981 The New Republic, Inc. All reprinted by permission of *The New Republic*.

New Statesman, v. LX, October 8, 1960; v. LXVI, December 6, 1963; December 20, 1968; v. 89, May 9, 1975; v. 102, December 4, 1981; v. 103, June 4, 1982; v. 104, July 16, 1982; v. 107, January 27, 1984. © 1960, 1963, 1968, 1975, 1981, 1982, 1984 The Statesman & Nation Publishing Co. Ltd. All reprinted by permission.

New York Herald Tribune Book Review, February 11, 1951; April 13, 1952; November 29, 1953; May 30, 1954; May 15, 1955; September 9, 1956; October 5, 1958; March 8, 1959; November 1, 1959; August 14, 1960. © 1951, 1952, 1953, 1954, 1955, 1956, 1958, 1959, 1960 I.H.T. Corporation. All reprinted by permission.

New York Herald Tribune Books, February 7, 1926; October 10, 1926; October 21, 1928; February 5, 1933; February 25, 1934; February 10, 1935; March 1, 1936; August 2, 1936; August 23, 1936; April 11, 1937; March 20, 1938; April 30, 1939; July 28, 1940; June 15,

1941; January 18, 1942. © 1926, 1928, 1933, 1934, 1935, 1936, 1937, 1938, 1939, 1940, 1941, 1942 I.H.T. Corporation. All reprinted by permission.

New York Herald Tribune Weekly Book Review, March 21, 1943; May 27, 1945; January 26, 1947; May 16, 1948; August 15, 1948; August 22, 1948; October 10, 1948; October 24, 1948. © 1943, 1945, 1947, 1948 I.H.T. Corporation. All reprinted by permission.

New York Magazine, v. 17, February 27, 1984 for "Pop: The Way They Were" by Tom Bentkowski. Copyright © 1984 by News Group Publications, Inc. Reprinted by permission of the author.

The New York Review of Books, v. III, December 3, 1964; v. V, August 26, 1965; v. XXI, November 28, 1974; v. XXII, June 26, 1975; v. XXIII, June 24, 1976; v. XXIX, November 4, 1982; v. XXXI, June 14, 1984. Copyright © 1964, 1965, 1974, 1975, 1976, 1982, 1984 Nyrev, Inc. All reprinted with permission from *The New York Review of Books*.

The New York Times, April 9, 1971; December 13, 1972; August 22, 1973; April 27, 1979; January 17, 1981; December 14, 1981; February 9, 1983; October 14, 1984. Copyright © 1971, 1972, 1973, 1979, 1981, 1983, 1984 by The New York Times Company. All reprinted by permission.

The New York Times Book Review, June 11, 1916; January 12, 1919; October 24, 1920; October 21, 1928; February 24, 1929; August 3, 1930; September 14, 1930; February 7, 1932; July 17, 1932; February 18, 1934; February 10, 1935; April 11, 1937; May 31, 1936; January 1, 1939; December 3, 1939; April 7, 1940; March 21, 1943; May 16, 1943; May 30, 1943; January 26, 1947; October 17, 1948; January 30, 1949; November 19, 1950; May 6, 1951; March 16, 1952; March 23, 1952; January 4, 1953; November 29, 1953; March 27, 1953; April 10, 1955; March 18, 1956; September 9, 1956; September 29, 1957; February 9, 1958; March 23, 1958; August 31, 1958; November 16, 1958; January 18, 1959; March 29, 1959; September 13, 1959; February 7, 1960; October 22, 1961; October 29, 1961; January 7, 1962; April 1, 1962; June 17, 1962; April 14, 1963; May 26, 1963; January 19, 1964; August 16, 1964; September 20, 1964; June 27, 1965; August 29, 1965; January 23, 1966; April 24, 1966; June 19, 1966; April 9, 1967; October 15, 1967; October 29, 1967; March 24, 1968; July 7, 1968; August 18, 1968; August 25, 1968; November 3, 1968; January 26, 1969; November 15, 1970; February 28, 1971; September 12, 1971; July 23, 1972; November 5, 1972; March 11, 1973; January 21, 1973; September 30, 1973; November 4, 1973; May 26, 1974; November 10, 1974; March 30, 1975; May 4, 1975; July 20, 1975; November 2, 1975; January 18, 1976; May 2, 1976; May 16, 1976; June 27, 1976; August 8, 1976; October 3, 1976; May 22, 1977; October 30, 1977; April 29, 1979; June 17, 1979; August 19, 1979; September 16, 1979; October 7, 1979; January 6, 1980; January 20, 1980; April 20, 1980; April 27, 1980; September 28, 1980; November 9, 1980; May 10, 1981; May 17, 1981; July 12, 1981; October 18, 1981; February 14, 1982; February 21, 1982; April 11, 1982; April 18, 1982; April 25, 1982; May 23, 1982; May 30, 1982; June 13, 1982; August 29, 1982; November 7, 1982; November 28, 1982; January 6, 1982; January 23, 1983; February 27, 1983; May 22, 1983; September 26, 1983; November 6, 1983; November 13, 1983; November 27, 1983; January 1, 1984; January 22, 1984; April 1, 1984; May 20, 1984; June 10, 1984; May 5, 1985. Copyright © 1916, 1919, 1920, 1928, 1929, 1930, 1932, 1934, 1935, 1936, 1937, 1939, 1940, 1943, 1947, 1948, 1949, 1950, 1951, 1952, 1953, 1955, 1956, 1957, 1958, 1959, 1960, 1961, 1962, 1963, 1964, 1965, 1966, 1967, 1968, 1969, 1970, 1971, 1972, 1973, 1974, 1975, 1976, 1977, 1979, 1980, 1981, 1982, 1983, 1984, 1985 by The New York Times Company. All reprinted by permission.

The New Yorker, v. LVIII, December 6, 1982 for "Children's Books for Christmas" by Faith McNulty; v. LVIII, February 14, 1983 for "A Doctor's Life" by Jeremy Brustein. © 1982, 1983 by the respective authors. Both reprinted by permission./ v. XXXII, January 12, 1957 for "The Hateful Legacy" by Anthony West. Copyright © 1957 by the author. Reprinted by permission of Wallace & Sheil Agency, Inc./ v. XXXII, March 24, 1956; v. XXXIX, November 9, 1963; v. XLIV, October 5, 1968; v. XLV, December 6, 1969; v. LIV, July 10, 1978; v. LV, May 21, 1979; v. LVI, January 26, 1981; v. LIX, December 26, 1983; v. LIX, January 16, 1984. © 1956, 1963, 1968, 1969, 1978, 1979, 1981, 1983, 1984 by The New Yorker Magazine, Inc. All reprinted by permission.

Newsweek, v. LXXV, April 20, 1970; v. LXXXV, February 3, 1975; v. LXXXVII, January 12, 1976; v. XCII, December 18, 1978; v. XCVI, September 8, 1980; v. XCVII, January 12, 1981; v. XCIX, May 3, 1982; v. CIII, April 30, 1984; v. CIV, July 23, 1984; v. CV, April 29, 1985. Copyright 1970, 1975, 1976, 1978, 1980, 1981, 1982, 1984, 1985, by Newsweek, Inc. All rights reserved. Condensed by permission.

The North American Review, v. 242, Winter, 1936-37.

The Observer, January 10, 1971; November 28, 1971; July 22, 1973; September 25, 1977; March 26, 1978; December 10, 1978; March 22, 1981; April 18, 1982; December 4, 1983; April 1, 1984. All reprinted by permission of The Observer Limited.

Parents', v. 54, January, 1979. Copyright © 1979 Parents' Magazine Enterprises. Reprinted from *Parents'* by permission.

Parnassus: Poetry in Review, v. 8, Fall-Winter, 1979. Copyright © Poetry in Review Foundation. Reprinted by permission.

Philological Quarterly, v. 56, Spring, 1977 for "The Rationalization of the Arthurian 'Matter' in T. H. White and Mary Stewart" by Maureen Fries. Copyright 1977 by The University of Iowa. Reprinted by permission of the publisher and the author.

Poetry, v. CXXV, December, 1974 for "Traveling & Living" by Gerald Malanga. © 1974 by The Modern Poetry Association. Reprinted by permission of the Editor of *Poetry* and the author.

Popular Music & Society, v. 2, Winter, 1973 for a review of "Woody's Story" by R. Serge Denisoff. Copyright © 1973 by the author. Reprinted by permission.

Publishers Weekly, v. 190, October 3, 1966; v. 199, May 3, 1971; v. 202, August 14, 1972; v. 203, April 2, 1973; v. 203, May 7, 1973; v. 204, October 15, 1973; v. 205, April 15, 1974; v. 205, June 3, 1974; v. 206, August 12, 1974; v. 207, March 17, 1975; v. 208, August 18, 1975; v. 209, May 10, 1976; v. 210, July 26, 1976; v. 210, September 6, 1976; v. 212, August 22, 1977; v. 212, October 3, 1977; v. 213, January 2, 1978; v. 214, July 31, 1978; v. 214, October 30, 1978; v. 214, December 11, 1978; v. 215, February 5, 1979; v. 215, April 23, 1979; v. 215, May 21, 1979; v. 216, November 19, 1979; v. 217, January 11, 1980; v. 217, February 22, 1980; v. 217, March 28, 1980; v. 217, April 11, 1980; v. 218, July 25, 1980; v. 218, November 7, 1980; v. 219, February 13, 1981; v. 219, April 17, 1981; v. 220, November 20, 1981; v. 221, January 15, 1982; v. 222, August 6, 1982; v. 223, January 28, 1983; v. 223, March 18, 1983; v. 223, April 8, 1983; v. 223, July 1, 1983; v. 224, September 2, 1983; v. 224, September 8, 1983; v. 224, September 16, 1983; v. 224, October 28, 1983; v. 224, November 4, 1983; v. 225, January 6, 1984; v. 225, January 27, 1984; v. 225, February 24, 1984; v. 225, March 9, 1984; v. 225, May 11, 1984; v. 225, June 22, 1984. Copyright © 1966, 1971, 1972, 1973, 1974, 1975, 1976, 1977, 1978, 1979, 1980, 1981, 1982, 1983, 1984 by Xerox Corporation. All reprinted from *Publishers Weekly*, published by R. R. Bowker Company, a Xerox company, by permission.

Punch, v. CCLV, September 11, 1968; v. 257, December 17, 1969; v. 281, July 22, 1981; March 23, 1983; August 15, 1984. © 1968, 1969, 1981, 1983, 1984 by Punch Publications Ltd. All rights reserved. None may be reprinted without permission.

Ramparts, v. 7, November 30, 1968; v. 9, April, 1971. Copyright, 1971, by Noah's Ark, Inc. (for *Ramparts* magazine). Both reprinted by permission of Bruce W. Stilson.

The Record, v. 70, March, 1969. Copyright © 1969, Teachers College, Columbia University. Reprinted by permission.

Record Review, v. 7, August, 1983. Copyright © 1983 by Ashley Communications, Inc. Reprinted by permission.

The Reporter, v. 32, January 14, 1965 for "It's Been Good to Know Him" by Nat Hentoff. © 1965 by The Reporter Magazine Company. All rights reserved. Reprinted by permission of the author.

Rigel Science Fiction, n. 3, Winter, 1982 for a review of "Wave without a Shore" by Debbie Notkin. Copyright 1982 by the author. Reprinted by permission of the author.

Rolling Stone, i. 164, July 4, 1974 for a review of "Seven" by Dave Marsh; i. 202, December 18, 1975 for a review of "Shaved Fish" by Dave Marsh; i. 215, June 17, 1976 for "Bob Seger's 'Bullet': Right on Target" by Dave Marsh; i. 267, June 15, 1978 for "Not a Stranger Anymore" by Dave Marsh; i. 317, May 15, 1980 for "Bob Seger's 'Wind' Is Mostly Hot Air" by Dave Marsh. All reprinted by permission of the author./ i. 28, March 1, 1969; i. 58, May 14, 1970; i. 7, January 7, 1971; i. 86, July 8, 1971; i. 99, January 6, 1972; i. 100, January 20, 1972; i. 134, May 10, 1973; i. 135, May 24, 1973; i. 138, July 5, 1973; i. 151, January 3, 1974; i. 187, May 22, 1975; i. 188, June 5, 1975; i. 199, November 6, 1975; i. 213, May 20, 1976; i. 230, January 13, 1977; i. 235, March 24, 1977; i. 310, February 7, 1980; i. 322, July 24, 1980; i. 347, February 19, 1981; i. 361, January 21, 1982; i. 370, May 27, 1982; i. 373, July 8, 1982; i. 384, December 9, 1982; i. 388, February 3, 1983; i. 393, April 14, 1983; i. 413, January 19, 1984; i. 416, March 1, 1984; i. 418, March 29, 1984; i. 426 & 427, July 19 & August 2, 1984; i. 428, August 16, 1984; i. 436, December 6, 1984; i. 437 & 438, December 20, 1984 & January 3, 1985. By Straight Arrow Publishers, Inc. © 1969, 1970, 1971, 1972, 1973, 1974, 1975, 1976, 1977, 1980, 1981, 1982, 1983, 1984, 1985. All rights reserved. All reprinted by permission.

Saturday Review, v. XLI, November 15, 1958; v. XLIII, January 23, 1960; v. XLIII, February 6, 1960; v. XLIV, November 18, 1961; v. XLIX, May 14, 1966; v. L, November 4, 1967; v. LI, July 13, 1968; v. LI, October 19, 1968; v. LII, August 16, 1969; v. LIII, May 2, 1970; v. LIII, May 9, 1970; v. LIII, May 30, 1970; v. LV, May 20, 1972; v. 8, January, 1981. © 1958, 1960, 1961, 1966, 1967, 1968, 1969, 1970, 1972, 1981 *Saturday Review* magazine. All reprinted by permission.

The Saturday Review, New York, v. XXXV, April 5, 1952; v. XXXVI, September 26, 1953./ v. XLI, February 6, 1958. © 1958 *Saturday Review* magazine. Reprinted by permission.

The Saturday Review of Literature, v. III, April 9, 1927; v. V, March 2, 1929; v. VII, August 23, 1930; v. VII, September 27, 1930; v. VIII, February 13, 1932; v. IX, February 18, 1933; v. X, December 2, 1933./ v. XI, February 9, 1935; v. XIV, August 1, 1936; v. XIV, August 22, 1936; v. XV, April 10, 1937; v. XVII, March 19, 1938; v. XXI, December 2, 1939; v. XXI, April 13, 1940; v. XXII, July 27, 1940; v. XXV, January 31, 1942; v. XXVI, April 17, 1943; v. XXVIII, June 2, 1945; v. XXIX, September 28, 1946; v. XXXI, August 14, 1948; v. XXXI, October 9, 1948; v. XXXII, August 6, 1949; v. XXXIII, November 18, 1950. © 1935, 1936, 1937, 1938, 1939, 1940, 1942, 1943, 1945, 1946, 1948, 1949, 1950 *Saturday Review* magazine. All reprinted by permission.

The School Librarian, v. 28, December, 1980; v. 30, September, 1982; v. 30, December, 1982; v. 31, December, 1983; v. 32, March, 1984. All reprinted by permission.

School Library Journal, v. 21, May, 1975; v. 22, April, 1976; v. 24, October, 1977; v. 24, February, 1978; v. 25, October, 1978; v. 25, December, 1978; v. 25, January, 1979; v. 25, March, 1979; v. 25, April, 1979; v. 25, May, 1979; v. 26, May, 1980; v. 26, August, 1980; v. 27, May, 1981; v. 28, November, 1981; v. 28, December, 1981; v. 28, March, 1982; v. 28, April 15, 1982; v. 28, May, 1982; v. 29, September, 1982; v. 29, December, 1982; v. 29, February, 1983; v. 29, April, 1983; v. 30, September, 1983; v. 30, October, 1983; v. 30, November, 1983; v. 30, December, 1983; v. 30, January, 1984; v. 30, March, 1984; v. 30, April, 1984; v. 30, May, 1984; v. 30, August, 1984; v. 31, October, 1984. Copyright © 1975, 1976, 1977, 1978, 1979, 1980, 1981, 1982, 1983, 1984. All reprinted from *School Library Journal*, published by R. R. Bowker Co./ A Xerox Corporation, by permission.

School Library Journal, an appendix to *Library Journal*, v. 14, February, 1968; v. 15, November, 1968; v. 17, November, 1970; v. 18, May, 1972; v. 20, April, 1974; v. 20, May, 1974. Copyright © 1968, 1970, 1972, 1974. All reprinted from *School Library Journal*, published by R. R. Bowker Co./ A Xerox Corporation, by permission.

Science, v. 161, August 30, 1968. Copyright 1968 by the AAAS. Reprinted by permission of the publisher.

Science Fiction & Fantasy Book Review, v. I, June, 1979; n. 7, August, 1979; n. 9, October, 1979. Copyright © 1979 by The Borgo Press. All reprinted by permission./ n. 2, March, 1982; n. 6, July-August, 1982; n. 8, October, 1982; n. 16, July-August, 1983; n. 17, September, 1983; n. 18, October, 1983. Copyright © 1982, 1983 by Science Fiction Research Association. All reprinted by permission.

Science Fiction Review, v. 7, July, 1978 for a review of ''Well of Shiuan'' by David A. Truesdale; v. 8, May, 1979 for a review of "WYST: Alastor 1716" by John Shirley; v. 12, February, 1983 for a review of "2010: Odyssey Two" by Gene Deweese; v. 12, November, 1983 for a review of ''The Lazarus Effect'' by Stuart Napier; v. 13, February, 1984 for a review of ''Cugel's Saga'' by Darrell Schweitzer; n. 52, Fall, 1984 for a review of ''1984: Spring, a Choice of Futures'' by Karl Edd; v. 14, February, 1985 for a review of ''Bearing an Hourglass'' by Neal Wilgus. Copyright © 1978, 1979, 1983, 1984, 1985 by the respective authors. All reprinted by permission of the respective authors.

Science-Fiction Studies, v. 3, November, 1976; v. 6, July, 1979. Copyright © 1976, 1979 by SFS Publications. Both reprinted by permission.

Sing Out!, v. 14, January, 1965. © 1965 Sing Out! Magazine, Inc., Box 1071, Easton, PA 18044. Excerpted with permission.

Southwest Review, v. L, Winter, 1965. © 1965 by Southern Methodist University. Reprinted by permission.

The Spectator, v. 142, March 9, 1929; v. 156, June 19, 1936./ v. 198, May 24, 1957; v. 202, February 20, 1959; v. 204, March 18, 1960; v. 218, June 30, 1967; v. 223, November 1, 1969; v. 231, August 18, 1973; v. 239, December 24, 1977; v. 246, May 9, 1981; v. 247, September 5, 1981; v. 249, July 17, 1982; v. 252, January 14, 1984. © 1957, 1959, 1960, 1967, 1969, 1973, 1977, 1981, 1982, 1984 by *The Spectator*. All reprinted by permission of *The Spectator*.

Stereo Review Magazine, v. 28, January, 1972; v. 30, April, 1973; v. 31, August, 1973; v. 32, March, 1974; v. 34, March, 1975; v. 34, May, 1975; v. 35, October, 1975; v. 36, January, 1976; v. 38, March, 1977; v. 38, May, 1977; v. 45, September, 1980; v. 46, February, 1981; v. 46, March, 1981; v. 47, February, 1982; v. 47, June, 1982; v. 48, June, 1983; v. 49, April, 1984; v. 49, October, 1984. Copyright © 1972, 1973, 1974, 1975, 1976, 1977, 1980, 1981, 1982, 1983, 1984 by CBS Magazines. All reprinted from *Stereo Review Magazine* by permission.

Studies in the Literary Imagination, v. I, April, 1968. Copyright 1968 Department of English, Georgia State University. Reprinted by permission.

Time, v. 95, April 20, 1970; v. 115, February 25, 1980; v. 117, January 26, 1981; v. 118, July 27, 1981; v. 124, August 6, 1984. Copyright 1970, 1980, 1981, 1984 Time Inc. All rights reserved. All reprinted by permission from *Time*.

The Times Educational Supplement, n. 3389, June 5, 1981; n. 3524, January 13, 1984. © Times Newspapers Ltd. (London) 1981, 1984. Both reproduced from *The Times Educational Supplement* by permission.

Top of the News, v. 27, April, 1971. Copyright © 1971 by the American Library Association. Reprinted by permission.

TV Guide ® Magazine, v. 29, June 13, 1981 for ''Ethnic Slurs Are Back'' by Jean Bergantini Grillo; v. 33, June 1, 1985 for ''For Its Audacity, Its Defiantly Bad Taste and Its Superb Character Studies'' by Joyce Carol Oates. Copyright © 1981, 1985 by Triangle Publications, Inc. Radnor, PA. Both reprinted by permission of the publisher and the respective authors.

Variety, November 24, 1971; February 20, 1980; January 21, 1981; June 9, 1982; February 22, 1984. Copyright 1971, 1980, 1981, 1982, 1984, by Variety, Inc. All reprinted by permission.

The Village Voice, v. XVIII, January 18, 1973 for ''John and Yoko Coming Unmorred'' by Stuart Byron; v. XIX, June 27, 1974 for ''The Lives of a Cell'' by Martin Washburn; v. XXIII, June 5, 1978 for ''Growing Up Is Hard to Do'' by Lester Bangs; v. XXIV, September 3, 1979 for ''Message from the Eggman'' by Carol Flake; v. XXV, March 3, 1980 for ''Prince Who?'' by Georgia Christgau; v. XXV, July 2-8, 1980 for ''Paul McCartney Is Afraid of the Dark'' by Tom Carson; v. XXV, December 10, 1980 for ''John Lennon, 1940-1980'' by Robert Christgau; v. XXV, December 17-23, 1980 for ''Rock's New Prince'' by Pablo Guzman; v. XXVI, January 14, 1981 for ''Symbolic Comrades'' by Robert Christgau; v. XXVI, December 2, 1981 for ''Genius of Love'' by Vince Aletti; v. XXVII, January 27-February 2, 1982 for ''Hill Street Cutes'' by James Wolcott; v. XXVII, May 11, 1982 for ''Paul Carries That Weight'' by Davitt Sigerson; v. XXVII, November 16, 1982 for ''Dream Lover Takes It to the Floor'' by Marjorie Spencer; v. XXVII, November 23, 1982 for ''Deep in the Heart of 'Dallas''' by Tom Smucker; v. XXVII, December 28, 1982 for a review of ''Christmas at Fontaine's'' by Brandon Judell; v. XXVIII, June 7, 1983 for ''The Last Labor of Pink Floyd'' by John Piccarella; v. XXVIII, November 29, 1983 for a review of ''Late Night Thoughts on Listening to Mahler's Ninth Symphony'' by Mark Caldwell. Copyright © News Group Publications, Inc., 1973, 1974, 1978, 1979, 1980, 1981, 1982, 1983. All reprinted by permission of *The Village Voice* and the respective authors.

The Virginia Quarterly Review, v. 59, Summer, 1983. Copyright, 1983, by *The Virginia Quarterly Review*, The University of Virginia. Reprinted by permission.

VLS, n. 12, November, 1982; n. 23, February, 1984. Copyright © 1982, 1984 News Group Publications, Inc. Both reprinted by permission.

Voice of Youth Advocates, v. 3, February, 1981; v. 4, August, 1981; v. 4, October, 1981; v. 4, February, 1982; v. 5, April, 1982; v. 5, June, 1982; v. 5, August, 1982; v. 5, December, 1982; v. 5, February, 1983; v. 6, April, 1983; v. 6, June, 1983; v. 6, August, 1983; v. 6, December, 1983; v. 6, February, 1984; v. 7, April, 1984; v. 7, June, 1984; v. 7, August, 1984; v. 7, October, 1984; v. 7, February, 1985. Copyrighted 1981, 1982, 1983, 1984, 1985 by *Voice of Youth Advocates*. All reprinted by permission.

The Wall Street Journal, June 9, 1972. © Dow Jones & Company, Inc. 1972. All rights reserved. Reprinted by permission of *The Wall Street Journal*.

West Coast Review of Books, v. 10, May, 1984. Copyright 1984 by Rapport Publishing Co., Inc. Reprinted by permission.

Western American Literature, v. XVIII, May, 1983. Copyright, 1983, by the Western Literature Association. Reprinted by permission.

Western Folklore, v. XXI, October, 1962; v. XXV, October, 1966. © 1965, 1966, by the California Folklore Society. Both reprinted by permission.

Wilson Library Bulletin, v. 50, October, 1975; v. 52, December, 1977; v. 56, March, 1982; v. 58, June, 1984. Copyright © 1975, 1977, 1982, 1984 by the H. W. Wilson Company. All reprinted by permission.

World Literature Today, v. 56, Autumn, 1982. Copyright 1982 by the University of Oklahoma Press. Reprinted by permission.

The Writer, v. 83, May, 1970 for "Teller of Tales" by Mary Stewart. Copyright © 1970 by The Writer, Inc. Reprinted by permission of the author and Hodder & Stoughton Limited.

The Yale Review, v. XXIX, December, 1939. Copyright 1939, renewed 1967, by Yale University. Reprinted by permission of the editors.

THE EXCERPTS IN CLC, VOLUME 35, WERE REPRINTED FROM THE FOLLOWING BOOKS:

Arbuthnot, May Hill, Sutherland, Zena, and Monson, Dianne L. From *Children and Books*. Sixth edition. Scott, Foresman, 1981. Copyright © 1981, 1977, 1972, 1964, 1957, 1947 by Scott, Foresman and Company. All rights reserved. Reprinted by permission.

Attebery, Brian. From *The Fantasy Tradition in American Literature: From Irving to LeGuin*. Indiana University Press, 1980. Copyright © 1980 by Brian Attebery. All rights reserved. Reprinted by permission.

Baskin, Barbara H. and Karen H. Harris. From *Notes from a Different Drummer: A Guide to Juvenile Fiction Portraying the Handicapped*. Bowker, 1977. Copyright © 1977 by Barbara H. Baskin and Karen H. Harris. All rights reserved. Reprinted by permission of the R. R. Bowker Company.

Bellamy, Joe David. From an introduction to *The Purple Decades: A Reader*. By Tom Wolfe. Farrar, Straus & Giroux, 1982. Copyright © 1982 by Farrar, Straus & Giroux, Inc. All rights reserved. Reprinted by permission of Farrar, Straus & Giroux, Inc.

Brizzi, Mary T. From "C. J. Cherryh and Tomorrow's New Sex Roles," in *The Feminine Eye: Science Fiction and the Women Who Write It*. Edited by Tom Staicar. Ungar, 1982. Copyright © 1982 by Frederick Ungar Publishing Co., Inc. Reprinted by permission.

Brown, John Mason. From *Two on the Aisle: Ten Years of the American Theatre in Performance*. Norton, 1938. Copyright © 1938 by W. W. Norton & Company, Inc. Copyright renewed © 1966 by John Mason Brown. Reprinted by permission of the Literary Estate of John Mason Brown.

Cadogan, Mary and Patricia Craig. From *You're a Brick, Angela! A New Look at Girl's Fiction from 1839 to 1975*. Victor Gollancz Ltd., 1976. © Mary Cadogan and Patricia Craig 1976. Reprinted by permission of the authors.

Cameron, Eleanor. From *The Green and Burning Tree: On the Writing and Enjoyment of Children's Books*. Atlantic-Little, Brown, 1969. Copyright © 1962, 1964, 1966, 1969 by Eleanor Cameron. All rights reserved. Reprinted by permission of Little, Brown and Company in association with The Atlantic Monthly Press.

Clareson, Thomas D. From "The Cosmic Loneliness of Arthur C. Clarke," in *Voices for the Future: Essays on Major Science Fiction Writers, Vol. I*. Edited by Thomas D. Clareson. Bowling Green University Popular Press, 1976. Copyright © 1976 by The Popular Press. Reprinted by permission.

Close, Peter. From "Fantasms, Magics, and Unfamiliar Sciences: The Early Fiction of Jack Vance, 1945-50," in *Jack Vance*. Edited by Tim Underwood and Chuck Miller. Taplinger Publishing Company, 1980. Copyright © 1980 by Tim Underwood and Chuck Miller. All rights reserved. Reprinted by permission of the author.

Davis, Arthur P. From *From the Dark Tower: Afro-American Writers, 1900 to 1960*. Howard University Press, 1974. Copyright © 1974 by Arthur P. Davis. All rights reserved. Reprinted by permission of Howard University Press.

Donelson, Kenneth L. and Alleen Pace Nilsen. From *Literature for Today's Young Adults*. Scott, Foresman, 1980. Copyright © 1980 Scott, Foresman and Company. All rights reserved. Reprinted by permission.

Egoff, Sheila A. From *Thursday's Child: Trends and Patterns in Contemporary Children's Literature*. American Library Association, 1981. Copyright © 1981 by the American Library Association. All rights reserved. Reprinted by permission.

Gardner, R. H. From *The Splintered Stage: The Decline of the American Theater*. Macmillan, 1965. Copyright © R. H. Gardner 1965. All rights reserved. Reprinted with permission of Macmillan Publishing Company.

Gitlin, Todd. From *Inside Prime Time*. Pantheon Books, 1983. Copyright © 1983 by Todd Gitlin. All rights reserved. Reprinted by permission of Pantheon Books, a Division of Random House, Inc.

Hellmann, John. From *Fables of Fact: The New Journalism as New Fiction*. University of Illinois Press, 1981. © 1981 by the Board of Trustees of the University of Illinois. Reprinted by permission of the publisher and the author.

Human—And Anti-Human—Values in Children's Books: A Content Rating Instrument for Educators and Concerned Parents. Edited by the Council on Interracial Books for Children, Inc. Racism and Sexism Resource Center for Educators, 1976. Copyright © 1976 by Council on Interracial Books for Children, Inc. All rights reserved. Reprinted by permission.

Jemie, Onwuchekwa. From *Langston Hughes: An Introduction to the Poetry*. Columbia University Press, 1976. Copyright © 1973, 1976 Columbia University Press. All rights reserved. Reprinted by permission of the publisher.

Lenz, Joseph M. From "Manifest Destiny: Science Fiction and Classical Form," in *Coordinates: Placing Science Fiction and Fantasy.* George E. Slusser, Eric S. Rabkin, Robert Scholes, eds. Southern Illinois University Press, 1983. Copyright © 1983 by the Board of Trustees, Southern Illinois University. All rights reserved. Reprinted by permission of Joseph M. Lenz.

Marsh, Dave. From *Fortunate Son: Criticism and Journalism By America's Best-Known Rock Writer.* Random House, 1985. Copyright © 1985 by Duke and Duchess Ventures, Inc. Reprinted by permission of the author.

McLean, Susan. From "A Question of Balance: Death and Immortality in Frank Herbert's Dune Series," in *Death and the Serpent: Immortality in Science Fiction and Fantasy.* Edited by Carl B. Yoke and Donald M. Hassler. Greenwood Press, 1985. Copyright © 1985 by Carl B. Yoke and Donald M. Hassler. All rights reserved. Reprinted by permission of Greenwood Press, a division of Congressional Information Service, Inc., Westport, CT.

Miller, David M. From *Frank Herbert.* Starmont House, 1980. Published and copyright © 1980 by Starmont House, P.O. Box 851 Mercer Island, Washington 98040. All rights reserved. Reprinted by permission.

Sadker, Myra Pollack and David Miller Sadker. From *Now Upon a Time: A Contemporary View of Children's Literature.* Harper & Row, 1977. Copyright © 1977 by Myra Pollack Sadker and David Miller Sadker. All rights reserved. Reprinted by permission of Harper & Row, Publishers, Inc.

Scanlan, Tom. From *Family, Drama, and American Dreams.* Greenwood Press, 1978. Copyright © 1978 by Tom Scanlan. All rights reserved. Reprinted by permission of Greenwood Press, a division of Congressional Information Service, Inc., Westport, CT.

Schraufnagel, Noel. From *From Apology To Protest: The Black American Novel.* Everett/Edwards, Inc., 1973. © 1973 by Noel Schraufnagel. All rights reserved. Reprinted by permission.

Silverberg, Robert. From an introduction to *The Eyes of the Overworld.* By Jack Vance. Gregg Press, 1977. Introduction copyright © 1977 by Robert Silverberg. Reprinted by permission of Robert Silverberg.

Smalley, Webster. From an introduction to *Five Plays.* By Langston Hughes, edited by Webster Smalley. Indiana University Press, 1963. Copyright © 1963 by Langston Hughes. All rights reserved. Reprinted by permission.

Spinrad, Norman. From "Jack Vance and 'The Dragon Masters'," in *Jack Vance.* Edited by Tim Underwood and Chuck Miller. Taplinger Publishing Company, 1980. Copyright © 1976 by Norman Spinrad. Reprinted by permission of the author.

Sternlicht, Stanford. From *C. S. Forester.* Twayne, 1981. Copyright 1981 by Twayne Publishers. All rights reserved. Reprinted with the permission of Twayne Publishers, a division of G. K. Hall & Co., Boston.

Thompson, Raymond H. From *The Return from Avalon: A Study of the Arthurian Legend in Modern Fiction.* Greenwood Press, 1985. Copyright © 1985 by Raymond H. Thompson. All rights reserved. Reprinted by permission of Greenwood Press, a division of Congressional Information Service, Inc., CT.

Tiedman, Richard. From *Jack Vance: Science Fiction Stylist.* R & J. Coulson Publications, 1965. Copyright © 1965 by Richard Tiedman. Reprinted by permission of the author.

Underwood, Tim. From an introduction to *Jack Vance.* Edited by Tim Underwood and Chuck Miller. Taplinger Publishing Company, 1980. Copyright © 1980 Tim Underwood and Chuck Miller. All rights reserved. Reprinted by permission of the author.

West, Rebecca. From a preface to *Selected Poems of Carl Sandburg.* Edited by Rebecca West. Harcourt Brace Jovanovich, 1926. Copyright 1926, 1954 by Rebecca West. Reprinted by permission of Harcourt Brace Jovanovich, Inc.

Wilder, Thornton. From a preface to *Three Plays: Our Town, The Skin of Our Teeth, The Matchmaker.* Harper and Brothers, 1957. Copyright © 1957 by Thornton Wilder. Reprinted by permission of Harper & Row, Publishers, Inc.

Willard, Mark. From "Tschai: Four Planets of Adventure," in *Jack Vance.* Edited by Tim Underwood and Chuck Miller. Taplinger Publishing Company, 1980. Copyright © 1980 by Tim Underwood and Chuch Miller. All rights reserved. Reprinted by permission of the author.

Wyld, Lionel D. From *Walter D. Edmonds, Storyteller.* Syracuse University Press, 1982. Copyright © 1982 by Lionel D. Wyld. All rights reserved. Reprinted by permission.

Yurchenco, Henrietta. From a foreword to *A Mighty Hard Road: The Woody Guthrie Story.* By Henrietta Yurchenco with Marjorie Guthrie. McGraw-Hill, 1970. Copyright © 1970 by Henrietta Yurchenco and The Guthrie Children's Trust Fund. All rights reserved. With permission of McGraw-Hill Book Co.

Cumulative Index to Authors

This index lists all author entries in the Gale Literary Criticism Series and includes cross-references to other Gale sources. References in the index are identified as follows:

AITN: *Authors in the News,* Volumes 1-2
CAAS: *Contemporary Authors Autobiography Series,* Volumes 1-2
CA: *Contemporary Authors* (original series), Volumes 1-115
CANR: *Contemporary Authors New Revision Series,* Volumes 1-14
CAP: *Contemporary Authors Permanent Series,* Volumes 1-2
CA-R: *Contemporary Authors* (revised editions), Volumes 1-44
CLC: *Contemporary Literary Criticism,* Volumes 1-35
CLR: *Children's Literature Review,* Volumes 1-8
DLB: *Dictionary of Literary Biography,* Volumes 1-39
DLB-DS: *Dictionary of Literary Biography Documentary Series,* Volumes 1-4
DLB-Y: *Dictionary of Literary Biography Yearbook,* Volumes 1980-1984
LC: *Literature Criticism from 1400 to 1800,* Volumes 1-2
NCLC: *Nineteenth-Century Literature Criticism,* Volumes 1-10
SATA: *Something about the Author,* Volumes 1-39
TCLC: *Twentieth-Century Literary Criticism,* Volumes 1-18
YABC: *Yesterday's Authors of Books for Children,* Volumes 1-2

Author Index

Author Index

Author Index

Author Index

Author Index

Author Index

Cumulative Index to Critics

Critic Index

Critic Index

Critic Index

Critic Index

Critic Index

Critic Index

Critic Index

Critic Index

Critic Index

Critic Index

Critic Index

Critic Index

Critic Index

Critic Index

Critic Index

Critic Index

Critic Index

Critic Index

Critic Index